# THE NEW PENGUIN DICTIONARY OF MODERN HISTORY

Duncan Townson was educated at Keighley Boys' Grammar School and at Sidney Sussex College, Cambridge. He taught at Sevenoaks School, where he was Head of the History Department, and was a Leverhulme Fellow at the School of Oriental and African Studies, University of London. A keen cricketer – he was an opening batsman for Cumberland and Westmorland – and opera buff, his passion for Islamic art and architecture has taken him to Egypt, India, Central Asia and, overland with his wife and three children, to Morocco, Turkey and Iran. He is the author of several books, the latest of which is *France in Revolution*.

# THE NEW PENGUIN

## DICTIONARY OF
## MODERN HISTORY
### 1789–1945

Duncan Townson

PENGUIN BOOKS

PENGUIN BOOKS

Published by the Penguin Group
Penguin Books Ltd, 27 Wrights Lane, London w8 5tz, England
Penguin Books USA Inc., 375 Hudson Street, New York, New York 10014, USA
Penguin Books Australia Ltd, Ringwood, Victoria, Australia
Penguin Books Canada Ltd, 10 Alcorn Avenue, Toronto, Ontario, Canada m4v 3b2
Penguin Books (NZ) Ltd, 182–190 Wairau Road, Auckland 10, New Zealand

Penguin Books Ltd, Registered Offices: Harmondsworth, Middlesex, England

First published 1994
Reprinted with minor revisions 1995
3 5 7 9 10 8 6 4 2

Filmset in 10/12 Monotype Bembo
Typeset in England by Datix International Limited, Bungay, Suffolk
Printed in England by Clays Ltd, St Ives plc

FOR LESLEY

# INTRODUCTION

This book covers the same period as the earlier *Dictionary of Modern History* by Alan Palmer and is primarily a dictionary of political and economic history. It begins with the French Revolution, an event of European significance, and ends with the Second World War, which had major repercussions throughout the world. The present dictionary differs from its predecessor in that there are many more extra-European entries and more too on topics which cut across national boundaries, such as **nationalism** and **Industrial Revolution**. To make this possible, entries on individual countries have been omitted. As in the previous dictionary there are no entries on scientists, artists, musicians or literary figures. Entries have been arranged alphabetically, according to the key word in the title: the **battle of Waterloo** appears as **Waterloo, battle of**. Kings, queens and emperors are given in their English form (e.g. William II, not Wilhelm II). For Chinese names pinyin, the official romanization system in the People's Republic of China, has been used. As the Wade–Giles system will be more familiar to many readers (*Chiang Kai-shek* rather than *Jiang Jieshi*), many entries are given first in pinyin, followed in brackets by the Wade–Giles equivalent. Russians used the Julian calendar up to February 1918, so Russian dates are twelve days behind those in the West in the nineteenth century and thirteen days in the twentieth century up to 1918. When a word or phrase appears in bold type this indicates that the subject has an entry of its own.

I am deeply indebted to Dr Nigel Townson, who wrote all the entries on Spain and Portugal and some on Latin America; to Dr David Killingray, who gave me considerable assistance with the entries on Africa; to Ian Walker, for his help with British history; and to my wife, Lesley, who did all the typing. She had the onerous task, which she performed impeccably, of deciphering my illegible script, though in the process she became convinced that the days of slavery were not yet over.

Duncan Townson

Sevenoaks
January 1994

**Abd al-Aziz ibn Saud** (1880–1953). Founder of the state of Saudi Arabia. In 1902 he took control of Riyadh and proclaimed himself *imam* ('leader') of the **Wahabis**, a puritanical Islamic sect. In 1912 he founded the *Ikhwan* ('Brothers'), whom he sent among the bedouin to persuade them to lead strict, ascetic lives according to the *sharia* (Muslim law). With his followers, Abd al-Aziz began a systematic conquest of Arabia which involved him in fighting **Husayn**, sherif of Mecca and ruler of the Hijaz, from 1919–25. In 1924 he captured Mecca; Husayn was forced to go into exile and in 1926 Abd al-Aziz proclaimed himself King of the Hijaz. Britain recognized him as King in 1927 and in return he recognized the Hashemites, Abdullah and Feisal (sons of Husayn), as rulers of Transjordan and Iraq. In 1932 he assumed the title King of Saudi Arabia, with control of the whole peninsula except for the British-protected Gulf sheikhdoms and the mountainous kingdom of Yemen. Once Abd al-Aziz became King the *Ikhwan* were an embarrassment, as they objected to modern innovations such as motor cars and telephones, and came into conflict with Britain in their fanatical campaign against unbelievers in Iraq and Transjordan. Abd al-Aziz therefore destroyed the movement he had created: most of the *Ikhwan* were killed at the battle of Sabila in 1929. Yet the *sharia* continued to be the basis of the Saudi state and modernization took place within this framework. The most backward of the Arab countries (its oil wealth was developed only from 1938), Saudi Arabia under Abd al-Aziz was the only one to gain full independence between the two world wars.

**Abd al-Qadir** (*c*. 1808–83). An Algerian military leader who led the fifteen-year resistance to the French in the 1830s and 1840s. In 1830, French military forces occupied Algiers, several other ports on the Algerian coast and a small inland zone. Resistance among Arabs and Berbers began in 1832, mainly in western Algeria around the city of Oran, where Abd al-Qadir organized an army of 12,000 men. The son of a marabout ('holy man') from Morocco, he declared a *jihad* against the French and assumed the title of 'Commander of the Faithful'. His aim was not simply to resist the infidel invader by forming a temporary coalition of tribes, but to found a Muslim state governed strictly according to the laws laid down by the Prophet Muhammad. For nearly ten years he was able to unite some of the Algerian tribes, hold back the French and extend the region under his control. The French ruthlessly and systematically crushed resistance, but to do so they had to increase their army from 18,000 men in 1831 to 108,000 in 1846. In 1847 Abd al-Qadir was captured, and he went to live in exile in Damascus. The war led to great bitterness between Algerians and French, which was increased by the arrival of 100,000 French settlers who took the fertile coastal lands. Abd al-Qadir is regarded as one of the founders of the Algerian nation, and identified with resistance to the French, which did not cease until 1879, by which time the French army had subdued all tribes between the sea and the desert.

**Abd al-Qrim** (*c*. 1880–1963). Berber chieftain who fought the Spaniards and the French in the Rif war of 1920–26. The son of a chief in northern Morocco, he resented the harsh Spanish rule established in 1912 and raised a revolt in 1920. His first operations were guerrilla strikes from the Rif mountains, but in July 1920 his forces inflicted a disastrous defeat on the Spanish army at the battle of Anual, killing 12,000 Spaniards, indirectly bringing down the Spanish government and enabling **Primo de Rivera** to become dictator. Abd al-Qrim then began to organize an independent Rif republic in the mountains. The French intervened when it seemed as if he might become the leader of a movement to liberate Morocco from French control. In 1924 **Lyautey**, the French Commander, moved his troops into the southern Rif, where they clashed with Abd al-Qrim's forces. By September 1925 French and Spanish armies totalling nearly 500,000 men and backed by tanks and aircraft, under the command of General Primo de Rivera and Marshal **Pétain**, took the offensive against the Rif republic. Within eight months Abd al-Qrim was defeated and surrendered. He was deported to the island of Réunion, where he remained until 1947 when he was given permission to live in France: at Suez he escaped from the ship that was carrying him, and spent the rest of his life in exile in Egypt.

**Abdication crisis** (1936) resulted in King **Edward VIII** surrendering the British throne. Since 1934 his closest companion had been Mrs Wallis Simpson, an American who was already divorced when she married Ernest Simpson in 1928. Edward mixed openly with Wallis after becoming King in January 1936, and in August accompanied her on a cruise along the Yugoslav coast, an event widely reported in the American and European press. Newspapers in Britain maintained a self-imposed censorship and, with sycophantic zeal, falsely portrayed Edward as a hard-working King. In November 1936, Edward made it clear to Stanley **Baldwin**, the British Prime Minister, that he intended to marry Wallis as soon as she was divorced from Ernest Simpson. As Edward was Supreme Governor of the Church of England, which did not recognize divorce, Baldwin, the Archbishop of Canterbury and the leaders of all the major political parties agreed that Edward should not marry Mrs Simpson. As he wanted both to retain the throne and marry Wallis Simpson, Edward suggested a morganatic marriage, whereby Wallis would not be Queen and any children resulting from the marriage would forfeit the right of succession. This proposal was rejected by the Cabinet and by the Prime Ministers of the **dominions**, who were also consulted. Edward was therefore left with the options of either renouncing Wallis, abdicating, or marrying her and causing a constitutional crisis in which the existence of the monarchy would be at stake, as the government would resign and the opposition parties would refuse to take office. On 10 December 1936 he abdicated; one day later, as Duke of Windsor, he left England for the Continent, where he spent most of the rest of his life. When James Maxton, leader of the **Independent Labour Party** (ILP), proposed an amendment to the Abdication Bill that the monarchy should be abolished, it was defeated by 403 votes to five.

**Abduh, Muhammad** (1849–1905). Egyptian religious leader and reformer. For supporting **Urabi Pasha** he was exiled and subsequently joined **al-Afghani** in Paris but their views differed, so he left al-Afghani and went to Beirut, where he lectured in theology. He was allowed to return to Egypt in 1888 but did not take an active part in politics. Unlike al-Afghani he did not believe in revolution and did not actively oppose the British occupation of Egypt. Lord **Cromer**, the British Consul-General, warmly approved of him and supported his becoming *mufti* (Chief Justice) in Egypt in 1889, a post he held until his death. Abduh wanted to reconcile Islam with modern science and thought, by preserving the essentials of Islam whilst discarding the additions which had been made over the centuries. He accepted the Quran and the *hadith* (reports of the sayings and deeds of the Prophet Muhammad made by his companions), but he thought that individual reason should be applied in matters which they did not discuss specifically. Abduh did not believe that Islam should provide a detailed, rigid and eternal blueprint for society which could never be changed, but general guidelines which should be reinterpreted in each age. His liberal and humane ideas led Cromer to regard him as 'the chief hope of Liberal Islam in Egypt'.

**Abdulhamid II** (1842–1918). Ottoman Sultan (1876–1909). He became Sultan when his brother Murad V went mad, and on condition that he granted the **Ottoman Empire** a constitution. A liberal constitution was therefore issued which limited the Sultan's autocratic powers and provided for the election of a legislative assembly. Within a year Abdulhamid had dismissed his reforming Grand Vizier, Midhat Pasha, and in 1878 he dissolved the assembly and suspended the constitution. For the next thirty years he ruled as an autocrat, keeping all power in his own hands and ending the autonomy of local governors. Hard-working and intelligent, he was prone to nervous collapses and was intensely suspicious. His main appeal to his Arab subjects was as a leader of Islam: he revived the title of Caliph, protector of Muslims throughout the world. Strict in his religious observances, he surrounded himself with *ulama* (religious leaders), built mosques and supported Muslim missionary activity in Asia and Africa. He did not show the same concern for his Christian subjects. When the Christians in Armenia demanded autonomy, he decided to annihilate them and began the Armenian massacres of 1894–6, in which tens of thousands of Armenians were killed. During his reign the Ottoman Empire became increasingly dependent on foreign loans. By 1882 it could no longer pay the interest on its debts and had to accept a foreign debt administration: henceforth foreign bankers controlled the Ottoman economy. The Empire continued to decline in size: after the **Russo-Turkish War** of 1877–8 Abdulhamid had to recognize the independence of Serbia, Montenegro and Romania, and the loss of part of the Caucasus to Russia, at the Treaty of **San Stefano**. Later in 1878, at the **Berlin Congress**, Austria was granted military occupation of the Ottoman provinces of Bosnia and Hercegovina. The **Young Turk** revolution of 1908 compelled Abdulhamid to restore the constitution of 1876 and an elected parliament; when he attempted a counter-revolution a year later he was deposed.

**Aberdeen, George Hamilton Gordon, 4th Earl of** (1784–1860). British Prime Minister (1852–5). A ward of **Pitt** the Younger, whom he greatly admired, Aberdeen became an earl in 1801 and therefore never sat in the House of **Commons**, the training ground for most politicians. He entered the **Lords** as a Scottish representative peer in 1806 and remained there for the rest of his life. As Foreign Secretary (1828–30) in **Wellington**'s government, he helped to create an independent kingdom of Greece in 1830. In **Peel**'s second administration (1841–6) he was again Foreign Secretary; he fixed Canada's boundary with the USA (and in so doing settled the **Oregon boundary dispute**) and restored good relations with France, rejecting the confrontational policy of **Palmerston**. A devoted follower of Peel, he resigned with him in 1846 following the split in the **Conservative Party** after the repeal of the **Corn Laws**. When Peel died in 1850 Aberdeen became leader of the Peelites and formed a coalition government of Peelites, Liberals and Radicals on the collapse of **Derby**'s government in 1852. Aberdeen knew that he was not suited to be Prime Minister, as he was a poor speaker and not forceful enough to control a wayward Cabinet, but his strong sense of duty led him to accept the post. His ministry was dominated by the **Crimean War** (1854–6), for which he must bear some responsibility, as he gave Russia the impression that Britain agreed with her and did not indicate early enough that he was prepared to go to war. He allowed Britain to drift into a war he did not want and then waged it incompetently. Aberdeen resigned when the Commons appointed a select committee to inquire into the conduct of the war, but from 1855 until his death in 1860 he played an active if unobtrusive role by seeking to ensure that **Gladstone** became leader of the **Liberal Party**, which emerged from the fusion of **Whigs** and Peelites.

**Abolitionists**. People in the United States who demanded the complete abolition of slavery. Abolitionism first became a powerful political force in 1831 when William Lloyd Garrison founded his magazine *The Liberator* in Boston. Southern politicians blamed abolitionist propaganda for Nat Turner's rebellion in 1831 and some, like John C. **Calhoun**, said that it might be necessary for the South to secede from the Union if the abolitionists were not silenced. Southerners loathed abolitionists, but even in the North the abolitionists were denounced as 'nigger-lovers' whose actions threatened the existence of the Union. They remained a comparatively small group until the 1840s, when the extension of slavery to new territories became a burning issue. Many moderates found themselves on the same side as the abolitionists in opposition to the annexation of **Texas** in 1845 and the **Mexican–American War** of 1846. In 1852, Harriet Beecher Stowe depicted the struggle against slavery as one of good against evil in her novel *Uncle Tom's Cabin*. This sold 1.5 million copies within a year and deeply affected public opinion in the North. Slavery was now regarded as a moral rather than a political or economic issue. The **Republican Party** was founded in 1854, largely in opposition to the expansion of slavery, and in 1860 its candidate, Abraham **Lincoln**, was elected President. In 1863, during the **American Civil War**, he signed a proclamation freeing slaves in the rebel states. At the end of the war in 1865, the abolitionists saw their cause triumph when the thirteenth amendment to the Constitution banned slavery in the USA.

**Aborigines**. An Australoid people who lived in Australia and Van Diemen's Land (later called Tasmania) before white convicts and settlers arrived. There were possibly 750,000 in Australia and 50,000 in Tasmania, who spoke 200 languages and lived by gathering food, catching fish and killing kangaroos. They came into conflict with whites, particularly on the open grasslands to the west of the

Blue Mountains, as sheepowners and Aborigines competed for the same land. The struggle was one-sided, as spears were no match for firearms and the tribes did not unite but fought each other as well as the whites. Massacres took place on both sides: the most famous was that at Myall Creek in New South Wales in 1838, when at least twenty-two Aborigines – men, women and children – were tied together and executed. The incident became well known, not because Aborigines were killed but because, unusually, seven whites were tried for their murder and hanged. This did not stop the killing of Aborigines, which continued until 1928 when police shot thirty-one in the Northern Territory. Though many whites in the south and east were outraged, no one was brought to trial. The highest estimate of the number of Aborigines killed in conflict with the whites in the nineteenth century is 20,000: many more died from European diseases such as smallpox and measles, so that by 1900 the Aborigines were reduced to about 50,000. In Tasmania they were wiped out completely, the last Aborigine dying in 1888. In the 1930s Reserves were set up in areas where labour was scarce, in which Aborigines were compelled to live unless they were granted permission to take up employment with whites. The government separated children who had Aborigine mothers and white fathers from their parents, in a brutal attempt to integrate them into white society. Aborigines were not recognized as Australian citizens until 1948: until then they did not receive old-age pensions or any of the benefits which were reserved for whites.

**Abyssinian War** (1935–6), see **Ethiopian War**

**Action Française.** An extreme right-wing nationalist movement, founded in 1899 to promote **anti-Semitism** and reflect the views of those who opposed **Dreyfus**. It had supporters in the middle and upper classes but its main appeal was to the *petite bourgeoisie* (the lower-middle classes) and it made no attempt to win over the working class. Its influence was due mainly to the writings of its leader, Charles **Maurras**, and his journal, *L'Action Française*, which became a daily newspaper in 1908. The movement was never important in parliament and its advocacy of a violent overthrow of the **Third Republic**, to be replaced by a monarchy, had few adherents. It anticipated and inspired many Fascist ideas (see

**Fascism**) but suffered a severe set-back in 1926, when Pope **Pius XI** publicly condemned the organization. Action Française was banned in 1936 but its newspaper was allowed to continue: it opposed France's entry into the **Second World War** and, after the fall of **France**, supported collaboration with the Germans. The movement revived under the **Vichy** regime, which it supported, but came to an end with the Liberation.

**Adams, John Quincy** (1767–1848). Sixth President of the USA (1825–9). He was a son of the second President, John Adams, and a typical New England Puritan, with strong principles, yet self-righteous and overbearing. A representative of his country abroad from 1794–1802 and again from 1808–17, at the Hague, Berlin, St Petersburg and London, he helped to draw up the Treaty of Ghent (1814), which ended the **Anglo-American War**. On his return he became President **Monroe**'s Secretary of State from 1817–25. He was very successful: he made a treaty with Britain which fixed the border with Canada as far west as the Rockies; he persuaded Spain to cede Spanish Florida to the USA in 1819; and he was the inspiration behind the **Monroe Doctrine**. **Jefferson** and **Madison** favoured an informal alliance with England, suggested by the British in 1823. Adams was against this. His views prevailed with Monroe, who issued a declaration stating that the USA no longer regarded the Americas as a legitimate field for European colonization. Adams was an expansionist, who believed that providence intended the USA to possess the whole North American continent.

Adams's brilliant run of success came to an end when he became President in 1825. He appeared to be the best-qualified candidate to succeed Monroe but the vote was split in the electoral college amongst four candidates, none of whom had a majority. Adams became President only with the support of Henry **Clay**, whom he made his Secretary of State. This laid Adams open to the charge of being corrupt. His reputation under attack and faced with a hostile Congress, he could do little as President and was defeated by Andrew **Jackson** in 1828.

**Aduwa.** A battle in southern Ethiopia in 1896 in which the Ethiopian army of King **Menelik II** defeated an invading Italian force. The Italians occupied the coastal region of Eritrea in the mid-

1880s and hoped to extend their control over the Ethiopian interior. Menelik came to the throne of Ethiopia in 1889 with Italian help and two years later signed a pact of friendship, the Treaty of Ucciali (Wichale), with Italy. The Italian version of the treaty was different from the Amharic one: in the Amharic version, Italy agreed to help Ethiopia in her relations with foreign countries; according to the Italian version, Menelik recognized an Italian protectorate over Ethiopia. Menelik subsequently denounced the treaty, and this led to war between the two countries in 1895. The Italians invaded Ethiopia with an army of 20,000 men. At Aduwa, on 1 March 1896, they were decisively defeated by an Ethiopian army of 110,000. In October 1896, in the Treaty of Addis Ababa, Italy agreed to recognize Ethiopian independence.

**African National Congress** (ANC). The first nation-wide African political organization in South Africa. It was formed in 1912 as the South African Native National Congress, and changed its name to the ANC in 1923. It opposed the racialist laws of the white Union parliament, and hoped to end racial discrimination by educating white opinion and petitioning parliament. Its leaders were part of the small black middle class, who stressed moderation and gradualism, looked down on the lower classes and wanted to make themselves acceptable to the whites. They rejected revolution and mobilization of the masses, and had little influence in the 1920s and 1930s. A younger generation, incensed by **Hertzog**'s 1936 bill which ended the Cape franchise for non-whites, was more militant and in 1943 formed the Congress Youth League. Among its members were Nelson Mandela and Walter Sisulu, but the leading influence was that of Anton Lembede from 1944 until his death three years later. He wanted blacks to be proud of being black, rejected co-operation with whites and wanted Africans to win liberty by their own efforts. It was largely due to Lembede that the ANC adopted a Programme of Action in 1949 (the **National Party** had come to power in 1948, pledged to apartheid) which committed it to strikes, boycotts and civil disobedience.

**Afrikaners.** A name applied in the twentieth century to white South Africans whose language is Afrikaans. In the nineteenth century they were often called Boers (Afrikaans, 'farmers'). They were descendants of mainly Dutch, but also French and German, immigrants. Calvinists, they believed that they were God's chosen people, superior to Africans, and sought to maintain their identity by a deep devotion to the Dutch Reformed Church and by adherence to their language, Afrikaans. Some sought to escape British rule in the **Great Trek** in the 1830s and formed the independent republics of the Orange Free State and Transvaal in the interior. They fought against Britain in the **South African Wars** of 1881 and 1899–1902. In the twentieth century they have formed between 54 and 58 per cent of the white population and have been a dominant influence in South African politics since the Union of 1910.

**Aga Khan, Sultan Muhammad Shah** (1877–1957). (Turkish *aga*, 'master' and *khan*, 'ruler'.) Aga Khan is the title held by leaders of the eastern branch of the Ismaili sect of Shiite Muslims. The first Aga Khan (d. 1881) fled to Sind after leading an unsuccessful revolution against the **Qajars** in Iran in 1838. The third Aga Khan, Sultan Muhammad Shah, played a crucial role in Muslim politics in India. He was closely associated with the Aligarh movement of **Sayyid Ahmad Khan**, and was co-founder of the **Muslim League** and its first President (1906–13). There was, he wrote, no hope 'of a fair deal for us [Muslims] within the fold of the Congress Party or in alliance with it . . . we asked that the Muslims of India should not be regarded as a mere minority but as a nation within a nation'. He resigned from the presidency because he disapproved of what he saw as the League drawing closer to the mainly Hindu **Indian National Congress**. When the Congress boycotted the Simon Commission in 1928 as there was no Indian representative on it, he returned to political life, demanding separate electorates for Muslims and Hindus and rejecting the Nehru Report, with its demand for a strong central government. 'Each Indian province', he declared, 'should have the freedom to proclaim independence.' He was the leading Muslim delegate to the Round Table Conference (1930–32), whose discussions resulted in the **India Act** of 1935. An Anglophile, the Aga Khan was best known in England for breeding racehorses, five of which won the Derby. The British government made him India's representative to the Disarmament Conference in

1932, and to the Assembly of the **League of Nations** (1932, 1934–7), of which he was President in 1937. He then retired from politics, spending most of his time in Europe, where he died in 1957.

**Al-Afghani, Jamal al-Din** (1839–97). Islamic reformer. A Persian Shiite by birth, he claimed to be an Afghan Sunni (hence his name) so that he could appeal to the majority of Muslims. He saw Islam as a rational religion: the Quran should be interpreted according to reason and was open to reinterpretation by individuals in every age. Deploring the passivity and resignation of Muslims, he wanted a dynamic and secular approach to the problems of the age and has been regarded by some as an agnostic. 'The centre of attention', he wrote, 'is no longer Islam as a religion; it is rather Islam as a civilization.' Al-Afghani wanted all Muslims to unite in a Pan-Islamic movement to resist European expansion, but he realized that this idea was too abstract to be popular, so he emphasized loyalty to one's homeland and the danger of adopting a foreign language and culture. His revolutionary methods, including assassination of despots, made it impossible for him to stay in one place for long. From 1871–9 he was in Egypt, where his followers included Muhammad **Abduh** and Saad **Zaghlul**. Expelled from Egypt, he went to India, France and Persia, where he became an adviser to the Shah, before he was forced to leave in 1891 for organizing popular opposition to the Shah's granting of economic concessions to Europeans. **Abdulhamid** then invited him to Istanbul, where he was a virtual prisoner of the Sultan, though he was still able to arrange for the assassination of the Persian Shah who had expelled him. Al-Afghani influenced Muslims in North Africa, Central Asia. Turkey and India and directly inspired the revolt of **Urabi Pasha** in Egypt in 1882. He spread an active and secular attitude to politics, which prepared the way for the rise of Arab nationalism.

**Alamein, El, battles of** (1–26 July and 23 October–4 November 1942). Decisive battles of the **North African Campaigns** between the German *Afrika Korps* and Italian forces on the one side, and the British and Commonwealth Eighth Army on the other. In the spring and summer of 1942 British forces had been driven back by **Rommel** from Gazala in Cyrenaica to El Alamein in Egypt, where defensive lines had been prepared. This was the only place in the western desert where the line could not be outflanked, as there was the sea in the north and the Qattara Depression in the south, a salt marsh below sea level at the bottom of cliffs. General Auchinleck, British Commander-in-Chief, Middle East, took over personal command on 23 June, as he found that the Eighth Army faced 'complete catastrophe' with Rommel's forces poised to advance to Cairo and the Suez Canal. In the first battle of Alamein Rommel tried to break through Auchinleck's centre and then envelop his wings, but he was halted by heavy fire on his flanks. Auchinleck counter-attacked on 9 July against Italian forces to the west, so that Rommel had to abandon his own offensive to help the Italians. In one sector after another Auchinleck attacked Italian units, so that Rommel had to use up his last German reserves to prevent the collapse of his front. Rommel had been halted and Egypt saved, but Auchinleck failed in his attempt to force the Germans to retreat, as the attacks of his infantry and armour were not coordinated. In August, Lieutenant-General **Montgomery** was put in charge of the Eighth Army and foiled a second attempt of Rommel to break through the British lines at Alam Halfa (31 August–3 September). Rommel, with his supply lines overstretched and unlikely to receive further supplies owing to allied control of the Mediterranean, was no longer able to mount another offensive. By October 1942 Montgomery greatly outnumbered Rommel in troops, tanks, anti-tank guns and aircraft. On 23 October the third battle of Alamein began with a British artillery barrage on a six-mile front from the sea inland. Rommel, who was in Germany recovering from exhaustion, flew back on 25 October to resume command, but there was little he could do. The battle raged for a week, with Montgomery skilfully probing the German lines so that their fuel, reserves and ammunition were used up. On 2 November a corridor was cleared through the German minefields for British armour to move through. With only thirty-five tanks left Rommel had to retreat, abandoning his Italian allies but extricating some of the *Afrika Korps*, as Montgomery was slow in following up. Rommel had lost most of his tanks and 59,000 men, many of whom were captured: the Eighth Army had 13,000 casualties and had 432 of its tanks knocked out. These battles prevented **Axis** forces overrunning Egypt and the Suez Canal, and were the first serious defeats the German army had suffered outside Russia. They began a German retreat which ended 1,500 miles later in Tunisia.

**Alaska, purchase of** (1867). Alaska had been discovered in 1741 by Vitus Bering, a Dane employed by the Russians. They were more interested in exploiting the fur trade than in settlement, but the fur trade declined in the mid-nineteenth century. At the same time Russia's defeat in the **Crimean War** made her aware that Alaska could not be defended against English or American attack, so she sold it to the United States for 7.2 million dollars, a sale widely condemned there as the territory was regarded as a barren waste.

**Albert** (1819–61). Prince Consort of England and Ireland, husband of Queen **Victoria** and father of **Edward VII**. A son of the Duke of Saxe-Coburg-Gotha, Albert married his cousin Victoria in 1840. He was never given a British peerage and became Prince Consort only in 1857. Although the Queen adored him, he was never popular with the public in England (he remained, in his own words, 'a true German') or with the Queen's ministers, who resented his interference in their affairs. When **Melbourne** retired in 1841, Albert became the Queen's confidential adviser, drafting her letters and seeing ministers with her or on his own. Albert had very ambitious and unrealistic plans for the monarchy: he wanted it to control the government and play a major part in running the country, and was on particularly bad terms with **Palmerston**, who refused to allow him to decide what English foreign policy should be. Yet Albert was the most gifted, well-educated and humane member of the royal family in the nineteenth century. He had a discerning interest in the arts, designed Osborne House on the Isle of Wight, patronized Winterhalter and Landseer, collected early German and Italian paintings and was an accomplished musician. The Prince Consort was also interested in the sciences and industry and was chairman of the commission that planned the **Great Exhibition** of 1851. When he died after four years of illness, probably from stomach cancer, Victoria was distraught and withdrew from public life.

**Alexander I** (1777–1825). Tsar of Russia (1801–25). Alexander was a son of the mad Tsar Paul and was implicated in his murder.

He had been educated by a Swiss tutor who was sympathetic to the ideas of the **French Revolution**, so many expected Alexander to be a reformer. As late as 1818 he hinted at radical reform when he told the Polish Diet that he hoped 'to extend free institutions to all countries under my care'. Yet Alexander did not have the determination to push through serious reforms. He was attracted by new ideas but soon lost interest in them. Little was done for the serfs, as Alexander felt that to emancipate them would be a leap in the dark, which might destroy the foundations of Russian society and the autocracy too. Though there were some hesitant improvements in higher education (more universities and secondary schools), elementary education was neglected and it is unlikely that more than 2–3 per cent of Russians were literate during his reign. His achievements as a social or political reformer were negligible.

Alexander took part in the struggle against **Napoleon Bonaparte** but after defeats at **Austerlitz** and Friedland he made peace at **Tilsit** in 1807. He was compelled to join Napoleon's **Continental Blockade**, which adversely affected the Russian economy as it ended exports to Britain. However, he was given a free hand in the north and the south: he seized Finland from Sweden and **Bessarabia** from Turkey, and after a long war with Persia acquired a large area between the Black and Caspian seas, which was later to be valuable for its oil. After Alexander withdrew from the Continental Blockade Napoleon invaded Russia in 1812, won a Pyrrhic victory at the battle of **Borodino** and captured a deserted Moscow. Napoleon expected Alexander to make peace but he refused, so Napoleon had to retreat to avoid being cut off from his sources of supply by the Russian winter. Alexander, against the advice of many of his generals, decided to pursue him beyond Russia's border and took part in the Allied victory at **Leipzig**. After Napoleon's defeat, Alexander was a dominant figure at the Congress of **Vienna**, at which Russia obtained most of Poland; Russia's frontiers in the west were to remain the same until 1914, except for some changes in Bessarabia. Alexander was determined to crush popular revolutions against legitimate monarchs and offered to send Russian troops to subdue risings in Spain and Italy in 1820–21. France and Austria declined his offer but crushed the risings themselves. During the **Greek War of Independence** he was torn between his sympathy for the Greeks as Orthodox Christians and his dislike of rebels. In the end he condemned the Greek rebellion, though this made him unpopular at home. Alexander often spoke about his intention to abdicate and spent many hours in religious contemplation. He reputedly died in 1825 whilst visiting the Crimea, although there were rumours that he had gone to Siberia and become a hermit. To disprove these rumours his coffin was opened in 1865: it was empty. All this seemed to confirm Pushkin's assessment of him as 'the sphinx who took his riddle with him to the grave'.

**Alexander II** (1818–81). Tsar of Russia (1855–81). The eldest son of **Nicholas I**. The reforms of Alexander were the only significant ones to be carried out in Russia in the whole of the nineteenth century. This is at first sight surprising, as Alexander showed his father's liking for autocracy and had no intention of allowing any of his powers to pass to a popularly elected parliamentary assembly. Alexander did not have the drive or conviction of a reformer and seldom took the initiative. It was not always clear what his personal views were, as he kept in office for years, and at the same time, men with opposing views, such as the liberal Milyutin (Minister of War 1861–87) and the reactionary Tolstoy (Minister of Education 1866–80). Why then were there so many reforms? The main reason was the disastrous **Crimean War**, which destroyed the myth of Russia being a great military power and showed just how backward her serf-based economy was. The reforms began in 1861 with the **emancipation of the serfs** but this necessitated other changes, as the structure of local government, the army and the judicial system had all been based on **serfdom**. *Zemstva* were therefore set up to provide local government. The corrupt, expensive and ponderous courts were swept away. New courts at the local level were run by Justices of the Peace and provided cheap, quick and impartial justice. At higher-level courts judges were well trained and paid, juries were introduced and trials were held in public. This was one of the most successful of the Great Reforms and lasted as long as the Tsarist regime. Milyutin improved the efficiency of the army, provided army schools to make recruits literate and in 1874 introduced conscription. Service in the army had previously been for twenty-five years: this was now reduced to six years, with nine in the reserves. Great advances in education were made at all levels when Golovnin was Minister of Education (1861–6). Secondary education was opened to all classes, and the percentage of commoners in secondary education increased from 18 per cent in 1853 to 44 per cent in 1885. 80 per cent of these students went on to universities, which became self-governing. In Finland, Alexander ruled with the advice and consent of the elected Diet, the only part of his Empire where he was prepared to do so. This was in marked contrast to the repression in Poland which followed the revolt of 1863.

The reign of Alexander saw the beginning of Russia's economic expansion. **Railways** were the key to economic advance as they stimulated growth in the coal, iron and engineering industries. In 1855 Russia had 660 miles of railways; by 1881 there were 14,000 miles. Manufacturing and grain-producing areas were linked to the major ports such as Odessa, to facilitate trade with Western Europe. The iron industry developed in the Ukraine, the coal industry in the Donetz basin and oil production began in the Caucasus. Banking was expanded and for the first time there was a central treasury and a budget.

During the Crimean War Alexander turned against Austria: he felt that Austria had betrayed him and so Russia helped to ease Prussia's path in uniting Germany. He also took advantage of the **Franco-Prussian War** to repudiate the Black Sea clauses of the Congress of **Paris**. Alexander became involved in a war with Turkey in 1877 and made substantial gains at the Treaty of **San Stefano** in 1878, though many of these had to be given up at the **Berlin Congress**. In contrast to his limited successes in Europe, Alexander extended Russia's frontiers considerably in Asia and at last pacified territory she had earlier acquired in the Caucasus. Russia took advantage of China's weakness during the **Taiping rebellion** to seize the Amur–Ussuri region, which greatly extended her Pacific coastline. China was forced to accept these changes at the Treaty of Beijing in 1860. Russia advanced remorselessly in **Central Asia**, south and east of the Aral Sea, conquering the great Muslim cities of Samarkand (1868), Khiva (1873) and Bukhara (1876). Her conquests took her to the borders of Afghanistan. This worried Britain greatly, as she saw these Russian advances as a threat to her position in India. The expansion under Alexander made Russia one of the great imperial powers of the nineteenth century. The only territory that Russia gave up was **Alaska**, sold to the United States in 1867.

Alexander's reforms and successes abroad did not end discontent. The Populist movement grew (see **Populists**) and, after its failure to appeal to the peasants, turned to terrorism. The organization 'Land and Liberty' was formed in 1876, and five years later Alexander was assassinated.

**Alexander III** (1845–94). Tsar of Russia (1881–94). Alexander was an impressive figure, a giant of a man with enormous self-confidence. He disapproved of his father **Alexander II**'s reforms, as he felt they had weakened the monarchy, so there was to be no further dabbling with liberal ideas. His reign was, therefore, a period of reaction, in which he not only rejected further reform but did his best to limit the effectiveness of many reforms which had taken place earlier. His tutor, **Pobedonostsev**, confirmed his prejudices and regarded democracy as 'the biggest lie of our time'. The 'counter-reforms', designed to tighten the grip of the government, began in 1881 with the 'temporary regulations', which were never repealed. These gave officials the right of arbitrary arrest if public order was threatened. This could be followed by imprisonment, exile or trial by court martial. The universities, which had been granted self-government in 1862, were brought under government control in 1884. Owing to continued peasant unrest, land-captains were appointed from the local nobility to control all peasant self-government. The position of nobles in the *zemstva* was also strengthened. There was persecution of those who were not members of the Orthodox Church and **pogroms** against the Jews. Alexander fervently believed in **Russification** and imposed Russian as the only language of instruction in schools throughout his multinational Empire. Reaction was not total: the poll tax on the peasants was abolished and a Peasant Land Bank set up. Under the Finance Minister **Witte** Russia's industrial boom of the 1890s began, with heavy investment in industry and railways, including the **Trans-Siberian Railway**.

Alexander's foreign policy was cautious, as the **Russo–Turkish**

**War** of 1877–8 had ruined Russia's finances and there was fear that another war would lead to revolution at home. Yet Russia almost went to war with Austria-Hungary. Bulgaria owed its existence as a state to Russia's defeat of Turkey but refused to act as a Russian satellite and in 1887 elected Ferdinand of Saxe-Coburg, who had served in the Hungarian army, as its ruler. **Bismarck** forced both Austria-Hungary and Russia to keep the peace by publishing the terms of the **Dual Alliance**. After Bismarck's fall in 1890 German policy became more anti-Russian, so Alexander moved towards France and concluded the **Franco-Russian Alliance** in 1894.

**Algeciras Conference,** see **Moroccan crisis** (1905–6)

**Allenby, Edward Henry Hynman, 1st Viscount** (1861–1936). British field marshal. Known from his violent temper and physique as 'The Bull', he gained a reputation as a cavalry leader in the **South African War** of 1899–1902. On the Western Front during the **First World War** his greatest achievement was at Arras (April 1917), when his Third Army advanced three and a half miles on the first day, further than any other army since **trench warfare** began at the end of 1914. In June 1917 he was sent to Palestine as Commander of the Egyptian Expeditionary Force. He broke through the Turkish lines at Gaza and was in Jerusalem by Christmas. The British government wanted him to advance north and knock the Turks out of the war, but in March 1918 the **Ludendorff offensive** began in France, and Allenby had to send some of his troops there. He was not able to resume his advance until September, when many of his British troops had been replaced by Indians. Allenby had far better artillery, cavalry and aircraft than the Turks and was assisted by an Arab revolt in the Hejaz, organized by British officers such as T. E. **Lawrence**. He defeated the Turks at Megiddo, occupied Damascus and advanced 360 miles in thirty-eight days, destroying three Turkish armies before the Turks signed an armistice on 30 October 1918. From 1919–25 Allenby was British High Commissioner in Egypt, where he showed great statesmanship. When there was a violent nationalist revolt against the British, who had declared Egypt a Protectorate, he persuaded the Foreign Office to release the main nationalist leader, Saad **Zaghlul**, from internment in Malta. He soon realized that the Protectorate could not be maintained and convinced the British government that it should be abolished. In 1922 Britain issued a declaration which recognized Egypt as 'an independent sovereign state' but retained for Britain control of the Suez Canal, the right to keep troops in the Canal Zone and the condominium in the Sudan.

**Alphonso XIII** (1886–1941). King of Spain (1902–31). From 1886 until 1902, Alphonso's mother, the Austrian Archduchess María Cristina of Habsburg (1858–1929), acted as Regent. The loss in 1898 of the final remnants of Spain's empire to the United States in the **Spanish–American War** created a cry for the 'regeneration' of a 'decadent' nation. The failure of Alphonso XIII to resolve the prolonged political crisis triggered off by the 'Disaster of 1898' eventually resulted in the loss of his throne in 1931. From the beginning of his reign, Alphonso displayed a marked taste for political intrigue and interference. His conservative outlook was partly responsible for the thwarting of liberal reform efforts prior to the **First World War**. He was a devout defender of the Catholic Church, though his greatest affection and interest was reserved for the army. In 1909 the King forced the resignation of Prime Minister Antonio **Maura**, after the call-up of military reserves in Barcelona for the Moroccan War led to the rioting and brutal repression of the 'Tragic Week'. In so doing, Alphonso disrupted the oligarchical rotation in power of the two monarchist parties that had distinguished the **Restoration system** under both his father and mother. During the crises of 1917 and 1918–21 the King was in constant conflict with the politicians. While becoming increasingly dissatisfied with the constitutional system, he became more and more absorbed by the concerns and outlook of the army. After the catastrophic defeat of the Spanish army at Anual in Morocco in 1921, Alphonso's anti-parliamentary stance became more pronounced. Parliamentary scrutiny of the causes of the defeat at Anual (including the King's own responsibility) helped prompt a *coup d'état* and the establishment of the military dictatorship of **Primo de Rivera** in 1923.

The complicity of the King in the dictatorship severely undermined the monarchy's prestige and legitimacy. Once Primo de Rivera fell from power in 1930, the King was soon abandoned by all sections of Spanish society. Monarchist losses in the municipal elections of April 1931 triggered his departure from Spain and the establishment of the **Spanish Second Republic**. From exile in Italy, Alphonso collaborated with the monarchist opposition within Spain to destabilize the new regime. Although the Republic was destroyed by the **Spanish Civil War** (1936–9), a monarchist restoration was rejected by the nationalist victor, General **Franco**, for a personal dictatorship. Alphonso abdicated in favour of his son, don Juan (1913–93), not long before he died in Rome. Alphonso XIII's personal failings undoubtedly played an important role in the collapse of the monarchy: his love of political intrigue undermined the continuity of government policy, while his closeness to the army militated against the constitutional system. Accordingly, the transition from the oligarchical politics of the Restoration to a democracy was made not by the monarchy but by the Republic.

**Alsace-Lorraine.** Provinces of north-eastern France, west of the Rhine. All of Alsace and most of Lorraine became part of Germany after the **Franco–Prussian War** (1870–71). There was widespread popular demand in Germany for annexation, but strategic considerations probably carried most weight: with memories of French invasions during the **French Revolutionary** and **Napoleonic Wars**, **Bismarck** felt that the provinces would protect Germany. The annexation played a major role in shaping Bismarck's foreign policy: he knew France would seek to recover the provinces at the first opportunity and so spent much of his time trying to keep her isolated. The rich deposits of iron ore and potash in Alsace-Lorraine, combined with a thriving textile industry, contributed greatly to Germany's economic growth, but Germanization was resented. The territories were returned to France in 1919 at the Treaty of **Versailles**, and although they were made part of Germany in 1940, they became French again in 1945.

**American Civil War** (1861–5). The war began because President Abraham **Lincoln**, elected in 1860, was determined to preserve the Union, which was threatened by the issue of slavery. The North was growing rapidly in wealth and population, and it was clear to the Southern slave states that the North would eventually be strong enough to carry a constitutional amendment abolishing slavery. The **Republican Party** had been formed in 1854 partly to oppose slavery, and so Southern leaders decided that when a Republican President was elected, they should secede from the Union. Consequently, when Lincoln became President, seven states seceded, formed the **Confederate States of America** and elected Jefferson **Davis** as their President. On 12 April 1861 Confederates bombarded Fort Sumter in Charleston harbour, one of only two federal properties in the South to remain in Union hands: this marked the start of the Civil War. The North had by far the greater population (twenty-two million compared with the South's nine million, which included three and a half million slaves) and resources, including most of the nation's mineral wealth, manufacturing, grain and shipping. Cotton was the South's one great asset, which it threw away by forbidding its export in 1861 in order to put pressure on Britain, the main importer of American cotton, to recognize and support the Confederate States. Britain did not comply, and found alternative cotton supplies in India and Egypt. The South had little industry and was dependent on imports from Europe, which the North cut off by blockading the coast.

Union forces invaded Virginia, confidently expecting victory, but were defeated at Bull Run (Manassas) on 21 July 1861 in the first major battle of the war. The demoralized troops retreated in disorder to Washington, but the Confederates were too disorganized to follow up their victory. After this disaster Lincoln appointed General McClellan to command the Union forces. He made the Army of the Potomac into a disciplined force but was inactive in the winter of 1861–2. Meanwhile, Ulysses S. **Grant** forced the Confederates to relinquish Kentucky and most of Tennessee. New Orleans, the largest Confederate port, was captured in April 1862, which left only Vicksburg and Port Hudson on the Mississippi in Confederate hands. If they fell, all the states to the west of the Mississippi would be cut off from the rest of the Confederacy. McClellan finally advanced in March 1862 and by the end of May was within five miles of Richmond, the Confederate capital. However, he was pushed back by Robert E. **Lee**, who moved north to defeat a Union army at the second battle of Bull Run in August. Lee then decided to invade the North for the first time, crossed the Potomac and met McClellan at Antietam (Sharpsburg) in September: Lee lost a quarter of his men and had to retreat to Virginia.

In May 1863, Lee won his most brilliant victory when facing an army twice his size at Chancellorsville, but he lost his right-hand man, 'Stonewall' **Jackson**, who was accidentally shot in the twilight by his own men, and died. Lee decided to invade the North for a second time: if he could win a victory he hoped that the war-weary North would end the war. He crossed the Potomac and was invading Pennsylvania when, in July, he came across a Union army at **Gettysburg**. There the greatest battle of the Civil War took place, ending with Lee's defeat. This was a decisive battle – Lee would never again be strong enough to take the offensive. In the same month, Grant captured Vicksburg; a few days later Port Hudson, the last Confederate stronghold on the Mississippi, fell. Union armies had gained control of the whole river and had split the Confederacy in two.

The Confederate cause was now hopeless, though Lee fought brilliantly a series of defensive battles against Grant in the woods of Virginia in 1864. He was gradually forced back to Petersburg, south of Richmond: if Grant kept up the pressure he was doomed. When **Sherman** captured Atlanta in September 1864, the way was open for him to split the Confederacy yet again. Sherman moved south into Georgia, destroying everything in his path, and on 13 December reached the Atlantic. He then swung north, continuing his destruction in the Carolinas, but before he could link up with Grant the war was over. Lee's army, pinned down by Grant at Petersburg, was at breaking-point by April 1865. Lee evacuated Petersburg and Richmond to avoid being surrounded, and on 9 April surrendered to Grant at Appomattox in southern Virginia. The war ended when the remaining Confederate army surrendered to Sherman on 26 April. Lincoln, however, was not to enjoy the peace, as he was assassinated on 14 April 1865 in a Washington theatre.

The Civil War was the most destructive war of the years between the **Napoleonic Wars** and the **First World War**: there were a million casualties, of whom 650,000 died, whilst much of the South was devastated. The beneficial results were that slavery was abolished and the Union preserved. The United States would be one nation, in which sovereignty lay with the federal government and not with the states.

**American Federation of Labor** (AFL). Founded in 1881 by craft unions, the AFL was reorganized in 1886. It was a loose federation of national unions, each of which had considerable autonomy, rather than a large, centrally controlled union. It consisted of skilled workers and had purely economic aims: to improve wages, hours and conditions of work. It rejected **socialism** as 'un-American' and did not seek political reforms. From 1886 until his death in 1924 it was dominated by its first President, Samuel **Gompers**. The AFL was prepared to use strikes to achieve its aims but was not a militant organization and was never a threat to the capitalist system, which it accepted. During the **Great Depression** and the **New Deal** public opinion increasingly favoured labour unions. There was a great opportunity to organize the unskilled and the semi-skilled in the mass-production industries, but the AFL made little attempt to do so. Hostility between craft unions organized according to trade, and 'vertical' unions organized according to industry, split the union in 1935, when John L. **Lewis**, President of the United Mineworkers, formed the Committee (later Congress) of Industrial Organizations (CIO), to unionize workers involved in mass production. In 1937 the AFL expelled nine unions which supported Lewis. The split was not healed until 1955, when the AFL and CIO merged with a total of fifteen million members.

**Amiens, peace of** (March 1802), provided an interlude in the **Napoleonic Wars** between France and Britain. The British, war-weary and heavily taxed, made a peace in which nearly all their overseas conquests were to be handed back, including the West Indian sugar islands of Martinique and Guadeloupe to France, Tobago to Spain and the Cape of Good Hope to the Dutch. Malta, Britain's only base in the eastern Mediterranean, was also to be given up. Britain retained only Spanish Trinidad and Dutch Ceylon. In Europe France's effective control of northern Italy, Holland and Spain was accepted. **Canning** condemned 'the gross faults and omissions, the weakness . . . and stupidity that mark this treaty'. The peace could not last, particularly when **Napoleon Bonaparte** refused to allow British manufactured goods into the areas of Europe under his control. When a British ultimatum that France should evacuate Holland and Switzerland and recognize British control of Malta was rejected, war was resumed in May 1803.

**Amritsar massacre** (13 April 1919). The government of India chose to retain its special wartime powers of press censorship and imprisonment without trial by passing the Rowlatt Acts in 1919. The resulting protests in the Punjab led to the imposition in Amritsar of martial law, which forbade large gatherings. An unarmed crowd of about 10,000, led by local political leaders, decided to ignore this and met in the walled area of Jallianwallah Bagh, which had only four or five narrow entrances, each three or four feet wide. General Dyer marched his fifty Gurkha and Baluchi troops into the Bagh and, without warning, ordered them to fire at point-blank range on the men, women and children amassed there. People were unable to escape through the crowded exits, and 1,650 rounds were fired in ten minutes. Firing stopped only when the ammunition ran out. According to official figures, 379 people were killed and nearly 1,000 wounded. Dyer admitted during the court of inquiry that he was not trying to restore order but to 'teach the crowd a lesson'. The Indian government forced him to resign but he was treated as a hero in Britain; he received an address from the House of Lords, was presented with a jewelled sword inscribed to the 'Saviour of the Punjab', whilst most newspapers took the view that his action was justified because of 'revolt' in the Punjab. All this shocked Indian opinion almost as much as the massacre itself. The freedom movement in India received a great boost; millions of Indians who had been loyal supporters of the **Raj** became nationalists. **Gandhi** declared that 'cooperation in any shape or form with this satanic government is sinful' and began his **non-cooperation movement**. 'Plassey', he said, 'laid the foundations of the British Empire; Amritsar has shaken it.'

**Anarchism** (from the Greek *anarkhia*, 'absence of rule'). The basis of all anarchist thought lies in Rousseau's 'Man is born free but is everywhere in chains.' This is, he thought, because man's natural goodness has been corrupted by the institutions of the state. Anarchism rejects the state and all forms of coercive authority – Churches, armies, bureaucracies – and seeks the destruction of the state, which will be replaced by a society in which all are treated equally and cooperate voluntarily with each other. The state is regarded as a repressive institution which allows a small ruling class to exploit the vast majority of citizens. The first to call himself an anarchist was **Proudhon**, who wanted peaceful change, but it was with **Bakunin**, who supported violent revolution, that anarchism became the most serious rival of **Marxism**. This rivalry reached its peak from 1869–72, when **Marx**'s and Bakunin's followers fought for control of the First International, and ended with the International breaking up. Marx wanted to replace capitalism with a classless society, but first there would be a transitional revolutionary state of the dictatorship of the proletariat. Bakunin wanted the destruction of the state from the very beginning, along with capitalism, as any state would become a source of privilege and oppression. A socialist state, which controlled all economic life, would, he maintained, be the most oppressive of all. Because of their attitude to the state, anarchists opposed all attempts to reform society through parliament, though all their attempts to use other methods ended in failure. In the 1880s and 1890s they tried 'propaganda by the deed': individual acts of terror and murder. Between 1893 and 1901 President Carnot of France, **Cánovas**, the Prime Minister of Spain, Empress Elizabeth of Austria-Hungary, King Umberto of Italy and President **McKinley** of the USA were assassinated. Yet these isolated incidents never threatened any government and were supported by only a small minority of anarchists. A more effective form of action, which involved the working class directly, was to ally with **syndicalism**. Anarcho-syndicalism looked to the trade unions to lead the revolutionary struggle by calling a general strike. Anarchists had a prominent role in the French trade-union federation **CGT** (*Confédération Générale du Travail*), but they failed to bring about a general strike. Its Spanish equivalent, the **CNT** (*Confederación Nacional de Trabajo*), was more successful, particularly during the **Spanish Second Republic** (1931–6) and the **Spanish Civil War** (1936–9), the only occasion when anarchists were able to put into practice their communal, anti-authoritarian ideas. Many factories and villages were collectivized with some success. Since **Franco**'s victory there have been no large-scale anarchist organizations.

**Anderson, Elizabeth Garrett** (1836–1917). English physician. As medical schools would not accept women students. Elizabeth

Anderson studied medicine with private tutors and in 1865 passed the examination of the Society of Apothecaries, thus qualifying as a doctor. She gained an MD from the Sorbonne in 1870, opened the New Hospital for Women in London in 1872 and was the first woman to be elected to the British Medical Association. From 1875–97 she was a lecturer at the London School of Medicine for Women, which in 1902 became a college of London University, thus ensuring the future training of women doctors. To overcome the hostility of male doctors Anderson needed great courage and determination, qualities she showed in her other activities. She was the first woman to be elected to the London School Board in 1871, supported the moderate suffragist movement led by her sister Millicent Fawcett and in 1908 followed her father and husband in becoming mayor of Aldeburgh, the first woman mayor in Britain.

**Andrássy, Gyula, Count** (1823–90). Hungarian statesman. A member of the radical reform party under **Kossuth**, he entered the Hungarian **Diet** in 1847 and in the **Revolutions of 1848** fought against Austria. On Hungary's defeat he fled into exile and was condemned to death in his absence, but took advantage of an amnesty in 1857 and returned to Hungary. He supported Deák in the negotiations leading to the *Ausgleich* (1867) and was the first Hungarian Prime Minister (1867–78) in the Dual Monarchy. From 1871–9 he was Austro-Hungarian Foreign Minister. A great admirer of **Bismarck**, he regarded Russia, the patron of the Orthodox Slavs, as the real enemy and wanted to preserve the **Ottoman Empire** to prevent Russia's expansion. He insisted on Austro-Hungarian neutrality during the **Franco-Prussian War** (1870–71) and saw the future of the monarchy in its economic penetration of the Balkans. When Russia greatly extended her influence in the Balkans at the Treaty of **San Stefano** (1878), Andrássy persuaded Britain and Germany to revise this treaty and reduce Russia's gains at the **Berlin Congress** (1878). Emperor **Francis Joseph** wanted to annex Bosnia-Hercegovina, to prevent it joining Serbia at some future date, but Andrássy was more cautious and settled for military occupation, as he did not want to add more Slavs to the Habsburg Empire. His last service to the Empire was to negotiate the **Dual**

**Alliance** (1879) with Germany on terms favourable to Austria-Hungary: Germany would come to the aid of the **Dual Monarchy** if it was attacked by Russia but Austria-Hungary was not obliged to support Germany if she was attacked by France. This alliance was renewed regularly and was the keystone of Austro-Hungarian foreign policy until 1918.

**Anglo-Afghan Wars** (1838–42, 1878–80, 1919). Britain feared Russia's southern expansion as a threat to India and was determined to keep Afghanistan out of Russian control. She wanted a friendly Afghan state under a puppet ruler and tried to impose one in 1838. **East India Company** (EIC) troops occupied Kabul, the Afghan capital, and replaced the ruler Dost Mohammad with Shah Shuja, who had lived in India for thirty years. In 1840 Dost Mohammad surrendered, but it soon became clear that Shah Shuja did not have the support to rule effectively, so an early British withdrawal was impossible. In 1841 the Afghan army rebelled and forced the Company army of 16,500 to begin the perilous retreat to Peshawar, in which all but one soldier perished. The Company then sent an army of retribution, which defeated the Afghans and reached Kabul before withdrawing. Dost Mohammad was released and reoccupied his throne. After four disastrous and costly years, in which British prestige suffered severely, the EIC left Afghanistan as they found it.

The second war too was fought to exclude Russian influence, after **Alexander II** had made extensive gains in **Central Asia** by defeating the Muslim khanates of Bukhara, Khiva and Samarkand. The British demanded that the Afghan ruler should sever all communications with Russia and accept a British Resident (adviser) in Kabul. When the British declared war in 1878 the Afghans appealed to Russia for help, but she did not wish to become involved, having just ended a war with Turkey (1877–8), which had left her almost bankrupt. Four British armies invaded Afghanistan, occupied Kabul and imposed the Treaty of Gandamak (1879), by which Britain gained control of the Khyber Pass: the Afghans accepted a British Resident in Kabul and gave the government of British India control of their foreign policy. Once again there was a rising in Kabul, in which British officials and the garrison at the residency were massacred. The British struck back and under Sir Frederick (later Lord)

Roberts defeated the Afghans at Kandahār in 1880; but it was clear that the guerrilla tactics of the tribesmen made close control of Afghanistan impossible, so peace was hastily made. In 1919, the third Anglo-Afghan War broke out after Afghanistan threw off the remains of British control and declared her independence. The British had far superior military forces but were preoccupied with nationalist agitation in India and so made peace at Rawalpindi, accepting Afghanistan as a completely independent, sovereign state.

**Anglo-American War** (1812–14). During the **Napoleonic Wars** Napoleon forbade neutral ships to trade with Britain, who responded with Orders in Council which prohibited neutral trade with France. In enforcing the Orders the British behaved arrogantly in stopping American ships, seizing their cargoes and press-ganging over 5,000 American sailors to serve in the British navy. The British were also accused of inciting Indians in the north-west to murder American settlers. The Americans did all they could to avoid war but British provocations continued, so that John Quincy **Adams** concluded that the only alternative to war was 'the abandonment of our right as an independent nation'. The War Hawks, led by Henry **Clay**, Speaker of the House of Representatives, persuaded Congress to declare war on Britain in June 1812. Only four days later the British suspended the Orders in Council, so the main reason for the war disappeared. It continued because Britain would not renounce the principle of impressment. Both sides were unprepared for war. The USA had only 6,700 troops, no ships of the line and almost no money. Britain had only 4,500 troops guarding the long Canadian frontier and few reserves (Canada had a population of half a million, the USA of seven and a half million). Jefferson thought that Canada would be easy prey and that its conquest would be 'a mere matter of marching'. However, the USA was deeply split by the war: nearly all **Republicans** in Congress backed it, but not one **Federalist**. The South and West supported the war; most of New England was against it, and some New Englanders even talked of secession. When President **Madison** wanted to use the New England militia to invade Canada, they refused and condemned 'Mr Madison's war'. Throughout the war most New England states never called up their militias and continued to trade with the British in Canada.

The war lasted two and a half years and did not go well for either side. Two US invasions of Canada failed, though a victory on Lake Erie in 1813 gave America command of the Great Lakes. In the same year General Harrison defeated the British and their Indian allies at the battle of the Thames in Upper Canada and secured north-west America from invasion. At sea, American privateers captured 1,300 British ships, but by 1814 the Royal Navy had tightly blockaded the US coast. When the Napoleonic Wars were over and the British could send reinforcements to Canada, the Americans were forced on to the defensive. In June 1814 a British force landed in Chesapeake Bay, moved north to Washington and set fire to the Capitol and other public buildings, in retaliation for the burning of public buildings in York (Toronto) by the Americans in 1813. (When the President's residence was rebuilt it was painted white and has been known as the White House ever since.) After this the British withdrew but prepared an assault on New Orleans. There, on 8 January 1815, they were crushingly defeated by Andrew **Jackson** – the British lost 2,000 troops, the Americans thirteen – though by this time the war was over. Peace had been made at Ghent on 24 December 1814: neither side lost any territory.

For England the war had been nothing more than an irritation. For Americans it was much more important: it was the only time since independence that the USA had been invaded. The war roused American nationalism and produced 'The Star-Spangled Banner', which Francis Scott Key, a Washington lawyer, composed whilst watching the British bombard Baltimore. The song was immediately successful, although it did not become the American national anthem until 1931. During the war Jackson defeated the Creeks at Horseshoe Bend in 1814, destroying Indian power east of the Mississippi and easing the way for white settlement.

**Anglo-Burmese Wars** (1824–6, 1852, 1885). The first war began when two advancing empires clashed. The Burmese had extended their control over Arakan and were preparing to invade Bengal. The **East India Company** (EIC), having defeated the Marathas in 1818, wanted to secure its eastern frontier and in 1824 invaded

Burma. Progress was slow owing to ignorance of the topography, poor communications and incompetent leadership. Out of 40,000 Company troops 14,000 were killed and 18,000 died of disease, so this became one of the most expensive Company wars. After its hard-won victory, the Company acquired Arakan and Tenasserim, territories recently conquered by the Burmese and centres of flourishing trade. The second Anglo-Burmese War occurred in 1852 when the Governor-General of India, Lord **Dalhousie**, accused the Burmese of maltreating British merchants. This time the war was short – Pegu (Rangoon and the Irrawaddy delta) was annexed, so that the EIC now controlled the whole coast and sea-trade of Burma. Upper Burma depended on the trade of Pegu, which had fertile soil and was rich in resources, especially teak, so the end of Burmese independence was in sight. It took place when the French began to secure a foothold in Upper Burma from their new base in Indo-China. The British countered this threat by conquering Upper Burma in ten days in 1885 and adding it to British India, though it took five years and an army of 40,000 to pacify the north.

**Anglo-French Entente** (*Entente Cordiale*) (1904). There had been friction between France and Britain since 1882, when Britain occupied Egypt, and this had almost led to war at **Fashoda** on the Nile in 1898. Britain had regarded France and Russia as its main rivals but this changed when **Tirpitz** began building a large German navy which could be aimed only at Britain. The need now was to end Anglo-French colonial rivalry and this was achieved by the French and British Foreign Ministers, **Delcassé** and Lansdowne. The Entente was a settling of colonial differences, particularly the recognition by France of Britain's dominant position in Egypt and by Britain of France's pre-eminence in Morocco. Siam (Thailand) was accepted as an independent buffer state between French Indo-China and British Burma; British claims to Madagascar were abandoned and the New Hebrides were put under a joint administration. Although the Entente was not an alliance, it was seen as an anti-German move. German attempts to break it up in the **Moroccan crisis** of 1905–6 failed and led to closer cooperation between Britain and France.

**Anglo-German agreement** (1890). An attempt by Germany to bring Britain closer to the **Triple Alliance**. Britain gave Germany the island of Heligoland in the North Sea, which she had seized from Denmark during the **Napoleonic Wars**, and a small strip of territory which gave German South-West Africa (present-day Namibia) access to the Zambezi river. In return, Germany recognized a British protectorate over Zanzibar, an island off the east coast of Africa, and accepted British claims to vast territories in East Africa, which gave her possession of the sources of the Nile and access to them from the coast.

**Anglo-German naval agreement** (1935). The British government had decided that the Royal Navy could not fight Japan and a strong European fleet at the same time, and did not want a naval race with Germany like the one before 1914. It therefore invited Germany to naval talks, where it was agreed that Germany could have a navy that was 35 per cent of the strength of the British and Commonwealth navies, and equal in numbers of submarines. As Germany did not intend to build a bigger fleet than this, Britain was allowing her to break the disarmament provisions of the Treaty of **Versailles** without gaining anything in return. Britain had not consulted either the **League of Nations** or her **Stresa** partners, France and Italy, before making the agreement, which caused great offence and weakened the Stresa Front shortly after it had been formed.

**Anglo-Irish Treaty** (1921). **Lloyd George** wanted to bring the **Anglo-Irish War** (1919–21) to an end, so he called a conference in London. As **de Valera** refused to attend, the Irish delegation was led by Arthur **Griffith** and Michael **Collins**. Both were prepared to compromise and made an agreement which established an 'Irish Free State', which was to be a self-governing **dominion** within the British Commonwealth. Members of the Irish parliament had to take an oath of allegiance to the British Crown, as it was part of the Commonwealth; the British navy had bases in certain Irish ports; and Northern Ireland could be excluded from the Irish Free State, if it so wished, and retain its status within the United Kingdom. This was not what Irish Republicans had wanted but Griffith saw that it gave the substance of independence and that the only alternative was a renewal of the war. The Dail Eireann (Irish Assembly) accepted the treaty by sixty-four votes to fifty-seven, though de Valera rejected it and so began the **Irish Civil War** (1922–3).

**Anglo-Irish War** (1919–21). In the 1918 elections **Sinn Fein** won seventy-three out of the 105 Irish seats and so could claim to represent Irish opinion. Its members refused to sit in the British parliament in London and set up a Dail Eireann (Irish Assembly) in Dublin. Eamon **de Valera** was elected President and appointed a ministry which claimed to be the government of Ireland. This was bound to lead to a clash with the British government, which ruled Ireland. There were some isolated attacks in 1919 on the Royal Irish Constabulary (RIC) by the Irish Republican Army (**IRA**), led by Michael **Collins**, and more extensive action in 1920. Collins wanted to avoid the mistakes of the **Easter Rising** (1916) and so did not try to hold any particular areas or clash openly with British forces. Instead he used guerrilla tactics, making raids and ambushes with flying columns of fifteen to thirty men, in order to make government impossible and force the British to withdraw. **Lloyd George** did not want to admit there was a war in Ireland, so he relied on police rather than troops to combat the IRA. Many of the RIC resigned, owing to attacks on them and the boycotting (see **Boycott**) of their families, so the British government raised men in England, mainly ex-soldiers. As sufficient police uniforms were not available, they wore khaki uniforms with police caps and belts and so were known as Black and Tans. The IRA could surprise their opponents as they did not wear a uniform, and they executed anyone, irrespective of age or sex, who was suspected of being a police informer. Atrocities were committed by both sides and reached their peak on 21 November 1920, when Collins murdered eleven unarmed British officers in Dublin: later the same day Black and Tans fired into a football crowd, killing twelve. 'The struggles', as they were known, did not spread to the whole of Ireland but were concentrated in Munster and on the Ulster borders. Lloyd George tried to end the conflict by passing the fourth Home Rule Bill (the Government of Ireland Act, 1920 – see **Home Rule for Ireland**), which divided the country into Northern Ireland (or six Ulster counties) and Southern Ireland (the remaining twenty-six counties), each of which was to have its own parliament and responsible ministry, though overall authority remained with the British parliament. The south flatly rejected this Act but it established a division of Ireland which still persists. As the Republicans were coming to the end of their resources and British public opinion strongly demanded peace, Lloyd George called a conference in London in 1921, which negotiated the **Anglo–Irish Treaty** and ended the war.

**Anglo-Japanese Alliance** (1902). Both Britain and Japan were alarmed at Russia's expansion in **Manchuria** and her interest in China. Britain had also become aware of the disadvantages of her 'splendid isolation', as most European powers were hostile to her during the **South African War** (1899–1902). She realized too that her navy was overstretched in trying to dominate all the oceans of the world: a Japanese alliance could enable her to reduce her naval strength in the Far East. The Japanese were divided on whether to make friends with Britain or Russia. **Ito Hirobumi** favoured the latter, as he thought that Britain's 'strength was failing'. However, the Prime Minister Katsura Taro, supported by **Yamagata Aritomo**, felt that a Russian alliance would not last, as Russia would not stop at Manchuria but would 'inevitably extend into Korea' and 'there is bound to be a clash in the end'. In the alliance Britain and Japan agreed that if either was at war with one other power in the Far East, the other would be neutral; but if two or more powers were involved, then Britain and Japan would support each other. The alliance ended Britain's 'splendid isolation' and was regarded as a triumph in Japan, as it put her on an equal footing with the other great powers for the first time. It also enabled her to fight Russia in the **Russo-Japanese War** (1904–5) without the fear that France would support Russia, as France would not want to be involved in a war with Britain. The treaty remained in force until the **Washington Conference** of 1922.

**Anglo-Maori Wars** (1845–72). Polynesians living in New Zealand took the name Maori (meaning 'normal' or 'ordinary') when confronted by European settlers. Maoris welcomed trade with Europeans but resisted settlement on their lands. Attacks on settlers began in the 1840s, and in 1854 a Maori nationalist movement began when different tribes met in Taranaki to coordinate their opposition to the sale of Maori lands: in 1858 they elected a Maori King. Maoris had courage and cunning, knew the land better than the settlers and were well-equipped for guerrilla warfare. 3,000 British troops were used against them before a truce was made in 1861, by which time settler farming had almost ceased in North Island. Sir George **Grey**, brought back as Governor, allowed the confiscation of three million acres of Maori land. The war resumed in 1863 and was prolonged by a new religious movement, *Pai marire* ('goodness and peace'), which gave new hope to the Maoris, combining elements of Christianity and Maori religion and reviving cannibalism. Grey and the British troops were recalled in 1868, so the settler militia carried on the war until it ended in 1872. About one thousand Europeans and friendly Maoris had been killed, and perhaps a further 2,000 Maoris. The wars broke the Maori will to resist, destroyed the authority of their natural leaders and led to the sale of most of their land. Without the land on which they had relied, the Maoris lost their self-respect and became demoralized, an easy prey to the diseases which Europeans brought with them, so that from 1800 to 1896 the Maoris had been reduced in number from 100,000 to 42,000.

**Anglo-Russian Entente** (1907). Throughout the nineteenth century Britain and Russia had been rivals in the Middle East and the Far East, but by 1907 they both wanted to bring their traditional rivalry to an end. Britain was anxious to make an agreement because of the naval race with Germany. Russia was weak after the **Russian Revolution** of 1905 and her defeat in the **Russo-Japanese War**, and wanted to concentrate on internal reform without distractions abroad. Their outstanding colonial disputes were settled in the Anglo-Russian Entente. Most important was the agreement over Persia: Russia was to dominate the north, Britain the south, and there was to be a neutral zone in the middle to separate the two sides. Both powers agreed not to interfere in the internal affairs of Tibet, which was recognized as being under Chinese suzerainty. Afghanistan was to remain under British influence but was not to be annexed. The Entente was not an alliance and did not commit either side to support the other in case of war, but Germany was disturbed, as it appeared to strengthen the **Franco-Russian Alliance** and gave rise to feelings of Germany being 'encircled'.

***Anschluss*** ('connection'). The union of Austria and Germany in 1938. When Germany was united in 1871, German-speaking Austria was excluded from the **German Empire**. After the collapse of the **Austro-Hungarian Empire** at the end of the **First World War**, most Austrians wanted to unite with Germany but they were forbidden by the Treaty of **Versailles**. In 1931 Germany and Austria intended to form a customs union but this was abandoned owing to opposition from France and the **Little Entente**, who rightly regarded it as a first step to *Anschluss*. After **Hitler** came to power in 1933 demands for union increased, and in July 1934 Austrian Nazis staged a ***Putsch***. They seized the Chancellery in Vienna and murdered the Chancellor **Dollfuss**, but the *Putsch* was put down by the Austrian army. **Mussolini** immediately sent troops to the Brenner Pass and told the new Chancellor, Schuschnigg, that he would defend the independence of Austria. This support was withdrawn during the **Ethiopian War** (1935–6), when Mussolini's **Stresa** partners, France and Britain, reluctantly supported **League of Nations** sanctions against Italy. As Hitler did not apply sanctions, Mussolini moved closer to Germany and in November 1936 announced a Rome–Berlin **axis**. In April 1937 he told Schuschnigg that he could no longer undertake to defend Austria. When a Nazi plot to seize power in Austria was discovered, Schuschnigg sought an interview with Hitler, which took place in February 1938. Hitler ranted about the 'intolerable conditions' in Austria and threatened to use force if Schuschnigg did not agree to his demands, which would make Austria a German satellite. Seyss-Inquart, a Nazi supporter, was to be made Minister of the Interior, all Nazi prisoners were to be freed and Austria had to coordinate her economic and foreign policies with those of Germany. Schuschnigg was browbeaten into accepting this ultimatum and Hitler was now convinced that Austria would soon be absorbed by Germany. He had to act more quickly than he expected when Schuschnigg announced that there would be a plebiscite on 13 March 1938 asking Austrians if they wanted their country to be free and independent. As the socialists told their supporters to vote 'Yes', it seemed likely that Schuschnigg would gain a majority, possibly a large one. Hitler could not tolerate such a set-back to his plans, so he told Seyss-Inquart to demand a postponement of the plebiscite. Schuschnigg, already deserted by Italy, turned to France and Britain but they refused to help, so he called off the plebiscite; **Goering** now made a new demand – Seyss-Inquart should replace Schuschnigg as Chancellor. The Austrian President at first refused, then gave way, but by this time Hitler had ordered his troops to invade Austria on 12 March. There was no resistance and Hitler himself received a rapturous reception at Linz. This persuaded him to announce *Anschluss* on 13 March – there was now a German Reich of seventy million people. It was Hitler's greatest triumph so far and greatly increased his prestige, as he had once again success-fully defied Britain and France. There were several important strategic implications of *Anschluss*: Czechoslovakia's western de-fences were outflanked, Germany now had control of the middle-Danube basin and she had a common frontier with Italy, Hungary and Yugoslavia. The Little Entente was dead. A further result of *Anschluss* was that Hitler's confidence grew enormously – he became bolder and more aggressive, as the **Czechoslovakian crisis** later in the year showed.

**Anthony, Susan Brownell** (1820–1906). American feminist. A Quaker, Anthony worked for temperance and anti-slavery move-ments in the 1840s and attended the first women's rights convention at Seneca Falls, New York, in 1848. In 1850 she met Elizabeth Cady **Stanton**, who became her lifelong friend. From 1856–61 she was an agent for the American Anti-Slavery Society, at the same time canvassing for women's suffrage and for the Married Women's Property Act (1861). After the **American Civil War** she concen-trated on votes for women and, from 1868–70, edited *Revolution*, a journal demanding female suffrage and equal educational and em-ployment opportunities for women, and encouraging women to form trade unions. In 1869, with Stanton, she formed the National Woman Suffrage Association, which in 1890 joined with another organization to become the National American Woman Suffrage Association, of which Anthony was President from 1892–1900. For half a century she was a leading figure in the movement for women's rights in the USA and this was recognized when the nineteenth amendment to the Constitution, which gave women the vote in 1920, was called the Anthony Amendment.

**Anthracite coal strike** (1902). Miners in the Pennsylvania coalfields of the USA worked in deplorable conditions and were poorly paid. When the owners rejected claims by the United Mine Workers Union for higher wages, an eight-hour day and recognition of the union, the miners went on strike. The owners responded by closing the mines, refused to go to arbitration and asked for the use of federal troops to break the strike. Public opinion was on the side of the miners, as the strike was orderly and the miners were willing to go to arbitration. President Theodore **Roosevelt** called both sides together in Washington and urged a compromise. The miners' union offered to cooperate but the owners were intransigent. The President, furious at their arrogance, threatened to send federal troops to take over the mines. The miners went back to work in March 1903 and were awarded by the Anthracite Coal Commission a 10 per cent wage increase and a reduction in hours, though not an eight-hour day or recognition of the union. Previous presidents had intervened in labour disputes only to break strikes, as Cleveland had done in the **Pullman strike** of 1894. Roosevelt had intervened to get a negotiated settlement and his prestige rose.

**Anti-clericalism.** Hostility to the influence of the clergy in political and social affairs and a desire to subordinate the Church to the State in non-religious matters. The origins of anti-clericalism lie in the opposition to the Church's wealth and power and to its support for the ruling classes. During the **French Revolution** anti-clericalism was widespread, as the Roman Catholic Church was seen to support the monarchy and the aristocracy. The privileges of the Church were abolished, its land was confiscated and sold, ties with the Pope were cut in the **Civil Constitution of the Clergy** (1790) and in 1793 a **dechristianization** campaign began. In the nineteenth century Liberals attacked the Catholic Church for supporting despotic governments and for opposing scientific thought, particularly when **Pius IX** in the Syllabus of Errors (1864) condemned **liberalism** and **nationalism**. Powerful anti-clerical movements and parties arose which wanted to suppress religious orders, separate Church and State (and thus make the Church dependent financially on the contributions of its members), establish civil marriage and divorce and State control of education. In the **Third Republic** (1870–1940) in France **Ferry** and Combes sought to deprive the Church of its influence in education, whilst the hostility of the Church to **Dreyfus** increased anti-clericalism and led to the separation of Church and State in 1905. The struggle between Church and State in Germany took the form of **Bismarck**'s *Kulturkampf* (cultural struggle) from 1871–8. There was considerable anti-clericalism in Latin America in the nineteenth century, especially in Mexico under **Juárez**. In the twentieth century anti-clericalism has been mainly associated with totalitarian regimes (see **Totalitarianism**), such as those of the Nazis and the Communists. In all communist countries the Church was separated from the State, education was secular, marriage was a civil ceremony and churches were closed down. This movement was most successful in states where the Greek Orthodox Church was established: where Catholicism was strong, as in Poland and Hungary, anti-clericalism made little headway. In Spain the Catholic Church was attacked in the 'Tragic Week' of 1909 in Barcelona, as it was the most visible manifestation of the repressive old regime. The Church's backing for **Franco**'s 'Crusade' against the **Spanish Second Republic** during the **Spanish Civil War** intensified the anti-clericalism of many Republicans. In Britain, anti-clericalism took a different form and was an attack on the official status and privileges of the Church of England, which Nonconformists wished to end: they were successful in obtaining the disestablishment of the Church of Ireland (1869) and Wales (1914), but did not succeed in England.

**Anti-Comintern Pact** (November 1936). Germany and Japan agreed to oppose the activities of the **Comintern**. A secret protocol stated that if either Germany or Japan fought the USSR, the other would end any activities beneficial to the Soviet Union. Italy joined the pact in 1937. This ended Japan's isolation caused by the **Manchurian Incident**. Admiration for Germany's military successes at the beginning of the **Second World War** and fear of American involvement in the **Sino-Japanese War** (1937–45) led to a full alliance with Germany and Italy in the Tripartite Pact (September

1940). This pledged assistance to any signatory attacked by a country which was not currently involved in the European or Chinese wars.

**Anti-Corn Law League.** A movement founded to obtain repeal of the **Corn Laws**, which imposed duties on grain imported into Britain. When food prices rose in the late 1830s, supporters of *laissez-faire* argued that the Corn Laws damaged the economy as they pushed up wages, which were spent on expensive food rather than on manufactured goods. Higher labour costs, it was maintained, made British manufacturers less competitive in world markets. As foreigners exported less corn to Britain owing to the Corn Laws, they could buy fewer manufactures from Britain, thus causing unemployment. Anti-Corn Law associations were formed in several towns in 1838: they joined together to form a national organization in 1839, with Richard **Cobden** as its leader. The Anti-Corn Law League was mainly an urban, middle-class body, opposed to working-class **Chartism**. Unlike Chartism it was never short of funds, which came mainly from donations. Its petitions gained almost as many signatures as those of the Chartists; it sent pamphlets to every elector and MP, and organized lectures and mass meetings. From 1841 Cobden and **Bright** gave much of their time to the activities of the League, so that nearly every large town in England and Scotland was visited by a leader of the movement. A special Free Trade Hall was built in Manchester to accommodate between 8,000 and 9,000 people for League meetings. The League was anti-aristocratic – it regarded the Corn Laws as an indication of the aristocracy's domination of parliament – but was not revolutionary, even though in 1842 some of its leaders were prepared to use the threat of violence to force the hand of the government. The League kept the issue of the Corn Laws before the public, but it was not responsible for their repeal, in spite of **Peel** attributing this to Cobden. Peel disliked pressure from extra-parliamentary groups and was determined not to bow to it. His belief that repeal was in the national interest was one that, as a supporter of free trade, he had long held. What precipitated his repeal was the **Irish Famine** (1845–9), which had nothing to do with the League. The Corn Laws were repealed by the House of Commons, most of whose members were landowners and opponents of the League. Peel justified repeal as a 'conservative' measure: by defusing working-class discontent, it would preserve the existing political system, in which the aristocracy had a leading role.

**Anti-Semitism.** Ever since the diaspora ('dispersion') which followed the sack of Jerusalem by the Romans in AD 70, Jews have been scattered as minorities in numerous countries. Held responsible for the crucifixion of Christ, they were persecuted in the Middle Ages, excluded from most occupations and from ownership of land, and therefore became merchants and money-lenders (Christians were not allowed to lend money at interest). In the nineteenth century Jewish families, such as the **Rothschilds**, became wealthy bankers and industrialists and the object of envy, though most Jews were not rich. In Russia, where five million Jews (one fifth of the world's Jewish population) lived in **ghettos**, they were used as scapegoats by the government to divert discontent away from the Tsarist regime. **Pogroms** took place from 1881, when **Alexander II** was assassinated, which led to three million Jews emigrating before 1914, half of them to the USA. Anti-Semitism was most violent in Russia before the **First World War** but it was widespread too in Germany, where the United Association of Anti-Semitic Parties proposed the '**Final Solution**' as early as 1899. The Jewish problem, it said, would have to be 'solved in the end by the complete exclusion and ... finally, annihilation of the Jewish people'. Though France had a Jewish population of only 80,000 (0.2 per cent of the population), anti-Semitism was surprisingly virulent there, as the **Panama scandal** and the **Dreyfus case** showed. After the war anti-Semitism increased in Germany, as Jews were blamed for the '**stab in the back**' and Germany's defeat. Hatred of the Jews figured prominently in **Hitler**'s *Mein Kampf* and as soon as he came to power in 1933 he began to exclude Jews from public life; in the Nuremberg Laws (1935) he denied them German citizenship and forbade them to marry Germans. These laws were copied by **Mussolini** in 1938 but met with no support from the Italian people, of whom less than 0.1 per cent were Jews. Hitler's attempt to eliminate the Jews entirely in the Holocaust did not take place until the **Second World War** had begun, when six million Jews were murdered in **extermination camps** such as

Auschwitz. This discredited anti-Semitism, though it still survives in parties such as the National Front in Britain and France.

**Anti-socialist law** (1878). **Bismarck** disliked socialists as they supported revolution and equality, and he was horrified at what he regarded as the excesses of the **Paris Commune** in 1871. The international character of the working-class movement led him to believe that socialists were enemies of the Reich. When the **Social Democratic Party** (SPD) was formed in Germany in 1875 Bismarck was determined to crush it, though it gained only twelve seats in the **Reichstag** elections of 1877. After an attempt on the Emperor's life in May 1878, Bismarck put before the Reichstag a bill to ban the SPD, but the **National Liberals** opposed it and so it was defeated. A week later the Emperor was wounded in a second assassination attempt. Although the SPD had nothing to do with either attack, Bismarck dissolved the Reichstag, called another election and vilified the socialists. They lost only three seats in the election but there was a move to the **Right** which enabled Bismarck, this time with the support of the National Liberals, to pass an anti-socialist law: meetings and publications of the Social Democrats were banned, though they were allowed to stand in elections. Socialist trade unions and working-class clubs were dissolved. Bismarck's anti-socialist crusade was as much a failure as were his attacks on the Catholic Church in the *Kulturkampf*, as support for the SPD continued to grow. In 1890 the Reichstag refused to renew the anti-socialist laws, and the SPD increased its number of seats from eleven to thirty-five in the elections, receiving over one million votes.

**Appeasement.** The policy of settling disputes by peaceful means and compromise rather than by resort to war. Appeasement is usually associated with Neville **Chamberlain** and was used in a pejorative sense from the time of the **Czechoslovakian crisis** (1938–9), but its origins go back to the Treaty of **Versailles** (1919). Many, particularly in Britain, felt that Germany had been badly treated, as **reparations** were too high and as the principle of self-determination had not been applied to areas where there were German majorities, as in Austria, Danzig and the **Sudetenland**. There was a readiness, therefore, to meet genuine German grievances, reinforced by a desire to avoid a repetition of the horrific loss of life in the **First World War** and by an awareness of Britain's relative economic decline. Britain could not afford to pay for both social reforms and large defence forces, particularly as the national debt had increased eleven-fold from 1914–18: by the late 1920s interest payments on it accounted for 40 per cent of government expenditure, compared with 12 per cent in 1913. Britain's global commitments in defence of her Empire were another strong motive for appeasement, especially when she was faced with simultaneous threats from the members of the **Anti-Comintern Pact** in 1936. 'We cannot foresee the time', wrote the Chiefs of Staff in 1937, 'when our defence forces will be strong enough to safeguard our trade, territory and vital interests against Germany, Italy and Japan at the same time.' Japan took control of **Manchuria** in 1931 with no effective response from Britain or the **League of Nations**. With the **Anglo-German naval agreement** (1935), Britain agreed to Germany ignoring the limitations imposed at Versailles on the size of her navy. In the same year Britain tried to appease **Mussolini** during the **Ethiopian War**, when the **Hoare–Laval Pact** offered him much of the country, though the pact had to be abandoned when a public outcry followed its being leaked to the press. A year later, when Germany militarily reoccupied the **Rhineland** (again, contrary to Versailles), Britain and France did nothing. When Chamberlain became Prime Minister in 1937 he continued a policy of appeasement which was well established. He did not believe that France or the USA would act against Germany, he had a deep distrust of Russia and felt that **Hitler** was a rational man with whom he could do business. *Anschluss* with Austria could not, indeed should not, be stopped, as it was simply a matter of Germans uniting with one another. When the Czechoslovakian crisis (1938–9) arose, Chamberlain did not think that the British public would go to war 'because of a quarrel in a far-away country between people of whom we know nothing'. He felt that as the Sudetenland was populated by Germans it should be part of Germany, and managed to bring this about at Munich without war. On his return to London he was rapturously acclaimed for bringing 'peace with honour'.

Only in March 1939, when Germany occupied the rest of Czechoslovakia, did it become clear that Hitler's expansionist plans extended beyond territory where the population was German. Appeasement now ended and Britain joined France in pledging to support Poland if she were attacked: similar guarantees were soon given to Romania and Greece. A belated and half-hearted approach was made to Russia for cooperation against Germany, but this failed with the **Nazi–Soviet Pact** in August 1939. The effects of appeasement were the reverse of those Chamberlain intended. Far from satisfying Germany, appeasement persuaded Hitler that Britain and France were not likely to act when Poland was invaded. It therefore led directly to general conflict in 1939, which none of the great powers wanted.

**April Theses** (1917). When **Bolshevik** leaders **Stalin** and **Kamenev** had returned to **Petrograd** in March, from exile in Siberia, they had taken the orthodox Marxist position that a *bourgeois* revolution would have to take place and develop capitalism fully before a socialist revolution could occur. They were, therefore, prepared to give limited support to the **Provisional Government** of Russia. Lenin changed all this when he arrived, with German help, at the Finland Station in Petrograd in April. In his April Theses he was uncompromising: there should be no support for the Provisional Government or for continuing the war; power should pass to the **Soviets**; land and banking should be nationalized. Many Bolsheviks were shocked by this programme and only reluctantly did the Central Committee accept it, though it was to be the basis of Bolshevism's mass appeal in the months ahead.

**Arabi Pasha,** see **Urabi Pasha**

**Aristocracy, decline of.** Throughout the nineteenth century in Europe the landed nobility had enormous prestige and authority, even in the leading industrial nations. Only in France was their political power permanently reduced by **Louis Philippe** (1830–48): the Prefect, who supervised local government, was rarely a noble after 1830. In Germany the *Junkers* retained their political dominance, even when their economic position was declining. As late as 1913 three-quarters of the members of the Upper House of the Prussian *Landtag* were nobles and one quarter of the Lower House. The wealthiest of all landed aristocracies was in England. In 1875 a quarter of the land of England and Wales was held by 710 land-owners and 80 per cent of the British Isles by 7,000 families. Half the land in Britain was entailed in the 1850s, so that it could be passed to one heir, thus ensuring that the great estates would not be broken up. Until the 1880s most MPs were landowners or their relatives, in the **Commons** as well as the **Lords**: they held the majority of posts in the Cabinet, whether this was **Liberal** or **Tory**. The British landed aristocracy controlled rural local government until the County Councils were formed in 1888, and they held top posts in many professions – the law, church, civil service and the armed forces. Their power in Ireland disappeared between 1885 and 1914 as a result of the **Irish Land Acts**. In Britain they were subject to death duties from 1894, low at first but rising to 60 per cent on the largest estates by 1930. One quarter of the land in England was sold immediately after the **First World War**, a revolution in land ownership not seen since Henry VIII's dissolution of the monasteries. By the end of the war their political power had almost gone. The **Parliament Act** (1911) drastically reduced the influence of the House of Lords. Since 1885 the aristocracy had been in a minority in the Commons and after **Salisbury** they ceased to control govern-ments. The three Tory Prime Ministers between the wars – Bonar **Law**, Stanley **Baldwin** and Neville **Chamberlain** – were all businessmen. In Russia the nobility lost much of its power and most of its functions with the **emancipation of the serfs** (1861) and, constantly in debt, sold much of its remaining land before it was wiped out in the aftermath of the **October Revolution** (1917). In central and eastern Europe the power of the nobility declined with serf emancipation during the **Revolutions of 1848** in the Habsburg Empire, and in Poland after the revolt of 1863. The Habsburg government in Hungary and the Russian government in Poland wanted peasant support, so emancipation was carried out on terms unfavourable to the landlords. The aristocracy was one of the greatest sufferers from the **First World War**, as a result of which it lost its political power in Germany and much of its wealth everywhere.

**Asante** (Ashanti) **wars** were fought in West Africa in the nineteenth century by the Asante against their Fante neighbours and against the British. Asante was one of the richest and most powerful African states in the eighteenth and nineteenth centuries. In 1850 it controlled an area of 125,000 square miles, with a population of between three and five million, in what is now Ghana. The chiefs provided the *asantehene*, or King, with tribute and fighting men. The main trade in the eighteenth century was in slaves and gold, exchanged at the coast for firearms. The Fante states stood astride the routes to the coast and they were in a position to influence the volume of trade and the prices of goods exchanged with Europeans. By the early nineteenth century Asante was determined to gain control of the coastal trade while the Fante were equally determined to protect their position as middlemen. The British had abolished the slave trade in 1807 and they were opposed to Asante political control over the coast. In the nineteenth century Asante fought several wars with the Fante states and this led to conflict with Britain. Although Britain's authority was restricted to the coastal forts, the British upheld the Fante in their refusal to pay tribute to the Asante. In the war of 1824 the British Governor of the Gold Coast was killed before the Asante were defeated. To Europeans, Asante was a militaristic and barbaric state, owing to the ritual sacrifice of prisoners of war and criminals, although a succession of *asantehene*, anxious to maintain the Empire and its trade, attempted to solve disputes with Britain by diplomatic means rather than by war. In the mid-nineteenth century Britain began to consolidate its control over the Fante states. She also tried to weaken the Asante Empire and its control over the trade of the interior by encouraging tributary states to secede. Following an Asante invasion of the Fante states in 1871, a British military force of 2,500, under Sir Garnet **Wolseley**, invaded the country, sacked the capital Kumasi and forced the *asantehene* to make peace. Although Asante power was weakened the state remained powerful, and a further British military expedition in 1895–6 was required to depose the *asantehene* and place a British Resident in Kumasi. Four years later, the Asante rose in revolt and the country was conquered and annexed to become part of the Gold Coast. The Asante Confederacy was re-established in 1935 under Britain's policy of **indirect rule**.

**Asquith, Herbert Henry, 1st Earl of Oxford and Asquith** (1852–1928). British Prime Minister (1908–16). Born into a Yorkshire wool manufacturing family, Asquith gained a first-class degree at Oxford before becoming a barrister and **Liberal** MP in 1886. Home Secretary under **Gladstone** and Rosebery from 1892–5, Asquith differed from the Liberal leader, **Campbell-Bannerman**, in supporting the **South African War** (1899–1902). He nevertheless became Chancellor of the Exchequer in Campbell-Bannerman's ministry (1905–8), when he introduced non-contributory pensions for many over the age of seventy and imposed higher tax rates on unearned incomes. Asquith's Liberal administration, after Campbell-Bannerman retired owing to ill health in 1908, is one of the most important in modern British history, as it produced a series of far-reaching reforms both at home and abroad. In 1909 Asquith accepted a proposal for uniting the Boer states of Transvaal and the Orange Free State with the British colonies of the Cape and Natal to form the Union of South Africa, whilst in India the **Morley–Minto reforms** increased Indian membership of the legislative councils. Winston **Churchill** at the Board of Trade introduced Labour Exchanges, and provided minimum wages in 'sweated' trades such as tailoring through the Trade Boards Act (1909). The boldest reforms came from the Chancellor of the Exchequer, **Lloyd George**, particularly the **People's Budget** of 1909, which increased taxation on the wealthy in order to pay for social reforms and the building of **Dreadnoughts**. This '**New Liberalism**' was rejected by the **Lords**, so Asquith called an election in January 1910, which he won with a reduced majority. The Lords now passed the budget but Asquith had decided to reduce their powers, which he did in the **Parliament Act** of 1911. Lloyd George's **National Insurance Act** (1911) protected many workers from the effects of sickness and unemployment, but it did not prevent an escalation of strikes, **suffragette** violence or Ulster resistance to Home Rule (see **Home Rule for Ireland**). As Asquith was dependent on Irish nationalist support after the 1910 elections, he introduced a Home Rule Bill, which passed the Commons and was rejected by the Lords three times between 1912 and 1914, but the outbreak of the **First World War** led to its suspension.

Asquith had allowed his departmental heads (like Lloyd George and Churchill) a free rein but this relaxed attitude was not suitable for running a war. There was a crisis in May 1915, when **Fisher**, the First Sea Lord, resigned after disagreements with Churchill over the **Gallipoli** campaign, and there were reports of shell shortages on the Western Front. Asquith therefore formed a coalition government with the **Conservatives**, but he did not consult his colleagues about this and divided the Liberals, as he did again by introducing conscription in 1916. He lost Irish support by the brutal suppression of the **Easter Rising** and at the end of 1916 was faced by a demand from his Cabinet colleagues for a small war committee, of which he would not be Chairman. This indication of a lack of confidence in his leadership led Asquith to resign, and Lloyd George became Prime Minister. As Asquith refused to serve under him, the Liberals were split with two leaders: Lloyd George as Prime Minister and Asquith as Leader of the Opposition. In the 1918 election Asquith lost his seat, whilst his followers were reduced to twenty-six (136 Liberals supported Lloyd George). Asquith became an MP again in a by-election in 1920, and in 1923 joined with Lloyd George to oppose **Baldwin**'s campaign for **tariff reform**. In 1926 he retired owing to illness.

**Atatürk,** see **Kemal Atatürk**

**Atlantic, battle of the** (1939–45). Struggle between German and Allied navies and air forces for control of the shipping routes to Britain during the **Second World War**. When war broke out in 1939 the German surface fleet had four battleships, three 'pocket' battleships, four heavy and six light cruisers. It could not risk an action against the British fleet of eighteen battleships, ten aircraft carriers, fifteen heavy and sixty-two light cruisers. The German navy used its capital ships at first as commerce raiders but they met with little success and suffered losses, as when the *Graf Spee*, after an inconclusive action against British cruisers, was scuttled in Montevideo harbour. After the sinking of the *Bismarck* in May 1941 the Germans kept their fleet in their Norwegian and French bases. The main threat to Britain's supply lines, on which she was dependent for food and war material, was the U-boat (*Unterseeboot* or submarine), which could use Norwegian and French bases from the summer of 1940. The British introduced **convoys** but in 1940 they could be escorted only 400 miles west of Ireland, a distance increased to 1,200 miles – over half-way across the Atlantic – when bases in Iceland were secured in May 1941. The British were short of escort vessels and their radar (Asdic) worked only against submerged vessels. The submarines, which moved faster on the surface than the convoys, therefore attacked at night and on the surface. Another threat to British shipping was the German long-range Condor bombers and reconnaissance planes. **Doenitz**, the Commander-in-Chief of the German U-boats, organized them in 'wolf packs' to attack convoys with devastating effect. 1942 was the worst year of the war for Allied shipping losses and November the worst month, when 725,000 tons were sunk.

New tactics and inventions in 1943 ended the dominance of the submarine. Centimetric (short-wave) radar was the most important of the new devices, as it could pick up U-boats on the surface, so they could be located both night and day. Submarines which were forced to stay under water had a short range and low speeds. High-frequency direction finding, which indicated where submarines were from the signals they made, was standard in all escort vessels; long-range aircraft which could patrol a thousand miles from their base were used to hunt U-boats; escort carriers accompanied convoys; the 'hedgehog' enabled depth charges to be thrown ahead of attacking vessels. In May 1943 Doenitz told **Hitler** that the battle of the Atlantic would have to be broken off, at least for the time being, as U-boat losses amounted to 30 per cent of those at sea. Between May and September 1943 not one Allied ship was sunk by submarines in the Atlantic. The Germans introduced the '*schnorkel*' breathing apparatus to allow their submarines to remain submerged, but between January and June 1944 one million American soldiers and 1.9 million tons of war material came across the Atlantic almost without loss. The battle of the Atlantic had been won by the Allies, and though German U-boats bravely continued their patrols, their expectation of survival was one and a half missions. During the battle 2,500 Allied ships and 781 U-boats (out of the 1,200 used) were sunk.

**Atomic bomb.** In 1939 scientists in the USA, England and Germany informed their governments that it was theoretically possible to make an atomic explosion. In 1940 two American physicists published an account of the process, so there was no secret about the principles behind the bomb: the problem was to apply them. It was in Britain that an atomic bomb was first seen as a weapon which could win the war. In March 1940 O. R. Frisch and R. F. Peierls, Nazi refugees, wrote a memo to show how an atom bomb could be constructed from uranium-235 and outlined the lethal effects from its explosion and the accompanying radiation. The British now gave a high priority to nuclear research, as did the Americans when the USA entered the war in December 1941. By 1945 the USA had produced an atom bomb which used uranium, and one which used a man-made fissionable material, plutonium. A uranium bomb was dropped on **Hiroshima** on 6 August 1945 and a plutonium bomb on Nagasaki three days later. Other countries soon produced their own atomic bombs: the Soviet Union in 1949, Britain in 1952, France in 1960 and China in 1964.

**Attlee, Clement Richard, 1st Earl** (1883–1967). British Prime Minister (1945–51). Unusually for a leader of the **Labour Party**, Attlee came from a prosperous middle-class family (his father was a successful City solicitor) and went to a public school, Haileybury, before reading history at Oxford. In 1905 he went to help with a boy's club in Stepney and spent the next seven years among the London poor. This experience changed his whole career. Instead of practising as a barrister he did social work, joined the Stepney **Independent Labour Party** in 1907 and five years later gained a lectureship at the London School of Economics. When the **First World War** began he enlisted in the army, rose to the rank of major and took part in the **Gallipoli campaign**, where he was severely wounded. After the war he returned to Stepney, became mayor and in 1922 was elected as MP for the Limehouse constituency of Stepney, which he represented until it was abolished in 1950. He served in both of **MacDonald**'s Labour governments: in 1924 as Under-Secretary at the War Office, in 1931 as Postmaster-General, the only time he ran a department. In the 1931 election most Labour leaders were defeated and Attlee found himself one of only forty-six Labour MPs. A dull speaker, he did not impress, as his talents for running committees with quiet efficiency were unobtrusive. It was a surprise, therefore, when he was elected as leader of the Labour

Party to succeed George Lansbury in 1935; he was fortunate that more dynamic candidates with Cabinet experience, such as Herbert Morrison, had become unpopular. **Bevin** and **Dalton** rather than Attlee were responsible for the Labour Party abandoning **appeasement** and disarmament, and it was not until the **Second World War** that Attlee really made his mark. Patriotic in the fight against **Hitler**, he pressed for the removal of **Chamberlain** as Prime Minister. When Winston **Churchill** formed a coalition government in 1940, Attlee entered his War Cabinet and remained a member till the end of the conflict, being officially recognized as Deputy Prime Minister in 1942. The Labour Party gained its first majority in the 1945 election, so Attlee became Prime Minister in the most talented and successful of all Labour governments so far. He was the first Labour leader to accept a hereditary earldom.

**August Decrees** (1789). With the **Great Fear** anarchy reigned in the French countryside. To bring it to an end and gain the support of peasants for the **French Revolution**, it was clear that the **Constituent Assembly** would have to give them at least part of what they wanted. On 4 August, therefore, liberal nobles proposed that obligations concerning personal servitude should be abolished without compensation: these included serfdom and the *corvée* (unpaid labour on the roads). Other dues paid by peasants such as *champart* (harvest dues) were regarded as a form of property and were to be redeemed (their abolition paid for by the peasants). As these were the dues which affected peasants most severely, they were not pleased by the limited nature of the changes. The reforms, however, did not stop there, as noble deputies queued up to renounce their privileges in a spirit of patriotic fervour. The tithe (part of the harvest given to the church) and seigneurial courts were abolished, as were all venal offices, financial privileges and those of provincial estates. 'All citizens, without distinction of birth, are eligible for all offices.' The August Decrees marked the end of noble power and the privilege of birth in France. All Frenchmen now had the same rights and duties, could enter any profession and paid the same taxes, though equality in theory was not the same as equality in practice. The career open to talent benefited the *bourgeoisie* rather than the peasant or worker, as the latter did not have the education to take advantage of it.

Another effect of the August Decrees was to attach the peasants to the Revolution. They did not like having to redeem some feudal dues and many stopped paying them until they were finally abolished, without compensation, in 1793. Some, in areas such as Brittany and the Vendée (see **Vendean revolt**), became active opponents of the Revolution, but for most the Revolution marked the end of the feudal system and they feared that if they did not support it, aristocratic privilege and the tithe would return and they would lose all they had gained. The August Decrees swept away institutions such as the provincial estates and cleared the way for a national, uniform system of administration, which the Assembly set up in the next two years.

**Ausgleich** ('compromise') (1867) resulted from negotiations between Emperor **Francis Joseph** of Austria and the Magyar ruling class in Hungary. It was made necessary by Austria's defeat in the **Austro-Prussian War** (1866), which resulted in her giving up control of the **German Confederation** and losing Venetia to Italy. With the prestige of the Habsburg monarchy at its lowest point, it was essential to attach Hungary to the **Habsburg dynasty**. The *Ausgleich* created the **Austro-Hungarian Empire** (Dual Monarchy), in which the two states of Austria and Hungary were recognized as equal and in most respects independent of one another. Each had its own **Diet** but with a restricted suffrage that largely excluded non-Germans in Austria and non-Magyars in Hungary. Each had its own government and Prime Minister, responsible to their common ruler, Francis Joseph, who was Emperor of Austria and King of Hungary. The two states were to have a common army, Minister of Foreign Affairs and finances to pay for them. A commercial union, negotiated at the same time, was renewable every ten years.

The different nationalities in the Empire had not been consulted about the *Ausgleich*, which ignored their interests. 'Dualism', said **Kossuth**, 'is the alliance of the conservative, reactionary . . . elements in Hungary with those of the Austrian Germans who despise liberty, for the oppression of the other nationalities and races.' It was an alliance of Germans and Magyars against the Slavs, to ensure the dominance of the former, and was followed by ruthless

Magyarization of the administration, justice and education in Hungary and by Germanization in Austria. In the short term the *Ausgleich*, by satisfying the Magyars, strengthened the monarchy, but it made the national question, which was to dominate Habsburg history until the fall of the Empire, more volatile.

**Austerlitz, battle of** (December 1805), was fought by **Napoleon Bonaparte** against Russia and Austria. Alarmed at Napoleon making himself King of Italy, Austria had joined Russia in the Third Coalition. Napoleon immediately moved his troops from Boulogne, where they had been waiting to invade England, to the Danube, where they outflanked the Austrian General Mack at Ulm and forced him to surrender with 33,000 troops. Napoleon took Vienna and then moved north into Moravia (modern Czechoslovakia) where the Austrians and Russians had linked up. With long lines of communication, the approach of winter and the possibility that Prussia would join the Third Coalition, Napoleon wanted the Allies to fight. He persuaded them to do so by feigning weakness, asking for an armistice, withdrawing his troops from the village of Austerlitz and the Pratzen Heights, and exposing a weak right flank. **Alexander I**, Tsar of Russia, with the advantage of 85,000 Allied troops facing 73,000 French soldiers, ordered an attack on the French right flank. When enough Allied troops had been drawn from the Pratzen Heights into the attack, Napoleon stormed the Heights, captured them and then swept down on the flank and rear of the Allied right wing. It was Napoleon's greatest set-piece victory, in which the Allies suffered 27,000 casualties (including 11,000 prisoners), the French 8,500. The next day Austria sued for peace and at Pressburg (Bratislava) was forced to give up most of her possessions in Italy and Germany.

**Australian Commonwealth Act** (1900) united the six Australian states (formerly colonies) of New South Wales, Queensland, South Australia, Victoria, Western Australia and Tasmania and provided a federal government and legislature. Demands for federation had grown as railways linked the colonies, trade unions represented workers throughout Australia and many businessmen wanted a large continental market without internal tariff barriers. A conference of leaders from all the colonies to discuss federation was held in

1890, but another ten years and two referenda were needed before all the colonies, spurred on by the efforts of Sir Henry Parkes and Alfred **Deakin**, approved. The Act, which the British parliament passed in 1900, set up a legislature consisting of a House of Representatives and a Senate. State governments retained sovereignty in internal affairs, the federal government dealing with customs, postal services, currency and immigration. The Governor-General retained (until 1931) responsibility for defence and foreign affairs. The Commonwealth parliament met in Melbourne until 1927, when the capital was transferred to Canberra.

**Austrian Empire** (1804–67). Emperor Francis II of the Holy Roman Empire (abolished in 1806) ruled as Emperor Francis I of Austria from 1804. After the defeat of **Napoleon Bonaparte**, Austria gained at the Congress of **Vienna** (1815) Venetia and the Dalmatian coast and gave up the Austrian Netherlands (Belgium), so that she had for the first time a contiguous belt of territory, centred on the basin of the middle Danube which flowed into the Black Sea. The Austrian Empire consisted of the hereditary Habsburg lands of Austria, Bohemia, Hungary, Croatia and Transylvania, Galicia (once part of Poland) and Lombardy in north Italy. It was a mosaic of eleven peoples, who were so intermixed that it was often impossible to draw a line between one ethnic group and another. There were Slavs in the south (Slovenes, Serbs, Croats), in the west (Czechs), in the centre (Slovaks) and in the east (Ruthenians or Ukrainians) of the Empire. Italians lived in Lombardy-Venetia and on the Adriatic coast, where they mixed with Slovenes and Croats. North of the Carpathian mountains in Galicia there were Poles and Ruthenians. In Bohemia Romanians, Ruthenians and Germans lived with Czechs, whilst in Transylvania there were Magyars, Romanians and Germans. Some nationalities – Czechs, Slovaks, Slovenes, Croats and Magyars – were found only in the Austrian Empire. Other nationalities – Germans, Italians, Poles, Ruthenians, Romanians and Serbs – also existed outside the Empire. The only real unity was provided by loyalty to the **Habsburg dynasty**.

Austria dominated Italy and exerted a great deal of influence in Germany through the **Diet** of the **German Confederation**, over which she presided. Both **Metternich** and Francis I were determined to oppose change, which they equated with revolution, and imposed on the Empire a centralized form of government in which all important decisions were made in Vienna. When Francis died in 1835, he was succeeded by Ferdinand, who was retarded and an epileptic and totally unsuited to rule. This further weakened an Empire whose finances were in disarray (from 1815–48 30 per cent of the annual revenue went to pay the interest on the state debt). The **Revolutions of 1848** affected most parts of the Austrian Empire – Italy, Hungary, Bohemia and Austria itself – and were the most serious threat the monarchy faced in the nineteenth century. The Empire survived, though it had to call on Russian help to put down the revolution in Hungary. **Francis Joseph** replaced Ferdinand as Emperor and brushed aside attempts to give Austria a constitution which limited his power: there were no representative institutions. Austria's betrayal of Russia in the **Crimean War** (1854–6) was a disaster for the Empire, as Russia now supported France in Italy and Prussia in Germany. Defeated by France in 1859, Austria lost Lombardy. This forced Francis Joseph in 1861 to allow a parliament, with the power to pass laws and approve the annual budget. Austria's dominance in Germany had already been undermined by Prussian leadership of the *Zollverein* (customs union). It came to an end completely in the **Austro–Prussian War** (1866), when Austria lost her remaining possessions in Italy and was pushed out of Germany. The German Confederation was dissolved and replaced by the **North German Confederation** under Prussia: the Habsburgs thus gave up the position they had held in the German lands for 600 years. **Nationalism** had triumphed in Italy and Germany: it was to win another victory in Hungary with the *Ausgleich* (1867), which replaced the Austrian Empire with the **Austro-Hungarian Empire**, in which both parts had equal status.

**Austro-Hungarian Empire** (Dual Monarchy) (1867–1918) was created by the *Ausgleich*, which made Austria and Hungary autonomous states with a common sovereign, **Francis Joseph**. The mixture of nationalities was the same as in the **Austrian Empire**. In the Hungarian part of the Empire the Magyars comprised less than half the population but they were dominant economically, politically and culturally. They held nearly all the seats in the Hungarian parliament: almost all state officials and teachers were Magyar. A policy of Magyarization was followed, which allowed no autonomy for other ethnic groups, except for the Croats.

The Austrian part of the Empire was much more liberal than the Hungarian. A series of reforms in the 1870s made education compulsory, free and secular; ended the Concordat of 1855, which had given the Catholic Church control of education and family law; and allowed trade unions to be formed and to strike. In the 1880s, following **Bismarck**'s example, old-age pensions, sickness insurance and accident insurance were introduced and conditions in mines and factories were regulated. Attempts to give the Czech and German languages equal status in Bohemia in 1871 and 1897 had to be abandoned, owing to the violent opposition of Germans and Magyars. National discontent was defused to some extent by the granting of universal male suffrage in Austria in 1907, which meant that the Germans lost their majority in parliament.

There was no challenge to the monarchy between 1867 and 1914 as serious as that posed by the **Revolutions of 1848**. The subject nationalities remained loyal: the danger to the Empire resulted from its foreign policy. Excluded from Germany in 1866, the Dual Monarchy's attention turned to the Balkans, where her main enemy was Russia. **Andrássy**, the Foreign Minister, made the **Dual Alliance** (1879) with Germany, which remained the keystone of Austro-Hungarian foreign policy for as long as the Empire lasted. Relations with Serbia rapidly deteriorated after the Karadjordjevic dynasty came to power in 1903. Austria-Hungary felt threatened by the doubling in size of Serbia after the **Balkan Wars** (1912–13) and seized on the assassination of the heir to the Habsburg throne at **Sarajevo** to declare war on Serbia. All nationalities supported the Empire and though many wanted to reorganize it as a federal state, with autonomy for the different national groups, few wanted to see it break up. Not until the military defeat of Germany and Austria-Hungary in 1918 did Czechs, Yugoslavs, Magyars and Poles proclaim their independence. By the time that Emperor Charles (Francis Joseph had died in 1916) abdicated in November 1918, the Austro-Hungarian Empire had ceased to exist.

**Austro-Prussian War** (1866). **Bismarck** made skilful diplomatic preparations for war against Austria. He secured the neutrality of **Napoleon III** by hinting that France would receive territory on the Rhine if Prussia expanded in Germany, and also made a secret alliance with Italy by promising her Venetia. Austria would then have to fight on two fronts. At stake was Austria's domination of the **German Confederation**. War broke out when Bismarck proposed that it should be abolished. Many expected a long war and an Austrian victory, as she had the support of the larger German states, but the war was over in seven weeks. Austria's only successes were against Italy, whom she defeated on land at Custozza and at sea off Lissa. Owing to **Moltke**'s brilliant planning, Saxony, Hanover and Hesse-Cassel were occupied by Prussian troops in three days. The decisive battle took place at **Sadowa** (Königgrätz) in Bohemia, where Austria suffered a resounding defeat. Peace was made at **Prague** in August. The Austro-Prussian War was one of the most important wars in the nineteenth century. The balance of power in central Europe was overturned, as Prussia's gains made her richer and more populous than all the other German states combined. Her leadership of the *Zollverein* and of the **North German Confederation** now made the unification of Germany under Prussia more likely. Austria, ejected from Germany and Italy, was severely weakened and compelled to concede equality to Hungary in the *Ausgleich*. The only area where she remained a great power was in the Balkans: here her expansionist tendencies were to lead to the **First World War**. Within Prussia the power and prestige of Bismarck were greatly increased: the **Diet** passed an Indemnity Act which legalized the collection of taxes and reorganization of the army (see **Roon**), which Bismarck had carried out without the Diet's approval. The Liberals never really recovered from the victory of Bismarck and authoritarianism in the constitutional conflict.

**Axis powers.** In October 1936 Italy and Germany agreed to oppose the Republican government in Spain, and in November **Mussolini** referred to Rome–Berlin as 'an axis round which may cooperate all Europeans animated by a will to collaboration and peace'. This became a formal alliance in 1939 with the Pact of Steel, when Germany and Italy promised to support each other in case of war. The 'axis' was extended to Tokyo when Japan, who had formed an **Anti-Comintern Pact** with Germany in 1936 (Mussolini signed it a year later), made a Tripartite Pact with Italy and Germany in September 1940, by which each of them agreed to help, if one was attacked by a power not already in the **Second World War**. The term 'axis powers' was used in the war to indicate Germany and her allies: Italy, Japan, Hungary, Romania and Bulgaria.

**Azaña, Manuel** (1880–1940). Prime Minister (1931–3 and 1936) and President (1936–9) of the **Spanish Second Republic**. From a liberal family, Azaña was an exceptional student, who eventually joined the Ministry of Justice as a member of the élite notary corps in 1910, but his intellectual energies were centred more on writing and scholarship than the law. He published novels, plays, journalism and translations, and won the National Prize for Literature in 1926. Under the dictatorship of **Primo de Rivera** (1923–30), Azaña was co-founder of Republican Action, a progressive Republican Party. He was also a signatory to the anti-monarchical Pact of San Sebastian in August 1930. Upon the proclamation of the Second Republic in April 1931, Azaña was made Minister of War. Although relatively unknown, his superb oratory and ministerial ability led him to become Prime Minister in October 1931. He was to remain in power until September 1933. As Minister of War, he retired about half the bloated officer corps in an effort to keep it out of politics, though his contemptuous attitude greatly antagonized it. As Prime Minister, he endeavoured to transform Spanish society from a Catholic and backward nation into a secular and modern one. His achievements were many: Catalan autonomy, a greatly expanded education system, the curbing of the Church's influence, and agrarian and trade-union reform. However, the Republican–Socialist coalition failed, partly owing to the government's own shortcomings. In particular, Azaña, as a Madrid intellectual, tended to neglect pressing economic and social problems, especially the agrarian question, for cultural and institutional change. Yet the main reason for the failure of the Azaña administrations lay in the resistance of the conservative classes at all levels to the new regime.

In October 1934 Azaña was wrongfully and maliciously arrested as an accomplice in the general strike and rising of that month. His imprisonment won him renewed support, especially in view of the Centre-Right's destruction of the reformist achievements of the first two years. He returned to power as the architect of the **Popular Front** coalition, which narrowly defeated the 'anti-revolutionary' coalition of the **Right** in the general election of February 1936. During the spring of 1936 Azaña was overwhelmed by the demands of the **Left**. To combat the rising protest of the Left and increasing threats from the Right, he was elevated to the presidency in May 1936, so that the moderate Socialist Indalecio Prieto could become Premier. This strategy failed, because of the opposition of the left-wing Socialist Largo Caballero. Instead, a weak left-Republican Cabinet was appointed. As social strife and political disorder mounted, Azaña lapsed into paralysis. The left-Republicans' vacillating leadership allowed the military rising of July 1936 to develop into a civil war. Azaña played a relatively limited role in the **Spanish Civil War**. His numerous attempts to achieve a negotiated end to the war failed. Convinced by December 1937 that the Republic could not possibly win the war, he had become increasingly remote and miserable, taking refuge in his writing. He was extremely critical of the communist-influenced Prime Minister Juan **Negrín** and tried to remove him in August 1938. In February 1939 Azaña fled to France, before resigning as President. He died in Montauban on 3 November 1940. Vilified by the **Franco** regime because of his remorseless critique of the Spanish old regime, Manuel Azaña was the outstanding figure of the Second Republic.

**Babeuf Plot** (1796). Gracchus Babeuf was the son of a poor clerk, became a radical journalist during the **French Revolution** and spent most of the **Terror** in prison. He believed that the Revolution should secure equal enjoyment of life's blessings for all. As private property produced inequality, the only way to establish real equality was 'to establish the communal management of property and abolish private possession'. These ideas were more radical than those of the **Jacobins** and have led many historians to regard Babeuf as the first communist. He was novel too in the way he thought of organizing his Conspiracy of Equals. A rising, Babeuf realized, would not come about spontaneously but must be prepared by a small group of dedicated revolutionaries. Through propaganda and agitation they would persuade key institutions, such as the army and police, to support them. After seizing power, the revolutionary leaders should not hand it over to an elected assembly but should establish a dictatorship, in order to make fundamental changes in the organization of society. Marxist historians see Babeuf's importance in his theories, arguing that through Buonarroti (a fellow conspirator) his ideas passed to **Blanqui** in the nineteenth century and thence to **Lenin**. Babeuf's significance in the French Revolution itself was slight: his plot to overthrow the **Directory** was soon revealed by another conspirator. He received no support from the *sans-culottes* and little from former Jacobins. He was arrested in May 1796 and, with one other member of the Conspiracy, was executed a year later.

**Baden-Powell, Robert Stephenson Smyth, 1st Baron** (1857–1941). English general and founder of the Boy Scouts and Girl Guides. He served in the **Asante war** (1895–6) in West Africa and became a national hero when he successfully defended Mafeking for 217 days during the **South African War** (1899–1902). Before he retired from the army in 1910 he had set up the Boy Scout and Girl Guide movements (1908 and 1909 respectively). Baden-Powell encouraged outdoor recreations, self-reliance, fitness and commitment to public service. Both movements spread rapidly in Britain and abroad and were seen as a means of promoting racial and religious harmony between peoples, an ideal exemplified by the great international camps or Jamborees held after 1920.

**Bakunin, Mikhail** (1814–76). The son of a Russian noble landowner and founder, with **Proudhon**, of **anarchism** as an international revolutionary movement. He took part in the 1848–9 revolutions in Paris, Prague and Dresden, where he was imprisoned for seven years. He was then sent back to Russia, where he was exiled to Siberia. From there he escaped in 1861, fled to Western Europe and never returned to Russia. Bakunin was **Marx**'s main opponent in the First International, and helped to split it. He believed that the state and its authority should be abolished during a social revolution. He disagreed with Marx that there should be a dictatorship of the proletariat, as he thought that this would become a dictatorship *over* the proletariat and produce a new, more powerful and oppressive system. He also rejected Marx's belief that the proletariat should form a political party and work within the parliamentary system to gain benefits for the workers. Bakunin believed that all political parties were 'varieties of absolutism'. Peasants and workers should overthrow their oppressors by their own direct action and then build a new society based on the free association of workers. Bakunin's main influence was in Spain, southern Italy and parts of France, though his belief that 'the passion for destruction is also a creative passion' was shared by the Russian **nihilists**.

**Baldwin, Stanley, 1st Earl** (1867–1947). British Prime Minister (1923, 1924–9, 1935–7). The son of a rich ironmaster in the Midlands, Baldwin spent twenty years in the family firm before he followed his father as Conservative MP for Bewdley in 1908, a seat he retained until he went to the **Lords** in 1937. He first joined the Cabinet in 1921 as President of the Board of Trade but was highly critical of 'the morally disintegrating effect of **Lloyd George** on all whom he had to deal with' and particularly disliked his sale of honours. Speaking out strongly against the **coalition government**, he helped to bring it to an end and became Chancellor of the Exchequer in Bonar **Law**'s administration. When Law resigned in 1923 owing to ill health, Baldwin became Prime Minister in preference to **Curzon**, as leading Conservatives and **George V** felt that the leader of the government should be a member of the **Commons**. Baldwin was convinced that tariffs were necessary to protect British industry, but Bonar Law had promised not to introduce them without the nation's approval, so Baldwin called an election in 1923. He was much criticized for this unforced error, as the Conservatives lost their overall majority (with 258 seats instead of 344), though they were still the largest party. This allowed the **Labour Party** to form a (minority) government for the first time. Conservative fortunes were restored at the 1924 election, when they won an overwhelming victory (with 419 seats out of 615) and Baldwin became Prime Minister again.

Humane and liberal, Baldwin detested 'the hard-faced men who looked as if they had done well out of the war' and did not share the contempt for Labour of Conservatives such as Neville **Chamberlain**. 'He is out to develop a democratic **Conservatism**', wrote **Haldane**, 'and he has a great deal of sympathy with the aspirations of Labour.' Baldwin's relaxed style of leadership – he usually allowed his ministers to run their departments without interference – was accompanied by decisive intervention when he thought it necessary. In 1925 he stopped the attempt of some **Tories** to ban the trade-union political levy and a year later he forced through the nationalization of the electricity supply industry by creating the Central Electricity Generating Board, which many Conservatives regarded as a socialist measure. Baldwin's ministry was the most reforming Conservative administration since the 1870s. The British Broadcasting Corporation was another nationalized enterprise; pensions were extended to widows and orphans; the **Poor Law** Boards were abolished, their functions passing to County and Borough Councils, who were given a block grant; business rates were drastically reduced. The Franchise Act of 1928 gave the vote to all women over twenty-one – the same age as for men. Winston **Churchill** was welcomed back to the **Conservative Party** after twenty years with the Liberals and became Chancellor of the

Exchequer. His return to the **gold standard** in 1925, regarded as the best way to restore financial stability, was a controversial measure which reduced British exports and helped to bring about the **General Strike** of 1926. Baldwin refused to take the repressive measures suggested by some of his colleagues, but with a combination of tact, patience and firmness he carried public opinion with him in ending the strike. However, the effort exhausted him and he allowed the Trades Disputes Act (1927), which many regarded as a vindictive attack on the trade unions, to go through. Foreign policy he left to Austen **Chamberlain**, whose main success was at **Locarno**.

With unemployment rising, Baldwin lost the 1929 election, but joined the **National Government** under Ramsay **MacDonald** in 1931 and let it run for four years, in spite of the Conservatives' clear majority in the 1931 election. When MacDonald resigned in 1935, Baldwin began his last period as Prime Minister. He fought the 1935 election campaign with the promise of 'no great armaments' but this, with support for the **League of Nations** and collective security, was in tune with the isolationist mood of the country, so the Conservatives were returned with a huge majority. Baldwin approved of the **Hoare–Laval Pact** with **Mussolini**, but when this was leaked to the press there was such an uproar that his Foreign Secretary, Sir Samuel Hoare, was forced to resign. With the German occupation of the **Rhineland** more attention was paid to Britain's defensive needs, so in 1936 Baldwin began a programme of aircraft construction which in three years added 8,000 of the latest aircraft (Hurricanes, Spitfires and Blenheims) to the RAF, enabling it to win the battle of **Britain** in 1940. Baldwin collapsed in the summer of 1936 and would have retired but for the **abdication crisis**. He persuaded **Edward VIII** that he could not remain King if he married a divorced woman, but the strain was too much for him, so he resigned after the coronation of George VI and went to the **Lords**. When the **Second World War** began Baldwin's reputation plummeted: he was denounced as one of the 'guilty men' who had failed to rearm or to oppose **Hitler**.

**Balfour, Arthur James, 1st Earl** (1848–1930). British Prime Minister (1902–5). Nephew of the Marquess of **Salisbury**, Balfour came from the landed aristocracy. He was an intellectual, with a deep love of music, art, literature and philosophy. His great personal charm and languid manner concealed his occasional ruthlessness. Beatrice **Webb** described him as 'strong-willed, swift in execution, utterly cynical and honestly contemptuous of that pitiful myth "Democracy"'. Balfour entered the **Commons** in 1874 as a Conservative and made a success of a post which had ruined many reputations, Chief Secretary for Ireland (1889–91). A strong opponent of **Home Rule for Ireland**, his use of troops to keep order earned him a reputation as 'Bloody Balfour', but he succeeded where **Gladstone** had failed in enabling tenants to buy land with the **Irish Land Acts** of 1888 and 1891.

Balfour was groomed by his uncle for the post of Prime Minister from 1891, when he became Leader of the Commons and First Lord of the Treasury. When he duly succeeded Salisbury in 1902, he strongly supported the **Education Act** (1902), which extended secondary education throughout the country, and he was the driving force behind the *Entente Cordiale* (1904) with France; but his administration split over **tariff reform**, which offered protection to British industries facing severe foreign competition. Joseph **Chamberlain** resigned from the government in 1903 to take his campaign to the country. Balfour tried to keep the **Conservative Party** together by not committing himself, but could not prevent tariff reform being the dominant issue in the 1906 election. The **Liberals** presented it as a tax on bread, which resulted in the Conservatives suffering a crushing defeat.

As Leader of the Opposition, Balfour used the Conservative majority in the **Lords** to block or mutilate Liberal legislation, including the **'People's Budget'** of 1909. This led to a constitutional crisis in which **Asquith** introduced a **Parliament Bill** to curb the powers of the Lords, and obtained the consent of King **George V** to create enough Liberal peers to ensure its passage. At this stage Balfour realized the futility of rejecting the bill and persuaded the Lords to pass it. He then resigned as leader of the Conservative Party. His career revived during the **First World War**, when there was a **coalition government**. The only Conservative offered a senior post by Asquith, Balfour became First Lord of the Admiralty (1915–16) and then Foreign Secretary (1916–19) under **Lloyd**

**George**: in this post he issued the **Balfour Declaration** (1917), which gave the support of the British government for a national home for the Jews in Palestine. Balfour continued to hold public office till he was eighty as Lord President of the Council (1919–22 and 1925–9), and led the British delegation to the **Washington Conference** (1921–2).

**Balfour Declaration** (November 1917). A statement of British government policy in Palestine, which took the form of a letter from A. J. **Balfour**, the Foreign Secretary, to a leading British Jew, Lord **Rothschild**. 'His Majesty's Government', it said, 'view with favour the establishment in Palestine of a National Home for the Jewish people . . . it being clearly understood that nothing shall be done which may prejudice the civil and religious rights of existing non-Jewish communities in Palestine.' It was not clear what this meant. The British could argue that it simply offered Jews a home in Palestine, where they had lived for centuries (according to the British census of 1918 there were 700,000 Arabs and 56,000 Jews in Palestine), and that they had no intention that the Jews should take over the whole of Palestine or found a Jewish state there. Yet this was precisely what **Zionists** wanted, as they attributed their misfortunes to their world-wide minority status. The Declaration was included in the **Palestine mandate**, which the **League of Nations** assigned to Britain in 1920.

**Balkan Wars** (1912–13). Russia played a major role in persuading Serbia and Bulgaria to form an alliance in February 1912, in order to prevent an Austrian advance southwards. However, when Italy attacked **Tripoli**, the two countries saw an opportunity to attack Turkey and divide Macedonia between them. They were joined by Greece and Montenegro, in what became known as the Balkan League. When they attacked Turkey in October 1912 and defeated her, the Great Powers became alarmed, especially Austria, who did not wish to see Serbia gain part of the Adriatic coast. The powers therefore met in London in 1913 and created a new state, Albania, to prevent Serbia reaching the Adriatic. As she was denied this prize, Serbia demanded a larger share of Macedonia. This brought her into conflict with Bulgaria (Macedonia had formed part of the Greater Bulgaria set up at the Treaty of **San Stefano** in 1878 but had been returned to Turkey at the **Berlin Congress** in the same year), who declared war on Serbia and Greece in June 1913, thus beginning the second Balkan War. This was a war not against Turkey but among the victors of the first Balkan War. Romania joined Serbia and Greece, who crushingly defeated Bulgaria. At the Treaty of Bucharest (August 1913) most of Macedonia went to Serbia, the rest (and Western Thrace) to Greece. Bulgaria had to give up the southern Dobrudja to Romania. Izvolsky, the Russian Foreign Minister, had warned in October 1912 that a victory of the League over Turkey would be 'fraught with threatening consequences for the general peace; it would bring forward ... the struggle of Slavdom ... with Germanism. In this event one ... must prepare for a great and decisive general European War.' Austria was alarmed, as Serbia had doubled in size and there were many Serbs in the Habsburg Empire who wanted to join her. This threat to the Empire's stability led some Austrians, including the Chief of Staff, Conrad, to seek an excuse for a war against Serbia: this was provided by the assassination of the heir to the Austrian throne, the Archduke Franz Ferdinand, at **Sarajevo** in June 1914. Another result of the Balkan Wars was that Turkey lost all her European possessions, except for the small area between Adrianople (Edirne) and Constantinople (Istanbul), which she still holds.

**Barbarossa, Operation** (1941). The code-name for the German invasion of the Soviet Union in the **Second World War**. **Hitler** had talked of gaining *Lebensraum* ('living-space') in the east as early as 1924, when he wrote the first volume of *Mein Kampf*. In 1940 he decided to invade the Soviet Union in May 1941, although Britain had not been defeated. He realized that the USA might come into the war on the side of Britain and that he might therefore be faced with a two-front war, but he reckoned that he could defeat the Russians in two months. Hitler delayed his attack until 22 June so that he could first conquer Yugoslavia and Greece (where his ally **Mussolini** badly needed help). Stalin had ample warning of the attack from the British and from Richard **Sorge**, a Russian spy in Japan, but he did not believe them and was caught by surprise. The Germans began with a three-pronged attack on an 1,800-mile front. Army Group North was to move through the

Baltic states and seize Leningrad, Army Group Centre was to head for Moscow and Army Group South for the Ukraine and the Caucasus. The aim was to eliminate most of the Red Army in six weeks by *Blitzkrieg*, with Panzer groups encircling Russian armies. The Soviet army had suffered severely from the **Great Purges** in 1937, when most of its high-ranking officers had been executed, and therefore responded slowly and unimaginatively to the invasion, but it was better in some respects than the Germans expected. Its élite force was the artillery, excellent in both equipment and men. The Russians had 1,500 new tanks – heavy KVs and T34s (the best tank in the war), which were too heavily armoured to be knocked out by German tanks or by any anti-tank gun except the 88mm. Above all, the Russians appeared to have inexhaustible supplies of troops. Halder, the German Chief of Staff, wrote in August, 'the Russian colossus has been underestimated by us . . . we had expected 200 enemy divisions. Now we have already counted 360.' At first the *Wehrmacht* (German armed forces) made rapid advances, but by August it had become clear that the objectives of Barbarossa could not be met before the autumn rains. In spite of appalling casualties, the Red Army had not been destroyed, whilst partisans behind the front disrupted German supplies. One of the three prongs must be given priority. The German High Command wanted to concentrate on Moscow, the capital and hub of communications in the Soviet Union. Hitler did not agree. He wanted to consolidate his control of the Baltic in the north, and in the south to seize the Crimea, the food of the Ukraine and the industries of the Donetz basin. As Army Group South had advanced less quickly than Army Group Centre there was a large Russian salient at Kiev. Hitler ordered his centre to send its right wing, including **Guderian**'s Panzer group, to cut off the salient, which it did in one of the greatest victories of the war. Five Russian armies were encircled, yielding 665,000 prisoners, 884 tanks and 3,700 guns. Army Group South was then able to capture Kharkov on 24 October, advance to Rostov and occupy the Crimea; the Germans then resumed their advance on Moscow. When **Zhukov** took over the defence in October he had only 90,000 men, but when Sorge reported that the Japanese would not attack Russia, eight Soviet divisions with a thousand tanks and a thousand aircraft were moved from the Far

East to Moscow. By this time the Germans were having supply problems, as rain had turned the roads into mud. In November the ground became frozen and this made movement possible again, but by the end of the month temperatures were so low that the oil in vehicles froze (the Russians, equipped with winter oil, were unaffected) and the German tanks could not move. The Russians, with well-equipped and fresh troops from the east, began a counter-attack early in December which pushed the Germans back from Moscow. Barbarossa had produced for Germany some of the biggest victories in the history of warfare, in which the Russians had lost over four million men, but it had failed to attain its major objectives, the capture of Moscow and Leningrad. The Soviet Union had survived, and in so doing it had prevented Hitler from dominating the whole of Europe and made possible his eventual downfall.

**Barnado, Thomas John** (1845–1905). British social reformer. Born into a Spanish Protestant family in Dublin, he went to London in 1862 and qualified as a doctor. Barnado became superintendent of a 'ragged school' (free school for poor children) in the East End, where he set up a home for destitute boys in 1870, to be followed by one for girls in 1876. Over ninety 'Dr Barnado's Homes' were built during his lifetime, which cared for 60,000 children. They still thrive.

**Bastille, fall of the** (14 July 1789). When the **Estates-General** met in May 1789 there was conflict between the Crown and the privileged Estates (clergy and nobles) on the one hand and the Third Estate on the other, particularly when the latter claimed the right to manage the affairs of the nation and called itself the National Assembly in June. **Louis XVI** increased the number of troops round Paris with the apparent intention of using them to dissolve the Assembly. This was prevented by the revolt of the people of Paris. They began seizing arms but were short of gunpowder and cartridges, so they marched on the fortress of the Bastille. The government would have used its troops to crush the rising but they proved unreliable and some French Guards deserted to join the Parisians besieging the Bastille. When the crowds entered the inner courtyard the Governor, de Launay, ordered his troops to fire. Ninety-eight of those laying siege were killed before the French

Guards, using cannon, broke in: de Launay, forced to surrender, was decapitated. Those who attacked the Bastille were not the wealthy middle class but *sans-culottes* – master craftsmen and journeymen of the working-class districts. At the height of the rebellion about a quarter of a million Parisians were under arms. The fall of the Bastille had far-reaching results. The King had lost control of Paris, so the Assembly could now draw up a constitution safe from the threat of being dissolved by the King. Real power had passed from the King to the elected representatives of the people. When news of the Bastille's fall spread throughout France, the authority of the King collapsed in most French towns, as it had done in Paris, whilst in the countryside the peasant revolution, which had already begun, was extended and intensified. The revolt of Paris also began the emigration of some nobles, led by the King's brother, the Comte d'Artois (the future King **Charles X**): 20,000 fled abroad in two months. Gouverneur Morris, later US ambassador to France, wrote to George Washington, 'You may consider the revolution to be over, since the authority of the King and the nobles has been utterly destroyed.'

**Batlle y Ordóñez, José** (1856–1929). President of Uruguay (1903–7, 1911–15). The son of a former President, Batlle founded a daily newspaper *El Dia* in 1886, in which he called for honest elections and administration and appeared as a champion of the working class, demanding a shorter working week and the right to strike. As President he made Uruguay the first **Welfare State** in Latin America, providing an eight-hour working day, minimum wages, old-age pensions, compensation for industrial accidents and regulation of working conditions. He also introduced free and compulsory primary and secondary education, university education for women and a divorce law (he was the first Latin American statesman to call publicly for women's rights). Batlle set up public corporations to reduce foreign economic influence in Uruguay and nationalized electric power and the telephone services. As the Constitution did not allow a President to hold office for two consecutive sessions, he travelled to Europe in 1907 to study governmental systems and was particularly impressed by that of Switzerland. Convinced that executive power in the hands of one man leads to dictatorship, Batlle wanted Uruguay to replace the office of President with a National Council, whose members would represent all shades of political opinion. The Constitution of 1918 reached a compromise, retaining a President but also creating a National Council. It provided too for separation of Church and State, as Batlle wished. His ideals, *batllismo*, continued to have a wide following long after his death.

**Beaverbrook, William Maxwell Aitken, Baron** (1879–1964). British newspaper proprietor. The son of a Scottish Presbyterian minister in Ontario, Beaverbrook made a fortune by amalgamating all the cement companies in Canada before moving to England in 1910. Elected as a Conservative MP in the same year, he rarely spoke in the **Commons** and did not become prominent until he bought the *Daily Express*, a rival to **Northcliffe**'s *Daily Mail*, in 1916. He was owner of Express Newspapers until his death and had complete editorial control of the *Daily Express, Sunday Express* and the London *Evening Standard*, which he used to publicize his belief in the British Empire. By 1936 the *Express* had a circulation of two and a quarter million, the largest in the world at that time. From 1929–31 Beaverbrook used his newspapers unsuccessfully in a campaign to remove **Baldwin** as leader of the **Conservative Party** and was savaged by Baldwin for exercising 'power without responsibility, the prerogative of the harlot throughout the ages'. Beaverbrook again unsuccessfully adopted a lost cause when he sought to gain support for **Edward VIII**'s proposed morganatic marriage to Wallis Simpson during the **abdication crisis** (1936). He held office in both world wars, in 1918 as Minister of Information, in 1940 as Minister of Aircraft Production, when he was credited with tripling the number of aircraft built between May and August 1940, though this was possible only because of action taken before he became minister. As **Churchill**'s closest friend for much of the war, he held other government posts (Minister of Supply 1941–2, Lord Privy Seal 1943–5), retiring from political life in 1945.

**Bebel, August** (1840–1913). Co-founder of the German **Social Democratic Party** (SPD) and its most popular leader for nearly forty years. Bebel's father was a Prussian army corporal, his mother a domestic servant, so he grew up in extreme poverty and became a metal turner. In 1865 he met Wilhelm Liebknecht, who converted him to **socialism**. In 1867 Bebel entered the Reichstag of the **North German Confederation** as a member of the Saxon People's Party. This and similar parties united in 1869 to form the German Social Democratic Workers Party. Bebel and Liebknecht were the only ones to vote against a war loan for the **Franco-Prussian War** (1870–71), and both condemned the annexation of **Alsace-Lorraine**. Tried for high treason, they were imprisoned for two years.

In 1875 Bebel's followers and those of Lassalle joined to form the German **Social Democratic Party** (SPD). Bebel made the SPD into a Marxist party committed to revolution, and rejected **Bernstein**'s revisionism, refusing to cooperate with *bourgeois* parties. This led him to clash in the **Second International** with the French socialist Jean **Jaurès**, who was prepared to support *bourgeois* governments. 'I want to remain', Bebel said in 1903, 'the deadly enemy of this *bourgeois* society . . . and to eliminate it entirely.' Yet his revolutionary rhetoric was at odds with his political practice. He courageously condemned German action in the **Moroccan crisis** of 1911 and declared that expansion of the German navy was the 'real danger' to the German people, but he rejected Rosa **Luxemburg**'s call for revolution. Under his leadership the SPD increased its membership to over one million, and in the 1912 Reichstag election it won more seats than any other party.

**Beneš, Edvard** (1884–1948). Foreign Minister and President of Czechoslovakia (1935–8, 1945–8). Beneš escaped from Austria-Hungary in 1915 and joined Tomáš **Masaryk** in Paris, where they led the movement for Czech independence. As Foreign Minister of the new state of Czechoslovakia, he attended the **Paris Peace Conference** (1919), where he opposed the union of Austria and Germany. In 1921 he formed the **Little Entente**, with Yugoslavia and Romania, to make sure that Hungary observed the terms of the Treaty of **Trianon** (1920). A strong advocate of the **League of Nations**, Beneš supported the Soviet Union's entry into the League (1934) and in 1935 made a pact of mutual assistance with her. He succeeded Masaryk as President in 1935 but resigned in 1938 when Czechoslovakia was 'disgracefully betrayed' by Britain and France at **Munich**. Beneš went into voluntary exile, becoming head of the Czechoslovak National Committee in London. At the end of the **Second World War** he returned to Czechoslovakia to become President again, in the only government-in-exile allowed to return to Eastern Europe. As communist influence spread he had to accept Klement Gottwald as Prime Minister, but he refused to agree to a new Soviet-style constitution and resigned in June 1948. He died, a broken man, shortly afterwards.

**Bennett, Richard Bedford** (1870–1947). Canadian Prime Minister (1930–35). Bennett became leader of the Conservative Party in 1927 and in the 1930 election accused the Liberals of 'timidity and vacillation' and of doing little to cope with the **Great Depression**. Promising a public works programme and higher tariffs, he won the election and became Prime Minister. Bennett persuaded parliament to vote twenty million dollars for emergency relief work and increased the tariff by nearly 50 per cent. As a result, Canada had a surplus in her trade balance because there were fewer imports, but he made exporting more difficult by refusing to devalue the dollar and so kept prices high. Bennett presided over the Imperial Economic Conference at Ottawa in 1932, at which Canada made tariff-reducing agreements with Britain and other Commonwealth countries. As the recession deepened, the government was blamed. Bennett reacted at first by repression. During his first four years in office he appeared to be creating a police state: spies were sent to labour-union meetings; marches of the unemployed were broken up by Mounties; agitators were arrested. These measures did nothing to ease the impact of the Depression, so in January 1935, in a series of radio broadcasts, he announced a New Deal for the Canadian people. Conservative MPs, who had not been consulted, were astonished when he told his listeners, 'you have been the witnesses of grave defects and abuses in the capitalist system'. Major acts provided for social and unemployment insurance, minimum wages and maximum hours of work in industry. Bennett appeared to be acting more like a socialist than a conservative. Mackenzie **King** exploited the divisions in the Tory Party and accused Bennett of being a dictator, who had not even consulted his own Cabinet and who had made the Depression worse with his high tariff. In the 1935 election the Tories won only thirty-nine seats, the Liberals

171. Bennett later settled in England and in 1941 became a member of the House of **Lords**.

**Bentham, Jeremy** (1748–1832). English philosopher and reformer. The founder of utilitarianism, which held that the morality of an action should not be measured according to religious criteria but by 'utility' – its effect on people. The aim of government should be 'the greatest happiness of the greatest number'. His main concern was reform of the law, and as early as 1776 he ridiculed the reliance on precedent of Common Lawyers in *A Fragment on Government*. Between 1807 and 1810 he came, under the influence of his friend and neighbour James Mill, to believe that political reform was a precondition for all other reform, and he put forward demands for manhood suffrage, equal electoral districts and annual parliaments. A fervent believer in democracy, Bentham thought that politicians would serve the public good only if they were elected, as they would be rejected at the next election if they did not do so. Bentham accepted *laissez-faire* as the most efficient way of running the economy, but he was in favour of state intervention in social legislation by providing services such as schools, which the free market would largely ignore. By the 1820s Bentham had a reputation in Europe and Latin America as well as in England, where his ideas spread through the *Westminster Review* (founded in 1824). In 1828 he and his followers established a non-sectarian college as a rival to Oxford and Cambridge; it became University College, London in 1836. Bentham had a great influence on educated public opinion and on the political leaders and public servants (such as **Peel** and **Chadwick**) who sat on Royal Commissions and drafted laws, for example the **Poor Law** Amendment Act of 1834.

**Berlin Conference** (1884–5). An international conference to discuss African affairs of concern to the Great Powers. The conference was called by the German Chancellor, **Bismarck**, who was anxious to protect Germany's new commercial and territorial interests in Africa from British claims. The powers agreed that colonial territory could only be claimed if it was under effective occupation; that the rivers Congo and Niger should be open to free trade and navigation; and that every effort should be made to suppress the slave trade and slavery in Africa. Colonial powers later ignored these principles when they proved inconvenient. The most important outcome of the conference was the international recognition given to King **Leopold**'s Congo Free State. The conference speeded up the partition of Africa, as European powers felt compelled to stake out their claims formally.

**Berlin Congress** (1878). A conference of European powers, presided over by **Bismarck**, to revise the Treaty of **San Stefano**, which had ended the **Russo-Turkish War** of 1877–8. Austria was particularly upset at San Stefano, as Russian promises made to her at the Budapest Convention in 1877 had been ignored: a large Slav state, Bulgaria, had been established and Austria had not received Bosnia and Hercegovina. Britain sided with Austria, as she did not want to see Russian influence extend to the Aegean. The autonomous Bulgaria created at San Stefano was reduced to a third of its size and was cut off from the Aegean; Macedonia was returned to Turkey (conflict over this area was to lead to the **Balkan War** of 1912), as was Eastern Rumelia, Serbia, Montenegro and Romania retained their independence; and Russia kept her gains in **Bessarabia** and the **Caucasus**. Russia, therefore, had not done badly, but Tsar **Alexander II** was very angry, as Russia had done all the fighting against Turkey, yet states that had not fought at all made significant gains: Britain acquired Cyprus and Austria was given the right to occupy Bosnia and Hercegovina and Novipasar, which separated Serbia and Montenegro. This was the last piece of territory to be acquired by the Habsburgs, a move that was very unpopular with the people who lived there: there was a revolt which it took Austria three months and 200,000 troops to suppress. Alexander's claim that the congress had been a 'European coalition against Russia under the leadership of Prince Bismarck' soured his relations with Germany and led Bismarck to make the **Dual Alliance** (1879) with Austria.

**Bernadotte, Jean-Baptiste Jules** (1763–1844). Marshal of France and King of Sweden (1818–44). From a *petit-bourgeois* family, Bernadotte entered the royal army as a private in 1780. A fervent supporter of the **French Revolution**, he received rapid promotion, becoming a general in 1793 and a marshal in 1804. **Napoleon Bonaparte** gave him important commands at the battle of **Austerlitz** (1805), where Bernadotte was in charge of the central reserve, and at Jena (1806) (see battles of **Jena–Auerstädt**), where his failure to obey orders almost resulted in his being court-martialled. Bernadotte managed to redeem himself by vigorous pursuit of the Prussians to the Baltic, where he accepted their surrender and that of a Swedish division, which had been sent to help them. His courteous treatment of the Swedes, whom he allowed to return home, prepared the way for his future career. When he failed at Wagram (1809) to check an assault on his position by the Austrians, Napoleon relieved him of his command and he returned to France in disgrace. The Swedes, who had recently lost Finland to Russia, wanted a strong military figure as heir apparent (Charles XIII had no surviving children), so they offered Bernadotte the position in 1810. Napoleon allowed him to become Crown Prince as he thought Sweden would be a loyal satellite, but from now on Bernadotte put the interests of Sweden above those of France. After Napoleon seized Swedish Pomerania in 1812, Bernadotte brought Sweden into the coalition against France and fought at **Leipzig** with the Allies. He hoped to succeed Napoleon as ruler of France when the Emperor abdicated but his fellow marshals regarded him as a traitor, so he returned to Sweden and arranged for the annexation of Norway to Sweden at the Congress of **Vienna**. In 1818 he became King of Sweden, as Charles XIV, and showed that he was an enlightened reformer by accepting parliamentary control of taxation and the responsibility of ministers to the elected **Diet**, and by encouraging codification of the laws. His descendants remain on the thrones of Sweden and Norway.

**Bernstein, Eduard** (1850–1932). German socialist and critic of **Marx**. A Berlin Jew, Bernstein was the son of an engine driver. He joined the Social Democratic Workers Party in 1872, but **Bismarck**'s **Anti-socialist law** forced him to emigrate to England, where from 1882–1901 he was a close friend of **Engels** (whose literary executor he became), and was strongly influenced by the **Fabians**. From 1896–8 he published a series of articles, which attempted to revise the outdated ideas of Marxism and made him the leading exponent of revisionism. Bernstein argued that Marx's predictions about the development of capitalism had not come true and that this failure undermined the claims of Marxism to be a science. There had been no 'immiseration' of the workers, whose real wages had risen; the polarization of classes between an oppressed proletariat and capitalists had not taken place, as the middle class had expanded dramatically, particularly the lower-middle class of white-collar workers; instead of capital becoming concentrated in fewer hands, it had become more widely diffused through joint-stock companies; the contradictions of capitalism had not led to its early collapse, and it was stronger than ever. As these predictions were the basis of Marx's theory of revolution, Bernstein claimed that this should be discarded. Socialism was not the inevitable result of the collapse of capitalism, Bernstein believed, but should be regarded as a moral ideal, the successor to **liberalism**. The move to **socialism** should be gradual and workers should take control by peaceful and parliamentary means, through the ballot box. He called on the German **Social Democratic Party** (SPD) 'to appear what it in fact now is, a democratic, socialist party of reform'. Bernstein's ideas were strongly opposed by **Bebel** and the revolutionary **Left**, led by Rosa **Luxemburg**, and were always rejected at congresses of the SPD, though they were widely accepted by trade-union leaders and found support in socialist parties throughout Europe. Bernstein was an SPD deputy in the **Reichstag** from 1902–6, 1912–18 and 1920–28, and showed considerable courage in opposing Germany's declaration of war in 1914. He called for an early peace and in 1915 voted against war credits. In 1917 Bernstein left the SPD to join the more radical Independent Socialist Party (USPD), but rejoined the SPD after the war and took part in drafting its programme.

**Besant, Annie** (1847–1933). English feminist, socialist and theosophist. Brought up as an **evangelical** Christian, Besant became an atheist and was President of the Theosophical Society from 1907 until her death. At the age of eighteen she made a disastrous marriage with the Reverend Frank Besant, from whom she separated in 1873. She then came under the influence of the radical leader Charles Bradlaugh and joined his National Secular Society in 1874. Three years later Besant wrote a pamphlet on birth control, which sold 110,000 copies in ten years. In the 1880s she became a socialist, joined the **Fabian Society** and was strike leader in the London Match Girls' Strike (1888). She converted to theosophy, a system of beliefs derived from Hinduism and Buddhism, in 1889 and as a result went in 1893 to India, which became her home. In 1898 she founded the Central Hindu College, which later became Benares Hindu University. Besant did not take up politics again till 1913, when she supported Home Rule for India within the British Empire, but her appeal was always to the English-speaking middle classes rather than to the masses. In 1916 she formed a Home Rule League and was foolishly arrested by the Madras government a year later. This made Besant a martyr and popular hero, so that after her release she was made President of the **Indian National Congress**, one of only three Britons to hold this office. Annie Besant was disliked intensely by the British in India for her feminism, socialism and theosophy, as well as for her support for Indian independence. Her Home Rule campaign was largely responsible for the **Montagu–Chelmsford reforms** of 1919, but her influence was short-lived. She was soon eclipsed by **Gandhi** and his **non-cooperation movement**, of which she disapproved as she regarded it as anarchic. Her support for the government in the **Amritsar massacre** of 1919 alienated many former Indian supporters, so she gave up active politics.

**Bessarabia.** Territory lying between the rivers Prut and Dnestr. It formed part of the **Ottoman Empire** in Moldavia until 1812, when Russia annexed it after the **Russo-Turkish War** of 1806–12. The southern part was returned to Moldavia in 1856 after Russia's defeat in the **Crimean War**, but was regained by Russia after the **Russo-Turkish War** of 1877–8. Much of the population was Romanian, and Bessarabia was taken over by Romania in 1918, after the **October Revolution** in Russia. The **Nazi–Soviet Pact** of 1939 gave Russia a free hand there, and so in 1940 the Soviet Union gave Romania an ultimatum, demanding Bessarabia. Romania was forced to give it up but reoccupied it from 1941–4 after the German invasion of the USSR. After the victory of the Red Army Bessarabia returned to Russia and became the Moldavian Soviet Socialist Republic.

**Bethmann-Hollweg, Theobald von** (1856–1921). German statesman. Bethmann-Hollweg became Prussian Minister of the Interior (1905–7), filled a similar post in Germany (1907–9) and was German

Chancellor from 1909–17. This cautious, fatalistic and gloomy conservative was imbued with ideas prevalent in the German bureaucracy at the beginning of the twentieth century: he disliked democracy, as he thought it led to corruption, and was contemptuous of politicians in the **Reichstag**. He shared the common belief in *Weltpolitik*, as Germany's world position did not correspond with its military or industrial strength. Bethmann wanted to see a large German colonial empire carved out of the Belgian Congo and the Portuguese colonies, and a German-dominated *Mitteleuropa*. After the assassination of Archduke Franz Ferdinand at **Sarajevo** in June 1914, Bethmann wanted swift action by Austria against Serbia, so that the other powers would be presented with a *fait accompli* and there would be only a local war. He realized that this was 'a leap in the dark' and might lead to war with Russia, but he thought it a risk worth taking, as it would be better to fight Russia then rather than a few years later, when she would be stronger. 'The future belongs to Russia, which is growing and growing and imposes herself upon us like an ever-increasing nightmare.' When a general war did come, Bethmann did not share the view that it would strengthen the monarchy, but warned that 'a world war with its unforeseeable consequences will greatly strengthen the power of social democracy, since it preaches peace and will topple many a throne'. When war began he did not arrest all the socialist leaders, as the military wanted, since he had assured himself of the support of the **Social Democratic Party** by making it appear in the **July crisis** that Russia had started the war. Recognition that the workers would have to be granted concessions (such as abandoning the three-tier franchise in Prussia, which favoured the *Junkers*) as a reward for their sacrifices brought him into conflict with military leaders, as did his opposition to unrestricted submarine warfare, which he knew would bring the USA into the war. He resisted the unrestricted U-boat campaign until 1917 when, having lost support in the Reichstag on this issue, he finally and reluctantly gave way. When **Hindenburg** and **Ludendorff** threatened to resign if Bethmann remained in office, he decided to spare the Emperor any embarrassment by resigning in July 1917.

**Beveridge, William Henry, 1st Baron** (1879–1963). British civil servant and social reformer. The son of a judge in the Indian civil service, Beveridge went to Oxford and then became sub-warden (1903–5) at **Toynbee Hall**, where he began his investigation of social issues, such as unemployment, which was to be a life-long interest. In 1908 he entered the Board of Trade at Winston **Churchill**'s invitation and took part in drafting the Labour Exchanges Act (1909) and **Lloyd George**'s **National Insurance Act** (1911). He left the civil service in 1919 to become Director of the London School of Economics, where he remained until 1937, when he became Master of University College, Oxford. In the **Second World War** Beveridge was recalled to the Civil Service, and as Chairman of the Committee on Social Insurance (1940) he was asked to look into existing schemes of social security, which had grown up haphazardly, and make recommendations. The Report on Social Insurance and Allied Services (1942), known as the Beveridge Report, made wide-ranging suggestions. It proposed a free national health service, family allowances, government action to maintain full employment, and universal social insurance 'from the cradle to the grave'. This included unemployment, sickness and accident benefits, old-age and widows' pensions, funeral grants and maternity benefits. Beveridge proposed that a new Ministry of Social Security should coordinate the whole system. These benefits were to be paid for by contributions from employers and the state, a system that had been adopted in Lloyd George's Insurance Act of 1911. Although there was little new in the report, which was a synthesis of existing ideas, it received wide press coverage and enthusiastic public approval, selling 630,000 copies (including 50,000 in America). It received vigorous backing from most **Labour** and some **Conservative** MPs, which led to a series of government White Papers in 1944 accepting most of Beveridge's recommendations. These, with Butler's **Education Act** (1944) and the introduction of family allowances in 1945, laid the foundations of the **Welfare State**, which the Labour government of 1945–51 did so much to establish.

**Bevin, Ernest** (1881–1951). British **trade-union** leader and politician. Illegitimate, Bevin lived in poverty with his mother until she died in 1889, and then lived with a half-sister. He left school at eleven and had several poorly paid jobs before he became involved with the trade-union movement. Known as 'the dockers' KC' for arguing their case before wage tribunals, in 1922 he planned the amalgamation of eighteen unions into the Transport and General Workers Union (TGWU), which continued to absorb smaller unions until it was the largest in the country. As its General Secretary Bevin was the most powerful trade-union leader in Britain. In 1921 he had called for a General Council of the Trade Union Congress (TUC) and with Walter Citrine dominated that body in the 1920s and 1930s. He was a national leader of the **General Strike** (1926) and a member of the General Council which ended it. Bevin was responsible for building Transport House, completed in 1928, which became for a generation the home not only of his own union but of the TUC and the Labour Party. In 1929, as Chairman of the Board of the *Daily Herald*, he negotiated with Odhams Press for an infusion of capital, which enabled the paper's circulation to rise from 250,000 to two million by 1933. In theory the *Daily Herald*'s politics were controlled by the TUC and the **Labour Party**; in practice they were controlled by Bevin. As a member of the Macmillan Committee in 1930, he was convinced by **Keynes** that unemployment could be reduced by expanding, not by deflating, the economy. He therefore strongly opposed Snowden's proposed reductions in unemployment benefits in 1931 and thus helped to bring about the fall of **MacDonald**'s government. When MacDonald formed a **National Government** with **Liberals** and **Conservatives**, Bevin worked hard to have him replaced as leader of the Labour Party by Arthur **Henderson** and expelled from the party. Bevin and Citrine then arranged for the TUC to take control of the Labour Party. The National Joint Council, with representatives of the TUC, the Labour Party and the Parliamentary Labour Party (PLP), was re-formed so that the TUC appointed half its members. Bevin served on the National Council from 1931–7 and regarded the policy statements it made as binding on the leader of the PLP. His savage attack at the party conference in 1935 on the pacifist Lansbury for 'hawking his conscience around' led to Lansbury's resignation as leader of the PLP and his replacement by **Attlee**. A strong supporter of the **League of Nations** and collective security, Bevin was opposed to **Fascism** but refused to collaborate with the Communist Party in a 'United Front' against it. From the mid-1930s Bevin had heart trouble, and was considering retirement when Winston **Churchill** invited him to join his **coalition government** in 1940. He therefore became an MP at the age of fifty-nine and served with distinction as Minister of Labour from 1940–45, greatly expanding the labour force and persuading the trade unions to accept 'dilution', as Henderson had done in the **First World War**. At the end of the war Bevin was Foreign Secretary in Attlee's Labour administration.

**Biennio rosso** ('two red years') (1918–20). A period of chronic industrial and agrarian unrest in Italy which followed the **First World War**, caused by acute food shortages, inflation and unemployment, as two and a half million servicemen were demobilized. The bitterest clashes were in the industrial north-west and the agricultural regions of Emilia-Romagna and Tuscany. In Bologna, the capital of 'Red Emilia', there was a long agricultural strike, during which the harvest rotted in the fields. In other areas priests led peasants to occupy the lands of the great estates. The climax of the *biennio rosso* came in August 1920, when workers occupied factories in Milan, Turin and Genoa. Over 400,000 members of the Metalworkers' Union and 100,000 from other unions took part. There was no violence, though Red Guards (following the Russian example) patrolled the factories. Industrialists demanded government action but the Prime Minister, **Giolitti**, would not use force and allowed the protest to run its course. Industrialists feared a **Bolshevik** revolution, but socialists and trade-union leaders were unwilling to start such a revolution as they were not sure that the workers would support one. Giolitti brought both sides together in September, negotiated a settlement, and the workers evacuated the factories. This was a humiliating experience for the employers, who were convinced that the Liberal government could not cope with the threat of revolution, so they turned to **Fascism** for a political solution. The large landowners too turned to the Fascists, whose **Blackshirts** terrorized socialist strongholds in the countryside. The greatest beneficiary of the *biennio rosso*, therefore, was **Mussolini**.

**Bismarck, Otto von** (1815–98). Prussian Minister-President (1862–90) and German Chancellor (1871–90). Bismarck was a

*Junker* from Brandenburg. Vindictive and ruthless in his quest for power, he could never tolerate opposing views, all of which he regarded as personal attacks upon himself. He wished to strengthen monarchical absolutism in Prussia, maintain the dominant position of the *Junkers* and make Prussia the most powerful state in Germany. As Prussian representative at the **Diet** of the **German Confederation** from 1851 to 1858, Bismarck had come to believe that Austria must be deposed from leadership of the Confederation, as he did not consider her strong enough to lead a successful crusade against **liberalism** in Germany. He first came to prominence in 1862, when he was appointed Minister-President in Prussia in order to push through **Roon**'s army reforms. It was at this time that he made his famous remark: 'The position of Prussia in Germany will be decided not by its liberalism but by its power . . . not through speeches and majority decisions are the great questions of the day decided – that was the great mistake of 1848–9 – but by blood and iron.' Towards the end of his life, in his 'Reminiscences' Bismarck wrote as though every move which led to German unification in 1871 was part of a premeditated master plan. In fact he was quite pragmatic and seized opportunities for advancing the interests of Prussia as they arose, not knowing precisely where they would lead. 'Politics', he wrote, 'is not in itself an exact and logical science but it is the capacity to choose in each fleeting moment of the situation that which is least harmful or most opportune.' He first of all fought with Austria in 1864 against Denmark over **Schleswig-Holstein**. Then, after skilfully isolating Austria diplomatically, he defeated her in the **Austro-Prussian War** (1866) and founded the **North German Confederation**, which was dominated by Prussia. Only France now stood in the way of German unification. It appeared that this would be delayed for some time, as Prussia could not afford to appear the aggressor, but luck came to her aid in the shape of the **Hohenzollern candidature for the Spanish throne** and the stupidity of the French Foreign Minister, Gramont, which enabled Bismarck to publish the **Ems telegram**. This brought about the **Franco-Prussian War**, in which France was easily defeated: the **German Empire** was proclaimed in the Hall of Mirrors at Versailles in January 1871. There is no doubt that Germany would have been united at some time politically, as it was already united economically by the Prussian *Zollverein*, but it would not have been united at that time and in that way without Bismarck.

After unification Bismarck, as German Chancellor, dominated both the foreign and domestic policies of the new Reich. Abroad he pursued a cautious and realistic policy of avoiding war, as Germany had destroyed the balance of power in Europe. Germany dominated the Continent militarily and Bismarck knew that any attempt to increase her power would lead to a coalition being formed against her. He therefore sought to keep France isolated, so she would not wage war to recover **Alsace-Lorraine**, and to prevent Austria from coming to blows with Russia over the Balkans. France was isolated by such measures as the *Dreikaiserbund* (1871) the **Dual Alliance** with Austria (1879) and the **Triple Alliance** with Austria and Italy (1882). What Bismarck could not do was remove the causes of the recurring crises: France would remain hostile until she recovered Alsace-Lorraine, whilst the weakness of the Ottoman Empire ensured revolts within it, which neither Austria nor Russia fomented but which neither could ignore. The difficulty of Bismarck's position was shown at the **Berlin Congress** (1878), when his attempt to play the 'honest broker' greatly displeased Russia. Though Bismarck's elaborate system of alliances helped to maintain peace among the great powers, his preventing Russia from obtaining loans in Germany in the *Lombardverbot* pushed her towards France. A **Franco-Russian alliance** was not far off when Bismarck fell from office in 1890, and the differences of Austria and Russia in the Balkans had not been resolved.

Bismarck's policy at home was much more acerbic and much less cautious than his policy abroad. His aim was, he wrote, 'to preserve and to strengthen the position of the royal government *vis-à-vis* the power claims of the parliaments'. By trying to keep the **Reichstag** powerless and by refusing to give any position of authority to the leaders of political parties, Bismarck retarded Germany's political growth and postponed responsible government until well into the twentieth century. 'He left a nation', wrote Max Weber in 1917, 'accustomed to submit, under the label of constitutional monarchy, to anything that was decided for it.' Bismarck called groups who opposed him *Reichsfeinde*, 'enemies of the Reich', and persecuted them maliciously, as he did the Catholics in his *Kulturkampf* and the socialists with his **anti-socialist law**. In each case he failed, and the **Centre Party** increased in strength under persecution, as did the **Social Democratic Party**. In an attempt to counter the appeal of **socialism** he introduced **state socialism**, a series of reforms giving workers various forms of insurance, which marked the beginning of the **Welfare State**. As Bismarck was not a party leader, he had to rely on various coalitions to acquire a majority in the Reichstag. For most of the 1870s he relied on the **National Liberals**, but turned against them and towards the **Centre Party** when he moved to protection in 1879. In the 1880s, as socialist strength increased, Bismarck considered a *coup* and was prepared to destroy the constitutional system he had created rather than see it controlled by his enemies. He fell in 1890 when he clashed with the young Emperor, **William II**, who wanted to be a popular monarch and introduce labour legislation in favour of the workers, a move the Chancellor resolutely resisted.

**Black Codes.** An attempt by the Southern states after the **American Civil War** to keep the Negroes in a state of subjection to the whites. Slavery was abolished in the thirteenth amendment to the Constitution (1865), so Southern legislatures passed the Black Codes. These gave Negroes certain rights: they could hold property and get married (though not to whites) but they could not vote, testify against whites in court or serve on juries. Freedmen had to sign contracts of employment for a year and could not strike or leave their employment. Any black travelling without his employer's permission could be arrested. In most states Negroes were excluded from occupations where they would compete with whites, which often meant that they were confined to agriculture and domestic service. There was outrage in the North at these Codes, so Congress passed a **Civil Rights Act** in 1866 to make them illegal and later passed the fourteenth amendment (see **Reconstruction**), which gave Negroes 'the equal protection of the laws'.

**'Black Friday'** (15 April 1921). During the **First World War** the British railways and coal mines had been nationalized. In 1920, at the end of the post-war boom, when coal prices had fallen, **Lloyd George** decided to return the mines to private ownership on 31 March 1921. The owners announced heavy wage cuts (up to 49 per cent in part of Wales), and then locked the miners out when they refused to accept the cuts. The transport workers and railwaymen agreed to strike in support of the miners on 16 April. Just before this the government tried to reopen negotiations, but the miners refused. On 15 April, the leaders of the transport workers and railwaymen demanded that the miners should resume negotiations, and called off their sympathetic strike when the miners turned down this request. Feeling betrayed, the miners named 15 April 'Black Friday'. They continued their strike until June, when they were forced to accept wage cuts which averaged 34 per cent. This failure of working-class solidarity created great bitterness and contributed to the weakness of **trade unions** in Britain up to the **Second World War**.

**Black Hand.** A Serbian secret society, 'Union or Death', was founded in 1911 and later became known as the Black Hand. Its aim was to free all Serbs living under foreign occupation and to incorporate them into the Kingdom of Serbia. Its head was Colonel Dimitrijević ('Apis'), chief of the intelligence department of the Serbian General Staff. The Black Hand established links, without the knowledge of the Serbian government, with Serb secret organizations in foreign countries such as 'Young Bosnia', whose members 'Apis' trained in terrorist methods and then sent back to **Sarajevo** to assassinate the heir to the Austro-Hungarian throne, Archduke Francis Ferdinand, in June 1914. This led to the outbreak of the **First World War**.

**Blackshirts.** The colloquial name for *Squadre d'Azione* (Action Squads), paramilitary Fascist groups (see **Fascism**) formed in Italy in 1919, which played a decisive role in the rise to power of **Mussolini**. They were recruited from war veterans, students and lower-middle-class youth and received financial support from rich landowners and industrialists, who wanted to strike back at the **trade unions** and socialists for taking such a prominent part in the *biennio rosso* (1918–20). The police and army did nothing to stop them, as Blackshirt punitive expeditions terrorized the countryside, attacking and often burning down the offices of left-wing newspapers and parties, trade unions and Catholic peasant leagues. Between

1920 and 1922 the organization of socialist and Catholic trade unions was destroyed in much of central and northern Italy and their membership fell dramatically, whilst that of the Fascists increased. The violence of the Blackshirts was a powerful weapon in bringing Mussolini to power but became a liability after the **March on Rome** (1922), as the Blackshirts gave their allegiance to local leaders, whom Mussolini had difficulty in controlling, and they were anarchic. Their battle cry *Me ne frego* ('I don't give a damn'), taken from **D'Annunzio**, showed their contempt for all authority. With **Matteotti**'s murder the Blackshirts again went on the rampage and forced Mussolini to begin setting up a Fascist dictatorship in January 1925. Anxious to gain the support of industrialists, large landowners, the army and the monarchy, all of whom disliked the Blackshirts' lack of discipline, Mussolini had them disbanded and disarmed in October 1925.

**Blanc, Louis** (1811–82). French politician and Utopian socialist. In 1843 Blanc joined *La Réforme*, a left-wing republican newspaper, and played a prominent role in the banquet campaign (1847–8) which led to the fall of **Louis Philippe**. A member of the radical minority in the 1848 provisional government, he persuaded it to reduce working hours and set up National Workshops to provide work for the unemployed. Blanc was put in charge of the Luxembourg Commission to discuss workers' grievances, but this was closed down in May. After the failure of the **June Days** rising of the unemployed, he fled to England and did not return to France until 1871, after the fall of **Napoleon III**. Elected as a deputy of the National Assembly, Blanc refused to join the **Paris Commune** but tried to obtain an amnesty for those involved in the rising. His ideal society was expounded in *The Organization of Labour* (1839), which advocated control of industry by the workers in social workshops financed by the state, in which (anticipating **Marx**) workers would be paid not according to what they produced but according to their needs. Blanc's ideas influenced later social reformers, especially Ferdinand Lassalle.

**Blanqui, Louis Auguste** (1805–81). French communist and theorist of the strategy of revolution, who took part in the **July**

**Revolution** (1830) which deposed **Charles X**. In 1839 Blanqui staged an armed rising in Paris with 500 followers against **Louis Philippe**, but was defeated after four days. Sentenced to death, this was commuted to life imprisonment. Blanqui was freed just before the 1848 revolution, during which he took part in a workers' demonstration against the Republic in May and was sentenced to ten years' imprisonment. After the fall of **Napoleon III**, Blanqui twice tried to overthrow the provisional government for not resolutely opposing the German invasion of France during the **Franco-Prussian War** (1870–71). He was arrested again just before the **Paris Commune** was set up and was not released until 1879. Blanqui spent a total of thirty-three years in prison, during which he developed his ideas about the revolutionary seizure of power. He believed that a small, highly disciplined party, led by professional revolutionaries, was needed to seize control of the state, as spontaneous, popular risings were rarely successful. Once in power there must be a 'dictatorship of the proletariat' to confiscate the wealth of the church and large landowners, and to impose common ownership of industry and commerce. Eventually, self-governing 'communes' would replace the repressive state. Blanqui called this new society 'communism' and himself a 'proletarian'. He greatly influenced future revolutionaries, including **Lenin**.

**Blitz.** The English name for the bombing of London and other English cities in 1940–41. From 7 September 1940, during the battle of **Britain**, German bombers concentrated on London and for sixty-eight consecutive nights, with one exception, they attacked the capital. The main targets outside London were Liverpool, Birmingham, Plymouth and Coventry. 42,000 civilians were killed and 50,000 seriously injured. Two million houses were destroyed, 60 per cent of them in London, but the Blitz did not seriously disrupt British industry or communications, a lesson ignored when the **strategic bombing offensive** began against Germany.

*Blitzkrieg* ('lightning war'). A word used to refer to German methods of attack in the early stages of the **Second World War**. **Hitler** wanted short campaigns of rapid movement, so that the German economy would not be strained and the civilian standard of living could be maintained. Panzer divisions of tanks, with motorized infantry and artillery and supported by dive-bombers, were concentrated on one part of the enemy sector. After breaking through they would fan out and disrupt communications in the enemy's rear, causing confusion and panic. This method was used most successfully by **Guderian** in Poland and in the fall of **France**.

**Blood River, battle of** (16 December 1838). During the **Great Trek** some Boers moved into Natal, where a party led by Piet Retief was treacherously murdered by the Zulu Chief Dingane, when visiting his *kraal*. The Boers, determined on revenge, formed a commando of 468 trekkers under Andries Pretorius. When they encountered the Zulus near the Ncome river they formed a *laager* – their wagons tied together in a circle with cannon in the only three openings. 10,000 Zulus attacked but were shot down before they reached the *laager*. When they retreated, Boer horsemen cut them down; those who hid in a deep ravine were systematically killed. 3,000 Zulus died on that day; three Boers were wounded. December 16 has become a day of great emotional significance for **Afrikaners**, when they proclaim their faith that God will protect them from their enemies.

**Bloody Sunday.** On 9 January 1905 about 200,000 people gathered in the working-class districts of St Petersburg, then moved off, led by a priest, towards the Winter Palace. Whole families joined in, many carrying icons or pictures of Tsar **Nicholas II**, the 'Little Father' of the Russian people. They were carrying a petition to the Tsar, signed by 135,000 people, asking for the right to strike and a reduction of the working day to eight hours. They also asked for major political reforms: 'Order the election of a Constituent Assembly on the basis of universal, secret and equal suffrage.' They were convinced that when the Tsar knew what his people wanted, he would take action to meet their requests. Before the procession reached the Winter Palace troops barred the way. Then, without warning, they fired into the tightly packed crowd. About a thousand were shot down, of whom 150 were killed. The massacre did more than anything else to undermine the allegiance of the common people to the Tsar. 'All classes condemn the authorities and more particularly the Emperor', the US consul in Odessa reported. Immediately there was a wave of strikes and unrest – the **Russian Revolution** of 1905 had begun.

**Blücher, Gebhard Liberecht von** (1742–1819). Prussian field marshal. Bluff, honest and earthy, with a weakness for gin, Blücher was very popular with his men. In 1793 he proved to be a courageous and determined leader of cavalry when he fought in the **French Revolutionary Wars**. Prussia was at peace with France from 1795 to 1806. On re-entering the war she was crushingly defeated by **Napoleon Bonaparte** at Jena (see battles of **Jena–Auerstädt**), where Blücher fought bravely in charge of the rear-guard and retreated in good order before surrendering. Napoleon, who could dictate his terms after the Treaty of **Tilsit**, prevented Blücher from taking up a command; it was not till 1812 and Napoleon's retreat from Moscow (see **Moscow Campaign**) that Blücher returned to the Prussian army. He took part in the War of Liberation in 1813 and fought at Lützen, Bautzen and **Leipzig**: for his part in this battle he was made a field marshal. Blücher continued, with the Austrians and Russians, to drive Napoleon out of Germany into northern France. Napoleon fought a brilliant defensive campaign, often getting the better of Blücher, whose singleminded persistence paid off in the end by securing Napoleon's abdication. After Napoleon's escape from Elba, Blücher took charge of Prussian troops in Belgium. Defeated at Ligny (16 June 1815), he refused to retreat east along his own line of communications, as this would leave the British to fight Napoleon alone, but made a dangerous march north to Waterloo. This decision, made by Blücher's Chief of Staff, General Gneisenau, was later described by **Wellington**, with pardonable hyperbole, as 'the decisive moment of the century'. The Prussians entered the battle of **Waterloo** in the early afternoon of 18 June, attacked Napoleon's flank and so deprived him of the reserves he needed to break the British line. Blücher thus turned the possibility of defeat into a resounding victory.

**Blum, Léon** (1872–1950). French politician. The son of a wealthy Jewish manufacturer from Alsace, Blum passed into the highest ranks of the French Civil Service and also became a distinguished literary critic. In 1899 he joined the Socialist Party because of his admiration for **Jaurès** but did not become politically active (apart from his support for **Dreyfus**) until he was elected as a deputy in 1919. Blum was not a great orator, but his powerful intellect ensured his rapid rise in the Socialist Party. In 1920 he refused to accept **Lenin**'s twenty-one conditions for membership of the **Comintern** and at the party congress led the moderates, who believed in reform through parliament and loyalty to the **Second International**, against the extremist majority who supported world revolution and wanted to join the Third International (Comintern). The extremists broke away to form the Communist Party, but only thirteen out of sixty-eight socialist deputies joined them and local socialist parties remained faithful to Blum. He led the opposition to the governments of Millerand and **Poincaré**, disapproving of the French occupation of the **Ruhr**, but supported Herriot's Radical coalition, though he would not join the ministry as he was opposed to socialist participation in *bourgeois* governments. The demonstrations of the Fascist Leagues during the Stavisky affair (1934) led Blum to make a pact with the Communists (who had been his inveterate enemies since 1920) and with the Radicals, thus preparing the way for the **Popular Front** in June 1936. In the elections of that year the Socialists were the largest party, so Blum became the first Socialist to be French Prime Minister. The Matignon agreements, by which employers accepted many reforms demanded by the workers, were a great triumph for Blum, who began to nationalize the arms industry and brought the Bank of France under the control of the state. The **Spanish Civil War** divided French opinion: the Communists wanted to support the Popular Front in Spain, the Radicals were cautious, whilst the Catholics and Conservatives supported **Franco**. Blum, therefore, pursued a policy of non-intervention, as he said support for the Spanish Republic would bring about civil war in France. His government fell in 1937, as the Senate would not accept his attempt to ban the export of capital. Vice-Premier in the Chautemps government and Prime Minister again, briefly, in 1938, Blum would not serve under Daladier and condemned the **Munich agreement**. After the fall of **France** he opposed the **Vichy** government, was arrested in 1940 and spent the rest of the war in prison in France and Germany. Released in 1945, Blum negotiated in the USA for a loan to France, was head of a socialist caretaker government (December 1946–January 1947) and then retired from politics.

**Boer War,** see **South African War** (1899–1902)

**Bolívar, Simón** (1783–1830). A leader of the South American independence movements. From one of the richest **Creole** landowning families in Venezuela, Bolívar used **Napoleon Bonaparte**'s invasion of Spain (1808) to demand independence for Venezuela, which was proclaimed by a congress in 1811. Many Creoles were loyal to the Spanish throne, so the South American wars of independence were civil wars as well as wars against Spain. In 1812 royalist forces drove Bolívar out of Venezuela to New Granada (Colombia). From there he invaded Venezuela a year later and was acclaimed as 'Liberator'. Yet after the **Peninsular War** (1808–13) ended, Spanish troops were sent to Latin America and crushed the liberation movements, except in Buenos Aires. Bolívar fled to Jamaica and then Haiti where, with the support of the Negro ruler, he planned another invasion of Venezuela. He saw that it would be futile to attack the Spaniards where they were strongest, at Caracas and in the populous north, so in 1817 he landed in the Orinoco estuary. From there, with the aid of the *llaneros* ('cowboys') and some British veterans of the **Napoleonic Wars**, he was able to take control of the central plains and move west to New Granada. After a difficult crossing of the Andes, he defeated the royalists at Boyacá (1819) and captured Bogotá. At this time Bolívar was helped by an army revolt in Spain (1820), where the new liberal government ordered the colonial authorities to seek a truce with the rebels. Now most Creoles rejected loyalty to Spain and sought independence. In 1821 Bolívar defeated the Spaniards at Carabobo, Caracas fell and the whole of Venezuela was freed. Bolívar was now proclaimed as President of Gran Colombia: the union of Venezuela, New Granada and Ecuador (not yet liberated). He then turned south and with General Sucre conquered Ecuador. In 1822 Bolívar met **San Martín**, who had moved into Peru after subjugating Chile, at Guayaquil. It is not clear what they discussed in their secret conversations but San Martín left for Europe, never to return. Bolívar then took command in Peru, where Sucre won the decisive battle of Ayacucho, 9,000 feet above sea level, in 1824. Sucre overcame the last royalist resistance in Upper Peru, which he made a separate state and named after Bolívar. The Liberator wanted to form a union of all South

American states (like the United States of America) and called a congress at Panama in 1826 with this intention, but nothing came of it. There was little enthusiasm also for his idea of an Andean Confederation of Gran Colombia, Peru and Bolivia. Even his state of Gran Colombia disintegrated, with Venezuela and Ecuador declaring their independence. In despair, Bolívar prepared for self-imposed exile in Europe, but he died from tuberculosis on the coast of Colombia.

**Bolsheviks.** Russian revolutionary party. When the Russian Social Democratic Workers' Party split in 1903, the group which gained control of the party newspaper *Iskra* ('the Spark') became known as Bolsheviks ('members of the majority'). They differed from their **Menshevik** rivals on three main issues: the role of the party; the part to be played by peasants in a socialist revolution; and the speed with which such a revolution could come about. Owing to conditions in Tsarist Russia, where police could easily infiltrate large parties, **Lenin**, the Bolshevik leader, wanted a small, disciplined, centralized party (see **Leninism**), with only those who were dedicated revolutionaries as members. The Mensheviks accused Lenin of turning the party into a collection of generals without an army and wanted a broadly based party. Lenin saw that in Russia, the peasants (who formed the vast majority of the people) would be needed to support the workers if a revolution was to be successful. The Mensheviks, on the other hand, looked down on the peasants as *petit bourgeois*, who were conservative rather than revolutionary. Mensheviks took the orthodox Marxist line that a socialist revolution could not take place until capitalism was fully developed. This was likely to take a long time, as capitalism was in its infancy in Russia. Lenin wanted to shorten this period by involving the workers in the government as soon as the Tsar was overthrown. The Bolsheviks played little part in the **Russian Revolution** of 1905, as their leaders were in exile, but their influence grew among the workers, particularly after the **Lena Goldfields Massacre** in 1912, the year in which they became a separate party. After the fall of the Tsar in the **February Revolution** of 1917 the Bolshevik leaders returned from exile, but it was not till Lenin arrived at **Petrograd** in April that they began to play a dynamic role. Party membership rose from 20,000 in February 1917 to 200,000 by October; the majority of members were workers. The Bolsheviks seized power in the **October Revolution**, and in 1918 changed their name to the **Communist Party of the Soviet Union** (Bolsheviks). From this time Bolshevik was widely used as a synonym for communist.

**Bonapartism** was a political movement, a system of government and a set of political principles. As a political movement it supported the descendants of **Napoleon Bonaparte** and dated from the election of Louis Napoleon Bonaparte (later **Napoleon III**, the nephew of Napoleon Bonaparte) as President of the **Second Republic** in France in 1848. The movement survived the fall of the Second Empire in 1870, continuing until the death of the Prince Imperial in 1879, after which it slowly died. As a system of government Bonapartism was based on a weak legislature and a powerful executive, at the head of which was the Emperor. Strong central control over the provinces, as under the **Committee of Public Safety** of the **Jacobins** during the **French Revolution**, was another feature of Bonapartist government, whereby local officials were appointed not elected. The ideas underpinning Bonapartism were never coherently set out, but combined populism, based on the doctrine of the sovereignty of the people, with authoritarianism, and were derived from Louis Napoleon's *Napoleonic Ideas* (1839). In these writings Napoleon appeared as the saviour of France, who had united the country, ended internecine struggle and the **Terror**, protected religion and given France stability, order and efficient government. He had also made France the dominant power in Europe and championed freedom for the oppressed peoples of Europe, whilst maintaining at home (and spreading abroad) the gains of the Revolution: the sale of Church lands, the career open to talent, the establishment of representative assemblies, the end of feudalism and of the privileges of nobles and the Church. **Guizot** claimed that Bonapartism was a symbol of national glory, a principle of authority and a guarantor of the Revolution. As such, it appealed to disparate groups, and was to influence French opinion well into the twentieth century. Its legacy – the belief in a strong leader who would provide order and discipline – was seen in the rise to power of General de Gaulle.

**Booth, William** (1829–1912). Founder of the Salvation Army. Born near Nottingham, Booth experienced a religious conversion at the age of fifteen and became a revivalist preacher, seeking to bring Christianity to the poor who lived in urban slums, beyond the reach of the churches. In 1865 he set up his own Church Mission at Whitechapel in London, which in 1878 became the Salvation Army. Its orders and regulations were based on those of the British army, with 'General' Booth in command until his death. His 'officers' (127 in 1889, 4,170 by 1899) were drawn mainly from artisans and the lower-middle class; men and women were treated equally. Greeted with derision by many, they preached at street corners in their military uniforms and marched behind brass bands. At first the police treated them with hostility and many salvationists were imprisoned for public order offences, but they gained acceptance in the 1880s. Booth originally concentrated on the spiritual salvation of the poor, but later combined preaching with social work, setting up hostels and soup kitchens in the inner cities. The relief work of the Salvation Army was of great value, though the Army was no more successful than the ordinary churches in converting the poor to Christian belief. In 1880 the Salvation Army spread to the USA, in 1881 to Australia and later to the Continent and to India.

**Borden, Robert Laird** (1854–1937). Canadian Prime Miniister (1911–20). Borden led the Conservative opposition from 1901–11, when it defeated the Liberals, and he succeeded Sir Wilfrid **Laurier** as Prime Minister. A man of great integrity, but inflexible, he lacked Sir John **Macdonald**'s ability to understand and sympathize with French-Canadian aspirations or working-class demands. His period of office was marked therefore by an intensification of industrial strife and increased ethnic bitterness. The **First World War** saw Canada become an important industrial nation, as she built ships and manufactured war material. The investment came mainly from the USA, which replaced Britain as the main source of capital. Farmers and workers suffered because of inflation: the cost of living rose by two-thirds during the war and surged ahead of wages and the price of farm products. There was resulting unrest, which culminated in 1919 in the Winnipeg general strike. Another result of the war was that, in 1918, Canadian women over the age of twenty-one were given the vote. Both parties and founding peoples had supported Britain's entry into the war but there was fierce resentment when Borden introduced conscription in 1917. Canada made a significant contribution to the Allied war effort (60,000 Canadian troops were killed) and this enabled Borden to obtain greater independence for the **dominions**. At the Imperial War Conference (1917) he and **Smuts** submitted a declaration, which was accepted unanimously, calling for 'a full recognition of the dominions as autonomous nations' with the right to 'an adequate voice in foreign policy'. At the end of the war he insisted, despite US opposition, that the dominions should be represented at the **Paris Peace Conference** and that they should be admitted as members of the new **League of Nations**. Borden retired from office in 1920.

**Borodino, battle of** (7 September 1812), fought by **Napoleon Bonaparte** against the Russian General Kutusov seventy miles west of Moscow. The Russians, with 120,000 troops, took up defensive positions on high ground near the village of Borodino, commanding the Moscow–Smolensk highway. Napoleon, with 130,000 troops, rejected Davout's suggestion of a southerly outflanking movement, as he lacked troops of sufficient quality for such a manoeuvre, and chose instead a frontal assault. The Russians repulsed wave after wave of attacks on their main position until late in the afternoon, when they withdrew to another defensive line. As Napoleon refused to send in the Imperial Guard the fighting petered out indecisively, with both sides exhausted. During the night Kutusov withdrew his troops in good order, so the French claimed a victory; however Napoleon, in exile at St Helena, described Borodino as 'the most terrible of all my battles'. A quarter of the French troops and a third of the Russians who took part were casualties.

**Bose, Subhas Chandra** (1897–1945). Indian politician and nationalist. Bose took a degree at Cambridge and passed the examination for entry to the Indian Civil Service but resigned within a year, owing to his abhorrence of the **Amritsar massacre** (1919). After becoming a radical member of the **Indian National Congress** of Bengal he was arrested in 1924 on suspicion of being involved in terrorism. Released three years later, in 1928 he and **Nehru** demanded the complete independence of India and tried to make

Congress take a more militant anti-British line. Bose joined **Gandhi**'s civil disobedience movement, but he differed from Gandhi in that he was prepared to use violence to get rid of the British. In 1938 he became Congress President but failed to replace Gandhi as leader of the national movement. In 1940, during the **Second World War**, he was placed under house arrest but escaped in January 1941 and appeared in Berlin. In 1943 Bose went by submarine to Singapore, where, with Japanese help, he formed an Indian government in exile and, in imitation of the *Führer*, took the title *Netaji* ('beloved leader'). He also formed an Indian National Army (INA) from 20,000 prisoners of war and 40,000 Indian volunteers from South-East Asia. The INA invaded India from Burma with the cry 'Chalo Delhi' ('On to Delhi'), used by sepoys in the **Indian Mutiny** of 1857. It fought alongside the Japanese at Imphal and then joined in the Japanese retreat through Burma, surrendering at Rangoon in May 1945. Bose escaped, but was killed in an air crash in Taiwan in August 1945. He has since become a popular hero in India, owing to his armed resistance to the British **Raj**.

**Bosnian crisis** (1908–9). The Austrian occupation of Bosnia and Hercegovina had been recognized at the **Berlin Congress** of 1878, though the area remained nominally part of the **Ottoman Empire**. In 1908 the **Young Turk** revolution aimed to make Turkey a stronger and more efficient state. To prevent the return of effective Turkish rule to Bosnia and Hercegovina, Austria annexed the provinces in October 1908. This angered the Serbs, as most of the population in Bosnia were Serbs, and also the Russians, who resented any increase in Austrian power in the Balkans. The crisis worsened in January 1909, when Germany saw that an opportunity had arisen for Austria to crush Serbia, whilst Russia was still too weak after the **Russo-Japanese War** (1904–5) to face another conflict, and offered her full support to Austria. This led Austria to demand that Russia and Serbia should accept the annexation: if this was not done she would invade Serbia. Russia's attempt to get Germany to mediate resulted in Germany brutally calling for the immediate and unconditional acceptance of Austrian demands. Russia and Serbia were forced to give way, resentfully. The **Central Powers** appeared to have triumphed, but Russia learnt the lesson that she would have to strengthen her links with the other Entente powers, Britain and France. She could not afford another humiliation at Germany's hands and this determined her attitude in the **July crisis** of 1914. Another effect of the incident was that the Balkans, after twenty years of comparative tranquillity, once again became the powder keg of European politics. 'Here', wrote the Austrian Ambassador in Belgrade, 'all think of revenge, which is only to be carried out with the help of the Russians.'

**Botha, Louis** (1862–1919). Boer general and statesman. Botha was an opponent of **Kruger** but fought bravely against the British in the **South African War** (1899–1902), when he defeated General Buller at Colenso. As Commandant-General in the Transvaal, he kept up the guerrilla war until the situation was hopeless. In 1905 he founded *Het Volk* (Dutch, 'the people') to demand self-government for the Transvaal and the Orange River Colony. When the British government granted this in 1907, *Het Volk* gained a majority in the first election in the Transvaal and Botha became Prime Minister. With **Smuts** he followed a policy of reconciling **Afrikaner** and Briton and supporting a union of the four British colonies in South Africa. When this was achieved in 1910 he became the first Prime Minister of a united South Africa, a post he held until his death. Botha founded, with Smuts, the South African Party in 1911 and supported the entry of South Africa into the **First World War** on Britain's side. The invasion of German South-West Africa (Namibia) by South African troops and the suppression of an Afrikaner rebellion in 1914–15 lost him the support of many of his ex-colleagues. Botha attended the **Paris Peace Conference** but died shortly after returning to South Africa.

**Boulanger, Georges Ernest** (1837–91). French general and politician. He fought in Algeria, against Austria in Italy in 1859 and in the **Franco–Prussian War** (1870–71), and became known as a republican general. **Clemenceau** and the Radicals insisted on his appointment as Minister of War in 1886 in return for their support of the **Opportunist** government. Boulanger was popular with both the troops and the public, who saw in him a strong man who would support *revanche* ('revenge') against Germany and the recovery of **Alsace-Lorraine**. The government, alarmed at his popularity, fearing a military *coup* like that of Louis Napoleon Bonaparte (later **Napoleon III**) in 1851 and frightened that he would provoke war with Germany, dismissed him from office in 1887. It sent him to a provincial command and in 1888 discharged him from the army. This was a mistake, as Boulanger was now free to stand in by-elections, where he won some remarkable victories (candidates were allowed to stand in more than one constituency), culminating in a triumph in Paris in January 1889. By this time his main supporters were on the **Right**, monarchists and **Bonapartists** and all who were discontented with the **Third Republic** and sought to discredit it. His followers urged him to seize power but he refused, either because he lost his nerve or because he felt that he would come to power legally by winning the 1889 general election. The government, determined to act before that election, threatened Boulanger with prosecution for treason, whereupon he fled to Brussels, where in 1891 he committed suicide on the grave of his mistress. About forty Boulangist deputies were elected in 1889, though most were defeated in 1893 and the movement disintegrated, some members becoming socialists, others backing the nationalists and the army in the **Dreyfus case**.

**Bourbon dynasty.** The ruling house, at various times, in France, Spain and part of Italy. The Bourbons inherited the French throne in 1589 when the last Valois, Henry III, was succeeded by his distant relative the King of Navarre, who became Henry IV of France. In 1792, during the **French Revolution**, the monarchy was abolished, and **Louis XVI** was executed the next year. The Bourbons returned to the throne in 1814 after the defeat of **Napoleon Bonaparte** but ruled only until 1830, when **Charles X** was overthrown in the **July Revolution**. **Louis Philippe**, Duke of Orleans, a descendant of Louis XIV's brother, then became King but he too was removed by revolution in 1848. When the **Habsburg** Charles II died childless in 1700, Louis XIV claimed the throne of Spain for his second son, who became King of Spain as Philip V. Bourbons have ruled Spain intermittently ever since: from 1700–1808, 1813–68, 1870–73, 1874–1931 and from 1975. One of Philip V's sons became King of Naples and Sicily in 1735. Napoleon deprived the Neapolitan Bourbons of their throne in 1806 but they recovered it in 1816 and held it until 1861, when Naples was absorbed in the new kingdom of Italy.

**Boxer Rising** (1899–1900), a popular movement in north China against the **Qing dynasty** and foreign influence in China. The movement started in the province of Shandong, where Germany had seized Qingdao (1897) in the '**scramble for concessions**' and where the import of foreign goods had caused severe unemployment. In north China there was constant peasant unrest (between twelve and thirteen million people had died in the great famine of 1876–9), made worse by the use of Western technology (boatmen were ruined by steamships). The gentry too were disaffected: they were hostile to foreign missionaries, who threatened their traditional role as leaders of society. Concessions to foreigners were also deeply resented, especially after the disaster of the **Sino-Japanese War** (1894–5), which showed that the Qing dynasty was unable to defend China. The rising took its name from the ritual self-defence exercises known as 'harmony fists'. The Boxers wrote on their banners 'Exterminate the foreigners'; they killed Christian missionaries and their Chinese converts and destroyed everything associated with the hated foreigner, such as railway and telegraph lines. When the movement spread to Zhili, in which the capital Beijing (Peking) lay, the Empress Dowager **Cixi** sought to direct hostility from the dynasty by declaring war on the European powers in 1900. However, this rash decision was not supported by provincial governors, like **Li Hongzhang** in Guangzhou. By guaranteeing to protect foreign lives and property they ensured that the rebellion would be confined to the north. The German ambassador in Beijing was killed and the foreign legations were besieged for two months, before being relieved by a force of 20,000 troops from eight nations in August 1900. Beijing was laid waste. Meanwhile, Cixi and the Emperor had fled to Xian, from where they did not return until January 1902. The Peace Protocol of September 1901 imposed harsh terms on China: she had to pay a huge indemnity, which gave foreigners even greater control of Chinese revenues, and foreign troops remained in occupation of many strategic points, including the Inner City of Beijing, now known as the Legation Quarter. Leading Boxers were to be executed. Russia took the opportunity to massacre many Chinese in the Amur–Ussuri region ceded to Russia in 1860, on the grounds that she feared a rising there. Russia also seized the whole of Manchuria, which increased Japanese hostility and was to lead to the **Russo-Japanese War** of 1904–5. The fanaticism of the Boxers – they believed that foreign bullets would not affect them – may have saved China from a partition by the European powers, which was widely expected, as it became clear that any such attempt would meet massive popular resistance. A final effect of the Boxer Rising was that the prestige of the Qing dynasty disappeared completely – it was only a matter of time before the Manchus fell, as they did in the **Chinese Revolution** (1911).

**Boycott.** A policy of ostracism used in the **Irish Land War** (1879–82) and named after Captain Boycott, an English land agent in Ireland. When he refused to lower rents and evicted tenants who refused to pay their full rents, **Parnell** advised everyone to have no communication with him or his family. The policy was successful and Boycott was forced to return to England.

**Brest-Litovsk, Treaty of** (3 March 1918). Germany began peace talks with Russia in the Polish town of Brest – Litovsk in December 1917. **Trotsky** dragged out negotiations, hoping for proletarian revolutions in the West, and adopted the unrealistic attitude of 'neither war nor peace': the Russians would not wage war, but neither would they accept German peace terms. The Germans tired of this and in February 1918 resumed their advance, moving rapidly and deeply into Russia. The Left Communists, led by **Bukharin**, wanted to resist the Germans and fight a guerrilla war. **Lenin** saw this was futile and that if the Germans continued to advance, the Bolshevik regime would be overthrown. He therefore decided to sacrifice space to gain time, and by threatening resignation forced the Bolshevik Central Committee to accept the terms of the Central Powers. Russia gave up Finland, the Baltic states (Estonia, Latvia, Lithuania), Russian Poland, the Ukraine and part of Belorussia, all territories outside its control. She also gave up territory in the **Caucasus** (Kars, Ardahan and Batum) to Turkey. Russia lost a third of her agricultural land, 80 per cent of her coal mines and half her industries; she was pushed back from the Black Sea and virtually cut off from the Baltic.

This was a disastrous peace for Lenin and a great gamble, as it would have crippled Russia had it been maintained. It was only the defeat of the Central Powers by the Allies that saved Russia from the worst effects of the treaty, though even after Germany's surrender she did not recover Poland, the Baltic states or Finland. The treaty had widespread effects. In Russia the Left **Socialist Revolutionaries** called it 'a betrayal' and left the government, so that Russia became a one-party state. Opposition to the treaty was so strong that it helped to bring about the **Russian Civil War**. Russia's withdrawal from the war enabled the Germans to move many divisions from the Eastern to the Western Front and made possible their spring offensive. It also led to Allied troops being landed in Russia in an attempt to revive an Eastern Front.

**Bretton Woods Conference** (July 1944). A United Nations meeting of representatives from forty-four states in New Hampshire, USA. The conference was called to devise measures to prevent a financial collapse after the war, such as the one that occurred during the **Great Depression**. It drew up a plan for the International Bank for Reconstruction and Development (World Bank), which would make long-term loans to countries for development projects, and for an International Monetary Fund (IMF), which would finance short-term deficits in a state's balance of payments. The World Bank and IMF still exist as agencies of the UN.

**Briand, Aristide** (1862–1932). French politician. Briand began his political career as a man of the extreme **Left** and took up a **syndicalist** position in 1894, when he persuaded the trade unions to adopt the general strike as a political weapon. Later he was associated with a group of socialists led by **Jaurès**, whom he helped to found the socialist newspaper *L'Humanité* in 1904. Two years earlier he had become a deputy and won his first great success by drafting the law (1905) which separated Church and State in France. This led to his appointment as a minister in 1906 and to his expulsion from the Socialist Party, which was opposed to members taking part in *bourgeois* governments. From 1906–32 Briand was Prime Minister eleven times (but for only fifty-eight months) and held twenty-six ministerial posts. When he became Prime Minister for the first time in 1909 he appeared as a moderate, appealing for support from 'men of goodwill' in all parties, but he increased the hostility of his former comrades by calling up railway workers for military service in order to end a rail strike in 1910. After the **First World War** Briand was a fervent supporter of the **League of Nations** and collective security. In 1925 he became Foreign Minister and held this post in fourteen consecutive governments for seven years, longer than anyone else in the **Third Republic**. An advocate of Franco-German reconciliation, his greatest success was the **Locarno treaties** (1925), by which Germany reaffirmed acceptance of her western frontiers, fixed at the Treaty of **Versailles** (1919). The Kellogg–Briand Pact (1928) was a *succès d'estime*, as eventually sixty nations agreed to outlaw war as an instrument of national policy, but in practice it amounted to little. Briand retired in 1932, after failing to become President of the Third Republic.

**Bright, John** (1811–89). English radical and politician. The son of a Quaker who owned a cotton mill in Rochdale, Lancashire, Bright was deeply influenced by his religion and by the attitudes of the manufacturing middle class. Education at Quaker schools made him see political problems in moral terms and, he maintained, made him a Radical. 'Belief in the equality of all men in the sight of heaven . . . naturally leads to a strong sympathy with the great body of the people.' Yet Bright did not believe that the State should act to improve the condition of the people, except by removing impediments to liberty. His belief in *laissez-faire*, self-help and independence led him to oppose **trade unions, factory acts** and public health reform. He saw the landed aristocracy as the great enemy, against whom both the middle and working classes should combine. Bright first took part in political activity outside Lancashire when he joined the **Anti-Corn Law League** and became an MP in 1843. After the repeal of the **Corn Laws** in 1846 his popularity plummeted, along with that of Richard **Cobden**, when they opposed the **Crimean War**, which Bright saw as 'a war in which we have a despot for an enemy [Russia], a despot for an ally [France] and a despot for a client [the Ottoman Empire]'. War and diplomacy he regarded as 'a gigantic system of outdoor relief for the aristocracy of Great Britain'. Bright's effigy was burnt in Manchester, where he came bottom of the poll in the 1857 election, though he was returned unopposed for the Radical stronghold of Birmingham, which he represented until he died. During the **American Civil War** (1861–5) he was a strong supporter of the North, where 'there is no privileged class'. He saw the war as a struggle between aristocracy and democracy, which would prepare the way for the extension of democratic rights in England. From 1865 he led the campaign for **parliamentary reform**, addressing a crowd of 200,000 in Birmingham in 1866. In favour of household rather than manhood suffrage – 'I do not pretend to be a democrat' – he claimed the credit for **Disraeli**'s Reform Act of 1867, which doubled the size of the electorate. Bright served three times in **Gladstone** ministries (1868–70, 1873–4, 1880–82) without making much impression, though he helped to shape the **Irish Land Acts** of 1870 and 1881. By rejecting **Home Rule for Ireland** he broke with Gladstone in 1886. Bright was one of the most important Victorian Radicals, but his opposition to social reform was remembered long after his death. The Rochdale Trade Council refused to send representatives to celebrate the centenary of his birth because 'John Bright was a capitalist and an employer of labour, who opposed industrial legislation and was against shortening the hours of labour for children'.

**Britain, battle of** (July–October 1940). The attempt by the German air force (*Luftwaffe*) to win air superiority over the English Channel as a prelude to a German invasion of Britain (Operation Sealion). After the fall of **France**, **Churchill** told the British public that 'The battle of France is over. I expect that the battle of Britain is about to begin.' **Hitler** expected that Britain would make peace with Germany, but when this did not happen he ordered Operation Sealion to be carried out. As Britain had command of the sea he had to defeat the RAF, so that the *Luftwaffe* could provide air cover for an invasion and prevent interference from the Royal Navy. In France, Belgium and Holland the Germans had 1,150 bombers and 630 fighters; the RAF had 600 fighters to oppose them. Many of the German planes were ME109s, the best all-round fighter, as fast as the Spitfire and much faster than the Hurricane; they also climbed faster and had greater fire power but were less manoeuvrable than the British planes. The British had the advantage that they were nearer their home bases – German fighters could stay over southern England only for half an hour and over London for ten minutes – and radar stations along the coast gave them advance warning of German attacks. From 10 July to 12 August 1940 the *Luftwaffe* attacked shipping in the Channel and British ports, but the main battles took place from 13 August to 6 September, when the Germans switched their attack to airfields and communications centres in southern England. This was the critical stage, which almost overwhelmed the RAF: the fighters could be replaced but pilots were being lost at twice the rate of replacement. Once again the Germans changed targets. After a British raid on Berlin, Hitler ordered the *Luftwaffe* to concentrate on bombing London and this allowed the British airfields to recover. This move was, at least in part, the result of overconfidence: both sides exaggerated enemy losses and the Germans thought that the RAF was crippled – the bombing of London might end the war and make an invasion unnecessary. On 7 September the *Luftwaffe* began to bomb London and met unexpected resistance from the RAF. Heavy German losses showed that the RAF had not been destroyed, so on 12 October Hitler postponed Operation Sealion until the spring of 1941; in effect it was abandoned. During the battle of Britain the RAF lost 792 planes, the *Luftwaffe* 1,389. Of the 3,000 British aircrew involved, 500 were killed. They had averted the invasion of Britain and almost certain defeat, and thus justified Churchill's tribute, 'Never in the field of human conflict was so much owed by so many to so few.'

**British North America Act** (1867) was passed by the British parliament to form the **dominion** of Canada. There had been widespread dissatisfaction in Canada since the Act of Union in 1840 (see **Canada Acts**), as there was an economic depression. The repeal of the **Corn Laws** (1846) in Britain ended Canada's protected market for wheat, and the Erie Canal siphoned off trade to New York which had previously gone through Montreal. There was a political problem too. The population of English-speaking Canada West (Upper Canada) had outgrown that of French-speaking Canada East (Lower Canada), and so the English-speaking Canadians wanted a larger say in political affairs, which the French Canadians resisted. Some Reformers thought that prosperity would return if Canada was annexed by the United States, but the French Canadians did not want this as they feared they would lose their cultural identity. In 1864 the leader of the Reformers, George Brown, proposed a coalition which would lead to a Confederation; **Macdonald**, the Conservative leader, and **Cartier**, the leader of the French Canadians, agreed. Macdonald led a Canadian delegation to London in 1866, which persuaded the government to pass the British North America Act. This united the provinces of Canada West (Ontario) and Canada East (Quebec) with the colonies of New Brunswick and Nova Scotia to form 'one dominion under the name of Canada'. There were to be two Houses of Parliament: an elected House of Commons and an appointed Senate. The Senate was supposed to represent the regions but it hardly served this purpose, as its members were appointed by the government in Ottawa (the administrative capital). The existing system of responsible government continued, with the Cabinet responsible to parliament and not directly to the Governor-General. This Act formed the basis of the Canadian Constitution until 1982. The Pacific coast province of British Columbia joined the Confederation in 1871 and Prince Edward Island in 1873, but Newfoundland did not become a member until 1949.

**British South Africa Company.** The Chartered Company which controlled Southern Rhodesia (Zimbabwe) from the 1890s to 1923. In 1889 various British and South African commercial interests, led by Cecil **Rhodes**, secured from the British Crown a royal charter which authorized them to establish a government in central Africa north of the Limpopo river. Rhodes and his associates hoped that the area possessed mineral wealth and would be settled by Europeans. The British government had already recognized the sovereignty of the Ndebele King, Lobengula, and the charter appeared to contradict that agreement. A white 'pioneer' column entered Zimbabwe and established the Company headquarters at Fort Salisbury (modern Harare) in Mashonaland. Eventually, in 1893, war broke out between the white settlers and the Ndebele, who were defeated and lost land and cattle to the whites. Three years later, in 1896–7, a serious rising by the Ndebele and Shona was suppressed with considerable violence. The Chartered Company governed Southern Rhodesia until 1923 when, following a referendum, the European settlers gained a measure of self-government with an elected white parliament. In 1891 the Company had been allowed to expand north of the Zambezi, which became Northern Rhodesia (Zambia), lands in which rich copper seams were found. This area was administered by the Company until 1924, when it became a Protectorate. The only part of central Africa excluded from the Company's control was Nyasaland (Malawi), where British missionaries and traders were hostile to the British South Africa Company. Nyasaland became a Protectorate under the direct control of the British government in 1891.

**Broederbond** (Afrikaans, 'band of brothers'). An organization to promote **Afrikaner** interests in South Africa. Formed in 1918, it became a secret organization in 1921. Members have to be church goers and their children have to attend Afrikaner schools. In the 1930s (it had 1,400 members in 1935) the Broederbond infiltrated nearly all political, economic and cultural bodies. **Hertzog** and **Smuts**, who were not members, clashed with the Bond, which supported Malan's Purified **National Party**. Malan became a member in 1933 and was, in 1948, to be South Africa's first Broederbond Prime Minister. Since then all prime ministers have been members. The Bond aimed to unite all Afrikaners, rich and poor, in one *volk* ('nation') and to this end promoted Afrikaans, which was recognized as an official language in 1925. The Bond's Federation of Afrikaans Cultural Organizations (1929) soon dominated Afrikaner cultural life, whilst its economic organizations moved into what had been an English preserve. A people's bank, *Volkskaas*, formed in 1934, became the third largest banking group in the country, whilst the *Spoorbond* (union of railwaymen) attracted Afrikaner workers.

**Brown, John** (1800–1859). US **abolitionist**. Brown was born into a religious New England family, which was strongly affected by insanity, and became convinced that he had been chosen by God to abolish slavery. In 1856, together with a party of Free Soilers, he murdered five pro-slavery settlers at Pottawatomie Creek in Kansas. Three years later he decided to stir up a slave rebellion in the South, which he hoped would lead to a collapse of the whole system. In October he and twenty-one followers raided the federal arsenal at Harper's Ferry in Virginia, but the slaves failed to rise and the local militia, reinforced by US troops under Robert E. **Lee**, stormed the arsenal and forced Brown to surrender. At his trial he impressed many by his great dignity and refusal to plead insanity, for which there was plenty of evidence. He was found guilty of murder and was executed along with six others on 2 December 1859. On the day of his execution funeral bells tolled throughout the North. Emerson regarded Brown as 'a new saint awaiting his martyrdom' and he became a cult figure amongst abolitionists. Thomas Bingham Bishop, the composer of 'Gone to be a Soldier in the Army of the Lord', added some new words which Union soldiers would soon be singing: 'John Brown's body lies a-mouldering in the grave, but his soul goes marching on'. The effect of John Brown's escapades was very different in the South: Northern approval of the raid convinced Southerners that the North intended to abolish slavery and that the South should therefore secede as soon as a Republican President was elected.

**Bruce, Stanley Melbourne, Viscount** (1883–1967). Australian Prime Minister (1923–9). Bruce went to Cambridge University and served in the British army during the **First World War**, fighting at **Gallipoli**. An Anglophile, he seemed more English than Australian with his Rolls-Royce, spats and Oxford accent. Bruce was made Treasurer by **Hughes** in 1921 but intrigued to bring about his fall in 1923. In the same year he became Prime Minister, with a policy of 'men, money and markets' designed to populate rural areas with settlers and provide markets for their produce. Negotiations with Britain resulted in 260,000 Britons emigrating to Australia in the next decade, 80 per cent of whom were assisted. Faced with strikes, some by public servants, Bruce introduced legislation in 1926 to curb trade-union power and increase that of the Arbitration Court. The unions strongly opposed this: there were riots in Melbourne in 1928 and strikes throughout Australia. Bruce, therefore, changed course and introduced a bill to give general control of industrial matters to the states. Hughes saw his opportunity for revenge and introduced an amendment to the bill, which was defeated by one vote. Calm, confident and superior, Bruce called a general election in 1929, which he lost. He later served as High Commissioner in London (1933–45) and as the first Chancellor of the Australian National University. In 1947 he was the first Australian to be awarded a Viscountcy. Bruce died in London, but at his request his ashes were scattered in Canberra, which he had helped to make the Federal Capital in 1927.

**Brumaire, *coup d'état* of** (November 1799), brought an end to the **Directory** in France. **Sieyès**, a Director, wanted to strengthen the Executive but he knew that one of the legislative councils, the Council of Five Hundred, would not accept this and so army support would be needed for a *coup*. **Napoleon Bonaparte** agreed to take part, so Sieyès persuaded the councils to move from Paris to St Cloud, on the pretext of a terrorist plot. Once there, it became clear on 19 Brumaire (10 November) that the only plot was one organized by Sieyès himself. When Napoleon reluctantly agreed to address the councils, he was shouted down in the Five Hundred and was physically attacked. His brother Lucien, President of the Five Hundred, came to his rescue by telling troops that some deputies were trying to assassinate their general. At this they cleared the hall. A rump of the councils then approved a decree abolishing the Directory and replacing it with a provisional government of three consuls, including Napoleon and Sieyès. The population accepted the *coup* apathetically, but few realized its significance. The **French Revolution** was over: the **Consulate** had begun.

**Brüning, Heinrich** (1885–1970). German Chancellor and Foreign Minister (1930–32). A Catholic leader of the **Centre Party**, Brüning became Chancellor during the **Great Depression**, when unemployment in Germany was at three million and rising. He sought to deal with this by deflation, increasing taxes and cutting government expenditure. When it became clear that he would not have a majority in the **Reichstag** for these measures, he enforced them by Article 48 of the Constitution (see **Weimar Republic**), by which the President could issue decrees with the force of law in an emergency. As Brüning never had a majority in the Reichstag, he became dependent on President **Hindenburg**. When a socialist motion demanding a withdrawal of the decrees was passed, Brüning dissolved the Reichstag and called for fresh elections. The September election of 1930 dashed all the Chancellor's hopes, as extremist parties increased their representation considerably: the Communist Party won seventy-seven seats, but the greatest shock was the rise of the **Nazi Party**, whose seats increased from twelve in 1928 to 107, making it the second largest party in the Reichstag, after the **Social Democratic Party** (SPD) with 143 seats. 40 per cent of Germans had voted for parties opposed to the Weimar Republic. Brüning could rely only on his Centre Party, but the SPD gave him tacit support so as to avoid another election and further gains for the Nazis. Brüning continued his policy of deflation, as unemployment rose to over six million. He disliked the Nazis, and when there were street clashes between Nazi stormtroopers and their opponents, he banned the **SA** and **SS**. To prevent **Hitler** becoming President, Brüning persuaded Hindenburg, much against his will, to stand for re-election when his term of office expired in 1932. Hindenburg regarded it as demeaning to stand against an ex-corporal (Hitler) and a communist (Thalmann), particularly when nearly half of the Germans voted against him, and he never forgave Brüning. In 1932, the Chancellor at last decided to reduce unemployment with a public works programme, which included breaking up some bankrupt East-Prussian estates and settling 600,000 unemployed on them. This infuriated the *Junkers*, who persuaded Hindenburg that Brüning was 'an agrarian Bolshevik', so Hindenburg refused to sign new emergency decrees. Brüning therefore resigned and in 1934, after the Nazi take-over, feeling that his life was in danger, he fled to the USA before the **Night of the Long Knives**, when he would probably have been killed. He became a professor at Harvard University and remained in the USA till he died, apart from three years in the 1950s when he lectured at Cologne. Brüning was a man of great integrity and ability, but his governing by decree marked the end of parliamentary democracy in Germany and prepared the way for the Nazis to take power.

**Brusilov offensive** (4 June–10 August 1916). One of the few offensives in the **First World War** to be named after a commander, the Russian General Alexei Brusilov. After the great retreat of 1915 the Russians had withdrawn in good order to a line which stretched for 500 miles from Riga on the Baltic to the Romanian frontier. In 1916 they were called upon to attack the Austrians on this front to aid their allies, France and Italy, as the Germans threatened to break through the French defences at **Verdun** and the Italians were in great difficulties with the Austrians in northern Italy. When Brusilov attacked, the Austrians, caught by surprise, went into a headlong retreat and lost half of their forces in the east within a week. **Ludendorff** had to send German units south to aid the Austrians in Galicia, and the Germans had to move thirty-five divisions from France to the Eastern Front. They halted the Russian attack, which had advanced fifty miles on a 200-mile front, though the Russian losses of a million men were horrendous. Brusilov's offensive had destroyed the fighting spirit of the Austro-Hungarian army in the east, and without German intervention would have knocked them out of the war. By drawing German troops away from the Western Front, Brusilov may have prevented the Allies from losing the war. His success persuaded Romania, who wanted the Romanian-speaking areas of Transylvania from Austria-Hungary, to join the war on the allied side in August. However, this was of little benefit, as the German General **Falkenhayn** had overrun Romania by December, thus extending the Russian front to the Black Sea.

**Bryan, William Jennings** (1860–1925). US politician. Bryan was a Protestant fundamentalist and teetotaller. Born in Illinois, he practised law in Nebraska and throughout his life spoke for rural America. He shared many ideas with the **Populist Party**, which supported him in the 1896 presidential election, when he was the **Democratic** candidate. At thirty-six, he was the youngest man ever to be nominated by a major party for President. Bryan became famous during his election campaign by reviving **Jefferson**'s belief in the primary importance of agriculture, and by attacking the gold standard in Biblical language: 'You shall not press down upon the brow of labour this crown of thorns, you shall not crucify mankind upon a cross of gold.' He was a great popular orator, who travelled

18,000 miles stumping the country: he made 600 speeches and was heard by five million people during the campaign. He did not try to win over the masses in the East, which he called 'the enemy's country', and alienated many wealthy Democrats and city bosses by his declaration of war on the rich and powerful. The urban workers did not like his advocacy of free silver, which would lead to inflation, and his attack on high tariffs, which, they felt, protected their jobs. He did not win one state in the industrial North-East, though he won overwhelmingly in the South and carried most of the West. He lost the popular vote by only 600,000 (out of 13,900,000) to **McKinley**. After the election, Bryan kept his hold on the Democratic Party. He was a candidate in the 1900 presidential election, when he opposed **imperialism** and the annexation of the Philippines after the **Spanish–American War**, but he was again defeated by McKinley. After a further defeat in 1908, Bryan supported **Wilson** in his successful campaign to become President in 1912. He became Wilson's Secretary of State in 1913, but broke with him when the President threatened Germany with war over the sinking of the *Lusitania*. Bryan resigned in 1915 and became a firm supporter of American neutrality. His last years were spent supporting **Prohibition** and campaigning against Darwinism, which contradicted the Bible: he became prosecuting counsel in the **Scopes trial** of 1925 in Tennessee, when a young schoolmaster was prosecuted for teaching Darwin's theory of evolution, which was forbidden by a state law. Bryan died of a heart attack while recovering from the stress of the trial.

**Buffalo Bill** (William Frederick Cody, 1846–1917). A frontiersman and a trapper, at the age of thirteen Cody was prospecting for gold in Colorado, and a year later was carrying messages for the Pony Express across the continent. In 1867 he became a buffalo hunter in Kansas, supplying meat for railway workers: in seventeen months he claimed to have killed 4,280 buffalo and so became known as 'Buffalo Bill'. He served as cavalry scout in the Sioux War of 1872–7, when he gained a great reputation for his marksmanship and bravery. In peacetime Cody was friendly with Indians, was liked by them and defended them. 'The defeat of Custer [at **Little Big Horn**] was not a massacre,' he wrote. 'The Indians were being pursued by skilled fighters with orders to kill . . . They had their wives and little ones to protect and they were fighting for their existence.' His way of life, like that of the Indians, disappeared as farms and railroads spread across the plains, so from 1883–1916 he toured the USA and Europe with his 'Wild West' shows. With his shoulder-length hair, buckskin clothing and goatee beard he symbolized for millions the American West. His shows included Indians like Sitting Bull, simulated attacks on stage-coaches and sharpshooting by himself and Annie Oakley.

**Bukharin, Nikolai Ivanovich** (1888–1938). The son of a Moscow schoolmaster, who joined the **Bolsheviks** in 1906 and took over the leadership of their Moscow organization in 1908. He was arrested the same year, but escaped abroad in 1911. Returning to Russia in 1917, he became a member of the Bolshevik Central Committee three months before the **October Revolution**; he remained a full member until 1934 and was a candidate-member from 1934–7. Bukharin opposed the Treaty of **Brest-Litovsk** and wanted to continue a revolutionary war against the Germans, an unrealistic idea. In spite of opposing **Lenin** on this issue, he retained his influence: he was editor of *Pravda*, the party newspaper, from 1917–29 and a member of the *Politburo* from 1924–9. He thought that there was no short cut to industrialization and that agricultural prosperity was a necessary prerequisite, as it would provide a market for industrial goods. Rapid industrialization, he believed, would lead to an all-powerful state, repression and terror. Bukharin wanted a gradual move to socialism and said that the state 'must come riding into socialism on a peasant nag'. He therefore became a fervent advocate of **NEP** (New Economic Policy), which allowed private peasant farms and some free trade, and even called on the peasants in 1925 to 'Enrich yourselves, accumulate, develop your economy.' This roused much opposition in the party, as it appeared that Bukharin was giving primacy to the capitalist rather than the socialist sector of the economy. After Lenin's death he supported **Stalin** against **Trotsky** in the leadership struggle, and was a leading advocate of 'socialism in one country', first put forward by Stalin in 1924. He was rewarded by replacing **Zinoviev** as Chairman of the **Comintern** in 1925. When Stalin abandoned his support for NEP in 1929 in favour of rapid industrialization, which would be paid for by raising 'tribute' from the peasants, Bukharin opposed him. He joined with the Prime Minister, Rykov, and head of the trade union, Tomsky, to form a Right opposition to **collectivization**. Accused of being a 'Right deviationist', he was removed from *Pravda*, the Comintern and the *Politburo*. He managed to rehabilitate himself to a limited extent – he played a large part in drafting the new Soviet Constitution in 1936 and was editor of the official government newspaper, *Izvestia*, from 1934–7. In 1937, however, he was expelled from the party as a Trotskyite and was arrested. Bukharin became a victim of the **Great Purges** in the third and last of the Moscow show trials, in 1938. Among the ridiculous charges laid against him was that of plotting to kill Lenin. Like all other defendants in these trials, he was found guilty and was executed.

**Bulgarian crisis** (1885–8). When Alexander of Battenberg, a nephew of the Tsar, was elected to the Bulgarian throne with Russian approval in 1879, it appeared that Bulgaria would be a Russian satellite. However, Alexander, headstrong and independent, refused to accept a wholly subordinate role, and in 1885 annexed the Turkish province of Eastern Rumelia (see **Berlin Congress**) without Russian approval. The Russians thought they would lose all control over Bulgaria and so kidnapped Alexander and forced him to abdicate. They intended to impose a Russian nominee on the Bulgarian throne, but the Bulgars chose instead Ferdinand of Saxe-Coburg, who had served in the Habsburg army. It appeared that Austria-Hungary and Russia would go to war, but **Bismarck** prevented this by publishing the terms of the **Dual Alliance** – this made clear to Russia that if she attacked Austria-Hungary she would have to fight Germany too. It also served as a warning to Austria-Hungary that if she attacked Russia she would fight alone. The crisis brought to an end the *Dreikaiserbund*.

**Bulge, battle of the** (15 December 1944 – 7 February 1945). **Hitler**'s last offensive in the West during the **Second World War** and the greatest pitched battle in American history, with 600,000 US troops fighting 500,000 Germans. As the Allies prepared to cross the Rhine at the end of 1944, it appeared that the war would soon be over. No Allied commander believed that the Germans were capable of mounting an offensive, but Hitler decided to use his last reserves in a desperate gamble. Striking through the Ardennes, as in 1940 (see fall of **France**), he aimed to divide the British and American armies, cross the Meuse and then move north to seize the port of Antwerp. Attacking in thick snow and heavy cloud, which meant that Allied aeroplanes could not be used, Hitler completely surprised the Americans, made a salient in the US line (hence the battle's name), separated two American armies and on 21 December surrounded US troops at Bastogne, an important road junction. The situation was serious, but the Germans were running out of fuel, their mobility was impaired as they used a mixture of motorized and horse-drawn transport, and on 23 December the skies cleared and Allied air forces could be used. **Montgomery** moved quickly to prevent Germans crossing the Meuse, whilst **Patton** rapidly moved his armour seventy-five miles from Alsace to relieve Bastogne on 2 January 1945. By 7 February the salient had been eliminated. The Germans had lost 100,000 troops, the Americans 81,000, but the Germans had also lost tanks and aircraft which could not be replaced. Their defeat in the Ardennes made it impossible for them to halt the Allied offensive, which led to Germany's surrender in 1945.

**Bülow, Bernhard von** (1849–1929). German Foreign Minister (1897–1900) and Chancellor (1900–1909). Bülow aimed to become popular by supporting Emperor **William II**'s *Weltpolitik*, but his foreign policy was disastrous. He rejected any attempts to form an Anglo-German alliance, as he believed that this was incompatible with naval expansion and with Germany's desire for colonies. He asked the Kaiser to visit Tangier in 1905 and then insisted on an international conference to discuss Morocco (see **Moroccan crisis**, 1905–6), confidently believing that the majority of powers would support the independence of Morocco and that the **Anglo-French Entente** would break up. On both counts he was wrong. During the **Bosnian crisis** of 1908, when Austria-Hungary annexed Bosnia and Hercegovina, Bülow told her that Germany would approve of any action she considered necessary against Serbia, thus reversing **Bismarck**'s policy. He also humiliated Russia by issuing an ultimatum forcing her to accept the annexation, and so left Germany more distrusted and isolated than when he came to power. At home he was faced by mounting deficits, owing to the vast sums spent on the army and navy, and was defeated in the **Reichstag** in 1908, when he sought to increase taxation. In the same year he joined in attacks on the Emperor's 'personal' government. William never forgave the Chancellor who had 'betrayed' him.

**Burke, Edmund** (1729–97). British politician. Born and educated in Dublin, Burke went to London where he became Private Secretary to Lord Rockingham in 1765, a post he retained until Rockingham's death in 1782. Burke soon became the main spokesman of the Rockingham **Whigs**, whom he supported in parliament when he became an MP in 1784. In his 'Thoughts on the Present Discontents' (1780) he justified the concept of 'party' (an unpopular idea in the eighteenth century), which he defined as a body of men united by common principles. Burke saw MPs as independent representatives, who should follow their own judgement and conscience in acting for the common good and who should not be constrained by instructions from their constituents. Burke supported the Americans in their War of Independence, as the colonists were defending the traditional rights of Englishmen in rejecting taxation without representation. Attacking corruption (he played a leading role in the impeachment of Warren Hastings) and calling for parliamentary control of royal patronage, Burke gained a reputation as a Whig reformer.

His *Reflections on the Revolution in France* (1790) caused great surprise, as it showed the fundamentally conservative nature of his thought and established him as a theorist of counter-revolution. He ridiculed abstract natural rights and the rationalism of the Enlightenment and stressed the importance of instinct and emotion, custom and habit. He believed that the best constitutions are those which are the product of many minds over a long period of time, being far superior to theories which are produced by a single, limited intelligence: 'the individual is foolish but the species is wise'. Defending 'a constitution, whose sole authority is, that it has existed time out of mind', Burke saw the need for tradition, rank, property and religion, owing to the weakness and imperfections of human nature. In supporting the *status quo* he was not entirely opposed to change, but thought this should be limited to removing particular evils, and should not attempt to change the whole of society: 'We must reform in order to preserve.' Burke's account of the origins of the **French Revolution** was ill-informed – he saw it as a conspiracy of the 'moneyed interest' and a 'literary cabal' of *philosophes* committed to the destruction of Christianity – yet his prophecies about its course proved remarkably accurate. He foresaw that *nouveaux riches*, made wealthy by acquiring confiscated estates, would rule France, that *assignats* would produce bankruptcy, that terror would arise from the ensuing anarchy and that this would end when 'some popular general . . . who possesses the true spirit of command, shall draw the eyes of all men upon himself'. The *Reflections* was immediately translated into French, German, Italian and Spanish and became a best-seller. Burke's condemnation of the French Revolution ended his friendship with **Fox** in 1791 and split the Whigs, most of whom followed Burke in supporting **Pitt**. Burke retired from parliament in 1794 and died three years later, but his influence long outlived him. His work influenced statesmen like **Metternich**, as it was fully in tune with the reaction that followed the Revolution, and his influence lasted well into the nineteenth century.

**Burton, Sir Richard** (1821–90). British scholar, linguist and explorer. From 1842–9 Burton served in the army in India, and learned Arabic and a number of Indian languages. In 1851–3 he travelled in disguise to the Muslim holy city of Mecca in Arabia, which was closed to all non-Muslims: discovery would have meant almost certain death. The next year, in the company of J. H. Speke, he went to Ethiopia and Somalia and visited Harar, another forbidden Muslim city. Both Burton and Speke wanted to discover the source of the river Nile. In 1856 they marched inland from the coast of East Africa and explored a large part of western Tanzania and southern Uganda. Their discoveries and theories sparked off a bitter geographical debate: Burton claimed that the Nile flowed out of Lake Tanganyika while Speke, who alone had gone north to Lake Victoria, said that he had found the true source of the river. Speke's claim was correct, but it was not finally verified until the 1870s. Burton was made British Consul on the West African island of Fernando Po (1861–5), and from there he made several journeys into the Cameroons and Dahomey. From the late 1860s to his death Burton was a British diplomat in South America, Syria and Europe. He was a brilliant linguist and claimed to speak thirty languages fluently. He wrote numerous books about his travels, twenty of them on Africa, and also translated important books from Portuguese and Arabic, including an unexpurgated version of *The Arabian Nights*, which shocked the Victorians.

**Bushrangers.** Outlaws of the Australian bush, who robbed stagecoaches, banks, homesteads and small towns. From 1789 to the 1850s they were nearly all escaped convicts, but were later joined by many freemen who failed to find rich pickings in the **gold rush** of the 1850s. 'Bush telegraph' quickly informed them of police movements and enabled them to use their fast horses to retreat to the mountains. Most died young, either shot by police or hanged. Many were ruthless killers; others became famous in Australian folklore for the humane treatment of their victims or for sharing their booty with the poor, as did the gang led by Ben Hall, who held the township of Canowindra for three days in 1863 and entertained the locals to free food and drink. The last and most famous of the bushrangers was Ned Kelly, who was wounded and captured in his suit of home-made armour in 1880, and was hanged later that year.

**Cacique.** Spanish party boss, the term deriving from the Caribbean Indian for 'chief'. The influence of such bosses generally derived either from their economic power, usually rooted in land ownership, or their role as an intermediary between the locality and the region or state: thus they were often either landowners or lawyers. By these means they came to control local institutions such as the town council, the judiciary and the Civil Guard. They can be seen not only as a product of the isolation of rural communities and the stark inequalities of the Spanish class system, but also of the need to underpin the weakly integrated central state, following the decline of royal absolutism. After the Restoration of 1875, the *caciques*' role as intermediaries of the state became institutionalized. They controlled political life by fixing elections, so that the Liberal and Liberal–Conservative parties rotated in power in a pre-arranged manner, otherwise known as the *turno pacífico* ('peaceful rotation'). The *caciques* thereby became the cornerstone of the **Restoration system**. With their economic and social power, they controlled every aspect of local life. Not surprisingly, *caciquismo* was attacked by reformers as the prime obstacle to modernization. The fraudulent parliamentary system of the Restoration survived until the establishment of the dictatorship of General **Primo de Rivera** in 1923. Although the monarchist parties were disbanded by the dictatorship, the socio-economic power of the *caciques* often remained intact in rural Spain. Consequently, under the **Spanish Second Republic** of 1931–6 they proved a severe obstacle to the implementation of the democratic and liberal reforms of the new regime.

**Cairo Conference** (22–26 November 1943). A meeting between **Roosevelt**, **Churchill** and **Jiang Jieshi** (Chiang Kai-shek), after which a joint declaration was issued, stating that war with Japan would continue until she surrendered unconditionally. Japan would then lose all the Pacific islands she had seized since 1914; Manchuria, Taiwan and the Pescadores Islands would be returned to China; and Korea would become independent. All this was later included in the **Potsdam Declaration**.

**Calhoun, John Caldwell** (1782–1850). US politician. Calhoun, from South Carolina, was the most persuasive leader of the white South, a fervent supporter of states' rights and slavery. John Quincy **Adams** described him as being a man of 'clear and quick understanding, of cool self-possession . . . and of an ardent patriotism'. In the House of Representatives (1811–17) Calhoun was a leading nationalist, who helped to push President **Madison** into the **Anglo-American War** of 1812. Secretary of War (1817–25), he became Vice-President, first under Adams in 1824, then under Andrew **Jackson** four years later. Abandoning hope that Congress would lower the tariff to what he regarded as a tolerable level, he wrote the South Carolina Exposition (1830), in which he put forward the doctrine of **nullification**: that states had the right to prevent the enforcement of a federal law within their borders if they considered the law to be unconstitutional. Calhoun gave up his vice-presidency in 1832 and spent nearly all the rest of his political life in the Senate. He joined Henry **Clay** in the mid-1830s to found the **Whig Party**, but returned to the Democrats when he felt that they were better able to defend slavery. He served as President Tyler's Secretary of State from 1844–5, when he strongly supported the annexation of **Texas**. On 4 March 1850, when Calhoun was old and bent and hardly able to walk, a colleague read out in the Senate what was to be his last speech, in which he opposed the **Compromise of 1850**. After this he seemed to realize that his aims would not be achieved. 'It is difficult to see', he said about the North and South, 'how two peoples so different and hostile can exist together in one common Union.'

**Campbell-Bannerman, Sir Henry** (1836–1908). British Prime Minister (1905–8). 'C.B.', as he was known, was the son of a wealthy Glasgow wholesale draper and became **Liberal** MP for Stirling Burghs in 1868, a constituency he represented for the next forty years. As War Secretary in **Gladstone**'s Cabinets of 1886 and 1892–5 he showed only modest competence before he was unexpectedly chosen to lead the Liberal Party in the **Commons** in 1899. He found a quarrelsome party, which divided over support for the **South African War** (1899–1902). C.B. was denounced as a traitor by the Tory press for condemning the setting up of **concentration camps** in South Africa as 'methods of barbarism', and also upset the Liberal imperialists. Yet by tact, good humour and patience he managed to reunite the Liberal Party and found opposition to **tariff reform** a cause on which they could all agree. When **Balfour** resigned in 1905, C.B. rejected a move by the Liberal imperialists (**Grey**, **Haldane** and **Asquith**) for him to go to the **Lords**, and soon established his authority over the Cabinet and the Commons.

In 1906 C.B. led the Liberals to a landslide victory, with a majority of 222 over the Conservatives (the largest for over eighty years) and eighty-eight over all other parties combined. His achievements as Prime Minister were remarkable, as he was prostrated by his wife's illness and death in 1906 and then by his own poor health. He insisted on giving self-government to the Boer states of Transvaal and Orange Free State, which prepared the way for the Union of South Africa in 1910 and turned **Botha** and **Smuts** into friends of England. C.B. asserted himself again over the Trades Disputes Bill (1906), by ensuring that the Labour version of the bill, which freed trade unions from liability for damages caused as the result of a strike, was accepted. Though he was largely indifferent to social reform, C.B.'s ministry made it possible for local authorities to provide free school meals for needy children, and school medical inspections. The Children Act (1908) abolished the practice of sending children to prison and established juvenile courts. Care for the elderly came belatedly with the introduction of state pensions (ten countries already provided this). He firmly supported Haldane's army reforms and the **Anglo-Russian Entente** (1907), arranged by Grey. Some Liberal bills were rejected by that annexe of the **Tory Party**, the House of Lords, so C.B. suggested restricting their powers, a proposal later carried out in the **Parliament Act** (1911). As he wished to keep the Liberal Party united, he favoured a step-by-step approach to Ireland, which meant postponing **Home Rule for Ireland**. He had a heart attack in the autumn of 1907 and another at the beginning of 1908, so effective leadership of the government passed to Asquith several months before C.B. retired in March 1908.

**Canada Acts** (1791, 1840). The Act of 1791 sprang from loyalist demands for a legislative assembly. The province of Quebec was divided into two along the Ottawa river. West of this was Upper Canada (now Ontario), populated mainly by Britons, loyalists from the American colonies who had moved north after the American War of Independence (1775–83) and Iroquois. East of the Ottawa river was Lower Canada (now Quebec), the heartland of the old French Empire in Canada, where the population was overwhelmingly French-speaking and the Catholic Church was strong. Power was held by a Governor appointed by the British Crown. There was to be an elected legislature in each province, but legislative power was to be shared with an appointed upper house. Land was set aside in each province for the establishment of a 'Protestant clergy', a move which greatly angered the French Canadians.

The Act of Union of 1840 followed the **Durham Report**. It united Upper (West) and Lower (East) Canada into a single province with one legislature, in which both parts had equal representation. This was done to prevent French Canadians, who were assumed to be the majority, from dominating the assembly. Immigration soon made the English-speaking Canadians the majority, so they were left with a sense of grievance. Canadians did not get the responsible government they wanted but Lord John **Russell**, the British Colonial Secretary, did not reject it completely: he told the Governor of the Union to choose advisers from those who had the confidence of the assembly.

**Canadian Pacific Railway.** Work began in 1880 on Canada's transcontinental railroad, which was to become the longest in the world. To induce capitalists to invest in the railway, the Conservative government of Sir John **Macdonald** offered them millions of acres of fertile land alongside the track, subsidies and exemption from taxes. British Columbia would not join the Canadian Confederation in 1871 until it was promised a transcontinental railway. The difficulties of building track across largely uninhabited territory were immense: temperatures well below zero in winter; tunnels to be blasted through the Rockies; and bridges to be built across the rapids of the Columbia and other rivers. The Canadian Pacific Railway was completed in 1885 and had enormous political and economic importance. As the boundary with the USA – the 49th parallel – was unmarked and undefended, the railway ran just north of the border to ensure that the USA did not penetrate that area. The railway made the settlement of the prairies possible, encouraged immigration, and extended the trade and industry of the St Lawrence valley westwards to the Pacific. It also encouraged **urbanization**, as towns like Winnipeg, Calgary and Vancouver grew up along the route.

**Canning, George** (1770–1827). British statesman. Like **Castlereagh**, Canning began his political life as a **Whig**, but with the **French Revolution** he became a supporter of **Pitt**, under whom he held junior office before resigning with Pitt in 1801 over the issue of **Catholic emancipation**. He became Foreign Secretary in 1807, ordered the destruction of the Danish fleet at the second battle of **Copenhagen** (1807) and took the decision which led to Britain waging the **Peninsular War** (1808–13) against **Napoleon Bonaparte**. After a duel with Castlereagh in 1809, Canning resigned. When **Liverpool** became Prime Minister in 1812, Castlereagh, who was Foreign Secretary in the previous administration, generously offered to make way for Canning. The arrogant and abrasive Canning refused, as Castlereagh would remain Leader of the House of **Commons**, so he kept himself out of high office for the next decade. He had just become Governor-General of India when Castlereagh committed suicide and so, fortuitously, Canning was able to return to the Foreign Office in 1822. He disliked the Congress System, for which Castlereagh was largely responsible, as it involved Britain too much in European affairs. 'Every nation for itself and God for us all' was his motto. The Spanish colonies had broken away from Spain during the **Napoleonic Wars**. Canning recognized their independence, and that of Brazil, so that they could become economic dependencies of Britain. 'Spanish America is free', he said in 1824, 'and if we do not mismanage our affairs, she is English.' He supported the **Monroe Doctrine**, as Britain wanted trade not territory, though in practice it was the British rather than the US navy which would prevent the intervention of other powers in Latin America. In 1826 he arranged with Russia to recognize the autonomy of Greece when the **Greek War of Independence** ended. On Liverpool's resignation in 1827, Canning became Prime Minister. He was a supporter of Catholic emancipation but an opponent of Repeal (of the Test and Corporation Acts, which denied Dissenters full political rights) and of **parliamentary reform**, which he thought would 'end in national destruction'. The 'Protestants' who opposed Catholic emancipation, led by **Wellington** and **Peel**, refused to serve under him, so he had to turn to the Whigs to form a government. The stress was too much for him – feeling 'quite knocked up', he died in August 1827.

**Cánovas del Castillo, Antonio** (1828–97). Spanish Prime Minister (1875–81, 1884–5, 1890–92 and 1895–7). Cánovas remained aloof from both the Revolution of 1868 and the Spanish First Republic of 1873–4, but he cultivated his political position within the monarchist camp to the extent that, after the Martínez Campo rising of December 1874 against the Republic, he exercized virtual dictatorial power in Spain for six years. His outstanding achievement was the creation of the **Restoration system**, which survived until the dictatorship of **Primo de Rivera** in 1923. Physically unattractive and an enormous eater, Cánovas was known by his opponents as 'the Monster'. He based his political pre-eminence on an unusual capacity for work, intellectual prowess and his outstanding parliamentary oratory. From 1876 Cánovas alternated in power with the Liberal Party under Sagasta. By the 1890s the regime was beset by difficulties at home and abroad. When Cánovas returned to office in 1895 a major rebellion was in progress in Cuba. The harsh response of his government to opposition in Cuba and the Philippines played an important role in precipitating the **Spanish–American War** of 1898 and the end of Spain's empire. Domestic protest finished Cánovas' own life, when an anarchist assassinated him on 8 August 1897. Cánovas' stabilization of the monarchy and the preservation of the political power of the predominantly landowning élite was achieved at the expense of the lower classes. In the absence of democratic reform lay the origins of revolutionary and republican opposition. Cánovas was, therefore, not only responsible to a great extent for the 'Disaster of 1898', but also for many of Spain's subsequent problems.

**Capone, Al** (1899–1947). US gangster. Alphonse Capone was born in Naples but grew up in Brooklyn, New York. Known as

'Scarface', he became the right-hand man of Johnny Torrio, boss of Chicago's underworld, and took over as head of his organization in 1925, after Torrio was badly wounded in a gangland attack. Capone thrived at a time of **Prohibition** by controlling illicit stills, distributing liquor, running protection rackets and bribing politicians and police. Prostitution and gambling were further sources of his enormous income. Al Capone was the world's most famous gangster, who removed rivals by intimidation or murder, using new weapons like the machine-gun rather than the sawn-off shotgun. He is held to be responsible for 400 murders, the most notorious of which took place on St Valentine's Day 1929, when his men, dressed as police, lined up and machine-gunned the Bugs Moran gang, his Irish rivals. He cut a distinctive figure, dressed in striped yellow suit and spats, and was well known to a fascinated public. Al Capone was finally jailed in 1931 for not paying taxes. When he was released in 1939 he was suffering from paralysis, the effect of syphilis.

**Caporetto, battle of** (24 October–23 November 1917). A crushing defeat of the Italian army in north-east Italy by Austro-German forces in the **First World War**. The Italian front stretched from the Swiss frontier in the west to the river Isonzo, which enters the Adriatic Sea west of Trieste, in the east. The whole length of the front, except for fifteen miles (twenty-four kilometres) at the southern end of the Isonzo front, was mountainous, with Austrians holding the high ground. Between June 1915 and August 1917 the Italians made eleven attacks on the Isonzo and gained only seven miles. Their commander, General Cadorna, was a ferocious disciplinarian who made repeated frontal assaults. The morale of his troops was therefore low when the Austrians, reinforced by seven German divisions, attacked after a heavy bombardment at Caporetto. Confusion and panic spread throughout the Italian ranks, and the Italians began a retreat which did not end until they reached the river Piave, seventy miles away. Of Cadorna's troops, 40,000 were killed and wounded, 275,000 had been captured by the Austrians and many had deserted. Austro-German losses totalled 20,000. British and French troops were rushed to Italy to hold the new line of the Piave. This battle, the most humiliating Italian defeat in the war, revived the dying Habsburg Empire.

**Caprivi, Leo Graf von** (1831–99). German Chancellor (1890–94). When Caprivi succeeded **Bismarck** he pursued a New Course, which involved reconciliation with opponents of the government at home, favouring industry at the expense of agriculture and closer relations with Britain abroad. He refused to renew the **Reinsurance Treaty** with Russia, as he felt that if its terms became known Britain, Italy and Austria-Hungary would be offended. This was a crucial decision, as Russia consequently moved towards France and made the **Franco-Russian Alliance** in 1894, although Bismarck's *Lombardverbot* had first pushed Russia in that direction. The **Anglo-German agreement** with Britain in 1890 was an attempt to gain British support in Europe in return for concessions in Africa, and alarmed Russia, as it brought Britain closer to the **Triple Alliance**. Caprivi also wanted to form a Central European customs union, dominated by Germany, and so in 1892–3 he made a series of commercial treaties, by which Germany reduced her tariffs on foreign agricultural goods in return for reduced duties on German industrial exports. This pleased the workers, as grain prices fell by 50 per cent, but incensed the powerful *Junkers*, who were also strongly opposed to Caprivi's other measures to improve the lot of the workers. The Chancellor refused to renew the **anti-socialist law** and persuaded the **Reichstag** to pass laws forbidding Sunday work and limiting working hours. Courts, with representatives of both workers and employers, were set up to deal with industrial disputes. The Emperor **William II** became alarmed when the socialists gained more votes than any other party in Reichstag elections, and contemplated a *coup* to reduce the Reichstag's powers. Caprivi dissuaded him from this and then resigned, bringing the New Course to an end.

**Cárdenas, Lázaro** (1895–1970). President of Mexico (1934–40). A *mestizo* (of Indo-European stock) from a poor family, Cárdenas began work at the age of twelve and joined the revolutionary armies in the **Mexican Revolution** when he was sixteen. By 1920 he was Governor of his native province, Michoacan, where he had a reputation for being honest and hard-working. He held several Cabinet posts under Calles before he was elected President in 1934. It was expected that he would be another puppet President dominated by Calles, but he showed considerable independence by replacing Calles's supporters with his own in the Cabinet, the army and all branches of government. In April 1936, he had Calles and his closest supporters expelled from the country, thus (unusually for Mexico) eliminating a *caudillo* without bloodshed. Cárdenas then widened his power base by gaining the support of peasants and workers, and sponsoring the formation of the Confederation of Labour and of Mexico's first National Confederation of Peasants. He was the first Mexican President to bring about a major social revolution by reviving agrarian reform, which Calles had almost abandoned. Eighteen million hectares (forty-four million acres) of land were redistributed to three-quarters of a million peasant families: twice as much as under all previous governments. The results were not all beneficial, as many peasants resorted to subsistence farming and production fell. Yet Cárdenas had gone a long way to assuaging the land hunger of the peasants. Nearly half the land was now held by *ejidos* (Indian village communities), thus vastly reducing the power of the *haciendas* (large estates). Cárdenas tended to support the trade unions when there was labour unrest, and this led to confrontation with foreign oil companies when they refused to accept wage claims. The response of the President, who had nationalized the railway companies (which had been largely foreign-owned) in 1937, was to nationalize the oil companies a year later. Many expected the USA to take action but President Franklin D. **Roosevelt** was planning his **'Good Neighbor'** policy and would not interfere. The major oil companies boycotted Mexican oil for the next thirty years, but nationalization made Cárdenas a hero in Mexico. His government was certainly the most radical to emerge from the Mexican Revolution, though his aim was always to balance social reform with the strengthening of the capitalist economy. In accord with the Constitution, he did not seek re-election.

**Cardwell, Edward, Viscount** (1813–86). British military reformer. As Secretary of State for War in **Gladstone**'s first administration (1868–74), Cardwell carried out the most important reforms of the British army until those of **Haldane**. The British inefficiencies shown in the **Crimean War** (1854–6) and Prussia's success against Austria (1866) prompted a series of changes. Cardwell ended the purchase of commissions: entry to and promotion in the officer corps was to be by competitive examination, though in practice the social origins of officers changed little. The Army Enlistment Act of 1870, inspired by the Prussian example, introduced short-term enlistment to be followed by a period in the reserves. In 1872 a localization scheme began, though it was ten years before it was fully worked out. Every regiment had a recognized territorial area (and was later given a territorial name), from which it drew most of its recruits. Each infantry regiment would consist of two linked battalions, one stationed abroad and one at home: reinforcements needed overseas would be drawn from the home battalion. Cardwell also equipped the army with breech-loading rifles and made life less barbarous for the ordinary soldier by ending flogging and the branding of deserters with a large D. His reforms enabled the British army to fight colonial campaigns successfully in the last quarter of the nineteenth century, though the second **South African War** (1899–1902) revealed weaknesses which necessitated further reforms.

**Carlism.** A Spanish political movement of the extreme **Right**, whose name derived from Charles Maria Isidro of Bourbon (see **Bourbon dynasty**). Following the death of his brother Ferdinand VII in 1833, Charles disputed the right to the throne of his niece Isabel II. This led to the civil wars of 1833–40, 1846–9 and 1872–6. The Carlists' failure to establish themselves beyond their strongholds led to defeat on each occasion. Conservative and fervently Catholic, the strength of the Carlist cause lay in its defence of local traditions and customs. It thereby drew on opposition to secularism, the extension of capitalism, and the increasing involvement of the state in regional and local life. Its heartland lay in the Basque region and Navarre, but extended to parts of Castile, Aragon, Catalonia and Valencia. After the defeat of 1876, Carlism was no longer a source of widespread anti-capitalist protest, retreating to Navarre and the Basque country. The movement struggled to survive during the monarchist Restoration of 1876–1931, principally because the Alfonsine monarchy undermined Carlism's conservative appeal. Just as the anti-clerical Spanish First Republic had revived Carlism in 1873, so the Second Republic of 1931 gave it a new lease of life in the 1930s. Many Conservatives rallied to the Carlist banner because of the Republic's secular and liberal reforms, but also because of the general demoralization and disorganization of the non-republican Right. The Carlists aimed to overthrow the Republic for the 'traditional monarchy'. Although limited in support and lacking a definite plan, the counter-revolutionary activism of the Carlist movement nevertheless played an important role in the polarization which destroyed the **Spanish Second Republic**. It strongly influenced the Catholic Right by helping to create a shared ideological outlook that superseded strategic differences. The Carlists played a key role in the rising of 17–18 July 1936 against the Republic. During the **Spanish Civil War** of 1936–9 they contributed greatly to the Nationalist war effort, with as many as 100,000 military volunteers. However, in April 1937 General **Franco** forcibly fused the Carlists with the **Falange** to form the National Movement, which was to provide the basis of his single party. Disillusioned with this result, many Carlists withdrew from political life after the war. The movement split into warring groups, a situation worsened by the unresolved succession that arose on the death of the Carlist leader Alphonso Charles in 1936. Although eclipsed as an independent political force, Carlism's main ideological goals were achieved during the early years of the Franco dictatorship.

**Carnegie, Andrew** (1835–1919). US industrialist. The son of a Scottish hand-loom weaver, Carnegie went to America when he was thirteen. He worked in a cotton mill, as a telegraph operator and on the Pennsylvania Railroad, of which he became superintendent. In 1865 he turned to iron manufacture, which made him a millionaire, and then to steel. Carnegie had no engineering training but he had enormous energy and drive, which swept aside competitors and **trade unions** alike. His Homestead plant was the scene of a bitter strike in 1892 (see **Homestead strike**), in which he defeated the Steelworkers' Union. Carnegie was quick to apply new methods, such as the open-hearth process for making steel, and with Henry Clay Frick made the first huge vertical combine to include coalfields, coke ovens, iron mines, ships and railroads. He then controlled all sources of supply and distribution. The Carnegie company soon dominated the steel industry and made its owner one of the richest men in the world. Carnegie received 447 million dollars for his holdings when his company was merged with others in 1901 to form the United States Steel Corporation, which produced 60 per cent of the country's steel.

Carnegie then retired to devote himself to philanthropy. His *Gospel of Wealth* (1889) expressed the view that personal fortunes should be used to benefit society as a whole, an idea he put into practice from the 1880s. Over 2,500 libraries in the USA, Britain and Canada were founded by Carnegie, the first being in his home town of Dunfermline in 1882. He set up the Carnegie Institute of Technology in Pittsburgh in 1912, which is now part of the Carnegie-Mellon University. Carnegie endowed many charitable institutions and gave away 350 million dollars.

**Carnot, Lazare Nicolas Marguerite** (1753–1823). French revolutionary and general. A military engineer and officer in the royal army when the **French Revolution** broke out, Carnot was elected to the **Committee of Public Safety** in August 1793, and from then until September 1797 was the government's chief military adviser. He organized the *levée en masse* (conscription) and the setting up of state factories to make arms and ammunition, and he drew up military plans for the fourteen armies raised by the Republic. Carnot combined new and old regiments (the *amalgame*) to make the army more efficient, took part in the victory at Wattignies (October 1793) and was responsible for the army's success in driving the invaders out of France by the end of that year. When the **Directory** was formed in 1795 Carnot became a Director, but he was distrusted by the generals, as he was prepared to give up territory in order to make a lasting peace. In the *coup d'état* of Fructidor (1797) he was sentenced to deportation to Guiana, but he escaped and fled abroad. After the *coup d'état* of **Brumaire** he returned as **Napoleon**'s Minister of War (1800–1801), but soon retired, as he disapproved of Napoleon becoming Consul for life and later Emperor. Carnot was recalled to the army in 1814 during the **Hundred Days** and was sent to defend Antwerp against **Bernadotte**'s Swedish army, which he did skilfully. As a Regicide (he had voted for the execution of **Louis XVI**) he was exiled by **Louis XVIII** and died in Magdeburg.

**Carpetbaggers.** Northerners who came South after the **American Civil War**. They were derisively called carpetbaggers because many of them allegedly arrived carrying all their possessions in one bag. Along with ex-slaves and local collaborators (**scalawags**) they formed state governments under Republican control in the period of **Reconstruction**. Some wanted only to make their fortune and acquire power, but others genuinely wanted to help the South to overcome the ravages of civil war. All were deeply disliked by Southern whites as 'foreign' intruders. When Reconstruction ended and federal troops were withdrawn from the South in 1877, the influence of the carpetbaggers declined rapidly.

**Carson, Edward Henry, Baron** (1854–1935). Anglo-Irish statesman. Born in Dublin, Carson gained a great reputation at the English bar, where his cross-examination of Oscar Wilde in 1895 secured Wilde's conviction for homosexuality. In 1892 he was elected as **Liberal Unionist** MP for Dublin University, a seat he held until 1918; from 1918–21 he was an MP for Belfast. Solicitor-General in **Conservative** ministries from 1900–1905, he became leader in 1910 of the anti-Home Rule Unionists. Convinced that an Ireland separated from Britain could not survive economically, he wanted to keep the whole of Ireland within the union with Britain. He opposed **Asquith**'s Home Rule Bill (see **Home Rule for Ireland**), and in a public ceremony in Belfast in September 1912 signed the Covenant, a pledge to use 'all means which may be found necessary to defeat the setting up of a Home Rule Parliament in Ireland'. In 1913 Carson raised a private army, the Ulster Volunteers, to resist Home Rule and made plans to stage a *coup*, declare the independence of Ulster and set up a provisional government the day Home Rule became law. By the spring of 1914 the Ulster Volunteers had 23,000 armed men, who in April received 25,000 rifles and three million rounds of ammunition, which were landed at Larne. Carson claimed in the **Commons** the responsibility for this gun-running and appeared to be leading Ulster on the path to civil war. This did not happen, as the **First World War** began and the Home Rule Act was suspended for the duration. Carson reluctantly agreed in 1914 to Home Rule for southern Ireland but insisted that Ulster, including the counties of Tyrone and Fermanagh, where Catholics were in the majority, should remain united with Britain. His near-treasonable activities did not prevent him from taking office, as Attorney-General in 1915 and First Lord of the Admiralty in 1916. He joined the Cabinet in 1917 but resigned a year later when he found **Lloyd George** preparing a Home Rule Bill for the whole of Ireland. Carson accepted the **Anglo-Irish Treaty** (1921), which established the Irish Free State, as Ulster was allowed to opt out, and he resigned as Unionist leader. From 1921–9 he was a Lord of Appeal.

**Cartels** (or trusts). The cooperation of firms to control prices, quantity of goods produced and marketing of the finished product. Cartels appeared at the end of the 1870s in response to low prices, overproduction and the Great Depression of 1873–96, and took the form of setting prices and fixing quotas for production, thus providing economic stability, regular growth and secure profits. They eliminated competition, risk-taking and the free play of the market. Cartels could be either horizontal or vertical: horizontal cartels were groups of firms producing the same product; vertical cartels controlled all stages of production from buying the raw material to selling the goods produced. Cartels could be used to promote exports: by keeping prices high at home goods could be dumped abroad. Cartels spread most rapidly in Germany: in 1875 there were eight cartels there, in 1905 366 and in the 1920s over 3,000. **I. G. Farben** (1925) became the largest cartel in Europe, with a monopoly of synthetic dyes and nitrogen production and with extensive interests in the chemical industry. Siemens had a virtual monopoly in electrical goods and there were cartels too in iron and steel, cement, coal and shipping. German prosperity depended on a few huge cartels. In the USA, the Standard Oil Company in 1880 controlled 90–95 per cent of the oil refined there, and US Steel (the 'one billion dollar trust') produced 63 per cent of American steel in 1901. There were (ineffective) anti-trust laws in the USA, but in Germany cartels had legal protection and were encouraged by the state, as they promoted German trade and exports. Cartels flourished in the depression of the 1930s.

**Cartier, Sir Georges-Étienne** (1814–73). French-Canadian states-man and Co-Premier in the **Macdonald**–Cartier administration (1857–62). Cartier believed that the French Canadians would be able to maintain their cultural identity only in cooperation with the British. He therefore worked hard to persuade them to support westward expansion (he had a financial interest in the Grand Trunk railways system and other businesses), which the English-speaking Canadians wanted in return for British acceptance of the French language and civil law, the Catholic religion and Catholic schools. The Catholic Bishops in Canada East gave Cartier their full support, as they thought that the main threat to the Church and French Canadians came from the United States: annexation of Canada by the USA should therefore be avoided at all costs. Cartier was a leading figure in the campaign for unification which came about with the **British North America Act** (1867) and had immense influence, as the electors of Canada East followed his lead.

**Casablanca Conference** (14–24 January 1943). With the **North African Campaign** going well, **Churchill**, **Roosevelt** and their Chiefs of Staff met to plan the next offensive. The conference was mainly concerned with a **Second Front** in Europe, which **Stalin** had long been demanding, to help the Soviet Union. The American service chiefs, led by General Marshall, favoured a cross-Channel invasion of France in 1943, but the British said this was too early and wanted to invade Sicily and Italy. The US naval Commander-in-Chief, Admiral King, said that if France could not be invaded then all available resources should be concentrated in the Pacific against Japan. There were heated arguments but in the end Roo-sevelt sided with Churchill, and the British plan for the invasion of Sicily (Operation Husky) was approved. This was the last time that the British were able to determine overall Allied strategy. The conference also agreed on a **strategic bombing offensive** over Germany and that unconditional surrender should be demanded from the **axis powers**.

**Casement, Roger David** (1864–1916). Irish nationalist. Born near Dublin, Casement was a British Consul in Africa and South America from 1892–1911 and gained an international reputation for his reports on atrocities in the Congo (which led the Belgian government to take over control of the Congo from **Leopold II**). He was knighted and retired to Ireland where, in spite of coming from an Ulster Protestant family, he supported the Irish nationalists. In 1913 Casement joined the Irish Volunteers, a paramilitary force, and a year later went to the USA to seek financial aid for it. When the **First World War** began he went to Berlin to persuade the Germans to invade Ireland and tried, unsuccessfully, to form a brigade of Irish prisoners of war to fight against England. Failing to get any German officers to lead the **Easter Rising** (1916), which he thought was essential for its success, he landed in Ireland from a German submarine in order to seek a postponement of the rising. He was captured and sentenced to death as a traitor. As a reprieve was sought, the government allowed the 'Black Diaries', which revealed that he was a homosexual, to be circulated. Hanged in August 1916 after being received into the Catholic Church, Casement became an Irish martyr.

**Castlereagh, Robert Stewart, Viscount** (1769–1822). British statesman. Born in Dublin, Castlereagh entered the Irish parliament in 1790 as a **Whig**, but visits to France turned him against the **French Revolution**. He became a Member of Parliament in 1794 as a supporter of **Pitt**, who made him Irish Secretary in 1797. In this post Castlereagh had to deal with the suppression of the **Irish Rebellion** (1798), and used bribery to secure the passage of the Act of **Union** (1800) through the Irish parliament. Like Pitt, he thought that **Catholic emancipation** should follow Union and resigned with his leader in 1801 when **George III** would not allow this. In 1802 he returned to office as President of the Board of Control for India which, in Pitt's last administration, he combined with the secretaryship for war. Criticism of his conduct of the war against **Napoleon Bonaparte** by **Canning** led to a duel between them in 1809 and to both men resigning their offices.

Castlereagh went to the Foreign Office in 1812 and remained there until 1822, becoming one of Britain's greatest Foreign Secretaries. In 1813 he feared that the coalition against Napoleon would collapse, as earlier ones had done, and that Austria would make a separate peace with France which would ignore English interests. He prevented this at Chaumont (1814), when Austria, Prussia and

Russia agreed not to make a separate peace with France. His influence at the Congress of **Vienna**, after Napoleon's defeat, was enormous, and he got his way on nearly all the major issues, giving France peace with honour yet surrounding her with states strong enough to resist a French attack. Britain's interests abroad were strengthened by the acquisition of colonies, particularly the Cape of Good Hope and Ceylon. Castlereagh persuaded the other powers to form the Quadruple Alliance and to meet at regular intervals to consider means for 'the maintenance of the peace of Europe'. This was the beginning of the Congress System, though Castlereagh increasingly differed from the other powers, particularly when Prussia and Russia agreed in the Troppau Protocol not to recognize any regime established by revolution, and to restore 'legitimate' governments which had been overthrown. Castlereagh wrote in 1820 that the Alliance 'never was intended for the Superintendence of the Internal Affairs of other States'. He did not think that **liberalism** or **nationalism** could be crushed by force of arms, and distinguished between intervention on principle and intervention where the great powers' essential interests were concerned. When Austria intervened to suppress a rising in Naples, Castlereagh did not object, as Italy was in Austria's area of influence.

At the same time as he was Foreign Secretary, Castlereagh was Leader of the House of **Commons**, and as such he had to justify to the House the **Peterloo massacre** and introduce the repressive legislation of **Liverpool**'s government, such as the Six Acts (1819), at a time of economic depression and unrest. He therefore gained the undeserved reputation of being a reactionary and became the butt of writers like Shelley and Byron. **Wellington** wrote in the summer of 1822 that Castlereagh was 'in a state bordering on Insanity'. On 12 August 1822 he committed suicide by cutting his throat.

**Catholic emancipation.** The granting of full political and civil rights to Catholics in Britain and Ireland. Much legislation against Catholics had been repealed in 1791 but they were still not allowed to vote, sit in parliament or hold public office. Catholics were allowed to vote for members of the Irish parliament in 1793, though they could not become MPs. **Pitt** thought that Catholic emancipation should follow the Act of **Union** (1800) but **George**

**III** would not allow this, as he felt it contradicted his coronation oath, so Pitt resigned over the issue in 1801. The matter arose again in 1828 when Daniel **O'Connell** was elected for County Clare, but as a Catholic was not allowed to take up his seat. It seemed that if the law was not changed there would be civil war in Ireland. To avoid this, **Wellington**, supported by **Peel**, decided that emancipation would have to be granted, in spite of opinion in England being overwhelmingly against it. The Catholic Emancipation Act (1829) allowed Catholics to sit in parliament and hold any public office except that of Lord Chancellor or Lord Lieutenant of Ireland, but the Tory government needed Whig support to pass the bill, as 173 **Tories** in the **Commons** and 109 peers in the **Lords** voted against it. This split in the Tory Party allowed the **Whigs** under Earl **Grey** to come to power and pass the **Reform Act** of 1832.

**Cato Street Conspiracy** (1820). A plot to murder members of the British Cabinet whilst they were at dinner. The period following the **Napoleonic Wars** was one of great unrest, as there was a slump with high unemployment and political agitation (eleven people were killed in the **Peterloo massacre** in 1819). The conspiracy to assassinate the Cabinet was infiltrated by a government spy, so that plotters were arrested as they gathered in Cato Street in London. All were tried for high treason: five were executed and five transported for life. The belief that a general rising would follow was reinforced by outbreaks in Scotland and Yorkshire soon after the plot failed. An unsuccessful attempt to seize Glasgow resulted in three leaders being executed and others being transported. There was no real threat to the government, though there were considerable disturbances in 1819 and 1820 in London, Lancashire, Yorkshire and central Scotland.

**Cattle trails** in the USA ran from the open prairies to the railheads. As Americans moved into Texas in the early nineteenth century they took with them their cattle, derived from English stock. They bred these with Spanish cattle to produce the wiry Texan Longhorn, which had long legs suitable for moving vast distances over the prairies. By the end of the **American Civil War** there were five million on the Texas ranges; if they could be driven to the railheads, from where they could be taken to meat markets in cities like Chicago, their value would increase tenfold. In 1866 some Texans began the first of the 'long drives': **cowboys** drove the cattle a thousand miles to Sedalia on the Missouri–Pacific railroad. A year later the more accessible Abilene was chosen; 35,000 cattle were taken there in 1867, 700,000 in 1871. New trails were opened as the 'long drive' pushed West, and new railheads like Dodge City arose. From 1866 to 1888 between six and ten million cattle were driven to these 'cow towns', the number reaching a peak from 1880–85. By this time most Indians had been forced on to reservations, whilst the slaughter of the buffalo left the plains open for cattle grazing. Railways were extended, refrigerated cars were built, beef was exported to Europe (from 1875) and prices were high. Yet by 1885 the range had begun to shrink, as the **Homestead Act** lured farmers to the West and as beef prices fell because the ranges had been overstocked. Ranchers and sheep farmers fenced in their farms — the days of the 'long drive' were over.

**Caucasus, Russian conquest of**. Russia acquired this territory, between the Black and Caspian Seas, piecemeal from the **Ottoman Empire** and Persia in the first half of the nineteenth century. Georgia was annexed in 1801, and after a war with Persia (1804–13) Russia acquired the eastern Caucasus, including Baku and part of Azerbaijan. Persia renounced these concessions in 1826, but was defeated again, and in 1828 gave up Persian Armenia and the rest of Azerbaijan. Russia was now free to turn to the western Caucasus: after defeating Turkey she extended her control of the Black Sea coast, but found it hard to subdue the mountainous areas inland. From 1834–59 Russia was involved in a prolonged *jihad*, waged by the Caucasian Muslims under their *imam*, Shamil, and it was not till 1864 that the area was pacified. Russia was then able to concentrate on the subjugation of other Muslim peoples in **Central Asia**.

*Caudillo.* A military dictator in Latin America. After the long wars of independence against Spain (1810–26) in Latin America, the breakdown of law and order, economic depression and the rise of military leaders all contributed to *caudillismo*. Charismatic leaders, with the support of the army, built up a patronage network. Many *caudillos* (such as Francía in Paraguay, Rosas in Argentina) were brutal in suppressing opposition, executing, torturing or imprisoning opponents. *Caudillos* operated at all levels of national life, in the provinces as well as the capital cities, and were often popular with certain groups, particularly the *hacendados* (owners of large estates), who considered them to be a force against anarchy. All Latin American states were ruled at one time or another by *caudillos*. Some, such as **Díaz** in Mexico (1876–1910) and Gómez in Venezuela (1908–35), retained power for a considerable time. In Spain, **Franco** applied the name to himself, using it as a title like *Führer*.

**Cavour, Camillo Benso, Count** (1810–61). Italian statesman, who made a major contribution to the *Risorgimento*. A Piedmontese aristocrat, whose native language was French (like **Garibaldi**, he spoke Italian imperfectly), in 1847 Cavour became editor of the newspaper *Il Risorgimento*, which preached that Italian rulers should cooperate to throw Austria out of Italy. The **Revolutions of 1848**, in which Cavour played no active part, made it clear that this could not be done without foreign help. In 1850 Cavour entered the Piedmontese government, becoming Prime Minister in 1852, a post he held until his death, except for six months in 1859. A secularist and free trader, monarchist and opponent of revolution, who hated **Mazzini**, Cavour reduced the power of the Church, made commercial treaties with several European countries, began to expand the railway network and to turn Piedmont into a progressive state. He used parliament to check royal authority, and controlled it by bribery.

Cavour entered the **Crimean War** to please **Victor Emanuel II**, though Piedmont gained nothing from the war. In 1858, without consulting his Cabinet, Cavour made an agreement with **Napoleon III** at **Plombières**, by which a successful war with Austria would be followed by Piedmont gaining Lombardy and Venetia, whilst France would receive Nice and Savoy from Piedmont. The war of 1859 was over in two months. The French defeated Austria at Magenta and Solferino, but losses on both sides were heavy, so Napoleon suddenly made peace at Villafranca without conquering Venetia. Piedmont therefore gained only Lombardy (France did not acquire anything, as the terms agreed at Plombières had not been fulfilled) and so Cavour resigned in a fury. Meanwhile, in central Italy the rulers of Tuscany, Parma and Modena had fled and had been replaced by provincial governments, whose leaders wanted Piedmont to annex them. Cavour, returning to power in January 1860, saw his opportunity and made another deal with Napoleon. After plebiscites in the central Italian states were in favour of annexation to Piedmont, Napoleon allowed this to take place in return for the acquisition by France of Nice and Savoy. Piedmont had now doubled in size, but Cavour still had no idea of uniting Italy. This was made possible only by Garibaldi's invasion, which Cavour tried to prevent, of Sicily and then of Naples. Cavour was now in a difficult situation: if Garibaldi marched on Rome, Napoleon III would defend Pope **Pius IX**. In a desperate gamble, Cavour decided to invade the Papal States before Garibaldi did, ostensibly to block his advance on Rome. The ruse worked, as Britain supported the action of Piedmont. Plebiscites in Sicily, Naples and the Papal States voted for annexation to Piedmont, to whom Garibaldi handed over his conquests. Cavour, with the indispensable help of Garibaldi, had united Italy, with the exception of Rome and Venetia. He was not to enjoy his triumph for long, as he died four months after becoming Italy's first Prime Minister.

**Central Asia, Russian conquest of.** In the nineteenth century Russia expanded south to the great mountain chains which separated it from Persia, Afghanistan, India and China. Much of this area of Central Asia was desert populated by nomads, with settled Muslim communities on the rivers Amu Darya and Syr Darya, which flowed into the Aral Sea. As the nomadic tribes raided Russian settlements, the Russians began to move into the steppe between the Caspian and Aral Seas in the 1820s. East of the Aral Sea they crossed the Ili river and founded Verny (Alma-Ata) in 1854. Gorchakov, the Russian Foreign Minister, did not want to advance on the settled khanates of Khiva and Kokand and the emirate of Bukhara, as he was more concerned with events in Europe, but Russian generals on the spot were difficult to control and the expansion continued. In 1864 General Chernyaev, acting on his own initiative, attacked the Kokand capital of Tashkent. This led the Emir of Bukhara to declare a *jihad* against Russia, which resulted in the creation of the new Russian province of Turkestan (1866) and the establishment of Russian Protectorates over Kokand and Bukhara

(1868) and later Khiva (1873). These last two remained Protectorates till 1917, but Kokand was annexed to Russia after a rising in 1875. Russian attention now turned to the Turkoman tribes south-east of the Caspian Sea, who were defeated. By 1885 Russia's border extended south to Afghanistan, a cause for tense relations with Britain, who regarded Russia's advance as a threat to India. Russia's expansion in Central Asia, the **Caucasus** and the Far East made her one of the great imperialist powers of the nineteenth century, as all these territories were occupied by non-Russian peoples.

**Central Powers.** A term which referred to the members of the **Triple Alliance** (1882): Germany, Austria-Hungary and Italy. As Italy did not join Germany in the **First World War**, the phrase was applied from 1914 to Germany and her allies, Austria-Hungary, Turkey and later Bulgaria.

**Centre Party.** A Roman Catholic political party in the **German Empire** and **Weimar Republic**. Most Catholics had wanted a Greater Germany which would include Austria, so they were regarded as enemies of the Reich by **Bismarck** in the predominantly Protestant empire (Catholics formed 37 per cent of the population). The Centre Party opposed Bismarck's attack on the Catholic Church in the *Kulturkampf*, defended confessional schools and supported greater autonomy for the states. As Catholic areas were generally made up of economically backward small towns and countryside, the Centre Party came to represent small farmers, artisans and the *petite bourgeoisie*. It therefore supported Bismarck when he moved to protection in 1879 and approved of his **State Socialism**, but it remained a party of opposition until Bismarck's fall in 1890. After that, with usually about 100 out of 347 seats in the **Reichstag**, its support was needed by the government to pass legislation and it formed part of a dominant 'Blue-Black Block' (of Conservatives and Catholics) from 1893 to 1906. During this time the Centre Party went into opposition to bring about the fall of **Caprivi** in 1894, as it disapproved of his lowering agricultural tariffs, but it generally supported the government on such issues as **Tirpitz**'s Navy Laws of 1898 and 1900 and the tariff of 1902. When the Centre Party attacked the government's colonial administration, **Bülow** tried to form a majority without it, but failed when the Centre Party and the Conservatives joined to defeat his attempt to increase taxation in 1909. The 'Blue-Black Block' was then reformed and supported the new Chancellor, **Bethmann-Hollweg**. The Centre Party's hostility to the socialists continued, so that in 1914 a leading member of the party, Matthias Erzberger, could still regard 'the decimation of the gigantic power of Social Democracy' as the greatest task of the Reich. Not until 1917 did the Centre Party join with the Left Liberals and the SPD to pass the Erzberger Peace Resolution, calling for a peace without annexations, and later form a Centre–Left Weimar Coalition. Like the SPD, the Centre Party had its own sub-culture, with mass organizations such as the People's Association for Catholic Germany, which had 800,000 members by 1914. It also had its own trade union, though this was only a tenth of the size of the socialist trade-union movement. During the Weimar Republic the Centre Party took part in nineteen out of twenty-one Cabinets and became increasingly right-wing, particularly when **Brüning** was Chancellor (1930–32). When **Hitler** came to power it feebly voted for the **Enabling Act** (1933), which removed all power from the Reichstag, and then dissolved itself on 5 July 1933.

**Cetshwayo** (c. 1825–84). Last King of the independent Zulu state in South Africa. When Cetshwayo became King in 1872, Zululand was united with a powerful army, and was almost alone in retaining its independence from whites. Yet there were threats from the British in Natal and the Boers in the Transvaal. Cetshwayo tried to play them off against each other, but in 1877 the British annexed the Transvaal. When they demanded that he should disband his army of 40,000 Cetshwayo refused and reluctantly went to war. The British invaded Zululand in 1879 and suffered a severe reverse at Isandhlwana when a column of 1,200 troops was wiped out. This was the Zulus' last success. When British reinforcements arrived, the Zulus were defeated at Ulundi and Zulu power in Natal was broken. Cetshwayo was captured and exiled to Cape Town, whilst Zululand was divided among thirteen chiefs under a British Resident. Allowed to go to London to plead his cause, Cetshwayo was reinstated in 1883 in a kingdom reduced in size, without an army and weakened by internal unrest. In 1884 civil war broke out;

Cetshwayo had to flee and was probably murdered shortly afterwards. Zululand was annexed by Britain in 1887 and became a part of Natal ten years later.

**CGT** (*Confédération Générale du Travail*). French trade-union federation, formed in 1895. It was a rival to the *Bourses du Travail* (labour exchanges, which became trade-union centres and brought workers of different trades together) until they joined together in 1902. From 1902–10 the CGT was controlled by revolutionary **Syndicalists**, who rejected reform through parliament in favour of direct action, particularly in the form of the general strike, to bring about the downfall of capitalism. Its officials were forbidden to enter parliament. In 1906, when the CGT called a general strike, only 800,000 of France's seven to eight million industrial workers were trade-union members, 200,000 of whom were affiliated to the CGT (a number which rose to 700,000 by 1912). The strike was a failure, as **Clemenceau** sent in the troops and arrested the CGT leaders. From then until the **First World War** the CGT was in disarray, but in 1914 it supported the war effort. After the war there was a conflict within the CGT between the moderates, who were prepared to cooperate with the government, and a revolutionary wing led by communists. The latter broke away in 1921 to form a separate organization, but rejoined the CGT in 1934 in order to oppose **Fascism**. In 1936 the CGT supported the **Popular Front** government of Léon **Blum** and negotiated the Matignon agreements with employers, which brought substantial gains for workers and greatly increased the prestige and membership of the CGT. After the outbreak of the **Second World War** in 1939 the CGT expelled its communist members because of the **Nazi–Soviet Pact**, but was itself dissolved by the **Vichy** government in 1940. Communists controlled the CGT when it was reconstituted after the war.

**Chaco War** (1932–5) was fought by Bolivia and Paraguay for control of the Chaco area, a waste of scrub and white sands, forests and swamps between the rivers Pilcomaya and Paraguay. Bolivia had lost its coastal area on the Pacific in the **Pacific War** (1879–83) and so turned towards the Atlantic, to which it sought access via the rivers of the Chaco. Rumours of petroleum deposits in the area intensified the rivalry between Bolivia and Paraguay. When war began in 1932 it appeared that Bolivia would win, as she had a larger army and population than Paraguay, but Indian conscripts from the Bolivian highlands could not cope with the heat of the Chaco. They were driven back to the Bolivian foothills before a truce was made. Peace in 1938 gave most of the disputed territory to Paraguay. The war was a catastrophe for two poor countries: 50,000 Bolivians and 35,000 Paraguayans were killed. It put the army in control in Paraguay; in Bolivia it stimulated demands for social change which culminated in the rebellion of 1952.

**Chadwick, Sir Edwin** (1800–1890). English social reformer. A friend and follower of Jeremy **Bentham**, Chadwick was largely responsible for the Poor Law Amendment Act (1834), which insisted that poor relief should be given only in workhouses, which should be made as uncomfortable as possible. As Secretary of the Royal Commission on the **Poor Laws** he became convinced that the main cause of poverty was not idleness but illness, which could result in premature death and so make all dependants reliant on the Poor Law Unions. Chadwick collected information from doctors and Poor Law officials in order to write his seminal *Inquiry into the Sanitary Condition of the Labouring Poor* (1842), which showed that much illness was due to the conditions in which people lived and worked, and could be prevented. Civil engineers were needed to provide pure water supplies and sewers. His report was a best-seller and provided the basis for the Public Health Act (1848), which enabled (but did not compel) local authorities to supply water and sewerage. Chadwick was a Commissioner of the Board of Health from 1848–54 but became very unpopular owing to his self-righteousness. *The Times* in 1854 described him and Dr Southwood Smith, the Board's medical officer, as 'firmly persuaded of their own infallibility, intolerant of all opposition, utterly careless of the feelings and wishes of the local bodies'. Chadwick was dismissed in 1854 but his work was carried on by other devoted public servants.

**Chamberlain, Arthur Neville** (1869–1940). British Prime Minister (1937–40). The younger son of **Joseph Chamberlain** and half-brother of Austen, his father decided that Neville should go into business. After studying metallurgy at Birmingham, he was sent to grow sisal in the Bahamas. On his return he worked as a businessman in Birmingham, became a city councillor in 1911 and was elected mayor four years later. In 1918 he became a Unionist (Conservative) MP, and when **Lloyd George**'s coalition government fell in 1922 he took office under Bonar **Law** in various posts. When **Baldwin** succeeded Law as Prime Minister in 1923, Neville Chamberlain unexpectedly became Chancellor of the Exchequer. This ministry lasted for only a short time, but when Baldwin returned to power in 1924 he made Chamberlain Minister of Health (1924–9). In this post he made his political reputation by showing great energy, decisiveness and self-confidence in encouraging the building of council houses and in reforming the **Poor Law**. He played a leading part in the negotiations which led to the formation of a **National Government** under **MacDonald** in 1931, in which he was Chancellor of the Exchequer, a post he held until 1937. *Laissez-faire* was abandoned in 1932, when protective duties were imposed on imports, a policy of **tariff reform** his father had advocated in 1903. At the Ottawa Conference (1932) preferential agreements were made with the **dominions** and later with the colonies, which increased both exports to and imports from the British Empire. Chamberlain's policy of low interest rates and cheap credit led to a housing boom (300,000 new houses were built in 1934) and aided the development of new industries (motor cars, electrical engineering, rayon), mainly in the Midlands and the South, so parts of Britain began to recover from the **Great Depression**.

In 1937 Baldwin retired and Chamberlain was the natural choice as Prime Minister. Winston **Churchill** later wrote of Chamberlain that he 'had, as Chancellor of the Exchequer, not only done the main work of the government for the five years past but was the ablest and most forceful minister'. Smugly self-righteous, he was an authoritative leader who believed in firm government. He is usually identified with the policy of **appeasement**, though this preceded him, and in making concessions to **Hitler** he had the full support of his Cabinet and the Chiefs of Staff. Chamberlain developed his own form of 'shuttle' diplomacy by flying to see Hitler and bypassing the Foreign Office. The **Munich agreement** was immensely popular at the time and it has been claimed that it gave Britain a breathing-space, in which she developed her radar and built Hurricanes and Spitfires, which enabled her to win the **battle of Britain** in 1940. When Hitler invaded the rest of Czechoslovakia in May 1939, Chamberlain abandoned appeasement and, with France, gave a guarantee to Poland against attack, a commitment that the *Führer* did not think he would honour. After the **Second World War** began, Chamberlain showed naïve over-optimism in saying in April 1940 that Hitler had 'missed the bus'. The failure of the Norwegian campaign reduced his support dramatically in the **Commons**, so he tried to form a **coalition government**, but the **Labour Party** would not serve under him. He therefore resigned as Prime Minister and was replaced by Churchill in May 1940, though Chamberlain loyally served in the coalition government as Lord President of the Council. Remaining leader of the **Conservative Party**, he retired in September owing to ill health and died soon afterwards.

**Chamberlain, Joseph** (1836–1914). English politician. Born in Camberwell into a middle-class Unitarian family, Joseph was sent to Birmingham at the age of eighteen to work in the screw-manufacturing firm of Nettlefold and Chamberlain, founded by his father. He worked there for the next twenty years and was largely responsible for the rapid expansion of the firm. In 1869 he was co-founder of the National Education League, which wanted free, undenominational and compulsory elementary education for every child in the country, and was bitterly disappointed by Forster's **Education Act** (1870). Chamberlain retired from business in 1873 to devote himself entirely to politics and became Lord Mayor of Birmingham in the same year. 'By temperament he is an enthusiast and a despot', wrote Beatrice **Webb**, with 'a passionate desire to crush opposition to his will, a longing to feel his foot on the necks of others.' Dynamic and ruthless, his 'municipal socialism' in three years transformed Birmingham, where the local authority established gas, water, sewerage and lighting services, demolished slums and began the rebuilding of the city centre.

'Radical Joe' became a Liberal MP in 1876 and sought to remodel the **Liberal Party** by breaking the stranglehold of the landowning **Whigs** and by persuading it to adopt a radical programme, in which the state would play a positive role. He wanted to do this through the National Liberal Federation (1877), a national union of Liberal organizations centred in Birmingham. Democratically organized, with the 'direct participation of all members of the party in the direction of policy', but under strong central control, the caucus did not have much influence over the party leaders, particularly **Gladstone**. In the House of **Commons**, Chamberlain was a distinctive figure, always wearing a white waistcoat, eyeglass and orchid in his buttonhole. He was appointed President of the Board of Trade in 1880 but became frustrated with Gladstone's obsession with Ireland, which allowed no time for social reforms, so in 1885 he drew up his 'unauthorized programme', which called for the government to 'discharge its responsibilities and its obligations to the poor' and 'to remove the excessive inequality in social life'. The wide-ranging reforms it demanded, such as free elementary education, democratic local government for the counties, disestablishment of the Church of England, were to be paid for by a graduated income tax. By this time Chamberlain was the probable successor to Gladstone as leader of the Liberal Party, but he threw away his chances by opposing Gladstone over **Home Rule for Ireland**, thus dividing the party. He and his followers, with some Whigs, voted against the bill, which was defeated.

In the election which followed, Chamberlain stood as **Liberal Unionist** and remained leader of that group until he joined **Salisbury**'s Conservative government in 1895 as Colonial Secretary. He felt that **Afrikaner** nationalism was a threat to Britain's dominant position in southern Africa, so he covertly supported **Rhodes**'s attempt to overthrow **Kruger** in the **Jameson Raid** and was held by some to be partly responsible for provoking the Boers into starting the **South African War** (1899–1902). In 1903 he made **tariff reform** (the end of free trade) the great issue and resigned from the Cabinet so that he could campaign for it outside parliament. This split the Conservative Party and led to its overwhelming defeat in the 1906 election, so Chamberlain was responsible for dividing each of the major parties. In the same year he suffered a paralysing stroke, which ended his political career.

**Chamberlain, Sir Joseph Austen** (1863–1937). English politician. The elder son of **Joseph Chamberlain** and half-brother of

Neville, Austen's mother died at his birth. His father decided that he should go into politics, so in 1892 he entered the House of **Commons** as a **Liberal Unionist**. Completely dominated by Joseph Chamberlain, whom he copied by wearing a monocle and an orchid in his buttonhole, Austen followed him in joining the **Conservative Party**, and in 1902 joined **Balfour**'s Cabinet as Postmaster-General and later as Chancellor of the Exchequer. When Joseph retired in 1906, Austen was left to carry on the campaign for **tariff reform**, but he lacked his father's drive, self-confidence and ambition. He had a chance to become party leader in 1911 but withdrew from the contest in order not to split the party. During the **First World War** he served in the **coalition government** as Secretary of State for India, in **Lloyd George**'s War Cabinet (1918) and as Chancellor of the Exchequer when the coalition government continued after the war. He finally became Conservative leader when Bonar **Law** retired in 1921, and in February 1922 he was offered the premiership by Lloyd George but declined out of loyalty to the Prime Minister. Chamberlain favoured retaining the coalition to keep Labour out of power, but when the majority of Conservative MPs voted to end it, he resigned as party leader. He returned to office as Foreign Secretary in 1924 in **Baldwin**'s ministry and successfully negotiated the treaties of **Locarno** (1925), which guaranteed the western frontiers of France and Germany. Serving briefly in **MacDonald**'s first **National Government** as First Lord of the Admiralty, he retired after the 1931 election and, with Winston **Churchill**, warned of the danger to European peace of the rise of **Hitler**. Austen Chamberlain is the only leader of the Conservative Party in the twentieth century who has not become Prime Minister.

**Champ de Mars massacre** (July 1791). Radicals in France were appalled when **Louis XVI** was not dethroned or put on trial by the **Constituent Assembly** after the flight to **Varennes**. The **Cordeliers Club** took the lead in drawing up a petition for the King's deposition. On 17 July 1791 50,000 of the poorer members of the Paris population flocked to the Champ de Mars, on the outskirts of Paris, to sign a republican petition. Under pressure from the Assembly, the Commune, the local government of Paris, declared martial law and sent Lafayette with the National Guard (a middle-class citizens' militia) to the Champ de Mars. There the Guard fired on the peaceful and unarmed crowd, killing about fifty people. This was the first bloody clash between different groups in the Third Estate. Some popular leaders were arrested, others (**Hébert**, **Marat**, **Danton**) went into hiding or fled. It took nearly a year for the popular movement to recover.

**Charles X** (1757–1836). King of France (1824–30). A younger brother of **Louis XVI** and **Louis XVIII**, he fled from France as the Comte d'Artois in 1789, after the fall of the **Bastille**, and became leader of the counter-revolution. A libertine in his youth, Charles was a devout Catholic when he returned to France in 1814 and a prominent ultra-royalist. He was sixty-seven when he became King and immediately gave the impression that he wanted to undo all the work of the **French Revolution**. Nobles who had fled from France during the Revolution and had their property confiscated were compensated by '*le milliard*' – one thousand million francs (in fact 630 million francs were paid out). This irritated the *bourgeoisie*, as it was paid for by reducing the interest rates on state bonds by 40 per cent. Clerical and aristocratic influence continued to increase, nobles dominated the highest positions in the administration and army, and in 1829 Charles chose the reactionary Polignac to lead his ministry. When he called an election in 1830 the result was disastrous for the government: 274 opposition deputies were elected, 143 government supporters. Charles and Polignac responded on 25 July with the Four Ordinances, which brought back censorship of the press, reduced the number of deputies, dissolved the newly elected Chamber and ordered fresh elections. This precipitated the **July Revolution**, in which Charles lost his throne and was forced into exile again.

**Chartism.** The most important political movement of working men in Britain in the nineteenth century. Radical working-class politics dated back at least to the **Corresponding Societies** of the 1790s. In the 1830s it had its roots in the worst slump (1837–42) in the nineteenth century and in the reforms of the **Whig** government, which were seen as a persistent assault on the rights of the workers. The **Reform Act** of 1832 had not given the working men the vote, the **Factory Act** (1833) had ignored the demand for a ten-hour day, the new **Poor Law** (1834) was seen as a 'Starvation Law', whilst the police forces were 'plagues of blue locusts', designed to crush the workers. The workers' grievances would not be addressed, it was felt, as long as parliament was dominated by landowning aristocrats and capitalists, so the People's Charter (1838), drawn up by the London cabinet-maker William Lovett and the radical tailor Francis Place, put forward a political programme of six points: universal male suffrage; no property qualifications for Members of Parliament; annual parliaments; constituencies of equal size; payment of MPs; and vote by secret ballot. These demands had first been proposed in 1780 but they were now backed up by large rallies in the leading industrial towns, a national petition with 1.3 million signatures, and a National Convention. This met in February 1839 but its weakness was revealed in the divided reactions of the Chartists when the petition was rejected by parliament in May. Some supported 'physical force' (the use or threat of violence) but the majority would not go beyond 'moral force' (the use of persuasion only), so the Convention broke up in disarray. When there was an armed rising in **Newport** it was easily put down by troops, and many middle-class supporters of Chartism turned their backs on the movement.

In 1840 the National Charter Association (NCA) was formed by Feargus **O'Connor**, who dominated Chartism in the 1840s with his newspaper the *Northern Star*. He revived Chartism as the depression deepened; NCA membership grew to 50,000 and a second National Convention, organized by O'Connor, presented a petition with 3.3 million signatures, but parliament refused to consider it. After this second failure and with economic recovery Chartism declined, surviving in the next few years only through its cultural activities: Chartist schools, chapels, cooperative stores, burial clubs and temperance societies. Following poor harvests in 1846 and 1847 Chartism made its last direct challenge to the government in 1848. A mass rally was called in April on Kennington Common, London, from where there would be a procession to parliament with yet another petition. The government feared a revolution, so it gathered together 7,000 soldiers, 4,000 police and 85,000 special constables (mainly middle class), who outnumbered those attending the rally.

When the government banned the procession O'Connor asked his supporters to disperse peacefully, whilst he presented the petition alone. This humiliating blow to O'Connor's leadership was followed by the arrest of many Chartist leaders and the collapse of the movement. It had never been as serious a threat to the government as the radical movement in 1831–2, as the middle class was largely satisfied by the **Reform Act** of 1832 and did not want to extend the vote to the lower classes. The collapse of Chartism marked the end of democratic political protest. All the demands of the People's Charter except annual parliaments later became law, but their acceptance by parliament owed nothing to Chartism.

**Cheka.** Soviet secret police. 'The Extraordinary Commission for Combating Counter-Revolution, Sabotage and Speculation', known from the initials of its abbreviated Russian title as the Cheka, was set up in December 1917. **Lenin** was opposed by the *bourgeoisie*, peasants and socialist parties in his effort to set up a one-party state, and was faced with civil war and famine. He regarded the Cheka as essential for the survival of the Soviet regime. Outside the law and not accountable to any other authority, the Cheka soon acquired far greater powers than the Tsarist secret police, the *Okhrana*. It arrested suspects, staged trials, fixed sentences (including the death penalty) and carried them out. The Pole, Felix Dzerzhinsky, its first head (from 1917–26), stated, 'We stand for organized terror – this should be frankly stated.' After an attempt on Lenin's life Red Terror was proclaimed in September 1918. Latsis, Chairman of the Eastern Front Cheka, explained to his officers what this meant: 'We are not waging war against individual persons. We are exterminating the *bourgeoisie* as a class.' The first use of mass terror was in the summer of 1918, to suppress peasant risings which followed the requisitioning of grain under **War Communism**. In July the Cheka, under orders from Lenin, executed Tsar **Nicholas II** and his family. **Forced labour camps** under Cheka control were established in 1919 and were cleared from time to time by executing the inmates. The number of people executed by the Cheka is not known: Robert Conquest estimates that 200,000 were shot between 1917 and 1923 and that the Cheka killed another 300,000 in suppressing peasant risings, strikes and mutinies. With the **Red Army** it was the main instrument of Bolshevik dictatorship. In 1922 the Cheka became the GPU, in 1923 OGPU and in 1934 **NKVD**.

**Chernyshevsky, Nikolai Gavrilovich** (1828–89). Russian revolutionary, greatly admired by **Marx**. The son of a priest, Chernyshevsky hated injustice and in the late 1850s hoped that **Alexander II**'s reforms would transform the situation in Russia. He was so disappointed with the terms of the **emancipation of the serfs** that he came to believe that the Tsar would have to be overthrown. The lesson he drew from the **Revolutions of 1848** in Europe was that no hope could be placed in liberal reforms. His novel *What is to be Done?*, written in prison in 1863, expressed his ideas and was an inspiration for generations of Russian revolutionaries. In it he described the 'new men and women', freed from family ties and the constraints of conventional morality, who would dedicate themselves to a revolutionary struggle against all traditional authorities. 'It is a work which charges one up for the rest of one's life', **Lenin** told a friend. It was from Chernyshevsky that Lenin learnt that nothing could be achieved by reform and that liberals would always betray the working class. Chernyshevsky was arrested in 1862 and was in exile in Siberia until 1883.

**Chiang Kai-shek,** see **Jiang Jieshi**

**Chinese Revolution** (1911) brought about the fall of the **Qing dynasty**, which had ruled China since 1644, and ended an imperial tradition which went back to the third century BC. In a desperate attempt to preserve the dynasty, the Empress Dowager **Cixi** had supported reforms which included sending Chinese to study abroad, especially in Japan. There Chinese students were influenced by Western ideas of **nationalism** and democracy and became very critical of the Qing dynasty, which was blamed for the exploitation of China by foreign powers. Many joined **Sun Yixian**'s anti-Manchu *Tongmenghui* (Revolutionary Alliance), founded in Tokyo in 1905. When they returned to China they spread revolutionary propaganda and infiltrated the army (many officers had been trained in Japan). On 10 October 1911 there was an army mutiny at Wuchang, on the middle reaches of the Yangzi. It was soon followed by anti-Manchu risings in the central and southern provinces, where provincial assemblies, in alliance with army command-ers, declared their independence. Representatives of these provinces met in Nanjing to set up a Provisional Republican Government. Sun Yixian, who was in the USA raising funds, returned to China in December and was elected provisional President. Meanwhile, the Court had recalled **Yuan Shikai** to command the new army and crush the revolt. He besieged Wuchang but was unable to capture it and so, well aware that support for the dynasty was crumbling, made a deal with Sun, who agreed to hand over the presidency to Yuan if he would declare his support for the Republic. The revolutionaries knew that Yuan had the best army, and that if there was civil war the Western powers might intervene to protect their economic interests. In February 1912 Yuan obtained the abdication of the dynasty. This had been brought about mainly by provincial assemblies dominated by the gentry and by army commanders, who had made themselves provincial military governors. They, and not Sun's revolutionary party, held the real power, so a social revolution was unlikely to follow: the foundations of the Chinese Republic were very insecure.

**Churchill, Lord Randolph Henry Spencer** (1849–95). The third son of the Duke of Marlborough and father of **Winston Churchill**, he entered the House of **Commons** for the family borough of Woodstock in 1874. He first came to public attention with his attacks on **Gladstone** in 1880, and by mocking the inept Conservative leadership in the Commons. A leading advocate of **Tory Democracy** and founder of the **Primrose League** (1883), Churchill wanted to widen the base of Tory support, but his views were traditionally conservative and did not involve giving way to working-class demands. Churchill opposed **Home Rule for Ireland** but was in favour of local self-government and let **Parnell** know that he would oppose coercion in return for Irish support in the 1885 election. This enabled the Conservatives to gain power briefly, but when Gladstone pledged the **Liberal Party** to Home Rule, Churchill announced that 'Ulster will fight and Ulster will be right', which became a slogan in Northern Ireland. As Secretary of State for India in **Salisbury**'s administration (1885–6) he was largely responsible for the **Anglo-Burmese War** (1885), which ended with Britain annexing Upper Burma. In Salisbury's government of 1886 as Chancellor of the Exchequer and leader of the Commons Churchill was an impossible colleague, interfering in foreign policy and making major public speeches without consulting the Prime Minister. He made a serious miscalculation when, after only five months in office, he offered his resignation unless cuts were made in the army and navy estimates. Salisbury, glad to be rid of his overbearing Chancellor, gratefully accepted. This was in effect the end of what had seemed a promising career, as from 1891 there began a prolonged deterioration of mind and body, perhaps caused by syphilis, which lasted until his death.

**Churchill, Sir Winston Leonard Spencer** (1874–1965). British Prime Minister (1940–45, 1951–5). The elder son of Lord **Randolph Churchill** and grandson of the 7th Duke of Marlborough, Winston did badly at Harrow and scraped into Sandhurst at the third attempt. He charged with the Lancers at **Omdurman**, left the army and became a war correspondent in the **South African War** (1899–1902), where he was captured and escaped. In 1900 he became a Conservative MP but was opposed to **tariff reform** and so joined the **Liberal Party** in 1904. His rise after that was rapid: he became associated with the **New Liberalism** and in 1908 served in **Asquith**'s Cabinet as President of the Board of Trade. Churchill set up Labour Exchanges and, by the Trade Boards Act (1909), created machinery for fixing (and raising) wages in the 'sweated' trades such as tailoring. In 1910, as Home Secretary, he became unpopular with the **trade unions**, as he took a firm stand against industrial unrest. A leading advocate of smashing the power of the House of **Lords** in the **Parliament Act** (1911), Churchill moved in the same year to the Admiralty. There he continued **Fisher**'s work in expanding the navy to meet the German threat, building **Dreadnoughts** and converting the fleet from coal to oil. During the **First World War** he was blamed for the disaster of the **Gallipoli Campaign**, resigned from the Admiralty and commanded a battalion for a short time in France, before **Lloyd George** brought him back as Minister of Munitions (1917–18) in his **coalition government**. Remaining in the post-war coalition government (1918–22) in various posts, Churchill strongly urged intervention in the **Russian**

Civil War (1918–21) against the **Bolsheviks**, but he was overruled, as he was when he wished to take a stand against **Kemal Atatürk** at Chanak (Çannakale) in 1922.

Churchill rejoined the Conservatives in 1924 and was made Chancellor of the Exchequer, a post for which he was not suited. The return to the **gold standard** in 1925 at the pre-war parity, which was far too high, adversely affected British exports and led to a miners' strike and the **General Strike** of 1926. By this time Churchill had lost his earlier radicalism, was obsessed by the 'red peril' and organized government action to bring the strike to an end. The Conservatives lost office in 1929, and though they were back in power from 1931 as part of the **National Government**, Churchill was excluded. He had fallen out with **Baldwin**, as he bitterly opposed the negotiations leading to the **India Act** (1935), which gave Indians control of their provincial government. The **abdication crisis** (1936) was another occasion on which Churchill ploughed a lone furrow, as he supported **Edward VIII** and tried to form a King's Party. At this time he was mistrusted by all parties and particularly by the Conservatives, who regarded him as unstable and unreliable, 'not a safe man'. Consequently, his warnings about the threat **Hitler** posed to European peace and security were ignored. 'Germany', he said in 1934, 'is arming secretly, illegally and rapidly', and urged British rearmament. In 1938 he called Munich 'a defeat without a war', prophesied that the destruction of Czechoslovakia would follow and called for Russia to be brought into an anti-German alliance. When the **Second World War** began, Neville **Chamberlain** recalled Churchill to the Admiralty, his first ministerial post for ten years. He bore a major share of responsibility for the disastrous Norwegian campaign, but public and parliament blamed Chamberlain, who had to resign.

Consequently, at the age of sixty-five, Churchill was Prime Minister for the first time and immediately gained the confidence of the nation by facing up to the dangers ahead. 'I have nothing to offer', he told the **Commons** in his first speech as Prime Minister, 'but blood, toil, tears and sweat.' The **Labour Party** were given key posts in the **coalition government** which Churchill formed in 1940, with **Attlee** officially being recognized as Deputy Prime Minister in 1942. **Halifax** wanted to seek peace terms from

Germany after the fall of **France** but Churchill was adamant: 'We shall go on to the end . . . we shall never surrender.' Although he detested **communism**, he welcomed the Soviet Union as an ally in June 1941 and promised all possible aid, though he continued to resist **Stalin**'s demands for a **Second Front** until the Allies had built up overwhelming strength in the West. Churchill immediately saw the significance of the USA entering the war in December 1941 ('So we have won after all') and built up a very close relationship with President **Roosevelt**, whom he met nine times during the war. After the turning-point of the battles of El **Alamein**, Churchill persuaded the USA at the **Casablanca Conference** (January 1943) that the Allies should invade Sicily rather than north-west France, though this was opposed by the American Chiefs-of-Staff. It was the last time that Churchill was able to dictate Allied strategy. After that the Americans, with their vastly superior strength, called the tune. Deeply suspicious of Stalin and fearful of a communist domination of Eastern Europe, Churchill wanted the Americans to advance as far east as possible in the later stages of the war, but **Eisenhower** did not agree. When the war ended, the coalition broke up and Labour won a huge victory at the 1945 election. Churchill became Leader of the Opposition, but returned as Prime Minister for the second and last time from 1951–5.

**Ciano, Galeazzo, Count** (1903–44). Italian Fascist (see **Fascism**). The son of an admiral, Ciano entered the Italian foreign service in 1925 and in 1930 married **Mussolini**'s eldest daughter, Edda. This led to rapid promotion and his appointment as Foreign Minister in 1936 at the age of thirty-three, a move greatly resented by Fascist Party officials. Ciano followed Mussolini's policies of extending Italian influence in the Balkans and intervening in the **Spanish Civil War** but disagreed with Mussolini moving ever closer to Nazi Germany (see **Nazism**). He feared Germany, tried to prevent the Pact of Steel (1936) and aimed to create a barrier to German power in the Balkans. Albania was invaded, in response to Germany's seizure of Czechoslovakia in 1939, at Ciano's insistence and under his direction. Aware of Italy's military unpreparedness, he insisted in August 1939 that Italy should not enter the **Second World War** and was responsible for the policy of non-belligerency, which was followed until June 1940. Ciano's influence declined in 1940 because of German distrust and as the belief arose in Italy that Germany would win a complete victory, in which the Fascist regime would have no part. **Hitler**'s victories in the Low Countries persuaded Ciano to change his mind about intervention. When Italy entered the war he pressed for the invasion of Greece – 'Ciano's War' – which was a miserable failure. After that he had little influence on events and was dismissed as Foreign Minister in February 1943. Aware of conspiracies to overthrow Mussolini, Ciano voted at a meeting of the Fascist Grand Council in July for the motion which resulted in Mussolini being dismissed by King **Victor Emanuel III**. He later naïvely sought to escape from Italy via Germany, where he was held captive until the Italian Social Republic was set up in northern Italy. The Germans then handed Ciano over to the puppet government, which tried and shot him as a traitor in January 1944.

**Civil Constitution of the Clergy** (July 1790) was passed by the French **Constituent Assembly**. It adapted the organization of the Catholic Church to the administrative framework of local government. Dioceses were to coincide with departments, so the number of bishoprics would be reduced from 135 to eighty-three. There would not only be fewer bishops but fewer clergy generally, as all clerical posts, except for parish priests (*curés*) and bishops, ceased to exist. The attempt to extend democracy to all aspects of government was applied to the Church, as clergy were to be elected. A link with the Pope was cut, as he lost the right to confirm new bishops. All clergy had to reside in their diocese or parish. There had been no serious conflict with the Church during the **French Revolution** up to this time, but the clergy split when they were required to take an oath to the Civil Constitution in November: only seven bishops and 55 per cent of the clergy took the oath, and a few of these retracted when the Pope condemned the Constitution in 1791. The Civil Constitution had momentous results. There were now in effect two Catholic Churches in France. One, the Constitutional Church, accepted the Revolution and was rejected by Rome. The other, a non-juring Church (those who refused to take the oath were known as non-jurors or refractories), was approved by the

Pope but regarded by patriots as against the Revolution. One major effect of this split was that the counter-revolution (the movement which sought to overturn the Revolution) received mass support for the first time; before it had been supported only by a few royalists. Now, in the most strongly Catholic areas there was disaffection with the Revolution. This, combined with opposition to other measures of the Assembly (such as conscription), led to open revolt in 1793 in areas such as the Vendée (see **Vendean revolt**). Civil war was, therefore, one result of the Civil Constitution. Another was **Louis XVI**'s attempt to leave France in the flight to **Varennes** (June 1791), precipitating a series of events which was to bring about the downfall of the monarchy.

**Civil Rights Acts.** Federal legislation in the USA which gave equal rights to Negroes. When the **American Civil War** had ended, Congress passed an Act, over President Andrew **Johnson**'s veto, giving freed slaves the same rights as white citizens. This was the first in a series of civil rights Acts in the **Reconstruction** era which sought to nullify the **Black Codes**, which aimed to keep blacks permanently in a position of inferiority. The fourteenth amendment to the Constitution (see **Reconstruction**) gave all citizens 'equal protection of the laws', whilst the fifteenth, passed in 1869, said that a citizen's right to vote 'shall not be denied . . . on account of race, colour or previous condition of servitude'. Passing laws was one thing, enforcing them was another. Terrorist organizations like the **Ku Klux Klan** used intimidation to prevent Negroes from voting, so in 1871 Congress made it a crime to deny a citizen equal protection of the laws by 'force, intimidation or threat'. In 1875 Congress passed laws giving Negroes equal access to hotels and schools, but in 1883 the **Supreme Court** declared these laws unconstitutional. By this time states had found ways of avoiding civil rights legislation by passing **'Jim Crow' laws**.

Nothing further was done to give Negroes equal rights with whites until the middle of the twentieth century. The Civil Rights Act of 1964 and the Voting Rights Act of 1965 ended racial discrimination in voting for the first time since Reconstruction, and also forbade it in employment. Immediately blacks were elected to local offices, including that of mayor.

**Cixi** (1835–1908). Empress Dowager and real ruler of China from 1861–1908. Able and highly literate, Cixi was the only woman to exercise real power under the **Qing dynasty**. The daughter of a minor Manchu official, she was a concubine of the Emperor Xianfeng (ruled 1851–61) and was the only one to bear him a son. When the Emperor died Cixi's son, aged five, became the new Emperor, and Cixi became the power behind the throne as Empress Dowager. When her son died childless in 1874 she installed another boy Emperor, so that her regency would continue; she never gave up this position, except for a period of retirement from 1889–98. Her sole aim was to stay in power, which she did by a mixture of flattery, ruthlessness, corruption and the exercise of her strong will. She misused public funds (much of the money allocated to the navy was spent on rebuilding the Summer Palace, destroyed by the British in the second of the **Opium Wars**) and staged a *coup* in 1898 to bring to an end the **Hundred Days Reform**. She supported the **Boxer Rising**'s anti-foreign attacks and was forced to flee ignominiously from Beijing. After the failure of the rising, Cixi began a belated and desperate attempt to save the Qing dynasty by promoting a series of reforms very much like those she had denounced in the Hundred Days Reform. She died before her failure became apparent in the **Chinese Revolution** of 1911.

**Clausewitz, Karl von** (1780–1831). Prussian war theorist. Clausewitz fought in the Prussian army in the **French Revolutionary Wars** in 1793–4 and in 1806 was captured during the battles of **Jena–Auerstädt**, when fighting against **Napoleon Bonaparte**. On his release he assisted **Scharnhorst** in reforming the Prussian army and in 1812, like many other Prussian officers, defected to Russia rather than fight for Napoleon in his **Moscow Campaign**. Although he had never held a command, in 1818 he became Director of the Military Academy in Berlin and for the next twelve years worked on his *On War*, which was unfinished when he died in the cholera epidemic of 1831. Clausewitz's theories were based on his experiences during the French Revolutionary Wars and **Napoleonic Wars** (1792–1815). He believed that 'War is only a continuation of state [peace] policy by other means' and that wars could not be limited but should aim at the complete destruction of the enemy's main force in a decisive battle. To achieve this it was necessary, if an absolute superiority of forces was not available, that 'a relative superiority is attained at the decisive point . . . Surprise is the most powerful element of victory.' He saw that the French had roused the civilian population against them in the territories they had conquered and had therefore had to use many troops to quell internal unrest. 'The spontaneous cooperation of the people' is therefore 'in all cases most important'. Clausewitz recognized Napoleon as the greatest offensive general, yet maintained that the defensive was the stronger form of warfare, an idea reinforced by the development of firearms after his death. *On War*, published in 1832, contained much that was soon out of date, as it was written before the development of **railways** and of breech-loading rifled firearms, which transformed warfare. It might have been forgotten, if **Moltke** had not claimed after the **Franco-Prussian War** (1870–71) that it was the work which had influenced him most. After that, Clausewitz affected all military thinking: **Foch**'s *Principles of War* (1903) were those of Clausewitz. Yet the generals of the **First World War** ignored his belief that defence was stronger than attack and concentrated instead on another of his ideas: the need for a decisive battle to overthrow the enemy, whatever the cost.

**Clay, Henry** (1777–1852). US politician. Henry Clay was a very generous, witty and charming man, who was one of the most popular politicians in America, yet he never succeeded in becoming President. Clay was elected to the House of Representatives in 1810 and immediately became Speaker, a post he held for most of the time between 1810 and 1825. He was a nationalist, a supporter of **Westward expansion** and a leader of the War Hawks, who helped to bring about the **Anglo-American War** of 1812. He was also amongst those who brought it to an end by negotiating the Treaty of Ghent in 1814. After the war Clay promoted what he called the 'American System', which aimed to make the USA self-sufficient by providing federal aid for transport and protective tariffs for industry and by re-creating a national bank. Much of this resembled **Hamilton**'s earlier programme, but it was not based on close ties with Britain, as Hamilton's was, and did not seek to promote industry at the expense of agriculture. In 1816 Clay persuaded Congress to pass a tariff act to protect industries such as textiles and iron, which had grown up during the Anglo-American War and were threatened by the British dumping of cheaper goods after the war. When the charter of the first Bank of the United States expired in 1811, the **Republican Party** had refused to renew it. Soon there was monetary chaos, as state banks printed money much as they liked. By 1816 Clay saw that a new national bank was needed to provide a stable, uniform currency, so Congress gave the second United States Bank a charter. In 1820 Clay pushed through the House the **Missouri Compromise**, earning for himself in the process the title 'Great Pacificator'.

Clay sought the presidency in almost every election from 1824–48 and was nominated three times. In 1824 none of the four candidates obtained a majority, so the House of Representatives, according to constitutional procedure, had to choose between the three candidates with most electoral votes. Clay, in fourth place, supported John Quincy **Adams** and helped to ensure that he became President. When Clay became Adams's Secretary of State he was accused of having made a 'corrupt bargain'. He left the State Department in 1829 but was elected to the Senate in 1831, and for the next twenty years, as leader of the **Whig Party**, was largely responsible for establishing the two-party system in the USA. In 1833 there was controversy again over protection (the South felt that it was a burden round its neck, which benefited only the North), with South Carolina threatening to secede from the Union. Once again the 'Great Pacificator' came to the rescue by proposing a compromise tariff. As the crisis over slavery threatened to disrupt the Union, Clay for the third time helped to heal the rift in the nation by bringing about the **Compromise of 1850**. By this time he was suffering from tuberculosis, from which he died in June 1852.

**Clemenceau, Georges** (1841–1929). French Prime Minister (1906–9, 1917–20). From a landowning family in the Vendée, Clemenceau studied medicine and grew up a staunch anti-clerical (see **anti-clericalism**), opposing votes for women because so many of them were Catholics. Fearless (he fought many duels) and a passionate believer in France and the **Third Republic**, he entered the National Assembly in 1871 and soon became leader of the left-wing radicals, though he was a member of the Radical Party only in 1909. In the 1880s he opposed colonial expansion, as it distracted attention from *revanche* ('revenge') on Germany and the need to recover **Alsace-Lorraine**, and was mainly responsible for the fall of **Ferry** (the architect of French imperial policy) in 1885. As President Grévy would not make him Prime Minister, Clemenceau wielded power without responsibility, putting his own supporters in office and bringing about the fall of Cabinets of which he disapproved. He brought about the appointment of General **Boulanger** as Minister of War, though he later turned against him. Known as a wrecker, Clemenceau made many enemies, who used his association with a financier involved in the **Panama scandal** (1892) to attack him. Defeated in the 1893 election, he was not able to recover his influence until his defence of Dreyfus (see **Dreyfus case**) brought him to the fore again.

Elected to the Senate in 1902, Clemenceau first held office as Minister of Home Affairs, and then as Prime Minister at the age of sixty-five in 1906. He quickly fell out with the socialists by using troops ruthlessly to put down strikes, and tried to break up the **CGT** (trade-union federation) by arresting its leaders. When civil servants went on strike he reacted harshly: a postal strike was followed by mass dismissals. Clemenceau had begun his ministry with a programme of reforms, most of which were delayed in the Senate, so that measures introducing old-age pensions (1910) and income tax (1914) were not passed until he was out of office. During the **First World War** he constantly goaded the government to make greater efforts and in November 1917 he accepted **Poincaré**'s invitation to be Prime Minister again. At seventy-six he provided the will to victory, executed Mata Hari and other spies and traitors, and persuaded the Allies to accept **Foch** as overall commander. 'He possessed restless energy', wrote **Lloyd George**, 'indomitable courage and a gift for infecting others with his own combativeness and confidence ... by conviction and temperament he was an inexorable cynic ... His sole concern was for France.' Clemenceau presided over the **Paris Peace Conference** (1919) and wanted draconian terms imposed on Germany: she should pay the whole cost of the war; the Saar and its coalfields should become part of France; and the left bank of the Rhine should be detached from Germany and made independent. On all these points Clemenceau had to compromise, though he insisted that the Treaty of **Versailles** should be signed in the Hall of Mirrors, where **William I** had been proclaimed Emperor. The 1919 elections produced a conservative Assembly, which rejected Clemenceau as President, so he resigned as Prime Minister and, at the age of seventy-nine, retired.

**CNT** (*Confederación Nacional de Trabajo* – National Confederation of Labour). Spanish anarcho-syndicalist movement. The emergence of the CNT in 1911 provided Spanish anarcho-syndicalism with its first national framework. It was based on already existing **trade unions**, most of them in Catalonia, which were sympathetic to **anarchism**. Centred in Barcelona, Saragossa and rural Andalucia, the CNT became the largest trade-union movement in Spain during the socio-economic crisis which followed the **First World War**. The CNT's influence in Catalonia was at its greatest from 1918 to 1923. During this period it met with the resistance of employers who, with the zealous backing of the military authorities, defied the government's attempts at a negotiated wage settlement in an effort to crush the unions, whether through lock-outs, the promotion of Catholic 'free' unions, or the use of *pistoleros* ('gunmen'). The situation was exacerbated by the CNT's philosophy of 'direct action', rejecting any state intervention in its dealings with employers. The upshot was ferocious urban guerrilla warfare between the employers and the CNT (1919–23). Under the **Primo de Rivera** dictatorship of 1923–30 the CNT, unlike the collaborationist socialist trade unions, was severely repressed. In reaction against the military regime and increasing **syndicalism** within the CNT, the FAI (*Federación Anarquista Ibérica* – Iberian Anarchist Federation) was founded in 1927. This semi-secret group of activists, who came to exercise great influence within the CNT, aimed to preserve the revolutionary anarchist tradition. Although the CNT moderates were prepared to collaborate with the **Spanish Second Republic** (1931–6), their efforts were rejected by the new regime in favour of repression, thereby playing into the hands of the FAI. The FAI not only caused the movement to split in 1932 over the issue of revolutionary confrontation with the Republic, but also promoted a series of largely fruitless strikes and risings.

In response to the military rising of 17–18 July 1936, the CNT played a key role in retaining Barcelona for the Republic, though the anarcho-syndicalist strongholds of Saragossa and Seville both fell to the Nationalists. While the anarchist rural and industrial collectives during the **Spanish Civil War** often proved both a social and an economic success, the failure of the anarchist militia undoubtedly undermined the Republican war effort. The CNT's revolutionary conception of the war clashed with that of the Communists, Republicans and most Socialists. None the less, in November 1936 four anarchists joined a Socialist-led Cabinet (the only occasion on which anarchists have entered a government) with the objective of preserving the revolutionary gains. This they failed to achieve. The Communists were determined to control the Republic and, with the support of the Socialist Party and various Republican groups, crushed the CNT uprising in Barcelona in May 1937. After that the CNT was effectively marginalized: the CNT-dominated Council of Aragon was brutally repressed and the liquidation of the collectives accelerated. The CNT had suffered an eclipse from which it would never recover.

**Coalition governments** were formed in Britain from 1915–22 and from 1940–45. The **National Government** (1931–5) was also a coalition government. **Asquith** formed a coalition government in 1915 but did not show enough dynamism in directing the war effort, so he lost the support of his colleagues and was replaced as Prime Minister by **Lloyd George** in December 1916. He appointed a small War Cabinet of five (himself, Bonar **Law**, **Curzon**, **Milner** and the Labour leader **Henderson**) to prosecute the war vigorously. Lloyd George was very critical of military leaders like **Haig**, whose bloody offensives he regarded as senseless, but was unable to get rid of him, as he had the support of King **George V** and of the Conservative (Unionist) leaders. The Prime Minister drastically reduced shipping losses, which threatened to bring about a German victory, by insisting on the use of **convoys** from April 1917. The power of the state was extended to run the mines and railways, and in 1918 the Representation of the People Act increased the electorate by eight million, by giving the vote to all men over twenty-one and women over thirty.

When the war was over the **Labour Party** withdrew from the coalition but Lloyd George decided, with the support of Bonar Law, the Unionist leader, to continue it. He called an election, in 1918, which Asquith dubbed the 'Coupon' election, as Bonar Law and Lloyd George issued a letter of approval to coalition candidates. Most coalition Liberals and Conservatives agreed not to stand against each other. The result was a massive vote of confidence in Lloyd George, who was credited with winning the war. 526 coalition candidates (of whom only 136 were Liberals, the rest being Conservative) were elected, 57 Labour and 26 Independent Liberals under Asquith. Lloyd George was therefore dependent on Conservative support: all the leading ministers, except for himself and Winston **Churchill**, were Unionists. As Lloyd George had promised 'a land fit for heroes' he carried out some social reforms: a Housing Act led to 200,000 publicly subsidized houses being built (1919–22) and in 1920 unemployment insurance was extended to most workers. However, with a national debt which had risen from £706,000,000 in 1914 to £7,875,000,000 in 1920, there were demands for economy and a balanced budget, particularly when the post-war boom collapsed in 1921. Reluctantly, Lloyd George had to accept a government committee under Sir Eric Geddes to recommend economies. The 'Geddes Axe' slashed government spending on education and the social services and lost the coalition government much support. Lloyd George's reputation as a benefactor of the working man disappeared when he used troops to break strikes, refused to nationalize the coal mines and caused the collapse of the Triple Alliance on **Black Friday** (15 April 1921). His use of Black and Tans for repression in the **Anglo-Irish War** (1919–21) also shocked many, though he successfully negotiated the **Anglo-Irish Treaty** (1921), which ended the war and established the Irish Free State. Lloyd George's main concern after 1918 was foreign policy; he played a leading role at the Treaty of **Versailles**, tried to cut down **reparations** and at the **Washington Conference** agreed with the USA and Japan to limit the construction of capital ships. Many Conservatives could not see why they needed a coalition when they had a majority in the **Commons**. Their opportunity to break it up came with the Chanak crisis, when **Kemal Atatürk** defeated the Greeks in Asia Minor and overturned the Treaty of **Sèvres**. Lloyd George's threat of war with Turkey received no support from France, Italy or the **dominions**, and British public opinion was against him. When a majority of Unionist members voted to end the coalition, he resigned.

In Winston Churchill's coalition government (1940–45), two of the original five members of the War Cabinet were from the Labour Party. Churchill kept for himself the Ministry of Defence, so that he had a general oversight of the armed forces, and concentrated on winning the war, leaving others to manage the home front. **Bevin**, the most powerful trade-union leader, played a key role at the Ministry of Labour in persuading unions to give up restrictive practices. Committees were set up to make recommendations for post-war reconstruction, the most celebrated of which was the **Beveridge** Report, greeted enthusiastically by press and public, which proposed a free national health service, family allowances and social insurance for all 'from the cradle to the grave'. The Uthwatt Report (1942) suggested creating a 'green belt' round major cities, new controls over land use and the building of new towns to cater for the overpopulation of large cities. As early as 1940 the Barlow Report advocated industrial development in the areas distressed in the 1930s, and this was taken up by **Dalton** in his Distribution of Industry Act (1945), which began the economic regeneration of north-east England and south Wales. **Keynes** at the Treasury greatly influenced the Cabinet's economic thinking in proposing the nationalization of the Bank of England and was behind the White Paper of 1944, which committed the government to secure full employment. Education had been savagely cut back by the Geddes Axe of 1922, so that large numbers of working-class children had no secondary education at all. R. A. Butler remedied this with his **Education Act** of 1944, which laid the basis for secondary education for all, to be provided by secondary modern, grammar and technical schools. Paradoxically, Britain moved further to the left under the Conservative leadership of Churchill than at any previous time. The coalition ended with the war, and the election in 1945 gave Labour an astonishing landslide victory.

**Cobbett, William** (1763–1835). The most influential popular journalist in England in the early nineteenth century. A self-taught farm labourer from Surrey, in 1802 Cobbett began publishing his weekly *Political Register* as a supporter of the government and opponent of the **French Revolution**, but in 1804 he was convicted of libel for criticizing the government's conduct of the war. This personal experience of government repression slowly turned him into a radical. He blamed 'misgovernment' for the economic distress in England and attacked 'Old Corruption': the patronage system and the control of parliament by the landed aristocracy and gentry in their own interest. Cobbett was a passionate defender of the poor and unprivileged but he had no understanding of the forces transforming society. He hated the towns and factories of the **industrial revolution**, which he saw as depriving the worker of his freedom, and had a romantic attachment to a mythical past when the agricultural labourer lived happily, ate well and wove cloth in his own home. Yet he could see that machinery was not in itself responsible for the plight of the weavers, and in his *Letter to the Luddites* (1816) (see **Luddites**) he condemned attacks on machinery. In the 1820s Cobbett travelled through the North, the Midlands and East Anglia, condemning **enclosures** and defending the rural way of life which was dying; he described these travels in *Rural Rides* (1830). Cobbett became a supporter of **parliamentary reform** as he thought that the existing House of **Commons** would never carry out the reforms he wanted: abolition of sinecures and tithes, confiscation of Church property and Crown lands, and a massive reduction in the size of the army. A vain man, he thought that the effect of his writing was 'prodigious: the people everywhere on the stir in the cause of parliamentary reform'. When the **Reform Act** was passed in 1832, Cobbett was elected MP for Oldham but made little impression in the House and soon became disillusioned with politics. Outraged by the new **Poor Law** of 1834, which destroyed the remains of the old order he revered, he saw it as completing the demoralization of the poor by putting them in gaunt workhouses.

**Cobden, Richard** (1804–65). English radical and politician. The son of a poor farmer in Sussex, Cobden set up a calico-printing mill in Lancashire and made enough money to be able to devote his energies to the **Anti-Corn Law League** from 1839–46. A member of the **Manchester School**, he believed in *laissez-faire* and thought that the state should interfere as little as possible in the workings of commerce and industry. He believed that the repeal of the **Corn Laws** would be good for both the manufacturer and the worker, as it would provide cheaper food, open up markets and create more employment. Only the landlords, 'unprincipled, unfeeling, rapacious and plundering', prevented repeal, so the middle and working classes should unite against the landed interest to abolish the 'feudal order'. Cobden was a brilliant organizer who made the League the most efficient and successful of all nineteenth-century British pressure groups. Entering parliament in 1841, he successfully pressed **Peel** to take up repeal. In the campaign against the Corn Laws Cobden lost all his wealth, so he returned to the Sussex village where he had been born, and lived there for the rest of his life. His concern now was with 'financial reform': strict economy in government spending and low taxation. The popularity that he and John **Bright** had enjoyed in the 1840s disappeared when they opposed the **Crimean War**. Cobden hated the waste of men and money in war, which interfered with the free flow of commerce. He organized a petition in the House of **Commons** against the aggressive foreign policy of **Palmerston**, 'a venerable political imposter', and when this led to a general election in 1857 Cobden lost his seat. Two years later he re-entered the House and worked hard to bring about a commercial treaty with France in 1860, which lowered the duties on goods moving from one country to the other.

**Code Napoléon** was the name given in 1807 to the Civil Code of 1804. Before the **French Revolution** there were different legal systems in France, with customary law predominant in the north, Roman law in the south. Efforts had been made under the *ancien régime* and during the Revolution to codify the law and create a uniform system which applied to the whole of France, but none was successful. Napoleon provided the driving force by presiding at fifty-five of the 107 sessions of the Council of State which were called to discuss the Civil Code. The great gains of the Revolution were maintained: equality before the law, religious toleration, the abolition of privilege and of seigneurial dues. The revolutionary land settlement – the sale of Church and *émigré* lands – was confirmed, thus placing property owners firmly behind Napoleon. Property was to be inherited equally by male heirs, except for a proportion, varying from a quarter to a half, which could be reserved for one heir. Following the **Le Chapelier law**, trade unions and employers' associations were banned and strikes made illegal. The liberalism of the Revolution was rejected in the clauses which referred to women and children: the authority of the husband over his wife and children was emphasized, as was the inferior position of women. 'A husband owes protection to his wife; a wife owes obedience to her husband . . . Married women are incapable of making contracts.' Divorce remained, but while a wife could be divorced for adultery, a husband could only be divorced if he brought his mistress into the household. The Code, revised in 1904, has remained the basis of French civil law and was imposed in the **Napoleonic Empire**. It has influenced existing legal codes in Belgium, Holland, Switzerland, Italy and several countries outside Europe.

**Collectivization**. The compulsory transformation in the Soviet Union of individually owned peasant farms into large collective farms. The decision to enforce collectivization was taken in 1929, because the state needed reliable grain deliveries at low prices in order to feed the increasing number of workers needed for the **Five Year Plans**. The minority of rich peasants, *kulaks*, could hold the state to ransom as long as there was a free market by refusing to sell their grain if the price was too low and if there were no consumer goods to be bought, as had happened under **NEP**. **Stalin** wanted to end this and needed capital to invest in his Five Year Plans, which could come only from agriculture, by squeezing peasant consumption and by exporting grain. Collective farms would be more efficient than small, private farms, because they would have the tractors and combine harvesters that individual peasants could not afford. They would create on the land a surplus of labour, which could be used in the growing industries. There was also an ideological reason for collectivization: it would end ownership of private property and the inequality of incomes which had grown up under NEP.

The peasants fiercely resisted collectivization and reacted in the only way they knew: they reduced output and slaughtered their animals, so that livestock in the Soviet Union was reduced by half. The damage was not made good until the 1950s. The government responded by shooting hundreds of *kulaks* and sending hundreds of thousands to **forced labour camps** in Siberia. Collectivization continued relentlessly – 62 per cent of peasant households were in collectives by 1932, 93 per cent by 1937. Delivery quotas were high for the collectives – up to 40 per cent of the crop, two to three times what the peasant had marketed – and prices paid by the state were low. Even when there was a disastrous famine in the Ukraine in 1932–3, in which at least five million people died, the state continued its expropriations. The regime did make some concessions to the peasants: they were allowed to have a small plot and some animals for their own use. By 1937 50–70 per cent of the total production of vegetables, meat, fruit and milk came from these private plots. Collectivization was successful in that it enabled the government to feed the towns, finance the Five Year Plans and provide the workers which industry needed. Yet it left a legacy of bitterness, hatred of the regime and low productivity in the country-side. To many peasants, the major victims of forced savings, it seemed that **serfdom** had returned.

**Collins, Michael** (1890–1922). Irish nationalist. Charming, brave and ruthless, Collins fought in the General Post Office in the **Easter Rising** (1916) as a member of the Irish Republican Brotherhood and was imprisoned. Released in December 1916, he began to organize an underground military network. In the election of 1918 he was elected as a **Sinn Fein** MP but, with the others, refused to attend the British parliament at Westminster and formed a Dail (Assembly) in Dublin. The Dail created a government in which Collins was Minister of Finance. He raised large loans at home and in America, but his main achievement was to lead the guerrilla warfare against the British in the **Anglo-Irish War** (1919–21). Penetrating the Dublin Castle intelligence service, he knew what the authorities were planning and who were the informers. They were the first victims of his murder squad, known as the Twelve Apostles. As Commander-in-Chief of the **IRA** (Irish Republican

Army) and President of the Irish Republican Brotherhood (IRB), Collins was the most important Irish figure in the war: the British put a price on his head of £10,000 dead or alive. In 1921 he was a member of the Irish delegation which went to London and agreed to the **Anglo-Irish Treaty**, which ended the war and set up the Irish Free State. This was accepted by the Dail, and Collins became head of a provisional Irish government. When **de Valera** rejected the treaty and the **Irish Civil War** began, Collins commanded the Free State army against the Republican forces and was killed in an ambush in August 1922. More than anyone else, Collins was responsible for the creation of the Irish Free State.

**Colons.** A French name for white settlers in Algeria. Only about half the settlers were of French origin; the rest were mainly from the western Mediterranean (Spain, Italy, Malta). The French began their long occupation of Algeria in 1830: by 1871 Europeans there numbered 245,000; by 1912 they had increased to 800,000. The *colons* generally despised the indigenous Algerians and regarded the North African colonies as an integral part of France. As citizens of France they elected their own Deputies to the National Assembly in Paris. In 1896 direct control from Paris ended, and in 1898 an elected Assembly, with a European majority, was introduced. This and settler control of local government ensured that Algeria remained in the hands of the *colons*, who strongly opposed attempts by the French government to give Algerians political rights. In 1958, during the Algerian war of independence, *colons* cooperated with factions of the French army to bring down the government in France. They believed that the new President of France, General de Gaulle, would support their cause of keeping Algeria French. De Gaulle was more realistic and began negotiations with Algerian nationalists. A number of *colons* formed a secret terrorist organization, but this failed to prevent Algeria becoming independent in 1962. In the six months following independence 800,000 of the one million *colons* left Algeria.

**Combination Acts.** Laws passed by the British parliament in 1799 and 1800, which made **trade unions** and combinations of employers illegal. The acts were a response to political agitation during the **French Revolutionary Wars**, but workers' combinations in important industries had already been forbidden in the eighteenth century. The idea of a general act came from **Wilberforce**; it was supported by **Pitt** in order to prevent the spread of combinations to the populous textile areas of Lancashire and Yorkshire. The Acts failed to do this, as unions of skilled workers became stronger in the next twenty-five years, many thriving as **friendly societies**. Employers were often afraid to prosecute, and by the mid-1820s there was widespread support for repeal. Francis Place, the radical leader who had become an employer and was a supporter of *laissez-faire*, thought that wages should be determined by free competition in the labour market, which union activity could not affect. The repeal was steered through the House of **Commons** by the radical MP Joseph Hume and was not a government measure, although it was supported by Huskisson at the Board of Trade. There was little resistance to repeal in 1824, so trade unions were officially recognized by a state for the first time. Repeal coincided with an improvement in the economy and a wave of strikes, some violent, so a new Act in 1825 allowed combinations for peaceful collective bargaining over wages and hours, but for no other purpose. This remained the position for trade unions for the next fifty years but it did not protect the workers, who could be prosecuted under other laws: the **Tolpuddle Martyrs** were transported for taking illegal oaths.

**Comintern** (Third International) (1919–43). **Lenin** thought that the **Second International** had betrayed socialism, when most of its members supported their respective governments in the **First World War**. He was therefore alarmed to see it reviving when its leaders called a congress to meet in February 1919, as he did not believe that it would be at all revolutionary. Lenin therefore founded the Third International, known as the Communist International or Comintern, in Moscow in March 1919, to promote world revolution. Its first President was **Zinoviev**. The main decisions regarding its structure were taken at the second congress in 1920. This met at a time when there was widespread working-class unrest in many countries and it appeared that Europe was on the verge of a proletarian revolution. The Comintern consequently rejected any accommodation with '*bourgeois* democracy' or moderate socialists.

The Comintern was defined as a single world party, in which national parties were mere 'sections'. Twenty-one conditions of admission laid down that each member party must have an organization and rules similar to those of the **Bolsheviks**, based on centralization. 'Iron discipline' was necessary – the decisions of the Comintern were binding on all members. This in effect meant the subordination of all 'sections' to the **Communist Party of the Soviet Union**. By 1921, hopes of revolution in Europe had dimmed – an attempted communist rising in Germany had failed and the Bolsheviks had been defeated in the **Russo-Polish War**. Lenin therefore changed his tactics and called on communists to infiltrate *bourgeois* institutions. 'It is necessary', he wrote in 1920, 'to resort to all sorts of stratagems, double-dealing, illegal methods, concealment of the truth, if only they [communists] penetrate the **trade unions**.' Similarly, communists should take part in *bourgeois* parliaments, to undermine them from within.

From Lenin's death in 1924 the internal struggles of the Russian Communist Party were reproduced in the Comintern. The removal of people like **Trotsky** and Zinoviev from the Soviet Communist Party was accompanied by purges in the Comintern. In 1927, Trotsky was expelled from the Comintern Executive. In the same year Comintern policies produced disastrous results in China. On Comintern advice the Chinese communists had cooperated with the **Guomindang**, only to be decimated in the **Shanghai** *coup*. In 1928 there was another reversal of policy, when a united front with other socialist parties was rejected. This had unfortunate effects in Germany, where communist and socialist parties (**Stalin** called the German socialists 'social fascists') spent more time fighting one another than they did fighting the Nazis. This eased **Hitler**'s way to power. After the Nazis established their dictatorship, the Comintern changed course yet again and called for **Popular Fronts**, which were established in France and Spain, to stop the spread of **Fascism**. By this time the Comintern had become an organization whose main purpose was to rouse support for Soviet foreign and domestic policy. It gave full backing to Stalin's purges of 1936–8, in which most of its leaders, both Russian and foreign, were executed. The Comintern helped to rally support for the Republicans during the **Spanish Civil War**, and in 1939, following the **Nazi–Soviet**

**Pact**, made another of its famous about-turns and dropped its anti-Fascist stance. After Germany invaded the Soviet Union in 1941 the Comintern gave unqualified support to the anti-German coalition. It was dissolved in 1943, probably to please Stalin's allies.

**Committee of Public Safety** (1793–5). The name for the government of France at the height of the **Terror** during the **French Revolution**. In 1793 France faced problems which threatened to overwhelm the Revolution: the French General Dumouriez was defeated by the Austrians at Neerwinden in March and deserted to the enemy; there was a rising in the Vendée (see **Vendean revolt**) and there was also massive inflation. The **Convention** therefore set up in April a Committee of Public Safety (CPS) to supervise ministers, whose authority it superseded. After the *journée* of 2 June, when leading Girondin deputies were arrested, a new CPS was formed in which all twelve members were **Jacobins** or sympathizers. This Committee became the first strong government in France since the Revolution began. The CPS staged a series of celebrity trials, which ended with many executions, including those of **Marie-Antoinette** and thirty-one Girondin deputies. By December the CPS was overcoming its problems: the **federal revolts** had been crushed, inflation was falling and Allied armies were driven out of France. In December 1793 the Convention gave full executive powers to the Committee of General Security, responsible for police and internal security, and to the CPS, which had more extensive powers. It controlled ministers and generals, foreign policy and local government. The chief officials of the communes and departments, who had been elected, were placed under 'national agents', appointed by and responsible to the central government. All this was a reversal of the principles of 1789, when there had been decentralization, elections to all posts and the separation of legislative from executive authority. **Robespierre** justified this about-turn by saying that a dictatorship was necessary until the foreign and internal enemies of the Republic had been destroyed. The CPS ruthlessly stifled all criticism by executing **Hébert** and **Danton** and their followers. The Terror was speeded up by the Law of Prairial (10 June 1794), which resulted in the **Great Terror**. The Convention was now simply a passive instrument of the CPS.

The Great Terror sickened the population, yet the dictatorship of the two Committees was unassailable unless they fell out amongst themselves. This they proceeded to do, when Robespierre accused unnamed members of the Committee of 'a conspiracy against public liberty'. Some members of the Committees who felt threatened plotted against Robespierre in **Thermidor** (July 1794) and executed him and his supporters. The way was now clear for the Thermidorian reaction and the abolition of the CPS.

**Commons, House of.** The elected chamber of Britain's bicameral parliament. Its origins lie in the thirteenth century, when Edward I summoned knights of the shires and freemen (burgesses) of the boroughs to approve of increased taxation. In 1275 the King held his first general parliament when the knights and burgesses met with his leading advisers, earls, barons and bishops. In the fourteenth century the Commons met separately from the House of **Lords**. Attempts by the Stuarts to assert the divine right of kings by raising taxes without the consent of parliament led to the Civil War (1642–6), the execution of Charles I and, later, the replacement of James II by William of Orange. The supremacy of the Crown in parliament was recognized by the Bill of Rights (1689), which stated that the Crown could not make or dispense with laws or raise taxes without the consent of parliament. Before the **Reform Act** of 1832 the members of the House of Commons were elected on a very restricted franchise and were dominated by the aristocracy, who controlled **'rotten' boroughs** and whose younger sons often sat in the House. This Act and further **parliamentary reform** made the Commons much more representative of the population as a whole and led to the rise of highly organized political parties, **Conservative, Liberal** and later **Labour**. The leader of the party with a majority in the Commons formed the government, which was chosen from members of both Houses but increasingly from the Commons, whose pre-eminence was made clear by the **Parliament Act** (1911). Although the government is in theory dependent on the Commons for its money supply and for passing legislation, under a predominantly two-party system there is little to stop it from doing whatever it wishes between one election and another, unless there is a revolt within the party in power. The Commons had to be elected every seven years from 1716 until 1911, since when elections must be held every five years. The British parliamentary system has been widely copied in many European countries and in the British Commonwealth.

**Communications revolution.** The rapid increase in the speed with which information could be passed on was made possible by **electricity**. An electric telegraph was developed in 1837 by Charles Wheatstone in Britain and Samuel Morse in America, the latter sending messages by Morse code. This was the first example of a technological development which was based on a sophisticated scientific theory. Submarine cables were laid across the Channel in the 1850s to transmit these messages and across the Atlantic in 1865–6. By 1872 London was linked to Tokyo. Newspapers could now publish up-to-date international news, and European governments could exercise much greater control over their armies and empires (it had previously taken between one and two years to send a message from Britain to India and to receive a reply) **Moltke** used the telegraph to direct Prussian armies in the **Austro-Prussian War** (1866) from his headquarters in Berlin. The first transmission of direct speech was by the American Graham Bell, who patented his telephone in 1876. Subscriber dialling was invented in 1896, and by 1905 half a million miles of underground cable had been laid in Britain, where there was the same number of telephones. America led the way, with 2.3 million telephones in 1905 and 13.5 million in 1920, by which time there was a telephone for every eight people in the USA. Radio signals, which did not need electric cables, were transmitted in the 1890s by the Italian Guglielmo Marconi, but national radio networks did not appear until the 1920s. Once again, America showed the way: in 1922 the USA had 732 broadcasting stations, commercially run. In the same year the British Broadcasting Corporation (BBC) was formed, with **Reith** as General Manager. It had a monopoly of broadcasting in Britain and derived its revenue from licence fees, a system copied in Scandinavia. By 1926 there were two million 'wireless' sets in Britain. The importance of radio as a propaganda vehicle was soon realized in the Soviet Union and in Nazi Germany, where a Ministry of Propaganda was set up to control it. Television broadcasts began in

Britain in 1936 but were seen by only a small minority before the Second World War. Until 1945 newsreels, shown in all cinemas, informed people of international and domestic events.

**Communism.** A political system in which there is common ownership of property. The idea of a classless society, in which the means of production are owned by the community, is an old one which found expression in Thomas More's *Utopia* in the sixteenth century. It was given a new meaning by Karl **Marx**, whose *Communist Manifesto* (1848) saw communism as the inevitable outcome of history, which was a series of class struggles. In his utopian vision, communism was to succeed the dictatorship of the proletariat, which would result from the successful revolution of the industrial working class against *bourgeois* capitalism. For Marx the state was a form of class oppression. When there were no longer any classes there would be no need for the state, which would 'wither away' and be replaced by a communist society, in which the guiding principle would be 'from each according to his ability, to each according to his needs'. Such a theory has never been applied in practice. After the **October Revolution** (1917) in Russia the **Bolsheviks** adopted the name 'Communist'; however, the state under **Lenin** and **Stalin** did not wither away, but became a far more repressive institution than it had been under the Tsars. In 1919 the **Comintern** was formed to spread revolution world-wide, but it was dominated by the **Communist Party of the Soviet Union** and made all other communist parties satellites of the Russian party.

*Communist Manifesto* (1848). The clearest and most succinct exposition of **communism**. Written by **Marx** and **Engels**, it was intended to provide a programme for the Communist League, a working-class movement. It included, surprisingly, a paean of praise for the *bourgeoisie*, who it claimed had opened up the world with the discovery of America and the rounding of the Cape of Good Hope, which gave access to the Indian and Chinese markets. The feudal system, in which guilds restricted industrial production, was inadequate to cope with new markets, so it was replaced by capitalism, as steam power and machinery revolutionized production and giant industries arose. The *bourgeoisie* advanced politically as well as economically, ended the dominance of the landed aristocracy and set up free trade. 'It has accomplished wonders far surpassing Egyptian pyramids, Roman aqueducts and Gothic cathedrals.' The *bourgeoisie* needed a constantly expanding market, so it created a **world economy** by drawing raw materials from the remotest regions. With its improved means of transport (**railways**) and cheap prices, the *bourgeoisie* forced all nations to adopt capitalism, promoted **urbanization** and rescued much of the population 'from the idiocy of rural life'. The *Manifesto* states that 'The bourgeoisie, during its rule of scarcely one hundred years, has created more massive . . . productive forces than have all preceding generations together.' Yet 'the history of all hitherto existing society is the history of class struggles'. The *bourgeoisie* was considered to have created its own grave-diggers in the proletariat, the industrial working class. Monotonous tasks were seen to have made the worker 'an appendage of the machine', paid only what is necessary for his subsistence, whilst cyclical crises of over-production make his livelihood even more precarious. The lower middle class cannot compete with large-scale industry, and with the advent of machines their specialized skills are no longer needed, so they are pushed down into the proletariat. In the class struggle the workers form **trade unions** to increase their strength: the *Manifesto* foresees their victory as inevitable and predicts that, when they become the ruling class through revolution, they will take over the capital of the *bourgeoisie* and centralize production in the hands of the state. The *Manifesto* ends with the call: 'Working men of all countries, unite.'

**Communist Party of the Soviet Union** (CPSU). This party succeeded that of the **Bolsheviks**, when **Lenin** proposed in 1918 that the Russian Social Democratic Workers' Party (Bolshevik) should change its name to the Russian Communist Party (Bolshevik), which later became the CPSU. The party had come to power in 1917, following the **October Revolution**. At first it ruled with the support of some **Socialist Revolutionaries**, but when they left the government, as they disagreed with the Treaty of **Brest-Litovsk** (March 1918), the Communists ruled alone. All other parties were banned in 1922. The Party Congress elected a Central Committee but this was too large and unwieldy to determine policy, so in 1919 a ***Politburo*** was set up. Gradually power passed from the *Politburo* to the Secretariat, which controlled the appointment of party members to key posts throughout the country. The career of party officials therefore depended on their loyalty to the Chief Secretary, who could influence who was elected to the Party Congress, Central Committee and *Politburo*. **Stalin**'s role as Chief Secretary was crucial in his rise to dominance. The CPSU had enormous power, as it controlled the government, which consisted of the Council of People's Commissars, headed by its Chairman (who was Prime Minister). All ministers were party members. Through the *nomenklatura* system, by which party committees drew up lists of posts and candidates, the CPSU controlled public appointments at every level, both national and local. It also came to control foreign communist parties through the **Comintern** (Third International), as they had to adopt the same organization as the CPSU and take orders from it.

At first there was free and open debate within the party, but **Lenin** became impatient of criticism during the **Russian Civil War** and established an iron grip on the party. The Tenth Party Congress in 1921 banned 'factions', such as the **Workers' Opposition**. This effectively ended all serious criticism and dissension within the party. From time to time party members (who grew from 200,00 in 1917 to over 700,000 in 1921) were purged. At first this was to get rid of 'radishes' (red outside, white within), who had joined the party to further their careers rather than from conviction. Under Stalin, party members found that their lives, as well as their jobs, were at stake. The higher ranks of the CPSU were decimated in the **Great Purges**.

**Compromise of 1850.** An attempt to prevent the secession of the South from the United States of America by making a compromise on slavery. After the **Mexican–American War** of 1846–8, the question arose whether the new states, formed out of the territory acquired from Mexico, would be slave or free. California drafted a Constitution which forbade slavery and in 1850 applied for admission to the Union. This would give the Northern free states a majority in the Senate, which was likely to be permanent, as it did not appear that any other territory would become a slave state. The South realized that this might lead to a constitutional amendment abolishing slavery, so in 1849 a secession movement developed, especially in South Carolina and Mississippi, which had the largest slave populations. The Union was in danger, so Henry **Clay**, old and ill, proposed the Compromise, which Stephen A. **Douglas** saw through Congress. California was to be admitted to the Union as a free state. The rest of the territory taken from Mexico would be divided into two states, New Mexico and Utah, which would join the Union 'with or without slavery as their Constitutions shall prescribe'. To please the South a harsher Fugitive Slave Act replaced that of 1793: slave-owners could arrest suspected runaway slaves without a warrant; escaped slaves had no right to trial by jury or to give evidence on their own behalf; and there were heavy penalties for helping slaves to escape. The South accepted the Compromise reluctantly, as the North gained most from it. However, it did preserve the Union – if the South had seceded in 1850 it might have established its independence. Eleven years later, when the **American Civil War** began, the North was strong enough to maintain the Union by force. A result of the Compromise was that the **Whig Party** split and in the 1852 election voters abandoned it for the **Democratic Party**.

**Concentration camps.** Places of imprisonment for opponents of some regimes. They were first set up in Cuba during the **Spanish–American War** (1898) and were used by Lord **Kitchener** during the **South African War** (1899–1902) to deprive the Boers of civilian support. About 20,000 Afrikaner women and children died in the South African camps, mainly from disease caused by unhygienic conditions. Concentration camps were built in Germany soon after **Hitler** came to power, the main ones being at Dachau near Munich in the south, Buchenwald near Weimar in central Germany and Sachsenhausen near Berlin in the north. All 'opponents' of the regime – Jews, Marxists, gypsies, homosexuals and dissenters of all kinds – were incarcerated there. From 1934 the camps were under the control of the **SS**, who began a reign of systematic terror. When the **Second World War** began new camps were built, and from 1942 factories were erected near them by firms such as **Krupp** and **I. G. Farben**, so that they could make use of slave labour. The overcrowded and under-fed prisoners survived for an average of nine months before they were too weak to work, and were then gassed in the camps. In 1945 there were 714,000 inmates in German camps, mostly foreigners, compared with 25,000, mainly Germans, in 1939. During the war **extermination camps** were also built, whilst in Buchenwald and Dachau medical experiments on prisoners often resulted in death. It has been estimated that between 1933 and 1945 1.6 million people were sent to concentration camps, of whom one million died. Concentration camps were also set up in the Soviet Union (see **Forced labour camps**).

**Concordat** (1801). An agreement between Pope Pius VII and **Napoleon Bonaparte**. The Roman Catholic Church in France had been divided by the **Civil Constitution of the Clergy** (1790) into the constitutional Church, which accepted the Civil Constitution, and the non-jurors, who rejected it. Napoleon wanted to gain acceptance from the Pope, as this would help him to pacify areas of unrest like the Vendée (see **Vendean revolt**) and Brittany, would deprive royalism of support and would make his regime more acceptable in the Catholic areas of the **Napoleonic Empire**. The Pope wanted to unite the Catholic Church in France and recover his influence over it, so in 1801 he made the Concordat, recognizing the French Republic, accepting that Church lands seized during the **French Revolution** would not be restored to the Church and that clergy would be paid by the State. Catholicism did not become the State religion but was recognized as 'the religion of the great majority of citizens'. All existing bishops had to resign and a new episcopate, consisting of both constitutional and non-juring clergy, was appointed by Napoleon and confirmed by the Pope. Napoleon carried through the Concordat in spite of the opposition of most of his generals and advisers, but when it became law in France, in 1802, he added the Organic Articles without consulting the Pope. These weakened the Pope's influence in France by saying that no Papal bulls (decrees) could be issued in France without the permission of the government and by putting bishops firmly under the control of the prefects. The Concordat lasted until 1905, when Church and State were separated in France.

**Concordat** (1933). An agreement between **Hitler** and Pope **Pius XI**. Hitler despised Christianity and rejected its values of charity and mercy but he realized that an agreement with the Pope would make his regime acceptable to Catholics in Germany. In July 1933 a Concordat was negotiated by Cardinal Pacelli (later **Pius XII**) and von **Papen**: the Catholic Church was assured full religious freedom and bishops freedom to communicate with the Pope; religious orders could continue with their pastoral work; and Church schools could remain. In return the Church ordered bishops to take an oath of loyalty to the State, agreed to disband the Christian trade-union movement and the **Centre Party**, and prohibited clergy from taking part in political activity. Hitler soon ignored the Concordat by turning Church schools into non-denominational schools and by demolishing Catholic lay organizations. An open breach with the Church came in 1937 with the papal encyclical '*Mit brennender Sorge*', in which Pius XI attacked **Nazism**. Many priests were put in **concentration camps**, though persecution of Catholics in Germany ceased when the **Second World War** began.

**Confederación Nacional de Trabajo,** see **CNT**

**Confederate States of America.** After the election of Abraham **Lincoln** as President of the United States, six Southern states – South Carolina, Georgia, Florida, Alabama, Louisiana and Mississippi – seceded from the Union and formed the Confederate States of America on 8 February 1861. They were joined by Texas on 2 March, and finally by Virginia, North Carolina, Tennessee and Arkansas, after Fort Sumter was captured by Confederate forces in April 1861. The Confederate States adopted a Constitution like that of the United States, except that states' rights and slavery were guaranteed. Their capital became Richmond, Virginia, in June 1861, only 100 miles from the Union capital of Washington. Their first and only President was Jefferson **Davis**. From the beginning the Confederacy faced an almost impossible task, as it was much smaller in both population and resources than the North and therefore depended on imports from Europe, which the Union navy gradually cut off by imposing a blockade. Only foreign recognition and assistance could have enabled the Confederacy to survive, but this was not forthcoming, and with General **Lee**'s surrender at Appomattox on 9 April 1865, the Confederacy ceased to exist.

## Confédération Générale du Travail, see CGT

**Confederation of the Rhine** (1806–13) was created by **Napoleon Bonaparte** after his victory at the battle of **Austerlitz**, from states in south and central Germany which allied with France. After Prussia's defeat at **Jena–Auerstädt** (1806) and the Treaty of **Tilsit** (1807), the Confederation extended from the Rhine to the Elbe, as it included the Kingdom of Westphalia and the Grand Duchy of Warsaw. As an ally of France it suffered from the **Continental Blockade** and had to provide troops for Napoleon's **Moscow Campaign** (1812) and 1813 campaign. The Confederation broke up after the battle of **Leipzig** (1813), when its member states one by one deserted Napoleon and joined the Allies.

**Confucianism,** named after Confucius (a latinization of Kongfuzi, 'venerable master Kong') (551–479 BC), provided the dominant social and political ideas for most of Chinese imperial history. Little is known about Confucius, except that he was a minor official in the state of Lu, but his writings and those of his later followers such as Mengzi ('Master Meng', latinized as Mencius) (370–290 BC) appealed to the ruling dynasties of China because they stressed obedience to and reverence for one's 'superiors' (a subject for his ruler, a son for his father, a wife for her husband) and respect for the past, for one's ancestors and for the elderly. The ruler for his part had to be virtuous and act in the interests of his subjects. Mengzi developed the idea of the Mandate of Heaven by insisting that if a ruler was no longer virtuous he would lose the support of Heaven, and this would be shown by the revolt of his subjects, who would then accept as their next ruler the man chosen by Heaven. Successful revolution was, therefore, always justified. For just over one thousand years (until 1905) Confucianism was the chief subject of study for those who took the examinations for entry into the Chinese civil service, in which success depended on ability and not on birth (though no one who was poor could afford the arduous study which was necessary before taking the examinations). The scholar-officials who ruled China became a closed caste, with a vested interest in preserving a system from which they benefited. It was a very conservative and authoritarian system, in which tradition was praised and change condemned, but it provided stability. Nowhere else has government authority been based for so long on one set of ideas. The disadvantage of the system was that when rapid changes in the outside world began to affect China in the nineteenth century, the scholar-officials were unable to adapt quickly enough. The **Self-Strengthening movement** still tried to preserve Confucian values, whilst accepting Western technology. Its failure was shown by China's defeat in the **Sino-Japanese War** (1894–5), the abandonment of the traditional civil service examination in 1905 and the collapse of the imperial system in the **Chinese Revolution** of 1911. Yet Confucian ideas persist today in the minds of the rulers of communist China, as the events in Tiananmen Square in Beijing (1989) showed.

Confucianism also influenced Japan, which obtained from China her writing system and much of her culture. As late as the nineteenth century formal education in Japan consisted largely of a study of the Chinese Confucian classics. Confucianism appealed to rulers in Japan for the same reasons as in China. Throughout the **Tokugawa shogunate** Confucian values were dominant, and did not disappear, even when Japan had begun her process of modernization. Loyalty to one's superiors was reasserted in the 1880s as part of the **Emperor system**.

**Congress.** The legislative body in the USA. The Congress has two houses, the Senate and the House of Representatives. The two senators from each state who sit in the Senate are elected for six years; they were chosen by state legislatures until 1913, when direct popular election was introduced. The size of the House of Representatives changed as the population increased, until it was fixed in 1929 at 435 seats. Congressmen (as members of the House are called) are popularly elected for two years. Congress is authorized by the Constitution to pass laws concerning taxation, tariffs, national welfare and national defence, and its consent is needed to declare war. The Senate has to ratify treaties with foreign governments by a two-thirds vote. The authors of the Constitution thought that Congress would be more important than the executive branch of government, the presidency, but this has rarely been the case. The Executive has long initiated policy, whilst Congress's role has been to approve, modify or reject the President's proposals. Yet Congress has real power, as it can refuse to support action proposed by the President and may pass legislation of which the President disapproves by overriding his veto. This needs a two-thirds vote in each House. When conflict does take place it is usually when Congress is dominated by a party different from that of the President. During the presidency of Andrew **Johnson**, Congress exercised considerable power when it ordered the implementation of **reconstruction** policies which the President opposed. No President should take Congress for granted, and is likely to suffer a humiliating rebuff if he does: this was the fate of Woodrow **Wilson**, when the Senate failed to ratify the Treaty of **Versailles** and US entry into the **League of Nations**. Franklin **Roosevelt** also failed to obtain the approval of Congress for his proposal to enlarge the **Supreme Court** and had to withdraw it. Nevertheless, the President's power has increased and that of Congress has diminished with the growth of the party system, in which the President is a party leader, and with the steady expansion of presidential responsibilities (for war and peace and the national economy) in the twentieth century.

## Congress Party of India, see Indian National Congress

**Conservative Party** (Britain). The name was first used in 1830 of the **Tories**, as they wished to preserve existing institutions (see **Conservatism**). After the **Reform Act** of 1832 it was in common use, though Tory has continued to be a synonym for Conservative until today. Since Conservatives believed that the role of the state should be reduced to a minimum, this meant that social reform should, whenever possible, be avoided. The **Tamworth Manifesto** (1834) of **Peel** showed a realization that, if the Conservatives were not to remain permanently a minority party, they could not afford to turn their backs on reform completely. Peel won the 1841 election, but by insisting on the repeal of the **Corn Laws** he split the Conservative Party in 1846 and forced it into the wilderness, where it remained for a generation. The Conservatives were out of office from 1846–74, except for a short time when they formed three minority governments under **Derby**. In 1867 they passed the second Reform Bill (see **Parliamentary reform**). In that year they were the first party to create a national organization, soon controlled by a Central Office. In an effort to appeal to a wider electorate (which the Reform Act had doubled) **Disraeli** declared that the Conservative Party was 'the national party . . . the really democratic party of England' and the myth of **Tory Democracy** was born.

The Conservatives were given a great boost when **Gladstone** split the **Liberal Party** in 1886 over **Home Rule for Ireland**. The **Liberal Unionists**, led by Joseph **Chamberlain**, separated from the Liberals and later joined the Conservatives, who became the Conservative and Unionist Party (until the Irish Free State was established in 1922) and were known as Unionists as well as Conservatives. They were in power, under **Salisbury** for most of the time from 1886–1905, except for 1892–5. The **Primrose League** successfully mobilized working-class support, aided by the new, right-wing, mass-circulation newspapers like **Northcliffe**'s *Daily Mail*. Queen **Victoria**'s jubilees of 1887 and 1897, and the **South African War** (1899–1902), were used to bang the imperialist big drum and make the Conservatives appear as the patriotic party.

Conservative popularity ended with the **tariff reform** campaign of Joseph Chamberlain in 1903, which opponents portrayed as a tax on food. Chamberlain succeeded in dividing the Conservative Party, as he had earlier split the Liberal Party, enabling the Liberals to come to power in 1905. They remained in office until 1915, when **Asquith** formed a **coalition government** (later continued by **Lloyd George**) which included Conservatives. At the end of the **First World War** Lloyd George and the Conservative leader, Bonar **Law**, agreed to continue the coalition government, which won an overwhelming victory in the 1918 election. 526 coalition candidates were returned, but 374 of these were Conservatives. This began a period of Conservative dominance which lasted throughout the inter-war years. They were the largest party in the House of **Commons** from 1918–39, except for the period of Labour government from 1929–31. When Ramsay **MacDonald** formed a **National Government** (1931–5) it was mainly a Conservative administration, as the **Labour Party** rejected their former leader and formed the opposition. The governments of **Baldwin** (1935–7) and Neville **Chamberlain** (1937–40) called themselves National Governments, but were in fact Conservative. When Chamberlain fell in 1940 Winston **Churchill** formed a coalition government in which Labour leaders held important posts, **Attlee** being officially recognized as Deputy Prime Minister in 1942. In 1945 the electorate rejected the great war leader by returning a Labour government, which for the first time had a clear majority. Thus the long period of Conservative ascendancy came, temporarily, to an end.

**Conservatism.** A set of ideas and attitudes which emphasizes respect for tradition and historic institutions such as the Church of England, the British Empire, family, monarchy and private property. Conservatism takes an organic view of the state, which has evolved over many centuries and which it believes should be changed only gradually. Conservatives believe in *laissez-faire* and a minimalist state, which should not interfere with the free operation of market forces. They distrust abstract blueprints for society, such as declarations of rights, and take pride in practical, piecemeal reforms. Accepting social deference and inequality, conservatives are firm believers in law and order. Edmund **Burke** is the father of modern conservatism, Britain its birthplace. The strongest **Conservative Party** is also to be found in Britain.

**Constantinople agreements** (1915). During the **First World War** Britain and France feared that Russia would make a separate peace with Germany, unless she was offered significant territorial gains. They secretly agreed, therefore, that after the war Russia should receive Constantinople (Istanbul) and land along the **Straits**. This was a remarkable change in British policy particularly, as throughout the nineteenth century Britain had opposed Russia gaining control of the Straits. After the **October Revolution** the **Bolsheviks** rejected all agreements made by the Tsarist government and in 1918 published the terms of the secret treaties. This greatly embarrassed the British and French governments, who were condemned by public opinion at home and in the USA.

**Constituent Assembly** (July 1789–September 1791). On 7 July 1789 the **Estates-General** in France adopted the name National Constituent Assembly. Within a short time, beginning with the **August Decrees** and **Declaration of Rights**, it swept away most of the institutions of the old regime and produced reforms which were to be the most radical and lasting of the **French Revolution**. The privileges of nobles and Church disappeared, as did the administrative divisions and the entire financial and legal stucture of the *ancien régime*. The aim of the Assembly was to give France a uniform, decentralized, representative and humanitarian system of government. France was divided into eighty-three departments, subdivided into districts and communes (or municipalities), all run by elected councils. Before 1789, government officials ran the provincial administration: there was not one elected council. By 1790, there were no government officials at the local level. The unpopular indirect taxes were abolished and eventually replaced by a tax on land. Meanwhile, Church lands were sold for the benefit of the state, the greatest change in land ownership in France for hundreds of years, as a tenth of the land came on the market at the same time. As the deputies believed in *laissez-faire*, free trade was introduced and internal tariffs abolished, thus creating a national market for the first time. This was helped by the creation of a single system of weights and measures – the decimal system – which applied to the whole of France. Guilds were abolished in 1791, as they restricted entry to certain trades, and workers were prevented from forming trade unions and striking by the **Le Chapelier law**. Uniformity was also applied to the legal system: instead of different systems of law existing in the north and south, there were to be the same laws and lawcourts throughout France. Juries and Justices of the Peace were introduced and the penal code made more humane: torture and mutilation were abolished and the number of crimes for which death was the penalty was vastly reduced. For the first time in France justice became accessible, impartial and cheap. The organization of the Church was adapted to the new framework of local government in the **Civil Constitution of the Clergy** (July 1790) but this split the clergy and made counter-revolution possible. It also led to the King's flight to **Varennes** (June 1791), which resulted in popular demands for a Republic. An attempt to promote this was bloodily suppressed at the **Champ de Mars** (July 1791), as the deputies wanted to retain the monarchy but with limited powers. The Constitution of 1791 placed real power in the hands of an elected Assembly, as it passed laws which the King had to obey. When Louis reluctantly accepted the Constitution in September 1791, the Constituent Assembly was dissolved and replaced by the **Legislative Assembly**.

**Consulate** (1799–1804). The period in France between the *coup d'état* of **Brumaire**, after which **Napoleon Bonaparte** became First Consul, and his becoming Emperor. This was the time when Napoleon carried out most of his domestic reforms, as he was at peace from 1801–3, except with England, with whom he made the Peace of **Amiens** in 1802. The Constitution of 1799 gave Napoleon complete control of the Executive, as he was First Consul and could appoint all officials and ministers, who were responsible to him and not to the elected assemblies. The façade of democracy was maintained, as there was a Tribunate to discuss legislation and a Legislature to vote on it, but real power was in the hands of Napoleon, as legislation was proposed by the Council of State, which was picked by him. He used his power to carry out far-reaching reforms, which affected France throughout the nineteenth century. The First Consul got rid of elected councils which had been established during the **French Revolution**, and imposed a centralized, authoritarian system. Prefects, appointed by him, supervised all local government and they appointed the mayors in the communes. The *Code Napoléon* made the varied laws in France into a unified system, whilst the **Concordat** (1801) with the Pope ensured the support of most Catholics. To provide civil servants and army officers Napoleon set up *lycées* (state grammar schools), though the curriculum was surprisingly old-fashioned, concentrating on the classics rather than science. Napoleon reversed some of the changes of the Revolution by taking the first steps to re-create an aristocracy: in 1802 he established the Legion of Honour, which was a means of rewarding his army officers and high officials.

**Continental Blockade** (1806–13). An attempt by **Napoleon Bonaparte** to ruin Britain economically and so force her to make peace. This was the climax to a trade war with Britain which had begun during the **French Revolutionary Wars** (1792–9), when the British navy cut off French exports to, and imports from, her colonies. When the battle of **Trafalgar** (1805) made it clear that Napoleon would not be able to invade England, he tried to ruin her by cutting off English exports to Europe. The Berlin Decrees (1806) forbade France and her satellite states to trade with Britain, who replied by Orders in Council, which compelled neutral ships trading with France to call at a British port and pay a duty there. Napoleon's Milan Decrees (1807) made ships which called at a British port a lawful prize. There was a dual purpose to the Blockade. Napoleon hoped that by preventing British exports and re-exports to Europe, he would bring about a collapse of the British economy and so end British participation in the **Napoleonic Wars**. He also wanted to replace British industrial hegemony on the Continent by that of France. Goods from France to other parts of the **Napoleonic Empire** paid no duty, whereas manufactures entering France were taxed heavily. In order to make the Blockade more efficient, Napoleon compelled conquered countries to join it, such as Prussia and Russia at the Treaties of **Tilsit** (1807), and extended French frontiers by annexing Holland and part of the North German coast (1810–11).

The Blockade was never fully effective: there was extensive smuggling via Holland, Sweden, the Iberian peninsula and Malta, and Napoleon undermined it by granting licences for trade with Britain. In 1810, when the harvest failed in Britain and there was widespread unrest, Napoleon unwittingly came to the assistance of his enemy by allowing large shipments of grain from France. By making Britain pay in gold, he mistakenly believed that he would bankrupt her. The effects of the Blockade varied from one area to another. French sea ports suffered the most, but other areas benefited, as they were protected from British competition and could export to the captive markets of the Napoleonic Empire. The textile industries in Belgium and on the left bank of the Rhine (which were annexed to France and so had access to the French market) thrived. In France, textiles and war industries boomed, as did Strasbourg on the eastern frontier, as it handled a third of French exports. The Blockade contributed significantly to Napoleon's downfall as, to enforce it, he invaded Spain in 1808 and so began the disastrous **Peninsular War**. In 1812, as **Alexander I** had withdrawn from the Blockade, Napoleon invaded Russia and fought the **Moscow Campaign**, so beginning a series of events which ended with his defeat and abdication.

**Convention, the** (1792–5), succeeded the **Legislative Assembly** during the **French Revolution**. It contained at first about 200

**Girondins** and 100 **Jacobins**, but the majority of the deputies were uncommitted to either group and were known as the Plain, owing to the middle ground where they sat in the Assembly. The Convention's first act was to abolish the monarchy, and this was followed in January 1793 by the trial and execution of **Louis XVI**. The **French Revolutionary Wars** were extended when the Convention declared war on Britain and Holland in February 1793. Defeated by the Austrians at Neerwinden in March, the French lost Belgium and the left bank of the Rhine and there was fighting once again on French soil. At the same time there was civil war in the Vendée (see **Vendean revolt**), so the Convention set up the machinery of the **Terror**. A Revolutionary Tribunal to try counter-revolutionary suspects was established, as were watch committees in each commune to keep an eye on suspected traitors and a **Committee of Public Safety** (CPS) to supervise ministers. On 2 June 1793, a *journée* instigated by the *sans-culottes* intimidated the Convention and forced it to agree to the arrest of leading Girondin deputies. For the next fourteen months the Plain was the reluctant accomplice of the Jacobin minority in putting down the **Federal Revolt** and carrying out the Terror. As anarchy reigned in much of France, the Convention gave the CPS and the Committee of General Security dictatorial powers in December 1793, which they used to intensify the Terror, so that the Convention became simply a nominal parliament whose members went in fear of their lives. They were able to recover control after the execution of **Robespierre** in **Thermidor** (July 1794) and bring the Terror to an end. The Convention abolished price controls in December: the result was massive inflation and misery, which erupted in the rising of **Prairial** (20 May 1795). The Convention needed the army to suppress the rising. A new Constitution was drawn up to maintain the gains of the 1789 Revolution and to make impossible a dictatorship like that of the CPS. In an attempt to retain power in the new legislative Councils, the Convention decreed that two-thirds of the deputies in the Councils should be from the existing Convention. This precipitated the last rising of the Revolution, the rising of **Vendémiaire**, which the Convention once again used the army to suppress.

**Convoys.** Merchant ships sailing in groups with an armed naval escort. During the **First World War** Germany began unrestricted submarine warfare in February 1917, aiming to deprive Britain of food and war material and so force her to surrender. She almost succeeded. Shipping losses rose from 300,000 tons in January 1917 to 870,000 tons in April. The Admiralty opposed the use of convoys, which it regarded as death-traps, but **Lloyd George**, the British Prime Minister, insisted in April that convoys should be organized. By the end of October, 1,500 ships had reached Britain in convoys and only ten had been sunk. U-boat losses had risen sharply, so it was clear that convoys were not simply a defensive measure but acted as a bait to attract submarines, which could then be hunted and sunk by the escorts. In the **Second World War** convoys were used immediately in the battle of the **Atlantic**. Where they were not used there were disastrous shipping losses. The Americans, who did not use convoys in their coastal trade between January and July 1942, had 460 ships (two–three million tons) sunk. The Japanese too did not use convoys extensively in the **Pacific War** and had most of their merchant shipping destroyed by US submarines.

**Coolidge, John Calvin** (1872–1933). Thirtieth President of the USA (1923–9). Coolidge first came to national attention when, as Governor of Massachusetts, he intervened in the Boston police strike of 1919 and denied that the strikers had the right to have their former jobs restored. 'Silent Cal' made one of his few public statements on this occasion: 'There is no right to strike against the public safety by anybody, anywhere, anytime.' His reputation for upholding law and order brought him the vice-presidency when Warren Harding became President in 1921. Coolidge became President in 1923 when Harding suddenly died, and was re-elected in 1924. Dour, aloof and inscrutable, he saw the role of the President in a very negative way: the government should not interfere with free enterprise. 'The business of America is business' he proudly declared, and usually supported it by 'that masterly inactivity', to which the journalist William Allen White referred, 'for which he was so splendidly equipped'. In a period of general economic prosperity, Coolidge concentrated on cutting government expenditure. 'I am for economy', he said. 'After that I am for more economy.' Twice he vetoed bills that would have provided relief for hard-pressed farmers, though he cut income tax to aid the rich, whom he revered. He had a success abroad with the **Dawes Plan** of 1924, which made **reparations** a manageable problem. His administration was also responsible for the Kellogg–Briand Pact (1928), which renounced war as a means of settling disputes, though nearly all the major signatories ignored it in practice. Coolidge would probably have been re-elected for a third term but announced in a characteristically terse statement, 'I do not choose to run for President in 1928.'

**Cooperative societies** were owned by the members who used them, who received a share of the profits, according to the amount of their purchases, in the form of dividends. Robert **Owen** had tried to set up his own cooperative communities early in the nineteenth century, but the first successful cooperative society was that of the Rochdale Pioneers (1844). The movement rapidly spread in the industrial north of England and in Scotland, with different societies forming a federation, the Cooperative Wholesale Society (CWS) in 1864. By 1881 there were 971 societies with 550,000 members, which had grown to three million by 1914, when the CWS was the biggest single retailing group in Britain. The movement spread to other countries of Western Europe and to Scandinavia. One of the most successful cooperative movements was in Denmark, which had a thousand cooperative dairies by 1892: most Danish eggs, bacon, butter and milk were marketed by cooperatives.

**Copenhagen, battles of** (1801 and 1807). Fought by Britain against Denmark during the **Napoleonic Wars**. The Baltic powers (Russia, Prussia, Denmark and Sweden) had formed a League of Armed Neutrality to prevent Britain from interfering with neutral shipping trading with France, so the British, without declaring war, sent a fleet under Sir Hyde Parker to destroy the Danish navy at Copenhagen in 1801. The British fleet divided, Parker attacking from the north, **Nelson** from the south. In bad weather Nelson lost three ships but captured or sank all but three of the Danish vessels. This marked the end of the League. In 1807 Britain feared that **Napoleon Bonaparte** was about to seize the Danish fleet and exclude

Britain from the Baltic, so she sent a military and naval expedition to bombard Copenhagen. The attack turned Denmark into Napoleon's most reliable ally in enforcing the **Continental Blockade**, for which she was to pay at the Congress of **Vienna** (1815) by losing Norway to Sweden.

**Cordeliers Club.** A society founded in 1790 during the **French Revolution**, which was more radical than that of the **Jacobins**. It supported measures which the *sans-culottes* favoured – direct democracy, the recall of deputies to account for their actions and the right of insurrection. Though most of its leaders (**Danton**, Desmoulins, **Hébert**) were *bourgeois*, it had much support among the working class. As there were no political parties, the clubs played an important part in the Revolution, acting as pressure groups to influence deputies in the Assembly. In 1791 the Cordeliers Club took the lead in organizing a petition and demonstration at the Champ de Mars (see **Champ de Mars massacre**), which called for the end of the monarchy. After the execution of Hébert in March 1793, the Cordeliers Club was closed by the **Committee of Public Safety**.

**Corn Laws** in Britain applied to the import and export of grain, in order to control its supply and price. First passed in the Middle Ages, they caused a public outcry when in 1815, at the end of the **Napoleonic Wars**, parliament passed an Act prohibiting the import of wheat until the domestic price reached 80 shillings (£4) a quarter: above that price wheat could be imported free of duty. The Prime Minister, Lord **Liverpool**, maintained that this would preserve domestic production at a time of falling prices and prevent famine, but many saw it as a blatant piece of class legislation, passed by a parliament of landowners in their own interest. There were riots in London, during which troops were needed to protect parliament. The **parliamentary reform** movement was greatly helped by the Corn Laws, as many believed that only when parliament was more representative would such legislation be repealed. There were further Corn Laws in 1822, 1828 and 1842, which lowered duties and introduced a sliding scale. In 1839 the **Anti-Corn Law League** was formed to press for abolition and pursued a vigorous campaign, but it was **Peel** rather than the League who brought about abolition. A believer in free trade, he had introduced various *laissez-faire* measures in his budgets of 1842 and 1845 and was convinced that the Corn Laws would have to go. The **Irish Famine** (1845–9) was the occasion for the repeal, which split the **Conservative Party**. Agriculture did not suffer from the repeal, as an increase in population kept prices steady in the 1850s and 1860s. The working man did not benefit greatly until the 1870s, when American wheat started to flood the market and reduce the cost of living.

**Corporate State.** A Fascist system in Italy (see **Fascism**), which aimed to end class conflict between workers and employers and to replace it with class harmony, manifested in corporations in which workers, employers and managers were represented. This was not a Fascist invention but had both Catholic and syndicalist (see **Syndicalism**) origins. Pope **Leo XIII** (1878–1903) tried to bring employers and workers together in 'mixed unions' or corporations. Syndicalists wanted workers to bring about change through **trade unions** rather than through political parties: some Fascist syndicalists saw 'integrated corporations' as a means of promoting popular participation in the state. The cornerstone of the new system was the syndical law of April 1926, which allowed only one Fascist association of workers and employers for each branch of production. Strikes and lock-outs were forbidden and there was compulsory arbitration in industrial disputes. A Ministry of Corporations was set up in the same year to oversee the associations. In 1930 a National Council of Corporations – a sort of corporate parliament – was established, and four years later 'mixed corporations' of employers and workers were finally created, to decide wages and conditions in specific areas of economic activity. They were not impartial, as workers were represented by Fascist officials, who defended the interests of the employers. The Chamber of Fasces and Corporations, made up of members from the Fascist Grand Council and National Council of Corporations, replaced the moribund parliament in 1939. The Corporate State attracted great interest abroad, where its admirers included Sir Oswald **Mosley** in Britain and Juan Perón, the future dictator of Argentina. Yet its claim to provide a third way between capitalism and socialism and promote social harmony was undermined, as **Mussolini** refused to give the

corporations any real power. The Institute for Industrial Reconstruction (1933), a holding company for the large state-run industrial
sector, operated independently of the corporate system,

**Corresponding societies** were formed by skilled workers in
Britain in the 1790s to press for political reform. They were greatly
influenced by the **French Revolution**, in which aristocratic privileges had been destroyed and the powers of the King reduced,
before the monarchy was abolished completely. The most important
of these radical societies was the London Corresponding Society
(LCS), formed in 1792 by the shoemaker Thomas Hardy. It sought
universal manhood suffrage, equal parliamentary constituencies
(which involved the abolition of **'rotten' boroughs**) and annual
elections. It corresponded with similar societies throughout Britain
and sent 'fraternal delegates' to Paris, but it had no links with the
unskilled labourers or the very poor. When war with France began
in 1793, most members affirmed their loyalty to the King and the
Constitution, though they continued to press peacefully for reform.
The government regarded them as dangerous agitators and to make
their activities difficult suspended *Habeas Corpus* in 1794, thus
allowing imprisonment without trial, and in 1795 passed the 'Gag'
Acts, which forbade meetings of over fifty people without a magistrate's permission and made treasonable any criticism of the Constitution. These Acts were hardly ever applied, but they indicated the
government's concern and its serious repressive intent. Support for
the societies was highest at times of economic distress: in 1792–3,
when there was widespread unemployment, and in 1795–6, when
record food prices followed harvest failure. Yet the societies posed
no real threat to the government, though a minority of members
turned to conspiracy, violence and treason, which their leaders
repudiated. By the time the leading societies were banned in 1799,
they had already collapsed.

**Cosgrave, William Thomas** (1880–1965). Irish politician and
first President of the Irish Free State (1922–32). Cosgrave joined
**Sinn Fein** and, in 1913, the Irish Volunteers, a paramilitary organization. When this split a year later, he backed the minority who were
opposed to **Redmond**'s cooperation with Britain in the **First**

**World War**. After taking part in the **Easter Rising** (1916), he was imprisoned (1916–17) and in 1918 was elected as an MP. Together with other Sinn Fein members, Cosgrave refused to take his seat in the British parliament: they set up their own Dail (Irish Assembly) and Republican ministry, in which Cosgrave was responsible for local government. In the **Anglo-Irish War** (1919–21) he was to ensure that local authorities did not cooperate with the British. In 1921 he supported the **Anglo-Irish Treaty**, which set up the Irish Free State, and became Minister of Local Government in the new provisional government. When Arthur **Griffith** died and Michael **Collins** was killed in August 1922, Cosgrave became head of the Irish government, a position he retained for the next ten years. His was not a popular government, as the economy was weak and taxes were high. Unemployment benefit was cut in 1924 and other social benefits pegged at their pre-1922 level. He encouraged the spread of the Gaelic language, which became a compulsory part of the curriculum in state schools: some knowledge of it was required by all civil servants. This policy was not successful, as English continued to be spoken everywhere except in the remote west. In 1932 the **Fianna Fail** party of **de Valera** won the election and Cosgrave became leader of the opposition. To strengthen his own party, Cumaan, he joined with two smaller parties in 1933 to form **Fine Gael**, but he was not able to regain power before he retired in 1944.

**Cowboys** looked after cattle on the Great Plains of the USA. They originated in the Spanish ranches of north-east Mexico, where they developed their skills with horse, lariat and branding iron, and their functional costume of sombrero, leather chaps, high-heeled boots and spurs. The cowboy became the hero of many 'Western' films as a tough, independent man of action, who was quick on the draw. The reality was very different, as much of the cowboy's life was tedious and unpleasant. In the winter and spring he looked after cattle on the open range; in the late spring he rounded up and branded the cattle. When the 'long drives' started in 1866 (see **Cattle trails**) he spent two months in the summer driving the Longhorns, in a continuous cloud of dust, to the railheads. He could spend eighteen hours a day in the saddle and face many dangers on the way – stampedes, Indian attacks and rustlers. When paid he spent his money in the bars, brothels and gambling halls of cow towns like Dodge City. The heyday of the cowboy was between 1866 and 1890. By the later date there was no need to drive cattle to the railroads – the railroads had moved into the heart of the cattle country and much of the open grassland had been fenced off, after the invention of barbed wire in 1874. With the round-up and the 'long drive' ended, the cowboy became a farm hand.

**Crazy Horse** (1849–77). American Indian chief. One of the greatest war leaders the Sioux ever had, Crazy Horse was both feared and respected by the US army. He first made his mark by wiping out a force of eighty soldiers in 1866, and a year later attacked surveying parties on the Union Pacific Railroad. In 1868, when some Sioux chiefs agreed to move to a vast Great Sioux Reservation, Crazy Horse refused to go and led the resistance when prospectors moved into the Black Hills of Dakota, the sacred hunting ground of the Sioux, after gold was discovered there in 1874. He won two victories over the US army in June 1876: first at Rosebud river, then at the battle of **Little Big Horn**, where Custer and all his party were killed – the worst defeat suffered by the US army at the hands of the Indians. After the battle many Sioux fled to Canada to avoid US punitive expeditions. Crazy Horse decided to stay and fight, but after a winter of starvation he surrendered in May 1877. He was imprisoned by the army later in the same year because he refused to stay on a reservation. While in custody he was stabbed to death by a soldier or Indian scout.

**Creole.** The term has a number of meanings: in South America it referred to white people born in the Spanish colonies, while in the Caribbean islands it generally meant children of white and black parents, as it did in Senegal. In Sierra Leone, Creoles were the descendants of black settlers and liberated slaves who came to Freetown, the capital, from Britain and North America in the late eighteenth and early nineteenth centuries.

**Crimean War** (1853–6). With Turkey, Britain and France (and later Piedmont) all fighting against Russia, the Crimean was a war no one wanted. It sprang from a series of blunders and misunderstandings. **Napoleon III** had gained from the Sultan the right for

Catholics to look after the Holy Places in Jerusalem. **Nicholas I** saw this as an affront to Russia and the Orthodox Church, and in May 1853 demanded that the Sultan should recognize him as protector of all the rights of the Christians in the **Ottoman Empire** (40 per cent of the Sultan's subjects were Orthodox Christians). To back up his claim Nicholas invaded Moldavia and Wallachia (later Romania, then part of the Ottoman Empire). This led to Turkey declaring war on Russia in October. In November the Russians destroyed a Turkish fleet at Sinope on the Black Sea, a battle depicted as a 'massacre' by the anti-Russian British press. Britain and France now feared that Russia would seize Constantinople and the Bosphorus, and so sent their warships into the Black Sea in January 1854, and in March declared war on Russia.

In August 1854 Russia withdrew from Moldavia and Wallachia, as she feared that Austria would join the Allies. The threat to Constantinople was now removed, so the war could have ended, but Britain and France wanted a prestige victory. They landed troops in the Crimea but too far away from the naval base at Sebastopol, which they aimed to capture, and with three rivers to cross. They defeated the Russians at Alma and secured a good base by capturing the port of Balaclava. The Russians attacked at Inkerman in November and though they were beaten, losses on both sides were so heavy that a stalemate resulted. The Allies finally captured Sebastopol in September 1855, a useless victory as the Russians commanded strongly fortified positions above the port. In December Austria gave Russia an ultimatum: she would join the Allies if Russia did not end the war. Peace was made at the Congress of **Paris** in 1856. There were more casualties in the Crimean War than in any other war fought by European powers between 1815 and 1914. 675,000 died, 80 per cent from disease or infected wounds, in spite of the efforts of people like Florence **Nightingale**.

Russia's defeat was humiliating, as she had been regarded in 1815 as the greatest military power in Europe. 480,000 Russian soldiers had died, and Russia's backwardness was now evident to all. In January 1856 the State Council warned the Tsar that if the war continued Russia would be bankrupt. 'We cannot deceive ourselves any longer', the Grand Duke Konstantin Nikolayevich stated,

' . . . we are both weaker and poorer than the first-class powers.' The Crimean War, therefore, led **Alexander II** to carry out a series of reforms, in particular the **emancipation of the serfs**, which were designed to modernize Russian institutions and develop her economy.

**Crispi, Francesco** (1819–1901). Italian Prime Minister (1887–91, 1893–6). Born in Sicily, Crispi fought in Palermo in the **Revolutions of 1848** as a Republican Democrat, then spent ten years in exile, during which he was expelled from Turin by **Cavour** because he was a follower of **Mazzini**. He pushed **Garibaldi** into invading Sicily in 1860 and played an important part in the success of 'the Thousand' there. Crispi's main concern was national unity and this led him to become a monarchist in the 1860s, as 'The monarchy unites us, a republic would divide us.' He also sought, unsuccessfully, a reconciliation with the papacy, as this too would help to unite Italy. In 1886 he called for a 'strong man' to save Italy from anarchy and a year later was the first southerner to become Prime Minister. He also held the posts of Minister of the Interior and Foreign Minister. Seeing France as Italy's great rival in the Mediterranean, Crispi foolishly began a trade war with her in 1887, which deprived Italy of 40 per cent of her exports. In spite of the weakness of the economy he began an expansionist foreign policy, spent 38 per cent of the state's income on the army and navy, and in 1889 proclaimed that Eritrea was an Italian colony. By the time he became Prime Minister for the second time he had abandoned his early democratic beliefs and behaved dictatorially. When there was social unrest in Sicily in 1894 he declared martial law and sent 40,000 troops to restore order and suppress workers' organizations. In the same year he dissolved the Italian Socialist Party, removed a quarter of the voters from the electoral register and ruled, sometimes unconstitutionally, by decree. Parliament was suspended when it investigated the government's role in a banking scandal, and met for only eleven days in the twelve months after June 1894. There was surprisingly little resistance to Crispi's disdainful treatment of parliament, as there was much criticism of *trasformismo*, of the inefficiency and factionalism of the parliamentary system and its subordination of national to local interests. Crispi's downfall came when he decided to add Ethiopia to Italy's empire: an Italian army was destroyed at **Aduwa** in 1896 and he was forced to retire. He died a lonely and bitter man five years later.

**Cromer, Evelyn Baring, 1st Earl of** (1841–1917). British colonial administrator. Born into a famous banking family, he was trained as a soldier but disliked military service. When his cousin, Lord Northbrook, became Viceroy of India in 1872, Baring became his private secretary. He soon showed considerable ability in administration but patronized his subordinates and so became known as 'Over-Baring'. He first went to Egypt in 1877 as a representative of bondholders on the Debt Commission (see **Ismail**), returned to India (1880–83) and from 1883–1907 was British Agent and Consul-General in Egypt, the real ruler of the country. Baring (or Lord Cromer as he became in 1892) was very hard-working and an able linguist: he learnt Greek, Latin, French, Italian and Turkish but, surprisingly, not Arabic. He was a great imperialist, believing that native rulers were incompetent tyrants and that British rule was therefore needed to bring reform and just government. When he went to Egypt as British Agent, after **Urabi Pasha**'s revolt, Cromer was expected to reform the administration and then evacuate British forces, but he soon decided that if there was evacuation there would be no reform, so it would be better for the Egyptians if the British stayed. He therefore established a 'veiled protectorate' in Egypt – the Khedive was the ostensible ruler but all important decisions were taken by the British Resident. For Cromer, reform meant above all a sound financial system, which he successfully established, so that from 1889 there were budget surpluses. Agriculture was improved by extensive irrigation projects, the most important of which was the building of the original Aswan Dam (1896–1903), which stored enough water to irrigate the Nile valley all year round. For the first time in 5,000 years Egyptian agriculture ceased to be dependent on the variations of the annual Nile floods. Cromer further improved the condition of the peasants by abolishing forced labour for the clearing of the irrigation canals, but he did little for education, as he was suspicious of the Western-educated élite, which wanted more power than he was prepared to give them. As he grew older Cromer became more aloof and underestimated the importance of the nationalist movement which was arising in Egypt, though he was aware of the importance of the **Anglo-French Entente** (1904), which he did much to promote, as the French at last accepted the British occupation of Egypt.

**Crystal Night** (*Kristallnacht*, Night of Broken Glass, 9–10 November 1938). The occasion of an anti-Jewish **pogrom** in Germany. In spite of being violently anti-Semitic, the Nazi regime had moved with some caution in its early years, as it feared foreign reaction to attacks on the Jews and a disruption of the German economy. Jews had been removed from the civil service as early as 1933, and the Nuremberg Laws of 1935 had deprived them of citizenship and had forbidden them to marry Aryans or have extra-marital relations with them, but persecution of the Jews had been sporadic. In 1938 a Jewish youth murdered a German embassy official in Paris and this provided the excuse for a pogrom organized by **Heydrich**, commander of the **Gestapo**. 7,000 Jewish businesses were looted and destroyed; Jewish houses, schools and synagogues were burnt down; nearly a hundred Jews were murdered and thousands were beaten up; 20,000 Jews were arrested and sent to **concentration camps**. People abroad and many Germans were horrified, but the regime was now confident enough to begin a more sustained attack on the Jews. A fine of one billion marks was imposed on the Jewish community to pay for the destruction and this was followed by laws which confiscated Jewish industrial assets and completely separated Jews from other Germans: they were not allowed to own cars, enter cinemas or theatres; their children were expelled from schools and universities. Hitler hinted that this renewed persecution would lead to the **'Final Solution'** when he told the **Reichstag**, in January 1939, that if war broke out it would lead to the annihilation of the Jews in Europe.

**Curragh 'mutiny'** (1914). There was great opposition in Ulster to **Asquith**'s **Home Rule for Ireland** Bill, as the Protestants in Ulster would be a minority in a united, mainly Catholic, Ireland. A paramilitary force, the Ulster Volunteers (UVF), was formed to prevent this. The government had no plans to suppress the UVF but needed reinforcements in Ulster to keep order. Officers at the Curragh, near Dublin, were told that those who lived in Ulster could 'disappear': the rest would have to resign or be dismissed if they were unwilling to serve there. Fifty-seven cavalry officers said they were 'prepared to accept dismissal if ordered north'. The press called this a 'mutiny', which was untrue. This incident greatly encouraged the Ulster Unionists, as it appeared to show that they had the support of the British army. In England there was shock and concern that the army might prove to be unreliable.

**Curtin, John Joseph** (1885–1945). Australian Prime Minister (1941–5). The son of a policeman in an Irish Roman Catholic family, Curtin became a socialist in 1906 and a trade-union offical. He spent much time building up the **Labor Party** in Western Australia, before becoming its leader in 1935. In opposition until 1941, he rejected Menzies appeal for a National Government as the Japanese moved into Indo-China, and forced Menzies to resign. Curtin became Prime Minister before the **Pacific War** began in December 1941, but was soon faced with a situation in which Australia was threatened with invasion for the first time in its history. As early as 1936 he had said that reliance on Britain for Australia's defence was 'too dangerous a hazard', and in his end-of-year message in 1941 he declared that 'Australia looks to America, free of any pangs as to our traditional links or kinship with the United Kingdom.' In February 1942 Darwin was bombed by the Japanese but there was no invasion, partly because of the arrival of American armed forces from the Philippines under General **MacArthur**. Curtin, whom MacArthur called 'the heart and soul of Australia', saw the Japanese threat recede as they were driven back from Port Moresby in New Guinea in November 1942. Curtin had been imprisoned for opposing conscription in the **First World War**, but in 1942 he introduced conscription for the South-West Pacific zone. In the same year he won the election for the House of Representatives and the Senate, and began to establish the **Welfare State** policies which were applied in Australia after the war, setting up a Ministry of Post-War Reconstruction in 1945. Worn out by his efforts, he died shortly before the war ended.

**Curzon, George Nathaniel, 1st Marquess of** (1859–1925). British statesman and imperialist. Educated at Eton and Oxford, Curzon was a brilliant scholar, who became a Fellow of All Souls

College, Oxford, before turning to politics. In 1886 he became a Conservative MP and then Parliamentary Under-Secretary for India (1891–2) and Foreign Under-Secretary (1895–8). His knowledge of India and foreign affairs was increased by his extensive travels, especially between 1887 and 1894, when he visited Canada and the United States, China and Japan, India and Afghanistan, Russia, Central Asia and Persia. In 1898 Curzon became Viceroy of India and had real power for the first time. He was obsessed by the Russian menace to India and so strengthened the North-West Frontier by creating a new province there, which he used local levies to police, whilst troops were kept as a mobile reserve in bases behind the frontier. Tibet was invaded in 1904, as Curzon claimed that the Dalai Lama was seeking Russian support: there was little resistance and Lhasa was entered, but nothing was achieved. Curzon cared passionately for India and felt obliged to protect its land and people. He acted vigorously to suppress racialism, which made him unpopular with the army, and set up a new department to preserve India's archaeological and architectural heritage. 6,000 miles of track were added to the existing railways and 6.5 million acres of extra land were irrigated. Curzon worked exceptionally hard, largely because he would not delegate, and made 'efficiency' his watchword. It was this which in 1905 led him to partition Bengal, which he maintained was too large to be ruled effectively. This was his greatest blunder. Typically, he had not consulted Indian opinion and was surprised by the ensuing uproar. Arrogantly he believed that he knew what was best for India and showed nothing but contempt for the **Congress Party** and Indian nationalism. Curzon believed that a royal *darbar*, held in 1903 to commemorate the coronation of **Edward VII**, would impress the Indians and show the strength of the British **Raj**. He spent six months preparing it and centred the ceremony so much around himself (Edward VII did not attend) that it became known as the 'Curzonation' *darbar*. Shortly after becoming Viceroy for a second term, Curzon clashed with **Kitchener**, the Commander-in-Chief of the Indian army, over the military representative on the Viceroy's Council. As he felt that the British government was supporting Kitchener he resigned and was mortified when his resignation was accepted. In England he led an active public life, particularly as Chancellor of the University of Oxford, before entering the War Cabinet in 1915, becoming Foreign Secretary in 1919 and giving his name to the **Curzon Line**, the frontier proposed between Russia and Poland. He strongly opposed the **Montagu–Chelmsford reforms** as they would, he felt, lead to parliamentary government in India and undermine British rule there. When Bonar **Law** resigned as Prime Minister in 1923, owing to ill health, Curzon expected to succeed him, but he was passed over, partly because he was a member of the House of **Lords**, in favour of Stanley **Baldwin**. Although bitterly disappointed, he gave loyal support to the new Premier.

**Curzon Line.** In December 1919 the British put forward proposals for settling Poland's eastern frontier, which had been left undecided at the Treaty of **Versailles** in June. The Curzon Line, named after the British Foreign Secretary Lord **Curzon**, tried to divide the Catholic Poles from the Orthodox Ukrainians and White Russians. The Poles rejected the proposals and as a result of the **Russo-Polish War** (1920–21) obtained a frontier well to the east of the Curzon Line. In 1939 the Curzon Line became, roughly, the boundary between the German and Soviet areas of occupied Poland, which followed the **Nazi–Soviet Pact**. In 1945 it became the boundary between Poland and the USSR and has remained so.

**Czechoslovakian crisis** (1938–9) arose from the territorial demands made by **Hitler**, which led to the dismemberment of Czechoslovakia. As a result of the **Treaty of Versailles** there were over three million Germans living in Czechoslovakia in the **Sudetenland**, along the borders with Germany and Austria. After Hitler came to power in Germany in 1933, demands for their inclusion in Germany grew, particularly when the *Anschluss* (union) of Germany and Austria took place in March 1938. On 30 May, Hitler told his generals, 'It is my unalterable decision to smash Czechoslovakia by military action in the near future.' This might involve war with other powers, as both France and Russia were allied to Czechoslovakia, but the Russians could help the Czechs only by marching through Poland and the Poles would not allow this. France had shown, when Germany rearmed and sent troops into the Rhineland (see remilitarization of the **Rhineland**), that she was not prepared to stand up to Germany, so Britain came to play a leading diplomatic role. Neville **Chamberlain** was opposed to war, partly because of his memories of the **First World War** and partly because Britain was not militarily prepared for war, so he flew on 15 September 1938 to meet Hitler at Berchtesgaden. The *Führer* told Chamberlain that Czechoslovakia was the 'last major problem to be solved' and obtained his agreement that the areas of Czechoslovakia where over 50 per cent of the population was German should become part of Germany. Chamberlain returned home and obtained the approval of his Cabinet and that of the French government. **Beneš**, the Czech Premier, was in an impossible situation. He knew that these proposals would lead to the disintegration of his country, as they would be followed by Polish and Hungarian claims for territory (see **Paris Peace Conference**, 1919). Yet it had been made clear to Beneš that if he fought, he would fight alone against Germany, so he was forced to agree. The British Prime Minister saw Hitler again on 22 September at Bad Godesberg to inform him of his success, only to find that Hitler had raised the stakes. He now demanded that the Sudetenland should be occupied immediately and that Polish and Hungarian claims must be met: if his new demands were not accepted he would take military action. Hitler probably wanted war, so that he could crush Czechoslovakia, and expected the Czechs to reject his demands (he had told the Hungarian Prime Minister on 20 September that he was 'convinced that neither England nor France would intervene'). Chamberlain was prepared to recommend acceptance of the new demands but his Cabinet was opposed to them, so he told Daladier, the French Prime Minister, that Britain would support France if she backed Czechoslovakia. War seemed likely until Chamberlain persuaded **Mussolini** to act as mediator and arrange a meeting of Britain, France, Germany and Italy to resolve the situation. Czechoslovakia and the Soviet Union were not invited to attend. The meeting took place on 29 September at Munich and agreed to the demands Hitler had made at Bad Godesberg. German troops entered the Sudetenland early in October, thus depriving Czechoslovakia of her mountain defences and her most important industrial area. Polish troops occupied Teschen and Hungary acquired a strip of southern Slovakia and Ruthenia. Chamberlain flew home claiming that he had brought 'peace in our time' but others were not deceived. 'We have suffered a total and unmitigated defeat', Winston **Churchill** said, an opinion repeated by Clement **Attlee**, leader of the **Labour Party**: 'Without firing a shot . . . he [Hitler] has achieved a dominating position in Europe which Germany failed to win after four years of war.'

Hitler wanted to destroy the rest of Czechoslovakia. On 15 March he saw President Hacha, threatened to destroy Prague by air bombardment and bullied Hacha into saying that he 'confidently placed the fate of the Czech people and country in the hands of the *Führer* and of the German Reich'. German troops entered Prague on the same day, and on 16 March Hitler announced the German Protectorate of Bohemia and Moravia. Slovakia too accepted German protection and, when Hitler allowed Hungary to occupy Ruthenia, Czechoslovakia ceased to exist as an independent state. Memel, the Lithuanian port, was annexed by Germany on 23 March. The events of March had a marked effect on British public opinion. **Appeasement** was now discredited, as it was clear that Hitler aimed to dominate the whole of Europe (there were few Germans in Bohemia and Moravia). Chamberlain had never wanted peace at any price, and on 31 March 1939 offered Poland a guarantee of her independence.

**Daily Telegraph Affair** (1908). During a visit to England the German Emperor, **William II**, stayed with Colonel Stuart-Wortley, who wrote an article for the *Daily Telegraph* recounting his conversations with the Emperor. William was quoted as saying that many Germans were anti-British; that he had remained neutral in the **South African War** (1899–1902) in spite of much pro-Afrikaner feeling in Germany; that he had prevented the foundation of an anti-British coalition at that time; and that he supported the growth of a large German navy. Many people in both Britain and Germany were incensed by the article, although William had acted correctly in handing it to Chancellor **Bülow** for approval prior to publication. (Bülow, immersed in the **Bosnian crisis**, had passed the article without reading it.) All parties in the **Reichstag** therefore attacked Bülow for allowing publication and criticized the Emperor for interfering in government affairs. Bülow defended himself by joining the attack on the Emperor's 'personal government'. William was forced to give a written promise to respect the Constitution. He was deeply upset, as it became clear that he was unpopular with many Germans, and he talked of abdication, but quickly recovered his pride and never forgave Bülow for his disloyalty. This affair provided an opportunity for the Reichstag to insist on the increase of its powers at the expense of those of the Emperor, but nothing was done as the political parties did not remain united.

**Dalhousie, James Ramsay, 1st Marquess of** (1812–60). Governor-General of India (1848–56). One of the most able and innovative governors-general, and the youngest to hold this office, Dalhousie worked so hard that he ruined his health and died at the age of forty-eight. An imperialist, he believed that British rule was so superior to Indian that the more of India the British **Raj** ruled, the better it was for the Indians. He therefore sought to extend

British control, which he did partly by conquest and partly by using the doctrine of 'lapse'. **East India Company** troops entered the Punjab in 1848; after they defeated the Sikhs it was annexed a year later. Pegu (Lower Burma) was also taken over after the second **Anglo-Burmese War** (1852). What remained of Awadh (Oudh) was annexed in 1856 on the grounds of misgovernment. Other princely states were seized when their rulers died without a male heir: they 'lapsed' into Company control. The only states which retained a tenuous independence were those, like Hyderabad, which were surrounded by British territory and where 'paramountcy' applied. Influenced by the utilitarianism of Jeremy **Bentham** and John Stuart **Mill**, Dalhousie promoted popular education and passed laws against female infanticide. He wanted to create a modern administration and unify the subcontinent as far as possible, so he abolished internal trade barriers, began building railways and established a telegraph system to link the 'presidencies' of Bombay, Madras and Calcutta, with a trunk line up the Ganges from Calcutta to Delhi and Lahore. This would enable British goods to be sold in the interior and would make it possible for troops to be moved quickly from one part of India to another. Communications were further improved by introducing a cheap postal service. Dalhousie's greatest blunder was to annex Awadh, one of the richest areas of India, as the resulting discontent there contributed to the outbreak of the **Indian Mutiny** in 1857.

**Dalton, Edward Hugh Neale** (1887–1962). British politician. His father was a Canon of Windsor who had been tutor to the future **Edward VII**'s two sons, so Hugh Dalton grew up in the surroundings of the Court. His privileged life continued at Eton and Cambridge, where he became a socialist through the **Fabian Society** and mixed in homosexual circles which included J. M. **Keynes** and Rupert Brooke. He served in the **First World War** on the **Somme**, which gave him a permanent loathing of Germans, and in Italy, where he was awarded an Italian medal for bravery in the retreat from **Caporetto**. After the war Dalton lectured at the London School of Economics, but politics was his main interest, so he became an MP in 1924. Soon recognized as an expert in foreign affairs and public finance, he served in **MacDonald**'s Labour government (1929–31) as Under-Secretary of State for Foreign Affairs. He lost his seat in the 1931 election but used his time profitably to develop a theory of democratic socialism, which found expression in *Practical Socialism* (1935), a seminal book for the British Labour movement. In it, Dalton provided a detailed programme for the nationalization of industries and showed sensitive concern for the environmental aspects of planning, including proposals for National Parks and the National Trust. The programme put forward in this book was largely followed by **Attlee**'s administration from 1945–51. Dalton's views on foreign policy were equally important in determining the policies of the **Labour Party** from 1935, when he returned to the House of **Commons** and became party spokesman on foreign affairs. He had little sympathy for the Republicans in the **Spanish Civil War**, who aided **Franco** by fighting amongst themselves. More important for Dalton was the threat from Nazi Germany (see **Nazi Party**). From 1934 he was urging rearmament and an end to **appeasement** and in 1937 succeeded in stopping the Labour Party from voting against the arms estimates. When Winston **Churchill** formed a coalition government in 1940, Dalton became Minister for Economic Warfare and was responsible for the blockade of Germany and for encouraging **resistance** movements in German-occupied countries. In 1942 he was moved to the Board of Trade, where he was in charge of wartime controls and post-war planning. He saw through the Commons his Distribution of Industries Act in 1944–5, which planned for industries to be moved to depressed areas like South Wales and Durham: it was the basis for all post-war regional policy.

**D'Annunzio, Gabriele** (1863–1938). Italian poet and nationalist. D'Annunzio was in favour of Italian intervention in the **First World War** on the Allied side, as he wanted Italy to acquire territory populated by Italians in the **Austro-Hungarian Empire**. Although over fifty when the war began, he volunteered for service and risked his life on several occasions, lost an eye and received the Italian equivalent of the Victoria Cross. A popular hero at the end of the war, he claimed that Italy's victory was 'mutilated' at the Treaty of **Versailles**, as she did not acquire Fiume or Dalmatia. In September 1919 D'Annunzio led a band of war veterans, who seized Fiume without bloodshed and held it for over a year. His contempt for authority expressed in the phrase *Me ne frego* ('I don't give a damn') was taken up by the Fascists, as were his public parades with their salutes and uniformed participants. D'Annunzio was pushed out of Fiume in 1920 by **Giolitti**, who made an agreement with Yugoslavia making Fiume a 'free city'. In 1922 D'Annunzio endorsed **Fascism** but retired from active political life after the **March on Rome**. Fiume was acquired for Italy by **Mussolini** in 1924, when he renounced Italian claims to Dalmatia. It became part of Yugoslavia, with the name Rijeka, after the **Second World War**.

**Danton, Georges-Jacques** (1759–94). French revolutionary. Trained as a lawyer, Danton abandoned the law for politics in the summer of 1789, after the **French Revolution** had begun. He became a municipal official in Paris and a founder of the **Cordeliers Club**, where he worked with other radicals, including the journalists **Marat** and Desmoulins. A big, ugly man with a pock-marked face and loud, rasping voice, Danton was a moderate by temperament, who usually waited to see which side in a conflict would be successful before committing himself. By 1791 there were doubts about his honesty, as he lived well beyond his means and accepted political bribes from people such as **Louis XVI**'s cousin, the Duc d'Orléans. Danton helped to plan the attack on the **Tuileries** on 10 August 1792, which brought about the downfall of the monarchy, and became Minister of Justice after it. This marked the peak of his political power: he was the effective head of the government, raised volunteers for the army and speeded up the arrest of political suspects. When the **September massacres** occurred Danton refused to condemn them and claimed that he was the organizer. When he was elected to the **Convention** he resigned from office, as he could not be both a minister and a deputy. In April 1793 he was elected to the **Committee of Public Safety** (CPS) but was removed in July because he wanted to end the war, which he saw would be necessary if the divisions in the revolutionary movement were to be healed and the **Terror** brought to an end. The CPS came to regard Danton as a threat, because he had a large following in the Convention. His policies of peace and an end to Terror would, they felt, leave the door open for a return of the monarchy. Doubts about his honesty had reappeared – nearly 400,000 livres spent at the Ministry of Justice when he was in charge could not be accounted for – and he was accused of being bribed by foreign powers, a damaging accusation which had been levelled against **Hébert**. Condemned by the Revolutionary Tribunal, Danton was executed with many of his followers on 5 April 1794.

**Darbar** (*Durbar*)(Persian and Urdu, 'open court'). A term used by Mughal emperors for their public audiences, when they granted redress of grievances and showed their authority. The British held three *darbars* to manifest their dominance over their Indian subjects, in 1877, 1903 and 1911, to mark the accession of Queen **Victoria**, **Edward VII** and **George V** to the title Queen-Empress or King-Emperor of India. The ceremonies were designed to attach Indian princes to the British Crown and to impress public opinion at home and abroad. All were held on a special site north of Delhi; Queen Victoria and Edward VII did not attend, but George V crowned himself Emperor of India in the greatest of all *darbars*. 233 camps of the King-Emperor and his subjects covered twenty-five square miles of the Delhi plain. Two vast concentric amphitheatres were specially built, the outer one to hold 100,000 spectators, the inner one for the 70,000 guests – princes and notables – in the centre of which, on a dais, were the thrones of the King-Emperor and Queen-Empress. In his speech George V announced the end of **Curzon**'s partition of Bengal and the removal of the capital of India from Calcutta to Delhi, the old Mughal capital. Throughout, the British copied the Mughals by having a golden cupola over the thrones and by the King and Queen greeting the people from the walls of the Red Fort.

**Davis, Jefferson** (1808–89). President of the **Confederate States of America** (1861–5) during the **American Civil War**. Davis, like **Lincoln**, was born in a log cabin. He became a wealthy Mississippi planter and served in the **Mexican–American War** of 1846–8. He was Secretary of War (1853–7) in Pierce's administration and was responsible for the **Gadsden Purchase** from Mexico. When the Civil War began he was, as the leading Southern statesman since **Calhoun**, the obvious choice as President of the Confederate States.

Although he was headstrong, stubborn and self-righteous, he was also brave, intelligent and capable of inspiring intense devotion in those who knew him well. The South had no one who could have done his job as well. Davis worked unstintingly to preserve the independence of the South, introducing conscription and even suggesting that slaves should be armed to fight the Union armies. He was blamed, often unfairly, for the South's failures against a foe that commanded infinitely more resources than the beleaguered South. When the war was over he was charged with treason and imprisoned for two years, but was never brought to trial.

**Dawes Plan** (1924). A report on **reparations** issued by a commission, whose head was the American banker Charles Dawes. Reparations had been imposed on Germany at the Treaty of **Versailles**. German unwillingness and inability to meet these payments had led to the French and Belgian occupation of the **Ruhr** in 1923. This was followed by massive inflation and economic collapse in Germany. A commission was therefore set up to consider how to balance the German budget, stabilize its currency, fix an achievable level of reparations and make them secure. It recommended stabilization of the currency by creating a new bank of issue, run by a body of whom half would be non-Germans. The new mark would be backed by a foreign loan. The reparation total was unchanged but annual payments were to be made on a sliding scale, which would take into account Germany's ability to pay. Payments were assured by taking over some indirect taxes and bonds for state railways. A Reparations Agency, including Allied representatives, was to be set up to control these arrangements. Germans did not like the Plan because there was some foreign control of their finances and the reparations total was not reduced, but they accepted it, because they wanted backing for their currency and to get the French out of the Ruhr. The Plan had a marked effect on the German economy: loans were easily raised abroad, especially in the USA, the currency was stabilized and unemployment fell, but Germany had become excessively dependent on short-term American loans. By 1929 the German economy was again having problems, so a new commission under another banker, Owen Young (see **Young Plan**), was set up to reconsider reparations.

**D-Day** (6 June 1944). The invasion of France by Allied forces during the **Second World War**. From the beginning of 1944 the Germans knew that there would be an Allied attack on France, but they did not know when or where. **Rommel**, in charge of two German armies in north-west France, thought that it would be 'the most decisive battle of the war which would determine the fate of the German people'. Von Rundstedt, the German Commander West, had 2,000 miles of coast to defend and did not believe that a landing could be prevented. He therefore held strongly only the key ports and kept a powerful mobile reserve, which could move swiftly to counter any invasion. Rommel disagreed with him and said that any invasion would have to be defeated on the beaches, as Allied air forces would disrupt the movement of German reserves: 'The first twenty-four hours will be decisive.' Operation Overlord, the code-name for the invasion, was meticulously planned and involved three million men (one million combat troops, one million in logistical support and another million in the navies and air forces), under the control of General **Eisenhower**. The invasion was preceded by a massive aerial bombardment of German communications by 9,000 aircraft (the *Luftwaffe* had 300 aircraft with which to oppose them). 2,727 ships then sailed to the Normandy coast and on the first day landed 156,000 men on a front of thirty miles. On only one of the five beaches were there considerable difficulties for the Allies (although Caen had not been captured as planned), as von Rundstedt had expected an attack in the Pas de Calais and kept most of his troops there. By 9 June the bridgeheads had been consolidated: the **Normandy Campaign** had begun.

**Deakin, Alfred** (1856–1919). Australian Prime Minister (1903–4, 1905–8, 1909–10). Deakin first entered politics as a member of the Victorian Legislative Assembly (1879–1900), where he was able to apply his ideal of making Australia a place where the poor, sick and old would be protected and all white Australians would have equal rights. In 1896 he was responsible for legislation in Victoria to protect unskilled labourers in sweated industries, an example followed by Winston **Churchill** in Britain in 1909. Deakin was a fervent advocate of federation throughout the 1890s and saw his goal achieved in the **Australian Commonwealth Act** (1900). Elected to the first Commonwealth parliament in 1901, he remained there until 1913, shaping many of the policies of the new federation: social welfare, protection of domestic industry and support for a **White Australia policy**. As Prime Minister he increased tariffs in 1908 but linked this to his idea of New Protection: if Old Protection imposed tariffs in the interests of manufacturers, the New Protection should reciprocate by providing 'fair and reasonable' wages for employees. In the same year he introduced old-age pensions and sickness benefits. Deakin had relied on the support of the **Labor Party** to continue in office and when this was withdrawn in 1908 he fused his followers with others to form the Liberal Party. New Protection was declared unconstitutional by the Federal High Court after Deakin's third government had been defeated by Labor in 1910: he then led the opposition until 1913.

**Decembrist Conspiracy** (1825). During the **Napoleonic Wars** a large number of Russian nobles saw the West for the first time, as army officers. 'The campaigns of 1812–14', wrote Prince Volkonsky, 'brought Europe nearer to us, made us familiar with its forms of state, its public institutions, the rights of its people. By contrast with our own state of life, the laughably limited rights which our people possessed, the despotism of our regime first became truly present in our hearts and understanding.' All could see how far Russia was behind the West, economically and educationally. Secret societies were formed and by 1825 there were two main ones: northern and southern. The northern society wanted a Constitution like that of the United States, with the Tsar having similar powers to those of the US President. The southern society was more radical and wanted to replace the monarchy by a republic, after assassinating the imperial family. Both societies wanted to end **serfdom** and to introduce Western reforms, such as equality before the law and trial by jury. All the conspirators were gentry, who aimed at a palace revolution rather than a popular rising. They intended to stage a *coup* in 1826 but had to bring forward the date to December 1825 (hence they were later called Decembrists), owing to the death of **Alexander I**. Disorganized, they made no real preparations for a rising, but on 13 December decided to act when they found that they would be required to take an oath of allegiance to the new Tsar, **Nicholas I**, the next day. The rising collapsed because the nerve of the plotters failed. Some defected and when rebel and loyal troops faced each other in St Petersburg, no one fired. As a result of the investigations which followed, five were condemned to death and over 100 exiled to Siberia. The conspiracy had a traumatic effect on Nicholas, who never forgot that the rebels came from the ruling class whose loyalty had hitherto been unquestioned. As there was now no one he could trust, repression was intensified, though this further alienated the educated minority and encouraged some of them to take the path of revolution.

**Dechristianization.** An attack on the Catholic Church during the **French Revolution**. Non-juring priests, who refused to take the oath accepting the **Civil Constitution of the Clergy**, had been persecuted since 1790 but the main onslaught on the Church came in 1793, as priests were identified with royalism and with the **Federal Revolt**. The **Convention** introduced a new calendar, dated from 22 September 1792 (when the Republic was proclaimed), to replace the Christian calendar, so the period from 22 September 1792 to 21 September 1793 became year 1. The year was divided into twelve months of thirty days, with five supplementary days. Each month was given a new name appropriate to its season: thus Vendémiaire (the month of vintage) ran from 22 September to 21 October. The new calendar ignored Sundays and festivals of the Church. The main impulse for dechristianization came from the *sans-culottes* in the Paris Commune and the *armées révolutionnaires* and took many forms. Church bells and silver were removed, most churches in France were closed (the cathedral of Notre Dame in Paris became a Temple of Reason) and some priests were forced to marry. For many ordinary people outside the civil war zones, dechristianization was the aspect of the **Terror** which most affected them.

**Declaration of the Rights of Man** (August 1789) was passed by the French **Constituent Assembly** to lay down the principles on which a Constitution (finally passed in 1791) should be based. Its ideas derive from John Locke's *Second Treatise of Government* (1690), with its stress on natural rights, religious toleration and civil equality, and from the French Enlightenment. It declared that 'men are born free and equal in their rights' and that 'the natural and imprescriptible rights of man . . . are those of liberty, property, security and resistance to oppression'. Freedom of thought and expression was affirmed and no one was to be imprisoned without trial. Taxation was to be 'borne equally by all citizens in proportion to their means'. One of its most momentous statements, which disposed of the Divine Right of Kings, was that 'sovereignty resides in the nation'. The Declaration's principles could be applied throughout the world and have become the basis of Constitutions in many countries, including France's Fifth Republic. **Louis XVI** refused to accept the Declaration until he was forced to do so by popular pressure in the **October Days**.

**Delcassé, Théophile** (1852–1923). French Foreign Minister (1898–1905, 1914–15). A radical republican, Delcassé was determined on *revanche* (revenge) for the loss of **Alsace-Lorraine** in the **Franco-Prussian War** (1870–71). He became an ardent colonialist, supporting the acquisition of Tunisia (1881) and Indo-China, and in 1887 advocated a **Franco-Russian Alliance** to keep in check both Germany and Britain, France's main colonial rival. In 1889 he entered parliament, becoming Colonial Minister in 1893. Delcassé backed the journey of Marchand from the French Congo to the Nile and was Foreign Minister by the time Marchand confronted **Kitchener** at **Fashoda**. Faced with British military superiority in the Sudan, anxious to avoid war with Britain and convinced that Germany was the real enemy, Delcassé ordered Marchand to withdraw. This humiliation increased the Anglophobia which had been prevalent in France since Britain's occupation of Egypt (1882) and which found expression in French hostility during the **South African War** (1899–1902). Britain's isolation in that war convinced her that she needed friendly relations with France, which Delcassé did much to encourage, so that the **Anglo-French Entente** was signed in 1904. German attempts to break it up in the first **Moroccan crisis** (1905–6) brought Delcassé's fall: he had opposed a German request for an international conference on Morocco, so the German government demanded and obtained his resignation. This concealed Delcassé's success – when the conference was held at Algeciras, Britain supported France and the Entente was strengthened.

Another triumph for Delcassé was his bringing about a *rapprochement* with Italy. Franco-Italian relations had been poor since France made Tunisia a Protectorate in 1881 and Italy joined the **Triple Alliance** with Germany and Austria in 1882. The way was open for better relations after Italy's defeat by Ethiopia at **Aduwa** (1896) and the fall of the anti-French **Crispi**. Delcassé seized his opportunity, arranged a commercial treaty with Italy in 1898 and two years later made a secret agreement, by which Italy recognized French claims in Morocco in return for Italy being given a free hand in Tripolitania (Libya). When the Triple Alliance was renewed in 1902, Italy privately assured France that she would not take part in any aggressive war against her. Delcassé played an important part, therefore, in ensuring that Britain would enter the **First World War** as an ally of France and that Italy would be a friendly neutral. He later held various posts: Minister of the Navy (1911–13), when he arranged for cooperation with the British navy if war came; ambassador to Russia; Minister of War and Foreign Minister (1914–15). In this office he helped to negotiate the Treaty of **London** (1915), which brought Italy into the war on the Allied side.

**Democratic Party.** One of the two major political parties in the USA. The name goes back to 1792, when **Jefferson** and **Madison** founded the Democratic-Republican Party, which adopted its present name in the 1830s during the presidency of Andrew **Jackson**. The Democrats stood for states' rights and a weak federal government and were free traders opposed to high tariffs. Their support came from the 'solid South' and from those who were not well off: small farmers, urban labourers and immigrants, especially Irish Catholics. The Democratic Party held the presidency for all but eight years between 1828 and 1860, but split over slavery when the North and South wings of the party put forward different candidates in the presidential election of 1860. This let in Abraham **Lincoln**, the **Republican Party**'s first President. As most Confederate leaders were Democrats (see **Confederate States of America**), the Republicans appeared as the party of Union. The Democrat Andrew **Johnson** was selected as Lincoln's Vice-President in order to unite the nation, and became President (1865–9) when Lincoln was assassinated, but no Democrat was elected as President between 1865 and 1884. The Democrat Grover Cleveland was elected President in 1885 and again in 1893, though his policies differed little from those of his Republican predecessors.

Early in the twentieth century the Democrats adopted many policies of the **Progressive Movement**, such as lower tariffs and tougher anti-trust laws. Aided by a split between Theodore **Roosevelt** and **Taft** in the Republican Party, the Democrat Woodrow **Wilson** was elected President in 1912 and again in 1916. However, he failed to persuade Congress to join the **League of Nations**, and as Americans returned to **isolationism** again after the **First World War**, the Republicans once more returned to office in 1920. The Democratic Party was divided in the 1920s over **Prohibition** and civil liberties and did not return to power until the **Great Depression**, when many Americans became disillusioned with Herbert **Hoover**'s handling of the economy. The Democrats won control of Congress in 1932 and did not lose it until 1946. Also in 1932 Hoover was crushingly defeated by the Democratic presidential candidate, Franklin D. **Roosevelt**. Democrats had been the party of states' rights; now they became the party of strong federal government, as the **New Deal** sought to attack unemployment and get the economy moving again. Roosevelt's policies persuaded industrial workers, many Western farmers, and for the first time, Negroes, to vote for the Democrats. The **Second World War** enabled Roosevelt to be elected for an unprecedented four terms: Democrats retained the presidency until 1953.

**Derby, Edward George Geoffrey Smith Stanley, 14th. Earl of** (1799–1869). British Prime Minister (1852, 1858–9, 1866–8) and leader of the **Conservative Party** (1846–68). A highly intelligent man, Derby won the Chancellor's Latin-verse prize at Oxford, published a blank verse translation of the *Iliad* and with his enormous talents (he was a great orator) should have made a formidable politician, but he had bouts of indolence and would retire to his estates in Lancashire for weeks on end, shooting pheasants and nursing his gout. He entered the **Commons** in 1820 as a **Whig** and served in the administrations of **Canning**, Goderich and **Grey** from

1827–34. As War and Colonial Secretary (1833–4) Derby was responsible for the abolition of the **slave trade** in the British Empire. In 1834 he resigned, as he disapproved of the government's attack on the Protestant Church of Ireland, and joined the Conservative Party three years later. As Colonial Secretary under **Peel** he ended the **Opium War** with China and a dispute over Maori lands in New Zealand before resigning in 1845, as he opposed the repeal of the **Corn Laws**. This split the Conservative Party and left Derby, who had moved to the **Lords** at his own request in 1844, as leader of the protectionist wing. By the time he became Prime Minister in 1852, in the first of his three minority administrations, he had abandoned protection. Derby's government fell when the budget of his Chancellor of the Exchequer, **Disraeli**, was savaged by **Gladstone**. His second ministry (1858–9), though brief, was more successful: the property qualification for MPs was removed, Jews were admitted to parliament and the administration of India was transferred from the **East India Company** to the Crown. In his last ministry the Reform Act of 1867 doubled the size of the electorate, but a year later Derby resigned owing to ill health, after persuading the Conservatives to accept Disraeli as his successor.

**De Valera, Eamon** (1882–1975). Irish statesman and revolutionary. Born in New York, the son of a Spanish artist and an Irish mother, de Valera was brought up in Ireland by his grandmother and an uncle. He studied Gaelic, changed his name from Edward to Eamon and joined the Gaelic League (Irish language society). In 1913 he became a member of the paramilitary Irish National Volunteers and commanded one of its battalions in the **Easter Rising** (1916) in Dublin. The last to surrender, he was the only commander to avoid execution, owing to his American birth. After imprisonment, he was elected leader of the **Sinn Fein** Party in October 1917 and in November became President of the Irish Volunteers, so that both the political and military wings of the revolutionary movement were under his control. Arrested in May 1918, he was elected a Sinn Fein MP later that year. Michael **Collins** arranged his escape from Lincoln jail in February 1919, and in April de Valera became President of the Dail (Irish Assembly) set up by the seventy-three Sinn Fein MPs who refused to take their seats in the British parliament. In May 1919 he went to the USA to seek money and support and did not return until December 1920, so he was away for most of the **Anglo-Irish War** (1919–21). De Valera refused to accept the **Anglo-Irish Treaty**, which established the Irish Free State, as it required an oath of loyalty to the British Crown. When the Dail narrowly approved it, he resigned as President and fought against the provisional government in the **Irish Civil War** (1922–3). Defeated in the war, he formed his own party, **Fianna Fail**, in 1926, taking most Sinn Fein supporters with him.

In the 1932 election Fianna Fail became the largest party, so de Valera became head of the Irish government, a position he held continuously until 1948. His primary aim was to weaken the links with Britain and to get rid of the limitations to Irish sovereignty imposed by the Anglo-Irish Treaty. He began by removing the oath of allegiance to the Crown and refused to make payments to Britain for annuities collected under the **Irish Land Acts**. The British government responded by imposing tariffs on Irish goods entering Britain. The economic war hit both countries badly, as 96 per cent of Irish exports went to Britain. The 1937 Irish constitution effectively made Ireland a republic: the name Irish Free State was replaced by Ireland (Eire); the Crown had no role in internal Irish affairs but was merely a symbol of 'association' with the British Commonwealth; and the 'special position' of the Catholic Church was recognized, though it was not made the State Church. Strong Catholic influence was evident in that divorce was prohibited and working mothers denounced. The Constitution claimed to apply to the whole of Ireland 'pending the reintegration of the national territory' but did much to ensure that partition remained, as it reinforced fears in Ulster of Catholic domination. De Valera was an enthusiastic supporter of the **League of Nations** and in 1938 became its President. He brought the trade war to an end in 1938 by paying a lump sum to end the Land Act payments. He also secured the withdrawal of the British navy from the 'treaty ports', which he later regarded as his greatest achievement as it enabled Ireland to remain neutral during the **Second World War**.

**Díaz, Porfirio** (1830–1915). Mexican *caudillo* and President (1876–80, 1884–1911). A *mestizo* (of mixed race) from a poor family, Díaz joined the army, became a general and fought with distinction against the French forces of **Napoleon III**, playing a major role in the capture of Mexico City. This made him a national hero, though he twice failed to be elected President. He came to power in a *coup* in 1876 and ruled for the next thirty-four years, providing a stability unknown in Mexico (in the previous half-century governments had lasted on average for less than a year). He kept himself in power by a mixture of corruption and force. Army generals and regional *caudillos* were showered with honours and gifts; he appointed all public officials, rigged elections and eliminated all opposition. Díaz had the support of the Catholic Church, as he allowed it to regain much of the wealth and influence it had lost in preceding decades (see **Juárez**). The *hacendados* (great estate owners) also backed Díaz because he allowed them to take over most of the Indian communal lands and his *rurales* (mounted police) helped to eliminate banditry in the countryside. He revived Mexico's flagging economy by attracting foreign investment and by modifying Mexican laws in favour of foreigners. Large concessions were made to British and American oil companies to exploit the recently discovered oil, so that production rose from 10,000 barrels in 1901 to thirteen million in 1911 and Mexico became a leading exporter. Foreigners dominated the economy: US and British investors owned the oilfields, mines and public utilities, and US citizens bought millions of acres of land in the north, thus arousing violent xenophobia. A railway boom (640 kms of track in 1876 grew to 20,000 kms in 1910) opened up the country, enabling mining production of silver, gold, copper, zinc and lead to increase dramatically. Cash crops for export (sisal, sugar, coffee) stimulated agriculture and there was a long period of economic prosperity in the *Porfiriato*. Yet this affluence benefited mainly a small minority: most peasants owned no land and were in debt peonage. The survival of Díaz's dictatorship depended on a flourishing economy. A recession, beginning in 1907, led to inflation, falling wages, unemployment and major strikes, which were put down with great brutality, at least 200 strikers being killed by troops. The growing opposition finally erupted in the **Mexican Revolution** of 1910. Díaz resigned in 1911 and went into exile in France, where he died.

**Diet.** The name for the representative assembly of various countries. The **German Confederation** had a Diet, as had Prussia and different parts of the **Austrian Empire**, the Scandinavian countries and Japan.

**Directory** (1795–9). The government of France in the later stages of the **French Revolution**. The Directory was a product of the Constitution of 1795, drawn up by the **Convention**. This rigidly separated the legislative councils from the executive, the Directory. The five Directors faced a daunting task as the treasury was empty, paper money almost worthless, yet the **French Revolutionary Wars** had to be paid for. Most of the French did not expect the Directory to last more than a few months, yet it survived longer than any of the other revolutionary regimes. This was partly because its opponents were discredited: few wanted a return of **Jacobin**-led **Terror** and the royalists were divided amongst themselves. Public apathy also helped the Directory to survive: after six years of revolution and three years of war, revolutionary fervour had all but disappeared. The army supported the Directory, as a royalist restoration would mean an end to the war and therefore the end of opportunities for promotion and plunder. It was the army above all which enabled the Directory to overcome all challenges to its authority, as it did by the *coup d'état* of Fructidor (1797), when it purged the Councils of monarchists. The Directory's unpopularity grew as the military situation deteriorated in 1799 and as emergency measures were passed, including renewed conscription and a forced loan on the rich. Government administration in the provinces collapsed, which led to brigandage in many areas. **Sieyès**, one of the Directors, decided that the Executive should be strengthened, so he plotted with **Napoleon** to bring about the *coup d'état* of **Brumaire**, which abolished the Directory and ended the French Revolution.

**Disraeli, Benjamin, 1st Earl of Beaconsfield** (1804–81). British Prime Minister (1868, 1874–80). The son of a Jewish author, Disraeli was baptized a Christian and this enabled him to become an MP in 1837 (Jews at that time were not allowed to hold public office or to become Members of Parliament). In his *Vindication of the English Constitution* (1835) he defended the existing social order in which the aristocracy ruled owing to their wealth, leisure and education, though they had duties to their social inferiors. He wanted to strengthen the traditional institutions of the monarchy, Church of England and House of **Lords**. Rejecting abstract principles, he saw society as organic, growing stronger over the centuries by adapting to changing circumstances. According to **Derby**, he had an 'odd dislike of middle-class men'. Disraeli first made his mark as a brilliant orator in his opposition to **Peel**'s repeal of the **Corn Laws** in 1846, when he articulated the sense of betrayal felt by many Tory MPs. This conflict split the **Conservative Party** and was to leave them in opposition for a generation, except for the minority governments of 1852, 1858–9 and 1866–8. Disraeli became Conservative leader in the House of **Commons** in 1851 and Chancellor of the Exchequer in 1852, when his budget to help the landed interest by tax reductions was savaged by **Gladstone**. Not until 1867 was Disraeli able to take the initiative away from the **Liberal Party** by introducing a Reform Bill (see **Parliamentary reform**), which greatly increased the number of working-class voters in the boroughs whilst strengthening Conservative influence in the counties.

When Derby retired owing to ill health in 1868, Disraeli became leader of the Conservative Party and Prime Minister (for six months) but did not become head of a majority Conservative administration until 1874, by which time he was old and tired. His reputation as a social reformer went back to his novels of the 1840s, particularly *Sybil* (1845), in which he had written of the 'Two Nations', the rich and the poor, and put forward the ideal of 'One Nation', in which the interests of all would be looked after. The large number of measures in the first two years of his ministry seemed to endorse this: eleven Acts were passed concerning licensing laws, hours of work in factories, **trade unions**, workers' dwellings, education, public health, food adulteration, river pollution and merchant shipping. However, most of these measures were either inherited from the previous administration or were the work of ministers in which Disraeli took little interest, and nearly all were hedged around with restrictions or were not compulsory, so they had little effect. The Artisans' Dwellings Act, for example, enabled urban local authorities to buy slum housing and arrange for the building of better working-class accommodation, but since this would have meant an increase in rates, few authorities were willing to contemplate it. The measures which Disraeli did fully support (against much Cabinet opposition) and which were the most successful concerned labour legislation. Trade unions could no longer be prosecuted for conspiracy or for peaceful picketing and the penalties for workers breaking their contract were limited to civil damages.

Disraeli also gained an undeserved reputation as an imperialist who wished to expand the British Empire in order to increase national prestige, whereas in fact he had little interest in colonial policy and administration. He became involved reluctantly in the **Zulu Wars** on account of the activities of the British High Commissioner in South Africa, Sir Bartle Frere, and was remembered for the humiliating British defeat at Isandhlwana in 1879: troops had to be sent out at great expense before the war was won. An equally futile **Anglo-Afghan War** was fought from 1878–80, begun by the Viceroy of India, Lord Lytton, on his own initiative. Disraeli's main imperial success came in 1875 when he bought the shares of **Ismail**, Khedive of Egypt, in the **Suez Canal**, thus preventing France gaining control of the shortest route to India. In 1877 he made Queen **Victoria** Empress of India, an event celebrated in a great *darbar* in Delhi. His last great success in foreign policy was at the **Berlin Congress** (1878), which Disraeli attended and where he followed **Palmerston**'s policy of propping up the **Ottoman Empire** and keeping Russian influence out of the Mediterranean. His 'Peace with Honour' also obtained for Britain a valuable base in the eastern Mediterranean, Cyprus. Disraeli lost the 1880 election as a result of the deepening depression and the increased taxation needed to pay for the African and Afghan wars. By this time he was worn out and died a year later.

After his death Disraeli became a cult figure and the myth arose that he was the founder of **Tory Democracy**, making the Conservative Party the 'natural' party of government as it stood for 'One Nation', in which aristocratic leadership would best safeguard the interests of the people as a whole.

**Doenitz, Karl** (1891–1980). German Grand Admiral. Doenitz served in the **First World War** with the German U-boat fleet from 1916–18 and was captured when his submarine was sunk. In 1935, when **Hitler** had decided to ignore the Treaty of **Versailles** which forbade Germany to have any submarines, Doenitz was appointed to build up and command the new U-boat fleet. During the **Second World War** he played a vital role in the battle of the **Atlantic**, when his submarines came close to winning the war for Germany: they sank fifteen million tons of Allied shipping and brought Britain to the verge of starvation. He conceived the idea of wolf-packs, which for a time decimated convoys to Britain, but by 1943 he was losing submarines faster than they could be replaced. In January 1943, when Hitler ordered that the German navy's shipbuilding programme should concentrate on submarines, Raeder resigned and Doenitz became the Supreme Commander of the German navy. One of the few among the highest officers of the German navy convinced by **Nazism**, Doenitz was chosen by Hitler in his last will to succeed him as Reich President. Doenitz, to his surprise, was tried at Nuremberg for war crimes and was sentenced to ten years' imprisonment, which he served in full.

**Dollar diplomacy.** The use of US investments abroad to extend American influence. The phrase derived from a speech by President William Howard **Taft** to Congress in 1912, in which he described his foreign policy as 'substituting dollars for bullets'. The basis for this policy was laid by President Theodore **Roosevelt**. When the Dominican Republic defaulted on its debts to European investors, the investors demanded action by their governments. To avoid this, Roosevelt issued his Corollary to the **Monroe Doctrine** in 1904: as this doctrine prevented European powers intervening in the Caribbean, the USA must act as policeman there. 'Chronic wrong-doing or impotence', he said, 'may force the US . . . to the exercise of an international police power.' Roosevelt first applied this doctrine in 1905 when the Dominican Republic agreed to American financial control so it could pay off its debt. Taft went further. He put pressure on Caribbean republics to replace their European investments with American ones. In 1909 US bankers, with the encouragement of the State Department, took control of Nicaragua's finances. When a revolution broke out there in 1912 against the pro-American government and US investments were in danger, Taft sent in the Marines to crush it. His policy was criticized at home and abroad as a form of **imperialism**. It was rejected by President Woodrow **Wilson**, although interference to support American business interests continued to be a feature of US policy in Latin America.

**Dollfuss, Engelbert** (1892–1934). Austrian Chancellor (1932–4). Under five feet in height, the illegitimate son of a farmer's daughter, Dollfuss received eight awards for bravery on the Italian front during the **First World War**. A devout Catholic, he became leader of the Christian Social Party and Chancellor in 1932. The Social Democrats and National Socialists called for new elections, as the Christian Socials with their allies had a majority of only one. Rather than risk defeat in an election, in March 1933 Dollfuss ended parliamentary government and took full authority for himself. In the same month he turned against the socialists, the strongest party in Austria, and outlawed their paramilitary force, the *Schutzbund*, which went underground. In May the Communist Party was banned, and a month later the **Nazi Party**, which wanted union with Germany, was also banned. Detention camps were set up for all his opponents. Dollfuss was able to stay in power only because he had the support of the army, the police and *Heimwehr* (civilian militia) at home and of **Mussolini** abroad, but Mussolini demanded changes on Fascist lines (see **Fascism**) and the suppression of the socialists. *Schutzbund* leaders were arrested, so in February 1934 it took up arms and called a general strike. This was a miserable failure, as most workers ignored the call. There was fighting in Vienna, Graz and Linz, but after four days *Schutzbund* forces were defeated by the army. The Socialist Party was outlawed, socialist property confiscated and socialist trade unions dissolved. In May Dollfuss issued a new Constitution 'for a Christian, German, federal state on a corporate basis' (see **Corporate State**). Political parties were replaced by professional organizations (corporations), which were to advise in preparing legislation. Dollfuss did not long survive his Constitution. The Austrian Nazis, without the knowledge of **Hitler**, planned to seize control of the government and install a Nazi regime. They staged a *coup* on 25 July 1934, which failed as the government was forewarned and dispersed. The revolt was crushed by the army, but not before Dollfuss had been captured and shot by the rebels.

**Dominions.** The name used for countries in the British Empire which had some degree of self-government but still owed allegiance to the British Crown. Canada was the first country to be called a dominion (1867), followed by Australia, New Zealand, South Africa and, in 1921, the Irish Free State. Their independence was recognized at the Imperial Conference (1926) and their power to pass laws independently of the British government was confirmed by the Statute of **Westminster** (1931).

**Douglas, Stephen Arnold** (1813–61). American politician. Douglas, the popular 'little giant', was a **Democratic** Senator from Illinois from 1847 until his death. He became the leading spokesman for **Westward expansion**, a cause he was able to promote as chairman of the Senate Committee on Territories. A divisive issue was the expansion of slavery to new lands in the West. Douglas sought to avoid a conflict and tried to find a solution which would satisfy both the pro-slavery South and the anti-slavery North. He piloted the **Compromise of 1850** through Congress but this pleased neither side. In 1854 he drafted the **Kansas–Nebraska Act**, which he hoped would solve the problem of slavery by allowing whites in each territory to decide whether they wanted slavery or not. This he called 'popular sovereignty' but it failed to take into account the feelings of those who regarded slavery as a moral outrage. Douglas was appalled by the violence in Kansas which followed the passing of the Act. He constantly strove for reconciliation between North and South, as in his famous debates with Abraham **Lincoln** when both were standing in 1858 for election to the Senate. Douglas won this election but failed in the presidential election of 1860. Though Lincoln became President, Douglas's popular vote was only half a million less than Lincoln's. Douglas worked hard to avoid secession and civil war, but when they came he supported the Union and Lincoln, asking 'every American citizen to rally around the flag of his country'.

**Dowding, Hugh Caswell Tremenheere, 1st Baron** (1882–1970). British air chief marshal. Austere, humourless and a difficult colleague (known as 'Stuffy'), Dowding served as a pilot in the Royal Flying Corps in the **First World War**. In 1930 he became Air Member for Supply and Research in the Air Council and so was responsible for the development of aircraft with which the

RAF fought the **Second World War**. He disagreed with **Baldwin**'s view that 'the bombers will always get through' and thought that fighters could provide an effective defence. Responsible for building monoplanes such as the Hurricane and Spitfire, with eight-gun armaments and a much-improved Rolls-Royce Merlin engine, Dowding also understood the importance of radar. In 1936 he became Commander-in-Chief Fighter Command and fought hard for fighters to be given priority in aircraft construction. By 1940, owing to Dowding, Britain had a fighter force with an early warning radar system, and a sophisticated system of ground control. After the German invasion of France in 1940, Dowding was adamant that the RAF should retain sufficient fighters in Britain to defend her in case of German attack, though Churchill wished to send more fighters to help the French. This decision was of enormous importance and probably enabled Britain to win, narrowly, the battle of **Britain**. During this battle Dowding's tactics were to scramble fighters and attack German bombers before they could destroy his bases in Kent, as he knew that if Fighter Command had to move north of the Thames, a German invasion of the south coast was possible. Exhausted, he was replaced as head of Fighter Command in November 1940 and retired in 1942.

**Dreadnought.** A class of battleship named after HMS *Dreadnought* (1906), which was planned by Admiral Sir John **Fisher**. He used ideas of the Italian designer Cuniberti to build a ship which, at twenty-one knots, was faster than its rivals and could also outgun them. The Dreadnought used oil-fired turbines, faster and more reliable than coal-burners, and mounted ten twelve-inch guns instead of the usual four. A fleet of Dreadnoughts could defeat a fleet three times its own size, and made all other warships obsolete. This aided Germany, as Britain's overwhelming superiority in battleships was now useless, and gave the Germans a chance to compete on equal terms with the construction of new ships. The naval race was therefore intensified, with the Conservative opposition and much of the press in England demanding, with the slogan 'We want eight and we won't wait', that two Dreadnoughts be built for every German one (Germany was building four a year at the time). These ships were very expensive, so Britain twice suggested naval reductions, but Germany would agree only if Britain allied with Germany or promised that she would be neutral in the event of a war. Britain, however, would not abandon the Entente, so the naval race continued. When war began, Britain had forty-two ships of the Dreadnought class, Germany twenty-nine. The only time both fleets clashed during the war was at the battle of **Jutland** in May 1916.

**Dred Scott case** (1857). This case, brought before the US **Supreme Court**, was designed to test whether the laws regulating slavery in the states were constitutional. Dred Scott was an illiterate Missouri slave who was taken by his owner, an army surgeon, first to Illinois, a free state, and then to Minnesota, where slavery had been forbidden by the **Missouri Compromise** of 1820. Supported by **abolitionists**, Scott sued for his freedom on the grounds that residence on free soil automatically made him a free man. When the case of *Dred Scott* v. *Sandford* came before the Supreme Court a majority of the judges supported Chief Justice Taney, who said that the framers of the Constitution had regarded Negroes 'as beings of an inferior order . . . who had no rights which every white man was bound to respect'. Negroes could not be citizens of any state, slave or free, so Dred Scott could not sue in a federal court. Slaves were property and the fifth amendment to the Constitution guaranteed that **Congress** could not deprive a person of his property 'without due process of law'. Consequently, Congress had no right to pass a law forbidding slavery in any territory, so the Missouri Compromise was unconstitutional. This decision created a furore: it was greeted with joy in the South, with dismay and hatred in the North.

*Dreikaiserbund* (Three Emperors' League) (1873). After France's defeat in the **Franco-Prussian War** (1870–71) and the formation of the **German Empire**, **Bismarck** wanted to keep France isolated, as he feared she would seek a war of revenge to recover **Alsace-Lorraine**. He also wanted to prevent Austria-Hungary and Russia clashing in the Balkans, as this might lead to either country seeking an ally in France. The *Dreikaiserbund* was a vague agreement between Germany, Austria-Hungary and Russia to consult on matters of common interest and was not a formal alliance. Its weakness was shown in the 'War in Sight?' crisis of 1875, when **Alexander II** warned Germany not to go to war with France. It effectively came to an end with Austria-Hungary's alarm at Russia's gains at the Treaty of **San Stefano**, which ended the **Russo-Turkish War** of 1877–8. Austria-Hungary, with Britain, compelled Russia to modify the treaty at the **Berlin Congress** (1878).

After the assassination of Alexander II in 1881 Russia wanted to escape from her diplomatic isolation, and Bismarck wanted to reassure Russia, after Germany's **Dual Alliance** with Austria-Hungary (1879). Russia, Germany and Austria-Hungary therefore made the more formal but secret Three Emperors' Alliance, which was much more precise than the *Dreikaiserbund*. All agreed that if any of the three powers was at war with a fourth power, the others would remain neutral. In practice, this meant that Russia would be neutral in case of a Franco-German war and Germany would be neutral if there were a Russo-British war. The three powers also agreed not to permit change in the Balkans, except by mutual agreement. Bismarck hoped to prevent conflict there between Russia and Austria-Hungary by dividing it into spheres of influence: Russian in the east, Austrian in the west.

Germany and Austria-Hungary therefore agreed not to oppose the union of Eastern Rumelia and Bulgaria (a union which had been rejected at the Congress of Berlin) and Russia recognized Austria-Hungary's right to annex Bosnia and Hercegovina. The Three Emperors' Alliance was a triumph for Bismarck, as France's isolation was confirmed and Austria-Hungary and Russia appeared to have a *modus vivendi* in the Balkans. Yet the Alliance lasted for only six years – in 1887 Austria refused to renew it, owing to the **Bulgarian crisis** of 1885–8. Bismarck then had to resort to the **Reinsurance Treaty** (1887) to keep Russia out of the arms of France.

**Dreyfus case** (1894–1906). Alfred Dreyfus (1859–1935), a Jewish officer in the French army, was accused in 1894 of passing military secrets to Germany which were apparently written in his handwriting. He was condemned by court martial to life imprisonment on Devil's Island, French Guiana. When the new head of the army intelligence service, Colonel Picquart, found in 1896 that the real traitor was a Major Esterhazy, Picquart was promptly transferred to Tunisia. At the end of 1897, when Esterhazy was tried and acquitted, the Prime Minister Méline declared that 'there is no Dreyfus affair'. However, in January 1898 Emile Zola wrote an open letter, '*J'accuse*', in a newspaper run by **Clemenceau**, in which he accused the army of an anti-Semitic conspiracy to prevent justice (see **Anti-Semitism**). This forced the government to prosecute Zola and brought the details of the case to public notice. Zola, sentenced to a year's imprisonment, fled to England. The government still refused to reopen the case as documents, which appeared to prove his guilt, had been added to Dreyfus's file. When the additions were revealed as forgeries in August 1898, their author, Major Henry, committed suicide. A retrial was ordered in 1898; a military court again found Dreyfus guilty but with 'extenuating circumstances'. He was almost immediately pardoned by the President of the **Third Republic**, but not until 1906 was he declared innocent and reinstated in the army. *L'affaire*, as the case was known in France, could not be ignored by the general public, most of whom were convinced of Dreyfus's guilt. Only seven of the fifty-five daily newspapers in France were in favour of Dreyfus but the case split educated opinion. Some Catholic newspapers were violently anti-Semitic, as were nationalists and monarchists, who believed there was an international syndicate of Jews, Protestants and Freemasons, which was determined to discredit the army. The **Right** saw its anti-Dreyfus campaign as a patriotic defence of the nation, of authority and of legal decisions. The **Left** believed that the Catholic Church and army (many officers were Catholics and royalists) were conspiring to destroy the Republic, and that injustice was being tolerated so that the honour of the army would not be questioned. The strength of conservative opinion shocked the Radicals and revived **anti-clericalism**, which resulted in the Roman Catholic Church being disestablished in 1905. *L'affaire* marked the end of the cooperation of conservatives and moderate republicans in the 1890s and of the *Ralliement* and led to the **Opportunist Republic** being replaced in 1899 by the **Radical Republic**.

**Dual Alliance** (1879). A secret defence alliance between Germany and Austria-Hungary, which stated that they would help each other if either was attacked by Russia, and would be neutral if either was attacked by any other power. After the **Berlin Congress** there was a possibility that Germany would be isolated: France was hostile, as she wanted to recover **Alsace-Lorraine**; many Austrians resented Austria-Hungary's exclusion from Germany after the **Austro-Prussian War**; and **Alexander II** of Russia complained bitterly that **Bismarck** had abandoned Russia at the Berlin Congress. Bismarck feared an Austro–French–Russian Alliance. 'We,' he wrote in 1879, 'situated in the centre of Europe, must not be exposed to isolation.' An alliance with Austria-Hungary, with whom Germany had common ties of kinship and language, would prevent this and would also preserve peace, as Russia would not attack the two empires. Bismarck did not intend the alliance to be anti-Russian but he was taking a gamble. Its contents were not fully known, though other powers knew there was an alliance and this might have driven Russia, in self-defence, into the arms of France. **William I**, the German Emperor, regarded the alliance as anti-Russian and Bismarck had to force his acceptance by threatening to resign. The Dual Alliance became the cornerstone of German foreign policy and lasted until 1918. Bismarck sought to placate Russia by making the Three Emperors' League (see *Dreikaiserbund*) in 1881.

**Dual Monarchy,** see **Austro-Hungarian Empire**

**Du Bois, William Edward Burghardt** (1868–1963). Black scholar and civil-rights leader in the USA. Du Bois studied at Harvard and Berlin before becoming a professor of economics, history and sociology at Atlanta University. He spent his whole life fighting for Negro rights and was the main opponent of Booker T. **Washington**, whose politics, Du Bois said, would lead to 'humiliation and inferiority' for Negroes. In 1905 he and others founded the Niagara Movement, which demanded for the Negro 'every single right that belongs to a freeborn American, political, civil and social'. He also helped to found the National Association for the Advancement of Colored Peoples in 1909. This was the most important of the black pressure groups which fought in the courts for Negro rights, with only limited success, between the wars. Disillusioned with the slow improvement in the Negroes' position Du Bois joined the US Communist Party in 1961. In 1962 he renounced his American citizenship and settled in Ghana, where he died a year later. He was the author of several important works of history, including *Black Reconstruction* and *The Souls of Black Folk*.

**Duma.** Russian parliament, which **Nicholas II** had to concede owing to the **Russian Revolution** of 1905. The franchise was restricted by property qualifications, so that landowners were over-represented, peasants under-represented. Most urban workers had no vote. The powers of the Duma, elected for five years, were limited by the **Fundamental Laws**. All laws required the Duma's consent but it controlled only part of the budget, excluding the expenditure of the Court and the armed forces and the state debt. The first Duma (April–July 1906) was almost solidly opposed to the government, so was dissolved by the Tsar after only two months. The second Duma (February–June 1907) fared little better, so **Stolypin** produced a new electoral law, which increased the representation of landowners. This had the desired effect of producing a right-wing majority, so the third Duma (1907–12) lasted its full five years. The fourth Duma (1914–17) was also conservative, though the Tsar treated it with contempt and put no important legislation before it. He even contemplated getting rid of its legislative powers, but his ministers drew back from this step as it might start a new revolution. The Duma was weak because the Duma parties, the **Kadets** and the Octobrists, would not work together. They had no effective organization nationally and in practice they were confined to the educated classes of St Petersburg and Moscow. They had no links with the peasantry or working class and avoided economic and social reform, owing to their fear of anarchy. When war began the government intended to wage it without consulting the Duma at all. The Duma met only once between August 1914 and August 1915. All parties formed a **Progressive Bloc** in 1915 but the Tsar ignored it. The deputies in the Duma were helpless: they refused to take their case to the country, as this might start a revolution. The politicians played no part in bringing about the **February Revolution** of 1917 and simply reacted to events. As the Tsar's government collapsed, a Duma Committee set up a **Provisional Government** on 2 March.

**Dunkirk, evacuation of** (27 May–4 June 1940). The surrender of the Belgian army and the advance of German Panzers to the French coast (see fall of **France**) cut off the British Expeditionary Force (BEF) in northern France from the main French armies further south. On 26 May the British government gave the order for the BEF to be brought home. It had been helped, unintentionally, by von Rundstedt, the German Commander, who halted the advance of his Panzers on 23 May to allow his infantry to catch up and to preserve his armour for the conquest of the rest of France. The Germans, overconfident, believed that the *Luftwaffe* could prevent any evacuation from Dunkirk. **Hitler** approved and ordered the Panzer attacks to be resumed only on 27 May. In spite of this valuable respite Churchill thought that only 50,000 troops could be evacuated; 100,000 would be a miracle. 765 British ships went to Dunkirk, two-thirds of them civilian boats, and took off from the beaches and the harbour 338,000 men, of whom 140,000 were French. The French had ordered their troops to leave only on the fifth day of the evacuation, so the rearguard action, which prevented the Allied force from being wiped out, was mainly French in its later stages. Although the BEF had left all its equipment behind, the evacuation strengthened Britain's defence against invasion.

**Durham Report** (1839). After the Mackenzie and Papineau rebellions in Canada in 1837–8, John George Lambton, the 1st Earl of Durham, was sent to conduct an investigation into the North American colonies. He had played an important role in passing the 1832 **Reform Act** and had been nicknamed 'Radical Jack'. He arrived at Quebec in 1838 in impressive style: a vain man, the new High Commissioner and Governor of British North America disembarked in full dress uniform, riding a white horse. An enormous amount of silver plate and his race horses followed. Durham showed remarkable insensitivity and racist arrogance in dealing with the French Canadians, who were determined to retain their culture. He decided they should be anglicized. 'The error', he wrote in his Report, 'to which the present contest [between English-speaking and French-speaking Canadians] must be attributed, is the vain endeavour to preserve a French-Canadian nationality in the midst of Anglo-American colonies and states.' The French Canadians were, he wrote, 'an utterly uneducated and inert population . . . destitute of all that can invigorate and elevate a people', and so 'it must henceforth be the first and steady purpose of the British government to establish an English population with English laws and language ... and to trust no one but a decidedly English legislature'. Fortunately, Durham had brought with him leaders of the colonial reform movement, who were convinced that ministers should be responsible to an elected assembly rather than to a British-appointed Governor. The Report made three main proposals: that Upper and Lower Canada should be united; that there should be responsible government in Canada; but that this would be limited by imperial control of trade, foreign policy and defence. The British government was not prepared to go as far as the Report recommended: it accepted union but not responsible government (see **Canada Acts**).

**Dust Bowl.** The area of the Great Plains in the USA ravaged by dust storms in the 1930s. Farming had been depressed ever since the early 1920s, as American farmers had to face competition from Canada, Australia, Argentina and Russia. Conditions became even worse with the **Great Depression**: farm incomes fell by two-thirds between 1929 and 1932. For many who had managed to survive, the dust storms of 1933–6 were the last straw. Overplanting and overgrazing had broken the soil structure of the once-rich grasslands of the Great Plains, and after several years of drought the soil had become powdery. Storms blew away the topsoil, devastating 150,000 square miles in Oklahoma, Arkansas and neighbouring states. Ruined farmers, forced to abandon their homes, piled their families and belongings into ramshackle cars and set off for California; but they were to find no land of plenty there, as John Steinbeck showed in his novel *The Grapes of Wrath*. The US government began a programme of relief and recovery, planting trees to anchor the soil, and by 1941 the Dust Bowl was producing wheat again.

**Eastern Front** (1941–5). When three million German soldiers invaded the Soviet Union in June 1941 in Operation **Barbarossa**, they met Russian armies which were badly led and poorly trained, and had some spectacular successes, in which over four million Russian soldiers were captured or killed. They advanced to Leningrad (see siege of **Leningrad**) and Moscow, but were not able to take either city before the winter set in. In December the Russians under **Zhukov** counter-attacked and pushed the Germans back from Moscow. Their failure there led **Hitler** to replace all his army group commanders and thirty-five generals; Hitler himself became Commander-in-Chief. The Russians went on the attack in May 1942 with an attempt to recapture Kharkov but this was another disaster for the Red Army, as they were surrounded and 250,000 Russian troops were captured. Hitler planned his own offensive in 1942, one prong of which aimed to capture the industrial city and communications centre of Stalingrad on the Volga (see battle of **Stalingrad**), whilst the other advanced into the Caucasus and seized the Russian oilfields; this would knock the Soviet Union out of the war. After conquering the Crimea the main German offensive began on 28 June but, as in 1941, after initial rapid advances neither objective was attained. German troops did not reach the main oilfields, protected by the Caucasus mountains, while a Russian counter-attack at Stalingrad surrounded the German Sixth Army and led to a major defeat for the *Wehrmacht*.

Stalingrad marked the limit of the German advance in the Soviet Union. The Russians had been successful, in spite of losing much of their coal and steel capacity when German troops overran the Ukraine, as by a superhuman effort they had moved over 1,500 factories and one-and-a-half million truckloads of equipment beyond the Volga as the Germans advanced. Only 20 per cent of their weapons were produced in the east in 1941, 75 per cent in 1942. In

1943 Hitler tried to regain the initiative by making his third major offensive, this time against the Russian salient, at the battle of **Kursk**, but this, the biggest tank battle of the war, resulted in another massive German defeat. The German retreat continued, disorganized, as Hitler would not allow the planned retreat his commanders wanted. The Russians recaptured the Ukraine, crossed into Romania and Poland and lifted the siege of Leningrad. By 1944 the Russians had built up a superiority over the Germans of five to one in men, seven to one in aircraft and nine to one in tanks. They were therefore able to begin a carefully planned offensive, which inflicted the biggest defeats of the war on the German army. Employing tactics the Germans had used so successfully in 1941, the Russians surrounded German armies, aided by Hitler's insistence that the *Wehrmacht* should not retreat. Within two weeks of the Soviet offensive beginning on 22 June 1944, three German armies had been encircled and destroyed. The Russians reached the Vistula and the suburbs of Warsaw before they halted in order for supplies to be brought up (see **Warsaw Rising**). Romania surrendered in August and a month later Stalin declared war on Bulgaria and began the conquest of the Balkan states. The Russians took Warsaw in February 1945 and advanced beyond the Oder into Germany. Berlin was surrounded on 25 April and captured on 2 May, after Hitler had committed suicide. Germany surrendered unconditionally on 8 May 1945. The battles on the Eastern Front decided the outcome of the **Second World War**, as the Allies would not have been able to invade France on **D-Day** if most of the German armies had not been occupied in Russia. From 1941–3 the Soviet Union had to cope with the bulk of the German forces and it was there that the decisive battles of the war took place. Without the Soviet victories it is unlikely that Hitler would have been defeated.

**Eastern Question** was concerned with the problems arising from the decline of the **Ottoman Empire** in the nineteenth century. The Great Powers all had different interests in the Empire, which they were determined to preserve. Britain wished to prevent Russian warships gaining access to the Aegean from the Black Sea and managed to do this by making the Anglo-Turkish agreement of 1809, whereby the **Straits** would be closed to warships in peacetime, an agreement adhered to by other powers in the Straits Convention of 1841. She also wished to prevent the Balkan states, which sought their independence, from falling under Russian influence, which seemed probable as many there were Slavs and Orthodox in religion. Britain sought too to keep the short route to India, which involved going overland from Alexandria to the Red Sea or from the **Levant** to the Persian Gulf, in Ottoman (or British) hands. Russia, the only European power who went to war with the Turks in the nineteenth century, was adamant that the Straits, which gave her access to the Aegean and through which she could be attacked, should not be under the control of any other foreign power. Russia also wanted to extend her control in the Caucasus at Turkey's expense and her influence in the Balkans, though she did not usually aim at annexing Turkish territories there, as she knew that this might involve her in war with Austria. Her policy was therefore generally cautious and conservative, as was that of the **Austro-Hungarian Empire**, which sought to maintain the *status quo* in the Balkans. If the Balkan states revolted and became independent, they might encourage the subject nationalities of the Habsburg Empire to seek independence too. 'The end of the Turkish monarchy', wrote Gentz, **Metternich**'s Secretary, in 1815, 'could be survived by the Austrian for but a short time.' France was mainly interested in trade and influence in Egypt (a legacy of **Napoleon Bonaparte**) and the Levant.

Unfortunately for the Great Powers, the Balkan states and Ottoman vassals like **Muhammad Ali** of Egypt were not prepared to play a passive role and created situations which could not be ignored by the powers. The **Greek War of Independence** (1821–32) showed the weakness of the Ottoman Empire, as the Sultan had to ask Muhammad Ali for help and even so was no match for the European states when they joined in and secured Greece's independence. Muhammad Ali's defeat of Turkey and his acquisition of Syria further illustrated the decline of the Ottoman Empire. When the Sultan tried to recover Syria in 1839 he was again soundly defeated by Muhammad Ali; the Ottoman Empire was preserved only by the intervention of Britain and Russia, who insisted that Muhammad Ali should give up Syria. The Eastern Question surfaced again in the **Crimean War** (1854–6). This time Britain and

France came to the Sultan's aid, against what they saw as a Russian threat, and preserved the Empire. The Eastern Question then lay dormant for the next twenty years until, in 1875, there was a rebellion in Bosnia and Hercegovina, which was followed a year later by one in Bulgaria, soon joined by Serbia and Montenegro. Russia entered the war in 1877, having made an agreement with Austria-Hungary that she would not create a large Slav state in the Balkans and that Austria-Hungary would be allowed to occupy Bosnia and Hercegovina, terms which were ignored in the Treaty of **San Stefano**, which followed a Russian victory. Neither Austria-Hungary nor Britain would accept the treaty so, to avoid war, the **Berlin Congress** was called (1878), which greatly reduced Russia's gains and allowed Austria-Hungary to occupy Bosnia and Hercegovina. In doing this, Austria-Hungary was abandoning her traditional policy of preserving the Ottoman Empire. She brought the Eastern Question to the forefront of European politics again when she annexed Bosnia and Hercegovina in 1908, following the **Young Turk** revolution. Italy's occupation of Tripoli in 1911 revealed once again the weakness of the Ottoman Empire and tempted Serbia, Bulgaria, Greece and Montenegro to declare war on Turkey. In the **Balkan Wars** (1912–13) Serbia doubled its size, something which Austria-Hungary could not tolerate, as a powerful Serbia would act as a magnet for Serbs in the Austro-Hungarian Empire. When the heir to the throne of that Empire was assassinated in **Sarajevo**, Bosnia, in June 1914, Austria-Hungary took the opportunity to declare war on Serbia. Thus the Eastern Question helped to bring about the **First World War** which, in turn, ended the Eastern Question, as the Ottoman Empire disintegrated and the Turkey which emerged from the war at the Treaty of **Lausanne** (1923) was confined to Turkish-speaking provinces.

**Easter Rising** (April 1916) took place in Dublin, when 1,600 members of the Irish Republican Brotherhood (IRB), the Irish Volunteers and James Connolly's Citizens Army rose up against British rule. When the **First World War** began in 1914 **Asquith**'s **Home Rule for Ireland** Bill was suspended. This was accepted by John **Redmond**, leader of the Irish Nationalist Party in the **Commons**, and by most of the Irish, as the Irish economy boomed during the war. There were some, however, mainly in the IRB and **Sinn Fein**, who saw Britain's preoccupation with a foreign war as the best time to stage an armed uprising. They tried to get arms from Germany, using Sir Roger **Casement** as their agent, but relied on the Irish National Volunteers, a paramilitary force formed in 1913, for men. Its Chief of Staff was not in favour of a rising and when he found out what was planned he prevented any action outside Dublin. A German ship arrived with arms off the coast of Kerry but was captured by the British, as was Casement, who had been landed from a German submarine. When the IRB military command met on Easter Day, its members decided to carry out the rising on Easter Monday, though they knew that failure was inevitable and that they were likely to be shot. The British were taken completely by surprise when rebels seized the General Post Office, from where Padraic Pearse read a proclamation declaring the existence of a republic. By nightfall nearly all the city centre was in rebel hands, as was a cordon of fortified posts in the suburbs. When the British brought up artillery the rebels' position was hopeless, particularly as their strongholds were isolated from each other. Inaccurate British shelling destroyed much of the city centre; the GPO caught fire on Friday and had to be evacuated. The next day Pearse surrendered unconditionally. 450 people had been killed, 2,614 wounded; 116 soldiers and 16 police also died. The Dublin population had been shocked by the rising and had cheered government troops. All this changed when the government court martialled the rebel leaders and between 3 and 12 May executed fifteen of them, including Pearse and Connolly, an act which George Bernard Shaw described as 'canonizing their prisoners'. Irish opinion was horrified, turned against the government and the Irish Nationalist Party and supported the republican leaders, so that when an election was held in 1918, Sinn Fein gained seventy-three of the 105 Irish seats, the Nationalists seven. The Easter Rising, which had appeared to be such a complete fiasco, therefore began a series of events which ended in an independent Ireland.

**East India Company** (EIC) was granted a charter by Queen Elizabeth I in 1600, which gave it the sole right to trade with the East Indies (i.e. all countries east of the Cape of Good Hope and west of the Straits of Magellan). At first it was mainly concerned with the spice trade, which the Dutch controlled in what is now Indonesia. Indian silk and cotton goods could be exchanged for spices, so in the seventeenth century the Company established 'factories' (trading posts) in Madras, Bombay and Calcutta. These became 'presidencies' (local centres of the Company) with their own governors and councils. The EIC did not move far outside these areas until the second half of the eighteenth century, when the French were defeated in the Seven Years War (1756–63). In 1765 the Company was recognized by the Mughal Emperor in Delhi as the effective ruler of Bengal, India's richest province with twenty million inhabitants. With the revenues from Bengal the Company was able to expand: in 1799 the powerful state of Mysore was defeated and its leader, Tipu Sultan, killed. A large part of Awadh (Oudh) was annexed in 1801 to strengthen the Company's territory against the Marathas further west. They were finally defeated in 1818, by which time the Mughal Emperor had become a Company pensioner. The British were now dominant in India but sporadic annexations continued. Fear of instability in Afghanistan and the death in 1839 of the Sikh leader, Ranjit Singh, led the Company to take over Sind and the Punjab in the 1840s, in order to provide a stable northern and western frontier. The rest of Awadh was annexed in 1856 by Lord **Dalhousie**, the Governor-General, as were other states through the doctrine of 'lapse': Hindu rulers were not allowed to adopt heirs when their line died out, so their states 'lapsed' into Company hands.

By 1820 the Company had an army of 300,000, the most formidable in Asia, which not only was used to control India but which fought extensively abroad: in Egypt against **Napoleon** in 1801; in the **Anglo-Burmese Wars** of 1824–6 and 1852; and in the **Opium Wars** against China in the 1840s and 1850s. Its only major failure was in the **Anglo-Afghan War** (1838–42), when the Company suffered one of its worst military defeats. All the officers were British and the artillery was kept firmly out of Indian control, but there were rarely more than 40,000 Europeans in the Company army, which was therefore dependent on Indian troops. As Indian taxation paid for the army, this was a huge concealed subsidy to the British taxpayer. With the **Industrial Revolution** in Britain, Lancashire machine-made goods flooded into India, as they were both finer and cheaper than Indian hand-produced cotton. India therefore ceased to export cloth but became an exporter of raw materials – raw cotton, indigo and, above all, opium which, grown in Bengal, was a lucrative export to China. In 1813 the Company lost its monopoly of trade with India – only its China trade remained profitable but its monopoly here ended too in 1833. As a result of the **Indian Mutiny** (1857), control of India passed from the EIC to the British government.

**Ebert, Friedrich** (1871–1925). First President (1919–25) of the **Weimar Republic**, Ebert was a saddler who succeeded August **Bebel** as chairman of the **Social Democratic Party** in 1913. He supported revisionism in the Party (see **Bernstein**) and wanted socialists to come to power by the ballot box rather than by revolution. Ebert did not share Rosa **Luxemburg**'s faith in working-class spontaneity and wanted to avoid the violence and civil war that had taken place in Russia after the Bolshevik Revolution. He was even prepared to accept the monarchy and demanded the abdication of Emperor **William II** only when forced to do so by his supporters. 'If the Kaiser does not abdicate,' he said, 'social revolution is inevitable. I do not want it: I hate it like sin.' On 9 November 1918 Prince Max of Baden handed over his office as Chancellor to Ebert, convinced that he was 'a man determined to fight the revolution tooth and nail'. Ebert tried to steer a middle course between extreme **Right** and **Left**. During the **German Revolution** (1918–19) he allied with the army High Command to maintain order in the capital and used it and the **Free Corps** to crush the communist **Spartakist Rising** in 1919 and later to put down **Hitler**'s **Munich** (**beer-hall**) *Putsch* of 1923. He was condemned by the extreme Left for betraying the Revolution but this did not gain him the support of the Right, for whom he was a 'November Criminal', who had signed the armistice and got rid of the Kaiser in 1918 and later accepted the humiliating Treaty of **Versailles**.

**Education Acts** (British). Most elementary schools in the first half of the nineteenth century were run by the churches. The state made its first small grant for school building in 1833 but it was not until the 1867 Act that Robert Lowe told the **Commons** that it was 'necessary that you prevail on our future masters to learn their letters'. The National Education League, founded in Birmingham in 1869 by Nonconformists, including Joseph **Chamberlain**, wanted 'for every child free, compulsory, undenominational but not a Godless education'. Forster's Education Act (1870) rejected the League's programme as too expensive. 'Our object,' said Forster, 'is to complete the present voluntary system, to fill up the gaps.' In areas where voluntary schools had not been set up, elected school boards were to establish board schools, to be paid for by local rates. Education in these schools was to be undenominational but was neither compulsory nor free: religious schools continued to receive state aid. Yet the Act did recognize that education should be provided for all – in 1880 attendance was made compulsory from the ages of five to ten and in 1891 fees in elementary schools largely disappeared. Forster's Act did not affect secondary education, which was provided for the middle classes by fee-paying grammar and 'public' (i.e. private) schools. 'The existing educational system,' said **Balfour**, 'is chaotic, is ineffectual, is utterly behind the age, makes us the laughing stock of every advanced nation in Europe and America.' He therefore provided in his 1902 Education Act for the abolition of school boards: county and borough councils were made local education authorities with responsibility for both elementary and secondary education, so that secondary education expanded rapidly. Free places were introduced into secondary education in 1907; some working-class children could now gain a foothold on the educational ladder which led to university, though few did. The lower-middle class benefited most from the new system. The school leaving age was increased to fourteen in 1918 and to fifteen in 1944, with R. A. Butler's Education Act. This provided free, secondary education for all in three types of school (grammar, technical and secondary modern), selection for which was to be made by the 'eleven plus' examination. Free school milk, subsidized meals and free medical and dental inspections were also to be supplied.

**Edward VII** (1841–1910). King of Great Britain and Ireland, Emperor of India (1901–10). The eldest son of Queen **Victoria** and

Prince **Albert**, he did not have the seriousness or intellectual interests of his father, and reacted against his rigorous upbringing. As Prince of Wales he was not given any royal duties or responsibilities (he did not have access to reports of Cabinet meetings until 1892), so he devoted himself to social life, voracious eating, pleasure and self-indulgence. He loved foreign travel, horse-racing, shooting parties, yachting and the company of beautiful women. A compulsive womanizer, his home at Marlborough House became the hub of fashionable society. In 1863 he married Princess Alexandra of Denmark, who bore him five children, but his affairs continued. When he became King at the age of nearly sixty he did not give up any of his old pleasures or old friends but he brought colour and gaiety back to the Court, which had been in mourning for forty years since the death of Prince Albert. The long silence of the royal palaces was shattered by Court balls and lavish banquets. Edward loved pomp, ceremony and dressing up and was a stickler for protocol and correct dress on every occasion, a fetish he passed on to his son **George V**. He entertained heads of state, including the Kaiser **William II**, and went on a series of goodwill visits to the King of Italy, Pope **Leo XIII** (this was the first meeting of a British king and the Pope since the Reformation) and Tsar **Nicholas II**. The most famous of these trips abroad was to France in 1903, when his charm, affability and speeches in perfect French turned hostility into adoration and prepared the way for the *Entente Cordiale* (see **Anglo-French Entente**) of the following year. 'Good old Teddy' was a popular king, as he took every opportunity of showing himself to his people, who were delighted with his wins in the Derby in 1896, 1900 and 1909. Very conscious of his prerogatives, Edward wished to be consulted about government policy but A. J. **Balfour** brusquely rejected this. When the **Liberal** Prime Minister **Asquith** demanded that the King should create enough Liberal peers to ensure the passage of the **Parliament Bill** through the House of **Lords**, Edward considered asserting himself by inviting the **Conservative Party** to form a minority administration but he died before a decision had to be made.

**Edward VIII** (1894–1972). King of Great Britain and Northern Ireland, Emperor of India (1936). The eldest child of King **George**

V and Queen Mary, he became, as heir-apparent, Prince of Wales in 1911. He had a distant relationship with his parents and clashed with his father, whose obsession with dress and deportment and the minutiae of Court procedure he found outmoded. A lover of parties and heavy drinking, he led a dissolute life, in which most of his lovers were married women. The Prince of Wales shared many of the reactionary views of the time, taking the side of the officers in the **Curragh 'mutiny'** in 1914, referring to 'bloody **suffragettes**', showing a racialist hostility to Indians and Jews and an admiration for **Nazism**. In his short reign (January to December 1936 – he was never crowned) he showed little interest in affairs of state and was preoccupied by his relationship with Mrs Wallis Simpson, which precipitated the **abdication crisis**. When he married Wallis in France in June 1937, no member of the royal family was present. Effectively he was an outcast, whose title HRH was not extended to his wife. In 1937 he continued to ignore advice by visiting **Hitler** in Germany. He escaped from France to Portugal in 1940 but the British government, fearing he would be kidnapped by the Germans, persuaded him to become Governor of the Bahamas (1942–5). After the war he spent most of his time in France, where both he and his wife died.

**Eisenhower, Dwight David** (1890–1969). American general and thirty-fourth President of the USA (1953–61). A humane, warm and friendly man, Eisenhower's attitude to war was very different from that of **Patton**. 'I hate war,' he wrote, 'as only a soldier who has lived it can, only as one who has seen its brutality, its futility, its stupidity.' He first became widely known as Allied Commander-in-Chief for the invasion of North Africa in November 1942 (see **North African Campaigns**). He remained Supreme Commander of Allied forces in the Mediterranean during the conquest of Sicily (May 1943) and in the invasion of Italy (September 1943), until he was recalled in January 1944 to plan the invasion of France. During this time he showed a remarkable ability in coordinating the activities and securing the cooperation of ambitious generals of disparate views and of different nationalities. 'Ike' was a great conciliator, tactful and sensitive, reluctant to dominate but prepared to exert his authority when it was necessary, as it sometimes was with

**Montgomery**. He was an excellent administrator and planned the invasion of France on **D-Day** (6 June 1944) with meticulous care. After the success of the **Normandy Campaign** he disagreed with Montgomery on how best the **North-West Europe Campaign** should be conducted. Montgomery wanted all Allied forces to be concentrated on a single thrust across the Rhine and straight to Berlin. Eisenhower felt that this would be too dangerous, as its flanks would be exposed, and he did not believe it could be supplied. He therefore favoured an attack on a broad front to push the Germans back to the Rhine before advancing further. This was the policy successfully adopted, though it meant that the war dragged on until 1945. 'Ike' never had the chance to show his skill as a field-commander but he reacted with speed and determination in the battle of the **Bulge** (December 1944), when a German counter-attack caught the Americans unprepared. At the end of the war he was in charge of US occupation forces in Germany until he replaced General Marshall as US Chief of Staff in 1949–50 and took command of the newly created North Atlantic Treaty Organization (NATO) in 1951. In June 1952 he resigned to become the Republican candidate for the presidency of the USA: he won the election, was re-elected in 1956, and so was President from 1953–61.

**Electricity.** Its application, after a century of theoretical and practical advances, affected more people than any other discovery or invention during the **Industrial Revolution**. Volta's battery (1800), the statement of the law of the electric circuit by Ohm (1827), the experiments of Faraday and others which led to the discovery of electromagnetic induction (1831), provided theoretical knowledge for the electricity industry. It was another fifty years before it could be applied, as there was no cheap source of current. This was made possible by the electromagnetic generator (1866–7), efficient dynamos and Parsons' steam turbine (1879). The first electric power station was built in England in 1881. Because transformers (1890) allowed long-distance transmission, falling water could be used as a source of energy, so hydroelectric power stations were built from 1893 (by 1940 40 per cent of the world production of electricity came from water). The Central Electricity Board (1926) in Britain began a national grid, which by 1934 served most of the country.

In factories belts and shafts disappeared with the electric motor. Electricity provided power for lifts, winching gear in the mines and rolling mills in the steel industry. It was also used for traction in trams, trolleybuses, and electric and underground railways (see **Transport revolution**). Electricity gave rise to new industries (electrolysis was vital for the extraction of copper and aluminium and the production of caustic soda) and had a 'multiplier' effect on existing industries: thermally generated electricity meant an increased demand for coal, whilst electric transport required more rolling stock. The direct effect of electricity on people's lives was seen most clearly in the home. The incandescent light bulb, invented simultaneously by Swan in England and Edison in the USA in 1879, lit homes as well as factories, shops and streets. Electric sewing machines were followed by electric cookers (1891), toasters, kettles and fires by 1895 (the bar fire was produced in 1908). The vacuum cleaner, a great boon for the housewife, was a British invention of 1901. In the 1920s immersion heaters, electric mixers, washing machines, hair driers and fridges appeared, followed by the electric razor in the early 1930s. Electricity also produced the **communications revolution** – the electric telegraph, telephone, radio and television.

**Emancipation of the serfs** (Russia) (1861). **Alexander II**'s most ambitious and far-reaching reform. The serfs were freed because it was feared that they would revolt if they were not freed. 'It is better to abolish serfdom from above,' Alexander told a group of Moscow nobles, 'than to wait for the time when it will begin to abolish itself from below.' Serfs were given the right to marry, own property and set up in business, though they could not leave the *mir* without permission. The size of their holdings was supposed to be based on the amount of land they worked before emancipation, but in the black-earth regions of rich soil the landlords kept over a fifth of the land worked by the peasants. Most land now went not to the individual peasant but to the collective ownership of the *mir*, so the peasant simply changed one form of domination (that of the landlord), for another (that of the *mir*). The peasant had to pay for his land by redemption payments for the next forty-nine years. Emancipation did nothing to improve the productivity of farming, as the dead hand of the *mir* prevented innovation and the peasants lacked capital. Emancipation left the peasants discontented, owing to the redemption payments and the small size of their plots. During the rest of the century their position deteriorated further, as there was a population explosion: the population of rural Russia increased from fifty-five million in 1863 to eighty-two million in 1897. As a result plots became smaller and rents rose, so that peasants remained potentially rebellious.

**Emancipation Proclamations** (22 September 1862, 1 January 1863) freed slaves in the USA. When **Lincoln** became President he had promised not 'to interfere with the institution of slavery where it exists' but from the start of the **American Civil War** he was pressed by **abolitionists** to free the slaves. They were supported by some Union generals, who wanted to enlist Negroes in their armies. Lincoln did not want to alienate the four Union slave states but by the summer of 1862 had decided that emancipation was 'a military necessity'. On 22 September he therefore issued a preliminary Emancipation Proclamation, which stated that all slaves in areas still held by the rebels would be freed on 1 January 1863. This did not solve the problem of slavery, as it did not free slaves in the four Union slave states or in parts of the Confederacy already occupied by Union forces. It became effective therefore only as the Union conquered the South but it led to the employment of 186,000 Negroes in the Union armies. The final Emancipation Proclamation of 1 January 1863 demonstrated that the war was not simply about maintaining the Union but was about slavery and freedom too. This Proclamation prepared the way for the thirteenth amendment to the US Constitution, passed in 1865, which abolished slavery in the USA.

**Emigration.** The movement of people from one country to settle in another. Most European emigrants in the nineteenth century went to the USA (see **Immigration to the USA**), Canada, South America, Australia, New Zealand and South Africa. Between 1821 and 1850 they averaged 110,000 a year: this rose to 900,000 a year from 1881 to 1915 and fell in the 1930s to 366,000 a year. In the first half of the nineteenth century most emigrants came from Britain (two–three million) and Germany (1.1 million): in the second half of the nineteenth century Britain (nine million) and Germany (five million) were still in the lead but large numbers also came from Italy (five million), Scandinavia (one million), Belgium, Spain and the Balkan states. The British went to the USA and British colonies, Germans to the USA and Brazil, French to Algeria, Italians to the USA and Argentina, Spaniards to Argentina and Central America. There was also emigration from Asia: many Chinese settled in Siam, Java and the Malay peninsula and in smaller numbers in the USA and Australia. Indians went to Ceylon, Natal and East Africa, Japanese to the USA and Hawaii.

Some emigrants did not go freely – British and French convicts sent to the **penal settlements** in Australia, Guiana and New Caledonia in the Pacific; Negroes who went as slaves from Africa to America and the Caribbean islands and from Zanzibar to Arabia until the abolition of the **slave trade**. Indians and Chinese often went as **indentured labourers**. Russian Jews emigrated to escape persecution and **pogroms**. Many, particularly the Irish after the **Irish famine** of 1845–9, emigrated to avoid unemployment and destitution; others were attracted by the promise of a better life in a country where land was plentiful and cheap, or where employment could be found in the new, burgeoning industries. It is estimated that between 1800 and 1917, thirty-six million people emigrated to the USA, fifteen million to South America and five million to Canada. Without them, the economic development of these areas would have been seriously retarded.

There was a huge movement of peoples also as a result of the **First** and **Second World Wars**. Following the Treaty of **Lausanne** (1923) one million Greeks were moved from Turkey to Greece and 350,000 Turks were expelled from Greece. After the defeat of Poland in 1939 Germany expelled three-quarters of a million Poles from what Germany regarded as 'German' territory. **Stalin** did the same in the part of Poland the Soviet Union occupied as a result of the **Nazi–Soviet Pact**, transferring up to a million Poles to Siberian **forced labour camps**. To prevent possible collaboration with the invaders, Stalin also sent half a million German-speaking people of the Volga basin to Siberia. For alleged cooperation with the Germans 600,000 Crimean Tartars were forced to go to Siberia from 1944–6. When German troops retreated in

1944, German settlers fled before the advancing Russian armies and many were forcibly deported in 1945–6 from Czechoslovakia (especially the **Sudetenland**) and Poland. By 1947 ten million Germans had moved west into post-war Germany, the largest migration ever recorded.

**Emperor system** (Japanese *tennosei*). The name given to Japan's political system in which, up to 1945, the Emperor was the highest authority. In Japan there has been only one imperial dynasty, which claimed descent from the sun goddess Amaterasu. This made the Emperor a god. Under the **Tokugawa shogunate** (1603–1867) the Emperor had no power and was under the control of the Tokugawas but when they showed they were incapable of defending Japan against foreign intrusion (see **Perry** and **Unequal treaties**), the anti-Tokugawa forces united to revive the authority of the Emperor in the **Meiji Restoration** (1868). The **Meiji Constitution** (1889) declared that he was inviolable and sacred and gave him greater powers than those of the elected **Diet**. The official ideology was a mixture of Shinto, which stressed his divine origin, and **Confucianism**, whose influence was seen in the Educational Rescript (imperial declaration) of 1890. This said that loyalty to the Emperor and patriotism were the supreme virtues. Copies of this rescript were hung in all schools beside the Emperor's portrait: ceremonial readings were made from it from time to time. The Emperor did not normally make political decisions, as he had to be 'above the clouds' (apart from the stresses of government), so he reigned rather than ruled, the Showa Emperor **Hirohito** wishing to be seen as a constitutional monarch. The leading position of the Emperor was abolished in 1945 and he renounced his divinity in 1946. In the new Constitution (1947) the Emperor became 'the symbol of the state and of the unity of the people, deriving his position from the will of the people, with whom resides sovereign power'.

**Ems telegram** (13 July 1870). After the **Hohenzollern candidature for the Spanish throne** was withdrawn, the way was open for friendly relations between France and Prussia. However, Gramont, the French Foreign Minister, wanted to make the most of France's diplomatic success. He ordered Benedetti, the French ambassador to Prussia, to see **William I**, who was taking the waters at the spa of Bad Ems, and ask him for a promise that the candidacy would never be renewed. This insulting request was politely but firmly rejected by the King, who sent a telegram to **Bismarck** telling him what had happened. Bismarck saw his opportunity of bringing about war with France, a successful conclusion to which would bring about German unification. He published a shortened version of the telegram which made it appear that French demands had been peremptory and that William had, as a matter of national honour, curtly rebuffed the French ambassador and ended diplomatic relations with France. Public opinion in both France and Prussia was outraged. **Napoleon III** was reluctant to declare war but there was such an outcry in the French press, supported by the Empress, that France declared war on 19 July, thus beginning the **Franco-Prussian War**.

**Enabling Act** (23 March 1933). The Act gave the Nazi government of Germany the right to issue laws without the consent of the **Reichstag** and to change the Constitution. The idea was not completely new, as Enabling Laws had been introduced in the **Weimar Republic** in 1923, to deal with the crisis caused by inflation and by the French occupation of the **Ruhr**. From 1930 to 1933 laws passed by the Reichstag were increasingly replaced by government decrees, issued by the President under Article 48 of the Constitution: in 1932 there were sixty emergency decrees and only five Reichstag laws. The Act needed a two-thirds majority in the Reichstag, which it obtained easily by 444 votes to ninety-four, as the **Centre Party** voted for it: only the Socialists bravely voted against, in a hall filled with intimidating **SA** (stormtroopers). The Act marked the end of parliamentary democracy in Germany and the establishment of the Nazi dictatorship. The **Social Democratic Party** was dissolved on 22 June and the middle-class parties hastened to dissolve themselves: the Nationalists on 27 June and the Centre Party on 5 July. On 14 July the **Nazi Party** was proclaimed the only legal party in Germany. The Reichstag continued to meet but passed only seven more laws and was addressed only by Hitler and other Nazis.

**Enclosures** (Britain). The conversion of open fields, commons and waste land into closed fields, surrounded by fences, hedges or ditches. The open-field system was very inefficient, as all farmers had to grow the same crops and there was no flexibility: custom prevailed. Enclosures by agreement had been taking place since the Middle Ages but before 1760 there had been only 130 enclosures by Acts of parliament. Between 1760 and 1780 there were 900 parliamentary enclosures and 2,000 between 1793 and 1815, in order to take advantage of the rising price of corn. Acts of parliament were more expensive than enclosure by agreement, though the process was simplified by the General Enclosure Act of 1801, but they were quicker. Whereas earlier enclosures had mainly been in pastoral areas, the new ones were in the corn-growing regions of the Midlands, East Anglia and the northern Home Counties. One aim was to make farms larger, more compact and therefore easier to work and more efficient: farmers could experiment with new crops and crop rotations to increase output. Enclosures would also increase the cultivated area by including commons and waste land. These aims were generally realized, as was shown by the doubling of rents on enclosed farms. There was increased work in the short term on enclosed land, for hedging and fencing, but many had to give up valuable common rights, such as the pasturing of their animals and gleaning, which could provide enough corn for a family for six months. Squatters were no longer able to live on the commons. The loss of these rights made more of the rural population dependent on charity and the **Poor Law**, though increased rural poverty was also due to the rise in population and the depression which followed the **Napoleonic Wars**.

**Engels, Friedrich** (1820–95). German political philosopher and colleague of **Marx**. The son of a prosperous factory owner in the Rhineland, he left school at sixteen to work in the family firm. In 1842 he went to England, where his family was in partnership with some Manchester cotton spinners. He used his own observations and press reports to write *The Condition of the Working Class in England* (1845), in which he showed the degrading situation of the workers and supported communal control of the means of production. In 1844 Engels met Marx and began a friendship which lasted until Marx died in 1883. They joined the Communist League in 1847 and wrote the *Communist Manifesto* as a programme for the movement. Engels worked with Marx on a radical newspaper in Cologne but when the **Revolutions of 1848** failed in Germany, they both fled to England in 1849. Marx lived in London, doing research for his book on *Capital*; Engels lived in Manchester, until he retired as a partner in the family firm in 1870. He lived a double life, riding to hounds and mixing with the wealthy, whilst having two working-class sisters successively as his mistresses, living in separate accommodation. Engels, who was Marx's principal political and intellectual companion, supported Marx financially and in *Anti-Dühring* (1878) put forward his views on historical materialism. After Marx's death he spent much of his time editing the second and third volumes of *Capital*, which were published in 1885 and 1894. He also took an active part in forming the **Second International** (1889) and acted as informal adviser to leaders of the German **Social Democratic Party**. Engels did much more than Marx himself to popularize the ideas of **Marxism** and shaped the way Marx was interpreted, by offering a more accessible and simplified version of Marx's thought.

***Entente Cordiale,*** see **Anglo-French Entente** (1904)

**Erfurt Union** (1850). **Frederick William IV** of Prussia had rejected the crown of a united Germany, as it had been offered to him by a popularly elected **Frankfurt Parliament** and not by his fellow rulers. He wanted to unite Germany but with the agreement of the princes, so he persuaded seventeen states to join the Erfurt Union, though the larger states like Bavaria and Württemberg stayed outside, as they did not want to be dominated by Prussia. Austria saw the Erfurt Union as a threat to her commanding position in Germany, so at Olmütz forced Prussia to abandon it and to agree to the revival of the **German Confederation**, presided over by Austria.

**Estates-General.** An assembly which met in France in May 1789, which represented the First (clergy), Second (nobles) and Third (the rest of the population) Estates. It had last met in 1614. When **Louis XVI**'s ministers tried to impose taxes on privileged groups such as the clergy and nobility, they claimed that only an Estates-General would have the authority to do this. The King gave way but when the Paris *Parlement* (a law court with the right to register royal edicts) declared that the three orders should meet and vote separately, the leaders of the Third Estate would not accept this, as they would be outvoted by the two privileged orders. They demanded a doubling of Third Estate deputies and vote by head; this would give them a majority, as some lower clergy would vote with them. The King granted doubling but not vote by head, so there was confusion when the Estates-General met. On 17 June the Third Estate voted to call itself the National Assembly and claimed that, as it represented most of the nation, it had the right to manage its affairs and decide taxation. This was a direct challenge to the King and was reinforced by the Tennis Court Oath of 20 June, when the Third Estate took an oath not to disperse until they had given France a constitution. The King held a Royal Session (23 June) to break the deadlock but came down on the side of the privileged orders. After riots in Paris he changed his mind and on 27 June told the nobles and clergy to join the Third Estate and vote by head. This appeared to be only a tactical withdrawal on his part, when he surrounded Paris with troops, apparently with the intention of dissolving the Assembly. This was averted by the revolt of the people of Paris and the fall of the **Bastille** (14 July). On 7 July the Estates-General adopted the name of **Constituent Assembly**.

**Ethiopian War** (1935–6). War between Italy and Ethiopia. At the end of the nineteenth century Ethiopia was, apart from Liberia, the only part of Africa not under European control. The Italians tried to conquer it, as it would link up their colonies of Eritrea and Italian Somaliland but they were defeated at **Aduwa** in 1896. When **Mussolini** came to power in Italy he wanted to avenge this defeat and to show the strength of his Fascist regime (see **Fascism**). He considered invasion as early as 1925 but his troops did not invade Ethiopia, without declaring war, until ten years later in October 1935. The **League of Nations** condemned Italy and in November imposed sanctions on her: the export of arms, rubber and various metals to Italy was banned, there were to be no loans to Italy and no imports from her. However, oil, iron, steel and coal were excluded from the ban, as it was felt that a ban on oil might lead to a general war. France accepted sanctions reluctantly, as she did not want to push Mussolini into **Hitler**'s arms. She preferred, as did Britain, to negotiate a settlement with Italy at Ethiopia's expense. The **Hoare–Laval Pact** was therefore drawn up, giving much of Ethiopia to Italy, but there was a public outcry when its terms became known and it was abandoned.

The poorly armed and led Ethiopians were no match for Italy's modern weapons – aeroplanes, tanks, artillery and mustard gas: 400,000 troops were sent to East Africa. The invasion from Eritrea in the north and Italian Somaliland in the south was successful in seven months: Addis Ababa, the capital, was occupied in May 1936 and the Emperor **Haile Selassie** fled to England. In July sanctions were formally lifted. The war was a triumph for Mussolini: he had successfully defied the League, whose sanctions had united Italians behind him, and he had refused to give way, when international pressure was greater than expected. He now became bolder in his foreign policy, joined in the **Spanish Civil War** and moved closer to Hitler, who had not applied sanctions, and away from his Stresa partners, France and Britain (see **Stresa Front**). An unfortunate effect of the war was that the League of Nations, as a body for protecting weak nations and for maintaining peace, was now dead: there was a retreat from collective security into isolation, regional groupings or **appeasement**.

**Evangelical Movement.** Members of the Church of England in the late eighteenth and early nineteenth centuries, who stressed 'vital Christianity', the awareness of sin and the need for salvation through good works and a strict moral code. The Clapham Sect of William **Wilberforce**, Hannah **More** and others, named after the area where Wilberforce lived in the 1790s, forced Evangelicalism into the forefront of public life and had an influence out of all proportion to its numbers. Evangelicals thought that reform should begin in the Church of England, so that it could minister to all the people. There should be a resident clergyman in every parish, pluralism should be abolished and new parishes and churches built in the industrial towns. Many of these reforms were carried out by the Ecclesiastical Commission, set up by **Peel** in 1835. Evangelicals promoted humanitarian causes such as the abolition of the **slave trade** in 1807 (Wilberforce played a leading part in this campaign) and the ending of slavery in the British Empire in 1833, the restriction of child labour in the **Factory Acts** and the humane treatment of people in prison. Hannah More, in particular, called on the upper classes to reform and set an example to the rest of the population and managed to make respectability a hallmark of the middle classes. Evangelicals sought to spread their message abroad by founding the Church Missionary Society (1799) and the British and Foreign Bible Society (1804). They were not democrats and opposed the transfer of political power to the masses, Wilberforce maintaining that Christianity made 'the inequalities of the social scale less galling to the lower orders, whom she instructs . . . to be diligent, humble, patient; reminding them that their more lowly path has been allotted to them by the hand of God'. This was the message they tried to get across to the working class in their Sunday Schools where, along with a strict observance of Sundays and a knowledge of the Bible, they emphasized the virtues of submission, obedience, sobriety and the acceptance of one's station in life.

**Extermination camps.** Camps set up in Poland by the **Nazi Party** in 1941–2 in order to wipe out the Jewish population of German-occupied Europe. The decision to eliminate all European Jews in the '**Final Solution**' was probably taken by **Hitler** in the summer of 1941 and led the **SS** to seek a secret means of mass execution. Rooms filled with carbon monoxide gas had been used in 1940–41 to kill 70,000 German mentally handicapped children but Hitler abandoned this 'euthanasia programme' in August 1941, because it was condemned by the churches. The same method was used in the first mass gassing of Jews at Chelmno in December 1941. In 1942 special camps, of which Treblinka became the best-known, were opened in Poland for the rapid murder of large numbers of Jews. After arriving by train they undressed and were taken immediately to the gas chambers, often disguised as showers, where they were killed by carbon monoxide fumes. At Treblinka between 900,000 and 1.2 million Jews were killed. Some camps were not exclusively for extermination. At Auschwitz Jews were divided into the able-bodied, who were sent into the camps to be used as slave labour (see **Concentration camps**), and those who were unfit for work (including all children), who went immediately to the gas chambers. Pellets of hydrogen cyanide (trade name Zyklon, produced by **IG Farben**) were dropped into the chambers. 'We knew when the people were dead,' said the Auschwitz camp commander, Rudolf Hoess, at the Nuremberg trials, 'because their screaming stopped.' In the death camps between five and six million people were killed.

**Fabian Society.** Formed in 1884 and named after Quintus Fabius Cunctator, the Roman general who avoided pitched battles against Hannibal but gradually wore him down in a war of attrition. Its small membership (3,000 in 1914) included Sidney and Beatrice **Webb**, Annie **Besant**, George Bernard Shaw and H. G. Wells. Fabians believed that socialism would develop slowly, and without violent revolution, from capitalism by the 'permeation' of existing institutions, something Sidney Webb referred to as 'the inevitability of gradualness'. They rejected *laissez-faire* and thought that state intervention was necessary to get rid of poverty and provide a 'national minimum'. Although labour leaders like Keir **Hardie**, Ben Tillett and Tom Mann were members before the foundation of the **Independent Labour Party** in 1893, Fabians like the Webbs did not see the need for a separate party for the working class, though the Fabian Society was one of the groups which formed the Labour Representation Committee (the forerunner of the **Labour Party**) in 1900. Essentially a middle-class, élitist, London-based society, the Fabians were more concerned with detailed research into social problems and the suggestion of remedies, than with the elaboration of socialist theory. Their propaganda in the form of numerous pamphlets and *Fabian Essays* (1899) did much to make socialist ideas respectable. They drew closer to the Labour Party in the **First World War** and greatly influenced its 1918 constitution. Their most lasting influence in Britain has been in their approach to social questions: their collection of statistical and documentary evidence helped to create a public opinion in favour of the **Welfare State**.

**Factory Acts** (Britain). Laws to regulate conditions of work in factories. These began to grow up in the late eighteenth century in the north of England as a result of the **Industrial Revolution** and there were soon complaints about long working hours and unhealthy conditions. The campaign for reform was led by clergymen, doctors, some Tory (see **Tories**) manufacturers like the senior Sir Robert Peel, the Tory land steward Richard Oastler and **Evangelicals** such as Lord Ashley (later the Earl of **Shaftesbury**), whose interest was humanitarian and religious. They gained support from the Royal Commissions which investigated factories and found poorly ventilated buildings, severe penalties for unpunctuality, and sometimes brutal treatment of children: they showed that these conditions led to illness, deformity and early death. The first Factory Acts affected only children, as adults were held to be 'free agents'. The Act of 1802 promoted by Peel Senior limited the hours worked by children in textile factories to twelve hours a day but this and other Acts were easily evaded as no inspectors were appointed to enforce them. It was not until the 1833 Act that a breakthrough was made. Children under nine were not allowed to work at all in textile mills; those from nine to thirteen could work no more than nine hours a day or forty-eight a week; children from fourteen to eighteen could work up to twelve hours a day or sixty-nine a week. This time factory inspectors were appointed but there were only four, so that one had to cover 2,700 factories with a quarter of a million workers. Yet this was a start which made further advance easier. In 1842 women and boys under ten were forbidden to work in mines; the work of women was limited to twelve hours a day in 1844, whilst in 1847 the Ten Hours Act prevented women and children in textile mills working more than ten hours a day. The age below which children could not be employed rose to ten in 1874 and by stages to fourteen in 1920. Vast numbers of children in uncontrolled industries were not affected by the Acts and continued to work long hours in unhealthy conditions. The first government regulation in Britain of work for adult males did not take place until 1908, when the Coal Mines Act established an eight-hour day in the mines.

**Faidherbe, Louis** (1818–89). French general and governor of Senegal (1854–61, 1863–5). Faidherbe gave Senegal new roads, schools, forts and harbours, including Dakar, but realized that the colony could pay for itself only if it expanded into the region producing ground nuts. He therefore began the systematic conquest of the Senegal basin, using Senegalese soldiers. This brought him into contact with the Muslim states which arose from the local *jihads* (holy wars), especially the Tukulor Empire of al-Hajj **Umar**, which stretched from the Senegal to the Niger. Faidherbe drove him east and at a treaty in 1860 Umar recognized French control of the Senegal river. The basis for the French conquest of the western Sudan had been laid.

***Falange Española*** (Spanish Falange). Spanish Fascist movement. It was founded in 1933 by José Antonio, the son of the military dictator of the 1920s, General **Primo de Rivera**. Opposed to both the reactionary **Right** and revolutionary **Left**, its manifesto of 1934 condemned republicanism, party politics, Marxism and capitalism and proposed that Spain should become a **Corporate State** like that of **Mussolini**'s Italy. Up to the spring of 1936 the Falange lacked members, organization, leadership and a clear political strategy. Primarily reliant on student support, its strongholds were Madrid and Valladolid. In the general election of February 1936 the Falange won a mere 0.7 per cent of the vote. After the victory of the **Popular Front**, the Falange grew rapidly, as disillusioned middle-class youth abandoned the parliamentary parties. The Falange backed the military rebellion of July 1936 against the **Spanish Second Republic**. After the outbreak of the **Spanish Civil War**, the Falange became the dominant political movement in the Nationalist camp, mobilizing most volunteers. Through control of the press and of propaganda it also became the principal publicity force in the Nationalist zone. However, the mass influx into the Falange had diluted its radical spirit. With most of its principal figures in republican jails since March 1936, its leadership remained extremely weak. In particular, the execution of José Antonio in November 1936 left the Falange without an authentic leader. The fate of the Falange was sealed in April 1937, when **Franco** united it with the Carlists (see **Carlism**) to form the basis of his single party, the only one permitted in Franco's Spain. The Falangist movement – to which all public employees automatically belonged – served as the regime's administration, organizing the labour force. It performed a valuable function as the political cheerleader of the dictator, becoming one of the pillars of the Francoist state. In 1945 the Falange became widely known as the National Movement and the fascist salute was abolished.

**Falkenhayn, Erich** (1861–1922). German general. A Prussian *Junker*, he was intelligent, honest and self-reliant, becoming Minister of War in 1913 and Chief of Staff in November 1914, when Moltke had a nervous collapse. He realized that the Allies had greater resources than Germany and so Germany must win the war quickly, if she was to win it at all. The failure of his attacks in Flanders at Ypres, the hinge of Allied communications, in November 1914 made him pessimistic and he told a startled Chancellor, **Bethmann-Hollweg**, that a German victory was now impossible, unless either France or Russia was removed from the Allied coalition. In 1915, after Russian successes against the Austrians in Galicia, he turned to the Eastern Front and won one of Germany's greatest victories of the war when he routed the Russians at Gorlice and pushed them back 300 miles, but he believed that 'Victories in the east that are achieved only at the cost of weakening our position in the west are worthless.' He had no intention of allowing his armies to be caught up in the vast spaces of Russia, as **Napoleon**'s had been, so he called off the offensive in September and sent an army to the Danube where, with the aid of Bulgaria, it knocked Serbia out of the war. In 1916 Falkenhayn again sought victory on the Western Front by a massive attack on Verdun (see **Verdun,** battle of). When it failed, with heavy German as well as French casualties, Germany lost the initiative in the West, as the British attacked on the Somme (see battle of the **Somme**) (July–October 1916). Falkenhayn was dismissed as Chief of Staff in August but showed his brilliance as a field commander by quickly overrunning Romania when she joined the Allies.

**Falloux Law** (1850). Named after the deputy who proposed it in the French Legislative Assembly, the Falloux Law was a major event in the educational, religious and political history of France in the nineteenth century. It gave the Roman Catholic Church the right to run secondary schools in competition with state *lycées* and increased Church supervision of state primary schools. Similar bills had been rejected four times in the 1840s but after the rising of the **June Days** (1848) many *bourgeois*, such as **Thiers**, regarded the Church as 'the last bulwark of the social order'. It was a great clerical victory, as within a generation half the secondary school pupils in France were attending Catholic schools. This gave Catholicism a solid *bourgeois* base well into the twentieth century but it intensified the **anti-clericalism** of the **Left**, which became convinced that the Church wanted total control of education, so that it could control the state. It was repealed in 1905 by the anti-clerical ministry of Emile Combes.

**Fascism.** An extreme right-wing totalitarian ideology developed in Italy by **Mussolini**. Its name arose from the *fasces* or bundle of rods carried before magistrates of Republican Rome, which represented unity and authority. It was influenced by **Social Darwinism** and by the ideas of **Hegel**, **Nietzsche** and **Sorel**. From Hegel it derived the belief that the state is more than a collection of citizens and has an organic life of its own, which transcends individual morality. Giovanni Gentile, the leading Fascist philosopher, declared that 'for the Fascist everything is the State and nothing human or spiritual exists outside the State.' Fascism was therefore a totalitarian system, which sought to control all aspects of the life of its citizens: individuals, families and organizations of all kinds must be subordinate to the state. Parliamentary democracy was rejected, as political parties represented conflicting interests, which destroyed the unity of the state. From Sorel, Mussolini took the importance of myths, images which activate people. 'We have created our myth,' he wrote in 1922. 'The myth is a faith, it is passion. It is not necessary that it shall be a reality. Our myth is the greatness of the Nation.' Mussolini wanted to create a nation of virile warriors (Nietzsche's supermen) who would be prepared for violence and sacrifice. 'War is the only beautiful thing that makes life worth living.' The embodiment of the unity of the nation was the infallible *Duce* (the leader), an almost sacred figure who stood on a pedestal, towering above his people in the mass rallies, with their marches, uniforms, songs and torch-lit processions, which were such a characteristic feature of Fascism. *Mussolini ha sempre ragione* ('Mussolini is always right') was written on walls all over Italy, as was the regime's motto: 'Believe. Obey. Fight.'

Similar movements arose in **Nazism**, the *Falange Española* in Spain, *Action Française* in France, in Britain under Sir Oswald **Mosley**, with **Salazar** in Portugal, in the Balkan states and in Latin America. All were a product of the social and economic crises which followed the **First World War** and the **Great Depression**. All were different from one another but had certain common features: nationalism, the subordination of the individual to an absolute state, in which there would be only one party with a monopoly of power; the suppression of all autonomous institutions and opposition, often by the use of terror; a charismatic leader (*Führer*, *Duce*) with dictatorial powers; the belief in war and conquest as the national destiny. This was linked in Germany to racism and **anti-Semitism**, ideas which were shared by many Fascist movements but not by all (Italy rejected them, in spite of Mussolini's anti-Semitic laws of 1938). Support for Fascist movements came from war veterans, who could not settle down to the dull routine of civilian life; from the lower-middle classes, whose standard of living was threatened by inflation and unemployment; from nationalists and those who were attracted by the dynamism of Fascism. Defeat in the **Second World War** brought an end to most Fascist movements.

**Fashoda** (1898). An incident on the White Nile when British and French forces confronted one another and there was a danger of war. The French resented the British occupation of Egypt since 1882 and her claim to the Sudan, which was under the control of the **Mahdi** since the death of **Gordon** in 1885. In 1896 the British under **Kitchener** began the conquest of the Sudan and in September 1898 defeated the Mahdist forces at the battle of **Omdurman**. Meanwhile, the French had sent a small expedition under Major Marchand from Gabon, which after nearly two years reached the Nile at Fashoda, 400 miles south of Khartoum, shortly after Kitchener's victory. When Kitchener moved south and confronted Marchand there was talk of war between Britain and France but more sensible counsels prevailed. The British had by far the larger force on the Nile and so the French withdrew. An Anglo-French agreement of 1899 left Britain in control of the modern state of the

Sudan and France in control of an area from Darfur to Lake Chad. Other outstanding colonial disputes were settled in the **Anglo-French Entente** of 1904.

**February Revolution** (1917). The origins of this Revolution in Russia lie in the unpopularity of Tsar **Nicholas II** and particularly in the demoralization and dislocation brought about by the **First World War**. Russian losses between 1914 and 1917 were enormous: of fifteen million men called up, it is estimated that between seven and eight million were killed, wounded or taken prisoner. To pay for the war the government simply printed money. The result was massive inflation: prices had increased four-fold by 1916. There was also a shortage of grain in the towns, largely because the peasants would not sell it, as there were no consumer goods to buy. They chose instead to feed it to their animals, so that the ludicrous situation arose whereby the animals received more than the army and the towns put together. With inflation the worker found his real wages declining, so strikes increased sharply in 1916. The Tsar had taken personal command of the Russian armies in August 1915. This was a grave error, as he was held responsible for military defeats and the Tsarina and **Rasputin** were left to run the government. The result was 'ministerial leapfrog': in two and a half years there were four prime ministers, six ministers of internal affairs, three war ministers and three foreign ministers. By the end of 1916 even conservative circles in the nobility and the imperial family itself saw that change was necessary. Nicholas remained supremely unconcerned, so that many began to feel that the only way to save the monarchy was to get rid of the monarch. General Krymov told **Duma** members that the army would welcome 'the news of a *coup d'état* . . . A revolution is imminent and we at the front feel it to be so.' Surprisingly, the only people at the beginning of 1917 who did not expect a revolution were the revolutionaries. In January **Lenin**'s view was that 'We of the older generation may not see the decisive battles of this revolution.'

On 23 February, International Day, women in St Petersburg took to the streets demanding bread and called on factory workers to join them. On the 24th between 100,000 and 200,000 workers went on strike and political slogans calling for the overthrow of the Tsar appeared.

**Bolshevik, Menshevik** and **Socialist Revolutionary** agitators were now active, though most revolutionary leaders were in exile or abroad. By the 25th the strike was almost general and the city was paralysed. Troops fired into the crowds for the first time on the 26th, but mutinied on the 27th when they were ordered to shoot to kill. By 1 March almost the whole garrison had joined the rising. In 1905 the army had crushed the Revolution: in 1917 it ensured that it was successful. The Cabinet resigned on the 27th and so a Duma committee set up a **Provisional Government**. On 2 March Nicholas abdicated. 'All around me treason, cowardice and deceit,' he wrote bitterly in his diary. The Romanov dynasty, after ruling for 300 years, had fallen.

**February Rising** (1936). An attempt by young officers in Tokyo to carry out a military *coup*. On 26 February 1,400 soldiers, led by junior officers, took over the centre of Tokyo, seizing the **Diet** building and the War Ministry. They issued a statement calling for a *Showa Restoration* and saying that Japan's ills were due to the *genro* (elder statesmen), *zaibatsu* and political parties, and that those responsible must be killed. They also claimed that in taking direct action they were carrying out their duty as loyal subjects of the Emperor. Several ministers, including two former Prime Ministers, were killed and others wounded. Martial law was declared but the military authorities took no immediate steps to put down the mutiny. Only on 28 February, when it was clear that the *coup* did not have the support of the high command or of the Emperor, did the military authorities put on a show of force to persuade the rebels to return to barracks. Some of the leaders were arrested and others committed suicide. Of 124 people prosecuted, thirteen officers and four civilians were sentenced to death. **Kita Ikki**, whose ideas had strongly influenced the officers, was tried in August 1937 for complicity in the *coup* and was executed. There was no further attempt to establish direct military rule after this, perhaps because one was no longer felt to be necessary, as the army became more than ever the dominant force in politics, dictating the composition of new Cabinets and the proportion of the budget spent on the armed forces (it rose to nearly 50 per cent).

**Federalist Party.** US political party which formed the first government after the adoption of the Constitution in 1789 and remained in office until 1800. The party of George **Washington** and John Adams, it believed in a strong central government and adopted the economic policies of Alexander **Hamilton**, aiming to promote industry and keep the government, in Adams's words, in the hands of 'the rich, the well-born and the able'. Its main support came from the wealthy businessmen, financiers and landowners of New England. In 1800 the Federalists lost the presidency to Thomas **Jefferson** and never regained it. Their decline was hastened by their pro-British stance during the **Anglo-American War** of 1812–14, when some of them even threatened secession. They did not contest a presidential election after 1816 and finally disappeared in 1825.

**Federal Revolt** (1793). A revolt in the French provinces against the dominance of the Paris Commune over the **Convention**. The *journée* of 2 June 1793, when *sans-culottes* surrounded the Convention and insisted on the expulsion of **Girondins**, resulted in spreading the anti-**Jacobin** movement, which had already begun in Bordeaux, Lyon and Marseille. Sixty departments protested at the expulsion, though there was serious resistance in only eight. The Jacobins called these revolts 'Federalism' and said they were royalist plots to destroy the unity of the Republic. Initially the revolts had nothing to do with royalism but the rising in Toulon went further than intended, as the government cut off food supplies to the city. To obtain food the town authorities negotiated with the British, who insisted that the monarchy be proclaimed: British troops entered the town in August. As half the French fleet was lying off the coast at Toulon, this was a serious blow to the Republic. Many smaller towns in the Rhône valley and Provence followed the example of Toulon and Lyon in rejecting the Convention. Federalism appeared a serious threat to the government, which also had to face hostility to conscription, but federal forces were pitifully small: Marseille could raise only 3,500 men, Bordeaux 400 and none wanted to move far from home. There was little cooperation between the centres of revolt, so the government could pick off rebel areas one by one. Between August and December 1793 the regular army put down the revolt everywhere and began the **Terror** in the conquered areas. 800 were shot in Toulon without trial and a further 282 were sent to the guillotine by a Revolutionary Commission. In Lyon, the second city in France, people were mown down by cannon fire in front of previously dug graves and many others were guillotined, about 1,900 in all. It was in these rebel areas of the south-east and the Vendée (see **Vendean revolt**), which covered only five departments, that 70 per cent of total executions during the Terror took place.

**Feminist movements** sought the same rights for women as for men. They believed that women were oppressed by men and that this oppression should be ended: that women were not inferior to men and should not defer and be subordinate to them. Such movements were a product of Protestant, industrial societies in Europe and the USA and were overwhelmingly middle class. The first great feminist tract was Mary Wollstonecraft's *A Vindication of the Rights of Women* (1792), which said that women did not exist simply for child-bearing and for the pleasure of men but should have the same opportunities as men in education, work and politics. Elizabeth Cady **Stanton** called the first Women's Rights Convention at Seneca Falls, New York, in 1848 to demand a bill of rights for women. The movement for women's suffrage grew out of this, with the National Woman Suffrage Association, founded by Stanton and Susan **Anthony** in 1869. In Britain the **suffragettes** agitated, often violently, to gain the vote for women. Feminists played a leading part in temperance movements in the USA and in bringing about **Prohibition**. Yet outside the USA, Britain, the Low Countries and Scandinavia, feminist movements had little impact before 1945.

**Fenians.** Members of secret revolutionary societies in Ireland and the USA, who sought an independent Irish republic. They derived their name from the Fianna army in a medieval Irish saga. The Irish Republican Brotherhood (IRB), formed in 1858, was a society in Ireland, whilst the Fenian Brotherhood was a supporting organization of Irish emigrants based mainly in America but with branches in South Africa and Australia: the members of both societies were known as Fenians. They were opposed to constitutional methods, were influenced by the ideas of **Blanqui** and **Mazzini**, and looked forward to the time when Britain would be involved in a foreign war, giving them the opportunity to revolt. The IRB was never a popular movement, as it was anti-clerical (and so was opposed by the Catholic Church) and at first had little interest in land reform: at its peak it probably had about 50,000 members. Fenian invasions of Canada from the USA in 1866 and 1870–71 all failed. The movement received much publicity in England when it tried to seize Chester Castle and when twelve people were killed in London in 1867 in an attempt to rescue some prisoners. Several Fenians were executed and hundreds imprisoned. In the late 1860s the movement split up. Other organizations, such as the Home Rule League (see **Home Rule for Ireland**), the Irish Volunteers and **Sinn Fein**, appeared to replace it, though Fenians played an important role in all of them. The greatest success of the Fenians was in persuading **Gladstone** to devote so much of his time to the problems of Ireland.

**Ferry, Jules François Camille** (1832–93). French Prime Minister (1880–81, 1883–5). From a rich middle-class family Ferry became a lawyer and was Mayor of Paris (1870–71) at the time of the rising of the **Paris Commune**. His narrow escape resulted in his deep hatred of the **Left**. Authoritarian, cold and arrogant, he called in 1883 for 'a government which governs' but, like **Gambetta**, he was aware that peasant support was needed for the firm establishment of the **Third Republic**. Peasant ownership of land ensured that 'our social edifice is the most solid in Europe and the best sheltered against social revolutions'. Socially conservative, he was radical in his **anti-clericalism** and as Minister of Education from 1879 he tried to make sure that Frenchmen voted for the Republic by making primary education free (1881), compulsory (1882) and by putting it in the hands of laymen. 'Unauthorized' religious orders (mainly the Jesuits) were banned from teaching in France and nearly all male religious orders were expelled from their houses. State *lycées* (secondary schools) were set up for girls, Catholic universities were forbidden to confer degrees and clergy were not allowed to teach in state schools. Yet Ferry maintained the **Concordat** of 1801 with the Pope, as it gave the state control of clerical appointments. Ferry's second ministry (1883–5) passed many liberal reforms which have lasted to the present day: freedom of the press and of association was guaranteed, trade unions were legalized, mayors in the communes were to be elected and divorce was re-established.

Concern that the use of tariffs by European countries to protect their own industries would deprive France of her traditional markets made Ferry an imperialist: 'Colonial policy is the daughter of industrial policy.' In 1881, in order to forestall the Italians, a French force of 40,000 rapidly overran Tunisia, which became a French protectorate. This revival of **imperialism** divided the Republicans and was bitterly attacked by the Radicals for using up French energy and resources which ought to be devoted to recovering **Alsace-Lorraine**, lost in the **Franco-Prussian War** (1870–71). France strengthened her control of Madagascar from 1883–5, had her claims to the French Congo recognized at the **Berlin Conference** (1884–5) and declared a protectorate over Annam in Indo-China (Vietnam). This involved France in an undeclared war with China, which claimed suzerainty over Annam: it ended in 1885 with China accepting French claims. A minor reverse in Indo-China and a demand, rejected by the Chamber of Deputies, for more money to wage the war there, brought about Ferry's resignation. This was the effective end of his political career, though he narrowly failed to be elected President of the Third Republic in 1887.

**Fianna Fail** (Gaelic, 'soldiers of destiny'). Irish political party, sometimes called the Republican Party. Formed in 1926 by **de Valera** from those who opposed the **Anglo-Irish Treaty** (1921), which established the Irish Free State. Its aim was to create a united republic of Ireland. At first its members would not sit in the Dail (Irish parliament), as they would not take the oath of allegiance to the British Crown. They finally entered the Dail in 1927 and in the 1932 election became the largest party, forming a government with de Valera as Prime Minister. They remained in office until 1948, when **Fine Gael**, with the help of smaller parties, formed a minority government.

**Fifth Column.** A phrase coined by the nationalist General Mola during the **Spanish Civil War**. As his four columns were advancing on Madrid he said that it would be a 'Fifth Column', his supporters inside the city, who would bring about its fall. The term was widely used during the **Second World War** to indicate secret supporters of the enemy working behind the lines.

**'Final Solution'** (Holocaust). The attempted genocide of European Jews carried out by the Nazis between 1941 and 1945. **Hitler** had a pathological hatred of Jews, which he expressed in *Mein Kampf*, and thought that they aimed to enslave and destroy the Aryan race. As soon as he came to power in 1933 he began to exclude them from German society, removing them from their posts in the civil service, judiciary, the universities and the professions. The Nuremberg Laws (1935) deprived them of citizenship and forbade them to marry Aryans or to have extra-marital relations with them. Exclusion was followed by persecution, as in the **Crystal Night** (1938), when synagogues were burnt down and Jewish shops looted. The 'solution' to the Jewish problem at this time was to force them to emigrate and about half the 500,000 Jews in Germany and Austria fled abroad. Hitler indicated a worse fate when he said in a **Reichstag** speech in January 1939 that if war broke out it would lead to 'the annihilation of the Jews in Europe'. It is not known when Hitler gave the official order to exterminate all Jews but he told **Himmler** and **Goering** orally in March or April 1941. The mass extermination of Jews began after the invasion of Russia in June 1941. Four **SS** Action Groups (*Einsatzgruppen*), 3,000 men in all, followed the German armies to shoot Jews, Communist officials and partisans and had killed half a million Jews by the end of the year, with the help of Waffen SS combat troops and sometimes of the *Wehrmacht*. Many German officers thought that the shooting of Jews and prisoners was a stain on the honour of the German army, so it was decided to send all Jews to **extermination camps**. The Wannsee Conference held in Berlin in January 1942 worked out how this could be done and was told by **Heydrich** that 'The final solution to the Jewish problem in Europe will be applied to about eleven million people.' The deportation of German Jews to camps in Poland had begun at the end of 1941, and in 1942 Jews from all over Nazi-controlled Europe were sent there. This could not be done without some help from local authorities. The Dutch did what they were told but in Romania, Bulgaria and France most local officials refused to help and those who aided the Nazis did not believe that deportation meant death. The Danes and Italians did most to help their Jews, the Danes by helping them to escape to Sweden, the Italians by refusing to hand over any Jews to the Germans. Six death camps were set up in Poland, where it is estimated that at least five million Jews perished. The 'Final Solution' is the only attempt in recorded history made by a government to murder an entire people.

**Fine Gael** (Gaelic, 'united Ireland'). Irish political party. *Cumann na n Gaedheal* (Society of Gaels) was formed in 1923 by William **Cosgrave** from those members of the Dail (Irish parliament) who accepted the **Anglo-Irish Treaty** of 1921, which established the Irish Free State. Calling itself the party of peace and stability it won 41 per cent of the seats in the Free State's first election in 1923 and formed a minority government under Cosgrave. It remained in power until it was defeated by **de Valera**'s **Fianna Fail** in 1932. To create a larger party as a means of regaining power, Cosgrave joined Cumann with two smaller parties in 1933 to form Fine Gael, though this did not have enough electoral success to form a government until 1948. Regarded as a party which sought reconciliation with Britain, it created a sensation when it declared Ireland a republic and withdrew from the British Commonwealth.

**Finnish–Russian War** (November 1939–March 1940). The Soviet Union wanted her frontier moved back on the Karelian Isthmus to make Leningrad more secure, a long-term lease of the port of Hanko, which commanded the entrance to the Gulf of Finland, and some territory in the north near Petsamo to protect the sea-route to Murmansk. When the Finns rejected these demands, the Russians attacked without declaring war on 30 November 1939. Finland fought without help from the major powers, as Germany had made the **Nazi–Soviet Pact** and Britain and France were at war with Germany. The Finnish army of 300,000, 80 per cent of whom were reservists, was one of the weakest in Europe, with no tanks, little artillery and under one hundred aircraft. The Russians, with massive artillery and air support, attacked with a million troops on four fronts: round Petsamo; in the centre, where they hoped to cut through Finland's narrow waist to the Gulf of Bothnia; on the northern edge of Lake Ladoga; and against the Mannerheim Line in the Karelian Isthmus. They expected a quick victory but all their attacks were repelled and in the thick snow the Finnish ski troops (the Russians had no skis) manoeuvred brilliantly. Finnish resistance could not last: as Russian pressure mounted they were pushed back and, exhausted, surrendered on 12 March 1940. Finland had to concede Russia's original requests and even more territory, including Vyborg, but she retained her independence. The Soviet Union's military performance had been appalling, partly because she had lost the cream of her commanders in Stalin's **Great Purges**. Nearly 200,000 Russians were killed, 1,100 of their tanks knocked out and 684 aircraft shot down. Finnish losses were 25,000 men killed and sixty-one aircraft shot down. The weaknesses of the Soviet army exposed in this war encouraged **Hitler** to expect a quick German victory when he invaded Russia in June 1941 in Operation **Barbarossa**.

**First World War** (August 1914–November 1918). The war arose out of the **Eastern Question** and the collapse of Ottoman power in Europe, as was shown by her defeat in the **Balkan War** of 1912. Austria-Hungary felt threatened by the vast increase in the size of Serbia and was given an opportunity to strike at her when the heir to the Habsburg throne was assassinated at **Sarajevo** (28 June 1914). In the **July crisis** which followed Germany pushed Austria into war. Russia had been humiliated in the **Bosnian crisis** of 1908 and felt bound to support Serbia. Germany declared war on Russia on 1 August and on France, Russia's ally since the **Franco-Russian Alliance** of 1892–4, on 3 August. Britain had guaranteed Belgian independence since 1839 and declared war on 4 August when Germany invaded Belgium. The Allies – Russia, France, Britain and Serbia – were joined by Japan (1914), Italy (1915), Portugal and Romania (1916), the USA and Greece (1917). The Central Powers – Germany and Austria-Hungary – were supported by Turkey (1914) and Bulgaria (1915).

Both sides expected that the war would be over by Christmas. Germany, using the **Schlieffen Plan**, intended to knock out France in six weeks before the Russians could mobilize but her advance was thrown back at the battle of the **Marne** (5–8 September 1914). The German and Allied armies tried to outflank each other in Flanders but the German attempt to break through to the

Channel ports was stopped at the first battle of Ypres. By December there was stalemate on the Western Front: each side had a line of trenches (see **Trench warfare**) stretching from the Channel to Switzerland, protected by barbed wire and machine-guns. This line did not move more than ten miles either way in the next three years; attempts to break through it, such as the French offensives in Artois and Champagne in 1915, were costly failures. The Germans tried to bleed the French army to death by attacking **Verdun** in 1917 and though it resulted in horrendous losses, both French and German, it did not achieve its aim. The British offensive on the **Somme** (July–November 1916), Nivelle's offensive in 1917, which was followed by widespread mutinies in the French armies, and the third battle of Ypres (**Passchendaele**) all showed the futility of mass attacks against well-entrenched positions. On the Eastern Front the Russians invaded East Prussia in 1914 but were crushingly defeated at the battle of **Tannenberg** (26–9 August). They had success against the Austrians and won a great victory at Lemberg but German troops went to the aid of the Austrians. **Falkenhayn**, the German Chief of Staff, won a brilliant victory at Gorlice in 1915 and pushed the front back three hundred miles. A year later, in the **Brusilov offensive**, the Russians almost destroyed the Austro-Hungarian army but once again it was saved by German reinforcements.

There were attempts to break the stalemate by poison gas attacks, first used by the Germans at Ypres in April 1915, and by using tanks, which the British first produced in the later stages of the battle of the Somme, but both proved inconclusive. More successful for a time was the unrestricted submarine warfare which the Germans adopted in February 1917. This had the unfortunate effect, for them, of bringing America into the war but it almost brought Britain to her knees until the **convoy** system was adopted in May. The only major battle of the war at sea, the battle of **Jutland** in 1916, was indecisive. The Allies, therefore, sought success elsewhere. They tried to knock Turkey out of the war by the **Gallipoli Campaign** (April 1915–January 1916), which failed, but they did eventually gain success in the **Middle East campaigns**. In Africa and the Far East, Germany lost her colonies. South Africans conquered South-West Africa in 1915. British and

French troops took the Cameroons and Togoland, though a brilliant guerrilla campaign by the German General von Lettow-Vorbeck prevented the same success in East Africa. In the Pacific, Australian, New Zealand and Japanese troops captured German colonies in the first four months of the war: German concessions in China fell to Britain and Japan.

Russia ceased to play any effective part in the war in 1917, particularly after the **October Revolution**, when the **Bolsheviks** seized power and sued for peace, which was made in the Treaty of **Brest-Litovsk** in March 1918. The Germans could now move most of their troops to the Western Front, as Italy too was unlikely to give any trouble after her major defeat at the battle of **Caporetto** (October–November 1917). The **Ludendorff offensive**, aimed at victory before American troops arrived in strength, achieved early successes in 1918 but was hurled back by **Foch**'s counter-offensive on the Somme in August. With Germany's allies (Austria-Hungary, Bulgaria and Turkey) collapsing, Ludendorff on 29 September urged the government to ask for an armistice. There was a **German Revolution** in which the fleet mutinied, the Kaiser abdicated and the government accepted the armistice terms. Fighting stopped on 11 November 1918 and was followed by the **Paris Peace Conference**.

**Fisher, John Arbuthnot, 1st Baron** (1841–1920). British admiral, who became First Sea Lord, head of the Royal Navy, in 1904. Throughout his career he was interested in design and technology and from 1904–10 carried out a series of reforms which transformed the Royal Navy. He was responsible for building the **Dreadnought**, a battleship with heavy guns (ten twelve -inch) of only one calibre, powered by high-speed turbines, another innovation. These new ships made much of the fleet obsolete, so without hesitation Fisher scrapped 154 older ships, which 'could neither fight nor run away'. Battle-cruisers were another of his ideas. They were nearly equal in fire-power to the Dreadnought, with eight twelve-inch guns, but had less armour and so could move faster and act as scouts for the battleships. Fisher retired in 1910 but was recalled in 1914 when the **First World War** began. He believed in the army and navy working together in amphibious operations and favoured a totally unrealistic plan of sending a fleet into the Baltic and landing troops on the north German coast. When Churchill promoted the **Gallipoli Campaign** instead, Fisher resigned in May 1915.

**Five Year Plans.** The forced industrialization of the Soviet Union under **Stalin** from 1928 onwards. Industrialization had long been regarded as essential, if the Soviet Union was to be a major power. There was an added urgency from the late 1920s as the USSR expected to be attacked by capitalist powers. 'To slacken the tempo,' said Stalin in 1931, 'would mean falling behind, and those who fall behind get beaten . . . We are fifty or a hundred years behind the advanced countries. We must make good this distance in ten years. Either we do or we shall go under.' The first Five Year Plan (five years would allow for fluctuations of the harvest to be taken into account) was from 1928–32, the second from 1933–7 and the third from 1938–42. The first Plan was the most important, as it laid the foundations for future growth, but in all of them the emphasis was on heavy industry: iron and steel, machine tools, armaments and huge hydroelectric schemes, like that on the Dnieper river, to provide power. Consumer goods, housing, the chemical industry were all neglected: textile production actually declined during the first Plan. Much of the new industry was in the east, where the vast Ural–Kuznetsk complex began, based on steel from Magnitogorsk in the Urals and coal from the Kuznetsk basin in western Siberia. This made sense, as there were vast mineral deposits to be tapped there, but there was a political motivation too – these areas were far away from any possible attack from the West and enabled the USSR to survive **Hitler**'s attack in 1941.

The Plans were successful. Output in steel and coal quadrupled between 1928 and 1941: electricity generation increased ten-fold. The average annual growth rate for these years was 10 per cent, a remarkable achievement. This was made possible by a high rate of investment, by a massive increase in the work-force and by a ruthless use of state power. **Witte** had industrialized in the 1890s by borrowing heavily abroad. This was not possible for Stalin, who had to find the capital at home, which meant that it had to come from agriculture. Private agriculture under **NEP** could not provide enough funds, so Stalin decided that **collectivization** was necessary.

In this way the peasant could be squeezed and forced savings made by cutting internal consumption. Wages for industrial workers were kept low too, so the Five Year Plans were financed by a drop in living standards (which were already depressed), unprecedented in peacetime. Investment was, on average, 25 per cent of GNP (Gross National Product), a very high rate. Between 1928 and 1940 the industrial labour force trebled and was subjected to draconian discipline. In 1939 'absenteeism' was defined as being twenty minutes late for work, which could mean six months' 'corrective labour'. To make the Plans effective there was a vast extension of state power – private enterprise was almost eliminated and central planning agencies were set up to direct the economy. There was much coercion but also considerable enthusiasm, as many workers took pride in the achievements of the Soviet state, which in a decade became one of the greatest industrial nations. Without the Five Year Plans it is doubtful whether Russia would have been able to defend herself successfully during the **Second World War**.

**Foch, Ferdinand** (1851–1929). Marshal of France. Like many French soldiers, Foch thought that France had lost the **Franco-Prussian War** because she was too much on the defensive. In his *Principles of War* (1903) he argued that troops must have the will to conquer and must attack at all costs. His views were widely accepted in the French army (he was commandant of the *Ecole de Guerre* from 1907–11) and resulted in the disastrous attacks in Alsace and the Ardennes at the beginning of the **First World War**. As Commander of the French Ninth Army, Foch held up the massive German assault in September 1914 in the battle of the **Marne** and was appointed by **Joffre** to coordinate the French, British and Belgian armies in Flanders and so prevent German armies breaking through to the Channel ports, which he did successfully. Failure to use his reserves and to withdraw to a more defensive line at the second battle of Ypres (April–May 1915) dented his reputation but in May 1917 he replaced **Pétain** as Chief of Staff. His real fame came in 1918 when, in order to stem the **Ludendorff offensive**, he was made General-in-Chief of Allied Armies. He first held up the German advance and then counter-attacked to drive back German troops on a retreat which ended with the armistice of November 1918. As a recognition of his success he was made a marshal of France and was the only Frenchman to become an honorary field-marshal in the British army.

**Forced labour camps.** In Soviet Russia they were first set up on **Lenin**'s orders in 1918 (see **Cheka**). In remote areas, where there was a shortage of free labour by the late 1920s, the government used convicts. A special department of the **NKVD**, the Chief Administration of Camps (GULAG), was set up to organize convict labour. Its first big project was the White Sea–Baltic Canal (1931–3), to enable the Baltic Fleet to move quickly to the White Sea, but the canal was built in such haste that it was too shallow for that purpose. Prisoners were used in the timber, gold, coal and mineral industries. The original centre of camps was in Karelia on the White Sea coast; later centres were in the Arctic, Western Siberia, the Urals and, most notorious of all, in the Kolyma basin in the Far East. This was in the permafrost zone, cut off from the rest of Russia by hundreds of miles of barren waste: it could be reached only by sea. By the late 1930s there were camps all over the Soviet Union and convict construction sites in every major city. Rations depended on output, not of the individual but of the work-team, although normal rations were inadequate to sustain prisoners working ten to fifteen hours a day, often in freezing conditions. Consequently, many died. The death rate in the camps was 10 per cent in 1933 rising to 20 per cent in 1938. The total number of deaths is not known, although estimates range as high as fifteen to twenty million by 1950. Evgenia Ginsburg in *Into the Whirlwind* and Alexander Solzhenitsyn in his novel *One Day in the Life of Ivan Denisovich* vividly describe life in the camps.

**Ford, Henry** (1863–1947). US industrialist. Henry Ford was born on a Michigan farm. He became a watch-repairer and mechanic before building his first petrol-driven car, mainly from bicycle parts, in 1893. He formed the Ford Motor Company in 1903 and, at a time when automobiles were for the rich, conceived the idea of concentrating on one model and producing a cheap family car. His Model T (known as the 'Tin Lizzie') was produced in 1909 and remained the best-selling car until 1926. In 1913 he introduced assembly-line techniques, which cut production time by 90 per cent. Work was planned 'so that each man and each machine do only one thing,' he wrote. 'The thing is to keep everything in motion and take the work to the man and not the man to the work.' By 1925 Ford was producing a car every ten seconds and built fifteen million Tin Lizzies between 1909 and 1927, though there was no choice of colour. 'You can have any colour you like,' he said, 'so long as it is black.' Competition came from General Motors, who copied Ford's methods, had seven different and more stylish models and in a variety of colours. Ford had to replace the Model T by the Model A in 1928, which had improved features like shock absorbers and came in four colours.

Ford surprised everyone in 1914 by giving his workers a guaranteed minimum wage of five dollars a day (more than double the going rate), an eight-hour working day and a share of the profits, but he was implacably opposed to **trade unions**. He was a pacifist and isolationist, who bitterly opposed the USA's entry into the **First World War**, though this did not stop him building tanks, ships and vehicles for military use. In the **Second World War** he applied his mass-production techniques to the manufacture of bombers. In 1936 he established the Ford Foundation, which became the world's largest trust for educational, scientific, artistic and charitable purposes.

**Fouché, Joseph, Duke of Otranto** (1759–1820). French revolutionary. Educated by the Oratorians, he became a member of their order, which he renounced when the **French Revolution** took place. He became a **Jacobin**, was elected as a member of the **Convention** in 1792 and a year later was sent as one of their representatives-on-mission with wide-ranging powers to put down the **Federal Revolt**. At Lyon he was associated with Collot d'Herbois, a member of the **Committee of Public Safety**, in the savage repression in which 1,900 people were executed. As a leading exponent of the **Terror** Fouché encouraged **dechristianization**, forcing priests to marry, removing crosses from graveyards and, at Nevers, putting up a sign 'Death is an eternal sleep'. Recalled to Paris in the spring of 1794 he feared for his life, as **Robespierre** disapproved of dechristianization and excesses which turned people against the Revolution, so he plotted with others to overthrow him at **Thermidor** (July 1794). After a period in poverty and obscurity, his fortunes revived and he became Minister of Police in 1799, a post he also held under **Napoleon**, to whom his network of informers and spies was invaluable. Napoleon made him Duke of Otranto in 1809 but dismissed him a year later for making contacts with England. A devious intriguer, Fouché conspired with Napoleon and the Bourbons at the same time, helped to arrange the Bourbon Restoration yet became Napoleon's Minister of Police again during the **Hundred Days**. From July–September 1815 he was **Louis XVIII**'s Minister of Police, when he drew up a list of all those who had served Napoleon on his return from Elba: 'he left out none of his friends,' commented **Talleyrand**. In 1816 he was banished as a regicide (he had voted for the execution of **Louis XVI**) and he died in Trieste.

**Fourteen Points.** US President **Wilson** outlined the basis on which peace in the **First World War** should be made in an address to Congress on 8 January 1918. He wanted to show that the USA did not want a punitive peace and by so doing encourage Germany and her allies to end the war. Eight of the Fourteen Points dealt with territorial matters, such as the evacuation of territory in Belgium, Russia, France (including the return of **Alsace-Lorraine** to France), Romania, Montenegro and Serbia. An independent Poland should be created with access to the Baltic; the peoples of the **Austro-Hungarian** and **Ottoman Empires** should be granted self-determination. Five other points concerned international cooperation. There was to be open, rather than secret, diplomacy; 'absolute freedom of navigation upon the seas'; general disarmament; the removal of trade barriers; and the impartial settlement of colonial claims. The Fourteenth Point, by far the most important to Wilson, was the creation of a **League of Nations** to keep the peace, by arbitrating in cases of dispute and by guaranteeing the political independence and territorial integrity of all member states. The Fourteen Points were enthusiastically received in America but Wilson had made them without consulting his Allies. They were contrary to secret agreements Britain and France had made with Russia and Italy for the annexation of enemy territory (see

Constantinople agreements and Treaty of London, 1915), and the Allied desire for a peace with huge indemnities. Germany used the Fourteen Points as the basis for agreeing to the armistice of 11 November 1918 and complained bitterly when some of them were ignored at the Treaty of Versailles.

**Fox, Charles James** (1749–1806). English politician. When he entered the House of Commons at the age of nineteen, his skill in debate was immediately recognized, as he could absorb facts and arguments with remarkable speed. From the death of Rockingham in 1782 he was effectively leader of the Whigs. With his great charm and gift for making friends he was a popular figure but his hatred for Lord North, and then for George III and for Pitt the Younger, kept him out of high office for all but one and a half years of the thirty-seven he spent in parliament. After opposing the American War of Independence and Lord North's running of it, Fox surprised everyone by making a coalition with North in 1783 and, as Secretary of State, made the peace of Versailles which ended the War. George III loathed Fox and used his influence in the House of Lords to obtain a rejection of the coalition's Indian Bill. The King then dismissed Fox and North and appointed Pitt as Prime Minister, although he had no majority in the Commons. George therefore called a general election, which resulted in a majority for the new ministry. Fox became leader of the opposition, which he was to remain for all but the last seven months of his life. When the French Revolution occurred Fox welcomed it as 'the greatest event that ever happened in the world' and split the Whigs when he opposed war with France and supported Grey's proposal for parliamentary reform in 1793. He had already quarrelled with Burke over the Revolution and in 1794 saw the Duke of Portland and other Whigs join Pitt's government. Fox appeared as a defender of the liberties of Englishmen by opposing the 'Gag' Acts of 1795, which allowed the death penalty to be imposed for attendance at unofficial meetings of over fifty people and made any criticism of the Constitution treasonable. Courageously in 1797, a year of invasion scares and naval mutinies, Fox again supported Grey in his bill for parliamentary reform, which would have abolished some 'rotten' boroughs, though Fox was no democrat and was in favour of a property qualification for voting. By this time the Foxites numbered only about fifty in the Commons. When the bill was rejected, Fox and most of his followers seceded from the House and did not sit there between 1797 and 1801. Pitt's resignation over **Catholic emancipation**, which Fox supported, brought them back. Fox approved of peace being made in 1802, though he condemned the 'shameful surrender of all our conquests' at the peace of **Amiens**. He had come to regard **Napoleon** as the betrayer of the liberal ideals of the French Revolution and supported the resumption of war against France in 1803. When Addington fell in 1804 Pitt wanted to form a broad-based government which would include Fox but George III would not allow this. Only when Pitt died and Grenville became Prime Minister did the King reluctantly lift his veto on Fox, who became Foreign Secretary in the mainly Whig 'Ministry of All the Talents'. Fox promoted the bill for the abolition of the **slave trade** but died in October 1806 before it became law.

**France, fall of** (May–June 1940). When Germany attacked France on 10 May 1940 she was not greatly superior to her opponents in numbers or quantity of equipment, except in aircraft: 136 German divisions faced 125 French, British and Belgian divisions. The Germans had 2,500 tanks, half of which were obsolete: the Allies had 3,600 tanks, including some French tanks which were better than anything the Germans had. The difference between the sides was that the Germans massed their tanks in ten Panzer divisions, whereas the Allies scattered theirs amongst infantry units. The Germans were dominant in the air, as they had 3,000 aircraft, 2,000 of which were modern: the French had 1,000 aircraft and the British 400, many of them obsolete, as the British kept their best fighters for home defence. The Germans attacked, as the Allies expected, through Belgium and Holland and this drew Allied forces north, but it was not the main German assault. This, spearheaded by Panzers, came in the wooded Ardennes, which was regarded by the French High Command as unsuitable for tank warfare and was weakly guarded. The **Manstein** Plan, carried out by the Panzer commander **Guderian**, worked perfectly and was a decisive demonstration of *Blitzkrieg*. By 14 May the Panzers had crossed the

Meuse, opened up a fifty-mile gap in the Allied front and then, supported by Stuka dive-bombers, rushed along the valley of the Somme towards the Channel. This was a very daring move, as the Panzers were in long columns supported only by motorized infantry and were very vulnerable to counter-attacks from north and south. They never took place as Gamelin, the French commander, was paralysed by the audacity of the German attacks and was replaced by Weygand. On 20 May the Germans reached the Channel. By 28 May they were at Calais and had cut off the French, British and Belgian forces in the north from the rest of the French armies. As the Dutch and Belgian armies surrendered, the British moved to **Dunkirk** from where, against all expectations, they were able to evacuate 338,000 troops and take them to England. Weygand tried to hold a line along the Somme and Aisne but by this time he had only forty-five divisions against ninety-five German divisions, including ten Panzers. In a battle from 5–9 June this line was broken and the French fell back to the Loire, isolating those holding the **Maginot Line**. The Germans occupied Paris on 14 June and on 16 June Reynaud, the French Prime Minister and strongly anti-Nazi, resigned and was replaced by the fatalistic **Pétain**, who had no hesitation in accepting German surrender terms: Northern France and the Atlantic coast were to be occupied by German forces. De Gaulle, broadcasting from London on 18 June, asked the French to continue the fight abroad but few responded.

**Francis Joseph** (1830–1916). Emperor of Austria (1848–1916) and King of Hungary (1867–1916). He succeeded to the throne at the age of eighteen on the abdication of his uncle Ferdinand, during the **Revolutions of 1848**. Believing in the Divine Right of Kings, he looked on the **Austrian Empire** as a dynastic estate. Devoted to duty and well-informed, Francis Joseph in 1851 withdrew the promise of a constitution which had been given in 1849 but ten years later he had to accept a parliament with the right to pass laws and approve the budget, though he retained considerable power for himself, as he appointed ministers and controlled foreign affairs and the army. Austria's foreign policy during the **Crimean War** was his own and it was disastrous, as he lost the goodwill of Russia, who thereafter supported France in Italy, and Prussia in Germany.

Defeated by France in 1859 at Magenta and Solferino and by Prussia at **Sadowa** in 1866, Austria was pushed out of Germany and Italy. Consequently, Francis Joseph had to accept the *Ausgleich* ('compromise') in 1867, which gave Hungary equal status with Austria in what was now the **Austro-Hungarian Empire**. From this time he wanted peace at almost any price, as he might lose influence in the Balkans in a war with Russia. His first foreign policy success was at the **Berlin Congress** (1878), when he secured for Austria-Hungary the military occupation of Bosnia and Herce-govina, and a year later the **Dual Alliance**, which made Germany the protector of his Empire and was to be the foundation of his foreign policy for the rest of his life. After the annexation of Bosnia and Hercegovina in 1908, Conrad, his Chief of Staff, wanted to fight a preventive war with Serbia but Francis Joseph opposed this: 'My policy is that of peace.' Yet in 1914 he changed his mind because of Serbian gains in the **Balkan Wars** (1912–13) and decided on war after the assassination of the heir to his throne at **Sarajevo**. He died in 1916, before the military defeats which brought an end to his Empire and his dynasty.

**Franco Bahamonde, Francisco** (1892–1975). Spanish military dictator (1939–75). Born in the major naval port of El Ferrol in Galicia, Franco was the son of a naval paymaster. He entered the Military Academy of Toledo in 1907, graduating in 1910 as the 251st of 381 cadets. He had a meteoric rise through the ranks from 1912–26 in the Moroccan colonial wars. Militarily, he was distin-guished by his ability to command, imperturbability under fire, and fearless bravery. His often reckless courage probably compensated in part for his unprepossessing appearance, small stature (5ft 3ins), and high-pitched voice. Personally, he was reserved and serious, a loner who stood out as a soldier '*sin misa, sin mujeres y sin miedo*' ('without Mass, women or fear'). Indeed, his emotional life was to be character-ized by denial: of fear, pleasure, intimacy, emotion, and even of death. In 1926, Franco became, at thirty-three, the youngest general in Europe. He had become not only a favourite of King **Alphonso XIII**, but also of General **Primo de Rivera**, the military dictator of Spain from 1923 to 1930. Consequently, in 1928 Franco was chosen at the first director of the General Military Academy in

Saragossa. As a monarchist and conservative, Franco was ill-disposed to the **Spanish Second Republic** established in 1931. Under the left-wing governments of 1931–3, he fell from favour, the Saragossa Academy being closed. After the electoral victory of the **Right** in November 1933, he was rapidly restored to pre-eminence. He orchestrated the severe suppression of the Asturian rising in October 1934 as a special ministerial adviser, and was then named Commander-in-Chief of the armed forces in Morocco. Moreover, in May 1935 Franco was appointed Chief of the General Staff, using his position to counter liberal influence in the officer corps and to prepare the army for a *coup*. Following the victory of the **Popular Front** in February 1936, Franco was once again removed from the centre of power. He was posted to the distant Canary Islands. With typical caution, he joined the military rebellion of 17–18 July only days beforehand. At the beginning of the rising Franco was flown to Morocco to take command of the most powerful section of the Spanish army, the Army of Africa. By gaining the support of the Germans and Italians, he was able to transport the army across the blockaded Straits to the south of Spain – the first major airlift in military history. This avoided defeat for the Nationalists and established Franco as the leading military figure in the Nationalist camp. The swift advance of the Army of Africa through southern Spain (leaving a horrific trail of slaughter) consolidated his position. His decision to relieve the siege of the Alcazar in Toledo in September 1936 probably cost the Nationalists the conquest of Madrid at that time. But this internationally recognized incident, together with the backing of the **Axis powers**, greatly strengthened Franco's claim to overall leadership of the Nationalists. On 1 October 1936 he was proclaimed not merely the military commander of the Nationalists but also the head of state.

Franco rapidly unified the Nationalists under his control, neutralizing the mass-based **Falange**, partly through its fusion with the **Carlists** in April 1937 and partly by conniving in the death of its charismatic leader, José Antonio Primo de Rivera. Franco prolonged the **Spanish Civil War**, partly because of his conservative military outlook, but also to purge his opponents thoroughly and to consolidate his personal dictatorship. He treated his allies just as ruthlessly, sacrificing the Italians at Guadalajara in March 1937, so that **Mussolini**, following the success of the Italians at Malaga, did not diminish his own prestige and power. Yet Franco won the war above all because of the support of the Germans and Italians. He rejected all offers of mediation or compromise: victory was finally achieved unconditionally on 1 April 1939. Revenge not reconciliation characterized the regime ushered in by the Nationalist victory. Franco kept the hatreds of the Civil War alive as a means of maximizing his own control over Spanish society. Including the post-war repression, the Nationalists executed between 150,000 and 200,000 people, while the Republicans had shot between 20,000 and 50,000 during the war. The authoritarian Francoist state was based on corporatist principles, with the Catholic Church playing an important role of legitimation. Franco saw himself as a warrior-king, who would return Spain to the Catholic and imperial past of his hero Philip II. The appalling starvation and scarcities of the 1940s were exacerbated by Franco's decision to pursue a course of economic autarky, eventually abandoned in the 1950s because of its disastrous results. He retained power by skilfully balancing the various 'families' that made up the regime: the army, monarchists, Falangists, and church. From a wider perspective, he returned power to the landed and industrial ruling classes that had dominated Spain prior to the Second Republic. During the **Second World War** Franco provided the Axis powers with important strategic and material support, such as observation posts and radio interception stations, refuelling facilities, and exports of wolfram. At the Hendaye meeting with **Hitler** in October 1940 Franco was prepared to enter the war on Hitler's side, in exchange for French territories in North Africa but Hitler was not prepared to pay Franco's price, preferring instead to placate **Vichy France**. Meanwhile, the appalling shortages in Spain prompted Franco to accept the aid offered by the Allies. Yet Franco continued to support the Axis, believing in a German victory till late 1944. Moreover, the Spanish Blue Division sent a total of 47,000 soldiers to the Russian front (1941–4). Although ostracized at Potsdam in July 1945 (see **Potsdam Declaration**) by the major powers, the onset of the Cold War ensured the consolidation of Franco's regime, which survived until 1975.

**Franco-Prussian War** (1870–71). After the defeat of Austria in the **Austro-Prussian War** (1866) Prussia dominated north Germany, but unification seemed a distant prospect, as the Catholic south German states did not wish to be dominated by Protestant Prussia. **Bismarck** used French demands for territory on the Rhine to persuade Baden, Bavaria and Württemberg that France was their real enemy: he made secret alliances, which required them to put their armies under Prussian command in wartime and to aid each other if one of them was attacked. He came to realize that a successful war against France would bring about German unification, but the secret alliances would only be activated if France was clearly the aggressor. With the **Hohenzollern candidature for the Spanish throne** he thought his opportunity had arisen and when this was withdrawn he was in despair. Here Gramont, the French Foreign Minister, came to his rescue, by demanding a promise from King **William I** of Prussia that the candidacy would never be renewed. Bismarck's manipulation of the **Ems telegram** made it appear that both France and Prussia had been insulted and led to France declaring war on 19 July 1870. This deprived her of European support and enabled Bismarck to rouse the enthusiasm of the southern states for a great patriotic war in defence of the German Fatherland.

Owing to the efficiency of **Moltke**'s mobilization, 1.8 million troops were called up within eighteen days and 460,000 were transported by railway to the western front. **Napoleon III** intended to invade southern Germany and hoped to bring Austria and Italy into the war on his side but before his reserves could be gathered together Moltke had pushed through the Lorraine gap and got between Paris and the two main French armies. Bazaine was pushed back east and bottled up in Metz. **MacMahon**, joined by the Emperor, tried to go to his aid and was defeated at **Sedan**. The Emperor and 100,000 French troops were captured. This was the end of the Second Empire, as a Republic was proclaimed in Paris on 4 September. Bazaine surrendered at the end of October with 173,000 men but the war continued, as Bismarck had announced his intention of annexing Alsace and Lorraine (see **Alsace-Lorraine**). Paris was besieged from 19 September and when it fell on 28 January 1871, peace talks began. At the Treaty of Frankfurt, 10 May 1871, France lost Alsace and most of Lorraine and had to pay an indemnity of five billion francs: there would be a German army of occupation until it was paid. Meanwhile, on 18 January 1871, the **German Empire** had been proclaimed in the Hall of Mirrors at Versailles.

**Franco-Russian Alliance** (1894). Germany was convinced in 1890 that France and Russia would never become allies, as the Tsar regarded France as the home of revolutionary movements and unstable governments. Their interests were different too – Russia was mainly concerned with the Balkans, France with the recovery of **Alsace-Lorraine**. Yet Germany's actions helped to bring France and Russia together. In 1887 **Bismarck** had made it impossible for Russia to obtain loans in Berlin, so she had turned to France, who readily lent her the money she needed. After Bismarck's fall, Germany refused to renew the **Reinsurance Treaty** with Russia in 1890, thus leaving her diplomatically isolated. At the same time Germany moved to strengthen her ties with Britain and, if possible, persuade her to join the **Triple Alliance** of Germany, Austria-Hungary and Italy. When Britain and Germany signed the **Anglo-German agreement** in 1890 it seemed that this was about to happen. Russia, therefore, began negotiations with France in 1891, which were finally settled in 1894. It was agreed that if France was attacked by Germany, or by Italy supported by Germany, Russia would come to her aid. Similarly, France would assist Russia if she was attacked by Germany, or by Austria supported by Germany. If any member of the Triple Alliance mobilized, France and Russia would do the same: this would amount to a declaration of war. This agreement completed the alliance system, which is sometimes held responsible for the **First World War**, though its purpose was defensive.

**Frankfurt Parliament** (18 May 1848–18 June 1849). During the **Revolutions of 1848** some liberals called for the election of a parliament to unite Germany and provide her with a constitution. Such a parliament was elected by universal but indirect male suffrage and met at Frankfurt. It was not representative of the German people as a whole, as it was overwhelmingly a middle-class body (lawyers, civil servants, professors): only one peasant was elected and not one labourer. The weakness of the parliament was immediately apparent: it had no power to impose taxes and the separate states refused to give up control of their armed forces. A further weakness was that the members could not agree on what the boundaries of Germany should be: Protestants wanted a Little Germany, excluding Austria and led by Prussia, whereas Catholics wanted to include Austria and Bohemia in a Great Germany. The impotence of the parliament was demonstrated when Germans in **Schleswig-Holstein** asked it for aid, as the King of Denmark had incorporated the Duchies in Denmark. As the parliament did not have an army of its own it had to call on Prussia, who defeated Denmark but then gave up control of the Duchies, owing to pressure from Britain and Russia. The parliament had no choice but to accept this blow to its national pride and prestige. In March 1849 the parliament finally produced its Constitution. There were to be two houses, the upper house representing the states in Germany, the lower to be elected by universal male suffrage. Ministers were to be responsible to parliament and there was to be a hereditary emperor with a suspensive veto. The parliament offered the crown to **Frederick William IV**, King of Prussia, who rejected it, as it was not offered by his fellow princes. In fact he had no choice, as Austria was strongly opposed to any such increase in Prussian strength and Frederick William did not want a war with Austria, in which she would almost certainly have been supported by Russia. When he withdrew Prussia's deputies from the parliament (Austria had already done so) it moved to Stuttgart, where it was dispersed by Württemberg troops. The failure of the Frankfurt parliament showed clearly that if Germany was to be united, this could be done only with the support of Prussia or Austria.

**Frederick William IV** (1795–1861). King of Prussia (1840–61). A romantic, a lover of art and literature, Frederick William IV was sensitive to the intellectual currents around him and briefly took up the cause of German unification during the **Revolutions of 1848**, when he declared that 'Prussia is henceforth absorbed in Germany.' Yet he rejected the throne of a united Germany, when it was offered to him by the **Frankfurt Parliament**, as the offer did not come from his fellow rulers. His attempt to create a union of German states under Prussian leadership (the **Erfurt Union**) had to be humiliatingly abandoned in 1850, when he was faced with the opposition of Austria. His most lasting achievement was the Prussian Constitution (1848–50), which astonished his contemporaries, as it seemed so liberal. It established a bicameral **Diet**. The Upper House consisted of hereditary and life members (the latter appointed by the King). The Lower House was elected by male suffrage but in a three-tier system: the electorate was divided into high (5 per cent of the total), medium and low taxpayers, each group having equal representation. This ensured that the Diet would be conservative and dominated by *Junkers* and the wealthy. The Diet had some control over legislation and taxation but ministers were appointed by, and responsible to, the King, not the Diet. The King retained most power, as he could veto legislation, he controlled the army and he had extensive emergency powers. This Constitution was in force and unchanged until 1918. As the constituencies were never redrawn, the urban centres, which grew rapidly with industrialization, were underrepresented. In practice the Constitution enabled the *Junkers* to enjoy political control long after their economic power had declined.

**Free Corps** (*Freikorps*). Paramilitary organizations formed in Germany at the end of the **First World War**. They were led by former officers and NCOs and were composed of demobilized soldiers (who had difficulty in adjusting to civilian life), nationalists and unemployed youths. They sprang up all over Germany and were used to fight, with Allied approval, against **Bolsheviks** in Lithuania and Latvia; and to crush left-wing risings at home. They put down the **Spartakist Rising** in January 1919, murdering its leaders Karl Liebknecht and Rosa **Luxemburg**. They were also used to support right-wing *coups*, such as the **Kapp** *Putsch* in 1920. The *Freikorps* were disbanded in 1921 but some members continued to take part in murder squads, which assassinated politicians of the **Weimar Republic**, whom they accused of betraying the German people. Matthias Erzberger, the **Centre Party** leader, and Walther Rathenau were among their victims. In each case German courts imposed lenient sentences on those responsible. Many members joined the **SA** to continue their murderous activities.

**Free French.** Supporters of General de Gaulle, who continued the fight against Germany after France surrendered in 1940. De Gaulle, broadcasting from London in June 1940, proclaimed Free France with the Cross of Lorraine as its emblem but few French people heard the broadcast and even fewer knew who de Gaulle was. Nearly all French colonies remained loyal to the Vichy government (see **Vichy France**): in July 1940 the Free French had only 7,000 troops, partly owing to resentment at the British bombardment of the French fleet at Oran and Mers el-Kebir in North Africa, to prevent it falling into German hands. De Gaulle was rebuffed at Dakar (West Africa) in September 1940, when he tried to establish a base there but gradually colonial territories in Chad, the Cameroons, the French Congo and the Pacific joined him. He cooperated with the French **Resistance**, whose French National Committee (based in Algiers) developed into a provisional government for liberated France. Arrogant and aloof, de Gaulle was distrusted by the Americans, who excluded him and the Free French from their invasion of North Africa in November 1942 (see **North African Campaigns**). By this time the Free French, now known as Fighting French, had 400,000 troops, who played their part in the campaigns to liberate Western Europe from German occupation.

**French Revolution** (1789–99). Its origins lay in a financial crisis brought about by wars (France was at war for twenty years between 1740 and 1783), especially by French involvement in the American War of Independence (1778–83), which greatly increased the national debt. The privileged orders (the clergy and nobility) resisted attempts to tax them and demanded the calling of a representative assembly, the **Estates-General**. When it became clear in September 1788 that the privileged orders would be able to outvote the Third Estate in the Estates-General, the *bourgeois* leaders of the Third Estate began a struggle against the aristocracy. They sought equality and this involved destroying the privileges of the Church and the nobility and the setting up of a system where promotion to high office should be based on merit, not birth, where all paid taxes on the same basis and where the law was the same for all. The French Revolution was, above all else, a struggle for equal rights. In its struggle against **Louis XVI** and the privileged orders – for the two had combined to resist the *bourgeois* assault – the *bourgeoisie* needed the support of the Paris populace. In July 1789 the Crown prepared to use force to dissolve the **Constituent Assembly**, which the Estates-General had become. It was prevented from doing so by the rising of the *sans-culottes*, the artisans and workers of Paris who, in the first great *journée* of the Revolution, attacked the Bastille on 14 July (see fall of the **Bastille**). This saved the Assembly and ensured the success of the Revolution, as the King lost control of Paris and of the towns. The King lost control of the countryside too in a peasant revolution, which spread over most of France in the **Great Fear** (20 July–6 August 1789). To end this revolution the Assembly had to give the peasants much of what they wanted in the **August Decrees**, which also marked the end of noble powers and privilege. The **Declaration of the Rights of Man** laid down the principles on which a new constitution should be based but the King refused to accept either the August Decrees or the Declaration of Rights. He was forced to do so in the **October Days**, when he was brought, a virtual prisoner, from Versailles to Paris.

By sweeping away many of the institutions of the old regime, the August Decrees had prepared the way for the creation of a national, uniform and representative system of administration for France. This was achieved in 1789–91 by the Constituent Assembly, whose reforms were to prove the most radical and most lasting of the Revolution. There was little opposition to the Revolution until the **Civil Constitution of the Clergy** (July 1790) reformed the Catholic Church in France and severed its ties with the Pope. Now counter-revolution received mass support for the first time. The King, a devout man, was unhappy about the Civil Constitution and tried to flee. The flight to **Varennes** (June 1791) made it clear that Louis had not accepted the Revolution and was followed by demands for a republic. A demonstration demanding this was crushed at the Champ de Mars (see **Champ de Mars massacre**) in July but few believed the King when he took an oath to uphold the new Constitution, which drastically limited his powers, in September 1791. Yet it seemed likely that the Constitution and the monarchy would survive.

What prevented this was war with Austria, which began the **French Revolutionary Wars** in April 1792. This was one of the most important events of the Revolution, which affected nearly everything that happened in France afterwards. The King and

Marie Antoinette were suspected – with reason – of wanting an Austrian victory: on 10 August 1792 the palace of the **Tuileries** was attacked in another revolutionary *journée*, the King was imprisoned and in September a new Assembly, the **Convention**, abolished the monarchy. In the same month the Prussian invasion of France caused panic in the capital, where the **September massacres** took place, but the danger to Paris was averted by the French victory at the battle of **Valmy**. The King was tried and executed in January 1793 and a month later the war was extended, when the Convention declared war on Britain and Holland. The French were defeated at Neerwinden in March by the Austrians, there was a rising in the Vendée (see **Vendean revolt**) against conscription, and an economic crisis with huge inflation. It appeared that the Revolution might not survive, so the Convention set up a Revolutionary Tribunal, which was to become a main agency of the **Terror**, and a **Committee of Public Safety** which, after the fall of the **Girondins** in June 1793, was dominated by **Jacobins**. This Committee overcame the dangers facing France by driving out the invaders, crushing the **Federal Revolt**, controlling food prices and by executing enemies (real and imaginary) of the regime, including **Hébert** (March 1794) and **Danton** (April 1794) and their followers. **Robespierre** inaugurated the **Great Terror** when he persuaded a terrified Convention to pass the Law of Prairial, which denied anyone a fair trial, but he overreached himself in **Thermidor** (July 1794), when he accused unnamed members of the CPS of conspiracy. To save themselves they plotted to have Robespierre and his closest associates executed on 21 July.

By this time everyone was sick of the Terror, which was brought to an end and the Law of Prairial was repealed. In the provinces the **White Terror** sought revenge on ex-terrorists, whilst in Paris the abandonment of price controls led to the collapse of the paper currency and the rising of **Prairial** (May 1795), a *sans-culotte* gesture of despair, crushed by the army. The Convention came to an end in 1795 by establishing a new Constitution, which set up the **Directory**. In seeking to preserve their own power (by insisting that two-thirds of the deputies in the new Legislative Councils should come from the Convention), the deputies provoked the last of the *journées*, the rising of **Vendémiaire** (October 1795), which was again put down by the army. The Directors, to prevent royalists gaining a majority in the Councils, called in the army to purge them in the *coup d'état* of Fructidor (1797). By 1799 the Directory was extremely unpopular – conscription had been reintroduced, a forced loan imposed on the rich to pay for the war, local government had collapsed and brigandage was widespread. There was hardly a murmur, therefore, when the *coup d'état* of **Brumaire** brought the Directory and the Revolution to an end and began the long dominance of **Napoleon**.

**French Revolutionary Wars** (1792–9) began when France declared war on Austria in April 1792. This event had more decisive and far-reaching results than any other in the whole of the **French Revolution**. Almost everything that happened in France from that time was affected by it. The war finally destroyed the consensus of 1789 and led directly to the fall of the monarchy, to civil war and to the **Terror**. Prussia, who declared war on France in May, took the lead in the early campaign. By September the Prussians were at Verdun, the last major fortress on the road to Paris. The ensuing panic resulted in the **September massacres** but the capital was saved by the minor engagement at the battle of **Valmy**. French armies were able to take the offensive, defeat the Austrians at Jemappes and occupy most of Belgium. In the south, Nice and Savoy were conquered and annexed. The war was extended when France declared war on Britain and Holland in February 1793, and on Spain in March. To the surprise of the French the war went badly. The Austrians defeated them at Neerwinden in March, their leading general Dumouriez defected, they lost Belgium and there was fighting once more on French soil. Opposition to conscription led to a rising in the Vendée (see **Vendean revolt**). In the summer of 1793 the Allies had 160,000 men on the Netherlands' border with France, with a smaller French force opposing them. If York and Coburg, the Allied commanders, had joined forces and moved on Paris the French would have faced disaster. Fortunately for them, the Allies did not coordinate their plans. Pitt ordered the Duke of York to capture Dunkirk as a naval base, so he turned west. The Austrians turned east, and the Allied army broke in two. This enormous blunder saved France. The disunity of the Allies at this time was a major factor in France's survival. Prussia and Austria were quarrelling about Poland: the second partition took place in 1793, in which Austria gained nothing. Austria, fearing that Russia and Prussia would take even more territory in Poland, was unwilling to commit herself fully in the west.

By the end of 1793 the Allied troops had been pushed out of France: after their victory at Fleurus (June 1794) the French recaptured Belgium. This was the first of a series of successes which continued until all the members of the First Coalition, except Britain, had been knocked out of the war. Prussia made peace with France at Basle (April 1795) and handed over her territories on the left bank of the Rhine to France. The Dutch and Spaniards also made peace, so that only Britain and Austria remained in the war against France. The main French objective in 1796 was to defeat Austria. **Carnot** drew up the plan for a pincer movement. The main attack of Jourdan and Moreau, with 140,000 troops, was to march across Bavaria to Vienna. A secondary attack through northern Italy and then across the Alps into Austria was under the command of the twenty-seven-year-old General Bonaparte, with only 30,000 troops. **Napoleon**'s genius turned Italy into the major battleground against Austria. He defeated Piedmont and forced her to make peace and then won a victory over the Austrians at Lodi and entered Milan. The key to the passes over the Alps leading to Vienna was Mantua, which he captured in February 1797. As Moreau had been driven back to the Rhine, Napoleon signed an armistice with Austria at Leoben (April), whose terms were confirmed in the Peace of Campo Formio (October). He was now making his own foreign policy without consulting the **Directory**. Austria gave up Belgium to France and in return was granted Venice and part of the Venetian Republic.

Britain was now the only country fighting France. The French hoped to invade Britain, with the help of the Dutch and Spanish fleets, but these hopes were dashed by two British victories in 1797. In February the Spanish fleet was defeated off Cape St Vincent and the Dutch fleet was almost completely destroyed at Camperdown in October. The French continued to extend their influence by setting up satellite states in Switzerland (the Helvetic Republic) and Italy, and in March 1798 the Congress of the Holy Roman Empire ceded the left bank of the Rhine to France. Revolutionary France's power was at its height: it now dominated west, central and southern Europe. As Napoleon could not invade England, he decided to strike at her route to India by attacking Egypt. In May 1798 he sailed from Toulon, captured Malta on the way and in Egypt defeated the Mamluks at the battle of the Pyramids and took Cairo. This brilliant campaign was negated by Nelson's victory at the battle of the **Nile**, when he captured or destroyed eleven of thirteen French ships of the line. This British victory encouraged other countries to take up arms against France again and form the Second Coalition. This included Russia, who had not taken part in previous fighting against France. The French were pushed back to the Rhine by the Austrians in 1799, whilst the Russians advanced through northern Italy into Switzerland. It appeared that France would be invaded for the first time in six years but, as had happened before, France was saved by quarrels among the Allies. Austria, instead of supporting Russia in Switzerland, sent her best troops north to the Rhine. This allowed the French to move on to the offensive in Switzerland, where the Russians were compelled to withdraw in the autumn of 1799. The danger to France was over, though the war was still continuing when the *coup d'état* of **Brumaire** ended the Revolution and began Napoleon's long ascendancy.

**Friendly Societies.** The most common form of working-class organization in nineteenth-century Britain, which had more members than **trade unions** throughout the century. They were mainly concerned with providing insurance against accident, sickness and old age, so that members would not be dependent on charity. Nearly all members were skilled workers, the more affluent section of the working class, as the poor could not afford the regular payments. They emphasized the traditional artisan values of thrift, respectability and sobriety and often forbade involvement in politics. By 1899, 27,000 friendly societies, with 5.4 million members, were registered in Britain. **Lloyd George**'s **National Insurance Act** (1911) recognized them as 'approved' societies, a status they retained until 1946, when they had 8.6 million members. In France there were 2,000 friendly societies in 1840 and others were formed in

Spain in the 1840s, in Russia in the 1870s and in Germany. They were often persecuted by the state, particularly in Germany under **Bismarck**'s **Anti-socialist law** from 1878 to 1890, as their funds were sometimes used to support strikes and as some were front organizations for opposition to the existing political system.

**Fry, Elizabeth** (1780–1845). English humanitarian and prison reformer. The daughter of a wealthy Quaker banker, she married a London merchant and fellow Quaker, Joseph Fry, in 1800. She was recognized as a 'minister' by the Society of Friends in 1811, and two years later was shocked on visiting Newgate, the women's prison in London, where she found 300 prisoners in two wards, who slept on the floor without bedding in appallingly filthy conditions. She began a campaign to improve conditions there and made several recommendations: that there should be a classification of prisoners, female warders, and that useful employment and education should be provided. Her scheme received much publicity and she was invited to visit prisons and advise on reform in several European countries. Inspired by her work at Newgate a German pastor and his wife set up a refuge for women at Kaiserswerth, which grew to include a lunatic asylum and training hospital for nurses, which Florence **Nightingale** later attended. Elizabeth Fry was accused of neglecting her nine children in her absorption with improving the moral and material condition of women, which she saw as part of her religious calling.

**Führer** (leader). A title taken by **Hitler** in imitation of Mussolini, who called himself *Duce*. Its use became compulsory in 1931 in the **Nazi Party**, on the order of **Goebbels** and, like the greeting 'Heil Hitler', was designed to produce an unthinking adulation of the Party leader. In August 1934, when Hitler combined the offices of Chancellor and President, after **Hindenburg**'s death, *Führer* became his official title. The term implied that supreme authority was not in a popularly elected assembly (democracy) or in hereditary monarchy but solely in the person of the Leader. The *Führer* therefore stood above the law and indeed his word *was* law. The *Führerprinzip* (leadership principle), which Hitler stressed in his autobiography *Mein Kampf*, extended the idea of the Leader to all organizations in society. At all levels there should be leaders who give orders and subordinates who obey them without question: thus **Himmler** was the *Reichsführer* **SS**.

**Fukuzawa Yukichi** (1835–1901). Japanese reformer. A lower *samurai*, Fukuzawa hated the rigidly stratified society in which he was born. He studied Western sciences and in 1858 opened his own school in Edo (Tokyo), which became Keio University, one of the two earliest and greatest of Japan's private universities. Here he introduced the study of English, which he had learnt himself. In the 1860s he travelled in Europe and the USA on behalf of the **Tokugawa shogunate**. His *Conditions in the West* (1866–9) was the first systematic account of Western civilization written by a Japanese. He rejected his hereditary status, refused to join the government and spent his time promoting 'practical' education, particularly the sciences, though he believed that these would be of little use unless Japanese developed the spirit of independent initiative. He attacked **Confucianism**, which stifled initiative and encouraged unquestioning obedience and so provided the foundation for authoritarian government. Fukuzawa believed in an open and mobile society, in which ability would be rewarded and in which a democratic, constitutional government could be established. His writings and speeches were a major influence in spreading Western ideas in Japan, although from the 1880s he became less radical and supported the Meiji (see **Meiji Restoration**) government's policy of 'rich country, strong army' and its aggressive foreign policy.

**Fulani Empire of Sokoto.** A West African Islamic Empire. This arose out of the *jihad* (holy war) proclaimed in 1804 by **Uthman dan Fodio**, who conquered the Hausa states in what is now northern Nigeria with the aid of his mainly Fulani followers. The Empire spread south into Oyo, which became the emirate of Ilorin and a base for the steady spread of Islam among the Yoruba. By 1850 the Empire of Sokoto was the most extensive in tropical Africa, covering 150,000 square miles and stretching from the Sahara to the forest belt and from the north-west of Nigeria deep into the Cameroons. Sokoto was a great slave-owning state, which controlled many of the southern trans-Saharan trade routes. It consisted of about twenty provinces, which varied in size, wealth and ethnic population from Kano, the Hausa Kingdom of a million people with an elaborate system of administration before the Fulani conquest, to others with less than 50,000 inhabitants. The Empire was a confederation, as provincial governors (emirs) had almost complete autonomy in their own territories. Within the Empire there was greater peace and security than anywhere else in tropical Africa in the mid-nineteenth century. Later in the century the British began to intrude and the Empire came to an end in 1903, when they conquered Kano and Sokoto, although the emirates survived in the system of **indirect rule** introduced by the British High Commissioner, Lord **Lugard**.

**Fundamental Laws** (1906) defined the powers of the Tsar after **Nicholas II** was forced to grant a Constitution, following the **Russian Revolution of 1905**. They began: 'To the Emperor of all the Russias belongs supreme autocratic power.' This was not strictly true, as his powers were limited by the Constitution, but he had the right to introduce legislation and could veto laws passed by the **Duma**. Ministers were appointed by the Emperor and were responsible to him, not to the Duma, and he was in sole charge of military and foreign affairs, including the right to declare war. By Article 87 the Tsar could issue decrees with the force of law, if an emergency arose, though they had to be submitted to the Duma for approval within two months of its next session. This enabled him to by-pass the Duma, as it was almost impossible for the Duma to undo measures which had already been taken.

**Gadsden Purchase** (1853) When the **Mexican–American War** ended in 1848, the border between Mexico and what are now the states of Arizona and New Mexico was left unclear. Americans wanted this disputed territory, as it was on one of their projected routes for a **transcontinental railroad**. President Pierce therefore sent James Gadsden to negotiate the sale of the land, for which the USA paid ten million dollars. The Southern Pacific Railroad, completed in 1884, was built through this area of 30,000 square miles, which completed the present borders of the mainland USA.

**Gallipoli Campaign** (19 February 1915–9 January 1916). A combined operation of British and Commonwealth naval and land forces, which aimed to knock Turkey out of the **First World War**. This would open the supply route to Russia through the Black Sea and, it was hoped, persuade neutral Balkan states to join the Allies. Winston **Churchill**, the First Lord of the Admiralty, was convinced that the stalemate on the Western Front could not be ended and so he wanted decisive action elsewhere. The plan was for the British and French fleets to destroy the defences of the Dardanelles while troops conquered the Gallipoli peninsula. They could then advance on Constantinople (Istanbul), the Turkish capital, whose fall would lead to Turkey's surrender. The British drifted into the difficult amphibious operation and made no calculation of what resources would be needed to tackle it successfully. Secrecy was lost when a premature naval bombardment in 1914 made the Turks aware of the weakness of their defences, which were then strengthened. Even so, the naval bombardment in February–March 1915 was nearly successful, as the Turks used up almost all their shells. The British did not realize this and did not force entry to the Dardanelles, as three British battleships had been sunk by mines and three badly damaged. Landings were now planned to support the fleet. On 25

April, 78,000 Anzac (an acronym for the Australian and New Zealand Army Corps) and British troops landed on the Gallipoli peninsula but too far apart to support each other: the Anzacs were a mile north of their intended position and were faced with precipitous cliffs. Command blunders and indecision – Lord **Slim**, who fought there, described the Gallipoli Commanders as the worst since the Crimean War – led to both Anzac and British troops being pinned down. **Trench warfare** began and was to last for almost a year. Another landing in August at Suvla Bay was unopposed but the incompetence of the British Commander gave the Turks time to bring up reinforcements and another stalemate ensued. Naval support was withdrawn owing to mines in the **Straits** and submarines. Opposition in England grew and in December 1915 and January 1916 all the troops were evacuated – this was the most successful part of the operation. The campaign was a total failure and brought down the Liberal government, which was replaced by a **coalition** in which Churchill had no place. Bulgaria now joined the **Central Powers**, who appeared to be winning the war.

**Gambetta, Léon** (1838–82). French politician. The son of an immigrant Italian grocer, he became a lawyer and was elected to the Legislature of the Second Empire (1852–70) in 1869. As a radical republican he loathed the regime of **Napoleon III**. When it fell during the **Franco–Prussian War** (1870–71) Gambetta proclaimed the **Third Republic** from the Hôtel de Ville in Paris in September 1870. He was the key figure in the Government of National Defence, and escaped by balloon to carry on the war, when Paris was surrounded by Prussian troops. As Minister of War as well as Minister of the Interior he took all power into his own hands to raise an army but this failed to relieve Paris. Opposed to elections for a National Assembly, which he felt would be dominated by monarchists, he thought a dictatorship was needed to preserve the Republic. When his views were rejected by politicians such as **Thiers**, he resigned. Gambetta soon abandoned the radicalism of his early years and devoted all his energies to gaining acceptance of the Republic. He called himself an opportunist, who abandoned doctrine in favour of practical tasks, and wanted to convince the electorate that the Republic stood for moderation, stability, peace and national unity. Gambetta persuaded the Radicals to accept the 1875 Constitution, which included features they did not like, such as a bicameral legislature, so that the Republicans would not be divided and therefore weakened. In 1877 he looked forward to 'the fusion between the *bourgeoisie* and the workers, between capital and labour'. President Grévy distrusted Gambetta because of his supposed dictatorial tendencies and kept him out of office until 1881, when his administration lasted less than three months. Shortly afterwards he died from peritonitis at the age of forty-four.

**Game Laws.** Class legislation in Britain passed by a parliament of landowners in the early nineteenth century, so that no one would interfere with their favourite sport, the shooting of game. The laws became most punitive between 1816 and 1827. Anyone found at night with a net for poaching could be sentenced to seven years' transportation to a **penal settlement** in Australia: landowners were allowed to use spring-guns and man traps to maim poachers. Not only did landowners pass such legislation: they or their friends also enforced it as magistrates. Between 1827 and 1830 one in seven of all criminal convictions were for breaches of the Game Laws.

**Gandhi, Mohandas Karamchand** (1869–1948). Indian spiritual and national leader. Born into a prosperous merchant family (*gandhi* in Gujarati means 'grocer'), his father had become chief minister of the small state of Purbandhar. Gandhi was sent to England to qualify as a lawyer but on his return to Bombay he failed in his law practice, as he was painfully shy. He therefore went to South Africa in 1893 as representative of a business firm and was to remain there for over twenty years. It was in South Africa that he became the spokesman for Indian **indentured labourers** who suffered from racial discrimination, and it was there that he developed his political skills, in dealing with a large number of Indians and with the white authorities. *Satyagraha*, non-violent resistance, was the method he developed for coping with injustice. He was forty-five when he returned to India in 1915, a small, thin, bespectacled figure, who appeared the antithesis of a charismatic, national leader. Yet this is what he became within five years. Known as Mahatma ('Great Soul'), a name given to him by the poet Rabindranath Tagore, he became a *guru*, a Hindu holy man, who attracted followers by his personal sanctity. He discarded his European clothes and wore the peasant's *dhoti* and shawl. In 1919 he organized a *hartal* (stoppage of work) as a protest against the Rowlatt Act, which sought to continue repressive wartime legislation into peacetime, condemned the **Amritsar massacre** and persuaded Congress to support the *Khalifat* campaign, a massive Muslim movement of opposition to the dismemberment of the **Ottoman Empire** (Muslims regarded the Ottoman Sultan as *Khalifa* or spiritual leader of Islam). From this time Gandhi was the dominant personality in the **Indian National Congress**, who aimed to achieve *swaraj* (self-rule) for India by non-violent means. He began his **non-cooperation movement** in 1920 but abandoned it two years later, when some of his followers used violence. Gandhi was then arrested by the British authorities and on his release in 1924 retreated to his *ashram* (self-sufficient religious community) at Sabarmati, a suburb of Ahmedabad, the capital of Gujarat. It was not until 1928 that he returned to politics and 1930 before he began his campaign of civil disobedience to achieve *swaraj*. He chose to attack the government's monopoly and high tax on salt, as this was an issue which would appeal to the poorest. Gandhi marched 240 miles from Sabarmati to the sea at Dandi, where he made salt illegally by boiling sea-water. The government reacted by arresting Gandhi and 60,000 others, and by 1931 had recovered control, although civil disobedience continued, with interruptions, until 1933. Gandhi, released from prison in 1934, once more retreated to his *ashram*. When war came in 1939 he sympathized with the democracies but was not prepared to use force, even for the defence of India. When the Cripps mission in 1942 offered India independence after the war in return for full cooperation during the conflict, Gandhi rejected it as 'a post-dated cheque on a bank that was failing'. The Mahatma then began his last *satyagraha* campaign, the '**Quit India' Campaign**, which **Jinnah** deplored as an 'open rebellion'. This was suppressed with some bloodshed and Gandhi was again arrested. Released in 1944, his influence in Congress waned after the war. He was opposed to partition and distressed by the communal rioting, when Hindus and Muslims murdered each other. When independence was declared in August 1947, Gandhi deliberately stayed in Calcutta, far from the celebrations in Delhi. When he returned to the capital he was murdered by a Hindu fanatic.

**Garibaldi, Giuseppe** (1807–82). Italian leader of the *Risorgimento*. Born in Nice (then part of Piedmont), Garibaldi joined **Mazzini**'s Young Italy and in 1834 was forced to flee from Italy, after an unsuccessful plot in Genoa in support of Mazzini. He spent the next twelve years in South America, where he developed his skills as a guerrilla leader and adopted the *gaucho* costume – poncho and red shirt – which he retained for the rest of his life. On returning to Italy he took part in the **Revolutions of 1848** and in 1849 organized the defence of the Roman Republic against the French during a two-month siege, which ended with his retreat into exile again. This episode made him a popular hero in Italy.

Garibaldi played a crucial part in bringing about the unification of Italy. After Piedmont had acquired Lombardy and central Italy **Cavour** was prepared to stop but Garibaldi extended the movement for unification by invading Sicily with his Thousand (in fact there were 1,100) in May 1860. There were 30,000 Neapolitan troops in Sicily but Garibaldi's troops, aided by a peasant revolt, won a minor engagement at Calatafimi and this led to many Sicilians joining him. When the Bourbon (see **Bourbon dynasty**) troops were defeated at the Volturno and agreed to evacuate the island, Garibaldi was left as dictator of Sicily. He then decided to cross the Straits of Messina and invade Naples. Cavour, fearful that Garibaldi's prestige would overshadow that of **Victor Emanuel II**, tried unsuccessfully to stop him. Garibaldi landed in Calabria in August, defeated Neapolitan troops and entered Naples in September. Cavour now attempted to recover the initiative, which he had lost to Garibaldi, by invading the Papal States before Garibaldi could do so. In November, Garibaldi, never personally ambitious, met Victor Emanuel II and handed over his conquests to Piedmont. He therefore played a large part in the unification of Italy by conquering Sicily and Naples and by forcing Cavour to acquire the Papal States. Rome and Venetia still remained outside the new Kingdom of Italy, so in 1862 Garibaldi began a march on Rome from the toe of Italy but was held up and wounded by royal troops. A second attempt to seize Rome failed in 1867 when French troops stopped him at Mentana.

**General Strike** (Britain) (4–12 May 1926). When Winston **Churchill** put Britain back on the **gold standard** in 1925 coal exports fell, as the pound was overvalued. The miners objected when coal owners wanted to reduce wages and increase the hours of work, and asked the General Council of the Trades Union Congress (TUC) for help. Railwaymen and transport workers, conscious of their failure to support the miners on **'Black Friday'** in 1921, agreed in July 1925 to stop the movement of coal. At this stage the Prime Minister, Stanley **Baldwin**, intervened and agreed to subsidize miners' pay until 1 May 1926, whilst a Royal Commission, under Sir Herbert Samuel, inquired into the problems of the industry. In March 1926 the Samuel Commission recommended the rationalization of the industry into larger units and some reduction in wages, though it opposed longer hours and district rather than national wage agreements. The miners rejected the report and were faced with a lock-out by the mine owners when the subsidy ended on 1 May. The TUC set up a Strike Committee under Ernest **Bevin** and on 4 May the General Strike began.

It was a selective rather than a general strike, as the TUC called out a million and a half workers (to add to the million miners locked out) in transport, printing, iron and steel, and power. The aim was to bring industry to a halt whilst not affecting essential services, such as electricity for homes. There was an enthusiastic response from workers, as docks, railways, newspapers and some power stations closed. Baldwin said, 'The General Strike is a challenge to Parliament and is the road to anarchy and ruin' and was supported by the middle classes, who volunteered in their thousands as special constables and bus drivers. The Prime Minister feared civil war but, though some people were injured, there were few violent incidents. Ramsay **MacDonald**, the leader of the **Labour Party**, had declared just before the strike began that with 'general strikes and Bolshevism and all that kind of thing, I have nothing to do at all. I respect the Constitution.' This was the attitude of many TUC leaders, who were not at all revolutionary, were unhappy about a political strike and feared they would lose control of their more militant members. They looked for a way out and made contact with Samuel when he returned from abroad. He drew up a memorandum based on the Royal Commission's report, which the TUC Negotiating Committee accepted, though the government and mine owners had made no concessions. When the miners rejected the memorandum, the TUC called off the strike on 12 May, with the miners' dispute unresolved. It was a complete surrender, which surprised the strikers, as support had remained solid and industrial production had been greatly reduced. The miners, feeling betrayed as in 1921, stayed out, but had to accept total defeat in November: wages were cut and were fixed on a district basis, working hours were not reduced and there was no reorganization of the industry. The government rubbed salt in the wounds of a TUC which had lost prestige, by passing the Trade Disputes and Trades Union Act of 1927. This made sympathetic strikes illegal, forbade civil servants to join trade unions affiliated to the TUC and introduced 'contracting in' for trade-union members who wanted to pay the political levy to the Labour Party. The disunity and defeatism engendered by the General Strike, with massive unemployment, kept **trade unions** weak and on the defensive until the **Second World War**.

**George III** (1738–1820). King of Great Britain, Ireland and Hanover (1760–1820). George was slow to develop (he was eleven before he could read) and retained feelings of inadequacy all his life, though these were combined with stubbornness. When he came to the throne he was determined to rule as well as reign. He could choose his own ministers but found that they needed the support of a majority in parliament, so he set out to provide this by the use of royal patronage. George obstinately clung to Lord North as Prime Minister (1770–82) and prolonged the American War of Independence, possibly by as much as two years, in a vain attempt to prevent American independence. The most overbearing use of his powers came in 1783 when he ensured the defeat of his own government in the House of **Lords** by saying that anyone who voted for **Fox**'s India Bill would be his personal enemy. On the Bill being rejected by the Lords, he dismissed the Fox–North coalition and appointed **Pitt** as Prime Minister, though he did not have majority support in parliament. The King then called an election in 1784 in which a hundred of 'Fox's Martyrs' lost their seats and Pitt gained the majority he needed. In 1788 George had a mental collapse, but recovered within a year and interfered little with Pitt's policies until 1801. Following the Act of **Union** (1800) with Ireland Pitt supported **Catholic emancipation** in order to placate the Irish majority but George would not accept this, so Pitt felt that he had to resign, even though he had massive support in parliament. The King once again used his influence, in 1807, to get rid of the 'Ministry of All the Talents', as it sought to improve the position of Catholics. By this time George was nearly blind and in 1810 he became permanently insane, so that from 1811 until his death his dissolute son, the Prince of Wales (later **George IV**), acted as Regent.

**George IV** (1762–1830). King of Great Britain, Ireland and Hanover (1820–30). The eldest son of **George III**, he clashed with his father over his self-indulgent and extravagant life-style. A great gambler, he owed £600,000 by 1796 and was still £500,000 in debt when he became Regent in 1811. He had a passion for older mistresses who became almost as fat as he was. In 1785 he secretly and illegally married a Roman Catholic widow, Maria Fitzherbert, but this was ignored when he married his vulgar cousin, Caroline of Brunswick, ten years later. Both soon enjoyed other partners and separated after the birth of their only child, Princess Charlotte, in 1796. When George became King in 1820 he urgently sought a divorce, on the grounds of his wife's adultery, to prevent Caroline assuming the role of Queen. A bill to this effect passed the House of **Lords** by only nine votes, so the government abandoned it, as it would clearly be rejected in the **Commons**. This affair made Caroline undeservedly popular in London and enabled the cartoonists to pillory the King unmercifully as a hypocrite and libertine. The monarchy has never been so unpopular and so derided as it was then. When Caroline died of a fever in 1821, George rejoiced. The King's views were reactionary but of little consequence, as he would always give way to his ministers if they were persistent. Like his father he strongly opposed **Catholic emancipation** but, unlike George III, he was unable to prevent it.

As Regent (1811–20) and as King, George indulged his obsession with building and gave his name to the Regency style of architecture. John Nash designed for him Regent's Park, Regent Street, and Carlton House Terrace; Buckingham Palace was virtually rebuilt and Windsor Castle restored. The most unusual of his buildings was the Royal Pavilion, Brighton, inspired by Indian Islamic architecture and also designed by Nash. George was a connoisseur of art too, and built up a superb collection of seventeenth-century Dutch paintings and eighteenth-century French furniture. No modern monarch has equalled his artistic taste or his contribution to England's architectural heritage.

**George V** (1865–1936). King of Great Britain and Ireland, Emperor of India (1910–36). A son of **Edward VII**, his formal education ended when he was twelve. He never developed any intellectual curiosity and throughout his life was supicious of new ideas and bored by books, music and paintings. His only interests appeared to be in collecting stamps and shooting pheasants. An obsession with dress and Court etiquette he derived from his father. He became King in the midst of a constitutional crisis, when **Asquith**'s **Liberal Party** government was determined to reduce the power of the House of **Lords**. George V had to agree, reluctantly, to create enough Liberal peers for the **Parliament Bill** (1911) to pass in the Lords, though this proved unnecessary, as the Lords passed the bill to avoid their permanent **Conservative Party** majority being overturned. During the **First World War** he was a fervent patriot, supporting **Haig**'s policy of mass attacks on the Western Front and changing the royal family name to **Windsor**. The King was not highly regarded by his ministers: **Lloyd George** thought there was 'not much inside his head', whilst **Fisher** referred to the King and Queen as 'futile and fertile', but the King made great efforts to prevent his personal feelings from interfering with his role as a constitutional monarch. When the dying Bonar **Law** resigned as Prime Minister in 1923, George V took advice from leading Conservatives before asking **Baldwin** rather than **Curzon** to lead the government, as it was desirable that the Prime Minister should sit in the **Commons**. In 1931 he again consulted prominent politicians before persuading **MacDonald** to form a **National Government**. Surprisingly, as he detested **socialism**, he liked MacDonald the most of all his Prime Ministers. Whilst accepting his limited political role, he developed the monarchy as a symbol of national unity and strength. He took part in the royal *darbar* in Delhi in 1911, often toured the United Kingdom and was seen by more of his subjects than any previous monarch. His popularity was apparent in the genuine enthusiasm for his Silver Jubilee celebrations in 1935.

**George, Henry** (1839–97). American land reformer. In *Progress and Poverty* (1879) George described the existence of poverty in the midst of plenty as 'the great enigma of our times'. He found a solution to this problem in the abolition of all taxes, except for one on land values. George maintained that idle landowners saw the value of their property rise inexorably, because the increase in population and economic development led to a shortage of land. As this extra wealth was not the result of any effort on their part, this 'unearned increment' should be seized by the state in the form of taxation. His book was enormously popular, was translated into many languages and influenced the thinking of politicians such as Joseph **Chamberlain** and **Lloyd George**. Although George did not want to get rid of private property, he unintentionally popularized the idea of land nationalization.

**German Confederation** (or *Bund*) (1815–66). A grouping of mainly German states, formed at the Congress of **Vienna**. It contained not only Germans but Czechs (in Bohemia), Danes (in Holstein) and Italians (in Tyrol). Some parts of the *Bund* had foreign rulers: the King of England ruled Hanover until 1837, the Danish King was Duke of Holstein and the Dutch King Duke of Luxemburg. About half the Habsburg Empire was outside the *Bund*, as was East Prussia. Representatives of the thirty-nine states in the *Bund* met in the **Diet** at Frankfurt to discuss matters of common concern. They wanted to maintain the status quo and so met mainly when there was a threat to the established order. As the ruler of each state was very jealous of his sovereignty, the *Bund* was a means of maintaining the division of Germany, rather than of bringing about unification. The Diet could not impose taxes on the member states and though there was a small federal army from 1821, the separate states controlled their own contingents. This conservative body had, therefore, no teeth and was dominated by Austria, who sought to prevent change. The 1848 Revolution in Germany (see **Revolutions of 1848**) produced the **Frankfurt Parliament**, which tried to unite Germany, but this was opposed by both Prussia and Austria and the Parliament collapsed. Austria recovered her control of the *Bund* and was able at Olmütz (1850) to prevent Prussia from bringing some north German states under her control in the **Erfurt Union**. Not until **Bismarck** became Minister-President in Prussia in 1862 was there any real challenge to Austria's supremacy in the *Bund*. Prussia's victory in the **Austro-Prussian War** (1866) brought an end to the German Confederation. It was replaced north of the river Main by the **North German Confederation**, dominated by Prussia, and this was merged in the **German Empire** after France's defeat in the **Franco-Prussian War** (1870–71).

**German Empire** (1871–1918). **Prussia** united Germany by her victories in the **Austro-Prussian War** (1866) and **Franco-Prussian War** (1870–71) and it was Prussia who dominated the new German Empire. The Prussian King became the German Emperor, the Prussian Minister-President became the German Chancellor and Prussians seized the highest positions in the imperial administration. It was not a liberal Empire, as power remained in the hands of conservative *Junkers*, who dominated the ministries, the army and the civil service. The Constitution of the Empire did not make ministers responsible to the elected assembly, the **Reichstag**, as in Britain and France. They were appointed by and responsible to the Emperor, who had considerable power, as he was commander of the armed forces and had the sole right to conduct foreign policy. Political parties, therefore, never had much influence, although the government needed their support to pass legislation. **Bismarck** at first relied on the **National Liberal Party** until he moved to protection in 1879. After his dismissal a 'Blue-Black Block' of Conservatives and the Catholic **Centre Party** was formed, which provided support for most governments up to 1914, and was determined to prevent the **Social Democratic Party** (SPD) gaining influence. The socialists had been persecuted by Bismarck with his **anti-socialist law**. He tried to counter their appeal with his **State Socialism**, which provided social insurance for the workers, but, with industrialization and a growing working class, the SPD increased its strength until it became the largest party in the Reichstag in 1912.

The German Empire became a leading industrial power. Her coal output, which was about a third of that of Britain in 1871, had almost caught up by 1914. Steel increased even more dramatically: output was only 0.3 million tons in 1870 but the invention of the Gilchrist–Thomas process (1879) enabled the phosphoric ores of Lorraine to be used, so that by 1914 fourteen million tons were produced, much more than in Britain. The most impressive development of all came in the electrical and chemical industries. Electrical engineering began to expand in the 1880s and by 1913 Germany controlled half of the international trade in electrical goods. By 1907 the German chemical industry was the world's largest and produced 80 per cent of the world production of dyes. Germany was Britain's most serious competitor by 1913, when she had an almost equal share of world trade. This rapid advance had been brought about by a rise in population (from forty-one million in 1871 to sixty-eight million in 1914), which provided both labour and a large market; by investment banks, whose representatives sat on the boards of directors of industrial enterprises; by the spread of **cartels**, particularly after 1900; and by enterprising entrepreneurs, who adopted the latest techniques and equipment. German industry used specialized research teams but it also swiftly applied methods invented elsewhere; aniline dyes, electrical power and the Gilchrist–Thomas process were French and British discoveries.

After the wars which produced the German Empire Bismarck became 'a fanatic for peace', so that France, longing to recover **Alsace-Lorraine**, would not find an ally: he also tried to prevent Austria-Hungary and Russia clashing in the Balkans and so starting a war into which Germany might be drawn. He succeeded but at the cost of a complicated web of alliances (the **Triple Alliance** with Austria-Hungary and Italy) and agreements (the **Reinsurance Treaty** with Russia). His only foreign adventure was when he joined in the **Scramble for Africa** to acquire colonies for the Empire. When he was dismissed his successor **Caprivi** refused to renew the Reinsurance Treaty and so pushed Russia into a **Franco-Russian Alliance** (1894), the very thing Bismarck had tried to avoid. The foreign policy of the German Empire became ever more strident when *Weltpolitik*, supported by the unbalanced Emperor **William II** (1888–1918), was adopted. This involved looking for more colonies (though the pickings were meagre) and **Tirpitz** presiding over the building of a large navy. This brought about a naval race with Britain, who patched up her colonial differences with France and Russia, so that Germany was faced with a **Triple Entente**. Bismarck's restraint was abandoned, as Germany sought to break up the **Anglo-French Entente** in the first **Moroccan crisis** (1905–6) and failed. She then aggressivly compelled Russia to accept Austrian annexation of Bosnia and Hercegovina in the **Bosnian crisis** of 1908, with the result that Russia was determined to stand firm when Austria-Hungary attacked Serbia, after the assassination of the heir to the Austro-Hungarian throne at **Sarajevo** in June 1914. Germany pushed Austria into war during the **July crisis** and so was largely responsible for the outbreak of the **First World War**, a war which saw the defeat of Germany, the abdication of the Kaiser and the end of the German Empire, which was replaced by the **Weimar Republic**.

**German Revolution** (1918–19) began on 29 October 1918, when sailors at Kiel refused to obey orders to put to sea to do battle with the British fleet. This seemed to them a suicide mission, so they mutinied and set up sailors' councils. The mutiny had spread by 6 November to all the major cities and ports and to garrisons throughout Germany and on the Western Front. It was a bloodless revolution, as the old regime could not offer any resistance, and it was also moderate. There was no attempt to overthrow the existing social system; most members of the workers' and soldiers' councils, which had sprung up everywhere, were anxious to maintain law and order. In Bavaria, where people blamed the Berlin government for their hardships and for its failure to make peace, the Independent Socialists (USPD), a small minority, led by Kurt Eisner, seized the initiative, deposed the ruling dynasty of Wittelsbachs and declared a republic on 8 November. This was not a socialist revolution, as Eisner did not think that Germany was ready for one yet: imperial officials remained at their posts as elsewhere in Germany, and the government promised to protect private property. The Majority Socialists (as the **SPD** was now called) had a large following and were in a position to decide the course of the revolution but their leaders, **Ebert** and Scheidemann, were cautious. They wanted the SPD to come to power not by a bloody revolution but by receiving the largest number of votes at an election. They were patriotic (Ebert had lost two sons in the war) and were even prepared to accept the monarchy, until their own supporters pushed them into demanding the Emperor's abdication. When there was no response they called a general strike and this had the desired effect. The Kaiser abdicated and on 9 November the Chancellor, Prince Max of Baden, handed over his office to Ebert, who wanted to wait for a constituent assembly to decide whether or not to declare a republic. The decision was taken out of his hands by Scheidemann, who proclaimed a republic to a crowd outside the **Reichstag** building. To provide a broader base for his government he asked the USPD to join it, which it did, though its policies differed from Ebert's.

The SPD thought that the revolution was over when, in October, a government responsible to the Reichstag had been set up, in which ministers could be members of the assembly. The USPD was much more radical, as it felt that authoritarian habits had a firm hold over the German people. It wanted to break up the power structure of the old ruling classes by nationalizing key industries, dividing the vast *Junker* estates and by getting rid of aristocratic domination of the army, civil service and judiciary. As disorder continued in the capital, with demonstrations and strikes, Ebert decided to ally with the army to cope with the extreme **Left**, and this led to USPD members leaving his government in December. The Supreme Command offered its support to crush Bolshevism, which appeared a real threat when the **Spartakist Rising** took place in January 1919. The Communist Party declared the Ebert government deposed, so the Chancellor turned to the generals who, finding the regular army unreliable, used **Free Corps** volunteers to crush the rising and kill its leaders, Rosa **Luxemburg** and Karl Liebknecht. The German Revolution was not yet over. Workers were angered by the use of the Free Corps and the failure of the SPD to gain a majority in the January elections to the constituent assembly seemed to confirm the fears of the Independent Socialists, that democracy would be still-born. In March the USPD rejected parliamentary democracy and called for rule by workers' councils. With the call for a general strike a revolutionary situation was developing: there was disorder in Berlin and again the government called on the Free Corps. Order was restored after more than a thousand had been killed. In Bavaria unrest had revived and a soviet republic was proclaimed in April. The Bavarian government followed the example of Berlin and called on the Free Corps, who ended the republic in a 'white terror', in which hundreds of workers and all the communist leaders were shot. With the defeat of the Bavarian communists the German Revolution came to an end. It had achieved little. The structure of society had not been affected; the unreformed army, civil service and judiciary remained. The steps towards democracy which survived – universal suffrage, a government responsible to the Reichstag – had been made in October before the Revolution. The main losers, apart from the communists, were the socialists, who had become dependent on the army generals, enemies of democracy and **socialism**. The SPD leaders were blamed by the USPD and the communists for betraying the revolution: for the **Right** they were 'November criminals' who had 'stabbed the fatherland in the back' (see **'Stab in the back' myth**). This was an unfortunate legacy which the **Weimar Republic** inherited.

**Gestapo** (short form of *Ge[heime] Sta[ats]po[lizei]*: Secret State Police). Secret police in the **Third Reich**. It was set up by **Goering** in 1933, taken over by **Himmler** in 1934 and placed under the **SS**. In 1939 it was merged with the SD (Security Service), the intelligence branch of the SS, under **Heydrich**. Its purpose was to eliminate opponents of the Nazi regime – at first communists and social democrats, later the Jews – and to do this it could use whatever methods it liked, outside the jurisdiction of the law courts. It was the main agent of Nazi terror. By 1943 it had 45,000 members, 60,000 agents and 100,000 informers. As it was so much a part of the SS it was often difficult to tell which acts were carried out by the *Gestapo* and which by the SS. Between them they controlled the **concentration camps** and followed behind the advancing German armies in Russia to kill Jews, partisans and communist officials. They administered the slave labour programme and the **extermination camps**.

**Gettysburg, battle of** (1–3 July 1863). The greatest battle of the **American Civil War**. The Confederate General Robert E. **Lee**

decided to invade the North, for the second time, after his victory at Chancellorsville on 2 May 1863. It was a desperate gamble for high stakes. If he could capture Washington, Northern morale might crack, Britain and France might recognize the Confederacy and he would win the war for the South. In June he advanced up the Shenandoah valley, crossed the Potomac river and headed for Pennsylvania. On 1 July Lee, commanding 75,000 men of the Army of Northern Virginia, unexpectedly came upon the Union Army of the Potomac, 93,000 men under Major-General George Meade, at the little town of Gettysburg, Pennsylvania. Lee attacked and forced Meade back to strong defensive positions, where he held his ground. On the third day Lee ordered an assault by 15,000 men on the centre of the Union lines. After a bombardment of nearly two hours Confederate troops began their mile-long advance on Cemetery Ridge. Most were mown down by artillery or musket fire: only 150 reached the Union lines, where they were soon killed or captured. The Confederate army suffered 7,000 casualties in this one assault and 28,000 in the whole battle: Union losses were 23,000. On 4 July Lee's shattered army began to retreat, in the pouring rain, to Virginia. Meade's forces were too exhausted to pursue and destroy Lee's army, yet Gettysburg was the decisive battle of the Civil War. Lee would never again be strong enough to take the offensive.

**Ghetto.** The area of a city set apart where Jews were forced to live. The first was in Morocco in 1280: ghettos spread to Europe in the fourteenth and fifteenth centuries. They were normally enclosed by walls and gates, which were locked at night. In Western Europe ghettos were abolished in the nineteenth century but were revived by the Nazis (see **Nazi Party**) in Eastern Europe, in towns such as Warsaw. Since the Second World War 'ghetto' has been used to refer to urban slum areas, inhabited entirely by socially deprived groups, such as Negroes in the USA.

**Giolitti, Giovanni** (1842–1928). Italian Prime Minister (1892–3, 1903–5, 1906–9, 1911–14, 1920–21). Like **Cavour**, Giolitti came from Piedmont, but unlike Cavour he was not from the aristocracy but from a middle-class family of magistrates and civil servants. Elected to the Chamber of Deputies in 1882, he served under

**Crispi** at the Treasury before becoming Prime Minister for the first time in 1892. As a result of financial scandals he resigned in 1893. Returning to office in 1901 as Minister of the Interior, he dominated Italian politics up to the First World War, for most of the time as Prime Minister. He maintained a majority by *trasformismo*, using corruption and patronage, but appreciated the importance of the emergent political forces of **socialism** and Catholicism and wished to integrate them into the parliamentary system. This policy of 'tolerance' involved a refusal to interfere in industrial disputes. Giolitti did not introduce any major social legislation but took the first steps in protecting female and child labour and in limiting working hours. In foreign policy he maintained the **Triple Alliance** with Austria and Germany but also improved relations with France, recognizing French interests in Morocco in return for a French acceptance of Italian claims to Libya. Nationalist pressure pushed him into war (1911–12) with the **Ottoman Empire** over Libya, a conflict which was very popular in Italy, except with the socialists. Giolitti lost the support of conservatives and nationalists, which he had gained in the Libyan War, by granting almost universal male suffrage in 1912, thereby trebling the electorate to nine million. He opposed Italy's entry into the **First World War**, as he thought she was unprepared for a major war. He was Prime Minister for the last time in 1920–21, when he forced **D'Annunzio** out of Fiume and brought an end to the workers' occupation of the factories in the *biennio rosso*. Completely misjudging the danger from the **Fascists**, whom he thought he could 'tame' and 'constitutionalize', he made an electoral pact with **Mussolini** in 1921, which enabled thirty-five Fascists to become deputies (they had not won any seats in the 1919 election). He therefore helped unwittingly to prepare the way for the Fascist seizure of power. Though shocked by Fascist violence, he refused to join the Aventine Secession after the murder of **Matteotti** but he withdrew his support for the Fascist government at the end of 1924.

**Girondins.** A group of deputies in the French **Legislative Assembly** and **Convention**, several of whom came from the Gironde department in south-western France. They were sometimes known as Brissotins, after their leader Jacques Brissot, who helped to persuade the Assembly to declare war on Austria in April 1792, as he thought a successful war would rouse enthusiasm for the Revolution. The history of the Convention until 2 June 1793 is that of a struggle between Girondins and **Jacobins**. Neither group was a party but they agreed with each other on most policies. Both strongly believed in the Revolution and the Republic, hated privilege, were anti-clerical and wanted free trade. They differed in the sources of their support and in their deep suspicions of one another. The Girondins had most of the Paris press on their side and had much support in the provinces but they earned the hatred of the Parisian *sans-culottes* by their opposition to the attack on the **Tuileries** (10 August 1792). The Girondins supported federalism – the right of the provinces to run their own affairs without interference from Paris – which was the policy of the **Constituent Assembly** from 1789–91. When **Louis XVI** was tried in January 1793, they tried to save his life by proposing a referendum on his fate and were therefore branded as royalists by the Jacobins. When Dumouriez, who had close links with the Girondins, was defeated by the Austrians at Neerwinden in March 1793 and tried to march on Paris to restore the monarchy, the Girondins were greatly weakened. On 2 June *sans-culottes* surrounded the Convention and demanded the expulsion of Girondins from the Assembly, which was forced to agree to the arrest of twenty-nine Girondin deputies and two ministers. On 31 October they were executed, victims of the **Terror**.

**Gladstone, William Ewart** (1809–98). British Prime Minister (1868–74, 1880–85, 1886, 1892–4). The son of a Liverpool merchant who was wealthy enough to send him to Eton and Oxford, Gladstone thought of becoming an Anglican clergyman but his father persuaded him to become a politician instead. He entered parliament in 1832 as a Tory MP (see **Tories**) and in the 1830s opposed almost every reform of the **Whig** government, including the abolition of slavery (see **Slave trade**) and the **Factory Act** of 1833. This reactionary phase ended when he served in the Board of Trade and the Colonial Office in **Peel**'s **Conservative Party** ministry (1841–6) but Gladstone remained throughout his life socially conservative, anxious to preserve the hierarchical social order.

In 1878 he told Ruskin that he was 'a firm believer in the aristocratic principle – the rule of the best. I am an out-and-out inequalitarian.' The vote was not a right for all men but a privilege for those who had shown they could use it responsibly. Gladstone showed his conversion to *laissez-faire* when he became Chancellor of the Exchequer under **Aberdeen** (1852–5) and **Palmerston** (1859–66). He continued Peel's tariff reforms by reducing 150 duties and abolishing nearly 140 in 1853 and in his budgets of 1860 and 1861 he almost completely abolished duties on imports. Good government for Gladstone was cheap government, which should remove hindrances to economic activity but should not play a more positive role by providing services.

Having become a Peelite after Peel split the Conservative Party in 1846 over the repeal of the **Corn Laws**, Gladstone did not commit himself to either of the major parties between 1846 and 1859. In the end he joined the Liberals, partly because he had 'a strong sentiment of revulsion' for the Conservative **Disraeli** and partly because the Liberal leaders, Palmerston and **Russell**, were old and would soon retire. Palmerston died in 1865 and Russell retired two years later, so Gladstone became leader of the **Liberal Party** and in 1868 formed his first administration. He fought the election with the slogan 'justice for Ireland', as this would unite Radicals, Irish Catholics and Protestant Nonconformists. The Church of Ireland, which had only 700,000 members (there were four and a half million Catholics in Ireland), was disestablished in 1869, a third of its wealth going to various charities and education. In 1870 the **Irish Land Act** attempted to give security of tenure to tenants but had little effect in practice. The Irish Universities Bill (1873) was another attempt to redress Irish grievances by proposing a new University of Dublin but this was defeated in the House of **Commons**. The Irish bills were accompanied by other measures which made Gladstone's first ministry one of the greatest in the nineteenth century, though the Prime Minister took little part in the other reforms and actively disliked some of them. Forster's **Education Act** (1870) sought to provide elementary education throughout the country, **Cardwell**'s reforms were designed to make the army more efficient, and entry to most of the civil service was to be by competitive examination. Gladstone accepted the secret ballot (1872) with 'lingering reluctance', and disliked the Licensing Act (1872), which limited the hours public houses could be opened. In 1871 he gave protection to the funds of **trade unions** but in the Criminal Law Amendment Act retained as criminal offences 'obstruction', 'intimidation', and 'threat', terms which were so vague that trade unions did not feel secure.

After his defeat in the 1874 election Gladstone resigned as leader of the Liberal Party but said that he would return if he was needed for 'arresting some great evil'. He found such an evil in Disraeli's support for Turkey in the **Eastern Question** and the massacre by Turks of thousands of Christian Bulgars in 1876, which he denounced in *The Bulgarian Horrors and the Question of the East*. Gladstone loved to fight general elections on a single issue, which he could present in moral terms, and he chose Disraeli's foreign policy for his **Midlothian Campaign** in 1879. A Liberal victory, which probably owed more to an agricultural depression than to the Midlothian Campaign, provided Gladstone with his second administration. This was dominated by Ireland, where the Land War (1879–82) threatened British control. Gladstone passed another Irish Land Act, which failed to diminish support for the nationalists. The only other significant piece of legislation concerned **parliamentary reform**. The third Reform Act (1884) gave the vote to all male householders, so that two-thirds of all adult males now had the vote, instead of one third. Abroad, Gladstone was faced with problems which led to a decline in his popularity. The Boers in the Transvaal sought to recover the independence they had lost in 1877, so the first **South African War** (1880–81) began, in which the British were defeated at Majuba Hill. Gladstone decided to grant independence to the Transvaal rather than send out British forces to avenge the defeat. A British army went to Egypt to put down a nationalist revolt led by **Urabi Pasha**. General **Wolseley** defeated him but Gladstone then found he was unable to withdraw from Egypt as he intended, as the **Mahdi** had revolted in the Sudan. General **Gordon** was ordered to evacuate Anglo-Egyptian forces from the Sudan but was killed in Khartoum by the Mahdi and Gladstone was blamed. The GOM (Grand Old Man) became the MOG (Murderer of Gordon). By this time Gladstone had decided that Home Rule, though not complete independence, would have to be given to Ireland (see **Home Rule for Ireland**) but when he introduced a bill to this effect he split the Liberal Party and the bill was defeated. A third of his followers, led by Joseph **Chamberlain**, deserted him in 1886 to form the **Liberal Unionists** but they soon joined the Conservatives. When out of office from 1886–92 Gladstone made no attempt to reunite the Liberal Party and remained aloof, 'not in touch with the new order of things', according to Rosebery. When the Liberals returned to power in 1892 and Gladstone formed his last ministry, he was obsessed with Ireland, which was now a millstone round the neck of the Liberal Party. Another Home Rule bill passed the Commons in 1893 but was rejected by the Lords. Gladstone's colleagues were relieved when he finally retired.

*Gleichschaltung* (literally 'putting into the same gear': coordination) refers to the establishment of a dictatorship in Nazi Germany by getting rid of independent institutions and by coordinating or centrally controlling those that remained. The process began in February 1933, when civil liberties were suspended. In March the **Enabling Act** made Hitler completely independent of the restraining power of the **Reichstag**. The rights of the separate states (*Länder*) were then removed: eighteen commissioners, all Nazis, were put in charge of their governments and later the *Landtage* (state parliaments) were abolished. Elected bodies were replaced by party nominees and in practice the sovereign powers of the *Länder* were transferred to the Reich Minister of the Interior. In April 1933 the civil service was purged of Jews and those who were politically unreliable: **Nazi Party** members took over the senior posts. A month later the trade unions were swallowed up in the Labour Front, run by the *Gauleiter* (district boss) of Cologne, Robert Ley. Independent political parties ceased to exist: the **Social Democratic Party** was dissolved on 22 June 1933, the Nationalists dissolved themselves on 27 June, as did the **Centre Party** on 5 July. The Nazi Party became the only legal political party. The *Reichsrat* (Federal Council) was abolished in 1934, so that only an emasculated Reichstag, which represented the Nazi Party alone, remained of the **Weimar Republic**'s political system.

*Gleichschaltung* applied to everyone in one way or another, as it was almost impossible to avoid involvement in a Party organization.

The **Hitler Youth** was the only youth organization allowed. At the age of nineteen men had to spend six months in the Labour Service on public works and military training and this was followed by two years of compulsory military service. There were separate Nazi organizations for doctors, civil servants, lawyers, university lecturers, students and farmers. All the communications media – radio, press, cinema, the arts – were coordinated by **Goebbels** in his Reich Chamber of Culture. He was responsible, by his control of propaganda, for making *Gleichschaltung* acceptable to the public, by stressing the need for national unification against Germany's enemies. This would overcome class differences and bind people together, under the guiding hand of the Nazi Party, in selfless devotion to the Reich. By 1934 only two institutions retained sufficient independence to be a possible danger to the *Führer*: the army and the **SA** in the Nazi Party. Both dangers were removed at the same time in the **Night of the Long Knives** (30 June 1934). The power of the SA was smashed and the *Gleichschaltung* of the army began with its oath of loyalty to Hitler, a process completed in 1938, when Hitler purged the army High Command and became Commander of the armed forces.

**Gobineau, Joseph Arthur, Comte de** (1816–82). French diplomat and ethnologist, who published his *Essay on the Inequality of Human Races* in 1853–5. Gobineau recognized only three races, white, black and yellow. He thought that the white race was superior to the others and within it the Aryan held the highest place. The race which remained superior would be the one that kept its racial purity intact: degeneration set in when a pure race mixed its blood with that of inferior races. His book was almost unnoticed when it was published in France but by the end of the century it was known throughout Europe, especially in Germany. His ideas were taken up by Richard Wagner and by Wagner's son-in-law, Houston Stewart Chamberlain, and appeared in **Hitler**'s *Mein Kampf*, where the importance of keeping the Aryan race pure was stressed. Gobineau was therefore the unlikely founder of the racial ideology of Nazi Germany.

**Godoy, Manuel** (1767–1851). Dictator of Spain (1792–1808). As an obscure guardsman from Extremadura, Godoy rapidly became a

Court favourite through his allegedly amorous relationship with Queen Maria Luisa and his role as confidant to King Charles IV. After the fall of Floridablanca as chief minister in 1792, Godoy, at the age of twenty-five, effectively became dictator of Spain. He was to rule for the next sixteen years. Godoy came to power shortly before relations between Spain and France reached their nadir because of the execution of **Louis XVI**, a relative of Charles IV. In 1793 the twenty-year alliance with France gave way to war. From the beginning Godoy sought an understanding with his powerful neighbour, finally securing a peace settlement in 1795. He was henceforth dubbed 'the Prince of Peace'. In 1796 Godoy took the relationship a step further by forming an alliance with the **Directory**. This confronted England with Spain and led to war the following year. The conflict with England proved extremely costly, above all for the Spanish economy. To meet the mounting crisis, the state administration was further centralized, thereby enhancing Godoy's own power. By the turn of the century, Spain was more under French influence than ever, a virtual satellite. Godoy was not only forced to go to war with the Portuguese and British, but also had to raise major loans for Napoleon's war effort. The accumulated burdens resulted in the loss of the American market, damaging inflation, and an economic depression, with Catalonia suffering the most. By the time **Napoleon** invaded Spain in 1807, Godoy was involved in secret negotiations with the French Emperor, above all to secure a kingdom of his own in the Portuguese territory of the Algarve. By 1808 the unpopularity of the vain and ostentatious Godoy had spread throughout Spain. He was overthrown by his principal enemy, the Prince of Asturias (the future Ferdinand VII), in alliance with aggrieved nobles. The imprisonment of Godoy in France in 1808 was to mark the end of his political career. After the War of Independence (**Peninsular War**) of 1808–14 with France was over, Godoy lived out his life in Rome and Paris. Although rehabilitated by Isabel II in 1847, he died in Paris without returning to Spain. The alliance of Spain, under his mild dictatorship, with the French had devastating consequences for the Spanish Empire and trade, undoubtedly hastening the decline of an enfeebled nation.

**Goebbels, Paul Josef** (1897–1945). Propaganda chief in the **Nazi Party**. Goebbels came from a working-class family in the Rhineland and was rejected for military service in the **First World War** because of a crippled foot, the result of having polio. He was totally different from the tall, blond Aryan superman of Nazi mythology, as he was small with black hair and throughout his life felt physically inadequate. Joining the Nazi Party in 1922 and disliking *bourgeois*, capitalist society, he was at first on the left of the Party. In 1926 he became *Gauleiter* (district leader) of the Party in Berlin, where he organized parades and street brawls and made the Party a much more powerful organization in north Germany. Consequently **Hitler** made him propaganda leader of the Party. Goebbels created the *Führer* myth of Hitler as a Messiah-like figure who would save Germany from Jews and Marxists: as the Leader was infallible, he deserved unquestioning obedience. In the 1932 election campaign Goebbels' mastery of the techniques of mass persuasion helped to bring about a Nazi victory, so after Hitler became Chancellor in January 1933, he made Goebbels Reich Minister for Public Enlightenment and Propaganda, which gave him control of communications media: radio, the press, publishing, the cinema and the arts. On 10 May 1933 he staged a ritual 'burning of the books' in Berlin, when the works of Jewish and Marxist writers were publicly burnt. He put the press directly under Nazi control, as he amalgamated all the various agencies into one official German News Bureau and he made journalists responsible to the state for what they wrote. At daily press conferences he told journalists what line to take on each issue. His propaganda on the radio was not confined to Germany, as he increased the stations making foreign broadcasts from one in 1933 to 130 ten years later. Goebbels became a great Jew-baiter, encouraging the **Crystal Night** pogrom (9–10 November 1938) and supporting the '**Final Solution**' for the extermination of the Jews. During the **Second World War** his influence increased, particularly from 1943, when Germany's military situation deteriorated. He seized on the unconditional surrender demand of the Allies to tell Germans that they would become slaves if they lost the war, and spurred them on to make greater sacrifices. In July 1944 Hitler made him General Plenipotentiary for Total War, with wide powers to direct the civilian population, but by this time it was too late. He was now the *Führer*'s most loyal supporter and spent the last days of the war with Hitler in his bunker in Berlin. After Hitler's suicide Goebbels had his six children killed by a lethal injection and then shot himself and his wife on 1 May 1945.

**Goering, Hermann Wilhelm** (1893–1946). **Nazi Party** leader. In the **First World War** Goering became a fighter pilot, was credited with shooting down twenty-two British planes and was awarded Germany's highest honour, the Iron Cross (First Class). He joined the Nazis in 1922 and was appointed by **Hitler** to command the **SA**, whom he led in the abortive **Munich *Putsch*** of 1923, when he was seriously wounded. He fled from Germany for four years to avoid arrest and returned when there was a general amnesty, becoming a Nazi Party deputy in the **Reichstag** in 1928 and its President in 1932. When Hitler became Chancellor in January 1933 Goering was one of only three Nazis in the Cabinet, holding the posts of Reich Minister without Portfolio and Prussian Minister of the Interior. In Prussia he set up the secret police, the *Gestapo*, and with **Himmler** established **concentration camps** for political opponents. He exploited the **Reichstag Fire** (February 1933) by imprisoning communists and socialists and by banning the left-wing press and directed operations in Berlin during the **Night of the Long Knives** (June 1934), when leaders of the SA were murdered. In March 1935 Goering became Commander-in-Chief of the *Luftwaffe* and was responsible for its rapid expansion. His powers were further increased in 1936, when he was given control of a Four Year Plan to prepare Germany for war and to reduce her dependence on imported raw materials, such as petrol and rubber, by producing substitutes. This was very costly and was only partly successful: in 1939 Germany still imported a third of the raw materials she needed. Whilst he had almost total control of the German economy Goering used his position to amass an enormous fortune and live ostentatiously. He was the most popular of the Nazi leaders, as he appeared a jolly extrovert, who laughed uproariously at jokes against himself. Yet there was another side to Goering – brutal and ruthless – which he showed after the **Crystal Night** pogrom (November 1938), when he imposed a fine of a billion marks on the

Jewish community, ordered their removal from the German economy and warned of a 'final reckoning with the Jews' if war came. Goering was named as Hitler's successor in September 1939 and directed the successful *Luftwaffe* campaigns against Poland and France. A new position of Reich Marshal was created for him in June 1940. He seemed at the height of his power but 1940 saw the beginning of his fall from grace. He failed to defeat the RAF in the battle of **Britain** and made a serious mistake when he switched attacks from British airfields and radar stations to the bombing of London. Fighter Command, which was near to collapse, was given precious time to recover. Hitler never forgave him for this, as he had to abandon his projected invasion of Britain. Goering's influence and prestige further declined when he failed to supply by air the German Sixth Army at **Stalingrad** and when he was unable to prevent massed air attacks on German cities. He became isolated and overtaken in influence by **Himmler**, **Goebbels** and **Speer**. After Germany's defeat he was put on trial at Nuremberg, where he recovered his panache and gave a scintillating performance, which made him the dominant personality among the defendants. Sentenced to death, he committed suicide by taking poison, which incredibly his captors had failed to find, two hours before he was due to be hanged on 15 October 1946.

**Gokhale, Gopal Krishna** (1866–1915). Indian politician. A Brahmin from western India, he became a professor of English literature and mathematics, who was deeply influenced by European liberal thought: he disparaged caste and supported the emancipation of women. He was a severe critic of British rule in India, believing that it was economically disastrous, and he demanded abolition of the salt duty, cuts in army expenditure and the Indianization of the public services. Gokhale was nevertheless a great admirer of the British system of government, its law and order and the administrative unity it had imposed on India. Self-government for India was his goal but he thought this could best be achieved by working within British institutions, by cooperating with the **Raj** and by making constructive criticisms. A member of the Bombay Legislative Council, he also became a leading figure in the Indian Legislative Council, established by the **Morley–Minto reforms** in 1910. He opposed non-cooperation with the British as it encouraged indiscipline in the masses. Gokhale became President of the **Indian National Congress** in 1905 and for the next ten years dominated the Congress Party; he was prepared to see the Party split in 1907 rather than follow the 'extremism' of **Tilak** and prevented any reconciliation with the extremists. **Gandhi** called Gokhale his *Rajaguru* and though Gandhi and **Nehru** provided Congress with a more dynamic leadership, Gokhale's ideals of a humane, secular and democratic nationalism remained the beliefs of the Congress Party.

**Goldie, Sir George** (1846–1925). British imperialist, who established commercial and political control over a large part of Nigeria. In the 1870s Goldie went to Southern Nigeria, where European merchants were competing fiercely with each other to control the trade from the interior to the coast. He realized that unless the British companies amalgamated, they would not be able to stand up to the competition of their French or German rivals or to resist the demands of the African chiefs, who levied duties on trade passing through their territory. By 1879 Goldie had succeeded in uniting the British traders into a single corporation, the United Africa Company. He also signed treaties with African rulers and gradually extended the commercial control of the UAC over a large part of the lower Niger. In 1885 Britain claimed the Niger Delta as the Oil Rivers Protectorate. In the following year Goldie's company received a royal charter and became the Royal Niger Company, with control over the area north of the Delta. Goldie created a trading monopoly on the lower Niger by excluding the French and by deposing any African rulers who attempted to challenge his trading system. The Royal Niger Company extended its commercial and political interests into Northern Nigeria: its forces under Frederick **Lugard** captured Nupe and Ilorin in 1897. It also became involved in incidents with the French, who were advancing down the Niger and up the coast from Dahomey. These operations were too costly and dangerous for a private company, so in 1899 the RNC's charter was revoked and two years later the British government took control of the Company territory in Nigeria. Goldie was compensated and retired a rich man.

**Gold rushes.** In 1848 gold was discovered in California, which attracted 80,000 'Forty-niners' from all over the world. The surface diggings, where prospectors used primitive techniques of panning gravel from a stream, were soon worked out. Most of the gold was in deep and hard veins of quartz, which needed capital and expensive machinery for extraction, so big business took over. Gold was found in the Colorado Rockies in 1858 and a year later in Nevada, where there was the greatest single deposit of gold and silver ever found in the USA. Minor strikes in Idaho and Montana (1862) and Arizona (1863) preceded the last great gold rush in the USA in the Black Hills of Dakota, a Sioux reservation, in 1874. Deadwood, its one street lined with saloons, brothels and gambling dens, became one of the wildest places in America. Gunfights and stagecoach robberies took place almost every day and it was there that 'Wild Bill' Hickok was murdered in 1876. Violence and crime did not prosper for long: when the federal government could not keep law and order, local communities did so with their vigilantes. The goldfields stimulated the building of the **transcontinental railroads** and speeded up the settlement of the West.

Rich deposits of gold were found in Australia in 1851, near Bathurst in New South Wales, and at Ballarat, Victoria, whose population grew in the 1850s from 80,000 to half a million. Forty per cent of the world production of gold came from Australia in the 1850s: it was a more valuable export than wool until the 1870s. The goldfields were extended in the 1870s to Queensland, where the country's richest gold mine was, and in the 1880s and 1890s to Northern and Western Australia. As a result, the population of Western Australia quadrupled. New Zealand, too, increased its population after the discovery of gold in Otago (1861), many miners coming from Australia, and for several years it was New Zealand's major export. The richest goldfields in the world were found on the **Rand** in South Africa, where mining began in 1886 and transformed the Transvaal from the poorest state in South Africa into the richest. British attempts to control this area led to the **Jameson Raid** (1895) and the **South African War** (1899–1902). The last great gold rush was the Klondike, 300 miles from the Arctic Circle in Canada in 1896.

**Gold standard.** The backing of paper money by gold. Britain was the first country to adopt the gold standard when in 1821 people were allowed to convert their money into gold on demand. In the 1870s the gold standard was adopted by France, Germany and the USA and from the 1890s was a currency system used throughout the world. Gold could be used as an international currency for settling debts and was supposed to provide an automatic mechanism for adjusting a nation's balance of payments (the difference between the amount of goods imported and the amount exported). A balance of payments surplus would lead to an inflow of gold, fall in interest rates and an economic boom. Yet more money circulating would increase prices, suck in imports and lead eventually to a balance of payments deterioration. When there was a deficit, the outflow of gold reduced economic activity, unemployment rose but imports and the prices of exports fell and so the balance of payments would improve. The **First World War** disrupted the gold standard. Britain returned to it in 1925 and it was re-established by 1928, though gold coins were no longer in circulation. The **Wall Street Crash** (1929) and the ensuing **Great Depression** led to the abandoning of the gold standard by Britain in 1931, and the USA in 1933. By 1937 not one country remained on it.

**Gompers, Samuel** (1850–1924). American labour leader. Gompers was born in London of Dutch–Jewish parents and went to the USA in 1863. By the age of twenty-four he was head of a cigar-makers' union and in 1886 became a founder, and first President, of the **American Federation of Labor** (AFL). He was to retain this position, except for one year, for the rest of his life. Gompers accepted the capitalist system and rejected **socialism** and the idea that there should be a separate political party representing labour. He was against direct involvement in politics but believed that workers should use their votes to support parties which promoted their interests. Though he was prepared to use strikes to attain purely economic ends, he preferred to get what he wanted by negotiating with the bosses. Gompers believed in 'voluntarism': that unions should voluntarily look after their members in sickness and old age, rather than rely on compulsory insurance organized by the state, which he regarded as socialist. As nearly all his ideas were conservative, Gompers and the AFL were accepted in American society and during the **First World War** he was invited to serve on several government boards concerned with national defence.

**'Good Neighbor' policy.** US policy of conciliation in dealing with Latin American countries in the 1920s and 1930s. In his inaugural address in 1933 Franklin D. **Roosevelt** promised: 'In the field of world policy I would dedicate this nation to the policy of the good neighbor – the neighbor who resolutely respects himself and, because he does so, respects the rights of others.' Though it was meant to be generally applied, the 'good neighbor' policy was associated primarily with Latin America. Roosevelt did not begin this policy but simply continued what Calvin **Coolidge** and Herbert **Hoover** had begun. After the USA acquired the **Panama Canal** zone in 1903, the Caribbean became a US lake. Most Latin American countries were economic dependencies of the USA and, as a result of Theodore **Roosevelt**'s use of 'the big stick', US troops occupied Cuba, Haiti, the Dominican Republic and Nicaragua in 1918. In the 1920s American economic control increased but the USA withdrew her troops from Cuba in 1922 and from the Dominican Republic in 1924. Hoover went further. In the Clark memorandum of 1930 he rejected Theodore Roosevelt's Corollary to the **Monroe Doctrine**, which claimed for the USA a police power in the western hemisphere. Unlike Theodore Roosevelt, **Taft** and **Wilson**, he did not intervene when revolution broke out in Brazil, Cuba and Panama in 1930–31, or when Latin American countries defaulted on their loan repayments. American Marines left Nicaragua in 1933. At a Pan-American conference at Montevideo in 1933 the USA signed a convention which said that 'no state has the right to intervene in the internal or external affairs of another.' Franklin Roosevelt honoured this in 1934 by cancelling the **Platt Amendment**, which allowed American intervention in Cuba. When American Marines left Haiti (where they had been since 1914) in 1934 there was no part of Latin America under US occupation for the first time in a generation. The USA maintained its financial and economic dominance in these areas, yet the 'good neighbor' policy did mark a real change. When there were disputes with Latin American countries, in which there were considerable US investments, the USA did not send in the Marines. In 1937

Bolivia confiscated the holdings of the Standard Oil Company; in 1938 Mexico took over nearly all foreign-owned oil companies; in 1939 Venezuela demanded higher royalties from US companies. On each occasion the oil companies demanded US intervention but there was to be no return to the 'big stick', although the US government insisted on compensation.

**Gordon, Charles George** (1833–85). British general. Gordon served in the **Crimean War** and distinguished himself by his bravery at Sebastopol. He then took part in the second **Opium War**, was present at the occupation of Beijing (Peking) in 1860 and personally directed the burning of the Emperor's Summer Palace. In 1862 he commanded the Chinese 'Ever-Victorious Army' of 3,500 troops, which played a small role in helping the **Qing dynasty** to defeat the **Taiping rebellion**: his success here made him known in Britain as 'Chinese' Gordon. At the request of the Khedive **Ismail** of Egypt he went in 1873 to open the Upper Nile to commerce and by 1876 had set up trading stations as far south as Lake Albert. As an evangelical Christian (see **Evangelical Movement**) Gordon also decided to suppress the slave trade, which was widespread in that area. Ismail made him Governor-General of Equatoria (the Upper Nile) where he remained until 1879, when he returned to England. When the **Mahdi** rebelled against the Egyptians and destroyed a force sent against him by the Khedive, **Gladstone** decided to withdraw British and Egyptian troops from the Sudan and in 1884 sent Gordon to supervise the withdrawal. Instead, Gordon stayed in Khartoum, where he was besieged by the Mahdist forces. Ever since Lytton Strachey's *Eminent Victorians* some historians have maintained that he deliberately refused to evacuate. Khartoum fell after a long and spirited defence and Gordon was killed in his residence on 26 January 1885, two days before a relief column under General **Wolseley** arrived. Gordon became a national hero, whilst Gladstone was much criticized for not sending a relief force earlier and this helped to bring down his government.

**Gramsci, Antonio** (1891–1937). Italian Marxist and a founder of the Italian Communist Party. Born in Sardinia, the son of a minor public official, Gramsci had an unhappy childhood; he was hunchbacked and his father was imprisoned for corruption. In 1911 he won a scholarship to Turin University and two years later joined the Italian Socialist Party (PSI), writing regularly for socialist newspapers such as *Avanti*. Inspired by the **October Revolution** (1917) in Russia, he took an active part in the workers' occupation of factories in the *biennio rosso* (1918–20) and saw the need for workers and peasants to unite to resist the power of industrialists and large landowners. Dismayed by the caution of the PSI and its failure to take advantage of what he saw as a revolutionary situation in Italy, he broke away from it in 1921 and, with the support of the **Comintern** and **Lenin**, was a founder of the Italian Communist Party. He became its General Secretary and, in 1924, a member of parliament. Arrested by the Fascists (see **Fascism**) two years later, he spent the rest of his life in prison.

Whilst he was there he wrote his major work: a huge collection of notes and unfinished essays, published posthumously as *Prison Notebooks* (1929–35), which established his reputation as one of the most important Marxist theorists since Marx. In the *Notebooks* he declared that Marxism was not a scientific description of 'objective' reality and that it must be constantly changed to take account of historical experience. He ridiculed those who turned Marxism into a closed system, with immutable laws underlying human development. Such determinism, he said, was false, as it did not explain why capitalism still existed. There was nothing inevitable about the rise of **socialism** from capitalism. By reducing thought to a 'reflex' of productive forces, Marxists underestimated the power of myths and ideas. The hegemony (the spiritual and cultural supremacy) of the ruling classes was, he maintained, based on their control of institutions such as the press, radio, churches and trade unions, through which their own values could be imposed on society as a whole. Gramsci rejected the belief that conflict between employers and workers was inevitable, as he saw that many workers accepted capitalism. This led him to reject Lenin's belief that revolution could be brought about by a small, dedicated minority, as he thought that this could work only in backward countries like Russia. Revolution would have to come 'from below', when the mass of workers wanted it. By emphasizing the need for persuasion, consent and doctrinal flexibility Gramsci later came to have a profound effect on the Eurocommunists.

**Grant, Ulysses Simpson** (1822–85). Union general in the **American Civil War** and eighteenth American President (1869–77). Grant served in the **Mexican–American War** of 1846–8 but resigned his commission to avoid being court-martialled for drunkenness. His fortunes then plummeted and he was working as a clerk when the Civil War gave him the opportunity of pursuing a more exciting career. In February 1862 he showed his ability by seizing Forts Henry and Donelson on a tributary of the Mississippi but in April his military career almost came to an end. Confederate troops surprised him at Shiloh and inflicted heavy losses before being driven back. Only President **Lincoln** saved him from dismissal. 'I can't spare this man,' he said. 'He fights.' Lincoln's faith in him was justified when Grant forced Vicksburg to surrender in July 1863. This was a turning-point in the war, as the whole of the Mississippi was soon in Union hands and the Confederacy was cut in two. Lincoln made Grant Union Commander in the West in October. A month later he smashed a Confederate army besieging Chattanooga and drove it from Tennessee. The next step was to break through the mountains into the Confederate heartland of Georgia but Grant was removed from this theatre and given command of all the Union armies, with the rank of Lieutenant-General (the first general to hold that rank since Washington). Now Grant showed that he was a first-rate strategist. He left **Sherman** to advance into Georgia and cut the Confederacy in two again, whilst he relentlessly drove **Lee** back through the woods of Virginia to the Confederate capital of Richmond. This campaign, in which Lee manoeuvred brilliantly, saw some of the heaviest fighting of the war, in which Grant lost more men than Lee. Gradually Lee was pushed back to Petersburg, twenty miles from Richmond, and was there besieged in the winter of 1864–5. Grant prepared his final offensive, which began on 31 March 1865 and ended in Lee's surrender at Appomattox on 9 April. Generous in victory to the Confederate forces, Grant decreed that 'each officer and man will be allowed to return to his home, not to be disturbed by the US authorities.'

Grant was now a military hero and was nominated for President by the **Republican Party** in 1868. He was elected by a large majority but was out of his depth and was an ineffective President. His **Reconstruction** programme in the South collapsed and there were several financial scandals involving members of his administration. Grant was personally honest but surrounded himself with corrupt and incompetent cronies, whom he protected. After his retirement he invested his money unwisely and was in debt. He spent the last months of his life writing his memoirs, which provided for his family and became a classic.

**Great Depression** (1929–39). The world economic crisis which followed the **Wall Street Crash**. The collapse of American share prices meant that dollar loans to European countries were called in, the USA raised her tariffs so that imports declined and this was accompanied by a fall in agricultural prices, which preceded the Crash and made the depression worse. Rural communities could not afford industrial goods, so factories closed, shops went bankrupt and there was rising unemployment (three million in Britain, six million in Germany and thirteen million in the USA by 1932). As industry declined there was a fall in demand for raw materials which affected Africa, Asia and Latin America and as prices of all goods fell, so did profits and share prices, so that banks could not obtain repayment of their loans. In 1931 the Kredit-Anstalt, the great Austrian bank, failed and this was followed by the disintegration of the banking system in Central and Eastern Europe. Banks in the USA and Germany closed, as customers withdrew their savings. Britain came off the **gold standard** (in 1931), as did other countries, and *laissez-faire* policies gave way to protection.

The economic effects of the depression were uneven. The USA suffered the worst: millions lost everything, their jobs, homes and possessions. Starvation was a real threat in the greatest food-producing country in the world, as prices were so low that grain was left to rot in the fields, as were slaughtered animals, because farmers could not afford to feed or ship them. By 1939 the USA had not regained the level of output of 1929: not till the **Second World War** did the need for armaments pull it out of the depression. Germany, which had relied on American loans, was also badly hit. It could not pay its **reparations**, which were quietly abandoned in 1932, but the German economy began to recover from 1933, when **Hitler** started rearming. The effect of the recession in Britain was very patchy – old industrial centres in the North and North-East suffered severely but new industries, such as motor cars, grew up in the Midlands and the South and the country as a whole was beginning to recover by 1935. France suffered less than other industrial countries, as she was largely self-sufficient in food. The Soviet Union was the one country which did not appear to be affected at all, as it was isolated from the world economy: her economic growth continued throughout the 1930s. The depression brought the end of democracy, as well as the end of economic liberalism, in many countries. The **Weimar Republic** broke down and was followed by the rise of **Hitler** and the **Nazi Party** dictatorship. **Dollfuss** came to power in Austria in 1933, and was followed by fascist (see **Fascism**) regimes in most of Eastern Europe. Japan, having lost her American markets, turned to **imperialism** and in 1931 invaded **Manchuria** in a search for markets and raw materials. Capitalism, which seemed about to break down in the USA, survived with the help of **Roosevelt**'s **New Deal** policies. The Great Depression helped, indirectly, to bring about the **Second World War**, as it enabled Hitler to come to power, although by 1939 economic recovery was well under way in many countries.

**Greater East Asia Co-Prosperity Sphere.** In August 1940 the Japanese Foreign Minister first spoke of creating a Co-Prosperity Sphere, which would be an economically self-sufficient area. It would include Japan, China, **Manchukuo** and the Dutch, British and French colonies in South-East Asia. After Japan had conquered these colonies early in the **Pacific War** (1941–5), the Co-Prosperity idea was used to justify Japanese expansion, which made the area militarily secure against threats from the USA and the European powers. The ideal was Asiatic harmony and unity, in which all the nations of Asia would cooperate under the benign leadership of Japan. In practice Japan used her conquered territories as a source of supplies and of forced labour and by the end of the war the local populations regarded the Co-Prosperity Sphere with loathing and as a form of Japanese **imperialism**.

**Great Exhibition** (1851). 'The Great Exhibition of the Works of Industry of all Nations' was held in Hyde Park, London, and was the first large exhibition held anywhere in the world. It was designed to show the industrial supremacy of Britain who, with her Empire, contributed over half of the 14,000 exhibits. The centrepiece was the enormous iron and glass, prefabricated structure of the Crystal Palace – 1,848 feet long, 408 feet broad and 66 feet high – designed by Joseph Paxton, a gardener who had taught himself engineering. Ruskin thought it vulgar: others, including many of the six million visitors who came in the five months of the exhibition (the **railways** ran cheap excursions from all over Britain), found it awe-inspiring. Prince **Albert**, who had chosen the site and was closely involved in the planning of the exhibition, saw it as a triumph of peace and progress. With the profits a site in South Kensington was bought, where the Victoria and Albert Museum, the Science Museum, and the Natural History Museum were to be built. Paxton's style of architecture was to influence other buildings in London, particularly the arches over the railway lines at King's Cross (1851–2) and St Pancras (1868) stations and the dome over the Circular Reading Room at the British Museum (1854–7). The Crystal Palace was re-erected in South London but was destroyed by fire in 1936.

**Great Fear** (20 July–6 August 1789). After the fall of the **Bastille** (14 July) there were riots against taxes, the tithe and feudal dues throughout France, so that it appeared that law and order had collapsed everywhere. The price of grain was high, owing to the bad harvest of 1788, so *châteaux*, where grain collected as rents, feudal dues and tithes was stored, were attacked. These attacks were caught up in the Great Fear, which began in local rumours that bands of brigands, in the pay of the aristocracy, were going to destroy the harvest. The peasants took up arms to await the brigands and when they did not appear, turned their anger against the landlords. The Great Fear spread the peasant rising throughout most of France, except for some areas on the periphery, such as Brittany, Alsace and the Basque region, which were unaffected. It also pushed the **Constituent Assembly** into meeting at least some peasant demands in the **August Decrees**.

**Great Purges.** The arrest, trial and often execution of millions of people in the Soviet Union, particularly in the years 1936–8. **Stalin** wanted to get rid of all his actual and potential rivals and used the murder of **Kirov** in 1934 as an excuse to do so. The high point of the purges were the three show trials in Moscow, when the Revolution devoured its creators, just as the **Terror** had done during the **French Revolution**. In the first part of the trials in August 1936, **Kamenev**, **Zinoviev** and fourteen others were accused of taking instructions from **Trotsky** to murder Stalin and other party leaders. All were condemned to death and executed. Their confessions implicated the trade-union leader Tomsky, who committed suicide, and **Bukharin**. Bukharin was arrested but released for lack of evidence. This was not good enough for Stalin, who blamed the head of the secret police (**NKVD**), Yagoda, for incompetence. He was therefore replaced by **Yezhov**, who was responsible for the second trial in January 1937, when Radek and others confessed to links with foreign intelligence services. Some were executed: Radek was sentenced to ten years' hard labour and died in a prison camp. In the final trial in March 1938 Bukharin and Rykov confessed to planning with foreign powers for the downfall of the USSR and were executed. Yezhov prepared the sentences in advance and Stalin approved them, as he did with nearly 400 such lists in 1937-8. Of the fifteen members of the original Bolshevik government, by 1939 ten had been executed, four had died and only Stalin remained. In all these trials the only evidence produced was the confessions of the victims, though it often took weeks to obtain them. The NKVD broke prisoners down by continuous interrogation for days and nights, so that they became so exhausted and disorientated that they would sign anything. Threats against their families were also used: if they confessed, their families would be unharmed. Others were promised that their lives would be spared if they confessed.

Only seventy people were tried in public. Most of the victims of the purges were tried secretly and it was these trials that decimated those who held high positions in society. The high ranks in the Communist Party were a main target – 70 per cent of the Central Committee at the Party Congress in 1934 were executed in the following five years. Of the ordinary delegates, 1,108 out of 1,966 were arrested or executed in the same period and only fifty-nine reappeared at the next Congress in 1939. The armed forces suffered one of the most severe purges – three out of five marshals, fourteen out of sixteen army commanders, 169 out of 280 corps and divisional commanders disappeared. A third of all officers were arrested. Similar purges took place in the air force and navy, where only one senior commander survived. Foreign communist leaders who had sought refuge in Russia, such as Bela **Kun**, were also executed.

As the number of victims grew the terror developed a momentum of its own. Officials who coveted the positions of their superiors were encouraged to denounce them and no NKVD officer could ignore such accusations, however flimsy, in case he himself was accused of a lack of vigilance. Once he had arrested someone he needed a confession and more denunciations, in order to further his career (or even save his life). Relations, acquaintances and colleagues of those accused became suspects themselves. Even members of the NKVD became victims of the purges they promoted, as they provided perfect scapegoats for the excesses of the regime. Yagoda and Yezhov were both executed. A KGB report to the **Politburo** in the 1960s said that between January 1935 and June 1941, 19.8 million people were arrested, of whom seven million were shot.

The purges were successful in crushing all opposition to Stalin and in producing a climate of fear and suspicion, in which any criticism of the regime was impossible. The worst of the purges came to an end in 1939, after Beria replaced Yezhov, though they never stopped entirely. **Trotsky** was the last illustrious figure to be hunted down, in Mexico, and murdered in 1940.

**Great Terror** (1794). The peak of the **Terror** during the French **Revolution**. After attempts had been made to murder **Robespierre** and Couthon, they drafted the Law of Prairial, which was passed by the **Convention** on 10 June 1794. 'Enemies of the people' were defined as 'those who have sought to mislead opinion . . . to deprave customs and to corrupt the public conscience'. These terms were so vague that almost anyone could be included. No witnesses were to be called and judgment was to be decided by 'the conscience of the jurors' rather than by any evidence produced. Defendants were not allowed defence counsel and the only verdicts possible were death or acquittal. This law removed any semblance of a fair trial and was designed to speed up the process of revolutionary justice. In this it succeeded. More people were sentenced to death by the Revolutionary Tribunal in the nine weeks after 10

June than in the previous fourteen months of its existence. Many of them were from the upper classes: 38 per cent of nobles, 26 per cent of clergy and nearly half the wealthier *bourgeoisie* who were victims of the Terror were executed at this time. No one dared criticize the **Committee of Public Safety**. 'The Revolution is frozen,' Saint-Just commented.

**Great Trek.** The movement of Boer farmers northwards out of Cape Colony into the Orange Free State, Natal and Transvaal in the 1830s. Throughout the eighteenth century in South Africa there were small groups of Dutch, or Boer, farmers who moved (trekked) by ox-cart in search of land. These *trekboers* lived a semi-nomadic life, slowly extending the frontier of white settlement, remote from the control of any government. When the British took over the Cape from the Dutch at the end of the **Napoleonic Wars** in 1815 many Boers resented their new rulers. In particular they disliked new laws which ended slavery (though few of the *trekboers* owned slaves) and provided for equal treatment of blacks and whites in the courts. Each *trekboer* required a large area of land for his cattle and by the 1830s most of the land in Cape Colony had been divided up into farms. Therefore *trekboers* wanted not only to get away from British rule but also to find more land and new sources of labour. Starting in 1835 an organized migration of several thousand people moved northwards across the Orange river and into lands controlled by African peoples. These *voortrekkers* (pioneers, those who travel ahead), who by 1845 numbered about 14,000, with as many 'Coloured' and African servants, left in different parties. Once north of the Orange river they tended to unite for protection. One group went to Mozambique; another under Piet Retief entered Natal in 1837 only to be killed by the Zulu King Dingane. In 1838 their deaths were revenged, when a Boer force under Andries Pretorius defeated the Zulu army at the battle of **Blood River**. A short-lived Boer republic was set up in Natal (1838–43) but the British would not allow Boers to control harbours on the Indian Ocean and so sent troops to Port Natal (Durban) and annexed Natal in 1843. Most of the Boers there went to the high veld, where they defeated the Ndebele and set up two republics: the Orange Free

State, between the Orange and Vaal rivers, and Transvaal, between the Vaal and the Limpopo.

**Greek War of Independence** (1821–30). Most Greeks were peasants, but the educated minority had great influence in the **Ottoman Empire** as bankers, bishops of the Orthodox Church, governors of the Principalities (the Turkish provinces of Moldavia and Wallachia, later to form Romania), and as merchants. It was amongst these Greeks, who lived outside Greece itself, that the ideas of the **French Revolution**, liberty and **nationalism**, spread. The Philike Hetairia (Society of Friends), a secret society mainly respons-ible for the revolt of 1821, was founded in the Russian grain port of Odessa. The revolt for Greek independence did not begin in Greece at all but in the Principalities. The Greek leaders here – landlords, bishops, merchants – revolted but the mass of the people, the peasants, were not Greek and did not support the rebellion, which failed miserably within a few months. It was then that the Philike Hetairia called on the local chieftains in Greece itself to rise up against the Turks. The rising was successful. By the end of 1821 the Turks had lost control of the Greek mountains and countryside and held only the towns, which were themselves besieged, in the Morea (Southern Greece): the Greeks had command of the sea.

At first the Great Powers opposed the revolt: Austria and Russia did not wish to encourage rebellion against established rulers, whilst Britain and France wanted to keep the Ottoman Empire intact as a barrier against Russian expansion. Support amongst European peoples, however, was widespread. Volunteers from many countries went to help the Greeks, the best known of whom is Lord Byron, who became a Greek hero when he died at Missolonghi, though from disease and not in the fighting. By 1824 it was clear that the Sultan would lose Greece unless he called on the help of his greatest commander **Muhammad Ali**, *pasha* (governor) of Egypt. His son Ibrahim captured Crete and then conquered the Morea. It looked as if the Greeks would be crushed, but when the Turks massacred Greek Christians the Great Powers decided to impose a settlement. Britain, France and Russia agreed to send their fleet to blockade the Morea when the Sultan refused to accept their mediation. When they arrived at Navarino Bay a battle took place in which the

Turkish and Egyptian fleets were destroyed. This ended Muhammad Ali's involvement in the war – Egyptian forces were withdrawn in 1828. In the same year Russia declared war on Turkey, defeated her in a year and made peace at Adrianople, when the Turks accepted the creation of an autonomous Greek state. In 1830 Britain and France persuaded Russia that Greece should be independent rather than autonomous, with a frontier stretching from the Gulf of Arta on the Adriatic to the Gulf of Volo on the Aegean. This left Thessaly and Crete still under Ottoman rule, with a majority of Greeks living outside the new state. In 1832 Otto of Bavaria became the first King of Greece.

**Grey, Charles, 2nd Earl** (1764–1845). British Prime Minister (1830–34). Grey was elected a county MP for Northumberland at the age of twenty-two and joined the Foxite **Whigs**. In 1793 and 1797 he introduced bills for **parliamentary reform**, proposing to get rid of some **'rotten' boroughs**, but they were defeated. Grey first took office in the 'Ministry of All the Talents' (1806–7), as Foreign Secretary after **Fox**'s death, and saw through parliament Fox's bill for the abolition of the **slave trade**. When the Ministry fell he began a period of twenty-three years in opposition, during which he became leader of the Whigs in 1821. He disliked politics, which he described as a theatre of 'base passions, little jealousies and sordid interests', and was no happier in the **Lords** (of which he became a member in 1807, on his father's death) than in the House of **Commons**. Increasingly, he became a nominal leader of the opposition, spending much of his time in Northumberland with his wife and fifteen children. He took few initiatives and became Prime Minister in 1830, at the age of sixty-six, largely as a result of a split in the Tory Party (see **Tories**) over **Catholic emancipation**, rather than through his own efforts.

His government was pledged to parliamentary reform and was responsible for the **Reform Act** of 1832, though Grey's purpose here was conservative: by promoting moderate reform he hoped to make more radical measures unnecessary. 'The principle of my reform is,' he told the Lords in 1831, 'to prevent the necessity for revolution . . . there is no one more dedicated against annual parliaments, universal suffrage and the [secret] ballot than I am.' Above all he wanted to preserve government by men of property. The Reform Act was only one of many reforms during his ministry. Slavery was abolished throughout the British Empire in 1833, a **Factory Act** in the same year limited child labour in textile mills, a Government of India Act ended the **East India Company**'s trading monopoly, the Bank Charter Act limited the Bank of England's issue of notes to the size of the gold reserve, a Judicial Committee of the Privy Council was set up to deal with appeals from the colonies and the Poor Law Amendment Act (see **Poor Laws**) was passed in the Commons, although it did not pass the Lords until after Grey resigned. Yet Grey took little part in promoting these measures and it seemed that all he wanted to do was retire. His contemporaries were not impressed by his achievements. 'I am surprised,' wrote J. C. Hobhouse in 1836, 'how, by mere fluency of speech and arrogance of manner, this really inferior man has contrived to connect his name imperishably with the most splendid triumphs of British legislation.'

**Grey, Sir Edward, Viscount Grey of Fallodon** (1862–1933). Liberal Foreign Secretary (1905–16). Related to Earl **Grey** of the **Reform Bill** (1832), Grey came from a Northumberland landowning family. In 1885 he became an MP for Berwick-upon-Tweed, which he represented until he accepted a peerage in 1916. During the **South African War** (1899–1902), which split the **Liberal Party**, Grey supported the British government and came to be seen as a Liberal imperialist, though he did not want further imperial expansion. When he became Foreign Secretary in 1905 (and held the post longer than anyone else) he continued the policy of his predecessor, the Conservative (see **Conservative Party**) Lord Lansdowne, in accepting the **Anglo-French Entente** (1904) and in seeing a large German navy combined with the largest army in Europe as a threat to Britain. 'If the German fleet,' he wrote, 'ever becomes superior to ours, the German army can conquer this country. There is no corresponding risk of this kind to Germany.' When Germany tried to break up the *entente* in the first **Moroccan crisis** (1905–6), Grey supported France. In January 1906 he wrote that 'An *entente* between Russia, France and ourselves would be absolutely secure. If it is necessary to check Germany it could then be done.' Consequently he made in 1907 the **Anglo-Russian Entente**, which settled differences between the two countries, though this was very unpopular in England, where autocratic Russia was greatly disliked. The second **Moroccan crisis** (1911–12), in which Grey again supported France, brought the two countries closer together and led to military and naval cooperation. During the **Balkan Wars** (1912–13) Grey persuaded the Great Powers to meet with him as chairman, in London. This was seen as a great triumph for Grey but it did not prevent the further weakening of the **Ottoman Empire** or the increase in strength of Serbia, both of which contributed to bringing about the **First World War**. When Germany declared war on Russia and France in August 1914 Grey was in favour of declaring war on Germany, as he did not want to see one power dominating the Continent. He was able to carry the Cabinet with him when Germany invaded Belgium but he was strongly criticized for not making Britain's position clear earlier, as it was felt that this would have prevented war. This is unlikely. Grey had to gain the support of parliament, the Cabinet and the country but this was not forthcoming until Belgium was invaded. An early declaration of British support for France and Russia would not have stopped Germany, who expected that the war would be over before Britain could raise an effective army. Grey, his eyesight failing, lost office in 1916 when **Lloyd George** became Prime Minister.

**Grey, Sir George** (1812–98). British Colonial administrator. Educated at Sandhurst, Grey served in the army (1830–37) and explored Western Australia (1837–9), before becoming Governor of South Australia. It was as Governor of New Zealand (1845–52), however, that his influence was at its greatest. He maintained the Crown monopoly of buying Maori lands established in the Treaty of **Waitangi** (1840), and managed to provide enough land for most settlers, whilst still protecting the interests of the Maoris. He was also mainly responsible for the democratic New Zealand Constitution of 1852. All members of the provincial councils and the national House of Representatives were elected, though the members of the Legislative Council (the upper house) were appointed for life by the Governor. Parliament could revise the powers of the provincial councils and amend the Constitution. From 1853–9 Grey was Governor of Cape Colony but was recalled to New Zealand as Governor from 1861–8. In dealing with the **Anglo-Maori Wars** he allowed the confiscation of three million acres of Maori land. In England he campaigned for state-aided emigration and then settled in New Zealand, where he was a member of the House of Representatives (1874–94) and Prime Minister (1877–9). His Trade Union Act (1878) gave legal recognition to trade unions. In 1894 he returned to England.

**Griffith, Arthur** (1872–1922). Irish nationalist. Trained as a printer, Griffith made his name as a journalist, editing *The United Irishman*. He favoured passive resistance to the British: the withholding of taxes, the refusal of Irish MPs to sit at Westminster and the setting up of an Irish parliament in Dublin. At first he rejected both violent revolution and the constitutional methods of the Irish Parliamentary Party as useless. In 1905 he was a founder of **Sinn Fein**, changed his attitude to violence and moved to a strong nationalist position. Griffith opposed the Home Rule Bill of 1912 (see **Home Rule for Ireland**), joined the paramilitary Irish National Volunteers (1913) and took part in gun-running. Opposing Irish participation in the British war effort, he was imprisoned (May–December 1916), though he had not taken part in the **Easter Rising**. After the Sinn Fein victory in the 1918 election he, with other Irish MPs who refused to sit in the British parliament, met in Dublin as the Dail (Irish Assembly) and declared a republic, with **de Valera** as President and Griffith as Vice-President. As de Valera was in the USA for eighteen months (1919–20) during the **Anglo-Irish War**, Griffith acted as head of the Irish Republic. He led the Irish delegation to London in 1921 and accepted the **Anglo-Irish Treaty**, which ended the war and set up the Irish Free State. A provisional government was set up, led by Michael **Collins**, and Griffith was elected first President of the Irish Free State (1922). Opposition to the treaty by people such as de Valera ended in the **Irish Civil War** (1922–3), during which Griffith died from a cerebral haemorrhage.

**Guderian, Heinz** (1888–1954). German general and a prime creator of modern mechanized warfare. Guderian realized in the 1930s that tanks could play a decisive role as the core of a combined attack force, which would also include mobile artillery and infantry in a subordinate role. His ideas were not taken very seriously until **Hitler** came to power and in 1934 agreed to the *Blitzkrieg* tactics, first applied when Poland was invaded in 1939. Tanks were used not only to support infantry but to pierce the enemy's line and cause confusion by disrupting communications. After success in Poland, the same tactics were applied in France, when in May 1940 Guderian's Panzers emerged from the wooded Ardennes, smashed through the French defences at Sedan and then drove across France to reach the Channel in a week, thus bringing about the fall of **France**. Guderian showed the same skill and panache when Operation **Barbarossa** began in June 1941. He advanced rapidly to within 200 miles of Moscow, when he was ordered to join the Panzers in Army Group South. Together they helped to encircle four Soviet armies in September 1941. Guderian fell out with Hitler, as he maintained that German advanced positions could not be held in the Russian winter, and was dismissed in December 1941. Inactive until February 1943, he was then recalled as Inspector-General of armoured forces. After the retreats at the end of 1943 he began to see that Germany's military position was hopeless and discussed the possibility of removing Hitler, without committing himself to the **July Plot** (1944). When this failed Guderian was promoted to Chief of the General Staff and was appointed to be a member of the court of honour, which investigated officers involved in the conspiracy. He continued to disagree with Hitler, wanting to transfer troops from the Western to the **Eastern Front** to prevent a complete collapse there and early in 1945 he argued strongly for an immediate armistice. This led to his dismissal in March 1945. Guderian was a brilliant strategist and tactician and the most successful tank commander of the **Second World War**.

**Guizot, François Pierre Guillaume** (1787–1874). French statesman. A Protestant intellectual, whose father was executed in the **Terror** during the **French Revolution**, he served **Louis XVIII** after the **Bourbon dynasty** was restored in 1814. In the ultra-royalist reaction following the murder of the Duc de Berry, the son of the future **Charles X**, in 1820, he lost his post in the Council of

State and joined the liberal opposition. He supported **Louis Philippe** becoming King after the **July Revolution** (1830) and as his Minister of Public Instruction (1832–7) increased the number of primary and secondary schools and of teacher training colleges, so that the number of pupils almost doubled in 1833–47, though education was neither free nor compulsory. In 1840 he became Foreign Minister and for the rest of the reign was the dominant figure in the government. Press and public were hostile, as he was accused of being too pro-British, because he accepted the British solution to the **Muhammad Ali** affair. His fragile friendship with Britain ended in 1846, when Guizot arranged for one of Louis Philippe's sons to marry the heiress to the Spanish throne. To avoid France being isolated he now moved closer to **Metternich** and the conservative powers, and this too was unpopular. When there was civil war in Switzerland in 1847 between the liberal majority in the Diet and the conservative Catholic Cantons (the *Sonderbund*), Guizot supported the *Sonderbund*. He believed in maintaining the status quo at home and throughout the 1840s complacently rejected bills to extend the franchise to a larger proportion of the middle class. This 'immobilism' was reinforced when the government gained a majority of 100 in the 1846 election, though corruption was held to be responsible for this result (200 deputies held official posts). 'Personally incorruptible,' wrote Victor Hugo, 'yet he governs by corruption.' Dissatisfaction led to a banquet campaign calling for reform and this erupted into a full-scale rising, when troops fired into a crowd. Louis Philippe dismissed Guizot on 23 February but it was too late to save his throne. Both the King and his minister went into exile.

**Guomindang (Kuomintang).** Chinese Nationalist Party led by **Sun Yixian** (Sun Yat-sen) and after his death by **Jiang Jieshi** (Chiang Kai-shek). The party was formed by Sun in 1912, after the fall of the **Qing dynasty**. It was suppressed in 1913 by **Yuan Shikai** but re-formed by Sun in 1920. In 1923 Sun established a base for his party in Guangzhou (Canton) and in the same year received Soviet aid, in return for allowing members of the Chinese Communist Party (CCP) to join the Guomindang as individuals. The **United Front** of the Guomindang and CCP, against the **warlords**

who ruled China, worked amicably as long as Sun lived. The Guomindang became a centralized and disciplined party, in which communists acquired influential positions. At the first National Congress of the Guomindang in 1924 communists, including **Mao Zedong** (Mao Tse-tung), were elected to the Central Executive Committee. The Congress adopted Sun's 'Three Principles of the People' as the party's ideology. The Whampoa Military Academy was established, also in 1924, to train officers for a Nationalist Army under the direct control of the Guomindang. Jiang was the Academy's commandant, so he was in a strong position when Sun died in 1925. He began the **Northern Expedition** in 1926 to unite China under the Guomindang but a year later, in the **Shanghai coup**, he turned on his communist allies and massacred them, thus ending the United Front. The Guomindang, which had been a radical party under Sun, now became much more conservative. The Northern Expedition ended with the capture of Beijing (Peking) in 1928 and the establishment of a new Nationalist Government in Nanjing. The Guomindang appeared to rule the whole of China but in fact warlords, who kept their own armies, still controlled much of it. The communists survived and so the Guomindang became involved in a civil war with the CCP, which did not end until the **Xi'an incident** of 1936, when Jiang was compelled by his own troops to make another United Front with the CCP in order to resist the Japanese. As the **Sino-Japanese War** (1937–45) developed the Guomindang abandoned its capital at Nanjing and retreated to the safety of Chongqing behind the Yangzi gorges. With the defeat of Japan in the **Pacific War**, a further civil war began between the Guomindang and the CCP, which ended with a communist victory in 1949. Jiang and Nationalist forces fled to Taiwan, where the Guomindang still forms the government.

**Habsburg (or Hapsburg) dynasty.** The ruling house of Austria from 1282 to 1918. From 1526 to 1918 Habsburgs ruled Hungary and Bohemia and held the Crown of the Holy Roman Empire from 1452 to 1806, except for the years 1740–45. For nearly two centuries (from 1504–6, 1516–1700) Habsburgs also reigned in Spain and the Spanish Empire, and in Italy were Dukes of Modena (1803–60) and of Tuscany (1737–1860).

*Haganah* (Hebrew, 'defence') (1920–48). Zionist (see **Zionism**) military organization, which aimed to defend Jewish settlements in Palestine against Arab attacks. During the Arab rebellion (1936–9) it increased greatly in size and organized illegal Jewish immigration. Its members served part-time until, in 1941, a full-time commando force, the Palmah, was formed. Until 1945 it was moderate and opposed the actions of Jewish terrorist groups such as the **Stern Gang** and Irgun. When Britain refused to allow unlimited Jewish immigration after the **Second World War**, the *Haganah* turned against Britain as well as against the Arabs. It became the defence force of the Jewish state when Palestine was partitioned in 1947, clashed with the British army and defeated the Palestinian Arabs and their supporters. In May 1948 it became the national army of the state of Israel.

**Haig, Douglas, 1st Earl** (1861–1928). British field marshal. Haig first saw active service during **Kitchener**'s advance to Omdurman (see **battle of Omdurman**) in 1898 and then during the **South African War**. After the **First World War** began he criticized French's command of the British Expeditionary Force (BEF), intrigued for his removal and replaced him as Commander-in-Chief in December 1915. Aloof and self-disciplined, Haig rarely discussed strategy and tactics with his commanders, who were afraid of him. A deeply religious Catholic, he believed that he had God's support and that all his decisions were therefore right. He strongly believed that the only way to destroy the enemy's army was to take the offensive and show the stronger will. This led him to order pointless frontal attacks, in which losses were horrendous: there were 56,000 casualties on the first day of the battle of the **Somme** (June–November 1916). By October the area was a sea of mud and it was clear that the offensive had failed but Haig, over-optimistic and stubborn, persisted in continuing the assault until November, so that yet more lives were wasted. The BEF suffered 400,000 casualties on the Somme, for a maximum gain of eight miles. **Lloyd George**, the British Prime Minister, was so alarmed at the carnage that in February 1917 he put Haig under the temporary command of the French Commander-in-Chief Nivelle, but his offensive was a disaster and led to mutinies in the French army. Haig was therefore allowed to strike north-east from the Ypres salient at the Belgian coast. The third battle of Ypres, commonly known as **Passchendaele** (July–November 1917), repeated the experience of the Somme: useless slaughter, 300,000 BEF casualties and a gain of five miles, soon lost in the **Ludendorff offensive**. This was first directed against Haig's armies in March 1918 and only by desperate resistance was it held up at Arras. **Foch** was appointed, with Haig's blessing, as Allied generalissimo and prevented the BEF from being cut off from the French army. Fortunately for Haig, Ludendorff struck at the French line on the Aisne in May and this gave the BEF time to rest and refit. On 8 August Haig began a counter-attack with the French and the Americans which recovered most of the spring losses. Their advance continued until the armistice of 11 November. After the war Haig spent much of his time looking after the welfare of soldiers and it was largely owing to him that the various ex-servicemen's organizations were united in one body, the British Legion. Haig has been much criticized for using methods which were suitable in colonial wars but not against armies in a technological age, and for destroying his own armies in pursuit of unattainable objectives.

**Haile Selassie** (1892–1975). Last Emperor of Ethiopia (1930–74). Baptized as Tafari Makonnen, a Coptic Christian, his father Rao (Prince) Makonnen was a cousin of Emperor **Menelik II**. The young Tafari was appointed governor of Harar province shortly before Menelik's death in 1913. The Christian Amharic ruling class feared that the new Emperor Iyasu was trying to promote Islam and so in 1916 Tafari led the *coup* which deposed him. Menelik's daughter Zawditu became Empress, with Ras Tafari as prince regent and effective ruler of Ethiopia. Regarded as a reformer, Ras Tafari brought Ethiopia into the **League of Nations** in 1923. On Zawditu's death he became Emperor, taking the name of Haile Selassie (Power of the Trinity). In 1935 the **Ethiopian War** began when **Mussolini** invaded Ethiopia. Haile Selassie appealed unsuccessfully for help to the League of Nations and was forced to flee when his army was defeated: from 1936–40 he lived in exile in England. When Italy entered the **Second World War** he had the support of British-led troops, who enabled him to reconquer his country in 1941. After the war he united the former Italian colony of Eritrea with Ethiopia, encouraged economic development with foreign aid and set up a modern educational system. However, he kept power largely in his own hands with the support of a strong army, which suppressed an attempted palace *coup* in 1960. He played an active and leading role in African diplomacy, especially when Addis Ababa became the headquarters of the Organization of African Unity in 1963. The slow pace of reform failed to satisfy the new educational élite, which he had done much to create, and there was also increasing unrest from ethnic minorities, such as Eritreans, who resented the centralizing policies of the Ethiopian state. In the early 1970s rapid inflation, and a serious drought followed by a disastrous famine, which killed about 400,000 people, led to rural unrest and serious strikes. Workers, students and the military were all disaffected and in 1974 there was a military revolution. Haile Selassie was deposed and died a year later in mysterious circumstances, while under house arrest.

**Haldane, Richard Burdon, Viscount** (1856–1928). British politician. An intellectual with a life-long interest in philosophy, Haldane became a **Liberal Party** MP in 1885 and War Secretary (1905–12) in **Campbell-Bannerman**'s administration. The **South African War** (1899–1902) had shown the poor state of the British army, so Haldane set about making it more efficient. He introduced a General

Staff to organize military planning and created a small 'expedition-ary force', which could be quickly sent abroad. For a reserve he abolished the old militia and volunteers and established a new Territorial Army, whose members would have part-time training for four years. Consequently the British army entered the **First World War** (1914–18) much better organized than in the South African War. From 1912–15 in **Asquith**'s government Haldane was Lord Chancellor, a post he occupied again in 1924 in the **Labour Party**'s first administration. Haldane was passionately concerned with education, becoming a founder of the London School of Economics, President of Birkbeck College for nine years and an enthusiastic supporter of the Workers' Educational Association.

**Halifax, Edward Frederick Lindley Wood, 1st Earl of** (1881–1959). English statesman. A devout Christian and scholar, after Eton and Oxford Halifax became a Fellow of All Souls and sat in the **Commons** from 1910–25, when he was created Lord Irwin. An unambitious politician, his most fruitful work was as Viceroy of India (1926–31). He realized that conciliation was necessary if British rule in India was to continue. Irwin persuaded **MacDonald**'s **Labour Party** government in 1929 to call a round table conference in London of British and Indian representatives to discuss India's future Constitution and to declare that **dominion** status was the aim for India. These talks, and the long conversations he had with **Gandhi**, helped him on his return to England to prepare the **India Act** (1935), which gave Indians control of provincial government. In 1937 he visited **Nazi Party** leaders and returned with the conviction that 'the Germans had no policy of immediate adventure.' When Eden resigned as Foreign Secretary in 1938 Halifax succeeded him but played a subordinate role to Neville **Chamberlain**, who wished to conduct his own foreign policy, and did not accompany the Prime Minister on his visits to **Hitler**. A supporter of **appeasement** and of the Munich agreement (see **Czechoslovakian crisis**), he realized the extent of German ambitions when Hitler occupied the rest of Czechoslovakia in March 1939 and insisted that Poland's independence should be guaranteed. When Chamberlain lost support in 1940, he wanted Halifax to succeed him but Halifax felt unsuited for the post of Prime Minister and rejected the suggestion. In May 1940, at the time of the evacuation **of Dunkirk**, he wanted to find out German terms for ending the war, though these would have left Hitler as master of Europe. **Churchill** refused and in 1941 sent Halifax as ambassador to the USA. This was a role he did not like, particularly as Churchill had close personal relations with Franklin D. **Roosevelt** and Halifax was largely ignored.

**Hamilton, Alexander** (1755–1804). American politician and founder of the **Federalist Party**. Hamilton was born in the West Indies and came to New York when he was seventeen. Though an admirer of Britain, he fought against her in the Revolutionary War, during which he was **Washington's** *aide-de-camp* from 1777–81 and took part in the attack on Yorktown in 1781. He led the demand for a Constitutional Convention and did much to secure the ratification of the Constitution by the states, by his contributions to the Federalist Papers (1777–8).

Hamilton had no use for states' rights but wanted a strong national government, based on sound monetary policies and an alliance between business and government. He was openly élitist and spurned democracy, believing that 'the rich and well-born' should control the government. In 1789 he became Washington's Secretary of the Treasury and was henceforth the driving force of the administration. In his *Report on Public Credit* (1790) he proposed that the federal debt should be paid in full, that the Federal Government should take over the states' debts and that a Bank of the United States, modelled on the Bank of England, should be set up. To finance these reforms he proposed to impose import duties and excise taxes. All these measures were passed, though the excise tax on rye whisky led to the Whisky Rebellion of 1794, when Pennsylvanian farmers refused to pay the tax. This was the first challenge to Federal authority. Hamilton, with Washington's support, used Federal troops to suppress the rising, thus making clear that Federal authority would be upheld. Hamilton's financial measures restored public credit and ensured the success of the new government. Hamilton was at his most brilliant in the last of his state papers, the *Report on Manufactures* of 1791, when he put forward a plan for industrialization through protective tariffs and subsidies, which would make the United States self-sufficient, although Congress was not yet prepared to act on those proposals.

**Jefferson** clashed with Hamilton, as he came to believe that Hamilton's ideas were 'adverse to liberty'. Hamilton favoured industrialization and a hierarchical society: Jefferson wanted a republic of small, independent farmers. The conflict between them had led by the mid-1790s to the formation of two political parties: Hamilton's Federalist Party and Jefferson's Democratic-Republican Party. Although Hamilton was a bitter opponent of Jefferson, he ensured the latter's success in the presidential election of 1801. In the electoral college Jefferson and Aaron Burr received the same number of votes, so the decision was made by the House of Representatives where, owing to Hamilton's influence, Jefferson was finally successful. Hamilton once again used his influence, to prevent Burr becoming Governor of New York in 1804. Burr, incensed, challenged Hamilton to a duel, in which Hamilton was shot and died on 11 July 1804.

**Hanover.** An electorate which became a kingdom in 1815, as part of the **German Confederation**. The Elector became King of England in 1714 as George I but the connection was purely dynastic and Hanover was never ruled by England. When **Victoria** became Queen of England in 1837 she was not able to be sovereign in Hanover, as the Salic Law there prevented a woman inheriting the throne. Her uncle, the Duke of Cumberland, became King of Hanover, which was annexed by **Prussia** in 1866, after Austria's defeat in the **Austro-Prussian War**.

**Hardie, James Keir** (1856–1915). British socialist and founder of the **Independent Labour Party** (ILP). Born in Lanarkshire, the illegitimate son of Mary Keir, it was not clear who Hardie's father was. The drinking of his stepfather, David Hardie, kept the large family poor and made Keir a supporter of temperance. He began work at the age of eight, went down the mines two years later and eventually became a trade-union official. In 1878 he was converted to Christianity and thereafter saw socialism as an expression of brotherly love. 'More inspiration for the work,' he later claimed, 'has been drawn from the teachings of Jesus than from any other source.' He was never much interested in theory and read Carlyle,

Ruskin and Dickens rather than Marx. To defend the miners' interests he became a journalist and strongly advocated the need for a separate working-class party. Defeated in a by-election at Mid-Lanark in 1888, he became secretary of the new Scottish Labour Party and in 1892 was elected as the first independent Labour MP for West Ham. A year later he was the main force in forming the ILP. Hardie saw that trade-union financial support was necessary for a viable working-class party, so he persuaded **trade unions** and socialist societies to join together in forming the Labour Representation Committee in 1900, which became the **Labour Party** in 1906. Defeated in the 1895 election, he was an MP again from 1900–1915 and was elected as first chairman of the parliamentary Labour Party (1906–8), persuading **Asquith**'s **Liberal Party** government to pass the Trade Disputes Act (1906), which removed the restrictions placed on trade-union activity by the **Taff Vale case** (1901).

Hardie showed great passion and courage in championing causes which were often unpopular. Outspoken in his attacks on Queen **Victoria** and the royal family, he wanted the abolition of the House of **Lords** in 1911 rather than the limitation of its powers which the **Parliament Act** provided. A staunch supporter of the **suffragettes** (Sylvia Pankhurst was probably one of his mistresses), he defended civil liberties in the period of industrial unrest from 1910–14 and condemned the use of the police and army, when workers were killed at Liverpool and Tonypandy without any public inquiry being set up. Favouring devolution of power, he wanted self-government for Wales, Scotland, Ireland and India, where he spoke at home rule meetings in 1907. He encouraged nationalist movements in Africa and Asia and had his meeting broken up in Johannesburg when he spoke in favour of African rights. In all he did, Hardie was a constitutionalist, who rejected class war and the violent overthrow of capitalism by revolution. As an internationalist he attended the inaugural meeting of the **Second International** in Paris in 1889 and in 1910 tried unsuccessfully to persuade it to organize an international general strike if war began. A pacifist, he opposed both the **South African War** (1899–1902) and the **First World War** (1914–18), for which he was greatly reviled. He was deeply depressed when socialist parties everywhere supported their home governments, and died in 1915 sad and lonely.

Keir Hardie was a towering figure in working-class politics before 1914, who did more than anyone to establish an independent Labour Party in Britain.

**Haussmann, Georges Eugène, Baron** (1809–91). French civil servant. Prefect of the Seine from 1853, Haussmann was responsible for the substantial rebuilding of Paris under **Napoleon III**. Supported by the Emperor, he destroyed the working-class areas of the inner city and built much of the Paris we see today: the great *boulevards*, parks like the Bois de Boulogne, the Opéra, Les Halles (central market place which survived until the 1960s), the Palace of Justice and the Louvre–Tuileries complex. The workers were pushed out into the suburbs, so the rich centre was surrounded by a Red Belt, which affected Parisian politics well into the twentieth century. Haussmann also provided a sewerage system, a clean water supply which eliminated the worst diseases such as cholera, and better municipal housing for workers at low rents.

**Haymarket Square riot** took place in Chicago in 1886. A small anarchist movement (see **Anarchism**) there was led by German immigrants, who called for violent revolution. On 3 May police clashed with strikers at the McCormick Harvester plant, killing one striker and wounding several more. Union leaders called for a mass rally the next day in Haymarket Square to protest at police brutality. During the rally someone threw a bomb which killed one policeman and six other people and injured sixty-seven. Police opened fire, killing four more. Eight anarchists, all but one foreign-born, were charged with conspiracy to murder. There was no evidence of their involvement in the bomb-throwing but all were convicted and seven were sentenced to death. Two had their sentences commuted to life imprisonment, one committed suicide and four were hanged. In 1893 the liberal governor of Illinois pardoned the three anarchists who were still in prison, as he said that a miscarriage of justice had occurred. There was a furious public reaction, which increased hostility to the labour movement.

**Hearst, William Randolph** (1863–1951). American newspaper proprietor. The son of a millionaire industrialist, Hearst was given the *San Francisco Examiner* by his father in 1887. He saw that the large number of uneducated or poorly educated people wanted some excitement brought to their hard and drab lives. He therefore went in for sensational journalism to boost sales: 'muck-raking' campaigns, sex and scandal. In 1895 he bought the *New York Journal* and used the Cuban revolution, which began in the same year, to build up his circulation by giving lurid accounts of Spanish atrocities and thus stirring up war fever. 'How Do You Like the *Journal's* War?' was the headline in his newspaper, when the **Spanish–American War** began. The circulation of the *Journal* soared to over one million a day. By 1922 Hearst owned twenty newspapers, thirteen magazines, two motion-picture companies, eight radio stations, a rich art collection and vast estates in California, New York City, Mexico and Wales. He was politically ambitious but failed in his attempts to become mayor and governor of New York. In 1932 he helped to obtain the Democratic presidential nomination for Franklin D. **Roosevelt**, a move he later deeply regretted, as Roosevelt's policies clashed with his conservative and isolationist beliefs. Hearst was the model for *Citizen Kane*, one of the most famous of all American movies.

**Hébert, Jacques-René** (1757–94). French journalist and revolutionary. Hébert's newspaper *Le Père Duchesne* was scurrilous and earthy and very popular with the *sans-culottes*. In 1791 he became a member of the radical **Cordeliers Club** and after the attack on the **Tuileries** (10 August 1792) he was elected to the Paris Commune. He supported the **Jacobins** against the **Girondins** and when they came to power after the *coup* of 2 June 1793, he expected high office. When he did not get it, he turned against the Jacobins, accused the **Committee of Public Safety** of tyranny and tried to obtain power for himself by becoming a champion of popular discontent. He organized a *sans-culottes* invasion of the **Convention** on 5 September to obtain a reduction of food prices, supported the **dechristianization** campaign in the winter of 1793–4 and called for an intensification of the **Terror** and a redistribution of property. Hébert had few supporters in the Convention but many in the Cordeliers Club, the Commune, the Paris revolutionary army and the popular societies. When he announced in the Cordeliers Club in March that an insurrection was necessary 'that shall bring death to those who oppress us', **Robespierre** decided to destroy him. Hébert and eighteen supporters were arrested on the night of 12–13 March, accused of being foreign agents, who wanted a military dictatorship (charges that would discredit them in the eyes of the *sans-culottes*) and were guillotined.

**Hegel, Georg Wilhelm Friedrich** (1770–1831). German idealist philosopher, who rejected the empiricism of the classical tradition. Hegel's ideas were taught in German universities from the 1820s and deeply influenced the bureaucracy and the educated middle class. He idealized the State, seeing it as all-important compared with the individual, who became totally free only when subordinate to the State. 'The State is objective spirit itself,' he wrote in *The Philosophy of Right* (1821), 'and the individual has objectivity, truth and morality only in so far as he is a member of it.' The World Spirit does not care about the happiness or unhappiness of individuals and it is useless to deplore the crimes of the past, as everything has a purpose. Whatever happens is the only thing that could have happened and all who failed in life deserved their fate. Success indicates superiority, so might is right. Hegel defended the ruthless use of power and despised those who thought that right was more important than might. He was a great admirer of **Napoleon** up to the battle of Jena (see battles of **Jena–Auerstädt**) (1806) – later, right was on the side of the Allies, as they were successful. Hegel's worship of power and authority could easily be used to identify the State with the Prussian Crown and its institutions, especially the bureaucracy and army. For the neo-Hegelians the **Reichstag** symbolized party conflict, which destroyed the unity of the State: this could be brought about only by an impartial authority, the Crown, which stood above party. This ideology of the State dominated German politics until 1918 and even beyond.

**Henderson, Arthur** (1863–1935). English politician. Probably the illegitimate son of a domestic servant, Henderson left school at the age of twelve and was eventually an official and then President of the Iron Founders Union. An evangelical Christian (see **Evangelical Movement**), he became a Methodist lay-preacher and fervent teetotaller. In 1900 his union was affiliated to the Labour Representation Committee (which became the **Labour Party** in 1906) and

Henderson was elected as an MP in 1903. In 1912 he joined the **Fabian Society** and became secretary of the Labour Party, a post he held until 1934. When the **First World War** began he supported the war effort and replaced Ramsay **MacDonald**, an opponent of the war, as chairman of the Parliamentary Labour Party. He joined **Asquith**'s coalition government in 1915 as President of the Board of Education with a seat in the Cabinet and persuaded the reluctant **trade unions** to accept 'dilution' (the use of unskilled labour in skilled jobs) for the duration of the war. His importance as a link between the trade unions and the government was shown when he was appointed a member of **Lloyd George**'s small War Cabinet. Lloyd George sent him to Russia after the **February Revolution**, 1917, to persuade the Russians to stay in the war. His opposition to **Bolshevism** led to his condemnation by **Lenin** in *Left-Wing Communism: an Infantile Disorder* (1920) as a *petit-bourgeois* opportunist. On his return Henderson suggested that a negotiated peace should be made with Germany and that delegates, representing all the belligerent countries, should attend an International Socialist Congress at Stockholm. This led to a rebuke from Lloyd George and his resignation.

Henderson used his considerable skills as an administrator to reorganize the Labour Party, building up local branches nationwide, making it possible for individuals to become full members and bringing in intellectuals like Sidney **Webb** to draft policy statements. The 1918 Constitution for the first time committed the Labour Party to **socialism**, with its Clause Four calling for 'the common ownership of the means of production'. At a time when the **Liberal Party** organization was collapsing, Henderson ensured that the Labour Party was in a position to replace the Liberals as one of the two major parties. Ramsay MacDonald (who returned as leader of the Labour Party in 1922) disliked Henderson and tried to keep him out of the first Labour government in 1924 but had to find a place for him as Home Secretary. In the second Labour government (1929–31) Henderson insisted on being Foreign Secretary and was extremely irritated by MacDonald's interference in foreign affairs. Yet he remained loyal to the Prime Minister until 1931 and even when MacDonald formed a **National Government**, Henderson opposed a complete break with him and replaced Mac-

Donald as leader of the Labour Party unwillingly. Henderson lost his seat in the 1931 election and resigned as leader of the Party a year later. Determined, honest and unselfish, he was one of the major figures in making the Labour Party a party of government.

**Hertzog, James Barry Munnik** (1866–1942). Boer general and Prime Minister of South Africa (1924–39). Hertzog was born in the Orange Free State, studied law in the Netherlands, returned home and became a judge. In the **South African War** (1899–1902) he was a Boer general and made commando raids into Cape Colony. After the war Hertzog became a politician in order to work for the restoration of self-government in the Orange River Colony and the Transvaal. When this was achieved in 1907 he became a minister in the government of the Orange Free State (OFS). In 1910 the OFS became part of the Union of South Africa and Hertzog became Minister of Justice in the new government headed by **Botha**. He opposed Botha's policy of close cooperation with Britain and in 1912 left the government. Strongly opposed to South Africa entering the **First World War** on Britain's side, he formed a new, exclusively Afrikaner (see **Afrikaners**) **National Party** (NP) in 1914. As leader of the opposition he made a pact with the Labour Party in 1923, promising more **segregation** and legislation to protect white workers against cheap black labour. The pact won the 1924 election and Hertzog became Prime Minister, a position he retained until 1939. In 1925 Afrikaans was recognized as an official language for the first time. Hertzog became one of the main architects of apartheid, as he feared that the more numerous Africans would overwhelm the white population. 'The European is severe and hard on the African,' he wrote, 'because he is afraid of him. It is the old instinct of self-preservation.' He wanted to remove the fear by separating the races and wished to get rid of the Cape franchise, the only area in South Africa where some Africans qualified for the vote (in 1909 they were 4.7 per cent of the Cape electorate). For this he needed a two-thirds majority at a joint sitting of the two houses of parliament. In the 1929 election the National Party gained a majority (but not a two-thirds majority). In the **Great Depression** Hertzog's government became unpopular, as it cut wages and increased taxes, so he had to seek support from **Smuts**, leader of the

South African Party (SAP). In 1934 the NP and the SAP 'fused' to become the United Party. This split the old NP, a section of which led by Malan broke away to form a 'Purified' National Party. The alliance with Smuts gave Hertzog the two-thirds majority he had long wanted, so in 1936 he passed the Natives Representation Act, which ended the Cape franchise. As compensation to the Africans, land in the native reserves was to be increased from 7.5 per cent to 13 per cent of the total land in South Africa. When the **Second World War** began in 1939 Hertzog favoured neutrality, whilst Smuts wanted South Africa to join Britain against Germany. Hertzog was narrowly defeated in parliament, so Smuts replaced him as Prime Minister. Hertzog joined the Purified National Party but left it in 1940, when it rejected cooperation with English-speaking South Africans, and retired from politics.

**Herzen, Alexander Ivanovich** (1812–70). Russian revolutionary and journalist. The illegitimate son of a rich noble, Herzen emigrated to Western Europe in 1847, living mainly in London, like his contemporaries **Marx** and **Mazzini**, and in Geneva. In 1857 he founded the first anti-Tsarist newspaper, *The Bell*, in London, 'devoted to the task of Russian freedom and to propagating within Russia free ideas'. He became disillusioned with Western liberals after their failure in the **Revolutions of 1848** and disliked the greed and inhumanity of the capitalist societies around him. Herzen saw in the egalitarianism of the Russian peasant commune or *mir* a means of passing directly from feudalism to socialism, overtaking the decadent capitalist West. This was to be a major theme of the Russian intelligentsia, especially the **Populists**, for much of the rest of the century. The revolution, when it came, must be a peasant revolution, which would change autocratic Russia into a society of self-governing village communes. His main aim was freedom for the Russian people, though he realized that the masses were indifferent to it. 'They want . . . a government to rule for their benefit,' he wrote, 'but to govern themselves doesn't enter their heads.' Herzen's call for educated Russians to go to the people, to learn as well as to teach, was a central feature of Russian populism.

**Herzl, Theodor** (1860–1904). Founder of **Zionism**. The son of a wealthy Jewish merchant in Budapest, Herzl moved with his family to Vienna, where he became a writer and journalist. At first he believed in the assimilation of Jews to the country in which they lived but his experiences in the 1890s in Paris, where as a journalist he reported the **Dreyfus case**, convinced him that Jews should have their own homeland. The Dreyfus case, he later said, made him a Zionist. In 1896 he published his pamphlet *Der Judenstaat* (*The Jewish State*) and a year later organized the first World Zionist Congress at Basel in Switzerland, where 200 delegates, mainly from Russia and Eastern Europe, met. The Congress declared that 'Zionism aspires to create a publicly guaranteed homeland for the Jewish people in the land of Israel.' Herzl became the first President of the World Zionist Organization, set up by the Congress, though he had little knowledge of Palestine, calling it a 'land without people' which should be given to the Jews as 'a people without land'. His tireless efforts and propaganda made Zionism a world-wide movement.

**Hess, Walther Richard Rudolf** (1894–1987). Deputy leader of the **Nazi Party** (1933–41). Hess joined the Party in 1920, took part in the **Munich Putsch** (1923) and was imprisoned with **Hitler**, who dictated the first volume of *Mein Kampf* to him. Hess was introverted, insecure and not very intelligent but he showed a dog-like devotion to Hitler and was his private secretary from 1925–32, although he held no official party post at this time. His loyalty was rewarded when, almost unknown, he became deputy leader of the Party in 1933. He reached the height of his career in 1939, when he was appointed successor to Hitler and **Goering**. In May 1941 he flew a Messerschmitt fighter to Scotland and baled out, apparently in the hope that he could persuade King George VI to dismiss Winston **Churchill**, make peace with Germany and join her in the impending struggle against Russia. By this time he had lost touch with reality and Hitler declared him insane. He was interned until the war ended, when he was tried at Nuremberg and sentenced to life imprisonment. After 1966 he was the sole prisoner in Spandau prison, Berlin, as the Russians would not agree to his release, and he remained there until he supposedly committed suicide at the age of ninety-three.

**Heydrich, Reinhard Tristan Eugen** (1904–42). Leading organizer of the **'Final Solution'**, the extermination of the Jews. Heydrich's father, a well-known musician, appeared in Hugo Riemann's *Musiklexikon* (1916) as 'Heydrich, Bruno, real name Süss', which indicated that he was a Jew, a fact which tormented Reinhard all his life. He served as an officer in the German navy in his early twenties but was dismissed in 1931 for dishonourable conduct towards a young woman. In the same year he joined the **Nazi Party** and the **SS**. Tall, blond, blue-eyed and an excellent sportsman (he could also play the violin at concert level), he was the archetypal Aryan of Nazi mythology. He was disciplined and a good organizer and became **Himmler**'s right-hand man. Both Himmler and **Hitler** were aware of his Jewish descent but this knowledge gave them a hold over Heydrich, which meant that he was entirely dependent on them and would obey orders blindly. Ruthless, cold and cynical, he trusted no one and perpetrated the most inhuman acts without compassion. Heydrich played a leading part in the **Night of the Long Knives** (1934), when the **SA** leadership was murdered. In 1939 he was appointed head of the Reich Main Security Office, which incorporated the *Gestapo*, the Security Service and the criminal police. He was in charge of Jewish affairs before the war, though emphasis then was on forced emigration, rather than extermination, and was one of the instigators of the **Crystal Night** pogrom in 1938. After the war began he organized the setting up of **concentration camps** and, with Adolf Eichmann, the mass deportation of Jews to them. When Germany invaded the Soviet Union in 1941, **Goering** ordered him to carry out 'a total solution of the Jewish question in those territories of Europe which are under German influence'. His *Einsatzgruppen*, SS murder squads, killed a million Russian and Polish Jews, as well as numerous Soviet officials. In September 1941 he was appointed Deputy Reich Protector of Bohemia and Moravia and it was on the outskirts of Prague that he was wounded by the Czech resistance and died a few days later, in June 1942. Barbarous reprisals followed. The village of **Lidice** was destroyed and all its male inhabitants executed: 860 Czechs were condemned to death by German courts martial in Prague and 395 in Brno.

**Hill, Sir Rowland** (1795–1879). Originator of the modern postal system. He suggested that a low, uniform rate of postage would greatly increase the volume of mail, which should be pre-paid by using a postage stamp. His proposals were adopted in England in 1840 and later spread throughout the world.

**Himmler, Heinrich** (1900–1945). Head of the **SS** in Nazi Germany. He joined the **Nazi Party** in 1921 whilst still an agricultural student and had already formed his racialist views. Himmler regarded the struggle between Aryans and Jews as the key to world history and believed that Germany needed *Lebensraum* ('living-space') and must extend her boundaries by settling German peasants in the east, especially in the Baltic states and western Russia. He looked, with his rimless glasses and receding chin, frail and timid and suffered from psychosomatic illnesses all his life but this concealed a great ambition and drive for power. He was an able administrator, with a meticulous care for detail, and had an enormous capacity for work. His first important post was in 1929, when **Hitler** put him in charge of his personal bodyguard, the SS. Himmler made it into an élite force, with its black uniform, and raised its numbers from 280 in 1929 to 50,000 in 1933. When Hitler came to power in January 1933, Himmler took control of the police in Bavaria and within months controlled the police in all states except Prussia: in April 1934 he also became head of the Prussian secret police, the *Gestapo*. With the secret police under his control, he played a leading part in murdering **SA** leaders on the **Night of the Long Knives** (30 June 1934). Hitler rewarded him by making the SS, which had been part of the SA, an independent body, responsible only to himself and to Himmler. Two years later all the separate police forces in Germany became one body under Himmler. By 1939 Himmler's influence overshadowed that of the Nazi Party: he was one of Hitler's most trusted advisers and feared throughout Germany. His power grew even greater during the **Second World War** as the SS was responsible for security in German-occupied Europe. The number of prisoners in **concentration camps** rose from 21,000 in 1939 in six camps to 800,000 in twenty-two camps by 1945. Himmler was responsible for running them and masterminded the **'Final Solution'** when six million Jews were gassed or killed in other ways. He was also in charge of the slave labourers, whom he worked to death in factories supporting the German war effort. 'Whether other peoples live in comfort or perish of hunger,' he told SS group leaders in 1943, 'interests me only in so far as we need them as slaves.' From 1943–5 he was Minister of the Interior, which gave him control of the courts and civil service. The height of Himmler's power came in 1944 when, after the failure of the **July Plot** to assassinate Hitler, he was made Commander-in-Chief of the new reserve army and the regular army was put under SS supervision. Next to Hitler he was the most powerful man in Germany. Towards the end of the war Himmler saw that Germany could not win and so he approached the Allies for peace negotiations, which led an enraged Hitler to strip him of all offices. He was arrested by British troops in May 1945 but committed suicide by taking poison before he could be put on trial.

**Hindenburg, Paul von** (1847–1934). German field marshal and President of the **Weimar Republic** (1925–34). Hindenburg came from the same East Elbian *Junker* and Lutheran state as **Bismarck** and was the son of an officer, who traced back his family's tradition of military service to the thirteenth century. He served in the **Austro-Prussian War** (1866) and won the Iron Cross at **Sedan** in the **Franco-Prussian War** in 1870. He gained steady rather than rapid promotion to the post of general and retired in 1911. He was recalled in 1914 to take command of the Eighth Army in Prussia, which was threatened by two converging, and larger, Russian armies. In a week one Russian army was encircled and annihilated at the battle of **Tannenberg** and a fortnight later the second was heavily defeated at the Masurian Lakes and driven out of Prussia. Hindenburg was given credit for these victories and became a national hero, although the man chiefly responsible was General Hoffmann, a Staff Officer of the Eighth Army. The Kaiser made Hindenburg a field-marshal and supreme commander of the German and Austrian armies on the Eastern Front. He remained there with his Chief of Staff, **Ludendorff**, for the next two years, complaining bitterly that the Commander-in-Chief **Falkenhayn** prevented him winning a decisive victory, which would have knocked Russia out of the war, by refusing to move large numbers of troops from the Western to the Eastern Front. In August 1916 Hindenburg replaced

Falkenhayn as Chief of the General Staff and with Ludendorff mobilized the economy for total warfare. They insisted on **Beth-mann-Hollweg** resigning as Chancellor in 1917 and on unrestricted submarine warfare, which brought the USA into the war. They were jointly responsible for the harsh terms imposed on Russia in the Treaty of **Brest-Litovsk** in March 1918 and for the final offensive on the Western Front. Its failure led Hindenburg to sue for peace and call on the Kaiser **William II** to abdicate.

Hindenburg then retired but was persuaded by nationalists and conservatives to stand for President of the Weimar Republic when Friedrich **Ebert** died in 1925. He was elected, though not by a wide margin, obtaining 14.6 million votes compared with 13.8 million for his **Centre Party** opponent. A monarchist rather than a republican, Hindenburg nevertheless acted with the utmost propriety as President, at least for his first five years in office. In 1930, with the **Great Depression** getting worse, he appointed **Brüning** as Chancellor and, as he could not obtain a majority in the **Reichstag**, allowed him to use Clause 48 of the Constitution of the Weimar Republic and rule by presidential decrees. When his term of office expired in 1932 Hindenburg, physically and mentally exhausted at the age of eighty-five, wanted to retire to his estates but Brüning insisted that he stood for re-election as the only alternative to **Hitler**. The President felt it was humiliating to stand against an ex-corporal (Hitler) and a communist (Thalmann) but was elected on the second ballot by 19.3 million votes to Hitler's 13.4 million. He never forgave Brüning and replaced him first with von **Papen** and then with **Schleicher**, in a vain attempt to provide Germany with a strong government. In the 1932 elections the Nazis became by far the strongest party and Hindenburg was persuaded by von Papen to agree in January 1933 to a coalition government, in which Hitler would be Chancellor and von Papen Vice-Chancellor. A month later, after the **Reichstag Fire**, Hindenburg accepted Hitler's demand for a decree suspending civil and political liberties, an act which marked the end of democracy in Germany and the beginning of the Nazi dictatorship. By this time Hindenburg was senile: after Hitler had murdered many of his opponents in the **Night of the Long Knives**, he sent a telegram congratulating him on 'saving the German nation from serious danger'. He died a month later.

**Hirohito** (1901–89). Japanese Emperor (1926–89), who took the reign name Showa (Enlightened Peace). The son of Crown Prince Yoshihito (1874–1926), who became the Taisho Emperor (1912–26), Hirohito was the first member of the Japanese imperial family who was allowed to travel abroad. In 1921 he visited the USA and Europe and shortly after his return he became regent, as his father was declared insane. Austere, hard-working and frugal, he ended the long tradition by which the Empress's ladies-in-waiting served as the Emperor's concubines. Although he was the key figure in the **Emperor system**, his divinity placed him above party politics. He was a silent presence at all Cabinet meetings but followed the convention by which it was the Emperor's duty to accept his ministers' advice when that was unanimous, so that he could be a focus of national unity. As he played such a passive role, it is difficult to assess what his opinions and influence were. There were at least two occasions when he effectively expressed his personal views, as his ministers were not agreed on what action to take. He insisted on the suppression of the **February Rising** (1936) and he took the decision to surrender in 1945. When an **atomic bomb** fell on Nagasaki an imperial conference was called. Civilian ministers wanted to end the war at any price but three out of four military advisers wished to continue fighting, if the Allies would not guarantee to preserve the imperial throne. The Prime Minister, therefore, asked the Emperor to decide what should be done. Hirohito said that 'we must bear the unbearable' and on 15 August 1945 addressed his people for the first time, on radio, to announce Japan's surrender, although he knew that he might be tried as a war criminal and that his dynasty, the oldest in the world, might be brought to an end. Many Chinese, Australians and New Zealanders, who had fought against the Japanese, wanted him tried as a war criminal but General **MacArthur**, Supreme Allied Commander in Japan, refused, as he required a conservative figurehead to act as a bulwark against the spread of **communism** in Japan. In 1946 Hirohito publicly renounced his claim to divinity and ruled as a constitutional monarch, acting as a symbol of the state and appearing occasionally at ceremonial functions. Modest, studious and withdrawn he lived in seclusion, devoting much of his time to his favourite hobby of marine biology.

**Hiroshima.** A military base and port in the north of Honshu Island, Japan, which had a population of 300,000 in 1945. When President **Roosevelt** died suddenly on 12 April 1945, his Vice-President, Harry S. Truman, knew nothing about the atom bomb, yet he had to decide what to do with it. Fierce Japanese resistance in the islands such as during the invasion of **Okinawa**, as the Americans approached Japan, indicated that hundreds of thousands of lives would be lost in the invasion of Japan itself. When the **Potsdam Declaration**'s call on 26 July for Japan's unconditional surrender was rejected, Truman and his advisers decided that an **atomic bomb** should be dropped without warning on a military target in a densely populated area. On 6 August 1945, a B29 bomber set off from Tinian in the Marianas and at 8.15 a.m. released its bomb from 32,000 feet. Forty-five seconds later it exploded 1,850 feet above Hiroshima. Many were killed immediately by the explosion: the heat was so intense that where the bomb fell only the outlines of people remained, etched in the pavements or walls. After the heat came the blast, a fireball with the force of a 500 mile an hour wind, which generated a temperature of 6,000 degrees centigrade. In a circle two miles across everything was reduced to rubble and buildings were flattened throughout the city. Many who escaped the initial blast suffered from radiation sickness and died later. It is estimated that 100,000 people died from the dropping of that single bomb. On 9 August a second bomb fell, on Nagasaki, and on 14 August 1945 Japan surrendered.

**Hitler, Adolf** (1889–1945). *Führer* of the German Reich (1933–45). Hitler was the son of an Austrian customs official. Morose and unstable, he hated his authoritarian father and from 1907–13 tried, unsuccessfully, to make his living as an artist in Vienna. It was here that he picked up his **anti-Semitism**, his belief in the superiority of the Aryan race and his hatred of **Marxism**. In the **First World War** he served in the German army as a lance-corporal and was awarded the Iron Cross (First Class) for his bravery, an unusual distinction for an ordinary soldier. After the war he joined the German Workers' Party (which had forty members), changed its name to the National Socialist German Workers' Party (see **Nazi Party**) and became its leader in 1921. He chose for the Nazi Party its **swastika** symbol, organized Stormtroopers (**SA**) to protect his meetings and had a personal bodyguard in the blackshirted **SS**. Convinced that the **Weimar Republic** was about to collapse, he staged the **Munich** *Putsch* in 1923. This failed and Hitler was imprisoned but he learnt the lesson that he must come to power legally. Whilst in prison he wrote the first part of *Mein Kampf* (*My Struggle*), in which he put forward ideas he was later to apply, such as the elimination of Jews from German life and the need for **Lebensraum** ('living-space') in the east. After his release at the end of 1924 he spent his time building up the Nazi Party, aided by Josef **Goebbels**, whom he put in charge of propaganda in 1928.

The Nazis made little impact on German politics – in the 1928 elections to the **Reichstag** they gained only twelve seats – until the **Great Depression** hit Germany, producing six million unemployed. Hitler made an alliance with the Nationalist Alfred Hugenberg and through his newspapers was able to reach a mass audience for the first time. In the 1930 elections the Nazis won six million votes and 107 seats: they were now the second largest party in Germany. Much of this support was attracted by the charismatic figure of Hitler and by his message. His harsh voice and violent tirades seemed to indicate an indomitable will, which was at the service of the German people. He told them what they wanted to hear: that they had a right to feel dissatisfied with the 'criminals' who had signed the Treaty of **Versailles** and with the Marxists and Jews who were responsible for Germany's ills. The Nazis moved to first place in July 1932, when 13.7 million people voted for them and they gained 230 seats. Hitler won the support of big industry by promising to smash the **trade unions** and democracy, and rearm Germany. With the aid of conservative politicians, such as von **Papen**, he became German Chancellor in January 1933. He used the **Reichstag Fire** to suspend all political and civil liberties and in the 1933 elections gained 288 seats but, with 44 per cent of the vote, had still not achieved a majority. He nevertheless persuaded the Reichstag to pass an **Enabling Act**, which freed him from all dependence on the elected legislature. Totalitarian control of the country was obtained by a process the Nazis called *Gleichschaltung* ('coordination'), whereby political parties and trade unions were abolished, and Nazis took control of all institutions. A challenge to

Hitler could now come only from within his own party or from the army. The SA, under **Röhm**, talked about a 'second revolution', which would impose the socialist side of National Socialism and which would also bring the army under its control. This alarmed industrialists and generals, whose support Hitler needed to arm Germany and to carry out an expansionist foreign policy. On the **Night of the Long Knives** (June 1934), therefore, Hitler ordered the murder of the SA leadership. This brought him army support, so that when President **Hindenburg** died on 2 August 1934, Hitler succeeded him with the title of *Führer* and Reich Chancellor and the army took an oath to Hitler personally, as their new Commander-in-Chief. After that Hitler's authority was unchallenged, so that he could devote most of his time to foreign affairs.

At first he gave the appearance of moderation by pursuing the same aims as all other German governments since 1919: to get rid of the unfair restrictions imposed on Germany at the Treaty of Versailles (1919). He condemned the failure to grant equal armaments to Germany at the Disarmament Conference and withdrew from it, and from the **League of Nations**, in 1933. In 1934 he surprised everyone by his reasonableness in making a Non-Aggression Pact with Poland. The Saar returned to Germany after a plebiscite in January 1935 and in March Hitler revealed the existence of a German air force and said that he would increase the army to 550,000 troops, thus contravening the Versailles treaty. In June he made an **Anglo-German naval agreement**, which allowed for a larger German navy, and in March 1936 sent troops into the demilitarized **Rhineland**. These moves were accepted, reluctantly, by Britain and France, as was *Anschluss* (union) with Austria in 1938 and the transfer of the **Sudetenland** to Germany (see **Czechoslovakian crisis**, 1938–9). Only when Hitler moved into the rest of Czechoslovakia in March 1939 did Britain and France realize that Hitler was aiming at European domination. This prompted them to guarantee Poland's independence, though the *Führer* did not think they would honour their pledges when he had made the **Nazi–Soviet Pact**. To his surprise they declared war on Germany when he invaded Poland and so began the **Second World War**.

Up to this time Hitler had been remarkably successful: the unemployment of six million people had become full employment;

the restrictions of Versailles had been removed and Germany had become the dominant military power in Europe. No German leader since **Bismarck** had enjoyed such popularity – Hitler was regarded as his country's saviour. Germany was not prepared for a long war (her economy was not completely geared to war produc-' tion until 1942) but Hitler did not expect one. He relied on *Blitzkrieg* tactics, which were successful in bringing quick victories. in Poland in 1939 and in Norway, Denmark, the Low Countries and France in 1940. His first set-back was in the battle of **Britain**, when he had to abandon his projected invasion of England. He showed boldness and flair in supporting the plans of some of his generals; he backed **Guderian** in his formation of Panzer divisions and approved of **Manstein**'s daring strike through the Ardennes, which led to the fall of **France**. Hitler's biggest gamble was in his invasion of Russia in June 1941, Operation **Barbarossa**. When it failed to take Moscow and the Russians counter-attacked in December, the *Führer* took control of all military operations himself. He made another enormous blunder in December 1941, when he declared war on the USA, after the Japanese attack on **Pearl Harbor**, thus ensuring that the economic might of the strongest power in the world would aid his enemies. As Commander-in-Chief Hitler made many errors: he did not concentrate his forces on one objective in Russia, and refused to allow his armies to retreat, even when their position was hopeless, as at the battle of **Stalingrad**. Hitler neglected the Mediterranean, when more support for **Rommel** might have brought victory there. After the British success at the battles of **El Alamein** and the surrender of the Sixth Army at Stalingrad, Germany began a retreat which continued until the war was over. An attempt to kill Hitler in the **July Plot** (1944) failed and so the war was prolonged into 1945. Hitler, suffering from extreme nervous exhaustion, retired to his Berlin bunker. From 1941 he had tried to annihilate European Jews in the '**Final Solution**' and now he turned his wrath on the German people, who had been unworthy of his genius, and ordered the destruction of German industry, an order which Albert **Speer** refused to carry out. On 30 April, 1945 after marrying Eva Braun, who had been his mistress for many years, Hitler shot himself.

**Hitler Youth.** **Nazi Party** organization for German boys from the ages of fourteen to eighteen. It was formed in 1926, and in 1933, as part of the process of *Gleichschaltung*, absorbed all other youth organizations except the Catholic. When this was banned in 1936 the Hitler Youth was the only legal youth organization for boys. Hitler wanted all German non-Jewish boys and girls to join the Young Folk organization at the age of ten, where they would enjoy outdoor activities like sport and camping and be indoctrinated with Nazi ideas. At fourteen the boys would enter the Hitler Youth, where they would wear a uniform and there would be semi-military discipline. The *Führer* made clear what he wanted: 'A violently active, dominating, brutal youth – that is what I am after. Youth must be indifferent to pain . . . I will have no intellectual training.' There were varied activities to appeal to all tastes – arts and crafts, modelling, music, hiking, camping, attending demonstrations – which took precedence over formal education. There was a parallel organization for girls, the League of German Maidens, where they learnt about motherhood and domestic duties. By 1938 there were 7.7 million members in the Hitler Youth, although the attempt to enrol every boy and girl failed and there was constant conflict between the Hitler Youth and schools, as educational standards dropped, owing to the length of time spent on HY activities. Universities complained that students did not have the basic skills or work habits and failure rates were high.

**Hoare–Laval Pact** (December 1935). An attempt by the British Foreign Secretary, Sir Samuel Hoare, and the French Foreign Minister, Pierre **Laval**, to end the **Ethiopian War** (1935–6) by making concessions to Italy. They proposed that Italy should take Ethiopian territory next to her colonies of Eritrea and Italian Somaliland and that she should have 'a zone of economic expansion and settlement' in southern Ethiopia. A strip of British Somaliland would be given to Ethiopia, so that she would have access to the sea. The British Cabinet approved the plan, which was to be put to **Mussolini**, **Haile Selassie** and the **League of Nations**, but when it was leaked to the press in Paris there was uproar. It appeared that Italy was to be rewarded for her unjustified aggression. The British Cabinet changed its mind and Hoare was forced to resign. Two of the major powers, whose duty it was to support the League, had fatally undermined it.

**Hohenzollern candidature for the Spanish throne.** When a revolution in Spain in 1868 drove Queen Isabella off the throne, the Spaniards looked for a new ruler and approached Leopold of Hohenzollern-Sigmaringen, a Catholic member of the ruling Prussian dynasty. The King of Prussia, **William I**, was not keen on the offer, as he knew France would be alarmed with a Prussian as King of Spain, but **Bismarck** secretly urged Leopold to accept, which he did in June 1870. Historians disagree as to whether Bismarck wanted to provoke a war with France, though there is no doubt that his risky policy might end in war. In July Gramont, the French Foreign Minister, said that the move would not be tolerated so, under pressure from William I, the Hohenzollern-Sigmaringens renounced the candidacy. This was a diplomatic triumph for France, which made Bismarck and **Moltke**, the Prussian Chief of Staff, extremely depressed. The crisis would have been over but for Gramont's stupidity in seeking from William a promise that the candidacy would not be renewed. Bismarck seized his opportunity and, by publishing the **Ems telegram**, helped to bring about the **Franco-Prussian War**, which could so easily have been avoided.

**Hohenzollern dynasty.** The ruling family in Prussia from 1701–1918 and in the **German Empire** from 1871–1918, when the last Emperor, **William II**, abdicated. Prince Charles of Hohenzollern-Sigmaringen, a member of a branch of the family, became King Carol of Romania in 1881. The offer of the Spanish Crown to his brother Leopold helped to bring about the **Franco-Prussian War** of 1870.

**Holocaust,** see 'Final Solution'

**Home Rule for Ireland.** A movement which at first sought the re-establishment of an Irish parliament responsible for internal affairs but later wanted complete independence for Ireland. In 1870 Isaac Butt, a Protestant barrister strongly opposed to **O'Connell**'s campaign to repeal the Act of **Union** (1800), founded the Home Rule League to make the Union more effective. He wanted an Irish parliament in Dublin but final authority would remain with the

United Kingdom parliament in London, in which Irish representation would be unchanged. Butt hoped this would appeal to both Catholics and Protestants. In the 1874 election fifty-nine Home Rulers were elected and decided to form an independent Irish party, which was soon dominated by **Parnell** (Butt died in 1879). **Gladstone**, with Parnell's support, introduced a Home Rule Bill in 1886, which provided for an Irish parliament with much control of domestic affairs, but it ignored the problem of Ulster, where there was a pro-British Protestant majority, who opposed Home Rule, as this would mean domination by the Catholic majority. The bill split the **Liberal Party**, ninety-three **Liberal Unionists** led by Joseph **Chamberlain** voting against the bill, which was defeated. In 1893 Gladstone tried again, introducing the second Home Rule Bill but this was defeated in the **Lords**. Conservatives (see **Conservative Party**) were strong supporters of the Union and tried to kill Home Rule by passing **Irish Land Acts**, which enabled tenants to buy their farms. When the Liberals returned to power in 1905 they ignored Home Rule until the 1910 election, when they became dependent on the support of Irish MPs to obtain a majority in the **Commons**. **Asquith** therefore introduced a third Home Rule Bill in 1912, after the **Parliament Act** of 1911 ensured that the Lords could not prevent it becoming law for more than two years. This caused a great outcry in Ulster, where Unionists, led by Sir Edward **Carson**, formed a paramilitary force, the Ulster Volunteers, and prepared to seize power as soon as the Home Rule Bill became law. They were recklessly supported by the Conservative leader, Bonar **Law**. Civil war looked likely when the Home Rule Act was passed in September 1914, but was averted by the **First World War**, as the operation of the Act was suspended. The repression that followed the **Easter Rising** of 1916 led to much Irish opinion favouring a republic, as was shown by the victory for **Sinn Fein** in the 1918 election. The **Anglo-Irish War** (1919–21) forced **Lloyd George** to bring in a further Home Rule bill in 1920, which divided Ireland into two: Northern Ireland made up of six counties in Ulster and Southern Ireland made up of the remaining twenty-six. Each was to have its own parliament, though the United Kingdom parliament was still supreme and there were to be Irish MPs at Westminster. A Northern Ireland parliament was set up in Belfast but the Act was rejected in the South. To bring the war to an end Lloyd George called a conference in London in 1921, when an **Anglo-Irish Treaty** set up an 'Irish Free State', as a self-governing **dominion** within the British Empire. Though this did not provide the complete independence many wanted, it was approved by the Dail (Irish Assembly) by sixty-four votes to fifty-seven. **De Valera** refused to accept this and so was largely responsible for the **Irish Civil War** (1922–3) which followed.

**Homestead Act** (1862) was intended to encourage settlement of the West in the USA. It gave to any citizen over twenty-one or head of a family a homestead (farm) of 160 acres, which would be his when he had lived there for five years. Between 1862 and 1900 the government awarded 600,000 claimants eighty million acres but many of these claimants were not farmers but people acting for speculators: 160 acres was too small for a farmer to make his living on the Great Plains. More important in opening up the West were the lands made available to settlers by the states and the railroads, which were given 521 million acres by the federal government. Railroads needed settlers to generate rail traffic, so they sold off much of their land.

**Homestead strike** (1892) was one of the most bitter and violent in the USA. It took place when the President of the Carnegie Steel Co., Henry Clay Frick, imposed wage cuts at the company's Homestead works, near Pittsburgh. The Steelworkers' Union rejected the cuts, so Frick said he would close the plant and reopen it with non-union labour. He employed 300 Pinkerton men (Pinkerton was a detective agency, which provided spies, gunmen and strike-breakers for industrialists) to protect the plant. When they arrived from Pittsburgh there was a pitched battle with the workers, in which ten men, both Pinkerton detectives and strikers, were killed. Frick then appealed to the Governor of Pennsylvania, who sent in the National Guard to eject the strikers. Frick reopened the plant on 12 July. Public opinion was at first on the side of the workers, as Pinkerton men were detested, but this changed when there was an attempt on Frick's life. On 20 November the steel union called off the strike. Other steel companies, encouraged by Frick's victory, refused to recognize the steel union, which was crushed. There was no effective union in the steel industry until the United Steelworkers were organized in the 1930s.

**Hoover, Herbert Clark** (1874–1964). Thirty-first President of the USA (1929–1933). The son of a Quaker blacksmith, Hoover was orphaned at eight and became the archetypal self-made man. He graduated as a mining engineer, managed mines in different parts of the world and was a millionaire by the age of forty. In the **First World War** he became head of Allied relief operations and when America entered the war in 1917 President **Wilson** made him National Food Administrator. In the immediate post-war years he was responsible for distributing food to the starving millions in Europe. He became Secretary of Commerce in 1921 under Harding and continued under **Coolidge**, chairing commissions that led to the construction of the Hoover Dam and the St Lawrence seaway. He was the natural Republican choice for President when Coolidge refused to stand, and was elected by a large majority. On taking office in March 1929 he announced that 'In no nation are the fruits of accomplishment more secure.' Seven months later came the **Wall Street Crash**, which led to the worst depression America had known. To reduce foreign competition he allowed Congress to raise tariffs to an all-time high in 1930. This was one of the worst things he could have done: the Depression deepened, as European countries, unable to export to America, could not afford to buy American goods and retaliated by raising their own tariffs. A more sensible move to boost exports was a moratorium on war debts declared by Hoover in 1931. Hoover did not believe in federal relief for the growing army of unemployed, as he thought that it would unbalance the budget, weaken local and state governments and make people permanently dependent on public hand-outs. The state, he felt, should not take on responsibilities which belonged to the individual. Not until the third winter of the Depression (1931–2) did he relent and decide that federal action would have to be taken. He set up the Reconstruction Finance Corporation (RFC) in January 1932 to lend money to banks and businesses in trouble and he released gold to support the dollar and increase credit. His Relief and Construction Act allowed the RFC to lend one and a half billion dollars to state and municipal governments for public works and another 300 million dollars for relief. These steps showed him interfering in the economy more than his predecessors had done but they were not enough. He was still strongly opposed to direct federal aid to the unemployed: this was left to private charity, which could not cope. The shanty towns which grew up round the big cities were known as 'Hoovervilles'. Bitterness mounted, as people could not understand why it was right to use federal money to help industrialists and financiers and wrong to use it to feed the hungry. Hoover appeared cold and callous, which he was not. He worked eighteen hours a day, wearing himself out trying to solve the nation's problems. In the presidential election of 1932 he was crushingly defeated by the **Democratic Party** candidate, Franklin D. **Roosevelt**. During the **Second World War** he became involved in relief work again and in 1946 President Truman made him coordinator of food supplies to avoid the threat of post-war famine. He chaired two commissions (1947–9, 1953) to improve the efficiency of the federal government and did not retire from politics until the age of eighty.

**Hopkins, Harry Lloyd** (1890–1946). US public servant. From 1912–27 Hopkins was a social worker in New York and spent some years with the Association for Improving the Condition of the Poor. He worked with the Red Cross towards the end of the **First World War**. At the height of the **Great Depression** in 1931 the Governor of New York, Franklin D. **Roosevelt**, put him in charge of emergency relief. When Roosevelt became President in 1933, Hopkins advised him on **New Deal** relief programmes and became head of several federal agencies: the Federal Emergency Relief Administration (1933–5), the Works Progress Administration (1935–6) and from 1938–40 he was Secretary of Commerce. He believed in providing work for the unemployed rather than giving them the dole, so he spent vast amounts on building roads and hospitals and on slum clearance. He was accused of being a spendthrift but he helped more Americans during the Depression than anyone else, except the President. In 1941 he was put in charge of the Lend-Lease programme (see **Lend-Lease Act**), which provided military supplies for the Allies. During the **Second World War** he was Roosevelt's personal representative on visits to Europe and negotiated with **Churchill** and **Stalin** on arms supplies and military strategy. He advised President Truman after Roosevelt's death but was forced to retire owing to his poor health (he was a chain-smoker) and died shortly afterwards.

**Horthy de Nagybanya, Miklos** (1868–1957). Regent of Hungary (1920–44). From a Protestant noble family, Horthy served in the **First World War** in the Austro-Hungarian navy and was its last Commander-in-Chief. In 1919 he organized an army which, with the help of Romanian forces, overthrew the communist regime of Bela **Kun**. A year later the Hungarian parliament voted to restore the monarchy and elected Horthy as regent but he thwarted all efforts of King Charles to recover the throne and ruled as a dictator. His main concern was to recover territory lost at the Treaty of **Trianon** (1920) and, with Nazi (see **Nazi Party**) help, he succeeded in regaining parts of Czechoslovakia and Romania (1938–40). Horthy disliked **Hitler** but approved of his crusade against Bolshevism and in 1941 took part in the German invasion of Yugoslavia and declared war on the USSR. In October 1944, as he sought a separate peace with the Allies, he was imprisoned by the Nazis. After the war the Americans refused to hand him over to Yugoslavia for trial as a war criminal. He went into exile in Portugal, where he died.

**Hughes, William Morris** (1864–1952). Australian Prime Minister (1915–23). Born in London, Hughes emigrated to Australia in 1884 to become a seaman, sheep shearer and actor. Later he studied law, organized strikes as a trade-union leader in the 1890s and helped to found the New South Wales **Labor Party**. In 1894 he was elected to the New South Wales legislature and in 1901 became a member of the first federal parliament, retaining a seat there for the rest of his life. Small, prickly and autocratic, Hughes had enormous energy and was twice Attorney-General before he became Prime Minister in 1915. He had a fierce loyalty to Australia and to the British Empire and whole-heartedly supported the war effort. In 1916 he tried to introduce conscription, which was twice rejected in national referenda, and split the Labor Party on the issue. When it passed a motion of no confidence in him, he left the Party and formed the Nationalist Party, with the support of some of his former colleagues and the parliamentary opposition. Hughes remained Prime Minister as leader of the Nationalist Party and Labor now became the opposition. In 1917 he called an election with the slogan 'Win the War' and won twice as many seats as Labor. At the **Paris Peace Conference** (1919) he established Australia's right to sign the peace treaty as an independent country. He protested vehemently at Japan's request for a declaration of racial equality, which would undermine the **White Australia policy**, so Woodrow **Wilson** refused to accept the proposal. Hughes objected unsuccessfully when Japan claimed and was given a **mandate** of the north Pacific islands, which had been held by Germany, but Australia was granted German colonies in the South-West Pacific as mandates. Accepted as a great imperial statesman, he received a tumultuous welcome on his return home. After the war he relied on the Country Party to keep his minority government in power and so tried to please both agricultural and industrial interests, by giving subsidies to farmers and by imposing tariffs. In 1921 he made Stanley **Bruce** his Treasurer. Though Bruce had openly pledged to support Billy, as Hughes was known, he intrigued with the Country Party leader Earle Page, who withdrew his support for Hughes and thus brought about his fall in 1923. Hughes never forgave Bruce for this betrayal and in 1929 helped to bring to an end Bruce's premiership. In 1931 Hughes was a founder of the United Australia Party and served in the Cabinet in various posts from 1934–41, in the administrations of Joseph **Lyons** and Robert Menzies. During this time he saw that Japan was the great danger to Australia, who could no longer rely on the British navy for her defence, and helped to persuade Lyons to expand the Australian army and air force.

**Hundred Days** (20 March–28 June 1815). The period between **Napoleon**'s arrival in France after his escape from Elba and the second restoration of **Louis XVIII**. Napoleon landed near Fréjus on 1 March and was warmly greeted as he advanced north through Lyon. Marshal **Ney**, sent to arrest Napoleon, joined him with his army: Louis XVIII fled from Paris shortly before Napoleon reached the capital. The Allies had 100,000 troops under **Wellington** and 120,000 Prussians under **Blücher** in Belgium. Napoleon decided to strike rapidly before they could link up and before Austrian reinforcements could reach them. He almost succeeded. The Allies were taken by surprise, as Napoleon advanced between the forces of Blücher and Wellington. Blücher was forced back from Ligny by Napoleon but boldly retreated north to keep in touch with Wellington and by so doing enabled the Allies to win the battle of **Waterloo** on 18 June. Four days later Napoleon abdicated: Louis XVIII was restored to his throne on 28 June. One result of the Hundred Days was the imposition on France of more severe peace terms at the second Treaty of **Paris**.

**Hundred Days Reform** (1898). An attempt to preserve the **Qing dynasty** by reforming Chinese institutions on Western lines. Scholar-officials in China had introduced reforms to modernize their army and navy in the 1860s and 1870s in the **Self-Strengthening movement** but their failure was evident in China's defeat in the **Sino-Japanese War** (1894–5). China's weakness encouraged European powers to seize, or lease, Chinese territory in the 'scramble for concessions' and this persuaded officials like **Kang Youwei** that more drastic reforms were needed. His followers gained the Emperor's ear and for a hundred days, from mid-June to September 1898, many reform edicts were issued. They proposed that the traditional civil service examinations, based on the Confucian classics (see **Confucianism**), should be replaced, that sinecures should be abolished, industry developed and that a national school system should be established, in which Western learning would be included in the curriculum. Conservative scholar-officials in the provinces and at Court were appalled, as they felt their dominant position in society was threatened. They looked for a lead to the Empress Dowager **Cixi** who, supposedly in retirement, still retained much power by controlling Court officials. The reformers appealed to **Yuan Shikai**, Commander of the new Chinese army, for support but he betrayed them to Cixi. On 21 September she carried out a *coup*, repudiated the reform edicts and made the Emperor a prisoner in his own palace. Six prominent reformers were put to death, although Kang Youwei and **Liang Qichao** escaped: many others were imprisoned or exiled.

**Hungry Forties.** A rather misleading term for unrest in Britain which began before the 1840s with the depression of 1837 and which ended (except in Ireland) in 1842. The years 1837–42 saw the most severe and prolonged depression since the **Industrial Revolution** began. Bad harvests, high prices and unemployment combined to reduce workers to a degree of poverty and starvation never subsequently equalled. There was unrest in fourteen English, one Welsh and eight Scottish counties, in which factories, workhouses and private houses were attacked. In the Plug riots in Yorkshire strikers, wanting higher wages, pulled out the boiler plugs to put out the fires and bring the factories to a halt. The *Westminster Review* wrote 'of a general, bitter, deep-rooted discontent, pervading a vast proportion of the working population of Great Britain'. Most of the available military force was used to contain the disorder. In some places troops opened fire and rioters were killed but there was no general rising, as soldiers used their weapons only when attacked and the government acted with moderation, often blaming the mill-owners rather than the workers for what **Peel** called their 'just and peaceable demands for a rise in wages'. Seven hundred rioters were tried: none was executed and eighty were transported to Australia (less than a fifth of the number after the **Swing riots** of 1830–31). After 1842 unemployment declined sharply and the danger of revolution disappeared, aided by the repeal of the **Corn Laws**. In Ireland there was further distress with the failure of the potato crop and the disastrous **Irish Famine** (1845–9). Depression and hunger returned, after bad harvests, in 1847–8 and enabled the Chartists (see **Chartism**), led by Feargus **O'Connor**, to make their last challenge to the government but the movement collapsed after the failure of the rally on Kennington Common in London in 1848.

**Husayn, ibn Ali** (1856–1931). Sharif of Mecca and Arab political leader. Husayn was a member of the Hashemite family in Arabia and a descendant of the Prophet Muhammad. When the **First World War** began and the British tried to persuade him to rise up against the Turks, he saw his opportunity to become King of an Arab state, Caliph (head of all Muslim peoples) and the leader of an Arab nationalist movement which had developed independently of him. He negotiated with Sir Henry M$^c$Mahon, British High Commissioner in Egypt, and proposed that Britain should accept as independent an area that included the present states of Syria, Lebanon, Iraq, Jordan and the Arabian peninsula, except for Aden. McMahon excluded the *vilayets* (districts) of Basra and Baghdad and an area on the Syrian coast north of Palestine but said, in October 1915, that, with these exceptions, 'Great Britain is prepared to recognize and support the independence of the Arabs in all the regions within the limits demanded by the Sharif of Mecca.' The British, however, were making other agreements, which conflicted with the promises made to Husayn, such as the **Sykes–Picot agreement** with France in May 1916. Husayn began his revolt in June 1916, soon captured Mecca and Jedda and in 1917 moved out of the Hijaz and operated on **Allenby**'s flank as he advanced into Palestine. At the end of the war he was frustrated and bitter, as the Allies recognized him only as King of the Hijaz and he was driven out of there after a conflict from 1919–24 with **Abd al-Aziz ibn Saud**. His sons Feisal and Abdullah became Kings of Iraq and Transjordan respectively but Husayn felt betrayed by Britain and France, who had left only Arabia as a truly independent Arab area. He died in Transjordan in 1931, a pathetic and sad figure.

**Ibn Saud,** see **Abd al-Aziz ibn Saud**

**IG Farben** (shortened form of *Interessen Gemeinschaft Farbenindustrie*, 'community of interests of dye industries'). A **cartel** formed after the **First World War** by the leading chemical companies in Germany, including BASF, Bayer and Hoechst. It was the largest cartel in Germany between the wars, controlled 500 firms in ninety-two countries and made 2,000 cartel agreements with businesses such as Standard Oil (USA), ICI (Britain) and Mitsui (Japan). IG played a vital role in the 1930s in trying to free Germany from dependence on imported raw materials. She produced nearly all Germany's synthetic lubricating oils, petrol and rubber, poison gases, explosives, dyes and nickel. To increase synthetic oil and rubber production, IG Auschwitz was set up in 1943, the largest plant in the world. It was built and operated by slave labourers from the neighbouring **concentration camp**, who were gassed in the camp, when they were too weak to work, by an IG product Zyklon-B. At the Nuremberg trials many directors were found guilty of war crimes and the cartel was broken up into its three major parts.

**Immigration (to the USA).** Between 1815 and 1914 there was the largest peaceful migration in history, when over thirty million immigrants entered the USA: there were five million between 1815 and 1860 (more than the entire population of the USA in 1790) and a five-fold increase to twenty-six million between 1865 and 1914. Until 1880 nearly all came from north and west Europe: mainly from Britain, Ireland and Germany. They came because there was a rise in population throughout Europe in the nineteenth century and many could not find work: some suffered appallingly in natural disasters, such as the **Irish Famine** of 1845–9, when a million people died and another million emigrated. The USA attracted immigrants as it needed workers in its growing industries and new land was available in the West as **transcontinental railroads** opened up the country. After 1880 there were fewer German and English immigrants, as the **Industrial Revolution** at home provided work. In 1914, 85 per cent of immigrants came from south and eastern Europe: Italy, the **Austro-Hungarian Empire** and Russia. Smaller numbers arrived in California from China and Japan. Most immigrants went to towns in the north and east, where industrialization was increasing rapidly, and joined America's slum-dwellers. By 1910 two-thirds of the population of America's twelve largest cities were immigrants or the children of immigrants. New York had more Italians than Naples, twice as many Irish as Dublin and more Jews than the whole of Europe.

The vast influx of immigrants created tensions in American society. Until 1830 the USA was almost wholly Protestant: by 1860 there were three million Catholics, many of Irish and German origin. Later immigrants, often illiterate, were regarded as even more difficult to assimilate and were blamed for the increase in crime. The US Congress therefore began to restrict immigration. Chinese had been effectively kept out since 1882 and Japanese since 1907. In 1917 literacy tests were required for immigrants and in 1912 the Quota Act allowed entry to only 3 per cent of the numbers of each nation who were listed in the 1910 census, which favoured immigrants from Western Europe. A maximum of 150,000 were to be admitted each year. A 1924 Act based quotas on 1890 immigration figures and reduced the percentage to two. The result, aided by the **Great Depression**, was a marked drop in the number of immigrants: four million in the 1920s, half a million in the 1930s, the lowest total for over a century. Half of them were refugees fleeing from Nazi persecution (see **Nazi Party**) and included eminent people such as Albert Einstein and Thomas Mann.

**Imperialism.** The political or economic domination, direct or indirect, of one state by another. Imperialism has existed for millennia but in the nineteenth century European powers appeared to take little interest in it until the late 1870s. Before then Britain was the only major industrial and naval power and expanded her Empire to protect the 'jewel in the crown', India, and the routes to it. The

**Opium War** (1839–42) with China, fought to defend the export of opium from India, resulted in Britain acquiring Hong Kong. France occupied Algiers in 1830 and under **Faidherbe** moved inland from Senegal in West Africa in the 1850s. Russia, in the reign of **Alexander II**, became a major imperial power when she gained land from China between the Amur and Ussuri rivers and the Pacific in 1860 and when she pushed south into Central Asia (see Russian conquest of **Central Asia**).

All these gains were a preliminary to the massive imperial expansion of the years 1879 to 1914, when the **Scramble for Africa** and the 'scramble for concessions' in China took place. At this time new imperial powers appeared: Germany and Italy in Africa, the USA in the Pacific and Caribbean, following the **Spanish–American War** (1898), and Japan in Asia and the Pacific, after her successes in the **Sino-Japanese War** (1894–5) and **Russo-Japanese War** (1904–5). In this period, too, France completed her conquest of Indo-China and the Dutch of the East Indies (Indonesia). Between 1870 and 1900 the British Empire increased by five million square miles, to cover a fifth of the world. This vast expansion was made possible by **medical advances** (quinine was used as a prophylactic against malaria from the 1850s), advances in communications (see **communications revolution**), and transport (see **transport revolution**) and above all by more lethal weapons (see **Warfare: on land**).

The spread of imperialism has been explained in economic, political and strategic terms. Economic explanations concentrate on the need of European countries for markets and raw materials (see **World economy**) during the Great Depression (1873–96). As Britain was overtaken as an industrial power in some key industries by Germany and the USA, and as many states introduced protective tariffs, she looked on colonies as a necessity. Jules **Ferry** in France and King **Leopold** of Belgium also believed in the economic benefits of having colonies, though they did not in fact provide lucrative markets. In 1902 J. A. Hobson, in his book *Imperialism*, put forward the view (adopted by **Lenin**) that capital could more profitably be invested abroad, where interest rates were higher, than at home: European governments would then annex territories to protect their investments. This theory fitted British experience in

Egypt and South Africa but not elsewhere. Britain was the largest foreign investor but she loaned money mainly to the USA, Canada, Australia, South Africa and South America. She lent little to African colonies, as did France and Germany, whilst some imperial powers (Russia, Italy, Portugal) did not have any money to invest abroad.

Some historians think that political motives were more important than economic motives in the spread of imperialism. Colonies were acquired, they maintain, in order to ensure the security of existing empires. This motive is linked to the strategy of denial: colonies, needed to protect trade routes, were seized by one power to prevent a rival grabbing them first. Singapore (1819), Aden (1839) and Natal (1844) were all annexed by Britain in order to protect the trade routes to India. The strategy of denial played an important role in Britain's seizure of Egypt (to defend the **Suez Canal**) and in her acquisition of East Africa, the Sudan and Upper Burma. It worked too in Germany's African Empire. **Nationalism** and the belief that having an empire is a necessary sign of great power status was another driving force of imperialism. Many in France, after defeat in the **Franco-Prussian War** (1870–71), looked for prestige in colonial conquests. Italy seized barren areas of Africa so she could look like a great power, whilst Portugal extended her existing Empire in Mozambique and Angola, which were an economic burden to her, purely for prestige. Nationalism connects with **Social Darwinism**, some of whose adherents saw Europeans as being naturally superior to other races and as having the moral right, indeed the duty, to rule over them. This doctrine was widespread in Germany and influenced imperialists such as Joseph **Chamberlain**, **Rhodes** and **Milner** in England.

The 'turbulent frontier' theory is another which attempts to account for imperialism. This maintains that imperialism arose out of local crises (which drew in the great powers reluctantly) and not from drives within Europe. The revolt of **Urabi Pasha** (1882) persuaded the British to move into Egypt. Once there, the rising of the **Mahdi** made it impossible for them to get out and led eventually to the conquest of the Sudan. Discovery of gold on the **Rand** in 1885 changed the balance of power in South Africa in favour of the **Afrikaners**: Rhodes's attempt to counter this led to the establishment of Northern and Southern Rhodesia. In West Africa the **Asante** threat to the British Fante protectorate led to war and the extension of British control in the Gold Coast. Other examples of local crises which resulted in the spread of imperialism can be found in New Zealand (annexed in 1840 to protect the Maoris), Burma, Malaya, the Fiji Islands and Russia's conquest of Central Asia. One form of local crisis occurred when soldiers or officials took action without the consent of their governments, which were unable to repudiate the gains made. This is the case in the British conquest of Sind and the Punjab in the 1840s, in Russia's expansion in China in the 1850s and in the treaties the German adventurer Karl Peters made with chiefs in East Africa. Some historians think that the concept of imperialism should be widened to include the indirect control ('informal' empire) of one country dominating the trade and economy of another, as Britain did in Argentina and Brazil in the nineteenth century and as the USA has done in South and Central America and much of the Caribbean.

**Indentured labour.** A system in which poor people were contracted (indentured) to work for a number of years overseas, in return for pay, accommodation and return passage. Following the abolition of slavery in the islands of Mauritius and Réunion, 450,000 Indians between 1835 and 1923 came on five - year contracts to work in the sugar plantations: about 160,000 eventually returned to India. When sugar was first grown in Natal there was a shortage of labour, as Zulus had no wish to work on the plantations, so from 1860 Indians were brought in on a three-year (later five-year) contract. After further residence for five years as 'free' labourers, they could then return on a free passage to India or be given a small grant of Crown land in Natal. Few returned to India. By the time the practice ended in 1911, 152,000 Indians had come to Natal. Indian indentured labourers also worked on plantations in British Guiana, Trinidad, Malaya and Fiji and in Uganda, where they built the railway from Mombasa to Lake Victoria between 1898 and 1904. Chinese also came as labourers to the **Rand** in the 1890s to work in the mines. They were little better than slaves, as they lived in cramped and insanitary compounds and could be flogged, fined or imprisoned by their employers for laziness or inefficiency. The system was so strongly criticized in both South Africa and Britain that it was ended in 1910.

**Independent Labour Party** (ILP). The first two working-class MPs were elected in 1874 as 'Lib-Labs' (Liberal-Labour) but local **Liberal Party** associations were unwilling to select working-class candidates, so Keir **Hardie** and others decided that a separate working-class party was needed. The ILP, whose aim was the 'collective ownership of the means of production, distribution and exchange', was set up in Bradford in 1893 but was short of money and poorly organized, so that in 1895 all twenty-eight ILP candidates were defeated. It did much better in local government elections and in 1898 gained a majority in West Ham Borough, where it introduced a minimum wage for council workers, two weeks' paid holiday a year and an eight-hour working day. In 1900 some ILP members, with trade unionists and Fabians (see **Fabian Society**), set up the Labour Representation Committee, which in 1906 changed its name to the **Labour Party**. The ILP dominated the Labour Party from 1906–14 but after the **First World War** it differed increasingly from it, as the ILP supported pacifism, showed sympathy for the Communist Party and wanted a more Marxist policy. In 1932 the ILP separated from the Labour Party and thereafter declined, its membership falling from 17,000 in 1932 to 4,400 in 1935, when only four ILP candidates were elected. After the death of its leader, James Maxton, in 1946, the two remaining ILP MPs joined the Labour Party in 1947.

**India Act** (1919), see **Montagu–Chelmsford Reforms**

**India Act** (1935) was passed by the British parliament for the government of India. It gave the provinces autonomy, providing for Indian ministers responsible to the electorate, with control of all provincial government. The franchise was enlarged to thirty million (from 3 per cent to 14 per cent of the population). At the centre there was to be an elected Council of States and Federal Assembly with control of internal affairs, though Britain retained control of the army and foreign policy. There was also an attempt to set up a federal system, by including the princely states as well as British India. The princes would be guaranteed a third of the seats in the lower House of Assembly and 40 per cent in the upper Council of States but half the princes had to agree to this. As this never happened, this part of the Act was not implemented and the princes lost any say in deciding what form the new India was to take. Members of the **Conservative Party**, such as Winston **Churchill**, attacked the Act for giving Indians too much power and spoke of 'the undue exaltation of the principle of self-government' but Congress leaders saw they could have power in the provinces and so abandoned their campaign of civil disobedience. When the Act was implemented in 1937 Congress won control of six provinces, which they ruled until the outbreak of war in 1939.

**Indian Mutiny** (1857–8). A rebellion against British rule in north and central India. The immediate cause of the rebellion was the issue of cartridges to be used with the new Lee Enfield rifle. They were greased with beef and pork fat, polluting to Hindus and Muslims respectively, and had to be bitten off before being put in the rifle. The punishment at Meerut on 10 May 1857 of eighty five sepoys (**East India Company** soldiers), who refused to use the cartridges, began the mutiny but there were other causes too. The Governor-General, **Dalhousie**, had annexed Awadh (Oudh) in 1856 for alleged misgovernment and several other states under the doctrine of 'lapse'. Princes and nobles who had suffered from the **Raj** joined in the rebellion, which assumed a popular character in the Gangetic plain and central India, where small landowners and peasants had to pay heavy land taxes. The rebellion therefore involved civilians as well as the military but it was very patchy. Only one of the Company's three armies mutinied, that of Bengal: those in Madras and Bombay remained loyal, as did the whole of southern India.

The mutineers at Meerut, forty miles from Delhi, marched on the old Mughal capital, where they forced the last Mughal Emperor, eighty-two-year-old Bahadur Shah, to become their leader. The mutiny rapidly spread through the Bengal army, so that within weeks all the major stations in the North-West provinces and Awadh were controlled by the rebels. The major centres of rebellion were Delhi, Lucknow (in Awadh) and Cawnpore (Kanpur), where the Marathas sought to restore the authority of the old Maratha states. In Cawnpore the garrison of about a thousand surrendered in June, having been offered safe passage by boat to Allahabad, but they were fired on and only four escaped. Delhi fell to the British in September and from then the rebellion ceased to be a major threat to the Raj.

The rebels failed because they had no effective leadership or common goal and no funds, and because they were unable to cut the British lines of communication between Calcutta and Delhi. The Company used its Madras army, Sikhs from the Punjab and Gurkhas from Nepal, as well as British troops, to put down the rebellion. In doing so they behaved with ferocious savagery, General Neill instructed his troops attacking Cawnpore: 'slaughter all the men; take no prisoners.' Captured mutineers were blown to pieces by cannon to which they had been strapped and entire villages were razed, simply because they were near Cawnpore. The learned and mild Bahadur Shah was exiled to Rangoon, where he died miserably a year later, whilst his sons were murdered by a Captain Hodson, thus ending the Mughal dynasty. The Indian Mutiny had far-reaching effects. The governing of India passed from the East India Company to the British Crown. The doctrine of 'lapse' was rejected, to prevent another rebellion, so 560 autocratic princely states remained in India until independence. The Indian part of the army was cut from 238,000 in 1857 to 140,000 in 1865, the British part increasing from 45,000 to 65,000. Recruitment, too, changed: Sikhs and Gurkhas replaced sepoys from Awadh. So that the army could be moved to trouble spots quickly, there was a vast increase in railway construction: 432 miles of track in 1859 had grown to 5,000 a decade later and 25,000 by the end of the century.

**Indian National Congress** (INC). The main political party in India. It was formed in 1885 by a group of educated, high-caste Indians, who wanted more Indian participation in the governing of their country. They were loyal to the British **Raj** and did not, at this stage, seek independence for India. Congress was more a debating society, which met annually, than a political party, had no mass support and had little appeal for Muslims. In 1907 a split occurred between the 'moderates', led by **Gokhale**, and the 'extrem- ists', led by **Tilak**, who wanted complete independence for India and a less deferential attitude to the Raj. Gokhale managed to keep control of Congress until his death in 1915 but the INC adopted a more aggressive attitude when **Gandhi** became a dominant figure in 1919. Congress ceased to be an élite club and became a mass party, with a Constitution (1930), largely drawn up by Gandhi, which gave it the clear aim of *swaraj* (self-rule) and an effective organiza- tion, with a hierarchy of committees (district, provincial, All-India). The All-India Committee had 350 members, so an inner cabinet held the real power and negotiated with the British and other parties. It supported Gandhi's civil disobedience campaign but when the **India Act** (1935) was passed, it took part in the elections under the Act and won control of six out of the eleven British-ruled provinces. Congress, therefore, had considerable power at the provin- cial level in 1937 but at the beginning of the **Second World War** the government declared war on Germany without consulting Indian opinion. Congress was outraged, ordered all its provincial ministries to resign and demanded complete independence. In 1942 Congress's call for a **'Quit India' Campaign** led to the arrest of all its leaders and the banning of the Congress Party. The ban was lifted in 1944. Congress (and the **Muslim League**) negotiated with Britain from 1945–7 for India's independence and became by far the largest party in the new state.

**Indian reservations** (USA). The Northwest Ordinance of 1789 declared that 'the utmost good faith shall always be observed towards the Indians: their lands and property shall never be taken from them without their consent.' Such admirable intentions did not survive the greed for land, as white settlers moved west across the continent. President Andrew **Jackson** assured the Creeks in 1829 that when they moved to new territory: 'There your white brothers will not trouble you; they will have no claim to the land and you can live upon it, you and all your children, for as long as the grass grows and the water runs . . . It will be yours for ever.' All such promises were broken, as the white man pushed the Indians west across the Mississippi and then followed them into the Great Plains (see **Westward expansion**). It was in 1850 that Orlando Brown, the

Commissioner for Indian Affairs, recommended that each tribe should be confined to a reservation, which should be 'a country adapted to agriculture, of limited extent and well-defined boundaries; within which all ... should be compelled to remain.' A year later at Fort Laramie, at a meeting of the US government and Indian chiefs, the Plains Indians were, for the first time, restricted to particular areas where, they were told, they could live for ever. Some tribes resisted (see **Indian Wars**) but by 1867 they were ready for peace. They were forced to give up the land granted to them at Laramie and were moved to smaller reservations. In the next twenty years all Indians were rounded up and moved on to reservations. Even then their land was not safe from white predators. In 1887 Congress passed an Act giving Indians who renounced their tribal allegiance 160 acres of reservation land and US citizenship. What remained, the 'surplus' land, would be bought by the US government and sold to white settlers. By 1906, 60 per cent of reservation lands were in white hands.

Life on the reservations was harsh. The soil was often barren, so the Indians had to struggle to survive. Their religions were banned. In 1924 all Indians were granted US citizenship and in 1934 the Wheeler–Howard Act returned to tribal ownership some 'surplus' lands which had been up for public sale. Indians on the reservations are among the country's poorest citizens. They have the lowest income and the highest rates of unemployment, suicide, alcoholism and infant mortality.

**Indian Wars** were the result of resistance by the American Indians to white encroachment on their hunting grounds. Immediately after the American War of Independence, military expeditions were sent to the Ohio valley. At Fallen Timbers (1794) they defeated the Indians, who ceded most of the present state of Ohio to the USA. Tecumseh, a Shawnee chief, tried to form a confederation of Indian tribes and fought on the side of Britain in the **Anglo-American War** of 1812 but Indian power in the old Northwest was finally destroyed at the battle of the Thames (1813), when Tecumseh was killed. As white settlers moved west of the Allegheny Mountains they made numerous treaties with Indian tribes, who gave up their lands east of the Mississippi river in return for land to the west.

Most tribes were too small to resist but there were two minor wars. The Black Hawk War (1832–5), when the Sacs and the Foxes tried to hold on to their ancestral lands in Illinois, became a war of extermination. The Seminole War (1835–42), when the US tried to remove the few hundred Seminoles from the Florida swamps, was almost as brutal. Their chief, Osceola, was captured under a flag of truce but his followers continued fighting until they were almost wiped out.

The Indians had been given lands in the West 'for as long as the grass shall grow and the water flow' but such guarantees were ignored when miners and settlers crossed the Mississippi and invaded the Great Plains. The Plains Indians, such as the Sioux, Cheyennes, Apaches and Comanches, were nomadic and the most warlike of the Indian tribes. They were superb horsemen, brave and skilful with their short, powerful bows, though only 24,000 lived in the Plains in 1860. They were not united and fought one another for hunting grounds, which weakened their opposition to the whites. The superior numbers and technology of the whites – the railway, the telegraph, the repeating rifle – ensured their victory in the end but it was the buffalo, on which the Indians depended for food, clothing, shelter and fuel, which sealed their fate. In 1865 there were thirteen million buffalo on the Great Plains – between 1872 and 1874 professional hunters killed three million a year, so that the buffalo were almost wiped out. Savagery on both sides marked the wars in the Plains from the 1860s to the 1880s. The Sioux went on the warpath in Minnesota in 1862 and killed 500 settlers before they were hunted down by the militia: 300 Indians were publicly hanged. In 1864 the Sand Creek Massacre took place, when Cheyennes, who had made peace and were under the protection of the US army, were shot by the Colorado militia. The federal government sent a Peace Commission to the Plains in 1867, which put most of the blame for the wars on the whites. 'Have we been uniformly unjust?' it asked. 'We answer unhesitatingly, yes ... when the progress of settlement reaches the Indians' home, the only question considered is "how best to get his lands".' Yet **Congress** made little attempt to restrain the advancing settlers and instead tried to concentrate the Indians in two reservations, one in the Black Hills of Dakota and one in Indian territory (later Oklahoma). Even the reservations were not a safe haven for the Indians. When gold was discovered in the Black Hills in 1874, prospectors poured in and the last serious Indian conflict began. The Sioux War of 1876 became famous for 'Custer's Last Stand' at the battle of **Little Big Horn** in 1876, when Custer and his party were wiped out by **Crazy Horse** and his warriors. However, the Sioux could not sustain a large force and by 1880 they had all surrendered. West of the Rockies, the Nez Perces in 1877, under Chief Joseph, retreated for 1,300 miles before they were forced to surrender just short of their destination, the Canadian border. The last Indians to carry on fighting were the Apaches of the South-West: it took 500 troops fifteen years to defeat them. With the capture in 1886 of their chief Geronimo and his few warriors, Indian resistance ended. A tragic postscript to the Indian Wars occurred in 1890. An outburst of religious fervour, centring round the Ghost Dance, broke out on the Sioux reservation in South Dakota. The authorities feared a rising and sent in the troops, who fired indiscriminately on the Indians at Wounded Knee, killing 300.

**Indirect rule.** A method of colonial administration used mainly by the British, by which colonial powers ruled through indigenous chiefs. The idea was not new. The great African empires had been run in this way: the Asante, for example, ruled their conquered territories through local chiefs. Indirect rule was first used by the British in Buganda, developed in Northern Nigeria and then extended to other colonies in Africa. By the terms of the Uganda Agreement of 1900 the Bugandans were to be governed by their hereditary rulers, who made laws with the consent of the British Governor. The system of indirect rule developed by **Lugard** in Northern Nigeria was a practical means of administering a vast territory with limited men and money. Lugard used the existing structure of local emirs as rulers but real power lay with the British Governor. Traditional laws (e.g. Islamic law, in Northern Nigeria) were maintained, except for those aspects that were thought to be barbaric, and enforced by 'native' courts and a local police force. Lugard believed that chiefs should be given responsibility for both raising and spending taxes and for local law and order. A proportion of revenue (a half in Nigeria) would be passed on to the colonial government to spend on services best provided by Europeans, such as health and railways: the rest could be spent by chiefs on local needs at their own discretion. Lugard saw indirect rule as a road to political independence. 'Liberty and self-government,' he wrote, 'can best be secured to the native population by leaving them free to manage their own affairs through their own rulers.' In Northern Nigeria where there were well-established emirs, it was relatively easy to create a structure of indirect rule. In the regions east of the river Niger most societies had no system of centralized authority. The British appointed local chiefs but these were often very unpopular and rejected by the people. In the 1920s and 1930s the idea of indirect rule became a generally accepted principle of British colonial administration. The system was extended by various British colonial Governors, notably in Tanganyika, 1925–31. Indirect rule was criticized by a few colonial administrators because it tended to strengthen traditional rulers and often hindered economic and social progress; it was disliked by educated Africans because it held back the development of elected representative government and left them without political influence. After the **Second World War**, the British abandoned the system of indirect rule and gradually replaced it with an elected system of local and central government.

**Industrial Revolution.** The change from an agrarian to an industrial economy, in which there are new sources of power (steam power, **electricity**, oil), new forms of organization (the factory system, the joint stock investment bank), new industries (electrical, chemical), new means of transport (**railways**, the motor car) and **urbanization**: growth becomes self-sustaining and the standard of living rises. The first Industrial Revolution began in Britain in the late eighteenth century, as she was well endowed with natural resources (coal, iron, tin and copper), had an efficient transport system (navigable rivers, canals), good harbours and no part of the country was far from the sea. The Lancashire climate was ideally suited to the manufacture of cotton goods, which became the leading sector of the early Industrial Revolution, as machines – rapid, tireless and regular – were used to produce yarn far finer than that of the most skilful Indian spinner. The coal (used as fuel for the steam engine and later for the railways) and iron industries also grew rapidly when coke was used for smelting. On the Continent Belgium, which had the same advantages as Britain (a small country with natural resources and good communications), was the only country to industralize before 1850. The expansion of railways was essential for the growth of industry in larger countries (France, Germany, Russia), where vast new coalfields began to be developed in the 1850s in the **Ruhr** and Pas de Calais. Tariff barriers were removed in Germany by the *Zollverein* and after unification in 1871 industry developed rapidly there.

Old industries expanded – coal, iron, textiles – but it was in new industries – chemicals, electricity and in steel – that Germany took the lead. Steel had been almost a precious metal but a series of inventions made it cheaper and greatly increased output. Bessemer blew hot air through the molten metal to get rid of impurities in 1856 and this was followed by the Siemens-Martin open hearth process (1864). Both these methods used non-phosphoric ores to absorb impurities, which could then be removed. World output of 80,000 tons in 1850 rose to twenty eight million tons by 1900. Electricity was a new source of power and spawned a variety of industries. The chemical industries which developed after 1870 depended, like electricity, on scientific advances. Soda, used in the soap and glass industries, was made from ammonia, a coal tar product. Aniline dyes were also made from coal tar, as were plastics. Synthetic nitrogen and phosphates were used for making explosives and fertilizers; other products of the chemical industry included drugs, insecticides, perfumes, films and artificial fibres (art silk and later nylon). The two German **cartels** which dominated the chemical industry united in 1925 to form **IG Farben**. Germany took the leading part in this second Industrial Revolution, overtaking Britain in the production of steel in 1893 and of iron in 1903. Another form of energy was the internal combustion engine, with petrol or diesel oil as fuel. Oil produced in the USA, Russia and later the Middle East contributed to the **transport revolution**, by providing power for motor cars, lorries and ships.

By 1900 the USA had become the greatest industrial power in the world. Railways had made possible **westward expansion**, the opening up of the prairies (which made America the world's biggest agricultural producer) and the exploitation of her natural resources. Between 1860 and 1900 pig iron production rose from

800,000 to fourteen million tons, steel from almost nothing to eleven million tons, more than the combined production of Germany and Britain. Russia too was industrializing rapidly, by exploiting the coal and iron of the Donets Basin, and had a growth rate of 8 per cent per annum in the 1890s but she started from a low base and was in fact falling further behind the leading industrial countries. The only non-Western nation to industrialize on a large scale before 1945 was Japan, determined after the **Meiji Restoration** to catch up with the West. At first traditional industries such as textiles grew and though there was more concentration on heavy industry from 1895, textiles were still her largest export in the 1930s.

From 1850 there has been a steady rise in living standards in industrial countries, at least for skilled workers, partly because of the growth of the **world economy**, which brought cheap imports of food from the USA, Australasia and Argentina. Workers spent less of their income on food and more on clothes, consumer goods and entertainment. Hours of work fell, as did prices. Yet most people, even in Europe, were still engaged in agriculture: much of eastern and southern Europe was underdeveloped. The rest of the world was largely untouched by the Industrial Revolution.

**International Brigades** (1936–8). Volunteers for the republican cause in the **Spanish Civil War**. The International Brigades were organized from September 1936 by the **Comintern**, though they included people of other political persuasions. Of the 59,380 volunteers from fifty-three countries (with around 15,000 serving at any one time), the great majority were from the working classes, the participation of middle-class writers such as George Orwell often having given a false impression. Communist control of the Brigades made them a source of suspicion for other factions in the republican camp. Nevertheless, the Brigades played an important role in the crucial defence of Madrid in November 1936. They also had leading roles in the battles of Jarama and Guadalajara – where the Garibaldi Battalion vanquished Mussolini's **Blackshirts** – in early 1937. But the Brigades' losses were heavy: by June 1937, 70 per cent of those at Madrid were either dead or in hospital. Huge losses were suffered in the battle of Teruel of 1937–8 and in the Republic's last major offensive at the battle of the Ebro, July–August 1938. In

September 1938 the republican Prime Minister Juan **Negrín** declared that the International Brigades would be unilaterally withdrawn from Spain, but General **Franco**'s German and Italian backers failed to reciprocate.

**Iqbal, Muhammad** (1877–1938). Indian Muslim poet and political leader. One of India's greatest thinkers and literary figures, a poet in both Urdu and Persian, he is best known for putting forward the idea of a separate Muslim state in India. He took little part in politics until the late 1920s, when he became concerned at the **Indian National Congress**'s Nehru Report of 1929, which seemed to reject any safeguards for the Muslim minority. In 1930 he presided over the annual session of the **Muslim League** and declared that 'the formation of a consolidated Muslim state appears to me to be the final destiny of the Muslims at least of North-West India.' Although Bengal was not mentioned, this speech was the forerunner of the Pakistan resolution in 1940, when the Muslim League pledged itself to the creation of a separate state for India's Muslims. About the same time as Iqbal was making his speech in 1930, Indian Muslim students in Cambridge issued a pamphlet, in which they used the name 'Pakistan' for an Indian Muslim state. An Urdu word meaning 'Land of the Pure' (Pak means 'ritually pure'), it was also an acrostic: P for Punjab, A for Afghania (North-West Frontier Province), K for Kashmir, S for Sind and 'tan' for the last part of Baluchistan.

**IRA (Irish Republican Army).** A terrorist organization fighting for a united, republican Ireland. Originally created by **Fenians** in the USA, it was revived in 1919 as a successor to the paramilitary Irish Volunteers. Its object was to use armed force to get rid of British rule in Ireland and establish a republic. The same aim was followed politically by **Sinn Fein**, to which many IRA members belonged, though the IRA acted independently of Sinn Fein. In the **Anglo-Irish War** (1919–21) the IRA, led by Michael **Collins**, successfully used guerrilla tactics against British forces. In 1921 an Irish delegation, which included Collins and Arthur **Griffith**, negotiated the **Anglo-Irish Treaty**, which set up an independent Irish Free State. The treaty split the IRA, as many members objected to the oath of allegiance to the British Crown. The group which supported the treaty became the Irish Free State army. Opponents of the treaty organized armed resistance to the new, provisional Irish government and were known as Irregulars. In a bitter **Irish Civil War** (1922–3) the Irregulars were defeated. The IRA kept its arms and did not disband, so it remained a threat to the government. Recruiting and illegal drilling, with sporadic acts of violence, continued, so the Irish government banned the IRA in 1931. In 1939 the IRA was responsible for bombings in England, where many of its members were imprisoned. During the **Second World War** many IRA members were imprisoned without trial in Ireland and five were executed for atrocities. Since then the IRA has continued as an underground movement to agitate for the union of the Protestant North with the rest of Ireland.

**Irish Civil War** (1922–3). The Dail (Irish parliament) in January 1922 ratified the **Anglo-Irish Treaty**, which ended the **Anglo-Irish War** (1919–21) and set up an Irish Free State, by the narrow margin of seven votes. Eamon **de Valera** refused to accept it, as it required an oath of allegiance to the British Crown. He resigned as President and was replaced by Arthur **Griffith**. A provisional Irish government was formed, with Michael **Collins** at the head, the evacuation of British troops began and the **IRA** (Irish Republican Army), as the army of the provisional government, replaced them. This split into pro- and anti-treaty factions and in March those who opposed the treaty formed a separate force, the Irregulars. De Valera formed a new republican party and began a propaganda campaign to encourage resistance to the new government by force of arms. Collins at first was reluctant to use violence, even when the Irregulars occupied the Four Courts, the headquarters of the Irish judiciary in Dublin, in April. After the June elections, in which government supporters gained fifty-eight of the 128 seats (to the thirty-five of de Valera's party), he decided to take strong action and attacked the Four Courts, which surrendered in two days. This marked the beginning of the Civil War, which spread throughout the country to areas not involved in the Anglo-Irish War. The murders of Free State judges and officials were followed by massive retaliations, in which there were summary executions and thousands were imprisoned. Most of the country wanted peace and supported the government, as did the Roman Catholic hierarchy, which called the republican campaign 'a system of murder and assassination'. Griffith died and Collins was killed in an ambush in August 1922, so **Cosgrave** became head of the government and brought the war to a successful conclusion when de Valera, with little support left, proclaimed a cease-fire in May 1923.

**Irish Famine** (1845–9). The population of Ireland had grown to over eight million by 1840, partly because enough potatoes could be grown on small plots to feed an increasing number of people. About half the population subsisted almost entirely on the potato and were devastated when a fungus caused the crop to rot in 1845 and affected the yield up to 1849. The British government, influenced by *laissez-faire* doctrines, at first left relief to voluntary organizations, though it did begin some public works schemes. As deaths from starvation increased it changed its mind in 1847 and provided food for three million Irish. By taking direct action so late it was held responsible for the misery and deaths which resulted from the famine. One effect of the famine was a marked decline in the population, which fell by two and a quarter million between 1845 and 1851. Probably a million died from starvation and disease: the rest emigrated, particularly to the USA, where large numbers of Irish-Americans grew up with a hatred of Britain and were therefore willing to give financial support to revolutionary activity in Ireland. The population decline began before the famine and was to continue long after it (there were 5.5 million people in Ireland in 1871, 4.4 million by 1911) but there is no doubt that the famine speeded up the process. The Gaelic language also declined, as most emigrants came from Irish-speaking areas. As there were fewer people, the size of holdings increased and enabled those who remained to survive more easily. The part of Ireland least affected by the famine was Ulster, less dependent on the potato, where the linen industry expanded, thus widening the gap between the largely Protestant north-east and the rest of Ireland.

**Irish Land Acts** (1870–1903). The myth arose in the second half of the nineteenth century that Irish farming was backward owing to an impoverished Catholic peasantry, who were in constant fear of eviction and who paid exorbitant rents for small plots to absentee,

Protestant landlords living in England. The picture was more accurate in the period before rather than after the **Irish Famine** (1845–9), as farming was generally prosperous between 1850 and the depression which began in 1877 and lasted to the mid-1880s. In 1870 only 13.3 per cent of landlords (owning 23 per cent of the land) lived in England, evictions were few (1.36 per thousand holdings per year in 1854–80), most rents lagged behind the rise in prices of agricultural produce and many tenants were substantial farmers with secure and long leases. It was the landlords who were invariably in debt, as they suffered during the famine from a loss of income and increased expenditure for poor relief. When **Gladstone** decided to pass his first Land Act (1870) his motives were as much political as economic. Alarmed by **Fenian** outrages in England in 1867, he thought that land reform would bring prosperity and peace to Ireland and with it an acceptance of British rule. He also hoped that it would unite his divided **Liberal Party**. The Act gave legal recognition to tenants' customary rights, provided that landlords should pay compensation for any improvements to tenants leaving their farms and that compensation should be paid to anyone evicted, unless this was for non-payment of rent. Tenants wishing to buy their farms could borrow two-thirds of the cost from the government, paying off the debt at 5 per cent interest over thirty-five years. This Act was almost completely ineffective: tenants could not afford the deposit if they wanted to buy, whilst landlords could raise rents to avoid paying compensation. The main demand of tenants for rent control was ignored. Gladstone's second Land Act (1881) was a response to the **Irish Land War** (1879–82) and did much to give the tenant what he wanted by granting the 'Three Fs': 'fair' rents to be fixed by new courts; free sale (the right of a tenant to sell his 'interest' on leaving a farm); and fixity of tenure (security that he could not be evicted so long as he paid his rent). This Act was extended a year later to cover tenants in arrears with their rents and ended Liberal attempts at land reform. It helped to bring the Land War to an end and was successfully used to bring down rents but did nothing to make agriculture more efficient. The Conservatives (see **Conservative Party**), again looking at political rather than economic effects of land reform, thought that if tenants were able to buy their farms, support for **Home Rule for Ireland** would fall away. The Ashbourne Act (1885) therefore provided five million pounds for tenants who wanted to buy their farms: they could borrow the full price of their farms, to be paid off at 4 per cent over forty-nine years. The Irish Land Purchase Act (1903) reduced the rate of interest and extended the length of time over which loans could be repaid. These Acts drastically changed Irish land ownership: in 1870 70 per cent of Irish land was rented; by 1914 two-thirds of farmers owned their land. It was the Conservatives, therefore, who ended landlordism in Ireland.

**Irish Land War** (1879–82). There was an agricultural depression in Ireland in the late 1870s, when the potato crop failed for several years from 1877. Large tenant farmers and smallholders joined to seek a reduction of rents and to resist evictions. **Fenians** like Michael Davitt saw their opportunity to strike at Britain and formed the Land League in 1879, to defend the interests of tenants: **Parnell** became its leader. The League's tactics varied: in the west haystacks were burnt, cattle maimed and there were attacks on landlords and their agents. Generally the more peaceful method of the **boycott** prevailed: rents were withheld, farms from which tenants were evicted (there were 14,000 evictions in 1879–83, more than in the previous thirty years) were kept empty and landlords were ostracized. **Gladstone** responded by a mixture of conciliation and coercion. He met most of the demands of the tenants in his **Irish Land Act** of 1881, arrested Parnell and banned the League. The result was an increase in outrages in the winter of 1881–2, so Parnell and the British government came to an agreement, by which he would be released and would help to bring the disorders to an end, in return for futher concessions to the tenants. The war made Parnell the undisputed leader of the Irish nationalists, enabled his party to win eighty-five Irish seats (out of 103) in the 1885 election and politicized much of rural, Catholic Ireland.

**Irish Rebellion** (1798). An attempt to end English control of Ireland and set up an independent Irish Republic. The Society of United Irishmen tried to organize a rebellion in Ireland but the government was well informed of its activities through spies and in March 1798 arrested most of its leaders in Dublin. The society had therefore little control over the rising which broke out in May

1798, which was largely a popular, Catholic rebellion against Protestants and landlords. Its only real success was in Wexford, where rebels took control of almost the whole county. In Ulster the uprising was a Protestant affair but many defected when they heard of the Catholic nature of the rising in the South and the Ulstermen were defeated in ten days. There were horrible atrocities on both sides before the rebels were finally routed, largely by Catholic militia, at Vinegar Hill on 21 June. Wolfe **Tone** persuaded the French to invade but they did not land 11,000 men in County Mayo until the rebellion had been defeated. They bravely marched through Connaught and defeated a British force but failed to rouse the Irish peasantry, and surrendered when they were held up on the way to Dublin. A second small French fleet was captured by the British in October off Donegal. One of those on board was Wolfe Tone, who was sentenced to death but committed suicide before he could be hanged. Between thirty and forty thousand Irish were killed in the rebellion, which was one of the most violent events in Irish history.

**Irish Republican Army,** see **IRA**

**Irredentism.** Italian patriotic movement which aimed to acquire for Italy all 'unredeemed' lands (i.e. lands inhabited by Italians but held by the **Austro-Hungarian Empire**). Italy made the Treaty of **London** (1915) and entered the **First World War** on the Allied side to acquire these territories. She was largely successful at the Treaty of **Versailles** (1919), when she gained the Trentino, Trieste, the Alto Adige and Istria. Fiume (occupied by **D'Annunzio** for a year) and Dalmatia were not awarded to Italy.

**Ismail** (1830–95). Ruler of Egypt (1863–79) who was given the title Khedive (King) by the Ottoman Sultan in 1867. Ismail spoke French fluently, as he was educated in France, and was deeply imbued by Western ideas. He continued the modernization of Egypt begun by **Muhammad Ali** by building roads, railways, docks and by completing the **Suez Canal**. One million acres were reclaimed from the dessert and the export of cotton expanded. State schools increased from 185 to 4,817, including the first girls' school in the **Ottoman Empire**. These reforms benefited the peasants little, as they were heavily taxed, conscripted for the army and compelled to perform forced labour, so there was considerable rural impoverishment. To pay for his innovations and extravagant life-style, Ismail borrowed heavily and in 1875 sold his 44 per cent of the shares in the Suez Canal to the British government. As his debts had risen to £100,000,000 by 1876 he had to set up a Debt Commission, which consisted of representatives from Britain, France, Austria and Italy, to organize the servicing of the debt. Later in the year, under pressure from the bondholders, he appointed British and French controllers to supervise Egypt's finances. Thus began the Dual Control, by which Egypt effectively lost her independence. In 1878 the British and French governments decided that he should give up his vast estates (20 per cent of Egypt's cultivated land) in return for a fixed salary and that he should hand over some of his power to a ministry, which included an English and a French representative. They attempted to raise money by taxing the wealthy landowners and to cut expenditure by reducing the size of the Egyptian army. Three powerful groups, the army, the landowners and the *ulama* (religious leaders), who resented Christian influence, were now united against foreign control. In 1879 Ismail placed himself at the head of this opposition, dismissed his foreign ministers and overthrew the controls. Britain and France therefore persuaded the Turkish Sultan to depose Ismail. Anglo-French financial control of Egypt was restored and in 1880 two-thirds of Egypt's revenue was assigned to the Debt Commission to service the debt.

**Isolationism.** The policy of the USA which aimed at avoiding alliances with other countries or becoming involved in the affairs of other continents. It went back to George **Washington**, who advised Americans in his Farewell Address 'to steer clear of permanent alliances with foreign nations'. Thomas **Jefferson** endorsed this policy when he became President in 1801: 'Peace, commerce and honest friendship with all nations; entangling alliances with none.' Isolationism was confirmed by the **Monroe Doctrine** (1823), which warned other powers not to interfere in the American continent and said that the USA had no intention of intervening in the affairs of European powers. America's entry into the **First World War** in 1917 saw the abandonment of isolationism for a brief period. After the war Americans again turned their backs on the outside world and rejected President **Wilson**'s plea to join the **League of Nations**. In the 1930s, preoccupied with the **Great Depression**, the USA refused to take a stand when Japan invaded **Manchuria** (1931), Italy attacked Ethiopia (1935) and **Hitler** overturned the Treaty of **Versailles**. The **Neutrality Acts** of 1935–7 marked the triumph of isolationism in America. This policy was modified when the **Second World War** began in 1939. President Franklin D. **Roosevelt** did all he could to aid Britain, short of declaring war on Germany, by such measures as the **Lend-Lease Act**. It was the **Axis powers** who ended America's isolation; Japan by attacking the American fleet at **Pearl Harbor** on 7 December 1941, Germany and Italy by declaring war on the USA four days later.

**Italian Campaign** (July 1943–May 1945). After their success in the **North African Campaign** the Allies had to decide what to do next. General Marshall, head of the Combined Chiefs of Staff, did not want to invade Italy, as it would take away troops needed for the invasion of France. **Churchill**, however, thought that Italy was the 'soft underbelly of the Axis'. An invasion of Italy would be a threat to the Balkans and would force Hitler to dissipate his forces. At the **Casablanca Conference** (January 1943) Churchill persuaded **Roosevelt** to support an invasion of Sicily, which began on 10 July 1943, when 2,590 ships landed 180,000 men in the largest sea-borne operation of the war. Sicily was conquered in thirty-eight days, although the Germans were able to retreat in good order to Italy. Success encouraged the Americans to agree that Italy should be invaded, provided that Operation Overlord (the invasion of France, see **D-Day**) had priority and that the British agreed to a landing in southern France. After the conquest of Sicily eight of the best divisions, four British and four American, were sent to Britain in preparation for Overlord. On 25 July **Mussolini** was overthrown and on 3 September the invasion of Italy began when **Montgomery** and the Eighth Army crossed the Straits of Messina. Italy surrendered on 8 September, though this had little effect, as the Germans promptly took control of the country. The main invasion of Italy began on 9 September, with an Anglo-American landing at Salerno, near Naples. The Germans had been expecting a landing there, as fighter cover from Sicilian airfields could not be provided further north, so resistance was fierce. The Allies might have been defeated before Montgomery reached them on the 15th but for a supporting naval and air bombardment. On 12 September Mussolini was rescued by the **SS** and made a puppet ruler in northern Italy. The Germans evacuated Corsica and Sardinia and retired to a strong defensive Winter (Gustav) Line, based on the rivers Garigliano and Rapido and the monastery of Monte Cassino. Churchill wanted to outflank this by a landing behind the Gustav Line, which would threaten communications with it and produce a German withdrawal without a costly assault on the Line itself. Two Allied divisions therefore landed at Anzio sixty miles behind the Line on 22 January 1944 but troops were quickly sent from Germany and France to trap the Allies in the beachhead. The Allied spring offensive began on 11 May and five days later the Germans withdrew from Monte Cassino. US forces at Anzio now struck north to cut off the retreat of the German Tenth Army but their general, Mark Clark, then headed for Rome, vainly wishing to be the first Allied general to enter the capital, and allowed the Tenth Army to escape. Rome fell in June and the Germans retreated to another defensive line, the Gothic, north of Rome and astride the Apennines. It is likely that General Alexander, commander of Allied forces in Italy, could have driven over the Line and across the river Po in summer but seven of his divisions were withdrawn for the invasion of southern France on 15 August. This gave Kesselring, the German Commander who had fought a brilliant defensive campaign, time to recover. He now received eight extra divisions and held the British attack in the mountains south of Bologna in October. Another winter stalemate ensued, with Alexander having to send five divisions to France. He now had fewer divisions (seventeen) than the Germans (twenty-three), yet his attack in April 1945 was a great success. Mussolini was executed by Italian partisans on 28 April and a day later German forces in Italy surrendered unconditionally. The Italian Campaign had achieved all its aims: it had knocked Italy out of the war, drawn German troops to Italy and kept them there, while the Allies invaded Normandy. This was vital, as D-Day could be successful only if the number of German mobile forces in France was limited.

**Ito Hirobumi** (1841–1909). Japanese reformer and politician. Ito was a lower *samurai* from Choshu, whose ideas were shaped by foreign travel, which began with a visit to England in 1863. He took part in the movement which overthrew the **Tokugawa shogunate** and became a member of the government after the **Meiji Restoration**. From 1881 he had an unchallenged position in the government and was a leading figure in Japanese politics until his death. He visited Europe in 1882 to study Western constitutions and was responsible for the introduction of a new peerage in 1884 and of cabinet government a year later. He became Japan's first Prime Minister from 1885–8, a post he held again from 1892–6 and in 1900–1901. Other senior posts he held were President of the Privy Council (1888–90 and 1903–5) and President of the House of Peers (1890–92). Ito believed that the move towards popular participation in government was irreversible – 'all despotic conduct,' he wrote in 1880, 'must be abandoned and there can be no avoiding a sharing of the government's power with the people' – but that it should be controlled. As main architect of the **Meiji Constitution** (1889), therefore, he ensured that the elected **Diet** had a subordinate role to that of the Emperor. He explained his belief in 'transcendental' (non-party) government in 1889: 'The Emperor stands above the people and apart from every party. Consequently, the government cannot favour one party or the other. It must be fair and impartial.' Yet to make the Constitution work he was prepared to cooperate with parties in the Diet and in 1900 he formed his own party, the *Seiyukai*, which supported the government in return for some Cabinet posts. This brought about a split with **Yamagata Aritomo**, who relied for support on the army and civil service, and marked the beginning of what became a civilian–military rivalry in government. Ito, like Yamagata, favoured Japanese expansion in Asia (he was Prime Minister at the time of the **Sino-Japanese War** (1894–5) but differed with him over the desirability of an alliance with England. He opposed the **Anglo-Japanese Alliance** (1902), as he regarded England as a declining power, and wanted an understanding with Russia, on the basis of recognizing Japan's rights in Korea and Russia's in **Manchuria**. As ambassador in St Petersburg he tried to prevent the **Russo-Japanese War** (1904–5). In his later years Ito became a *genro*, an elder statesman, who was a personal adviser to the Emperor and so had a large measure of control over appointments to the government, Privy Council, House of Peers and High Command of the army. From 1905–9 Ito was resident-general of Japan's protectorate in Korea and was assassinated by a Korean in 1909.

**Iwakura Mission** (1871–3). A delegation from Japan, led by Prince Iwakura Tomomi, which included some leading members of the government such as **Ito Hirobumi**, was sent to Europe and America, to persuade the Western powers to revise the **unequal treaties**. It was not successful in this but the Mission had a profound effect on Japan, as its members were able to see just how backward in science and technology Japan was. They realized that Japan would have to compete with the West on its own terms and would have to adapt Western legal, political and economic systems to Japanese requirements. The result was the extensive reform programme of the **Meiji Restoration**. Another effect of the Mission was a split in the ruling oligarchy. Saigo Takamori had remained in Japan and wanted to send a military expedition to Korea, which had refused to agree to diplomatic relations with Japan and was trying to maintain a policy of seclusion, which Japan had only recently abandoned (see *Sakoku*). The members of the Mission rejected Saigo's plan, and insisted that Japan must build up her strength at home before waging war abroad. Saigo therefore left the government, returned to his domain and became the focus for anti-government dissent, which led to the **Satsuma rebellion** of 1877.

**Jackson, Andrew** (1767–1845). Seventh President of the USA (1829–37). Born in South Carolina, the son of an Ulsterman, he first became renowned as a soldier, fighting against the Creek Indians, when his men called him 'Old Hickory'. He defeated the Creeks at Horseshoe Bend (1814) and took half their lands. His victory opened up much of Alabama, Mississippi and Georgia to white settlement. He showed his abilities as a general also in the **Anglo-American War**, when he routed the British at New Orleans in January 1815. This made him a national hero. Jackson's military success made him wealthy, as he bought cheaply some of the lands he had conquered and he became a large slave-owner.

In 1828 he stood for President and, with **van Buren**'s help, won convincingly. The Presidents of the USA had been either Southern aristocrats or wealthy New Englanders, well educated and cultured. Jackson had risen from poverty and wanted to give the common man a greater say in government. Many of his ideas derived from **Jefferson**, particularly his belief that the federal government had limited powers and that he should prevent 'all encroachments upon the legitimate sphere of state sovereignty'. He thought 'that government is best which governs least' and opposed the use of public funds for 'internal improvements' (roads, canals, railways). Jackson speeded up what Jefferson had begun, the removal of all Indian tribes to land west of the Mississippi, and supported the state of Georgia when it defied the **Supreme Court**'s ruling that the removal of the Cherokee Indians from their lands was unconstitutional. Although he was a defender of state rights, Jackson implacably opposed anything which was likely to break up the Union, as he showed in the crisis of 1832–3 which resulted from the **Nullification Doctrine**. The suppression of the nullification movement in South Carolina, by which he avoided civil war for nearly thirty years, was his greatest achievement. The other major dispute during his presidency concerned the Second Bank of the United States. Jackson saw in the bank an institution dominated by the New England mercantile interests he so disliked. He vetoed a renewal of the bank's charter in 1832, withdrew federal funds from it and deposited them in state banks. The President saw in this conflict a struggle between big business and the rest of society for control of the state and regarded federal power as something to be used in the interests of the people as a whole. This was an essential part of the appeal of Jacksonian democracy.

Jackson greatly increased the authority and prestige of the President and vetoed twelve bills, more than all his predecessors had done. He also, with van Buren, organized the first modern, mass-based and nation-wide party, the **Democratic Party**, which he strengthened by use of the **spoils system**. His opponents soon had to copy his methods, so that the nature of American politics was permanently changed.

**Jackson, Thomas Jonathan ('Stonewall')** (1824 63). Confederate (see **Confederate States of America**) general in the **American Civil War**. A Virginian like **Lee**, Jackson joined the Confederate army when Virginia seceded from the Union in 1861 and became one of the most dashing and inventive commanders on either side. He showed his great physical courage in the first battle of the war at Bull Run, July 1861, when his troops repulsed a fierce Union attack. 'Look at Jackson's men,' said an admiring commander, 'standing like a stone wall.' In May 1862 Union troops were five miles from Richmond, the Confederate capital, waiting for reinforcements for a final assault. They never received them, because Lee sent Jackson up the Shenandoah valley in May–June, where he defeated three separate Union armies which were three times stronger than his own. Jackson then moved back to assist Lee and forced the Union armies to retreat in the Seven Days' Battles. Jackson also took part in the Confederate victory at the second battle of Bull Run (August), which enabled Lee to invade the North. This invasion was defeated at Antietam (September), which compelled Lee to retreat to Virginia, but further victories at Fredericksburg (December 1862) and Chancellorsville (May 1863) enabled him to go on the offensive again. Jackson played a large part in Lee's most brilliant victory at Chancellorsville, when he fought an army twice the size of his own, by his flank attack on Union troops and by his successful surprise attack in the twilight. As it was getting dark Jackson's party was mistaken for Union troops by his own soldiers. He was shot and died eight days later.

**Jacobins.** A political group during the **French Revolution**. They derived their name from the premises rented in Paris from the Dominicans, who were nicknamed Jacobins. As the club had a high entrance fee, its members came mainly from the wealthiest sections of society. The dominant members of the club up to the summer of 1791 were liberal constitutional monarchists. **Robespierre** was the leader of a minority group of radical Jacobin deputies. A national network of Jacobin clubs soon grew up: eventually there were 5,500, which were especially strong in the south-east. After **Louis XVI**'s flight to **Varennes** the Paris club split: those who did not want the King deposed (and this included nearly all who were deputies) left the club, so that Robespierre was in charge of a radical rump. It seemed that the Jacobins had destroyed themselves but few Jacobin clubs in the provinces defected. The Marseille Jacobin Club sent *fédérés* (provincial National Guards) to Paris, who played an important part in the attack on the **Tuileries** (10 August 1792), which led to the downfall of the monarchy. When the **Convention** was elected in September 1792, there were about 100 Jacobin deputies, who became known as *Montagnards* or the Mountain or simply the **Left**. The Jacobins increasingly depended on the *sans-culottes* for support and insisted on the trial of the King. Louis's execution in January 1793 was the first Jacobin victory in the Convention and began an ascendancy which they did not lose until Robespierre was executed in **Thermidor** (July) 1794. The peak of their power followed the arrest of the leading **Girondins** in June 1793: when a new **Committee of Public Safety** was formed between July and September 1793, all twelve members were either *Montagnards* or sympathizers. During the **Terror** Jacobin clubs in the provinces were responsible for purges of the local administrations, for arresting political suspects and for ensuring food supplies: they were vital props to the Revolution. After Robespierre's execution the Jacobin clubs were abolished during the Thermidorian Reaction of 1794–5.

**Jameson Raid** (1895). The discovery of gold on the **Rand** in 1885 transformed the Transvaal from the poorest to the richest state in South Africa and increased the rivalry of Boer and Briton. Foreign expertise was needed to mine the gold, so many foreigners (*uitlanders*) went to the Transvaal, where they were not allowed any political rights. Cecil **Rhodes**, Prime Minister of Cape Colony, planned to use *uitlander* discontent to stage a rising, which would overthrow the government of President **Kruger**. He secretly arranged for his close friend, Leander Jameson, an administrator in Rhodes's **British South Africa Company**, to lead a force of mounted men from Bechuanaland (Botswana) into the Transvaal, where there would simultaneously be a rising of *uitlanders*. Joseph **Chamberlain**, the British Colonial Secretary, was aware of what was going on, although he later denied this. The Raid was a fiasco. Jameson and 500 men entered the Transvaal but an *uitlander* rising did not take place: Jameson's force was surrounded and had to surrender. He was sent to Britain for trial, where he was sentenced to fifteen months' imprisonment but served only four. Rhodes had to resign as Prime Minister of the Cape. The Raid convinced Boers that Britain aimed at the destruction of their republic and brought about a deterioration in relations which led to the **South African War** (1899–1902). The Raid also brought about a worsening of British relations with Germany, as Kaiser **William II** sent Kruger a telegram congratulating him on suppressing the rebellion 'without having to invoke the help of friendly powers'. The British press regarded this as insufferable interference in British imperial affairs and began a virulent anti-German campaign. 'If the government had wished for war,' wrote the German ambassador in London, 'it would have had the whole of public opinion behind it.'

**Jaurès, Jean** (1859–1914). French socialist. A brilliant student at the élite *Ecole Normale*, Jaurès became a philosophy lecturer at the University of Toulouse and in 1890 declared that he was a socialist. When the miners of Carmaux went on strike in 1892 he became their spokesman and a year later was elected as one of thirty-seven socialist deputies: he soon became their leader. Jaurès believed that

**socialism** was a realization of the principles of the **French Revolution** and the Enlightenment. Power should not be seized by a revolutionary minority but should be won peacefully by obtaining a majority in parliament. Many French socialists kept aloof from the **Dreyfus case**, which they regarded as a quarrel amongst the *bourgeoisie*, but Jaurès saw that important principles were at stake and became a passionate Dreyfusard. He supported the socialist Millerand when he accepted office in the '*bourgeois*' Cabinet of Waldeck-Rousseau in 1899 and was one of the main organizers of the *Bloc des Gauches* (Left Bloc) in the Chamber of Deputies, which helped to keep in power the anti-clerical (see **anti-clericalism**) but socially conservative ministry of Combes. In 1904 he started the socialist newspaper *L'Humanité*, in the same year as the Congress of the **Second International**, meeting in Amsterdam, condemned socialists taking part in *bourgeois* governments. Jaurès loyally accepted this decision, so that when he united various socialist factions in the SFIO (French Socialist Party) in 1905, it became a party of opposition and the *Bloc des Gauches* came to an end. Believing that nations should resolve their differences peacefully by arbitration, he opposed the extension of the French Empire to Morocco and wanted the workers of all nations to unite to prevent their governments bringing about war. He opposed the extension of military service from two to three years in 1913 and was shot and killed by a fanatical nationalist as the **First World War** was about to begin.

**Jefferson, Thomas** (1743–1826). Third President of the USA (1801–9). Jefferson had an insatiable intellectual curiosity and a greater range of interests and abilities than any other American President. In addition to being a politician and a diplomat, he was an inventor, philosopher, naturalist and architect. He collected paintings and loved music. His liberal ideas found their way into the Declaration of Independence but there was an uneasy juxtaposition between his precepts and his practice. He was a slave-owner, whose wealth and life-style were based on slavery, though he saw it as a dangerous evil. He believed in the political equality of all men but did not think that different races could easily live together as equals, particularly in the USA. His ideal American society was that of the small farmer – 'Those who labour in the earth are the chosen people of God,' he wrote – who worked his own land, though this vision clashed with the American reality, in which industries and cities were growing rapidly. By 1816 he realized this: 'Experience has taught me that manufactures are now as necessary to our independence as to our comfort.' Though he did not think that an aristocracy of birth and wealth should run America, he firmly believed that an élite of intellect and ability should do so.

Jefferson's mother was an aristocrat, through whom he gained access to the powerful cliques in the colony. He became a lawyer and joined the movement against British control of the American colonies. He was a Virginian representative at the Continental Congress (1775–6) and drafted the Declaration of Independence, a document that was to make him famous with its claim that 'All men are created equal' and that all have the right to 'Life, Liberty and the pursuit of Happiness'. When the war was over he went to Europe, where he became the US ambassador to France from 1785–9 and approved of the beginning of the **French Revolution**. He returned home to become the nation's first Secretary of State in **Washington**'s administration but soon clashed with the Secretary of the Treasury, Alexander **Hamilton**. Jefferson's vision of the USA as an agricultural country consisting of self-governing states was rejected by Hamilton, who saw the USA as an industrial and trading nation, which needed strong support from the central government if it was to be successful. Hamilton was contemptuous of democracy: Jefferson believed in obtaining the consent of the governed. Above all, they differed on what powers the federal government should have. Jefferson thought it could do only what the Constitution specifically allowed: Hamilton believed that it could do anything that was not specifically forbidden by the Constitution. Although Washington supported Hamilton's views, Jefferson remained a member of his government until 1793. By 1791 he realized that he needed to organize opposition to Hamilton, so he formed alliances with politicians like James **Madison**, which grew into the Democratic-Republican Party, from which the **Democratic Party** is descended. In opposition to them Hamilton and John Adams formed the **Federalist Party**. In 1796 Adams was elected President. Jefferson was elected Vice-President but took no part in the administration of his political opponent.

Jefferson became President in 1801. He behaved with moderation and did not indulge in the wholesale removal of Federalists from government office. He showed that a strong and powerful United States was as important to him as it was to Hamilton, when he negotiated the **Louisiana Purchase** (1803), which doubled the size of the country. Immediately he followed up by sending the **Lewis and Clark expedition** to find a route through the new territory to the Pacific. After the Purchase, Jefferson tried to persuade Indians east of the Mississippi to exchange their lands for others further west: they were not to stand in the way of white settlement.

He retired to his plantation at Monticello, where he planned and eventually (in 1819) founded the University of Virginia, whose buildings he designed.

**Jena–Auerstädt, battles of** (October 1806). Two of **Napoleon**'s greatest victories against the Prussians. Prussia did not join the Third Coalition until after the defeat of Austria at the battle of **Austerlitz** (1805). Instead of waiting behind the river Elbe for Russian reinforcements, the Prussians foolishly advanced. When Napoleon found the Prussian army at Jena in Saxony he ordered Marshals Davout and **Bernadotte** to move north to cut the Prussian line of retreat to the river Elbe. Napoleon, vastly superior in strength (with 96,000 troops to the Prussians' 53,000), routed the Prussians at Jena and was unaware that nine miles further north a major battle was taking place against the main Prussian army, in which the Prussians (63,500) greatly outnumbered Davout (27,000): Bernadotte had disobeyed his orders and did not take part in the battle. Davout, aided by Prussian confusion when their commander, the Duke of Brunswick, was mortally wounded, fought with great skill until Frederick William III ordered a Prussian retreat, which became a rout, as **Murat**'s cavalry cut to pieces the fleeing Prussians. The Prussians lost 46,000 men in the two battles, the French 12,700: a further 100,000 Prussian troops and 1,500 cannon were captured in the pursuit. The French soon overran three-quarters of Prussian territory, including their capital of Berlin, but Frederick William unexpectedly continued to fight, so the war did not end until the Treaties of **Tilsit** (July 1807).

**Jiang Jieshi (Chiang Kai-shek)** (1887–1975). Chinese soldier and leader of the **Guomindang** (Nationalist Party). The son of a merchant, Jiang went to Tokyo (1908–10) for military training and there became closely associated with **Sun Yixian** (Sun Yat-sen). During the **Chinese Revolution** of 1911, which saw the fall of the **Qing dynasty**, he fought in Shanghai and thereafter worked for Sun. He became Chief of Staff at Sun's headquarters in Guangzhou (Canton) and was sent by Sun to study military organization in the Soviet Union. When he returned he became head of the Whampoa Military Academy, where he built up, with Soviet help, a private army for the Guomindang. Sun had formed a **United Front** with the Chinese Communist Party (CCP) in 1923 and allowed communists to join the Guomindang. This was resented by business supporters of the Guomindang and by nationalist generals. Jiang made skilful use of this hostilty to the CCP by reducing communist influence in the Guomindang and at the same time increasing his own. He mounted a successful **Northern Expedition** (1926–8) against the **warlords**, in an attempt to unite China, and after capturing **Shanghai** in 1927 carried out a *coup* against the communists, executing all he could find. In 1928 Beijing (Peking) fell to Jiang, who set up a nationalist government in Nanjing. Although China was now apparently united, much of it was in the hands of warlords who, whilst giving nominal allegiance to the nationalist government, retained their private armies. In 1930 Jiang turned again on the communists, who had formed the **Jiangxi Soviet**, and in five extermination campaigns (1930–34) drove them out of Jiangxi on the **Long March** to a new base at **Yanan** in the north. Meanwhile, Jiang's nationalist government made little attempt at social and economic reform, as most income was spent on the army. Jiang tried to provide an alternative appeal to communism with his New Life Movement (1934–7) but this was essentially conservative, stressing Confucian (see **Confucianism**) values such as obedience, propriety, discipline and frugality. This movement was a failure, as it did nothing for the peasant, whose taxation increased.

Jiang was widely criticized for spending more time fighting the communists than opposing Japan, who had seized **Manchuria** in 1931. In 1936 he was arrested by his own troops at **Xi'an** and forced to form a second United Front with the CCP, this time against Japan. Any chance Jiang had of creating a strong, centralized state disappeared when the **Sino-Japanese War** (1937–45) began. Within a year the Japanese had overrun eastern China, taking all China's main industrial centres and most fertile farmland and virtually cutting Jiang off from the outside world. Jiang had to leave his capital of Nanjing and retreat to Chongqing, a thousand miles up the Yangzi. As he had lost most of his sources of revenue he financed the war by printing money. This led to rapid inflation, distress and unpopularity for Jiang and the Guomindang. Jiang had more success with the Great Powers. In 1943 he persuaded them to abandon the **unequal treaties** imposed on China in the nineteenth century and China was recognized as one of the 'Big Four'. At the **Cairo Conference** in the same year the Allies agreed that all Chinese territories held by the Japanese would be restored. When the **Second World War** ended in 1945 Jiang was universally recognized as leader of the Republic of China but, overconfident, he would not agree to a coalition with **Mao Zedong** and the CCP. The result was a civil war (1945–9), which ended with Jiang's defeat and his withdrawal to Taiwan, where he remained President until his death, protected by the USA and building up a modern industrial state.

**Jiangxi Soviet**. The main base of the Chinese communists from 1929–34. After the **Shanghai** *coup* the communists, in order to survive nationalist attacks, had to disperse to remote rural areas throughout China, though they tried to maintain an underground urban organization in cities such as Shanghai. When **Mao Zedong** failed to capture Changsha, the capital of Hunan province, in the Autumn Harvest Rising, he took the remains of his force to Jingganshan, a remote mountainous area on the Hunan–Jiangxi border, in the autumn of 1927. Here he confiscated the land of landlords and rich peasants and distributed it amongst the poor and began to build up a military force, which became the Red Army. In January 1929 he moved to a mountainous area between Jiangxi and Fujian provinces, where he set up soviets (councils) of workers, peasants and soldiers. Here he followed policies which were designed not to upset the wealthier peasants, the real driving force in peasant society. **Jiang Jieshi** (Chiang Kai-shek) was determined to complete the destruction of the communists which he had begun at Shanghai, and in December 1930 he began the first of his extermination campaigns by attacking Jiangxi. Mao refused to take on the nationalists in open battle and responded by using guerrilla tactics: 'When the enemy advances we retreat; when he halts we harass him; when he retreats, we pursue.' The campaign failed, as did two others in 1931. The Japanese invasion of **Manchuria** in September 1931 gave the communists a brief respite, so they held a National Congress of the Chinese Soviet Republic at Ruijin in Jiangxi, when they set up a soviet government with Mao as chairman. There were now five soviets in Jiangxi, controlling nine million people, so Jiang tried again, unsuccessfully, to crush them. For his fifth campaign, which began in October 1933, Jiang used 700,000 troops and, on the advice of General Hans von **Seeckt**, head of the German military mission, changed his tactics. He abandoned costly frontal assaults and instead surrounded and blockaded the Soviet, gradually tightening the noose. It was clear that the communists would be destroyed if they remained in Jiangxi, so they decided in October 1934 to break out and move to a new base in the north-west. Thus began the **Long March**. The Jiangxi Soviet was only one of a dozen communist bases in China but it was the most important, as there the Red Army was formed, guerrilla tactics developed and new leaders, such as Mao, appeared.

*Jihad* (Arabic, 'striving'). A holy war of Muslims against unbelievers. It is a religious duty prescribed by the Quran for Muslims to fight the infidel until he either becomes a Muslim or accepts the protected status of those whose religion is based on written scriptures, such as Jews and Christians, 'peoples of the Book'. They were allowed to practise their old religion on payment of a special tax.

**'Jim Crow' laws** were passed by state legislatures in the USA mainly in the South, and were designed to maintain racial segregation and keep Negroes in an inferior position to whites. They were effective from the 1870s to the 1950s. **Reconstruction** ended when federal troops were withdrawn from the South in 1877. Soon Southern legislatures passed 'Jim Crow' laws to restore **segregation** of the races and to deprive Negroes of the rights guaranteed by **Civil Rights Acts** and constitutional amendments passed after the **American Civil War**. Races were segregated in every aspect of life – in schools, churches, housing, hotels and public parks. Negroes were also effectively prevented from voting, as they had to pay the poll tax before they could vote. The **Supreme Court** encouraged 'Jim Crow' laws when in 1883 it said that the Civil Rights Act of 1875 was unconstitutional. In 1896 it upheld a Louisiana law, which required railroads to provide 'equal but separate accommodation for the white and coloured races'. This decision was not overthrown until 1954, when the Supreme Court abolished segregation in public schools. This was followed by Civil Rights Acts in the 1950s and 1960s, which banned all forms of racial discrimination.

**Jingoism.** A mood of aggressive and hysterical nationalism. In 1878, after the Treaty of **San Stefano** increased Russia's influence in the Balkans, it appeared that Britain might go to war with Russia. This gave rise to a music-hall song:

> We don't want to fight;
> But, by jingo, if we do,
> We've got the men, we've got the ships,
> We've got the money too.

War was averted but jingoism reappeared at times of national crisis abroad. The relief of Mafeking in 1900, during the **South African War** (1899–1902), was greeted in London by 'seething crowds, waving flags, blowing horns and howling in a frenzy of delight', according to the *Anglo-Saxon Review*. At the end of the nineteenth century jingoism was whipped up by cheap newspapers like the *Daily Mail* and was most common amongst the lower-middle class of white-collar workers.

**Jinnah, Muhammad Ali** (1876–1948). Indian Muslim leader and founder of Pakistan. Jinnah studied law in England (1892–6) and on returning to India became a 'moderate' member of the **Indian National Congress** and an admirer of **Gokhale**. At this time he opposed special representation for Muslims and worked hard to bring about cooperation between Congress and the **Muslim League**. He joined the League in 1913, while still a member of Congress, and in 1917 became a supporter of Annie **Besant**'s Home Rule movement. Jinnah strongly disapproved of **Gandhi**'s **non-cooperation movement** (1920–22) as 'it must lead to disaster' and saw it as an example of Hindu revivalism, which was a threat to Muslims. Consequently, he resigned from Congress and the Home Rule League. In 1930 he went into self-imposed exile in England, from where he returned in 1935 to take over the leadership of the Muslim League. It had few members, no national network and no money. Jinnah, with his dominating personality and iron will, changed all this but it took time and in the 1937 elections the League fared very badly, gaining under a quarter of the seats reserved for Muslims. He was prepared to work in provincial governments with Congress ministers but his offer was declined and by 1939 his breach with Congress was complete. The Second World War gave him an unexpected opportunity, as Congress leaders resigned from provincial governments and from 1942, following the **'Quit India' Campaign**, were in jail. Jinnah now had British support, as he supported Britain, and persuaded the Muslim leaders in states with large Muslim populations to support the League. This success was astonishing, as he was an impassive, aloof, Westernized lawyer, who refused to adopt Indian dress and did not speak Urdu. Yet there was no doubting his achievement when, in the 1945 elections, the League won 90 per cent of the reserved seats. He then negotiated with Congress and the British about the future of India. According to the Viceroy, Mountbatten, he was the one man who prevented India gaining independence as a unified state. Jinnah did not get all he wanted: he had to accept a 'moth-eaten' Pakistan, as much of the Punjab and Bengal was left in India, when independence came in 1947. He became Governor-General of Pakistan but was already suffering from tuberculosis and died a year later.

**Joffre, Joseph Jacques Césaire** (1852–1931). Marshal of France. He took part as a junior engineer officer in the defence of Paris during the **Franco-Prussian War** (1870–71) and then continued his career in the French colonial service. In 1911 he became Vice-President of the Higher War Council, responsible for war plans, and aimed to launch an offensive across the Franco-German frontier if war broke out. When Germany invaded Belgium, Joffre immediately went on to the offensive and committed a third of the French army to disastrous attacks in Lorraine and the Ardennes. Ponderous and taciturn, his great strength was his calmness in a crisis, which he showed when the French were driven back with heavy losses. He cleverly transferred troops from his right wing to form fresh armies on his left, which enabled him to mount a counter-attack at the battle of the **Marne** and win a decisive victory. After that he managed to prevent a German breakthrough to the Channel ports in the first battle of Ypres. Both his major offensives in 1915, in Artois and Champagne, failed, and he was blamed for the neglect of Verdun's defences in 1916 (see battle of **Verdun**). Although he deployed his reserves skilfully to contain the German attack, Pétain and Nivelle got most of the credit. Joffre was replaced as Commander-in-Chief by Nivelle in November 1916 and took no further part in the war.

**Johnson, Andrew** (1808–75). Seventeenth President of the USA (1865–9). Like **Lincoln**, Johnson was born in a log cabin. He is the only President who never went to school and who learnt to read only after he was married. He became a spokesman for the poor, white farmers of the South, who were opposed to the slave-holding planter aristocracy, entered the US Senate in 1857 and was the only Southern Senator who supported the Union when the **American Civil War** began in 1861. From 1862–5 he was Governor of Tennessee, where he purged the administration of Confederate (see **Confederate States of America**) supporters and kept the state within the Union. In 1864 Lincoln supported his nomination for the post of Vice-President, because, as a Southerner and a Democrat, he could help to reconcile North and South after the Civil War. When Lincoln was assassinated in 1865 Johnson automatically became President, a Democrat in charge of a Republican administration. He was totally unsuited to the role which was thrust upon him, as he was a firm believer in white supremacy. 'This is a country for white men,' he wrote, 'and by God, as long as I am President, it shall be a government for white men.' He believed in states' rights and opposed most of what the Republicans stood for. Once the Southern states had abandoned slavery, repudiated the Confederate debt and accepted the Union, he felt that they had done all that could be reasonably expected of them. Congress, he thought, had no right to pass legislation affecting the South until Southern representatives sat there. He therefore opposed the **Reconstruction** Act of 1867, which was passed over his veto by obtaining two-thirds majorities in both houses of Congress. In the same year the Tenure of Office Act was passed, which prevented a President dismissing high officials without the approval of the Senate. Johnson thought this was unconstitutional, deliberately ignored it and was therefore impeached by the House of Representatives. The case was heard by the Senate, where the impeachment failed by one vote to get the necessary two-thirds majority. One of his few successes was the purchase of **Alaska**.

**Journées.** Days during the **French Revolution** when the Parisian *sans-culottes* took to the streets, often to intimidate the elected Assembly and change the course of the Revolution. The great *journées* were on 14 July 1789, the fall of the **Bastille**; on 5–6 October 1789 (the **October Days**), when **Louis XVI** was brought from Versailles to Paris; on 10 August 1792, the attack on the **Tuileries**, when the monarchy effectively ended; and on 31 May–2 June 1793, the time when the leading **Girondin** deputies were arrested and the **Jacobins** were forced to give way to *sans-culottes* demands. The last *journée* was on 20 May 1795 (the rising of **Prairial**), which failed. After this the Paris populace did not play an important political role again until the **Revolution of 1830**.

**Juárez, Benito** (1806–72). Mexican statesman. A Zapotec Indian, Juárez became a lawyer before being elected Governor of his native province, Oaxaca (1848–52), where he provided honest, efficient administration. When the conservative *caudillo*, Santa Anna, became President again in 1853, Juárez was exiled to the USA. He returned to Mexico when there was a liberal revolution in 1855 and became Minister of Justice. Believing that Mexico could be spared further dismemberment by the USA (see **Mexican–American War**) only by bringing the army and the Catholic Church under civilian control, he abolished special courts for the Church and military and supported the law which forced the Church to sell its property. In 1858 the conservatives seized power again and so Juárez and his liberal supporters retired to Veracruz. In the civil war which followed (1857–60), the Church supported the conservatives, so Juárez issued several decrees to curb its power. Church and State were separated, Church property nationalized, monasteries closed, civil marriage established and religious liberty guaranteed. After a liberal victory in the civil war Juárez was elected as the first civilian President (1861) in the country's history. As Mexico was bankrupt, he defaulted on payment of her foreign debt. This gave the French Emperor **Napoleon III** the excuse to send French troops to Mexico and to impose a **Habsburg** prince, Maximilian, as Emperor of Mexico. Juárez led the resistance and, following the withdrawal of French troops in 1870, he defeated the remaining imperial forces and had Maximilian executed. Mexico now had a secular state but Juárez was faced in his last years with peasant unrest (many of their communal lands had been sold to the great landowners) and with the revolt of regional *caudillos*. It was one of his most successful commanders, Porfirio **Díaz**, who became a major political opponent and, after Juárez's death, dictator of Mexico.

**July crisis** (1914). When the Archduke Franz Ferdinand, the heir to the Austro-Hungarian throne, was murdered on 28 June 1914 at **Sarajevo** in Bosnia, by Serb nationalists, Austria-Hungary had the opportunity she wanted for making war on Serbia. Much depended on Germany's reaction, as Russia might support Serbia and Austria-Hungary could not take on Russia alone. Kaiser **William II** reacted violently and on 5 July gave Austria a *carte blanche*, promising to support her whatever she did. The German government went further and pressed the Austrians to take immediate action, so that the other powers would be presented with a *fait accompli*. The Kaiser believed that Tsar **Nicholas II**, shocked by the murder of a fellow monarch, would not act. The Austrians, however, were incapable of taking swift action, as it would take time to mobilize their army, and the Hungarian Prime Minister, Count Tisza, insisted that Serbia should first be given an ultimatum. This was delayed until the French President **Poincaré** had ended his state visit to Russia and was delivered on 23 July. The ultimatum contained demands, such as that Austrian officials should be allowed into Serbia to suppress agitation against the Habsburg monarchy, which Serbia was expected to reject. Sazonov, the Russian Foreign Minister, regarded war as unavoidable when he saw the ultimatum, as Austria-Hungary clearly intended to attack Serbia: if Russia did not support her she would become a second-rate power and her prestige in the Balkans would 'collapse utterly'. The Serbian reply on 25 July in fact accepted nearly all Austria-Hungary's demands and convinced the volatile Kaiser that war was no longer necessary. He asked for his message to be passed on to Austria-Hungary but **Bethmann-Hollweg**, the German Chancellor, delayed doing this until Austria-Hungary had declared war on Serbia on 28 July. Bethmann-Hollweg was now concerned that if Russia came into the war, she should appear as the aggressor, so the **Social Democratic Party** and the workers would support the war effort. This meant waiting for Russia to mobilize before Germany did so. The German General Staff became impatient and agreed to delay mobilization only until noon on 31 July. Just before that Bethmann-Hollweg heard that Russia had mobilized, so on 1 August Germany declared war on Russia. 'Atmosphere brilliant,' wrote Admiral von Müller in his diary. 'The government has had a lucky hand in being able to depict us as the victims of aggression.' On 3 August Germany declared war on France, who had played little part in the crisis but was the ally of Russia. The British Cabinet and public opinion was divided on whether Britain should join in but the **Schlieffen Plan** led to Germany invading Belgium, whose integrity Britain was pledged to defend. Britain therefore declared war on Germany on 4 August. The **First World War** had begun.

**July Days, 1917.** A demonstration of workers, soldiers and sailors in **Petrograd** against the **Provisional Government**. Bolshevik propaganda had undermined discipline in the army and called for an end to the war. By the summer the Petrograd garrison, which had mutinied during the **February Revolution**, supported the **Bolsheviks**. When the government tried to move some regiments from the capital to the front, there was a mass demonstration on 3 July. This placed the Bolsheviks in a dilemma. They did not want to attempt to seize power, as they thought this would be unsuccessful, yet if they did nothing they were likely to lose support amongst the workers and soldiers. On the 4th, therefore, they tried to take control of a movement they could not stop. The demonstrators, joined by sailors from Kronstadt, demanded that the **Soviet** should take power but when it was clear that this would not happen, they did not know what to do. On the 5th, loyal troops, swayed by government propaganda that Lenin and the Bolsheviks were German agents, cleared the streets. The episode appeared a disaster for the Bolsheviks, who were now half-heartedly persecuted. **Lenin** fled to Finland and the Party went underground. The Bolsheviks recovered surprisingly quickly owing to the **Kornilov affair**.

**July Monarchy** (1830–48), see **Louis Philippe**

**July Plot** (1944). An attempt by senior army officers to assassinate **Hitler**. General Beck, who had resigned as army Chief of Staff in 1938, and Goerdeler, ex-mayor of Leipzig, decided that only the assassination of the *Führer* would release the army from its oath of allegiance to Hitler and make a successful *coup* possible. After Hitler's death they planned to set up a provisional government and make peace with the Allies but politically they were looking backwards and wanted to return to a monarchical, authoritarian system, like that in 1913. Colonel von Stauffenberg placed a bomb in the conference room at Hitler's headquarters in East Prussia on 20 July 1944. The bomb exploded but Hitler survived with minor injuries. **Himmler** and loyal army officers acted quickly and arrested the conspirators. Stauffenberg was shot and Beck was allowed to commit suicide. A 400-strong **Gestapo** team then set to work to uncover how extensive the plot was and arrested 7,000 people. Of these about 5,000 were executed: some were strangled by piano wire, others, like Field Marshal **Rommel**, were told to commit suicide. Hitler, enraged, removed the last remains of the *Wehrmacht*'s independence. Himmler was made Commander-in-Chief of the home forces, so the army passed under **SS** control. The plot had no popular support and was condemned by most Germans, who were still prepared to follow their *Führer*.

**July Revolution** (1830) in France brought about the fall of **Charles X** and the accession to the French throne of **Louis Philippe**. The Four Ordinances of 25 July, which brought back censorship of the press, reduced the number of deputies, restricted the franchise, dissolved the newly elected Chamber of Deputies and ordered fresh elections, were a rejection of the wishes of the electorate, who had just returned a Chamber in which there were twice as many opposition deputies as there were government supporters. This was an exceptionally foolish and overconfident act of Charles X and his unpopular chief minister Polignac, as the best of the army was in Algiers (there were only 12,000 troops in the Paris area) and there were no military plans to cope with a rising. Workers began protesting on 26 July. They were not directly affected by the Four Ordinances, as they did not have the vote, but there had been an economic recession since 1826, in which increased food prices owing to poor harvests had reduced the demand for manufactured goods and caused widespread unemployment. Over a quarter of the Paris population of 750,000 was receiving public assistance in July 1830. On the 27th barricades went up and there were violent outbreaks in which several demonstrators were killed. Charles lost control of the capital in *les Trois Glorieuses* ('three glorious days'), 27–29 July, as 20 per cent of the troops deserted. Only on the 29th did he dismiss Polignac and annul the Four Ordinances but by this time it was too late. **Thiers** was calling for his abdication and the succession of his cousin, the Duke of Orleans, who was proclaimed King Louis Philippe by parliament. Thus the Bourbon restoration (see **Bourbon dynasty**) ignominiously came to an end.

**June Days** (1848). A rising of unemployed workers in Paris when the National Workshops were closed down. National Workshops had been set up after the February Revolution, which saw the downfall of **Louis Philippe** and the July Monarchy and the establishment of the **Second Republic**. They were to provide work for the unemployed but by June 1848, 118,000 (about half the adult, male working-class population of Paris) were out of work, whilst the workshops could provide work for only 14,000. The rest were given outdoor relief. The *bourgeois* members of the government found the workshops expensive and also dangerous, as a concentration of large numbers of idle workers in the capital was a threat to public order. They therefore closed the workshops, told the unmarried unemployed to join the army and the rest to go and drain marshes in the provinces. The result was a popular, spontaneous rising of artisans and unskilled labourers. About 50,000 rose in rebellion (only a quarter of the total number of workers) but it was not a class war, as some workers fought on the government side and the Mobile Guard, responsible for much of the savagery of the repression, was entirely working class. General Cavaignac used 50,000 troops and the same number of Mobile and National Guards, many brought from the provinces, to put down the rising in four days. About a thousand of the government forces were killed and between 1,500 and 3,000 rebels, as there was summary execution of prisoners in the brutal reprisals. There was no support for the rising in the provinces. The June Days doomed the Second Republic, as the workers turned against it, whilst the *bourgeoisie* were haunted by the possible return of **Jacobins** and the **Terror** and looked for an authoritarian leader, whom they soon found in Louis Napoleon (later **Napoleon III**).

**Junkers.** Prussian landowning aristocracy in provinces east of the river Elbe. They reached the peak of their economic power between 1840 and 1876, when they exported wheat to England, after the repeal of the **Corn Laws** in 1846. When Russian and American grain exports ate into their markets, they turned to protection in 1876 and formed a *Sammlung* (see ***Sammlungspolitik***) with industrialists (the alliance of 'iron and rye') to maintain their privileged position and keep tariffs high. Though only a small minority of the population, they dominated the highest ranks of the civil service, the army and the Court and maintained this position, even when there was a relative decline in their economic fortunes, until 1918 and to a certain extent up to 1945. The great East Elbian estates finally disappeared with the Russian invasion of 1945 and the establishment of a communist state in East Germany (GDR).

**Jutland, battle of** (31 May–1 June 1916). Fought in the North Sea, this was the only major action between the British and German battle fleets in the **First World War**. Admiral Beatty, with six battle cruisers, scoured the North Sea looking for Admiral Hipper's force of five battle cruisers, which he knew had left port. When they met, Hipper's ships showed superior gunnery – they found the range more quickly than Beatty and blew up two of his ships, which had inadequate armour and no flash-tight magazines. The German High Seas Fleet, with sixteen **Dreadnoughts** under Admiral Scheer, was lured by Beatty north towards the stronger British Grand Fleet, with twenty-eight Dreadnoughts commanded by Admiral Jellicoe. When he saw this Scheer ordered an about-turn and, under a smoke screen laid down by his destroyers, escaped from the trap into which Beatty had led him. As night fell the British fleet lay between Scheer and his base but he managed to cross astern of Jellicoe's ships in the darkness and so made a remarkable escape. Both sides could, and did, claim victory, the British because the Germans had fled back to port, the Germans as they sank more ships. The British lost three battle cruisers, three cruisers and eight destroyers, the Germans one pre-Dreadnought battleship, one battle cruiser, four light cruisers and five destroyers.

**Kadets** (Constitutional Democrats). Russian political party, founded during the **Russian Revolution of 1905**. They were the largest party in the first **Duma** and represented the majority of the professions and the *zemstva*. They wanted universal, equal and direct suffrage and a government responsible to the Duma. They also favoured taking over private land, with compensation to the owners, for distribution to the peasants but they were not revolutionary. Under their leader **Milyukov** they tried to work with the Tsar in the **Progressive Bloc**. After the fall of the monarchy they played a leading part in the **Provisional Government** between February and May 1917. Their main weakness was that they had little contact with, or appeal to, the peasants and the workers. In the elections to the Constituent Assembly in November 1917 they won only seventeen seats. They were destroyed soon after the **October Revolution** by the arrest, murder or exile of their leaders.

**Kamenev, Lev Borisovich** (1883–1936). Son of a Jewish railway engineer, he joined the **Bolsheviks** in 1903. He was exiled to Siberia for opposing Russia's entry into the **First World War** and returned to **Petrograd** after the **February Revolution**, giving conditional support to the **Provisional Government**. He opposed **Lenin**'s call for revolution in 1917, as he thought it was premature, and wanted to rule in coalition with other socialist parties after the success of the **October Revolution**. As Lenin would not do this, Kamenev resigned from the Central Committee of the Bolshevik Party. He was re-elected to the Central Committee and to the *Politburo* in 1919 and became Party boss in Moscow. On Lenin's death he joined with **Stalin** and **Zinoviev**, in the so-called triumvirate, to prevent **Trotsky** taking over. Both Kamenev and Zinoviev feared Trotsky as a potential Bonaparte and felt they had nothing to fear from Stalin. They supported the suppression of Lenin's 'last testament', which heavily criticized Stalin. When they became alarmed at Stalin's growing power and his (short-lived) support for **NEP**, they formed the Left Opposition. Kamenev lost his post in the *Politburo* and as head of the Party in Moscow. At the Party Congress in 1927 Kamenev was expelled from the Central Committee. In the first of the show trials of the **Great Purges** in 1936, he was falsely accused of **Kirov**'s murder and was shot.

*Kamikaze* ('Divine Wind'). The name given to Japanese suicide attacks on Allied fleets during the **Pacific War** (1941–5). Japan had only twice been threatened by invasion: by the Mongols in 1274 and again in 1281. On each occasion the invaders were repelled by storms, the *kamikaze*, which destroyed much of their fleet. At the battle of **Leyte Gulf** on 25 October 1944, Japanese pilots began *kamikaze* attacks when they crashed their explosive-laden aircraft on to American ships. Mass suicide attacks were made during the American invasion of **Okinawa** (April–June 1945). *Kamikaze* attacks sometimes took the form of rocket-assisted piloted bombs, manned torpedoes and motor boats filled with explosives. *Kamikaze* attacks sank twenty-five Allied ships and damaged over 250 but their danger did not last owing to the 100 per cent loss of pilots and planes. In the first mass *kamikaze* attack at Okinawa on 6 April there were 355 planes: in the last on 22 June there were forty-five. According to the Japanese, 4,615 *kamikaze* pilots were killed.

**Kang Youwei** (1858–1927). Chinese scholar and reformer. He alarmed conservative scholar-officials by portraying Confucius as a reformer (see **Confucianism**), who stood for the rights of the people as a check on the authority of the ruler. He believed that China's weakness, cruelly exposed by internal rebellions and the depradations of foreigners (see Treaty of **Shimonoseki** and **'scramble for concessions'**), could be overcome only by changing Chinese institutions and education. China, he thought, should learn from Japan, who had successfully adopted a constitution and become an important East Asian power. He bombarded the Emperor with proposals, many of which were approved in the **Hundred Days Reform** (1898). These reforms ended abruptly when the Empress Dowager, **Cixi**, staged a *coup*. Kang avoided arrest and execution with British help and spent the next fifteen years in exile. During this time he saw many of the changes he had advocated take place. Kang remained loyal to the **Qing dynasty** and when he returned to China in 1913 became a fierce critic of **Sun Yixian** (Sun Yatsen) and the Republic. He spent the rest of his life in a futile effort to restore imperial rule.

**Kansas–Nebraska Act** (1854) allowed settlers in the new territories of Kansas and Nebraska to decide whether they wanted slavery there. The author of the Act was Stephen **Douglas**, a Democratic Senator from Illinois, who had become the leading spokesman for **westward expansion**. As Chairman of the Senate Committee on Territories he introduced a bill to organize the area of the Great Plains west of Iowa and Missouri, territory which extended north to the Canadian border and west to the Rockies. This area was divided into two: Kansas and Nebraska. He also had an interest in the route of the **transcontinental railroad**. There were two possible routes: a southern one from New Orleans to Los Angeles and a northern one from Chicago to San Francisco. As a Chicago property-owner Douglas favoured the northern route but without Southern support his bill would not pass Congress. He therefore proposed to make concessions to the South in his Kansas–Nebraska bill. These territories were part of the **Louisiana Purchase** and were north of latitude 36° 30′, so were closed to slavery by the **Missouri Compromise** of 1820. Douglas proposed that the question of slavery in these territories should be decided by 'popular sovereignty', which meant by the white people living there. He claimed that this 'superseded' the Missouri Compromise, which was 'inoperative and void'. This bill opened to slavery an area from which it had been excluded, but Douglas saw no problem. He thought that it would satisfy the South without damaging the North, as he was convinced that the climate and soil in Kansas and Nebraska were unsuited to cotton cultivation, so slavery would not in fact be extended there. He also thought that the question of popular sovereignty would defuse the question of slavery, as each territory could decide for itself what it wanted. He failed to understand that for many Northerners slavery was a moral, not a practical, problem.

The bill was passed in May 1854 but both parties split on the issue. Every Northern **Whig** opposed it; nearly every Southern Whig supported it. In Douglas's own party the Southern Democrats supported it but only half of those in the North. A new and completely Northern political party was born on 6 July 1854, the **Republican Party**, pledged to oppose the extension of slavery. The passing of the Act, according to the *New York Times*, produced 'ineradicable hatred' and was followed in 'bleeding Kansas' by five years of violence, which horrified Douglas, between pro- and anti-slavery groups. Eventually Kansas entered the Union as a free state in 1861, Nebraska in 1867.

**Kapp** *Putsch* (13–17 March 1920). An attempt to overthrow the **Weimar Republic** by **Free Corps** units near Berlin and officers who were appalled at the reduction in the size of the German army, as a result of the Treaty of **Versailles**. The revolt was led by General von Luttwitz, commandant in Berlin, and Wolfgang Kapp, a Prussian civil servant and founder of the extreme right-wing Fatherland Party in 1917. Luttwitz and a Free Corps brigade marched into Berlin on 13 March and were greeted by their supporters, including General **Ludendorff**. The President of the Republic, Friedrich **Ebert**, called on the army Chief of Staff, General von **Seeckt**, to put down the rising but was told that 'troops do not fire on troops'. The government therefore withdrew to Dresden and a new government, with Kapp and Luttwitz at its head, was set up in Berlin. It looked as if the Weimar Republic had come to an end after only one year. It was saved by the workers, who went on strike and paralysed the city. Most army officers remained loyal and civil servants would not accept orders from Kapp, so after four days Kapp and Luttwitz fled and the *Putsch* collapsed. Little was done to discipline officers who had supported the *Putsch*, as the government needed the army to deal with disorder in the Ruhr. There, communists had formed a Red Army and taken over most of the industrial centres. When they would not disband Ebert called on Seeckt to restore order in the Ruhr. This time Seeckt, willing to fight against the **Left** but not the **Right**, acted promptly and with the aid of the Free Corps put down the rising brutally. When the Kapp conspirators were brought to trial they were lighty treated by the courts, as in all cases of right-wing attacks on the Republic. Kapp died in prison before his trial but Luttwiz was simply compelled to retire from the army.

**Katyn massacre.** Murder of Polish officers by the Soviet **NKVD** in 1940. When the Russians occupied Poland east of the **Curzon Line** in 1939, in accordance with the **Nazi–Soviet Pact**, they interned 15,000 Polish officers in three Russian camps. In April 1943 the Germans uncovered near Smolensk a mass grave, containing the bodies of over 4,000 Polish officers, all of whom had been shot in the back of the head. The Polish Red Cross and a German medical team concluded that they had been murdered, presumably by the NKVD at Katyn, in April 1940. The Soviet government indignantly rejected this and said that they had been murdered by the Germans, after they had conquered the area. When the Polish government-in-exile in London demanded an investigation by the International Red Cross, **Stalin** broke off relations with it. The British government knew the truth in 1943 but suppressed it so as not to offend Stalin, and Anthony Eden even supported the Soviet view in the House of Commons. The Tass news agency cleared up the mystery when it announced on 13 April 1990 that the Soviet Union had been responsible for the murder of 15,131 Polish officers, who had been executed by the NKVD.

**Kemal Atatürk (Mustafa Kemal)** (1881–1938). Turkish soldier and statesman. An imperious figure, with a very strong will, Mustafa Kemal had immense vitality, sometimes occupied in hard drinking and womanizing. He was Turkey's most successful soldier during the **First World War**, saved the capital Istanbul from capture during the **Gallipoli Campaign** and afterwards fought in the Caucasus against the Russians and in Palestine. At the end of the war Turkey was demoralized and the Sultan was prepared to accept any terms the Allies imposed on him. When the Greeks landed at Izmir (Smyrna) in May 1919, intent on annexing much of western Anatolia, where there were substantial Greek minorities, the Sultan ordered Turkish troops not to resist. Mustafa Kemal was sent to Samsun on the Black Sea and told to disband the Turkish Ninth Army. Instead he organized an army of national resistance to prevent the partition of Anatolia. In opposition to the Sultan's government a national assembly met in Ankara, elected Mustafa

Kemal President and rejected the harsh terms of the Treaty of **Sèvres** (August 1920), which would have deprived Turkey of some of her richest provinces. The bitter struggle against the Greeks culminated in a twenty-one day battle at Sakarya (August 1921), in which the Turks, led by Mustafa Kemal, won an overwhelming victory. After that the Turks were able to obtain much better terms from the Allies at the Treaty of **Lausanne**, which left Turkey independent, with her present boundaries.

With military victory behind him Mustafa Kemal rejected foreign adventures to concentrate on the reconstruction of Turkey, appearing in top hat and tails instead of a military uniform. In 1923 the Ottoman Sultanate was abolished and Turkey was declared a Republic by the National Assembly, with Mustafa Kemal named President for life. He was the head of the government (which moved to Ankara, the new capital in the heart of Anatolia) and of the Republican People's Party, formed in 1922 but, in spite of appearances, Turkey was a dictatorship. Opposition parties – the Progressive Party in 1924 and the Liberal Party in 1929–30 – were allowed for only brief periods, the Assembly representing only the Republican People's Party for most of the time. Mustafa Kemal thought that the only way to make Turkey strong was by Westernization, and this involved destroying Islamic institutions. The Caliphate was abolished in 1924, *waqf* (religious endowments) and the *ulama* (religious leaders) were put under government control and the Gregorian replaced the Muslim calendar. In 1925, after a Kurdish rebellion led by dervishes, all Sufi orders were abolished: their mosques and convents became museums. The wearing of the fez was forbidden and replaced by the hat, in which it was impossible to perform Muslim prayer. A new civil code, based on that of Switzerland, replaced the *sharia* (Muslim law). This abolished polygamy and the repudiation of a wife by her husband and replaced it by civil marriage and divorce, with equal rights for each party. The Constitution gave women the same rights as men in education and employment and in 1934 they were given the right to vote. A year later women were elected for the first time to the Turkish parliament. Arabic was the language of the Quran, so in 1928 a Latin script replaced Arabic for the writing of Turkish. All Turks were required to take surnames in the Western fashion in 1935, so that Mustafa Kemal became Kemal Atatürk (the National Assembly gave him the title 'Atatürk', meaning 'Father Turk'). Finally, Islam was disestablished and deprived of any role in public life. In addition to these cultural changes, Atatürk tried to modernize the Turkish economy. As Turkish capitalism was so undeveloped, the state played a leading role in economic development. Textile factories were built in the 1920s with Soviet loans and expertise. When export markets collapsed with the **Great Depression**, there was even more state control and planning, with a Five Year Plan (1929–33) on the Soviet model to promote consumer industries. This did not indicate approval of **communism** but was a purely pragmatic response to circumstances. Atatürk's dictatorship has been criticized for dividing town and country, for creating a highly educated urban and military Westernized élite which ran the state but which was totally divorced from the mass of rural peasants, whose allegiance was still to Islam. Yet there is no doubt that Atatürk helped the Turkish people to recover from a desperate situation at the end of the First World War and that he laid the foundations for a modern economy. Turkey still retains the secular institutions which he introduced.

**Kerensky, Alexander** (1881–1970). Russian revolutionary. A **Socialist Revolutionary** lawyer, he became a leading member of the **Soviet** in **Petrograd** and Minister of Justice in the **Provisional Government** after the fall of the Tsar in the **February Revolution**, 1917. In May he became Minister of War and in July Prime Minister, as a result of the **July Days**. Kerensky was a popular politician and spell-binding orator but he lacked **Lenin**'s singleness of purpose and ruthlessness. He was a sincere democrat and socialist and tried to hold together all the different factions in Russia, an impossible task in 1917. His failure to deal with pressing problems – the peasants' desire for land, the soldiers' wish to end the war and economic chaos – led to the **Bolsheviks** gaining more and more support. Kerensky's dispute with the Army Commander General **Kornilov**, about the means needed to suppress the Bolsheviks, weakened his position, as did Kornilov's attempted *coup*. When a rising was being openly prepared by the Bolsheviks, he fell into a state of fatalistic apathy and did little. After the **October Revolu-**

**tion** he was in hiding for several months before escaping to Western Europe. He emigrated to America in 1940 and spent the rest of his long life there.

**Keynes, John Maynard, Baron** (1883–1946). English economist and government adviser. Coming from an academic family in Cambridge (his mother was the first woman mayor of the city), he was educated at Eton and King's College, Cambridge, where he read mathematics. At Cambridge he was President of the Liberal Club and of the Union Society and a member of a select circle, the 'Apostles', which included homosexuals such as Lytton Strachey and Duncan Grant, with whom he had a close relationship (Keynes was bisexual). They later formed the nucleus of the Bloomsbury group. From 1908 Keynes taught economics at Cambridge and in the **First World War** worked in the Treasury, which he represented at the **Paris Peace Conference**. In June 1919 he resigned, owing to the heavy **reparations** imposed on Germany at the Treaty of **Versailles**, which he thought would make the economic recovery of Europe impossible. His criticisms were made public in his *Economic Consequences of the Peace* (1919). Financial deals made Keynes rich and in 1925 he married the ballerina Lydia Lopokova. He criticized the return to the **gold standard** in 1925 at its pre-war parity, as he thought that the overvaluation of sterling would increase unemployment. In the late 1920s he was involved in **Liberal Party** politics and helped **Lloyd George** to produce for the 1929 election a programme which included public works to reduce unemployment. When the **Labour Party** government was in power, he supported Sir Oswald **Mosley**'s plans to revive the economy.

From 1931 he devoted his time to economic theory, the fruits of which appeared in *The General Theory of Employment, Interest and Money* (1936). Keynes was concerned that unemployment could not be cured by applying classical economic theory. This said that unemployment would lead to falling wages and therefore lower costs of production, which in turn would produce a greater demand for goods and this would reduce unemployment. The government should not interfere by spending money on public works to stimulate employment, as this would divert funds to the public from the private sector. Left to itself the economy was self-adjusting and would produce full employment. Clearly this had not happened in the 1920s and 1930s, when high unemployment and unused industrial capacity had persisted. To deal with this problem Keynes devised a new economic theory, which took into account the institutional rigidities which classical economics ignored (for example, trade-union pressure might keep wages high and tariffs prevent competition). Keynes saw that a depression was caused by inadequate aggregate demand (i.e. the total spending of consumers, business and government). To counter this governments should lower interest rates (a 'cheap money' policy) and, if this did not stimulate investment sufficiently, they should substitute state action for inadequate private investment by granting subsidies or by undertaking a programme of public works, which would create employment and a demand for the products of industry. Thus, monetary policy and government spending would work together to produce full employment. Many regarded Keynesian economics as little different from **socialism**, whereas Keynes favoured a mixed economy and was offering capitalism a lifeline when it appeared to be drowning. Franklin D. **Roosevelt**'s **New Deal** was in line with Keynes's ideas, which were widely accepted in the **Second World War**. In 1940 he returned to the Treasury, where his influence was seen in the 1944 White Paper, which committed the government to seek full employment after the war. Increasingly Keynes was concerned with the international economy and played a leading part at the **Bretton Woods Conference** (1944), which helped to set up the International Monetary Fund and the World Bank. When Lend-Lease (see **Lend-Lease Act**) ceased at the end of the war he represented Britain in long and difficult negotiations to obtain a loan from the USA. The effort was too much for him – he had suffered a major heart attack in 1937 – and he died suddenly at Easter 1946.

**Kiangsi Soviet,** see **Jiangxi Soviet**

**King, William Lyon Mackenzie** (1874–1950). Canadian Prime Minister (1921–30, 1935–48). King became deputy Minister of Labour in the Liberal government of Sir Wilfrid **Laurier** in 1900. A podgy figure, who was not at all charismatic, he was chosen in 1919 as Liberal leader, on the death of Laurier, largely because he had not deserted his leader over the conscription crisis of 1917, when several leading Liberals joined the Union government (1917–20). He was thus acceptable to French Canadians and retained their support by making Ernest Lapointe his deputy. He was to be Prime Minister for twenty-one years, largely because he was a master of compromise and divided Canadians least. His main concern was for unity and this made him cautious: he consequently avoided social reforms, did not interfere with provincial rights and pursued an isolationist foreign policy. In dealing with the workers he seemed more concerned with social order than workers' rights. When there was a strike in Nova Scotia in 1922 – the British Empire Steel Corporation had cut wages by $37\frac{1}{2}$ per cent – King said the government had no constitutional right to intervene. He left the matter to the Nova Scotia government, which sent in police to break up the strike. King refused to establish a federal system of unemployment insurance, though he did secure the passage of an Old Age Pensions Act in 1927. The **Great Depression**, which began in 1929, hit Canada particularly badly, as she depended on her exports of grain and raw materials, but King resisted demands for federal action and was defeated in the 1930 election by the ebullient Conservative Richard **Bennett**.

At the Imperial Conference in 1923 King obtained for Canada complete independence in its foreign policy, when it was agreed that **dominions** could in future make their own treaties with foreign powers. In the same year Canada for the first time signed a treaty (with the USA about fisheries) without seeking British consent and in 1927 appointed a Canadian minister to Washington. King rejected appeals for collective security in the 1930s and followed a policy of 'no commitments', which fitted in well with the isolationist mood of many Canadians. The English-speaking Canadians assumed that Canada would support Britain in any major war and King thought this too, but if such a war broke out he wanted to bring Canada into it united. This he did in 1939, aided by Lapointe's promise that there would be no conscription for overseas service. He kept this pledge till November 1944, when 16,000 home defence conscripts were sent overseas. There were angry protests in Quebec but King survived. Industry boomed during the war – a million people worked directly in war industries, producing ships, aircraft, weapons and munitions. Another million served in the armed forces, of whom 42,000 were killed. After the war Canada became a member of the United Nations, though King showed as little enthusiasm for it as he had done for the **League of Nations**. King served as Prime Minister for longer than any other political leader in the Commonwealth. After his death his reputation suffered through revelations of his naïve enthusiasm for spiritualism.

**Kirov, Sergei Mironovich** (1886–1934), became the **Communist Party** boss in Leningrad in 1926. At the Party Congress in January 1934 Kirov condemned **collectivization** and 'extremism' in dealing with the peasants and was promoted. He was to move to Moscow to join **Stalin** in the Secretariat but before he could do that he was assassinated in December 1934. The most common view is that Stalin organized Kirov's murder in order to get rid of a rival: Khrushchev hinted in 1956 that his murder might have been organized from above. Mikoyan's memoirs, published in 1987, confirm that Stalin was alarmed at Kirov's growing popularity. His death is generally held to mark the beginning of the **Great Purges**, as Stalin accused other leading communists of being responsible for it. In the first of the show trials in 1936 **Kamenev** and **Zinoviev** made spurious confessions that they had organized Kirov's murder and were executed.

**Kita Ikki** (1888–1937). Japanese nationalist. Kita was a socialist before he became an ardent nationalist and never gave up his radical ideas. His influence was mainly through his writings, especially his *Outline Plan for the Reconstruction of Japan* (1919), in which he called for a military *coup*, suspension of the Constitution and a declaration of martial law. The supreme power under the Emperor should be held by the armed forces. He also advocated the confiscation of large personal fortunes, the nationalization of major industries and a welfare state, with profit-sharing for workers and participation in management. Only Japan, he thought, was capable of expelling the West from Asia, so he supported all moves to make her stronger, including expansion in Asia. Kita greatly influenced young army officers, who were often anti-capitalist as well as being fervent nationalists. He was accused of involvement in the **February Rising** in 1936 and was executed a year later.

**Kitchener, Horatio Herbert, 1st Earl** (1850–1916). British field marshal. An excellent linguist, he spoke fluent French as he was educated in Switzerland and learnt Arabic when he went to Palestine in 1874. He took part as a junior officer in the British occupation of Egypt in 1882 and in General **Wolseley**'s unsuccessful attempt to relieve **Gordon** at Khartoum in 1885. In 1889 he became Sirdar (Commander-in-Chief) of the Egyptian army and with it began the reconquest of the Sudan in 1896. He defeated the **Mahdist** forces at the battle of **Omdurman** in September 1898 and then moved south to confront the small French expedition which had reached the Nile at **Fashoda**. By a mixture of tact, courtesy and a show of superior force, he persuaded the French to withdraw. In 1889 he became Governor-General of the Sudan but in the same year the **South African War** (1899–1902) began. After initial British defeats Lord Roberts was sent to command British forces there, with Kitchener as his Chief of Staff. When the war was apparently over with the capture of the Boer capital of Pretoria, Roberts returned home in 1900, leaving Kitchener as Commander-in-Chief. He was faced, not with the end of hostilities, but with a guerrilla war, which went on for the next two years. To defeat the Boer commandos Kitchener adopted a scorched-earth policy and herded Boer women and children into **concentration camps**, where 2,700 of them died as well as many thousands of Africans. For this he was much criticized in both South Africa and Britain. From 1902–9 Kitchener was Commander-in-Chief of the Indian army, where he clashed with the Viceroy, Lord **Curzon**, over the extent of his authority and this led to Curzon's resignation. In 1911 Kitchener was promoted to field marshal and became Consul-General in Egypt, which meant that he was the effective head of the Egyptian government. On the outbreak of the **First World War** he was made War Secretary by **Asquith**, the first serving officer to hold this post. He startled the first Cabinet meeting he attended by informing his colleagues that the war would last for three or four years. His main contribution to the war effort was to raise a volunteer army of three million men: 'Your country needs YOU' he proclaimed in thousands of posters with a stern, admonitory finger. He had complete control of British strategy until the autumn of 1915 and insisted on total support for the

French in the battle of the **Marne**. Popular with the public, he was disliked by his colleagues as he was secretive and contemptuous of politicians, from whom he became increasingly isolated. Without friends, his authority waned when he vacillated over the evacuation of British and **dominion** troops from the **Gallipoli Campaign**. When Sir William Robertson became Chief of the Imperial General Staff in December 1915 he replaced Kitchener as the government's chief military adviser. In June 1916 the cruiser in which Kitchener was travelling to Russia was sunk by a mine and he was drowned.

**Know-Nothings.** American political party in the mid-nineteenth century. Native-born Americans became alarmed at the number of immigrants (there were three million in 1846–54), who were prepared to work for low wages, and the number of Catholics among them. Secret societies, many of which were specifically anti-Irish, were formed in the late 1840s to counter this menace. Their members, when questioned by outsiders, were supposed to say 'I know nothing.' Their aim was not to abolish immigration but to prevent Catholics and foreigners from holding public office; they also wanted stricter naturalization laws and literacy tests for voting. These societies merged and campaigned nationally in 1854 as the American Party with support from Protestants and small business-men. They had striking success and won 104 out of 234 seats in Congress. Lincoln was not impressed. 'I am not a Know-Nothing,' he said. 'How could I be? How can anyone who abhors the oppression of Negroes be in favour of defrauding classes of white men?' The Know-Nothings declined as rapidly as they had risen, largely because they split over the question of slavery. At the Party's first national convention in 1855 Southern Know-Nothings pushed through a motion supporting the **Kansas–Nebraska Act**, whereupon Northern delegates walked out. The Party nominated Millard Fillmore as President in 1856 but won only one state and soon disintegrated. Many joined the **Republican Party**, who quickly accepted Know-Nothing principles: it was to be the party of Protestants and the native-born well into the twentieth century.

**Kollontai, Alexandra** (1872–1952). Russian revolutionary. Kollontai joined the **Bolsheviks** in 1914 and became a member of the party's Central Committee in 1917. After the **October Revolution** she became the only woman in **Lenin**'s government, in which she was Commissar of Social Welfare and Director of the Women's Department of the Party. She disliked *bourgeois* morality and the nuclear family and promoted communal living. Her support for 'free love' was interpreted as promiscuity and earned her hostility both in the Soviet Union and abroad. As Commissar, Kollontai introduced laws to permit civil marriage, easy divorce and abortion. Many women took advantage of the new laws. As a member of the **Workers' Opposition** within the Bolshevik Party she articulated dissatisfaction with the bureaucracy, élitism and dictatorship of the Party. For this she was condemned by Lenin and in 1922 was banished to a diplomatic post in Oslo; from 1930–45 she was Soviet ambassador in Sweden. She remained loyal to the Party that rejected her ideas and became a source of inspiration to many feminists in the West.

**Königgrätz, battle of** (1866), see **Sadowa**

**Kornilov affair** (August 1917). After the failure of the **Brusilov offensive** and the disintegration of the Russian army, **Kerensky**, the Prime Minister, appointed General Kornilov as Commander-in-Chief on 18 July. He accepted on condition that discipline was restored and firm action was taken against the **Bolsheviks**. There is no evidence that Kornilov intended to establish a personal dictatorship, though he and Kerensky came to misunderstand the intentions of each other, as they communicated through intermediaries. After Riga fell to the Germans on 21 August, Kornilov proposed to march on **Petrograd** to prevent an expected Bolshevik rising. He thought Kerensky had agreed to this. However, the Prime Minister, who was also vice-chairman of the **Soviet**, realized that this would not have the support of the Soviet and might provoke a popular rising. He therefore dismissed Kornilov, who nevertheless continued his advance. He was stopped by railwaymen, who halted the troop trains, and by a hastily formed workers' militia. The Soviet organized the resistance but Bolshevik militants led it; Kornilov was forced into a humiliating surrender and was arrested. The affair left the High Command demoralized and resentful. However, the most important effect was the revival of Bolshevik fortunes, which had been at a low ebb after the **July Days**. In September the Petrograd and Moscow Soviets had their first Bolshevik majorities and it was clear that the Bolsheviks would be the largest party when the All-Russian Congress of Soviets was elected in October. These moves gave **Lenin** the confidence to organize the **October Revolution**.

**Kossuth, Lajos** (1802–94). Hungarian nationalist and revolutionary. A poor, Protestant, Hungarian noble, he led Hungary's struggle for independence from the **Austrian Empire** during the **Revolutions of 1848–9**. Elected to the Hungarian **Diet** in 1847, he put forward a radical programme, which was passed by the Diet in 1848. The March Laws gave Hungary virtual independence, as she had her own parliament, to which ministers were responsible, and her own army: the only connection with the Austrian Empire was that the Emperor of Austria was also King of Hungary. The nobles lost their exemption from taxation, the peasants were emancipated, there was equality before the law and the censorship of the press was abolished. These liberal measures were accompanied by others designed to ensure Magyar dominance within Hungary (other nationalities – Croats, Serbs, Romanians, Slovaks and Germans – formed over half the population), as Transylvania and Croatia lost their own Diets and candidates for the Hungarian Diet had to speak Magyar. The Emperor Ferdinand, preoccupied with revolution in Vienna, accepted the March Laws but Kossuth lost the support of half the population by refusing to recognize the equality of all nationalities. The Croats, led by Jellacić, revolted against the Magyars in July and in October Ferdinand declared war on the Hungarian regime. In April 1849 Hungary declared its independence and elected Kossuth as Governor. Hungarian forces had at first considerable success against the Austrians but they never linked up with the Viennese or Italian rebels and their fate was sealed when Tsar **Nicholas I** sent 150,000 troops to help the Austrians put down the rebellion. In August 1849 the Hungarians surrendered to the Russians and Kossuth fled to Turkey and later to France, Britain and the USA. He remained an exile for the rest of his life and strongly opposed the *Ausgleich* (1867). Yet he was revered as a national hero: when he died in 1894 his body was brought back to Hungary and buried amidst nation-wide mourning.

*Kristallnacht*, see **Crystal Night**

**Kronstadt Rising** (1921). Kronstadt was a Russian naval base, where the Baltic fleet had its headquarters on an island in the Gulf of Finland, twenty miles from **Petrograd**. The Petrograd sailors had become revolutionaries in 1905, when they first set up a **Soviet** and they played a vital part in the **Bolshevik** seizure of power in the **October Revolution**. They saw Soviets as free, self-governing communities but had a Bolshevik dictatorship imposed upon them. When the **Russian Civil War** was over their discontent with the rule of political commissars led them to return to their 1917 programme: 'All power to the Soviets and not to Parties.' A delegation of sailors met Petrograd workers and reported back to a large meeting at Kronstadt on 1 March. Among its demands were freedom of speech and of the press, for 'workers and peasants, anarchists and left socialist parties', for multi-party elections to the Soviet, and for the abolition of the **Cheka** and **Communist Party** military units, as 'no single party should have special privileges'. **Lenin** denounced the revolt as a White Guard plot, which it was not. As the sea is frozen over in the winter the Red Army was able to storm Kronstadt over the ice. There were heavy losses on both sides, made worse as the Cheka afterwards shot hundreds of those involved.

This popular rising was a humiliation for the Bolshevik Party and showed its deep unpopularity but it was never a serious threat: not one member of the **Workers' Opposition** supported the rebels. It led directly to **NEP**, adopted on 21 March 1921, as Lenin realized the need for compromise on economic matters. There was to be no political compromise, however. **Mensheviks** and the **Socialist Revolutionary Party** were now formally outlawed and Lenin used the rising to defeat the Workers' Opposition.

**Kruger, Paul (Stephanus Johannes Paulus)** (1825–1904). Boer leader and a great hero of **Afrikaner** nationalism. Kruger was born in the Cape Colony into a landless farming family, who moved round the eastern Cape in search of grazing land. He disliked the British, especially with the abolition of slavery (his parents were slave-owners), and in 1836 joined in the **Great Trek** across the Orange river, where he fought against the Ndebele and Zulus. By 1850 he had settled in the Transvaal, where he became commandant-general (military leader) in 1863. He was a leading figure in opposing British annexation of the Transvaal (1877) and regained independence for his country in the first **South African War** (1881). In 1883 he became President of the South African Republic (SAR or Transvaal), a position he retained until 1900. The land-locked SAR was the poorest state in South Africa until gold was discovered on the **Rand** in 1885. This rapidly made it the richest state. Gold mining made the SAR wealthy but it presented problems for Kruger, as it led to the influx of many non-Boer whites (*uitlanders*) into the SAR. Kruger, a strict Christian and member of a conservative wing of the Dutch Reformed Church, had no intention of allowing pagan intruders to take control of his country and refused to give them any political rights. Capitalists on the Rand and in the Cape, led by Cecil **Rhodes**, decided to make use of *uitlander* discontent to overthrow Kruger, but the **Jameson Raid** (1895) was a miserable failure and left Kruger strengthened. The British High Commissioner, Alfred **Milner**, now stepped in to put pressure on Kruger to reform the political system in the SAR. When it became clear to Kruger that Britain wanted to take over control of the SAR, the second **South African War** (1899–1902) began. As the British approached Pretoria in 1900, Kruger left for Europe to seek aid for the SAR. He failed to find any and so lived in exile in the Netherlands, and died in Switzerland.

**Krupp family.** German industrialists based in Essen. The firm was founded in 1811 but was very small and did not expand greatly until the railway boom of the 1850s. In 1859 Krupps received its first order for cast steel cannon barrels from the Prussian government and soon became the largest arms supplier in the world. The firm also extended its activities to mining in the Ruhr and shipbuilding. Krupps were paternalistic employers, who introduced a welfare scheme for their workers (a sickness and burial fund in 1836, a pension scheme in 1855 and a housing fund in 1861) which acted as a model for **Bismarck's State Socialism**. On the death of Friedrich Krupp in 1902 the firm passed to his daughter Bertha (1886–1957), who in 1906 married Gustav von Bohlen (1870–1950). He was allowed to change his name to Gustav Krupp von Bohlen and was the effective head of the Krupp empire from 1909–43. During the

**First World War** Krupps supplied most of the arms for Germany and her allies, including the 'Big Bertha', which bombarded Paris from a distance of seventy miles. In 1933, when **Hitler** promised to increase the army and get rid of Marxists, Gustav Krupp became a Nazi supporter and provided them with money for their election campaign. During the **Second World War** Krupp used 100,000 slave labourers and Russian prisoners of war, in conditions which were hardly better than those in the **concentration camps** and where the death rate was almost as high. Alfried Krupp (1907–67), who had sole control of the firm from 1943, built a large fuse factory at Auschwitz, where Jews were worked until they were exhausted and then gassed. He was sentenced to twelve years' imprisonment at the Nuremberg trials and all his property was confiscated, but he served only three years and his property was returned. Krupps again became the leading steel producer in Germany, though financial difficulties during the recession of the mid-1960s led to control of the firm passing to the big German banks. Krupps recovered but was no longer a family firm.

**Ku Klux Klan.** An organization to preserve white supremacy in the South after the **American Civil War** and to make **Reconstruction** ineffective. 'Ku Klux' comes from the Greek word *kuklos*, 'drinking-bowl'. The Klan began in Tennessee in 1866, as a secret society with an elaborate ritual, and soon spread throughout the South. Members dressed up in white hoods and sheets and rode out at night carrying burning crosses. Their aim was to intimidate Negroes, drive them from their land and prevent them from voting. When intimidation did not work Klansmen turned to violence, not only against Negroes but against **carpetbaggers** and **scalawags** as well. Opponents were flogged, tarred and feathered, their homes burnt and many were lynched. The violence produced a backlash. Congress passed a Force Act in 1870, which imposed heavy fines for using force or intimidation to prevent people voting. In 1871 the Klan and similar organizations were outlawed. President **Grant** enforced the laws rigorously, proclaimed martial law and sent in troops. By the end of 1871 the Klan was effectively suppressed.

The Klan was resurrected in Georgia in 1915, aided by D. W.

Griffith's film *The Birth of a Nation*, which glorified the earlier Klan. This time it did not simply promote white supremacy but was also directed against minority groups, such as Jews, Catholics and immigrants. It spread in the North and Mid-West as well as the South, where flogging and branding returned, though most Klansmen kept within the law. By 1925 the Klan had over four million members, including some state officials and Congressmen. In the same year the Grand Dragon of the Indiana Klan, convicted of kidnapping and raping a secretary, who committed suicide, exposed the corruption of some leading state officials who were Klansmen. Thereafter there was a dramatic fall in membership, so that by 1930 there were only 10,000 Klansmen.

**Kulak.** The Russian word for 'fist' in the sense of 'tight-fisted', it was applied to the richer peasants, who hired labour, hired out their plough teams and loaned money to the poorer peasants. They tended to dominate the *mir*. **Stolypin**, with his 'wager on the strong', tried to create a large class of wealthy, independent farmers. War and revolution ended his plans, though *kulaks* thrived again under **NEP**. In 1929 Stalin decided on 'a policy of liquidating the kulaks as a class', as they stood in the way of his **collectivization** drive. They were not allowed to join the collectives but were deported thousands of miles to Siberia, the Urals or north Russia. The most common estimate is that one million households (about five million peasants) were deported, although some historians double the figure. *Kulaks* who actively resisted, sometimes by taking up arms, were either shot or sent to **forced labour camps**, where they formed the first large group of convicts.

**Kulturkampf** ('cultural struggle'). An attack by **Bismarck** between 1872 and 1887 on the Catholic Church in Germany. Bismarck regarded the Catholics, who were a powerful minority in Germany (37 per cent of the population), as enemies of the Reich, particularly as they supported the Poles and Alsatians, discontented groups within Germany. Traditional opponents of Protestant **Prussia**, they were *großdeutsch* and in favour of Austrian inclusion in Germany. Bismarck accused them of taking their orders from a foreign power (the Pope). 'The question that confronts us,' he said in 1873, 'becomes ... distorted ... if it is looked on as a confessional or religious one. It is essentially political.' As education and religion were state rather than Reich responsibilities, the struggle was waged mainly in Prussia, though some measures, such as compulsory civil marriage and the banning of Jesuits, affected the whole of Germany. The climax of the campaign came with the May Laws, passed in Prussia in 1873, when nearly all aspects of Church life were subjected to state regulation. In 1875 Pope **Pius IX** condemned all the measures of the *Kulturkampf*. Bismarck responded by removing all clergy who would not accept them, so that by 1876 every Prussian bishop was in prison or exile and 1,400 parishes (about a third of the total) had no priest. Far from crushing the Catholic Church, the *Kulturkampf* united all Catholics in opposition to Bismarck's policies: this was shown in the 1874 **Reichstag** elections, when the Catholic **Centre Party** doubled its vote and won ninety-five seats. By the late 1870s Bismarck was prepared to abandon the *Kulturkampf*, as he wanted to free himself from his dependence in the Reichstag on the **National Liberal Party**, especially as he wanted to move to a policy of protection and an alliance with Austria. These policies were opposed by the Liberals but supported by the Centre Party. Bismarck was helped in his change of course by a new Pope, **Leo XIII**, in 1878, who wanted friendly relations with Germany. The conflict officially ended in 1887, by which time most of the anti-Catholic laws had been repealed: only state inspection of schools, civil marriage and the banning of Jesuits remained.

**Kun, Bela** (1886–1937). Hungarian communist. A middle-class Jew and journalist, Kun served in the Austro-Hungarian army in the **First World War** and was captured by the Russians in 1916. After the **October Revolution** (1917) he joined the **Bolsheviks** and returned to Hungary in 1918 to found the Hungarian Communist Party. In 1919 he persuaded the Social Democrats to join the Communists in a coalition government. Although the Communists had only 7,000 members, they dominated the government. Kun was Commissar for Foreign Affairs and established a dictatorship, using terror in imitation of the **Cheka**. He nationalized industry and the large estates (thus losing the support of the peasants, who wanted the land for themselves) and formed a Red Army, which fought successfully in Slovakia and set up a Soviet regime there.

Faced with invasion by Czechs and Romanians and a counter-revolutionary army organized by **Horthy**, only help from the Bolsheviks could have saved him but they were occupied with the **Russian Civil War** (1918–21). After four and a half months the regime – the only communist government outside Russia at that time – collapsed. Kun fled to Vienna and then to Moscow, from where, as a member of the **Comintern**, he tried unsuccessfully to stir up revolutions in Austria and Germany in the 1920s. He was executed in the **Great Purges** of **Stalin**, probably in 1937.

**Kuomintang,** see **Guomindang**

**Kursk, battle of** (July 1943). The last major German offensive on the **Eastern Front** and the greatest tank battle ever fought. Two million men, 6,000 tanks and 4,000 aircraft were involved. After the defeat of the German army at **Stalingrad**, **Hitler** wanted to recover the initiative. At Kursk, which the Russians had recaptured in February, there was a salient 100 miles deep and 150 miles wide. The Germans were tempted to attack from both north and south, cut off the salient and trap five Russian armies. The Russians were well aware of what the Germans would try to do and knew the details of their plan from intelligence sources. The attack was planned for May but was put off for two months so the Germans could bring up more tanks. This delay gave the Russians time to build eight concentric lines of defence and to mass 1.3 million men and nearly all their armour in the salient. A great asset was the appearance for the first time of two new Russian tanks, the SU122 and SU152, which were superior to all the German tanks. When the Germans attacked on 5 July they were able to gain only six miles in the north. **Manstein** did better in the south, advancing twenty-five miles before he was stopped. On 12 July, the day the Russians counter-attacked, Hitler ordered some troops to be moved to the west, where the Allies had invaded Sicily on 10 July. By the 23rd the Germans were back where they had started and defeat turned into rout, as the German armies were in danger of being cut off by Russian attacks north of the salient towards Orel and south towards Kharkov. The Germans lost 70,000 men, 3,000 tanks and 1,400 planes in the battle. Soviet losses are not known but were probably slightly less, although the Russians could make good their losses and the Germans could not. This was as big a disaster for the *Wehrmacht* as Stalingrad: with such heavy losses the Germans could not mount another offensive on the Eastern Front.

**Labor Party** (Australia). Labour groups, with various names, arose in the 1880s and 1890s in the different Australian colonies. They did not believe in the violent overthrow of capitalism by revolution but favoured social reform through parliament and the maintenance of a **White Australia policy**. The state organizations entered national politics with the first federal elections in 1901, though they did not adopt the name Australia Labor Party until 1918. The Labor Party was the first party to win a majority in both Houses of Parliament in 1910 and in the next three years carried out a wide-ranging programme of reform. A Commonwealth Bank was founded and a national currency introduced, old-age pensions were extended and sickness and maternity benefits brought in, though only for whites. The first Australian coins (which replaced English ones) were minted and the first Australian postage stamps were issued, when the Commonwealth took over postal services from the states. A land tax on unimproved properties (inspired by Henry **George**) raised a lot of revenue and a start was made on a railway line from Port Augusta in South Australia to Kalgoorlie in Western Australia, which would link east and west. The Labor Party, in power again in 1915, was divided by **Hughes** over conscription. When he left Labor and formed his own Nationalist Party, whilst remaining as Prime Minister, Labor became the opposition. They were further weakened when their left wing broke away in 1920 to form the Communist Party and did not become a government again until 1929. Faced with the **Great Depression**, Labor increased taxes, cut defence expenditure and raised tariffs but split over the decision to cut pensions and salaries of civil servants by 20 per cent. **Lyons** left them to join with the Nationalist Party in forming the United Australia Party, which kept Labor out of office until 1941, when **Curtin** became Prime Minister. Labor remained in power for the rest of the war.

**Labour Party** (Britain). An **Independent Labour Party** (ILP) had been formed by Keir **Hardie** and others in 1893 but it was very weak and all its candidates were defeated in the 1895 election. Some ILP members and trade unionists therefore demanded that the Trade Union Congress (TUC) should call a conference of trade unions, cooperative and socialist societies to promote labour representation in parliament. The Labour Representation Committee (LRC), which included representatives of the ILP and the **Fabian Society** as well as of the unions, was therefore formed in 1900. Only two of its candidates were successful in the 1900 election, so in 1903 its secretary, Ramsay **MacDonald**, made a secret agreement with the Liberal chief whip by which about thirty Labour candidates were given a clear run. As a result of this 'Progressive Alliance', twenty-nine Labour candidates were returned in 1906, the year in which the LRC changed its name to the Labour Party. The **Osborne judgment** in 1909 was a severe blow to the Labour Party, as it prevented **trade unions** from contributing to Party funds, but this was largely overturned by **Asquith**'s **Liberal** government in 1913. The Labour Party remained weak up to the **First World War** and appeared dependent on its 'alliance' with the Liberals. Most Labour MPs supported the war but MacDonald did not, so he was replaced by Arthur **Henderson** as leader of the Parliamentary Labour Party (PLP). In 1918 Henderson and Sidney **Webb** drew up a new constitution, which for the first time committed the Labour Party to **socialism**, whilst Henderson used his considerable organizational skills to give the party a strong centralized structure with local branches throughout the country. The PLP withdrew from the **Coalition Government**, in which Henderson had been a member of the War Cabinet, in 1918 but won only fifty-seven seats in the election of that year.

Four years later they became the main party of opposition when, with 142 seats, they had more than the Liberal Party. When **Baldwin** surprisingly called another election in 1923 the **Conservative Party** lost its majority and the PLP, once again under MacDonald, was able to form the first Labour government, though it was dependent on Liberal support. In 1929 with rising unemployment, the PLP won 188 seats and for the first time was the largest party in the House of **Commons** but it had still no clear majority and so formed another minority government. MacDonald had no effective policy to cope with unemployment, and when American bankers demanded cuts in civil service pay and unemployment benefits in return for a loan, nine members of his Cabinet opposed these measures (twelve were in favour) as did the TUC. MacDonald therefore resigned but, without consulting his colleagues, agreed to form a **National Government** with Liberal and Conservative support. Only seven members of the PLP followed him, so the majority, feeling betrayed, became a party of opposition. MacDonald, removed as leader of the PLP and expelled from the Labour Party, further embittered his former colleagues by calling an election in 1931, in which the PLP was reduced to only forty-six MPs. As most Labour leaders lost their seats, the pacifist George Lansbury became leader of the PLP until he was replaced by Clement **Attlee** in 1935. In that year Labour won 154 seats and under the influence of **Dalton** and **Bevin** (who was not an MP but was a powerful figure in the TUC) moved away from its earlier pacifism to support rearmament and an end to **appeasement**. When the **Second World War** began the PLP refused to serve under **Chamberlain** but joined **Churchill**'s coalition government in 1940, Attlee being officially recognized as Deputy Prime Minister in 1942. Labour members of the government gained valuable ministerial experience and were able to develop policies which could be applied when the war ended. In 1945 the PLP surprised everyone by winning 393 seats which gave it for the first time a clear majority (of 146) over all other parties.

**Labour Party** (New Zealand). Formed in 1910 and reconstituted in 1916, its share of the vote rose steadily and in 1925 it replaced the **Liberal Party** (New Zealand) as the offical opposition. To broaden its appeal to farmers it dropped its demand for land nationalization and proposed cheap credit for farmers. In 1935 Labour said nothing about nationalizing the means of production and won the election with the second largest majority in the country's history. It was to remain in power continuously until 1949. The first major reforms since those of the Liberals in the 1890s made New Zealand into a **Welfare State**. Compulsory arbitration in industrial disputes was restored, a minimum wage introduced and a large public works programme undertaken to provide employment on full wages. Houses built by the government were let at low rents. The Social Security Act (1938) increased pensions, extended family allowances and began a national health service and maternity benefits, providing the first comprehensive social security system in the world. Progressive taxation redistributed income from the rich to the poor and from single to married people. Farmers were helped by guaranteed prices for their dairy produce and by the state marketing their exports. Industry was protected against foreign competition by restrictions on imported goods. Broadcasting, internal airlines and the Reserve Bank were nationalized as, in 1945, was the Bank of New Zealand. The Labour government also sought to raise the living standards of Maoris by promoting land development schemes for them. There was a change too in foreign policy, as New Zealand at last played an active role in the **League of Nations**. In 1936 she was elected to the League Council and supported collective security and economic sanctions against aggressors. Alone of the Commonwealth countries she refused to recognize the Italian conquest of Ethiopia.

**Laissez-faire.** This doctrine, that free trade is preferable to protection and that the state should not normally interfere in economic affairs, dominated economic thought in the nineteenth century. The most cogent exposition was in Adam Smith's *Wealth of Nations* (1776), which maintained that tariffs held back world trade and living standards in all countries. Free trade provided competition and so ensured that goods would be of high quality and cheap. This benefited the consumer but the manufacturer gained too, as he became more efficient and made more rational use of his labour by specialization, whereby workers were trained to do fewer jobs more effectively. Although the manufacturer is guided by self-interest, aiming to increase his profit, he benefits society as a whole, as 'he is led by an invisible hand to promote an end which was no part of his intention'. This applied only in a free market: protection and monopolies pushed up prices. The doctrine of *laissez-faire* had important political effects, as it influenced the new **Poor Law** of 1834, the budgets of **Peel** and **Gladstone**, which reduced duties on most imported goods, and the repeal of the **Corn Laws** (1846). The

**Manchester School** in the 1840s was a fervent advocate of *laissez-faire* yet it was not to be applied at all times: the state had to provide services which private enterprise would find unprofitable, such as national defence, the protection of life and property, education and public health. Adam Smith was under no illusion about the class nature of the state: 'Civil government is in reality instituted for the defence of the rich against the poor, or of those who have some property against those who have none at all.' It was therefore the duty of the state to help those who could not protect themselves, such as children working in factories. Most European countries, except Britain, abandoned *laissez-faire* in favour of protective tariffs from the 1870s (Austria–Hungary in 1874, Russia in 1877, Germany in 1879, Italy in 1887, the USA in 1890, France in 1892). Joseph **Chamberlain** unsuccessfully tried to introduce protection to Britain with his **tariff reform** campaign in 1903 but Britain did not abandon free trade until 1932, during the **Great Depression**.

**Lateran Treaties** (1929) were made by Pope **Pius XI** and **Mussolini**. Since 1860, when the Papal States had been incorporated in the new united Kingdom of Italy (to which Rome was added in 1870), the Papacy had refused to recognize the new Kingdom. The hostility of Church and State in Italy came to an end with the Lateran Treaties. The Pope was granted sovereignty over the Vatican territory that had been in his possession since 1870: he recognized Rome as the capital of Italy and renounced all claims to the former papal states. As recompense for the loss of this territory he was given a large sum of money. All Italian bishops were to be appointed by the Pope, though they had to be approved by the State, which agreed to pay the salaries of clergy, who were forbidden to belong to any political party. The Catholic Church was given a privileged position in Italy: Catholicism was recognized as 'the sole religion of the state', religious education was allowed in secondary schools, state recognition was given to religious marriages and the independence of Catholic Action (the only non-Fascist organization allowed to exist) was guaranteed. The treaties were greeted enthusiastically by Catholics everywhere; they did much to increase Mussolini's prestige internationally and his support at home. The Lateran Treaties are recognized in the Constitution of the Italian Republic.

**Laurier, Sir Wilfrid** (1841–1919). The first French Canadian to become Prime Minister (1896–1911) of Canada. Laurier entered politics in Quebec as an anti-clerical Liberal but soon made Liberalism dominant there by making his peace with the Catholic Church. Like **Cartier** he believed that French Canadians would be secure only by being tolerant and by rejecting communal isolation in favour of cooperation with English-speaking Canadians: he set an example by speaking fluently in both languages. He entered the Canadian House of Commons in 1874 and retained a seat there until his death forty-five years later. In 1887 he became leader of the Liberal Party and in 1896, after a Liberal victory, became Prime Minister, a post he held until 1911. Laurier was anxious to reassure the English-speaking business community that there would be no real change in economic policy, so he ended Liberal support for free trade. He was aided by the recovery of world markets after the depression of 1873–96 and by the discovery of gold in the Yukon (see **Gold rushes**) in 1896. Canada's rich mineral reserves – lead and zinc in British Columbia, nickel, silver and copper in Ontario – began to be developed, along with a new paper-making industry, based on the forests of British Columbia and central Canada. Heavy American investment contributed to the boom, in which agriculture shared: two new provinces, Alberta and Saskatchewan, were established in the wheat belt in 1905. Laurier kept tariffs high to protect industry, subsidized wages and was responsible for Canada supporting Britain in the **South African War** (1899–1902), in which Canadian troops fought. He made his greatest political mistake when he made an agreement with the USA for the reciprocal lowering of tariffs in 1911 – businessmen accused him of handing control of the Canadian economy to the USA and he lost the election in the same year. During the **First World War** he refused to serve in a coalition government, as he opposed conscription, although he supported Canada's entry into the war.

**Lausanne, Treaty of** (1923), was between Turkey and the victorious Allies in the **First World War**. It revised the Treaty of **Sèvres** (1920), which Turkish nationalists led by **Kemal Atatürk** had never accepted, and was made after the Greeks had been driven out of Anatolia. Some of the terms of Sèvres (those relating to the Arab lands of the **Ottoman Empire** and to Italian control of the Dodecanese Islands) were maintained but Turkey recovered from Greece Eastern Thrace and territory round Izmir (Smyrna) in Anatolia: this re-established Turkish sovereignty in nearly all the territory included in the present Turkish Republic. The **Straits** were no longer under the **League of Nations** but they were to be demilitarized and freedom of passage allowed through them. Turkey was not to pay any reparations. It was agreed that there was to be an exchange of populations between Greece and Turkey: in the end about a million Greeks were forced to leave Turkey and 350,000 Turks were expelled from Greece. By this treaty Turkey alone of the defeated powers in the First World War was able to reject the dictated peace imposed on her and to negotiate a settlement which was acceptable to her.

**Laval, Pierre** (1883–1945). French politician. The son of a butcher, Laval joined the Socialist Party in 1903, before becoming a lawyer and making a name for himself by defending trade unionists. Elected as a deputy for a Parisian working-class suburb, he was a pacifist who opposed the military service law and lost his seat in 1919. He left the Socialist Party in 1920, became a deputy again in 1924 and a senator in 1927. Holding various government posts from 1925, he was Prime Minister from 1931–2 and 1935–6, when he was also Foreign Minister. Laval was anxious to have good relations with **Mussolini**, so he negotiated the **Stresa Front** (1935), with Italy and Britain, to maintain the independence of Austria. When the **Ethiopian War** (1935–6) began, he made the **Hoare–Laval Pact**, which would have given Mussolini much of what he wanted, but this came to nothing, owing to the outcry when it was leaked to the press. Laval then, as France was a leading member of the **League of Nations**, half-heartedly applied sanctions against Italy, which alienated Mussolini and pushed him into the arms of **Hitler**. His ministry fell just before the **Popular Front** victory in 1936. After the fall of **France** (1940) Laval joined **Pétain**'s government and persuaded parliament to dissolve itself, thus ending the Third Republic in July 1940. Certain of an ultimate German victory, he thought the best course for France was to collaborate with Hitler. Other ministers distrusted him and suspected him of wanting to seize power, so he was dismissed and arrested in December 1940. In April 1942 he was released at Hitler's insistence and made Prime Minister of the Vichy government (see **Vichy France**). 'I desire the victory of Germany,' he declared, 'for without it Bolshevism would install itself everywhere.' Laval allowed French men and women to be sent to Germany as forced labourers and Jews to be deported, in the vain hope that the Germans would make concessions, such as the release of prisoners of war. His trial for treason after the liberation was a disgrace, as his lawyers were not allowed to introduce evidence in his defence. He was condemned to death and shot in October 1945.

**Law, Andrew Bonar** (1858–1923). British Prime Minister (1922–3). The son of a dour Presbyterian minister of Ulster origin, Bonar Law was born in New Brunswick but was brought up in Scotland by his mother's family. He became a self-made businessman in the iron trade in Glasgow before he was elected as a **Conservative Party** MP in 1900. In 1902 he was Parliamentary Secretary to the Board of Trade, the only office he held before becoming leader of the opposition in 1912, when **Balfour** resigned. Bonar Law was an unusual choice, as he was neither an Anglican nor a landowner and was a solitary figure, but he was the least unpopular candidate. He tried to unite the Conservative Party, split over **tariff reform** since 1903, by opposing **Home Rule for Ireland** and in doing so he behaved irresponsibly. His public statement that he could 'imagine no length of resistance to which Ulster can go in which I should not be prepared to support them' seemed to be an encouragement to civil war. More successful was his reorganization of the Conservative Party, which by 1912 had a new chief whip, chairman, treasurer, national agent and press adviser. The Conservative and **Liberal Unionists** fused in 1912 as the Conservative and Unionist Party. During the **First World War** the Conservatives formed a coalition with the **Liberal Party** under **Asquith** in 1915, Bonar Law taking the junior post of Colonial Secretary. A year later, when Asquith was replaced by **Lloyd George** as Prime Minister, Bonar Law became Chancellor of the Exchequer (1916–19) and Leader of the Commons and was in effect deputy Prime Minister for the next five years. When the war ended he agreed to continue the coalition, as

Lloyd George was a popular leader credited with winning the war. Law was Lord Privy Seal from 1919 to 1921, when he resigned owing to ill-health. **Tory** backbench feeling against the coalition was growing and at a meeting of Conservative MPs in October 1922 Bonar Law spoke out against the coalition. When the meeting passed a motion calling for an end to the coalition Lloyd George resigned and Bonar Law found himself Prime Minister. His ablest Conservative colleagues – Austen **Chamberlain**, Balfour, Winston **Churchill** – resentful at the break-up of the coalition, refused to serve in his 'government of the second eleven' but, suffering from throat cancer, Bonar Law resigned in May 1923 and died five months later.

**Lawrence, T. E.** (Thomas Edward) (1888–1935). British soldier and orientalist, known as 'Lawrence of Arabia'. His father Thomas Chapman, from a well-connected Anglo-Irish family, eloped with his daughter's governess, adopted the name Lawrence and settled in Oxford. Lawrence gained a first in history at Oxford University and then in 1911 went on an archaeological expedition to Syria, where he learnt Arabic and studied the history and customs of the Arabs. He worked in the Middle East for four years before joining British Military Intelligence in Cairo in 1915. A year later he collaborated with **Husayn**, Sharif of Mecca, and his son Feisal in the Arab rising against Turkish rule. By mastering guerrilla tactics, wearing Arab dress and learning to ride camels superbly, Lawrence was accepted as a bedouin leader. Arab forces played a valuable role in tying down Turkish troops, in attacking the Medina–Damascus railway, in capturing the port of Aqaba and in operating on **Allenby**'s flank as he advanced from Egypt into Palestine but they could not have defeated the Turks on their own. It was the British army led by Allenby which was mainly responsible for victory.

Lawrence wanted the Arabs to be self-governing within the British Empire – 'our first brown **dominion**, not our last colony', as he wrote to Lord **Curzon**. At the **Paris Peace Conference** he tried unsuccessfully to gain Arab self-government in Syria and Mesopotamia but these areas were handed over to France and Britain as **mandates**. In 1921 Winston **Churchill**, appointed to the Colonial Office, took Lawrence as his adviser on Arab affairs. Together they provided a large measure of self-government for Iraq under Feisal and for Transjordan under Abdullah, both of whom were sons of Husayn. In 1922 Lawrence resigned from the Colonial Office and enlisted in the ranks of the RAF, first under the name of J. H. Ross and later in the Tank Corps (1923–5) as T. E. Shaw. During the following years he spent much time writing *Seven Pillars of Wisdom*, an account of his experiences in the Middle East. He retired from the RAF after twelve years' service and shortly afterwards received injuries in a motor-cycle accident from which he died.

**League of Nations.** An international organization set up after the **First World War** 'to promote international cooperation and to achieve international peace and security'. Several statesmen during the war had suggested such an organization: Lord Robert Cecil in Britain, Jan **Smuts** in South Africa, Léon Bourgeois in France. Woodrow **Wilson**, the American President, included it as the last of his **Fourteen Points** and insisted that the Covenant (Constitution) of the League, drawn up by an international committee, should be included in each of the separate peace treaties. The Covenant called for collective security and the peaceful settlement of disputes by arbitration: anyone resorting to war would be subjected to economic sanctions. The main organs of the League, which met in Geneva, were the General Assembly, the Council and the Secretariat, which prepared the agenda and reports. The Assembly consisted of representatives of all the member states and decided on general policy but it met only once a year. The Council met more often to decide on specific disputes as they arose and consisted of four permanent members (Britain, France, Italy and Japan – the USA should have been a fifth) and four (later nine) others elected by the Assembly for three years. Decisions in the Assembly and the Council had to be unanimous. There were also subsidiary bodies, such as the Permanent Court of International Justice, which met at The Hague in Holland to deal with legal disputes between states; the International Labour Organization (ILO); and commissions to deal with such issues as **mandates**, refugees, health, drugs and child welfare. These organizations carried out some of the most valuable work of the League, particularly the ILO, which worked hard to persuade governments to fix minimum wages and maximum working hours, and the Refugee Organization, under the Norwegian explorer Fridtjof Nansen, which helped to settle half a million people. Not all these bodies were successful – the Disarmament Commission made no progress at all in persuading member states to reduce armaments. Initially the League had forty-two members (fifty-five by 1926) but it was gravely weakened by the refusal of the USA to join. Germany was a member only from 1926–33, the Soviet Union from 1934–9.

Although it had no armed force at its disposal, the League enjoyed considerable prestige in the 1920s as it prevented or quickly ended several conflicts and all but two of its decisions were accepted. In 1920 it decided in favour of Finland in a dispute between Finland and Sweden over the Aaland Islands; when Greece invaded Bulgaria in 1925 the League persuaded Greece to withdraw; Turkey's claim to Mosul was rejected, so it remained part of Iraq. The League also settled disputes in South America between Peru and Colombia and between Bolivia and Paraguay. Yet the League was twice overruled by the Conference of Ambassadors in Paris. In 1920 the League supported Lithuania in her claim to Vilna, which had been seized by Poland, but the ambassadors awarded it to Poland. When **Mussolini** bombarded Corfu (1923), after three Italians were killed, Greece appealed to the League but the ambassadors ordered her to pay the compensation Italy demanded.

A major power was not involved in any of the disputes in which the League intervened successfully. When a great power was at the centre of a conflict, the League members were unwilling to take any effective action. China asked the League for help when Japan invaded **Manchuria** in 1931 but there was little response, apart from the setting up of the **Lytton Commission**. The League's authority collapsed completely in the **Ethiopian War** (1935–6), when the leading members (Britain and France) attempted to do a deal with Mussolini (the **Hoare–Laval Pact**) and applied sanctions half-heartedly. The League was not consulted and remained silent when **Hitler** seized Czechoslovakia, Mussolini invaded Albania and both took part in the **Spanish Civil War**. It rose from its torpor by expelling the Soviet Union when it attacked Finland in December 1939, but did not meet after that and was dissolved in 1946, to be replaced by the United Nations.

**Lebensraum** ('living-space'). The idea that Germany was over-populated and needed to expand territorially was used before the **First World War** to justify the desire for colonies. **Hitler** rejected the need for colonies and wanted living-space in the east, at the expense of 'Jewish–Bolshevik' Russia and the inferior Slav races, who would be pushed aside or made into slaves of the master race. He wanted a new Reich from the Atlantic to the Urals and told his army commander, within three days of taking office in 1933, that rearmament was his first priority for the conquest of *Lebensraum* in the east and its 'ruthless Germanization'.

**Le Chapelier Law** (1791). Named after the deputy who proposed it, the le Chapelier Law was passed by the French **Constituent Assembly**. It forbade trade unions and employers' organizations, collective bargaining, picketing and strikes. No one in the Assembly objected to this piece of class legislation, which was a response to the petitions of manufacturers. Strikes remained illegal until 1864: the ban on trade unions was not lifted until 1884.

**Lee, Robert Edward** (1807–70). Confederate (see **Confederate States of America**) general in the **American Civil War**. He came from a well-known Virginia family: his father was at one time Governor of the state. Lee served in the US army during the **Mexican–American War** and captured John **Brown** at Harper's Ferry in 1859, when Brown tried to start a slave uprising. Lee was opposed to secession, had freed his slaves and was in a dilemma when the Civil War began. He was offered command of the Union armies but ties with his native state were too strong, so he joined the South, where the Confederate President, Jefferson **Davis**, made him his military adviser in March 1862. In June he took command of the Army of Northern Virginia and immediately took the offensive against Union troops, who were threatening Richmond, the Confederate capital. In the Seven Days Battles (June–July) he forced them to retreat and then defeated another Union army at the second battle of Bull Run. This enabled him to invade the North but he was held up on 17 September in the bloodiest day of the war at Antietam, when Lee lost nearly 14,000 men, a quarter of his force. He was forced to retreat to Virginia but recovered to win victories at Fredericksburg (December 1862) and Chancellorsville

(May 1863), which prepared the way for his second invasion of the North. This was brought to an abrupt halt by his worst defeat at the battle of **Gettysburg** on 1–3 July 1863. After this all hope of defeating the North by offensive action had disappeared. Lee was now continually on the defensive, though his brilliance as a tactician was nowhere more apparent than in his retreat through Virginia. **Grant**, the Union Commander, suffered heavy losses in some of the bitterest fighting of the war, but Grant's losses could be replaced; Lee's could not. Grant failed to outflank and destroy Lee's army but pinned him down at Petersburg only twenty miles from Richmond in the winter of 1864–5. In February 1865 Davis made Lee Commander-in-Chief of the Confederate armies but it was too late. On 31 March Grant attacked. Lee's troops were in rags, hungry, short of ammunition and too weak to resist. Lee evacuated Petersburg and Richmond and on 9 April surrendered to Grant at Appomattox Court House. After the war he lived in retirement, urging acceptance of the Union and reconciliation between North and South.

**Left, the.** A name which originated during the **French Revolution**, when the **Jacobins** sat in the **Convention** on the left of the President's chair. It came to be associated with those who held radical views, believed in the sovereignty of the people, wanted a republic rather than a monarchy and were **anti-clerical**. With the **Industrial Revolution** the Left was identified with the interests of the working class and with those who wanted the state to intervene in the free market to bring about social change. In the twentieth century the Left refers to socialist and communist parties and to proponents of the **Welfare State**.

**Legislative Assembly** (October 1791–September 1792) succeeded the **Constituent Assembly** in the **French Revolution**. It changed the whole course of the Revolution by declaring war on Austria in April 1792, thus beginning the **French Revolutionary Wars**, which continued as long as the Revolution itself. When the war went badly at first, **Louis XVI** was suspected of intriguing with France's enemies and there were increasing demands from the *sans-culottes* for the abolition of the monarchy. When the Assembly refused to depose the King, the *sans-culottes* seized the initiative, set up a revolutionary Commune in Paris and made an attack on the **Tuileries** (the King's palace). This bloody *journée* gave effective power to the Commune, which forced the Assembly to agree to the election of a National **Convention** to draw up a new democratic constitution. To win the support of the peasants, the Assembly abolished feudal dues without compensation, something the peasants had wanted since the **August Decrees** of 1789. The King was suspended: it was left to the Convention to abolish the monarchy.

**Leipzig, battle of** (16–19 October 1813). Also known as the battle of the Nations, it was the climax of **Napoleon**'s 1813 campaign in the **Napoleonic Wars**: 177,000 troops of France and her German allies faced 257,000 Allied troops (Austrian, Russian, Prussian and Swedish), who grew to 365,000 during the battle. Napoleon's failure to win on the first day was decisive, as the arrival of Allied reinforcements, including **Bernadotte**'s Swedish soldiers, gave them an advantage of three to two in numbers and two to one in artillery. On 18 October Napoleon's Saxon allies deserted him and a day later he ordered a retreat before all his troops were surrounded. French losses, including prisoners, were 73,000, Allied casualties 54,000. For the second year running Napoleon had lost over 400,000 troops. The Allies were now able to seize control of Germany from the French, who retreated rapidly to the Rhine. France was about to be invaded for the first time since 1794.

**Lena Goldfields massacre** (1912). In February 5,000 miners went on strike in Siberia, protesting against low wages, appalling conditions and a working day from 5 a.m. to 7 p.m. After a month troops were called in, killed 170 miners and wounded 372. This massacre had the same effect as **Bloody Sunday** in 1905. 'From a peaceful economic strike on the Lena river to political strikes in Russia,' wrote **Stalin**. In April 1912, 500,000 men went on strike in sympathy – more than in the previous four years. The strike movement continued to gather momentum up to the outbreak of war in 1914.

**Lend-Lease Act** (March 1941). By the end of 1940 Britain was in desperate straits, as France had been defeated and she was fighting Germany alone. She badly needed American war supplies but was running out of money, so President Franklin D. **Roosevelt** suggested lending goods. The Act allowed the President to lease or lend arms, war supplies and food to any country whose defence was deemed vital to that of the USA, on the understanding that their value would be returned after the war. By the end of the war the USA had lent fifty million dollars, 60 per cent to Britain and 20 per cent to the Soviet Union. The Act was vital to Britain, as it enabled her to continue fighting. It was important to the USA too, as American industry began to switch to wartime production. This made her the 'arsenal of democracy', ended the **Great Depression** in the USA and began her transformation into a super-power. Lend-Lease ended in August 1945.

**Lenin, Vladimir Ilyich** (family name Ulyanov) (1870–1924). Russian revolutionary, founder of the **Communist Party of the Soviet Union** and of the **Comintern**. Lenin was a son of the chief Inspector of Schools in Simbirsk province on the middle Volga and trained as a lawyer. He became a revolutionary when his older brother was hanged in 1887 for plotting to assassinate Tsar **Alexander III**. Persecuted as a revolutionary, Lenin was exiled to Siberia from 1897 to 1900, where he adopted the name Lenin from the river Lena: he lived in Western Europe from 1900–1917, except for a brief period in 1905–6. At the Second Congress of the Russian Social Democratic Party, held in Brussels and London in 1903, Lenin split the Party with his demand for a small, centralized party (see **Leninism**). His supporters became known as **Bolsheviks**. Lenin, like most revolutionaries, was unprepared for the **Russian Revolution of 1905** and did not return to St Petersburg until November, by which time it was almost over. He hoped that the **First World War** would produce proletarian revolutions in the major industrial countries and was disappointed when **nationalism** was more powerful than working-class solidarity and that socialist parties everywhere supported their governments. The **February Revolution** of 1917, like that of 1905, caught the Bolshevik leaders by surprise. The Germans decided that if Lenin returned to Russia he would disrupt the war effort, so they allowed him to pass through Germany in a sealed train. He arrived at **Petrograd** in April and immediately began to change the whole course of the

Revolution. The Bolsheviks had been giving limited support to the **Provisional Government**. Lenin stopped all that in his **April Theses**, by identifying himself with popular demands for an end to the war and 'all power to the **Soviets**'. His aim was now to gain enough popular support to seize power. In spite of the débâcle of the **July Days**, Bolshevik support continued to rise, especially after General **Kornilov** failed in his attempted *coup*. By October the Bolsheviks were a mass party and Lenin persuaded the Central Committee, much against its will, that the time was ripe for them to seize power. Without Lenin there would have been no **October Revolution**.

After the Revolution many Bolsheviks expected that their party would rule in coalition with other socialist parties. Lenin had other ideas. He announced that the Council of People's Commissars, all of whom were Bolsheviks, would be the new government, though he had to allow some Left Socialist Revolutionaries to join it, when transport and other workers threatened to go on strike. Lenin now had the problem of retaining power: the Bolsheviks were a minority in the country, as the elections to the Constituent Assembly showed (they polled 25 per cent of the vote). He therefore adopted policies in which he did not believe, such as granting all land to the peasants. He insisted, against considerable opposition within the party, that the war should be ended and that the Treaty of **Brest-Litovsk** should be signed in March 1918, though this gave to Germany large amounts of Russian territory. The Left SRs now left the government, so Lenin had what he had always wanted: one-party rule (the Constituent Assembly had been closed down after it had met for one day in January 1918). The dictatorship of the Bolshevik Party was reinforced by the activities of the **Cheka**, whose ruthlessness Lenin did much to encourage. He approved of 'real, nationwide terror, which reinvigorates the country and through which the great **French Revolution** achieved glory'. The result of one-party rule and a humiliating peace was the **Russian Civil War**, in which **Trotsky** rather than Lenin was the directing force. In order to cope with economic collapse Lenin introduced **War Communism**, by which the state sought to control all aspects of the economy. This was so unpopular, especially with the peasants, who resented requisitioning, that Lenin abandoned it in 1921 in favour of **NEP**, which allowed a partial return to a market economy. In May 1922 Lenin had his first stroke, followed by a second one in December, which partly paralysed him. He had a third stroke in March 1923, which deprived him of speech. In April 1922 **Stalin** had become General Secretary of the Communist Party, with Lenin's approval. Lenin expressed doubts about his fitness for this post in his dictated 'testament' in December 1922 but this was suppressed. He died on 21 January 1924.

Lenin's dynamism, decisiveness and thoroughness gave him un-equalled prestige, which enabled him to overcome opposition within his own party at crucial times. Without him it is doubtful if **communism** would have become established in Russia. He, more than anyone else, changed the face of world politics in the twentieth century.

**Leningrad, Siege of** (September 1941–January 1944). The 890-day siege of Russia's second city by the German army. When Operation **Barbarossa** began the German Army Group North moved through the Baltic states to Leningrad, which was cut off from the rest of Russia on 15 September. **Zhukov** arrived to organize the defence and by the end of the month the Germans, finding resistance so fierce, had given up the idea of storming the city and settled down to besiege it. Not until December could an ice road be used by the Russians across Lake Ladoga but this was a precarious lifeline. There had been little attempt to evacuate civilians, so starvation took its toll, aided by a constant air and artillery bombardment: estimates of the total number of civilian deaths vary from 800,000 to 1.5 million. Leningrad's survival was made possible by the Finns, who recovered the territory they had lost during the **Finnish–Russian War** but would not go beyond their original frontier and attack Leningrad. In January 1943 the Russians reconquered a thin corridor south of Lake Ladoga which gave Leningrad a tenuous link with the rest of Russia. The siege was completely lifted in January 1944, when the Moscow–Leningrad railway was reopened.

**Leninism**. The theoretical application of **Marxism** to conditions in an under-developed country like Russia. 'Without a revolution-ary theory, there can be no revolutionary movement,' **Lenin** wrote. Central to his theory is the role of the Party in bringing about revolution. In 1902 Lenin set forth his ideas in a pamphlet *What is to be Done?* Here he maintained that 'The history of all countries shows that the working class, solely by its own forces, is able to work out merely trade-union consciousness,' by which he meant that workers would often be satisfied with economic gains, such as better working conditions and higher pay, whilst working within the capitalist system. For Lenin the most important thing was to smash capitalism and for this 'a strong organization of revolutionaries' was required. These professional revolutionaries should be a small, tightly knit body, which must accept orders from the Party leadership without question. The idea of a mass party in a Tsarist state was ridiculous, as it would easily be infiltrated by police informers and would therefore become useless.

At the Second Congress of the Russian Social Democratic Party held in Brussels and London in 1903, Lenin's ideas were attacked, as his view of the party would widen the gap between the intellectual leadership and the mass of the workers. Lenin's views were élitist, it was said, and would lead to dictatorship, a view endorsed by **Trotsky**, who warned (in 1904) that the Party would substitute itself for the working class: 'the Party organization substitutes itself for the Party, the Central Committee substitutes itself for the organization and finally a "dictator" substitutes himself for the Central Committee.'

A second feature of Lenin's theory concerned the strategy of the revolutionary struggle. Orthodox Marxists believed that socialism could arise only from a *bourgeois*–capitalist society, in which capitalism is fully developed and in which there is a large proletariat. As Russia was still a pre-industrial country, with a small working class and a vast number of peasants, the first revolution to overthrow the Tsarist autocracy must be a *bourgeois* one. It might take years after that before capitalism developed and there could be a socialist revolution. Lenin rejected this in *Two Tactics of Social Democracy*, written in 1905. He did not accept that the *bourgeoisie* were the natural leaders in an anti-Tsarist revolution, as he thought they would betray the revolution and seek a compromise with the ruling class. He did not share the **Mensheviks**' scepticism about the *petit-bourgeois* nature of the peasant. The revolution must be led by the working class, in alliance with the peasants. When the Tsar was overthrown there would be a 'provisional government' with the workers taking part. The last battle would then take place between the *bourgeoisie*, who would have moved over to counter-revolution, and the workers, who, with the support of proletarian revolutions in Europe, would be successful. In this way the time taken to close the gap between the *bourgeois* and socialist revolutions, which the Mensheviks admitted might be long, would be shortened dramatically.

In setting out his ideas about the sort of society which would arise out of revolution, Lenin distinguished **socialism** from **communism**. The latter would be an equal, classless society in which there would be no need for repressive institutions of state, such as the police. However, this would not arise immediately, as there would be a great deal of opposition to the revolution, which would have to be overcome before communism could be established. Meanwhile, there would be socialism, based on the dictatorship of the proletariat. This would be exercised on behalf of the workers by the **Communist Party** in a one-party state. This situation would last for a long time and could be ended quickly only by world revolution.

Leninism has had an enormous impact, as communist parties everywhere have modelled themselves on Lenin's idea of the Party, which must seize and retain power on behalf of the proletariat. For **Stalin** 'Leninism is the theory and tactics of the dictatorship of the proletariat.' It became a doctrine which subordinated communist parties throughout the world to that of the Soviet Union, as it did in the **Comintern**. That dominance was not broken until the late 1980s.

**Leo XIII** (1810–1903). Pope (1878–1903). A great humanist and scholar, Leo XIII was more sensitive and sympathetic to changes taking place than his predecessor, **Pius IX**. His encyclicals restated Catholic social doctrine in terms relevant to modern society, without compromising on the essentials of the Catholic faith. Leo wanted to improve the Papacy's strained relations with the governments of France, Germany and Italy, so he negotiated with **Bismarck** an end to the *Kulturkampf*, stopped papal support for French monarchists and urged French Catholics to be loyal to the **Third Republic**, a call which resulted in the *Ralliement*. 'None of the several forms of government is condemned in itself,' he said in the encyclical *Immortale Dei* (1885). He was unable to come to an agreement with the anti-clerical (see **anti-clericalism**) **Crispi**, so he repeated Pius's injunction that Catholics in Italy should not take part in political activity. In 1891 the encyclical *Rerum Novarum*, whilst affirming that private property was a natural right, said that its use could rightly be limited in order to protect the weak and the poor. Employers were reminded of their moral duty to pay adequate wages. Materialistic **Marxism** was condemned but Christian Socialism was welcomed and the formation of Catholic **trade unions** encouraged.

**Leopold II** (1835–1909). King of the Belgians (1865–1909). Leopold was energetic, widely travelled and wanted overseas possessions. In 1876 he became President of the African International Association, which sent out expeditions to Central Africa, and used this as a cover for his own activities. H. M. **Stanley**, in crossing the African continent, followed the Congo river from the heart of Africa to the Atlantic Ocean. In 1879 Leopold employed Stanley, who in the next five years established land and water communications from the Congo estuary to Stanley Falls, a thousand miles inland. As the Belgian parliament would not support his desire for African colonies, Leopold decided to form a personal empire but for this he needed the support of the great powers, Britain, France and Germany. By skilful diplomacy he persuaded them that it would be preferable to make the Congo a free trade area under his 'international' regime, rather than let it fall into the hands of one of their rivals. At the **Berlin Conference** (1884–5) the Congo Free State, with Leopold at its head, was recognized as a sovereign state. In effect this meant that a large part of Equatorial Africa had become the private estate of a European king. Leopold never visited the Congo but he wanted to make money out of it, so he allowed his officials to demand fixed amounts of rubber or ivory from each village. Those who did not fulfil their quota were flogged, mutilated by having hands or feet cut off, or even executed. When this reign of terror became known there was a public outcry, which forced the Belgian government to take control of the Congo from Leopold just before his death.

**Levant** (from the French *lever*, to rise, as in sunrise, meaning the east). The term referred to the countries on the eastern shore of the

Mediterranean, Anatolia and Syria, and which now include Lebanon and Israel.

**Lewis, John Llewellyn** (1880–1969). US labour leader. The son of an immigrant Welsh coal miner, Lewis became a miner himself at the age of fifteen. By 1920 he had become President of the United Mine Workers (UMW), a post he retained until 1960. During the 1920s the industry declined, owing to overmanning, over-production and underinvestment. The **Great Depression** made things worse, so that by 1933 the UMW had only 150,000 members. With the pro-labour legislation of the **New Deal**, the UMW, along with other unions, revived. The UMW belonged to the **American Federation of Labor** (AFL), which represented craft unions and was not interested in organizing unskilled workers in the mass-production industries. Lewis was frustrated by this and so helped in 1935 to form the Committee of Industrial Organizations (CIO) which aimed at organizing all workers in an industry into one union. When the AFL expelled nine CIO unions in 1937, Lewis reorganized them as the Congress of Industrial Organizations and became its first President. He then began a vigorous campaign to organize workers in the steel, automobile and other mass industries and had such success that the Congress soon had more members than the AFL. Lewis was at first a supporter of Franklin D. **Roosevelt** but in 1937 clashed with him over a steel strike and in 1940 supported the **Republican Party** presidential candidate. When Roosevelt won, Lewis resigned as CIO President and in 1942 withdrew the UMW from the CIO. During the **Second World War** Lewis continued to be militant on behalf of the miners, which made him very unpopular. His aggressive policies led to anti-labour legislation, such as the Taft–Hartley Act of 1947, which weakened union power by such measures as forbidding the closed shop. Although he was a strong opponent of **communism**, Lewis refused to take an oath, which the Taft–Hartley Act required of union leaders, that he was not a communist. He was probably the most powerful and successful labour leader in the USA.

**Lewis and Clark expedition** (1804–6). After the **Louisiana Purchase**, President **Jefferson** wanted to send an expedition to explore the new territory and to find a route to the Pacific. He put his private secretary, Captain Meriwether Lewis, and another officer, William Clark, in charge. They set off from St Louis in May 1804, followed the Missouri river to its headwaters and then crossed the Rockies. After descending the Clearwater, Snake and Columbia rivers they reached the Pacific coast in November 1905. They had travelled 4,000 miles. They arrived back in St Louis in September 1806 with maps, botanical specimens and much information on Indian customs. The expedition strengthened the USA's claim to Oregon and stimulated the fur trade and western settlement.

**Leyte Gulf, battle of** (23–26 October 1944). A naval battle, in which the Japanese sought to prevent the American reconquest of the Philippines but which finally destroyed Japan's naval power. On 20 October 1944, US troops began invading Leyte Island. The Japanese realized that American success in the Philippines would cut Japan off from her oil supplies and raw materials in South-East Asia, and therefore they were prepared to throw all their available ships into battle, although they were heavily outnumbered. The Americans had 134 ships, including twenty-six aircraft carriers, the Japanese sixty-nine, with only six carriers, in what was the biggest naval battle of the **Second World War**. Japanese forces were divided into three groups. The first, with all the aircraft carriers, was far to the north, hoping to lure the fastest and most powerful American ships away from the Gulf. In this it succeeded, as Admiral Halsey dashed off in pursuit with his fleet of carriers and battleships. The remaining American capital ships moved south to deal with another Japanese force and fought the only classical naval battle of the **Pacific War**, with surface ships firing at each other. The Americans, with their radar-controlled guns, won this battle comprehensively. With Halsey in the north and their other capital ships in the south, the Americans were left with only sixteen slow escort carriers and their destroyer support to defend the beachheads on Leyte when Admiral Kurita's main fleet, with four battleships and six battle cruisers, appeared. Kurita found that he would be without his southern force and withdrew. In response to a call for help Halsey moved back, after sinking four Japanese carriers, too late to intercept Kurita. In the conflict the Japanese lost four aircraft carriers, three battleships, ten cruisers, eleven destroyers, a submarine and 500 planes. American losses were three carriers, three destroyers and 200 planes. The battle of Leyte Gulf ended as a resounding American victory but it had been a near disaster, as the Americans had failed to coordinate their operations. Admiral Kurita could have destroyed US forces on the beachheads if he had shown more determination. This was the last great sea battle of the Pacific War.

**Liang Qichao** (1873–1929). Chinese scholar and reformer, who held a mid-way position between that of **Kang Youwei** and that of **Sun Yixian** (Sun Yat-sen). Liang rejected Kang's idea that reform could take place within the Confucian tradition (see **Confucianism**), as he did not believe that China could simply borrow Western technology and retain Chinese thought and institutions. A society, he wrote, 'cannot make use of new institutions with an old psychology'. Attitudes as well as institutions must change. Yet he did not accept Sun's idea of a democratic revolution, as he did not think the Chinese were ready for democracy and because he thought revolution might end in a dictatorship and with foreign powers partitioning China. He wanted a constitutional monarchy, which would make gradual progress possible. Liang was a prolific and brilliant writer, who greatly influenced the intelligentsia. He was behind the **Hundred Days Reform** (1898) and, with the help of the Japanese legation in Beijing (Peking), narrowly escaped arrest and execution when the Empress Dowager, **Cixi**, staged a *coup* and aborted the reforms. He continued to campaign for reform while living in Japan. After the fall of the **Qing dynasty** (1911) he returned to China and took part in **Yuan Shikai**'s and later governments, although he opposed Yuan's attempt to make himself Emperor. He became disenchanted with Europe after a visit following the **First World War**, but did not find **Marxism** attractive either. By this time his influence had waned: he was too moderate to appeal to a new generation of intellectuals, who wanted to smash the old order.

**Liberalism.** The creed of those who believe in freedom: of speech, association, religion and of trade. Many liberals supported natural rights such as those embodied in the **Declaration of the Rights of Man** (1789). They sought to prevent government becoming despotic by the separation of powers (an executive, legislature and judiciary all independent of one another, as in the US) and by making governments responsible to freely elected parliaments. Believing in *laissez-faire*, some liberals did not want the state to interfere with the free market, whilst others wanted the state to have a more positive role in protecting the poor and weak. Liberals tended to be reformers, opponents of tradition and of **conservatism**. Britain was the birthplace of modern liberalism: its philosophy was derived from John Locke, its economic ideas from Adam Smith. In the late nineteenth century the **Liberal Party** in Britain was for many years the strongest party, reaching its heyday in the decade before 1914, when it laid the foundations of the **Welfare State**. Since the First World War, liberal parties have been in decline, their ideas appropriated by other parties.

**Liberal Party** (Britain) was descended from the **Whigs** and nonconformist radicals. Historians use the term 'Whig' or 'Liberal' to describe the same political group in the period 1832–67. **Gladstone** was leader of the first government (1868–74) generally called Liberal, but only with the National Liberal Federation (1877) did the structure of a mass party begin to appear. Gladstonian liberalism was committed to removing restrictions on political, religious and economic life, which involved abolishing the privileges of the Church of England and promoting *laissez-faire*. It was concerned with political rather than social reform and with 'retrenchment' in government, which meant keeping taxes low and eliminating waste in the administration. Abroad, it favoured arbitration as a way of settling disputes and thought that force should be used only as a last resort. Gladstone split the Liberals over **Home Rule for Ireland** in 1886, when a Liberal Unionist group led by Joseph **Chamberlain** broke away and later joined the **Conservatives**. From 1886 to 1905 the Liberals were out of office, except in 1892–5, when Gladstone again unsuccessfully introduced a Home Rule Bill. There was a further Liberal split during the second **South African War** (1899–1902), when **Lloyd George** and his followers opposed it, whereas **Asquith** supported it. They were able to reunite in opposition to **tariff reform** and in 1906 won an overwhelming electoral victory with 400 Liberal MPs returned.

In the next decade, influenced by the '**New Liberalism**', which approved of more extensive state intervention, they carried out a wide-ranging programme of social reform. In the 1910 December election they won 272 seats, the same number as the Conservatives, so they were then dependent on **Labour** and Irish support. In 1915, during the **First World War**, Asquith ended ten years of Liberal rule by forming a coalition government. There has never been another Liberal administration. The Liberals divided again, disastrously, in December 1916, when Lloyd George, with the help of the Conservative leader Bonar **Law**, replaced Asquith as Prime Minister. About half the parliamentary Liberal Party followed Asquith into opposition. At the end of the war Lloyd George and Bonar Law decided to continue the coalition and fought the 1918 election on a common platform. The result was a massive vote of confidence in Lloyd George – over 520 coalition candidates were returned (including 136 coalition Liberals), but the Liberal Party in the country was destroyed, only twenty-eight Asquithian Liberals winning seats. 'Liberal Associations perished,' wrote the Liberal chief whip, Herbert Gladstone. 'Masses of our best men passed away to Labour. Others gravitated to Conservatism or independence ... There was an utter lack of enthusiasm.' After that the Liberals never looked like becoming a party of government again. The Labour Party replaced the Liberals as the official opposition in 1922, and though the Liberals reunited again in 1923 under Asquith to oppose **Baldwin's** tariff reform and won 159 seats, Labour had 191. A decline followed: 40 seats in 1924, 59 in 1929, 21 in 1935 and only 12 in 1945. The Liberals lost working-class support after the war, as Lloyd George and Churchill were prepared to use troops to break up strikes and refused to nationalize the mines. Radicals switched their support to the Labour Party. The Liberal Party enabled minority Labour governments to survive in 1923 and 1929 and took part in Churchill's wartime coalition (1940–45). This was the only way Liberals could return to office.

**Liberal Party** (New Zealand) dominated politics from 1890–1911 and passed a series of wide-ranging reforms which anticipated those of the British Liberal governments in the decade before the **First World War**. **Reeves** (Minister of Labour) and **Seddon** (Prime Minister) were mainly responsible for the reforms, which greatly increased the powers of the state. Liberals took part in the wartime coalition government but never recovered their pre-war power. Sir Joseph Ward (1856–1930) tried to broaden the appeal of the Party, which he named the United Party. In 1928 he won a narrow election victory but Liberals could not cope effectively with the **Great Depression**, and in 1935 the Labour Party won a landslide victory. To provide a strong opposition to Labour, the Liberals merged with the Reform (Conservative) Party in 1937 to form the National Party.

**Liberal Toryism** refers to the period of **Liverpool**'s administration, which followed the suicide of **Castlereagh** in August 1822 and lasted until Liverpool's resignation in 1827. The reforms at home and a more liberal policy abroad were contrasted with the 'reactionary' years 1812–21, when there was popular unrest and government repression. This contrast, however, is misleading, as there were no fundamental changes in either men or measures. In the five months after Castlereagh's death, six out of thirteen Cabinet posts changed hands – **Canning** became Foreign Secretary, **Peel** became Home Secretary and Huskisson went to the Board of Trade – but all had held junior posts earlier. Liverpool's aim had always been to preserve the political dominance of the landed interests, and this did not change. The government was opposed to **Parliamentary reform**, and when Lord John **Russell** introduced a bill to disfranchise 100 **'rotten' boroughs** the government opposed it and it was easily defeated. As there was a split in the government over **Catholic emancipation** – the 'Protestants' led by Peel and **Wellington** opposed it, the 'Catholics' led by Canning supported it – nothing was done about this, nor was there any attempt to repeal the Test and Corporation Acts and so give full political equality to Dissenters. Liverpool was not a reformer, but he was not a reactionary either and supported his more able colleagues in bringing about moderate changes. Huskisson relaxed the Navigation Acts a little, allowing the colonies some direct trade with Europe, and reduced the numerous customs regulations to a simple code. These measures were to strengthen the economy, as was Canning's recognition of the independence of Spain's Latin American colonies and of Portuguese Brazil, which were now open to British trade and could become part of her 'informal' empire. Peel consolidated and amended English criminal law and reduced the number of capital offences, though most of these had ceased to be punished by execution. In 1824 the **Combination Acts** were repealed and **trade unions** made legal, but this was a backbench and not a government measure. There were, therefore, some modest reforms under Liberal Toryism, many of which were a continuation of earlier policies.

**Liberal Unionists.** Members of the **Liberal Party** who broke away from it in 1886, as they opposed **Gladstone**'s **Home Rule for Ireland**. Ninety-three Liberals, including Hartington, leader of the **Whigs**, and the radical Joseph **Chamberlain**, voted against the bill, which was defeated. In the election of 1886 the **Conservative Party** agreed not to oppose the Liberal Unionists, seventy-seven of whom were returned. Gladstone made little effort to entice them back into the Liberal Party, so they formed a separate group, which gradually drifted towards the Conservatives. In spite of having a Conservative majority, **Salisbury** formed a coalition with them in 1895, Chamberlain becoming Colonial Secretary. In 1912 the Conservative Party changed its name to the Conservative and Unionist Party when the Liberal Unionists finally joined the Conservatives.

**Lidice.** A Czech mining village near Prague. The Nazis claimed that the villagers had assisted **Heydrich**'s assassins, so they shot all the men and older boys and sent all the women and children to **concentration camps**, where many died. The village was destroyed on 9 June 1942. The village of Lezaky was also demolished. The site has become a national monument and museum, to remind people of the barbarity of Nazi rule in occupied Europe.

**Li Hongzhang** (1823–1901). Chinese scholar and statesman. A pupil of **Zeng Guofan**, he was in military service from 1853–68, when he played a leading role in suppressing the **Taiping** and Nian rebellions. He gained the favour of the Empress Dowager **Cixi** and from 1870 to 1895 was governor-general of Zhili province (in which the capital Beijing lay) and virtual Prime Minister. He was a leader of the **Self-Strengthening movement** and had explained to the government as early as 1864 that foreign domination, based on the superiority of their weapons, presented China with her greatest crisis since its unification under the first Emperor in 221 BC. He established arsenals, factories, telegraph lines and China's first modern navy and sent students abroad to study, but there was no overall plan. He did not see the value of European institutions and thought that Chinese culture and education were superior to those of the West. His failure was shown in the ease with which Japan destroyed his 'modern' navy in the **Sino-Japanese War** (1894–5). He negotiated the Treaty of **Shimonoseki** with Japan in 1895, a secret alliance with Russia against Japan a year later and, with Russia and other European countries, the Protocol of 1901 after the **Boxer Rising**. He was one of the ablest scholar-officials, with an unequalled prestige among foreigners in China, but he followed the standard practice of his day in diverting public funds for his private use: he left a large fortune.

**Lincoln, Abraham** (1809–65). Sixteenth President of the United States (1861–5), who saved the Union, freed the slaves and was the staunchest defender of democracy. Born in Kentucky, the son of a poor backwoods farmer, Lincoln spent less than a year at school and moved with his family to Illinois in 1830. There he ran a general store, became a lawyer and in 1846 was elected as a **Whig** to the US House of Representatives, where he opposed the **Mexican–American War** of 1846–8. He did not seek re-election in 1848 and had almost retired from politics when he was brought back by his opposition to the **Kansas–Nebraska Act** of 1854, which allowed slavery into what had been free territory. In 1856 he joined the new **Republican Party** and in 1858 was its candidate for election to the Senate. Slavery was the dominant issue and Lincoln showed his awareness that it could split the nation in a speech accepting his nomination: 'A house divided against itself cannot stand. I believe that this Government cannot endure permanently half-slave and half-free.' His opponent in the election to the Senate was the **Democrat** Stephen **Douglas**. Lincoln challenged him to a series of debates on slavery, which he said was 'a moral, social and political wrong'. Lincoln was not an abolitionist. He accepted that the Constitution allowed slavery in the states but he was opposed to its extension. Lincoln lost the election to the Senate but his debates with Douglas made him a national figure.

In the presidential election of 1860 he was chosen by the Republicans as their candidate, as he had shown himself to be a moderate on slavery and, born in a log cabin, could be put forward as representing the people. The election showed the deep divisions within the nation. Lincoln carried most of the states in the North and West but not one in the South. This tall, gaunt man with a high-pitched voice was now to be President of the United States, but before he took office seven states seceded from the Union. When Lincoln ordered that the beleaguered Federal garrison in Fort Sumter should be relieved, the **American Civil War**, which he had not wanted, began. Once the war had started he acted decisively and showed rock-like strength to bring it to a successful conclusion. He declared a blockade of the South, called for volunteers (and later conscription), and issued an **Emancipation Proclamation**, freeing the slaves in Confederate-held territory. This was the first step to the abolition of slavery in the USA. Lincoln's belief in freedom and equality was forcefully expressed in November 1863, when he gave an address at the new national cemetery at **Gettysburg**: 'We here highly resolve that ... this nation, under God, shall have a new birth of freedom – and that government of the people, by the people, for the people, shall not perish from the earth.' By the time Lincoln became President for a second time, in 1865, the Confederate armies were on the point of collapse. He could now look beyond the war to a peace in which there would be no vindictiveness. He called on all Americans to act 'with malice to none; with charity for all ... to bind up the nation's wounds ... to achieve ... a just and lasting peace among ourselves and with all nations.' Lincoln, tragically, was not able to preside over such a peace. On 14 April 1865, five days after Robert E. **Lee**'s Confederate army had surrendered, Abraham Lincoln was shot by John Wilkes Booth, an actor, while attending a theatre in Washington. He died the next day.

**List, Friedrich** (1789–1846). German economist who put forward a powerful case against *laissez-faire*. He argued that Britain's commitment to free trade was simply a means for maintaining

British economic supremacy and that her condemnation of state interference in the economy was hypocritical. British industry in the **Industrial Revolution**, he said, had been protected: the success of the Lancashire cotton industry had been possible only by keeping Indian cotton goods out of England. Britain had prohibited foreign manufactures from entering her colonies (including America before she became independent), so that British industry would have a captive market. Britain's enthusiasm for free trade, List said, came only after she had a dominant position. He favoured the unification of Germany, creating a large internal market for German industry that should be protected. List was the architect of the *Zollverein* and of a railway system covering the whole of Germany. His ideas lay behind **Bismarck**'s move to protection in 1879 and deeply influenced Sergei **Witte** in Russia in the 1890s.

**Little Big Horn, battle of** (1876). In 1868 the US government had signed a treaty with Sioux chiefs granting them sole use 'forever' of the Black Hills of Dakota, which were their traditional hunting grounds and also sacred, as warriors spoke there with the Great Spirit. When gold was found in the Black Hills in 1874 the US army could not keep prospectors out or protect them against Indian attack. The government, therefore, decided to buy the Black Hills, but the Sioux Chief Sitting Bull refused to sell and prepared to defend his lands. He and the war leader **Crazy Horse** set up a huge camp of Sioux, with their Cheyenne allies, near the Little Big Horn river in Montana. There were nearly 12,000 men, women and children, of whom 2,000 were warriors. Lieutenant-Colonel George Armstrong Custer, of the US Seventh Cavalry, was sent to find the Indians' position. When he saw the Indian camp he decided to attack, ignoring his scouts' warning that he would be greatly outnumbered; he refused to wait for reinforcements, which were a day's march away. On 25 June he split his command into three columns, one of which, with 265 men, he led in a direct charge against the Indians. His fatal overconfidence cost him his life and that of every member of his party. It was the Indians' greatest victory against the whites, and their last. The Sioux could not supply a large force for long, so they split up into small bands, which were hunted down by the US army or driven into Canada.

By 1880 most had surrendered and been moved to **Indian reservations**.

**Little Entente** (1920–38). An alliance between Czechoslovakia, Romania and Yugoslavia that aimed to preserve the post-war settlement in Eastern Europe, which had been established by the Treaties of **St Germain** (September 1919) and **Trianon** (June 1920). It was directed mainly at Hungary who, it was feared, might seek to recover her considerable losses. France became linked to the Entente, when she made a treaty to defend Czechoslovakian independence in 1924. In the 1930s the Entente fell apart, particularly when Yugoslavia and Romania in 1937 refused to assure Czechoslovakia of military aid if she was attacked by Germany. The Entente collapsed completely when Britain and France abandoned Czechoslovakia at Munich in 1938 and the **Sudetenland** was annexed by Germany.

**Litvinov, Maxim Maximovich** (1876–1951). Soviet diplomat. He was Foreign Minister from 1930–39, when he followed a policy of collective security against Germany and Japan. Litvinov established diplomatic relations with the USA in 1933, made the USSR a member of the **League of Nations** in 1934 and arranged a defence pact with France in 1935. As a Jew he was hostile to the Nazis, so Stalin replaced him with **Molotov** before signing the **Nazi–Soviet Pact** in 1939. When Germany invaded the Soviet Union he became ambassador to the USA (1941–3). He was one of the few Jews to hold high office in the USSR, though he never became a *Politburo* member.

**Liverpool, Robert Banks Jenkinson, 2nd Earl of** (1770–1828). British statesman and Prime Minister continuously for sixteen years (1812–27), a period exceeded only by Walpole and **Pitt** the Younger. He entered parliament at the age of twenty and by 1809 had held all three secretaryships – Foreign, Home and War. As Foreign Secretary (1801–4) he was responsible for making the peace of **Amiens** with France. When he became Prime Minister, reluctantly, on the assassination of Spencer Perceval, Britain was suffering greatly from Napoleon's **Continental Blockade** and there was widespread Luddism (see **Luddites**) and discontent, with wheat prices at their highest point in the whole of the nineteenth century. He was able to survive partly owing to **Wellington**'s successes in the **Peninsular War** but the end of the war brought an economic slump and further unrest, as 300,000 soldiers and sailors were demobilized. The **Corn Laws** (1815) provoked more agitation, as they were seen by many as a piece of class legislation, passed by landowners in their own interest. Parliament's refusal to renew income tax in 1816 left the government with an income of £12 million and expenditure of £30 million, so there were drastic reductions in posts and salaries. There were mass demonstrations calling for reform, at one of which, in Manchester, the **Peterloo massacre** took place. The government responded with repressive legislation. The agitation ended as economic prosperity returned, and from 1822–7 there was the period of **Liberal Toryism**, when economic and legal reforms were carried out by Huskisson and **Peel** and the **Combination Acts** were repealed. Liverpool held his Cabinet together through all vicissitudes, as he was tactful, good-tempered and honest – difficult colleagues like **Canning** would serve under him but with no one else. He was helped by a divided opposition – the **Whigs** were demoralized when the Grenvillites, who had usually voted with them, joined Liverpool in 1822. Liverpool was the first Prime Minister to accept the designation 'Tory', but he saw himself as a defender of more than the landed interest and the Church of England. After a stroke in 1827 he resigned and was a physical and mental wreck until he died a year later. His indispensability to the Tory Party was seen in the way it broke up in the next three years under Canning and Wellington.

**Livingstone, David** (1813–73). Scottish missionary and explorer. The son of a tea tradesman, Livingstone started to work at the age of ten in a cotton factory, where he worked six days a week, fourteen hours a day until he was twenty-three, voluntarily attending the company school between eight and ten o'clock at night. It is a tribute to his extraordinary dedication that he was to go to Glasgow University, where he studied Greek and Divinity, and then to London, where he became a doctor. Whilst working in London hospitals he joined the London Missionary Society and was ordained in 1840. Livingstone intended to go to China as a medical missionary but was prevented by the **Opium Wars**, so he went to Africa instead. In 1841 he arrived in Bechuanaland (Botswana), where he devoted himself to missionary work, marrying the daughter of a missionary in 1845. Tiring of missionary work, he concentrated on exploration and crossed the Kalahari three times, twice with his wife and children. In 1852 he sent his family to Britain where they lived in penury, whilst he began the search for a route to West Africa via the Zambezi, which could be used by traders and missionaries. On his return journey he followed the Zambezi to reach the Indian Ocean in 1856. On these journeys he had discovered that the interior of Africa was not an unpopulated desert, as Europeans thought, but 'a well-watered country, with . . . fine fertile soil covered with forest and beautiful grassy valleys, occupied by a considerable population'. When he returned to England and published an account of his journeys in 1857 he became a popular hero. In 1858 he was sent to lead an expedition up the Zambezi to find if it was navigable and suitable for British settlement and cotton cultivation. This was disappointing, as it showed that the Zambezi was not navigable far inland. Livingstone set out on his last journey in 1866 and spent seven years wandering between Lakes Nyasa and Tanganyika and in the upper reaches of the Congo. His reports on the East African slave trade led directly to British pressure on the Sultan of Zanzibar to abolish it, which in 1873 he agreed to do. During these wanderings **Stanley** found him, 'a mere ruckle of bones' according to Livingstone, at Ujiji. Worn out by travelling 30,000 miles in Africa on foot and constantly suffering from tropical diseases, his faithful servants found him dead on 1 May 1873. They buried his heart, embalmed his body and carried it in a hammock slung on poles for a thousand miles before they reached the coast eleven months later. His body was taken to England, where Livingstone became the only explorer to be given a funeral in Westminster Abbey. He had shown remarkable powers of endurance and perseverance, but he has been criticized for neglecting his children for most of his long years in Africa and for taking his wife on strenuous and dangerous journeys in 1850–51 when she was pregnant.

**Lloyd George of Dwyfor, David, 1st Earl** (1863–1945). British Prime Minister (1916–22). Born in Manchester, Lloyd George's father died when he was a baby, so he was brought up in north Wales by his mother and an uncle, Richard Lloyd, a self-educated shoemaker and co-pastor of a Baptist chapel. David, who spoke Welsh with his family throughout his life, left school at fourteen, trained as a solicitor and supported Nonconformist objectives, such as temperance and the disestablishment of the Anglican Church in Wales. In 1890 he was elected as MP for Caernarvon Boroughs, a seat he retained until 1945. He first came to national notice by his courageous opposition to the second **South African War** (1899–1902), for which he was bitterly attacked.

In 1905 he began the first of seventeen consecutive years in office when he was appointed President of the Board of Trade, becoming Chancellor of the Exchequer (1908) when **Asquith** took over the premiership. His conversion to the '**New Liberalism**' was shown in his '**People's Budget**' of 1909, which the Conservatives denounced as '**socialism**'. Its rejection by the House of **Lords** led to the **Parliament Act** of 1911, which severely curtailed the powers of the upper house. Lloyd George continued the great series of Liberal reforms with his **National Insurance Act** (1911), which provided sickness and unemployment benefits, and his scheme for land reform (1913). This established land courts, which could fix higher wages for labourers and lower rents for tenants, though the **First World War** began before it could be applied. His political career almost came to an end in 1912, when he was accused of speculation in the shares of the Marconi Company, which was under contract to the government. A select committee, which investigated the affair, absolved him, as it had a Liberal majority and voted on party lines. During the First World War Lloyd George was Minister of Munitions, a new post in which he acted energetically to end the shell shortage in France. A **coalition government** was formed, first under Asquith and then, from December 1916, under Lloyd George. This split the **Liberal Party**, as **Asquith** refused to serve under Lloyd George. When the war ended and Lloyd George's popularity was at its height, he decided to continue the coalition and fought the 'coupon' election of 1918 on a joint programme with the **Conservatives**. This was a triumph for Lloyd George, as more than 520 government supporters were returned. The coalition continued until 1922, during which time the

Prime Minister largely neglected domestic in favour of foreign affairs, but both Liberals and Conservatives became disillusioned with it, and when a majority of Conservative members voted against its continuation in 1922, Lloyd George resigned.

He was never to hold office again, as both **Baldwin** and **MacDonald** disliked him. In the 1924 elections only forty Liberals were elected, a result Sidney **Webb** described as 'the funeral of a great party'. In the late 1920s Lloyd George collaborated with reformers and economists like Seebohm **Rowntree**, **Beveridge** and **Keynes** to produce policies which called for more state intervention to reduce unemployment. In a revival of 'New Liberalism', *We Can Conquer Unemployment* (1929) demanded a massive public works programme to build roads and houses, a stark contrast to Baldwin's 'safety first' campaign. In 1929 the Liberals increased from forty to only fifty-nine seats (**Labour** had 287). Lloyd George's last campaign had failed. In the 1930s he supported the **League of Nations**, condemned the British government for failing to apply sanctions against **Mussolini** and called for support for the Republicans in the **Spanish Civil War**, but politically he was a spent force. He had helped to divide the Liberal Party, which had been overtaken by Labour as an alternative government to the Conservatives, but he had also laid the foundations of the **Welfare State** and greatly extended state intervention in economic and social affairs.

**Lobengula** (*c.* 1836–94). The last King (1870–94) of the Ndebele (Matabele) state in what is now Zimbabwe. He was a son of Mzilikazi, who founded the Ndebele state in the 1830s, when he fled with his people from the Zulus during the *Mfecane* and then from the Boers. The danger to Lobengula in the 1880s came from competing Britons, Boers, Portuguese and Germans, as his kingdom lay across the route into central Africa. The most serious threat came from Cecil **Rhodes**, who wanted control of Ndebele and Shona lands, as he was convinced that there was gold there. In 1888 Lobengula signed the Rudd Concession, which gave Rhodes's **British South Africa Company** exclusive mining rights in Ndebele territory, but he was deceived. Lobengula could not read or write, so he signed with a cross. According to a missionary, the Reverend

Charles Helm, who was at the King's *kraal*, promises made to Lobengula (that, for example, few white men would work in his land) did not appear in the document. When he realized that mining was to be on a large scale and that there would be white settlers, he tried to renounce the agreement, but Rhodes obtained from the British government a royal charter for his company to govern the concession lands. In 1890 an armed column of the company entered Ndebele country, crossed into Mashonaland and raised the British flag at Fort Salisbury (Harare). Lobengula tried to preserve peace but was forced into a war he could not win. His capital Bulawayo was captured and burnt to the ground. Defeated, he fled and died a fugitive in the Zambezi valley. The British annexed the whole of the Ndebele state, which became part of Southern Rhodesia.

**Local government** (British). Democratic control of local government began with the **Municipal Corporations Act** (1835), which provided for elected councils in many boroughs. The Victorians preferred local to central control and set up numerous local bodies with particular powers. It was not a very efficient system, as there was much overlapping and little coordination. G. J. Goschen, President of the Local Government Board in 1871, called it 'a chaos as regards authorities, a chaos as regards rates and a worse chaos than all as regards areas'. There were parishes, boroughs, sanitary districts, Poor Law Unions and highway districts, to which school boards were added in 1870. County administration was controlled by the landed gentry, meeting as Justices of the Peace in Quarter Sessions. **Salisbury** reformed county government in 1888, by putting it in the hands of elected county councils. A new London County Council was also set up, so that for the first time there was an elected authority for London as a whole. In 1894 the counties were divided into a network of parish, rural district and urban district councils, all elected. The **Education Act** of 1902 merged school boards with the local authorities, which now provided a range of services, such as education, water, gas, electricity, transport and, in some areas, working-class housing, often collectively referred to as 'municipal socialism'. The independence of local government bodies was reduced in the twentieth century, as central government expanded its activities, beginning with the **'New Liberalism'** of **Asquith** and **Lloyd George**, whose social services covered the whole nation and were controlled and financed centrally. The state, rather than local poor relief, came to care for the unemployed, the old and the sick, whilst local government increasingly came to rely on government grants rather than the rates for financing its services.

**Locarno, treaties of** (1925). The German Foreign Minister, Gustav **Stresemann**, proposed that France, Germany and Belgium, with Britain and Italy as guarantors, should recognize as permanent their frontiers with one another fixed at **Versailles** and the demilitarized zone of the **Rhineland**. Germany and France renounced war as a means of solving their future differences. Stresemann refused to guarantee Germany's eastern frontiers with Poland and Czechoslovakia but agreed that any change there must come peacefully. France sought to give Poland and Czechoslovakia the security they needed, by signing treaties of mutual guarantee with them. The Locarno treaties opened the door to Germany's entry into the **League of Nations** in 1926 and were regarded as a great triumph for Stresemann and for the French Foreign Minister, Aristide **Briand**. For Germany the danger of an anti-German coalition being formed was removed, as was the possibility of future incidents like the French occupation of the **Ruhr** in 1923. France now had a British guarantee of her frontier with Germany and the recognition by Germany that the return of **Alsace-Lorraine** to France was permanent. In 1936 **Hitler** declared the treaty null and void and sent troops into the demilitarized **Rhineland**.

*Lombardverbot.* The closing of the German stock market, ordered by **Bismarck** in November 1887, to the placing of Russian loans and the acceptance of Russian securities. Bismarck was acting under pressure from the army, the landowners and the industrialists. **Moltke**, the Chief of Staff, was convinced that war with Russia was inevitable and wanted to strike first. He feared that German loans were financing the strengthening of Russia's army and railway network. Industrialists wanted retaliation against the high Russian import duties on German goods (German exports to Russia had fallen by half between 1880 and 1887). Both German landowners and industrialists complained about scarce capital and high interest rates and wanted more money invested at home. Bismarck was strongly opposed to a preventive war but depended on the support of agrarian and industrial interests. The *Lombardverbot* undid much of the good work of the **Reinsurance Treaty**, which sought to attach Russia to Germany. Russia was beginning to industrialize rapidly and desperately needed capital. When she could not get it from Germany she turned to France, whose bankers were only too willing to lend. Loan agreements were followed in 1891 and 1892 by political and military agreements, and what Bismarck had feared, and tried to prevent, for so long came about: a **Franco-Russian Alliance**, the roots of which lay in the *Lombardverbot*.

**London dock strike** (1889). A strike, led by Ben Tillett, which demanded the 'dockers' tanner' (6 pence instead of 5 pence per hour and 8 pence instead of 6 pence for overtime) and an end to the system whereby casual labourers at the dock gates had to fight for a ticket, which would bring them one day's work. When the port employers rejected these demands there was a sympathetic walkout by skilled stevedores and watermen: trade unionists such as Tom Mann and John Burns, leader of the Amalgamated Society of Engineers, joined in leading the strike. They gained national support by well-organized and peaceful marches, which sometimes attracted 100,000 people, through the City of London. When funds were low Australian trade unionists sent £30,000. The Lord Mayor of London and Cardinal Manning acted as sympathetic mediators and ended the strike after five weeks, with most of the dockers' demands granted.

**London Naval Conference** (1930). A conference attended by Britain, the USA, Japan, France and Italy. Japan hoped that all would agree to her having 70 per cent of the number of British and American auxiliary warships, but this did not happen. The conference simply extended the 5:5:3 ratio on capital ships, agreed at the **Washington Conference** (1921–2), to auxiliary vessels and extended the ban on building capital ships to 1935. Many Japanese thought this inferior position of Japan should not be accepted but the Hamaguchi Osachi Cabinet enforced ratification, in spite of fierce opposition from the Naval Chief of Staff, who resigned, and from the Privy Council. The outcry against what was regarded as civilian interference with the 'independence of the supreme command' led to the shooting of Hamaguchi in November 1930 (he died from his wounds in August 1931).

**London, Treaty of** (April 1915). A secret agreement by which Russia, Britain and France promised Italy some significant territorial gains if she joined the Allies in the **First World War**. She was promised the Trentino, south of Tyrol (which would give her a frontier on the Brenner pass), Trieste, Istria and a portion of the Dalmatian coast, all of which were part of the **Austro-Hungarian Empire**; control of Albania; the Turkish Dodecanese Islands and the region of Adalia, if Turkey was partitioned; and compensation in Africa, if Britain and France gained the German colonies there. Several of these promises were broken after the war: Albania became fully independent, the Dalmatian coast went to Yugoslavia and Italy received no territory in Africa. This made Italians very bitter and aided the rise to power of **Mussolini**.

**Long, Huey Pierce** (1893–1935). US politician and demagogue. Highly intelligent and energetic, he passed a three-year law course in eight months and was a practising lawyer at twenty-one. When he became a railroad commissioner in Louisiana, he set himself up as the poor man's friend by forcing the railroads to reduce their rates. In 1927–8 he ran for governor with the slogan 'Every man a king but no man wears a crown'. His promise of higher public expenditure, to be paid for by taxing the rich, appealed to the impoverished rural workers, who were the majority of voters, and he was elected. Immediately he made full use of the **spoils system**, making his own men state officials at all levels. Bribery, threats and violence were used to silence his political opponents. Men were imprisoned without appearing in court and police brutality was condoned by judges. His own agents supervised elections and counted the votes, so that in elections in two counties more people voted for Long than there were electors; the result was allowed to stand. Huey Long taxed the railroads and the oil companies to pay for his public works and social-welfare schemes: roads were built, education improved and he ensured the support of the poor – both white and black – by abolishing the tax on small properties and ending the poll tax qualification for the vote. Having become supreme in Louisiana, Long was elected to the US Senate in 1931 and began to rival the **New Deal** with his grandiose reform proposals. His 'Share Our Wealth' movement promised a national minimum wage, old-age pensions and the confiscation of large fortunes. He planned to run against Franklin D. **Roosevelt** in the presidential election of 1936 but was assassinated in September 1935. His legacy of corruption and intimidation was an unhappy one – it continued in Louisiana long after his death.

**Long March** (1934–5). The march of Communist forces from the **Jiangxi Soviet** in the south of China to **Yanan** in the north. **Jiang Jieshi**'s (Chiang Kai-Shek's) fifth extermination campaign forced the Communists to abandon their base in Jiangxi in October 1934. About 80,000 men and thirty-five women moved west. At Zunyi, January 1935, **Mao Zedong** (Mao Tse-tung) became effective leader of the Chinese Communist Party (CCP) when he was elected to the Politburo of the CCP and made head of the important Military Affairs Committee. The Communists then moved south-west into Yunnan before turning north into the wild and mountain-ous provinces of Sichuan and Xikang (eastern Tibet), in an attempt to avoid constant attacks by **Guomindang** and **warlord** armies. At Luding bridge, high over the Datong river, one of the most daring and courageous actions of the Long March took place. The only crossing of the swift wide river was by a chain suspension bridge covered with planks. Most of them had been removed, so 200 Communist troops went 100 yards hand over hand across the chains to storm positions on the other side. The rest of the force then crossed the river safely. An exhausting march across the 'Great Snow' mountains, 16,000 feet high in places, followed, in which many had limbs amputated owing to frostbite. After a rest Mao's force struggled yet further north across the marshlands of the Qinghai–Gansu border. In bogs like quicksand they groped their way forward by holding on to thin grass ropes laid on the ground by scouts. Owing to the wet ground it was impossible to sleep except standing up. Thousands died from illness and exhaustion.

Leaving the swamps behind there were further hazards ahead (mountains, enemy troops) before the remnants, about 8,000 in October 1935, reached Yanan in north Shaanxi, where they were protected by barren mountains. They had covered 6,000 miles in eleven provinces at an average of seventeen miles a day, in spite of crossing numerous rivers and mountains. The Nationalists hailed the Long March as a disaster for the Communists, who had lost nearly all their bases in the south and east, but they had survived. Without the March they would not have been able to build up their strength in Yanan and there would have been no Chinese People's Republic proclaimed in 1949.

**Lords, House of.** The upper chamber of the British parliament, which consists of hereditary peers (the majority), life peers since 1958, Lords of Appeal (the House is the Supreme Court of Appeal in the United Kingdom) and twenty-six archbishops and bishops. For most of the nineteenth century British Prime Ministers sat in the Lords and most members of their governments were drawn from that House. In theory they were of equal status with the **Commons**, as bills had to pass both Houses before they could become laws. As the Commons was more democratically elected with a widening of the franchise, the balance of power tipped in favour of the Commons. From the late nineteenth century there has been a permanent **Conservative** majority in the Lords, which was used to reject, amend or mutilate bills in every **Liberal** administration from 1868 to 1914. In 1893 it rejected **Gladstone**'s **Home Rule for Ireland** bill, though the Liberals had fought a general election with Home Rule at the top of their agenda. The Lords had become, said the Liberal leader **Campbell-Bannerman** in 1907, 'a mere annexe of the Unionist [Conservative] Party'. When it rejected **Lloyd George**'s **People's Budget** in 1909, **Asquith** decided to reduce its powers, which he did in the **Parliament Act** (1911); the Lords could not reject money bills passed by the Commons and could hold up other legislation only for three sessions (two years, reduced in 1949 to one year). The Lords was now clearly in a subordinate role, recognized by the convention that a Prime Minister and most of his Cabinet must sit in the Commons (the last Prime Minister to sit in the Lords was the Earl of **Salisbury**).

**Louis XVI** (1754–93). King of France (1774–92). Louis was a clumsy and awkward figure in public, who did not inspire respect, though most Frenchmen looked on him with affection until 1789, in spite of his having little knowledge of the country over which he ruled or of its people: only once before the Revolution did he move outside the Paris–Versailles area, to inspect a new harbour at Cherbourg. A devout man, he took seriously his duty, imposed by God, to rule in the interests of his subjects, but he lacked self-confidence and drive. 'The weakness and indecision of the King,' wrote the Comte de Provence (later **Louis XVIII**), the elder of his two brothers, 'are beyond description.' His failure to support the reforms of ministers like Necker and Brienne helped to bring about the **French Revolution**. He ignored Necker's advice at the Royal Session in June 1789 by coming down firmly on the side of the privileged orders (the nobles and clergy) and then made a revolution almost inevitable by surrounding Paris with troops. It was now impossible to doubt that the King intended to dissolve the National Assembly, by force if necessary. This precipitated the attack on the **Bastille**, which resulted in the King losing control of Paris. Louis refused to accept the **August Decrees** and **Declaration of Rights**, passed by the **Constituent Assembly**, until he was forced to do so in the **October Days**, when the King and the royal family were brought from Versailles to Paris. From this time Louis was virtually a prisoner in the **Tuileries**. His disapproval of the **Civil Constitution of the Clergy** led to his flight to **Varennes**, which demonstrated to all that he was opposed to the Revolution and could not be trusted. What remained of his popularity disappeared – royal inn signs and street names were removed all over Paris – and there were demands that the monarchy should be replaced by a republic. When the **French Revolutionary Wars** began in April 1792 with a declaration of war on Austria, suspicion of Louis increased, as it was believed that he was intriguing for an Austrian victory. On 10 August 1792 the *sans-culottes* attacked the Tuileries, the King was suspended and when the **Convention** met in September the monarchy was abolished. The **Jacobins**, fearing that Louis would be a threat to the republic as long as he lived, insisted that he be brought to trial. In January 1793 he was sentenced to death and executed.

**Louis XVIII** (1755–1824). King of France (1814–24). The elder brother of **Louis XVI**, as the Comte de Provence he escaped to Brussels in 1791 at the same time as the King's ill-fated flight to **Varennes**, and spent the next twenty-three years in exile. On the abdication of **Napoleon**, **Talleyrand** persuaded him to accept the Charter of 1814 in order to recover his throne. Sensibly he kept unaltered the institutions of the **French Revolution** and the Empire: the *Code Napoléon*, the **Concordat** (1801), the sale of Church lands and Napoleon's administrative system, though Catholicism was recognized as the state religion and the white flag of the Bourbons replaced the *tricolore* as the national flag. The franchise for the elected Chamber of Deputies was restricted to the richest landowners (72,000), only 15,000 of whom were qualified to become deputies. Louis ignominiously fled during the **Hundred Days** but was restored to his throne after the battle of **Waterloo**. The indemnity imposed at the second Treaty of **Paris** was paid off and the Allied army of occupation withdrawn in 1817. France was recognized as an equal of the great powers again, a status she demonstrated in 1823 when a French army restored Ferdinand VII of Spain to his throne, after a liberal revolution there. At home Louis acted with moderation and caution until the murder of the Duc de Berry, son of the Comte d'Artois (later **Charles X**), in 1820, when he gave way to pressure from the ultra-royalists by further restricting the franchise and by increasing the control of the Roman Catholic Church over education.

**Louisiana Purchase** (1803). **Napoleon** had made a treaty with Spain in 1800, which returned Louisiana to France. This huge territory stretched from the mouth of the Mississippi river to the Rockies and northward to Canada and included the port of New Orleans. The French never took possession of Louisiana before Napoleon sold it to the United States in 1803. This doubled the size of the United States – over 2 million square kilometres (828,000 square miles) were acquired at less than 3 cents an acre. It was **Jefferson**'s greatest achievement as President. From then on it seemed certain that the USA would one day stretch from the Atlantic to the Pacific.

**Louis Philippe** (1773–1850). King of the French (1830–48). A descendant of Louis XIII (1601–43) and eldest son of Philippe, Duc d'Orléans, Louis Philippe ostentatiously supported the **French Revolution**, voted for the execution of **Louis XVI** and took the name of Philippe Égalité. He fought in the **French Revolutionary Wars** at **Valmy** and Jemappes in 1792 but with his commander, Dumouriez, became involved in an unsuccessful plot to restore the constitutional monarchy and defected to the Austrians in April 1793. This led to the arrest and execution of his father in November 1793. In exile until 1814, Louis Philippe became one of the wealthiest men in France on his return and benefited from the *milliard* of **Charles X**, compensation given to *émigrés* whose lands had been sold during the Revolution. He was the epitome of *bourgeois* domesticity, with his ten children, top hat and rolled umbrella, and mixed freely with Parisians.

When Charles X fell in the **July Revolution** (1830) Louis Philippe was proclaimed King by the French parliament, after accepting a revised Charter that allowed parliament to initiate legislation and doubled the electorate to 170,000 (still only 2.8 per cent of the male population over twenty-one). Roman Catholicism ceased to be the state religion but was recognized, as in **Napoleon**'s **Concordat**, as the religion of the majority of French citizens. The *tricolore* became the national flag again. Louis Philippe firmly believed that political power should be in the hands of the wealthy, so there was no change in the composition of the élite of officials who ran the country: it was based, as before, on land and included both the upper *bourgeoisie* and aristocracy. The King, conscious of being regarded as a parvenu by other European monarchs, pursued a cautious foreign policy. He made no effort to seize territory in Belgium when there was a revolt there, refused the offer of the Belgian throne for one of his sons and did not attempt to help the Poles when they rebelled against Russia in 1831. Although there was little social legislation – an education Act in 1833 and a limitation on child labour in 1841 – and fifteen governments in ten years gave the appearance of ministerial instability, there were no serious threats to the July Monarchy. Workers were alienated when the army was called in to crush the violent protest of silk weavers in Lyon over wage cuts in 1831 and 275 people were killed. A further 300 were killed in Lyon in 1834 during another strike, but when anarchists tried to seize power in Paris in 1839 they received no popular support. There was no support either for **Bonapartism**, as the attempts of Louis Napoleon (later **Napoleon III**) to seize power in 1836 and 1840 showed. France came close to war with England in 1840, when **Thiers** backed **Muhammad Ali** in his struggle with the **Ottoman Empire**, but Louis Philippe forced Thiers to resign and the danger was averted.

**Guizot** as Foreign Minister dominated the government from 1840 but was very unpopular owing to his foreign policy and his refusal to extend the franchise to the *petite bourgeoisie*. The 'immobilism' of Louis Philippe and Guizot caused great discontent among the middle classes and led to a banquet campaign (to avoid the restrictions on public meetings) from August 1847 to February 1848, in which the government was denounced and franchise reform demanded. The organizers of these banquets did not want a revolution and when the government banned a banquet to be held in Paris on 22 February, they accepted this. The situation, however, moved out of their control, when students and workers, suffering from an economic depression (half the working-class population of Paris was out of work), took to the streets. Barricades were set up and on 23 February troops fired into a crowd on the Boulevard des Capucines and killed fifty-two people. Some of the dead were piled in carts and dragged through the working-class districts of Paris, bringing about a huge, popular uprising. Louis Philippe, aware of the fate of Louis XVI, uncertain of the loyalty of the army and genuinely wishing to avoid bloodshed, abdicated and retired to England, where he died.

**Luddites.** Skilled workers in Nottinghamshire, West Yorkshire and South Lancashire, who attacked industrial machinery between 1811 and 1816. They derived their name from the signature 'Ned Ludd', appended to letters denouncing the introduction of machines. The violent protests took place only when petitions to parliament had been ignored. Attacks on machinery had taken place earlier, in the 1770s in Lancashire, when spinning jennies and water frames were destroyed. In 1811–12 there was an economic crisis owing to **Napoleon**'s **Continental Blockade**, which closed most European markets to British exports, and the **Anglo-American War** (1812–14), which affected exports to the USA. The workers took to 'collective bargaining by riot' in order to force mill-owners and magistrates to uphold the 'moral economy' of just wages, fair prices and customary work practices. Wage cuts coincided with a steep rise in the price of bread in 1812 to produce the peak of Luddite activity, when highly organized bands, who enjoyed much local sympathy, attacked employers and their mills. The government feared that revolution was planned and hastily made machine-breaking a capital offence. There were certainly some armed Luddites in Lancashire and Yorkshire in 1812, and evidence of secret oaths, drilling and preparations for a rising, but it is doubtful if many were involved. Luddites were not typical of working men – the unskilled majority did not take part – and their activities declined from 1813, as economic conditions improved. They failed in their attempts to stop mechanization but they frightened the government into using 12,000 troops to cope with the disturbances.

**Ludendorff, Erich** (1865–1937). German general. His dynamism and great physical and mental energy ensured his promotion to the General Staff. When the **First World War** began he showed great courage in leading his troops to capture the Belgian fortress of Liège. As a result he was promoted to Chief of Staff of the Eighth Army under General **Hindenburg**, who had been recalled to deal with the Russian invasion of East Prussia. A master of strategy, Ludendorff helped to bring about the defeat of two Russian armies at **Tannenberg** and the Masurian Lakes. He maintained German supremacy on the Eastern Front until September 1916, when **Falkenhayn** was dismissed and Hindenburg became Supreme Commander, with Ludendorff as his Senior Quartermaster-General. To allow for recovery after the attack on **Verdun**, Ludendorff withdrew German troops to the Hindenburg Line and went on to the defensive. For the next two years he exercised more influence on domestic affairs in Germany than the Chancellor and became virtually a military dictator. He demanded the total mobilization of the civilian population for war: compulsory labour for women, restriction of workers' rights and the closing of universities. **Bethmann-Hollweg**, the Chancellor, complained of his 'dictatorial thirst for power and a consequent intention to militarize the whole political scene'. A Supreme War Office was set up and given wide powers over industry and labour: it increased munitions production three-fold.

Ludendorff pushed for unrestricted submarine warfare, which began in February 1917, and he was partly responsible for the decision to allow **Lenin** to pass through Germany to Russia in a sealed train to start a revolution and so bring about Russia's withdrawal from the war. After the **October Revolution** Ludendorff insisted on the punitive terms of the Treaty of **Brest-Litovsk** (March 1918), which showed the Allies what to expect if Germany won the war. In the spring of 1918 he began the **Ludendorff offensive**, in order to secure a German victory before American troops arrived in France in sufficient numbers to tip the balance in favour of the Allies. Three and a half million troops were involved in five separate offensives between March and July 1918. All failed after initial successes, and so Ludendorff asked the Chancellor to approach President **Wilson** for an armistice based on his **Fourteen Points**. As a democratic Germany might gain better terms from the Allies, Ludendorff, who had opposed all reforms, now proposed that Germany should become a parliamentary democracy. He resigned in October so that a civilian government would have to take responsibility for the armistice and the peace, and then 'we can climb back into the saddle, and govern according to the old ways'.

After the war Ludendorff encouraged opposition to the **Weimar Republic**, took part in the right-wing **Kapp** *Putsch* (1920) and promoted the '**stab in the back**' legend. He led the 'march in the **Munich** *Putsch* (1923), and when the police fired he alone did not fling himself to the ground but marched calmly on. Tried and acquitted, he became a **Nazi** deputy to the Reichstag from 1924–8. Increasingly eccentric, he maintained that supernatural forces had brought about the events of November 1918, so that he ended up as an embarrassment to the Nazis he had supported.

**Ludendorff offensive** (March–July 1918). A massive assault on the Western Front which aimed to bring victory for Germany in the **First World War**. When fighting stopped in Russia in February 1918 **Ludendorff** moved a million men and 3,000 guns to the Western Front, so that he had 3.5 million soldiers there. He wanted a decisive victory in the west as his allies, Austria-Hungary and Turkey, could not last out much longer and because there was discontent in Germany, where food was in short supply and half a million workers had gone on strike in Berlin in January. American troops were arriving in France and so Ludendorff wanted to attack before their numbers decisively tilted the balance in favour of the Allies. If he broke through where the British and French armies met, he expected to split the opposing armies, as the British would retreat to the Channel ports and the French south-west to defend Paris. Ludendorff first attacked the British between Arras and the Oise river with three armies on 21 March, supported by a massive artillery bombardment. He made a spectacular breakthrough and advanced forty miles on a front of the same length, but on 29 March the Germans were strongly repulsed at Arras. By early April this attack had petered out just short of the vital railway junction of Amiens. The British, with some French support, had held up the greatest offensive ever launched, which led to **Foch** being appointed to coordinate the activities of all Allied armies on the Western Front, the first time the Allies had unity of command. On 9 April Ludendorff launched a second attack, this time in Flanders, which again met with limited success before desperate resistance brought it to a halt. Ludendorff's third offensive struck at the French on the Aisne river and broke through to reach the Marne, forty miles from Paris. American troops were now arriving in France at the rate of 250,000 a month and played a great part in preventing the Germans crossing the river. On 15 July German armies attacked in force on each side of Rheims, but three days later Foch struck at the exposed German flank between the Marne and the Aisne and forced the Germans to abandon the Marne salient. British, French, Canadian and Australian troops, with 700 tanks, smashed the German lines near Amiens on 8 August – Ludendorff called it 'the black day' for the German army. By the end of August German troops were back at the Hindenburg Line, from where they had started five months earlier, after suffering 800,000 casualties. This line was stormed by the British at the end of September and from then the German armies retreated, in good order, over the whole front. When the armistice was signed in November they were holding a line from Antwerp to the Meuse, still outside Germany.

**Lugard, Frederick Dealtry, 1st Baron** (1858–1945). British soldier, imperialist and colonial administrator, who was responsible for extending British control over Uganda and a large part of Nigeria. Lugard joined the army and fought in India, Burma and the Sudan, before he took a job with the African Lakes Company in Nyasaland in 1888 and fought against slave traders. The next year he was employed by the British Imperial East African Company, first to explore Kenya and then to lead a military force into Uganda. By a mixture of bluff and force Lugard gained a treaty with the Kabaka of Buganda and established a British protectorate. His book *The Rise of our East African Empire*, published in 1893, helped to persuade the British government to maintain its position in East Africa. In 1894 Lugard took charge of the military forces of the Royal Niger Company at a time of serious rivalry between Britain and France. By moving his forces rapidly north and making treaties with local chiefs as he went, he secured a large area of Nigeria for Britain. When a British protectorate was established over Northern Nigeria in 1900, Lugard became the first High Commissioner. From 1901–6 he conquered the Sokoto Caliphate and consolidated British control over the North. With few administrators Lugard was forced by necessity to develop a system of **indirect rule** in Northern Nigeria. From 1907–12 he was Governor of Hong Kong. He returned to Nigeria as Governor in 1912 with the task of uniting the North and the South. Unification was achieved in 1914, and Lugard became the Governor-General (1914–19) of Nigeria. He then attempted to extend the system of indirect rule and direct taxation to the South, but this led to unrest and a serious rising among the Egba in 1918. Lugard retired in 1919. Three years later he completed *The Dual Mandate in British Tropical Africa*, which became an influential guide for colonial administrators in the inter-war years.

**Luxemburg, Rosa** (1871–1919). Polish Marxist and revolutionary. From a middle-class Jewish family, Luxemburg had to flee from her native Poland in 1889 because of her revolutionary activities and in 1898 settled in Germany, where she remained for the rest of her life. She became the foremost representative of the **Left** in the German **Social Democratic Party** (SPD), vigorously attacking **Bernstein**'s revisionism and advocating a working-class revolution. From 1905 she favoured the mass strike to give free play to working-class 'spontaneity'. She believed that workers should rely on their own efforts and should not be dominated by a 'vanguard' party, as **Lenin** wished. She spent most of the **First World War** in prison for her opposition to the war effort and there wrote *The Russian Revolution*. This praised the **October Revolution** but thought that the **Bolsheviks** were wrong to dissolve the Constituent Assembly: 'freedom . . . only for members of one party . . . is no freedom at all. Freedom is always and exclusively freedom for the one who thinks differently,' and she called for 'the most unlimited, the broadest democracy and public opinion. It is rule by terror which demoralizes.' She predicted that when the Bolshevik Party had established its dictatorship and destroyed multi-party democracy, the dictatorship of the party would become that of a group within the party, and that in turn would become the dictatorship of an individual. She was freed during the **German Revolution** (1918–19), and in December 1918 formed the German Communist Party with Karl Liebknecht. A month later she led the **Spartakist Rising** against the government of Friedrich Ebert. Luxemburg and Liebknecht were captured by the **Free Corps**, who put down the rebellion, and were murdered on their way to prison.

**Lyautey, Louis Hubert** (1854–1934). Marshal of France and colonial administrator. A cultured man with great intellectual curiosity, who learnt Arabic, Lyautey was strongly influenced (in Indo-China) by another great colonial administrator, Galliéni. Galliéni believed in seizing the most important towns in a country: from these 'zones of attraction', pacification would spread outwards by building roads, railways, schools and hospitals. The institutions and customs of the inhabitants must be respected and they must be won over to accept French authority by persuasion rather than force. 'Force should be displayed in order to avoid using it.' The aim should be to create peace and prosperity, which would benefit both the indigenous peoples and France. After working under Galliéni in Indo-China, Lyautey went with him to Madagascar, when this was annexed by France in 1897, where the same methods were applied. From 1903–10 he served in Algeria and moved to Morocco in 1912 as Resident-General, when it became a French protectorate. He remained there until 1925, apart from a brief spell as War Minister in France in

1916–17. When he went to Morocco he found it 'submerged in a wave of anarchy'. The Sultan, the traditional religious leader, had effective control only of the rich coastal strip and not of the mountainous interior, inhabited by Berber tribes. Lyautey was able to pacify the tribes and persuade them to accept French authority, in return for recognizing the *Grands Caids* as autonomous rulers in their own areas. He understood and respected the religion and customs of Islam and did not wish to interfere with them. His methods had more in common with the **indirect rule** of **Lugard** in Nigeria than with the assimilation attempted in most of the French colonial empire, and they were successful. Lyautey also began the economic development of Morocco by building roads, schools, hospitals and a port at Casablanca and by extracting phosphates, discovered in 1922. He resigned in 1925 in protest at the French government not sending him the reinforcements he had asked for in order to fight **Abd al-Qrim** in the Rif war.

**Lyons, Joseph Aloysius** (1879–1939). Australian Prime Minister (1932–9). A **Labor Party** politician in Tasmania (1909–29), Lyons was Premier there from 1923–8, when he sponsored bills to provide welfare benefits for public employees. Elected to the federal parliament in 1929, he was a member of the Labor government until 1931, when he resigned and with some Nationalists formed a new party, the United Australia Party, backed by business interests. His party won the election of 1931 and so he became Prime Minister in the middle of a depression, determined to balance the budget. Salaries were cut but economic recovery owed more to the rising gold and wool prices in the world markets than to the policies of Lyons. Unemployment declined, industry diversified and prospered and there was a budget surplus. Lyons was a pacifist, who opposed conscription and supported **Chamberlain**'s policy of **appeasement**, but he could see the threat from Japan and so in 1934 he began to expand the Australian army and air force, as a defensive measure. He led a simple life with his wife and large family and died of a heart attack in 1939, a much loved figure.

**Lytton Commission** (1932). After the **Manchurian Incident** in 1931, when Japan invaded Manchuria, China complained to the

**League of Nations**, who appointed a commission headed by Lord Lytton to investigate the affair. Before its report was published in October 1932 Japan had turned Manchuria into the puppet state of **Manchukuo**. The Lytton Report was intended to be conciliatory as far as Japan was concerned but it rejected her version of events. When the League of Nations accepted the report in 1933, Japan withdrew from the League, although it had offered no real help to China.

**MacArthur, Douglas** (1880–1964). US general. The son of an **American Civil War** hero who became governor of the Philippines, MacArthur graduated from West Point Academy in 1903. Aide-de-camp to President Theodore **Roosevelt** (1906–7), he became Chief of Staff to a US division in France during the **First World War**, where he distinguished himself by leading attacks personally. From 1930–35 MacArthur was US army Chief of Staff, the youngest holder of that post. He retired from the US army in 1937 and became military adviser to the Philippine government. In 1941 he was recalled to the US army to command US and Filipino troops defending the Philippines against Japan. He fought a stubborn, defensive campaign, his troops holding out in Bataan and Corregidor until May 1942. By this time MacArthur had left for Australia, where he became Supreme Allied Commander in the South-West Pacific. He became the greatest master in the world of combined operations, skilfully coordinating amphibious landings with naval bombardment and air attack. He and Admiral **Nimitz** devised the policy of island-hopping, capturing small islands as bases and by-passing those which were larger and more heavily defended. In this way they could cut Japanese supply routes with South-East Asia and creep closer and closer to Japan. MacArthur was flamboyant and arrogant and disagreed with the Combined Chiefs of Staff, who gave greater priority to the defeat of Germany than to that of Japan. He also disagreed with Nimitz, who wanted to by-pass the main Philippine island of Luzon. After the capture of the Solomon Islands and New Guinea by the spring of 1944, MacArthur got his way and the reconquest of the Philippines began at **Leyte Gulf** in October. In February 1945 Manila fell to the Americans. MacArthur became Supreme Commander of all US forces in the Pacific in April 1945, by which time Iwo Jima had been captured and **Okinawa**, the largest of the Ryukyu Islands next to Japan, had been invaded. After the dropping of **atomic bombs** on **Hiroshima** and Nagasaki, MacArthur accepted the Japanese surrender on 2 September 1945.

From 1945–51 he was Supreme Commander for the Allied Powers during the occupation of Japan, and played an active role in drafting a new democratic Japanese constitution. In 1950, when the Korean War (1950–53) began, he became Commander of UN troops in Korea. Early victories of communist North Korea threatened to overwhelm the South until MacArthur carried out an amphibious landing at Inchon, behind enemy lines, and forced them to withdraw. North Korea, supported by China, again moved into South Korea in November 1950. MacArthur wanted to extend the war by bombing China and blockading Chinese ports but President Truman feared that this would lead to another world war, and so he dismissed MacArthur in April 1951.

**Macartney Mission** (1793). The first British diplomatic mission sent to China. The Chinese regarded their country as the Central Kingdom in the universe: other countries were peripheral and unimportant. The Chinese Emperor was the son of Heaven and so superior to all other rulers: he would not have diplomatic relations with other countries and would receive diplomatic missions only when they came bearing tribute. All trade with Europe was restricted to the port of Guangzhou (Canton) after 1760, where European traders had to deal only with licensed Chinese merchants. The British found these restrictions irksome, so the **East India Company**, with the agreement of the British government, decided to send Lord George Macartney, an experienced diplomat, who had served at the Court of Catherine the Great in Russia and had been administrator of Madras in India, to the Court of the Chinese Emperor Qianlong. He reached Guangzhou in June 1793 bearing expensive gifts and was allowed to go to Tianjin. From there he was taken to Beijing (Peking), as a bearer of tribute. Macartney was courteously received by Qianlong, although he had refused to prostrate himself full length on the ground before the Emperor in the ritual *kowtow* and was allowed instead to bow on one knee, as he would in front of King **George III**. He asked for a British diplomat to be allowed to reside in Beijing, for the end of the restrictive trading system at Guangzhou, for other ports to be opened to international trade and for the fixing of fair tariffs for foreign goods. The Emperor would not grant any of his requests and sent a letter to George III saying that China could not increase its foreign trade, as it did not require anything from other countries. 'We have never valued ingenious baubles,' wrote Qianlong, 'nor do we have the slightest need of your country's manufactures.' Macartney had to leave China by the appointed route to Guangzhou, noting in his journal that this awe-inspiring Empire had weaknesses which could destroy it. He described China as 'an old, crazy first-rate man-of-war' which, under rulers less able than Qianlong, would be 'dashed to pieces on the shore', as it was 'in vain to attempt arresting the progress of human knowledge'. The deficiencies which Macartney noted became apparent in the ease with which Britain defeated China in the **Opium War** (1839–42), as a result of which the British were able to obtain the concessions which Qianlong had rejected.

**MacDonald, James Ramsay** (1866–1937). British Prime Minister (1924, 1929–35). The illegitimate son of a servant girl and farm labourer in north-east Scotland, MacDonald took clerical jobs and studied in the evening. Intelligent and hard-working, he rose rapidly after joining the **Independent Labour Party** in 1894 and, with Keir **Hardie**, played an essential role in forming in 1900 the Labour Representation Committee (which became the **Labour Party** in 1906). He was its first secretary and made a secret electoral pact in 1903 with Herbert Gladstone, the **Liberal Party** chief whip, which enabled the Labour Party to win twenty-nine seats in the 1906 election and become a significant parliamentary party for the first time. MacDonald became an MP himself in 1906 and established himself as Labour's leading theorist. Like Keir Hardie, he rejected violent revolution and class war and saw an evolutionary and peaceful route to **socialism**, whereby the functions of the state would be gradually extended. Socialism would, he wrote, retain 'everything that was of permanent value in **Liberalism**, by virtue of being the hereditary heir of Liberalism'. His wife was a great support and influence; when she died in 1911 he was devastated, never recovered from the blow and never remarried. In the same year he became chairman of the Parliamentary Labour Party, which he completely dominated until 1914. When the **First World War** began he opposed British involvement and resigned as leader of the Labour Party. Courageously he coped with the savage abuse, which accused him of being unpatriotic, and lost his seat in the 1918 election. He was not re-elected until 1922, by which time he was seen as a man of principle and once again became leader of the Labour Party. For the rest of the 1920s he was the dominant personality in British politics, who made the warring factions of the Labour Party into an effective political force, which replaced the Liberals as one of the two leading parties.

In 1924 he became Prime Minister of the first Labour government, but depended on Liberal support to give him a majority in the **Commons**. MacDonald was his own Foreign Secretary and was very successful in obtaining acceptance of the **Dawes Plan**, which dealt with **reparations** and enabled the French to withdraw from their occupation of the **Ruhr**. He also recognized, and made a trade treaty with, Soviet Russia, but this was unpopular with both Liberals and Conservatives and helped to bring his short-lived government to an end. When MacDonald again became Prime Minister in 1929 the Labour Party was for the first time the largest party in the Commons, though it did not have an overall majority. MacDonald, whose interest remained in foreign rather than domestic affairs, had no policy to cope with the **Great Depression** and unemployment, which rose from one million to three million between 1929 and 1931. His Chancellor of the Exchequer, Philip Snowden, refused to abandon the **gold standard** and, to meet American conditions for a loan, proposed in 1931 to cut civil-service pay and unemployment benefits. As the Cabinet accepted this by only twelve votes to nine and the TUC, led by **Bevin**, was resolutely opposed, MacDonald saw that he could not continue. He resigned on 23 August but on the next morning accepted **George V**'s urgent plea to form a **National Government**, which would include Liberals and **Conservatives**, as he saw the national interest as more important than that of his party. His astonished Labour colleagues had not been consulted and regarded this as a betrayal. Only seven Labour MPs remained faithful to MacDonald, who was replaced as leader of the Labour Party by Arthur **Henderson** and was expelled from the party. MacDonald's treachery was, in Labour eyes, magnified when he called a general election in October 1931, in which 556 National Government candidates were elected. He had a personal following of only thirteen National Labour MPs, so he was entirely dependent on the Conservatives. MacDonald continued as Prime Minister, reviled and ostracized by his former Labour colleagues, until 1935, when he lost his seat. In **Baldwin**'s administration he served as Lord Privy Seal from 1935–7, but he was a broken man and died suddenly on a voyage to South America. The events of 1931 have clouded Ramsey MacDonald's reputation as a great leader of the Labour Party. Yet for thirty years he was an outstanding politician, who turned Labour from a party of protest into a party of government.

**Macdonald, Sir John Alexander** (1815–91). Canadian Prime Minister (1867–73, 1878–91). Macdonald became leader of the Conservative Party, which emerged in 1854 and dominated Canadian politics from that time until his death in 1891. His success was due to his timely concessions to both the English-speaking and the French Canadians. Supporting the former in their desire for economic and westward expansion, he recognized that the latter were afraid of losing their cultural identity. Macdonald worked closely with the French Canadian leader Georges-Etienne **Cartier** in secularizing the Clergy Reserves (see **Canada Acts**), and in bringing about the **dominion** of Canada through the **British North America Act** (1867). He saw that the connection with Britain was essential to finance and protect the Canadian Far West from American encroachment. He was careful to have representatives from each province in his Cabinet and kept the Conservatives in power from 1867–96, apart from one Liberal administration from 1873–8. The way was clear for the opening of the West when, in 1869, the Hudson's Bay Company gave up its Rupert's Land charter and its trading monopoly in the North-West Territory, where there was a settled population of only 7,000. Opposition by Indians and *Métis* (French-Indians) erupted in the **Riel rebellion** (1869–70), but in 1870 Manitoba joined the dominion. After that Macdonald turned his attention to the Pacific coast. British Columbia joined the Confederation in 1871, on being promised a transcontinental railway. Two years later Macdonald lost the general election owing to the 'Pacific Scandal', when it became known that railway promoters had contributed handsomely to Conservative election funds. He was back in office again in 1878, supporting the building of the **Canadian Pacific Railway** and the drive for immigrants to fill the prairies. This led to another Riel rebellion in 1885, which was easily put down; but Macdonald made an uncharacteristic misjudgement in executing Riel, who was regarded by French Canadians as a defender of their rights. This began a decline in Conservative fortunes, and though Macdonald won his last election in 1891, it was with a greatly reduced majority. He died in 1891, exhausted by the election. John Macdonald was one of Canada's greatest statesmen. In spite of his emotional appeal to English-speaking Canadians in 1891 ('a British subject I was born, a British subject I will die') he genuinely wanted, and worked for, a partnership with French Canadians. He successfully prevented Canada from being absorbed by the USA and he presided over the westward expansion of Canada to the Pacific coast.

**Mackenzie, Alexander** (1764–1820). Canadian explorer. At the beginning of the nineteenth century Scottish merchants in Montreal had established the North-West Company as a rival to the Hudson's Bay Company for fur-trapping in Canada, especially in the region beyond the Great Lakes towards the Rockies and the Pacific Ocean. Canadian explorers set out on behalf of the Company to open up the continent for trade. From Lake Athabasca Alexander Mackenzie, with a tiny party of French Canadians and Indians, found the river which is named after him and in 1789 sailed down it in his birch-bark canoes to the Arctic. In 1793 he followed the Peace river from Lake Athabasca to the Rockies and then went over the mountains to the Pacific coast. Another explorer, Simon Fraser, opened up new Pacific territory in 1804 by exploring the Fraser river, as it wound its way through the gorges of the Rockies. These voyages of exploration strengthened British claims to the north-west part of the American continent.

**McKinley, William** (1843–1901). Twenty-fifth President of the USA (1897–1901). McKinley was bitingly described by the journalist William Allen White as 'on the whole decent, on the whole dumb, who walked among men like a bronze statue determinedly looking for a pedestal'. He was certainly not dynamic but he was intelligent and pious and genuinely devoted to public service. He first came to public attention as a Congressman in 1890, when he was responsible for the McKinley tariff, which imposed the highest duties up to that date on imports into the USA. He was the **Republican** candidate in the presidential election of 1896, when he fought a 'front-porch' campaign, staying at home to address visitors whilst his opponent, William Jennings **Bryan**, stumped the country making over 600 speeches. McKinley's support for the **gold standard** and high tariffs and his promise to restore prosperity after the depression, which began in 1893, brought him success. He carried out his promises by raising tariffs even higher in 1897 and by putting the nation on the gold standard in 1900. He promised 'no wars of conquest' but gave way to public opinion by declaring war on Spain in 1898. After the **Spanish–American War** he annexed the Pacific island of Guam, Puerto Rico and the Philippines. He hoped 'to educate the Filipinos, uplift them and civilize and Christianize them', apparently unaware that they were already Christian. His Presidency saw further additions to the American empire: Hawaii in 1898, Wake Island and part of Samoa (shared with Germany) in 1899. McKinley began his **'open-door' policy**, by which he tried to ensure that all nations would be able to trade with China on an equal basis and sent troops there as part of an international force to crush the **Boxer Rising**. He was re-elected in 1900, defeating Bryan again, but on 6 September 1901 he was assassinated by an anarchist.

**MacMahon, Marie Edmé Patrice Maurice, Comte de** (1808–93). Marshal of France and President of the **Third Republic** (1873–9). MacMahon took part in the conquest of Algeria and in the **Crimean War** and was mainly responsible for the victories over the Austrians at Magenta and Solferino in 1859. In the **Franco–Prussian War** (1870–71) his army was defeated at **Sedan**, where he was captured with the Emperor **Napoleon III**. After his release he commanded the government troops which defeated the **Paris Commune**. A devout Roman Catholic and a conservative, he was elected President of the **Monarchist Republic** by a royalist Assembly, which hoped that he would restore the monarchy. He accepted reluctantly – he disliked politics – from a sense of duty and in 1877 brought about the *Seize Mai* crisis, when he dismissed the republican Prime Minister and replaced him by a monarchist, the Duc de Broglie. As Broglie could not command a majority in the Chamber of Deputies, MacMahon called a general election but his gamble failed: a majority of republicans was once again returned. Some of his advisers wanted him to stage a military *coup* but he refused, as this might bring about civil war. When the Senate also gained a republican majority in 1879, MacMahon resigned, though his term of office had nearly two years to run.

**Madison, James** (1751–1836). Fourth President of the USA (1809–17). Madison played a greater part than any other American in forming his country's political institutions. Many Americans, including Madison, recognized that the Articles of Confederation, which held the states together in a loose Union from 1781–9, did not give the central government any real power and were unworkable in the long run. Madison therefore supported the call for a Constitutional Convention, which was held at Philadelphia in 1787. The Constitution, which provided for a strong central government, reflected his views. The Federalist papers, to which he made a major and brilliant contribution, still remain the best commentary on the Constitution and the only classic of political thought yet written by an American. Madison played a crucial role in persuading Virginia, the largest state, to ratify the Constitution. In 1791 he proposed the Bill of Rights, a series of amendments to the Constitution, which guaranteed freedom of speech, religion, the press and assembly. His work on the Constitution marked the peak of his career.

He was, with **Jefferson**, co-founder in 1792 of the Democratic-Republican Party, the forerunner of the **Democratic Party**. As Jefferson's Secretary of State from 1801–9 and as President, he was largely concerned with trying to defend the rights of American shipping against French and British predators during the **Napoleonic Wars**. As the British seized American ships trading with France and insisted on impressing American sailors into the British navy, relations between the two countries deteriorated to such an extent that the War Hawks, led by **Clay** and **Calhoun**, pushed

Madison into the **Anglo-American War** in 1812. This war divided the nation and saw Madison's popularity fall sharply. It revived with the economic prosperity that followed the end of the war in 1814, a prosperity to which Madison contributed by permitting the setting up the second Bank of the United States in 1816 and the first protective tariff in US history.

**Mafia.** A Sicilian word for a clandestine criminal organization, deeply rooted in Sicilian society. It administered its own law and justice, based on *omertà*, a code of silence, which demands that there should be no resort to, or cooperation with, the legal authorities of the state. Landowners paid protection money to it, farmers borrowed from it. Opponents were murdered and few murders were solved, because of fear and corruption. **Mussolini** declared war on it and greatly reduced its power, but he did not destroy it. In the 1880s many Sicilians emigrated to the USA and set up the Mafia in New York and Chicago. They were active in the **Prohibition** era and by the 1930s had developed the most powerful organized crime syndicate in the USA, which adopted the name *Cosa Nostra* (Our Affair).

**Maginot Line.** A French system of fortifications along the Franco-German border begun in 1929 and named after the Minister of War, André Maginot. It was not a continuous line but a series of fortified zones, with anti-tank defences and pill-boxes in front of bomb-proof artillery placements. Its aim was to deter Germany from attacking across the Rhine through Lorraine but it left the 200 miles of France's frontier with Belgium unfortified; consequently it could be outflanked (and was, in May 1940).

**Mahan, Alfred Thayer** (1840–1914). American naval officer. In *The Influence of Sea Power upon History, 1660–1783*, published in 1890, Mahan argued that a country could never be a world power without sea power, which had in the past been more important than land power and always would be. In order to be successful commercially, the USA would have to expand her merchant marine and build a powerful navy to protect it. He thought that overseas colonies were vital for a nation's prosperity and that island bases were more useful than the control of large land masses. The USA must therefore acquire overseas bases and colonies, especially in the Caribbean and Pacific. His ideas had considerable influence in the USA on politicians like Theodore **Roosevelt**, who became Assistant Secretary of the Navy in 1897. Mahan's doctrines were responsible at least in part for the enlargement of the US navy (in 1880 it hardly existed; in 1900, with seventeen battleships and six cruisers, it was inferior only to those of Britain and Germany), for the building of the **Panama Canal** and for the annexation of Hawaii. In Britain he influenced Winston **Churchill** and in Germany **Tirpitz**'s strategy owed much to him. Kaiser **William II** ordered that a copy of his book should be placed on every German warship.

**Mahdi.** An Islamic title meaning 'the divinely guided one'. It was usually applied to a religious leader who was expected to end corrupt practices and restore the purity of Islam as in the time of the Prophet Muhammad. Since the tenth century a number of self-proclaimed Mahdis have appeared in the Sudanic region and North Africa. The best known in Europe is Muhammad Ahmad (1840–85), who claimed descent from the Prophet and declared himself to be the Mahdi in 1881. He was rebelling against a Muslim government, that of Egypt, which had been profoundly influenced by heretical European influences. As the Egyptian government was preoccupied in 1882 with **Urabi**'s revolt and the British occupation, the Mahdi was able to take over the whole of the Sudan. He defeated a force under General Hicks in 1883 and when **Gladstone** sent General **Gordon** to arrange for the evacuation of the Sudan, the Mahdi captured Khartoum in 1885, killing Gordon. The Mahdi himself died shortly afterwards, although the Mahdist state he had set up survived until it was destroyed by **Kitchener** at the battle of **Omdurman** in 1898.

**Mahmud II** (1785–1839). Ottoman Sultan (1808–39). The reform movement in Turkey appeared to be destroyed when Selim III, who had formed a European-style army, was deposed in 1807 and later murdered by the janissaries, the infantry élite of the Ottoman army. Mahmud, who wished to continue Selim's reforms, had therefore to act cautiously. He began by establishing central control over the provinces, where many *pashas* (governors) had become independent potentates, although he was not able to do this in Egypt, where he had to recognize the autonomy of **Muhammad Ali**. During the **Greek War of Independence** (1821–32), when a modern army was needed, Mahmud ordered the formation of a new army with European training. When the janissaries tried to prevent this in 1826 they were annihilated, and a conscript army, trained by Prussian officers and under the control of the Sultan, was introduced. This made possible the reforms which Mahmud had long wanted and which laid the basis for further reforms later in the nineteenth century. The power of the Sultan was increased as feudal fiefs – land granted in return for military service – were abolished in 1831 and the *ulama* (religious leaders) were weakened when their *waqfs* (religious endowments) were taken over by the state, and their courts and schools came under the control of new state-ministries. They were to offer little resistance to future reforms. European-type schools were set up to train the new élite of army officers and civil servants. Mahmud's attempt to control his Empire was less successful than his domestic reforms. Greece became independent in 1832, whilst Ibrahim, Muhammad Ali's son, conquered Syria and defeated the Turks in Anatolia. Mahmud had to grant Syria and Adana to Muhammad Ali in 1833. When he tried to recover them six years later he was again defeated, at Nezib in Syria, and his fleet defected to Muhammad Ali. At this time Mahmud died. His Empire survived only because the great powers came to its rescue and forced Muhammad Ali to give up Syria.

**Malta, Siege of** (1940–43). Malta was Britain's only military base in the central Mediterranean, sixty miles from Sicily. It became particularly important after the fall of **France** and Italy's entry into the war, as it was the only place from which Italian supply routes to North Africa could be attacked by air. It was poorly defended, as the British government had decided before the war that it was indefensible. The Italians could probably have taken Malta in 1940 and won control of the Mediterranean, but they were too timid to invade the island. From December 1941 to May 1942 the *Luftwaffe* bombed Malta day and night, so that hardly any aircraft remained on the island and only two merchant ships reached Malta in the first half of the year. The people were on the verge of starvation and many had to live in caves. Kesselring, the German Commander in the Mediterranean, promised **Hitler** that he would 'wipe Malta off the map', but in May sixty Spitfires arrived from carriers and shot down many attacking aircraft. As Rommel advanced into Egypt in the summer of 1942, attacks from Malta reduced his supplies to a trickle. British air superiority was established over the eastern Mediterranean, and at the end of 1942 convoys reached Malta without difficulty. With the Allied invasion of Sicily in June 1943 the siege ended. Rommel had said in February 1941 that 'Without Malta the **Axis** will end by losing control of North Africa,' and this had happened. The cost to Britain was high in losses of ships and aircraft and 1,500 Maltese civilians were killed, but Malta probably saved the Allies in North Africa.

**Malthus, Thomas Robert** (1766–1834). English economist. A Fellow of Jesus College, Cambridge, Malthus took holy orders in 1796 and then shot to national attention with *An Essay on the Principle of Population* (1798), which received wide publicity. He argued that population growth is not necessarily beneficial to the nation, as man's capacity to reproduce himself is greater than his ability to increase the means of subsistence. To prevent population from exceeding subsistence, 'checks' are needed. These are of two types: positive checks, the most important, are the result of disease, famine or war; and there are preventive checks, from conscious choice, such as delayed marriage or contraception. As the 'perpetual tendency' of mankind was 'to increase beyond the means of subsistence', poverty was man's inescapable lot. Because Malthus was so gloomy, economics was called 'the dismal science'. His ideas rapidly became part of current economics and helped to justify a theory of wages that made the minimum cost of subsistence for the wage-earner the standard. Malthus had a great impact on social policy. He condemned the Elizabethan **Poor Law**, still in force, as he said that it produced rather than alleviated poverty by keeping people alive without increasing the means for their support. Workhouses could be justified for the most unfortunate but the 'fare should be hard', an idea adopted in the Poor Law Amendment Act (1834). The market alone, he thought, should determine wage levels, so he condemned outright the artificial raising of wages by the **Speenhamland system** (1795). Although he was accused by **Cobbett** of being inhumane and lacking Christian charity, his ideas were generally accepted by political economists in England and spread abroad. His reputation in Europe was such that in 1833 he was elected to the French Academy and to the Royal Academy in Berlin.

**Manchester School.** A name given by **Disraeli** to a group of businessmen and politicians in Britain in the 1840s. Led by John **Bright** and Richard **Cobden** and based in Manchester, the centre of the cotton industry, they followed the *laissez-faire* doctrines of Adam Smith and David Ricardo. They believed in a minimalist state, which should not interfere in the free market by, for example, passing legislation restricting hours of work in factories. Their influence declined in the 1860s, with increased state intervention in economic affairs, but revived under Margaret Thatcher in the 1980s.

**Manchukuo** ('land of the Manchus') (1932–45). The name given by Japan to the 'independent' state set up in Manchuria in March 1932, after the **Manchurian Incident**. Only Germany and Italy of the major powers recognized the new state. In 1933 the Japanese advanced into the Chinese province of Jehol and this was added to Manchukuo. The state council and ministers were headed by Chinese, but real power was in the hands of Japanese vice-ministers and the Commander of the Guandong army. There was no elected assembly. **Puyi**, the last Emperor of China, was made Emperor of Manchukuo in 1934. The Japanese invested in industry and mining (coal and iron ore), which developed rapidly, and in 1935 bought from the USSR the Chinese Eastern Railway, which cut across northern Manchukuo to Vladivostok. Immigrants came from Japan but not on a large scale, as there was a lot of anti-Japanese guerrilla activity, particularly during the **Sino-Japanese War** (1937–45). This was fuelled by unpopular Japanese rule, which imposed heavy taxes, labour conscription and enforced purchase of land for Japanese immigrants. In August 1945 Soviet troops occupied Manchukuo, which was returned to China. The Japanese there were repatriated.

**Manchuria.** The original home of the **Qing dynasty** of China. When Russia seized the sparsely populated Amur–Ussuri region (see **Alexander II**), China feared that Russia would next occupy Manchuria, which had a population of only three million in 1850.

Chinese settlers were therefore encouraged to go to Manchuria, so that by 1900 the population had risen to nine million. Japan too had her eye on Manchuria, where there was much fighting in the **Sino-Japanese War** of 1894–5. At the Treaty of **Shimonoseki**, which ended the war, Japan acquired the Liaodong peninsula but Russia, Germany and France forced her to give it up. In 1896 Russia obtained Chinese permission to build a railway across Northern Manchuria to link up with the **Trans-Siberian Railway** and two years later leased part of the Liaodong peninsula, including Port Arthur (Lushun), from China. Japan was furious, especially when Russia used the excuse of the **Boxer Rising** to send troops into other parts of Manchuria. Japan feared that a permanent Russian occupation of Manchuria would threaten her interests in **Korea** and block her route into China. Russia's failure to withdraw her troops was one of the reasons for the **Russo-Japanese War** (1904–5), which was fought in Manchuria. It ended with the Treaty of **Portsmouth**, when Japan took over the Russian lease of southern Liaodong and the South Manchurian railway. Japanese militarists wanted complete domination of Manchuria, as security against a possible Russian attack, so when it appeared that **Jiang Jieshi** (Chiang Kai-shek) would effectively unite China, members of the Japanese Guandong army in the Liaodong peninsula engineered the **Manchurian Incident** in 1931. This led to a Japanese occupation of Manchuria and the setting up there of an ostensibly independent state, **Manchukuo**, which remained under Japanese control until 1945, when Manchuria again became part of China.

**Manchurian Incident.** Japan's military action in Manchuria in 1931–2. By the Treaty of **Portsmouth**, which ended the **Russo-Japanese War** (1904–5), Japan acquired the lease of Port Arthur (Lushun) and part of the South Manchurian railway. The Japanese Guandong army was stationed in the Liaodong peninsula and Japan had the right to station troops along the South Manchurian railway, which gave her effective control of half of Manchuria. By 1931 Manchuria was very important to Japan: 82 per cent of Japan's foreign investment was in China, two-thirds of it in Manchuria, which was a vital source of minerals (coal and iron ore), necessary for Japan's industrial development. With the **Great Depression**, and the catastrophic fall in Japan's exports, Manchuria became even more important for Japan and was regarded as a suitable place for Japanese emigrants. The Japanese High Command thought that war with the USSR was inevitable and so favoured a Japanese take-over in Manchuria, but the liberal government in Tokyo was pacific. It was junior officers in the Guandong army who took action by blowing up part of the railway line outside Mukden on 18 September 1931. Claiming that Chinese troops were responsible, they then occupied Mukden and in five months, with the aid of Japanese troops in Korea, who joined in without gaining permission from the Japanese government, they overran Manchuria. The Japanese government was shocked but, faced with a *fait accompli*, could do little, particularly as the Guandong army had the backing of the War Ministry and General Staff in Tokyo. China appealed to the **League of Nations**. In March 1932 Japan set up the 'independent' state of **Manchukuo** before the **Lytton Commission**, sent by the League, arrived to investigate. Its report condemned Japan as the aggressor, and although the League took no action, Japan left the League in protest in 1933. The Manchurian Incident began a train of events that led to the triumph of militarism in Japan: it also showed how ineffective the League was as a force for maintaining world peace.

**Mandates.** A system by which the government of colonies taken from Germany and the **Ottoman Empire** after the **First World War** were entrusted to the victorious powers by the **League of Nations**. Mandates were divided into three groups: in Group A were the former Ottoman territories of Mesopotamia (Iraq) and Palestine (part of which became Transjordan), which were allocated to Britain, and Syria, which became the French mandates of Syria and Lebanon. These territories were to be prepared for independence as soon as possible. Groups B and C were the former German colonies: most of Tanganyika (Tanzania) went to Britain, the rest to Belgium; Togoland and the Cameroons were divided between Britain and France; South Africa became the mandatory power for South-West Africa (Namibia); Germany's Pacific islands north of the equator were allocated to Japan and those south of the equator to Australia and New Zealand. All B and C territories were regarded as too backward to be prepared for independence, though they were to be administered in the interests of the inhabitants. In all the colonies the wishes of the inhabitants were ignored. Each mandatory power was supposed to be accountable to the Permanent Mandates Commission of the League, but neither the Commission nor the League had the authority to coerce a recalcitrant mandatory power.

**Manifest Destiny.** A phrase used by a New York editor, John L. O'Sullivan, in 1845 to justify US control of the whole of the North American continent. He wrote that no nation on earth should be allowed to interfere with America's 'manifest destiny to overspread the continent allotted by Providence for the free development of our yearly multiplying millions'. He was writing to urge the annexation of **Texas** but it was soon used to justify the occupation of **Oregon** (see **Oregon boundary dispute**) and the large part of Mexico seized after the **Mexican–American War** of 1846–8. Originally a Democratic slogan, it was soon taken over by Republicans, when **Alaska** was purchased and the USA fought in the **Spanish–American War**. Idealism was mixed up with greed in Manifest Destiny, as there was a genuine conviction that as American territory spread, so would democracy.

**Mannerheim, Carl Gustav Emil, Baron von** (1867–1951). Finnish field marshal and statesman. From a Finno-Swedish noble family, Mannerheim was born a Russian subject and became a major-general in the Russian army, serving in the **First World War**. When the **October Revolution** broke out in 1917 he returned to Finland, which declared its independence, to lead the White forces to victory over the **Bolsheviks** in a bloody civil war. Failing to be elected President in 1919, he retired from politics until he was recalled in 1931 to head the National Defence Council and reorganize the Finnish army. In the **Finnish–Russian War** (1939–40) he led the Finns in a skilful defence against overwhelming odds and held up the Russians for four months before the exhausted Finns were compelled to surrender. When Germany attacked the Soviet Union in Operation **Barbarossa** (June 1941), Mannerheim waged war along with Germany to recover territories lost to Russia in 1940, but he refused to go beyond this limited aim and would not join in the German attack on **Leningrad**. As Finland's President (1944–6) he obtained terms from Russia at the end of the **Second World War** which left Finland independent.

**Manstein, Erich von** (1887–1973). German field marshal. At the beginning of the **Second World War** Manstein was Chief of Staff to General von Rundstedt and drew up the plan for the invasion of France which **Hitler** accepted and which was brilliantly successful. The main German attack came through the wooded Ardennes, where Panzer units caught the French by surprise, crossed the Meuse and then headed for the Channel coast, cutting the French armies in two (see the fall of **France**). He was put in charge of troops to invade England but when the invasion did not take place he was moved to East Prussia in command of a Panzer corps. When Operation **Barbarossa** began, Manstein's corps invaded the Soviet Union and advanced 200 miles in four days to the river Dvina and then on to **Leningrad**. In September he was promoted to command the Eleventh Army on the south-eastern front and from 1942–4 was Commander-in-Chief in this region. He defeated the Red Army in the Crimea with smaller forces, captured 430,000 prisoners and then took Sebastopol in June 1942 after a 250-day siege. In an attempt to relieve the German Sixth Army at **Stalingrad** he was held up thirty miles short of his target and then organized an orderly retreat to the Dnieper. He counter-attacked in the spring of 1943, drove the Red Army back to the Donetz river and captured Kharkov. Manstein wanted to nip off the Russian salient at **Kursk** quickly but Hitler waited until it was too late and suffered a major reverse there. The Germans had now lost the initiative, so Manstein conducted a skilful retreat to Poland. He was in favour of controlled retreats which allowed the Russians to advance in one sector, so that they could be cut off in flank attacks by Panzers. Hitler was opposed to this policy and when Manstein wanted to retreat again in March 1944, Hitler dismissed him. He retired to his estates until the war ended, when he was tried by a British military court in Hamburg. Sentenced to eighteen years' imprisonment in 1949, he was released in 1953 on health grounds. Manstein is considered by many to have been the ablest German commander of the Second World War, a view shared by his fellow generals, who wanted him as Commander-in-Chief in 1941 when Hitler removed Brauchitsch, taking over the role himself.

**Mao Zedong (Mao Tse-tung)** (1893–1976). Chinese communist leader and first chairman of the People's Republic of China. Mao was the son of a peasant, who became involved in the **May Fourth Movement** demonstrations in Beijing (Peking). Rejecting Confucian respect for authority and seemly behaviour, he turned to Western ideas and became a Marxist when working as a library assistant at Beijing University. He was a founder-member of the Chinese Communist Party (CCP) in 1921. When the CCP, on orders from the **Comintern**, made an alliance with **Sun Yixian**'s (Sun Yat-sen's) **Guomindang** (Nationalist Party) in 1923, Mao worked enthusiastically in the **United Front** in several Guomindang organizations. After visiting Hunan in 1926 Mao wrote a report on the peasant revolution there, which marked his first move away from orthodox Marxism and towards its adaptation to Chinese circumstances. Orthodox Marxists regarded the peasants as conservative and *petit bourgeois* and thought that revolution would not originate with them but with the urban proletariat. Mao maintained that the real revolution in China, where there were few industrial workers, was taking place in the countryside and that the CCP should become involved in it. 'The Chinese revolution,' he wrote, 'has only this form [a peasant revolution] and no other.' When **Jiang Jieshi** (Chiang Kai-shek) turned on, and massacred, his communist allies in the **Shanghai** *coup* of 1927 and destroyed the workers' movements in the cities, the CCP was forced to seek survival in the countryside. Mao and Zhu De helped to form the **Jiangxi Soviet** and saw it expand to cover an area with a population of nine million. Jiang felt this threatened the nationalist control of China, so he waged five extermination campaigns (1930–34) against the Jiangxi Soviet, finally forcing Mao and 80,000 followers to break out in 1934 on the **Long March**, which ended a year later with only 8,000 reaching the safety of **Yanan** in the north. During the time Yanan was the capital of communist China (1937–47), Mao established his ascendancy in the CCP as both political leader and ideologist. During this period the CCP enormously increased its membership and popularity, as it was seen as the chief opponent of Japan in the **Sino-Japanese War** (1937–45). In this war Mao and Zhu De used the tactics they had developed during Jiang's extermination campaigns, avoiding head-on conflict but tying down vast numbers of Japanese troops by guerrilla warfare behind their lines. The CCP had made a second United Front with the Guomindang to fight the Japanese, but there was distrust on both sides and the CCP continued to extend its influence in north China, so that when the war with Japan ended there were about ninety-six million people in areas under communist control. In 1945 Jiang, recognized as leader of China by all the Great Powers, was in no mood to compromise with Mao and the CCP and refused to form a coalition government with them. The result was civil war (1945–9), which ended with a crushing communist victory and the proclamation by Mao in Beijing (October 1949) of the People's Republic of China.

**Marat, Jean-Paul** (1743–93). French journalist and revolutionary. A failed doctor, Marat became the chief spokesman for the popular movement during the early years of the **French Revolution**, through his newspaper *L'Ami du Peuple* ('The Friend of the People'). In it he attacked the **Constituent Assembly** for not abolishing feudalism entirely and for giving the vote only to 'active' citizens (who paid taxes equivalent to three days' labour a year). He wanted power to be given to a dictator (himself) and called for the execution of all opponents of the Revolution. Marat had a strong following amongst the Parisian *sans-culottes*, but in the provinces and by the government he was regarded as dangerous and mad, so he spent much of his time in hiding. In August 1792 he became a member of the Paris Commune and in September was elected to the **Convention**, where he was attacked by the **Girondins** for encouraging the **September massacres** earlier in the month. When **Louis XVI** was put on trial in January 1793 Marat ensured that he would be condemned to death by proposing that a decision should be reached by '*appel nominal*' (each deputy was to annouce his decision publicly), 'so that traitors in this Assembly may be known'. In April 1793 he called on the *sans-culottes* to take up arms to remove the Girondins from power in the Convention. For this he was tried before the Revolutionary Tribunal but was acquitted with much public rejoicing. Two months later the *sans-culottes* did intimidate the Assembly into arresting the leading Girondins. On 13 July he was stabbed to death in his bath by a Girondin sympathizer, Charlotte Corday, an event made famous by David's painting.

**March on Rome** (1922). The intended seizure of power by **Mussolini** and his Fascist **Blackshirts** (*squadristi*). The inspiration was the armed occupation of Fiume by **D'Annunzio** and his followers in 1919. The occupation of public buildings in the towns of north and central Italy was to be followed by three columns of Blackshirts marching on Rome. Fascist squads seized public buildings in nearly all north Italian cities, but there was no real threat to the capital, as the *squadristi* were no match for the army. The Prime Minister, Facta, decided to oppose them and on 27 October asked King **Victor Emanuel III** to sign a declaration of martial law, obliging the army to stop the march. The King agreed but on the following morning changed his mind, as he feared civil war, was uncertain about the army's loyalty and felt, as did many liberal politicians, that Mussolini should be offered a post in the government. Facta immediately resigned. Mussolini would not join any government he did not lead, so when he arrived in Rome by train on 30 October the King made him Prime Minister. Defeat for Mussolini would have marked the end of **Fascism**, but his bluff had worked. The Chamber of Deputies, in which Fascists were a small minority, gave his new government a massive vote of confidence by 306 votes to 116. Mussolini's followers never marched on the city, but 15,000 arrived by train to take part in a ceremonial parade on 31 October.

**Marie-Antoinette** (1755–93). Queen of France (1774–92). The daughter of the Habsburg Empress, Maria Theresa, Marie-Antoinette was a symbol of the unpopular alliance with Austria, which had led to France's defeat in the Seven Years War (1756–63). She had the determination that her husband, **Louis XVI**, lacked ('the only man in the family', Mirabeau called her) but she was regarded as wilful, frivolous and arrogant. Her brother-in-law, the Comte de Provence (later **Louis XVIII**), called her Madame Deficit, owing to her enormous gambling debts. When Louis accepted the Constitution of 1791, which severely limited his powers, Marie-Antoinette was determined to overthrow it at the first opportunity. 'Conciliation is out of the question now,' she wrote to her brother Leopold. 'Armed force has destroyed everything and only armed force can put things right.' She hoped for a war in which France would be defeated, so that Louis could recover his old powers. When France declared war on Austria in April 1792, the Queen sent details of French military plans to the Austrians. After the attack on the **Tuileries** in August 1792, she was imprisoned with her family. She behaved with great dignity at her humiliating trial, before she became another victim of the **Terror** on 16 October 1793.

**Maritime Strike** (1890). A misleading name for a clash in Australia between capital and labour, which mainly affected New South Wales, Victoria and South Australia. As **trade unions** became more powerful and demanded the closed shop, employers called for 'freedom of contract' (the right to employ non-union labour). In June 1890 the Steamship Owners' Association (SOA) granted an eight-hour day and the closed shop to the Sydney Wharf Labourers' Union, which prompted the Marine Officers' Association to claim pay increases. These were rejected by the SOA, so many officers went on strike. Other workers became involved: coal miners would not supply coal to ships manned by non-union labour, whereupon the owners locked out the miners. In September work was suspended at Broken Hill, as the mine owners said they could not move the ore owing to the strikes, which were on a scale never seen before in Australia. The sheep shearers joined the strike, as did the Sydney road transport drivers; 'scabs' were intimidated and mounted police charged the strikers, some of whom were imprisoned. 3,000 middle-class Australians, shocked by the violence, enrolled as special constables. Unemployed labour was used to break the strike, which collapsed in October, the employers gaining the right to employ non-union labour, even in some industries where the closed shop had operated. Between 25,000 and 30,000 workers had been involved in the most important confrontation between capital and labour in Australia in the nineteenth century. The trade unions had overestimated their strength and were severely weakened, so that they were unable to resist pay cuts. Their defeat helped to bring about the formation of the Australian **Labor Party**.

**Marne, battle of the** (5–10 September 1914). The river Marne, a tributary of the Seine east of Paris, marked the furthest advance of the German army into France during the **First World War**. The **Schlieffen Plan** aimed to knock out France in six weeks, before the Russians could mobilize their vast army, by advancing in strength through Belgium, by-passing the French defences along the German border. German armies would sweep down to encircle Paris and then attack French armies in the rear. This plan might have worked if von Moltke, the German Chief of Staff, had not weakened it by transferring troops from the German right wing (rather than from Lorraine, where they could have been spared) to East Prussia, which the Russians had invaded. Yet the Germans made swift progress sweeping through Belgium and northern France, whilst the French made futile and costly attacks on German forces in Lorraine and the Ardennes. On 1 September the German First Army, under von Kluck, on the right wing had crossed the Oise and was only thirty miles from Paris. The French expected an attack on the capital and were astonished when air reconnaissance showed them that von Kluck was moving south-east across the Marne to support the Second Army. This exposed his flank, which the French attacked on 5 September, and so began the battle of the Marne. When von Kluck pulled back two of his corps from south of the Marne to meet the attack, he left a gap of twenty miles between his army and the German Second Army. **Joffre**, the French Commander, saw his chance and seized it, for opposite the gap was the British Expeditionary Force. The British advanced through it and came up behind the German First Army. The German armies retreated to the river Aisne and the battle of the Marne was over but at tremendous cost: the Allies suffered 250,000 casualties, the Germans even more. In the three weeks since the war began each side had lost half a million men, including a high proportion of their officers. Joffre had won one of the most important battles since **Waterloo**. Paris was saved and the Schlieffen Plan was dead. There was now no hope of knocking out France quickly, and Germany was condemned to fight a war on two fronts, which she dreaded. By the end of the year the Western Front stretched from the Channel to Switzerland as both sides dug into prepared positions – the period of **trench warfare** had begun.

**Marshall, John** (1755–1835). Chief Justice of the US **Supreme Court** (1801–35). One of John Adams's (President, 1797–1801) last appointments was to make his Secretary of State, John Marshall, Chief Justice of the Supreme Court. Marshall was a Federalist, with ideas similar to those of Alexander **Hamilton**. As the **Federal Party** never won another presidential election, Marshall served under five Presidents who belonged to other parties. He had no previous judicial experience but became the greatest American Chief Justice, who dominated the Supreme Court as no one has done since. His judgments interpreting the Constitution have profoundly affected the American political system, the role of the Supreme Court and American society.

In 1803 in the case of *Marbury* v. *Madison* he extended the jurisdiction of the Supreme Court to review Acts of Congress and declare them void if they violated the Constitution. He extended this power of judicial review to state legislatures in the case of *Fletcher* v. *Peck* (1810). In judgments like these Marshall made the Supreme Court a powerful and prestigious political institution. He also extended the power of the federal government at the expense of that of the states. In his most famous case, *McCulloch* v. *Maryland*, he decided that the Constitution contained 'implied powers', which the Congress could use to establish such institutions as the Bank of the United States. The Congress could use any means it liked to exercise its powers, if these were not explicitly forbidden by the Constitution. In the case of *Dartmouth College* v. *Woodward* he said that the New Hampshire legislature could not arbitrarily amend the Dartmouth College charter to bring it under state control. This judgment not only protected private endowments but in effect prevented state legislatures from interfering with business corporations.

**Martí, José** (1853–95). Cuban revolutionary. A poet, intellectual and journalist, Martí spent much of his life in exile, on account of his anti-Spanish activities in Cuba. He became so well known throughout Latin America for his journalism and poetry that Uruguay appointed him as its Vice-Consul in New York. From 1880 to 1895 Martí lived in the USA, where he united the diverse factions of a Cuban independence movement to form the Cuban Revolutionary Party (PRC). His *Cuba Libre* campaign culminated in the invasion of Cuba in 1895, thus beginning the country's war of independence against Spain. Shortly after the invasion Martí was killed fighting Spanish troops, though the rebellion he had begun was carried to a successful conclusion, with the aid of the USA in the **Spanish–American War** (1898). In the 1930s Martí's writings were extensively published: he was seen not only as one who had sought the independence of Cuba from Spain but as a visionary with wider horizons. His cry for Latin America to proclaim its 'second independence', this time from the USA, invoked the Pan-American tradition derived from the 'Liberator' of early nineteenth-century South America, Simón **Bolívar**. Martí was a major source of inspiration for Fidel Castro's Cuban revolution of 1959.

**Marx, Karl Heinrich** (1818–83). German social theorist and revolutionary. A Jew, whose father was a lawyer in Trier, Marx studied philosophy and history at university before becoming a journalist. In 1843 he moved to Paris, where he became a communist and met **Engels**, thus beginning a lifelong friendship. Expelled from Paris in 1844, he went with Engels to Brussels, where he developed his concept of historical materialism. He joined the Communist League and was commissioned, with Engels, to write the *Communist Manifesto*, the shortest and clearest statement of his ideas. When the **Revolutions of 1848** broke out Marx went back to Germany, but after the paper he was editing was suppressed he fled to London, where he remained for the rest of his life. Living in great poverty in Soho (three of his six children died there), he spent his time in the British Museum studying the development of capitalism. Engels provided his main source of income, though this was never sufficient until 1870, when Engels moved to London. Volume one of *Das Kapital* was published in 1867, and though volumes two and three were largely completed in the 1860s, they were not published till after his death. Much of Marx's time from 1864 to 1872 was taken up with the First International, in which Marx clashed with **Bakunin**. Marx was an enthusiastic supporter of the **Paris Commune** (1871) and wrote *The Civil War in France* after its suppression. In the last decade of his life his health declined and he was incapable of sustained effort, though he opposed the linking up of his German supporters (led by **Bebel**) with those of Lassalle to form a united German **Social Democratic Party** in 1875. Marx never set out his views clearly and systematically, but his followers, particularly Engels, turned his ideas into a comprehensive system, **Marxism**. As the most important social and political theorist of the nineteenth and twentieth centuries, Marx's influence was immense. Marxism became the ideology of the Soviet Union, of China under **Mao** and of communist parties everywhere, deeply influencing socialist parties and a wide range of academic disciplines. Almost half the world came to live under regimes which claimed to be Marxist, until the collapse of **communism** in the 1990s.

**Marxism.** An economic, social and political theory derived from the works of **Marx** and **Engels** and later developed by their followers. As Marx never set out his ideas in a lucid and comprehensive way, there has been considerable disagreement about what he really meant. Engels claimed that Marx's Russian disciples 'interpret passages . . . in the most contradictory ways, just as if they were texts from the classics of the New Testament'. At the core of Marx's teaching is his concept of historical materialism, which regarded economic forces as more important than any others in the formation of society. In each epoch the forces of production have been controlled by a minority, which has exploited the majority. This gave rise to class struggles, which centred on the ownership of the means of production. All political institutions and cultural beliefs, Marx thought, were shaped by the holders of economic power – the ruling class – who used them to legitimize their rule and keep themselves in power. Engels claimed that this view – that the economic base determines the political and ideological superstructure – 'explains all historical events and ideas'. He later (in 1890) denied that he and Marx had ever maintained that all historical development could be reduced to economic causes alone, though he thought they 'are finally decisive'. Marx regarded *bourgeois* capitalism as inherently unstable and, as early as the *Communist Manifesto* (1848), predicted its collapse. Capitalism produced its own grave-diggers in the proletariat (the industrial working class), whose alienation, as the worker became an 'appendage of the machine', and immiserization, would lead to revolution. The attempt of capitalists to keep wages low was an internal contradiction of capitalism, as it restricted the purchasing power of the worker and thus limited production, which would lead to cyclical crises, unemployment and bankruptcies. The workers would become stronger as they organized in **trade unions** and political parties and would seize power, by violent revolution in countries (such as Germany) with authoritarian traditions; in countries with democratic traditions (e.g. Britain and the USA) the transition could be peaceful. Proletarian revolution would begin in the most industrially advanced countries and would then spread internationally. Following revolution there would be the dictatorship of the proletariat, a transitional socialist stage to the development of a communist society. The state (for Marx, always an instrument of class oppression) would continue to exist, but for the first time it would be ruled by the majority, the workers, and goods would be distributed according to the contribution of each individual. When there were no longer any classes there would be no need for a state, which would 'wither away', and the principle for the distribution of goods would be 'from each according to his ability and to each according to his needs'.

Nearly all Marx's predictions have been proved wrong. Capitalism has not collapsed and the worker has become better off, so revisionists such as **Bernstein** adapted Marxism to take account of these changes. **Lenin** too saw that the worker was unlikely to become revolutionary, so he put forward a doctrine (**Leninism**) which stressed the importance of the revolutionary party in bringing about revolution, a view which was criticized by Rosa **Luxemburg** for its dictatorial tendencies. **Gramsci** elaborated the concept of hegemony, the way the ruling class sought to legitimize its domination, whilst **Mao Zedong** adapted Marxism to Chinese conditions by stressing the importance of the peasantry. In the Soviet Union under **Stalin**, Marxism became a rigid and ossified doctrine, criticism of which was not allowed, thus ignoring Marx's favourite motto *de omnibus dubitandum* (doubt everything).

**Masaryk, Tomáš** (1850–1937). First President of Czechoslovakia

(1918–35). Masaryk's parents were German-speaking Slavs, his father a coachman. Highly intelligent and industrious, he learnt Czech and Slovak and could soon read French, Russian and English. In 1879 he taught philosophy at the University of Vienna and three years later became a professor at the Czech University in Prague. A member of the Austrian parliament for the first time in 1891, at that time he did not think an independent Czechoslovakia was possible, owing to the 'unfavourable geographical position' of Bohemia. 'We want a federal Austria,' he wrote in 1909. 'We cannot be independent outside of Austria, next to a powerful Germany, having Germans on our territory.' Unlike most Czech and Slovak nationalists, who were **Slavophiles**, he was an ardent westerner. 'The fate of our nation is quite logically linked with the West and with its modern democracy.' During the **First World War** he became convinced that an independent Czechoslovakia was possible and went to Paris, London and New York to persuade the Allies to accept this. In 1917 he travelled to Russia to form a Czech Legion from prisoners of war, to fight with the Allies. He was rewarded when Czechoslovakia was recognized as an independent state and he was elected as its first President. He had a difficult task, as there were national minorities (particularly Germans and Hungarians) in the new state, which was also divided religiously (most Czechs were Protestants, most Slovaks were Catholics). The result was a large number of political parties, which Masaryk sought to bind together in a coalition by respecting the rights of minorities. One of his greatest achievements was to enable Czechoslovakia to survive as the only democracy in Eastern Europe in the inter-war period. Conscious that Czechoslovakia's fate depended on outsiders, he was a strong supporter of the **League of Nations** and sought friendly relations with Germany. He resigned, at the age of eighty-five, so that a younger man could cope with the growing **Nazi** menace.

**Massey, William Ferguson** (1856–1925). New Zealand Prime Minister (1912–25). A Presbyterian from Ulster, Massey emigrated to New Zealand in 1870, farmed in North Island and became spokesman for the small dairy farmer. Elected to parliament in 1894, he was leader of the conservative opposition to **Liberal Party** ministries from 1903 and a founder of the Reform Party

(1909). This reflected the ideas of the dairy farmers, who wanted to change leasehold into freehold, halt 'socialist' legislation and curb militant trade unions. Massey and the Reform Party came to power in 1912 and immediately turned leaseholds into freeholds. Faced with strikes of the **'Red Feds'**, Massey crushed them harshly and so unwittingly helped to promote the formation of the **Labour Party** in 1916. During the First World War Massey was head of a coalition government. At the end of the war New Zealand signed the Treaty of **Versailles**, became a member of the **League of Nations** and made commercial treaties with other states but Massey was unhappy with the independence which **dominion** status had given to New Zealand in 1907. He talked of 'partnership' with Britain and of 'the British Empire as a single, undivided unity' and was content to follow British leadership.

**Matteotti crisis** (1924). A turning-point in the history of Fascist Italy. Giacomo Matteotti, a socialist deputy in the Italian parliament, condemned intimidation by the **Blackshirts** in the 1924 election. In June he was seized by a gang of Fascists and stabbed to death, though his body was not discovered until August. There were demonstrations and demands for **Mussolini**'s resignation, as he was blamed for Matteotti's murder, and it appeared that the Fascist government would collapse. However, King **Victor Emanuel III**, fearing a socialist and communist revival, did not ask Mussolini to resign. Many socialist, liberal and Catholic deputies as a protest withdrew from parliament in the Aventine Secession, but this simply meant that they were not in a position to influence events. Mussolini was now faced with mutiny in his own party. Local party bosses wanted to use the crisis to get rid of the opposition and demanded in December that Mussolini should take steps to set up a dictatorship or they would depose him. On 3 January 1925, in his most important public speech, Mussolini made clear that this was his intention. He accepted responsibility for **Fascism** but did not admit involvement in Matteotti's murder.

**Maura, Antonio** (1853–1925). Four times Prime Minister of Spain, Maura dominated Spanish politics for much of the first decade of the twentieth century. Born into a Mallorcan lower-middle-class family, he studied law in Madrid, and became a deputy to the

Cortes in 1881. Autocratic and clerical, with a formidable personality, Maura became the outstanding parliamentary orator of his generation. Rejecting liberal parliamentarianism (universal suffrage represented 'mob politics'), he favoured a constitutional system centred on the throne and church, with a limited suffrage.

As Colonial Minister in the early 1890s, he fought hard to avoid the loss of Spain's remaining American colonies, by granting a certain measure of autonomy to the Cuban and Puerto Rican administrations, but the parliamentary opposition forced him to abandon the project and he resigned. With the loss of Spain's Empire in the **Spanish–American War** of 1898, he joined the diffuse if widespread clamour for the 'regeneration' of Spain. Maura pursued a vague 'revolution from above', with the aim of mobilizing the Catholic and often apolitical middle classes. Having entered the Conservative Party in 1902, he served as Minister of the Interior from 1902–3. As a would-be 'regenerator' he refused to fix the election through the use of *caciques*. As a result, the regionalist and republican parties made considerable gains in the cities.

In 1903 Maura became leader of the Conservative Party and formed his first Cabinet. He made a determined effort to destroy *caciquismo* through a new local-government law that would introduce an indirect franchise. Opposed by both **Right** and **Left**, the King dismissed him at the end of 1904. He was in power again from 1907 to 1909, when he reintroduced the local-government law. Maura was forced to resign by King **Alphonso XIII**, after the Tragic Week of July 1909 in Barcelona, a popular revolt against conscription, whose brutal suppression by the government led to an international outcry. The subsequent split in the Conservative Party all but destroyed it, and Maura was never again to serve as Prime Minister in a single-party government. He was Prime Minister again (in a national government) in 1918 and in 1921, but on each occasion his administration fell after only a few months. Maura lived to greet **Primo de Rivera**'s military dictatorship as the final triumph over liberalism. Both Primo de Rivera and **Franco** undoubtedly drew upon his authoritarian example.

**Maurras, Charles** (1868–1952). French nationalist, who felt that Dreyfus's guilt or innocence was irrelevant (see **Dreyfus case**), as

France needed a strong army, whose prestige would be undermined by a reopening of the case. A leader of the nationalist movement *Action Française*, he believed that the nation was more important than the individual and gave everyone a loyalty which transcended class and sectional interests. To stop the decline of the French nation it was necessary to reject all that the **French Revolution** and the **Third Republic** stood for, including the theory of natural rights and parliamentary democracy. Representation should be on a corporate (see **Corporate State**) or professional basis under a restored monarchy, which was the only regime that could unite the nation and provide it with an authoritarian, stable and permanent government, which did not change at elections. The nation had to be protected against the enemy within: the 'Four Confederated Estates' (Jews, foreigners, Freemasons and Protestants), all of whom were to be excluded from French public life. An arch-conservative, Maurras was seen as the ideologist of **Vichy France**. From 1940–44 he encouraged violent **anti-Semitism**, praised Vichy's racial laws and fought against the **Resistance** and the Allies. In 1945 he was sentenced to life imprisonment for collaboration with the Germans but was released on health grounds shortly before his death.

**May Fourth Movement** (1919). A movement in China aiming to modernize and strengthen the nation, so that it could reject foreign infringements of its sovereignty. China had declared war on Germany in August 1917, in the expectation that she would be represented at the peace conference and would be able to get rid of the **unequal treaties**. When the Great Powers decided at **Versailles** to give Germany's concessions in Shandong to Japan, there was an outburst of anger in China, which led to student demonstrations in Beijing (Peking) on 4 May 1919. When the police suppressed these, there were demonstrations, strikes and a boycott of Japanese goods in other cities. For the first time large numbers of merchants and urban workers, as well as students, took part. As a result, Chinese representatives at Versailles refused to sign the treaty. These demonstrations were part of a wider movement that began before 1919 and blamed traditional Chinese culture for China's backwardness. In 1915 the journal *New Youth* was published in Shanghai, which attacked **Confucianism**, especially its emphasis on respect for the old and on the inferior status of women. 'Overthrow Confucius and sons' was its slogan. It advocated westernization, democracy and a scientific outlook. Beijing University became a centre for disseminating Western liberal ideals and encouraging intellectual inquiry. After Versailles many advocates of Western liberalism became disillusioned and turned to Russia, which became popular, as the Soviet government promised to give up all the privileges the Tsarist regime had gained from China. The **October Revolution** was looked on as a model and increasing numbers of students became interested in **Marxism**, as it offered a programme of action. Marxist study groups formed in Beijing and other cities, and in 1921 the first congress of the Chinese Communist Party met in Shanghai: twelve delegates represented fifty communists. The May Fourth Movement also led to a revival of support for the **Guomindang**.

**Mazzini, Giuseppe** (1805–72). Italian revolutionary. Born in Genoa, the son of a doctor with radical views, Mazzini became a member of the secret society the Carbonari and from then on devoted his life to preparing for a revolution which would unite Italy. Exiled from Genoa and Piedmont in 1831, and disillusioned with the ineffectiveness of the Carbonari, he formed Young Italy in Marseille. Mazzini believed that Italy should be united as a republic (as sovereignty resides in the nation), which meant a rising of the people against all the rulers of Italy, both native and foreign. Italians should do this themselves and not rely on foreign aid. He realized that the support of the people could be obtained only by offering them material benefits, though these should be subordinated to the struggle for national unity and independence. Everything – family and friends – had to be sacrificed to the cause. Although he rejected Christianity, which he regarded as an ally of kings and despots, he was deeply religious and saw a divine purpose in the development of the national state, which would be only a stage on the road to a united Europe and the unity of mankind. No revolution could succeed without mass support or without middle-class leadership. He therefore opposed class conflict, because it was divisive and would result in a revolutionary dictatorship like that of the **Jacob-**

**ins**. 'We abhor fraternal bloodshed,' he wrote. 'We do not want terror created into a system.'

Expelled from Switzerland and France, Mazzini made London his base from 1837. He was able to inspire a few risings, all of which failed, and was sentenced to death in his absence in 1833 (fourteen of his followers were executed) for trying to persuade the Piedmontese army to revolt. In the **Revolutions of 1848** Mazzini became a triumvir of the Roman Republic, set up when Pope **Pius IX** was forced to flee, but it was crushed in 1849 by French troops. In the 1850s, after several abortive risings, his influence declined, as many moderates looked to Piedmont to unite Italy. Mazzini introduced **Garibaldi** to revolutionary activity but looked on his conversion to a united Italian kingdom under **Victor Emanuel II** as a betrayal. Depressed and embittered, Mazzini saw the **Risorgimento** as a failure. Yet his dedication and bravery – he repeatedly risked his life in clandestine visits to Italy – inspired revolutionaries and he helped to push **Cavour** into taking action which led to unification.

**Medical advances.** In 1800 ideas about disease were not very different from those held by the Ancient Greeks. Scientists thought that germs were a result and not a cause of disease and that they arose spontaneously out of decaying matter. Sanitation and drainage had improved little since the Middle Ages and there was no understanding that diseases such as cholera spread through polluted water supplies. Problems of pain, bleeding and infection limited surgery and ensured that most patients died from their operations. Surgery was revolutionized with the use of anaesthetics after 1850 – first ether, then chloroform – and of antiseptic chemicals, such as carbolic acid, to clean wounds. Joseph Lister, Professor of Surgery at Glasgow, first used carbolic acid in 1865, but he was not widely followed until the 1890s. After this there was an attempt to exclude microbes – aseptic surgery – rather than kill those already there, by boiling surgical instruments and by using rubber gloves.

In 1796 Jenner, a Gloucestershire country doctor, devised a safe method (which he called vaccination) of protection against smallpox. However, the great age of bacteriology came after 1870, when Louis Pasteur showed that airborne microbes caused disease and Heinrich Koch discovered that chemical dyes could be used to stain germs and make them visible. Between 1879 and 1900, twenty-one diseases were discovered and vaccines were produced to prevent many of them. The problem now was to cure those already infected, as in 1900 the only major infectious disease for which there was an effective cure was diphtheria (in 1890 the German Behring had cured diphtheria by injecting an anti-toxic serum – a blood product from an animal which had recovered from the disease – into a patient). In 1909 Dr Hata, one of a team led by Paul Ehrlich, found that some arsenic compounds would kill syphilis. These were developed into the drug Salvarsan, and anti-infective chemotherapy was born. Sulphonamide drugs were developed from coal tar to cure pneumonia, scarlet fever and tonsillitis. Yet drugs were powerless against many other germs until penicillin was discovered by Alexander Fleming in 1929. This was of little use until it could be turned into a mass-produced drug. The money to do this was not forthcoming until the USA entered the **Second World War**, when there was an urgent need to treat septicaemia (blood poisoning) amongst the wounded.

In the nineteenth century the great killer diseases had been infectious diseases, such as smallpox, tuberculosis, scarlet fever and diphtheria. By 1945 they had been largely overcome by new drugs and better public health. The main killer diseases were now non-infectious – heart disease, thrombosis, cancer – for which cures had still to be found.

**Mediterranean Agreements** (1887). Britain was anxious to stop French interference in Egypt and so **Salisbury**, the British Prime Minister and Foreign Secretary, negotiated an agreement with Italy by which they would preserve the status quo in the Mediterranean, Aegean and Adriatic. When Austria, encouraged by **Bismarck**, joined in March 1887, the first Mediterranean Agreement was made. Later that year Ferdinand of Saxe-Coburg was elected ruler of Bulgaria (see **Bulgarian crisis**) and it appeared that Russia would intervene, so in December a second Mediterranean Agreement was signed. Britain, Austria and Italy agreed to maintain the status quo at the **Straits** and in the Near East, Asia Minor and Bulgaria, and to assist Turkey if Russia attacked her. By associating Britain with the **Triple Alliance**, it was felt that these agreements would deter Russia and France from provocative actions in the Mediterranean. This pleased Bismarck, who was not directly involved, as others were doing his work for him: keeping Russia and France in check. The agreement lapsed in 1892, when Rosebery became British Foreign Secretary.

**Mehemet Ali,** see **Muhammad Ali**

**Meiji Constitution** (1889). The call for a constitution in Japan began in 1870 after the **Meiji Restoration** (1868). The ruling élite saw one as necessary to gain the support of the Western powers, and so in 1881 the government announced that there would be a constitution and an elected assembly from 1890. **Ito Hirobumi** was sent to Europe to study government systems and to draft a constitution. Before it was promulgated other Western institutions were introduced. A new peerage was created in 1884; a year later came a Cabinet with a Prime Minister at its head, and in 1888 a privy council was set up, as the highest advisory body to the Emperor. The Constitution, which operated from 1890, was a conservative document, greatly influenced by the Prussian example, which aimed to keep the greatest power in the hands of the Emperor and the ruling élite. The first sentence said that Japan 'shall be reigned over and governed by a line of emperors unbroken for ages eternal'. The Emperor was 'sacred and inviolable' and 'exercises the legislative power with the consent of the Imperial **Diet**'. He could issue ordinances with the force of law but these 'are to be laid before the Imperial Diet at its next session' and were invalid if the Diet did not pass them. The Cabinet was appointed by the Emperor and was responsible only to him: its members need not be taken from the majority party in the Diet. The army and navy were directly responsible to the Emperor and outside the control of the Cabinet and Diet. This part of the Constitution provided the legal underpinning for the **Emperor system**. The Diet consisted of two houses. There was a House of Peers designed, in Ito's words, to check 'the despotism of the majority' in the House of Representatives. It had the same powers as the lower house and could veto legislation passed there. The House of Representatives passed laws but could not initiate them. It was elected at first by large property owners (only 1 per cent of the population in the early years) and from 1925 by all males over twenty-five. It could be dissolved by the Emperor on Cabinet advice at any time. If the Diet rejected the budget 'the government shall carry out the budget of the preceding year'. The Constitution granted freedom of speech, of writing, of religion and of association, but all these rights were qualified. As the Meiji Constitution provided the framework in which military governments took power, the Occupation authorities imposed a new Constitution in 1947, which they hoped would provide a sounder basis for democracy.

**Meiji Restoration.** Meiji ('Enlightened Rule') was the reign name of the Japanese Emperor Mitsuhito, who ruled from 1868–1912. Following the fall of the **Tokugawa shogunate**, a group of anti-Tokugawa *samurai* declared in January 1868 that the shogunate was abolished and that power had been formally returned to the Emperor. Many *samurai* wanted to see Japan strong enough to resist Western domination and to get rid of the **unequal treaties**, which gave Westerners a privileged position in Japan. They realized that to do this, Western ideas and institutions would have to be adopted, as these had made European countries so powerful, and so there began a series of reforms which profoundly affected all aspects of Japanese life, political, economic and social. These changes continued throughout the Meiji period and have led some historians to talk about a Meiji Revolution, rather than a Restoration, which implies a return to the past. One of the most remarkable aspects of the Revolution was the surrender by the *daimyo* (feudal lords) of their lands to the Emperor, as this was carried out without bloodshed and with little resistance. This made possible the setting up of a centralized administration, based on the shogunal capital of Edo, renamed Tokyo in 1868. As the imperial government had no armed forces of its own, conscription was introduced in 1872. This marked the end of the *samurai* monopoly of military power but most accepted the new regime, as they found posts in the new Meiji administration and army and, as advisers to the Emperor, retained considerable political power. Some conservative *samurai*, who could not accept the new ways, rebelled, but the crushing of the **Satsuma rebellion** (1877) by the imperial conscript army marked the end of military resistance.

Western knowledge and technology were needed to make Japan strong, so in 1868 the Emperor declared in his Charter Oath that 'knowledge shall be sought all over the world'. Japanese went to Europe and the USA, and foreigners came to Japan to teach and act as financial and military advisers. Compulsory elementary education was proclaimed in 1872, with the result that Japan became the most literate society in Asia, with almost 100 per cent literacy by 1900. Cabinet government, with a Prime Minister at its head, was introduced in 1885, and five years later the **Meiji Constitution** provided a bicameral legislature, with an elected House of Representatives, although most power was retained by the Emperor and his advisers. From 1893 entry into the higher civil service was by examination and the legal system was remodelled on Western lines, as were the armed forces. No single country was taken as the model in these reforms. Britain and Germany were the model for civil and commercial law, whilst the criminal law was a mixture of Japanese feudal law and the *Code Napoléon*. Prussian influence was uppermost in local government, French and German in the army, British in the navy.

Industrialization seemed to be the basis for Western strength, but this was slow to take off in Japan, as there was little private capital. In the early years, therefore, nearly all industries were founded by the state, which sold them off cheaply in the early 1880s: this eventually led to the foundation of the *zaibatsu*. Textiles – silk and cotton – were the most important industries in the Meiji period, and silk employed more workers than any other industry until the 1930s. By 1914 Japan accounted for a quarter of the world's cotton-yarn exports. Heavy industry – iron and steel, engineering – did not grow much before 1914, owing to foreign competition and a shortage of capital. Up to 1914 most of the equipment needed for Japanese factories, railways and mines was imported. The Bank of Japan was founded in 1882 and this, with commercial banks, played an essential role in financing industrialization. Japan's modernization enabled her to defeat China in the **Sino–Japanese War** (1894–5) and become a colonial power at the Treaty of **Shimonoseki**. She managed to get rid of the unequal treaties by the end of the century and was recognized for the first time as an equal of the European powers when she made the **Anglo–Japanese Alliance** (1902). This new status was amply confirmed, when she shocked European opinion by defeating Russia in the **Russo-Japanese War** (1904–5). Yet this war was very expensive: it increased Japanese borrowing and gave her a serious balance-of-payments deficit, from which she was rescued only by the **First World War**.

***Mein Kampf*** (*My Struggle*). A book by **Hitler** which set out his political programme and proved to be an accurate guide to what he intended to do. The first part, published in 1925, was written whilst he was in prison, after the failure of the **Munich *Putsch*** (1923): the second volume was published in 1928. In it Hitler put forward his ideas on race, **anti-Semitism**, *Lebensraum* ('living space') and life as a continual struggle. Following writers like Houston Stewart Chamberlain, he regarded the Aryan race (undefined) as the founder of civilization: it must keep its purity by not mixing with other races, so that it could fulfil its destiny of world supremacy. The lowest race was the Jewish, the destroyer of civilization, which was responsible for the **First World War** and Bolshevism. 'There is no making pacts with Jews; there can only be the hard: either–or.' All German-speaking peoples must be gathered together in one Reich and this involved *Anschluss* ('union') with Austria, but they also needed living-space in the east at the expense of 'Jewish–Bolshevik' Russia. *Mein Kampf* became a best-seller only after Hitler came to power in 1933: by 1939 it had sold over five million copies and had been translated into eleven languages.

**Melbourne, William Lamb, 2nd Viscount** (1779–1848). British Prime Minister (1834, 1835–41). Melbourne had an undistinguished political career and was nearly fifty before he first held office as Secretary for Ireland (1827) in **Canning**'s short-lived ministry. Although a **Whig** and supporter of **Catholic emancipation**, he held basically conservative views and was more interested in literature and theology than in politics. His view of society was paternalistic: he would do his duty by the lower classes, provided they accepted their lowly place in society. If they did not, they would be treated harshly, as he showed when he was Home Secretary (1830–34) in his support for the heavy penalties passed on the Swing rioters (see **Swing riots**) and, as Prime Minister, on the **Tolpuddle Martyrs**. Melbourne was not ambitious: he became Prime

Minister reluctantly and had no majority in the House of **Commons**, so he relied on the support of radicals and Irish MPs led by **O'Connell**. He disappointed these groups, as he was not a reformer. The main measure passed in his administration, the **Municipal Corporations Act** (1835), originated under his predecessor **Grey**. The compulsory civil registration of births, marriages and deaths provided reliable statistics for the first time on the population, and London University received a royal charter, but reforming legislation was sparse. In the British Empire the **Canada Act** (1840) united Upper and Lower Canada and began the move towards responsible government; in the same year New Zealand was annexed. When **Victoria** came to the throne in 1837 Melbourne became her mentor and had a very close relationship with her until he retired.

**Menelik II** (c. 1844–1913). Emperor of Ethiopia (1889–1913). He made Ethiopia strong enough not only to retain its independence during the **Scramble for Africa** but to take part in it. The Christian Church was a unifying influence in Ethiopia, which created a small group of educated people who were aware of what was going on in Europe. Menelik equipped his army with modern weapons and it was these which enabled him to defeat the Italians at **Aduwa** in 1896, when they invaded Ethiopia from their colony of Eritrea. They also enabled him to unite the provinces of Tigre, Amhara and Shoa and to extend Ethiopian rule over the Muslim and pagan tribes to the south and east, so that he doubled the size of his country. After defeating Italy, which recognized the independence of Ethiopia, he made treaties with foreign powers to settle his frontiers. Menelik began the building of a railway from French Djibouti to his new capital of Addis Ababa, and established a telegraph system, postal services, schools and hospitals. He issued a new currency in 1909 – the first coins in Ethiopia for a thousand years – and founded the Bank of Abyssinia. All these reforms he carried out without becoming indebted to European governments and so he avoided the foreign intervention in internal affairs that took place in Egypt and Tunisia.

**Mensheviks.** Russian revolutionary party. When the Russian Social Democratic Workers' Party split in 1903, the group which failed to gain control of the party newspaper *Iskra* ('the Spark') became known as Mensheviks ('members of the minority'). They differed from their successful rivals, the **Bolsheviks**, on three main issues: the role of the party; the part to be played by peasants in a socialist revolution and how a *bourgeois* revolution would turn into a socialist revolution (see **Bolsheviks** for a discussion of these differences). Mensheviks played a leading part in most **Soviets** during the **Russian Revolution** of 1905, especially in St Petersburg. They became a separate party in 1912. In 1914 most Mensheviks condemned the war, though a right-wing minority supported national defence against Germany. After the **February Revolution** in 1917 they, with the **Socialist Revolutionaries** (SRs), founded and controlled the **Petrograd** Soviet, but the disarray within the party continued. The Mensheviks had always rejected the idea that socialists should join a *bourgeois* government, yet this is precisely what they did in May 1917, when they joined with **Kadets** and SRs to form a coalition government. This decision was opposed by left-wing Mensheviks, led by Martov. It was Tsereteli, Menshevik Minister of the Interior in the coalition government, who ordered the arrest of **Lenin** and imprisoned **Trotsky** after the **July Days**. Mensheviks in the government turned a deaf ear to peasant cries for land and peace and consequently became unpopular. Bolsheviks took control of the Soviets, which the Mensheviks had dominated. The slump in their popularity was shown in the elections to the Constituent Assembly in November 1917. They polled under 3 per cent of the votes, compared with the Bolsheviks 24 per cent.

The Mensheviks united to condemn the **October Revolution** and a month later accepted Martov as leader. The majority loyally supported the Bolsheviks in the **Russian Civil War** (at the same time condemning Bolshevik terror), though a minority of right-wing Mensheviks took part in anti-Bolshevik provincial governments. The Mensheviks continued as a legal opposition until the **Kronstadt Rising** of 1921, after which all non-Bolshevik parties were suppressed. There was no execution of Menshevik leaders, who were allowed, even encouraged, to go abroad, which they did.

**Metaxas, Ioannis** (1871–1941). Greek dictator. Trained as an army officer in **Prussia**, Metaxas fought against the Turks in 1897 and in the **Balkan Wars** (1912–13), becoming Chief of Staff in 1913. He opposed Greece entering the **First World War** and went into voluntary exile in Italy when she declared war on Germany in 1917. After the war he condemned **Venizelos**'s attempt to conquer western Anatolia and led the opposition to Venizelos in the Greek parliament. Metaxas helped to restore the monarchy in 1935 and was rewarded by being made Prime Minister in 1936. Parliament gave him a vote of confidence and agreed to adjourn and to allow him to govern by decree. It did not meet for another ten years, as Metaxas persuaded the King to suspend key parts of the Constitution in August 1936 and to establish a dictatorship. Political parties were banned and strikes made illegal. Metaxas never built up a mass following, as **Hitler** and **Mussolini** did, though he admired the dictators and shared their loathing for liberalism, parliamentary democracy and communism. He took the title *Archigos*, leader, in imitation of the *Führer* and the *Duce*, and copying Hitler's **Third Reich**, claimed to be leader of the Third Hellenic Civilization (the first two being Ancient Greece and Byzantium). His National Youth Organization copied the **Hitler Youth** in bringing children of all classes together to provide military training for boys and to teach girls how to be good housewives. There was great emphasis on the family, religion, the social order and stability. Metaxas worked especially hard – as Minister of Foreign Affairs and of the armed forces and from 1938 Minister of Education, as well as Prime Minister – to reduce corruption and make the Greek army the most efficient in the Balkans. When the **Second World War** began he kept Greece neutral until October 1940, when he rejected an ultimatum from Mussolini. Italian troops invaded, but within weeks the Greeks pushed them out of their country and entered Albania. He died in January 1941 before Germany came to the help of her Italian ally.

**Metternich, Clemens von, Prince** (1773–1859). Austrian Foreign Minister (1809–48). Born at Coblenz on the Rhine, the son of a diplomat in Habsburg service (see **Habsburg dynasty**), Metternich entered the Austrian diplomatic service in 1801. Foreign Minister from 1809 to 1848, he regarded the years 1809–15 as the most important period of his life. After Austria's defeat at Wagram

(1809), Metternich favoured close collaboration with France and promoted the marriage of Marie Louise, daughter of the Emperor Francis I, to **Napoleon**. With the failure of the **Moscow Campaign** (1812) and Napoleon's retreat from Russia, Metternich regarded Russia as a greater threat than France to Austria and was prepared for Napoleon to retain the French throne. Only after Napoleon rejected Metternich's offer of a negotiated peace did Austria join the Allied coalition in August 1813 and fight at **Leipzig**. Metternich presided over, and was a major influence at, the Congress of **Vienna** (1815). The peace settlement there was a triumph for him, as the size of the **Austrian Empire** increased by a half and Austria dominated the **German Confederation** and Italy.

Metternich's main object after 1815 was to maintain the existing international and social order. This meant preserving centralized monarchical government and the dominance of the aristocracy and opposing **nationalism**, revolution and all liberal reforms. Metternich had considerable success in Germany and Italy. Austrian leadership of the German Confederation enabled him, with the support of **Prussia**, to pass through the **Diet** the Carlsbad decrees (1819), which increased government control of the universities, student societies and the press. When there were risings against repressive regimes in Naples and Piedmont in 1820–21, he used Austrian troops to put them down and persuaded Russia and Prussia to join him at the Congress of Troppau (1820) in asserting the right of the Great Powers to intervene in the internal affairs of other states. In 1831 there were revolutions in central Italy – in Parma, Modena and the Papal States – and once again Metternich sent Austrian troops to suppress them. Within the Habsburg Empire he centralized much of the administration, so that the influence of the Diets in Lombardy–Venetia and Hungary was reduced and important decisions were taken in Vienna.

Yet there were severe limitations to Austria's power and to that of Metternich. The finances were in a parlous state, so that to balance the budget military expenditure (which took 40 per cent of revenue in normal times) had to be cut. Peace was therefore a necessity for Austria, so Metternich became dependent on the support of the other conservative powers, Prussia and Russia. He did not have a decisive voice in European diplomacy in the 1830s and 1840s. Belgian independence was decided by Britain and France, the **Eastern Question** by Britain and Russia; Metternich's Catholic allies were defeated in the *Sonderbund* war in Switzerland in 1847. Even in Germany, leadership passed to Prussia through the *Zollverein*, which Austria was not strong enough to join. Metternich could see the danger and predicted that 'the links which bind Austria to the other states of the German Confederation will gradually become loosened and in the end will break entirely, thanks to this barrier,' but he could do nothing about it. Others could see that Metternich's resistance to change was likely to end disastrously. 'Your repressive and suffocating policy,' **Palmerston** told the Austrian ambassador in London, 'is also a fatal one and will lead to an explosion just as certainly as would a boiler that was hermetically sealed and deprived of an outlet for steam.' Metternich was one of the first victims of the **Revolutions of 1848**, but even after his fall he told **Guizot** that it had never entered his head that he might be wrong. He fled to England in 1848, returning to his castle on the Rhine three years later.

**Mexican–American War** (1846–8). US President **Polk** was a firm believer in **Manifest Destiny**, and after he was elected in 1844 he decided to acquire California and New Mexico, both of which were part of Mexico. He wanted Mexico to sell the territory, but when she refused he sent General Zachary Taylor into territory which both Mexico and the USA claimed, north of the Rio Grande. Taylor defeated the Mexicans at Palo Alto in May 1846, by skilful use of artillery, though his 6,000 troops were heavily outnumbered by an opposing force of 23,000. This set the pattern for the rest of the war – the Mexicans fought bravely but never won a battle. Taylor drove them across the Rio Grande and only then did **Congress** declare war. The American people were not united in its support. The Northern **Whigs** opposed it as a Southern plot to add new slave states to the Union. Others condemned it as a war of aggression, the Massachusetts legislature describing it as a 'war of conquest . . . hateful . . . a crime'.

The Mexicans were confident of winning the war, as their army of 32,000 was four times as large as that of the USA but it was poorly led and organized. Polk took charge – the first American President to act as Commander-in-Chief – and decided the strategy of the war. In the north Taylor won a series of victories, culminating at Buena Vista (February 1847), which ended the war in northern Mexico. The Mexicans would still not admit defeat, so Polk decided to advance on their capital, Mexico City. The route from the north was 500 miles long, much of it over deserts and mountains. Polk therefore sent General Winfield Scott with a seaborne expedition to land at Veracruz. Scott captured the port after an eighteen-day siege and then began the difficult advance of 280 miles on Mexico City. After several battles Scott, with his army of 10,000, half of them untrained volunteers, captured Mexico City in September. Meanwhile, the Americans had captured San Francisco and ended Mexican rule in California.

Peace was signed on 2 February 1848 at Guadalupe Hidalgo. Mexico gave up about half her territory, which was later formed into the States of California, Arizona, Utah, Colorado, Nevada and New Mexico. She also recognized the Rio Grande as her boundary with Texas. The Americans agreed to pay $15 million for the territory they had acquired. The USA had added half a million square miles to her territory, including the excellent harbour of San Francisco (through which she could trade with the East), and now spanned the whole continent.

**Mexican Revolution** (1910–40). There was considerable discontent in the last years of Porfirio **Díaz**'s rule when power was concentrated in the hands of a small élite of landowners; the middle class, peasants and urban workers were excluded from the political process and foreigners were allowed to dominate the economy. Yet there was no organized party behind the revolution, which began when Francisco Madero rejected Díaz's election in 1910 as President, demanded genuine democracy and called for rebellion. Peasants in the north rose under the leadership of the former bandit 'Pancho' Villa, whilst in the southern state of Morelos, Indians led by Emiliano **Zapata** rose to reclaim communal lands which had been taken from them. Díaz was forced to go into exile in 1911 and Madero was elected President, but the revolt did not end there. Madero would not sanction a massive transfer of land to the Indians and so peasant discontent persisted. In 1913 Victoriano Huerta, a general who had the support of the landowners, staged a *coup* against Madero, who was arrested and murdered.

The civil war increased in intensity in 1913–14 to cover the whole country. The radical forces of Villa and Zapata combined with the Constitutionalist army, led by the landowner Venustiano Carranza and his most successful general, Alvaro Obregón. Aided by the US President Woodrow **Wilson**, whose troops seized Veracruz and so deprived Huerta of arms supplies, the Constitutionalists compelled Huerta to flee abroad in 1914. The successful coalition now broke up, as Carranza did not want to carry out the radical social reform demanded by other revolutionary factions. Obregón and Carranza, who set up a government in Veracruz, fought against Villa and Zapata, who for five months controlled the capital, Mexico City. The turning-point came in April 1915, when Obregón, in the bloodiest battle in Mexican history, defeated Villa at Celaya. Villa retired to the north, where he kept the rebellion going until 1920, but his hold on national power had gone. Zapata's army withdrew from Mexico City and his activities were now confined to his home state of Morelos.

Carranza did not want much social change, but Obregón and others saw the need to appeal to peasants and workers and so produced the radical Constitution of 1917. This completely separated Church and State; authorized the break-up of the *haciendas* (great estates) and the return of lands to the Indian communities; gave workers extensive rights, such as to form trade unions and to strike; and asserted the state's control of the subsoil, which was to lead to a clash with foreign oil companies. If the Constitution had been strictly carried out there would have been a social revolution, but Carranza did not want to see any transfer of power to the lower classes. Zapata was murdered in 1919 and a year later Carranza was also assassinated. He was replaced by Obregón as President (1920–24), and the most violent phase of the revolution came to an end – Villa was granted a large *hacienda* by the government in 1920 and ceased his murderous activities (he too was assassinated three years later). A period of reconstruction began under Obregón, which was to make Mexico the most stable state in Latin America. Peasants were organized in Agrarian Leagues, industrial workers joined the trade-union confederation (CROM). All these organizations were controlled by the government. Obregón's successor, Plutarco Elías Calles, ruled as President (1924–8) and then through puppet presidents from 1928–34. He sought to further the process of consolidation through the development of the economy, the strengthening of the state and the formation of the National Revolutionary Party, an association of labour and peasant confederations, and middle-class and women's organizations. Its successor, the PRI, was still in power fifty years later. There was cautious land reform under Obregón and Calles, but not until the presidency of Lazaro **Cárdenas** (1934–40) were there radical changes, which saw the culmination of the social revolution.

**Mfecane** ('the crushing'). The name given in the Zulu language (*Difaqane* in Sotho) to the series of wars and disturbances in the 1820s and 1830s which affected much of southern Africa. Bantu-speaking people had lived for centuries in the coastal plains between the Drakensberg mountains and the Indian Ocean, an area where the monsoon made the land much more fertile than in the high veld of the interior plateau. In the early nineteenth century, owing to an increased population which followed the introduction of maize, there was a land shortage, exacerbated by overuse of land and severe droughts. Some chiefs therefore sought to expand their territory. The best land was along the coast south of the Fish river but **Boers** held this, so a movement began north and west. The Zulu leader **Shaka** played a leading part by uniting various Nguni chiefdoms into a strong centralized state with a fearsomely efficient army. As the Zulus preyed on their neighbours, those they displaced attacked others in turn, so that nearly all the peoples living in the northern half of South Africa became involved. Out of the disruption of the *Mfecane* some major new states arose: Mzilikazi founded the Ndebele kingdom in western Zimbabwe and **Moshweshwe** the Sotho kingdom of Basutoland. Millions of Africans gained new identities – as Zulus, Swazis, Ndebele – which would be long-lasting. The *Mfecane* brought destruction and hardship to many and depopulated large areas, so the Boers were given the opportunity of moving inland from Cape Colony on the **Great Trek** without meeting any effective resistance.

**Middle East.** A term first used in 1902 by the American naval historian Alfred **Mahan** to indicate the area between Arabia and

India, with its centre in the Persian Gulf. Since then its use has been extended to cover an area from Turkey to the Yemen (north to south) and from Egypt to Iran (west to east), thus including part of North Africa and South-West Asia.

**Middle East campaigns** (1914–18) were fought in Palestine and Mesopotamia during the **First World War** by British and Indian troops against the Ottoman Turks. To protect the Suez Canal the British sent a force from Egypt through the Sinai Desert to Palestine, where it was stopped at Gaza. **Allenby** eventually broke through the Turkish lines at Gaza in 1917 and occupied Jerusalem, aided by the Arab revolt of Sharif **Husayn** of Mecca, in which T. E. **Lawrence** and other British officers took part. In 1918 Allenby went on to defeat the Turks at Megiddo in Syria and occupy Damascus. A second campaign was fought in Mesopotamia (Iraq) to protect the Persian oil-fields, which were under British control. An Anglo-Indian force occupied Basra and then moved north, but it had to surrender at Kut in April 1916. 600,000 British and Indian troops were sent to the Middle East: they recaptured Kut in February 1917 and Baghdad a month later, and had reached the oil-fields of Mosul when an armistice was made in 1918.

**Midlothian Campaigns** (1879–80). **Gladstone** was the first English politician to address huge crowds on public-speaking tours, but in doing so he was addressing the whole nation, as his speeches were reported in the newspapers. These tours, begun in 1862 in the north of England, made him, according to Lord Randolph **Churchill**, 'The greatest living master of the art of personal political advertisement'. In 1879 Gladstone felt it was his Christian duty to attack **Disraeli**'s support for the **Ottoman Empire** and thought this could be done best by contesting the Conservative-held seat of Midlothian, near Edinburgh. At the end of 1879 and again in 1880 he made a series of speeches in Scotland – 'stumping the provinces' *The Times* called it – attacking Disraeli's foreign policy, not only on the **Eastern Question** but also for his part in the **Anglo-Afghan** and **Zulu Wars**. Gladstone also put forward fundamental principles which should guide British foreign policy: the pursuit of peace, respect for the rights of small nations and a commitment to the Concert of Europe, which would settle disputes by international agreement rather than by war. His campaign was enormously successful. He defeated the Conservative candidate at Midlothian and the **Liberals** were returned in the 1880 election with a majority, though this had probably more to do with the agricultural depression than with the Midlothian campaigns.

**Midway, battle of** (3–6 June 1942). Aircraft-carrier-based battle in the **Pacific War** (1941–5), which resulted in a crushing American victory over Japan. It was the second, and greatest, carrier battle. The first, in the Coral Sea (4–8 May 1942), began a new type of sea battle when the opposing fleets never saw each other or exchanged gunfire and the fighting was carried on entirely by aircraft. In that battle each side had lost one carrier and had another badly damaged. **Yamamato**, the Japanese Commander-in-Chief, thought through faulty intelligence that two American aircraft carriers had been sunk and that the USA would not therefore be able to oppose effectively a strike at Midway Island in the Central Pacific. He gathered together an enormous fleet of 165 ships, including eleven battleships, which should have ensured success in a concentrated attack, but he made several errors. Two Japanese aircraft carriers were sent to cover a diversionary attack on the Aleutian Islands and might have proved decisive if they had joined the main carrier force at Midway. The Japanese fleet was so dispersed that only two of the five forces were close enough to support each other: the fleet which should have provided the carriers with cover from anti-aircraft batteries was 400 miles away at the time of the battle. The Americans, on the other hand, had learnt to use their fleet as escorts for aircraft carriers. Admiral **Nimitz**, the American Commander-in-Chief, knew what the Japanese were going to do, as the Americans had broken the Japanese code. He therefore concentrated all his available ships (three carriers, eight cruisers and fifteen destroyers) against the four Japanese carriers attacking Midway. The Japanese had an early success when they attacked Midway Island, destroying many American aircraft on the ground and shooting down thirty-three planes for the loss of only six of their own. The American Commander ordered his carrier planes to attack the Japanese when he calculated that their planes would be refuelling and rearming on their aircraft carriers: in five minutes American dive-bombers destroyed three Japanese aircraft carriers. The fourth, the *Hiryu*, sailing apart from the others, was able to strike at the Americans and knocked out the *Yorktown*, which was abandoned and sunk by a Japanese submarine on 6 June. The *Hiryu* itself was badly damaged and was scuttled on 5 June. American losses at Midway were one aircraft carrier, a destroyer and 132 planes. This battle did not determine the course of the war, as Japan still had two fleet carriers and six smaller ones, whilst the USA had three large carriers and a smaller one. Japan was still superior in battleships and battle cruisers. More important in wearing down Japan was the lengthy struggle for the Solomons, when the Japanese lost 3,000 aircraft. The real significance of Midway was psychological – the Japanese navy had suffered its first major defeat.

**Mill, John Stuart** (1806–73). British philosopher and reformer. Subjected to a rigorous education at home by his father James Mill (a friend of Jeremy **Bentham**), John Stuart supposedly read Greek at the age of three but he had no friends, no holidays and played no games. Intellectually he developed rapidly but was emotionally stunted until embarking on his long friendship with Mrs Harriet Taylor, which ended in marriage in 1851 after her husband's death. The greatest intellectual radical of the mid-Victorian period, Mill believed that ideas should have a practical application. A supporter of the **Reform Act** of 1832, he wanted a secret ballot, payment of MPs and universal suffrage, though his belief in the latter became more muted after reading de Tocqueville's *Democracy in America* (1840), which argued that democracy could lead to the 'tyranny of the majority'. Mill retained his belief that the rights and interests of the governed can only be protected when they themselves elect the governors, who, unchecked, would behave selfishly and corruptly, but he also wanted to protect the rights of minorities. He saw proportional representation as a means to this end, as it would ensure the representation of every minority opinion according to its strength. His obsession with freedom was apparent in *On Liberty* (1859), immediately recognized as a masterpiece. A summary of his ideas, 'which I have been working up during the greater part of my life', came in *Considerations on Representative Government* (1861). From 1865–8 Mill was a **Liberal** MP, but by this time he had moved towards **socialism**, rejecting capitalism because the workers were not self-governing and favouring a competitive economy with worker-owned companies. *The Subjection of Women* (1869), which declared the 'perfect equality' of men and women, was Mill's tribute to the influence of his wife.

**Milner, Alfred, 1st Viscount** (1854–1925). British imperialist and civil servant. A brilliant scholar, with a first in Classics at Oxford, his interest in finance led to his serving in the Egyptian finance ministry (1889–92) and then as chairman of the Board of Inland Revenue in London. Joseph **Chamberlain** appointed him to be British High Commissioner in South Africa and Governor of Cape Colony, at a time (1897) when relations between Britain and the Boer government of the South African Republic (SAR) were very strained. The British wanted to prevent the SAR, which was the richest state in South Africa since the discovery of gold on the **Rand** in 1885, from dominating the 'British' colonies of the Cape and Natal. Milner therefore put pressure on President **Kruger** of the SAR to grant political rights to the *uitlanders*, white foreigners who had flocked into the SAR with the gold boom. Kruger refused, as he realized that it was not simply the vote for *uitlanders* that Milner wanted but control of the SAR, and for that he was prepared to go to war. After the British victory in the **South African War** (1899–1902) Milner was conciliatory to the Boers, as he firmly believed in white supremacy. 'A political equality of white and black is impossible,' he wrote. 'The white man must rule.' He therefore, at the Treaty of **Vereeniging**, persuaded Chamberlain to agree that the vote would not be given to blacks in the ex-republics before the restoration of self-government. In the period of reconstruction after the war Milner wanted to ensure British dominance in South Africa by encouraging British settlement and by insisting on education in English for the Boers. This policy failed, as few Britons settled in South Africa. At the same time Milner tried to gain **Afrikaner** confidence by re-settling them in their farms and by paying them £19 million in war damages and loans. As the mining industry was depressed he rescued it by allowing in cheap Chinese **indentured labour**. Milner returned to England in 1905 and opposed Liberal measures such as the **'People's**

**Budget'** (1909) and the reform of the House of **Lords**. During the **First World War** he held office in the War Cabinet (1916–18), and as Colonial Secretary from 1918–21 he held negotiations with Egyptian nationalist leaders, which led to the Anglo-Egyptian settlement of 1922. Recognizing that the Protectorate could not be maintained, he wanted the British to grant Egypt independence whilst protecting British interests by keeping troops there to protect the Suez Canal. As the British government would not at first accept his proposals he resigned.

**Milyukov, Paul** (1859–1943). Russian politician and historian. A stern critic of the Tsarist regime, Milyukov was leader of the **Kadets** (Constitutional Democrats) in the Russian **Dumas** from 1906–17. He typified the weakness of liberals in pre-revolutionary Russia. Believing in British-style parliamentary government, he was frightened of revolution and was therefore not prepared to take a strong stand against the Tsar. He was the leader of the **Progressive Bloc** in 1915, though this was no threat to the government. 'Milyukov is the greatest bourgeois of all,' Sazonov (Foreign Minister) told his fellow ministers, 'and fears a social revolution more than anything else.' Following the **February Revolution** in 1917 he became Foreign Minister in the **Provisional Government**. His commitment to continue the war and his wish to preserve the monarchy were unpopular. Milyukov resigned in May, owing to the uproar when it became known that he wanted Russia to annex land along the **Straits** (see **Constantinople agreements**). After the defeat of the Whites in the **Russian Civil War** he spent the rest of his life in France.

**Mir.** Russian peasant commune, which dominated rural life throughout the nineteenth century. In most communes land was owned by the community and redistributed every few years between households to take account of changing membership. The *mir* also controlled the rotation of crops and common pasture. On the **emancipation of the serfs** in 1861 its functions were extended, as the government needed it as an unpaid civil service to collect redemption dues and state taxes and to control the passport system. Land was given to the *mir* rather than to the individual peasant. The Tsar hoped that it would act as a conservative bulwark of the regime in the countryside, but the **Russian Revolution** of 1905 showed that this was not so. **Stolypin**, therefore, tried to undermine it by persuading peasants to set up as independent farmers and leave the *mir* but with only partial success. Following the Russian Revolutions of 1917 (see **February Revolution, October Revolution**), most peasants who had left the *mir* returned to it, in order to obtain greater security. It was abolished in 1930 when **Stalin** embarked on the **collectivization of agriculture**.

**Missouri Compromise** (1820). Missouri was part of the **Louisiana Purchase** and had been settled mainly by Southerners with their slaves. The North had outstripped the South in population and had a majority in the House of Representatives, but there was equality in the Senate – eleven free and eleven slave states – which the South was determined to maintain. In 1819 it was proposed to admit Missouri to the Union as a slave state. Northerners in **Congress** objected, though the balance of power in the Senate would not be upset as Maine, an outlying part of Massachusetts, could be admitted at the same time as a free state. Henry **Clay** persuaded Congress to accept the Missouri Compromise: slavery would be forever excluded from all parts of the Louisiana Purchase north of latitude 36° 30′ but it would be allowed in Missouri. Maine and Missouri would be admitted to the Union at the same time. The Compromise did not settle the question of slavery. It was revived again with the **Mexican–American War** of 1846–8 and there was another attempt to settle it with the **Compromise of 1850**. The Missouri Compromise was repealed by the **Kansas–Nebraska Act** of 1854, though the question of slavery was not finally decided until the **American Civil War**.

**Mitsubishi.** An important Japanese conglomerate (*zaibatsu*). Mitsubishi began as a shipping line under the control of the Iwasaki family. It bought cheaply from the government in 1884 the Nagasaki shipyards, the largest in the country, and a year later merged with its greatest competitor to form the NYK (Japan Shipping Company). This became one of the largest shipping lines in the world and carried much of Japan's trade. In 1880 Mitsubishi formed its own bank. Shipping, shipbuilding and insurance were the most important of Mitsubishi's activities, but after the **First World War** it diversified into heavy industry, engineering and chemicals. By 1930 its holding company controlled 120 enterprises. It played an important part in developing the war economy of the 1930s and 1940s. In 1945 the Occupation authorities were determined to break up the *zaibatsu*. The Iwasaki family lost control of the group, which was split into its separate units; these were later re-formed, with the Mitsubishi Bank playing a leading role. From the 1960s its heavy industrial interests were rebuilt.

**Molly Maguires.** A secret terrorist organization of Irish miners in the anthracite coalfields of Pennsylvania. To fight for better working conditions the miners formed a secret society, the Molly Maguires, named after an anti-landlord organization in Ireland. They turned to terror when the mine-owners tried to bring in cheap labour in the 1870s: plants were sabotaged, police and mine officials murdered. When they organized a 'Long Strike' in 1874–5, the mine-owners decided to destroy them. They employed an Irish-born private detective to infiltrate the organization and produce evidence which led to nineteen Molly Maguires being hanged (1875–7). The organization disintegrated. The anthracite miners did not gain any of their main demands until the United Mineworkers Union (formed in 1890) organized the **anthracite coal strike** in 1902.

**Moltke, Helmuth, Graf von** (1800–1891). Prussian field marshal. He became Chief of the Prussian General Staff in 1857 and in collaboration with the War Minister, General von **Roon**, increased the size and efficiency of the Prussian army. He was the effective field commander in the **Austro-Prussian War** (1866) and **Franco-Prussian War** (1870–71) and as a reward for his success was made a count and field marshal. When Germany was united he became the first German Chief of Staff, a post he retained until 1888. His greatest military innovation was in completely reorganizing the General Staff. As armed forces became larger, the problems of moving and supplying them increased the need for specialized staff officers. Moltke made them the military élite, who alternated between staff and command posts. Most of the revolutionary changes in warfare for which he is given credit – the rapid mobilization of resources, the use of **railways** for movement and supply, the use of massed artillery – he owed to others. Moltke brilliantly applied, often for the first time in Europe, the lessons learnt elsewhere and adapted the methods of **Napoleon** and the theories of **Clausewitz** to new technical developments. American generals had shown the value of railways in the **American Civil War**; Moltke made them the most important part of his strategy, so that his troops could be mobilized more quickly and in greater strength than those of the enemy. He was one of the first to realize that the breech-loading rifle gave infantry on the defensive such fire-power that frontal assaults would be suicidal: this had been made clear in the **Crimean War** and American Civil War. Envelopment must therefore be the aim and massed artillery used to defeat the enemy, as at **Sedan**. As armies were growing larger and transport quicker, Moltke realized that detailed planning could not go beyond the start of a battle. After that, local commanders must act on their own initiative and command must be decentralized. After 1871 Moltke's methods − conscription, strategic railways and a General Staff − were copied in most European countries.

**Monarchist Republic** (1871–9) in France. After the capture of **Napoleon III** at **Sedan**, a republican Government of National Defence was set up in Paris to continue the **Franco-Prussian War** (1870–71). An election was held in February 1871, whilst Paris was blockaded by the Prussian army, and produced a monarchist majority in the National Assembly, as republicans wanted to continue the war. **Thiers**, an Orleanist, was made head of the executive and made peace by ceding **Alsace** and part of Lorraine to Germany. Republican opponents of this move formed a **Paris Commune**, which rejected the authority of the government and was crushed by the army under Marshal **MacMahon**. In by-elections in 1871 republicans won 99 of the 114 seats. Thiers became convinced that a Republic divided Frenchmen least and so he sought to win acceptance for it by paying off the indemnity imposed after the Franco-Prussian War, which was followed by the withdrawal of the Prussian army of occupation. Thiers' conversion to republicanism was unacceptable to the monarchists who dominated the parliament, so they replaced him as President in 1873 by Marshal MacMahon and as Prime Minister by the Duc de Broglie, an Orleanist. A royalist restoration now seemed possible, but the royalists could not agree amongst themselves: the Legitimists supported the Comte de Chambord, grandson of **Charles X**, whereas the Orleanists backed the Comte de Paris, grandson of **Louis Philippe**. He was prepared to accept Chambord, who was childless, as king if he could then succeed him, but Chambord would not agree to this and lost much support when he insisted that the white flag of the **Bourbons** should replace the *tricolore* as the national flag. This ended hopes of a royalist restoration, and justified Thiers' jibe that Chambord would go down in history as the French George Washington, the real founder of the Republic. The monarchists still tried to cling to power by arranging, in the constitutional settlement of 1875, for a strong President (who appointed the Prime Minister) and a bicameral legislature. When the Chamber of Deputies was elected by universal male suffrage in 1876 the republicans gained a decisive victory, winning 340 seats: there were 153 monarchist deputies, of whom 75 were Bonapartists (see **Bonapartism**). **Gambetta** was now the obvious choice as Prime Minister but MacMahon refused to appoint him and in 1877 made the Duc de Broglie Prime Minister again. This *Seize Mai* (**16 May**) **crisis** was followed by a new election in which the republicans retained their majority. Two years later the monarchists lost their majority in the Senate too, so MacMahon resigned and was replaced by the moderate republican Grévy. The Republic was now in the hands of republicans, who celebrated by moving the parliament from Versailles to Paris, adopting the *Marseillaise* as the national anthem, and by making 14 July (the date of the fall of the **Bastille** in 1789) a national holiday.

**Monroe Doctrine** (1823). President **Monroe** was disturbed by rumours that the Holy Alliance (a loose association of European powers, except Britain) was prepared to help Spain to recover her South American Empire. He was also concerned by a Russian proclamation in 1821 extending the boundary of Alaska into Oregon county and claiming the west coast of North America as a possible area for Russian colonization. In 1823 George **Canning**, the British Foreign Secretary, proposed to Monroe an alliance of Britain and the USA to resist any attempt by the Holy Alliance to reconquer Spain's former colonies. John Quincy **Adams**, Monroe's Secretary of State, was against it and persuaded the President to issue what became known as the Monroe Doctrine in a message to **Congress**. This stated 'that the American continents . . . are henceforth not to be considered as subjects for future colonization by any European power', and that European interference in the New World would be regarded by the USA as an unfriendly act. The doctrine also stated: 'Our policy in regard to Europe . . . is not to interfere in the internal concerns of any of its powers', or interfere with their existing New World colonies. This was the message of **isolationism** and of **Washington**'s Farewell Address in 1796, when he advised Americans 'to steer clear of permanent alliances with foreign nations'. Canning thought it was impertinent, as the USA was too weak to enforce it against a great power. It was the Royal Navy, in order to preserve Britain's domination of the New World markets, which would keep other powers away from the American continent for most of the century.

Monroe's message received little attention at the time in the USA and it was not till the **American Civil War** that there was a serious challenge to the Doctrine, when the French put Maximilian, a **Habsburg** archduke, on the Mexican throne. This was a short-lived challenge, as French troops were hastily withdrawn when the Civil War was over. By the end of the century the USA felt strong enough to extend the Monroe Doctrine, when President Theodore **Roosevelt** said in 1904 that the USA would feel free to interfere in any Latin American state guilty of 'chronic wrong-doing'. His policy, known as 'the big stick', led the USA to intervene in several Caribbean and Central American states in the next twenty years. For many Latin American countries the Monroe Doctrine, which is still a basic part of American policy, signifies US domination.

**Monroe, James** (1758–1831). Fifth President of the USA (1817–25). Like so many early Presidents, Monroe came from Virginia. In a varied career as a diplomat his one great success was to negotiate the **Louisiana Purchase** in 1803. He was **Madison**'s Secretary of State (1811–17) and largely kept the government going during the **Anglo-American War**. When he became President the question of the extension of slavery into the newly acquired territories arose. Monroe recognized that slavery was evil but he was not an **abolitionist** and accepted the **Missouri Compromise** of 1820.

He enthusiastically supported sending freed Negroes to Liberia, whose capital Monrovia was named after him. Monroe's greatest impact was in foreign policy, which was strongly influenced by John Quincy **Adams**, his Secretary of State (1817–25). In 1818 he made a treaty with Britain which fixed the boundary between Canada and the USA at the 49th parallel and agreed to share with Britain access to Oregon Territory beyond the Rockies. A year later he persuaded Spain to give up her part of Florida to the USA, which then controlled the whole of Florida. In 1823 he put forward the **Monroe Doctrine**, which has been an integral part of US foreign policy ever since.

**Montagu–Chelmsford reforms** (Government of India Act, 1919). Constitutional changes in India named after Edwin Montagu, the Secretary of State for India, and Lord Chelmsford, the Viceroy (1916–21). India played an important role in the **First World War**: 1.2 million Indians were recruited for the British forces and taxes were increased to fund the war effort, so Indians expected some reward for their efforts. Montagu therefore announced in August 1917 that Britain aimed at the 'increasing association of Indians in every branch of administration, the gradual development of self-governing institutions, with a view to the progressive realization of responsible government in India as an integral part of the British Empire'. It was not intended to grant independence, as British control was considered to be permanent, but for the first time something like colonial self-government was proposed for a non-white colony. The Act gave Indians a much larger role in government, as central and provincial legislatures were enlarged and no longer had official majorities. Control of certain affairs (military and foreign policy, taxation) was retained by the government of India, whilst other areas (local government, health, education) were handed over to the provinces, and it is here that the real changes occurred. There was to be a system of 'dyarchy' in the provinces, by which some responsibilities were to be 'transferred' to the control of Indian ministers accountable to the legislature, whilst others were 'reserved' for the governor and his Council. Certain revenue sources were given to the provinces, so they could pay for their new tasks. The franchise was increased but included only about a tenth of the male population: communal electorates, granted in the **Morley–Minto reforms** of 1909, were retained. There was also provision for an inquiry into the working of the Act after ten years, which suggested that further change was possible.

**Montgomery, Bernard Law, 1st Viscount** (1887–1976). British field-marshal. When Montgomery became Commander of the Eighth Army in North Africa in August 1942, he found the troops dispirited, but he revived their morale with his pep-talks and his constant visits, wearing his distinctive beret and battle-dress. Auchinleck had halted Rommel's advance at the first battle of El **Alamein** in July 1942 and had made a defensive line there and at Alam Halfa. When **Rommel** attacked at Alam Halfa (31 August–6 September 1942) Montgomery repulsed him. He then built up an overwhelming superiority in tanks and planes before attacking at El Alamein in October 1942, when he defeated Rommel's *Afrika Korps*, though he failed to follow up rapidly to destroy the remnants of Rommel's forces. Yet he had produced the victory the British so badly needed and was rewarded by a knighthood and promotion to full general in November 1942. Montgomery planned the successful invasion of Sicily but had to work under **Eisenhower** and was furious when he was given a secondary role in the invasion of Italy.

In December 1943 he was recalled from Italy to help prepare for Operation Overlord, the invasion of France, for which he was made land Commander under Eisenhower. He made an important contribution to the planning of the invasion by securing agreement for a wide front for the **D-Day** landing (6 June 1944). His conduct of the **Normandy Campaign** has roused much controversy: his attempted break-out from the bridgehead at Caen (18–20 July) was a costly failure, but he did succeed in attracting the German armour to his left flank so that the Americans could advance at Avranches on the right. After the success of the Normandy campaign Monty felt that he should be in charge of all Allied land forces for the invasion of Germany. He resented Eisenhower taking over direction of land operations in August, as he thought that the Supreme Commander's 'ignorance as to how to run a war is absolute and complete' and that therefore he, Monty, 'must run the land battle for him'. Monty's assertion that he was alone responsible for the successes in Normandy irritated the Americans, as did his constant demands that American generals should be put under his command. Montgomery, made a field marshal in September, wanted a narrow-front strategy, by which all available forces would be put under his command for a crossing of the Rhine and then a strike direct for Berlin. Eisenhower insisted on a broad-front approach to the Rhine, but he did allow Monty to gamble on a seizure by paratroops of bridges across the Rhine at Arnhem in Holland. This was a disastrous failure in September 1944 (see **North-West Europe campaign**) and Montgomery's reputation suffered. It was improved somewhat by his prompt help in relieving the Americans from the north in the battle of the **Bulge** (December 1944) and in his set-piece crossing of the Rhine in February 1945. Eisenhower forbade any advance on Berlin, leaving this to the Russians, so Montgomery was left to clear German forces from Holland and Denmark and received the surrender of German forces in the north at Luneburg Heath on 4 May 1945. 'Monty' then became governor of the British zone of Germany until he replaced Sir Alan Brooke as Chief of the Imperial General Staff in June 1946. When the North Atlantic Treaty Organization (NATO) was formed in 1951, Montgomery became deputy to the Allied Supreme Commander, a post he held until he retired in 1958. There is no agreement on Montgomery's merits as a commander. Some see him as the greatest British general since **Wellington** (a view Monty partly endorsed: when asked who had been the three greatest generals of all time, he replied that the other two were Alexander and Napoleon) and one of the most successful generals of the **Second World War**. Others regard him as competent but over-cautious and unimaginative, one whose successes were based on superior force and on the orthodox set-piece battle.

**More, Hannah** (1745–1833). English Evangelical. The daughter of a schoolmaster, Hannah More was attracted to the **Evangelical Movement** by her friend William Wilberforce, whom she met in 1787, and joined him in attacking the manners and morals of the rich, who, she thought, ought to set an example to the rest of the population. She set up Sunday schools where poor children were taught to read the Bible but not to write, as this would give them ideas above their station in life. When the **French Revolution** began she was convinced that traditional values and the social order must be supported at all costs and so she and her friends produced *Cheap Repository Tracts* at the rate of three a month for three years (1795–8). They were written in a homely style for distribution by the gentry to their labourers and taught the virtues of sobriety, hard work, deference to one's superiors and trust in God. Over two million were distributed in three years. Her extreme social conservatism was shown in her attitude to women, who should be chaste, modest and pious and firmly under the control of men: freedom would be harmful to them. 'To be unstable and capricious, I really think, is but too characteristic of our sex,' she wrote to Horace Walpole, 'and there is, perhaps, no animal so indebted to subordination for its good behaviour as women.' The most influential woman of her day, she promoted conformity and the high moral seriousness which was to be characteristic of Victorian Britain.

**Morgan, John Pierpont** (1837–1913). American financier. The son of a rich international banker, Morgan made a fortune investing in railroads after the **American Civil War** and founded his own investment banking house, J. P. Morgan and Co., in 1895. He symbolized finance capitalism, whereby financiers came to control the economy. In the 1890s he helped companies, particularly railroads, through difficult times and in return insisted on putting his own representatives on their boards of directors. He disliked inefficiency and cut-throat competition and forced many capitalists to combine. Between 1893 and his death he was behind all mergers in railroads, shipping, electricity and telephone systems. His most spectacular combination was the formation of United Steel in 1901, the first billion-dollar trust, which has dominated the steel industry ever since. He exercised his influence through interlocking directorships: 341 in 112 corporations, with assets of over $22 billion in the early twentieth century. He and his partners virtually controlled the American economy: by 1910 all leading American capitalists were associated either with him or with J. D. **Rockefeller**. J. P. Morgan built up a great art collection, much of which he left to the Metropolitan Museum of Art, New York, of which he had been President.

**Morley–Minto reforms** (Indian Councils Act, 1909). Constitutional changes in India, named after John Morley, the Secretary of State for India (1906–10), and Lord Minto, Viceroy (1905–10). The British were dependent on the cooperation of Indians in ruling India, as they relied on Indian revenues and civil servants. They therefore made a determined effort to secure the support of Indian politicians. Morley was the driving force and was greatly influenced by **Gokhale**, who persuaded him that if rational argument did not work, then violent revolution would follow. The elective principle was introduced into the Indian Legislative Council, though officials remained a majority. Twenty-seven of the sixty-one members were to be elected and they were allowed to question civil servants on budgetary and other matters. In the provincial councils official majorities were abandoned and there was to be separate representation of Muslims (at the request of the All-India **Muslim League**), large landowners, chambers of commerce and universities. Indians have always regarded this as an example of 'divide and rule', and the **Aga Khan** later wrote that 'its final, inevitable consequence was the partition of India and the emergence of Pakistan.' Morley maintained that 'a parliamentary system in India is not at all the goal to which I for one moment aspire,' but **Curzon** more far-sightedly saw this as the 'inevitable result' of the new scheme.

**Mormons.** American religious sect. Joseph Smith, a farm boy from New York, allegedly had visions from the age of fourteen, which convinced him that he was a prophet of the Lord. In one of these visions he was visited by the angel Moroni, who led him to a hiding place where there were tablets of gold, on which were written the Book of Mormon. Smith, with divine help, translated this from the original 'reformed Egyptian'. This Book, with the Bible, was the foundation of the Mormon faith. Smith founded the Church of Jesus Christ of the Latter-Day Saints in 1830 and soon made converts, assuring his followers that they were the chosen people of God. All Mormon business ventures were cooperative and Smith insisted that Mormons could have dealings with Gentiles (those who were not Mormons) only through his church. With their discipline and unity the Mormons were successful. Their prosperity was resented by others, who also disliked their sense of superiority and above all the

Mormon practice of polygamy. They had to move from Ohio to Missouri and then to Illinois, where Joseph Smith and his brother were murdered by a hostile mob in 1844. The Mormons almost disintegrated as a movement but were held together by Brigham **Young**, who moved them to the safety of what became Utah and Salt Lake City, where they flourished. Utah could not become a state of the Union as long as polygamy was practised there. In 1890 the Mormon Church abandoned polygamy and in 1896 Utah joined the Union.

**Moroccan crisis** (1905–6). Germany was encouraged by the **Russian Revolution of 1905** and Russia's defeat in the **Russo-Japanese War** (1904–5) to pursue a more aggressive foreign policy and, if possible, break up the **Anglo-French Entente** (1904). Although Germany had not hitherto objected to French penetration of Morocco, **Bülow**, the Chancellor, persuaded Kaiser **William II** to visit Tangier in March 1905. There he told the Sultan that Germany considered Morocco an independent state. This alarmed the European powers, particularly when Bülow demanded an international conference to discuss Morocco. He firmly believed that the other states would support Moroccan independence, France would be humiliated and the Entente would come to an end. **Delcassé**, the French Foreign Minister and the architect of the Entente, opposed the conference but was overruled by his colleagues and resigned, thus giving Germany a great diplomatic victory. However, when the conference met at Algeçiras in Spain in January 1906, Germany suffered a severe set-back. Moroccan independence was affirmed but France was given control of the Moroccan police and the state bank. Germany, deserted by her **Triple Alliance** partner Italy, was supported only by Austria-Hungary. Germany, not France, was humiliated, her isolation made apparent and the Entente strengthened rather than weakened. British suspicions of Germany had been increased, so that in 1906 'military conversations' were held to discuss how Britain could help France, if she were attacked by Germany. **Grey**, the British Foreign Minister, also decided that an **Anglo-Russian Entente** should also be made, so that 'If it is necessary to check Germany, it could then be done.'

**Moroccan crisis** (1911). In May 1911 French troops occupied the Moroccan capital of Fez, at the Sultan's request, when there was a revolt against him. Many thought that this would be followed by French annexation of Morocco, so in July a German gunboat called at the Moroccan port of Agadir. Germany hoped to intimidate France into granting her substantial compensation, in return for recognizing a French protectorate over Morocco, and demanded the whole of the French Congo. The French rejected this demand. Britain joined in when **Lloyd George**, the Chancellor of the Exchequer and hitherto the most pro-German member of the Cabinet, gave a speech at the Mansion House in which he said that Britain would find it intolerable, if she were treated, 'when her interests were vitally affected, as if she were of no account'. Though Morocco was not mentioned, his speech was understood as a warning to Germany not to use force. **Moltke**, the German Chief of Staff, wanted war but was opposed by Kaiser **William II** and **Tirpitz**. **Bethmann-Hollweg**, the Chancellor, agreed 'that the people need a war' but settled for a small part of the Congo, as Germany's partners in the **Triple Alliance**, Austria-Hungary and Italy, were unwilling to go to war. German public opinion was outraged at this climb-down. 'It is false that in Germany the nation is peaceful but the government bellicose,' wrote the French ambassador Jules Cambon. 'The exact opposite is true.' This second Moroccan crisis consolidated the **Triple Entente** of Russia, France and Britain and led to an increase in armaments on all sides. It also provided a favourable moment, by occupying the attention of the other powers, for Italy to invade **Tripoli**. In Germany there was anger and bitterness and a widespread feeling that war was inevitable.

**Moscow Campaign** (1812). **Napoleon**'s invasion of Russia was, in his eyes, made necessary by **Alexander I**'s withdrawal from the **Continental Blockade** in 1810. It was a great gamble, as his army of nearly 700,000 troops (of whom only a third were French) was too big to be fed and supplied adequately, particularly as the Russians carried out a scorched-earth policy as they retreated. Napoleon hoped that the Russians would give battle, would be defeated and would make peace. This did not happen. The Russians steadily retreated, drawing the French further into Russia and extending their supply lines. In two months (June–August) no serious battles were fought, yet Napoleon lost 150,000 soldiers through sickness and desertion. At Smolensk, 280 miles from Moscow, his generals advised him to turn back, but Napoleon could not afford such a blow to his prestige. The Russians did eventually stand and fight at **Borodino**, seventy miles from Moscow, where the French suffered heavily and the Russians retreated in good order, leaving Moscow to the French. Napoleon entered the deserted Russian capital on 14 September: a day later a fire began which burnt down three-quarters of the city. Napoleon waited vainly for Alexander to sue for peace, before deciding on 19 October to retreat, so that he would not be cut off by the Russian winter. The Russians under Kutusov forced him at the battle of Maloyaroslavets to take the route to Smolensk, which was already devastated. By the time the French reached Smolensk in November snow had begun to fall, the temperature had plummeted and Russian armies moving from north and south were preparing to cut off the French retreat at the river Beresina. By building pontoon bridges across the river, French engineers enabled most of what remained of the *Grande Armée* to escape: 25,000 men, plus 70,000 from the flanking armies, finally escaped from Russia. The Moscow campaign was Napoleon's biggest disaster: he had lost 570,000 men (370,000 killed and 200,000 taken prisoner), 200,000 horses and 80 per cent of his artillery. The horses could not be replaced, so that in his 1813 campaigns he did not have the cavalry that might have ensured his survival.

**Moshweshwe** (Moshoeshoe) (*c.* 1785–1870). African leader. The son of a village headman in South Africa, Moshweshwe became the first paramount chief of the Sotho and the founder of the state of Basutoland (Lesotho). In 1822 when the Nguni began to devastate Sotho territory in the *Mfecane*, he was a chief of only 2,000 people in the lowlands of north-east Lesotho. To survive he led his people on a long and heroic march far to the south to Thaba Bosiu ('mountains of the night'), a flat-topped stronghold protected by sheer cliffs on the edge of the Drakensberg mountains. From there he expanded his kingdom to the plains around and paid tribute to nearby tribes to avoid being attacked. The number of his followers grew from 25,000 in 1836 to 80,000 in 1848, as he offered protection to those fleeing from the *Mfecane* and was a humane and tolerant ruler in his loose-knit state. In the 1840s a new threat appeared, when the Boers invaded his territory and settled on his land. At first Moshweshwe fought successfully against them, as he had obtained rifles to protect his kingdom, but by the late 1860s he realized that to avoid Boer domination he would have to place his people under British protection. This he did in 1868, when Basutoland became a British protectorate, with frontiers that are almost the same as those of modern Lesotho. Moshweshwe was one of the greatest African statesmen of his time who, unlike nearly all his Bantu neighbours, managed to preserve the independence of his people.

**Mosley, Sir Oswald Ernald** (1896–1980). British fascist leader (see **Fascism**). He began his political career as a **Conservative** MP (1918–22), was elected as an Independent in 1922 and joined the **Labour Party** in 1924. As a member of **MacDonald**'s Labour government (1929–31) he was greatly influenced by the ideas of J. M. **Keynes** and proposed to deal with unemployment by restricting imports, expanding purchasing power and by using banks to finance industrial development. When this programme was rejected he resigned in 1930 and a year later set up his own New Party: all its candidates failed in the election of that year, including Mosley himself. In 1932 he went to Italy, where he was greatly impressed by **Mussolini**, so on his return he dissolved the New Party and replaced it by the British Union of Fascists (BUF). This was organized on paramilitary lines, with an emphasis on youth, physical fitness and unquestioning loyalty to the leader. Blackshirted stewards silenced hecklers at his meetings and gained a reputation for violence which, with Mosley's **anti-Semitism**, turned many middle-class supporters against the movement. The Public Order Act (1936) was a further blow to the BUF, as it banned political uniforms and allowed the police to prohibit marches. As the economy picked up in the late 1930s, support for the BUF fell away and as conflict with **Hitler** looked more likely it appeared to be unpatriotic. During the **Second World War** Mosley was imprisoned from 1940–43 and was then under house arrest until the end of the war. After the war he founded and led the Union movement, which was in favour of

European unity, tried unsuccessfully to become an MP again and lived for most of the time abroad.

**Muhammad Ali** (Mehemet or Mehmet Ali) (1769–1849). Viceroy (*pasha*) of Egypt (1805–48) and founder of the dynasty which ruled Egypt until 1952. Muhammad Ali was born in Macedonia, a part of the **Ottoman Empire**, of Albanian parents. In 1801 he arrived in Egypt as leader of a small Albanian military force, part of the Ottoman army fighting against **Napoleon**'s Egyptian expedition. By 1805 he had taken control of the country and became Viceroy or Ottoman governor. He then set out to consolidate his control over Egypt, extend its territory and gain his independence from the Sultan. The Mamluk *beys* (princes), who had ruled Egypt since 1250, were a threat to his authority, so Muhammad Ali dealt with them in a typically ruthless and treacherous fashion. In 1811 he invited 300 of them to a banquet at the citadel in Cairo; as they were returning home they were shot down in a narrow alley. The basis of his power lay in the army, which, by using Italian and French instructors, he made into the most efficient in the Ottoman Empire. In the 1830s it numbered 100,000 men, with 18,000 in the navy (60 per cent of Egypt's revenue was spent on the armed forces). New land was irrigated, and cotton, sugar and grain were grown for export to pay for imported arms. The modernization of Egypt continued with a new system of collecting taxes, whereby salaried officials replaced tax-farmers. The power of the *ulama* (religious leaders) was broken when their tax-farms and *waqfs* (religious endowments) were confiscated: they became dependent on the ruler for their income, lost all political influence and became obedient subjects. Educational institutions were founded, not for the whole population but for the élite of army officers and civilian officials, where technical subjects and foreign languages were taught. For all his reforms Muhammad Ali used foreign instructors but never became indebted to European bankers or under the control of European powers. The price of all these reforms was paid by the peasants, who were heavily taxed, conscripted and compelled into forced labour: they fell into debt and throughout the 1820s there was a series of peasant revolts.

In 1811 the Sultan asked Muhammad Ali to send an army to

Arabia to quell the puritanical Islamic movement of the **Wahabis**, who had rejected Ottoman control of the Holy Places of Mecca and Medina. It took him seven years to capture the Hijaz and destroy the Wahabi strongholds. Muhammad Ali then turned to the Sudan, which he conquered. Meanwhile, the **Greek War of Independence** had begun. When Sultan **Mahmud** asked Muhammad Ali for help, Ali sent his son Ibrahim, a military leader of genius, to the Morea, where he was so successful that European powers decided to intervene to prevent the destruction of the Greeks. In 1827, at Navarino, the Europeans annihilated the Egyptian fleet, so Ibrahim's army was withdrawn. When Mahmud refused to make Ibrahim governor of Syria as a reward for his support in the Greek War, Ibrahim seized Syria and advanced into Anatolia, where he defeated the Turks near Konya. He could have gone on to take Istanbul and bring about the fall of the **Ottomans** but Muhammad Ali acted cautiously, because he did not want the European powers to intervene as they had done in Greece. He therefore accepted from Mahmud the Syrian provinces and Adana as a Turkish vassal. The uneasy peace between Mahmud and Muhammad Ali lasted for only six years. In 1839 Mahmud invaded Syria but was defeated at Nezib. Once again Muhammad Ali had been too successful. Britain did not want the disintegration of the Ottoman Empire or it falling to Muhammad Ali, as he was supported by Britain's rival France. In 1840 Britain made the Convention of London with Russia, Austria and Prussia, by which Muhammad Ali had to withdraw from Syria and the conquered provinces: in compensation, his descendants were made hereditary viceroys of Egypt. This marked the end of Muhammad Ali's empire-building. He had been remarkably successful in making Egypt a major Mediterranean power and had been prevented from overthrowing the Sultan only by the European powers.

**Munich agreement** (1938), see **Czechoslovakian crisis** (1938–9)

**Munich (beer-hall)** *Putsch* (8–9 November 1923). An attempt by **Hitler** to seize power in Bavaria, prior to marching on Berlin, where the **Weimar Republic** would be overthrown and a Nazi regime set up. On 8 November 1923 a meeting of right-wing politicians was being held in a Munich beer hall, when Hitler surrounded the building with 600 brownshirts (**SA**) and burst in.

He declared that the Bavarian and Reich governments were dissolved and that he was leader of a national government: he named General **Ludendorff** as the new army chief. The next morning he and Ludendorff led 3,000 Nazis through the city: police fired on the marchers, sixteen of whom were killed, and the *Putsch* collapsed. Hitler, Ludendorff and eight others were put on trial in 1924; Ludendorff was acquitted, much to his disgust. Hitler was given the minimum sentence of five years but was released in nine months. He used his time in prison to dictate the first volume of his autobiography *Mein Kampf* (*My Struggle*). Although the *Putsch* was a fiasco, it made Hitler's name known throughout Germany and it taught him a lesson: that the way to power did not lie through a *coup*. He would have to win over the people to his cause and come to power legally.

**Municipal Corporations Act** (1835). A corollary of the **Reform Act** of 1832. Borough corporations were as much controlled by oligarchies as the unreformed parliament and were regarded as corrupt Tory and Anglican strongholds. The Act imposed a uniform system on 178 old corporate boroughs: councillors were to be elected for three years by all male ratepayers over twenty-one (this was a much more democratic franchise than that of the Reform Act). There was a property qualification for councillors, who elected aldermen for six years and a mayor for one year. Corporations had to set up police forces, paid from the rates, and were given general powers for lighting and cleaning the streets. Most working men did not get the vote as their houses were not rated. Towns not included in the Act could apply for incorporation and many did so, including Manchester and Birmingham. The Act enabled **Liberal** councillors to take over from the **Tories** in most of the large towns in the North and Midlands.

**Murat, Joachim** (1767–1815). Marshal of France and King of Naples (1809–15). The son of an inn-keeper, Murat joined the cavalry in 1787 and spent five years in the ranks before being commissioned. He provided the guns **Napoleon** needed to crush the rising of **Vendémiaire** (1795) and became his brother-in-law when he married Caroline Bonaparte in 1800. A brave and dashing cavalry commander, who was idolized by his men, he led cavalry in each of Napoleon's great campaigns from 1800–1807, and at Essling (1807) his massed cavalry charge prevented disaster. He brutally suppressed the *dos de Mayo* (2 May) rising in Madrid in 1808 and two months later succeeded Joseph Bonaparte as King of Naples. There he could indulge in his vain passion for extravagant uniforms, which he designed himself. He remained at Naples until the **Moscow campaign** of 1812, when he commanded the cavalry at Smolensk and **Borodino** and the whole of the *Grande Armée* after Napoleon's departure. In 1813 he fought at Dresden and **Leipzig** on the retreat through Germany. After Napoleon's first abdication he remained on his throne, but when Napoleon escaped from Elba in 1815 and the **Hundred Days** began, he tried to raise the Italians in support of Napoleon. Defeated by the Austrians in Italy, he escaped to France, where Napoleon foolishly rejected his offer to lead the cavalry at **Waterloo**. Following Napoleon's second abdication he landed in Calabria in an attempt to recover his throne of Naples but was captured and shot.

**Muslim Brotherhood.** Muslim organization in Egypt. After the carnage of the **First World War** there was considerable disillusionment in Egypt with the Western democracies and with the regime at home, which had failed to obtain full independence. There was a revival of popular commitment to Islam, which owed little to the traditional *ulama* (religious leaders) but was led by young teachers, who wanted to restore the supremacy of Islamic practices in public life. The Muslim Brotherhood, founded in 1928, was the most important of the youth organizations that were formed. It had a wide following amongst those with a traditional Muslim education – clerks, civil servants, shopkeepers – and it organized mosques, schools and clinics and in the 1930s turned to political activity. Paramilitary groups were formed and volunteers sent to support the Arab rising in Palestine in 1936–9. During the **Second World War** economic distress in Egypt increased – living standards fell and unemployment rose – so the Brotherhood became the leading opponent of British influence, organized violent demonstrations and strikes and turned to terrorism.

**Muslim League.** Indian political party. Formed in 1906, the Muslim League was like the early **Indian National Congress**, in that membership was restricted to the educated and the affluent, it was loyal to the British **Raj** and its organization was virtually confined to its annual meetings. It was ignored by most Muslims until the **First World War**, when it made the Lucknow Pact (1916) with Congress, which recognized separate electorates for Muslims and reserved seats in Muslim minority provinces, in return for the League's acceptance of Congress's aim of self-government. At the end of the war many League members took part in the *khilafat* campaign against the British government. Indian Muslims regarded the Ottoman Sultan as their *Khalifa*, spiritual leader, and objected to the dismemberment of the **Ottoman Empire** at the end of the war. They became involved in **Gandhi**'s **non-cooperation movement**, but the *khilafat* campaign collapsed when **Kemal Atatürk** abolished the caliphate in 1923. The League then sank into its earlier torpor and in 1927 had only 1,330 members. It began to revive after the return to India in 1935, after his self-imposed 'retirement' in England, of Muhammad Ali **Jinnah**, who had the same impact on the League as Gandhi had on Congress. He found the League poor and disorganized, so that in the provincial elections in 1937, held under the **India Act** of 1935, it gained only 22 per cent of the seats reserved for Muslims. Jinnah set up branches in all parts of the country and made the League, which had three million members by 1944, a political force in India second only to Congress. By the end of the war he had persuaded Muslim leaders in the majority areas of Punjab and Bengal, who had acted independently, to support the League, which had become a mass political party. Its success was shown in the 1945 elections, when it won 90 per cent of the seats reserved for Muslims. The League's Pakistan Resolution of 1940 had demanded 'independent states', where Muslims were in a majority. This was brought about when India was partitioned in 1947, though the League was almost annihilated in the first elections in Pakistan.

**Mussolini, Benito** (1883–1945). Founder of **Fascism** and Italian dictator. The son of a socialist and republican blacksmith in the Romagna, Mussolini was named Benito after Benito **Juárez**, the anti-clerical Mexican leader (see **Anti-clericalism**). Mussolini qualified as an elementary school teacher, then spent two years in Switzerland (1902–4) before returning to take part in trade-union activity. He became a leader of the revolutionary wing of the Italian Socialist Party (PSI) and editor of the party newspaper *Avanti*. By supporting Italian involvement in the **First World War** he broke with the PSI's policy of neutrality, had to resign from *Avanti* and was expelled from the party. After the war he founded the *Fascio di Combattimento* (Combat Group) with a socialist programme, advocating the abolition of private property and that workers should run the factories, and pledging to defend the 'values of war' and the 'rights of Italy'. Initially he supported **D'Annunzio**'s seizure of Fiume, but he made no impact in the general election of 1919 and won no seats. His movement was saved from collapse by financial support from large landowners and industrialists, who used his **Blackshirts** to terrorize the countryside and destroy trade-union and peasant organizations in the *biennio rosso* (1918–20). By this time Mussolini had abandoned his socialist beliefs and in 1921, the year in which the *Fasci* became a political party, he made a political pact with **Giolitti**, who thought he could 'constitutionalize' and absorb Fascism. As a result Fascists won thirty-five seats in the 1921 election and joined Giolitti's 'national bloc'.

Mussolini came to power a year later through the **March on Rome** and King **Victor Emanuel III**'s unwillingness to oppose Fascists, who were a small minority in the Chamber of Deputies. His Cabinet was a coalition, which included all parties, except the Socialists and Communists. In the 1924 elections, in which there was much violence and intimidation by Blackshirts, the Fascists polled 66 per cent of the votes and won 374 out of 535 seats. Criticism of the conduct of the election by the Socialist deputy Matteotti led to his murder by Fascists and a crisis, in which Mussolini would have fallen but for the failure of the King to act and the withdrawal of many deputies from the Chamber in the Aventine Secession (see **Matteotti crisis**). Local Fascist Party bosses now insisted that Mussolini should become a dictator, which he did in 1925–6. A law of December 1925 gave him total power, which he used to ban political opposition and **trade unions**, censor the press, purge the administration of anti-Fascists, replace elected mayors in local government by appointed officials and set up a secret police and special courts to try political offences. The *Duce* ('leader') realized the need for mass support, so in 1929 he made the **Lateran Treaties** with Pope **Pius XI**, which ended the antagonism of Church and State in Italy, which had persisted since the **Risorgimento**. Mussolini now had to cope with the **Great Depression**, in which prices and production fell and unemployment rose. He began public works schemes, rebuilding much of Rome, drained the Pontine marshes and financed industry through the IRI (*Istituto per la Ricostruzione Industriale*) (1933), ignoring the institutions of the **Corporate State**. From 1935 the state's role in industrialization constantly increased, so that by 1939 it controlled four-fifths of Italy's shipping and three-quarters of its pig-iron production. Italy's public sector was second only to that of the Soviet Union.

Mussolini pursued a cautious foreign policy up to 1935, cooperating with his **Stresa Front** partners (France and Britain) to maintain the status quo in Europe, but the **Ethiopian War** (1935–6), in which Britain and France half-heartedly imposed sanctions on Italy, pushed him towards **Hitler**. The **Axis** was formed in 1936; both Italy and Germany intervened in the **Spanish Civil War** on the side of **Franco**, and in 1938 Mussolini accepted the union of Austria and Germany in the *Anschluss*. Mussolini's subservience to Germany was shown at home too, when anti-Semitic laws in 1938 excluded Italian Jews from teaching and from the civil service and their right to hold property was restricted. At Munich (1938) (see (**Czechoslovakian crisis**) Mussolini was clearly a junior partner to Hitler and pathetically copied Germany's seizure of Czechoslovakia in 1939 by annexing Albania. Although committed by the Pact of Steel (May 1939) to join Germany in the **Second World War**, **Ciano**, Mussolini's Foreign Minister, realized the weakness of Italy's armed forces and kept her out of the war until 1940. Hitler had to rescue Mussolini from his disastrous invasion of Greece, and in North Africa **Rommel** was given command after Italian reverses. Mussolini's subordination to Hitler was now complete – he sent Italian troops to Russia and in December 1941 declared war on the USA. As the Axis powers were pushed out of North Africa and Sicily was invaded in 1943, members of the Fascist Grand Council in July 1943 asked the King to resume command of the armed forces. He dismissed Mussolini, who was arrested but rescued by German paratroopers and installed as a German puppet ruler in the Italian Social Republic in northern Italy. As the Allies advanced, Mussolini was captured by the Italian **Resistance** and was shot with his mistress on 28 April 1945.

**Nanjing, Rape of.** Japanese troops entered Nanjing, the Chinese capital, in December 1937, shortly after the **Sino-Japanese War** (1937–45) had begun. There they took part in an uncontrolled orgy of murder, rape and looting. It is estimated that in the first six weeks of Japanese occupation, at least 60,000 and possibly as many as 200,000 Chinese civilians and prisoners-of-war were murdered and that a third of the city's buildings were destroyed. News of the atrocity was not reported in the Japanese press, although there were numerous foreign protests, which the Japanese ignored. The 'Rape of Nanjing' gave Japanese troops a reputation for barbarity and cruelty that lasted until 1945. At a military tribunal after the war, the Japanese general who was in command at Nanjing in 1937 was sentenced to death for war crimes.

**Nanjing, Treaty of** (1842). The first **Opium War** between Britain and China was ended by the Treaty of Nanjing. Four ports, in addition to Guangzhou (Canton), were opened to foreign trade; the Chinese agreed to pay an indemnity and Hong Kong was given to Britain in perpetuity. This was the first of many **unequal treaties**. Surprisingly, the import of opium, which had been a major cause of the war, was not mentioned.

**Napoleon Bonaparte** (1769–1821). Emperor of the French (1804–14). Born in Corsica, the son of a minor noble, Napoleon became an artillery officer in the French royal army and gained his first war experience in the **French Revolution** at the siege of Toulon (1793), where his artillery forced the British to withdraw from the port. In 1795 he put down the rising of **Vendémiaire** against the **Directory** and was rewarded by being given command of the army of Italy. His success there (see **French Revolutionary Wars**) made his reputation as a general and gave him the confidence to pursue his own foreign policy by making peace with Austria at

Campo Formio (1797). A year later he was despatched to Egypt but his army was cut off by **Nelson**'s victory at the battle of the **Nile**, so he returned to France in time for the *coup d'état* of **Brumaire** (1799), which made him First Consul.

During the **Consulate** he carried out major reforms in France, bringing the provinces under central control by instituting prefects, preserving the gains of the Revolution in the *Code Napoléon* and making a **Concordat** (1801) with the Pope. In 1804 he crowned himself Emperor and soon established an imperial nobility. When the peace of **Amiens** (1802) came to an end in 1803, he planned to invade England but was thwarted at **Trafalgar** (1805). By this time the Third Coalition had been formed against him, so in a brilliant series of campaigns (1805–7) he defeated Austria and Russia at **Austerlitz**, Prussia at **Jena–Auerstädt** and Russia at Friedland, finally making peace at the Treaty of **Tilsit**. His success was not due to any major innovations he made, as the weapons and methods he used had all been developed under the monarchy and during the Revolution. The use of widely spread columns, which could live off the land and therefore free him from dependence on slow-moving baggage trains, was the key to his success and enabled him to surprise the enemy by the speed of his advance. His defeat of the Third Coalition enabled him to enlarge the **Napoleonic Empire**, which by 1811 extended from the Baltic to the Adriatic, with client states in Germany (the **Confederation of the Rhine**), Italy and Poland.

The **Continental Blockade**, which aimed to destroy Britain economically by depriving her of her European markets, led Napoleon to make his two greatest blunders, the invasion of Spain in 1808, which began the **Peninsular War**, and the **Moscow Campaign** of 1812. Henceforth Napoleon was on the defensive, and after defeat at **Leipzig** (1813) was pushed back into France, where he once again showed his brilliance as a general in some small-scale battles. His refusal to compromise (the Allies were offering him peace terms as late as February 1814) led to his downfall, abdication and exile to Elba. The **Hundred Days** followed his escape from there and came to an end with the battle of **Waterloo**, after which Napoleon spent the rest of his life as a prisoner on St Helena. His influence long outlived him. The map of Europe was permanently changed with the disappearance of the Holy Roman Empire, the republics of Genoa and Venice and the free cities and ecclesiastical states in Germany, where the number of territories was reduced from 234 to forty. Where Napoleon abolished feudalism it was nowhere re-established. The *Code Napoléon* survived not only in France but in the legal systems of Belgium, the Italian states and the Rhineland.

**Napoleon III** (Charles Louis Napoleon Bonaparte) (1808–73). Emperor of the French (1852–70). Son of Louis Bonaparte, King of Holland (1806–10) and **Napoleon Bonaparte**'s brother, Napoleon III was forced to leave France in 1815 and lived in exile, mainly in Switzerland. On the death of Napoleon's only son in 1832, he became the Bonapartist pretender to the French throne and twice tried unsuccessfully to overthrow **Louis Philippe**, the first time in 1836 when he failed to raise the garrison at Strasbourg. After the second attempt, at Boulogne in 1840, he was imprisoned but escaped to England in 1846. He returned to France after the February revolution in 1848, but the government forced him to leave. Elected to the Assembly, he was finally allowed to take his seat in September and made good use of the Napoleonic legend to gain popularity. Appearing as the saviour who would end internal strife, protect the Catholic Church, and provide firm and efficient government, whilst maintaining the gains of the **French Revolution**, he was elected as President of the **Second Republic** in December 1848 by an overwhelming majority (he gained 5.4 million votes, his nearest rival 1.4 million). As the Constitution did not allow him to hold office for a second term, he staged a *coup* in December 1851 which made him President for ten years, and a year later he replaced the Second Republic with the Second Empire, with himself as hereditary Emperor. A plebiscite produced 7.8 million votes in favour of the change, 250,000 against it.

Napoleon III wanted to establish his dynasty firmly by healing the divisions in French society, by promoting economic prosperity and by giving France a leading role in Europe again. He therefore encouraged massive railway construction, which gave a great boost to the iron, steel and coal industries, created employment and, by linking northern France to the Mediterranean, provided easier access to the North African and Middle Eastern markets, making Marseille a centre of Mediterranean trade. The building of the **Suez Canal** increased French financial and commercial penetration of Egypt. Railways also opened up new markets for agriculture, made the peasants more prosperous and firmly attached them to the regime. More roads were built too, so great progress was made in making France a unified nation and market. This expansion was funded by investment banks, such as the *Crédit Mobilier* of the Péreire brothers, which tapped the savings of small investors. Public works, including the rebuilding of Paris by Baron **Haussmann**, also increased employment. To make French industry more efficient and reduce the cost of living Napoleon favoured *laissez-faire*, and in 1860 made a commercial treaty with England that reduced the duties on goods traded between the two countries. In an attempt to gain support from the working class he granted the right to strike in 1864 and the right to form **trade unions** in 1868. Napoleon was dependent on the *notables* – the land-owning and professional élite – and as they wanted a stronger parliament (which they controlled), he was prepared to make concessions to them. The Legislative Body was given complete control of finance in 1861, and in the new Constitution of 1870 it was allowed to initiate legislation and ministers were made responsible to it. The Constitution was approved in a plebiscite by 7.2 million people, with 1.5 million voting against, which prompted **Gambetta** to remark that 'The Emperor is stronger than ever.' Yet within four months the Empire had ended and the **Third Republic** had begun.

This unexpected outcome was brought about by the failure of Napoleon's foreign policy. His involvement in the **Crimean War** had ended in triumph, as Russia was defeated and the peace conference was held in Paris. France was successful too in expanding her Empire in Senegal under **Faidherbe** and in Indo-China. But Napoleon's support of **Cavour**, arranged at **Plombières** (1858), and the subsequent war with Austria, was unpopular in France, though France eventually gained Savoy and Nice. Napoleon's prestige suffered greatly from his interference in Mexico, where he put a **Habsburg**, Maximilian, on the throne in 1863 and then withdrew French troops in 1867, leaving Maximilian to be captured and shot by **Juárez**. His greatest blunders, however, were in his dealings with Prussia. Constantly out-manoeuvred by **Bismarck** and under-estimating Prussian strength, he failed to get any compensation for France after Prussia's victory in the **Austro-Prussian War** (1866) and then by inept diplomacy enabled Bismarck to lead him into the **Franco-Prussian War** (1870–71), which brought about the defeat of France and Napoleon's overthrow.

**Napoleonic Empire.** This consisted not only of countries annexed to France but of satellite states which **Napoleon** set up. The doctrine of natural frontiers for France (the Rhine, the Alps and the Pyrenees) had been put forward during the **French Revolution**: Belgium had been annexed in 1795, to which the left bank of the Rhine was added in 1801. Further German territory – Hamburg and part of the north German coast – became part of France in 1810–11, in order to make the **Continental Blockade** more effective. In Italy Piedmont was annexed to France in 1802, followed by Parma, Tuscany, the Papal States and the Illyrian provinces on the Dalmatian coast by 1809. Napoleon created satellite states on or near France's borders, such as the Helvetic Republic (Switzerland), many of which became kingdoms ruled by members of Napoleon's own family. The Kingdom of Holland was under Louis Bonaparte from 1806–10, when it was annexed to France, as Louis refused to apply the Continental Blockade rigorously; Napoleon himself became King of Italy in 1805; Joseph Bonaparte ruled Naples from 1806–8 (when he was succeeded by **Murat**, Napoleon's brother-in-law) before becoming King of Spain; Jérôme Bonaparte was King of Westphalia, formed mainly from Prussian lands west of the Elbe at the treaty of **Tilsit** (1807). The **Confederation of the Rhine**, a group of German states allied to France, was formed in 1806, and the Grand Duchy of Warsaw, under the King of Saxony, was created a year later. Napoleon therefore controlled nearly all of continental Europe west of the **Habsburg Empire** and Prussia. He intended to rule his Empire efficiently and make it popular by introducing reforms that had been applied in France, many of which were encapsulated in the *Code Napoléon*: careers open to talent, equality before the law, the end of feudalism, guilds and tithe and the sale of Church lands. These reforms were carried out most successfully in Holland, the Rhineland and north-east Italy, but they were accompanied by measures which made his rule unpopular. The prime purpose of the Empire was to serve France, so it was plundered to provide estates for his generals and conscripts for French armies and was heavily taxed to pay for the **Napoleonic Wars**.

**Napoleonic Wars** (1799–1815). When **Napoleon Bonaparte** became first Consul in 1799 France was at war with Britain, Austria and Russia. Austria, defeated at Marengo (1800) in Italy by Napoleon and by Moreau at Hohenlinden in Bavaria, made peace at Lunéville (1801), recognizing the left bank of the Rhine as French territory. The Tsar, resenting the British seizure of Malta and Austria's failure to support Russian troops in Switzerland, withdrew his forces from Western Europe. Both Britain and France were exhausted and so made peace at **Amiens** in 1802, though the peace did not last, as Britain refused to withdraw from Malta, whilst France strengthened her control in Italy and Switzerland. Napoleon's hopes of invading Britain were destroyed at **Trafalgar** (1805), by which time a Third Coalition of Britain, Austria and Russia had been formed against France. Swiftly Napoleon moved his troops from Boulogne to the Danube, surrounded General Mack at Ulm and forced him to surrender, captured Vienna and then advanced into Moravia to defeat the Austrians and Russians at **Austerlitz** (1805), in one of his greatest victories against superior numbers. Austria made peace at Pressburg (1806) and was deprived of her remaining possessions in Italy and Germany. Prussia, alarmed at Napoleon's power in Germany, belatedly took up arms against France and was crushed at **Jena–Auerstädt**. Against the Russians Napoleon suffered a reverse at Eylau in February 1807, but gained the decisive victory he needed at Friedland in June. Both Russia and Prussia made peace at **Tilsit**, thus leaving only Britain fighting France.

Napoleon tried to strike at Britain by cutting off her trade with countries under his control in his **Continental Blockade**. As Portugal refused to take part he decided to seize the Iberian Peninsula, and so began the **Peninsular War** (1808–13). This was one of his greatest blunders, as it was a constant drain on his manpower and resources and encouraged resistance to France in central and eastern Europe. Austria entered the war again in 1809 and defeated

Napoleon on the Danube at Aspern–Essling before losing narrowly at Wagram and making peace. When **Alexander I** withdrew from the Continental Blockade Napoleon made his second major error in deciding to invade Russia in 1812. The **Moscow Campaign** was a disaster. Napoleon, unable to win a decisive victory at **Borodino**, saw his army melt away through desertion and disease, so that of nearly 700,000 of his troops who invaded Russia, less than 100,000 returned. This did not necessarily mean the collapse of the Napoleonic Empire, as the Russians too were exhausted and the Austrians, fearing Russia more than France, were not anxious to re-enter the conflict. Prussia joined Russia in February 1813, and though Napoleon defeated her at Lützen and Bautzen he did not have enough cavalry to mount an effective pursuit. As Napoleon would make no concessions – 'My domination will not survive the day when I cease to be strong and therefore feared' – Austria joined in the fight, so that at **Leipzig** Napoleon faced for the first time the combined armies of Austria, Russia and Prussia. After his defeat there he had to retreat from Germany, at the same time as **Wellington** was invading southern France from Spain. Fighting was taking place on French soil again for the first time since 1794. Napoleon's brilliance as a general returned, as he defeated the over-extended Austrians and Russians three times in five days in minor engagements, but the appetite for war had disappeared in France, and when his Marshals deserted him he had to abdicate. The first Treaty of **Paris** (1814) imposed lenient terms on France, which were made more severe when Napoleon escaped from Elba and in the **Hundred Days** sought to recover control of France, an attempt which failed at **Waterloo**.

**National Governments.** British coalition governments from 1931–5. In August 1931 the **Labour** government of **MacDonald** split, as nine ministers opposed a cut in unemployment benefit, which was needed to secure an American loan. As the Trades Union Congress also strongly condemned the cuts, MacDonald resigned. The **Liberal** leader, Herbert Samuel, suggested that he should form 'a government of national salvation' with the **Conservatives** and Liberals. Pressed to do this by King **George V**, MacDonald accepted, feeling that he was putting the needs of the nation before those of his party, but he did this without consulting his Labour colleagues and so divided the Labour Party. Only seven members of the Parliamentary Labour Party stayed with MacDonald and the National Government, the rest forming the opposition. As sterling continued to fall Britain abandoned the **gold standard**. MacDonald called a general election in October, which further increased the hatred of the Labour Party for its former leader; 556 National Government candidates were returned (473 of whom were Conservatives – only thirteen were Labour supporters of the Prime Minister). The Labour Party was reduced to fifty-one seats, with most of its leaders being defeated. The new National Government was therefore dominated by Conservatives, particularly by Neville **Chamberlain** as Chancellor of the Exchequer. The government abandoned *laissez-faire* and at the Ottawa Conference (1932) established a system of tariffs and imperial preference which lasted until the 1970s. Chamberlain forced down interest rates, which enabled a home-building boom to take place. New industries (motor cars, electrical engineering, rayon) helped by cheap credit grew up, mainly in the Midlands and South, so that Britain began to recover from the **Great Depression**, except in the north.

The government nationalized London Transport by taking over a bill prepared by the Labour Minister of Transport, Herbert Morrison, in 1931, which created the London Passenger Transport Board to control London's buses, trains and 'tubes' (underground railways). Other measures begun by the Labour government were continued, such as Marketing Boards to guarantee prices for agricultural products. The **India Act** (1935) gave responsible government to the Indian provinces, a move to which MacDonald was personally committed. When that was passed he resigned and was replaced as Prime Minister by the Conservative **Baldwin**. The governments of both Baldwin (1935–7) and Chamberlain (1937–40) called themselves National but were in fact Conservative administrations.

**National Insurance Act** (1911). Passed by **Asquith**'s **Liberal** government when **Lloyd George** was Chancellor of the Exchequer, the National Insurance Act gave unemployment benefit to workers in selected industries such as building, shipbuilding and engineering (this was extended to cover nearly all industries in 1920). Sickness benefit was provided for all manual workers, except the self-employed, and was paid for by compulsory contributions of four pence per week from employees, three pence from employers and two pence from the government: Lloyd George called it 'nine pence for four pence'. Sickness benefit was for twenty-six weeks, backed up by medical, maternity and sanatorium care. The three-tier system of contributions went back to **Bismarck**'s **State Socialism** and was to be used again by the **Labour** government after the **Second World War**. This act was a significant move towards the **Welfare State** and marked a huge increase in government intervention.

**Nationalism.** The feeling of loyalty to a group united by race, language and history. As people identified with the nation, nationalism became the most powerful force in modern history. During the **French Revolution** nationalism was associated with popular sovereignty, the **Declaration of the Rights of Man** (1789) stating that 'sovereignty resides in the nation'. This was not the case in the European monarchies, where nationalism was a reaction to French domination. The popular rising in Spain during the **Peninsular War** (1808–13) was not in favour of the sovereignty of the people, but was a conservative movement of loyalty to the **Bourbon dynasty** and to the Catholic Church. In Germany Herder and Fichte stressed the importance of language in forming national character and looked forward to the unity of all Germans, but people like them were a small minority. The Congress of **Vienna** (1815) ignored nationalism in its concern for the balance of power, so that Belgium was given to the Dutch, Venice to Austria, and Norway to Sweden; Poland was divided amongst Russia, Prussia and Austria. **Metternich** was determined to resist nationalism, which would lead to the break-up of the **Austrian Empire**, and succeeded in doing so between 1815 and 1848. The only two countries where nations won their independence in those years were Belgium and Greece, and this was possible only because Britain and France aided Belgium and the Great Powers fought against the **Ottoman Empire** in the **Greek War of Independence** (1821–32).

There was no mass support for nationalism (except in Ireland) as, with poor communications, few people moved far from the district where they were born and so had local or, at most, regional loyalties. In countries like Italy language also bred particularism, since French was spoken in the north and various patois in the rest of the country – Italian was a literary language spoken by hardly anyone. In Poland and Hungary peasants regarded the leaders of the national movement, the gentry, as their oppressors and therefore refused to help them in the struggle against Russian and Austrian domination. In areas of mixed population nationalist movements were in conflict with each other and this weakened them, as it did in Hungary in the **Revolutions of 1848**, when **Kossuth** refused to give to Croats and Romanians the same rights he was claiming for the Magyars. The attempts to unite Italy and Germany and to make Hungary independent all failed in 1848–9 and showed clearly that spontaneous, popular risings would achieve little.

Nationalism would triumph in Italy and Germany only if, as in the case of Belgium and Greece, it was supported by one or more of the Great Powers. This took place in Italy in 1859–60 when Piedmont, supported by **Napoleon III** of France, took the lead, and in Germany when **Bismarck** and **Prussia** defeated Austria in the **Austro-Prussian War** (1866) and France in the **Franco-Prussian War** (1870–71). In both cases unity was imposed from above as a result of war and was not the result of popular pressure. Nationalism was an artificial not a spontaneous growth, so institutions (schools, bureaucracy and conscript army) had to be established to create a nation and a feeling of loyalty to the nation state. Schools could foster patriotism (as in the USA, where the day begins with homage to the flag) and ensure that all speak the same language (there were even attempts to revive languages which were almost dead, as in the Gaelic League (1893) in Ireland). Mass loyalty to the nation state was thus created and was accompanied by a more aggressive form of nationalism, fostered by **Social Darwinism** and the racial theories of writers such as **Gobineau**. The success of Italy and Germany encouraged nationalists elsewhere, particularly in the Ottoman Empire. Serbia, Montenegro and Romania were recognized as independent at the **Berlin Congress** (1878) and Bulgaria declared her independence in 1908. These states deprived Turkey of most of her European territory in the first **Balkan War** (1912) and then fought each other for the spoils in the second Balkan War, as a result of which Serbia doubled in size. Austria-Hungary regarded the enlarged Serbia as a threat, as it would act as a focus of attraction for Serbs in the **Dual Monarchy**, and so began the **First World War** by attacking Serbia. There were eleven nationalities in the **Austro-Hungarian Empire** but they all remained loyal until 1918, when military defeat brought about the disintegration of the Empire.

The treaties which ended the war appeared to be a triumph for nationalism. Independent nation states were created in Yugoslavia, Poland, Czechoslovakia, Finland, Latvia and Lithuania, but the seeds of future conflict were already sown, as there were large national minorities in these states: Hungarians in Czechoslovakia, Romania and Yugoslavia, Germans in Poland and Czechoslovakia. **Hitler** combined elements of late nineteenth century nationalism – an emphasis on racial purity, a belief in the superiority of the Aryan race and in violence – with a claim to embody the will of the German nation: *Ein Volk, ein Reich, ein Führer*. In seizing what he claimed were German lands – Austria in the *Anschluss* (1938), Czechoslovakia in 1938–9 and part of Poland in 1939 – he unleashed the **Second World War**.

Outside Europe, nationalism took an aggressive form in Japan's attack on China in the **Sino-Japanese War** (1894–5) and later in her seizure of **Manchuria** (1931) and invasion of China (1937). Elsewhere, nationalism was usually a reaction to Western rule or exploitation, as in the xenophobic **Boxer Rising** in China (1900) and in the **May Fourth Movement** (1919), which followed the award to Japan of Germany's former colonies in China. In India, where there was no racial, linguistic or religious unity, national movements were small and led by a Western-educated élite (**Nehru** was educated at Harrow and Cambridge) until **Gandhi** created a mass following with his policy of **non-cooperation**. In the Middle East, disappointment that promises of independence made to Arabs during the First World War were not kept led to the formation of the *Wafd* in Egypt in 1919 under Saad **Zaghlul**. In the Dutch East Indies (Indonesia) *Sarekat Islam*, founded in 1911, became a mass movement after the war (with two and a half million members in 1919), demanding independence. All these national movements were to succeed, like others before them, as a result of war: the

**Second World War** brought the European empires crashing down and saw independent national states rise out of their ashes.

**National Liberal Party.** German political party, which was formed in 1867 to support **Bismarck**'s bid for German unification. From 1867 to 1879 it was the largest party in the **Reichstag**. It was more nationalist than liberal and weakly agreed that the military budget should be passed for seven years, a measure which effectively removed the army from parliamentary control. The National Liberals betrayed their own liberal beliefs by supporting Bismarck in his persecution of the Catholic Church in the *Kulturkampf* and in his attacks on the socialists in the **anti-socialist law**. In the late 1870s Bismarck wanted to free himself from dependence on the National Liberals, particularly as he wanted to move to a policy of protection, which both *Junkers*, faced with competition from Russian wheat, and industrialists were demanding. As most National Liberals were supporters of free trade, Bismarck turned to the **Centre Party** for support in his move to Protection in 1879. This split the National Liberal Party, some of whose members broke away to form a new party, whilst those who remained favoured tariffs and cooperation with the Conservatives. By 1887 the National Liberals had only thirty-seven seats in the Reichstag. They never recovered their former position and became increasingly conformist and conservative, supporting an aggressive foreign policy and naval expansion, accepting the views of the military and fearful of the growth of **socialism**.

**National Party** (NP). South African political party formed in 1914 by Barry **Hertzog** to promote **Afrikaner** interests. 'In our attitude towards the Natives,' said Hertzog, 'the fundamental principle is the supremacy of the European population in the spirit of Christian trusteeship, utterly rejecting any attempt to mix the races.' At first the NP served Afrikaner farming interests and then those of the poor whites in industry, especially in the mines. The NP gained greatly from the savagery with which the **Rand** revolt of 1922 was put down by the government. The backlash came in 1924, when there was an election: Hertzog, the NP leader, was able to form a government by making a pact with the Labour Party. In 1929 he had a clear majority, but with the **Great Depression** South Africa suffered severely, and so Hertzog formed a coalition with **Smuts** in 1933; a year later the National Party and Smuts' South African Party 'fused' to become the United Party. The National Party had therefore ceased to exist but many Afrikaners, led by Daniel Malan, would not accept this. They formed a new 'Purified' National Party, which became the official opposition, though in the 1938 election it gained only thirty-eight seats. Ten years later, though it had only 37 per cent of the (white) vote, it was able to form a government. This was a turning-point in South African history, as the NP campaigned with a programme of *apartheid* (see **Segregation**) and had close ties with the Dutch Reformed Church and the **Broederbond**. It remained in power up to the 1990s.

**Naval mutinies** took place in British fleets in 1797. The causes were poor pay, which had not changed for a century, cramped, unhealthy conditions on board and ferocious discipline. Petitions for redress had been ignored by the Admiralty, so there was a widespread mutiny at a time when there was the possibility of a French invasion of England. In April the Channel fleet at Spithead refused to sail until its grievances had been rectified, though the men said they would sail if the French navy appeared. The government hastily promised to increase pay, so the Channel fleet put to sea in May. In the same month the North Sea fleet at the Nore mutinied. This was a more serious mutiny than that at Spithead, as the sailors were better organized and made greater demands. They elected two delegates from each ship to a central committee whose chairman was Richard Parker, a member of the London Corresponding Society, who sought to familiarize the seamen with **Paine**'s *Rights of Man* (see **Corresponding societies**). When the mutineers blockaded the Thames, public opinion turned against them and they were proclaimed rebels in June, with a pardon promised to those who submitted, except for the ringleaders. One ship after another surrendered, so the mutiny was over by the end of June. Thirty-six leaders, including Parker, were executed. The government had been alarmed that radical agitators were at work among the mutineers and it is clear that the United Irishmen, who wanted separation from England, and who felt that a mutiny in the British fleet would improve the chances of a successful French invasion of Ireland, had contacts with the fleet, as had the London Corresponding Society. Yet most seamen were concerned only with pay and conditions: when these were redressed the mutiny quickly collapsed.

**Nazi Party** (National Socialist German Workers' Party (NSDAP)) (1920–45). The NSDAP became known as the Nazi Party from the first syllable of *NAtional* and the second syllable of *SoZIalist*. It was originally the German Workers' Party, which **Hitler** joined in 1919 and which changed its name in 1920. The party programme of 1920 called for the union of all Germans in a greater Germany, rejected the treaty of **Versailles**, demanded *Lebensraum* ('living space') in the east and said that citizenship should be decided by race: no Jew could be a German. It also contained 'socialist' measures which were later abandoned, such as the abolition of unearned income and the nationalization of **cartels**. Hitler took over as leader of the party in 1921, with a following of ex-soldiers and middle-class youth, who were organized as a paramilitary force in the **SA**. After the failure of the **Munich** *Putsch* in 1923, the party was banned. When it was re-formed in 1925 Hitler was determined to gain power legally by winning elections. Before 1928, when the party gained only 3 per cent of the vote and twelve seats in the **Reichstag**, the party membership grew only slowly, as the workers maintained their allegiance to the **Social Democratic Party** and many Catholics to the **Centre Party**. Most of the middle class found the party too radical and did not like the words 'Socialist' and 'Workers' in its name.

The breakthrough came between 1928 and 1930, partly owing to the **Great Depression** and partly because the Nazis allied with nationalists in a campaign against the **Young Plan** for **reparations** payments, and this helped to make them acceptable to the middle class. In the 1930 elections the Nazi Party won 107 seats, with 18 per cent of the vote, and became the second-largest party. From 1930–33 it became a genuine mass party, as it broadened its social base, which the Social Democratic and Communist parties were unable to do. It did best in the rural areas and small towns of Protestant north and east Germany, where the most traditional section of society – peasants, self-employed artisans and small traders – felt themselves squeezed between the power of the **trade unions** and that of big business. Yet the attraction of the Nazi Party did not end there, as it skilfully appealed to each social group. It gained both middle-class and significant working-class support (in 1933 32.5 per cent of workers voted for the Nazis) and it attracted the young. They were impressed by the dynamism of the movement and its charismatic leader and its idealism in calling for the rebirth of Germany. The Nazi Party became a broadly based popular party without precedent in German history, and this was shown by its success at the polls. In July 1932 it won 230 seats with 37 per cent of the vote and became the largest party, yet the Nazi Party did not come to power by winning a majority in the Reichstag. In November 1932 its share of the vote fell by 4 per cent to 33 per cent and it was saved only by the decision of conservative politicians to replace parliamentary government by an authoritarian system. In the elections of March 1933, after Hitler became Chancellor, the Nazi Party had 43 per cent of the vote. It became the only legal party in July. Its membership rose dramatically from 75,000 in 1927, to 850,000 in January 1933 and reached 6.5 million in 1943. It came to dominate all aspects of German life through *Gleichschaltung* ('coordination') and affiliated organizations, such as the **SS**, **Hitler Youth** and the Labour Front, which became the main instruments of **totalitarianism**. In 1945 the NSDAP ceased to exist and its revival was forbidden by the Constitution of the German Federal Republic.

**Nazism.** The ideology of the **Nazi Party**. Nazism did not have a coherent programme, but its main features were hostility to both democracy and **communism**, violent **anti-Semitism** and a belief in the superiority of the Aryan race. The finest Aryan product was the German people, the master race, who had a right to *Lebensraum* ('living space') at the expense of inferior races in Eastern Europe, such as the Slavs. Much of Nazism's anti-Semitism was derived from writers such as Joseph **Gobineau** and Houston Stewart Chamberlain. The Jewish race was regarded as parasitic and responsible for most of the ills affecting Germany: the **First World War**, the **'stab in the back'** of the German armed forces and the peace of **Versailles**. They were to be excluded from German society: when Germany invaded Russia in 1941 **Hitler** decided on their complete extermination in the **'Final Solution'**. Another feature of Nazism was an aggressive nationalism. The aim was to establish a dictatorship and create a new social order, in which class conflict would disappear and be replaced by national solidarity: each individual would put the interests of the nation before self-interest. There was a belief that life was a struggle for survival, in which the weak went to the wall (see **Social Darwinism**). This struggle took place between nations and races, as well as between individuals; Germans, as the master race, were destined to throw off the shackles of Versailles and dominate Europe, if not the world. These ideas were to be found in the 1920 programme of the National Socialist Party, along with some socialist ideas that were later discarded, but their fullest expression was to be found in Hitler's *Mein Kampf* (*My Struggle*) (1925–8), which became the bible of the Nazi movement.

**Nazi–Soviet Pact** (23 August 1939). A non-aggression pact between Germany and the Soviet Union. When Germany reoccupied the rest of Czechoslovakia (she had been given part of it at Munich, – see **Czechoslovakian crisis**) in the spring of 1939, Britain and France guaranteed Polish independence but to defend Poland against a German attack they would need the Soviet army. Britain and France therefore negotiated with the USSR, though progress was slow, as **Chamberlain** disliked **communism** and was not convinced of the value of an alliance, since most Russian generals had been executed in the **Great Purges** of 1936–8. **Stalin** was wary of Franco-British approaches, fearing that in a war with Germany the USSR would be left with the bulk of the fighting. He was anxious to keep out of a European war, as from May to September 1939 the USSR was fighting Japan on the Mongolian border (see **Nomonhan Incident**). Stalin realized that the USSR would not be able to cope with a war on two fronts. He also wanted to make his western frontier more secure by acquiring territory Russia had lost in the **First World War**. Britain and France could not help him to realize either of these aims; Germany could. Like the USSR, she did not want a two-front war when she invaded Poland, so she needed an agreement with Stalin. On 23 August **Hitler** sent **Ribbentrop**, his Foreign Minister, to Moscow to sign a non-aggression pact with the Soviet Union. There were secret agreements at the same time, by which Germany and the USSR divided much of eastern and northern Europe between them. Germany recognized the USSR's paramount interest in Finland, Estonia, Latvia and eastern Poland. The USSR recognized Germany's interest in Lithuania and the rest of Poland. This agreement was amended on 28 September: Lithuania was to go to Russia and Germany was to get more of Poland. There were economic agreements too: Germany was to import raw materials from the USSR and to export weapons and machinery to her.

The **Second World War** began on 1 September when Germany invaded Poland. On 17 September the USSR invaded eastern Poland and seized territory with a population of thirteen million, of whom seven million were White Russians and Ukrainians. Estonia, Latvia and Lithuania were incorporated into the Soviet Union, and after the **Finnish–Russian War** of 1939–40 Finland had to give up territory which strengthened Leningrad's defences. The USSR had acquired a buffer zone in the west and had been given more time in which to rearm. For Stalin it was a very good bargain.

**Negative integration.** A description of **Bismarck**'s method of uniting supporters of the **German Empire**, by attacking those he held to be enemies of the Reich (i.e., on a negative basis). Such enemies were Catholics, whom he attacked in the *Kulturkampf*, foreigners who lived within the Reich (such as Poles and Alsatians, who were also Catholics), and socialists, whom he persecuted in his **anti-socialist law**. His policies divided people into 'friends' and 'foes' and, according to the historian Hans-Ulrich Wehler, help to explain why Germans could so easily accept the physical extermination of 'enemies' of the Reich, such as the Jews, by **Hitler**.

**Negrín, Juan** (1892–1956). Spanish Prime Minister (May 1937-March 1939) during the **Spanish Civil War**. Born into a wealthy business family in the Canary Islands, Negrín, a man of immense intellectual and physical energy, studied medicine in Germany. He became professor of physiology at the University of Madrid and a noted scientist. During the **Spanish Second Republic** (1931–6) he was elected to the Cortes as a Socialist deputy. After the outbreak of the Spanish Civil War, Negrín was appointed Minister of Finance in the Largo Caballero government of September 1936. He was responsible for overseeing the transfer of the Bank of Spain's gold to the Soviet Union, a measure forced on the Republic by the advance of the Nationalists on Madrid. Unlike many fellow Socialists, Negrín was prepared to sustain a close alliance with the Spanish Communist Party (PCE), through which the crucial Soviet aid was channelled. After the abortive revolutionary rising of the **CNT** and dissident communist POUM in Barcelona in May 1937, Negrín suppressed the POUM, as the PCE had demanded. The paralysis of the Socialist Party (**PSOE**) – crippled by internal divisions by December 1937 – led Negrín to rely on the PCE in his drive to centralize the state and army and thereby replicate Franco's single command structure in an effort to win the war.

In April 1938 Negrín became Minister of Defence, replacing his old ally Indalecio Prieto, now a vehement opponent of the Communists. On 1 May 1938 Negrín announced his 'Thirteen Points' as the basis for a peace settlement with the Nationalists, but it was rejected outright by **Franco**. Negrín's unilateral withdrawal of the **International Brigades** in October 1938 failed to induce a reciprocal response from the **Axis powers**. After the failure of the Ebro campaign (July–November 1938) and the fall of Catalonia in February 1939, Colonel Casado led a rebellion against Negrín, setting up a National Council of Defence in Madrid that attempted vainly to negotiate a settlement with Franco. As Negrín perceived, Franco was only interested in unconditional surrender. On 1 April 1939 the Civil War was officially declared over. Negrín's resourcefulness and unyielding determination made him an outstanding war leader, but his ruthlessness in sacrificing political allies, and his alliance with an ultra-Stalinist Communist Party, inevitably intensified divisions in the republican camp and demoralized many non-communists. After the Civil War, Negrín took refuge in Britain and France, where he died.

**Nehru, Jawarahlal** (1889–1964). India's first Prime Minister. Often called 'Pandit' (Hindi, 'teacher'), Nehru came from a rich, Brahmin family and was educated in England, at Harrow and Cambridge University. Here he developed a lasting interest in English literature and political philosophy, especially that of John Stuart **Mill**. He returned to India in 1914, became more radical during the **First World War** and was outraged by the **Amritsar massacre** (1919). Nehru greatly admired **Gandhi**, though he did not share his ideal of a

587

society based on self-sufficient villages, and was 'filled with shame . . . at the degradation and overpowering poverty of India'. Support for Gandhi's **non-cooperation movement** (1920–22) led to his first spell in jail (he spent nine years there between 1920 and 1945). In 1928 he joined with Subhas Chandra **Bose** to demand complete independence for India and a year later persuaded the **Indian National Congress** to adopt this as its aim. Handsome, intellectually brilliant and charming, he became, with Gandhi's backing, the youngest President of Congress in 1929, a post he had the rare distinction of holding three times. In the 1936–7 provincial elections, held under the **India Act** (1935), Nehru was largely responsible for Congress gaining control of six (and eventually eight) of the eleven states of British India, but he made a great blunder in rejecting **Jinnah**'s offer of coalition governments with the **Muslim League**. This turned Jinnah towards partition, to which Nehru was opposed. He made another blunder when he withdrew Indian provincial ministries in 1939, after the Viceroy declared war without consulting Indian opinion. Congress now lost all political influence, especially after the **'Quit India' Campaign**, when its leaders were arrested. On his release Nehru became Congress's chief negotiator with the British and developed a close rapport with the Viceroy Mountbatten and his wife, which prepared the way for a smooth transfer of power. He reluctantly agreed to the partition of India in August 1947, as Jinnah would accept nothing else and because 'we were tired men'. Nehru then became the first Prime Minister of an independent India, a post he held until his death.

**Nelson, Horatio, Viscount** (1758–1805). England's greatest admiral. The son of a Norfolk parson, he entered the navy at the age of twelve and at twenty was a captain. When Britain went to war with France in 1793 he was given a command in the Mediterranean, where he was blinded in his right eye during a successful attack on Corsica in 1794. Under Jervis he played a major part in the British victory over the Spanish fleet at Cape St Vincent (1797) and so helped to make Britain safe from foreign attack. In the same year he was promoted to rear-admiral and lost his right arm in an unsuccessful attempt to capture Santa Cruz de Tenerife in the Canary Islands. The French fleet at Toulon managed to elude

Nelson in 1798 and carried a French invasion force under **Napoleon** to Egypt. Nelson eventually discovered the fleet anchored in Abou-kir Bay, near Alexandria, and there won one of his most comprehensive victories at the battle of the **Nile**, which showed his tactical daring. He then captured Naples from the French and began an affair with Lady Hamilton, the British ambassador's wife, which lasted for the rest of his life. Back in England he was sent on an expedition in 1801 to destroy the Danish fleet in **Copenhagen** harbour: it was during this battle that he raised a telescope to his blind eye, so that he could ignore the signal of his superior, Sir Hyde Parker, to break off the battle. When the peace of **Amiens** ended in 1803 Nelson was sent to blockade the French fleet in Toulon but it managed to break out. The French commander Villeneuve was supposed to link up with other French and Spanish squadrons in the West Indies, return to seize command of the Channel and enable Napoleon to invade England. The plan went awry. Shortly after Villeneuve returned from the West Indies, Napoleon abandoned his invasion plan and ordered Villeneuve to sail for Naples. When he left Cadiz, Nelson confronted him and won his greatest victory at the battle of **Trafalgar** (1805), during which he was killed by a musket shot.

**NEP (New Economic Policy).** The economic strategy adopted by **Lenin** in March 1921 to replace **War Communism**, which had led to peasant risings. 'Only by coming to an agreement with the peasants,' Lenin wrote, 'can we save the socialist revolution.' A tax on peasant production replaced requisitioning. This encouraged the peasants to grow more food, as they could sell on the open market all their produce after they had paid their tax. This meant a restoration of private trade and of some private industry, which would supply the peasant with consumer goods. By 1923 76 per cent of retail trade was privately controlled, though most wholesale trade and all foreign trade was in state hands. Most industries were handed back to private owners, so that only 8.5 per cent remained nationalized. Yet these employed 84 per cent of the work-force, so 'the commanding heights of the economy' were still state-owned. The currency was reformed to halt inflation: a new, partly gold-backed, rouble was introduced by 1924 with a banking system to control the money supply. Lenin called the mixture of state and private enterprise in NEP 'State Capitalism' and described it as 'one step backwards in order to take two steps forward'. From the mid-1920s private enterprise began to be cut back as the economy recovered, though this had little effect on agriculture, where state and collective farms were responsible for only 2 per cent of farm production.

Lenin's last writings show that he did not regard NEP as a temporary measure to obtain a breathing-space. It would last 'not centuries but generations', as the **Bolsheviks** had taken power when the population was not ready for **socialism**. There was to be a period in which the peasants would learn the value of cooperation, but this should not be forced on them. Yet many communists did not like the partial return to a free market. To them it was like **Thermidor**, when the degeneration of the **French Revolution** began. Workers resented the profits of private traders and the inequality of living standards. There was, therefore, much support for **Stalin** when he introduced the first of his **Five Year Plans** and ended NEP in 1929.

**Neutrality Acts** (1935–9). Laws intended to keep the USA out of foreign wars. In the 1930s **isolationism** spread widely in the USA. There were laws in 1935, 1936 and 1937, which prohibited the sale of arms or the granting of loans to belligerents; banned US vessels from entering combat zones; forbade the arming of American merchant ships; and enabled the President to insist that belligerents should pay in cash for purchases in the USA and carry them in their own ships. **Roosevelt** did not like the Acts, because they gave the President no freedom of choice and because they treated aggressors and victims in the same way. When the **Second World War** began in 1939 the Neutrality Acts favoured the Nazis, as they did not need ships, planes and guns from the USA, while Britain and France did. A new Neutrality Act was therefore passed in 1939, designed to aid the Allies. The arms embargo was repealed: belligerents could buy arms on a 'cash and carry' basis, although the ban remained on loans to nations at war. Gradually the other restrictions of the Neutrality Acts were abandoned, except for that on loans, but Roosevelt found a way round that with his **Lend-Lease Act**.

**New Deal.** A phrase used by US President Franklin D. **Roosevelt**, which refers to the policies of his first two administrations. When he took office in 1933 the economy was collapsing, so Roosevelt began by putting the banks under federal control in order to restore confidence in them. He then, between March and June 1933, pushed through Congress fifteen major bills in a flurry of legislative activity. He did not follow any particular theory. 'It is common sense,' he said in 1933, 'to take a method and try it. If it fails, admit it frankly and try another.' He accepted, as his predecessor Herbert **Hoover** had not, that unemployment relief was a federal responsibility that could not be left to the inadequate resources of private charity. Various government agencies were set up to provide work for the unemployed: the Civilian Conservation Corps used them on conservation projects, whilst the Public Works Administration under Harold Ickes built schools, hospitals, roads and bridges. The best known of these projects was the **Tennessee Valley Authority**, which sought to bring prosperity to a very backward and depressed area. Apart from helping the unemployed, there was a need to aid those still working and the industrialists who employed them. The National Industrial Recovery Act (NIRA) suspended the anti-trust laws, in return for promises from employers to reduce working hours, pay a living wage, end child labour and allow workers to organize and bargain collectively. Each industry was to draw up a code of conduct. Agriculture as well as industry was to be helped. The Agricultural Adjustment Act (AAA) tried to raise farm prices by cutting production. Farmers would be compensated if they cut back on the crops they grew and had fewer animals; a quarter of the cotton crop was therefore destroyed and six million pigs slaughtered. This wanton destruction of food when so many were hungry was widely condemned. By 1935 farm incomes had doubled, but this was partly because dust storms (see **Dust Bowl**) and devaluation of the dollar pushed up prices. Most of the benefits of the AAA went to the large farmers: the tenants and share-croppers often became worse off and many left the land. A further reform aimed to prevent another **Wall Street Crash**: a commission was set up to regulate stock exchanges, and buying stocks 'on margin' (on credit) was forbidden.

All these reforms were welcome, except to capitalists (who did not like government interference in the economy and were appalled at the large budget deficits and the cost of relief), but they did not go far enough. There were still eleven million unemployed at the end of 1934, and so more radical legislation was passed in 1935. The Works Progress Administration, under Harry **Hopkins**, replaced earlier relief agencies and in eight years employed eight and half million people on public works and spent $11 billion. There was also an attempt to bring the USA up to Western European standards of social welfare. The Social Security Act created a compulsory system of old-age pensions and unemployment insurance, paid for by contributions from workers and employers. The system was seriously flawed: the federal government made no contribution; unemployment pay was low and was to run for only twenty weeks; many groups, like farm labourers, were excluded; and there were no sickness benefits. However, it provided a base which could be built upon. A wealth tax increased income tax and surtax and levied an excess-profits tax. The rich were now overwhelmingly hostile to the New Deal and regarded Roosevelt as a traitor to his class, a feeling which became more intense with the **Wagner Act**, which gave support to **trade unions**.

Roosevelt's landslide victory in the presidential election of 1936 gave him a mandate for more reform: in his inaugural address he referred to 'one third of a nation ill-housed, ill-clad, ill-fed'. Yet there was little legislation at first, because the President was involved in 1937 in a bruising battle with the **Supreme Court**. Dominated by conservatives, the Court was hostile to government intervention in economic and social affairs, and had declared illegal several of the most important acts of the New Deal, particularly the NIRA and AAA. Roosevelt responded in 1937 by proposing to **Congress** that the President should be able to appoint more (liberal) judges to the Supreme Court. There was a storm of protest: judges were seen as guardians of the Constitution and he was accused of trying to undermine judicial independence. When the President saw that there was no chance of Congress passing the bill he abandoned it. This was Roosevelt's first major defeat, but the Court had learned a lesson too. Under threat it changed course and upheld New Deal measures such as the Social Security Act and the Wagner Act. New Acts in 1937 and 1938 allowed the federal government to lend money to sharecroppers and tenants to buy their farms; provided federal aid for slum clearance; replaced the illegal A A A by a new one; established a minimum wage and a maximum working week of forty-four hours (to be reduced to forty); and forbade child labour. All these were welcome improvements, but in 1939, when manufacturing had returned to its 1929 level, there were still nine and a half million unemployed (17 per cent of the work force). There was no return to full employment and prosperity until 1941, when, with a change-over to war production, the USA became the 'arsenal of democracy'.

## New Economic Policy, see NEP

**'New Liberalism'.** A movement in Britain away from the Gladstonian conception of Liberalism to a belief in a more interventionist state. **Gladstone** saw the role of the state as that of removing impediments to liberty by making possible free trade and the free exercise of religion and by removing privileges and inequalities before the law. Writers such as L. T. Hobhouse, in his book *Liberalism* (1911), and J. A. Hobson saw that the state should make a more positive contribution to welfare, as people were often poor through no fault of their own and had no control over impersonal market forces. They therefore wanted the state to provide services (such as old-age pensions and sickness benefit) that the free market would not supply and to establish what the **Webbs** called a 'national minimum'. Hobhouse wrote that the 'right to work' and to a 'living wage' were 'just as valid as the rights of person and property'. The idea that the state's functions should be extended was not new. Since the 1870s the 'municipal socialism' of politicians such as Joseph **Chamberlain** in Birmingham, where the local authority provided water, gas, sewerage and transport, had been widely copied. The policies of the 'New Liberalism', which Winston **Churchill** described as 'the cause of the left-out millions', were to be paid for by redistributive taxation, by distinguishing between earned and unearned income and by taxing the latter heavily. Gladstone's ministry in 1894 had begun this by introducing death duties. It could be continued by taxing the 'unearned increment' on land, whose value increased through no effort on the owner's part. This was anathema to **Conservatives**, who objected to graduated taxation and wanted to restrict government expenditure to basic administration. 'New

Liberalism' was the source of the reforms of **Campbell-Bannerman**'s and **Asquith**'s administrations from 1906–14, which constitute the greatest reform programme in Britain before the **Second World War**. Much of what passes for **socialism** today is simply a revised version of the 'New Liberalism'.

**Newport Rising** (1839). After the National Convention of the **Chartists** was dissolved, 7,000 armed colliers and iron workers from Glamorgan marched on Newport. It is not clear what their aims were. Some think that they wanted to capture key towns, start a rising in the valleys and establish a republic. Others regard the rising simply as a mass demonstration to promote Chartist demands and protest against the arrest of some of their leaders. The authorities, forewarned, used a few dozen troops to kill twenty-four insurgents (twice the number of those killed in the **Peterloo massacre** in 1819) in a short, fierce skirmish. John Frost, their leader, a radical draper and magistrate, had urged caution but was sentenced to death with other leaders, sentences commuted to transportation for life to Australia. This minor affair, which was never any danger to the government, was the most important armed rising in Britain in the nineteenth century.

**Ney, Michel** (1769–1815). Marshal of France. The son of a cooper, Ney enlisted in the royal army in 1787 and was commissioned after the outbreak of the **French Revolution**. He became a general in 1798 and played an important part in Moreau's victory at Hohenlinden (1800) and at Ulm in 1805, when he prevented the Austrians from escaping. In 1807 he made a decisive contribution to **Napoleon**'s victory over the Russians at Friedland. Ney commanded the rearguard in the retreat from **Moscow** (1812) and was reputedly the last French soldier to leave Russian soil. Dubbed 'the bravest of the brave' by Napoleon, he was wounded for the sixth time at Lützen in 1813, fought at **Leipzig** and then in France in 1814 before he took an oath of allegiance to the Bourbons. When Napoleon returned from Elba in the **Hundred Days**, Ney was sent to arrest him and promised to 'bring him back in an iron cage'. Instead he changed sides and was given command of the left wing of Napoleon's army in the invasion of Belgium. There he fought the British at Quatre Bras and was in effective command at **Water-**

**loo** of the whole army, which he led in the thick of the fighting, having four horses killed under him. Arrested by the Bourbons for treason, he was tried by five fellow marshals and shot. He himself gave the firing party its orders.

**Nicholas I** (1796–1855). Tsar of Russia (1825–55). A younger brother of **Alexander I**, Nicholas had to deal with the **Decembrist Conspiracy**, which tried to dethrone him. This turned him against reform and convinced him that military discipline was needed to control Russia. He always wore military uniform, loved parades and surrounded himself with army officers. Nicholas had a great sense of duty – 'I consider the whole of human life as service to the State,' he once wrote – and wore himself out trying to keep control of every decision that was made. The motto of his reign was 'Orthodoxy, Autocracy, Nationality', a phrase coined by his Minister of Education, Count Uvarov. He wanted to keep all power in his own hands and so expanded the Imperial Chancellery, the Third Section of which became notorious for its secret police, which sought to stamp out all opposition to the regime. He was intelligent enough to appreciate the threats to social stability and described **serfdom** as 'a powder cellar under the State'. He set up nine secret committees to discuss serfdom but each time failed to take decisive action, as he feared that anarchy might follow abolition and this would threaten the existence of the monarchy. Reform, he felt, always led to further demands and so should be avoided. He was unwilling to expand education, as universities were the source of subversive ideas. The fall of **Charles X** in the 1830 revolution in France and the Polish rising of 1830–31 confirmed his opposition to change. The 'ungrateful' Poles lost their autonomy and representative institutions.

Russian armies could do well against minor powers – part of Armenia was taken from Persia in 1818 and some territory was gained from Turkey in the Caucasus in 1829. Nicholas intervened in the **Revolutions of 1848** by helping the Habsburgs to crush the rising in Hungary, but Russia's real weakness was shown in the **Crimean War**, when she was defeated on Russian soil by France and Britain, whose bases were thousands of miles away. In the 1780s Russia had produced twice as much pig iron as Britain. In 1855

Britain was producing fourteen times as much as Russia, and even Belgium was producing more. This was the real measure of Russia's relative decline under Nicholas I.

**Nicholas II** (1868–1918). Tsar of Russia (1899–1917). Nicholas was a contrast in many ways to his father **Alexander III**. Whereas Alexander was tall, decisive and confident, Nicholas was small and diffident. He was isolated from everyone outside his narrow court circle and unaware of what his subjects were thinking. Influenced by **Pobedonostsev**, he opposed change at a time when other Great Powers were changing rapidly and so helped to ensure that Russia was left behind. The ancestor he most disliked was Peter the Great, who Westernized Russia. When decisive action and vision were required he took refuge in a fatalistic religious belief that he was in God's hands. Nicholas was aware that he always agreed with the person he had seen last and that he was temperamentally unfit to rule. 'I always give in and in the end am made the fool,' he wrote, 'without will, without character.' Yet this uncertainty made him more determined than ever to uphold the power of the throne. In 1895 he received a delegation from the *zemstva* (town and noble assemblies), but referred to their modest request, to be allowed to tell the Tsar what the people were thinking, as 'a senseless dream'. 'I . . . shall safeguard the principles of autocracy,' he told them, 'as firmly and unswervingly as did my late, unforgettable father.' In the St Petersburg salons there was a joke that Russia did not need a constitution to limit the monarchy, as she already had a limited monarch. The leadership of the Tsar was essential in the Russian system of government, yet Nicholas not only failed to provide it, he also prevented anyone else from doing so.

The industrialization of Russia continued, particularly under Nicholas's Minister of Finance Sergei **Witte**, but at the cost of imposing heavy strains on Russian society. Tensions built up and erupted in the **Russian Revolution of 1905**, sparked off by the massacre of unarmed demonstrators on **Bloody Sunday** and by Russia's defeat in the **Russo-Japanese War**. Nicholas was compelled, much against his will, to make concessions in the October Manifesto, including the convening of a **Duma** with the power to make laws. The October Manifesto satisfied many in Russia and led to the collapse of the revolution, so Nicholas managed to retain considerable authority for himself in the **Fundamental Laws** of 1906. He treated the Duma with contempt but found a minister of vision in Peter **Stolypin**, who tried to improve agricultural productivity by persuading peasants to leave the *mir* and set up as independent farmers. By 1914 Russia was the fourth industrial power in the world, though this concealed serious weaknesses. She had the largest foreign debt in the world, was greatly dependent on foreign expertise and was still basically an undeveloped country. In spite of her efforts she was falling further behind her major competitors, particularly Germany.

Nicholas managed to end Britain's hostility in the **Anglo-Russian Entente** of 1907 but was humiliated in the Bosnian crisis of 1908, when he was forced to accept Austria-Hungary's annexation of Bosnia and Hercegovina. The Balkans remained the centre of conflict and it was the Austro-Hungarian invasion of Serbia which brought Russia into the **First World War**. Nicholas made the mistake of taking command of Russia's armed forces in 1915, leaving the government in the hands of his unstable wife Alexandra and of **Rasputin**. Military defeat was accompanied by massive inflation and food shortages, as the peasants refused to sell their grain for worthless money. The result was the **February Revolution** of 1917 and the abdication of Nicholas. The Romanov dynasty had come to an end after 300 years. Nicholas and his family were murdered in July 1918 at Ekaterinburg by the **Bolsheviks**, who feared that advancing White armies would free them.

**Nietzsche, Friedrich Wilhelm** (1844–1900). German philosopher. The son of a pastor in Saxony, Nietzsche was brought up a strict Protestant. He became Professor of Classics at the University of Basel at the age of twenty-five and remained an academic for ten years before his health broke down, possibly from a syphilitic infection. After that he lived as a writer, seeking health and sunshine in Italy and France. He wrote several philosophical works between 1873 and 1888, the most famous of which were *Thus Spake Zarathustra* (1883–5) and *Beyond Good and Evil* (1885–6). In 1889 he went mad and was looked after by his sister until his death. In his writings he attacked *bourgeois* morality and belief in the progress he saw around him and exposed the power structure on which the social order was based. He had lost his faith in Christianity and believed that the 'Will to Power' (a phrase he took from Schopenhauer) was the source and meaning of life. Nietzsche thought that the highest goal of humanity was the breeding of a superman – a 'blond beast' – who would discard sentimental inhibitions and use violence to produce a new and better world. He did not identify his superman with any particular people, especially the Germans, whom he despised: 'It [the Germany of his day] represents the stupidest, most depraved and most mendacious form of the German spirit.' Nietzsche extolled violent action: 'You say, a good cause justifies any war: I say, a good war justifies any cause.' He condemned Christian compassion for the poor and the weak: 'War and courage have done more great things than love of one's neighbour.' His thought was full of contradictions: he glorified power but believed that 'power makes people stupid'; he believed in great men but detested **Bismarck**; there were racialist undertones in his 'supermen', yet he was horrified at the persecution of the Jews and referred to the 'whole range of monstrosities including the anti-semitic'. The idea of an Aryan race was a 'mendacious swindle'. His influence came after his death, when his works were plundered for aphorisms by radicals and nationalists. To some his approval of violence appealed, as it did to **Mussolini** in 1908: 'To understand Nietzsche we must envisage a new race of "free spirits", strengthened in war, in solitude, in great danger.' Gavrilo Princip, who assassinated the Archduke Franz Ferdinand at **Sarajevo** in 1914, loved to read his poem *Ecce Homo*, with its line: 'Insatiable as flame, I burn and consume myself.' Others were attracted by his attack on *bourgeois* society and his call for each person to 'Become what you are'. His sister, Elizabeth Forster Nietzsche, who married a notorious anti-Semite, became his literary executor. She put together from his notes *The Will to Power*, published in 1908, the text most used by the **Nazis**. Nietzsche's writings affected a whole generation, not least because they could be interpreted in different ways.

**Nightingale, Florence** (1820–1910). Founder of nursing as a profession for women. Born into a well-off family, she had a religious vocation to care for the sick and wished to break away from the constraints of the Victorian family by leading a life of her own. She had an opportunity when press reports during the **Crimean War** showed the high mortality rate among the sick and wounded, owing to the appalling conditions in military hospitals. Florence Nightingale, with the backing of her friend Sidney Herbert, War Secretary, sailed in 1854 to Scutari, where she was to be in charge of nursing the troops. She found the hospitals infested with rats, sanitation hardly existing and a severe shortage of beds, linen and medicines. She had to show great courage, passionate determination and extraordinary will-power to counter the hostility of the doctors, and she used much of her own money to provide supplies. Many hours a day were spent in the wards, where she was idolized by the soldiers, becoming known on her night rounds as the 'Lady with the Lamp'. Mortality rates dropped dramatically with the improvement in hygiene. When she returned home after the war she was a national heroine and used the money raised by public subscription to set up in 1860 the Nightingale School for Nursing at St Thomas's Hospital, London, the first of its kind in the world. Her health was shattered on her return and she appeared to suffer from psychosomatic illnesses for the rest of her long life, much of which was spent bed-ridden. This did not prevent her from beginning training for midwives or from taking part in the reform of workhouses. In 1907 she became the first woman to receive the Order of Merit.

**Night of the Long Knives** (30 June 1934). The time when leaders of the **SA** were murdered on **Hitler**'s orders. The SA and its chief Ernst **Röhm** had become very disgruntled after Hitler became Chancellor in January 1933, as they were not given the spoils of office they expected. They therefore called for radical measures against industrialists and *Junkers* and Röhm wanted the army to be merged with the SA under his command. This alarmed the generals, whose support Hitler needed if he was to become President when **Hindenburg** died. There was opposition too to the SA within the **Nazi Party**, as **Goering** and **Himmler** saw Röhm as a rival in the struggle for power. They persuaded Hitler that Röhm was plotting a *Putsch* against him, and so Hitler, in Munich, ordered the execution of Röhm and other SA leaders on 30 June 1934. The purge was carried out in Berlin and north Germany by the **Gestapo**, under the control of **Heydrich**, and Himmler's **SS**. The army helped by providing transport and weapons. The purge continued for three days with no resistance: hundreds were killed, including people who had nothing to do with the SA but whom Hitler disliked. General von **Schleicher**, the Chancellor before Hitler, who had tried to split the Nazi Party, was one victim, as was Gregor Strasser, at one time in charge of Nazi Party organization, who had broken with Hitler in 1932. The purge was greeted with relief by many Germans, as Nazi propaganda made it appear that Hitler had saved Germany from civil war. General von Blomberg issued an order of the day to the army on 1 July, in which he spoke of Hitler's 'soldierly decision and exemplary courage' in wiping out 'mutineers and traitors'. Hitler got what he wanted when Hindenburg died on 1 August, as the army raised no objections when he immediately combined the offices of Chancellor and President and took the new title of *Führer*. Soon all officers and men (and civil servants too) were required to take an oath of loyalty to Hitler. This made later resistance by the army to the Nazi regime almost impossible. The SA now became a harmless organization – there would be no future opposition to Hitler within the Nazi movement. A further, and sinister, effect of the purge was the rise in power of the SS, which had been part of the SA and now became a separate organization. Terror, instead of being spontaneous, became institutionalized and controlled.

**Nihilists**. Russian revolutionaries. Bazarov in Turgenev's novel *Fathers and Children* (1862) describes himself and his friends as 'nihilists', as they rejected all traditional values, including those of religion and family life. They were disillusioned with the pace of reform in Russia and wanted to destroy all that remained of the old order. 'What can be smashed must be smashed,' wrote Pisarev (1840–68), portrayed as Bazarov in the novel. This attitude owed much to **Bakunin**, who saw destruction as a creative act.

**Nile, battle of the** (1 August 1798). Fought by British and French fleets near Alexandria. The French fleet had evaded **Nelson**'s blockade of Toulon and took an invasion force under **Napoleon** to

Egypt. Nelson eventually found fifteen French ships anchored in a solid line across Aboukir Bay, about thirteen miles from Alexandria. There was no way he could break through the line but there was a narrow gap between the last French ship and the shore. He therefore divided his fourteen ships-of-the-line: one group sailed on the outside of the French line, the other sailing through the gap on to the inside, so that the French fleet was attacked simultaneously from both sides. This dangerous and daring manoeuvre brought total victory for Nelson, who captured ten French ships. The French expedition was now marooned in Egypt, where its remnants surrendered to the British in 1801.

**Nimitz, Chester William** (1885–1966). American admiral. President Franklin D. **Roosevelt** chose him to take command of the US Pacific Fleet after the disaster at **Pearl Harbor** in December 1941. He quickly realized that aircraft carriers were the key to success in the Pacific and by using them won the decisive battle of **Midway** (June 1942), which he directed from his headquarters at Pearl Harbor. In 1942 the Pacific was divided into two commands. Nimitz was put in charge of Allied forces in the Pacific Ocean and Central Pacific Commands, with General **MacArthur** in control of the Southwest Pacific Command. Nimitz thought that the best way to defeat Japan was to mount amphibious attacks on Japanese-held islands and so move closer and closer to Japan, so that she could be bombed from the air and invaded. MacArthur preferred to attack the Philippines first. The Joint Chiefs of Staff (JCS) agreed with Nimitz, so successful assaults were made on Guadalcanal, the first large-scale American amphibious operation of the war, the Gilbert Islands, Saipan and Guam. MacArthur finally persuaded the JCS to approve an attack on the Philippines in late 1944. It was during this attack that Nimitz won one of his greatest victories at **Leyte Gulf** (October 1944), when the Japanese navy was destroyed. Nimitz was responsible for the successful invasion of the islands of Iwo Jima and **Okinawa**, which took the American fleet within striking distance of Japan. The invasion of Japan was made unnecessary by the dropping of **atomic bombs** on **Hiroshima** and Nagasaki. Nimitz, an immensely popular figure in the American forces, was promoted to Fleet Admiral in December 1944.

**NKVD** (the first letters in Russian of 'People's Commissariat for Internal Affairs'). Soviet secret police (1934–46), successor to the **Cheka** and OGPU. It was responsible for running the **forced labour camps** and for the **Great Purges**.

**Nomonhan Incident** (1939). In May 1939 the Japanese Guandong Army on the Manchurian–Outer Mongolian border clashed at Nomonhan with Mongolian troops, who called for Soviet help. The Japanese government tried to stop the fighting spreading but a major battle took place. The Russians under **Zhukov** combined tanks, artillery, aircraft and infantry in an integrated offensive for the first time and won a major victory, the Japanese suffering heavy losses. The defeat of the Japanese army was a severe shock to its leaders, who recognized that war with the Soviet Union must be avoided. When Germany invaded Russia in Operation **Barbarossa** in 1941, **Ribbentrop** urged Japan to attack the Soviet Union, but Nomonhan was a major reason for her refusal to do so.

**Non-cooperation movement** (1920–22). A campaign against the British government in India, organized by **Gandhi** and supported by the **Indian National Congress**. After the **Amritsar massacre** of 1919 Gandhi decided that the Indian government was 'satanic' and persuaded Congress to approve a 'policy of progressive, non-violent, non-cooperation until *swaraj* ('self-rule') is established'. There was to be a **boycott** of law-courts and schools and of the elections to be held under the **Montagu–Chelmsford reforms**. Gandhi called his movement 'a state of peaceful rebellion' and there was an enthusiastic response. For the first time there was a national and popular campaign in which, in 1921 and early 1922, Britain almost lost control of India, as there were widespread rural disturbances combined with demonstrations in the towns. Then suddenly, in February 1922, Gandhi called off the campaign, as some policemen had been murdered in northern India. Congress was sharply split by this decision: in the resulting resentment and confusion the British authorities saw their opportunity and arrested Gandhi. The movement had failed to produce *swaraj* but it had made Gandhi a national figure, the successor of **Tilak**, and had seen Congress become a more popular and powerful party, which could now take on the **Raj**. It had also introduced the idea of *satyagraha* into Indian political life.

**Normandy Campaign** (June–August 1944). The conquest of northern France by Allied forces in the **Second World War**. After **D-Day** the Germans still kept many of their forces in the Pas de Calais, as they expected another invasion there. The British absorbed most of the German pressure round Caen, where seven of the eight Panzer divisions were involved, and progress was slow. The Americans captured Cherbourg on 20 June but it was so badly damaged that it could not be used as a port until the end of July. As they cleared the Cotentin peninsula, **Montgomery** captured Caen on 8 July. The real Allied breakthrough began at Avranches on 25 July, when **Patton**'s tanks surged south then west, taking most of Brittany, before turning east to the Loire. **Hitler** had now to decide whether to withdraw from Normandy or to counter-attack and try to seal off the Avranches bottleneck. He chose to counter-attack on 7 August and failed on the first day. As the Germans moved west, the Americans were advancing east below the German spearhead. They turned north to Argentan as the British and Canadians attacked south from their beach-head towards Falaise. The gap was closed on 19 August, leaving twelve German divisions in an area seven miles by six, continuously bombarded by artillery and from the air. Between 20,000 and 40,000 escaped, 50,000 were captured and 10,000 killed. This débâcle forced the Germans into a hasty retreat, which made the Allied landing in southern France on 15 August unnecessary. In the north German troops began to withdraw from Belgium and Luxemburg and most of France. On 24 August American and French troops reached Paris, where General Cholitz, ignoring Hitler's orders to destroy the city, surrendered with Paris almost undamaged. Since D-Day the Allies had landed two million men in France and had inflicted half a million casualties on the Germans for a loss of 225,000 of their own men. France had been freed.

**North African Campaigns** (June 1940–May 1943). Fought by Allied forces against the **Axis powers**. When Italy entered the **Second World War** she had 300,000 troops in North Africa, the British 50,000. The Italians advanced sixty miles into Egypt, but in December 1940 and January 1941 they were driven back 340 miles by General O'Connor, who captured 130,000 prisoners. If he had been allowed to continue it is possible that he would have captured Tripoli and driven the Italians out of North Africa, but **Churchill** withdrew 60,000 British and Commonwealth troops and sent them to Greece, which had been invaded by Italy. Within three weeks they had to be evacuated, as German forces overran Greece. Meanwhile **Rommel**, who had been sent to prop up the Italians, surprised and defeated the British at El Agheila on 31 March and pushed them out of Cyrenaica, except for Tobruk. Rommel halted just over the Egyptian border, as he had run out of supplies. **Malta** was the key to success or failure in North Africa, as from there the British could attack Rommel's supply lines across the Mediterranean. This often left him short of tanks and fuel and enabled the British to drive him back over 300 miles at the end of 1941. He was also handicapped by **Hitler**'s reluctance to give him the troops and tanks he needed, as Hitler regarded North Africa as a side-show compared with the Russian front. As soon as he had received more tanks Rommel staged another offensive in 1942 and pushed the British back into Egypt again, capturing Tobruk and 30,000 prisoners on the way. By 30 June Rommel had reached the British defensive line at El **Alamein**, forty-five miles from Alexandria, after an advance of 570 miles. The Germans had been remarkably successful, partly owing to Rommel's unorthodox and brilliant leadership. There were other reasons too for Germany's success: their artillery, infantry and tanks worked closely together; their tanks were superior to anything the Allies had, until the American Sherman tanks arrived in September 1942; the British 2-pounder anti-tank gun was useless and infinitely inferior to the German 88mm anti-aircraft gun converted for use against tanks; and the ME 109F outclassed all Allied planes until the arrival of the Spitfire in the spring of 1942. In July Rommel tried to break through the British lines in the first battle of El Alamein but was held up by Auchinleck. In August, **Montgomery** became Commander of the Eighth Army and pushed back Rommel when he tried again to break through the British lines at Alam Halfa (31 August – 4 September). Montgomery was able to build up a far greater force of tanks, guns and aircraft than Rommel possessed and so was able to win a decisive victory at the third battle of El Alamein (23 October – 4 November 1942). This ended the Axis threat to Egypt but Montgomery was over-cautious in following up his victory and allowed the remnants of the *Afrika Korps* to fall back on Tunis.

The fate of the Axis powers in North Africa was sealed when a British and American force under General **Eisenhower** landed in French North-West Africa on 9 November. The Americans, sailing directly from the USA, landed on the Atlantic coast of Morocco; forces sailing from Britain landed at Oran and Algiers. Rommel was now squeezed between this force advancing from the west and the Eighth Army advancing from the east. The Axis sent reinforcements from Sicily and so were able to continue resistance until 4 May, when 150,000 Germans and 90,000 Italians surrendered. The Desert War had succeeded in diverting high-quality German troops and aircraft from Russia and had cost the Axis powers one million soldiers killed or taken prisoner. It had also protected the supply route to Russia through Iran and the oilfields of Iran and Iraq, although their loss would not have forced Britain out of the war, as by the summer of 1941 82 per cent of her oil came from the American continent.

**Northcliffe, Alfred Harmsworth, Viscount** (1865–1922). British newspaper owner. Born in Dublin, the son of a barrister, Harmsworth left school at sixteen determined to be a journalist. He began by writing for *Titbits*, published his own weekly, *Answers*, in 1888 and followed this by *Comic Cuts* and other popular titles. Within five years the weekly sales of all his publications reached one and a half million. With his brother Harold (1868–1940), the future Lord Rothermere, he became a millionaire. His breakthrough into mass journalism came with the *Daily Mail* in 1896. Mechanical typesetting and new presses enabled him to cut production costs by half, so that he could sell the *Mail* for a halfpenny instead of the penny charged for other newspapers. Harmsworth deliberately appealed to the lower middle class of office workers, small tradesmen and skilled artisans by avoiding long articles and by giving much space to gossip about the famous, sport, racing tips and columns specially for women. As in other newspapers, the front page was for advertisements, which became more important than circulation in providing income. The *Mail* reached the highest circulation of any newspaper up to that time, averaging 750,000 copies daily in the Edwardian Age. It became the first paper to be floated as a public company, Associated Newspapers Limited, in 1905. In 1903 he published the *Daily Mirror*, a one penny paper written by gentle-women for gentlewomen. This failed but Harmsworth saved it by changing it in 1904 into an illustrated paper, the first to make regular use of half-tone photographs. The *Mirror* overtook the *Mail* in circulation in 1911, when its sales were a million copies a day. Northcliffe (he was made a Baron in 1905) moved into the quality newspaper market when he bought *The Observer* in 1905, which under the editor J. L. Garvin increased its sales to 60,000 by 1911, when he sold it so that he could concentrate on *The Times*. He had bought this ailing newspaper in 1908 and saved it (increasing its sales from 38,000 in 1908 to 150,000 in 1914), without changing the tone of the newspaper or its editorial independence. Northcliffe loved power – he liked to be known as 'The Napoleon of Fleet Street' and was called 'The Chief' by his staff. In his last months he became mentally unbalanced.

**Northern Expedition** (1926–8). A campaign led by **Jiang Jieshi** (Chiang Kai-shek) to wrest control of China from the **warlords**. The National Revolutionary Army had Russian military advisers, owing to the **United Front** of the **Guomindang** and the Chinese Communist Party (CCP), when it moved north from Guangdong province in June 1926. By the autumn it had reached the Yangzi. On the way it received mass support from peasants and workers, who prepared the way for the Nationalist Army by striking in all the major industrial cities. Jiang moved east along the Yangzi to capture Nanjing and Shanghai early in 1927. At Shanghai the United Front came to an end, as Jiang carried out a *coup* (see **Shanghai** *coup*), killing as many CCP supporters as he could find. He then continued the Northern Expediton, captured Beijing (Peking) in June 1928 and forced the warlord **Zhang Zuolin** to flee to his homeland in Manchuria. A new national government was formed, with its capital at Nanjing. Jiang appeared to have united China but in fact controlled effectively only a part of east and central China. In the rest of the country he relied on the cooperation of the warlords, who were often given high positions in the Guomindang, whilst still keeping control of their own armies.

**North German Confederation** (1867–71). **Prussia** and the German states north of the river Main were united, as a result of Austria's defeat in the **Austro-Prussian War** of 1866. Prussia dominated the Confederation. The King of Prussia became President: he alone could make war or peace, was responsible for foreign policy and was Commander-in-Chief. All laws required his approval. As Prussia was feared and disliked in the smaller states, their princes remained on their thrones. The states were governed according to their own laws and constitutions and had their own parliaments, judiciary and civil service. Administration, religion and education were the responsibility of the states and were paid for by state taxation. A Bundesrat or federal council, which consisted of representatives from the states (Prussia had seventeen of the forty-three votes), was the most important institution. It was presided over by the Chancellor, who was appointed by the King and responsible to him, not to the Bundesrat. There was also a popular assembly, the **Reichstag**, elected by universal male suffrage. It passed legislation, although this also had to be approved by the Bundesrat and the King. The Confederation was absorbed by the German Empire, when this was formed in January 1871, after Prussia's victory in the **Franco-Prussian War**. The Confederation's Constitution formed the basis of that of the **German Empire** and as such survived until 1918.

**North-West Europe Campaign** (September 1944–May 1945). The advance of Allied troops from France, which, with the Soviet invasion of Germany from the east, ended the **Second World War**. After the **Normandy Campaign** German troops withdrew from most of France. British troops entered Brussels on 3 September 1944 and Antwerp a day later, although the port could not be used until 28 November, as German troops still had to be cleared from the mouth of the Scheldt. **Montgomery** then wanted all the Allied troops, except those in the south of France, to be concentrated under his command for a thrust across the Rhine north of the Ruhr, which would be cut off from the rest of Germany, and then they could move on to Berlin. **Eisenhower**, Allied Supreme Commander, would not agree to this. The Germans had left garrisons in French ports such as Calais, so 75 per cent of British and American supplies had still to come from the **D-Day** beaches and the rest from Cherbourg, 300 miles away, and they had to come by road, owing to the destruction of the French railways. Eisenhower did not feel that Monty's advance could be supplied. He favoured clearing the left bank of the Rhine first, by attacking on a broad front, though he allowed Montgomery to go ahead with his attempt to seize bridges over the Rhine at Arnhem in the Netherlands. On 17 September British paratroops were dropped at Arnhem ahead of advancing troops but ran into two Panzer divisions and suffered heavily: only 2,400 paratroops out of 9,000 were able to escape south. In November six Allied armies attacked on a broad front (Montgomery later maintained that the attack was on several fronts, which were uncoordinated) and made little progress.

To the surprise of all Allied commanders, the Germans counter-attacked in December 1944, but after initial successes were defeated in the battle of the **Bulge**. After that they were too weak to resist effectively the Allied Rhineland Campaign (February–March 1945), when **Hitler**'s order that German troops should fight west of the Rhine rather than retire over it resulted in 250,000 being taken prisoner. On 7 March the Americans found intact a bridge over the Rhine at Remagen, near Bonn, which had been kept for retreating Germans, and captured it before it could be blown up. **Patton** crossed the Rhine on 22 March between Mainz and Worms and swiftly advanced deep into Bavaria. The main offensive was launched across the Rhine on 23 March by Montgomery. Instead of heading for Berlin, Eisenhower ordered him to go north-west to Hamburg and Lübeck. General Bradley was to direct the main advance to Leipzig and Dresden, which left the Russians to take Berlin. There was little opposition in the drive east from the Rhine: the Americans reached the Elbe on 13 April, sixty miles from Berlin, where they halted. On 2 May the British reached the Baltic at Lübeck: by this time German troops were fleeing from the **Eastern Front** to surrender to the British and Americans rather than to the Russian's. The German forces in north-west Europe surrendered to Montgomery at Lüneberg Heath on 4 May, to be followed three days later by a general German surrender.

**Nuffield, William Richard Morris, Viscount** (1877–1963). English motor manufacturer and philanthropist. The son of an Oxfordshire farmer, Nuffield established a bicycle assembly and repair business at the age of sixteen, moved to motor bikes and in 1907 set up Morris Garages to sell and repair motor cars. Seeing the demand for cheap mass-produced cars, he built his first model, the two-door Morris Oxford, in 1913, the first British car planned for family use. To avoid high capital investment he bought his components from specialist firms. He built a new factory at Cowley to make the larger Cowley model in 1915 and in the 1920s became Britain's leading motor manufacturer, extending his range with the MG and buying up Wolseley. Nuffield used American assembly-line production methods, with standardized parts, and bought out many of his suppliers such as the body builder Pressed Steel. His share of the British car market dropped in the 1930s, as there was a demand for smaller cars and as Nuffield was devoting more of his time to politics and charitable activities.

A right-wing nationalist, Nuffield gave money to **Mosley**'s New Party and supported rearmament. Much of his fortune went to medical and, surprisingly, educational charities (he was largely self-taught and preferred as managers in his company those who had worked their way up from the shop floor rather than those with university degrees). Nuffield College, Oxford, and the Nuffield Foundation (1943), to promote education and the health, social well-being and care of the poor, were two of his benefactions. In 1952 the Nuffield Organization merged with Austin to form the British Motor Corporation, which was the third largest in the world at that time. Nuffield stayed only a year as President of BMC before retiring.

**Nullification Doctrine.** This was first put forward in the USA in 1798 by James **Madison** and Thomas **Jefferson**, who claimed that states had the right to prevent the application of federal laws within their borders, if they considered a law to be unconstitutional. The most celebrated example of nullification came when **Congress** imposed heavy tariffs on imports in 1828 and 1832. The South maintained that they benefited northern industry and were harmful to the interests of the South, which depended for its prosperity on trade with Britain. Prosperity was not the only issue for the South, which had been shocked by the Nat Turner rebellion and the strength of the **abolitionists** in the North and feared that Congress might seek to abolish slavery. Nullification, therefore, was meant to limit the federal government's power over slavery. South Carolina, following **Calhoun**, 'interposed her state sovereignty' and 'nullified' the tariffs in its own territory in November 1832, threatening secession if the federal government used force against it. President **Jackson** responded promptly with his Nullification Proclamation in December, which said that nullification was an 'impractical absurdity' and 'incompatible with the existence of the Union'. He asked Congress for a Force Bill to allow him to enforce the tariff but at the same time was conciliatory enough to ask Congress to reduce the tariffs. Henry **Clay** stepped in as mediator and suggested a gradual reduction of tariffs. This was passed, with the Force Act, and approved by the President in March 1833. Both sides claimed victory: Jackson had shown that no state could reject federal authority, yet nullification had brought about a change in federal policy.

**O'Connell, Daniel** (1775–1847). Irish nationalist leader. A successful and affluent barrister, O'Connell opposed the Act of **Union** (1800) of England and Ireland, which had not affected the Protestant Ascendancy. Protestants continued to dominate the executive, local government, justice, the civil service and the police. O'Connell therefore founded the Catholic Association in 1823, which pressed for reforms beneficial to the Catholic majority in Ireland, especially for **Catholic emancipation**, which would allow Catholics to sit in the British parliament. It was a popular body, with its roots in the rural masses. The parish was its unit of organization and the priest its agent, who collected the 'Catholic rent', a subscription of a penny a month, from the peasantry. By propaganda and 'monster meetings' O'Connell brought pressure to bear on the government. In 1828 he was elected MP for County Clare but was unable to take his seat, as he was a Catholic. This caused a crisis and a threat of civil war, which the government of **Wellington** avoided by granting Catholic emancipation in 1829.

O'Connell was now the leading figure in Irish politics, with an international reputation. After emancipation he was able to become an MP at Westminster, where he built up his own party of Irish MPs, which he used to obtain reforms in Ireland. In 1835 he joined the **Whigs** to get rid of **Peel**'s government and kept them in power for the next six years. He was rewarded by some reforms: a national system of elementary education was established in Ireland, a new **Poor Law** provided support for the destitute for the first time, whilst municipal reform began the transfer of local government control to the Catholics. Yet O'Connell was disappointed with what he saw as half-hearted Whig reforms – tithe remained and money was not diverted from the revenues of the Protestant Church of Ireland to secular purposes – so in 1840 he founded the Repeal Association to bring an end to the Union. He revived his mass agitation and in 1843 he called another of his 'monster meetings' at Clontarf, outside Dublin, in an attempt to intimidate the British government. Peel, however, stood firm and banned the meeting, whereupon O'Connell cancelled it (he had always opposed violence whilst using the threat of mass disobedience to obtain his ends) to prevent any disturbances. Many of his followers felt disillusioned by this climb-down, from which O'Connell's reputation never recovered. Some broke away from the Repeal Association to found Young Ireland, a movement which was prepared to take up arms to end the Union. O'Connell died in Genoa when he was making a pilgrimage to Rome. Known as the 'Liberator', he became the object of a Catholic cult and was described by **Gladstone** as 'the greatest popular leader whom the world had ever seen'. He established in Ireland a nation-wide tradition of political action, on which **Parnell** was later able to draw. Perhaps his greatest legacy was to link indissolubly the cause of Irish nationalism with that of the Catholic Church, so that Unionism became a predominantly Protestant movement.

**O'Connor, Feargus Edward** (1794–1855). Chartist leader and Irish radical whose father was a leader of the United Irishmen. O'Connor became a barrister and in 1832 an MP for Cork as a supporter of **O'Connell** but in 1835 he was deprived of his seat, as he could not meet the property requirements for an MP. This was a turning-point in his career; he went to England and became involved in working-class politics. A demagogue, his speeches were often incoherent but they made a powerful impression, with their mixture of threats, jokes and self-praise and his ability to adapt what he said to the mood of his audience. Tall, redheaded, with a powerful voice, he was an imposing figure, who soon had thousands of followers in the north of England. His newspaper, the *Northern Star*, founded in Leeds in 1837, sold more copies (50,000 in 1839) than any other provincial paper: nearly all his readers were working class. By 1838 he was a national leader of **Chartism** but he divided the leadership by his blustering and threatening speeches. O'Connor wanted to frighten the government into making reforms: others such as Lovett, who had drawn up the People's Charter in 1838, wanted to show that working men were responsible and respectable and therefore deserved the vote. This split in the National Convention led to its early demise in 1839. O'Connor was imprisoned in 1840, released fifteen months later and then put all his energies into the National Charter Association, which in 1842 presented a monster petition, signed by 3.3 million people, to parliament demanding **parliamentary reform**. When this was rejected, the support for Chartism fell away and O'Connor occupied himself with his Land Scheme. This aimed to return labourers to the land by providing them with allotments, to which Chartists subscribed through the Chartist Land Company. The scheme was a fiasco: there were 70,000 subscribers but only 250 received land before the Company was wound up in 1851. O'Connor was elected as MP for Nottingham in 1847, the only MP ever to be elected as a Chartist, and a year later began to organize another national petition to parliament. This was to be delivered by a procession from a monster demonstration on Kennington Common. When the government forbade the procession O'Connor lost his nerve and asked his followers (O'Connor claimed half a million were present: *The Times* estimated 20,000) to disperse peacefully. He never recovered from this humiliation, which was the effective end of Chartism. As a result of his stressful failure and his heavy brandy drinking, his health deteriorated and in June 1852 he was confined to a lunatic asylum, where he died three years later.

**October Days** (1789). A turning-point in the **French Revolution**. When **Louis XVI** refused to approve the **August Decrees** and the **Declaration of the Rights of Man**, passed by the **Constituent Assembly**, there were demands in Paris that he should be brought from Versailles to the capital. At the same time there was a food shortage in Paris, so between six and seven thousand Parisian women set off on the five-hour march to Versailles on 5 October. Later in the day they were followed by 20,000 National Guards (citizens' militia). When the women reached Versailles they invaded the Assembly and sent a deputation to the King, who agreed to provide Paris with grain and to approve the August Decrees and Declaration of Rights. On 6 October, at the request of the crowd, the King and Queen appeared on a balcony and were greeted with cries of 'To Paris'. That afternoon the royal family left Versailles for the Tuileries and was followed by the deputies of the Assembly. In Paris both the King and the deputies regarded themselves as prisoners of the Paris mob, which could impose its will on them by another *journée*. 'The city of Paris has assumed the role of King in France', wrote the Austrian ambassador. It was to dominate the Revolution for the next five years.

**October Revolution,** 1917. The **Bolshevik** seizure of power in Russia. After the **July Days** the Bolsheviks were half-heartedly persecuted. **Trotsky** and **Kamenev** were arrested, **Lenin** went into hiding in Finland. They recovered quickly owing to the **Kornilov affair**, when General Kornilov failed in his attempt to set up a military dictatorship. By September the Bolsheviks had a majority in the **Petrograd** Soviet and soon afterwards in the Moscow **Soviet**. Lenin now prepared to seize power and on 12 September called from Finland for an immediate rising but the Bolshevik Central Committee feared another failure, like that of the July Days, and agreed reluctantly only on 10 October. A day earlier the Petrograd Soviet had set up a Military Revolutionary Committee (MRC) to organize the defence of the capital against a possible military *coup*. This committee was under the control of Trotsky, who had earlier joined the Bolsheviks, and provided the military force for the rising. The Bolsheviks knew that if they rose in the name of their party they would get only limited support, so they used the slogan 'All power to the Soviets', as this would be more popular. There were rumours that the **Provisional Government** was going to leave Petrograd to the advancing Germans and move to Moscow and so the MRC took over the garrison from its commander and effectively took control of the capital a week before the rising on 24 October. The Prime Minister, **Kerensky**, was aware of Bolshevik plans but failed to act decisively. On the night of 24–25 October the MRC took over key points in the city and by the time the Congress of Soviets met on the evening of the 25th only the Winter Palace was holding out, guarded solely by a women's battalion and some officer cadets. It fell that night. Contrary to popular myth, the October Revolution was not a mass rising like that in February and there was little bloodshed. Five soldiers, one sailor and no defenders were killed.

The October seizure of power was not the end of the Bolshevik Revolution but the beginning. It was not clear what form of government there would be. The rising had been in the name of the Soviets, though the Petrograd Soviet and the Congress of Soviets had taken no part in it. Most Bolsheviks, such as **Kamenev** and **Zinoviev**, assumed that power would pass to the Soviet and that there would be a coalition government of socialist parties. To everyone's surprise Lenin announced the creation of a new body, the Council of People's Commissars, consisting entirely of Bolsheviks, to take over the government. At a heated meeting of the Soviet, Bolshevik moderates declared: 'It is vital to form a socialist government from all parties in the Soviet . . . We consider that a purely Bolshevik government has no choice but to maintain itself by political terror. We cannot follow this course.' Some Bolshevik Commissars resigned but within a few days Lenin had recovered his authority and the idea of a coalition government was abandoned.

**Oder–Neisse Line.** The frontier formed by these two rivers between Poland and Germany, which had been the western frontier of medieval Poland. This was provisionally agreed by **Stalin**, **Roosevelt** and **Churchill** at the **Yalta Conference** (February 1945) and was confirmed at the **Potsdam Conference** (July 1945). This meant giving much pre-war German territory to Poland and resulted, after the war, in the expulsion of six million Germans from this area and their replacement by Poles. The GDR (East Germany) accepted the frontier in 1949, the German Federal Republic (West Germany) in 1970.

**Okinawa, invasion of** (1 April–22 June 1945). Okinawa, sixty miles long and from three to fifteen miles wide, is the largest of the Ryukyu Islands between Taiwan and Japan. As the Americans intended to use it as a springboard for the invasion of Japan, the hardest fighting and most fanatical resistance of the **Pacific War** took place there. The Japanese had carefully prepared defensive lines, with deep dug-outs and well concealed artillery, so US progress was slow and costly. The Japanese tried to destroy the invading fleet and American beachheads by air and sea suicide attacks. The superbattleship *Yamato*, the largest battleship ever built, with eighteen-inch guns, was sent with enough fuel for only a one-way trip, but was sunk by US carrier-based planes before reaching Okinawa. *Kamikaze* pilots lost over 4,000 planes in attempting to crash them on to American ships, thus destroying what remained of Japanese air power. 107,500 Japanese troops were killed defending the island. American losses were over 7,000 killed and 32,000 wounded, but another 26,000 suffered from combat fatigue and breakdown, owing to the stress of the battle. Thirty-six American ships were sunk and 763 planes shot down. The invasion of Okinawa showed how high the cost of invading the Japanese mainland would be and may have influenced President Truman's decision to drop an **atomic bomb** on **Hiroshima**.

**Omdurman** (**Karari**), **battle of** (1 September 1898), was fought by **Kitchener**'s Anglo-Egyptian force against the **Mahdist** state in the Sudan. After the death of **Gordon** at Khartoum in 1885 the British made no attempt to recover control of the Sudan until the Ethiopian Emperor **Menelik II** defeated the Italians at **Aduwa** in 1896. The British government feared that he might help the French to reach the Upper Nile, so **Salisbury** ordered Kitchener to invade the Sudan. Meticulous preparations accompanied Kitchener's thousand-mile move south from Cairo. Troops and stores were transferred 500 miles up the Nile to the First Cataract. From there a military railway was built to within 200 miles of the twin cities of Khartoum and Omdurman, the Mahdist capital. When 50,000 Sudanese peasant soldiers attacked Kitchener's army of 25,000, most never reached the Anglo-Egyptian lines, as they were mown down by artillery and machine guns: 10,000 Sudanese were killed and 10,000 wounded, with only 500 casualties amongst Kitchener's troops. An Anglo-Egyptian Condominium was set up in the Sudan, which in practice meant that Britain ruled there.

**'Open-door' policy.** In the 1890s the USA became alarmed at what was happening in China. Japan had gained control of Korea after the **Sino-Japanese War** (1894–5) and European powers had rushed in to seize key ports in China (see **Scramble for concessions**). American interests in the Far East increased after the **Spanish–American War** of 1898 and the acquisition of the Philippines and Guam. Businessmen wanted to expand their trade with China, so in 1899 **McKinley**'s Secretary of State, John Hay, tried to protect

American interests by asking all the Great Powers to allow trade within their spheres of influence in China to all nations on an equal basis. Their replies were noncommittal but Hay announced that they had given their 'final and definite' consent to the 'open-door' policy. This remained the basis of US policy towards China for the next thirty years, though it had little effect. China escaped partition because the Great Powers could not agree on how the spoils should be divided, not because of the 'open-door' policy. Japan's invasion of **Manchuria** in 1931 showed how ineffective this policy was.

**Opium Wars.** The first (1839–42) was fought by Britain against China, the second (1856–60) by Britain and France against China. Foreign trade with China was allowed at only one port, Guangzhou (Canton). Foreigners were not permitted to travel inland or make contact with any Chinese except for officially licensed merchants. These restrictions were regarded as insufferable by the British, who wanted to open up China to foreign trade. The Chinese were more determined than ever to prevent this, owing to the opium trade. This was banned in 1800 but Chinese officials connived at imports, brought by British merchants from India, and some estimates put the number of Chinese addicts as high as ten million by 1830. Opium was imported on such a large scale that there was an outflow of silver, which threatened to destabilize the currency. High Commissioner Lin Zexu was therefore sent to Guangzhou to deal with the problem. He seized and destroyed over 20,000 chests of opium, whereupon Britain decided to go to war. The Chinese were confident they could defeat the 'insignificant and detestable race' but their war junks were no match for the steam-powered British gunboats. The British blockaded the coast to the mouth of the Yangzi and then advanced to Tianjin, thus threatening the capital Beijing (Peking). In 1842 they captured Shanghai and cut the Grand Canal, a vital artery between the capital and the richest provinces of the south. This was the most decisive defeat the Manchus had ever experienced. British and Indian troops had superior fire-power but they never numbered more than 15,000 and therefore could not have gone far inland. The Chinese, however, had lost the will to resist and made peace at **Nanjing**, the first of the **unequal treaties**.

China had agreed to renegotiate the Treaty of Nanjing twelve years later but she always avoided this, so an Anglo-French expedition was sent to enforce ratification of a new treaty. The ostensible cause of war was China's refusal to apologize when the British claimed that their flag had been insulted but the real reason was that Britain and France wanted to force China to accept the residence of their diplomats in Beijing and to extend foreign trade to more ports. The English bombarded and captured Guangzhou and then moved up the coast to take Tianjin, under 100 miles from Beijing. The Chinese therefore made peace at the Treaty of Tianjin in 1858. China agreed to open ten new ports, pay an indemnity and allow foreign legations in Beijing. Britain and France also obtained the right of inland navigation, and their missionaries were allowed to travel, preach and own land in the interior, where they would have the privilege of extraterritoriality (see **Unequal treaties**). Russia and the USA obtained similar treaties, because of their 'most-favoured nation' status. The allied representatives withdrew but when they returned in 1859 for ratification of the treaty, they were met by armed resistance. They moved therefore on Beijing, where the British destroyed the exquisite Summer Palace (the French refused to take part in such an act of barbarism). The Treaty of Beijing (1860) confirmed the arrangements made at Tianjin, and ceded Kowloon, on the mainland opposite Hong Kong, to Britain.

**Opportunist Republic** (1879–99) in France. The political power of the old aristocracy came to an end in 1879, after which they were kept out of governments. For the next twenty years moderate republicans ruled France and were known as Opportunists, as they did not follow an ideological programme but carried out piecemeal reforms as circumstances allowed. Republicans were divided into Opportunists (led by **Gambetta**, who died in 1882, and **Ferry**) and Radicals (led by **Clemenceau**). The civil service was purged of monarchists and then Ferry carried out a series of reforms, which guaranteed individual liberty and which have lasted to the present. He also made a determined effort to provide a secular education, removed from the control of the Roman Catholic Church, though his **anti-clericalism** did not extend to getting rid of **Napoleon**'s **Concordat** (1801). Government investment in **railways**, canals and ports began in 1878, in order to attach business interests to the Republic. Ferry's colonial expansion, particularly in Indo-China (Vietnam) and Tunisia, was also designed to benefit industry by providing markets and raw materials, but **imperialism** was bitterly attacked by Clemenceau as a diversion from *revanche* (revenge) on Germany and from the recovery of **Alsace-Lorraine**.

The workers became disillusioned with the Opportunists, as there were no social reforms to ameliorate the effects of the depression which began in 1882, whilst the **Right** gained the support of Catholics, who disliked Ferry's anti-clericalism. In the election of 1885, therefore, the Opportunists with 201 deputies lost their majority (there were 203 conservatives and 180 Radicals). For the first time they were dependent on the Radicals and had to grant them government posts. It was the Radicals who inadvertently provided a threat to the Republic by insisting that General **Boulanger** be made Minister of War in 1886. Boulanger's timidity enabled the Republic to survive without too much difficulty. In the 1890s the increasing strength of **socialism** (socialist deputies increased from twelve to forty-nine in 1893) and the militancy of **trade unions**, coupled with anarchist (see **Anarchism**) bomb outrages (which killed President Carnot in 1894), convinced many moderate Republicans that the danger was on the **Left**. They therefore sought cooperation with Catholics in the *Ralliement*, a move made even more desirable by the **Panama scandal** of 1892. The only Radical government at this time, that of Léon Bourgeois in 1895–6, was the only one which attempted to carry out social reforms (a limitation of the working day, accident insurance and pensions for workers, and a progressive income tax) but these were rejected by the Senate. Méline's protectionist tariff of 1892 had appealed to both industrialists and peasants, so he returned to lead an Opportunist government from 1896–8. The **Franco-Russian Alliance** (1894) had increased French prestige and ended France's isolation but colonial differences with Britain remained unresolved and France almost went to war with her when **Kitchener** confronted Marchand on the Nile at **Fashoda** in 1898. The Radicals gained ground during the **Dreyfus case** (1894–1906) and in 1899 replaced the Opportunists as the party of government – they were rarely out of office up to 1940.

**Oregon boundary dispute** (1843–6), between Britain and the USA over the ownership of Oregon territory. Oregon country was a vast area stretching north from California to Alaska and west from the Rockies to the Pacific Ocean. British claims were based on Captain Cook's charting of part of the coast in 1778. American claims were based on the discovery in 1792 of the Columbia river by the American Robert Gray and on the **Lewis and Clark expedition**. In 1818 Britain and the USA agreed on 'joint occupation', though by 1820 the British-owned Hudson's Bay Company was in effective control. In the late 1830s American trappers reported that it was an exceptionally fertile land. Almost overnight Oregon became a land of promise, with settlers from the east following the **Oregon Trail**. By 1845 there were 5,000 American settlers there who were demanding that Oregon should become a part of the USA. In the 1844 presidential election the **Democratic Party** had campaigned with the slogan 'Fifty-four forty (54° 40′) or fight'. James **Polk** won the election but in 1846 settled with Britain for a frontier with Canada along the 49th parallel from the Rockies to the Straits of Vancouver, where it has remained to the present day. Vancouver Island was to remain British.

**Oregon Trail.** The hazardous 2,000 mile trail from the Missouri river to Oregon, which from 1843–60 was the route of the greatest land migration in American history. Settlers, attracted by the rich grasslands, travelled in their covered wagons across prairies, desert and mountains. They had to cross the Snake river on rafts and the almost impassable Blue Mountains to reach their destination. On the way they suffered from hunger, exhaustion and Indian attack. When the railroads were built the trail was no longer used and had been abandoned by 1870.

**Osborne judgment** (1909). The second important case in eight years (the first being the **Taff Vale case** in 1901) which adversely affected the rights of **trade unions** in Britain. In 1903 the Trades Union Congress (TUC) had imposed on affiliated unions a compulsory levy, which was used to finance an independent **Labour Party**. In 1909 a branch secretary of the Amalgamated Society of Railway Servants, W. V. Osborne, a member of the **Liberal Party**, brought an action to prevent his union contributing to

Labour Party funds. Judgment went against Osborne in the High Court but this was reversed on appeal and the House of **Lords** upheld the appeal. An injunction prevented the Railway Servants raising a political levy, on the grounds that the support of a political party was not among the functions of a trade union. This was a great blow to the Labour Party, which lost most of its income, so it looked to the Liberal government, which it supported in parliament, for redress. In 1911 the Liberals introduced a bill for the payment of MPs in return for Labour backing **Lloyd George**'s **National Insurance Act**. Two years later the Trade Union Act overturned the Osborne judgment by allowing unions to charge political levies, providing a majority of their members had approved in a secret ballot. Individual members could 'contract out' if they did not wish to pay the levy, which must be kept separate from other union funds.

**Ottoman Empire.** A small Turkish principality was founded in north-west Anatolia at the beginning of the thirteenth century by Osman, whose followers were called *Osmanli*, who in Europe became known as Ottomans. From this base Ottomans expanded to conquer Byzantine territories in the rest of Anatolia and the Balkans before taking the Byzantine capital, Constantinople, in 1453. They then turned on the Arab lands, seizing most of North Africa, Mesopotamia and Arabia, including the Muslim holy cities of Mecca and Medina. At the height of its power in the sixteenth century the Ottoman Empire stretched from the gates of Vienna to the Indian Ocean and from the Crimea to Algiers. By the end of the eighteenth century the Empire was in decline and had lost the Crimea and territory on the Black Sea coast to Russia. The problems arising from this decline gave rise to the **Eastern Question**. There were attempts to reverse this decline and make the Ottoman Empire a stronger and more Western society by **Mahmud II** (1808–39) and in the **Tanzimat** reform movement (1839–78) but this momentum was not maintained by **Abdulhamid II** (1876–1908), so that he was deposed by the **Young Turks**. European provinces of the Empire broke away, beginning with Greece after the **Greek War of Independence** (1821–30) and followed by Serbia, Montenegro and Romania, all of which were recognized as independent at the

**Berlin Congress** in 1878, when Britain acquired Cyprus. Bosnia and Hercegovina were annexed by the **Austro-Hungarian Empire** in 1908 and in the same year Bulgaria declared its independence. Most of what remained of the Ottoman Empire in Europe was lost in the **Balkan Wars** (1912–13). Meanwhile, the Empire's Arab provinces had been whittled away; the French seized Algeria in 1830 and Tunis in 1881, Britain occupied Egypt in 1882 and the Italians conquered Tripolitania in 1911. The defeat of the Ottoman Empire in the **First World War** resulted in the complete dismemberment of the Empire, which lost all its non-Turkish provinces, out of which the new states of Syria, Lebanon, Jordan and Iraq were to arise. The Treaty of **Sèvres** (1920) even attempted to remove part of Anatolia from Turkish control but a nationalist rising led by **Kemal Atatürk** forced the Greeks out of Anatolia: the present frontiers of Turkey were recognized by the Treaty of **Lausanne** (1923). In the same year the last Ottoman Sultan, Mehmed VI, was overthrown and Turkey became a republic.

**Owen, Robert** (1771–1858). British industrialist and social reformer. Born in Wales, Owen made a fortune as a cotton manufacturer in Manchester and in 1799, with some Quaker colleagues, bought New Lanark Mills in Scotland, which they ran on enlightened but strictly supervised lines. Welfare services were provided for workers – better housing, sanitation, shops, free and compulsory education for their children – which were unknown elsewhere. The 'muncipal socialism' of the last quarter of the nineteenth century originated in New Lanark, as did many of the ideas of the **Welfare State**. Owen's ideas were expressed in his *New View of Society* (1813), which emphasized the value of cooperation rather than of competition and maintained that human character was largely formed by environment, an irreligious notion which the Church condemned. By 1817, during the depression which followed the **Napoleonic Wars**, he had formed the ideas which were to lead to **socialism** and the **cooperative movement**. He wanted public authorities to set up 'Villages of Cooperation' for paupers and the unemployed, in which work and its products would be shared in common. To put his beliefs into practice he went to the USA in 1824 and bought 20,000 acres to found a settlement at New Harmony, Indiana, but this was not a success, so he returned to England in 1828 nearly ruined. He now became involved in the **trade union** movement, encouraging small unions to unite into large units, and founded the Grand National Consolidated Trade Union (GNCTU) in 1834, which was the first to include both skilled and unskilled workers and soon had half a million members. Owen wanted it to establish cooperative production and refuse to work in the capitalist system but the opposition of government and employers was too much for him: the GNCTU floundered after a few months and the transportation to Australia of the **Tolpuddle Martyrs** (1834). Owen's desire for gradual, peaceful change – he had no time for class war – earned him the condemnation of **Marx** for being a 'Utopian dreamer'.

**Oxford Movement.** A group of scholars in the Church of England who wanted to purify the Church from within and opposed secular interference in Church affairs. Most of its leaders were Oxford men: J. H. Newman, Vicar of the University Church, E. B. Pusey, Professor of Hebrew, R. H. Froude and John Keble were all Fellows of Oriel College. The Movement began in 1833, when the first of many short pamphlets, called *Tracts for the Times*, appeared; its members were henceforth known as Tractarians. They sought a return to the 'catholic' thought and practice of the early Church and favoured the increase of ceremonial and ritual. Many saw the Tractarians as moving towards Rome. Newman at first denied this but in 1841 he tried to show that the Thirty-nine Articles were not contrary to Roman Catholic doctrine. This caused an uproar in the Anglican Church, which resulted in Newman joining the Catholic Church in 1845. In 1846 he was ordained as a priest and in 1879 became a cardinal. The Tractarians who remained in the Church of England stressed the pastoral obligations of the clergy and established Anglican monastic communities for men and women but they were unable to prevent secular intervention in the Church, embodied in **Peel**'s Ecclesiastical Commission.

**Pacific War** (1941–5). From the beginning of the **Sino-Japanese War** (1937–45) Japan's main concern was to defeat China. To do this she was tempted to expand into South-East Asia, so that she could control the raw materials on which she depended (oil from the Dutch East Indies and Burma, tin and rubber from Malaya) and cut off China's supply routes from the south, though this was likely to involve her in conflict with the USA. She could not move south as long as there was a danger that Russia would attack in Manchuria, particularly after the Russians badly mauled the Japanese army at Nomonhan (see **Nomonhan Incident**) in 1939. This danger was averted by a neutrality pact with Russia in April 1941 and by Operation **Barbarossa**, **Hitler**'s invasion of the Soviet Union in June. Japan had acquired bases in northern Indo-China, in agreement with the Vichy government (see **Vichy France**), and in July 1941 demanded bases in the south, which appeared to be the prelude to an attack on Malaya and the Dutch East Indies. The USA responded by banning oil and iron exports to Japan, as did Britain and the Dutch. Negotiations between Japan and the USA failed, as the USA insisted on Japanese withdrawal from China, and so, on 7 December, without declaring war, Japan attacked the main base of the American Pacific Fleet at **Pearl Harbor**. Simultaneous attacks made on British, Dutch and American territories in the Pacific and elsewhere were successful. The American colonies of Guam and Wake Island fell in December, Hong Kong surrendered on Christmas Day and Singapore, after the rapid conquest of Malaya, in February 1942 (see fall of **Singapore**). In the battle of the Java Sea (27–28 February) an Allied fleet lost eleven of its fourteen ships without sinking one Japanese vessel. In the Indian Ocean the Japanese bombed Ceylon, sank a British aircraft carrier and two cruisers and forced the Royal Navy to retire to the Persian Gulf. The Dutch East Indies were overrun by March, whilst the last British forces withdrew from Burma in May, after the longest retreat in British history, thus closing the Burma Road, China's main supply route. Resistance also ended in the Philippines in May. Japan's remarkable success – in only four months she had acquired a vast empire – was due to her air and sea superiority and the unpreparedness of her opponents, rather than to the number of her well-trained troops, as only eleven divisions were used (thirteen remained in Manchuria and twenty-three in China).

Yet the Japanese victory was not complete, as the US fleet was not destroyed (US carriers were not in harbour when Pearl Harbor was attacked) and they made a series of errors which allowed the Americans to regain the initiative. Overconfident, they decided to extend their defensive perimeter of island bases to include the Solomon Islands and New Guinea. In an attempt to take Port Moresby in New Guinea they suffered their first reverse in the battle of the Coral Sea (May 1942), the first sea-fight in which opposing ships neither saw nor fired at each other. It was conducted entirely by carrier-based planes: each side suffered the loss of one aircraft carrier but the Japanese abandoned their attempt to take Port Moresby. Over-elaborate plans, known as the 'octopus complex', led to a more serious reverse at the battle of **Midway**, a month later, when Japanese naval dominance of the Pacific ended with the loss of four carriers. After Midway the Americans began the conquest of Japanese-held islands with an attack on Guadalcanal in the Solomons in August (it was not captured until February 1943). By 1943 the Americans had sea and air domination in the Pacific, so they could land where they liked in a process of island-hopping, by-passing the islands which were most strongly defended and leaving them to 'wither on the vine', whilst they captured 'softer' targets. In the central Pacific Admiral **Nimitz** moved from the Gilberts (November 1943), to the Marshalls (January 1944) and the Palau Islands (September 1944), whilst General **MacArthur** advanced into the Bismarck Archipelago (January 1944) and then along the New Guinea coast. Twice the Japanese fleet challenged American sea supremacy. The first time, in the battle of the Philippine Sea (June 1944), they tried and failed to prevent the capture of Saipan in the Marianas, from where American bombers could attack Japan. The second Japanese naval challenge was at the battle of **Leyte Gulf** (October 1944), when the forces of MacArthur and Nimitz had combined to reconquer the Philippines. This battle crippled the Japanese navy and allowed the Americans to get nearer to Japan with the conquest of Iwo Jima (February 1945) and **Okinawa** (April–June 1945).

Attacks on Japanese shipping by American submarines had meanwhile destroyed her economy, by depriving her of the raw materials on which her industry depended: in 1940 Japan imported thirty-seven million barrels of oil – in 1944 only seven million barrels reached Japan. She had few escort vessels and sank only forty American submarines, 18 per cent of those used in the Pacific (in the Atlantic Germany lost 781 submarines, 71 per cent of those in service). From November 1944 the USA, using the Mariana Islands as bases, bombed Japan's major cities, causing massive destruction. In one raid on Tokyo, on 9 March 1945, when high winds spread the flames and kept them alight for twelve hours, the Japanese government estimated that 197,000 people were killed or missing. To prevent the hundreds of thousands of American casualties expected in an invasion of Japan, President Truman authorized the dropping of **atomic bombs** on **Hiroshima** and Nagasaki on 6 and 9 August 1945. This, combined with Russia's declaration of war on Japan on 8 August and her invasion of **Manchuria**, persuaded Emperor **Hirohito** to accept the unconditional surrender the Allies demanded.

**Pacific, War of the** (1879–1883) was fought by Bolivia and Peru against Chile. In the Atacama Desert, on the boundary between Chile and Bolivia, were rich nitrate deposits – nitrate being valuable as a fertilizer. They were exploited mainly by Chileans, who objected when Bolivia imposed new taxes on nitrate exports. Chilean troops forced Bolivia to withdraw from the Atacama. Chile then declared war on Bolivia and on Peru, which was allied to Bolivia. A decisive Chilean victory in 1880 resulted in Bolivia's withdrawal from the war. A year later Chile attacked Lima, the Peruvian capital, which fell after bloody fighting. Peru accepted severe peace terms in 1883, ceding to Chile the province of Tarapaca. Tacna and Arica were handed over to Chile for ten years but as they were not given back, relations between Chile and Peru were embittered for half a century. A compromise was not reached until 1929, when Peru recovered Tacna but Chile retained Arica. A truce with Bolivia in 1884 left Chile in control of the Atacama Desert but there was no peace until 1904, when Bolivia finally ceded to Chile its Pacific coastline and the Atacama. Bolivia thus lost her access to the Pacific and became a landlocked nation.

**Paine, Thomas** (1737–1809). English radical. With little education Paine began work at thirteen, drifted from one job to another and had two unsuccessful marriages before he went to America in 1774. There he published *Common Sense* in 1776, which supported the American demand for independence and established him as a writer who was lucid, rational and who had a lively style intelligible to the masses. His book sold half a million copies in a few months. In 1787 he left for Europe, became incensed by **Burke**'s *Reflections on the Revolution in France* and wrote *The Rights of Man* as a reply. Part One (1791) attacked Burke's reverence for tradition and privilege and accused him of being concerned only with the fate of the King and of forgetting the distress of the ordinary citizen. 'He pities the plumage but forgets the dying bird.' Paine thought that each generation must act for itself and should not be bound by what had happened in the past. The aim of government should be the happiness of all, not that of a privileged minority, and this could only be brought about by truly representative democracy, which would provide for universal male suffrage, equal electoral districts, secret ballots, the payment of members of parliament and the abolition of property qualifications for MPs. Part Two (1792) put forward practical policies for governments to follow, and was remarkable in anticipating the **Welfare State** of the twentieth century: free education, family and maternity allowances and old-age pensions were advocated. These reforms would be paid for by cutting defence expenditure (wars were the result of conflicting interests of monarchs, not of peoples) and by imposing progressive income and wealth taxes. **Corresponding societies** made the book a best-seller, particularly when Part Two was issued in a cheap sixpenny edition: 200,000 were sold in a year. The government became alarmed and banned the book. To avoid arrest, Paine went to France, where he had been elected as a member of the National

**Convention**. He supported the abolition of the monarchy in France but opposed the execution of **Louis XVI**, favouring banishment instead. When Paine opposed the **Terror** he was imprisoned (December 1793–November 1794) and until the fall of **Robespierre** was in danger of being guillotined. Whilst in prison Paine began writing the *Age of Reason*, an attack on organized religion which made many regard him as an atheist. In 1802 he returned to the USA but remained a social outcast, because of his religious views, until his death.

**Palacky, František** (1798–1876). Czech historian and nationalist. A leader of the Czech national and cultural revival, Palacký began in 1832 his history of the Czech nation, which he saw as a 'conflict between the Slavs on the one hand and Rome and the Germans on the other'. When the **Revolutions of 1848** began, he was invited to attend the **Frankfurt Parliament**, which was preparing for German unification, but he declined, because he saw that the Czechs would be swallowed up if they were included in a greater Germany. Only the **Austrian Empire**, he thought, could protect the Czechs against German or Russian expansion: 'if the Austrian state had not existed for ages, it would have been necessary for us . . . to endeavour to create it.' He wanted an autonomous Czech state, formed from the union of Bohemia, Moravia and Austrian Silesia, within the Austrian Empire. He organized a Pan-Slav Congress in Prague in June 1848 but it was not a success, as the different Slav groups fell out with one another and could reach no common agreement. After the suppression of the revolutions, Palacky retired from politics until 1861, when he became a deputy in the Austrian **Diet**. He warned against the *Ausgleich*, the union of Austria and Hungary, as it would be at the expense of the other nationalities and would be 'destructive for the whole monarchy'. After it took place in 1867 he advocated complete Czech independence. His influence on later Czech leaders was enormous. 'My guide and master was Palacký,' wrote Tomáš **Masaryk**, 'the father of the fatherland.'

**Palestine mandate.** After the **First World War** Palestine, territory west of the river Jordan, which included the holy places of Jerusalem and Nazareth, was granted to Britain as a **mandate** of the **League of Nations**. Included in the mandate was the **Balfour**

**Declaration** (1917), in which the British government favoured the establishment of a national home for the Jews in Palestine. The Jews had settled in their promised land about 1200 BC but, in AD 70, after a revolt against the Romans, their temple in Jerusalem was burnt down and after a second revolt in AD 135 they were scattered throughout the world in the Diaspora, without a homeland but retaining their identity as Jews, and hoping to return one day to Palestine and to their holy city of Jerusalem. The Arabs did not accept the British mandate, as they wanted self-government immediately and began attacks on Jews in 1920. The Jews responded by forming their own defence force, the **Haganah**, so an escalating cycle of violence began. After **Hitler** came to power in Germany in 1933 there was a vast increase in Jewish immigration, which led to an Arab revolution in 1936. The Arabs not unnaturally regarded the Jewish problem as a European one, caused by the persecution of Jews in Europe, and bitterly rejected any suggestion that their land should be used to solve the problem. In 1937 the British government set up a commission of inquiry under Lord Peel. He concluded that the interests of the two sides could not be reconciled and that the mandate was unworkable: he recommended the formation of both an Arab and a Jewish state in Palestine, with a small area round Jerusalem remaining under British control. Both Arabs and Jews rejected this idea. As the Arab revolt continued and war in Europe drew nearer, the British government tried to appease the Arabs by issuing a White Paper in May 1939. This proposed the creation of an independent state of Palestine within ten years and the limitation of Jewish immigration to 15,000 per annum for the next five years. After that there was to be no immigration 'unless the Arabs of Palestine are prepared to acquiesce in it'. As Arabs were still two-thirds of the population, the Jews did not want an independent state in which they would be in a minority and so for the first time the Jews became anti-British.

They were in a dilemma when war began, as most Jews felt that Britain should be supported against their common enemy Germany, though the **Stern Gang**, a Jewish terrorist organization, did not take this view and attacked both British and Arab targets. When the war ended there was illegal Jewish immigration on a large scale and a Jewish terrorist campaign, during which the British headquarters at the King David Hotel in Jerusalem was blown up in July 1946. The British government decided that it could not cope any longer and handed the problem over to the United Nations. A UN Commission in 1947 recommended the division of Palestine into Jewish and Arab states, with Jerusalem under international control. It was a grossly unfair settlement, as the 608,000 Jews in Palestine, who held 10.6 per cent of the land, were allotted 56.5 per cent of Palestine as their new state. The 1.3 million Arabs, holding 89.4 per cent of the land, were granted 43.5 per cent. When the UN Assembly accepted the proposal of its commission, Britain declared that its mandate would end on 15 May 1948 and left the Jews and Arabs to fight over the spoils.

**Palmerston, Henry John Temple, 3rd Viscount** (1784–1865). British statesman and Prime Minister (1855–8, 1859–65). Palmerston's family were English country gentry from Palmerston, near Dublin: much of their wealth came from their Irish estates. He entered the House of **Commons** in 1807 as a Tory (see **Tories**) and remained there for fifty-eight years, during which time he was in office for forty-eight years and in the Cabinet for thirty-eight. Good-looking, amusing and hard-working, he made little impression as Secretary at War (1809–28). Throughout his life he had many affairs and lived with Lady Cowper, **Melbourne**'s married sister, who bore him several illegitimate children before he married her in 1839 after Lord Cowper's death. He joined the **Whigs** when the old Tory party was breaking up and became Foreign Secretary from 1830–41. During **Aberdeen**'s ministry Palmerston was Home Secretary (1852–5), becoming Prime Minister in 1855 at the age of seventy, a post he retained (apart from a short interval) until his death.

His aim was the advancement of British interests and this could involve him in supporting independence movements at one time, dictators at another. Britain had no permanent friends or enemies, he told the Commons in 1848. Although he gained a reputation for being, according to the Radical MP Thomas Attwood, 'a bully to the weak and a coward to the strong', his foreign policy was generally cautious. The Belgian Revolt in 1830 was the first breach in the settlement made at the Congress of **Vienna** in 1815.

Palmerston's object was to prevent Belgium becoming a French dependency, so he persuaded all the Great Powers at the Treaty of London (1831) to accept Belgian independence and to guarantee her neutrality, thus protecting her from any French attack. When **Muhammad Ali** threatened the **Ottoman Empire** in 1839 Palmerston joined with Austria and Russia to force him to give up Syria. This almost involved Britain in war with France, a supporter of Muhammad Ali, but Palmerston was convinced that 'France will not go to war with the other Great Powers of Europe to help Mehemet Ali' and he was right. In spite of his cooperation with Russia against Muhammad Ali, Palmerston was a Russophobe, who saw Russia as a threat to India. To counter Russian influence in Afghanistan, he fought a disastrous **Anglo-Afghan War** (1838–42) which ended with the annihilation of the British army as it retreated from Kabul. In 1839 the **Opium War** began against China to force open her doors to British trade, and was not concluded when the Whigs lost office. Two years after Palmerston returned to the Foreign Office the **Revolutions of 1848** took place in Europe. Palmerston gave moral support to the revolutions in Italy and so was regarded by Austria and Russia as a dangerous radical but he was not anti-Austria. 'Anything which tends to weaken and to cripple Austria,' he told the Commons in 1849, 'must be a great calamity for Europe.' He simply thought that Austria would be stronger if she was out of Italy: he regretted the rising in Hungary, though he complained of the severe Austrian repression when it was put down.

The Don Pacifico affair in 1850 showed Palmerston's gunboat diplomacy at its worst. Don Pacifico was a Portuguese Jew born in Gibraltar but living in Greece, whose house in Athens was looted during anti-Jewish riots. Palmerston ordered a British fleet to Piraeus, where Greek ships were seized until compensation had been paid. This incident was much criticized both at home and abroad but it made Palmerston the personification of John Bull, and made him very popular with the British public. He was not responsible for the **Crimean War** but he extended it unnecessarily for two years. When Russia withdrew from Moldavia and Wallachia in 1854 Aberdeen thought that peace should be made but Palmerston insisted that Britain would 'lose caste in the world' if she ended the war 'with only a small result' and that it was necessary to deal 'some heavy blow' to Russia by capturing Sebastopol. In the same year that the Crimean War ended, Britain began another war with China after a trivial incident, when the Chinese arrested the crew of a ship, registered in Hong Kong, on suspicion of piracy. **Cobden** proposed a vote of censure on Palmerston, which was passed in the Commons. Palmerston therefore called a general election, which showed his enormous popularity with the public, as he gained the first clear majority for a party since 1841: his chief critics, Cobden and **Bright**, lost their seats. Palmerston enhanced his reputation as a liberal by supporting Italian unification, as he thought that a strong Italy would be a barrier to French expansion, but he rejected **Napoleon III**'s suggestion of a European congress to discuss the Polish Revolution of 1863 against Russia. The rebels were encouraged but nothing was done to help them – 'Meddle and muddle', **Derby** called it. During the **American Civil War** (1861–5) Britain came close to war when two Southern politicians were seized from a British steamer by Union forces. Palmerston's bluster in sending troops to Canada worked, as the politicians were released, but it was a reckless gamble. His bluff did not work in 1864 when he told the Commons that if the duchies of **Schleswig-Holstein** were seized by the Prussians 'it would not be Denmark alone with which they would have to contend'. When **Bismarck** ignored Palmerston's warning and, with Austria, grabbed the duchies, Britain did nothing and suffered a humiliating defeat, which showed just how powerless she was on the Continent.

'In his policy abroad . . . a Liberal,' declared the *Morning Herald* in 1853, 'at home a Tory.' Palmerston did carry out some penal reforms when he was Home Secretary, substituting imprisonment for transportation and setting up the first parole system, but his nine years as Prime Minister were almost devoid of legislation, except for **Gladstone**'s budgets and the Matrimonial Causes Act (1857), which made possible divorce through the courts instead of by a private and expensive Act of Parliament. He was a steadfast opponent of **parliamentary reform**.

**Panama Canal.** There had been talk for a long time of building a canal across the isthmus of Panama to link the Caribbean with the

Pacific Ocean. The French began building a canal in 1881 but this project was ended in 1889 by bankruptcy and because so many workers died from yellow fever. The **Spanish–American War** of 1898, when there was fighting in both the Caribbean and the Pacific, showed the USA just how beneficial a canal would be for them. Colombia ruled Panama, so in January 1903 the USA drew up a treaty which would give her a lease on a canal zone, in return for ten million dollars and an annual rent. When the Colombian Senate rejected this treaty President Theodore **Roosevelt** was furious and thought of taking the area by force. This proved unnecessary, as the Panamanians revolted. Roosevelt hastened to recognize the rebel government and ordered US Marines to prevent Colombian forces from suppressing the revolution. Secretary of State John Hay signed a new treaty on similar terms to those rejected by Colombia: the USA leased a canal zone ten miles wide in perpetuity. Building through the fever-ridden swamps and jungles began in 1907 and was completed in 1914. Panamanian hostility to US control of the Canal led President Jimmy Carter to obtain the approval of Congress in 1977 for a treaty by which the USA will give up total control of the Canal Zone to Panama by the year 2000 but will ensure the Canal's perpetual neutrality.

**Panama scandal** (1892). Ferdinand de Lesseps, builder of the **Suez Canal**, formed a Panama Canal Company to link the Pacific Ocean with the Caribbean and attracted the savings of many small investors. Difficult terrain and disease caused problems, which journalists were bribed to conceal. Members of the Chamber of Deputies in Paris were also bribed, in order to obtain parliamentary approval for an issue of lottery bonds. This did not prevent the Company going bankrupt and the bribes were revealed. **Anti-Semitism** increased, as two Jewish financiers had been involved. Only one deputy was convicted but the scandal ended the political careers of several more and interrupted that of **Clemenceau**. Associated with one of the Jewish financiers, he lost his seat as a deputy in 1893 and was in the political wilderness until the **Dreyfus case** revived his career.

**Pankhurst, Emmeline** (1858–1928). Leading English **suffragette**. The beautiful daughter of a Manchester cotton manufacturer, in

1875 she married a lawyer of socialist-radical opinions. Pankhurst joined the **Independent Labour Party** (ILP) in 1893 and after her husband's death in 1898 came under the influence of her strong-willed eldest daughter, Christabel. To promote women's suffrage they formed the Women's Social and Political Union (WSPU) in 1903, which at its height had eighty-eight branches, mainly in London and the South-East. Emmeline was an efficient organizer but was, like her daughter, dictatorial and demanded complete obedience and loyalty, whilst refusing to be accountable to the members of the WSPU. As politicians and the press took little notice of the WSPU, the Pankhursts decided to draw attention to their cause by becoming more militant, holding public meetings, at which Emmeline was a brilliant speaker, and setting fire to public buildings, country houses and railway stations. Christabel left for Paris in 1912, whilst Emmeline spent much time in prison, where she would go on hunger strike, be forcibly fed, released and rearrested when she had recovered. In 1913 she was sentenced to three years in prison for accepting responsibility for a bomb explosion in a house being built for **Lloyd George**, though she was released in under a year. The violence of their methods had the opposite effect to that intended and turned many, including former supporters, against the WSPU. By 1914 the Pankhursts' campaign had run into the ground. Emmeline was saved by the outbreak of war, which enabled her to abandon her campaign for **women's suffrage** and to encourage women to go into the armed forces or industry. It was women's services during the war rather than the work of Emmeline Pankhurst which did most to bring the vote to women over the age of thirty in 1918. After the war Emmeline left the ILP and lived in Canada from 1919–26. She moved more to the **Right**, and in 1929 agreed to stand as a **Conservative Party** candidate but died before the election took place.

**Panslavism** meant different things to different Slav groups. For Panslavs in Russia, where the ideology developed, it meant freeing the Slavs in the Habsburg and **Ottoman Empires** and then imposing on them Russian political control. The novelist Dostoevsky looked for 'assimilation of the Slavs under the rule of Russia'. This did not appeal at all to other Slavs, who did not want to replace

Turkish or Austrian domination with Russian. They wanted the Russians to liberate them, so that they could form independent states. The Bulgars were not prepared to accept Russian control after the Russians had freed them from Turkish rule in 1878. Panslavism was never the official doctrine of the Russian state. The Tsars could not support revolutions against legitimate rulers and, as they had a multi-national empire themselves, they could not encourage **nationalism** and the break-up of empires. Panslavism, therefore, had little effect on Russian foreign policy, though it did help to bring about the **Russo-Turkish War** of 1877–8.

**Papen, Franz von** (1879–1969). Chancellor in the **Weimar Republic** (1932) and **Hitler**'s Vice-Chancellor (1933–4). A Catholic aristocrat, von Papen had connections with the army, as at one time he was a General Staff officer, and with big business, as he married the daughter of a wealthy Saarland industrialist. He was a lightweight politician, who wanted to preserve the dominance in Germany of the old *Junker* and industrial élite, and progressed no further than representing the **Centre Party** in the Prussian Legislature from 1921–32. Then he was appointed by President **Hindenburg** to succeed **Brüning** as Chancellor. The French ambassador in Berlin recalled how the news was received: 'It was greeted at first with incredulous amazement. Everyone smiled. There is something about von Papen that prevents either his friends or his enemies from taking him entirely seriously.' His government was called 'the cabinet of barons', as it consisted mainly of titled landowners and businessmen. It could not command a majority in the **Reichstag**, so von Papen tried to strengthen his position and his appeal to the **Right** by staging a *coup*, to take control of the Socialist-Centre government of Prussia. On 20 July 1932 he declared a state of emergency, made himself Reich Commissioner in Prussia and dismissed the ministers there, on the grounds that they favoured the communists and could not keep order. The Centre Party and socialists weakly accepted the situation.

In the July elections to the Reichstag the Nazis increased their seats from 107 to 230 and became by far the largest party. Von Papen therefore offered Hitler a post in his Cabinet but Hitler would be satisfied with nothing less than total power and the post of

Chancellor for himself. Von Papen rejected this and called another election in September 1932, in which the Nazis lost two million votes, but the Chancellor was as far as ever from having a majority in the Reichstag. He therefore asked Hindenburg to declare martial law, until a new and more authoritarian constitution could be introduced. Hindenburg was prepared to do this, until **Schleicher** told him that the army could not support a move which might lead to civil war. Schleicher replaced von Papen as Chancellor but he too could not gain a Reichstag majority, so von Papen intrigued with Hitler to replace him, foolishly believing that he could control Hitler and that real power would be his, in a Cabinet where Hitler was Chancellor and von Papen Vice-Chancellor. This came about on 30 January 1933 but it was not long before von Papen realized that he had badly miscalculated. On 17 June 1934 he gave a speech calling for an end to the terrorist activities of the **SA**. Hitler was enraged and von Papen was lucky to escape with his life on the **Night of the Long Knives** (30 June). He resigned his post as Vice-Chancellor shortly afterwards but was soon working with the Nazis again as ambassador to Vienna, where he played a large part in arranging the *Anschluss*. Von Papen continued to serve Hitler loyally and was ambassador to Turkey from 1934–44. Tried at Nuremberg as a war criminal, he was acquitted but was classified as a 'Major Offender' by a German de-Nazification court and was sentenced to eight years' imprisonment in 1947. He was released on appeal two years later.

**Paraguayan War** (War of the Triple Alliance) (1864–70). War fought by Paraguay against the combined forces of Brazil, Uruguay and Argentina. Essentially, it was the result of the intense political and economic rivalry between the nations involved and of the instability which the river Plate region had long suffered. Uruguay had been created in 1828 as a buffer state between Argentina and Brazil. The Paraguayan *caudillo*, Francisco López, feared that Brazil would take over Uruguay and when Brazil invaded that state in 1864 López sent his troops into the Mato Grosso and across Argentina to attack Brazil's southern province of Rio Grande do Sul. Argentina therefore declared war on Paraguay, as did the puppet government of Uruguay, thus forming the Triple Alliance. In 1866 their forces invaded Paraguay: fierce fighting produced high casualties on both sides until López was killed in battle in 1870, after which the war ended. Paraguay was devastated: her population of 525,000 had shrunk to 220,000, with a dramatic decrease in the number of males, and she lost much of her territory. Over 100,000 Allied soldiers died from fighting or disease: the war was the bloodiest in Latin America's history.

**Paris Commune** (March–May 1871). After the defeat and capture of **Napoleon III** at **Sedan** a provisional, republican government of National Defence was set up in Paris but it was unable to stop the Prussian invasion of France. Elections in February 1871 produced a monarchist National Assembly, which made **Thiers** head of the government. He immediately negotiated the Treaty of Frankfurt with **Bismarck**, by which France lost Alsace and part of Lorraine. Those events led to the repudiation by Paris of the government, particularly when on 18 March Thiers sent in the regular army to seize the cannon of the National Guard, a citizens' militia formed to defend Paris against the Germans. As this move was unsuccessful, Thiers moved the government and the army to Versailles. In Paris a Commune was elected by universal male suffrage to run the city: thirty-five of its eighty-one members were workers, the rest middle class. It was not a socialist body (only one member was a Marxist (see **Marxism**) and had no clear aims apart from preserving the republic. The gold reserve of the Bank of France was not seized and only abandoned workshops were taken over. A conflict might have been avoided but Thiers had no intention of making concessions. On 21 May government troops invaded Paris and began *la semaine sanglante* ('bloody week'), during which much of the centre of Paris was destroyed. The army under Marshal **MacMahon** systematically shot prisoners and killed about 25,000 defenders, whilst the *communards* shot hostages, including the Archbishop of Paris. Of 40,000 people arrested, 10,000 were convicted and 5,000 sent to the penal colony of New Caledonia in the Pacific. The Commune had been crushed by a republican government and this reassured conservatives that a republic was not synonymous with radicalism and revolution. It therefore helped to establish the **Third Republic**.

**Paris, Congress of** (1856). The peace conference which ended the **Crimean War**. Russia gave up southern **Bessarabia** (acquired in

1813), which cut her off from the mouth of the Danube, to Moldavia and Kars to Turkey. The Straits Convention of 1841, which did not allow any warships to pass through the Bosphorus, was reaffirmed. The most serious clause for Russia was that neutralizing the Black Sea: neither Russia nor Turkey was allowed warships or naval bases there. Russia regarded this as a serious threat to her security in the south, as in wartime British and French warships could rapidly enter an undefended Black Sea. She took advantage of France's defeat in the **Franco-Prussian War** (1870) to repudiate this clause. Russia also gave up her claim to act as protector of the Orthodox Christians in the **Ottoman Empire**.

**Paris Peace Conference** (1919–20). A meeting of representatives of the 'Allied and associated powers' after the end of the **First World War**. It resulted in treaties with the defeated **Central powers**; **Versailles** (June 1919) with Germany, **St Germain** (September 1919) with Austria, Neuilly (November 1919) with Bulgaria, **Trianon** (June 1920) with Hungary and **Sèvres** (August 1920) with Turkey. Much of what happened at the Conference had been decided beforehand, as treaties had been made earlier in the war, such as the Treaty of **London** (1915) with Italy, which promised territory to countries which joined the Allies. Action had also been taken by states breaking away from the Habsburg Empire, so that new states (e.g. Czechoslovakia and Yugoslavia) already existed. There was a marked contrast between Western and Eastern Europe in the changes brought about. In the West there were few frontier changes, except that **Alsace-Lorraine** was returned to France, whereas in the East all frontiers changed and many new countries were created, or resurrected. Estonia, Latvia and Lithuania appeared as new states out of the ruins of the Russian Empire; Poland became an independent country again for the first time since 1795; Austria-Hungary split up into separate states much reduced in size; Czechoslovakia and Yugoslavia arose out of the **Habsburg** Empire, although the core of Yugoslavia already existed in Serbia. Some existing countries enlarged their territories (France, Belgium, Italy, Romania, Greece), others became smaller (Germany, Bulgaria) and this largely decided who was satisfied with the peace settlement and who was not. There had been some effort to apply President **Wilson**'s principle of self-determination (although it was ignored in some cases, particularly in that of Austria) but it was impossible to avoid having national minorities in each of the states, as population was so mixed. There were one and a half million Magyars in Transylvania, which was given to Romania, but many of these were in the eastern part, far removed from Hungary itself. Altogether nineteen million people were national minorities in nine states with a total population of ninety-eight million. Czechs were less than half the population in Czechoslovakia. The problem of national minorities was a daunting one for the countries of Eastern Europe. It was a source of great instability which could be used, as it was by **Hitler**, to undermine and then destroy newly independent states such as Czechoslovakia. A further source of instability was that some of the supposed partners in the new states felt that they were treated unfairly: Slovaks in Czechoslovakia maintained that all the highest posts went to Czechs and in Yugoslavia Croats made the same complaint about the Serbs. The Ukrainians (called Ruthenians in the West) did not even have a state of their own but lived in Russia, Poland and Czechoslovakia. General **Smuts** had seen as early as March 1919 that the peace would be unstable, as Poland and Czechoslovakia would not be able to survive without German goodwill. It was clear that Russia and Germany, which had dominated Eastern Europe before the war, would recover their power and then they could be resisted only if the countries there stood together. Owing to the minorities problem and the nationalist economic policies followed by the various states, this did not happen.

**Paris, Treaty of** (May 1814). After the defeat of **Napoleon** the Allies (Britain, Russia, Austria and Prussia) made a peace with France which was extremely generous. As France was still regarded as the main danger to European peace, they wanted to prevent future French aggression and saw the best way to do this was to treat France leniently, so she would not have a sense of grievance and want to overthrow the settlement. They also did not want to make the **Bourbons** unpopular in France by forcing on them a harsh and unpopular peace. Her boundaries were to be those of 1792, which meant that, although France gave up most of her conquests during the **French Revolutionary** and **Napoleonic Wars**, such as Belgium and the left bank of the Rhine, she retained Avignon and parts of Flanders and Savoy. She lost some of her colonial islands (Tobago, St Lucia and Mauritius to Britain, part of San Domingo (Haiti) to Spain) but she did not have to pay an indemnity or suffer an army of occupation.

**Paris, Treaty of** (November 1815). After the first Treaty of **Paris** (1814) was concluded **Napoleon** escaped from the island of Elba and in the **Hundred Days** recovered control of France. Britain and Prussia ensured his defeat at the battle of **Waterloo** and then the Allies imposed another peace treaty on France. Her boundaries were now reduced to those of 1789 (though she retained Avignon), an indemnity of 700 million francs was imposed and there was to be an army of occupation until this was paid. Though these terms were more severe than those of 1814, they were not unreasonable: the indemnity was paid off and the army of occupation withdrawn in 1818.

**Parliament Act** (1911). Following the rejection of the **'People's Budget'** (1909) by the House of **Lords**, the **Liberal** Prime Minister **Asquith** announced that he would reduce the powers of the upper house. A Parliament Bill was introduced in 1910 to deprive the Lords of all authority over financial bills passed by the House of **Commons**: they could hold up other legislation for two years only. The duration of parliament was to be reduced from seven years to five. When the Lords rejected this bill Asquith called for a general election in December 1910, the second that year, and obtained from a reluctant King **George V** the promise that, if the Liberals were successful at the election, he would be prepared to create Liberal peers to ensure the passage of the Parliament Bill through the Lords. The election produced little change in party strength, the Liberals again having a comfortable majority with **Labour Party** and Irish Nationalist support. There was no need to create Liberal peers as **Balfour**, the Conservative leader, realized that resistance to the bill was futile and would ensure the Conservatives losing their majority in the Lords. Some Conservative peers, led by Lord **Curzon**, therefore supported the Liberals in passing a bill of which they strongly disapproved, which permanently reduced the authority of the upper house. Three months later Balfour resigned as leader of the **Conservative Party**.

**Parliamentary reform.** At the beginning of the nineteenth century the British House of **Commons** represented only a small proportion of the population, as there were many **'rotten' boroughs**, whilst large industrial towns like Leeds and Manchester did not return any MPs at all. The 1832 **Reform Act** got rid of many 'rotten' boroughs and redistributed their seats to the industrial towns and the counties. It also extended and made uniform the franchise in the boroughs but even so only 18 per cent of adult males had the vote compared to 11 per cent before, the main beneficiary being the middle class. **Disraeli**'s Reform Act of 1867 doubled the size of the electorate and made working-class voters a majority in the boroughs, though this did not give rise to working-class candidates, as election campaigns were expensive and MPs unpaid. The Ballot Act (1872) helped to make elections more representative of voters' wishes by providing for secret voting, which largely eliminated bribery and intimidation. **Gladstone**'s Representation of the People Act (1884) extended the vote to agricultural labourers and made uniform the franchise in boroughs and counties, so that 60 per cent of adult males had the vote, a situation that remained unchanged until 1918. The Redistribution of Seats Act (1885) removed 142 seats from the smaller boroughs and gave them to the counties and larger towns, nearly all of which were divided into single member constituencies. These two acts of Gladstone, with the Corrupt Practices Act (1883), which limited the amount of election expenses for candidates, constituted the most extensive parliamentary reform of the nineteenth century.

Reforms too were made in the procedure of the House of Commons, which speeded up the transactions of business and gave the government greater control over it. To counter the disruptive tactics of **Parnell** and the Irish Nationalists, the Speaker was allowed to close a debate: the 'closure' soon became the 'guillotine', by which the government could end a parliamentary debate after a specified time. Government control of parliamentary time was almost complete in 1902, when private members were left with only Friday afternoons for their own business.

In the late nineteenth century the House of **Lords**, with its permanent Conservative majority, rejected or amended the bills of Liberal governments, so **Asquith** reduced its powers by the **Parliament Act** (1911), making it clear that power lay overwhelmingly with the Commons. In the same year MPs were paid, so working-class candidates could now afford to enter parliament. The most dramatic extension of the franchise came in the Representation of the People Act (1918), when all males over twenty-one and all women ratepayers (i.e. with property) over thirty were given the vote, thus adding eight million (six million women and two million men) to the electorate. Discrimination against women ended in 1928, when they were given the vote at twenty-one and the property qualification was abandoned, so they enjoyed the franchise on the same terms as men for the first time.

**Parnell, Charles Stewart** (1846–91). Irish Nationalist. A Protestant landlord from an old Anglo-Irish family, Parnell derived his hatred of England from his American mother. Tall, handsome, arrogant, a good shot and fine horseman, he appeared a typical country gentleman but he turned his back on the Protestant Ascendancy, joined the **Home Rule** League and became an MP in 1874. To draw the attention of the British parliament to Irish affairs and to wring concessions from the government, he and other Irish MPs began filibustering, making inordinately long speeches to disrupt the work of parliament. He almost succeeded in bringing it to a halt, before new rules of procedure were adopted. By sheer force of personality (he was a poor speaker) he dominated the Irish MPs and saw an opportunity to put further pressure on the government when the **Irish Land War** (1879–82) began. Parnell became President of the Land League, formed to defend the interests of the tenants, and joined with the **Fenians** to make an extremely successful tour of the USA, which established him as the greatest Irish leader since **O'Connell**. **Gladstone**'s response to the Land War was to pass his second **Irish Land Act** in 1881, which gave the tenants much of what they wanted.

Many of Parnell's followers urged him to abandon his parliamentary opposition, return to Ireland and set up a separate parliament, as **Sinn Fein** was to do forty years later. If he had done this civil war would probably have resulted, as the Fenians wanted. Parnell rejected their advice but Gladstone, thinking that he intended to wreck the Land Act, put him in Kilmainham jail, Dublin. As outrages increased in the winter of 1881–2, Parnell and the British government sought a compromise, reached in the Kilmainham Treaty of 1882. In return for his release and the extension of the Land Act to include tenants in arrears with their rent, Parnell agreed to do all he could 'to put a stop to the outrages which are unhappily so prevalent'. The brutal murder of the Chief Secretary for Ireland and one of his officials in Phoenix Park, Dublin, just after Parnell's release, did not deflect him from his cooperation with the Liberal government, in spite of renewed coercion.

In the 1885 election eighty-five Home Rule MPs were elected, many chosen by Parnell and all under his iron control. They were in a powerful position, as they held the balance of power between the two major parties, and helped to convert Gladstone to Home Rule. He introduced a Home Rule Bill in 1886 but in so doing split the **Liberal Party**, with the **Whigs** and the Radicals under Joseph **Chamberlain** breaking away and ensuring that the bill was defeated. When *The Times* tried to implicate Parnell in the Phoenix Park murders, the government set up a Special Commission, which in 1889 completely vindicated him. Parnell was now very popular in England, 'the uncrowned King of Ireland', and appeared to be in an impregnable position. Then disaster struck with the O'Shea divorce.

Parnell had met Katherine O'Shea, the wife of a Captain O'Shea, in 1880. She became his lover, mother of his children and lived with him continuously from 1886, though it was not until December 1889 that Captain O'Shea filed for divorce citing Parnell as corespondent. Parnell did not contest the case. His popularity disappeared in England, where Gladstone made it clear that the Irish MPs would have to choose between Home Rule and Parnell. The party split, the majority rejecting Parnell, who would not admit defeat. In Ireland the Catholic Church and the more respectable members of his party turned against him. Worn out by the unrelenting struggle, Parnell died on 6 October 1891. He had not achieved

Home Rule but his success had nevertheless been remarkable. A Protestant who became the leader of a Catholic nation, he had presided triumphantly over a campaign for land reform, had persuaded the Liberal Party to commit itself to Home Rule and he had done this whilst pursuing a constitutional path which rejected violence. The myth, encouraged by Yeats and Joyce, of Parnell as a potential revolutionary, betrayed by his followers under pressure from the English enemy, was how many Irish preferred to see him.

**Pašić, Nikola** (1845–1926). Prime Minister of Serbia and a founder of Yugoslavia. Elected to the Serbian parliament in 1878, he opposed the authoritarian Obrenović monarchy and in 1881 became founder and leader of the Radical Party. He appeared as a dominant figure in Serbia only after the Obrenović dynasty was bloodily overthrown in 1903 and replaced by the Karadjordjević dynasty, which came to the throne with Pašić's help. For most of the time from 1904–18 he was Prime Minister of Serbia and had to cope with steadily worsening relations with Austria-Hungary, who began the 'Pig War' in 1906 by preventing Serbian exports (mainly agricultural produce – 70 per cent of Serbia's exports went to Austria-Hungary) from entering the Empire. This was in response to Serbia placing orders for armaments in France rather than with the Skoda works in Bohemia. Pašić was responsible for Serbia taking part in the **Balkan Wars** (1912–13), which doubled the size of Serbia. Austria-Hungary seized the opportunity created by the assassination of Archduke Francis Ferdinand at **Sarajevo** in 1914 to blame Pašić and the Serbian government for the murder and to declare war on Serbia. After Serbia's defeat a government-in-exile, with Pašić as premier, was established in the Greek island of Corfu. There Pašić agreed in 1917 with the Yugoslav Committee of South Slav exiles from the **Austro-Hungarian Empire** (Serbs, Croats, Slovenes) to form after the war a single kingdom under the Serbian Karadjordjević dynasty. Pašić represented the new kingdom at the Treaty of **Versailles** and became Prime Minister after elections in 1920. He pushed through parliament a constitution which established a strong centralized state by abolishing the traditional autonomy of the provinces and in which power was largely in the hands of the Serbs. The Croats never accepted this (in the kingdom, which took the name of Yugoslavia in 1929, 43 per cent of the population were Serbs, 23 per cent Croats and 8.5 per cent Slovenes). The struggle between Serbs and Croats, during which Pašić imprisoned the leaders of the Croatian Peasant Party for a short time, paralysed the state and led to Pašić's resignation in 1926, shortly before his death.

**Passchendaele** (Third battle of Ypres, July–November 1917). An attempt by **Haig**, the British Commander in France, to push the Germans out of northern France and Belgium and capture their submarine bases there. He felt that, with mutinies in the French army, he needed to take pressure off the French. Haig was absurdly optimistic and thought that the German army was on the point of collapse. He may also have been influenced by Admiral Jellicoe's gloomy prediction that unless the U-boat bases at Ostend and Zeebrugge were captured, Britain would not be able to continue the war into 1918. A massive bombardment, which preceded the attack, shattered the drainage system on the low-lying ground and turned it into a quagmire, as the experts had predicted. Heavy rain fell on the first day of the battle, so that British troops were bogged down in no man's land, an easy target for German machine-guns, and some were drowned in the mud. After the failure of the initial assault, limited attacks on a narrow front continued until most of the Passchendaele ridge, which overlooked British positions in the Ypres salient, had been taken. Rain in October made further attacks useless but Haig rejected the advice of his generals and refused to call off the offensive until November. By then the British had advanced five miles, which made their line stick out in a more awkward salient than before: the land gained was abandoned when the Germans attacked in 1918. British losses were 300,000, German 260,000. Haig had consistently underestimated the strength of German forces and believed in a breakthrough when it was no longer possible. He had failed in all objectives, had condemned his troops to appalling suffering and had used up his reserves, so that the tank victory at Cambrai on 20 November could not be followed up. Owing to the enormous losses, **Lloyd George** starved Haig of reinforcements, so weakening the British army when it had to face the **Ludendorff offensive** in March 1918.

**Patton, George Smith** (1885–1945). American general. 'Compared to war, all other forms of human endeavour shrink to insignificance', he once said. 'God, how I love it!' An egoist, flamboyant (he loved to wear an ivory-handled pistol) and intolerant, he first commanded a tank brigade in France towards the end of the **First World War**. Between the world wars he was an outspoken advocate of tank warfare and had his first opportunity of using tanks on a large scale in the **North African Campaign** (1942–3), when he fought successfully. In the invasion of Sicily (1943) he captured Palermo in a spectacular advance of 100 miles in three days but received much adverse publicity when, on visiting a hospital, he slapped a GI suffering from battle fatigue and accused him of cowardice. He was moved aside and did not take part in the **Italian Campaign** but **Eisenhower** did not wish to be without the services of his most dynamic commander, so he was sent to France in July 1944, a month after the **D-Day** invasion, and played a leading part in the **Normandy Campaign**. His tanks broke out of the bridgehead at Avranches and rapidly moved towards the Loire but his advance was halted when he ran out of supplies. He maintained that if he had been given the supplies allocated to **Montgomery** (whose cautious and systematic policy he disliked) he could have reached Germany before the winter of 1944 and perhaps ended the war. In September–October he suffered reverses when he twice failed to take Metz, as he attacked on a broad front and did not concentrate his forces. The battle of the **Bulge** saw him at his best again: the swift deployment of his armour helped to bring about an American victory. In the spring offensive of 1945 his Third Army raced to the Rhine at Koblenz before sweeping up the left bank, cutting off German forces and taking many prisoners. He then pushed his troops across the Rhine south of Mainz without support or artillery and raced across northern Bavaria to Czechoslovakia, covering a greater distance than any other Allied commander. This was a typically bold move but could have been disastrous, as he rushed ahead of the main Allied armies without protecting his flanks. Patton had no interest in organizational skills so necessary for success in war and was too impulsive to be a good strategist: he needed firm control from his superiors. Yet he was supreme as a field commander and was the Allied general the Germans respected most. He died from injuries received in a road accident in Germany.

**Peace Police Law** (1900). Law passed in Japan to reduce anti-government protests. The political activity of women, the police and the armed forces was banned, as were labour organizations and strikes. The Home Ministry had the right to prohibit any association and the police could forbid any demonstrations or meetings. It was under this law that Japan's first left-wing party, the Social Democratic Party, was banned as soon as it was formed in 1901, as its leaders would not abandon their programme of reform, which called for equality and universal suffrage. This law was not abolished until 1945, although it was largely replaced in 1925 by the Peace Preservation Law. This was passed to protect the government from any danger which might result from giving the vote to all males over twenty-five, which had increased the electorate from three to 12.5 million. The new law banned any organization which wanted to abolish private property or change the status quo. As the law was so vague it could be used not only against communists and the **Left** but against any opponent of the government. In 1928 the law was made harsher by allowing the death penalty to be imposed.

**Pearl Harbor** (7 December 1941). A surprise attack, without declaring war, by Japanese carrier-based planes on the main US naval base in the Pacific at Hawaii. **Yamamato**, Commander-in-Chief of the Japanese fleet, realized that in a long conflict Japan would lose, owing to the industrial strength of the USA, so he aimed at a knock-out blow. Admiral Nagumo's fleet, which was to attack Pearl Harbor, included six aircraft carriers; 275 miles north of Hawaii 360 planes took off and were detected by American radar on the island but the warnings were ignored. This negligence ensured that in ninety minutes two of the eight US battleships in harbour were sunk and the rest badly damaged; three light cruisers and three destroyers were also sunk; 261 American planes were destroyed, most of them on the ground. Japanese losses were twenty-nine aircraft and three midget submarines. This was a well-planned and successful attack but it was not decisive, as the three US carriers of the Pacific Fleet were not in harbour at the time. Nagumo failed to launch a mission to find and destroy them. He also failed to destroy the shore installations, particularly the oil storage bunkers. Success here would have put the American Pacific Fleet out of action for months. Three of the damaged battleships soon, and three others eventually, rejoined the fleet. One effect of 'a day which will live in infamy', as President Franklin D. **Roosevelt** called it, was that the American **Congress**, with only one vote against, declared war on Japan. Germany and Italy had not known of Japan's intention to attack but supported their ally and declared war on the USA on 11 December. Thus the attack on Pearl Harbor not only started the **Pacific War** but ensured that American might would also be used against the **Axis powers** in Europe.

**Peel, Sir Robert** (1788–1850). British Prime Minister (1834–5, 1841–6). Born in Lancashire, Peel was the son of an industrialist who had made a fortune in the cotton industry and who was responsible for the **Factory Act** of 1802. He entered Parliament as a Tory (see **Tories**) in 1809 and in **Liverpool**'s administrations became Secretary for Ireland (1812–18) and Home Secretary (1822–7), a post he held again (1828–30) under **Wellington**. Although he was not a great orator, he soon established a reputation for his efficiency and mastery of detail, and carried out unprecedented reforms of the legal system, removing obsolete laws and abolishing the death penalty for nearly a hundred offences. In 1829 he set up the Metropolitan Police Force, the first uniformed, disciplined and professional body in the country, which became the model for police forces elsewhere. The outstanding 'Protestant' in the government and supporter of the Orange Order in Ireland – he was once known as 'Orange Peel' – he resigned in 1827 when **Canning**, a supporter of **Catholic emancipation**, became Prime Minister. Returning to office when Canning died, he became convinced, after **O'Connell**'s success in the County Clare election, that there would be civil war in Ireland unless emancipation was granted, so he piloted the bill for Catholic emancipation through the House of **Commons**, a move which many Tories regarded as a great betrayal. He opposed the **Reform Bill** of 1832 and **Grey**'s coercion of the House of **Lords** but realized that the **Conservative Party** would be forever a party in opposition if it opposed all change, so in the **Tamworth Manifesto** (1834) he sought to give it a broader appeal. When he became Prime Minister, briefly, in 1834, he set up the Ecclesiastical Commission, the most important measure affecting the Church of England in the nineteenth century, which enabled the Church to reform itself. All ecclesiastical legislation henceforth originated with the Commission, a mixed clerical and lay body.

The 1841 election, the first in which an organized opposition defeated the government of the day, gave Peel a majority of seventy-six and began a decade in which he was the dominant politician. As there had been deficits for the last three years he began by reforming the financial system. He reintroduced income tax, a very unpopular measure, so that he could then reduce the taxes on consumer goods to benefit the population as a whole. Duties on corn and on about 600 other goods were reduced in his budget of 1842, a year which saw some of the worst social disturbances of the century and Peel's rejection of the second Chartist petition (see **Chartism**). In the same year the bill of Lord Ashley (later Earl of **Shaftesbury**) was passed, forbidding the employment of women and boys under ten in coal mines. A Factory Act of Peel's Home Secretary, Graham, in 1844 limited the hours women and children could work. Financial reform continued with the Bank Charter Act (1844), which linked the power to issue bank notes to the bullion reserves and was to be the basis of currency policy for the next eighty years. Peel's budget of 1845 saw further tariff reductions (about half the duties were abolished completely) but in that year the Conservative Party began to split over Ireland.

Peel had reacted to O'Connell's movement to repeal the Act of **Union** by banning the Clontarf meeting in 1843 (see **O'Connell**) but he realized that 'Mere force . . . will do nothing as a permanent remedy for the social evils of that country.' He wanted to improve relations between the government and the Catholic middle class in Ireland and proposed that the grant to the Catholic seminary at Maynooth (set up by Act of Parliament in 1795) should be trebled. The strength of opposition from the Anglican Church, dissenters and Conservative MPs was so great that he had to rely on **Whig** support to pass his bill. Peel had always believed that he should govern in the national interest and that the party of which he was leader should not dictate policy but the Maynooth bill split the Conservative Party (159 voting for it, 147 against). This split was deepened by Peel's decision to repeal the **Corn Laws**. This was precipitated by the **Irish Famine** and, like the Maynooth Bill, was passed with Whig support: only a third of Conservatives voted for repeal. For the Ultras (extreme Conservatives) this was his third betrayal, so they joined with the Whigs to bring down his government. This division amongst the Conservatives lasted until the 1860s and helped to keep the **Liberal Party** in office for most of the time between 1846 and 1886.

In opposition Peel's prestige was so great that he was consulted by the Whig government (and by Prince **Albert**). His death after a riding accident in London was mourned by all classes. Along with **Pitt** and **Gladstone** he was one of the three greatest Prime Ministers of the nineteenth century, who gave the Conservative Party a wider basis of support than the landed interest and the Anglican Church by appealing to the business community from which he came. When the Conservatives were in power again under **Disraeli** it was Peelite policies that he followed.

**Penal settlements.** Britain sent some convicts to her American colonies from the seventeenth century and when they became independent in 1783, she looked for a new place of transportation. In 1786 **Pitt**'s government chose Botany Bay in Australia: the first convicts arrived there in 1788 but after a few days sailed north to the magnificent harbour of what became Sydney. Convicts provided the main basis of settlement for the next fifty years and in 1812 were sent to Hobart in Van Diemen's Land (which became Tasmania in 1855). Most of the prisoners had been sentenced for petty theft but some were political prisoners, particularly the Irish: 300 who had taken part in the **Irish Rebellion** (1798) were transported, as were sixty **Fenians** in 1867. Sixty **Luddites** were transported in 1812, 481 involved in the **Swing riots** in 1831 and the six **Tolpuddle Martyrs** in 1834. At first they were used on public works but were later assigned to free settlers, especially in pastoral farming. After seven years many became 'emancipists': they were freed, given land and even other convicts to work for them. The House of **Commons** recommended in 1838 that transportation to New South Wales and Van Diemen's Land be ended: the last convicts arrived at Sydney in 1840 and at Hobart in 1853. This did not end transportation to Australia, as Western Australian settlers asked for convicts to be sent there, so that from 1842–68 10,000 convicts went to Western Australia. Between 1788 and 1868, when the system was abandoned, 160,000 convicts had been transported to Australia. Other countries used penal settlements for their convicts, particularly France and Russia. The French established penal colonies in Africa, New Caledonia in the Pacific and French Guiana (Devil's Island was still being used in the Second World War). Russian Tsars used penal settlements in Siberia for political prisoners; these were massively extended in the **forced labour camps** of **Stalin**.

**Peninsular War** (1807–14). War fought by Anglo-Portuguese and Spanish armies against the French during the **Napoleonic Wars**. **Napoleon** invaded Portugal in 1807 to force it to accept his **Continental Blockade** and extended the war unnecessarily to Spain (which was allied to France) in 1808, when he forced the Spanish King to abdicate and placed his brother Joseph on the throne. As the Spaniards revolted and defeated a French army at Bailén, the British saw their opportunity to gain a foothold on the Continent, so a force under Sir Arthur Wellesley (created Viscount **Wellington** in 1809) landed in Portugal and defeated the French at Vimeiro. This led Napoleon to intervene personally for the only time in Spain. The British, now under Sir John Moore, as Wellington had been recalled to England, were pushed back and forced to embark at Corunna, where Moore was killed in January 1809.

Wellington returned in April and remained on the peninsula for the rest of the war, carefully husbanding his resources (he never had more than 60,000 troops) against superior French forces. At Talavera he defeated a French army twice the size of his own but was badly pressed when Napoleon, after the defeat of Austria at Wagram in 1809, sent Masséna with 100,000 of his best troops to Spain. Wellington retired to carefully prepared defensive lines at Torres Vedras, outside Lisbon, where he could be supplied by sea. When Napoleon withdrew troops from Spain for his **Moscow Campaign** in 1812 Wellington was able to go on the offensive. He successfully besieged the fortresses of Ciudad Rodrigo and Badajoz, which opened strategic passes into Spain, and won a battle at Salamanca (July 1812), where French losses were three times those of the

British and Portuguese. In 1813 the French were driven out of Spain after Wellington's victory at Vitoria and France was invaded.

Allied success in the Peninsular War would have been impossible without the contributions of the Spaniards and the Portuguese. The Spanish regular army of 100,000 at the beginning of the war was 160,000 by 1812 and kept many French troops occupied, so that they could not concentrate against Wellington. In 1810, when Masséna invaded Portugal, there were 325,000 French troops in Spain, but only a quarter could be used against Wellington. Spanish guerrillas, too, played a vital role, attacking French lines of communication and providing Wellington with invaluable intelligence. For Napoleon the war was an enormous blunder, in which the French suffered 164,000 casualties (half of them due to guerrillas) and which tied down vast numbers of French troops (there were never less than 200,000 in Spain) who were badly needed elsewhere. After the retreat from Moscow, when Napoleon was fighting for survival, he needed in central Europe the troops who were in Spain: they might well have brought about a French victory. The Peninsular War therefore played an important part in bringing about Napoleon's defeat; the Emperor himself was aware of this when he later wrote 'The Spanish ulcer destroyed me'.

**'People's Budget'** (1909). **Lloyd George**, as Chancellor of the Exchequer in **Asquith**'s **Liberal Party** administration, needed money to finance social reforms and to build more **Dreadnoughts**, so he presented a daring budget. This proposed increased taxation of higher earned, and all unearned, income, the introduction of a super tax on all incomes over £5,000 and a tax allowance for the less well-off. Death duties, liquor licences, tobacco and spirit duties were increased and there were taxes on cars and petrol for the first time. The most contentious part of his proposals was his assault on landowners, the value of whose land increased through no effort of their own. They were to pay 20 per cent on the unearned increment in land values after a new land survey (i.e. at some future date) and there was to be a capital tax on the value of undeveloped land and minerals. His proposals caused an outcry from the **Conservative Party** opposition, who denounced them as '**socialism**'. There was a constitutional convention that the House of **Lords** should approve all financial bills passed by the **Commons**, but this time they rejected the budget, so Asquith called a general election in January 1910, which was dominated by a 'Peers versus People' campaign. The Conservatives regained many seats but the Liberals were still the largest party and, with **Labour Party** and Irish Nationalist support, had a comfortable majority. The Lords therefore passed the budget but Asquith had decided that their powers should be clipped, so he introduced a Parliament Bill (see **Parliament Act**) to do this. The 'People's Budget' led, therefore, to a permanent diminution in the authority of the House of Lords.

**Perry, Commodore Matthew Calbraith** (1794–1858). American naval officer. Japan had been closed to foreign contact (see *Sakoku*) for over two hundred years when Commodore Perry entered Tokyo Bay in July 1853 with four 'black ships', two of which were steam-driven. The USA wanted to expand her trade in the Pacific and wanted coal supplies from Japan for American ships trading with China. Perry presented a letter from the American President demanding diplomatic relations with Japan and that US ships should be provisioned there. The Tokugawa authorities asked for time, so Perry agreed to return the next year. His ultimatum caused a crisis in Japan, as the shogun took the unprecedented step of asking the *daimyo* (feudal lords) for their opinion. When Perry returned in February 1854 with nine ships, the threat of military force compelled the shogun to make the treaty of Kanagawa. This provided two ports where American ships could buy necessities like coal and food from the authorities but there was to be no private trade. An American consul was permitted at Shimoda. Similar agreements were soon made with Britain and Russia but there were no full commercial relations until 1858 (see **Unequal treaties**). Perry's visits had enormous consequences in Japan: they showed that the Tokugawas were not strong enough to resist foreign demands and began a train of events which was to lead to the fall of the **Tokugawa shogunate**.

**Pétain, Henri-Philippe** (1856–1951). Marshal of France and Head of State (1940–45). The son of a prosperous peasant farmer, Pétain became professor at the *Ecole de Guerre* (Staff College), where he opposed the fashionable doctrine of all-out attack. During the

**First World War** he brilliantly defended Verdun (see battle of **Verdun**) in 1916 and became famous for his remark '*Ils ne passeront pas*' ('they shall not pass'). In May 1917 he replaced Nivelle as Commander-in-Chief and had to put down, by a mixture of tact and firmness, the mutinies in the French army which followed the failure of Nivelle's offensive. He did not get on well with the British and in 1918 at their request he was placed under **Foch**, General-in-Chief of Allied armies, although he continued to command French armies and prepared the great offensives of August and September 1918. He became a marshal at the end of the war. In 1925–6 he directed the campaign in Morocco which defeated **Abd al-Qrim** and in 1934 served as Minister of War.

When the **Second World War** broke out he was French ambassador in Spain, from where he was recalled in 1940 to become Deputy Prime Minister before replacing Reynaud as premier in June. Calm and fatalistic, Pétain made an armistice with the Germans which left 60 per cent of France under German occupation and became head of the Vichy government (see **Vichy France**) in unoccupied France. He was in favour of cooperating with the Germans but did not wish to go as far as **Laval** in collaboration and would not commit France to joining Germany against Britain in the war. When the Germans occupied the whole of France after the Anglo-American invasion of North Africa in November 1942 (see **North African Campaigns**) Pétain lost all influence. At the end of the war he was tried for treason and condemned to death, but de Gaulle commuted his sentence to life imprisonment. He was imprisoned alone on the Ile d'Yeu, where he died.

**Peterloo massacre** (16 August 1819). When 'Orator' Hunt was to address an open-air meeting in St Peter's Fields, Manchester, the local magistrates decided to stop it, as previous meetings had ended violently. After 60,000 people had assembled the magistrates ordered the local Yeomanry to arrest Hunt before he could speak. When they got into difficulties, owing to the density of the crowd and their own indiscipline, the Hussars, using sabres, were sent to rescue them. Eleven people were killed and over 400 injured, many of them trampled on in the panic. The government, which was not responsible for the massacre, felt bound to congratulate the magistrates to preserve their morale. The press seized this opportunity to attack the government, calling the events in St Peter's Fields the 'Peterloo massacre', in ironic reference to **Wellington**'s most famous victory. The **Whigs** took up the cause of **parliamentary reform** again, political unions were formed and protest meetings held in the industrial towns. The government responded with repression in the Six Acts, which restricted the right to hold public meetings and the freedom of the press.

**Petrograd.** The Russian name given to St Petersburg, which was too German-sounding, in 1914. It changed its name again, in 1924, to Leningrad, in honour of **Lenin**, who had just died.

**Pilsudski, Józef** (1867–1935). Polish nationalist. The son of an impoverished nobleman and subject of the Tsar, he hated Russia and worked for Polish independence. From 1887–92 he was banished to Siberia and on his return became a co-founder of the Polish Socialist Party (PPS) and editor of *Robotnik* ('worker'), until it was suppressed in 1900. He saw in the **Russian Revolution of 1905** an opportunity to begin a rising to gain independence for Poland and took charge of the Military Organization of the PPS, which raided banks and killed Tsarist police and officials. When it was clear by 1906 that there would be no revolution in Poland, Pilsudski regarded war between the powers (Austria-Hungary, Prussia and Russia) who ruled Poland as the only way of achieving independence. He organized a Polish army in Austrian Galicia, which joined Germany in the **First World War**, though Pilsudski refused to fight outside Polish territory. After the fall of the Tsar in 1917 he fell out with the **Central Powers**, as they would not guarantee the independence of Poland, and was imprisoned by the Germans from July to November 1917.

With the Allied victory Poland became independent for the first time in 130 years, as the largest and most powerful state in Eastern Europe. Pilsudski, as head of state and Chief of Staff of the army, fought against the **Bolsheviks** in order to extend Poland's boundaries in the east. In the **Russo–Polish War** (1919–20) he won, with French help, a decisive victory near Warsaw over the **Red Army** and at the Treaty of Riga (1921) added substantial parts of Lithuania, Belorussia and the Ukraine to Poland. He resigned as head of state in 1923 but soon became disillusioned with parliamentary government, as there was widespread corruption and inflation. In 1926 he staged a *coup* and established a limited form of military dictatorship: parliament, opposition parties and newspapers were allowed to continue, though in 1930 he ordered the detention and torture of eighty deputies who opposed him. Pilsudski had no ideology beyond a vague belief in order and national strength and was not leader of a party. He refused to become President and though he was twice Prime Minister (1926–8, 1930), he delegated most of his duties and attended few Cabinet meetings. In spite of his past links with the PPS he would not carry out social reforms. His main interest was in foreign policy. He appreciated the Nazi danger to Poland and when **Hitler** came to power suggested to France a preventive war against Germany. When this was rejected, he made non-aggression pacts in 1934 with Germany and the Soviet Union. Although personally honest and indifferent to wealth, he did nothing to eradicate the corruption of his colleagues. His health began to fail soon after he seized power: in his last years he was old, sick and demoralized and did not provide any effective leadership.

**Pitt, William** (Pitt the Younger) (1759–1806). British Prime Minister (1783–1801, 1804–6). A son of the Earl of Chatham, Pitt was twenty-four when he became Prime Minister, a post he was to hold continuously for seventeen years: for the first ten years he was the only member of the Cabinet in the House of **Commons**. He was a great believer in *laissez-faire* and in his early years supported **parliamentary reform**, introducing a bill in 1785 to get rid of **'rotten' boroughs** but this was defeated. He also concentrated on financial and administrative improvements. After the American War of Independence government expenditure vastly exceeded revenue. By 1792 Pitt had turned the deficit into a surplus, partly by reducing indirect taxes to make smuggling unprofitable, partly by getting rid of many sinecures and largely owing to the increasing wealth of the country. The Eden Treaty (1786) opened France to British manufactures and trade with America revived, so that by 1800 the USA was taking a quarter of British exports. Efficiency was Pitt's watchword. He sought to introduce this into imperial affairs too: his India Act (1784) brought the **East India Company**

more under the control of the British government, as a Board of Control was set up in London with its President a member of the Cabinet. The 1791 **Canada Act** divided the country into Upper and Lower Canada, with an elected legislature in each province, an arrangement that lasted for the next fifty years.

When the **French Revolution** broke out in 1789 Pitt was happy to see France bankrupt and divided, but his attitude changed with the **September massacres** and the execution of **Louis XVI**. Many **Whigs** too were alarmed at the French Revolution and split in 1794, when the Duke of Portland and other Whigs joined Pitt's government. Pitt always called himself a Whig but he was really a non-party man who thought that a government should be formed from the best men of all parties. Yet some historians see in the coalition of 1794 the rebirth of the Tory (see **Tories**) Party and the origins of modern Conservatism (see **Conservative Party**). After Britain went to war with France in 1793 Pitt began a policy of repression, as he feared a revolutionary upheaval in England. *Habeas Corpus* was suspended in 1794, so people could be arrested without trial, and in 1795 came the 'Gag' Acts, which made the death penalty possible for those holding unauthorized meetings of over fifty people: all who spoke or wrote against the Constitution were now guilty of treason. These ferocious Acts were hardly ever used but their existence terrified many and helped the government to stamp out most radical activity. In 1799 and 1800 the **Combination Acts** made trade unions illegal.

Pitt's conduct of the war has been much criticized, as he pursued the policy his father had so successfully applied in the Seven Years War (1756–63), concentrating on the colonies and leaving his allies to fight in Europe. The British lost 40,000 troops in the West Indies, mainly from yellow fever, but their capture of French islands there (1794–6) deprived France of much needed colonial imports. When Holland was forced to declare war on Britain, the Cape of Good Hope and Ceylon were captured, and were to remain valuable parts of the British Empire throughout the nineteenth century. Pitt's subsidies to Britain's allies were relatively modest – only £9.2 million before 1802. Pitt spent huge sums on the navy after the war began and so enabled Britain to dominate the seas. Victories over the Spaniards at Cape St Vincent and the Dutch at Camperdown in 1797 removed any danger of invasion and persuaded **Napoleon** to turn to Egypt, where his fleet was destroyed at the battle of the **Nile** (1798). The Armed Neutrality of the North, which threatened Britain's Baltic trade, was demolished when **Nelson** attacked the Danish fleet at the battle of **Copenhagen** (1801).

The **Irish Rebellion** (1798) persuaded Pitt to pass the Act of **Union** (1800) with Ireland but he wanted to go further and conciliate the Catholic majority there by granting **Catholic emancipation**. **George III** would not allow this so Pitt, who had a huge majority in both Houses, felt obliged to resign in 1801. He returned to office in 1804, saw Napoleon's hopes of invading England dashed at the battle of **Trafalgar** and the collapse of the Third Coalition after the battle of **Austerlitz** before he died in 1806.

**Pius IX** (1792–1878). Pope (1846–78). When he was elected Pope Pius IX seemed to have liberal ideas, as he relaxed the press censorship, freed political prisoners and set up a council of ministers which included laymen. The **Revolutions of 1848**, however, forced him to go further than he wanted in granting a constitution with a parliament, which had full legislative and financial powers. In November, when his Prime Minister was assassinated, Pius fled to Naples and a Roman Republic was proclaimed. He appealed to foreign powers for assistance and was restored by the French in 1849, convinced that **liberalism** and **nationalism** led to revolution. Constitutional government was not restored in the Papal States. Henceforth Pius appeared to be a reactionary opposed to the main intellectual, political and social changes of the time. In 1854 he issued the dogma of the Immaculate Conception of the Virgin Mary and encouraged the Marian cult. When the Papal States were seized to become part of the new Kingdom of Italy in 1860, Pius refused to accept the loss of his territories or to recognize the new state, and excommunicated all those who had been involved in setting it up: Catholics were forbidden to take part in elections. This began the division of Church and State in Italy, which lasted until the **Lateran Treaties** were made by **Pius XI** and **Mussolini** in 1929. In 1864 Pius issued the Syllabus of 'errors of our time', which denounced 'progress, liberalism and modern civilization'. It condemned freedom of conscience and of worship and the sovereignty of the secular state. This was a great blow to liberal Catholics, as was the Vatican Council of 1869–70, the first general assembly of the Roman Catholic Church for over 300 years, which proclaimed that the Pope was infallible on questions of faith and morals. The doctrine of Papal infallibility alarmed many governments, both Catholic and Protestant, as it seemed to imply clerical interference in politics. **Bismarck** used it to claim that Catholics in Germany owed allegiance to a foreign power and to justify his persecution of the Catholic Church in the *Kulturkampf*. In 1870 Italian troops occupied Rome, which became the capital of Italy, when French soldiers withdrew to fight in the **Franco-Prussian War**. Pius henceforth regarded himself as a prisoner and never set foot outside the Vatican again.

**Pius XI** (1857–1939). Pope (1922–39). Pius XI indirectly aided the destruction in Italy of the Catholic Popular Party, which he regarded as too radical, by forbidding it in 1924 to form an alliance with other parties opposed to **Mussolini**. In 1929 he made the **Lateran Treaties** with Mussolini, ending the dispute between Church and State in Italy, which went back to the unification of Italy in 1860. He protested in 1931 against the pagan worship of the state by **Fascism** and openly disagreed with Mussolini's **anti-Semitic** policies in 1938. Pius, with the assistance of Cardinal Pacelli (later Pope **Pius XII**), also made a **Concordat** with **Hitler** in 1933 but in 1937 issued the encyclical *Mit brennender Sorge* ('With deep anxiety'), protesting against Nazi (see **Nazism**) violations of human rights and accusing the Nazis of ignoring the terms of the Concordat.

**Pius XII** (1876–1958). Pope (1939–58). Eugenio Pacelli was born into a Roman family with a tradition of Papal service. Ordained a priest in 1899, he entered the Vatican administration in 1901. An excellent linguist, he became a skilled diplomat during his long period as Papal nuncio (ambassador) in Germany from 1917 to 1929. Shortly after becoming a cardinal in 1929, he was recalled to Rome to become Papal secretary of state, the highest office in the Vatican after that of the Pope. As chief adviser to **Pius XI** he played a leading part in negotiating the **Concordat** with **Hitler** in 1933 and in drawing up the Papal encyclical *Mit brennender Sorge*

(1937), which protested against the treatment of the Catholic Church in Germany. He visited several European and American countries before he succeeded Pius XI as Pope in March 1939. As the Nazis had reacted to the 1937 encyclical by intensifying their anti-clerical campaign, Pius tried a conciliatory approach, citing the example of **Leo XIII**, who had ended the conflict with **Bismarck** over the *Kulturkampf*. He wrote to Hitler and expressed his desire for friendly relations between Church and State. Pius did not condemn Germany's invasion of Poland, although he had no hesitation in denouncing the Soviet invasion of Finland. His attitude, he said, would be 'the most conscientious impartiality', though this did not mean 'insensitivity and silence where moral and human considerations demanded an open word'. He hardly lived up to these remarks, as he remained silent at the persecution of the Jews, though he knew what was going on in the death camps and he refused to excommunicate Catholics who were taking part in the **'Final Solution'**. It was later claimed that he was afraid to condemn Nazi atrocities in case there were reprisals against Catholics and as he might lose the loyalty of German Catholics. Pius regarded **communism** as much more dangerous than **Nazism** and in 1949 issued a general excommunication of all Catholics who were members of the Communist Party.

**Platt Amendment** (1901) to the Cuban Constitution made the island a US protectorate. It was drawn up by the American Secretary of War, Elihu Root, but received its name from its sponsor in the US Senate, Orville H. Platt. Cuba was not allowed to make treaties impairing her independence or grant concessions to foreign powers without US approval. The USA was given the right to intervene to preserve Cuba's independence or to maintain law and order. She was also granted the lease of Guantanamo Naval Base, which US forces still occupy. The Cubans were most reluctant to accept the Platt Amendment but were forced to do so, as this was the price of getting rid of American troops, who had occupied the island since the **Spanish–American War** of 1898. They went home in 1902. This Amendment soured relations between the USA and Cuba until it was revoked by the **'Good Neighbor' policy** of Franklin D. **Roosevelt** in 1934.

**Plekhanov, Georgi** (1856–1918). Russian revolutionary and 'the father of Russian **Marxism**'. Plekhanov began his political life as a **Populist** but came to believe that the urban workers rather than the peasantry would bring about revolution in Russia. He became a Marxist and though he was in exile in Geneva from 1880–1917, the influence of his writings spread widely and as late as 1920 **Lenin** acknowledged his debt to Plekhanov. Plekhanov believed that revolution would come in two stages. First there would be a democratic-*bourgeois* revolution against Tsarism, which would get rid of the dominance of the landed nobility. This would enable capitalism to develop fully and would produce a large proletariat (working class), which would make the second stage, a socialist revolution, possible. However, as capitalism was in its infancy in Russia in the 1880s, it might be a long time before there was a socialist revolution. As the Russian proletariat was both small and backward, the intelligentsia would have to organize and rouse the workers.

Plekhanov was a founder of the first Russian revolutionary Marxist organization (1883), which in 1898 merged with other groups to form the Social Democratic Workers' Party. When the party split in 1903 into **Bolsheviks** and **Mensheviks** he tried to bring the factions together again. He drew away from Lenin when Lenin stressed the importance of the peasants in Russian conditions in bringing about revolution. For Plekhanov this was a relapse into the illusions of Populism. He finally broke with Lenin during the **First World War**, when Lenin wanted to turn it into a civil war. Plekhanov supported the war effort and when he returned to Russia in March 1917 became a committed opponent of the Bolsheviks. He condemned their seizure of power in the **October Revolution**.

**Plombières** (July 1858). The site of a secret meeting between **Cavour**, Prime Minister of Piedmont, and the French Emperor **Napoleon III**, who wanted to replace Austrian influence in Italy by that of France. Ignoring the advice of his ministers, Cavour agreed to go to war with Austria, if Austria appeared to be the aggressor against Piedmont. If Austria was defeated Piedmont would acquire Lombardy, Venetia and the Romagna (part of the Papal States). France would acquire Nice and Savoy, which were French-speaking and had been temporarily seized by France during the **French Revolution**. In the war of 1859 the French defeated the Austrians at Magenta and Solferino but there was heavy loss of life, the war was costly and the Prussians were mobilizing on the Rhine. Napoleon, therefore, without consulting Cavour, made an armistice at Villafranca, by which Piedmont would receive Lombardy but not Venetia. As France had not fulfilled the terms of her agreement with Piedmont, she did not acquire Nice and Savoy. She was able to obtain these territories in 1860, in return for recognizing Piedmont's acquisition of central Italy.

**Pobedonostsev, Konstantin** (1827–1907). Pobedonostsev was a professor of law at Moscow University (1860–65) and procurator (chairman) of the Holy Synod (1880–1905), the body which supervised the Orthodox Church. At a time when so much was changing in Western Europe he saw support for Orthodoxy and aristocracy as the only way of preserving Russia's precarious stability. All who were not Orthodox would, he felt, inevitably be disloyal, so he regarded Jews, Catholics and Poles as enemy aliens. A bigoted nationalist, he encouraged the policy of **Russification**. He condemned all 'Western' innovations such as parliaments and freedom of the press, and these included some of the 'Great Reforms' of **Alexander II**. As tutor and adviser to **Alexander III** and **Nicholas II** his ideology was the dominant one in Russian government circles from 1882 to 1905. He had a malign influence in reversing the reforming trend of Alexander II's reign. By his total opposition to change he did most to encourage the revolutionary movements in Russia, which gained increasing strength during his lifetime.

**Pogrom** (Russian, 'devastation'). A virulent, popular outbreak in Russia against religious, racial or national minorities, especially Jews, in which their property was destroyed and many were killed. They were often encouraged by the Tsarist police. The first took place in the Ukraine after the assassination of **Alexander II**. They became more frequent towards the end of the nineteenth century, as the authorities sought to deflect anger directed at the government on to unpopular minorities. The worst pogrom of all took place in 1905, when 1,000 Jews were killed. Pogroms ceased after 1906, though the **anti-Semitism** of the Russian government did not. As a result of persecution many of Russia's seven million Jews (in 1914) emigrated to the USA or joined socialist and revolutionary parties.

**Poincaré, Raymond** (1860–1934). President (1913–20) of the **Third Republic** in France. The son of an engineer in Lorraine, Poincaré studied at the élite *Ecole Polytechnique* before becoming a lawyer and being elected to the Chamber of Deputies in 1887. He served in various ministries from 1893 and entered the Senate ten years later, becoming Prime Minister in 1912. His greatest fear was that France might be isolated as in 1870 and an easy prey for Germany, so he was determined to uphold the **Franco-Russian Alliance** and good relations with England. Elected President in 1913, in spite of the opposition of **Clemenceau**, when the **First World War** began he made a *union sacrée* (sacred union) of all parties. In 1917 he asked his old enemy Clemenceau to become Prime Minister, as he was the man most likely to lead France to victory. When his term as President ended in 1920 he returned to the Senate, where he supported the harsh Versailles settlement (see **Treaty of Versailles**). He became Prime Minister again in 1922 (the first ex-President to be Prime Minister), as he could be relied on to take a strong line against Germany. When she defaulted on payment of **reparations** in 1923, he sent French troops to occupy the **Ruhr**. This was not a success, as it proved costly, taxes had to be raised and the value of the franc fell. Out of office in 1924, he was recalled as Prime Minister in 1926, as the franc had continued to fall. He formed a *Union Nationale*, which included Radicals, and was given power by parliament to rule by decree to end the financial crisis. Poincaré devalued and stabilized the franc at a fifth of its former value, which allowed exports to increase, and began construction of the **Maginot Line** on the German border, all of which brought a modest prosperity to France for the next three years. He retired in 1929 owing to ill-health.

*Politburo.* The chief decision-making body of the **Communist Party of the Soviet Union**. In March 1919 the eighth Party Congress decided that the Central Committee of twenty-seven members was too large to make quick decisions, so a Political Bureau of five (increased to nine in 1925 and ten in 1930) was set up to do this. Its first members were **Lenin**, **Trotsky**, **Stalin**,

**Kamenev** and Krestinsky. In 1952 it was abolished and replaced by a Presidium of thirty-six members. After Stalin's death in 1953 the Presidium was reduced to ten members, very much like the old *Politburo*.

**Polk, James Knox** (1795–1849). Eleventh President of the USA (1845–9). An obscure former Congressman, Polk received the **Democratic Party** nomination for President in 1844 only because a former President, Martin **Van Buren**, was opposed to annexing **Texas**. He was elected at the height of **Manifest Destiny** and worked hard (often eighteen hours a day) to make his presidency a success. His main achievements were in foreign policy. In spite of campaigning with the slogan 'Fifty-four forty (54° 40′) or fight', he compromised with Britain over the **Oregon** boundary dispute and accepted the 49th parallel as the boundary between the USA and Canada in the west. Negotiations were unable to solve the boundary dispute with Mexico, so Polk went to war and at the end of the **Mexican–American War** he acquired a million square miles for the USA, including California and New Mexico, more than any other President obtained, except for Thomas **Jefferson** with his **Louisiana Purchase**. Polk was puritanical and unpopular (his wife banned drinking and dancing at the White House) and wore himself out with overwork. He did not seek re-election and died shortly after his presidency ended.

**Poor Laws** in Britain provided public relief for the destitute. The Elizabethan Poor Law (1597–1601), still in force at the beginning of the nineteenth century, made the parish responsible for supporting the old, sick and insane and for providing work in workhouses for the unemployed. Local rates paid for relief, supervised by unpaid and part-time overseers. In 1795 the **Speenhamland system** was introduced in many counties: it fixed relief on a sliding scale, according to the price of bread and the size of a labourer's family. By 1831, 80 per cent of the money from rates was used for poor relief, which was blamed by the Poor Law Commission for creating the poverty it was supposed to alleviate, as it led to early marriage and larger families. In fact poor relief was a response to population increase, unemployment and low wages rather than their cause, but the Poor Law Amendment Act (1834) reflected the Commission's ideas.

Parishes were to be grouped in Unions to provide workhouses, administered by paid officials under elected guardians of the poor. These local bodies were to be supervised by a central body, the Poor Law Commission, and its inspectors. In order to dissuade the able-bodied from seeking relief, conditions in the workhouses were to be 'less eligible' (i.e. more miserable) than those in the poorest labourer's dwelling. Inmates were therefore to lead a monotonous and regimented life, with harsh discipline. Wives were separated from their husbands and both from their children: they could see each other at meal times but they were not allowed to speak (until 1842). Carlyle saw this piece of class legislation as 'an announcement that whoever will not work ought not to live'. The new Act was based on the belief that people were poor because they were feckless and should therefore be punished for not helping themselves. The workhouses were regarded as little better than prisons and were soon called 'bastilles', places of terror and shame.

There was widespread opposition to the new Poor Law, especially in the north, as workhouses could not possibly cope with a slump in manufacturing industry, which put thousands out of work at the same time, so outdoor relief continued. The Poor Law remained throughout the rest of the nineteenth century, though it was increasingly seen to be inadequate, particularly when Booth in London and **Rowntree** in York showed that a third of the population was living in poverty. In the twentieth century the Poor Law was gradually dismantled, especially by the **Liberal** government (1906–14), which introduced a welfare system based on different principles: the **National Insurance Act** (1911) began social insurance which was gradually extended until it covered everyone in 1946. The **Beveridge** Report (1942) was the foundation of the **Welfare State**, established in Britain by the Labour government between 1945 and 1948. 'At last,' the Foreign Secretary, Ernest **Bevin**, exclaimed in 1948, 'we have buried the Poor Law.'

**Popular Front.** A coalition of **left**-wing parties in France and Spain to oppose the spread of **Fascism**. Fascist Leagues in France, including the *Action Française*, had taken advantage of the Stavisky affair (1934) to attack the Radical government and the **Third Republic**. Communists, who slavishly followed the commands of the **Comintern** and had bitterly attacked Socialists as 'social Fascists', were now ordered by the Comintern to cooperate with anti-Fascist parties. They, therefore, formed with Socialists and Radicals the Popular Front, which won the 1936 elections. As Socialists were the largest party in the coalition, Léon **Blum** was head of the government, the first Socialist to be a French Prime Minister. Immediately he was faced with a series of industrial strikes and sit-ins, which so alarmed employers that they were prepared to make concessions, when Blum brought them together with the **CGT** (trade union federation). The Matignon agreements provided great gains for the workers: wages were raised by an average of 12 per cent, workers were to have two weeks' holiday with pay each year, the working week was to be reduced to forty hours, trade unions were recognized by employers and labour disputes were to be submitted to compulsory arbitration. Blum made other reforms, bringing the Bank of France more under state control and nationalizing the arms industries. These reforms were costly, as was the rearmament programme, so Blum devalued the franc and in January 1937 announced a 'pause' in the reforms. This gave the Communists, who had not joined the ministry but had given it general support, an excuse to attack the government. They also wanted to support the Popular Front in Spain in the **Spanish Civil War**, which had begun in June 1936, and strongly disapproved of Blum's non-intervention. His government fell in June 1937, when the Senate refused to give Blum emergency powers to direct the failing economy. It was replaced by a Radical government, which meant an end to reform. The Popular Front broke down with the Munich agreement of 1938 (see **Czechoslovakian crisis**), condemned by both Socialists and Communists and finally came to an end with the **Nazi–Soviet Pact** (August 1939), when the French Communists obediently accepted the Moscow Line.

In Spain the Popular Front narrowly won the general election of February 1936. It included the Communist Party and the dissident Marxist POUM but its backbone was the Republican–Socialist alliance, which had been in power from 1931 to 1933. Its architect was the republican leader Manuel **Azaña**. Between February and July 1936 the Popular Front governments were undermined by weak republican leadership and by the refusal of the Socialist Party

(**PSOE**), the largest party in the alliance, to participate in the Cabinet. The outbreak of the **Spanish Civil War** in July 1936 transformed the Popular Front. With the disintegration of the republicans, a Socialist–Communist alliance dominated the Front but the bitter rivalry of these two parties undermined the war effort of the Republic and wrecked the Popular Front.

**Population growth.** World population appears to have been fairly stable between the collapse of the Roman Empire in the fifth century AD and the late eighteenth century. From that time there has been a dramatic increase, from 900 million in 1800 to 1,600 million in 1900 and 2,500 million in 1950. In Europe the population grew from 190 million in 1800 to 423 million in 1900 and 550 million in 1950, many of whom took part in **emigration** to North and South America, Australia, New Zealand, South Africa and Siberia. The USA witnessed the most spectacular growth, from four million in 1790 to 106 million in 1920. Whites formed 22 per cent of world population in 1800, 35 per cent in 1930.

Population grew so rapidly because the agricultural revolution produced more food, the **Industrial Revolution** provided more work and the **transport revolution** enabled the American prairies to be opened up and made possible the cheap and rapid transport of food around the world. The countries of Western Europe never faced famine after 1848, though this did not apply to Asia or Russia, where as late as 1892 five million people died of starvation. If the increase in the food supply was the main reason for the rise in population, it was not the only one. Lower death rates resulted from purer water supplies and better sewage disposal, as diseases from infected water (typhoid fever, cholera) largely disappeared: the last cholera epidemic in England was in 1866, in Germany in 1892. **Medical advances** also helped: antiseptics from the 1860s made child-birth safer, vaccination against smallpox and pasteurization of milk decreased infant mortality. From 1890 the birth rate in Western Europe began to decline, as contraception was more widely used and as the realization spread that a higher standard of living could be maintained by having smaller families. At the same time the birth rate was increasing in Asia, as a result of advances in hygiene and medicine and improvements in agriculture (the development of new strains of rice which produced bumper crops, increased irrigation and land reclamation and better transport). The population of Japan doubled between 1872 and 1930, that of India increased by eighty-three million between 1920 and 1940. These increases revived concern about the problems raised by **Malthus**: could food supplies be increased indefinitely to cope with the meteoric rise in population?

**Populist (People's) Party.** US political party (1892–1912). By 1890 the boom period for American farming was over. There was an international crisis of overproduction, with competition coming from Canada, Argentina, Australia and Russia. Farm prices fell and many farmers ran up large debts. Life was hard too in the South, where cotton prices dropped. The Populists appealed to disgruntled western farmers, Southern Negroes and poor whites, who blamed bankers and industrial magnates for their plight. Their 1892 platform called for the unlimited coinage of silver (the resulting inflation would enable the debt-ridden farmers to pay off their creditors), a graduated income tax, an eight-hour day for workers, public ownership of railways and telephones, restrictions on immigration, the secret ballot and the direct election of Senators by the people. All this seemed revolutionary, with its call for extensive government control of the economy. The Populists, as a third party in the 1892 presidential election, polled just over a million votes, under 9 per cent of the total. Populist demands influenced the **Democratic Party** during the depression which began in 1893. Western farming interests won control of the Democratic convention in 1896 and nominated William Jennings **Bryan** as presidential candidate. His Populist platform persuaded the Populists not to put up a separate candidate. The party leaders backed Bryan and Populists moved over to the Democratic Party. The People's Party ceased to exist after 1912, yet it had a lasting influence on the policies of the **Progressive Movement** and the **New Deal**.

**Populists** (*Narodniks*) were not a political party and did not have a coherent doctrine but they formed a widespread radical movement in Russia in the mid-nineteenth century. They arose after Russia's humiliating defeat in the **Crimean War**, grew in importance in the 1860s and 1870s and declined rapidly after the assassination of

Alexander II. They were influenced above all by **Herzen** and **Chernyshevsky** in their belief that Russia could and should avoid the evils of capitalism by building a socialist, democratic and egalitarian society based on the peasant commune or *mir*. The defeat of the 1848 Revolutions in Western Europe convinced them that political rights and parliaments were useless to starving men. As the literary critic Belinsky wrote, 'The people have a need for potatoes but not the least for a constitution.'

Their faith in the *narod*, or people, was a source of strength but also their greatest weakness, as the people continually refused to behave as the Populists expected. In 1874 between 2,500 and 3,000 of the young, educated élite went 'to the people' in the villages. Some went to persuade the peasants to rebel, others to teach them socialist principles. The peasants either ignored them or handed them over to the police. This convinced some Populists that an appeal to the people was useless, so they turned to terrorism, murdering government officials. In 1876 a revolutionary organization was formed which took the name Land and Liberty, though it never had more than 200 members. This split in 1879 over the issue of terrorism. One branch called itself the People's Will. Its members formed secret cells and became professional revolutionaries, obeying without question their leaders. The other group called itself Black Partition, as it wanted all land to be divided up amongst the peasants. Its leader, **Plekhanov**, rejected terror, as it was not likely to be successful and would produce reaction. He moved gradually towards **Marxism**. The greatest success of the People's Will, which had only forty members, was the assassination of Alexander II in 1881. Soon its leaders were executed, exiled or fled abroad and the group ceased to exist, though it greatly influenced later revolutionaries. **Lenin**, as he admitted, followed them in his organization of secret, dedicated revolutionary cells. The direct descendant of the Populists in the twentieth century was the **Socialist Revolutionary Party**.

**Porte, the Sublime,** was a term, used from the eighteenth century, which referred to the door of the grand vizier's official residence in Istanbul (Constantinople) and by extension to the Ottoman government.

**Portsmouth, Treaty of** (September 1905). This ended the **Russo-Japanese War** of 1904–5 and was signed in New Hampshire, owing to the mediation of the President of the USA, Theodore **Roosevelt**. Russia gave up to Japan half of the island of Sakhalin and her lease of Port Arthur, the Liaodong Peninsula and the South Manchurian Railway. Korea was independent, though Japanese supremacy there was recognized and she formally annexed it in 1910. Russia did not pay a war indemnity, as Japan wanted, but she lost all she had gained from China in the last ten years.

**Potsdam Conference** (17 July – 2 August 1945). The last Allied summit meeting of the **Second World War**, held outside Berlin. Since the **Yalta Conference** earlier in the year Franklin D. **Roosevelt** had died and Truman had become President of the USA. During the Conference **Churchill** was defeated in a general election and was replaced by Attlee, so only **Stalin** of the 'Big Three' remained. Germany's surrender in May focused attention on postwar Europe but the agreements reached were vague and tentative, as the Allies differed strongly on major issues. They agreed that an Allied Control Commission, with representatives of the Soviet Union, the USA, Britain and France, should coordinate policy in Germany and that its actions could be vetoed by any power. A body representing all the Allies was set up to administer Berlin. It was agreed that reparations, which were to be in kind, should be imposed on Germany but the amount was not fixed, as the Western Allies, learning the lesson of the Treaty of **Versailles** (1919), feared that if they prevented German economic development, the revival of the European economy would be held up. The territorial decisions reached at Yalta were confirmed: the six million Germans in Poland, Czechoslovakia and Hungary should be resettled in Germany. The Communist-dominated Polish government was recognized after Stalin agreed to include some members of the London-based government-in-exile. He also promised that there would be 'free elections' in all countries liberated by Soviet troops. An International Military Tribunal was to be set up to try war criminals.

**Potsdam Declaration** (26 July 1945) concerned Japan and was issued during the **Potsdam Conference**. It threatened her with 'prompt and utter destruction' unless she surrendered unconditionally, after which there would be a military occupation until a responsible and democratic government was set up. Japan would have to pay reparations, be demilitarized, her war criminals would be punished and she would lose territory in accordance with the Cairo Declaration (see **Cairo Conference**). When Japan rejected the Potsdam Declaration, **atomic bombs** were dropped on **Hiroshima** and Nagasaki to bring an end to the **Pacific War**.

**Potsdam War Council** (8 December 1912). This was called by Kaiser **William II** after he was warned by Lord **Haldane**, British War Secretary, that Britain 'would find it impossible to remain neutral in a continental war resulting from an Austrian invasion of Serbia. Britain was committed to upholding the balance of power in Europe and consequently could not tolerate the crushing of France by Germany's superior military strength.' Naval and military chiefs attended the meeting, to which the Chancellor, **Bethmann-Hollweg**, was not invited. The Kaiser wanted to declare war on England and France at once, whilst Moltke, the Chief of Staff, thought war was 'unavoidable' – 'the sooner the better'. **Tirpitz**, Secretary of State for the Navy, asked for a postponement for eighteen months, until the Kiel Canal was enlarged to take **Dreadnought** battleships and the submarine base was completed at Heligoland. Historians disagree as to the significance of this meeting. The absence of civilian ministers can be interpreted as showing either the dominance of the services in decision-making, or that the meeting was unimportant. Immanuel Geiss asserts that 'All participants at the conference knew that the basic decision for war had been taken and that implementation had only been postponed for practical reasons.' Others maintain that war did not arise in 1914 from deep-laid German plans but resulted from a sudden crisis, the assassination of Archduke Francis Ferdinand at **Sarajevo**.

**Prague, Treaty of** (August 1866), ended the **Austro-Prussian War**. **Prussia** annexed Schleswig-Holstein, **Hanover**, Hesse-Cassel, Frankfurt and Nassau and was now indisputably the dominant power in Germany. For the first time all her territories were in one unit. Austria lost only Venetia (to Italy), as **Bismarck** did not want to humiliate her and make her a permanent enemy. The **German Confederation**, which Austria had dominated since its formation in 1815, came to an end. The states north of the river Main were to form a **North German Confederation** under the leadership of Prussia, so the stage was set for the unification of Germany.

**Prairial, rising of** (1795). A gesture of despair by the *sans-culottes* in Paris. The **Convention** had got rid of price controls, which resulted in massive inflation, made worse by a poor harvest in 1794. There was enormous misery, suicides and death from malnutrition, as scarcity became famine. On 1 Prairial (20 May) 1795, housewives and some National Guards (citizens' militia) invaded the Convention, where there was complete chaos until some loyal National Guards arrived in the evening and cleared the Assembly. The next day 20,000 National Guards surrounded the Convention and aimed their cannon at it but no one was prepared to fire. The rebels presented a petition peacefully and retired after the President of the Convention had made some vague promises. On 3 Prairial the Convention took the offensive. Rebel suburbs were surrounded by 20,000 troops of the regular army, who forced them to give up their arms. A severe repression followed, in which forty-two militants were executed and 6,000 disarmed and arrested. Prairial marked the end of the *sans-culottes* as a political force in the **French Revolution**.

**Primo de Rivera, Miguel** (1870–1930). Military dictator of Spain (1923–30). Born into a well-to-do family in Jerez, Primo de Rivera rose rapidly through the army, partly through the patronage of an influential uncle, and partly through his valiant leadership in battle. Resolute and impulsive, he distinguished himself in the colonial wars in Morocco, Cuba and the Philippines. His wife, who died in childbirth in 1908, produced six children, including José Antonio, future leader of the *Falange Española*.

During the political turmoil of 1917 his uncomplicated political outlook and personal openness made Primo de Rivera an effective spokesman for the anti-élitist, if conservative, *Juntas de Defensa* (Defence Committees or army unions). After 1918, he held various important posts, including the captain-generalship of Valencia, of Madrid and finally of Barcelona. In 1921 he became the Marques de Estella on the death of his uncle and acquired the tax-free status of a grandee.

The political and social crisis after the **First World War** led Primo de Rivera to stage a *coup* attempt in September 1923, which succeeded because of the support of both the King and the army. The dictatorship was greeted with widespread approval. Primo believed that a strict military regime would eliminate corruption and 'social disorder' and establish the conditions for national regeneration. Accordingly, the Cortes and constitutional guarantees were suspended and martial law and censorship enforced.

The ninety-day Military Directory, which Primo had initially hailed as a 'brief parenthesis', lasted until December 1925. During this period there was little domestic reform, though the state administration was greatly centralized and in 1924 the official government party or *Unión Patriótica* (Patriotic Union) was formed. The most notable achievement was the conclusion of the Moroccan War. The victory at Alhumecas in September 1925, followed by the complete pacification of the Protectorate over the next three years, and the climate of economic prosperity, encouraged Primo to extend his rule still further by recasting the political institutions in an authoritarian mould. The Civilian Directory, established in December 1925, was imbued with an authoritarian, nationalist and Catholic-corporatist ideology, with the aim of winning over the conservative classes.

The regenerationist values of Primo and the corporate ideas of his young Finance Minister, José Calvo Sotelo, found expression in the regime's economic policies. Large-scale state intervention, involving public works, tariffs, subsidies, and state monopolies, fostered economic development. Drawing on the Italian Fascist model and eager to undercut the **Left**, the dictatorship also undertook a wide-ranging welfare and labour programme. The socialists collaborated in these schemes, only rejecting them once the dictatorship began to lose political and economic momentum in 1929.

The dictatorship endeavoured to finance its programmes through greater taxes on the propertied classes. The resulting middle-class backlash obliged the regime to resort to public loans, which relied on public confidence to be effective. This illustrated the extent to which the regime's reforms were limited by its social base. By the end of the decade, soaring deficits, inflation, and the fall of the peseta had greatly undermined the dictatorship.

Primo de Rivera was ultimately toppled by the rebellion of the army. His military reforms from 1925 caused many officers to join the civilian opposition and led to the risings of 1926 and 1929. Indeed, the loss of support from the army forced Primo to resign in January 1930. He died in Paris on 16 March from diabetes-related problems.

The Primo de Rivera dictatorship made a deep impression on Spain. The advent of the **Spanish Second Republic** in 1931 was facilitated by the political mobilization encouraged by the regime's rapid modernization, by its dismantling of the political system of the **Restoration**, and by the fact that it discredited the King and army. On the other hand, the ideology of the dictatorship not only inspired the authoritarian **Right** in opposition to the Republic, but also furnished General **Franco** with many of the concepts and principles of his own military regime.

**Primrose League.** Named after **Disraeli**'s favourite flower, it was formed in 1883 by Lord Randolph **Churchill** to promote **Tory Democracy** by mobilizing working-class support for the **Conservative Party** under the direction of the landed gentry. Conservative working-men's clubs had offered cheap 'baccy, billiards and beer'. The Primrose League offered tea and sandwiches on the lawns of country houses, where the lower classes could mix with the wealthy. Dances, brass bands and evening shows were organized in rural areas, where there was little entertainment. By 1900 there were 2,300 'habitations' (branches) with one and a half million members, nine-tenths of whom were working class. The League made no attempt to influence Conservative policy but was a valuable support for the Party, acting as its propaganda wing and canvassing for Conservative candidates at elections.

**Progressive Bloc.** A group of deputies from all parties in the Russian **Duma**, who joined together in 1915. With **Milyukov** as their leader, they asked the Tsar to appoint a ministry which would enjoy the confidence of the nation (not, as some wanted, a ministry responsible to the Duma). This had the support of most of the Tsar's ministers. Sazonov, the Foreign Minister, declared that 'For interests of State we have to support this Bloc, which is essentially moderate. If it falls apart, we shall have one far more to the **left**.'

**Nicholas II**, however, refused to make any concessions and on 3 September he prorogued the Duma. Milyukov later identified this as 'the precise moment' when revolution became inevitable.

**Progressive Movement.** A wave of reform that swept over the USA, affecting both major political parties, between 1900 and 1920. The origins of the movement lie in the 1890s: the concentration of capital and economic power in trusts, the spread of political corruption and the increasingly bitter conflict between capital and labour, as shown in the **Homestead Strike** of 1892. Most of the leaders of the movement were urban, affluent and educated: they did not want to overturn the existing political and economic system but wanted to make it fairer. Some of their ideas were derived from the **Populist Party**, though the Progressives were more concerned with the cities than the countryside. Though they tried to help the victims of industrialization – slum-dwellers and exploited workers – they were not socialists and did not form an organized and united movement. Their aims were varied: increased government regulation of the economy, tariff reduction, **Prohibition, women's suffrage**, municipal reform, the improvement of working conditions and the regulation or abolition of child labour.

They had some success in clearing up local government at state and municipal level. State legislatures passed laws to regulate industry and protect workers and to diminish the influence of political bosses and pressure groups. The initiative gave voters (if they were 5 per cent of the electorate) the right to insist on the consideration of particular measures: the referendum submitted legislative proposals to a direct, popular vote and recall allowed elected officials to be removed before their full term of office had ended. By 1918 twenty states had adopted the initiative and referendum, twelve the recall. The direct primary was even more widely adopted, first by Wisconsin in 1903: it allowed voters, rather than party bosses, to choose party candidates. Twenty-nine states had done this by 1912. An extension of this idea was the direct election of US senators, which became the seventeenth amendment to the Constitution in 1913. Child welfare was another important concern of the Progressive Movement. The 'Kids' Judge', Ben B. Lindsey of Denver, Colorado, treated young offenders not as criminals but as the product of a bad environment, who needed help rather than punishment. By 1910 children's courts modelled on his were in every major city. By 1925 twenty-five states had passed laws to restrict child labour. These changes marked the influence of new educational theories. John Dewey in *School and Society* (1899) rejected classroom authoritarianism and rote learning and stressed child-centred education, 'learning by doing', and the close ties of school and community.

At a national level the Progressive Movement was led by men like Theodore **Roosevelt** and Woodrow **Wilson**, who secured the passage of such measures as the Pure Food and Drugs Act, the Hepburn Act regulating the railroads and the constitutional amendments which provided for a federal income tax and votes for women. The election of Warren G. Harding as President in 1920 marked the end of the Progressive Movement for the time being. La Follette tried to revive it with his short-lived Progressive Party in 1924 but Progressive ideals had to wait for realization until the **New Deal** in the 1930s.

**Prohibition.** A movement to prevent the sale of alcohol in the USA. A Prohibition Party was formed in 1869 but the main pressure group at first was the Women's Christian Temperance Union (1874), founded by Frances Willard, who wanted to protect the home against drunken husbands and fathers. The wife of President Hayes supported it by refusing to serve alcoholic drinks at the White House and so became known as 'Lemonade Lucy'. Carry Nation, who used a hatchet to destroy saloons, was a more militant crusader. The American Anti-Saloon League, an organization of employers, became the most powerful pressure group. Many **Populist Party** and **Progressive Movement** reformers also supported Prohibition. By 1900 five rural states, all in New England, had adopted Prohibition and by 1915 two-thirds of the USA, with half its population, was 'dry'. When the USA entered the **First World War** patriotic arguments for Prohibition were added to religious and moral ones. It was said that Prohibition would conserve grain and make industry more efficient. The eighteenth amendment to the Constitution, prohibiting the sale and manufacture of alcohol, was passed by Congress in December 1917 and ratified by the states in January 1919: the Volstead Act of 1920 provided for its enforcement.

Thousands of illicit stills and millions of gallons of wine and spirits were destroyed but there were never enough agents to enforce the law: 1,520 in 1920 and 2,836 in 1930. They were badly paid, so many took bribes. 'Bootleggers' smuggled in liquor from the West Indies, Canada and Mexico and 'speakeasies' (illegal saloons) prospered under the protection of city bosses: there were 32,000 saloons in New York in 1929, twice the number than before Prohibition. The worst effect of Prohibition was that it led to a vast increase in organized crime. There were huge profits to be made, so gangsters established their own breweries, distilleries and distribution networks. Their gangs murdered competitors and blackmailed the owners of 'speakeasies' to pay 'protection' money. When they had established a monopoly of the liquor trade, they moved into gambling, prostitution and drugs. Their vast wealth enabled them to bribe police and judges and to dominate many city governments. Johnny Torrio, Chicago's underworld boss in the early 1920s, boasted: 'I own the police.' In the late 1920s Al **Capone** was the leading gangster and was responsible for many of the 500 gang murders in Chicago between 1927 and 1930. Nearly all were unpunished. Prohibition had another unfortunate effect in encouraging hypocrisy and disrespect for the law. President Warren Harding paid lip service to Prohibition but drank heavily in the White House: for the first time it became fashionable to defy the law.

As Prohibition could not be enforced effectively there was a growing demand for its repeal. Some objected to Prohibition because it was an infringement of personal liberty, others opposed it on economic grounds. The Association Against the Prohibition Amendment, financed by millionaire businessmen, thought a tax on alcohol would allow income tax to be reduced. The **Great Depression** provided more support for abolition, which would create thousands of jobs and benefit the farmer, while a liquor tax would increase state and federal revenues. In the 1932 presidential election the Democrats supported repeal – 'A New Deal and a pint of beer for everyone' – and when they had won passed the twenty-first amendment to the Constitution, which repealed the eighteenth. By December 1933 this was ratified and control of drinking passed to the states. Only seven, mainly in the South, voted to keep it, but all had abandoned Prohibition by 1966.

**Proudhon, Pierre Joseph** (1809–65). French anarchist. A *petit-bourgeois* – his father was an inn-keeper – Proudhon was completely self-educated. He took part in the 1848 revolution in Paris, won a seat in the Assembly and voted against the Constitution 'just because it was a constitution'. Disillusioned with the revolution, as it did not bring about any social changes, he spent three years in prison for a violent written attack on the President of the **Second Republic**, Louis Napoleon Bonaparte (later **Napoleon III**). On his release he continued to be a fearless journalist, who spent the years 1858–62 in exile in Belgium to avoid imprisonment in France. Proudhon put forward the first systematic arguments in favour of **anarchism**. He abhorred exploitation and authority and wanted liberty for all to do as they pleased, provided they did not harm others. By removing economic exploitation and government repression, people would be free. 'The ideal republic is positive anarchy,' he wrote. 'It is liberty free from all its shackles.' He wanted to destroy the machinery of the state, because the police, army and civil service were under the control of the *bourgeoisie*, whose rule was unjust and immoral. His most famous remark 'Property is theft' did not refer to personal property acquired by one's own labour for one's own use, but property based on interest, rent and the 'surplus value' of labour used in manufacturing. Proudhon's ideal society was a federal one of small communities, which cooperated to run their own affairs without any central state direction. Men and women would exchange the goods they produced for the goods they needed, so money would not be necessary. This classless society would be brought about not by revolution but by the voluntary agreement of the workers. The ideas of Proudhon were applied by the **Paris Commune** of 1871 and deeply influenced French socialist and anarchist thought for the rest of the century. His emphasis on decentralization, cooperation and the reduction of government power appealed to self-reliant peasant farmers and artisans who owned their own workshops. When the First International (1864) met not long before Proudhon's death, his followers clashed with those of the more authoritarian **Marx** and split the International.

**Provisional Government.** The Russian government in 1917 between the fall of the Tsar in the **February Revolution** and the **Bolshevik** seizure of power in the **October Revolution**. At first it was composed of liberals and dominated by the **Kadets** and their leader, **Milyukov**, who was Foreign Minister. There was only one socialist minister, the **Socialist Revolutionary Party** lawyer Alexander **Kerensky**, who was Minister of Justice. A **Soviet** was set up in **Petrograd** at the same time as the Provisional Government. Real power lay with the Soviet, especially after it issued Order Number One, which set up elected soldiers' committees. These, rather than officers, were to control arms and military discipline. Guchkov, the War Minister, sadly noted that 'The Provisional Government does not possess any real power: its directions are carried out only to the extent that is permitted by the Soviet, which enjoys all the essential elements of real power, since the troops, the railroads, the post and telegraph are all in its hands.' In the early months there was little conflict between the Provisional Government and the Soviet, as nearly all the demands of the Soviet were accepted: a political amnesty, abolition of the death penalty, freedom of the press, religion and association and the calling of a Constituent Assembly, to be elected by universal male suffrage, to decide the country's future. Conflict eventually arose over war aims: Milyukov wanted the war to continue so that Russia would obtain Constantinople and the **Straits**, as had been agreed by the Allies in 1915. The Soviet called a demonstration against this and rejected all annexations. Milyukov resigned and the crisis was resolved on 5 May only when leaders of the Soviet joined the government, which became a liberal–socialist coalition.

The crippling weakness of the Provisional Government was that it put off all important decisions until the Constituent Assembly met (elections were not held until November). Yet there were pressing problems: peasants wanted land, soldiers wanted an end to the war, the nationalities wanted independence or autonomy and the workers were becoming more militant, as the economic situation deteriorated. The Bolsheviks, on the other hand, after **Lenin** returned from Switzerland and issued his **April Theses**, put forward a radical programme with mass appeal and proposed immediate action.

Bolshevik influence spread rapidly. They dominated the factory committees in Petrograd by May and their influence increased in the army after the failure of the **Brusilov offensive**. They suffered a set-back in the **July Days**, when an anti-government demonstration was followed by persecution of the Bolsheviks, who were forced to go underground. They were saved and their reputation restored by the **Kornilov affair**, when General Kornilov failed in his attempt to establish a military dictatorship. This destroyed the reputation of Kerensky and the Provisional Government and led to the Bolshevik seizure of power in the **October Revolution**.

**Prussia.** In the eighteenth century Prussia was renowned for the size and efficiency of its army, especially under Frederick the Great. It was a poor, backward area, whose population was hard-working and disciplined. In 1815 Prussia was one of the greatest beneficiaries of the Congress of **Vienna** and became more of a German state, as she handed over most of her Polish territories to Russia and received part of Saxony, the Rhineland and Westphalia. Her population doubled. These areas were industrial and rich in minerals and, together with the *Zollverein* (which began as a Prussian customs union), enabled her to become the main economic power in Germany. The Kings of Prussia pursued a cautious and conservative foreign policy and accepted Austrian leadership of the Holy Roman Empire and later of the **German Confederation**. All this changed with **Bismarck**, who used the Prussian army to unite Germany, first by defeating Austria in the **Austro-Prussian War** of 1866, which added yet more territory to Prussia and set up the **North German Confederation**. The South German states joined the Confederation to form the **German Empire** after Prussia's victory in the **Franco-Prussian War** of 1870–71.

Although Germany was now united, she was still dominated by Prussia. The King of Prussia became the German Emperor, with the German army under his command; the Minister-President of Prussia became the German Chancellor and the imperial administration was staffed by Prussians. The Bundesrat, which represented the German states and had the sole right to initiate legislation, was under Prussian control, as her representatives had seventeen of the forty-three votes there. In size and economic power Prussia exceeded all the other states of the Empire put together. Within Prussia the small minority of *Junkers* dominated the army, the civil service, the judiciary and the Prussian parliament, where there was a three-tier franchise, based on property qualifications, so that the richest elected most of the deputies. The Prussian *Junkers* ensured that their dominance, and that of the Crown, continued in the Empire: they were able to imbue the whole of Germany with their military ethos of hierarchy, order and obedience. After Germany's defeat in 1918 the boundaries of Prussia were much reduced by the Treaty of **Versailles** but she was still the largest state in the **Weimar Republic**. She was a model republican government from 1920–32 under a coalition of the **Social Democratic** and **Centre Parties** until von **Papen** removed them from office. From 1933 Prussia was under **Nazi Party** control, like all the other *Länder* (states). The Prussian state was abolished in 1947, when much of its territory was divided between Poland, the Soviet Union and the German Democratic Republic.

**PSOE** (*Partido Socialista Obrero Español*) (Spanish Workers' Socialist Party). Spanish socialism was dominated until 1925 by the Madrid typographer, Pablo Iglesias. This austere and brooding figure founded the PSOE in 1879 and the UGT, the Socialist-led trade union movement, in 1888. During this period the party grew slowly, being characterized by its organizational rigidity and theoretical poverty.

As a result of an electoral alliance with the Republicans, in 1910 the PSOE was able to elect Pablo Iglesias as its first deputy to the Cortes. Although reformism dominated within the Socialist movement, the general crisis of 1917 led the Socialists to undertake a revolutionary general strike. Its failure and the harsh repression which followed unleashed a fierce three-year struggle between the reformists and the sympathizers of the Bolshevik revolution. In 1921 the revolutionaries left the PSOE to form the first Spanish Communist Party (PCE).

In the 1920s the UGT collaborated with the dictatorship of General **Primo de Rivera** (1923–30), in an effort to consolidate its position within the state and to enhance its support, at the cost of its anarchist and, to a lesser extent, communist rivals, both of whom were vigorously repressed by the regime. However, the Socialists distanced themselves from the dictatorship in time to join the broad anti-monarchical coalition embodied in the San Sebastian Pact of August 1930.

Under the **Spanish Second Republic** of 1931–6 the PSOE was the leading political party on the **Left**. The Socialists were divided over the Republic between 'worker corporativists', who saw improvements in trade-union conditions as the principal objective, and 'political reformists', for whom the establishment of liberal democracy was the overriding aim. From 1931–3 the PSOE formed the backbone of the reformist Republican–Socialist administrations that attempted to modernize Spain. Many Socialists were embittered by the failure of parliamentary reform, in the face of the opposition of the conservative classes. Consequently the PSOE withdrew from the Republican–Socialist alliance, and, without allies, lost over fifty seats in the 1933 general election.

Under the Centre-Right administration of 1933–5 many of the reforms of the Republic's first two years were reversed. In response sectors of the Socialist base became increasingly militant, leading to the agricultural strike of June 1934 and the general strike and Asturian Rising of October 1934. After the October defeat, divisions inside the Socialists hardened between the 'revolutionary' stance of Large Caballero and the moderate parliamentarianism of Indalecio Prieto. Although the PSOE formed part of the victorious **Popular Front** coalition in the general election of February 1936, the new all-republican government was undermined by the revolutionary posturing of the Socialist left-wing. The schism within the Socialist camp prevented the moderate leader, Indalecio Prieto, from accepting the premiership in May 1936, though this might have thwarted the military rising of July 1936, which led to the **Spanish Civil War**.

After the outbreak of Civil War, Largo Caballero formed a Socialist-dominated government in September 1936. However, badly divided amongst themselves, the Socialists were soon overshadowed by a united and disciplined Communist Party, whose reputation was enhanced by the Soviet aid to the Republic – all the more crucial in the absence of support from Britain and France. After Largo Caballero resigned as Prime Minister in May 1937, faced by the concerted opposition of Communists, moderate Socialists, and republicans, another Socialist, Juan **Negrín**, became Premier. He became increasingly reliant on the PCE, partly because of the necessity of guaranteeing Soviet military aid, and partly because of the paralysing division in the socialist ranks. Defeat in the Civil War was to devastate the socialist movement for decades.

**Pullman Strike** (1894). The Pullman Palace Car Company manufactured sleeping cars, which it hired to the railroads in the USA. During the depression of 1893–4 it cut the wages of its workers by 25 per cent. The workers went on strike and were supported by the militant American Railway Union, led by Eugene V. Debs. When the union boycotted railroads using Pullman cars, there was a major railroad strike, which paralysed traffic out of Chicago and spread across the country. The railroad companies appealed for the federal government to intervene, so the Attorney-General obtained a 'blanket' injunction prohibiting obstruction of the railroads or US mails. President Cleveland then sent in federal troops, in spite of the protests of the Governor of Illinois, who thought they had been sent in to break the strike rather than to preserve order. During rioting in Chicago seven strikers were killed by federal troops and the strike was broken. Debs was sent to prison for six months for defying the injunction and became a socialist. The strike showed that the government would support the employers in any clash with labour and it was the first time an injunction had been used to break a strike. Henceforth it was to be the employers' favourite weapon in labour disputes until it was outlawed by the Norris–La Guardia Act of 1932. The **trade unions** were incensed, as the federal court based its injunction on the Sherman Anti-Trust Act, saying that the American Railway Union was an illegal combination in restraint of trade.

**Putsch.** The German word for *coup*, which is usually used for right-wing attempts to seize power in Germany, such as the **Kapp** *Putsch* of 1920 or Hitler's **Munich** *Putsch* of 1923.

**Puyi** (1906–67). Last Emperor of the **Qing dynasty** in China. Puyi became Emperor at the age of two but was forced to abdicate in February 1912, after the **Chinese Revolution** of 1911. The Republican government allowed him to live in the Forbidden City, where he became the focus for a monarchist revival, and in July 1917 he became Emperor again for twelve days after a *coup*. When he was compelled to leave Beijing (Peking) in 1924, he was given protection by the Japanese, who made him head of their puppet government in **Manchukuo** in 1934. At the end of the **Pacific War** he was captured by the Russians, who handed him over to the Communist Chinese People's Republic in 1950. After a period of rehabilitation he became a Chinese citizen and worked as a gardener and librarian.

**Qajar dynasty.** Ruled Persia from 1794–1925. The Qajars came to power after a period of anarchy and never effectively consolidated their position. The provinces were divided into ethnic and tribal factions, in which chieftains were more important than the central government and were largely independent of state control, as they held the land and had the right to collect taxes. The *ulama* (religious leaders) were another severe constraint on the authority of the Shah. They claimed that only a scholar deeply learned in the *Sharia* (Muslim law) could rule and that they were the true leaders of the Muslim community. As they controlled education, justice and charities, Fath Ali Shah, who ruled from 1797 to 1834, deferred to them. In the nineteenth century the Qajars suffered from the attention of Russia and Britain. They lost Georgia and most of the Caucasus to Russia, changes which alarmed Britain, who wanted to keep Russia away from the Persian Gulf and the borders of India. In the **Anglo-Russian Entente** (1907) the two countries divided Iran into two spheres of influence: Russian in the north, British in the south, with a buffer zone in the middle. They effectively controlled Persia, though it retained a nominal independence. Western domination prompted the Qajars, especially Nasir al-Din Shah, who ruled from 1848 to 1896, to modernize and strengthen the state, just as **Muhammad Ali** had done in Egypt and **Mahmud II** in Turkey. He did not have a great deal of success. Tribal groups resisted centralization; the *ulama* opposed secular schools and law courts and concessions to Christian missionaries, which allowed them to set up schools and hospitals in Persia; merchants and artisans objected to European imports. *Ulama*, inspired by the **Russian Revolution of 1905**, took the lead in demanding the calling of a constituent assembly in 1905. This created a Constitution which lasted until 1979, in which the Shah was subordinate to parliament and Islam was declared to be the official religion. The government had to enforce the *Sharia* and a committee of *ulama* was to decide whether new legislation conformed with it. The new Constitution was opposed by wealthy landowners and the Shah, who in 1907–8 used Cossacks to close the parliament. Supporters of the Constitution resumed power from 1909–11 but the coalition of liberals and *ulama* soon broke up, as the liberals wanted to disestablish Islam and introduce secular education. In 1911 Russia intervened to destroy the new regime and restore the authority of the Shah. From 1911–25 there was near anarchy in Persia, which was occupied by British and Russian troops during the **First World War**. There was a succession of ineffective governments until Reza Khan (see **Reza Shah Pahlavi**), an officer in the Cossack Brigade, seized power and brought the Qajar dynasty to an end.

**Qing (Ch'ing or 'Pure') dynasty**. Ruled China from 1644 to 1912. They were Manchus, originally nomadic and hunting tribes of the north-east, beyond the Great Wall, with a different language and culture from those of China. The Qing, like earlier conquerors of China, were soon assimilated by Chinese civilization. Qing Emperors learned to speak and write Chinese and the Manchu language gradually ceased to be used: by the nineteenth century there was little to distinguish the Qing from a pure Chinese dynasty. They were soon accepted by the Chinese élite of scholar-officials, as they continued to recruit their own officials from the gentry. The Qing became one of the most successful Chinese dynasties by extending their control to Mongolia, Tibet and part of Turkestan (which later became the province of Xinjiang): none of these areas had been part of the Ming Empire (1368–1644) and no Chinese dynasty had previously held Tibet. Neighbouring kingdoms, Korea, Vietnam, Nepal and Siam, all sent tribute to the Qing. By the beginning of the nineteenth century the Chinese Empire was twice as large as it had been in the sixteenth century but the peace and prosperity which existed for most of the eighteenth century had resulted in a vast increase of population. Between 1700 and 1800 the population of China rose from 150 to 350 million and by 1859 it was 430 million. This far exceeded the amount of cultivable land available and by the early nineteenth century the Qing dynasty was in decline, made worse by corruption in the bureaucracy. Public works like irrigation channels were neglected and so natural disasters like floods and drought could not be contained. The result was a series of peasant insurrections, the most important of which was the **Taiping rebellion**, which the dynasty suppressed only with great difficulty and at the cost of enormous destruction. Another threat to the dynasty came from the Western powers, who demanded that China be opened up to foreign trade. Their defeat of China in the **Opium Wars** (1839–42 and 1856–60) and her defeat by Japan in the **Sino–Japanese War** (1894–5) showed just how feeble the Qing dynasty had become. Half-hearted efforts at reform in the **Self-Strengthening movement** were ineffective, so that the Qing were faced in the **Boxer Rising** (1899–1900) by an anti-Qing and anti-foreign movement. Belated efforts at reform by the Empress Dowager **Cixi** failed to prevent the collapse of the dynasty in the **Chinese Revolution** of 1911. The last Qing Emperor, **Puyi**, was forced to abdicate in 1912.

**Quisling, Vidkun** (1887–1945). Norwegian Fascist. Quisling was Minister of Defence (1931–3) in Norway but his dislike of democracy led to his forming the *Nasjonal Samling* (National Unity) movement in imitation of the Nazis (see **Nazism**). In the 1933 election his *Samling* party got only 2.2 per cent of the votes and no seats. He was the discredited leader of an almost extinct party when war broke out and was one of the few Norwegians to welcome the German invasion of Norway in 1940. For four and a half years he held office under the Germans and from 1942 was their puppet Prime Minister. Real power was exercised by German officials, with whom he quarrelled and who took no notice of him. Morose and stubborn, he was heartily disliked by his compatriots, membership of his party rising from 7,000 in 1939 to only 43,000 in 1943. Quisling helped to round up Jews for deportation and after the war was tried and condemned, as a result of retroactive legislation passed by the Norwegian government-in-exile. He was the first Norwegian to be executed since 1876, although the verdict was a popular one. 'Quisling' rapidly became synonymous with 'traitor' or 'fifth columnist' (see **Fifth Column**).

**'Quit India' Campaign** (1942). An attempt by the **Indian National Congress** to make India ungovernable and so secure independence from Britain. With Japan threatening India's borders, Congress saw its opportunity to put pressure on the British government of India, and in August 1942 adopted a 'Quit India' resolution, which sanctioned 'a mass struggle on non-violent lines'. **Gandhi** was put in charge of the movement but the government reacted quickly and within a week all Congress leaders had been arrested. Nevertheless, strikes and demonstrations paralysed the cities, whilst in the countryside railway lines were torn up. The Viceroy regarded the campaign as 'by far the most serious rebellion since that of 1857' (the **Indian Mutiny**). Yet there was no overall plan and by using the army the government contained the movement within four months, though at a cost, according to official figures, of 1,028 killed and 3,125 seriously injured. Unofficial figures put the dead at between four and ten thousand. Although the campaign failed, it was a warning to Britain that she could not hope to control India for much longer.

**Radetzky, Josef Wenzel, Count of Radetz** (1766–1858). Austrian field marshal. Radetzky fought against the Turks in the Balkans (1788–9), was wounded as a cavalry officer in the **Napoleonic Wars** at Marengo (1800), took part in the battle of Wagram (1809) and helped to plan the battle of **Leipzig** (1813). From 1809–29 he was Chief of the Austrian General Staff and then served mainly in Italy, where he was Commander-in-Chief from 1831. When there was a rising in Milan, during the **Revolutions of 1848**, Radetzky had to withdraw his troops from the city after five days of fighting: 'the most terrible decision of my life'. The Austrians were driven out of Venice too and Charles Albert of Piedmont declared war on Austria, so Radetzky withdrew to the Quadrilateral (the fortresses of Mantua, Verona, Peschiera and Legnano). There he built up his forces and when Charles Albert gave battle at Custozza, Radetzky crushed him in July, as he did at Novara in March 1849, when Piedmont re-entered the fray. He then starved Venice into surrender and so was responsible for the complete success of Austrian arms in northern Italy. Governor-General of Lombardy-Venetia until 1857, he was ninety-one when he retired. Adored by his troops, Radetzky was one of Austria's greatest generals.

**Radical Republic** (1899–1940) in France was one of the most stable and conservative societies in Europe, yet was noted for its rapid change-over of governments. Hardly any of these could be formed without the support of the Radicals, who were provided with the new doctrine of solidarism by Léon Bourgeois in *La Solidarité* (1896). In this book he sought a middle way between **socialism** and capitalism, in which cooperation would replace *laissez-faire*. The Radical programme, approved at the Radicals' Party Congress in 1907, rejected both class struggle and *laissez-faire* and approved of State intervention to provide social justice for the old and the sick. The Radicals were united only in their **anti-clericalism**, given a great boost by Combes (Prime Minister from 1902–5), who dissolved many religious orders, prohibited their teaching and prepared the way for the separation of Church and State. Socialists had supported Radical governments but the **Second International** condemned this policy, so from 1905 they were in opposition. This was the time when the **CGT** (trade-union federation) supported revolutionary **syndicalism**. There was a wave of strikes which Radical governments under **Clemenceau** and **Briand** crushed ruthlessly. After the fall of Briand (1911) there were seven Cabinets in three years, but when the **First World War** began party politics were suspended in the 'sacred union', and soon there were socialist ministers in the government. In the 1919 election there was a sweeping victory for the **Right** and a conservative majority in parliament for the first time since the Constitution of 1875. **Poincaré** wanted strict adherence to the Treaty of **Versailles** and occupied the **Ruhr** (1923) when Germany defaulted on **reparations**. This was costly for France, so in 1924 the *Cartel des Gauches* (a left-wing coalition) came to power and pursued a more conciliatory policy towards Germany, typified by the treaties of **Locarno**. The **Great Depression** affected France later than other European countries, but by 1934 the Action Française and Fascist leagues sought to take advantage of the Stavisky affair to undermine the **Third Republic**. The danger they represented brought together anti-Fascist forces, including the Communists, in the **Popular Front** (1936). In the elections of that year the Socialists became the largest party in parliament for the first time and Léon **Blum** became the first Socialist Prime Minister. After the fall of **France** the deputies who met at Vichy (see **Vichy France**) – and voted by 569 to 80 to end parliamentary democracy and the Third Republic in July 1940 – were the same deputies who had been elected in the Popular Front in 1936.

**Radical Republican Party** (Spain) (1908–36). The origins of the Radical Republican Party lie in the revolutionary working-class movement founded in Barcelona during the early years of the twentieth century by the Republican journalist and populist politician, Alejandro Lerroux. Mythologized by his fiery anticlerical demagogy, Lerroux created the first 'modern' political party in Spain. This brought to an end the desultory and faction-ridden politics of the Republican movement since the First Republic of 1873.

In 1908 Lerroux formed the Radical Republican Party. The climate of opinion which led to the Tragic Week of July 1909 was created to a great extent by the inflammatory anticlerical propaganda of the Radicals. The corruption scandal of 1910 over the Radical administration in Barcelona was the greatest single disaster in the party's entire history: it was expelled from the recently formed Republican–Socialist Coalition and its plans for a national organization suffered an irreversible setback.

During the **First World War**, the increasingly conservative Lerroux campaigned for intervention on behalf of the Allies. His pro-interventionist stance was partly designed to suit the varied business interests, to which he and his Barcelona entourage increasingly dedicated themselves. The Radical leader's conservatism became more marked during the widespread labour unrest of 1918–21, when he sought power as the saviour of the middle classes. In 1923 Lerroux offered to become the civilian figurehead of the military dictatorship established by General **Primo de Rivera**.

During the 1920s two new Republican parties emerged in reaction to the patronage politics and populist agenda of the Radical Party: Republican Action in 1925 and the Radical–Socialist Party in 1929. They aimed to provide the Republican movement with a more progressive and modern content. Yet on the advent of the **Spanish Second Republic** in 1931 the Radical Party remained the oldest and by far the largest of the Republican parties. It left the Republican–Socialist government in December 1931 over the continuing participation of the Socialists. From 1931–3 it was the principal source of opposition to the reforms of the progressive Republican–Socialist administrations under Manuel **Azaña**. Lerroux was even prepared to become the civilian figurehead of a military regime, had the *coup d'état* of General Sanjurjo in August 1932 proved successful.

From December 1933 to October 1935 the Radical Party ruled the Republic, in alliance with the non-Republican **Right**. In exchange for carrying out the minimum programme of the Right, the Radicals were granted privileged access to the public sector. But collaboration with the proto-fascist CEDA caused a major Radical split in May 1934. Moreover, the entry of the CEDA into the government, in October 1934, led to a general strike and a rising in Asturias. Unable to consolidate its support through constructive reform, the Radical Party was increasingly dominated by its right-wing allies. By the time it fell from power in late 1935, through financial scandals, the party was already on the verge of collapse.

The Radical Party played a pivotal role in the destruction of the Second Republic. The Radicals' inability to develop a strategy in line with their centrist appeal condemned them to an alliance with the non-Republican Right and ultimate political extinction. Consequently, the failure of Radical 'centrism' contributed significantly to the political polarization of the Republic. The resulting breakdown of the regime culminated in the **Spanish Civil War**.

**Railways.** The first railway that used a steam locomotive was the British Stockton to Darlington line (1825), followed in 1830 by the Liverpool to Manchester line, on which Stephenson's *Rocket* was put into operation. In the second half of the nineteenth century railways were built all over the world. The first **transcontinental railroad** was completed in the USA in 1869; there were four by 1893. By linking the Atlantic and Pacific coasts they created a huge market and made possible the exploitation of natural resources which made the USA the greatest industrial nation and the largest food producer in the world. The **Canadian Pacific Railway** (1885) had a comparable effect in Canada. The **Trans-Siberian Railway**, begun in 1891 but not completed until 1914, opened up Siberia and linked Moscow with Vladivostok on the Pacific. In 1870 railways were almost wholly confined to Europe and the USA: there were 60,000 miles of track in Europe; 56,300 in the USA and Canada, 9,100 in the rest of the world. This situation had changed by 1911, when 175,000 miles, out of a world network of 657,000 miles, were outside Europe and North America.

Railways had a marked effect on the **Industrial Revolution** and agricultural revolution. They provided a large market for the iron, steel and coal industries and stimulated the development of civil engineering (for bridges, tunnels, viaducts) and of mechanical engineering (for engines and rolling stock). As the railways could carry bulky goods (e.g. coal and iron ore) quickly and cheaply, they enabled industry to concentrate in certain areas, such as the Ruhr and the Ukraine. Capital, which had been tied up in the transit of goods (it took two years for the pig iron of the Urals to reach St Petersburg before the railways were built), was now freed. The railways also aided agriculture, as perishable goods (fruit, milk, vegetables) could be moved long distances quickly, thus opening new markets and making specialized production possible, such as dairy farming in Denmark. Wild price fluctuations were eliminated, as were the dangers of famine, last experienced in Western Europe in 1845–7. Success or failure in war came to depend, at least partially, on railways, as the **American Civil War** showed and as **Moltke** was quick to appreciate. By breaking down the isolation of communities, they helped to promote national consciousness and social mobility. Railways brought about the growth of suburbia and of dormitory towns round the great conurbations such as London and Paris. They also made the penny post possible in 1840 and the seaside holiday (the Brighton line was completed in 1841), and so affected the way people could spend their leisure.

**Raj** (Hindi, 'rule'). British rule in India, especially from 1858, when the Crown took over control from the **East India Company**, until independence in 1947. India was governed by a Viceroy in India and a Secretary of State in London and was administered by the Indian civil service. This was created in 1853 with entry by competitive examination, in which there was supposed to be no racial discrimination, but examinations were held in London so only a handful of Indians before 1914 held high-ranking posts, though they filled all the lower positions. A few thousand British officials could not hope to control millions of Indians (there were 305 million in 1921, 400 million in 1941) without the cooperation of their natural leaders. This was obtained in the princely states (30 per cent of the continent with about a quarter of the population) by leaving them in control of their internal affairs, bestowing honours upon their rulers and impressing them with the might of the Raj by occasional magnificent *darbars*. Muslims (about 20 per cent of the population) were encouraged by their leaders such as **Sayyid Ahmad Khan** to support the Raj, as a democratic, independent India would mean a Hindu India, in which the rights of Muslims might be ignored. High-caste Hindus, educated in English, who formed the **Indian National Congress** in 1885, admired much about British rule, especially its imposition of law and order, and at first sought a greater share in running the country rather than independence. Some nationalists like **Tilak** wanted more active opposition to the Raj but they failed in 1907 to take control of Congress, which remained under **Gokhale** and the 'moderates' up to the **First World War**.

India was of enormous benefit to Britain: the Indian army was, as Lord **Salisbury** told parliament in 1867, 'an English Barrack in the Oriental seas from which we may draw any number of troops without paying for them'. The Indian army, paid for by Indian taxes, was used by the Raj before 1914 in the **Anglo-Afghan War** of 1878–8, the **Anglo-Burmese War** of 1885–6, the expedition to Tibet in 1903–4 as well as in China, South Africa and the Pacific. India was important too to the British economy, as from 1840–1914 it was Britain's main trading partner, taking much of her cotton goods and heavy machinery and about 20 per cent of her overseas investment. Britain used Indian exports to other parts of the world to offset 40 per cent of her balance-of-payments deficit. 'We could lose all our **dominions** and still survive', said Lord **Curzon** in 1900, 'but if we lost India, our sun would sink.'

The First World War brought a dramatic change in India's relations with the Raj. 1.2 million Indian troops served in the Middle East and France. Demands for self-government increased, fuelled by war inflation and the slump that followed the ending of the war. This, and the **Amritsar massacre**, provided support for the **non-cooperation campaign** (1920–22) of **Gandhi**. The Raj responded to Indian demands and unrest by granting Indians a greater role in government through the **Montagu–Chelmsford reforms** (1919) and the **India Act** (1935), which enabled Congress to control eight of the eleven provinces of British India. The **Second World War**, like the First, had a traumatic effect on the Raj. Congress leaders refused to cooperate with the British and spent much of the war in jail. By 1946 it was clear to the Viceroy,

Wavell, that 'Our time in India is limited and our power to control events almost gone.' The Raj could not continue without Indian collaboration, and in any case the will to rule had disappeared. The Labour government was sympathetic to Indian independence and more concerned with problems at home in a war-weary Britain, so the British Raj came to an end in August 1947, when India and Pakistan became independent states.

***Ralliement*** ('rallying'). The reconciliation of Roman Catholics with the **Third Republic** in France. Catholic bishops and leading laymen had been monarchists until Pope **Leo XIII** asked them to accept the Republic so that they could join a conservative party (he did not want a separate Catholic party) to defend the interests of the Church by sharing in power. Many Catholics rejected his call – they remained opposed to 'Godless' schools and an atheist Republic – but some deputies formed a *Rallié* group and stood as republicans in the 1893 election. The moderate Opportunist governments of 1893–4 and 1896–8 (see **Opportunist Republic**) sought their support but gave nothing in return: no Cabinet posts or relaxation of the anti-clerical laws. The *Ralliement* therefore failed and suffered greatly from the **Dreyfus case**, when most Catholic opinion was against Dreyfus. This resulted in a revival of **anti-clericalism** and the separation of Church and State in 1905.

**Rand** (short form of *Witwatersrand*, Afrikaans, 'ridge of white waters'). Also known as the Reef, this ridge in the Transvaal, South Africa, has produced more gold than anywhere else in the world. The gold, discovered in 1885, is difficult to extract, as the seams dip steeply underground, so only wealthy companies like **Rhodes**'s Consolidated Goldfields could provide the capital and expertise needed. Within ten years the South African Republic (Transvaal) had been transformed from the poorest to the richest state in South Africa. The Rand, at the centre of which lies South Africa's largest city, Johannesburg, has remained the backbone of the South African economy.

**Rand revolt** (1922). A rising of white miners in the Transvaal, South Africa, in an attempt to preserve the job colour bar. Skilled jobs in the gold mines on the **Rand** had been reserved for whites and this had enabled them to earn ten times more than blacks. However, by 1921 nearly half the mines were running at a loss, so the owners announced pay cuts for whites and said that they would allow blacks to do the semi-skilled work previously reserved for whites, which would mean the loss of whites' jobs. The white workers, therefore, went on strike. Militant **Afrikaners** organized on commando lines took over the strike and marched through Johannesburg under the banner 'Workers of the World Fight and Unite for a White South Africa'. By 10 March they had seized control of almost the whole of Johannesburg and were calling for an armed rising to overthrow the government. **Smuts**, the South African Prime Minister, declared martial law and personally took control of 20,000 troops. Using tanks, artillery and aeroplanes he crushed the revolt in five days: 214 people were killed, including 76 workers and 78 troops, and 1,500 strikers were arrested. In the trials which followed eighteen were sentenced to death, four of whom were hanged. The mine-owners appeared to have won, as they were able to cut white wages and give semi-skilled jobs to black Africans, but the backlash came in 1924, when Smuts lost the general election and was replaced as Prime Minister by **Hertzog**. He appointed a committee of inquiry into mine labour, which decided that, in the interests of 'health and safety', blacks should have only unskilled jobs. The mining colour bar was then reimposed.

**Rapallo, Treaties of** (1920 and 1922). The first treaty, signed on 12 November 1920, settled the territorial differences between Italy and Yugoslavia. Italy was to have the Istrian peninsula; Dalmatia was to go to Yugoslavia. Fiume (now Rijeka) became a free city.

The second treaty was signed on 16 April 1922 by Germany and the Soviet Union, both of whom had been treated as outcasts by the victors of the **First World War**. Germany had been presented in 1921 with a reparations bill of 132 billion gold marks, which she was unable to pay, and had been deprived of much of the rich Silesian industrial area, which had been given to Poland. At Rapallo Germany and the USSR agreed to resume full diplomatic relations (Germany was the first country to give full recognition to the Soviet Union): both countries cancelled any claims against the other relating to debts or **reparations**; and it was agreed that 'the two governments will cooperate . . . in meeting the economic needs of both countries'. This was a triumph for Soviet diplomacy, which had ensured that an economic union of all capitalist states would not be formed against her. Britain and France were shocked. The deterioration in relations between France and Germany led to the French occupation of the **Ruhr** in January 1923.

**Rasputin, Grigori Yefimovich** (1869–1916). A Russian peasant from Siberia (his real name was Novykh), who acquired the reputation of being a *starets* (a holy man and healer). Tsar **Nicholas II** saw in him a representative of the simple, devout Russian peasant, but his real influence was due to the hypnotic effect he had on the heir to the throne, Alexei, who was a haemophiliac. Rasputin could stop his bleeding and therefore save his life. Consequently, the Tsarina Alexandra would not tolerate any criticism of him, though he was a debauchee (the meaning of his nickname 'Rasputin') and scandalized St Petersburg society, where his belief in redemption through sin was seen more as a way of life than as a doctrine. His main political influence came in 1915, when the Tsar left for the front and gave control of the government to Alexandra. She dismissed any ministers who criticized Rasputin, so the reputation of the royal family declined even further. Some extreme conservatives, led by Prince Yusupov, tried to preserve the monarchy by murdering Rasputin in December 1916.

*Realpolitik.* Word coined by a German liberal journalist in 1853. It came to be applied particularly to the policies of **Bismarck** and indicated that sentiment and conventional morality did not apply to politics, which was simply a struggle for power. Any means was justified, if it served the interests of the state; treaties were temporary expedients, which need not be observed when they had served their purpose.

**Reconstruction** (1865–77). The period which followed the **American Civil War**, in which there was an attempt to deal with two major problems: how to restore the rebel states to the Union and how to deal fairly with the freed slaves. **Lincoln** had put forward his own reconstruction plan in December 1863, when he offered reconciliation to the South. All white males, except Confederate officials, would become citizens of the USA by taking an oath of loyalty to the Union. When 10 per cent had done this, a state could form a government and send representatives to Congress, if it accepted emancipation of the slaves. Radical Republicans did not think this went far enough, as the plan did not insist on Negroes being given the vote. When Lincoln was murdered he was succeeded by his Vice-President, Andrew **Johnson**, who followed Lincoln's line. Once a state convention had repudiated secession and Confederate and state war debts and accepted emancipation, it could form a state government and join the Union. By the end of 1865 all the Southern states, except Texas, had done so, but the Republican majority in Congress was not prepared to accept this, as the Southern states had passed **Black Codes** which aimed to keep Negroes in permanent subjection. Radical Republicans, led by Thaddeus **Stevens**, insisted that blacks in the South should have the vote, as this would guarantee a Republican majority in Congress. In March 1866 Congress passed a **Civil Rights Act**, over the President's veto, which made the Black Codes illegal and in the Fourteenth Amendment to the Constititution gave equal protection of the laws to all citizens, who were defined as anyone 'born or nationalized in the US'. This included blacks and overturned the decision made in the **Dred Scott case**. Any state which did not give freedmen the vote would have its representation in Congress reduced. All the Southern states except Tennessee rejected the Amendment, which was nevertheless ratified by the necessary three-quarters of states by 1868.

Southern opposition made the Republicans more determined than ever to impose their will on what Stevens called the 'conquered provinces'. In 1867–8 Congress passed Reconstruction Acts, again over the President's veto. These divided the former **Confederate States** into five military districts, in which the commander could organize new governments. Before they could be readmitted to the Union the Southern states had to draft new constitutions, which gave the vote to Negroes, and state legislatures had to accept the Fourteenth Amendment. In 1870 the Fifteenth Amendment, the last great Radical reform, was ratified. It prevented the Southern states from denying the vote to citizens on racial grounds. By this time all the former Confederate States had joined the Union.

The Republican regimes imposed on the South consisted mainly of **carpetbaggers** from the North, **scalawags** from the South and freed Negroes. They carried out some useful reforms, passing new constitutions in which property qualifications for voting and office-holding were abolished. They also set up the first public system of education, for both whites and blacks, that the South had ever known, rebuilt railroads and provided poor relief. To bring an end to Republican rule, white terrorist organizations, like the **Ku Klux Klan**, intimidated Negroes to prevent them from voting. By 1876 many in the North were tired of reconstruction, whilst in the South only three states were still ruled by Republicans. In that year there was a disputed presidential election. A deal, known as the Compromise of 1877, was therefore made between Republicans and Democrats. The Republican candidate, Rutherford Hayes, would become President, and in return federal troops would be withdrawn from the South. This brought an end to reconstruction. The Union had been restored and though deep divisions between North and South remained, the North had largely washed its hands of the Negro problem.

**Red Army.** The Soviet army created at the end of 1917 to defend **Petrograd** against the Germans. It consisted mainly of Red Guards from the factories. In March 1918 **Trotsky** took command of the Red Army, and decided that if the **Bolsheviks** were to win the **Russian Civil War** they would have to create a disciplined and professional army of the old type. He abolished all elected soldiers' councils, ended the practice of electing officers and restored the death penalty. Conscription was introduced in the summer of 1918, so that by the end of the Civil War the army was five million strong, though desertion was a chronic problem (according to Soviet figures there were two million deserters in 1919 alone). Trotsky, overcoming much opposition in the Bolshevik Party, insisted that trained and experienced ex-Tsarist officers should be enlisted. Over 50,000, about 80 per cent of all officers, were taken. To ensure the loyalty of officers, political commissars were appointed to share command. 'By a combination of exhortation, organization and reprisals', wrote Trotsky, 'a wobbly, fluid mass became a real army.' Trotsky had no military experience and left matters of strategy to the experts but he provided the drive, ruthlessness and a will to victory, rushing from one front to another in his armoured train.

The top ranks of the Red Army were decimated in the **Great Purges** of **Stalin** and this helps to account for its poor performance in the **Finnish–Russian War** of 1939–40, and in the early stages of Hitler's attack on Russia in 1941. Russian casualties in the **Second World War** were enormous, perhaps seven million, but the Red Army was able to hold up and then reverse the German assault. It recovered its prestige and by 1945 was the most powerful military machine in the world.

**'Red Feds'.** Members of the National Federation of Labour in New Zealand, an association of militant unions formed in 1909. Their Constitution demanded the abolition of capitalism but, like the syndicalists (see **Syndicalism**), they wanted to achieve this through strikes and not through political action in parliament. They were opposed to arbitration as a way of settling industrial disputes, as this aimed to keep capitalism alive and to make strikes unnecessary. Only a fifth of trade unionists were 'Red Feds' but they were from the only strong unions (in the docks, mines and on the railways), in a country where there was no large-scale industry. When the Miners' Union began a strike in the gold-mining town of Waihi in 1912, the owners brought in strike-breakers and the government provided police to protect them. In the clashes which followed, one striker was killed, the strike leaders were imprisoned and the strike collapsed. A year later a lock-out in the Wellington docks led to a strike, which spread to other ports and mining towns. **Massey**'s government formed a force of special constables which, with naval and military units, was used to protect unionists who wanted to go to arbitration. The 'Red Feds' called a general strike but this was ignored, except in Auckland. The challenge to the arbitration system, established by **Reeves** in 1894, had failed. Since then New Zealand unions have worked peacefully through arbitration.

**Redmond, John Edward** (1856–1918). Irish Nationalist Party leader. A great admirer of **Parnell**, Redmond became an MP in 1881, dedicated to obtaining **Home Rule for Ireland** by cooperation with English politicians. When the Irish Nationalist Party split in 1890 after Parnell's divorce, Redmond became leader of a minority Parnellite faction and was not able to reunite the party until 1900. The 1910 elections put him in a strong position, as the Nationalist Party (with seventy MPs) held the balance of power between the **Liberal Party** and the **Conservative Party** in the House of **Commons**. Redmond supported **Asquith** in passing the **Parliament Act** (1911), which reduced the powers of the House of **Lords**, in return for a Home Rule Bill in 1912. The Lords could not delay this beyond 1914 but the **First World War** led to its postponement. Accepting the delay, Redmond pledged full support for the war effort. Thousands of Irishmen volunteered for service in the British forces, the economy boomed and all appeared to be going well for Redmond, until the brutal repression of the **Easter Rising** (1916) turned opinion away from the Nationalist Party in favour of more radical policies. In the 1918 election seventy-three **Sinn Fein** MPs were elected and only seven Nationalists.

**Reeves, William Pember** (1857–1932). New Zealand politician. Reeves claimed to be a Fabian socialist (see **Fabian Society**), spoke of 'the natural warfare between classes' and became Minister of Labour in 1891 in the New Zealand Liberal Party's first administration. In five years he was responsible for fourteen Acts, which regulated working hours, wages and factory conditions and prevented the exploitation of child labour. His Conciliation and Arbitration Act (1894) established the first compulsory system of arbitration in industrial disputes anywhere. Conciliation Boards, elected by owners and workers, were set up. If either side did not accept the Board's decision, they could appeal to an Arbitration Court (consisting of a Supreme Court judge and two assessors, one representing the employers and one the trade unions), whose award was legally binding. The Act led to a great increase in the number of unions, as workers at the Arbitration Court could be represented only by registered unions, and influenced legislation in other countries, particularly Australia. Reeves's measures gave New Zealand the most progressive labour code in the world. He left **Seddon**'s ministry in 1898, became New Zealand High Commissioner in Britain (1905–8), Director of the London School of Economics

(1908–14) and was Chairman of New Zealand's National Bank from 1917–31.

**Reform Act** (1832). A reform of the British parliament. The years 1829–32 were a period of great unrest in England: there was an industrial depression with low wages, unemployment, poor harvests and high food prices. Agricultural disturbances erupted in the **Swing riots** (1830–31). Social discontent added to the pressure for reform of a parliament which was not at all representative: there were many **'rotten' boroughs**, whilst large industrial towns like Birmingham and Manchester did not have any MPs at all. The **Whigs** came to power in 1830 pledged to reform, though their leader Earl **Grey** was no democrat: he was insistent on a property qualification for the franchise and opposed the secret ballot. Yet his bill of March 1831 shocked MPs, as it proposed that many boroughs should lose both their MPs and others should lose one: the vacant seats should be transferred to the main industrial towns and the most populous counties. In the boroughs there should be a uniform franchise: the £10 householder (i.e. anyone who occupied a house valued for rental purposes at £10 per annum) would have the vote. The 40 shilling freeholder (with property valued at 40 shillings per year) would remain the main franchise in the counties. A quarter of existing constituencies would disappear. This was far more radical than most MPs had expected and was passed in the House of **Commons** by only one vote. Grey therefore asked King William IV to call a general election, which produced a majority of 130 in favour of reform. A second bill very similar to the first was introduced in September 1831 but was rejected in the House of **Lords** in October. This led to riots in many towns in England and Wales – at Merthyr Tydfil twenty people were killed – and it appeared that public order would break down completely. As the King refused to create enough Whig peers to pass the bill in the Lords, Grey resigned. There was a great outcry in the country in favour of reform, with protest marches and demonstrations. When **Wellington** failed to form a government, Grey returned to office and the King reluctantly agreed to create new peers, but they were not needed. Most **Tories** stayed away from the Lords and the bill passed.

The Reform Act has been regarded as one of the most important pieces of legislation in modern British history, as it removed the threat of revolution, which occurred in most leading European countries in the 1830s and 1840s. Yet the same people ruled Britain after the Act as before it: between 70 and 80 per cent of those elected in the December 1832 election represented the landed interest. Though the middle classes now had the vote – the electorate rose from 366,000 to 652,000 in England and Wales, where 18 per cent of adult males had the vote instead of 11 per cent previously – they did not elect middle-class MPs, so aristocratic control of parliament continued until the 1870s. The working class was still without the vote but the Act had shown that non-violent change was possible and so the way was open for further moves towards democracy. The events leading up to the 1832 Act saw a marked reduction in the power of both the King and the House of Lords, who were no longer able to oppose successfully a determined House of Commons. One of the most radical changes the Act brought about was the fifteen-fold increase (from 4,500 to 65,000) in the number of electors in Scotland, where free elections were possible for the first time.

**Reichstag.** Legislature of the **North German Confederation** (1867) and later of the **German Empire** and **Weimar Republic**. The Reichstag was elected by all males over twenty-five and shared legislative power with the Bundesrat (Federal Council), an assembly of ambassadors from the various states, but it was the Bundesrat and not the Reichstag that initiated legislation. All that affected a citizen's daily life (health care, education, police, civil liberties) was under the control of the local **Diet** of the state, which alone had the right to impose direct taxes. Ministers could not sit in the Reichstag and were not responsible to it. It was difficult, therefore, for members to exercise real political power, though their consent was needed for all legislation. By rejecting legislation the Reichstag could have insisted on constitutional change, but it never used this power and never once vetoed the budget. Members were not paid, so the lower classes were effectively kept out of the Reichstag. It had greater power in the Weimar Republic, as government ministers were responsible to it, but the introduction of proportional representation made it unlikely that any party would have a majority. This made coalition governments and instability inevitable. With the rise of **Hitler** the Reichstag's authority was emasculated; it effectively brought about its own downfall by passing the **Enabling Act** in 1933.

**Reichstag Fire** (27 February 1933). When the **Reichstag** building in Berlin was burnt down, a mentally disturbed Dutch communist, van der Lubbe, was found there and arrested. The Nazis claimed that the fire was a signal for a communist rising, but there were rumours that the Reichstag had been set on fire by Nazis, to give them an excuse for attacking their opponents and declaring a state of emergency. Historians still do not agree about who was responsible, although an international commission under a Swiss, Walter Hofer, was strongly of the opinion that the fire was started by an **SS/SA** group, under the direction of **Himmler**'s assistant, Reinhard **Heydrich**. **Hitler** used the fire to obtain President **Hindenburg**'s agreement to a decree suspending most civil and political liberties, a 'temporary' measure which remained until 1945. This was the beginning of Hitler's dictatorship. Hundreds of communists and socialists were arrested, their meetings were disrupted and many were killed in street clashes with Nazi stormtroopers. In the electoral campaign which was under way the Nazis appeared as saviours, delivering Germany from **communism**. They increased their vote to 17.2 million (43.9 per cent), which gave them 289 seats, though this was still not a majority. Van der Lubbe was tried, found guilty and executed.

**Reinsurance Treaty** (1887). After Austria-Hungary refused to renew the Three Emperors' League (see *Dreikaiserbund*) in 1887, **Bismarck** sought to prevent Russia from turning to France by making the Reinsurance Treaty with her. Each agreed to be neutral if the other went to war with a third power, unless Germany attacked France or Russia attacked Austria-Hungary. Russia's dominant position in Bulgaria was recognized and Germany promised her diplomatic support for Russia's wish to gain access to the Aegean through the **Straits** for her warships. While Bismarck was pledging his support to Russia in Bulgaria and the Straits, he was secretly encouraging Britain, Austria-Hungary and Italy in the

**Mediterranean Agreements** to prevent any change there. The treaty did not benefit either side very much, as relations between Russia and Germany deteriorated in the same year, when Bismarck prevented Russia from obtaining loans in Germany (see **Lombardverbot**). After Bismarck's fall in 1890, the treaty was not renewed.

**Reith, John Charles Walsham, 1st Baron** (1889–1971). First Director-General (1927–38) of the British Broadcasting Corporation (BBC). The son of a Scottish minister of the United Free Church, Reith served an apprenticeship in engineering before moving to London. There he became General Manager of the BBC in 1922 and its Director-General five years later. Obstinate and autocratic, he was determined that the BBC should have a high moral tone and therefore insisted that entertainment must be strictly limited, that there should be religious programmes every day and that news, classical music and drama should predominate. As the BBC had a monopoly of broadcasting at that time, Reith had to ensure that it was impartial, and he was strong enough to resist pressure from the government. Reith was responsible for the BBC being a public service funded by a licence fee and began British television broadcasts in 1936. He left the BBC, and in 1939 became Chairman of Imperial Airways, which in the next year he merged with British Airways to form the British Overseas Airways Corporation (BOAC). In 1940 he became an MP and served in wartime governments in various posts, but he did not get on with **Churchill**, who dismissed him in 1942. A proud man, Reith bitterly resented what he regarded as undeserved treatment. After the war he was Chairman of the Colonial Development Corporation from 1950–59.

**Reparations.** At the end of the **First World War** the Allies demanded from Germany, Austria, Hungary and Bulgaria 'compensation for all damage done to the civilian population of the Allied . . . Powers and to their property'. A reparations commission was set up to decide how much should be paid and reported in 1921, claiming 132 billion gold marks (£6,600 million), to be paid in annual instalments. Germany claimed she could not pay such huge sums and was supported by J. M. **Keynes**, who claimed in *The Economic Consequences of the Peace* that reparations would put an intolerable strain on the German economy and that this would make impossible the economic recovery of Europe as a whole, as Germany was the greatest European industrial power. The Allies insisted on prompt payment of reparations, because they needed the money to pay their own wartime debts to the USA. Germany claimed she could not pay and when she defaulted on coal deliveries in 1923 French and Belgian troops carried out the occupation of the **Ruhr**. This was followed by massive inflation and a collapse of the mark. To sort out the problem of reparations the **Dawes Plan** (1924) was produced: it helped to stabilize the currency and made the steady payment of reparations possible again. The French withdrew from the Ruhr and Germany began a period of economic prosperity, but this was based on short-term American loans. When these were called in, Germany's ability to pay reparations was once more in question. The **Young Plan** was therefore devised in 1929: it reduced the total amount of reparations to be paid by about three-quarters and ended foreign interference in Germany's financial affairs. Before it could be applied the **Great Depression** led to payments being suspended for a year in 1931. Then, in 1932, an international conference at Lausanne, which included the creditor nations, agreed to abandon reparations. By this time Germany had paid one eighth of the sum originally demanded. The reparations question determined German financial policy in the 1920s and, as Keynes had foreseen, undermined her economy and stability.

**Republican Party.** One of the two major political parties in the USA. The party originated in opposition to the **Kansas–Nebraska Act** (1854), which allowed slavery in the new Western territories. **Whigs**, Free Soilers and discontented Democrats (see **Democratic Party**) joined to form the Republican Party, which opposed the extension of slavery. In 1860 **Lincoln** extended the party's appeal by promising high tariffs and subsidies for a **transcontinental railroad**, which appealed to businessmen, and free homesteads (farms), which attracted Western farmers. Republican support was therefore strongest in the Mid-West and New England: the slave-holding South was almost solidly Democratic. The Republicans' first success in a presidential election was in 1860, when Lincoln became President. This precipitated the **American Civil War**, during which the

Republicans were the party of Union and denounced the Democrats as traitors. After the Civil War, Radical Republicans imposed **reconstruction** on the South, which left it embittered for decades.

From 1868 to 1933 there were eleven Republican and only two Democratic Presidents, though Congress was often in Democratic hands. During this time the Republicans, the Grand Old Party (GOP), became increasingly identified with big business, supporting high tariffs and opposing labour unions, and claimed much of the credit for the prosperity which accompanied America's rise to become the major industrial power in the world. A split between Theodore **Roosevelt** and William Howard **Taft** enabled the Democrat Woodrow **Wilson** to become President in 1913, but he was rejected in the return to **isolationism** in 1921. Republicans presided over the boom of the 1920s, the greatest so far in American history, but made no attempt to control the speculation which led to the **Wall Street Crash** of 1929 and the **Great Depression**. Republican Presidents **Coolidge** and **Hoover** had benefited from the boom: now they were blamed for the depression, and Hoover was overwhelmed in the presidential election of 1932 by the Democrat Franklin D. **Roosevelt**. He won the support of Negroes, industrial workers, farmers, much of the middle class and the South, which kept the Republicans out of office for the next twenty years.

**Resistance.** Underground movements which fought against the **Axis powers** during the **Second World War**. They provided intelligence for the Allies, sabotaged German communications and military installations, helped Jews and prisoners of war to escape and, particularly in the later stages of the war, fought against the German army. The Resistance was strongest in Eastern Europe, in Russia, Poland and Yugoslavia. When **Hitler** invaded the Soviet Union in June 1941 partisans, led by soldiers who had been left behind by the German advance, attacked communications and tied down many German divisions. The Polish Home Army owed its allegiance to the government-in-exile in London and was persecuted by both Germans and Russians, as the **Katyn massacre** showed. The Home Army finally rose against the Germans in the **Warsaw Rising** of 1944 but was crushed, as the Russians did not come to its aid. In Yugoslavia the Germans and their Croat satellite government controlled effectively only the railways and main towns. The Resistance here was divided between the communists led by **Tito** and the Chetniks (from *ceta*, 'bands') under Mihailovich, an officer of the Royal Yugoslav Army, who wanted to restore the monarchy at the end of the war and maintain Serb domination within Yugoslavia. He did not wish to weaken his forces by fighting the Germans, in contrast to Tito, who fought a brilliantly successful campaign which freed his country from German control. The communists (ELAS) were most active in the Resistance in Greece too and harassed the Germans as they withdrew in 1944. When the Greek government-in-exile returned to Athens the communists refused to disarm and there was a civil war in which the British intervened to defeat ELAS.

In Western Europe few joined the Resistance at first. This changed in June 1941 when communists, who had followed the Soviet line of collaboration with the Germans, became ardent and active opponents when Germany invaded the Soviet Union. More French joined the Resistance when German troops occupied the whole of France after the Anglo-American invasion of French North Africa (November 1942) and when they were required to provide compulsory labour for Germany in 1943. 100,000 underground fighters took part in the liberation of France. In Italy a Resistance movement grew up from 1943, when Italy dropped out of the war, and in 1945 attacked the Germans as they withdrew, killing 10,000 fascists, including **Mussolini** and his mistress. It played a major role in liberating the Ligurian region and cities such as Turin, Milan and Venice.

Resistance was not confined to Europe. There were underground movements against the Japanese, usually led by communists such as Ho Chi Minh in Vietnam and by Chinese in Malaya. The most successful and large-scale Resistance to Japan was that of **Mao Zedong** and the Chinese Communist Party, which led to the foundation of the Chinese People's Republic in 1949.

**Restoration system** (1875–1923). Spanish political system. Established on the monarchist restoration of 1875, the system survived until the dictatorship of General **Primo de Rivera** in 1923. Two dynastic parties – the Liberals and the Conservatives – rotated in power through an institutionalized form of electoral corruption known as the *turno pacífico* ('peaceful rotation'). The elections were fixed by the Minister of the Interior through the local party boss (or *cacique*). This system strengthened the constitutional monarchy and obviated the interventionism of the army in politics. Its architect, Antonio **Cánovas**, thereby asserted the primacy of civilian and parliamentary government. However, the Restoration system was narrowly based, representing the landed and industrial oligarchy, and effectively excluded the non-monarchist opposition from the political process.

**Revolutions of 1830** took place in France, Belgium, Poland and Central Italy. In France the **July Revolution** overthrew **Charles X** and replaced him as King by **Louis Philippe**. The Austrian Netherlands (Belgium) had been united with Holland in 1815, at the Congress of **Vienna**, to form the United Kingdom of the Netherlands. Since then the Catholic Belgians had resented the dominance of the Protestant Dutch in the new state. Following the July Revolution in France there were riots in Brussels, which became a revolt when Dutch troops were sent to restore order. By September most of Belgium was in revolt, so the Dutch King William appealed to the Great Powers for assistance. Prussia, Russia and Austria were all opponents of revolution and supporters of monarchy, but if they sent troops to help the Dutch, French public opinion would almost certainly compel Louis Philippe to aid the Belgians. The Prussians, therefore, accepted a French proposal for non-intervention in October, after the Belgians had declared their independence. A London Conference of Ambassadors accepted Belgian independence but the French army and British navy were needed to force the Dutch out of Belgium, which they invaded in 1831. Not until 1839 did the King of Holland finally accept Belgian independence; the Great Powers then guaranteed Belgium's permanent neutrality. In Poland the Warsaw garrison revolted against Russian rule. At first Polish troops had some successes, as they outnumbered the Russians in Poland, but the rebels lacked mass support. Polish peasants suffered from the impositions of Polish landowners, the leaders of the revolution, and refused to support them. The Poles had assumed that the Western powers would help them, but this did not happen and in 1831 Russia crushed the rebellion. A harsh repression followed: the Polish **Diet**, universities and a separate Polish army were abolished and a policy of **Russification** began. In Italy there were revolts in Parma, Modena and the Papal States but all were suppressed by Austria within two months.

**Revolutions of 1848** took place in France, Italy, the **Habsburg** Empire and much of Germany. The discontent of the working classes which led to revolution was economic. The failure of the potato crop in 1845, followed by a poor cereal harvest in 1846 resulted in shortages and high prices, which in turn led to a reduced demand for manufactured goods and to unemployment. Artisans were also beginning to suffer from the competition of cheap, machine-made goods. The grievances of the middle class were political rather than economic: they resented their exclusion from power, and wanted constitutions which would limit the authority of monarchs and provide for elected parliaments. In France, where a parliament already existed, liberals sought an extension of the restricted franchise. **Nationalism** also played a part, particularly in Germany, where the **Frankfurt Parliament** aimed to create a united state out of all the German lands.

The first revolution, in January, was in Sicily, which resented being ruled by Naples, but it was the February revolution in Paris, which brought about the fall of **Louis Philippe** and the establishment of the **Second Republic**, which triggered off revolutions elsewhere. Demonstrations in Vienna and calls for a constitution ended with the flight of **Metternich** on 13 March and the promise of the Emperor Ferdinand to call a **Diet**. The Habsburg Empire appeared to be collapsing, as the Magyars led by **Kossuth** declared their autonomy in the March Laws, which Ferdinand was forced to accept. In Lombardy, **Radetzky** was driven out of Milan and Austrian troops were forced to withdraw from Venice. On 24 March, Piedmont declared war on Austria. In the rest of Italy all the states – Naples, Piedmont, Tuscany, the Papal States – had to grant constitutions. In Germany too it 'rained constitutions', as the small states in the west and south gave way to liberal demands and granted civil liberties and ministries responsible to parliaments. Also in March, after a clash between citizens and troops in Berlin in which 300 were killed (all but fifteen of them workers), **Frederick William IV** withdrew his troops from the capital, appointed a liberal ministry and declared that 'Prussia is henceforth merged in Germany'. The revolutions, which were urban and centred in the capital cities, had been successful everywhere, as the regimes lost their nerve. 'I am strong enough to take Berlin', said General von Prittwitz, 'but . . . the King has commanded us to play the part of the vanquished.'

When rulers recovered their confidence, the revolutions collapsed almost as rapidly as they had arisen. A working-class revolt in Paris was crushed in the **June Days**. Frederick William IV, with the help of his army, regained control of Berlin in November. In Italy the Neapolitan revolt was smashed as early as May. Austria reconquered Lombardy after defeating Piedmont at Custozza in July. There was really no threat to the Habsburgs in Bohemia, as the Czech leader **Palacký** did not seek independence. A rising of workers and students took place in Prague against his wishes and was easily put down when Windischgrätz bombarded the city in June, giving the counter-revolution its first victory in central Europe. Windischgrätz followed this up by bombarding Vienna and ending the revolt there in October.

Only in Hungary and parts of Italy did the revolutions continue into 1849. The revolution in Rome did not get under way until November 1848, when Pope **Pius IX** fled. A Roman Republic, in which **Garibaldi** and **Mazzini** took part, was declared in January 1849 but was overthrown by French troops in July. The revolt in Venice collapsed, through starvation and disease, in August. The Habsburgs had the greatest difficulty in Hungary, which declared its independence in April 1849. The Magyars were not prepared to allow autonomy to the other nationalities in Hungary, so they were faced by risings of Croats and Romanians against them, as well as by the Austrian army which, under Haynau, gradually regained control. The situation was serious enough for the Austrians to call on Russian support: Tsar **Nicholas I** sent 150,000 troops to ensure the defeat of the Hungarians but they were not needed. The Hungarians surrendered in August. There was no hope of the Frankfurt Parliament uniting Germany, when Frederick William IV rejected its offer of the crown of a united Germany.

There were many reasons for the collapse of the revolutions. Their middle-class leadership lacked mass support, as it concentrated on political and constitutional issues (representative assemblies, limitations on the power of monarchs) and ignored the economic demands of the workers. The liberal leadership was further weakened by a split in its own ranks: the moderates wanted to retain the monarchy and to have a restricted franchise, whereas the radicals wanted a republic and universal suffrage. The middle class turned against the workers when they became a threat to property: the August (1848) rising of workers in Vienna was put down by the *bourgeois* National Guard. The revolutions lacked support in the countryside because the Habsburgs promised the peasants an end to **serfdom** and feudal dues in April 1848 (the serfs were finally emancipated in September) – after that they lost interest in rebellion. Peasants in France, faced with increased taxation, soon turned against the revolution.

The success of counter-revolution was ensured when armies remained loyal to their rulers. They were helped by the lack of unity amongst their opponents: there was no coordination of one revolution with another, no cooperation between Viennese rebels and those in Budapest. There was not even an agreement on aims: deputies at Frankfurt were divided between those who wanted a Great Germany, which would include Austria, and those who favoured a Little Germany, which would exclude her.

The Revolutions of 1848 were the most extensive in Western and Central Europe in the nineteenth century. They failed comprehensively; only one ruler, Louis Philippe, lost his throne and many of the concessions granted early in 1848 were later withdrawn. However, the emancipation of the serfs remained, as did the constitutions and parliaments granted in Piedmont and in Prussia. After the revolutions democracy, **liberalism** and **nationalism** could no longer be ignored by the monarchies of the old regime.

**Reza Shah Pahlavi** (1878–1944). Shah of Iran (1925–41). As a boy, Reza looked after his father's sheep before joining the army. Rapid promotion enabled him to become head of the army and Minister of Defence, before he staged a military *coup* in 1925 which ended the rule of the **Qajar dynasty**. He then declared himself Shah and began to Westernize Iran. First Reza Shah built up a modern, conscript army, with officers trained in France; 33 per cent of the annual budget was spent on it. By using the army to overcome tribal opposition and by forcing the tribes to settle, he brought the whole country under control for the first time. His rule was authoritarian: parliament became a rubber stamp, the press was censored, the Communist Party and trade unions banned. The power of the *ulama* (religious leaders) was also curbed. A secular education system was introduced, religious schools were supervised by the government, the University of Teheran was founded (1935) and many students were sent abroad to study. Justice had been under *ulama* control, so in 1928 Reza Shah introduced new secular law codes, which replaced the *sharia* (Muslim law). Reza Shah was a great admirer of **Kemal Atatürk** and copied him in insisting that all men, except *ulama*, must wear Western clothes; from 1936 women had to go unveiled. He was determined that Iran should have a modern economy too: an Iranian National Bank was founded in 1927, with German advice; a railway was built (1926–38) between the Caspian Sea and Persian Gulf; postal, telegraph and air transport services were introduced; and the state promoted industrial projects. Oil, discovered in 1908, was developed from 1909 by the Anglo-Persian Oil Company (later British Petroleum), though foreign control was much resented as most of the profits went abroad. Yet Reza Shah was unable, despite all his efforts, to transform the Iranian economy. Agriculture, which occupied most of the population, remained backward, and modern industry small. A new Western-style élite of army officers, civil servants, lawyers and doctors had grown up but they were cut off from ordinary people, whose lives were dominated by their Islamic beliefs and who looked to the *ulama* for guidance. During the **Second World War** Britain and the Soviet Union occupied the country and forced Reza Shah to abdicate, owing to his pro-German sympathies. His son, Muhammad Reza Pahlavi, a minor, was made the new Shah. Reza Shah died in exile in South Africa.

**Rhineland, remilitarization of the** (1936). At the Treaty of **Versailles** the left bank of the Rhine and an area fifty kilometres deep on the right bank had been permanently demilitarized; this had been reaffirmed at the treaties of **Locarno** (1925), with

Britain and Italy as guarantors. All German governments had wanted to end the demilitarization, as it infringed German sovereignty and exposed the industrial heartland of Germany to French attack. **Hitler** intended to send his troops into the Rhineland in 1937 but changed the date to 7 March 1936, as the other powers were distracted by the **Ethiopian War** conducted by **Mussolini**. It was a gamble that succeeded, as Hitler, at the same time, offered to make non-aggression pacts with France and Belgium and with the countries of Eastern Europe. In France nearly all the press, trade unions and political parties renounced the idea of war and the general staff greatly overestimated German military strength, believing that a major war would be needed to push the German army out. The British thought that the Germans were simply moving into their own back yard and were not prepared to take any action. Later, Hitler said that if the French army had invaded the Rhineland German troops would have had to withdraw, but this is unlikely, as they were under orders to resist a French attack. The military occupation has been seen as a crucial step leading to the **Second World War**, as it encouraged Hitler to be bolder in his foreign policy. It showed that the French lacked the will to fight and this undermined her alliances with Eastern European countries and left the **Little Entente** in disarray: if France would not honour her pledges, should they come to terms with Germany? In Germany Hitler's popularity increased enormously.

**Rhodes, Cecil John** (1853 1902). English capitalist and ardent imperialist. 'I contend that we [the British] are the first race in the world,' he wrote, 'and the more of the world we inhabit the better it is for the human race . . . I believe it to be my duty to God, my Queen and my Country to paint the whole map of Africa red, red from the Cape to Cairo. That is my creed, my dream and my vision.' The son of an East Anglican clergyman, Rhodes was sent to South Africa in 1870 owing to his weak chest. A year later he moved to the diamond fields at Kimberley. He was an astute businessman, who by 1880 had established control of the diamond mines and formed the De Beers Mining Company. In 1888, by which time Rhodes was a millionaire, De Beers amalgamated with its main rival to become the largest company in southern Africa.

Rhodes also invested in the **Rand** and by 1895 his Consolidated Goldfields brought him even more money than De Beers. With this vast wealth he was able to pursue his ambition to extend British control over southern and central Africa. When the diamond fields were incorporated in Cape Colony (1880) Rhodes became a member of the Cape parliament and remained one for the rest of his life. He wanted a railway running through British territory from the Cape to Cairo and was delighted when Britain annexed Bechuanaland (Botswana) in 1885, as this kept the Boers out and enabled him to begin building his railway north from Kimberley, outflanking **Kruger**'s Transvaal.

In 1890 Rhodes became Prime Minister of Cape Colony and was responsible for the Cape taking over Pondoland, the only independent African area between the Cape and Natal. More important for him was the extension of British rule and settlement north of the Transvaal. Rhodes was convinced that there was gold in Matabeleland north of the Zambezi river, and in 1888 obtained a concession from **Lobengula**, the King of the Ndebele, for his **British South Africa Company** to have exclusive mining rights there. His Company obtained a charter from Queen **Victoria**, which gave it the right to rule the territory in which it operated. In 1890 Company troops and settlers entered Mashonaland and established themselves at Salisbury (Harare). They found little gold, so Rhodes decided to move into Matabeleland, where his troops defeated Lobengula and seized his kingdom, which became part of Southern Rhodesia. Company control was also established by treaty and conquest over Northern Rhodesia. Cattle levies, forced labour and a hut tax were imposed on the Ndebele. They rebelled in 1896, as did the Shona, but were defeated a year later. In South Africa Rhodes planned a rising of *uitlanders* ('foreigners') to overthrow Kruger and make the Transvaal a British colony, but the **Jameson Raid** (1895) failed and Rhodes had to resign as Prime Minister of the Cape. His health deteriorated from 1897 – he drank, smoked and ate excessively – and he died towards the end of the second **South African War**.

**Ribbentrop, Joachim von** (1893–1946). Foreign Minister (1938–45) in the **Third Reich**. The son of a middle-class officer, Ribbentrop was a wine salesman before he entered high society by marrying the daughter of the largest German champagne producer. He joined the **Nazi Party** late, in 1932, but soon made himself useful: it was at his palatial home that the negotiations with von **Papen** took place, which resulted in **Hitler** becoming Chancellor. Ribbentrop's noble prefix 'von' was fraudulent, but Hitler admired him as a man of the world and was repaid by flattery and subservience. Vain, snobbish and arrogant, Ribbentrop was detested by all the other leading Nazis. 'He bought his name,' said **Goebbels**, 'he married his money and he swindled his way into office.' Hitler distrusted the Foreign Ministry, which he regarded as conservative and opposed to his plans for expansion, so he made Ribbentrop his adviser on foreign affairs. In 1933 he set up the Ribbentrop Bureau, a rival organization to the Foreign Ministry, which carried out foreign policy initiatives independently of the Ministry. In 1935 Ribbentrop made the **Anglo-German naval agreement** and in 1936 the **Anti-Comintern Pact** with Japan. From 1936–8 he was German ambassador to Britain, where he was rejected by the upper classes and became an Anglophobe, regarding Britain as 'our most dangerous enemy'. Nevertheless, he persuaded Hitler that Britain would not oppose Germany's eastward expansion. Ribbentrop reached the height of his power when he became Foreign Minister in 1938 and a year later made the **Nazi–Soviet Pact**, which cleared the way for the invasion of Poland. When war began diplomacy became less important, although in 1940 Ribbentrop negotiated the Tripartite Pact with Italy and Japan, by which the three countries agreed to support each other if one of them was attacked by a power not already in the war. As his influence declined, he sought a more active role in the '**Final Solution**', pressing Germany's allies (Italy, Hungary, Bulgaria) to send their Jews to the **extermination camps**. By 1945 he had lost all influence. At the Nuremberg trial his craven performance was regarded with contempt by his co-defendants. Sentenced to death, he was the first of the Nazi leaders to be hanged in October 1946.

**Rice riots** (1918). The most serious popular protest against the government in Japan between the **Meiji Restoration** of 1868 and the end of the **Second World War**. The war boom of 1914–18 (see '*Taisho* democracy') had been accompanied by inflation, in which wages had fallen behind prices. In August 1918 the price of rice, the staple food, was three times what it had been in 1915. There were violent demonstrations against rice hoarding, which spread to become riots in much of the country. These lasted for several weeks and led to the imposition of martial law. Military force and tens of thousands of arrests were needed to bring the riots under control. 7,000 people were charged and some were sentenced to death. The government was forced to halve the price of rice and then resigned.

**Riel rebellions** (1869, 1885) in Canada led by the *Métis* (French-Indian) Louis Riel (1844–85). The territory south-west of Hudson's Bay in Rupert's Land had been slowly settled by Scottish colonists, *Métis* and Indians. In 1869 the Hudson Bay Company sold Rupert's Land to the new **dominion** of Canada (see **British North America Act**, 1867). Surveyors moved into the Red river area from Ontario, so the local settlers and Indians joined together to protect their lands and demand self-government. Many Scots Protestants rejected Riel's leadership and rose up against him: an outspoken young Orangeman from Ulster, Thomas Scott, was captured and executed by Riel. This outraged Protestant opinion in Ontario, so Sir John **Macdonald**, the Canadian Prime Minister, sent troops to put down the rebellion. Riel fled to the USA before they arrived. Macdonald negotiated with the settlers, which he had refused to do before, and removed many of their grievances in the Manitoba Act (1870). This made Manitoba a province of the dominion of Canada and gave it the same system of government as the other provinces except that, as in Quebec, French and English were guaranteed equality as official languages and there were to be denominational schools, both Catholic and Protestant.

After the 1869–70 rising the Indians and *Métis* had moved from the Red river to Saskatchewan, where they hoped to establish their traditional way of life based on buffalo hunting and subsistence farming. The westward migration of settlers soon caught up with them; most of their hunting lands were sold by the Canadian government and the buffalo were almost eliminated. Discontented settlers invited Riel, who was teaching in Montana, to come back and lead their resistance. He returned late in 1884 but by this time was mentally unstable: he claimed to have received a divine revelation. Once again Riel was deserted by the white settlers and the Catholic clergy, who were appalled by his idea of founding a new Church. Macdonald sent 7,000 troops on the **Canadian Pacific Railway** and soon defeated Riel, who was captured. He was tried and condemned to death for treason, although many believed that he was really hanged for the murder of Scott fifteen years earlier.

**Right, the.** A name applied in the nineteenth century to supporters of 'throne and altar', who believed in a monarchy, traditional religious dogma and a hierarchical society, in which the landed aristocracy had a leading role. It accepts class differences and inequality, believes in *laissez-faire* and a minimalist state, and prefers self-help and private insurance schemes to a state-organized social security system. The Right is fervently patriotic, strongly opposed to **socialism** and is associated with **conservatism**.

***Risorgimento*** ('resurrection'). The movement to unite Italy. In 1815 Austria was a formidable obstacle to the unification of Italy, as she dominated the peninsula, ruling Lombardy and Venetia: there were Habsburgs in Tuscany and Parma and an Austrian was Duke of Modena. None of the rulers of the eight states wanted to unite Italy and the mass of the population showed no interest. **Mazzini**, with his society Young Italy (1831), was the first to work for a united Italy but he wanted to remove existing rulers and set up a republic without foreign help. All the risings of his supporters failed. The **Revolutions of 1848**, when Charles Albert of Piedmont tried to drive out Austria and was defeated at Custozza (1848) and Novara (1849), showed that Austria could not be removed from Italy without foreign aid. **Cavour**, Prime Minister of Piedmont from 1852, realized this. In 1858 at **Plombières** he secured an ally in **Napoleon III**, who defeated Austria in 1859 at Magenta and Solferino and obtained Lombardy for Piedmont. Napoleon played a crucial part in the *Risorgimento*, as he began the train of events which, between April 1859 and December 1860, led to the unification of almost the whole of Italy. Without his defeat of Austria this would not have been possible. Cavour, too, played a vital role and arranged for the annexation of central Italy by Piedmont, a move which Napoleon accepted, as Cavour handed over Nice and Savoy to France. At this stage Cavour was thinking only of extending

Piedmontese control over northern and central Italy and did not consider uniting the whole of the peninsula. He was pushed in this direction by **Garibaldi**, the fourth towering figure in the *Risorgimento*. He conquered Sicily (aided by a peasant revolution) and Naples and gave Cavour the excuse to invade the Papal States, ostensibly to block Garibaldi's advance on Rome. Garibaldi selflessly handed over his conquests to **Victor Emanuel II** of Piedmont and the kingdom of Italy was proclaimed. Rome, where Pope **Pius IX** was protected by French troops, and Venetia (still under Austrian control) remained outside the new kingdom. In 1866 Italy joined **Prussia** in the **Austro-Prussian War** and though defeated by the Austrians on both land (at Custozza) and sea (at Lissa), gained Venetia owing to Prussia's victory in the war. Rome was added in 1870, and became the capital when French troops were withdrawn to take part in the **Franco-Prussian War**.

**'Roaring Twenties'.** A phrase which refers to the 1920s in the USA, a time of unparalleled prosperity for many, when industrial production doubled. It was the first great economic boom which was fuelled by the new mass market for consumer goods. Amongst these the automobile industry was pre-eminent: there were eight million cars in 1920, twenty-three million by 1930, by which time one in five Americans had a car, a position not reached in Britain until the 1960s. The electrical industry, aided by new sources of power like steam turbines and hydroelectric plants, expanded rapidly. Electrical consumption doubled and electrical household appliances came into general use: irons, cookers, toasters, refrigerators (production of which increased from 5,000 a year in 1920 to one million in 1930). Luxuries became necessities. Radio, which hardly existed in 1920, became an important new industry. The National Broadcasting Corporation (NBC) set up the first national network in 1926, followed a year later by the Columbia Broadcasting System (CBS). By 1930 40 per cent of American families had a radio. Aviation too was a new industry, boosted by the first non-stop solo flight across the Atlantic by Charles Lindbergh in 1927. US airlines were carrying half a million passengers by 1930. The construction industry benefited from the boom and changed the skyline of American cities with skyscrapers (buildings over twenty storeys high), made possible by steel-frame construction and the electric elevator. All this economic development resulted in high employment (unemployment was never above 5 per cent), rising wages and a great expansion of credit, in which hire-purchase became common.

With higher wages and more leisure, mass entertainment industries sprang up. 'Picture palaces' were built and going to the 'movies' became a national pastime, especially after the first full-length talking picture, *The Jazz Singer* starring Al Jolson, was shown in 1927. Crowds bigger than ever watched sport, and leading contenders like the baseball player 'Babe' Ruth and Jack Dempsey, world heavy-weight boxing champion from 1919–26, became national heroes. Jazz, originating in New Orleans with black musicians like 'Jelly Roll' Morton and Louis 'Satchmo' Armstrong, spread right across the country when it was taken up by white musicians, such as Jack Teagarden and 'Bix' Beiderbecke.

The 'roaring twenties' also saw the rejection by the young of traditional codes of behaviour. Many older people looked disapprovingly on the fast cars as 'brothels on wheels' or at least as providing an undesirable opportunity for 'necking'. 'Dating' became common: young women did not meet men in the security of their own houses with their parents present but were taken out alone. Jazz too, with the uninhibited nature of its new dances, seemed to contribute to the collapse of moral standards. Certainly many women rejected the conventional restrictions on their appearance and behaviour. They wore short skirts, used lipstick and some even drank and smoked in public and claimed the same sexual freedom as men. Yet appearances were deceptive. Most women in the twenties did not have sex before marriage, and half of those who did had intercourse only with their fiancés. Women's emancipation was very incomplete: they played little part in politics and those in work were predominantly in low-paid jobs. Few broke into 'male' professions like law and medicine.

The 'roaring twenties' had their bleaker side. The **Scopes trial**, which condemned the teaching of evolution, showed just how backward much of rural America still was, whilst the **Ku Klux Klan** (with five million members) was a witness to the intolerance and bigotry of many Americans. **Prohibition** ensured that a large number of Americans broke the law and led to the gangster domination of cities like Chicago. Not everyone benefited from the twenties' boom: farming was depressed for the whole period and inequality became more pronounced: 60 per cent of American families lived on or below the subsistence level.

**Robespierre, Maximilien Marie-Isidore** (1758–94). French revolutionary. The son of a lawyer, Robespierre became a lawyer himself and was known as the poor man's advocate when he was elected to the **Estates–General** in 1789, where he distinguished himself as a liberal and champion of the Rights of Man. Robespierre became a leader of the **Left** in the **Constituent Assembly** and the **Jacobin** club and demanded the trial of **Louis XVI** after his flight to **Varennes**. He was a lone voice opposing war in 1792, as he thought it would lead to a military dictatorship and did not share the belief that foreigners would rise up in support of a French invasion: 'no-one loves armed missionaries'. At the end of July 1792 he called for the overthrow of the monarchy, which took place after the attack on the **Tuileries** on 10 August. In the **Convention** Robespierre waged a bitter conflict with the **Girondins**, as he thought they would compromise with royalist forces, was a strong advocate of the execution of the King, and at the end of May 1793 invited 'the people to place themselves in insurrection against the corrupt [Girondin] deputies'. Another *journée* (31 May–2 June) saw the arrest of leading Girondins and a new **Committee of Public Safety** (CPS), dominated by Jacobins: Robespierre became a member on 27 July.

Self-righteous and suspicious, Robespierre was known as 'the Incorruptible' because he did not seek power or wealth for himself. To him principles were everything, to which human beings would have to be sacrificed. 'Terror is nothing other than justice, prompt, severe and inflexible; it is therefore an emanation of virtue.' Yet he was an extremely astute politician, who usually acted with caution. He associated himself with the risings of 10 August 1792 and 2 June 1793 only when he knew they would be successful and showed the same skill in revolutionary government, isolating his rivals before crushing them. It was his tactical skill which led him to ally with the *sans-culottes*, as he saw that their support was needed if the

Revolution was to survive. Like them he disapproved of excessive wealth, shared their ideal of small independent producers and thought that the state should 'provide for the subsistence of all its members'. Although popular with the *sans-culottes*, Robespierre was never one of them, as he dressed in the silk stockings, knee breeches and powdered wig of the old regime and never took part in a demonstration. Robespierre was a principal exponent of the **Terror**, who, after the **Federal Revolt** in Lyon, wanted 'inexorable severity', as humane measures would encourage new conspiracies. Anyone whom Robespierre regarded as a threat had to be eliminated, so in March 1794 **Hébert** and his supporters were executed and in June the Law of Prairial was drafted by Couthon and Robespierre. This ended any appearance of a fair trial and led to the **Great Terror**. On 26 July (8 **Thermidor**) 1794, Robespierre abandoned his usual caution and attacked his colleagues in the CPS. In self-defence they turned against him and had him executed. Some see Robespierre as a great revolutionary, who directed events and caused them to take place: it was on his initiative that the Revolutionary Tribunal and CPS were set up and that the Law of Prairial was passed and he was the inspiration behind the *journée* of 2 June 1793. The threats to the existence of the Revolution in the spring of 1793 – foreign invasion, civil war and economic crisis – had been removed or brought under control by the end of the year, but this was the work of the CPS as a whole. Other members such as **Carnot**, who successfully organized the prosecution of the war, played a larger part in bringing this about than Robespierre.

**Rockefeller, John Davison** (1839–1937). US industrialist. Like Andrew **Carnegie**, Rockefeller came from a poor background. The son of a patent medicine salesman, he worked first as a clerk and then as a meat dealer before turning to the new oil industry. He saw that oil producers were at the mercy of refiners and shippers, so he built up control of both so that he could dictate terms to producers. In 1870 he and others set up the Standard Oil Company of Ohio, which became the first of the trusts. He concentrated on efficient production, ploughing back profits, but also used the standard business practices of the day to drive competitors out of business: espionage, railroad rebates and price-cutting. He was so successful that by 1898 Standard Oil refined 83.7 per cent of all oil produced in the USA and produced 33.5 per cent of it. This Standard Oil Trust was copied in other industries, such as electricity, but was dissolved by the Ohio Supreme Court in 1892. The trust was promptly replaced by the Standard Oil Company cf New Jersey, until that too was outlawed (by the US **Supreme Court**) in 1911. By the time he retired in 1897, Rockefeller was the richest man in the world, with an estimated fortune of one billion dollars. Like Carnegie he gave away huge sums ($550 million in all) to the University of Chicago and for educational and medical research. He established the Rockefeller Foundation in 1913, so that his philanthropic activities would continue after his death.

**Röhm, Ernst** (1887–1934). Nazi leader and Chief of Staff of the **SA**. Röhm was an army captain, three times wounded during the **First World War**, who detested the respectable, *bourgeois* leaders of the **Weimar Republic**. He fought in the **Free Corps** to crush the communist government of Bavaria in 1919 and was employed by the army to form a special political intelligence unit. To infiltrate the German Workers' Party he recruited Adolf **Hitler** and it was from this group that the **Nazi Party** arose. He became a close friend of Hitler and took part in the abortive **Munich** *Putsch* (1923), which led to his dismissal from the army. In 1931 Hitler made him Chief of Staff of the SA, in which role he played an important part in Hitler's rise to power by intimidating opponents. When Hitler became Chancellor in 1933, Röhm expected the SA to be rewarded and was embittered when this did not happen. He thought that Hitler had become a tool of the old élites – **Junkers**, industrialists, bureaucrats and army officers – and talked of the need for a 'second revolution', which would destroy the power of the upper classes and adopt socialist measures, to which the party was in theory committed, to reduce unemployment. Hitler had no intention of acting on these issues, as he needed the support of capitalists for his rearmament programme. Röhm's most serious difference with Hitler was over the army, which Röhm regarded as a reactionary stronghold. He wanted to amalgamate it with the SA, to form a people's militia under his own control. This alarmed the generals, whose support Hitler needed for his aggressive foreign policy and so that he could become President when **Hindenburg** died. To Röhm's powerful opponents could be added **Goering** and **Himmler**, who regarded him as a rival for power in the party. Röhm did not help himself by his behaviour: he was a homosexual, often drunk and exceptionally indiscreet, as when he said early in 1934, 'Adolf is a swine, he will give us all away. He only associates with reactionaries now.' Hitler decided to get rid of his former friend and on the **Night of the Long Knives** (30 June 1934) ordered his execution.

**Rommel, Erwin** (1891–1944). German field marshal, known as the 'Desert Fox' for his mastery of desert warfare. Rommel served in the **First World War** in France, Romania and at **Caporetto**, where he led from the front in the thick of the fighting, as he was later to do in North Africa, and won the highest German award for bravery. Although never a member of the **Nazi Party**, he became an enthusiastic supporter of **Hitler** in his early days. During the invasion of France in 1940 he was in command of a Panzer division which advanced from the Ardennes to the Channel, when he used *Blitzkrieg* tactics. Popular with his men and with Hitler, he was sent to Libya in February 1941 to prop up the Italians, whose invasion of Egypt had ended in a disastrous retreat. As Commander of the *Afrika Korps* he acquired a legendary reputation as a brilliantly daring and inspiring leader. He defeated the British at El Agheila (March 1941) and pushed them out of Libya but he was starved of supplies, as the **North African Campaigns** were seen in Berlin as a sideshow and of little importance compared with the **Eastern Front**. In November 1941 Rommel was driven back to Benghazi with considerable tank losses by the British but when supplies of new tanks arrived he went on to the attack immediately and drove the British back to Egypt, seizing Tobruk in June 1942, whereupon Hitler made him a field marshal. The British fell back to prepared defences at El **Alamein**, which Rommel was unable to penetrate. Rommel, exhausted and ill, went to Berlin to recuperate but was recalled from his hospital bed when **Montgomery**, Commander of the Eighth Army, attacked with overwhelming strength at El Alamein. In November 1942 Rommel began a retreat which ended 1,500 miles later in Tunisia. Any hope of a German recovery was dashed when Anglo-American forces landed in Morocco and Algeria, though Rommel held them up until he was recalled in March 1943, leaving most of his troops to surrender in May.

After a brief spell in Italy, in January 1944 he became Inspector of Coastal Defences in France and commanded an army group under von Rundstedt. To counter an Allied invasion he wanted to prevent any landing and the formation of a bridgehead on the French coast rather than rely, as von Rundstedt intended, on a mobile reserve. Rommel spread his armour along the coastline, sited guns and laid four million mines. When the Normandy invasion took place on **D-Day** (6 June 1944) he was in Berlin. Recognizing Allied air superiority he twice begged Hitler in June 1944 to make peace, to no avail. He was not directly involved in the **July Plot** to assassinate Hitler but was in contact with the conspirators, who intended to make him Head of State when Hitler was dead. Seriously injured by a British plane on 17 July, he was recovering when an investigation which followed the failure of the Plot linked him with the conspirators. In October he was given the choice of committing suicide or facing trial. He took poison. The German public was told that he had died from his wounds: he was given a funeral with full military honours as a war hero so that the fiction could be maintained that he was a loyal Nazi.

**Roon, Count Albrecht von** (1803–79). Prussian War Minister at the time of the Constitutional Crisis of 1862. Roon put forward reforms for reorganizing the Prussian army, which would increase it in size: recruits would serve for three years instead of two with the line army, and for five years in the reserve, in which the *Landwehr* (a citizen militia, with mainly middle-class officers) would be incorporated. The Liberal majority in the Prussian **Diet** objected to the *Landwehr* changes and refused to pass the bill. The King, **William I**, would not give way and so the conflict became a constitutional one – was the King or parliament to rule? William considered abdicating before Roon persuaded him to call on Otto von **Bismarck**, who was appointed Minister-President. Bismarck maintained that if the government could not agree with the Diet, it should continue to raise taxes as in the last budget. He therefore levied taxes and spent money reorganizing the army, just as if the bill had been passed.

This defeat for the Liberals in the Diet (they were not prepared to tell people not to pay their taxes, as this might lead to revolution) greatly encouraged authoritarian and militarist attitudes in Germany, which persisted well into the twentieth century.

**Roosevelt, Anna Eleanor** (1884–1962). The most active and radical First Lady (wife of the President) in US history. A niece of Theodore **Roosevelt**, she married her cousin Franklin in 1905 and had six children. After he had an affair in 1918 they gradually moved apart, though she continued to support her husband in his political career, especially after he was paralysed by polio in 1921 and was wheelchair-bound. She lobbied hard to make him Governor of New York and, in 1932, President of the United States. On his behalf she undertook nationwide tours to promote his **New Deal** policies and claimed that she forced him to take a stand on controversial issues. Increasingly she became committed to women's causes and minority rights and campaigned throughout the 1930s – in the press, on the radio and in lectures – for civil rights. After her husband's death in 1945 President Truman made her a delegate to the United Nations, where she played a leading role in drafting the Declaration of Human Rights in 1948. Eleanor Roosevelt resigned her UN post when **Eisenhower** was elected President in 1953, and she opposed McCarthyism in the 1950s. Her last public position was as a member of the Commission on the Status of Women (1961–2).

**Roosevelt, Franklin Delano** (1882–1945). Thirty-second President of the USA (1933–45). Roosevelt was a member of an old, wealthy New York family and a distant cousin of Theodore **Roosevelt**. Charming, energetic and good-looking, he became a State Senator in 1910 and three years later Assistant Secretary of the Navy under President **Wilson**. In 1921 his career suffered what could have been an irreparable set-back when he was stricken with polio and was paralysed from the waist down, but he fought back with great courage and determination, encouraged by his wife **Eleanor Roosevelt**. In 1928 he was elected Governor of New York and in 1932 became Democratic presidential candidate. He promised a 'New Deal for the American people', who were suffering from the **Great Depression**, and won an overwhelming victory, carrying forty-two states to **Hoover**'s six. He faced a perilous situation: the banking system had almost collapsed; there were between twelve and fifteen million unemployed; farmers were in a desperate situation, as their income had fallen by two-thirds since 1929. Private charity could not cope with the demands made upon it, so many people starved. It appeared that revolution was imminent.

Roosevelt acted decisively and with great vigour. He told the nation that 'the only thing we have to fear is fear itself' and passed through Congress an Act which put all banks under federal regulation. He then gave the first of his 'fireside chats' on the radio and assured Americans that it was safe to bank their savings. The crisis was averted. There followed the 'Hundred Days', when fifteen **New Deal** bills were passed between March and June 1933. They were designed to reduce unemployment, control banking and credit and help agriculture and small-scale industry. They also aimed to protect the workers, at a time when employers were cutting wages. An even more radical programme began in 1935, when social welfare measures such as old-age pensions and unemployment insurance, long familiar in Western Europe, were passed. **Trade unions** were protected, the rich taxed more heavily and in the 1936 election Roosevelt won by a record margin, carrying every state except Maine and Vermont. The Democrats also won 75 per cent of the seats in the Senate and 80 per cent of those in the House of Representatives. By this time industrialists, alarmed at the cost of the New Deal measures and at the President's criticism of the greed and selfishness of industrialists – 'economic royalists', he called them – were hostile to 'that man in the White House'. They regarded him as anti-capitalist, which he was not: he was simply against the abuses of capitalism and, like his predecessor Theodore Roosevelt, felt they should be controlled. In 1939 Roosevelt turned his attention to national defence and the threat to world peace. For the first time foreign policy claimed a large share of his attention.

Roosevelt had sought good relations with Latin American countries in the 1930s with his '**Good Neighbor' Policy**, whilst maintaining a popular **isolationism** in the rest of the world. At the London Economic Conference in 1933 he rejected international cooperation to end the Depression and ignored the USA's obligations to help weaker nations. He disapproved of the **Neutrality**

**Acts** (1935–9), not because they would keep America out of wars but because they would reduce his room for manoeuvre as President. When **Mussolini** invaded Ethiopia and **Hitler** tore up the Treaty of **Versailles**, Roosevelt condemned the dictators but took no action. At the beginning of the **Second World War** in 1939 Roosevelt promised Britain 'all aid short of war' and was responsible for the **Lend-Lease Act** which provided her with war materials. America came fully into the war after the Japanese attack on **Pearl Harbor**. Roosevelt had close contacts with Winston **Churchill**, whom he met several times, and agreed with him that the fight against Hitler should have priority over that with Japan. The Allied invasion of France was delayed until 1944 at Churchill's request but Roosevelt had his way in insisting that it should take place on the Normandy beaches. Like Wilson before him, Roosevelt wanted to set up a world-wide organization – the United Nations – to maintain peace after the war. To obtain **Stalin**'s consent he was prepared, at the Teheran Conference and the **Yalta Conference**, to recognize Eastern Europe as a Russian sphere of influence, for which he was severely criticized. In 1940 Roosevelt became the first President ever to be elected for a third term, and was elected for a fourth term in 1944, in spite of his ill health. On 12 April 1945 he died after a cerebral haemorrhage.

Franklin D. Roosevelt was one of America's greatest presidents. During the Depression he preserved democracy in America, laid the foundations of the **Welfare State**, made capitalism more humane and gave more power to labour. He also increased greatly the activity of the federal government. 'The only sure bulwark of continuing liberty', he said, 'is a government strong enough to protect the interests of the people.' Along with this went the enhanced prestige and authority of the President. A further effect of his policies was that the **Democratic Party** became the normal majority party, winning eight presidential elections out of twelve between 1932 and 1976, and usually controlling both houses of Congress and many state governments.

**Roosevelt, Theodore** (1858–1919). Twenty-sixth President of the USA (1901–9). Born into a rich New York family, Roosevelt was thin and sickly when young but turned himself into a man of action by vigorous exercise – swimming, boxing and wrestling – and cultivated a manly image by always carrying a revolver. He was at various times a historian, rancher, big-game hunter in Africa, explorer in South America and a soldier. In 1897 he joined **McKinley**'s administration as Secretary of the Navy, but resigned when the **Spanish–American War** began in 1898 so that he could go on active service. He fought bravely in Cuba with his Rough Riders, a volunteer cavalry regiment, returned a hero and was elected mayor of New York, where his vigorous attack on corruption outraged the **Republican Party** bosses. They, therefore, helped him to become Vice-President of the USA, so as to remove him from New York. In September 1891 McKinley was assassinated and Theodore Roosevelt, 'that damned cowboy' as Mark Hanna called him, became President. At forty-two he was the youngest man ever to hold that office. He was also the most brilliant and intelligent president since Abraham **Lincoln** and the most active since Andrew **Jackson**.

Unlike all presidents since the Civil War, Roosevelt had abounding energy and remarkable self-assurance. He *knew* he was right in whatever he did and saw the President as 'the steward of the people bound actively . . . to do all he could for the people'. He saw it as his duty to do whatever the national interest required, if it was not specifically forbidden by the Constitution: he therefore made the position of the President more powerful, as Andrew Jackson had done. Roosevelt was prepared to act against big business if it was not serving the public interest and earned his name of 'trust-buster' by beginning proceedings under the Sherman Anti-Trust Act (1890) against forty-four corporations, including some of the largest, such as the American Tobacco Company and Standard Oil. He had more sympathy for **trade unions** than his predecessors, as the **anthracite coal strike** of 1902 showed, although he was opposed to the closed shop and sent troops to put down labour disturbances in Arizona and Colorado. He wanted a 'square deal' for both capital and labour. Roosevelt's bold and vigorous leadership was very popular and led to his election for a further term in 1904, after which reforms continued. The Hepburn Act (1906) allowed the Interstate Commerce Commission to fix minimum and maximum rates on the railroads: rebates were forbidden. This was the beginning of effective regulation of the railroads. There were also laws to protect public health. The Meat Inspection Act (1906) followed the muck-raking of Upton Sinclair's novel *The Jungle*: it laid down rules for running slaughterhouses and canning factories and set up a federal inspectorate to enforce them. The Pure Food and Drug Act (1906) forbade the manufacture or sale of adulterated food and drugs. Conservation also benefited from Roosevelt's action. A dam-building and reclamation programme brought irrigation to millions of acres in the West and the federal forest reserves were quadrupled. Many of his reforms – for a federal income tax and death duties, and for the regulation of child labour – were rejected by Congress as too radical.

In foreign policy Roosevelt's motto was 'Speak softly and carry a big stick.' He wanted the USA to break with its tradition of **isolationism** and assume international responsibilities. He was much influenced by Alfred **Mahan**'s ideas and wanted the USA to dominate the Pacific and the Caribbean. This meant a large navy (he added ten battleships and four cruisers to the fleet) and overseas bases. He worked hard for the annexation of Hawaii and thought the USA should take the Philippines from Spain. As President he encouraged the revolution in Panama and was responsible for building the **Panama Canal**. The Roosevelt Corollary to the **Monroe Doctrine** assumed the right of the USA to intervene in Latin America or Caribbean countries to maintain stability and protect American interests. He intervened in the Dominican Republic, with the effect that the USA gained effective control of its finances. Roosevelt also mediated between Russia and Japan to bring the **Russo-Japanese War** to an end with the Treaty of **Portsmouth**, for which he became the first American to receive the Nobel Peace Prize in 1906.

In 1908 Roosevelt respected the tradition by which a President did not seek a third term in office and did not run. Instead he used his control of the Republican Party to secure the nomination of his friend William Howard **Taft**, who was duly elected President. Roosevelt went off to tour Africa and Europe and returned in 1910 to find his party divided. The Progressives (see **Progressive Movement**) did not like high tariffs and thought Taft was insufficiently radical. Roosevelt came out more strongly than ever for progressive reform and in 1912 sought the Republican nomination for President.

The Republican bosses renominated Taft, so Roosevelt's followers formed a new Progressive Party and made Roosevelt their candidate, with a very radical programme which included votes for women, social welfare legislation and a federal income tax: Roosevelt called it 'The New Nationalism'. In the election the Republican vote was split: Roosevelt beat Taft but Woodrow **Wilson** for the Democrats beat them both. Roosevelt decided that his political career was over and urged the reunification of the Republican Party. In the **First World War** he supported the Allied side and was deeply offended when Wilson refused his request to raise and lead a division of volunteers. He had become a hero and a legend in his lifetime: a reminder of his enormous popularity is the Teddy Bear.

**Rothschild.** Jewish banking family that became established in the eighteenth century in Frankfurt. It made a fortune during the **French Revolutionary** and **Napoleonic Wars**, when it made loans to governments and traded, bypassing Napoleon's **Continental Blockade**. After the war it opened branches in all major European cities and dealt in government securities and industrial shares. The Rothschilds, as financial advisers to governments, had great political influence in the countries in which they settled. Lionel Rothschild was the first Jew to enter the British House of **Commons** in 1858 and in 1875 provided the four million pounds **Disraeli** needed to buy shares in the **Suez Canal**. His son Nathan became the first British peer who was a Jew. The head of the British branch was always considered the unofficial leader of British Jews and it was to Nathan's son, Lionel Walter, that the **Balfour Declaration** was addressed in 1917. The Rothschilds were distinguished as scientists and philanthropists as well as bankers.

**'Rotten' boroughs** were those boroughs described by the Earl of Chatham as 'the rotten part of the constitution', where there were few electors before the **Reform Act** of 1832. They were often the same as 'pocket' boroughs, constituencies which were at the disposal ('in the pocket') of patrons. Old Sarum, north of Salisbury, did not contain a single house but sent two MPs to Westminster. Voting rights there went with land owned by the Earl of Caledon. Dunwich in Suffolk was another notorious 'rotten' borough: once a thriving port, most of it was under the sea by 1831, when its thirty-two electors returned two MPs. As voting was open until the secret ballot of 1872, powerful magnates could put pressure on other voters to have their candidate elected. Often there was no need for an election in a 'pocket' borough: at Higham Ferrers, in Northants, where the MP was nominated by Earl Fitzwilliam, there was no election between 1702 and 1832. About a half of British MPs owed their seat to a patron before the 1832 Reform Act.

**Rowntree, Benjamin Seebohm** (1871–1954). English business-man and social investigator. Rowntree joined the family cocoa and chocolate firm in 1889, became its first labour Director and was Chairman from 1923–41. Following his family's Quaker tradition, he looked after the interests of the workers by introducing various welfare measures: an eight-hour day without a reduction in wages in 1896; a works doctor in 1904; works councils and a forty-four-hour, five-day working week in 1919; a supplementary insurance programme in 1921 and a profit-sharing scheme in 1923. Educational and recreational facilities were also provided for the workers. A friend of **Lloyd George**, he served in the Ministry of Munitions from 1915–18.

Rowntree was also concerned with investigating social questions such as poverty, unemployment and old age, and did for York in his *Poverty: a Study of Town Life* (1901) what Charles Booth had done for London. His methods were impressionistic in part but were an improvement on earlier techniques, especially in his concept of the life-cycle of poverty. Booth had given a static picture of the London poor. Rowntree gave a dynamic account, by showing how someone born in poverty would become more prosperous when he left school and began work; how there would be a decline when he married and had children; there would be an improvement as his children began to earn but then a return to poverty as children left home and he became old and infirm. 30 per cent of the people in York, Rowntree found, were living in poverty, which was not usually due to idleness or drinking. About half the working men in poverty in York were 'in regular work but at low wages'. One household in six or seven was in poverty owing to the death of the chief bread-winner. Rowntree's *Poverty* became a classic and was followed by further studies of York in 1936 and 1951. All showed the inadequacies of voluntarism in dealing with poverty and the need for state action, and influenced the social legislation of the Liberal government of 1906 (see **Liberal Party**) and that of the Labour government (see **Labour Party**) of 1945.

**Roy, Raja Ram Mohan** (*c.* 1772–1833). Hindu religious and social reformer. Whilst working for the **East India Company**, rising to the highest rank possible for an Indian by the time he retired in 1814, Ram Mohan Roy studied intensively and became an excellent linguist. His study of Christianity and Islam convinced him that there was a basic unity underlying these religions and Hinduism, which in its pure, original form in the *Vedas* was monotheistic. He put forward a social programme which boldly condemned many Indian practices, such as *sati* (*suttee*), child marriage, female infanticide, polygamy, idolatry and the caste system. Mass education, he felt, was necessary to get rid of these evils. Ram Mohan Roy pressed for the substitution of English for Persian as the official language and for a Western system of education with a scientific approach. In many ways he was more English than Indian in his thinking and thought that British rule was beneficial for India, as it would lead to a constitutional and more democratic form of government. In 1828 he founded the *Brahmo Samaj* ('Society of God') to propagate his views and a purified Hinduism. Branches grew up all over India and though the number of members was small – the society was too intellectual to have mass appeal – it made educated Indians aware of social issues and so made it easier for British governors-general to carry out reforms. Ram Mohan Roy died in Bristol when visiting England.

**Ruhr, occupation of the** (1923–5). The Ruhr, the centre of Germany's coal, iron and steel production, was occupied by French and Belgian troops in January 1923, when Germany defaulted on her **reparations** payment. Britain and America protested at the French action but **Poincaré**, the French Prime Minister, maintained that Germany could pay but did not want to: the occupation would make her pay and if she did not, the French would stay indefinitely to exploit the Ruhr. The Germans were outraged and began passive resistance in the Ruhr, refusing to cooperate with the French or

Belgians. The French responded by bringing in their own workers to operate the mines, declared a state of siege and imprisoned resistance leaders. Germany, therefore, suspended all reparation payments, whilst agitators began acts of sabotage by blowing up railway lines. One ex-**Free Corps** officer was court-martialled by the French and executed: he immediately became a national hero. The occupation of the Ruhr led to a collapse of the German economy, as German industry was deprived of vital raw materials (85 per cent of German coal came from the Ruhr), thus increasing unemployment in the rest of Germany. There was massive inflation, never seen before or since, as the German government felt bound to pay the wages of German workers and officials on strike in the Ruhr. In June 1923 the dollar was worth 100,000 marks; by November four billion. Gustav **Stresemann**, the German Chancellor, decided that this could not be allowed to continue, so in September 1923 he called off the passive resistance and began paying reparations again. French and Belgian troops finally withdrew from the Ruhr in 1925.

**Russell, John, 1st Earl** (1792–1878). British Prime Minister (1846–52, 1865–6). Known for most of his life as Lord John Russell (he became an earl in 1861), he entered the House of **Commons** in 1813 and soon established a reputation as a reformer. In the 1820s he was a leading advocate of **parliamentary reform** and of the removal of all religious disabilities: he urged in 1828 the repeal of the Test and Corporation Acts, under which no Catholic or Nonconformist could hold public office, and fully supported **Catholic emancipation**. He was largely responsible for drafting the bill which became the **Reform Act** of 1832. As Home Secretary (1835–9) he piloted the **Municipal Corporations Act** (1835) through the Commons and reduced the number of crimes punishable by death. During **Peel**'s administration (1841–6) he came out strongly in favour of free trade and supported Peel in his repeal of the **Corn Laws**.

Russell's **Whig** administration (1846–52) had an impressive reforming record. The Public Health Act (1848), for which **Chadwick** was the inspiration, enabled local authorities to provide pure water supplies and sewerage; the Ten Hours Act (1847) restricted the working day for women and children in textile factories; county courts were established; the Navigation Acts, which required all trade with the Empire to be carried in British ships, were repealed; and Australia was effectively made a self-governing **dominion**. In 1851 Russell dismissed his overbearing Foreign Minister, **Palmerston**, for welcoming the *coup d'état* of Louis Napoleon (later **Napoleon III**) and lost the support of Peelites and Irish MPs by attacking the Catholic Church.

After his resignation he served in **Aberdeen**'s coalition (1852–5) as leader of the Commons before retiring from public life from 1855–9. He returned to office as Foreign Secretary (1859–65) under Palmerston, refused to use the British navy to stop **Garibaldi** moving from Sicily to Naples and, without consulting the Cabinet, committed Britain to support Italian unification. By accepting a peerage as Earl Russell in 1861 he moved to the House of **Lords**, becoming Prime Minister on the death of Palmerston. His second Ministry (1865–6) was short-lived, as he divided the **Liberal Party** by introducing another bill for the reform of parliament. He never held office again.

**Russian Civil War** (1918–21). This war had its origin in the policies of the **Bolsheviks** after their seizure of power in the **October Revolution** of 1917. They insisted on ruling alone rather than in cooperation with other socialist parties, closed down the Constituent Assembly (the last to be freely elected in Russia) in January 1918 and they gave up to Germany large areas of Russian territory at the Treaty of **Brest-Litovsk**. All these events led their opponents to take up arms.

Full-scale war began in May 1918 when the Czech legion revolted. The Czechs had been in prisoner-of-war camps in the Urals when an independent Czech state was established and declared its support for the Allies. It was decided to return the 40,000 Czech prisoners to Western Europe via Vladivostok, so they could fight against Germany. On their way they clashed with Bolsheviks and took control of the **Trans-Siberian Railway** and large parts of the Ural and Volga regions. The Czechs gave military backing to the **Socialist Revolutionary Party** which had set up a government at Samara on the Volga. Siberia was lost to the Bolsheviks. In August

1918 Czechs and White (anti-Bolshevik) forces captured Kazan on the Volga, 400 miles from Moscow, with flat country and no significant Bolshevik forces in between. Here **Trotsky**, the Commissar for War, assembled a defence force, held up the White attack and recaptured Kazan.

There were two other attacks which posed a threat to the Bolsheviks in the autumn of 1919. General Denikin took advantage of a Cossack rising against the Bolsheviks to conquer most of the south and the Ukraine. By October he was at Orel, only 250 miles from Moscow. Meanwhile Yudenich was advancing from the Baltic and reached the outskirts of **Petrograd** but he had not received the help he had expected from Estonia and Finland, as he would not guarantee their future independence. With less than 20,000 troops he had to fall back on Estonia, where his army broke up. Denikin found that as his supply lines were extended they were exposed to attack from the anarchist army of Makhno and he did not receive the help he had hoped for from Poland. He therefore retreated to the Crimea and handed over to Wrangel, in April 1920. The Bolsheviks had begun 1919 on the defensive everywhere; by the end of the year they were in control on all fronts. In Siberia White generals had not liked the socialist policies of the democratic governments, so they had imposed Admiral Kolchak, who had been Commander-in-Chief of the Baltic fleet, as Supreme Ruler. He was pushed back and executed by the Bolsheviks after they captured Irkutsk in January 1920. Wrangel took advantage of the **Russo-Polish War** to make a despairing foray into the Ukraine in June but was driven back to the Crimea when the Polish War was over. The Civil War ended in 1921 when Bolshevik forces conquered the independent republics which had been set up in Georgia and Central Asia.

The Civil War was not simply a struggle of Reds and Whites. The Allies were concerned about Russia's withdrawal from the war against Germany and wanted to revive the Eastern Front. British troops were therefore sent to Murmansk and Archangel in May 1918, the French landed at Odessa on the Black Sea and the Americans and Japanese at Vladivostok. After the defeat of Germany most Allied troops were withdrawn in 1919, though the Japanese remained in Vladivostok till 1922. Allied troops took virtually no part in the fighting: total British, Australian and Canadian casualties were 180 killed. Their main effect on the war was to prolong it, by supplying the Whites with arms and equipment. They also created a permanent Soviet fear that the capitalist powers would, at the first opportunity, seek to overthrow the Bolshevik state. Why were the Bolsheviks victorious? The weaknesses of the Whites contributed a great deal to their defeat. They had no political unity and included both monarchists and Socialist Revolutionaries, who had nothing in common except hatred of the Bolsheviks. Denikin's conservative land policies lost him peasant support: he promised the return to the landlord of land seized by the peasants. His insistence on 'Russia one and indivisible' alienated his most natural allies, the Cossacks, who provided a large number of his troops, and deprived him of Polish support. The Bolsheviks had the unity the Whites lacked and also controlled the heart of Russia: Moscow, Petrograd, the main industrial centres and railways. Above all, the Bolsheviks had more resources than their enemies: their core area of one million square miles held sixty million people. By the end of 1918 they had half a million soldiers and a year later three million, about twenty times more than Denikin could raise.

The Russian Civil War had long-lasting effects. About 800,000 troops had died in the fighting or from disease but the total loss of population may have been as high as seven to ten million. The economy, already in chaos from revolution, was devastated and so **Lenin** adopted the policy of **War Communism**. The war also resulted in the establishment of a Bolshevik dictatorship and an acceptance in the Bolshevik Party of coercion, summary justice and a centralized administration, exemplified by the **Cheka**.

**Russian Revolution** (1905). The origins of the Revolution are to be found in the discontent of most sections of society with the Tsarist government. The peasants had been taxed mercilessly to pay for **Witte**'s industrialization, at the same time as rents were rising and grain prices falling. There were major peasant risings as early as 1902 in the Ukraine, the Volga region and Georgia. Urban workers, who were to be the driving force behind the Revolution, suffered from low wages and appalling living and working conditions. The non-Russian nationalities too were hostile (see **Russification**). However, the discontent of these groups does not account for the timing of the Revolution. Two events brought their grievances to a head: the **Russo-Japanese War** and **Bloody Sunday**. The fall of Port Arthur to the Japanese occurred in the same month, January 1905, as peaceful petitioners to the Tsar were mown down by soldiers on Bloody Sunday. Immediately there were strikes and demonstrations in all the major Russian cities and an outbreak of violence in the border areas (Poland, the Baltic, Finland). The middle-class intelligentsia also joined in, organizing strikes among salaried employees and professional people. Revolution even spread to the armed forces, when the crew of the battleship *Potemkin* mutinied at Odessa in June. By this time there were 500 peasant disturbances. In October there was an Empire-wide general strike, the first of its kind in Russia, in which railway workers prevented the government from moving troops.

With the government paralysed, **Nicholas II** had to take what he called 'this terrible decision' and grant a Constitution. The October Manifesto promised the first basic change in the Russian political system since Peter the Great. There was to be 'freedom of conscience, speech, assembly and association', and the Manifesto established 'the immutable principle that no law may come into force without the approval of the State **Duma**'. The precise terms of the Constitution had still to be worked out. There was nothing in the Manifesto to satisfy the peasants or the non-Russians in the Empire (no offer of autonomy, or independence in the case of Poland), so disturbances continued in the border areas and increased in severity in the countryside. There was also a dangerous challenge to the government in the capital. On the same day as the Manifesto was issued the central strike committee proclaimed itself the St Petersburg **Soviet** (Council) of Workers' Deputies and for nearly two months the capital was under two authorities: that of the government and that of the Soviet. Here was the origin of the dual power which was to reappear in February 1917. Though the government's difficulties continued long after October, the Manifesto marked a real break in the Revolution, as it split the opposition to the Tsar. Some felt that he had gone as far as could reasonably be expected and formed the Octobrist Party to support the Manifesto. The railways began working again and on 19 October the general strike was called off. By the end of the year the government felt strong enough to arrest the leaders of the Peasants' Union and the Executive Committee of the Soviet. The Moscow Soviet took up the fight in December and called for an armed uprising. In this the **Bolsheviks**, for the only time in 1905, played a leading part. The government reacted ruthlessly, shelling the working-class districts and shooting prisoners. 'On the politically blunted mind of the *muzhik* [peasant] who in his own village sets fire to the *barin*'s [landlord's] buildings, but who shoots the workers when dressed in a soldier's tunic – the first wave of the Russian Revolution was shattered', Trotsky concluded.

**Russian Revolutions** (1917), see **February Revolution** and **October Revolution**

**Russification**. A policy of imposing the Russian language, religion (Orthodoxy), laws and customs in all parts of the Empire. It was an attempt to maintain the dominant position of the Russians at a time when they were a minority of the population: in 1897 non-Russians formed 55.7 per cent of people in the Empire. Discrimination against Poles began in 1863 after they revolted but it was not until the end of the century that this policy was applied to the Baltic states, Georgia, Armenia and Finland. The effect was to turn local areas, especially Finland, into opponents of the regime.

**Russo-Japanese War** (1904–5). Russia and Japan were rivals in the Far East who wanted to take advantage of China's weakness, particularly in Manchuria and Korea. Japan had gained southern Manchurian territory, including Port Arthur, after defeating China in the **Sino-Japanese War** (1894–5) but France, Germany and Russia compelled her to return it to China. Japan was incensed when, in 1898, Russia leased Port Arthur from China and made it into an ice-free Russian naval base. Russia was also trying to extend her influence in Korea so Japan, to avoid a conflict, offered to accept Russian supremacy in Manchuria in return for Japanese supremacy in Korea. As Russia wanted both, no progress was made in the negotiations, so in February 1904 Japan attacked Port Arthur without declaring war.

The Russians were at first outnumbered, though there was no

need for them to surrender at Port Arthur in January 1905 as they did, because the defences there were excellent. Meanwhile, the Russians had sent their Baltic fleet half-way round the world, to gain command of the sea and cut off Japanese reinforcements and supplies to the mainland. On its way it fired on British trawlers in the North Sea, confusing them with Japanese torpedo boats. When it reached the Tsushima Straits between Japan and Korea, it was annihilated by Admiral **Togo** – only one cruiser and two destroyers reached Vladivostok. Mukden, the capital of Manchuria, was taken by the Japanese after a two-week battle but by this time Japanese forces were outnumbered and overstretched and Russia would probably have defeated Japan if she had continued fighting. Domestic events rather than military defeat brought an end to the war. With the threat of revolution in Russia, the Tsar decided to make peace in May 1905, a peace concluded at the Treaty of **Portsmouth**. Russia's defeat was totally unexpected in Europe – the last time an Asian power had defeated a major European country was nearly 700 years earlier, with the Mongol invasions. Defeat led, as it had done after the **Crimean War**, to the collapse of the government's prestige and authority, and helped to bring about the **Russian Revolution** of 1905.

**Russo-Polish War** (1920). Poland had become independent after the collapse of Germany in November 1918. Marshal **Pilsudski**, who became Head of State and Commander of the armed forces, regarded Russia as the main threat to Polish independence and saw Russia's weakness during the **Russian Civil War** as an opportunity to extend Poland's borders in the east. On 25 April 1920 he launched a surprise attack on the Ukraine, met little initial resistance and occupied Kiev. The **Red Army** then counter-attacked and forced the Poles back to the Polish frontier. **Trotsky** wanted to stop there but **Lenin** insisted on invading Poland, hoping to start a proletarian revolution there. Instead, the Russian invasion roused Polish **nationalism**. The Red Army was halted before Warsaw and pushed back well into Russia. Peace was signed at Riga in Latvia on 18 March 1921. The Polish–Russian frontier was fixed well to the east of the **Curzon Line**, and left Poland with six million Ukrainians and White Russians, in territory which the Russians regarded as their own. This territory was recovered by the Soviet Union in 1939 after the **Nazi–Soviet Pact**. It was lost in 1941 after the German invasion but became part of the USSR again in 1945.

**Russo-Turkish Wars** (1787–92, 1806–12, 1828–9, 1853–6, 1877–8). Russia was the only major European power to make war on Turkey in the nineteenth century. Her main aims were to extend her territory round the Black Sea, to help the Orthodox Slavs in the Balkans in their struggle against their Turkish overlords and to obtain for herself a dominant influence in the Balkans, which were part of the **Ottoman Empire**. After the first war (1787–92), fought largely over Russian penetration of the **Caucasus**, Russia acquired territory between the rivers Bug and Dniester and so strengthened her control on the northern shore of the Black Sea. It was here that the great port of Odessa was built, from which Russia could export her grain to Western Europe. The second war ended with the Treaty of Bucharest (1812), when Russia extended her frontier to the river Prut and the northern branch of the mouth of the Danube. This gave her most of **Bessarabia**. War was renewed in 1828 and after the fall of Adrianople (modern Edirne) in 1829, peace was made: Russia acquired southern Bessarabia and part of Armenia. After her defeat in the **Crimean War** Russia had to give back to Turkey, at the Congress of **Paris**, southern Bessarabia and part of the Caucasus. In 1875 a Balkan rising against the Turks began in Bosnia and spread to Serbia and Bulgaria. It was put down with great brutality by the Turks and this led Russia to intervene. After defeating the Turks the Russians made peace at the Treaty of **San Stefano** and recovered the territory they had lost at the Congress of Paris. All Russia's gains from Turkey were eventually retained, except for part of the Caucasus (the area round Kars), which Turkey recovered at **Brest–Litovsk** in 1918. Russia's involvement with Turkey formed part of the **Eastern Question**.

**SA** (*Sturm Abteilung*, 'storm detachments', stormtroopers). A Nazi paramilitary organization, formed in 1921 to protect Nazi meetings from disruption, break up the meetings of other parties and disseminate Nazi propaganda. Many of its members were ex-soldiers and **Free Corps**, who missed the camaraderie of the army and could not settle to the dull routine of civilian life after the **First World War**. The SA was modelled on the army, and had a distinctive brown uniform and military ranks. It was anti-capitalist, in that it was hostile to big business. When Ernst **Röhm** became Chief of Staff in 1931 it grew rapidly, so that by 1934 it had over four and a half million members, at a time when the army was limited to 100,000. The SA played a large part in bringing **Hitler** to power, by taking to the streets and intimidating his opponents. After he became Chancellor in 1933 the SA expected to be rewarded by well-paid posts but they were disappointed. As a result they became more radical and talked of a 'second revolution', which would seize the assets of *Junkers* and industrialists. The old élites and the army were alarmed, particularly when Röhm suggested that the army should be merged with the SA, under his command. Hitler needed the support of the army in order to become President on **Hindenburg**'s death and so, on the **Night of the Long Knives** (30 June 1934), he and his **SS** henchmen organized the execution of the SA leaders. After the purge the SA remained but it was now unarmed and unimportant, brought out only for demonstrations and parades.

**Saar.** An area of nearly a thousand square miles in Germany on the left bank of the Rhine. It had rich coal deposits, and iron and steel industries. From 1919–35 it was administered by the **League of Nations**: the French controlled the mines as recompense for the destruction of French mines when the Germans retreated from France at the end of the **First World War**. In 1935 the area was returned to Germany, after 90 per cent of the population voted for this in a plebiscite.

**Sacco–Vanzetti case** (1920–27). In May 1920 two Italian immigrants, Nicola Sacco and Bartolomeo Vanzetti, were arrested for robbing and murdering two men at a shoe factory in South Braintree, Massachusetts. The evidence during their trial in 1921 was inconclusive. The defence produced numerous witnesses to show that the accused were elsewhere when the murders were committed; the prosecution produced other witnesses to identify Sacco and Vanzetti as the murderers. One bullet was found to be 'consistent with' others fired from Sacco's gun. Judge Thayer was extremely biased and almost directed the jury to bring in a verdict of guilty, which it did. He condemned Sacco and Vanzetti to death and then boasted of what he had done to 'those anarchist bastards'. The verdict created a furore throughout the world, as it was felt that they had been condemned because they were immigrants, draft-dodgers and anarchists. There were demonstrations outside the American embassy in Rome and a general strike in Montevideo, whilst in Paris a bomb went off during a demonstration in favour of Sacco and Vanzetti and twenty people were killed. In America the trial became the equivalent of the **Dreyfus case**. As the appeals dragged on for seven years, writers and intellectuals petitioned for Sacco and Vanzetti's release and a Harvard law professor alleged that they were innocent victims of a 'Red Scare'. The Governor of Massachusetts appointed a committee of respected laymen, led by the President of Harvard University, to advise him whether there should be a pardon or re-trial. The committee found that Judge Thayer had behaved disgracefully but that the defendants were guilty. They were executed in the electric chair in August 1927. It is clear that on the evidence produced at the trial Sacco and Vanzetti should not have been convicted, but this is not to say they were innocent. New ballistic tests in 1961 appeared to prove that the murders had been committed with Sacco's gun.

**Sadowa** (Königgrätz) (3 July 1866). The main battle of the **Austro-Prussian War**, fought in Bohemia sixty-five miles east of Prague. The Austrian army was regarded as one of the best in Europe: its men enlisted for seven years, its cavalry was excellent and its rifled field-guns were better than those of Prussia. The main Austrian army of 270,000 under Benedek was in Bohemia, which was surrounded by mountains and hills. Benedek should either have held the passes or fallen back on the hills north of Brno. He did neither but stayed on the central Bohemian plain, which was served by only one railway. The Prussians could strike at him from Silesia in the north-east, or Saxony in the north, using five railway lines. **Moltke**, the Prussian Commander, struck from both directions. Benedek made no attempt to defeat either of the advancing armies but waited for them to attack. Moltke used Napoleonic tactics by attacking the Austrian right flank to weaken the centre, which then disintegrated. The Austrian artillery took a heavy toll of the Prussians but the Prussian breech-loading needle gun, which could be loaded lying down, was far superior to the muzzle-loading Austrian rifle, which had to be loaded standing up. This gave the Prussians a victory, which ended the war after only seven weeks and made Prussia the dominant power in Central Europe.

**St Germain, Treaty of** (1919). A peace treaty at the end of the **First World War** between Austria and the Allied powers. The **Austro-Hungarian Empire** had fallen apart by the time the **Paris Peace Conference** met and the separate states of Austria, Hungary, Czechoslovakia and Yugoslavia had appeared. The conference was, therefore, presented with a *fait accompli* and had to recognize much of what had already taken place. Austria lost her wealthy industrial provinces of Bohemia and Moravia to the new state of Czechoslovakia; Dalmatia, Bosnia and Hercegovina to another new state, Yugoslavia; Bukovina to Romania; Galicia to Poland; the south Tyrol (as far as the Brenner Pass), the Trentino, Istria and Trieste to Italy. This left Austria as a small republic, forbidden to unite with Germany, with a population reduced from twenty-two million to six and a half million, nearly a third of whom lived in the capital Vienna. Three million German-speakers lived in Czechoslovakia in the **Sudetenland**, a source of instability in the new state. Austria was now a basically agricultural country with severe balance-of-payments problems and had to be assisted by loans from the **League of Nations**.

***Sakoku*** ('closed country'). Between 1639 and 1854 Japan was cut off from contact with the rest of the world. The **Tokugawa shogunate** did not fear foreign conquest but an internal revolt against its rule. If foreign trade was allowed the *daimyo* (feudal lords) could become wealthy and buy arms abroad. The shogun also wanted to keep out Christian influences, which he regarded as disruptive. All foreign trade was therefore banned, except for a little with China and Holland, and this was strictly controlled by the shogunate at Deshima (Nagasaki). Japanese were not allowed to leave the country or, having left, to return. There was no serious attempt to end Japan's isolation until 1853, when the American Commodore **Perry** sailed into Tokyo Bay and demanded trade and diplomatic relations with Japan. The Japanese were undecided whether to maintain their isolation or accept Perry's ultimatum. They decided to do the latter, as seclusion for over 200 years had left them almost totally ignorant of Western technology and they had been astonished at the fire power of Perry's 'black ships'. Japan was compelled to open up her ports in a series of **unequal treaties** with foreign powers.

**Salazar, António de Oliveira** (1889–1970). Portuguese dictator (1932–68). Originally from the conservative, pious, smallholding peasantry of the north, Salazar was educated in a seminary before becoming a university lecturer in economics at Coimbra. Austere and reclusive, he led a simple life, rarely appeared in public and never left Portugal. His economic expertise led to his appointment in 1928 as Minister of Finance under the military dictatorship of General Carmona. Salazar pruned expenditure severely, introduced new taxes and achieved a budget surplus (a rare achievement in Portugal) in his first year and maintained this annually. The surplus was spent on public works (ports, irrigation, hydro-electric schemes), education and rearmament. Carmona made Salazar Prime Minister in 1932 and thereafter was content to act as a figurehead President until he died in 1951. In 1933 Salazar laid the foundations of the *Estado Novo* ('New State'), which he would dominate as dictator until 1968. 'The people', he said, 'has less need of being sovereign than of being governed.' The Constitution, which Salazar drew up, established a National Assembly (in which all seats went to government supporters), a mainly advisory body which met for only three months a year, and a Corporative Chamber (representing economic and professional corporations), whose members were government-nominated. The government did not rely on laws passed by the Assembly, as it could legislate by decree at any time. The *Estado Novo* entailed the abolition of political parties, trade unions and strikes, total censorship, and the glorification of the values of 'God, Country and Family'. Despite the trappings of **fascism** and of the **Corporate State**, the aim of the *Estado Novo* was mass depoliticization, rather than mobilization within a single party totally identified with the state. This heavily centralized and authoritarian state effectively allowed the old élite to retain political and social control.

In addition to being Prime Minister (1932–68) and Finance Minister (1928–48), Salazar was also Foreign Minister (1936–47) and War Minister (1936–44). During the **Spanish Civil War** (1936–9) he covertly backed the insurgent Nationalists, but during the **Second World War** (1939–45) he maintained a strict neutrality. The regime was underpinned by the army and the dreaded undercover security police, the PIDE (the Police of Vigilance and State Defence). The creation of a nationwide network of spies and informers effectively prevented the discussion of politics in public for nearly half a century.

**Salisbury, Robert Arthur Talbot Gascoigne-Cecil, 3rd Marquess of** (1830–1903). British Prime Minister (1885–6, 1886–92, 1895–1902). An aristocratic landowner and direct descendant of Elizabeth I's minister Lord Burghley, Salisbury was aloof, neurotic and an intellectual, who became a Fellow of All Souls College, Oxford, and of the Royal Society. Deeply pessimistic, he did not believe in progress or democracy and saw his role as that of defending the interests of the landed, educated, cultured minority. Realizing that he could not prevent change completely, he thought that it could be justified only if it prevented yet more radical change. He became an MP for the family borough of Stamford in 1853, moving to the House of **Lords** in 1868. In **Derby**'s government he became Secretary of State for India (1866), a post in which he showed little sympathy for the wish of Indians to have more say in the running of their country. As he strongly disapproved of the

Reform Act of 1867, which doubled the size of the electorate, he resigned from the government but returned, again as Secretary of State for India (1874–8), under **Disraeli**, becoming Foreign Minister (1878–80) and accompanying him to the **Berlin Congress**. On Disraeli's death in 1881 the leadership of the **Conservative Party** was split between Northcote in the House of **Commons** and Salisbury in the Lords: only in 1885 did Salisbury become undisputed leader of the party and Prime Minister, owing to Northcote's inept performance in opposing **Gladstone**.

As Prime Minister he made opposition to **Home Rule for Ireland** a main strand of Tory policy, in which he was supported by the **Liberal Unionists**. He disapproved of **Tory Democracy**, as he feared it might lead to the dispossession of the wealthy, but accepted 'Villa Toryism' (the support of suburban and lower-middle-class interests) and he attached business firmly to the Conservative Party by giving peerages and knighthoods to brewers, merchants and industrialists. For a short time Salisbury's hold on power was threatened by Lord Randolph **Churchill**, allied to the radical Joseph **Chamberlain**, but this danger was overcome when Churchill resigned as Chancellor of the Exchequer in 1886. Believing in *laissez-faire*, self-help and cheap government, Salisbury had little interest in change but accepted some reforms for tactical reasons. By the Ashbourne Act of 1885 (see **Irish Land Acts**) he hoped to gain the support of Irish tenants for the Act of **Union**. In 1897 a Workmen's Compensation Act provided compensation for accidents at work in most industries; democracy was extended to local government in the counties when county councils, elected by ratepayers, were set up a year later; elementary education was made free in 1891 and the 1902 **Education Act** made the county councils responsible for education and extended secondary education.

Salisbury was more interested in foreign policy and acted as his own Foreign Secretary from 1886–92 and from 1895–1900. Although he hated **jingoism** and did not wish to acquire colonies which would be an added burden to the British taxpayer, he was prepared to act to prevent other countries taking territory which threatened British interests. Salisbury therefore became involved in the **Scramble for Africa**. Britain acquired Kenya, Uganda, Nigeria and Rhodesia, the British hold on Egypt was strengthened, the

Sudan conquered by **Kitchener** and war with France was narrowly averted when the French were forced to retire from **Fashoda** on the Nile in 1898. The **Anglo-German agreement** of 1890 gave Britain control of Zanzibar in exchange for Heligoland, and in the **'scramble for concessions'** in China, Britain acquired Weihaiwei in 1898. She also became involved in the **South African War** (1899–1902), which made Britain's isolation clear. '**Splendid isolation**' was not Salisbury's aim. As he regarded France and Russia as rivals of Britain, he favoured 'leaning' towards the **Triple Alliance** of Germany, Austria and Italy, as he showed in the **Mediterranean Agreements** of 1887. Only when the naval race with **Tirpitz**'s fleet began did he turn against Germany and realize that the British fleet was over-extended in trying to control the oceans of the world. He therefore made the **Anglo-Japanese Alliance** (1902), so that part of Britain's Pacific fleet could be brought back to defend home waters.

***Sammlungspolitik*** ('the politics of rallying together'). This was a policy designed to secure the support of big business and large-scale agriculture for the German government and the Kaiser, by uniting all anti-socialist forces, in order to maintain the status quo and prevent democratic reform. The term was coined by the Prussian Finance Minister, Johannes Miquel, when he said in 1897, 'The great task of the present is ... to gather together all the elements which support the state and thereby to prepare for the unavoidable battle against the Social Democratic movement' (see **Social Democratic Party**). The idea of a *Sammlung* went back to **Bismarck**, who gained the support of both agrarians and industrialists for his policy of protection in 1879. From that time up to 1918 the alliance of 'iron and rye' became the key to German politics. **Caprivi**'s reduction of agricultural tariffs threatened to disrupt the *Sammlung* but after his fall in 1894 there was a return to high tariffs. The German historian Eckart Kehr saw three aspects of the *Sammlung*: for industry the building of a large fleet, beginning in 1898, and *Weltpolitik*; for agriculture high tariffs and the maintenance of the social supremacy of the *Junkers*; and for the **Centre Party** political hegemony, as it held the balance of power in the **Reichstag**.

**Samori Touré** (*c.* 1830–1900). West African military leader. Samori wanted to unite all Manding-speaking peoples under his leadership and revive the empire of Mali that had thrived in the fourteenth century. He gradually built up his state by skilful use of his army, equipped with modern firearms. By 1880 he ruled a vast empire from Upper Volta in the east to Futa Jallon in the west. To strengthen his control he took the title *almani*, religious leader of a Muslim state. He forbade pagan worship and the use of alcohol, forced conquered peoples to become Muslims, ordered mosques to be built in every town and insisted that children should be taught in Quranic schools. In the 1880s the French, advancing from Senegal, invaded his empire and forced him to move east to Upper Volta and the Ivory Coast, where he set up a new state between 1892 and 1896. For fifteen years he fought with great skill against the French. As Samori moved east he burnt and destroyed everything behind him. This scorched-earth policy held up the French but made him unpopular with the indigenous peoples, whom he often treated with great cruelty. In the end he moved into the rain forests of Liberia, where his army melted away. He was captured by the French in 1898 and exiled to Gabon, where he died. With his death the Muslim *jihads* ('holy wars') in West Africa came to an end. By 1900 all the Muslim states there had become part of European empires: the French conquered the state founded by **Umar** in 1893; the British defeated the **Fulani Empire of Sokoto** in 1903.

**Samurai.** The ruling class in Japan from the twelfth century. By the end of the eleventh century great warrior families were taking over power from the Emperor and the Court nobility. Following a struggle between the Minamoto and Taira families in the 1180s, the Emperor gave the victorious Minamoto Yoritomo the title of *shogun* (the Emperor's military deputy). He was ostensibly the servant of the Emperor, exercising power in his name, but in practice Yoritomo had absolute power and the Emperor was a figurehead. From this time to the **Meiji Restoration** of 1868 the rulers of Japan were all military men. They developed their own code of conduct, *bushido* ('the way of the warrior'), which stressed the virtues of bravery, loyalty and honour. A *samurai*'s (warrior's) main loyalty was to his lord, whose honour he had to defend. Rather than behave dishonourably he had to commit suicide painfully by *seppuku* ('belly-cutting'). In the sixteenth century a rigid caste system was imposed on Japanese society, which was organized into four groups, with the *samurai* at the top, followed by peasants, artisans and merchants. The fact that the lowest position was given to the merchants was an indication of *samurai* contempt for money-making and commerce. **Confucianism**, with its stress on a hierarchical society and loyalty, reinforced the position of the *samurai*.

The **Tokugawa shogunate** (1603–1867) brought 250 years of peace to Japan, so the *samurai* were not needed as a warrior class and were occupied in the administration of their domains, though they retained their *bushido* code, which permeated all sections of society. The Meiji Restoration was brought about by *samurai* from Choshu and Satsuma, who were enemies of the Tokugawas. As Japan needed a strong, central government the four-caste system was abolished in 1871. In the same year the domains of the *daimyo* (feudal lords) were taken over by the government and this was a further blow to the *samurai*, who formed about 6–8 per cent of the population, as their income was derived from a tax levied on the peasants by the domains. The government took over the burden of paying *samurai* stipends but this was so costly that in 1876 *samurai* were compelled to accept a once-and-for-all lump sum, instead of an annual payment. In the same year they lost their right to carry swords, signs of their prestige and status. By 1876, therefore, the *samurai* had lost their status and their income. They had also lost their monopoly of military power, as in 1872 conscription was introduced, in order to build up a modern, Western-style army. The resentment of many conservative *samurai* at these changes led to rebellions, the most serious of which was the **Satsuma rebellion** (1877), but many *samurai* were able to take advantage of the changes taking place. *Samurai* from Choshu and Satsuma, who had defeated the Tokugawas, dominated successive imperial governments up to 1918. Others were employed by the government in administration and the armed forces or became leading entrepreneurs. The influence of the *samurai* continued long after they had ceased to exist as a privileged class.

**Sandino, Augusto César** (1893–1934). Nicaraguan guerrilla leader. The illegitimate son of a prosperous landowner and an Indian domestic servant, Sandino was greatly influenced by the hostility to US **imperialism** of the **Mexican Revolution**, which began in 1910. While the Roosevelt Corollary (1904) to the **Monroe Doctrine** asserted the right of the USA to act as an 'international police power' in Latin America, the Knox Note of 1909 made explicit the USA's right to intervene directly in the affairs of Nicaragua. When US Marines landed there in 1909 they were following a pattern of intervention already established in Cuba (1898), Honduras (1905) and Panama (1908). From 1910 Nicaragua was a virtual protectorate of the USA. In 1925 the Marines withdrew from the country, only to return a year later after a Conservative *coup* led to civil war, in which Sandino fought for the Liberals. The USA negotiated an end to the civil war in 1927 but Sandino refused to lay down his arms until US troops had left Nicaragua. For the next six years the Sandinistas (named after Sandino), aided by the local population in the mountains, fought a successful guerrilla war with small, mobile units against 5,000 US Marines and the Nicaraguan National Guard who were trained by them. When the Marines withdrew again in 1933 Sandino accepted a ceasefire and began negotiations with the government, though his proposal for the redistribution of land to the peasantry was bitterly opposed by Anastasio Somoza García, the head of the National Guard. In February 1934, after attending a banquet at the presidential palace, Sandino was ambushed and killed by the National Guard. Somoza, a devoted ally of the USA, seized power in 1937 and established a brutal dynasty that ran Nicaragua until 1979, when it was overthrown by the Sandinista National Liberation Front. Sandino's popular patriotism, resistance to US imperialism, identification with the masses and martyrdom at the hands of a future dictator made him into a cult hero, renowned throughout Latin America.

**San Martín, José de** (1778–1850). An Argentine leader of the independence movement in South America. The son of a Spanish army officer, San Martín left South America when he was eight, as his father returned to Spain. Trained as a soldier, he fought against **Napoleon Bonaparte** from 1808–11. In 1812 he returned to Buenos Aires and joined the revolutionary regime there. Argentine independence could never be secure so long as there were Spanish armies on the other side of the Andes in Chile and Peru, the main Spanish stronghold. San Martín was determined to destroy them. In 1817 he crossed the 12,000-feet Andean passes with 5,000 men, took the Spaniards by surprise and defeated them at Chacabuco. He entered the capital, Santiago, and after his victory at Maipú (1818) declared the independence of Chile. As it was impossible to march across the Atacama desert to Peru, San Martín decided to go by sea. With the aid of a fleet commanded by the Scottish Admiral Cochrane, he landed on the Peruvian coast in 1820, after a thousand-mile sea voyage, and entered Lima unopposed. In 1821 he declared Peruvian independence but his position was not secure, as the Spaniards, undefeated, had retired to the mountains. San Martín carried out liberal reforms in the areas he had freed, ending Indian tribute and forced labour and gradually emancipating Negro slaves, but he was unpopular with the Peruvian **Creoles**, especially because he was not a Peruvian. His desire to establish a monarchy in Peru convinced many that he wanted to be King himself. Disillusioned, he sailed to Guayaquil to meet Simón **Bolívar**, seeking his aid to complete the conquest of Peru. Bolívar had no sympathy with his monarchist proposals, so San Martín left Peru and, finding the Argentine patriots quarrelling among themselves, sailed for Europe in 1824. He spent the rest of his life in retirement, mainly in France, where he died.

**Sans-culottes** (so called because they wore trousers rather than the knee-breeches of the upper classes) were the workers in the towns at the time of the **French Revolution**. They were not a class, as they included artisans and master craftsmen, who owned their own workshops, as well as wage-earners. They played an important part in the Revolution in 1789 by storming the **Bastille** and in bringing **Louis XVI** to Paris in the **October Days** but after that the *bourgeois* National Guard was used to keep them under control, as it did at the **Champ de Mars massacre** (July 1791). Their power was a product of the **French Revolutionary Wars**, which began in April 1792 when France declared war on Austria. The *sans-culottes* were needed to fight the war, so the National Guard was thrown open to all citizens in July 1792 and became a *sans-culotte* body. A month later they made the attack on the **Tuileries** and overthrew the monarchy. From the summer of 1792 to the spring of 1794 no one could control Paris without obtaining their support. They dominated the Sections (the forty-eight units of local self-government in Paris) and the Commune and could have seized power, but they chose instead to intimidate the **Convention**, never to replace it. On 2 June 1793 80,000 *sans-culotte* National Guardsmen surrounded the Convention, directed their cannon at it and demanded the arrest of the leading **Girondin** deputies. This brought to power the **Jacobins**, who had to recognize *sans-culotte* aspirations. The *sans-culottes* hated the aristocracy and anyone of great wealth and had a fierce devotion to equality, symbolized by their red caps (originally associated with freed slaves) and their use of the familiar 'tu' instead of the more polite 'vous' as a form of address. They also believed in direct democracy: the sovereignty of the people could not be delegated to representatives, whom the people should be able to change at any time. If the Assembly betrayed the people, they had the right of insurrection. The Assembly must be open to the public and deputies must vote aloud. A new Constitution in 1793 recognized the right of insurrection and gave all adult males the vote. As more soldiers were needed to fight the war, the Sections demanded conscription, which came with the *levée en masse* of August 1793. On 5 September the *sans-culottes* again marched on the Convention, as the economic situation had deteriorated, and forced it to proclaim 'Terror as the order of the day' and the setting up of a Parisian *armée révolutionnaire*, a civilian force of *sans-culottes* to requisition food in the countryside (fifty-six other *armées* arose in the provinces). The Convention also had to accept price controls by imposing a maximum on the price of bread and many essential goods. A conflict between the government and the *sans-culottes* was inevitable at some time, as there was anarchy in much of France as local revolutionary committees and *armées révolutionnaires* did as they pleased. In October 1793 the Constitution was suspended for the duration of the war (it was never put into operation), and in December the **Committee of Public Safety** was granted dictatorial powers and all *armées révolutionnaires*, except that in Paris, were to be disbanded. This and the execution of **Hébert** and leaders of the Commune in March 1794 marked the effective end of *sans-culotte* power. The bad harvest and harsh winter of 1794–5 reduced them to despair and the risings of Germinal and **Prairial** were crushed. After that the workers played no political role in the Revolution.

**San Stefano, Treaty of** (March 1878), ended the **Russo-Turkish War** of 1877–8 and brought about significant changes in the Balkans. Turkey saw her Empire in Europe dwindling, as she recognized the independence of Serbia, Montenegro and Romania. Russia gained southern **Bessarabia** from Romania and part of the **Caucasus** from Turkey. The most controversial feature of the treaty was the creation of the large state of Bulgaria, which included Macedonia and access to the Aegean Sea. Bulgaria was to be autonomous but pay tribute to Turkey, though all the Great Powers expected it to be a Russian satellite. This was unacceptable to Austria-Hungary and Britain, who forced Russia to abandon this part of the treaty at the **Berlin Congress**.

**Sarajevo**. The capital of the Austrian province of Bosnia where the Archduke Francis Ferdinand, heir to the Austro-Hungarian throne, was assassinated on 28 June 1914 by a Bosnian student. The murder had been planned by the Serbian terrorist organization, the **Black Hand**. After the assassination an official of the Austrian foreign ministry went to Sarajevo to investigate if the Serbian government had been responsible, and concluded that it had not. The German authorities came to the same conclusion. Former Chancellor **Bülow** later wrote that 'the Serbian government had neither instigated nor desired it. The Serbs were exhausted by two wars' (the **Balkan Wars** of 1912–13). This did not prevent Austria using the murder as an excuse to attack Serbia (see **July Crisis**, 1914) and so start the **First World War**.

*Sati* (suttee). Originally the Indian word for a virtuous woman, it came to refer to one who was so devoted to her husband that she immolated herself on his funeral pyre. In theory this was a voluntary act of the widow, anxious to rejoin her husband in death. In practice it was often enforced by relatives, who wanted the prestige of a *sati* in the family, wished to acquire her property or simply desired one less mouth to feed. The practice went back to 400 BC and was approved by most devout Hindus. It did not take place throughout India or among the lower castes, but at the beginning of the nineteenth century there were about 800 *satis* who took their lives each year in Bengal alone. Christian missionaries and Indian reformers like Ram Mohan **Roy** condemned the practice, which was made illegal in 1829, though it has continued on a small scale into the twentieth century.

**Satsuma rebellion** (1877). The most serious of the anti-government rebellions in Japan after the **Meiji Restoration**. Its origin lay in the discontent of *samurai* with the domestic reforms and foreign policy of the Meiji government. Their stipends had been compulsorily commuted for cash or bonds, which represented a considerable loss of income, and in 1876 they had lost their right to carry swords, the last symbol of their superior status. Saigo Takamori of Satsuma had left the government in 1873, as it had refused to send an army to compel Korea to end its seclusion and to trade with Japan. Saigo was a charismatic figure with all the *samurai* virtues of courage, generosity and lack of ostentation and soon had a devoted following in Satsuma. The government, fearing a revolt, tried to remove arms and munitions from the provincial capital of Kagoshima in southern Kyushu. This set off a rebellion, which Saigo soon joined and led. The rebels decided to march on Tokyo but they were held up by the garrison at Kumamoto. The government took six months to drive the rebels back to Kagoshima: it had to mobilize the whole of its standing army of 65,000 and spend 80 per cent of its annual budget to do so. Government forces suffered heavy losses with 6,000 dead and 10,000 wounded, but the modern weapons of their conscript army were superior to the swords and rifles of Saigo's *samurai* followers. Saigo, wounded, was beheaded on the battlefield, at his own request, by a close friend. This was the last of the military revolts against the government.

**Satyagraha** ('truth-force, soul-force'). A word coined by **Gandhi**, which he defined as 'the Force which is born of Truth and Love or non-violence'. He developed this idea in South Africa as a means of countering the racial injustice to which Indians were subjected. Non-violence (*ahimsa*) has deep roots in the Hindu and Jain traditions. For Gandhi it could take various forms, as in his **non-cooperation movement** from 1920–22; at its most extreme it became civil disobedience to unjust laws. Gandhi's followers were expected to practice *satyagraha*, a precondition of which was self-purification and self-discipline. Men and women in his *ashrams* (religious communities) led a simple life, shared all domestic chores, produced their own food and spun the yarn for their own clothes. They were to refrain from sexual intercourse, even if married. People of all religions and races were welcomed in his *ashrams*, where caste distinctions were ignored and men and women were equal in status.

**Sayyid Ahmad Khan** (1817–98). Indian Muslim leader and reformer. Convinced that British rule in India had come to stay, Sayyid Ahmad rejected the family tradition of serving the Mughals and instead worked for the **East India Company**. He wanted Muslims to compete with Hindus and Parsis for positions in the Indian civil service and so founded in 1877 the Muhammadan Anglo-Oriental College at Aligarh, between Delhi and Agra. Modelled on Cambridge University, this was a place where Muslims could study Western science without losing their religious roots. Soon Aligarh became the main centre for Muslim higher education in India and the breeding-ground for the **Muslim League** and Pakistan. Sayyid Ahmad discouraged Muslims from joining the **Indian National Congress**, as he felt that it expressed Hindu interests. Muslims could best pursue their own interests by being loyal to the British **Raj**: democracy would mean Hindu rule, as the Hindus were the majority. Sayyid Ahmad joined the Viceroy's Legislative Council, an advisory body, in 1878 and was the unquestioned leader of Indian Muslims in the later years of his life.

**Scalawags.** Southern white supporters of **Reconstruction**, which followed the **American Civil War**. It was a term of contempt, which was supposed to originate in Scalloway in the Shetlands, where undersized cattle and horses were bred. Scalawags were a diverse group. They included poor whites, who wanted to end the domination of the planter aristocracy (though the leaders were often wealthy businessmen) and pre-war Whigs (see **Whig Party**), who had opposed secession and saw in Radical Republican rule a chance to promote their interests. It was their opponents, former secessionists and determined white supremacists, who named them 'scalawags' and accused them of supporting the reconstruction governments solely to gain office for themselves.

**Schacht, Hjalmar** (1877–1970). German financier and **Nazi** minister. Schacht's skill as a financier was shown in 1923, when **Stresemann** gave him the task of ending inflation and stabilizing the currency, which he did by issuing a new mark backed by foreign loans. In December 1923 he was made head of the Reichsbank, took part in negotiations for the **Dawes Plan** (1924) and resigned in 1930 because he thought the **Young Plan** imposed too heavy a burden on Germany. He became an admirer of the **nationalism** of **Hitler** and persuaded some heavy industry – **Krupp** and **I G Farben** – to provide financial support for the Nazis in the elections of 1932–3. For these services Hitler made him Reichsbank President (again) in 1933 and Minister of Economics (1934–7). His job was to revive the economy, still suffering from the **Great Depression**, and provide funds for rearmament and the expansion of the army. Hitler's aim was autarky (national self-sufficiency), so that Germany would not be dependent on imported raw materials in case of war. In his New Plan Schacht sought to regulate imports by allocating foreign exchange only for essential raw materials, which were centrally purchased and distributed. He also made bilateral barter agreements, usually with Balkan or South American countries, by which German industrial goods were exchanged for raw materials. As foreign loans had dried up he introduced deficit financing. By these methods and public work schemes, such as the building of *Autobahnen*, Schacht reduced unemployment to one million by 1935; in 1939 there was an actual shortage of labour. In 1936 Hitler introduced his second Four Year Plan, this time with **Goering** not Schacht in charge. He aimed to put the economy on a war footing and replace imported raw materials, such as rubber, petrol and oil, with synthetic substitutes. Schacht opposed this as it was too costly and so resigned at the end of 1937 as Minister of Economics, although he remained President of the Reichsbank until 1939 and Minister without Portfolio to 1943. He gradually became disillusioned with the Nazis, made contact with the **Resistance** and was arrested after the **July Plot** (1944), which tried to kill Hitler. His direct involvement in the plot could not be proved and he was sent to a **concentration camp**, where he was freed by American troops. Schacht was charged with war crimes and acquitted by the Nuremberg Tribunal, but a German de-Nazification court sentenced him to eight years' imprisonment as a 'Nazi offender'. He was released on appeal in 1948. In the 1950s he began a new career as a financial adviser to developing countries, founded his own bank and made a fortune.

**Scharnhorst, Gerhard Johann David von** (1755–1813). Prussian general and military reformer. A Hanoverian, Scharnhorst joined the Prussian army in 1801 and was wounded fighting against **Napoleon Bonaparte** at Auerstädt in 1806. After Prussia's crushing defeat at Jena (see battles of **Jena–Auerstädt**), he was put in charge of rebuilding the army, a difficult task, as Napoleon insisted that the Prussian army should be limited to 42,000 men. Scharnhorst evaded this restriction by short-service training of recruits for three years, after which they moved into the reserve, so that by 1813 Prussia had 150,000 trained soldiers, who played an important part in the battle of **Leipzig** and in Napoleon's defeat. He also opened up careers in the army to the middle class, by persuading the King to award commissions for ability rather than birth. Napoleon compelled him to leave Prussian service in 1810, but with Napoleon's retreat from Moscow in 1812 (see **Moscow Campaign**) he returned as Chief of Staff to **Blücher**. He set up the *Landwehr*, a militia which elected its own officers and in which service was compulsory for all men of military age not called up into the army. Scharnhorst served in the war of liberation and was fatally wounded at Lützen in 1813. Some of his reforms – conscription for three years in the army with two in the reserve and a separate *Landwehr* – were incorporated in the Army Law of 1814, though the aristocracy was allowed to re-establish its dominance in the officer corps.

**Schleicher, Kurt von** (1882–1934). German general and last Chancellor (2 December 1932–28 January 1933) of the **Weimar Republic**. A born intriguer, Schleicher had great influence over President **Hindenburg** from 1930–33, as liaison officer between the government and the army. He recommended **Brüning** as Chancellor in 1930 but turned against him when he failed to produce strong and stable government, and brought about his dismissal in 1932. His friend Franz von **Papen** then became Chancellor but had little support in the **Reichstag**. In the July elections of 1932 the Nazis became by far the largest party with 230 seats. Von Papen and Schleicher offered **Hitler** a Cabinet post but he wanted to be Chancellor and demanded an Act which would allow him to rule by decree. They rejected these demands but when von Papen asked Hindenburg to declare martial law, Schleicher informed the President that the army could not approve of a policy that might lead to civil war. Schleicher, therefore, replaced von Papen as Chancellor and tried to gain support from the **Social Democratic Party** (SPD) and the **Centre Party** by a programme of public works, increase in wages and resettlement of the unemployed on bankrupt *Junker* estates. He also intrigued with the left-wing of the **Nazi Party**, led by Gregor Strasser, but Strasser proved indecisive, the Centre Party could not forgive him for bringing about Brüning's fall and the SPD distrusted him. As he could not get a majority in the Reichstag, he proposed to dissolve it, declare a state of emergency and ban the Nazis and Communists. It was now von Papen's turn to intrigue. He persuaded Hindenburg that Hitler was prepared to compromise and would, if he was made Chancellor, accept a subordinate position for other Nazis in the Cabinet. Hindenburg, therefore, rejected Schleicher's request for emergency powers. Schleicher resigned on 28 January 1933 and was replaced as Chancellor by Hitler on 30 January. On 30 June 1934 Schleicher, regarded as the most dangerous of Hitler's opponents, was murdered by Nazis on the **Night of the Long Knives**.

**Schleswig-Holstein.** Duchies in the south of the Jutland peninsula, linking Denmark and **Prussia**. The Danish King had been Duke of these territories since the Middle Ages, although they were not part of Denmark. Holstein was almost entirely German-speaking and so at the Congress of **Vienna** became part of the **German Confederation**. Schleswig, mainly Danish-speaking, remained outside it. During the **Revolutions of 1848** Denmark annexed the duchies but this was opposed by the German-speaking population, who appealed to the German states for help. Prussia invaded Denmark but was forced to withdraw by Britain, France and Russia, who were determined to maintain the 1815 settlement. In 1852 the great powers agreed that Schleswig and Holstein should be independent and in a personal union with the Danish King. Denmark also assured Austria and Prussia that neither duchy would be incorporated into Denmark. This assurance was ignored in 1864 when the new Danish King, Christian IX, annexed Schleswig. This led to Austria and Prussia invading Denmark and defeating the Danish army. The duchies were placed under the control of Austria and Prussia but after Austria's defeat in the **Austro-Prussian War** of 1866 they were annexed by Prussia and became part of the **German Empire**, when this was formed in 1871. After the **First World War** north Schleswig passed to Denmark after a plebiscite, the rest of the duchies remaining part of Germany.

**Schlieffen Plan** was devised by General Schlieffen, who became German Chief of Staff in 1891. When the **Franco-Russian Alliance** was made in 1894, Germany was faced with the prospect of fighting on two fronts, if there was a war with the Alliance. Schlieffen, therefore, devised a plan, of which there were several versions between 1895 and 1906, for defeating France quickly, before Russia had time to mobilize, so that Germany would effectively be fighting on one front only. Germany was to invade France through neutral Belgium and Luxemburg, cross the lower Seine, wheel east and attack the French fortresses from the rear. It was estimated that France would be defeated in six weeks, whilst Germany mounted a holding operation against Russia. After France's defeat, the whole of Germany's forces could be transferred from west to east. The plan failed in 1914, owing to **Joffre**'s counter-attack on the **Marne** and as Germany withdrew some divisions from the Western Front to stem Russia's advance into East Prussia.

**Scopes trial** (1925). Trial of a teacher in the USA accused of teaching the theory of evolution. American Protestants, who believed in the literal truth of the Bible, were strongest in the Mid-West and the South, where evolution seemed to threaten the basis of white supremacy. After the **First World War** fundamentalists, led by William Jennings **Bryan**, began a campaign for anti-evolution laws and in Tennessee such a law was passed in 1925. It prohibited the teaching in public schools of 'any theory which denies the story of the Divine creation of man as taught in the Bible and instead that man is descended from a lower order of animals'. Soon afterwards a young biology teacher, John T. Scopes, was arrested for breaking the law. His trial, which became known as the 'monkey trial', attracted enormous public attention. The trial was broadcast direct to the nation and many European journalists reported it, particularly the dramatic confrontation between Bryan, who acted for the prosecution, and Clarence Darrow, the country's leading defence lawyer and an agnostic. Darrow and the American Civil Liberties Union, which financed the defence, regarded the Tennessee law as 'an attack on all science and liberty of conscience'. The issue for them was academic freedom and tolerance. Fundamentalism was badly mauled, as Darrow's devastating cross-examination of Bryan revealed his inconsistency and his ignorance of the Bible, on which he claimed to be an expert. The outcome was never in doubt, as the judge ruled that the question was not whether or not evolution was correct but whether the law had been broken, which it clearly had. Scopes was fined. By 1929 six states had anti-evolution laws: that in Tennessee was not repealed until 1967.

**Scottsboro case** (1931). A celebrated civil rights case in the USA. One of two white girls travelling on an Alabama freight train claimed that she and her friend had been raped by nine Negroes, whose ages ranged from twelve to nineteen. The Negroes, after almost being lynched, were tried at Scottsboro, Alabama. The defending lawyers came to their aid only on the day of the trial. All were found guilty by the white jury and eight were sentenced to death: the jury could not decide whether the twelve-year-old should be electrocuted or imprisoned for life. The trial and sentences outraged many people and led to protest rallies in Northern cities. In 1932 the US **Supreme Court** overturned the convictions, as the defendants had not been given adequate counsel. Alabama was determined that the Scottsboro boys should not go free, so one of them was retried by the state in 1933. Although his New York lawyer showed that one of the alleged rape victims was a prostitute and the other 'victim' admitted that there had been no rape, he was convicted again. Once more the Supreme Court overturned the conviction, in 1935, as Negroes had been deliberately excluded from the jury. Alabama was still not prepared to give up. It retried the alleged ringleader and sentenced him to seventy-five years in jail, from where he escaped in 1948. The four youngest defendants were freed after being in prison for six years and the rest were eventually paroled.

**Scramble for Africa.** The partition of most of Africa by the European powers in the last quarter of the nineteenth century. In 1879 little of Africa was under European rule. In West Africa, only in Senegal and the Gold Coast did colonial administrations rule over a large number of Africans. The only deep penetration and settlement of Europeans in Africa was in South Africa, and to a more limited extent in the north, in Algeria. Yet by 1914 the only areas of Africa which were not under European control were Ethiopia and Liberia. This came about largely owing to the activities of colonial soldiers, explorers and administrators on the spot and the reaction of other governments to their activities: colonies were seized by one power to prevent rivals seizing them first. After France's defeat in the **Franco–Prussian War** (1870–71) and her loss of **Alsace-Lorraine**, some Frenchmen saw in colonial expansion a means of restoring France's prestige and prosperity. The French therefore pushed east from Senegal and dreamed of an empire which would link Algeria, Senegal and Lake Chad. This involved them in conflict with the Muslim Tukulor Empire for ten years (1883–92) and with **Samori Touré** for fifteen years (1883–98). The French explorer de Brazza made treaties with African chiefs in 1880 which gave France some territory on the Congo. **Leopold II** of Belgium also wanted an empire there and persuaded the Great Powers at the **Berlin Conference** (1884–5) to create the Congo Free State, of which he was the head. Germany too became a colonial power when **Bismarck** established protectorates in South-West Africa and the Cameroons in 1884. Unlike the others Britain had preferred informal influence to annexation but this changed with the actions of France and Germany, so that the lower Niger was brought under British protection by the end of 1884. As the French expanded across the western Sudan and Franco-British commercial rivalry in West Africa intensified, Britain occupied the hinterland of the Gold Coast in 1896 and northern Nigeria in 1898. The partition of West Africa was now complete.

In the north, France annexed Tunis, which bordered her existing colony of Algeria, in 1881. Britain was more concerned with

Egypt, because of its crucial position on the route to India, especially after the opening of the **Suez Canal** in 1869. When the Khedive **Ismail** got into debt and had to hand over control of Egypt's finances to the Dual Control of Britain and France, there was a nationalist revolt led by **Urabi Pasha** against foreign domination. Britain wanted joint action with the French to crush it but when the French Chamber of Deputies would not support such a move, she acted alone. General **Wolseley** defeated Urabi in 1882 and so began the British occupation of Egypt, still nominally part of the **Ottoman Empire**.

To protect Egypt and the headwaters of the Nile, Britain was dragged into East Africa. The German explorer Karl Peters had made treaties with African chiefs there in 1884, so in 1886 Britain made an agreement with Germany which divided the area between them: the north (what was to become Kenya and Uganda) was to go to Britain; the south (Tanganyika) to Germany. Two years later **Kitchener** defeated the Mahdist state (see **Mahdi**) at the battle of **Omdurman** and secured British control of the Sudan. Italy was the last of the powers to stake a claim in East Africa. She set up the colony of Eritrea in 1890 but her attempt to seize Ethiopia met with disaster at **Aduwa** in 1896, so that she was left with barren land which was a burden to her.

In southern Africa a threat to British interests appeared when Germany annexed South-West Africa. Bechuanaland, which **Rhodes** called South Africa's 'Suez Canal', was now sandwiched between German South-West Africa to the east and the Boer republics of the Transvaal and Orange Free State to the west. If Britain did not act quickly, her route to the north would be occupied by others, so Bechuanaland was brought under her control in 1886. British expansion north of the Limpopo river would have enormous strategic importance. It would prevent Portugal gaining a belt of territory across Africa from Mozambique to Angola, stop Germany linking up South-West Africa with Tanganyika and act as a barrier to Boer expansion north. In 1890–91 Rhodes moved north into what became Southern and Northern Rhodesia. Nyasaland, declared a protectorate in 1891, was a further British acquisition, this time through the activity of Scottish missionaries. The situation in South Africa changed dramatically when gold was mined on the

**Rand** in 1886 – Transvaal now became the richest area and Britain feared that **Kruger** would use his economic strength to dominate the whole of South Africa. To prevent this the British provoked the Boers into fighting the **South African War** (1899–1902) which brought the Boer republics under British control. The Scramble for Africa was now at an end, except in North Africa. After the **Moroccan crises** of 1905 and 1911, a French protectorate over Morocco was recognized by the other powers. The final partition of Africa took place when Italy occupied Libya in 1912.

**'Scramble for concessions'**. An attempt by European powers in the 1890s to carve up China into spheres of influence. After the **Sino-Japanese War** (1894–5) Japan acquired the Liaodong peninsula, including Port Arthur (Lushun), but Russia was building the **Trans-Siberian railway** and did not want Japan to be in a position to dominate **Manchuria**. She therefore persuaded France and Germany to join her in forcing Japan to give up the Liaodong peninsula. Russia provided a loan to enable China to pay the indemnity imposed at the Treaty of **Shimonoseki** and in return China allowed her in 1896 to build the Trans-Siberian railway across Manchuria to Vladivostok. In 1897 Germany seized Qingdao in the Shandong peninsula as a naval base and this was followed by other powers making their own demands. Russia obtained a twenty-five-year lease of the southern Liaodong peninsula and the right to build a railway from Port Arthur to Harbin, where it would link up with the Trans-Siberian railway. This irritated Japan exceedingly, as she had been forced to return this area to China only three years before. France obtained a lease of some territory in the south, near Indo-China. Britain first obtained a twenty-five-year lease of Weihaiwei in the Shandong peninsula and then a ninety-nine-year lease of the New Territories, on the mainland opposite Hong Kong. It appeared that China might be partitioned among the European powers, as Africa had been, but the **Boxer Rising** showed that they would face fierce resistance, so they satisfied themselves with spheres of influence: Russia in Manchuria and the north, France in the south, Britain in the Yangzi valley. The USA, which had no interest in seizing Chinese territory, insisted on an **'open-door' policy**, which would allow all nations to trade freely in China: all the Great Powers, except Russia, accepted this.

**Second Empire,** see **Napoleon III**

**Second Front.** A term used in the **Second World War**, which referred to an Allied attack on German-occupied France. Stalin was demanding this from August 1941 to take German pressure off the Russians, but the disastrous Dieppe raid of August 1942, when two-thirds of the Allied force was lost, showed how difficult an attack on France would be. The Americans wanted an assault across the Channel in 1943 but **Churchill** persuaded **Roosevelt** at the **Casablanca Conference** (January 1943) that this was not possible and that an attack on Italy should come first. The invasion of France finally took place on **D-Day**, 6 June 1944.

**Second International** (1889–1914). The First International Working Men's Association (1864–76) had been disrupted by clashes between **Bakunin** (and his anarchist supporters – see **anarchism**) and **Marx**. In 1889 two separate socialist conferences met in Paris to celebrate the centenary of the **French Revolution**. One consisted of Marxist revolutionary parties, the other of reformists, who believed that socialism could be brought about by parliamentary means. When they merged to form the Second International, it was clear that there would be sharp differences of opinion. Two main issues were to divide the delegates, who represented mainly the European labour movement. The first was whether socialists should take part in *bourgeois* governments, as Millerand did in 1899 when he joined the French government. Millerand was defended by **Jaurès**, the French socialist leader, but the congress at Paris in 1900 decided that such action was acceptable only as 'a temporary expedient'. This debate was extended in 1904 at the next congress in Amsterdam when the revisionist ideas of **Bernstein**, who wanted socialists to abandon revolution in favour of gradual and peaceful reform, were discussed. **Bebel**, leader of the German **Social Democratic Party**, the most powerful party in the International, took the lead in attacking Bernstein and in upholding Marxist orthodoxy. The congress condemned Bernstein, though revisionism continued to have many supporters in the International. The second major issue to dominate the proceedings of the International was the attitude, discussed at the Stuttgart Congress in 1907, that socialists should take if there was a major war. Bebel, Jaurès and most Western socialists wanted the workers to end the war quickly by opposing war credits, by a general strike and by sabotaging the war effort. This did not go far enough for **Lenin** and Rosa **Luxemburg**, who thought that socialists should use the crisis 'to rouse the people and thereby to hasten the abolition of capitalist class rule'. When war did begin in 1914 **nationalism** was stronger than working-class solidarity. All the socialist parties, except those of Serbia and Russia, supported the war waged by their own governments and in so doing brought the Second International to an end.

**Second Republic** (1848–52) in France began when **Louis Philippe** was overthrown and ended with the proclamation of the Second Empire. Concessions had to be made to the Parisian workers who had invaded the Chamber of Deputies and insisted on a republic, so all men over twenty-one were given the vote, the working day was reduced to ten hours in Paris (eleven hours elsewhere) and National Workshops were set up in Paris to provide work for the unemployed. These reforms had to be paid for, so the land tax was increased by 45 per cent, a burden which fell mainly on the peasants. The Second Republic began, therefore, by alienating the mass of the population. In the April elections – the first ever held in a major state by direct manhood suffrage – half of the deputies elected were monarchists and opposed to all social change. Disappointment with this result led the extreme republicans, led by **Blanqui**, to attempt a *coup* in May but this failed and prepared the way for a conservative reaction. When the National Workshops were closed there was a rising of Parisian unemployed in the **June Days**, which was brutally suppressed. A new Constitution in November gave complete executive power to the President; a month later Louis Napoleon Bonaparte (soon to become Emperor **Napoleon III**), the nephew of **Napoleon Bonaparte**, was elected as President by an overwhelming majority. He appeared as a symbol of order and authority, who would protect the Catholic Church, and skilfully used his position to appear as a defender of the rights of the people. When the conservative legislature, alarmed at the success of the **Left** in by-elections, deprived a third of the electors of their vote in May 1850, Louis Napoleon unsuccessfully attempted to have the law repealed. The Constitution allowed the President to take office for only one term: to change it a two-thirds majority was needed in the legislature. Louis Napoleon failed to obtain this, so he prepared for a *coup*. On 2 December 1851 troops occupied the main strategic points in Paris, the Assembly was dissolved and universal male suffrage restored. Under 2,000 attempted violent resistance in Paris, though 100,000 armed peasants and artisans protested in the provinces. The army restored order within a week. The Second Republic finally ended when Louis Napoleon proclaimed the Second Empire in November 1852, a decision given public support in a plebiscite, in which 7.8 million voted for the change, 250,000 against it.

**Second World War** in the West (1939–45). (For the war in the East see **Pacific War**.) As a result of the policy of **appeasement** by Britain and France, Hitler had been able to flout the restrictions imposed on Germany at the Treaty of **Versailles** in 1919. He had reoccupied the Rhineland (see remilitarization of the **Rhineland**), united Germany and Austria in the *Anschluss* and taken the **Sudetenland** from Czechoslovakia. Britain and France became convinced that his aims were not limited to acquiring territory where Germans lived when in March 1939 he occupied the rest of Czechoslovakia. It was clear now that Hitler aimed at European hegemony and that the next object of his greed would be Poland, as East Prussia had been cut off from the rest of Germany at Versailles by the 'Polish Corridor' and Danzig, a German town, had been made a Free City. Britain and France therefore guaranteed Poland's frontiers. Hitler was furious but did not think France and Britain would intervene on Poland's behalf when he made the **Nazi–Soviet Pact** in August 1939. This ended his fear of a war on two fronts and assured him of raw materials from the east.

In the invasion of Poland, which began on 1 September, Hitler successfully used *Blitzkrieg* tactics and by 19 September had overrun the country. Britain and France declared war on Germany but did nothing to aid Poland: the French behind their **Maginot Line** simply waited to be attacked. After the defeat of Poland there followed the 'Phoney War', in which little happened as Hitler regrouped his forces. The Soviet Union, having taken eastern Poland in accordance with the Nazi–Soviet Pact, attacked Finland in the **Finnish–Russian War** (November 1939) and though performing badly, overran the small Finnish army by March 1940, seizing some Finnish territory on her border. In June Stalin occupied Latvia, Lithuania and Estonia on the Baltic, as agreed with Germany. The 'Phoney War' came to an end in April 1940, when Germany conquered Denmark in a day and invaded Norway, in order to protect her iron-ore supplies from the ice-free port of Narvik and to acquire naval bases from which she could threaten Britain's Atlantic supply lines. British troops landed in Norway on 9 April but were withdrawn on 8 June. By this time Belgium, Holland and France had been invaded. As a result of the brilliantly conceived and executed German offensive in the Ardennes, followed by the dash of Panzer units to the Channel coast, the French armies were cut in two, the British had to evacuate their troops from **Dunkirk** and the fall of **France** followed in June. Much of France was occupied by German troops; the rest was controlled by the Vichy government (see **Vichy France**) under Marshal **Pétain**. Now only Britain stood in Hitler's way but Germany's first reverse of the war in the battle of **Britain**, when the *Luftwaffe* failed to destroy the RAF, led Hitler to abandon his planned invasion of England. **Mussolini** had entered the war on Hitler's side on 10 June 1940, so fighting now took place in the Italian colony of Libya in North Africa and in Ethiopia (see **North African Campaigns**).

Hitler had long intended to attack the Soviet Union but first conquered Yugoslavia, Greece and Crete before invading Russia in Operation **Barbarossa** (June 1941). This had remarkable initial success but it failed to capture either Moscow or Leningrad (see siege of **Leningrad**) before winter set in. The offensive was resumed in 1942, with the Germans sweeping to the Volga and south towards the oilfields of the Caucasus. Towards the end of the year Germany suffered her first major defeats, and from then was on the retreat until the end of the war. In October 1942 **Montgomery** defeated **Rommel** at the second battle of El **Alamein** in Egypt and a month later Anglo-American forces landed in Morocco; by May 1943 they controlled the whole North African coast. The

Russians counter-attacked at the battle of **Stalingrad** in November 1942 and by February 1943 had captured the remnants of the German Sixth Army. In July Anglo-American forces invaded Sicily and the Russians defeated the last German offensive in the east in the biggest tank battle of the war: the battle of **Kursk**. The **Italian campaign**, begun in September, was prolonged by fierce German resistance: it took the Allies eleven months to reach Rome. Stalin had long demanded a **Second Front** against the Germans and this took place on **D-Day** (6 June 1944), when Allied troops landed in France. The **Normandy Campaign** freed much of France, whilst the Russians conquered south-eastern Europe, knocking Romania and Bulgaria out of the war, but they failed to aid the **Warsaw Rising** (August–October 1944) which was crushed by the Germans. The Allies did not gain total victory in the **North-West Europe Campaign** of 1944 and the Americans were surprised by a German offensive in the Ardennes in December, which was defeated at the battle of the **Bulge**. The Allied attack resumed in 1945, and the Germans surrendered unconditionally in May that year.

There had been fighting too in the air and at sea. The Allied **strategic bombing offensive** devastated many German towns, whilst German U-boats almost brought disaster to Britain in the battle of the **Atlantic**. **Resistance** fighters disrupted communications and attacked German troops as they retreated. The war had been a total war, in which all the resources of the state were mobilized and civilians were affected more than in any previous war. Millions of slave labourers were taken to Germany and over ten million Germans were expelled from Eastern Europe or fled before the Russian advance. In the '**Final Solution**' the Germans murdered over six million Jews. It is estimated that fifteen million military personnel (including two million Soviet prisoners-of-war) were killed and thirty-five million civilians (twenty million of whom were Russian and 4.5 million Poles). When the war ended all European countries were devastated or bankrupt. The only country that became richer during the war was the USA, which enjoyed a boom and by 1945 was producing half the manufactured goods in the world. The USA and the Soviet Union, with its vast armies, emerged from the war as the two superpowers, who would dominate world affairs in the next decades.

**Sedan** (1–2 September 1870). The main battle of the **Franco-Prussian War**. When Bazaine retreated to Metz, Marshal **Mac-Mahon** decided to fall back on Paris but was ordered to relieve Bazaine. When he was held up sixty miles north-west of Metz, he decided to retire to the fortress of Sedan, near the Belgian frontier. Here **Moltke**, the Prussian Commander, saw his opportunity to surround the French forces. The superiority of the French *chassepot* rifle to the Prussian needle-gun persuaded him to rely on his artillery, which had been vastly improved since its poor performance in the **Austro-Prussian War** (1866). **Krupp** had produced new steel breech-loading field guns, which were superior to the French bronze muzzle-loading guns in range, accuracy and rapidity of fire. Sedan became the greatest artillery battle of the war: all French attacks were halted by Prussian field guns, most of them at 2,000 yards, a range far beyond that of the *chassepot*. The result was a crushing defeat for the French, who suffered losses more than twice as large as their attackers'. **Napoleon III** and 100,000 French troops were captured. This marked the end of the **Second Empire**, as the **Third Republic** was proclaimed in Paris. The balance of power in Europe had been overturned: Germany replaced France as the dominant military power on the Continent.

**Seddon, Richard John** (1845–1906). New Zealand Prime Minister (1893–1906). Born in Lancashire, England, Seddon went to the Australian goldfields before moving to New Zealand in 1866. He became the miners' spokesman, entered parliament and was Minister of Public Works in the Liberal Party's first administration in 1891. Two years later he was Prime Minister and from 1893 to 1906 New Zealand was governed by 'King Dick'. Beatrice **Webb** found him 'intensely vulgar' but also 'shrewd, quick, genial'. His government passed a wide range of radical legislation, much of it the work of William Pember **Reeves**, his Minister of Labour until 1896. Credit was provided at low interest for farmers, graduated land and income taxes induced large landholders to subdivide their properties, compulsory arbitration was provided in industrial disputes, women were given the vote, old-age pensions and free places in secondary schools were introduced. Seddon also bought much land from the Maoris to sell to white farmers and by providing something for everyone he retained his popularity for most of the time he was in office: there were no strikes between 1894 and 1906. Seddon was also an imperialist, who annexed the Cook Islands in 1901 and sent troops to support Britain in the **South African War** (1899–1902).

**Seeckt, Hans von** (1866–1936). Commander-in-Chief of the German army (1920–26). The son of a general, Seeckt served in the **First World War** mainly on the Eastern Front, where he planned the successful breakthrough at Gorlice. As a monarchist, he found difficulty in adjusting to the **Weimar Republic**, of which he had a low opinion. He considered that the army represented the 'national interest' and made it a 'state within the state', with its primary loyalty to the High Command, rather than to the political leaders of the Republic, whom he despised. This was made clear when he was asked by President **Ebert**, at the time of the **Munich (beer-hall)** *Putsch*, whether the army would obey the government or the rebels. 'Herr Reich President, the army will obey *me*', he replied.

He showed that his loyalty to the Republic could not be relied upon when he refused to use the army to crush the right-wing **Kapp** *Putsch* in 1920, though he was quite prepared to use it to put down communist risings in Saxony and the Ruhr. The Nazis hated him, as he had a Jewish wife and ordered the army commander in Bavaria to suppress **Hitler**'s beer-hall *Putsch* in 1923. His main object was to restore German military power by evading the limitations imposed on Germany's armed forces at the Treaty of **Versailles**. The General Staff, forbidden at Versailles, survived in the form of a Troop Bureau, where Seeckt continued to train staff officers. He overcame limitations on the size of the army by emphasizing speed and mobility and by short-term enlistment, which provided a large reserve. To ensure that the army had the latest weapons he did a deal with **Krupp** and other industrialists, who set up factories abroad: aeroplanes and chemicals were produced in Russia, submarines in Spain, tanks in Sweden and other weapons in Holland, Denmark and Switzerland. After the Treaty of **Rapallo** (1922) German pilots and tank crews were trained in Russia. Leading members of the government knew of these arrangements and approved. It was Seeckt who made the German army, which

Hitler was to use so successfully in France in 1940, into such a formidable fighting force.

**Segregation.** A term in common use in South Africa by 1910, which referred to the attempt to keep blacks and whites physically separate in a white-controlled state, in which Africans did not have the same rights as whites. After the **Second World War** it developed into *apartheid*. The Natives' Land Act (1913) aimed to separate whites and blacks territorially. Africans, though 70 per cent of the population, were allocated only 7.5 per cent of the land in South Africa as 'reserves' (this was increased to 13 per cent in 1936). These reserves were where they were supposed to live: when they came to work in the 'white' towns, they had to leave their families behind. They were not allowed to own land outside the reserves. The Natives (Urban Areas) Act of 1923 extended segregation to the towns: blacks were not allowed to live in white areas, but had to live in locations on the outskirts of the towns. All their movements were controlled by Pass Laws and they were prevented from entering white hotels, restaurants or beaches. They also had separate political institutions: blacks took no part in electing the parliament which governed the country but had government-appointed district councils in the reserves to look after their interests. The job colour bar prevented them from taking up skilled jobs in the mines and on the railways and ensured that they provided cheap unskilled labour (their wages were about 10 per cent of white earnings). The origins of segregation go back to slavery in the Cape and the **Afrikaners**' belief that they were God's chosen people and therefore superior to the Africans; but the real basis, as **Hertzog** freely admitted, was fear. If there was democracy in South Africa the whites would be swamped by the more numerous black Africans, whilst a free labour market would push down white wages.

Segregation was also practised in Southern Rhodesia, Kenya (where the White Highlands were reserved for Europeans) and the USA. There various **Civil Rights Acts** tried to protect the Negro but were unable to prevent segregation when the **Supreme Court** in 1896 upheld **'Jim Crow' laws**, provided that 'separate but equal' facilities were provided for Negroes.

*Seize Mai* (**16 May**) **crisis** (1877). The occasion when Marshal **MacMahon**, President of the **Third Republic** in France, dismissed the republican Prime Minister, Jules Simon, and replaced him with the monarchist Duc de Broglie. He then dissolved parliament and called a general election, in which the republicans lost thirty-six seats but still retained a comfortable majority. This crisis was of great constitutional importance. The President had acted within his powers but his humiliation at the polls ensured that he was the last French President to use his power of dissolving parliament and of appointing a Prime Minister who did not enjoy majority support in the Chamber of Deputies. The Legislature was henceforth more important than the President.

**Self-Strengthening movement.** A Chinese attempt to strengthen the **Qing dynasty** by adopting some Western techniques. The dangers to China, posed by her defeat in the **Opium Wars** and the initial success of the **Taiping rebellion**, led some scholar-officials like **Zeng Guofan** and **Li Hongzhang** to see what they could learn from the West. Their aim was basically conservative – to preserve the existing order rather than replace it. They wanted to 'learn the superior barbarian techniques to control the barbarians'. In the 1860s and 1870s they tried to increase their military strength by building Western-style arsenals and a modern navy. Chinese students were sent to Britain, France and Germany for training. This attempt at modernization was superficial, as it was based on the false premiss that Western technology could be accepted whilst maintaining the Confucian system of government and values (see **Confucianism**): 'Chinese learning for essential principles; Western learning for practical application.' The failure of the Self-Strengthening movement was shown in the ease with which Japan defeated China in the **Sino-Japanese War** (1894–5).

**September massacres** (1792), occurred in Paris, which was threatened by invading Prussians. As Verdun, the last major fortress on the road to Paris, was about to fall, thousands of *sans-culottes* volunteered to defend the capital and the Revolution. Once they had left for the front there was concern about the overcrowded prisons, where many priests and nobles, counter-revolutionary suspects, were held. A rumour arose that they were plotting to escape, murder the helpless population and hand the city over to the Prussians. **Marat**, a leading demagogue, called for the conspirators to be killed. The massacre of prisoners began on 2 September and continued for five days. Between 1,100 and 1,400 of the 2,600 prisoners in Paris jails were murdered. Only a quarter were priests and nobles: the rest were common criminals. Most deputies in the **Convention** were shocked, and regarded the *sans-culottes* as blood-thirsty savages – *buveurs de sang* ('drinkers of blood'). Just as the fortunes of war had brought about the September Massacres, they also brought an end to this part of the **Terror**. On 20 September French troops defeated the Prussians at the battle of **Valmy**: Paris was saved.

**Serfdom.** A system in which the peasant did not own land: he worked the land and in return either paid to the landlord dues in money or in kind, or carried out unpaid labour services for a certain number of days each year on the lord's estate. Where labour was scarce and markets distant, lords demanded labour services (called *Robot* in German-speaking areas, *barshchina* in Russia). Such areas were Prussia, Poland, the Danubian Principalities, southern Russia, and many parts of the **Austrian Empire**. Where there was a large population and sizeable local markets, landlords often let out their land and lived on rents and seigneurial dues, as they did in France, and west and central Germany. In both systems the serf was 'tied' to the land: he could not move or marry without his lord's consent and could not inherit or sell land. He was also subject to manorial courts, in which the lord was his own judge and jury.

In France personal servitude existed only in Alsace-Lorraine and this was abolished by the **August Decrees** of 1789. Compensation was supposed to be paid to the *seigneur* for ending some of the most onerous dues and services, but in 1793, to attach the peasants firmly to the **French Revolution**, the services and dues were ended without compensation. Serfdom was abolished in areas occupied by French armies, such as Savoy (1792), the left bank of the Rhine and Switzerland (1798), the Kingdom of Naples (1806), Westphalia (1807), Spain (1808) and parts of north Germany (1811) and was not reimposed after **Napoleon Bonaparte**'s fall. Following her defeat at Jena in 1806 (see battles of **Jena–Auerstädt**) Prussia abolished hereditary serfdom in 1807 (seigneurial courts remained) and in 1811 suppressed labour services and dues, though the peasants had to give up between a third and a half of their allotments to compensate the lords. Many peasants were no better off, as they were not left with enough land to provide for themselves and their families. They had therefore to sell their land and become wage labourers, at the mercy of market forces. The lord was no longer obliged to look after his peasants in bad times. In the Baltic provinces (part of the Russian Empire) serfs were emancipated (1816–19) without being given any land at all. Between 1815 and 1848 serfdom became a heavier burden in the Danubian Principalities and parts of the Austrian Empire, as more labour services were demanded. Emancipation came here as a result of the **Revolutions of 1848**. The Hungarian **Diet** hastily freed the serfs in March 1848, so they would be on the side of the Magyars. In the Austrian parts of the Empire serfs were freed in September, so that they would not join the rebels. The **emancipation of the serfs** took place in Russia in 1861, after her defeat in the **Crimean War**.

**Sèvres, Treaty of** (1920), was imposed on Turkey by the Allies after the **First World War**. Turkey gave up all her non-Turkish territories: the Hijaz was recognized as independent, Syria became a French **mandate**, whilst **Palestine**, Transjordan and Iraq became British mandates. Eastern Thrace and an area round Izmir (Smyrna) in Anatolia went to Greece, the Dodecanese Islands and Rhodes to Italy. The **Straits** were put under a **League of Nations** administration. This treaty was much harsher than the one imposed on Germany at **Versailles** and would have deprived Turkey of some of her richest provinces. The Ottoman Sultan accepted it but it was never applied, as it was rejected by Turkish nationalists led by **Kemal Atatürk**. In a two-year war they drove the Greeks out of Anatolia and obtained much more favourable terms at the Treaty of **Lausanne** in 1923.

**Seyyid Said** (1791–1856). Ruler (1806–56) of Oman and Zanzibar. Seyyid was more concerned with an economic than a territorial empire, so in 1818 he introduced the clove tree to Zanzibar from the East Indies and soon grew three-quarters of the world's supply of cloves on plantations worked by slaves. The slaves were obtained by trade rather than conquest, from African chiefs in the interior. After Seyyid transferred his capital from Muscat to Zanzibar in 1840, Arab traders went in increasing numbers to Lakes Nyasa, Tanganyika and Victoria and beyond to Katanga, where they exchanged cloth and guns bought from Europe for ivory and slaves. Seyyid made commercial treaties with Britain, Germany, France and the United States, so that Zanzibar became the central market for the whole of the East African coast and for much of the interior.

**Shaftesbury, Anthony Ashley Cooper, 7th Earl of** (1801–85), known from 1811–51 as Lord Ashley. English social reformer and supporter of the **Evangelical Movement**. A **Tory** MP from 1826, Shaftesbury was a defender of the landed interest, opposing the **Reform Acts** of 1832 and 1867 and the development of **trade unions**, as he felt they threatened that interest. Yet he believed that the aristocracy had duties and responsibilities as well as rights and this conviction was reinforced by his religion. A believer in the Second Coming of Christ and the infallibility of the Scriptures, he felt called by God to devote himself 'to the cause of the weak and the helpless, both man and beast'. This sombre, gloomy man, who showed some of the characteristics of a manic depressive, therefore spent much of his life promoting social reform.

His first parliamentary campaign was against the practice of *sati* (suttee) in India, the immolation of a Hindu widow on her husband's funeral pyre, which was made illegal in 1829. He then took an active part in bringing about the abolition of the **slave trade** in the British Empire in 1833 and in the same year helped to secure the passage of a **Factory Act**, which limited the hours of work of children in textile factories. In the House of **Commons** he promoted the Mines Act (1842), which forbade females and boys under ten to work underground, and the Ten Hours Act (1847), which limited the work of women and children in textile factories to ten hours a day. Public health was another of his concerns: he was responsible for the Lunacy Act (1845), which improved the treatment of the insane, and as a member of the Board of Health (1848–54) insisted that the government should sponsor low-cost housing for urban workers. For thirty-nine years he was President of the

Ragged Schools Union, which provided schools for children in slums and fought for the abolition of boy chimney sweeps. Shaftesbury also served as President of the British and Foreign Bible Society, founded many branches of the Young Men's Christian Association (YMCA) and financially supported missionary societies for Nonconformists as well as for the Church of England. As an Evangelical he disapproved of the **Oxford Movement** and the increasing ritual in the Church of England and assisted **Disraeli** in passing the Public Worship Act (1874), which halted the spread of Anglo-Catholic practices.

**Shaka** (c. 1787–1828). African Chief and founder of the Zulu nation. The Zulus were one of many small groups of Nguni who lived between the Drakensberg mountains and the Indian Ocean in what became Natal. There were no large states there until Shaka provided one. He was the illegitimate and unwanted son of a Zulu Chief and suffered many humiliations in his youth – his name in Zulu means 'beetle'. Dingiswayo, Chief of the Mthethwa confederacy, recognized Shaka's bravery and made him a regimental commander. Shaka despised the limited war which was customary, when the two sides lined up fifty paces apart, threw spears at one another and exchanged insults. He changed the fighting methods of the Zulus by introducing a short stabbing spear, the *assegai*, which was used to eliminate opponents in hand-to-hand fighting. Warriors had to 'wash their spears' in blood. His battle formation consisted of a 'chest', the main body, and the 'horns', which raced round to encircle the enemy so that it could then be wiped out. Shaka's methods were so effective that they spread terror everywhere and began the *Mfecane* ('the crushing'), when tribes attacked by the Zulus in turn fought against their neighbours, so a vast displacement of peoples began in Southern Africa. When Dingiswayo was murdered in 1818, Shaka became leader of the Mthethwa confederacy, and treated his subjects with remarkable ferocity. Shaka did not marry in case his heir plotted against him and he executed any of his concubines who became pregnant. He expanded his kingdom by incorporating conquered tribes in it and within ten years the Zulu kingdom covered 80,000 square miles. In 1828 Shaka was murdered by his half-brother Dingane but the kingdom he had founded survived, until it was destroyed by the British when they defeated **Cetshwayo** in 1879.

**Shanghai** *coup* (1927). An attempt by **Jiang Jieshi** (Chiang Kai-shek) to destroy the Chinese Communist Party (CCP). When Jiang began his **Northern Expedition** in 1926 to unite China, he was allied to the CCP in the **United Front**, but many of his conservative supporters were alarmed at communist influence in the **Guomindang** (Nationalist Party) and wanted to get rid of it. Many Nationalist generals and businessmen were strongly anti-communist, as were the Western powers and Japan, who feared that the communists would seize foreign settlements. The CCP was well-established in Shanghai: it controlled most of the labour unions, influenced the students and had many front groups. It had created paramilitary units to enforce strikes and assassinate opponents and had seized control of the city just as the Nationalist army was approaching. In April 1927, less than a month after being welcomed by the workers, Jiang turned on the communists. Using money supplied by the Japanese Consul-General and Chinese businessmen, Jiang employed members of Shanghai's underworld to round up and murder communists and their supporters. Zhou Enlai was one of those captured but he escaped. Jiang was not in Shanghai when the *coup* took place: he had gone to Nanjing to supervise a purge of communists there. The Shanghai *coup* is the subject of André Malraux's novel *La Condition Humaine* (*Man's Estate*).

**Sharecropping.** A system of farm tenancy which arose in the USA after the **American Civil War** to provide cheap labour on the plantations. Many planters had a lot of land but little cash for wages; most Negro ex-slaves were poor, illiterate and in desperate need of work. Planters therefore provided land, living quarters, animals and equipment, whilst the tenants provided their own and their family's labour, in return for a part of the crop, usually a half. Sharecropping was most common in the cotton states of the South, where overproduction in the 1890s led to falling prices, but was also found on the tobacco farms of Kentucky, Virginia and Tennessee. Sharecroppers – many of whom were poor whites – were little better off than slaves, as they were bound to their landlords by perpetual debt, on which they paid high interest rates. Their plight deteriorated in the **Great Depression** (1929–39), until the **New Deal** introduced by **Roosevelt** gave them some relief. The Farm Tenant Act (1937) provided loans to sharecroppers for the purchase of land and livestock. Although the number of sharecroppers declined there were still 750,000 (with their families, about three million people) in 1940, most of them living in extreme poverty.

**Sherman, William Tecumseh** (1820–91). Union general in the **American Civil War**. Sherman commanded a division at Shiloh and took a major part in **Grant**'s Vicksburg and Chattanooga campaigns in 1863. When Grant left to take charge of all Union armies in March 1864, Sherman took over his command in the West. After a long campaign he at last captured Atlanta in Georgia – a centre of communications and of the South's infant industries – on 1 September. He then decided to march from Atlanta to the sea, living off the land. He knew that the South's ability to wage war lay in its resources: if these were destroyed, and also the South's will to fight, the war would come to an end quickly. He therefore deliberately devastated the land through which he advanced, cutting a destructive path fifty miles wide and 250 miles long. Anything which might be of use to the enemy was destroyed – railways, bridges, food, livestock. Slaves were freed and the mansions of plantation owners burned down. He was determined 'to make Georgia howl'. After he had captured Georgia's capital, Savannah, he turned north to the Carolinas, where the destruction continued. He surprised his Confederate foes (see **Confederate States of America**) by the speed of his advance and marched 425 miles in fifty days, much of it through waterlogged land the Confederates thought was impassable. By February 1865 he had captured Charleston and moved to join up with Grant, but before he could do so the war was over. On 26 April Sherman accepted the surrender of the last Confederate troops. When Grant was elected President in 1868 Sherman became General-in-Chief of the US army, a position he held for fifteen years. A year after his retirement some Republicans wanted to nominate him for the presidency, a move ended by his famous retort, 'If nominated I will not run. If elected I will not serve.'

**Shimonoseki, Treaty of** (1895), ended the **Sino-Japanese War** (1894–5). Japan acquired Taiwan, the Pescadores islands and the

Liaodong Peninsula (including Port Arthur). Korea was to be independent, though Japanese influence was now dominant there and it was annexed by Japan in 1910. A huge indemnity was to be paid to Japan and more Chinese ports were opened to foreign trade. The treaty also provided for a Treaty of Commerce, concluded in 1896. This gave Japan 'most-favoured nation' treatment (she was given the same privileges in China as the Western powers) and allowed her and the European powers to set up their own industries in the treaty ports. France, Russia and Germany soon forced Japan to give up her claim to the Liaodong peninsula but her expansionist intentions in China had been clearly demonstrated.

**Showa** **Restoration.** *Showa* ('Enlightened Peace') was the reign name taken by the Emperor **Hirohito**. A *Showa* Restoration was the aim of several *coups* carried out by young right-wing officers and nationalists in the 1930s, who intended to restore the 'true relationship' between the Emperor and his people by getting rid of political parties and democratic institutions. Their grievances were both economic and political. Many junior officers came from the countryside, which suffered greatly from the depression of 1929–30, when the market for Japanese silk in America collapsed and cotton exports declined. They were anti-capitalist and criticized the wealth of the *zaibatsu* ('financial clique'), which they accused of serving its own interests rather than those of the nation. They hated the politicians who agreed to limit the size of the navy at the **London Naval Conference** (1930) and who sought to reduce the military budget. The result was the shooting of the Prime Minister Hamaguchi Osachi in November 1930: he died from his wounds the following year. In 1931 there was a plan to annihilate the Cabinet whilst it was in session, by an air attack, but the plot was betrayed. Its leaders were arrested but received absurdly mild punishments: reprimands and postings outside Tokyo. The assassination of Prime Minister Inukai Tsuyoshi by naval officers and army cadets was again followed by the mild sentence of four years' imprisonment. This demoralized the politicians and ended party Cabinets: no party politician served as Prime Minister again until 1945. The most serious *coup* attempt was the **February Rising**

of 1936, in which several ministers were killed. By this time politicians, fearful of assassination or of starting a military revolution, were not prepared to stand up to the army, which increasingly decided who should be in the Cabinet. After the start of the **Sino-Japanese War** (1937–45) all parties supported the armed forces. Some government ministers felt that the existence of political parties undermined national unity, so in 1940 all were disbanded and were not revived until 1945.

**Sian incident** (1936), see **Xi'an incident**

**Sieyès, Abbé Emmanuel Joseph** (1748–1836). French politician. A priest, Sieyès became well-known by writing political pamphlets, especially one entitled *What is the Third Estate?*, when **Louis XVI** announced the calling of the **Estates-General**. Sieyès attacked the privileges of the Church and nobility, advocated popular sovereignty and representative government and said that if the privileged orders refused to join the Third Estate in a common assembly, then the Third Estate, which represented the overwhelming majority of the people, should take the direction of the nation's affairs into its own hands. Carrying theory into practice, he proposed on 17 June 1789 that the Third Estate should take the title of National Assembly. Sieyès contributed to the Constitutions of 1791 (which imposed a property qualification for voting) and 1795, which aimed to maintain the gains of the **French Revolution** whilst making a dictatorship like that of the **Committee of Public Safety** impossible. Under the **Directory** he believed that the Executive needed strengthening and planned with **Napoleon Bonaparte** the *coup d'état* of **Brumaire**, which brought an end to the Directory. For a brief period in 1799 he was one of three Consuls, but gave up this position as Napoleon rejected so much of the Constitution Sieyès had drawn up. After Napoleon's fall he fled to Brussels but returned to France in 1830 on the fall of **Charles X**.

**Singapore, fall of** (February 1942). The surrender of the largest British-led force ever to lay down its arms was the most humiliating military defeat in British history. When the Japanese, led by General **Yamashita**, invaded Malaya and Siam (Thailand) on 8 December 1941, the British were unprepared. They had no tanks and few anti-tank and anti-aircraft guns. Yamashita had tanks, and air and sea superiority, particularly when the British battleship *Prince of Wales* and the battle-cruiser *Repulse* were sunk by Japanese carrier-based aircraft. The Japanese advanced mainly on roads and tracks and not through the jungle, bypassing British strong-points by seaborne landings. Instead of holding these defensible positions the British Commander, General Percival, abandoned them, so that Yamashita conquered Malaya more quickly than he expected. By 31 January 1944 the British had evacuated the mainland and concentrated their troops on the island of Singapore. Percival behaved with unbelievable complacency and ineptitude. Until 7 January he had refused to allow defences to be prepared on the northern coast of the island, as he believed such a move would be bad for morale. Yamashita began to cross the Johore Straits on 8 February after an intensive air bombardment. When Percival surrendered unconditionally on 15 February the British army, though short of food and water, had plenty of ammunition. Yamashita's forces by this time were a third of the British strength and they had almost run out of ammunition. 80,000 British, Australian and Indian troops were captured. Allied losses in the whole campaign were 138,700, of whom over 130,000 were taken prisoner. Japanese casualties were 9,824.

**Sinn Fein** (Gaelic, 'Ourselves Alone'). Irish political party which aimed to create a united, republican Ireland. Founded by Arthur **Griffith** in 1905, it had little importance until the **First World War**. The execution of leaders of the **Easter Rising** (1916) and **Lloyd George**'s attempt to enforce conscription in Ireland brought Sinn Fein much support and it became the focus of republican opposition to British rule. In October 1917, when **de Valera** became leader of the movement, there were 1,200 Sinn Fein clubs in Ireland with 250,000 members. Sinn Fein won an astonishing victory in the 1918 election, when seventy-three of its candidates were among the 105 Irish MPs elected. They refused to take their seats at Westminster and declared themselves to be the parliament of the Irish Republic (*Dail Eireann* or Assembly of Ireland). Though many members were in prison or on the run, they set up their own government of Ireland in rivalry to the official administration. Sinn Fein was the main anti-British political organization in the **Anglo-**

**Irish War** (1919–21), but many members refused to accept the **Anglo-Irish Treaty** (1921) which established the Irish Free State, as it was part of the British Commonwealth and required an oath of allegiance to the British Crown. De Valera, who opposed the treaty, set up his own party, **Fianna Fail**, in 1926 and this absorbed most Sinn Fein members, so that in the 1927 election Sinn Fein gained only 2.7 per cent of the votes and no seats. It did not contest an election again until 1957, when it won four seats. Sinn Fein's main importance since the 1920s has been its links with the **Irish Republican Army** (IRA), many of whose members belong to Sinn Fein, though the latter had little control over them.

**Sino-Japanese War** (1894–5). China's decline as a great power was apparent when other countries began moving into areas which had recognized Chinese suzerainty: France annexed Cochin China (south Vietnam) in 1862, and in 1864 declared a protectorate over Annam and Tonkin (central and north Vietnam). Japan annexed the Ryukyu islands in 1879 and Britain made Burma a protectorate in 1885. Japan was interested in Korea, China's most important tributary state, and in 1884 made an agreement with China which almost made Korea a joint protectorate. When the Korean government asked China for aid against rebels in 1894, Japan also sent troops and this resulted in clashes which led to war. Japanese forces proved to be far better equipped and trained than their Chinese opponents: the Chinese fleet was destroyed and Lushun (Port Arthur) captured, China's best troops were defeated at Pyongyang in Korea and the Japanese advanced into Manchuria, threatening Beijing (Peking), the Chinese capital. The Chinese were forced to seek peace at the Treaty of **Shimonoseki**. China's defeat was an unbearable humiliation, as Japan had once been a Chinese vassal, and had disastrous effects in China. The **Self-Strengthening movement** had clearly failed, as China had been defeated by a smaller Asian nation, whose modernization had begun only after the **Meiji Restoration** in 1868. More radical efforts at reform were therefore made in the **Hundred Days** (1898) but were thwarted by the Empress Dowager **Cixi**. Japan's success encouraged other powers to seize parts of China in the '**scramble for concessions**' and it appeared that China might be partitioned amongst the great powers. The prestige of the **Qing dynasty** plummeted still further and this contributed to the **Boxer Rising**. Another effect of the war was that Japan was now recognized as a major power in East Asia: a threat to Britain's maritime supremacy there and to Russia on land.

**Sino-Japanese War** (1937–45). Japanese troops had seized **Manchuria** after the **Manchurian Incident** (1931–2). After that there were small-scale clashes between Chinese and Japanese troops in north China, including one at the Marco Polo Bridge, near Beijing (Peking), on 7 July 1937. There was more serious fighting in Shanghai which led to full-scale war, though neither side declared war. The Japanese thought the war would be over quickly and this appeared to be confirmed by the speed of their early advance. By the end of 1937 they had captured Beijing, Shanghai and Nanjing, the Chinese capital, where there was an orgy of destruction (see Rape of **Nanjing**). The Nationalist government of **Jiang Jieshi** (Chiang Kai-shek) moved to the safety of Chongqing in Sichuan province, where it was protected by the Yangzi gorges. To delay the Japanese advance towards the great industrial complex of Wuhan, Jiang blew up the dikes of the Yellow river, thus flooding 4,000 villages and drowning many Chinese peasants. This changed the course of the Yellow river, which since the 1850s had flowed into the sea north of the Shandong peninsula: now it flowed further south across northern Jiangsu province. The Japanese captured Wuhan in October 1938 and also seized Guangzhou (Canton). Jiang had now lost all of eastern China from Manchuria to the semi-tropical south, with all the wealthy industrial cities and China's most fertile land.

The fall of Wuhan marked the end of the Japanese advance for the time being. They wanted China's resources for their own industrial development but did not want to tie down most of their army in occupying the whole of China. Instead they worked to set up puppet regimes, as in Manchuria. Japanese control of northern China and the lower Yangzi valley was therefore never completed and was centred on the main cities and the railway lines. There was a stalemate by 1939, which lasted until 1944. Jiang, after the **Xi'an incident**, when he was arrested by his own troops, had joined with **Mao Zedong** and the communists in a **United Front** against

Japan. It was the communists who carried on guerrilla warfare against the Japanese, often behind enemy lines, and gradually extended the territory under their control in north China. The Japanese responded brutally in their 'three-alls' campaign, 'kill all, burn all, destroy all', in a terroristic attempt to prevent peasants aiding the communists. Jiang, having lost his industrial base in the east, received little foreign aid until 1941, when the USA provided assistance under the **Lend-Lease Act**. As there was no railway at Chongqing, Jiang had to rely on the Burma Road (715 miles long, 600 of them in China), which opened in December 1938, for supplies. In 1942 the road was closed, as the Japanese conquered South-East Asia in the **Pacific War**. Jiang was therefore reluctant to launch a major offensive against the Japanese, particularly as he was fearful of communist gains in the north. Instead of fighting the Japanese, he used half a million troops to blockade the communist base at **Yanan**. The Pacific War placed an added strain on the Japanese, whose war in China drained them of men and money: from 1937 they had at least 700,000 troops in China, a number which had increased to 1.25 million (over half the number of Japanese troops overseas) by 1945. They had another 900,000 in Manchuria.

In 1944 Japan began her only major offensive since 1938, as in June 1944 the Americans had used Chinese airfields to bomb Japanese cities. The Japanese quickly overran the airfields in the south and then stopped, but Jiang's weakness and incompetence had been cruelly exposed. The American General Stilwell, attached to Jiang's command since 1942, had long complained of the inefficiency and corruption of the Nationalist government and now demanded that he be given command of Nationalist forces. Jiang would not accept this and Stilwell was recalled. Unrest was widespread in China, with peasants resenting increased taxes, grain levies and conscription, and there was famine in many areas. Only the Allied defeat of Japan saved Jiang from further humiliation. After accepting the **Potsdam Declaration**, the Japanese surrendered to Jiang on 9 September 1945.

**Slave trade, abolition of the.** The first states to abolish slavery were Quaker Pennsylvania and Puritan Massachusetts in 1780; by the end of the century they had been joined by all the north-eastern states of the USA. The Southern states depended almost entirely on slave labour to work the cotton plantations, so slavery continued there: the Mason–Dixon line between Pennsylvania and Maryland divided the two sides. In Britain the Society for the Abolition of the Slave Trade was formed in 1787 by William Wilberforce and Thomas Clarkson, members of the Clapham Sect, but even with the support of the Prime Minister, William **Pitt**, and the leader of the opposition, Charles James **Fox**, a bill for abolition was defeated in 1791. Most people regarded slavery as a form of property, which could not be touched. Not until there was a glut of sugar and a consequent fall in prices did some sugar planters come to regard free labour as more efficient than slave labour, as it required no capital outlay and could be laid off in a slump. In 1807 the slave trade was made illegal for British merchants: the Danes had already taken this action in 1804 and were soon followed by the USA and other countries. The status of existing slaves was not affected until 1833, when Britain abolished slavery in her Empire. 668,000 slaves were set free in the West Indies, about half of them in Jamaica.

Britain was the only country which strictly enforced laws against the slave trade and kept a permanent naval patrol in West African waters to stop it. It had only modest success. Between 1825 and 1865 130,000 slaves were set free from captured ships, but in the same period it is estimated that 1,800,000 slaves were exported from West Africa, mainly to the USA, Brazil and Cuba, where the demand for cotton and sugar caused the slave trade to expand. The economics of some West African states had become heavily dependent on the slave trade: their rulers refused to stop capturing and selling slaves. It was not British activity which ended the West African slave trade but the abolition of slavery in the USA in 1863 during the **American Civil War**, largely caused by the issue of slavery. Cuba (1886) and Brazil (1888) were forced to follow suit. Two regions of Africa were almost unaffected by the end of the Atlantic slave trade: the export of slaves to North and East Africa actually increased. When **Seyyid Said** transferred his capital from Muscat to Zanzibar in 1840, he expanded the clove plantations there, which were manned by slaves. Arab traders went as far as the Great Lakes of Central Africa to find slaves. Slaves were also exported to North Africa via the Nile and Sahara routes. Bornu constantly raided the area south of Lake Chad for slaves and in Kano (northern Nigeria) there were open slave markets. The Sultan of Zanzibar was persuaded by the British to end the slave trade in 1873 but in North and East Africa it did not finally come to an end until the twentieth century.

**Slavophiles** were members of the Russian intelligentsia in the mid-nineteenth century, who wanted Russia's development to be based on Russian institutions, particularly the Orthodox Church and the cooperative peasant commune or *mir*. They were opposed to the Westernizers, who, inspired by the **French Revolution**, wanted to imitate the West and introduce political freedom and constitutional government. The Slavophiles regarded Peter the Great's Westernizing policies, such as state control over the people and the Orthodox Church, as the source of all the evils in Russia. They were not opposed to reform and favoured emancipation of the serfs, civil liberties and an institution which represented the people. They had, therefore, much in common with the Westernizers. **Herzen** compared his followers and Slavophile opponents to the two heads of the imperial eagle, in whose breast the same heart beat, though the heads faced opposite ways. The Slavophiles were most active in the 1840s and 1850s. After the reforms of **Alexander II** the movement declined, though its principles were adopted by nationalists, Panslavs (see **Panslavism**) and **Populists**. The conflict between Slavophiles and Westernizers later reappeared in the division between Populists and Marxists.

**Slim, William Joseph, 1st Viscount** (1891–1970). British field marshal. Slim was commissioned from the ranks in the **First World War**, after which he transferred to the Indian army. When the Japanese attacked Burma in the **Second World War**, Slim was sent there and from March to May 1942 he conducted the longest retreat in British history of 900 miles from Rangoon to Imphal in India. There he built up a fighting force from demoralized troops, whom he trained to live and fight in the jungle and to survive for long periods when away from their bases. He mixed freely with his men and made them confident that they could defeat the Japanese in jungle warfare by using guerrilla tactics. When the Japanese attacked Kohima and Imphal (March–June 1944), he drove them back in bitter fighting and then began the reconquest of Burma. He crossed the Irrawaddy river by deceiving the Japanese, defeated them at Meiktila and was in the Burmese capital of Rangoon in May 1945. In their retreat from Burma the Japanese lost 350,000 troops: it was their greatest defeat in the **Pacific War**. After the war Slim became Chief of the Imperial General Staff (1948–52) and Governor-General of Australia (1953–60). Earl Mountbatten regarded him as the finest general of the Second World War.

**Smuts, Jan Christian** (1870–1950). South African soldier and Prime Minister (1919–24 and 1939–48). Smuts was at the centre of South African politics in the first half of the twentieth century and was the only South African up to the 1990s to be widely recognized as an international statesman. An **Afrikaner**, he was born in the Cape Colony and studied at the Universities of Stellenbosch and Cambridge (1889–94). In 1896, disgusted with the **Jameson Raid**, he moved to the South African Republic (Transvaal) and on the outbreak of the **South African War** (1899–1902) was given command of Boer troops operating in the Cape. He fought to the end of the war and, with Louis **Botha**, played a leading role in the negotiations which ended with the Treaty of **Vereeniging**. They were both founders in 1905 of an Afrikaner party, *Het Volk* ('the People'), which sought self-government for the Transvaal and the Orange River Colony. When the British government conceded this in 1907, Smuts became Minister of the Interior in the Transvaal and was a delegate to the National Convention in 1909, which led to the creation of the Union of South Africa (1910), under white minority rule but in the British Empire. Botha became Prime Minister, Smuts holding several ministerial posts under him.

Smuts and Botha formed the South Africa Party (SAP) in 1911 and favoured South Africa's entry into the **First World War**, though they were condemned by many Afrikaners for putting down the Afrikaner rebellion of 1914, which opposed the use of South African troops to conquer German South-West Africa. Smuts was then put in command of British forces fighting in East Africa and represented South Africa at the Imperial War Conference. His considerable energy and ability gained him a place in **Lloyd George**'s War Cabinet (1917–18). At the **Paris Peace Conference**

(1919) Smuts advocated a conciliatory peace with Germany, worked with Woodrow **Wilson** to set up the **League of Nations** and invented the **mandates** system.

With the death of Botha (1919), Smuts became Prime Minister. In 1922 he brutally suppressed the **Rand revolt** of white miners and as a result suffered in the 1924 election, when the SAP lost its majority and Barry **Hertzog** became Prime Minister. From then until 1933 Smuts led the opposition in the South African parliament. During the **Great Depression** Hertzog's government needed wider support, so he made a coalition with the SAP in 1933, Smuts becoming Deputy Prime Minister. A year later Hertzog's National Party (NP) and the SAP 'fused' to become the United Party. The price Smuts had to pay for this was that he had to agree to the ending of the Cape franchise for Africans, who no longer had even a limited say in electing white members of parliament. Smuts had long recognized that blacks were treated unjustly but was not prepared to do anything about it. As long ago as 1906 he had written, 'I sympathize profoundly with the native races of South Africa, whose land it was long before we came here to force a policy of dispossession on them', but weakly added, 'I feel inclined to shift the intolerable burden of solving the problem on to the ampler shoulders ... of the future'. Consequently he supported a policy of **segregation**.

When the **Second World War** broke out in 1939, Hertzog wanted South Africa to remain neutral; Smuts supported South Africa's entry into the war on Britain's side. Hertzog was narrowly defeated and Smuts became Prime Minister again. He played a leading role in wartime diplomacy as a close associate of Winston **Churchill** and wrote the preamble to the Charter of the United Nations in 1945. In his last years Smuts began to move away from segregation, though he thought there was plenty of time to bring about the necessary changes, and was shocked when the National Party, campaigning on a programme of *apartheid*, won the 1948 election. For the last two years of his life he led the opposition in the South African parliament.

**Social Darwinism.** The application to politics and society of what were believed to be Charles Darwin's biological theories of 'natural selection' and the 'survival of the fittest' (a phrase of Herbert Spencer) in the struggle for existence. The doctrine was used to justify the class system, the political status quo and the competitive capitalist system. Unrestricted competition was held to be in accordance with natural selection, in which wealth was a sign of success, poverty an indication of unfitness to survive. The state should not help the poor by social reform, as this would interfere with natural selection. Social Darwinism was applied to relations between states as well as to relations between individuals, as life was a constant struggle in which the fittest would survive. This led to *Weltpolitik* and **imperialism** and affected statesmen as varied as Lord **Salisbury**, Joseph **Chamberlain**, **Bethmann-Hollweg** and Theodore **Roosevelt**. Racialist theories also reflected Social Darwinist ideas. 'I contend', wrote Cecil **Rhodes**, 'that we are the first race in the world and the more of the world we inhabit the better it is for the human race.' Nazi racial theories (see **Nazism**) and **Hitler**'s conception of *Lebensraum* were influenced by Social Darwinism and were used as a form of **negative integration**.

**Social Democratic Party** (SPD). German political party. In 1875 Lassalle's General German Workers' Union and the Social Democratic Workers Party of **Bebel** and Liebknecht joined together at Gotha to form the German Social Democratic Party. The Gotha programme was a mixture of the ideas of **Marx** and Lassalle: its aim was to overthrow the existing order but it said that it would use only legal means to do so. Although it gained only twelve seats in the **Reichstag** election of 1877, **Bismarck** was determined to crush the new party and in 1878 introduced an **anti-socialist law**, which banned Social Democratic meetings and publications but still allowed their candidates to stand at elections. In spite of government harassment the SPD continued to grow, especially when the anti-socialist law lapsed in 1890. The SPD was the dominant force in the **Second International**, the largest and best organized of all the socialist parties in Europe: by 1912 it had 110 seats in the Reichstag, more than any other party. Kautsky, the party's theoretician, had introduced a more Marxist programme in 1891. Bebel refused to cooperate with *bourgeois*, liberal parties: this self-imposed isolation led to the SPD forming its own sub-culture. SPD newspapers, libraries, social and sports clubs were formed; there was a women's movement, a youth movement and even burial clubs. All these promoted self-reliance and pride in working-class culture but they were not revolutionary. In spite of its revolutionary rhetoric and its hostility to **Bernstein**'s revisionism, the SPD wanted to bring about change peacefully and in 1914 voted unanimously for war credits. During the war the SPD split: forty-two deputies left the party in April 1917 to form the Independent Socialist Party (USPD), which left sixty-eight Majority Socialists led by **Ebert**. The USPD called for an early end to the war and was supported by the Revolutionary Shop Stewards, who organized the great strike of January 1918 which the Majority Socialists condemned as unpatriotic. During the **German Revolution**, which began in October 1918, the SPD acted cautiously, and when Ebert became Chancellor he called in the army to deal with disturbances of the extreme left and bring the Revolution to an end. The SPD leaders were blamed by the USPD and the communists for betraying the Revolution. During the **Weimar Republic** the SPD, though the largest party, controlled the government only from 1928–30. The SPD offered no resistance to von **Papen**'s *coup* in Prussia in 1932, as it wanted to avoid civil war, but it was the only party to vote, courageously, against the **Enabling Act** (March 1933), which gave **Hitler** dictatorial powers. The Nazis banned the SPD in June 1933. It was re-formed in 1959 in West Germany as a non-Marxist party and between 1966 and 1982 took part in several coalition governments.

**Socialism.** The word was first used in 1827 to describe Robert **Owen**'s cooperative doctrines but when it came to be applied more widely in the 1830s it had no single meaning. Socialists wanted an alternative system to capitalism, in which cooperation would replace competition and there would be communal control of production and distribution. They believed in economic equality in the form expressed by Louis **Blanc**: 'from each according to his ability, to each according to his needs'. Few early socialists believed in revolution which, they thought, devoured its own children, as the **French Revolution** had done. This attitude was challenged by Karl **Marx**, whose *Communist Manifesto* (1848) encouraged violent revolution to overthrow capitalism. Henceforth, socialists were divided in their attitude to revolution and to the state, which Marx regarded as a means of class oppression. Some, such as Lassalle in Germany, wanted to use the state to achieve their ends peacefully, by working through elected parliaments to bring about social change. Orthodox Marxists, such as **Bebel** and other leaders of the **Social Democratic Party** (SPD) in Germany, opposed any cooperation with *bourgeois* governments and advocated revolution, though their revolutionary rhetoric was at odds with their practice. They condemned **Bernstein** but in effect accepted his revisionist doctrines. In Britain the **Fabian Society** and the **Labour Party** followed the parliamentary road to socialism. In France **Sorel** advocated the overthrow of capitalism by a general strike of trade unions but **syndicalism** failed there, as it did elsewhere. After the **October Revolution** (1917) in Russia, those who favoured revolution formed communist parties, leaving the socialists to pursue their aims through democratically elected parliaments. In the first half of the twentieth century some socialist ideals found expression in the **Welfare State**, particularly in Britain and in Scandinavian countries.

**Socialist Revolutionary Party.** Russian revolutionary party formed in 1901; it was an off-shoot of the **Populist** movement of the 1870s. Its leaders – urban workers and intelligentsia – came from the cities but they enthusiastically took up the cause of the peasantry. Land, they believed, should be the possession of the whole nation, and should be granted to the peasants according to their needs. The Socialist Revolutionaries (SRs) also believed in terrorism to destabilize the Tsarist regime and were responsible for the assassination of ministers such as Plehve in 1904. During the **Russian Revolution** of 1905 SRs played a leading role in the October general strike, which forced Tsar **Nicholas II** to agree to the election of a **Duma**. After the fall of the Tsar in the **February Revolution** of 1917 some SRs joined the **Provisional Government** in May and agreed to postpone all radical change, including land reform, until a Constituent Assembly was elected. This split the party. The Left SRs wanted a peasant revolution and in October 1917 formed a separate party and collaborated with the **Bolsheviks**. The SRs had widespread support among the peasants and when the Constituent

Assembly met in January 1918, they were by far the largest party. They bitterly opposed the dissolution of the Assembly by the Bolsheviks. The Left SRs were members of the Bolshevik government from December 1917 to March 1918 and left it because they considered the Treaty of **Brest–Litovsk** to be 'a betrayal'. They then resorted to terrorism again and tried, unsuccessfully, to seize power by a *coup* in Moscow in July 1918. Some SRs supported White forces during the **Russian Civil War** but Bolshevik success in that war brought an end to their activities. They were outlawed, with other parties, in 1922.

**Somme, battle of the** (24 June–18 November 1916). An attack by British troops under **Haig** and French troops under the command of **Joffre**, which aimed to break through German lines on the Somme. Owing to France's crippling losses at the battle of **Verdun** the British for the first time took the main part in the Western Front offensives. A seven-day barrage, so intense that it could be heard across the Channel, began the battle but it failed to destroy the deep German dug-outs or the barbed wire in front of their trenches. When the infantry went over the top in line abreast on 1 July, weighed down by their 66 lb. packs, they were mown down by German machine guns. 56,000 British and Empire troops were casualties on that first day, 19,000 of whom were killed, for trifling gains. South of the river French attacks failed to break the German lines. The British continued to make smaller-scale attacks until September, when Haig launched another major assault with twelve divisions, preceded by thirty-two tanks, which surprised the Germans but were too few and unreliable (some broke down, others stuck in the mud) to make much difference. By October rain had turned the ground into a quagmire, but still Haig pressed on with his attacks until November. By this time the British had gained a strip of land twenty miles wide and six miles deep, of no strategic importance, for losses of 400,000. The French losses were 200,000, the German perhaps half a million. A large part of the 'New Army', raised by **Kitchener** from volunteers, had been destroyed but the German army had also lost a large proportion of its junior officers and NCOs and had been considerably weakened.

**Sonderbund** ('separate league') (1845–7) was formed by seven Roman Catholic cantons in Switzerland to protect Catholic interests and preserve the autonomy of the cantons. The liberal Protestant cantons, which wanted to establish a more centralized government and had a majority in the Swiss **Diet**, persuaded the Diet in 1847 to dissolve the *Sonderbund* and expel the Jesuits. The Catholic cantons took up arms and appealed to **Metternich** and **Louis Philippe** for help, but they were defeated in less than a month, before foreign powers could intervene. The new federal Constitution of 1848 ended the sovereignty of the separate cantons.

**Sorel, Georges** (1847–1922). French theorist of **syndicalism**. Sorel combined **Marx**'s belief in the class struggle with **Nietzsche**'s idea of the will to power, to exalt the moral value of violence and action for its own sake. His *Reflections on Violence* (1908) put forward the general strike as the main weapon in the class war. Sorel argued that men are moved by 'myths', irrational beliefs that lead to action. The general strike was such a myth, which would be successful in overthrowing capitalism, if workers were really convinced of their own strength. The **CGT** (French trade-union federation) accepted the idea in 1906 but its attempt at a general strike failed. Sorel also adapted Nietzsche's idea of the superman in urging 'audacious minorities' to seize political leadership. Sorel's faith in the power of myth later influenced **Mussolini**.

**Sorge, Richard** (1895–1944). Russian spy. Born in Baku, the son of a German mining engineer, Sorge served in the **First World War** in the German army. After the war he became a communist and agent for the **Comintern** in the Far East, with his headquarters in Shanghai, where he worked as the editor of a German news agency. In 1933 he was sent to Tokyo with a cover job as correspondent for the *Frankfurter Zeitung*. There he established the first major spy ring in Japanese history, with Japanese collaborators who received highly confidential information from Cabinet sources. To prevent suspicion he posed as a loyal **Nazi** and worked as an agent for the German embassy. Sorge gave the Russians advance information of the **Anti-Comintern Pact** (1936) and was only two days out in his prediction of Hitler's invasion of Russia in June 1941, a warning Stalin ignored. After Operation **Barbarossa** had begun it was crucial for the Russians to know whether Japan intended to attack the Soviet Union (and so involve her in a two-front war), or the United States. At the end of August 1941 Sorge told them that there would be no attack on the Soviet Union, so they were able to move troops from Siberia to defend Moscow successfully. In October 1941 Sorge and a Japanese collaborator were arrested; they were held in prison until November 1944, when they were hanged.

**South African War** (1880–81). The first of two wars fought between British and **Afrikaners** in South Africa. In the 1870s the poverty-stricken Boer republic of the Transvaal (South African Republic or SAR), which had only 40,000 white inhabitants, could not cope with the wars with neighbouring African tribes. Britain annexed the Transvaal in 1877 and followed this up by defeating the Zulus under **Cetshwayo** in 1879. With the Zulu threat removed, the Boers under Paul **Kruger** wanted to recover their independence and took up arms in December 1880. British garrisons were besieged in Pretoria and other towns, whilst a relieving force from Natal was held up at the strategic pass of Laing's Nek. A few weeks later the Boers defeated a British force at Majuba Hill. The British government wanted peace and in August 1881 recognized the independence of the SAR, although its foreign relations remained under British control.

**South African War** (1899–1902). The second war fought between British and Afrikaners in South Africa. Ever since gold was discovered on the **Rand** in 1885, and the SAR (Transvaal) had become the richest state in South Africa, Britain had cast covetous eyes upon it. She was able to use the grievances of *uitlanders* ('foreigners'), who were denied the vote, to put pressure on President **Kruger** for reform, but what **Milner**, the British High Commissioner in South Africa from 1897, really wanted was to control the Rand. The Transvaal had formed a military alliance with the Orange Free State in 1896, so when war began Britain was fighting two Boer republics. The first phase of the war took place between October and December 1899 and saw an unbroken run of Boer successes. At first the Boers outnumbered British troops and invaded Natal to try to reach Durban before British reinforcements arrived. They did not succeed, owing to the caution of the Boer Commander Joubert, but they locked up 80 per cent of the British army in Natal in the siege of Ladysmith. Mafeking and Kimberley were also besieged and in the first week of December (Black Week for the British), the Boers won victories at Stromberg, Magersfontein and Colenso.

After these disasters, with the British pinned down from the northern Cape to Natal, Lord Roberts replaced General Buller as Commander, with **Kitchener** as his Chief of Staff. The second phase of the war, from January to September 1900, now began. Roberts relieved Kimberley in February and in the same month trapped 4,000 Boers at Paardeberg and forced them to surrender. Bloemfontein, the capital of the Orange Free State, was occupied, Mafeking relieved and the Orange Free State annexed by Britain. General Pretorius, pinned against the mountains, surrendered with a large part of the Orange Free State army. Roberts then resumed his move north, occupied Johannesburg and Pretoria and in September annexed the Transvaal. Convinced the war was over he went home, leaving Kitchener as Commander-in-Chief. The war, however, continued.

There had been divisions among the Boers between the *hensoppers* ('hands-uppers', those who surrendered) and the *bittereinders* ('bitter-enders', diehards who wanted to continue fighting). The *bittereinders* fought on, and so the war entered its third and last phase, from September 1900 to May 1902. They avoided pitched battles but in a guerrilla war used mobile commandos to attack British communications. **Hertzog** invaded the Cape at the end of 1900 and set off an **Afrikaner** rebellion there, and in 1901 was followed by **Smuts**, who came within sight of Cape Town. There was no effective occupation. Boers lived off the land and never had more than 30,000 armed men but they tied down 250,000 British troops, spread out over thousands of miles of communications. To deprive the Boers of food and of local support Kitchener turned to a scorched-earth policy, which had been used in the **American Civil War** and by Roberts in Afghanistan. There was a systematic destruction of Boer farms, crops and livestock, supplemented by block houses. The Boers from the farms were put in **concentration camps**, where many died from epidemics of measles and enteric fever. Of 136,000 Boers in the camps about 27,000 died, which led the **Liberal** leader of the opposition in Britain, **Campbell-Bannerman**, to refer to 'methods of barbarism'. 115,000 African servants were also put in camps, of whom at least 14,000 died. As the number of Boer commandos was reduced to 17,000 and the Pedi rose against their former masters, the Boers made peace at the Treaty of **Vereeniging**. 7,000 British troops had been killed; 35,000 Boers had died, including civilians.

**Soviet.** Russian council. During the **Russian Revolution** of 1905 striking workers set up the St Petersburg Soviet of Workers' Deputies. The Soviet had its own newspaper, *Izvestia* ('News'), and militia, but it did not try to overthrow the government. It spent most of its time coordinating strike action and negotiating with the authorities on behalf of the workers. Similar Soviets were set up in forty to fifty other cities. In December the government felt strong enough to arrest the leaders of the St Petersburg Soviet and destroyed it. The Moscow Soviet then took up the fight and prepared for an armed uprising, but this was crushed by the army.

With the fall of the Tsar in the **February Revolution** of 1917, Soviets (900 by October) were formed again in the major Russian towns. In **Petrograd** the Soviet, led by **Mensheviks** and the **Socialist Revolutionary Party**, saw itself as the watchdog of the Revolution and supported the **Provisional Government** only in so far as it carried out policies of which it approved. The Soviet could have taken control of the state but it did not wish to do so, as the Provisional Government had experienced politicians, who could command the loyalty of army officers and the provinces. The declaration of a Soviet government would have led to civil war. Yet real power lay with the Soviet, which in March reached an agreement with industrialists, which gave workers the right to strike, an eight-hour working day and recognition of their factory committees. In May some members of the Soviet joined the government, but this distanced them from the workers, who increasingly came to support the **Bolsheviks**. By September the Bolsheviks had a majority in the Petrograd and Moscow Soviets. It was the Military Revolutionary Committee of the Petrograd Soviet, led by **Trotsky**, which became the instrument for the Bolshevik seizure of power in the **October Revolution**. Though Lenin had used the slogan 'All power to the Soviets' to gain support, it was the Bolshevik Party rather than the Soviets that exercised power. The new communist state was formally based on elected Soviets at all administrative levels but this was a sham, as they became agents of the Bolshevik central government.

**Spanish–American War** (1898). The collapse of the sugar market, partly caused by the high US tariff of 1894, caused misery in the Spanish colony of Cuba and a rising, which began in 1895. US public opinion supported the Cubans, particularly when the popular American press gave lurid and one-sided accounts of Spanish atrocities. In 1896 Marshal Weyler invented the **concentration camp** (and its name) to deprive Cuban guerrillas of civilian support: many inmates died there. President **McKinley** wanted to avoid war, as the USA was just emerging from the depression which began in 1893, but public opinion forced his hand, particularly when the US battleship *Maine* was blown up in Havana harbour in February 1898, with the loss of 260 crew. It is still not clear what caused the explosion but Americans assumed that Spain was to blame. On 20 April Congress recognized the independence of Cuba and authorized the President to use armed force to expel the Spaniards from the island. It also passed the Teller Amendment, which said that the USA had no intention of annexing Cuba.

The US navy was the sixth largest in the world and vastly superior to Spain's but her army was small (28,000) and without recent fighting experience, except in the **Indian Wars**. 200,000 Americans volunteered but they were badly trained and equipped. Fortunately for the Americans, the Spanish army of 200,000 in Cuba was even more inefficient. The first fighting took place in the Far East, when the US forces destroyed a Spanish fleet in Manila Bay in May. An American expeditionary force, helped by Filipino rebels, captured Manila in August. In Cuba the fighting lasted only one month. An American force of 17,000 landed in June and moved towards Santiago, defeating the Spaniards at El Caney and San Juan Hill. The Spanish fleet in Santiago put to sea to avoid capture and was destroyed by the Americans. Spanish forces in Cuba surrendered in July, by which time Puerto Rico had been captured. According to the US Secretary of State John Hay it had been 'a splendid little war', with a string of US victories and fewer than 400 American casualties.

Victory gave a great boost in the USA to **imperialism**, which was reflected in the Peace of Paris, signed in December 1898. Cuban independence was recognized but the Philippines, Puerto Rico and the Pacific island of Guam all went to the USA. What had begun as a war to free a colonial people from oppression ended with America becoming a colonial power herself. There was much opposition in the USA. Many Americans felt they were abandoning their traditional foreign policy of avoiding foreign commitments; others said that it was against the spirit of the Declaration of Independence to rule foreign peoples without their consent. Imperialists had more support – they stressed the commercial and strategic importance of the Philippines and said that if the USA did not take them, another imperialist power would. Some stressed the benefit to backward peoples of American civilization and echoed Kipling's plea 'to take up the White Man's burden'. The treaty eventually gained the two-thirds majority needed for ratification in the Senate by one vote. Just before it was ratified in 1899 Filipino nationalists rose in rebellion against their unwanted masters: the USA needed 70,000 troops (4,300 of whom died) to suppress it. In doing so the USA reverted to the harsh methods which had so shocked American opinion when used by Spain: 'puking up their principles', the American philosopher William James called it. Cuba's independence was nominal – with the **Platt Amendment** Cuba was reduced to semi-colonial status.

**Spanish Civil War** (1936–9). The failure of the attempted military *coup d'état* against the **Spanish Second Republic** of 17–18 July 1936 led to a full-scale civil war. While the insurgents or Nationalists controlled much of the north, a number of cities in the south, including Seville, and Spanish Morocco, the Republic held on to Madrid, the chief industrial centres of Catalonia and the Basque country, and most of the south and east. Moreover, the Republic still had the bulk of the navy and air force behind it and much of the army and Civil Guard too. However, the conflict was transformed by the crucial intervention in July of Nazi Germany and **Mussolini**'s Fascist Italy on the side of the Nationalists. In the short term, this averted the defeat of the Nationalists as the most important section of the Spanish armed forces, the Army of Africa, was airlifted from Morocco to mainland Spain. In the long term, the **Axis powers**' material, financial and logistical support, including the prestigious Condor Legion and up to 100,000 Italian troops, was to ensure the Nationalists' victory.

In contrast, the Republic was abandoned by the two principal Western democracies, Britain and France. They were the principal architects of the Non-Intervention Agreement of August 1936, to which twenty-seven nations adhered, including Germany, Italy and the Soviet Union. In fact, the **Popular Front** in France provided some support for the Republic, but was greatly limited in its efforts by domestic pressures and changes in government. In Britain, the Spanish Civil War attracted more attention than any external event since the **French Revolution**. Successive Conservative governments were clearly sympathetic to the Nationalists and, despite their ostensible neutrality, provided secret diplomatic and economic support to the insurgents of a substantial nature. Non-intervention was not merely a farce but a policy of malevolent neutrality, which actively hindered the Republic. The only major power to support the Republic was **Stalin**'s USSR, which began supplying it from mid-October 1936. But Soviet aid was always conditioned by Stalin's foreign policy needs, above all by the formation of an alliance with France and Britain against the Axis powers. Stalin's support was critical to the Republic's survival but was sporadic and never enough to win the war. The **Cárdenas** government of Mexico backed the Republic wholeheartedly, but it lacked resources. (After the war, Mexico was the chief refuge for Republican exiles.)

During the first two months of the war, the Nationalists made rapid progress from both the north and the south in the advance on Madrid. General **Franco**'s diversion to Toledo, to relieve supporters besieged in the massive fortress called the Alcázar in September 1936, probably cost the Nationalists the conquest of the capital in that year. By the time the assault on Madrid began in October, the Republic had been bolstered by the arrival of Soviet arms and to a lesser extent by the **International Brigades**. The failure of the insurgents to take Madrid meant that what appeared destined to be a short war became a long one. The Nationalists thereby set about the piecemeal destruction of the Republic, with the main theatre of operations becoming the north. On 26 April 1937 the first saturation bombing of civilians in history occurred, as the German Condor Legion razed the sacred Basque *pueblo* of Guernica to the ground on market day. In June 1937 Bilbao fell to the Nationalists, followed in August 1937 by Santander. The Republic's loss of the north marked a significant shift in the balance of power to Franco's forces.

Whereas the Nationalist zone had been rapidly centralized under the command of General Franco from October 1936, the Republican war effort suffered at the outset from extreme internecine strife. Following the military rising of July 1936, much of the Republic was transformed by a largely spontaneous social revolution of unprecedented scope. Characterized by agrarian and industrial collectives, it reflected profoundly felt popular needs and ideals. For the anarchist–syndicalist **CNT**, POUM (dissident Marxists), and some left-wing socialists the triumph of the revolution was essential to victory in the war. By contrast, the communists, republicans and moderate socialists maintained that the revolution should be suppressed for the sake of the war. The socialist-led Largo Caballero government of September 1936 contained the revolution, re-established central state authority and created a conventional army, in the conviction that it would therefore be able to fight Franco on his terms. The Spanish Communist Party (PCE) became the major force in the republican camp, because it presented itself as united in a single-minded commitment to winning the war (compared to the socialists' deep divisions and the republicans' paralysis), because it was the conduit for Soviet aid, and because the PCE adopted a policy – in accordance with Soviet needs – of thoroughgoing suppression of the revolution, which it pursued more ruthlessly than either its socialist or republican allies. In May 1937, after the clash between the PCE and the CNT in Barcelona and in the face of mounting dissent from communists, socialists and republicans, Largo Caballero stepped down. He was replaced by another socialist, Juan **Negrín**, who worked closely with the PCE and centralized the state still further. Negrín oversaw the suppression of the POUM and the marginalization of the CNT.

Republican counter-attacks in 1937 and the winter of 1937–8 were unable to achieve a decisive breakthrough before the Nationalists cut the Republic in half in April 1938. On 1 May 1938 Negrín offered his 'Thirteen Points' as the basis for negotiation, but Franco rejected them outright. The battle of the Ebro, the Republicans' last, desperate counter-attack, lasted from July to November 1938 and was the bloodiest confrontation of the entire war. Negrín's unilateral withdrawal of the International Brigades, in October 1938, failed to produce a similar response from either the Germans or the Italians. With no other option – except unconditional surrender – Negrín fought on. He realized that if resistance could be maintained until the collapse of **appeasement**, then the ensuing European conflict could save the Republic. However, the Republic could not hold out. Catalonia fell in February 1939 and an internal *coup* led to Madrid's capitulation in March 1939.

The Spanish Civil War anticipated not only the struggle between democracy and **fascism** of the **Second World War**, but also the horrors of 'total war'. The outcome of the Civil War was a clerical and authoritarian dictatorship under General Franco that marked the successful defence by a predominantly landed oligarchy of its economic privileges against the reforming intentions of the Spanish Second Republic.

**Spanish Liberal Revolutions** (1812–68). Political liberalism, unlike economic liberalism, emerged rapidly in Spain. During the War of Independence of 1808–14 the Cortes of Cadiz staged an internal revolution by drawing up a liberal constitution. The Constitution of 1812 established a constitutional monarchy, embracing popular sovereignty, the division of powers, a unicameral Cortes, and the centralization of government. Supplementary texts abolished seigneurial jurisdiction, suppressed the guild system, provided for the sale of communal lands, and reduced the number of monasteries and religious orders. Although the Constitution preserved Catholicism as the state religion, the Church was alienated by the abolition of the Inquisition and by disentailment of its lands. From now on the struggle between the Church and the liberals became a central feature of Spanish political life. In vesting sovereignty in the people, the Constitution provided for a Cortes, elected by males over twenty-five, to draw up the laws, which the monarch would implement through ministers. The Cortes of Cadiz and the

Constitution of 1812 became leading symbols of **liberalism** throughout southern Europe and Latin America. In Spain, the Constitution of 1812 was regarded throughout the nineteenth century as the classic statement of liberalism and was revived on several occasions.

The reforms embodied in the Constitution of 1812 were abolished by the absolutism of Ferdinand VII, after he was restored to the throne in 1814. Once he was overthrown in 1820 the Constitution of 1812 was briefly re-established, only to be rejected once again upon Ferdinand's return at the hands of a French army in 1823. None the less, liberal influence remained at the highest levels, because Ferdinand's financial problems forced him to rely on liberal economic experts. On his death in 1833, the King's daughter Isabel was represented by the regency of Maria Cristina of **Habsburg**, thus provoking the first Carlist war of 1833–40, as Ferdinand's younger brother Charles laid claim to the Crown (see **Carlism**).

Between 1834 and 1868 Spanish politics were dominated by the rivalry between the Moderates and the Progressives. The liberal tradition was represented by the Progressive Party. It not only defended the legitimacy of revolution but also stood by popular, rather than monarchical, sovereignty. The Progressives also favoured reform of the Church, especially through the disentailment of its lands. By contrast, the Moderate Party was conservative and oligarchical, representing the large landowners and aristocrats. While in power from 1835–40 the Progressives reincorporated the principles of 1812 in the Constitution of 1837. They also undermined the Church by suppressing nearly all the male religious orders and by carrying out the greatest transfer of land since the Reconquest. Following the end of the Carlist War in 1840, they forced the disruptive and inconsistent queen regent into exile. They remained in power by gaining the support of the hero of the Carlist War, General Espartero. From 1843 to 1868 the unstable and authoritarian Queen Isabel II ruled Spain. Her reactionary governments of 1843–50 were dominated by General Narváez, as leader of the Moderates, who passed a conservative Constitution in 1845. The *modus vivendi* between the Church and the Moderates bore fruit in the shape of the Concordat of 1851, which governed the uneasy relations between Church and State until the **Spanish Second Republic** in 1931. However, in 1854 a middle-class revolt led to the return of the

Progressives under General Espartero and a further major pro-gramme of disentailment. Isabel's resistance to disentailment led her to rely increasingly on conservative generals. From 1858–60 the Liberal Union ruled under General O'Donnell, and from 1863–8 the Moderates returned to power under Narváez. Further unrest forced Isabel to flee in September 1868. The Constitution of 1869 resurrected the principles of the Constitution of 1812 (as well as establishing religious liberty for the first time) before giving way to the unstable reign of Amadeo I of 1870–73 and the Spanish First Republic in 1873.

**Spanish Second Republic** (1931–6). Spain's first democratic regime in nearly sixty years was established on 14 April 1931 amidst great popular expectation, following the disastrous policies of the monarchy. Yet the Republic had to overcome a formidable series of obstacles if it was to be consolidated, let alone fulfil the reformist hopes widely placed in it: the entrenched economic and institutional power of the ruling classes, the weakness of the state, the inherited debt and impact of the **Great Depression**, and the differences within the regime's own ranks.

The provisional government of April 1931 was returned to power by the general election of June 1931, when the Republicans and Socialists won an overwhelming victory. The **Right** was not only demoralized and disorientated by the fall of the monarchy, but also handicapped by poor organization and large-scale Catholic abstention. The Constitution passed in December 1931 embodied the principles of the Republican **Left** and of the Socialists. Shortly after, the largest of the Republican parties, the **Radical Republican Party**, left the government in protest at the continued participation of the Socialists, the two Catholic ministers having departed in October over the anti-clerical clauses of the Constitution.

The Left Republican-Socialist administrations of 1931–3, under Manuel **Azaña**, made the most determined effort yet to transform Spain from a reactionary and backward society into a modern and progressive 'European' state. An attempt was made to modernize and depoliticize the officer corps, but political favouritism and the bitterness of the reformers greatly antagonized the armed forces. State education was laicized and, expanded but suffered from a lack of resources, while anti-clerical measures did more harm than good by providing the Catholic Right with an all-embracing rallying cry: the defence of the Church. Following the abortive monarchist rising of August 1932, an agrarian reform bill and Catalan autonomy statute were passed. Yet reform of the land proceeded slowly, because of the landowners' resistance and sabotage by public officials and the Civil Guard. Its impact was also limited by insufficient money. Indeed, the entire modernization programme of the Azaña administrations was undermined by the lack of financial resources and the world depression.

The massacre at Casas Viejas (Andalusia) of twenty-two anarchists by Assault Guards in January 1933 underlined the shortcomings of agrarian reform and diminished the government's moral credibility. It also drew attention to the Republic's failure to win over the initially well-disposed, one-million strong anarcho-syndicalist movement (the **CNT**), through its harsh repression. The ruling majority declined throughout 1933, as the Socialists became increasingly frustrated at the left-Republicans' lack of commitment to socio-economic change and the oligarchy's power to thwart reform. The government was eventually dissolved in September 1933. Although the lack of unity, expertise, and resources within the ruling coalition had contributed to the failure of reform from 1931–3, the principal reason was the hostility of the conservative classes to meaningful change. This highlighted the difficulties of reforming a traditional society through a democratic parliamentary regime, especially at a time of economic crisis.

The course of the Republic was fundamentally altered by the general election of November–December 1933. While the right-wing CEDA won 115 seats and the Radical Party 104, the Socialists fell to fifty-eight and the Left Republicans to around forty. A parliamentary alliance was formed between the Radical Party and the CEDA, on the understanding that the Radicals would carry out the Right's minimum programme, in exchange for access to the patronage-spoils of the public administration. Although the Radical Party aspired to incorporate the non-Republican Right into the new regime through a conservative programme, the CEDA aimed to replace the Republic with a **corporate state**.

The Centre-Right administrations of December 1933 to October

1935 moved steadily to the Right, while demolishing the reforms of the first two years. This led to a major Radical schism in May 1934 and to mounting socio-economic conflict, as shown by the CNT strike in Saragossa of May 1934 and the extensive agricultural stoppage during the summer of 1934. The entry of three members of the proto-Fascist CEDA into the government, on 4 October 1934, resulted in a socialist general strike, a declaration of Catalan independence, and an armed rising in Asturias. The brutal repression of the October protest polarized the Republic to an unprecedented extent. As the CEDA gained more and more power at the expense of the Radicals throughout 1935, so the previously divided Left rallied to the banner of the **Popular Front**.

The disqualification from power of the Radicals in late 1935, as a result of two financial scandals, led President Alcalá Zamora, suspicious of the CEDA's democratic credentials, to dissolve the Cortes. The general election of February 1936 was a bitter contest between the National and Popular Fronts with the latter gaining a narrow victory. The political climate became increasingly volatile, as the weak Left Republican governments, bereft of Socialist support, proved unable to impose their political will. On the one hand landless labourers and workers took the law into their own hands in frustration at the slow pace of reform, while the Socialist leader Largo Caballero espoused a revolutionary rhetoric (although, as in 1934, he did little to prepare for an armed uprising). On the other hand the monarchists, Carlists (see **Carlism**), and the Falangists (see *Falange Española*) exacerbated the climate of confrontation through their aggressive propaganda and street violence. Immediately after the triumph of the Popular Front a section of the army began to prepare for a *coup d'état*. Largo Caballero's refusal to allow the moderate Socialist leader Indalecio Prieto to become Prime Minister in May 1936, as Manuel Azaña was elevated to the presidency, deprived the Republic of its best chance of containing the mounting conflict and preventing the planned military *coup*. With Azaña isolated as President and the ailing and complacent Casares Quiroga as Prime Minister, the Republic lacked resolute leadership. The military rising of 17–18 July 1936 resulted in the **Spanish Civil War**, which brought an end to the Second Republic.

**Spartakist Rising** (January 1919). A communist rising in Germany. The Spartakus League was named after a Roman slave who led a revolt. It was formed in 1916 and a year later became part of the Independent Socialist Party (USPD), which broke away from the **Social Democratic Party** (SPD). Its leaders, Karl Liebknecht and Rosa **Luxemburg**, rejected the socialist government of Friedrich **Ebert** as the enemy of the working class and called for government by workers' and soldiers' councils, the nationalization of all property and the reorganization of the army to give power to ordinary soldiers. On 30 December 1918 the Spartakists broke with the USPD and formed the German Communist Party. Russian revolutionaries wanted them to seize power immediately but Rosa Luxemburg was well aware that the communists did not have the support of a majority of the German working class and only reluctantly agreed to a revolution, when the shop stewards' movement promised the Spartakists armed support. On 6 January 1919 a revolutionary committee of shop stewards and communists announced the formation of a revolutionary government and armed supporters occupied public buildings in Berlin. The government acted promptly. As it found that many socialists were unwilling to fight for the republic, it turned to the generals. They realized after the sailors' revolution, when many soldiers had joined the revolutionaries in the **German Revolution** (1918–19), that the army was unreliable, so they called on irregular bands of volunteers, the **Free Corps**. They crushed the revolution by 13 January: about 100 rebels were killed, some of them summarily executed. Liebknecht and Luxemburg were captured and murdered on their way to prison. This shocked the socialists, who condemned the murders but were unable to control the Free Corps. The rising had not been a serious threat to the government but it left a bitter legacy: communists and socialists refused to cooperate and this later aided the rise of **Hitler**.

**Speenhamland system.** A method of outdoor relief for the poor in England, devised by Berkshire magistrates at the village of Speenhamland in 1795, a year of famine. They decided that relief would be paid out of rates to labourers (both those in employment and the unemployed) according to the size of their family and the price of bread. The system quickly spread to about half the counties of England, particularly those in the south, but not to the industrial areas. Political economists such as **Malthus** and Ricardo attacked the system, as it interfered with the 'fair and free competition of the market', which should alone determine wages. They also maintained that it encouraged early marriage and large families and by increasing population, created the problem it was designed to relieve; that it encouraged laziness, as the labourer knew his wages would be made up; and that farmers would pay low wages because the parish would increase them. Most of these criticisms were unjustified, as population did not increase faster in the Speenhamland counties than elsewhere; the allowance system was not a cause of low wages but a reaction to them and was a response rather than a stimulus to population growth. The Speenhamland system had almost died out before the **Poor Law** Amendment Act (1834) finished it off completely. Social discontent was widespread in spite of the system as the **Swing riots** (1830–31) showed, but would have been much worse without it.

**Speer, Albert** (1905–81). Nazi minister. Trained as an architect, Speer joined the **Nazi Party** in 1931, after hearing **Hitler** speak. From 1933 he was responsible for the artistic direction of the annual Party rally at Nuremberg. He designed and built the assembly site and stage-managed the event. Hitler was so impressed with his 'architect of genius' that he commissioned Speer to rebuild Berlin and other cities, in the neo-classical monumental style which he liked. Speer's main contribution to the **Third Reich** came when Hitler made him Minister for Armaments and War Production in 1942, where he showed exceptional ability in organizing the economy for total war. Until then there had been competing authorities (three agencies were responsible for equipping the armed forces), all of which Speer brought under his control by establishing a Central Planning Board. By 1943 he had control of the whole economy: production rose in spite of Allied bombing, so that Germany reached its highest level of arms and aircraft production in the second half of 1944. Speer managed to do this by central planning but also by pillaging occupied Europe: food from there ensured there was no drop in German living standards, whilst forced labour and sequestered raw materials kept the war industries going. Without Speer the war would almost certainly have ended much earlier but he could not prevent the economy collapsing, as Allied bombers disrupted communications and raw materials became scarce, when Allied forces occupied the territory from which they came. He told Hitler in January 1945 that the war was almost over and spent the next few months trying to protect German industry from Hitler's order that all areas likely to be captured by the advancing Allied armies should be destroyed. When he was tried at Nuremberg Speer, unlike other Nazi leaders, did not dispute the guilt of the regime and admitted his personal responsibility for using slave labour in the factories and for collaborating with the **SS**, which provided him with **concentration camp** prisoners. He was sentenced to twenty years' imprisonment. Released in 1966, he published his memoirs *Inside the Third Reich* in 1970 and exposed the inefficiencies which had resulted from rivalries within the Nazi hierarchy.

**'Splendid isolation'.** An expression first used in the Canadian parliament in 1886 and later in the same year by **Salisbury**. It was an inaccurate description of British foreign policy in the 1890s, when the European Great Powers, except for Britain, were grouped in two alliances: the **Franco-Russian Alliance** (1894) and the **Triple Alliance** (1882) of Germany, Austria and Italy. Britain certainly was isolated during the **South African War** (1899–1902), when there was talk in France and Russia of a continental coalition against her. When the German ambassador pointed this out, Salisbury asked, 'Have we ever felt that danger practically?' and observed that Britain had not been in real danger since the **Napoleonic Wars**. Yet Salisbury had offered to **Bismarck** in 1885 an alliance 'in the fullest sense of the term', which Bismarck had rejected, as he did not want to become involved in British conflicts with Russia. Joseph **Chamberlain** made further overtures to Germany in 1898 and 1899, and Lord Lansdowne, the Foreign Secretary, opened official negotiations with Germany in 1901. All failed and, as opinion in Britain turned against Germany owing to the naval race (see **Tirpitz**), Britain ended her isolation by making the **Anglo–Japanese Alliance** (1902), which enabled her to bring back part of her Pacific fleet to defend home waters.

**Spoils system.** The practice in the USA whereby, after every election in which power changes hands, whether at a local, state or national level, current office-holders are dismissed and replaced by supporters of the victorious political party. The phrase was first used in 1832 by Senator William Marcy, who said that he saw 'nothing wrong in the rule that to the victor belong the spoils of the enemy'. This system has continued into the twentieth century and also applies to the award of contracts, especially defence contracts, to those who contribute to party funds.

**Sport, spectator.** Most of the sports which are popular today – cricket, soccer, boxing, lawn tennis, rugby, athletics – were nurtured in the public (independent) schools and universities of Victorian England as amateur games. Cricket, played in England since the thirteenth century, became very popular in the British Empire. Its governing body, the Marylebone Cricket Club (MCC), was founded in 1787, though the first Test (international) Match did not take place until 1877, when the MCC (as the England team was known abroad) played Australia. England and Australia were the leading cricket countries until 1945, their rivalry reaching a peak in the bodyline series in Australia in 1932–3, when the practice of bowling at the batsman rather than at the wicket was first established. The distinction between amateurs (the captain was invariably an amateur) and professionals in English county cricket was carefully maintained until 1962, each group having its own dressing room and separate entry on to the field of play.

The rules of Association Football (soccer), which became the most popular spectator sport, were laid down at Cambridge in 1843. The Football Association (FA) was founded in England in 1863 (by 1940 40,000 clubs had joined it) and FIFA (*Fédération Internationale de Football Association*) in France in 1904. At the top it soon became a professional game and attracted crowds of 10,000 in England as early as the 1880s. The FA Cup Final was seen at Crystal Palace by 60,000 in 1897 and by 120,000 in 1913. Football pools (betting) spread in the 1890s. Soccer was almost entirely a working-class game. Its middle-class rival in England was rugby football, an amateur game begun at Rugby School in 1823. Like cricket, it spread mainly in the British Empire, though it was popular too in France (in the south and round Paris) and variations of the game were to be found in the USA and Australia. In

England a variant was Rugby League, a professional game played in the north of England, whose support came almost wholly from the working class. The first World Tennis Championship was organized by the All England Croquet Club at Wimbledon in 1877. Like horse-racing (which received much press coverage because of betting), it was seen by few until television made it a mass spectator sport. Athletics contests based on those of the Ancient Greeks took place in the Olympic Games, held every four years from 1896. Originally confined to track and field events, they eventually covered most amateur sports. Motor racing attracted huge crowds all over Europe and in the 1930s was dominated by German (Mercedes-Benz) and Italian (Alfa-Romeo, Ferrari) cars. In France cycling became a mass sport, as popular as football in England: the Tour de France, started in 1903, was the most popular cycle race in the world. Baseball, derived from the English game of rounders, took its modern form in the USA in 1845. The National League was formed in 1876, the American League in 1901. By the turn of the century it was the national game. Basketball, the only major world sport to originate in the USA, was created in 1891. It was an instant success in high schools and colleges, where it became the most widely played team sport. Its popularity has spread since throughout the world.

**SS** (*Schützstaffel*, 'defence echelon'). The élite force in the **Nazi Party**. It was founded in 1925 as a personal bodyguard for **Hitler** and was part of the **SA**. The SS became important when **Himmler** was put in charge in 1929: he built it up into a carefully selected and disciplined élite, whose aim was to find and destroy all enemies of Hitler. In 1929 it had 280 members – by 1933 there were 50,000 and this had risen to 240,000 by 1939. It was the SS which murdered the SA leaders, on Hitler's orders, in the **Night of the Long Knives** (30 June 1934) and was rewarded by being made an independent organization in the Party, responsible only to the *Führer* and to Himmler. He had set up the first **concentration camp** for political prisoners at Dachau, near Munich, in 1933, run by SS Death's Head detachments. Their number and size increased enormously during the war (there were six concentration camps with 25,000 prisoners in 1939, twenty-two camps with 714,000 prisoners in 1945) and it was here that the SS carried out mass murders, as Hitler decided on the '**Final Solution**' for eliminating the Jews. The Death's Head detachments became the nucleus of the Waffen SS, armed units which grew from three divisions in 1939 to thirty-five in 1945 and fought alongside the regular army. By this time (with 900,000 men, half of whom were non-German) it was a rival to the army. As the *Wehrmacht* invaded Russia in 1941 special SS units (*Einsatzgruppen*: 'combat groups') were attached to each division to control and terrorize the areas conquered: partisans were shot, hostages taken and executed for attacks on German soldiers and thousands of civilians were sent as slave labourers to Germany (there were nearly five million foreign workers in Germany in 1945), where the SS worked them to death.

**'Stab in the back' myth** spread the idea that the German army had not been defeated in 1918: traitorous politicians had cheated the army of victory and forced Germany to surrender. The **German Revolution** of 1918–19, it was said, had destroyed all discipline in the army and made further fighting impossible. The 'November criminals' were the coalition parties, especially the **Social Democratic Party**, who accepted the armistice and by their agitation for peace had brought about revolution. Later they signed the unpopular and dictated Treaty of **Versailles**. This myth was spread by army officers, civil servants, university professors and Church leaders. Friedrich **Ebert**, the Socialist Chancellor and one of the 'November criminals', contributed to it when he greeted the army in Berlin: 'I salute you who return unvanquished from the field of battle.' It was untrue, as it was not the military collapse which followed revolution but the revolution which was the result of military defeat. The myth, disseminated by the press, had the unfortunate effect of identifying the **Weimar Republic** and its democratic institutions with the loss of the war. **Hitler** made good use of the myth in bringing about the downfall of the Republic.

**Stalin, Josef Vissarionovich** (1879–1953). Stalin, 'man of steel', was the name he adopted in 1912. He was born Dzhugashvili, the son of a Georgian shoe-maker, and was one of the few **Bolshevik** leaders to come from the working class. He was expelled from the Tiflis (Tbilisi) Orthodox seminary in 1899 for his Marxist activities and became a full-time revolutionary in 1901. He was arrested six times between 1902 and 1913 and twice escaped from internal exile. He was in exile in Siberia from 1913–17 and returned to **Petrograd** after the **February Revolution**. After the **October Revolution** he joined the *Politburo* when it was formed in 1919 and helped to defend Tsaritsyn (later Stalingrad and now Volgograd) in the **Russian Civil War**. He was given jobs by Lenin which his more voluble and able colleagues did not want and which called for diligence rather than imagination. One such post, which was to be crucial in his rise to power, was that of General Secretary of the Communist Party, to which he was appointed in 1922. In this position he chose secretaries who headed local Party organizations: they elected delegates to Party conferences, who in turn elected the Party's Central Committee, *Politburo* and Secretariat. As General Secretary Stalin came to control all these bodies. **Lenin** regretted Stalin's accretion of power and in a secret memorandum of 4 January 1923 suggested that Stalin should be removed as General Secretary. He planned to work with **Trotsky** to oust Stalin at the Party Congress, which was to meet in April, but on 9 March Lenin had his third stroke from which he never recovered. This and the unpopularity of Trotsky, who was Lenin's obvious successor, saved Stalin. On Lenin's death in January 1924 **Kamenev** and **Zinoviev** persuaded the Bolshevik Central Committee to suppress Lenin's memorandum and supported Stalin against Trotsky. Stalin was a superb tactician, with a sharp eye for the weaknesses of others. He used his position of General Secretary first to isolate his rivals and then to secure their dismissal. He allied with **Bukharin** to force Trotsky, Kamenev and Zinoviev out of office and then turned against Bukharin. From 1929, when Trotsky was forced to leave Russia, Stalin was in a dominant position, though this did not become unassailable till the murder of **Kirov** in 1934.

Stalin realized that the Soviet Union was far behind her capitalist rivals economically and, as he feared attack from the Western powers, decided that this gap would have to be closed quickly. In 1924 he had put forward the idea of 'Socialism in one country', by which he meant that Russia could become strong by her own efforts. He began a period of rapid industrialization through the

**Five Year Plans**, which were successful in making the USSR one of the greatest industrial powers in the world. To finance this industrialization he abandoned **NEP** and introduced the **collectivization** of agriculture, though at enormous human cost in the murder or deportation of the *kulaks*. Such policies could only be carried through by centralizing power and by establishing a dictatorship. One-party rule had been set up by Lenin but Stalin carried this much further by establishing personal control of the Party, the government and the secret police and by using the latter to remove, not enemies of the regime, but former Bolsheviks. All who had disagreed with Stalin or whom he regarded as in any way a threat to his position were eliminated in the **Great Purges**. These did enormous damage to every sector of Soviet society and especially to the armed forces, whose officer corps was decimated. This almost led to the Soviet Union's defeat, when Germany invaded in 1941.

The Western democracies had been shocked by the about-turn in Soviet foreign policy, when Stalin abandoned his anti-Nazi stance and made the **Nazi–Soviet Pact** in 1939. This gave him two years to rearm before the German onslaught in Operation **Barbarossa** (1941). The Soviet Union managed to survive this partly by good luck (Japan did not attack in the east), partly owing to Hitler's mistakes in diverting troops from the attack on Moscow to the southern and northern fronts and partly because Russia was able to develop her industry beyond the Urals, out of the reach of the Germans: 1,500 individual enterprises and ten million people were moved from west to east, so that in the last two years of the war the USSR was producing more tanks, guns and aircraft than Germany. The costs were enormous – twenty million Russian dead and widespread devastation – but the USSR emerged from the war as one of the two superpowers and Stalin was able to impose regimes acceptable to him throughout Eastern Europe. In 1945 Stalin's prestige and popularity had never been higher. In 1941 he had become Prime Minister (a post he held until his death) and Commander of the armed forces. In 1943 he took the title Marshal and in 1945 that of Generalissimo. He had been a dominant figure at Allied conferences at Teheran (1943), **Yalta** (1945) and **Potsdam** (1945). The 'cult of personality', which involved extravagant praise for everything the 'great father' did, reached its height. All Soviet achievements were said to be due to his genius and inspiration. This did not bring any change in the regime. Stalin was obsessed, more than before, with both internal and external security. All those who had been under enemy occupation (and this included prisoners of war) were automatically suspected of being anti-Soviet. Consequently, most ex-prisoners of war ended up in **forced labour camps**, whilst hundreds of thousands of people were moved from their homelands to Siberia. There were further Five Year Plans (in 1946–50 and 1951–5) which, like those pre-war, concentrated on heavy industry, starving agriculture and consumer industries of funds. The results were impressive – by 1948 the war damage had been made good and there was rapid expansion after that but, for the mass of people, the privations of the 1930s and the war continued into the 1950s. In 1949 leading Leningrad Party officials were executed and it appeared that the purges of the 1930s were about to begin again. People disappeared, fear and suspicion returned, not least to Stalin's closest colleagues. Khrushchev was convinced that only Stalin's death in 1953 prevented the elimination of leading Bolsheviks.

**Stalingrad, battle of** (August 1942–February 1943). A German defeat on the **Eastern Front**, which was a turning point in the **Second World War**. In 1942 **Hitler** planned another major offensive, which aimed at the Caucasus oilfields, and at Stalingrad, a city which stretched for eighteen miles on the banks of the Volga. It was an important manufacturing and communications centre, producing a quarter of the Soviet Union's vehicles, and controlled traffic up and down the Volga. Hitler's generals told him that German forces were not strong enough to take both the Caucasus and Stalingrad but, encouraged by the capture of Sebastopol in the Crimea and of Rostov, he overruled them. The two attacks were too far apart to support each other and Hitler made another mistake when he ordered his only reserve in the south to go to **Leningrad**. The German advance across open country to Stalingrad was swift but there was ferocious resistance in the city, which was reduced to rubble by incessant shelling and bombing. This helped the defenders, so that each street and each house had to be fought for. The Germans reached the Volga in the city centre on 12 October, after fierce hand-to-hand fighting, but the Russians were still clinging to the west bank when winter arrived. The long German supply lines were vulnerable to attack, as were their extended flanks, protected by Romanian units. Meanwhile **Zhukov** was preparing for a counter-attack with fresh troops, which began on 19 November, preceded by a massive artillery bombardment. Attacking north and south of the city, the two prongs met in four days, encircling General Paulus and his Sixth Army of 270,000 men. They could probably have fought their way out of the trap but Hitler ordered them to stay where they were, believing **Goering's** assurance that he could supply the Sixth Army by air. **Manstein** was sent with a relieving force but was held up thirty miles short of Stalingrad. On his own authority he ordered Paulus to break out but he would not do so without permission from Hitler. Short of winter clothing, food and ammunition, Paulus ignored Hitler's order to fight to the last man and surrendered on 2 February 1943. Of the 270,000 Germans in Stalingrad, 34,000 were evacuated by air, 140,000 were killed and the rest, including Paulus and twenty-four generals, were taken prisoner: only 6,000 of these survived. The Germans also lost war material equal to six months' production. The defeat at Stalingrad was a disaster for the German army, which was no longer regarded as invincible. It began a retreat which did not end until Berlin fell in May 1945.

**Stanley, Henry Morton** (1841–1904). British journalist and explorer. An illegitimate son of a Welsh farmer, he was born John Rowlands. From 1847–56 he lived in a workhouse before sailing, in 1859, to the USA, where he took the name Stanley from the merchant who adopted him. He fought on the Confederate side (see **Confederate States of America**) in the **American Civil War** (1861–5) and in 1865 became a journalist. In 1871 the *New York Herald* sent him to find David **Livingstone** in Central Africa. Stanley travelled inland from Zanzibar and met Livingstone at Ujiji on Lake Tanganyika, a 'scoop' which gave him his international reputation. In 1873 he covered General **Wolseley**'s campaign in the **Asante** War and a year later began one of the greatest journeys of exploration in Africa. Backed by the *New York Herald* and the London *Daily Telegraph* he planned to cross equatorial

Africa from Zanzibar to the mouth of the Congo, trace the Congo from its origins to its mouth and map the great lakes of Central Africa. In a journey which lasted 999 days from 1874-7 he succeeded in all his aims and made the Congo Basin known to the outside world. Courageous and bold, he was brutal in his treatment of Africans and 'shot his way across Africa', as a contemporary noted. From 1879-84 he was an agent of **Leopold II** in setting up the Congo Free State. In 1888 he began his last great mission when he went to rescue Emin Pasha, the governor of Equatoria in the Sudan, who was threatened by forces of the **Mahdi** after the death of **Gordon**. In this final great exploration of Africa, Stanley travelled 6,000 miles across the continent, solving the mystery of the Nile's sources on the way, before reaching Zanzibar. He then retired, resumed British citizenship in 1895, was knighted and became a Member of Parliament, thus receiving the recognition he had always sought.

**Stanton, Elizabeth Cady** (1815-1902). American women's rights activist. In 1840 she married a prominent **abolitionist** and characteristically deleted the promise 'to obey' from her marriage service. She held a women's rights convention at Seneca Falls, New York State, in 1848 which adapted the American Declaration of Independence to state: 'We hold these truths to be self-evident: that all men *and women* are created equal.' It demanded for women the vote, property rights, and admission to higher education and Church office. In 1851 she joined Susan **Anthony** to lead the movement for women's rights for the rest of the century. They founded the National Woman Suffrage Association (1869-90), edited the feminist journal *Revolution* and campaigned to overthrow state laws which discriminated against women. When the leading women's organizations joined together in 1890 to form the National American Woman Suffrage Association (NAWSA), Stanton became its first President and was succeded by Susan Anthony when she retired in 1892.

**State Socialism**. **Bismarck** hated **socialism**, as it was a revolutionary doctrine, and he tried to destroy the **Social Democratic Party** with an **anti-socialist law** but he saw the need to put something in its place. He tried to wean the workers away from socialism by passing insurance legislation. In 1883 medical treatment and sick pay for workers were introduced, though two-thirds of the cost fell on the workers themselves (one third was paid by the employers). A year later accident insurance for industrial injuries, paid for wholly by the employers, was passed. Old-age pensions for those over seventy, to which the state contributed, as well as employees and employers, did not become law until 1889. These reforms had a limited impact: payments were low and many workers were not eligible. By 1900 only 600,000 had benefited from old-age pensions. Bismarck's aim had been political: he wanted to make workers loyal to the Reich and was not concerned with improving their pay or working conditions. He refused to abolish Sunday working, reduce the working day, introduce a minimum wage or restrict the use of female or child labour. Yet, in spite of its limitations, his system of social security was the first of its kind in Europe and laid the foundations of the modern **Welfare State**. After he fell from power in 1890, improvements were made slowly. In 1891 Sunday working was abolished and a minimum wage established. There was protection for child labour in 1903–5 and insurance for all salaried employees in 1911.

**Stein, Karl, Baron von** (1757–1831). Prussian statesman and reformer. Born in the Rhineland, Stein joined the Prussian civil service in 1780. After Prussia's disastrous defeat at **Jena** in 1806, King Frederick William III realized the need for reform and made Stein his chief minister in October 1807. Stein believed that, to combat **Napoleon** effectively, citizens would have to be more actively involved in the running of the state, as they were in France. He therefore abolished **serfdom** in 1807 and a year later ended the noble monopoly in the officer corps and made promotion dependent on merit. Non-nobles were allowed to buy noble land. Stein wanted local self-government in both town and country, an elected assembly in each province and finally a national assembly, working with a responsible government. These ideas were dangerously radical to the *Junkers* and to the King, so he was able to bring about self-government only in the towns. In 1808, inspired by the Spanish rising against Napoleon, Stein wanted the King to authorize a national rising against Napoleon and to rouse patriotic enthusiasm by granting a constitution. When Napoleon heard of this he insisted on Stein's dismissal. He returned to office in 1813, after Napoleon's retreat from **Moscow**, and tried to stir up a national rising against Napoleon, which would, he hoped, lead to a united Germany under Prussian leadership. He was thwarted in this aim by **Metternich**, who was able to maintain Austrian dominance in Germany at the Congress of **Vienna**.

**Stern Gang.** Zionist terrorist organization in Palestine founded by Abraham Stern (1907–42), after a split in the underground movement Irgun Zvai Leumi. As Jewish immigration increased in the 1930s, conflict with the Arabs intensified and led to the formation of Irgun, which carried out terrorist attacks, of which the moderate Jewish leadership disapproved, on Arabs. Stern was as much anti-British as anti-Arab and murdered British officials and police, who killed him in a gun-battle in 1942. The organization continued, and extended its operation outside Palestine, murdering Lord Moyne, British Minister of State in the Middle East, in Cairo in 1944. When the State of Israel was created in 1948 the group was suppressed, some units joining the Israeli army.

**Stevens, Thaddeus** (1792–1868). American politician. He was a fervent **abolitionist**, hater of Southern planters and a founder of the **Republican Party**. During the **American Civil War** he clashed with **Lincoln** who, he thought, was too soft with the **Confederate States**. He wanted planter estates to be confiscated and distributed among freed slaves. After the Civil War he was leader of the Radical Republicans and co-chairman (1860–68) of the Joint Committee on **Reconstruction**, where he fought for the fourteenth and fifteenth constitutional amendments, which gave full civil rights to freed slaves. He pushed through **Congress** measures which imposed military rule in the South and opposed President **Johnson**'s efforts to treat the Southern states leniently. He was chairman of the committee which impeached Johnson in 1868 but by this time he was very ill and died the same year. He was buried, at his own request, in an unsegregated cemetery.

**Stolypin, Peter** (1862–1911). Prime Minister of Russia (1906–11). Stolypin was a landowner, who became Governor of Saratov (on the Volga), the scene of some of the worst peasant revolts in

1905, which he crushed ruthlessly. As a minister (he became Minister of the Interior in April 1906 and Prime Minister three months later) he ended peasant disturbances, which continued after the **Russian Revolution** of 1905 into 1906 and 1907, by a reign of terror in the countryside, setting up field courts-martial, which were to pass sentence, often of death, and carry it out within a day. As the first two **Duma**s had anti-government majorities, he changed the electoral law in 1907, reducing the number of peasant electors and increasing that of the landlords, so that 1 per cent of the population controlled three-quarters of the seats in the Duma. After that the government had little trouble with the Duma. Stolypin saw that repression was not enough and that reforms were needed to gain support for the regime. His most ambitious project was to create a class of prosperous, independent farmers by destroying the *mir* or peasant commune, a class who would have a stake in maintaining the existing political system. In 1906 he issued a decree, which allowed the peasant to hold his existing land as private property and remove it from the control of the *mir*. This would make little difference if the old inefficient strip system continued, so more important was the decree which said that a peasant could ask for his strips to be consolidated into a compact holding. By 1916 a quarter of households owned their land individually and had left the commune: of these half had consolidated their holdings. Stolypin also sought to ease the peasant's lot by making more money available to the Peasant Land Bank and by encouraging over three million to emigrate to Siberia. Historians disagree about the effects of Stolypin's agricultural reforms. There is no doubt that there was a general improvement in Russian agriculture between 1900 and 1913: net income rose by 89 per cent, output by 34 per cent. Grain exports too rose sharply and were 50 per cent higher in 1911–13 than in 1901–5. Some credit Stolypin with the improvements, whilst others maintain that they were due to a rise in grain prices and a series of excellent harvests before 1914. Many peasants who had left the commune had moved back by 1914, as they lacked the capital to set up successfully as independent farmers.

Stolypin's reforms did not stop at agriculture. He put forward the most ambitious programme since the 1860s, for greater religious toleration, better treatment of Jews, the extension of primary education, increased peasant representation in the *zemstva* and further extension of local self-government to Poland. Unfortunately the *zemstva*, nobility, Church and employers' organizations made sure that all these reforms were rejected or watered down. Broken in health and spirit, Stolypin's fall was widely expected when he was assassinated in Kiev, apparently with the aid of the secret police, in September 1911.

**Stopes, Marie Charlotte Carmichael** (1880–1958). British pioneer of birth control. A fossil botanist, Stopes became famous with the publication of *Married Love* (1918), which tried to free women from the ignorance of sex which had made her own first marriage so unhappy. In the same year she published *Wise Parenthood*, which was a practical guide to methods of contraception. Interest in this subject had greatly increased during the **First World War**, because of the large number of illegitimate births, and as 20 per cent of British soldiers acquired venereal diseases. By 1924 she had sold 400,000 copies of *Married Love* and 300,000 copies of its successor. She was attacked by the press, churches and politicians but, undaunted, opened in 1920 the Mothers' Clinic for Constructive Birth Control, in Holloway, North London, which gave free contraceptive advice. With others she founded in 1930 the National Birth Control Council, which in 1939 became the Family Planning Association. Marie Stopes played a greater part than anyone else in England in transforming sex from a taboo subject into one openly discussed.

**Straits, the.** The Straits consist of the Dardanelles, the Sea of Marmara and the Bosphorus, which link the Aegean and Black Seas. Ever since she had first acquired territory round the Black Sea during the reign of Catherine the Great (1762–96), Russia had wanted access for her warships into the Aegean and Mediterranean and this meant passing through the Straits, which were controlled by the **Ottoman Empire** (Turkey). Britain was determined to prevent this and in 1809 made an agreement with Turkey that the Straits should be closed to foreign warships. The Straits Convention (1841) confirmed this. It was signed by all the Great Powers (Britain, Russia, Austria, Prussia and France), as well as by Turkey, who agreed that this settlement could be changed only by a European conference. This was the first time the Straits had been brought under international control and was a triumph for British diplomacy. The Straits remained closed to warships for the rest of the century and so bottled up the Russian Black Sea fleet, which was not able to go to the aid of her fleet at Vladivostok during the **Russo-Japanese War** in 1904–5. To encourage Russia to stay in the **First World War** in 1915, the Allies secretly agreed that she should control the Straits after the war (the **Constantinople agreements**). It was also in 1915 that the Allies staged an unsuccessful attack on the Dardanelles (the **Gallipoli Campaign**). After the war warships were allowed to use the Straits, control of which was restored to Turkey in 1936.

**Strategic bombing offensive.** Mass air attacks on military and civilian targets, which aimed to destroy the enemy's capacity to wage war and to shatter its morale. In the 1930s it was widely believed that air power could win wars and that the bomber would get through to destroy cities. German air attacks in the **Spanish Civil War** on towns like Guernica and Madrid seemed to confirm this. Yet, surprisingly, neither Britain, Germany, France nor the Soviet Union had any heavy bombers in 1939. The RAF ordered four-engined bombers, which came into service in 1941; the Germans did not. In the **Second World War** strategic bombing was first applied against England in 1940. In day bombing attacks on London in August the Germans lost so many planes that they changed to night attacks on London and other English cities in the **Blitz**, which went on until May 1941, when most German planes were moved to the east, in preparation for Operation **Barbarossa**. About three million homes were destroyed and 60,000 civilians killed in Britain but the bombing did not seriously interfere with industrial production or morale. In spite of the failure of the Blitz, the British Chiefs of Staff told the Americans in 1941 that they hoped to defeat Germany by bombing alone. The British, like the Germans, found day bombing too costly, so they switched to night attacks and at first tried to hit specific targets such as arms factories. Their navigational aids for night flying were inadequate and their bombing was wildly inaccurate, as aerial photographs showed. Consequently, 'Bomber' Harris, the new chief of Bomber Command in 1942, chose larger targets such as whole cities and went in for area bombing (the Germans called it terror bombing). When the four-engined Lancaster, with its great range and a bomb load of over six tons, became available, he mounted the first thousand bomber raid on Cologne on 1 May 1942, followed by others on the industrial Ruhr. In an attack on Hamburg on 27 July 1943 incendiary bombs set off a fire-storm which killed 50,000 people. The Americans disapproved of area bombing and favoured instead precision daylight bombing of military targets, but their losses mounted and when, in a raid on Schweinfurt on 14 October 1943, two-thirds of their planes were shot down or damaged, they had to suspend their bombing until long-range fighter cover could be provided. This came with the Mustang, operational from December 1943, a fighter which was superior to anything the Germans possessed. Not only did it enable American daylight bombing to be resumed in February 1944 but it smashed the German fighter force, so that when France was invaded on **D-Day** (6 June 1944) the Germans had few aircraft with which to oppose the landing.

German war production continued to increase in 1943 and 1944, in spite of the bombing, which increasingly destroyed Germany's capacity to wage war in 1944–5. RAF bombing of the Ruhr cut steel production there by 80 per cent and halved Germany's total production. The US attacks on German synthetic oil production led to a fall from 316,000 tons early in 1944 to 17,000 tons in September: aviation fuel was almost exhausted by the end of 1944. Attacks on the oil plants also affected production of derivatives: nitrates for explosives and synthetic rubber. From December 1944 production in all industries fell steadily, largely as a result of bombing. It is estimated that between 750,000 and a million German civilians were killed in bombing raids: aircrew losses were 50,000 for the RAF and about the same number for the Americans. Japan was another area for the strategic bombing offensive. This was made possible by the American capture of islands in the **Pacific War** and reached its peak in 1945. Here the Americans practised area bombing to spread terror and in a raid on Tokyo on 9 March a quarter of Tokyo's wooden buildings were destroyed, a million people made homeless and 80,000 killed. Between June 1945 and the end of the war fifty-five Japanese cities were attacked and half the built-up area in each was destroyed. With the dropping of

**atomic bombs** on **Hiroshima** and Nagasaki in July, the strategic bombing offensive ended.

**Stresa Front** (1935). After Germany announced conscription and the existence of a German air force, both of which had been forbidden by the Treaty of **Versailles** (1919), representatives of the British, French and Italian governments met at Stresa in Italy, reaffirmed the treaties of **Locarno** and declared that the independence of Austria 'would continue to inspire their common policy'. The Front did not last long. It was weakened when Britain made the **Anglo-German naval agreement** (1935) without consulting her Stresa partners and collapsed completely with the Italian invasion of Ethiopia (October 1935) (see **Ethiopian War**), as Britain and France felt bound to support the **League of Nations** in imposing sanctions on Italy. In November 1936 **Mussolini** announced a **Rome–Berlin Axis**.

**Stresemann, Gustav** (1878–1929). German Chancellor (1923) and Foreign Minister (1923–9). The son of a Berlin innkeeper, Stresemann became a **National Liberal Party** deputy in 1907. Highly intelligent, he was a brilliant speaker and had a dynamic personality. He was a great admirer of *Weltpolitik* and during the **First World War** uncritically supported the military and an annexationist policy, so that he was known as '**Ludendorff**'s young man'. A monarchist, he sympathized with the **Kapp** *Putsch* (1920) and became a defender of the **Weimar Republic** only after the murders of Erzberger, the **Centre Party** leader, and Rathenau, the Foreign Minister. He had formed his own small German People's Party in 1918 and became Chancellor in 1923 when German industry was collapsing, owing to the French occupation of the **Ruhr**. Stresemann saw that to restore the economy and end inflation drastic action was needed, so he ended passive resistance in the Ruhr, resumed the payment of **reparations** and established the Rentenbank to issue a new, strictly controlled, currency. He cut government expenditure by reducing the number of officials and the salaries of those who remained and he increased taxation. All of this was very unpopular but it was effective: confidence was restored, inflation disappeared and a period of stability began. When there was nationalist agitation in Bavaria (see **Munich** *Putsch*) and communist disorders in

Saxony and Thuringia, Stresemann sent in the army. This led to socialists resigning from his government and so his 'hundred days' as Chancellor came to an end, though he continued to serve the Republic as Foreign Minister.

His aims were to make Germany the dominant power in Europe again, to free her from the financial burdens imposed by reparations, get rid of foreign troops from Germany, gain military equality with the other powers, unite with Austria and change Germany's eastern frontier, so that she would recover Danzig, the Polish corridor and Upper Silesia. He did not succeed in achieving all his aims but he did make significant gains for Germany, as he was a patient, persistent and flexible negotiator. He accepted the **Dawes Plan** (1924) as it led to French withdrawal from the Ruhr and provided investment for Germany. The treaties of **Locarno** (1925) were a great diplomatic triumph, as they ended Germany's isolation, left him with freedom of action in the east and were a step towards Germany joining the **League of Nations** in September 1926. He was awarded the Nobel Peace Prize in 1926, an honour no other German politician had obtained. Stresemann was aware of Germany's secret rearmament in Russia, arranged by **Seeckt** to avoid the limitations imposed by the Treaty of **Versailles**, and turned a blind eye. In 1929 he accepted the **Young Plan**, as it reduced reparations and led to the removal of Allied troops from the Rhineland five years ahead of schedule. Before the negotiations were completed Stresemann, worn out by his efforts, died of a heart attack on 8 October 1929. He was the most outstanding politician of the Weimar Republic.

**Sudetenland.** A horse-shoe shaped area in Czechoslovakia on the borders of Germany and Austria, in which three million German-speakers lived. It had been part of the **Austro-Hungarian Empire** and was given to Czechoslovakia at the Treaty of **St Germain** (1919), in order to give her a defensible frontier (the Bohemian mountains) against Germany. After **Hitler** came to power in Germany in 1933 National Socialism (see **Nazism**) spread rapidly amongst the Sudeten Germans and was given a great boost by the *Anschluss* with Austria. In 1938 Hitler demanded the incorporation of the Sudetenland in Germany and threatened war with Czechoslovakia. This was averted at the Munich Conference (see **Czechoslova-kian crisis**), when the Sudetenland was handed over to Germany. This so weakened Czechoslovakia's ability to defend herself that Hitler was able to seize the rest of the country in March 1939. Czechoslovakia regained this territory in 1945 and was authorized by the Allies to expel the German-speaking inhabitants, which she did.

**Suez Canal,** 170 kilometres (106 miles) long, runs through Egypt from the Mediterranean to the Red Sea. Before the canal was built ships going from Europe and the Mediterranean to Asia had to use the long route around the tip of southern Africa. The canal route was shorter, quicker and cheaper. A concession to build the canal was given by the Egyptian Khedive to the French engineer Ferdi-nand de Lesseps in 1854. Britain at first opposed this, as she thought that control of the canal would enable France to threaten the route to India. A company was formed with finance raised mainly in France and Egypt: the Khedive was the largest shareholder, holding 44 per cent of the shares. Construction began in 1859 and was completed ten years later. The Khedive **Ismail**'s schemes to modern-ize Egypt, his lavish expenditure and the collapse of the cotton boom at the end of the **American Civil War** in 1865 made his country bankrupt. Faced with large foreign debts, he sold his shares in the Suez Canal Company to the British government in 1875 for four million pounds. The canal soon became of enormous commer-cial importance with the use of steamships, which were not depend-ent on wind to carry them through: 436,000 tons of shipping passed through it in 1870, twenty million tons by 1914. In 1882, when Britain occupied Egypt, over 80 per cent of this traffic was British. From 1882 to 1956, when the canal was nationalized by President Nasser, the Suez Canal Zone was under British military control.

**Suffragette.** A member of a British militant, feminist movement, which sought votes for women. The name was given by the *Daily Mail* to the followers of Emmeline **Pankhurst**, to distinguish them from the non-militant suffragists. The Women's Social and Political Union (WSPU) was a mainly middle-class organization founded by Emmeline Pankhurst in 1903. It was ignored by press and politicians, so in 1905 she decided to become more militant, by interrupting political meetings and breaking shop windows. In 1912 the **Liberal** government agreed to include female suffrage in a Franchise Bill but the Speaker ruled this out of order, as it would change the nature of the original bill. The suffragettes responded by increasing their militancy: almost every shop window in Regent Street and Oxford Street, London, was broken, paintings were slashed in art galleries and public buildings were set on fire. Emily Davison threw herself in front of the King's horse in the 1913 Derby and was killed. To prevent imprisoned suffragettes obtaining an early release by going on hunger strike, the Cat and Mouse Act (1913) allowed for their release in order to recover, followed by their re-arrest. All this violent agitation turned public opinion against the suffragettes, whose campaign came to an abrupt halt when war was declared in 1914. Now they concentrated on the war effort, encouraging the recruitment of soldiers and their replacement in industry by women. The Representation of the People Act 1918 gave the vote to all women over thirty (it was feared that if they were given the vote on the same terms as men, they would outnumber male electors). Much of what the suffragettes had wanted therefore came about, through the efforts of ordinary women during the war rather than through the suffragette campaign. Women over twenty-one got the vote ten years later.

**Sun Yixian** (Sun Yat-sen) (1866–1925). Chinese revolutionary and founder of the **Guomindang** (Nationalist Party). Born into a poor peasant family in the Guangzhou (Canton) area, he was educated at a missionary school in Hawaii, where an elder brother had settled, and at medical school in Hong Kong and became one of the earliest Western-trained intellectuals in China. By 1895 he was a full-time revolutionary, calling for a republic, but was forced into exile for sixteen years, after an attempted rising in Guangzhou failed. He spent much of this time visiting Chinese settlements in the USA and South-East Asia, raising money for secret society risings in China, all of which failed. In 1905 he was elected by Chinese students in Tokyo to be head of the *Tongmenghui* (Revolutionary Alliance). When the **Chinese Revolution** of 1911 overthrew the **Qing dynasty**, Sun was in the USA but returned to become President of a Provisional Revolutionary government. In order to gain the support for the republic of **Yuan Shikai**, who had the best army in China, Sun gave up the presidency in favour of Yuan. The *Tongmenghui* had in 1912 become a political party, the Guomindang, which became the largest party in both houses of parliament in the elections of 1912–13. Yuan felt threatened, so Sun was once again compelled to flee abroad. After Yuan's death Sun tried to set up his own government in Guangzhou but was twice evicted by local **warlords**. He therefore looked abroad for help and in 1923 accepted Russian support, in return for admitting communists into the Guomindang. Thus began the **United Front**, which lasted till the Shanghai *coup* of 1927. The Guomindang became a disciplined, mass party, opposed to warlords and **imperialism**, which based its ideology on Sun's writings. These proposed that after a successful revolution a military dictatorship should give way to party control, which should educate the people and prepare them for full parliamentary government. Sun also put forward his Three People's Principles – Nationalism, Democracy and the People's Livelihood, by which he appeared to mean **socialism**. To bring about the fall of the warlords, who dominated China after Yuan's death, Sun set up with Soviet help the Whampoa Military Academy, under **Jiang Jieshi** (Chiang Kai-shek), to train a party army but he died in 1925 before it had any success. Sun appeared to have failed: he never exercised real power and left China weak and divided. Yet he had inspired Chinese who wanted unity and Westernization and had set up institutions – the Guomindang and Whampoa Academy – which would give China a semblance of unity within five years.

**Supreme Court** (USA) was established by the Constitution as a third branch of government, independent of the legislative (**Congress**) and the executive (the President). Its members, nine since 1869, are appointed by the President with the consent of the Senate and hold office for life. The court soon established its right to decide whether laws passed by Congress or state legislatures were constitutional but it can do so only when cases arising from the laws are brought before it. As Chief Justice Hughes (1930–41) said: 'We are under the Constitution but the Constitution is what the judges say it is and the judiciary is the safeguard of our liberties and our property.' The court's decisions have played an important part in deciding whether power lies with the states or with the federal government and have affected the social and economic development of the USA. The court has no means of enforcing its judgments and relies for this on the President, who has sometimes ignored its decision.

Chief Justice **Marshall** was a liberal but many judges were not and, as their decisions often reflected their political attitudes, they could invalidate all kinds of progressive legislation. Marshall had declared many state laws unconstitutional but not till the **Dred Scott case** in 1857 did the Supreme Court declare an act of Congress illegal. The extraordinarily reactionary declaration of Chief Justice Taney that Negroes were 'beings of an inferior order', and the decision that Congress had no right to forbid slavery in any state, helped to bring about the **American Civil War**. After the war the fourteenth amendment to the Constitution gave Negroes 'the equal protection of the laws' but the Supreme Court showed hostility to Negro rights and in 1896 upheld the **'Jim Crow' laws**, which maintained racial **segregation**. From 1890–1930 the Supreme Court limited federal efforts to control trusts, to establish workers' rights to form unions, and to limit child labour. During Franklin D. **Roosevelt**'s first administration (1933–7) the court declared twelve **New Deal** laws unconstitutional. Roosevelt was incensed and asked Congress for a bill which would allow him to appoint more (liberal) judges to the court. He had to withdraw it, as there was too much opposition – Roosevelt was seen to be threatening the independence of the judiciary, which was guaranteed by the Constitution – but the judges, alarmed at this threat, changed their attitude. They upheld laws, such as the Social Security Act, which provided for old-age pensions and unemployment insurance and the **Wagner Act**, which aided labour unions.

**Swastika** (from the Sanskrit *svastika*, 'conducive to prosperity'). An ancient religious symbol in the shape of a hooked cross. It was used throughout the world as a symbol of good fortune: in ancient Mesopotamia as early as the fourth millennium BC, in early Christian and Byzantine art, in South and Central America and by Buddhists and Hindus in India. In 1910 a German poet Guido von List proposed it as a symbol for all **anti-Semitic** organizations, mistakenly believing that it was of Teutonic origin. It was used by some **Free Corps** in 1919 and became a Nazi emblem, featured in a white circle on a red background (red represented the blood of the **Nazi Party**, white the purity of the German nation and the swastika the triumph of the Aryan race over Judaism). In 1935 it became part of the national flag of the **Third Reich**.

**Swing riots** (1830–31). Agricultural disturbances in England. There was a slump in agriculture after the **Napoleonic Wars** ended in 1815, with unemployment and a fall in wages, made worse by the high prices which followed the poor harvests of 1829 and 1830. The disorders, which began in Kent in August 1830, spread rapidly as far west as Cornwall and as far north as Carlisle, but were most extensive in the 'Speenhamland' counties (see **Speenhamland system**), where wages were lowest. Scotland and Wales were not affected. The riots were named after the mythical Captain Swing, who was supposed to be leader of the movement and whose name appeared at the end of threatening letters. The disturbances took several forms: threshing machines were destroyed; hay ricks of farmers who paid low wages were burnt; clergymen, who as JPs dealt with local poachers, were threatened, as were harsh **Poor Law** overseers. Although there were 1,400 incidents no one was killed and they were nearly all over by December, except for renewed outbreaks in Kent and Norfolk in 1831. **Grey**'s **Whig** government, frightened by the **Revolutions of 1830** on the Continent, acted with great severity. 2,000 people were arrested and half were tried by Special Commissions rather than by the common law courts; nineteen were hanged, 481 (including two women) were transported to Australia and 644 imprisoned. The Swing riots contributed to the unrest of 1830–32, which helped to bring about the **Reform Act** of 1832 but they also led to some of the harsh provisions of the Poor Law Amendment Act of 1834.

**Sykes–Picot agreement** (1916). A secret agreement, named after the main negotiators, between Britain and France for the partition of the **Ottoman Empire** after the **First World War**. Britain was to have direct control of the Baghdad–Basra region in lower Iraq and France of the north Syrian coast. In the remainder of Mesopotamia and the Syrian interior, France would have indirect control in the north, Britain in the south. Palestine, apart from a section of the coast, which would go to Britain, would be under an international administration. Russia also became involved. In return for recognizing the agreement, she was to be given part of eastern Anatolia. The Sykes–Picot agreement conflicted, at least in spirit, with the **Husayn**–McMahon correspondence, which promised independence to Arabs in most areas. After the **October Revolution** (1917) in Russia the **Bolsheviks** published the text of the agreement, which embarrassed Britain and France and convinced the Arabs that Britain in particular had been double-dealing and was insincere in its promises.

**Syndicalism.** Derived from the French word *syndicat* (trade union), it was a movement which believed that the struggle of the working class against capitalism should be waged by **trade unions** through direct action, culminating in a general strike, rather than through the activity of political parties, which were under middle-class control. Influenced by **Proudhon** and **Blanqui**, it had some affinity with **anarchism** and in its militant form was called anarcho-syndicalism. The movement in France, the heart of syndicalism, was led by the **CGT**, France's largest federation of unions. Its attempt to promote a general strike failed and in the **First World War** it collaborated with the government, thus weakening the movement. The International Workers of the World (IWW), founded in the USA in 1905, planned to unite the American working class, which would eventually join with workers all over the world to wage class war against capitalism. It had some local successes in strikes in 1912 but never had more than 60,000 members. Syndicalists in Britain failed to persuade the trade unions to cut their ties with the **Labour Party** at the Trades Union Congress in 1912. Outside France syndicalism had most success in Spain with the **CNT** and in Italy the *Unione Sindicale* was popular until it was absorbed by Fascist organizations. The British **General Strike** was not led by syndicalists but its failure discredited their methods. A further blow to syndicalism was the decision of the **Comintern** to call for **Popular Fronts** of trade unionists and left-wing parties to halt the spread of **Fascism**.

**Taff Vale case** (1901) arose out of a strike and picketing by the Amalgamated Society of Railway Servants to prevent the use of blackleg labour by the Taff Vale Railway Company. The strike was settled after eleven days but the case continued until it reached the House of **Lords**, which decided that the union was liable for damages inflicted by its officials and awarded damages and costs against the union. This judgment appeared to overturn the Trade Union Act of 1871, which protected union funds, and was the most important case affecting **trade unions**, as it virtually destroyed their right to strike. Some union leaders were prepared to accept the judgment, as it would give them greater control over their militants, but the strength of rank and file protest compelled them to seek its reversal. This occurred when **Asquith**'s **Liberal** government passed the Trades Disputes Act (1906), which gave trade unions legal immunity to this type of action. Ramsay **MacDonald** wrote to the trade unions that the Taff Vale decision 'should convince the unions that a labour party in Parliament is an immediate necessity'. Trade-union application to join the Labour Representation Committee, the forerunner of the **Labour Party**, increased rapidly as a result of the case.

**Taft, William Howard** (1857–1930). Twenty-seventh President of the USA (1909–13). Taft was a tall, fat, friendly man, who never wanted to become President. He was a federal judge, civilian Governor of the Philippines (acquired in the **Spanish–American War**) and administrator of the **Panama Canal** Zone before he became Theodore **Roosevelt**'s Secretary of War. When Roosevelt decided not to seek a third term of office in 1908, he chose Taft to succeed him as President. Taft did not want to stand ('Politics, when I am in it, makes me sick', he had written to his wife in 1906) but yielded to pressure from his wife and Roosevelt. He was anxious to carry on Roosevelt's policies and did so. Abroad he supported American investors by his '**dollar diplomacy**', particularly in Nicaragua. At home he brought ninety prosecutions against trusts, (twice as many as Roosevelt), including some of the biggest, like Standard Oil and US Steel, continued the conservation of forests and oil reserves, granted government workers an eight-hour day and created the Department of Labor and the Federal Children's Bureau. These were considerable achievements for someone who was regarded in his time as a conservative. However, Taft lacked Roosevelt's political skills in keeping the various elements in the **Republican Party** together. He alienated the Progressives (see **Progressive Movement**), the most dynamic wing of the party, by raising the tariff on manufactured goods in 1909. Even more damaging was the Ballinger–Pinchot affair. Richard Ballinger was Taft's Secretary of the Interior, who put up for sale the rich coal lands in Alaska. This was opposed by Gifford Pinchot, head of the US Forest Service and friend of Teddy Roosevelt. Taft supported Ballinger and dismissed Pinchot. This led to a split in the Republican Party, with both Roosevelt (as a Progressive) and Taft running for President in 1912. The divided Republican vote enabled the Democrat Woodrow **Wilson** to become President. Taft then returned to his legal career. He became professor of constitutional law at Yale and in 1921 he was appointed Chief Justice of the Supreme Court (the only President to hold this position), where he remained till just before his death in 1930.

**Taiping rebellion** (1850–64) was the greatest peasant rising in China in the nineteenth century. During the eighteenth century the population of China rose from 150 to 350 million and by 1850 it was 430 million. The amount of cultivable land did not increase, so peasants became worse off. Many could not pay their taxes or rents and so were dispossessed. The result was a major series of peasant rebellions from 1850–70. From 1853–68 part of the North China Plain, between the Huai and Yellow rivers, was controlled by the Nian rebels. In Yunnan Chinese Muslims rebelled from 1862–73, whilst Miao tribesmen were in revolt in the mountains of Kweichow (1854–72). The most serious of these rebellions, that of the Taiping Tianguo or Heavenly Kingdom of Great Peace, began in the hinterland of Guangzhou (Canton), a port visited by Western merchants and missionaries. Its leader, Hong Xiuquan, came from a poor peasant family. He had hallucinations of ascending to heaven and, influenced by Protestant missionaries, believed that he was a young brother of Jesus. He accepted many elements of Christianity, such as the Ten Commandments and the divinity of Christ, and began to preach his new faith about 1845 in Guangxi province. He welcomed into his society the poor, such as landless peasants, handicraft workers, miners and charcoal burners: much of his appeal came from the system of primitive communism which he advocated. One of his edicts stated that 'land, food, clothing and money must be held and used in common, so that there is no inequality anywhere and nobody lacks food or warmth.' As the Taipings advanced through central China and the Yangzi valley, they put to death the wealthy, officials and unpopular landlords. In addition to being a movement of peasants against landlords, the Taiping was also a nationalist movement, which wanted to free China from the Manchus. In 1853 the Taipings captured Nanjing, which remained their capital for the next eleven years. If the Taiping had coordinated their rising with that of the Nian in the north and that of the Red Turbans in the south, the Qing could not have survived, as they were fighting Britain and France in the second **Opium War** from 1856–60.

In spite of having control of much of the Yangzi valley, the richest region in China, the movement began to break up. Two expeditions, aimed at capturing the capital, Beijing (Peking), were defeated; there were internal power struggles, in which most of the original leaders were killed; and the leaders led a life of luxury, with large harems, whilst expecting their followers to lead a frugal and monogamous life. In order to pay for running the area they controlled, they had to tax the peasants, who withdrew their support. Meanwhile their opponents recovered the initiative – loyal scholar-officials like **Zeng Guofan** raised well-paid and disciplined militias. The **Qing dynasty** was also helped by the Western powers. After they had defeated China they wanted a conservative and docile government, so Western officials trained imperial troops and foreign generals, such as Charles 'Chinese' **Gordon**, commanded mixed units. In 1864 Nanjing was recaptured – Hong died during the siege. Zeng reported to the Emperor: 'Not one of the 100,000 rebels in Nanjing surrendered when the city was taken but in many cases gathered together and burnt themselves ... Such a formidable band of rebels has been rarely known from ancient times to the present.' It is estimated that the destruction of central China was so great that many provinces had not fully recovered decades later. The Manchu (Qing) dynasty lost much prestige and power, which was transferred to local officials – here is the origin of the **warlords**.

**'Taisho democracy'** refers to the generally liberal trend in Japanese politics during the reign (1912–26) of the *Taisho* ('Great Justice') Emperor, when the influence of political parties became greater than at any time before 1945. Some see this beginning in 1918 when Hara Kei (1856–1921), the leader of the Seiyukai Party, became the first Prime Minister to hold a seat in the lower house and to head a Cabinet formed from the majority party in the **Diet**. He is therefore known as the 'commoner' Prime Minister, whose appointment began a decade (except for the years 1922–4) when there was party government. This did not lead to major reforms, as Hara was keen to be on good terms with the conservative élites – the military, Privy Council, *genro* (elder statesmen) – who had the ear of the Emperor. The only significant political reform in the *Taisho* period was the extension in 1925 of the franchise to all males over twenty-five, which increased the electorate from three to 12.5 million, but this was immediately followed by the Peace Preservation Law (see **Peace Police Law**). This enabled the authorities to suppress left-wing parties and imprison their members, if they were regarded as subversive. The result was that socialist parties, in order to remain active, were reluctant to criticize the government.

The Japanese took advantage of Western involvement in the **First World War** to make the humiliating **Twenty-One Demands** (1915) on China, which almost made Manchuria and Inner Mongolia into Japanese colonies, and they seized German possessions in China and the Pacific. Japan retained these at the Treaty of **Versailles** by threatening to withdraw from the **Paris Peace Conference** and the **League of Nations**. She had a seat on the League Council but was very bitter that a racial equality clause was not accepted in the

League Charter. The war benefited Japan economically as well as territorially. She supplied her allies with munitions and was able to gain a foothold in their export markets, replacing British cotton goods in China. She also secured part of the world carrying trade (her merchant marine fleet doubled during the war) and, when imports of goods (such as German chemicals) stopped, she had to produce them herself. The development of heavy industry in Japan – shipbuilding, electrical engineering, rolling stock – dates from this time, which saw a vast increase in production and soaring exports. Japan had entered the war a debtor nation: she ended it with a vast balance of payments surplus, although wartime inflation produced rural discontent, which erupted in the **Rice riots** of 1918.

**Talleyrand-Périgord, Charles Maurice de** (1754–1838). French statesman. A career in the army was closed to him as he had a club foot, so he became a priest, in spite of having no religious calling, and from 1780–85 was agent-general of the clergy of France. In 1788 he became bishop of Autun and a year later was elected as a noble deputy to the **Estates-General**. Worldly and notorious for his pleasure-loving life – he had a mistress and a son – Talleyrand was a cautious trimmer politically, who would see which side was likely to win before committing himself. He proposed the seizure of Church lands by the State in 1789, was one of only four diocesan bishops who took the oath to the **Civil Constitution of the Clergy** and consecrated many of the first elected bishops of the constitutional Church. In 1791 he left the Church and was French ambassador in London until the execution of **Louis XVI**, when he went to the USA, remaining there until the **Directory** was established. Involved in the *coup d'état* of **Brumaire**, which brought **Napoleon** to power, he was his Foreign Minister from 1799 to 1807, negotiating the **Concordat** with the Pope, the Peace of **Amiens** with England and establishing the **Confederation of the Rhine**. Alarmed at Napoleon's boundless ambition, he resigned a month after the Treaty of **Tilsit**. In 1814 he intrigued with the Allies, persuaded the Senate to depose Napoleon and, as head of a provisional government, recalled **Louis XVIII** to the throne. As Foreign Minister he represented France at the Congress of **Vienna**. Aware of the unpopularity of **Charles X**, Talleyrand negotiated to bring **Louis Philippe** to the throne in 1830 and was rewarded by being appointed French ambassador to London (1830–34) again. He played a vital part in the negotiations which led to the creation of an independent Kingdom of Belgium.

**Tamworth Manifesto** (1834), was an election address by Sir Robert **Peel** to his constituents at Tamworth, Staffordshire but was in effect a national appeal for support. After the overwhelming defeat of the **Conservative Party** in the first election after the **Reform Act** of 1832, Peel realized that unless Conservatives accepted the Act and the need for moderate reform, they were likely to remain permanently in opposition. In his manifesto he therefore recognized the Act as 'a final and irrevocable settlement of a great constitutional question' and promised to support a 'careful review of institutions, civil and ecclesiastical ... combining with the firm maintenance of established rights the correction of proved abuses and the redress of real grievances'. This gave the Conservative Party a much wider appeal than that of its traditional supporters, the landed aristocracy and gentry and the Anglican Church.

**Tannenberg, battle of** (20–31 August 1914). The Germans crushingly defeated numerically superior Russian armies at the beginning of the **First World War**. Germany's eastern frontier was lightly guarded in accordance with the **Schlieffen Plan**, which aimed at knocking out France before turning on Russia. Before mobilization was complete, two Russian armies, the First under Rennenkampf and the Second under Samsonov, invaded East Prussia north and south of the Masurian Lakes. There was no coordination between the two armies, which were too far apart to support each other if there was a German counter-attack. The German Commander, whose force was smaller than either of the Russian armies, wanted to retire to the river Vistula, so he was replaced by **Hindenburg**, called out of retirement, and **Ludendorff**. They adopted a plan drawn up by Colonel Hoffmann, chief of operations, to concentrate on Samsonov in the south. Incredibly Samsonov's wireless messages, giving his position and intentions, were not sent in code. The Germans surrounded the Second Army, which lost 125,000 men and 500 guns. Samsonov committed suicide. Hindenburg then turned against the First Army and fought the battle of the Masurian

Lakes (9–14 September 1914). A Russian counter-attack allowed Rennenkampf to withdraw across the Niemen river into Russia, though with the loss of another 125,000 men. German casualties in both battles were 20,000. These victories made Hindenburg a hero at home and gave Germany a dominance on the Eastern Front which she was never to lose. The Allies on the Western Front benefited, as von Moltke, the German Chief of Staff, withdrew troops from the armies in France at a critical time in order to help in East Prussia. They arrived too late to fight at Tannenberg but their removal from France helped **Joffre** to halt the German drive on Paris and so deprived Germany of a quick victory.

**Tanzimat** ('reorganization'). Period of reforms in the **Ottoman Empire** from 1839–78. Sultan Abdulmecid (ruled 1839–61) showed that he was determined to carry on the reforms of his father **Mahmud II**, when he issued the Noble Rescript (*Hatt-i Sherif*) in 1839. This marked a radical breach with Islamic tradition, which had always regarded non-Muslims as separate and inferior. The Rescript recognized the equality of all religious groups before the law. Equal treatment for Muslims and non-Muslims was again promised in the Imperial Rescript (*Hatt-i Humayun*) of 1856 and in 1867 Christians began to be appointed to state councils. The aim was to integrate them (40 per cent of the Sultan's subjects were Christians early in the century) in the Ottoman Empire and this meant replacing the traditional educational and legal systems, dominated by the *ulama* (religious leaders), by secular organizations. From 1840 Western-type law courts and codes were introduced and administration was centralized on the French model, with prefects and departments. A new educational system, with elementary and secondary schools to prepare students for higher technical education, grew slowly and painfully to create a new élite committed to reform. The economy was also improved, as land was reclaimed, new factories set up, postal (1834) and telegraph (1855) systems established and railways begun (1866). All these reforms were revolutionary, as they seemed to secure the triumph of the Christian enemy over Islam by imposing, often with the help of European advisers, European practices and institutions. Most Turks were unaffected by the Tanzimat – their lives, beliefs and loyalties were still dominated by Islam – but power had nevertheless passed to secular bureaucrats. This created an opposition in the 1860s known as the Young Ottomans, who wanted reform to continue to strengthen the Empire but did not want it to be anti-religious. They were alarmed too that the Tanzimat made the Sultan more of an absolute monarch than he had been before and so they wanted to curb his power. They did this by once again using a Western model, that of parliamentary government. The *coup* which brought **Abdulhamid II** to power in 1876 imposed on him a Constitution which limited his powers and set up an elected assembly. It did not last. When Abdulhamid suspended the Constitution in 1878 the Tanzimat came to an end and for the next thirty years the Sultan ruled the Empire as an autocrat.

**Tariff reform.** A campaign to end free trade and to impose tariffs on goods imported into Britain. In 1903 Joseph **Chamberlain**, deeply concerned at Britain's long-term industrial decline (in 1860 only 5.5 per cent of British imports by value were manufactured goods: this figure had risen to 25 per cent by 1900) and convinced that protection in the USA and Germany, Britain's main competitors, had strengthened industry there, began a campaign for tariff reform. He thought that it would unite the British Empire through imperial preference (lower rates of duty between member countries); that it would regenerate British industry by reducing foreign competition; and that it could be used to pay for social reforms like old-age pensions without raising taxes. Chamberlain split the Cabinet on this issue, so he resigned from office and carried his campaign to the country through the Tariff Reform League, which had hundreds of branches. This was modelled on the **Anti-Corn Law League** but it was unsuccessful in persuading the electorate, as tariff reform would lead to dearer food. In the 1906 election, fought largely over tariffs, the **Conservatives** were crushingly defeated and in the same year Chamberlain was forced to retire from politics, as he had a paralytic stroke. **Balfour** carried on the struggle for tariff reform but it declined in importance as **Home Rule for Ireland** became the leading topic in 1912. Tariff reform was rejected again in 1923 when **Baldwin** fought an election on this issue and failed to win a majority. It finally succeeded after the **Wall Street Crash** (1929) and the ensuing depression, when nearly all countries sought to protect their industries. **MacDonald**'s **National Government** adopted tariff reform in 1931.

**Tennessee Valley Authority** (TVA). US federal government agency, created as part of the **New Deal** programme of public works, designed to provide employment during the **Great Depression**. In 1916 the federal government had built a dam and two munitions plants on the Tennessee river in Alabama. This became part of a more extensive plan in 1933 to develop the Tennessee river basin, an area of 40,000 square miles in seven states. Dams and hydroelectric stations were built to provide cheap electricity, flood control, land reclamation and afforestation. Navigation was also improved by building locks and by enlarging and deepening the channel, which eventually made possible a seventy-fold increase in shipping on the river. Many people disliked the TVA, as it was publicly owned and therefore regarded as a product of **socialism**, but it was a great success. It created thousands of jobs and brought electricity to hundreds of thousands of homes for the first time.

**Terror, the** (1792–4). A response to the situation in France when the survival of the **French Revolution** seemed at stake: foreign armies were invading France, there was civil war in the Vendée (see **Vendean revolt**) and an economic crisis, with high prices and scarcity of grain. The **Convention** set up the machinery of the Terror between March and May 1793. A Revolutionary Tribunal was established to try counter-revolutionary suspects; representatives-on-mission were sent from the Convention to the provinces to speed up conscription and keep an eye on the generals; watch committees were set up in each commune to watch out for traitors and a summary execution decree provided for the trial and execution of armed rebels within twenty-four hours of capture. It provided many more victims than the Revolutionary Tribunal. The Terror took three forms. There was the official Terror, controlled by the **Committee of Public Safety** (CPS) and of General Security, which was centred in Paris and whose victims came before the Revolutionary Tribunal. There was the Terror in the areas of **Federal Revolt**, where the worst atrocities took place. There was also the Terror in other parts of France, which was under the control of watch committees and representatives-on-mission and the civilian *armées révolutionnaires* of the *sans-culottes*. **Robespierre** and the **Jacobins** staged a series of celebrity trials in late 1793, in which **Marie-Antoinette** and leading **Girondins** were executed, but the Terror in the provinces claimed far more victims when the federal revolt was put down. The CPS established a dictatorship in December 1793 and proceeded to eliminate all its real or imagined enemies, including **Hébert** and **Danton** and their followers. These executions terrified everyone, so that no one dared criticize the Committee, particularly when the **Great Terror** followed the Law of Prairial (June 1794) and ended any semblance of a fair trial. The Great Terror sickened the population and was brought to an end by the execution of **Robespierre** in **Thermidor** (July) 1794. One estimate of the Terror is that there were 17,000 official executions, most of them in Paris or in the areas of revolt. Most of the victims were peasants (28 per cent) and urban workers (31 per cent). If one adds the number of people executed without trial or who died in prison, the number is probably around 50,000.

**Texas, republic of** (1836–45). When Mexico became independent from Spain in 1821 there were few settlers in northern Texas, so the Mexicans offered liberal land grants there to Americans. By 1830 20,000 Americans, mainly Southerners with their slaves, had taken advantage of this offer. The Mexican government, alarmed, forbade further American immigration and tried to enforce laws against slavery, which had been made illegal in Mexico in 1829. In 1836 the Texans declared their independence and set up a republic, which the Mexican dictator Santa Anna was determined to crush. His troops overran the Alamo mission at San Antonio and killed every member of the garrison. 'Remember the Alamo' became a battle-cry for Sam Houston's small army, which defeated the Mexicans at San Jacinto, captured Santa Anna and forced him to recognize the independence of the 'lone star' republic. Texas immediately sought incorporation in the USA but there was much opposition to this in the North, as Texas would join as a slave state. It was not until 1845 that, as a result of the efforts of Secretary of State John C. **Calhoun** and President Tyler, Texas was admitted as the largest state in the Union.

**Thermidor** (1794). On 26 July (8 Thermidor, according to the revolutionary calendar) 1794, **Robespierre** abandoned his usual caution and in a speech in the **Convention** attacked his colleagues in the **Committee of Public Safety**, accusing them of 'a conspiracy against public liberty'. When he was asked to name the men he was accusing, he refused. Moderates like **Carnot** and terrorists like **Fouché** all felt threatened, so they joined together to plot against Robespierre. On 9 Thermidor the Convention voted for the arrest of Robespierre, Saint-Just and others. As they were taken to prisons controlled by the Commune (the local government of Paris, filled with Robespierre's supporters) they were soon released. The leaders of the Commune now called for an insurrection to assist Robespierre and for the National Guard (a citizens' militia, consisting mainly of *sans-culottes*) to mobilize. There was great confusion that evening, as the Convention also called on the National Guard to support it against the Commune. Only sixteen of the forty-eight Sections (units of local government in Paris) sent troops to aid the Commune, but they included some of the famous artillery units: for several hours the Commander of the National Guard had the Convention at his mercy. Only a failure of nerve by him and Robespierre saved the Convention. Robespierre had no faith in a popular rising, and while he waited passively the Convention outlawed the deputies, whose arrest they had previously ordered, and the leaders of the Commune, which meant they could be executed without trial. The decree of outlawry persuaded many Sections to support the Convention. Robespierre was re-arrested and on 28 July (10 Thermidor) he and twenty-one others were executed. In the next few days over 100 members of the Commune followed Robespierre to the scaffold. The **Terror** soon came to an end.

**Thiers, Louis Adolphe** (1797–1877). French politician and first President of the **Third Republic** (1871–3). A lawyer, journalist and believer in parliamentary government, he founded a newspaper *Le National* in 1830. This openly advocated a change of dynasty and welcomed **Louis Philippe** as the new French King, after the fall of **Charles X** in the **July Revolution** (1830). Thiers held various ministerial posts under the July Monarchy (1830–48) and in 1834, as Minister of the Interior, was responsible for the ruthless crushing of a rising by Lyon silk-workers, in which 300 were killed. As

Foreign Minister in 1840 his support for **Muhammad Ali** almost involved France in war with Britain but Louis Philippe pulled back from the brink and forced Thiers to resign. After the overthrow of Louis Philippe in 1848 he helped Louis Napoleon Bonaparte to become President of the **Second Republic** but turned against him after his *coup d'état* of 1851 and was in exile from 1852–3. From 1863 he was the leader of the opposition in the Legislature of the Second Empire (1852–70).

The elections for a National Assembly in February 1871, which followed the fall of **Napoleon III**, were a triumph for Thiers. His great prestige and experience resulted in his being elected in twenty-six departments. He was the obvious choice to become, at the age of seventy-three, Chief of the Executive Power of the French Republic and in August its President. Given a free hand to negotiate peace with **Prussia**, he had to accept the loss of **Alsace** and part of Lorraine and agree to pay a large war indemnity; there would be a German army of occupation until it was paid. Thiers also had to deal with the rising of the **Paris Commune**, which opposed the peace. He refused to make concessions and sent in troops to crush the revolt in *la semaine sanglante* ('bloody week'). The 'horrible sight' of piles of corpses would, he told his prefects, be a 'useful lesson' to keep the workers in their place. Previously an Orleanist, Thiers became convinced that a republic had the best chance of preserving social stability and national unity and that it was the regime that divided Frenchmen the least. In November 1872 he declared that he was in favour of a republic but stated that 'the Republic will be conservative or it will not exist'. By 1873 Thiers had paid off the war indemnity and seen the German army of occupation withdraw, but his conversion to republicanism was unacceptable to the monarchist majority in the Assembly. Consequently in 1873 he was removed from office and replaced by Marshal **MacMahon** as President and by a monarchist, the Duc de Broglie, as Prime Minister. The last years of his life were spent trying to gain acceptance of the **Third Republic**.

**Third International,** see **Comintern**

**Third Reich** (1933–45). The First Reich was the Holy Roman Empire of the German Nation, which began in 962 with the coronation in Rome of Otto the Great and was ended by **Napoleon Bonaparte** in 1806. The Second Reich was the **German Empire** (1871–1918), which began with the unification of Germany by **Bismarck** and ended with the collapse of the **Hohenzollern dynasty** in 1918. *The Third Reich* was the title of a book in 1923 by the German nationalist Moeller van den Bruck. The term was enthusiastically adopted by **Hitler** to indicate his intention of founding a new empire, which began with his seizure of power in 1933. He expected his Third Reich to be the greatest of all German empires and to last for a thousand years.

**Third Republic,** in France, see **Monarchist Republic** (1871–9), **Opportunist Republic** (1879–99), **Radical Republic** (1899–1940)

**Three Emperors' League,** see *Dreikaiserbund*

**Thugs** (Hindi *thag*, 'cheat'). Thieves and assassins in India, who posed as travellers and befriended their victims before strangling them with a scarf. Thuggee was widespread in the early nineteenth century, when it operated all over India but was dominant in the centre and north. It is estimated that a million people were killed by Thugs. They did not have any central or even regional organization and it is not clear whether or not they were worshipping, by ritual murder, the ferocious Hindu goddess Kali. Thugs were difficult to catch, as they were patronized by rich landlords, with whom they shared their booty. The **East India Company** therefore set up a special department in 1835 to wipe out Thuggee. It made arrests through 'approvers', members of a gang who turned king's evidence, and by the mid 1850s Thuggee had been virtually eliminated. It gave a new word to the English language.

**Tilak, Bal Gangadhar** (1856–1920). Indian nationalist. An orthodox Hindu, Tilak sought to rouse national pride and promote Hindu unity by reviving religious festivals and resurrecting forgotten national heroes, though this alienated Indian Muslims. Deeply conservative on social questions, he opposed limiting child marriage, the education of women and compulsory vaccination against the plague. He loathed the deferential attitude of the **Indian National Congress** to the British government and became convinced that direct action, rather than petitions to the **Raj**, was needed to bring about self-rule. **Boycott** and non-cooperation would, he felt, be effective, as the Raj depended on Indian cooperation for running the country. Tilak therefore supported the *swadeshi* (home industry) movement and boycott which followed the Bengal partition in 1905, and he tried to take over Congress in 1907. He and his 'extremists', with their demand for full Indian independence, were thwarted in this by **Gokhale** and the 'moderates', who retained control of Congress until Gokhale's death in 1915. In 1908 Tilak was arrested, deported to Burma and imprisoned. He was freed just before the **First World War** but was not able to re-enter Congress until Gokhale died. In 1916 he formed a Home Rule League, became undisputed leader of Congress and persuaded it to form a united front with Muslims in the Lucknow Pact of 1916, by which the **Muslim League** supported Congress demands for self-government, in return for Congress recognition of separate Muslim constituencies. Tilak set up the Congress Democratic Party in 1920 to campaign for *swaraj* (self-rule) but this 'giant of men', as **Gandhi** called him, died a few months later, leaving a legacy of aggressive **nationalism** which deeply affected the Indian radicals of the next decade.

**Tilsit, treaties of** (July 1807). Treaties made by **Napoleon Bonaparte** with **Alexander I** of Russia and Frederick William III of Prussia. **Prussia** was forced to give up her land west of the river Elbe, most of which was formed with other German states such as Hanover into the Kingdom of Westphalia, ruled by Napoleon's brother Jérôme Bonaparte. This completed Napoleon's control over north Germany. Prussia's Polish lands became the Grand Duchy of Warsaw, a French satellite under the nominal control of the King of Saxony. Prussia's humiliation was completed by her acceptance of a large war indemnity, a French army of occupation and by her joining the **Continental Blockade**. Russia was treated much better: she did not lose any territory, though she had to recognize the **Confederation of the Rhine** and had to join the Continental Blockade. She was given a free hand against Sweden, from whom she obtained Finland in 1809. Alexander began to ignore the treaty in 1810, when he opened his ports to neutral shipping and imposed duties on French goods, events which led to Napoleon's invasion of Russia and the **Moscow Campaign** of 1812.

**Tirpitz, Alfred von** (1849–1930). German admiral and Secretary of State for the Navy (1897–1916). Tirpitz was a supporter of *Weltpolitik*, which involved acquiring colonies, to protect which a navy was needed. A large fleet was also necessary, he felt, to prevent Britain from blocking Germany's entry into world markets. 'For Germany,' he wrote in 1897, 'the most dangerous enemy at the present time is England.' He aimed to challenge the British navy in home waters, 'between Heligoland and the Thames', but Britain's naval superiority was so great (in 1898 she had thirty-eight battleships and thirty-four cruisers; Germany had seven battleships and two cruisers) that this was a long-term project. 'The construction of a fleet,' he wrote, 'is the work of a generation.' His Risk Theory aimed to build a fleet strong enough to threaten British superiority in the North Sea, so that in attacking such a fleet Britain would take the risk of losing so many ships that it would be inferior to its other rivals (France and Russia). This would make Britain realize the necessity of coming to an agreement with Germany and would enable Germany to acquire an empire by peaceful means. Tirpitz hoped that his naval programme, begun with the Navy Laws of 1898, which provided for the building of nineteen battleships (a number doubled in the second Navy Law of 1900), would gain the support of the working class, by providing jobs and by appealing to their patriotism. This would counter the appeal of the **Social Democratic Party** and provide support for the conservative *Sammlung*, which would enable the *Junkers*, army officers and bureaucrats to retain their dominant position in the state. Tirpitz's plans were based on assumptions that all proved false. These were that Britain would never be able to concentrate enough of its fleet in the North Sea to meet the German challenge, owing to her world-wide commitments; that Britain would not spend enough to retain her superiority; and that she would never ally with any power except Germany. Tirpitz's Navy Laws were seen in England as the first serious threat to the dominance of the Royal Navy since the **Napoleonic Wars**. 'If the German fleet ever becomes superior to ours,' wrote Sir Edward **Grey**, the British Foreign Secretary, to

**Edward VII** in 1908, 'the German army can conquer this country. There is no similar risk . . . for Germany.' For Britain her fleet was a necessity, so there began a naval race, which became even more expensive and intense when Britain produced the **Dreadnought** in 1906 and Germany copied it. Far from bringing Germany and Britain closer together, Tirpitz's Navy Laws pushed Britain into the opposite camp, and led to her making the **Anglo-French** (1904) and **Anglo-Russian** (1907) **Ententes**. When war began in 1914 Tirpitz refused to risk his fleet on the high seas and became instead an advocate of unrestricted submarine warfare. He became more right-wing as he grew older, was a leading member of the nationalist Fatherland Party during the war and in 1924 was elected to the **Reichstag** as a deputy for the conservative German National People's Party.

**Tito** (born Josip Broz) (1892–1980). Yugoslav **resistance** leader and head of state. The son of a Croatian peasant, he was captured by the Russians in 1915, while serving in the Austro-Hungarian army. After the **October Revolution** in 1917, he joined the **Red Army** and fought against the Whites in the **Russian Civil War**. For the next twenty years he was an international communist agent. In 1920 he returned to Yugoslavia, where he was imprisoned from 1928–33 for his clandestine activities. On his release he went to Moscow to work in the **Comintern**'s Balkan secretariat. In 1936 he was in Paris organizing recruitment for the **International Brigades** in Spain and then worked in Yugoslavia again, supporting cooperation with Germany after the **Nazi–Soviet Pact** (August 1939), until **Hitler** invaded the Soviet Union in Operation **Barbarossa** (June 1941). Tito then became the leader of communist partisans, at first in cooperation with the royalist Mihailovich; but the latter was more concerned with preserving his forces for a royalist restoration at the end of the war than in fighting the Germans. The two soon parted company and from November 1943 Tito was recognized by the Western allies, as well as by the Soviet Union, as the leader of the Yugoslav resistance. In the mountains of Bosnia and Montenegro Tito, constantly on the move, fought a guerrilla campaign against the Germans and by 1943 had an army of a quarter of a million men, supported by the British. When Italy surrendered in 1943 Tito occupied the Dalmatian coast and came to control most of western Yugoslavia. In 1944 he went on to the offensive, besieged the Germans in Zagreb and other cities and tied down twenty-one German divisions. Tito's achievement among partisan leaders was unique, as he freed his country almost without foreign help. This ensured that he became head of the Yugoslav government after the war and enabled him, alone of East European communist leaders, to maintain his independence from Soviet control. He is one of the greatest guerrilla leaders in history.

**Togo, Heihachiro** (1848–1934). Japanese admiral. A *samurai*, Togo studied in England (1871–8) and commanded the Japanese fleet in the **Russo-Japanese War** (1904–5). His pre-emptive strike at Port Arthur in February 1904 was only partly successful: if he had pressed home his attack he might have destroyed the Russian fleet and ended the war quickly. After that he blockaded Port Arthur effectively and forced the Russian fleet to return to port in August when it tried to break out. A dour and usually cautious commander, he would take risks when he felt they were justified. His main claim to fame was the destruction of the Russian Baltic fleet, which had sailed half way round the world in order to reach Vladivostok. Togo attacked it in the Tsushima Straits between Korea and Japan, boldly turning on a course opposite and parallel to that of the Russians, exposing his ships to the heavier Russian guns. He was fortunate that the Russian crews were not fully trained, especially the gunners, and that a large proportion of the Russian shells failed to explode. With a 3–4 knot advantage Togo could outmanoeuvre the Russians and gained the greatest naval victory since **Trafalgar**, which earned him the title 'Nelson of Japan'. Thirty-four Russian ships were sunk or captured, only two destroyers and a light cruiser reaching Vladivostok. Japan lost only three torpedo boats. Togo became a popular hero in Britain and the USA, as well as in Japan. He was Chief of the Naval General Staff from 1905–9 and an influential figure in the Japanese navy, opposing the limitations imposed by the **London Naval Conference** of 1930, until his death.

**Tojo Hideki** (1884–1948). Japanese general and politician. Tojo was regarded as the leader of the extreme nationalist *tosei* faction, which wanted Japan to expand in China and **Manchuria**. In 1937 he became Chief of Staff of the Guandong army in Manchuria and helped to bring Inner Mongolia under Japanese control. As War Minister (1940–41) he built up Japan's armed force, advocated closer collaboration with Germany and Italy and was largely responsible for the Tripartite Pact with those countries. He persuaded **Vichy France** to allow Japan to occupy bases in Indo-China (July 1941) and regarded war with the United States as inevitable. Tojo helped to bring about the fall of the Prime Minister Konoye, whom he regarded as too conciliatory towards the USA, and replaced him as Prime Minister in October 1941; this marked the final triumph of the militarists in Japan. He gave the order to attack **Pearl Harbor** (December 1941) and so began the **Pacific War** (1941–5). During the war he gained more and more power with Japan's early successes, acting as War Minister and, for a time, as Home Minister, as well as retaining his post as Prime Minister. He was never a dictator, as he was always subordinate to the Supreme Command and had no control over the navy. Although he became Chief of Staff in February 1944, so that he could coordinate the planning of the war, his influence declined with Japanese reverses, and when Tokyo was in range of American bombers the Supreme Command forced his resignation in July 1944. Austere and known as 'the razor' for his ruthlessness, Tojo was the most hated figure in the Pacific War amongst Japan's enemies. He was tried as a war criminal, found guilty and hanged.

**Tokugawa shogunate.** The government of Japan from 1603 to 1868. In 1600 Tokugawa Ieyasu defeated his enemies at the battle of Sekigahara and three years later was given the title of shogun (*sei-i tai-shogun* meant 'barbarian-subduing great general') by the Emperor. The Tokugawa family's administration at Edo (Tokyo), rather than that of the imperial Court at Kyoto, was the effective government of Japan. The Emperor was virtually a prisoner in his palace, with no political influence. His court nobles had to swear allegiance to the shogun, who appointed all senior officials at the Court. The strength of the Tokugawas lay in their being the largest landowners in Japan (they owned 25 per cent of the land). The rest of the land was divided up amongst *daimyo* (feudal lords), whose lives were strictly controlled by the shogun. To prevent them from revolting there was a system of alternate attendance. Every *daimyo* had to spend half his time in his domain and half at Edo. When he was in his domain, he had to leave his wife and family in Edo as hostages. *Daimyo* were not allowed to visit the Emperor's Court at Kyoto. The Tokugawas promoted **Confucianism** to maintain their power and tried to prevent all change by cutting Japan off from nearly all foreign contacts (see *Sakoku*). All these measures were effective in maintaining Tokugawa dominance and internal peace until the arrival of the American Commodore **Perry** in 1853. He compelled the Japanese to open some ports to foreigners, and in 1858 the shogun had to make the first of several **unequal treaties**, which gave foreigners a privileged position in Japan. This indication of the shogun's weakness led to an anti-Tokugawa movement which sought to restore the authority of the Emperor and took as its slogan *sonno joi* ('respect for the Emperor and expulsion of foreigners'). By 1866 there was open rebellion by *daimyo* from Choshu and Satsuma, which led to the resignation of the last Tokugawa shogun in 1867 and the **Meiji Restoration** of 1868.

**Tolpuddle Martyrs.** The Friendly Society of Agricultural Labourers founded a new branch at the village of Tolpuddle in Dorset to obtain an increase in wages for its members. It was a peaceful not revolutionary organization, yet local magistrates arrested its leader George Loveless, a labourer and Methodist preacher, and five others. They were convicted in 1834, under an Act of 1797 that related to the **naval mutinies**, of administering unlawful oaths and were sentenced to seven years' transportation to Australia. Lord **Melbourne**, the **Whig** Prime Minister, fully supported the repression. On the initiative of the Grand National Consolidated Trade Union a committee was set up in London which organized protest meetings and petitions throughout the country. When Lord John **Russell** became Home Secretary the Martyrs were pardoned in 1836. All returned home, but later five migrated with their families to Canada. The trial showed just how little **trade unions** were protected by the repeal of the **Combination Acts**.

**Tone, (Theobald) Wolfe** (1763–98). Irish republican. A founder of the Society of United Irishmen, Tone wanted to unite the

Presbyterian minority and the Catholic majority in Ireland to get rid of religious discrimination and reform parliament. Although a Protestant, he organized a Catholic convention in Dublin in 1792, which pressured the Irish parliament into passing the Catholic Relief Act (1793). This gave Catholics the vote on the same terms as Protestants and allowed them to occupy most civil and military posts, though they could still not become members of parliament. When he was forced into exile in 1794 during the **French Revolutionary Wars**, he first went to the United States and then to France, where he sought French aid to overthrow British rule in Ireland. The **Directory** responded by sending one of its best generals, Hoche (Tone was his adjutant), with forty-three ships and 14,000 men to Ireland, but the expedition was dispersed by storms off the coast of Cork. The **Irish Rebellion** of 1798 gave Tone another opportunity, but he could persuade the French to send only a small force of 3,000 men. It was intercepted by the British off Donegal and Wolfe Tone was captured. He was sentenced to death but committed suicide before he could be hanged. Tone had underestimated the sectarian nature of political activity in Ireland in thinking that Catholic and Protestant would abandon their long-standing hatred to work for a common cause, but he established a revolutionary tradition in Ireland that has never died out.

**Tories.** A name used in the 1680s for those who supported the hereditary succession to the British Crown and were therefore in favour of Charles II's Catholic brother James becoming King. They were supporters of the royal prerogative, the divine right of kings and the privileges of the Church of England. With the Hanoverian succession many were regarded as traitors, who favoured a Stuart restoration, so they were kept out of power for the next fifty years. With the accession of **George III** their fortunes changed, as they accepted his right to choose ministers and have a say in policy and opposed **Catholic Emancipation.** The followers of **Pitt** the Younger were called Tories (though Pitt called himself a **Whig**) and during the **French Revolution** opposed **parliamentary reform** and placed order before liberty. Tories were continuously in power from 1783 to 1830, apart from a brief period in 1806–7. They came to be called Conservatives from the time of Peel, though the name Tory has continued to be used interchangeably with that of Conservative.

**Tory Democracy.** A response of the **Conservative Party** to the Reform Bill of 1867, which doubled the size of the electorate and made the working class a majority of voters in the boroughs. **Disraeli** proclaimed the Tory Party as 'the national party ... the really democratic party of England' and carried out some social reforms between 1874 and 1876. Randolph **Churchill** became the leading advocate of Tory Democracy in the 1880s, but this did not mean giving in to working-class demands. **Napoleon III** and **Bismarck** had shown that mass democracy could provide support for conservative governments which were not committed to widespread social reforms. Churchill held traditional conservative views and declared in 1885 that 'a hereditary monarchy and hereditary House of **Lords** are the strongest fortifications ... for the protection ... of democratic freedom'. Conservative policy changed little in the 1880s and 1890s: it was based on the maintenance of law and order, defence of property and the Church of England and resistance to **Home Rule**. **Salisbury**, the Prime Minister for most of the 1890s, distrusted democracy, disliked the **trade unions** and supported attacks on them, as in the **Taff Vale case**. Tory Democracy was therefore a reluctant and half-hearted response to a larger electorate which had a minimal effect on Conservative policy.

**Totalitarianism.** A word usually applied to the inter-war dictatorships of Fascist Italy, Nazi Germany and of **Stalin** in the Soviet Union. These regimes aimed at the total control of the lives of their citizens by means of a single party, the banning of opposition and by the denial of individual liberties and civil rights. The leader (*Führer*, *Duce*) was regarded as infallible. Obedience to him was ensured by terror, by propaganda and by mass rallies. In Italy particularly, totalitarianism was an ideal rather than a reality, as **Mussolini** had to compromise with vested interests – the monarchy, the army, the great landowners and industrialists, the Catholic Church in the **Lateran Treaties** (1929) – all of whom retained considerable independence.

**Toussaint L'Ouverture, François Dominique** (1743–1803). Haitian leader. The son of a slave, he organized a successful slave rising against French planters in Haiti (Hispaniola) in 1791 and was given the name *L'Ouverture* ('the Opening') in 1793, when his rapid campaigns freed the slaves. He briefly supported Britain and Spain when they went to war with France in 1793 (Spain controlled Santo Domingo, the eastern part of the island) but changed sides a year later when the French **Convention** abolished slavery, which the British and Spaniards refused to do. By 1795 he was recognized by the French as ruler of their part of the island, where freed labourers shared the profits on the plantations and racial tensions eased, as Toussaint wanted reconciliation with the whites, whose skills were needed. In 1801 he overran the Spanish part of the island, which was now united as a black republic, and freed the slaves there. Toussaint's independence did not last long. **Napoleon** in 1802 sent 40,000 troops to restore French control and reinstate slavery. Toussaint was seized when he went to negotiate with the French and was sent to France, where he was imprisoned and died.

**Toynbee Hall.** A 'settlement', supported by universities, in the East End of London, which aimed to help the poor. It was named after Arnold Toynbee (1852–83), a historian who gave a series of lectures to working men in 1881–2 on *The Industrial Revolution of the Eighteenth Century*, in which he said that middle-class wealth had been built on working-class suffering. His acute sense of guilt had led him to work in the East End with Samuel Barnett, Rector of St Jude's, Whitechapel. When Toynbee died Barnett opened the first 'settlement', linked with Balliol College, Oxford, in 1884, as a memorial to his friend. By 1913 there were twenty-seven 'settlements' in London and thirteen in the rest of England. They were run by Christian university students from the upper classes, who lived and worked for a time amongst the urban working class, collecting social data and providing adult education and various social services. Many of those responsible for later reforms – William **Beveridge**, J. M. **Keynes**, Clement **Attlee** – took part in the 'settlement' movement, which greatly influenced the work of the Liberal governments from 1906–14. Recently Toynbee Hall has provided a free legal-advice centre, help for alcoholics and teaching for adult immigrants and has been the headquarters of the Campaign Against Racial Discrimination.

**Tractarians,** see **Oxford Movement**

**Trade unions.** Organizations to defend the interests of workers. Trade unions arose in England in the late eighteenth century when skilled workers joined together, but they were declared illegal by the **Combination Acts** (1799). They survived, often in the guise of **friendly societies**, and spread when the Combination Acts were repealed in 1824. Most were formed in a single trade in one town and sought to maintain the standard of living of their members by restricting entry to their trade. Only with the New Model Unions, especially the Amalgamated Society of Engineers (1851), did national federations arise. These too were exclusive, with high subscriptions, and were confined to skilled workers. The unskilled did not become union members until after the success of the **London dock strike** (1889). The 1890s were a period of prolonged and bitter strikes, culminating in a six-month lock-out in engineering (1897–8), when workers demanded an eight-hour day and employers insisted on an end to restrictive practices. This was the first major national strike and lock-out in British history. The Trades Union Congress (TUC), formed in 1868 as a forum for all unions, had two million affiliated members (20 per cent of the male work-force) early in the twentieth century. As the **Taft Vale case** (1901) showed the vulnerability of union funds, the TUC joined with socialist societies to set up a Labour Representation Committee, to secure the election of workers to parliament: this became the **Labour Party** in 1906. The Trade Union Act (1913), reversing the **Osborne judgment** of 1909, legalized the political levy (money paid by unions to the Labour Party), from which union members could contract out. From 1910–14 the number of union members rose dramatically to four million and this was accompanied by industrial militancy unknown since **Chartism**, which caused *The Times* to state in 1912 'We are within measurable distance of civil war.' A million miners were involved in the national coal strike that year. The support of unions was needed for the war effort from 1914–18, so they grew in strength and influence, but they lost members in the post-war depression. **'Black Friday'** (1924), when transport workers failed to support the miners, was a blow to the trade-union movement, as was the **General Strike** of 1926, which failed miserably. It was followed by the Trade Union Act (1927), which limited the powers of unions by restricting picketing and by substituting contracting in for contracting out of the political levy.

With economic expansion there was a real growth of trade unions throughout Europe, in which national federations of labour were established. In France the **CGT** was founded in 1895, though most unions remained small: the average union in 1905 had only 170 members. **Syndicalism** dominated the CGT in the first decade of the twentieth century, when under 10 per cent of the French labour force were in trade unions. In 1921 the CGT split into communist and socialist organizations, but they came together again in the **Popular Front** in 1936, when membership increased from three-quarters of a million to four million in a few months. German trade unions were hampered by **Bismarck**'s **anti-socialist law** but were able to expand after its demise in 1890. The socialist Free Trade Unions, linked to the **Social Democratic Party**, with nine million members in the 1920s, were by far the largest, though there were also Catholic unions and company unions, run by large firms such as **Krupp**. All were destroyed by the Nazis in 1933. In Russia trade unions were not allowed until the **Russian Revolution of 1905**, and even then strikes were banned. After the **October Revolution** (1917) they became transmission belts for the orders of the Communist Party and ceased to have any independence. Trade unions developed more slowly in the USA than in Europe, because the workforce consisted largely of immigrants, divided by race, language and religion. The employers were prepared to use armed force to prevent labour organizing and could usually rely on support from the law courts. Many of the skilled workers joined together in the **American Federation of Labor** (AFL), formed in 1886, which was led for nearly forty years by Samuel **Gompers**. During the **Great Depression** (1929–39), Franklin Delano **Roosevelt** favoured the unions in his **New Deal**, but the AFL split when John L. **Lewis** formed the Congress of Industrial Organizations (CIO), to cater for unskilled workers in mass-production industries.

**Trafalgar, battle of** (21 October 1805). Fought between British and Franco-Spanish fleets off Cape Trafalgar in southern Spain. By March 1805 **Napoleon** had gathered an army on the northern coast of France ready for an invasion of Britain, so he ordered the French and Spanish fleets (Spain had allied with France in 1804) to evade the British blockade and sail to Martinique in the West Indies, where they would all combine into a formidable fleet, which could then return to take control of the Channel and escort the French troops across to England. The French fleet at Toulon, commanded by Villeneuve, and the Spanish fleet from Cadiz successfully reached the West Indies, but the Brest fleet was unable to break out of the British blockade. When he returned, Villeneuve did not feel strong enough to relieve the Brest fleet, so he sailed to Cadiz. Shortly afterwards on 27 August, Napoleon abandoned his invasion plan and began marching his *Grande Armée* from Boulogne to the Danube. On 28 September he ordered Villeneuve to enter the Mediterranean, disembark troops at Naples and then return to Toulon. When the French fleet had moved out of Cadiz it was attacked by **Nelson**, who divided his own fleet into two columns, one under Admiral Collingwood, which attacked the centre of the French line. This was a very dangerous manoeuvre, as it meant using his two flagships as battering rams to break through. They would have to take broadsides from five or six opposing ships and would not be able to return fire until passing through the line. The plan worked, though there was heavy damage to both flagships, and in the ensuing mêlée Nelson relied on superior British gunnery. This brought him his greatest victory, with nineteen enemy ships captured or destroyed, though many of these prizes were lost in storms which followed the battle. The greatest British loss was that of Nelson himself, killed by a musket shot. The battle of Trafalgar did not end Napoleon's plan to invade England – it had already been abandoned – but it gave Britain a supremacy at sea which she did not lose during the rest of the **Napoleonic Wars**.

**Transcontinental railroads** (US). By 1869 there were 30,000 miles (48,000 kilometres) of track in the USA. Four lines connected the Atlantic coast with the Middle West but there was no railroad across the continent, as there was no agreement about which route to follow. The North wanted a central route, the South a southern one, in the hope that it would ease the spread of slavery into the new territories. The **Gadsden Purchase** (1853) made a southern line possible, but hopes of this were dashed by the **American Civil War**. In 1862 Congress passed the Pacific Railway Act. This chartered the Union Pacific Railroad to build west from Omaha, Nebraska, and the Central Pacific Railroad to build east from Sacramento, California. There were great problems to be overcome, as the railroads passed through barren and uninhabited country. Everything – sleepers, rails, machinery, food for the labourers – had to be carried long distances. The mainly Irish labourers on the Union Pacific had sometimes to fight off Indian attacks. The Central Pacific, which used Chinese labour, had to cross the 7,000-foot Sierra Nevada. The two lines finally met in Utah in 1869. It was a remarkable engineering feat, made possible by land grants to the railways by federal and state governments and by federal loans. By 1893 there were four transcontinental railways, all of which built branch lines, so there was a North–South as well as East–West network. By 1900 the USA had 193,000 miles (308,800 km) of track, more than in the whole of Europe.

Railways were responsible for the rapid growth of the American economy after the Civil War. They made possible the settlement of the West by providing cheap land for settlers (the federal government gave 131 million acres to the railways, an area larger than that of France or Germany), so that towns, farms and factories grew up on what had been uninhabited plains. They linked the Pacific and Atlantic coasts and so created a single continental market and made possible the exploitation of America's vast natural resources. They also accounted for the rapid expansion of the coal, iron and steel industries, which provided fuel, rails and rolling stock. The railroads made the USA into a nation of town-dwellers (in 1860 five out of every six Americans lived in the country) and enabled her to become a self-sustaining continental economy, no longer dependent on overseas trade, and the greatest industrial nation in the world. By 1900 the USA was producing more coal and pig iron than Britain, more steel than Germany and more wheat than Russia.

**Transport revolution.** In 1800 wind, water and horse power were used for transport. When a cheap means of carrying bulky goods, such as coal and iron ore, was needed in Britain with the **Industrial Revolution**, a network of canals was built, which covered Britain by 1830. Canals were also built extensively in the USA (3,300 miles by 1840) and in Europe, but there was no new method of propulsion until the steamship was invented. It was used in the USA from 1807 on rivers, particularly the Mississippi, and for coastal traffic, but the first Atlantic crossing of a steamship did not take place until 1838, as these ships were unreliable and inefficient: their engines and fuel (coal) took up so much space that little was left for cargo. Not until the triple-expansion engine made more efficient use of steam in the 1870s did the steamship begin to replace the sailing ship: by the 1880s over half the world's merchant ships were steam driven and by 1914 nearly all of them were, greatly boosted by the opening of the **Suez Canal** (1869) and the **Panama Canal** (1914). As steel replaced wood in ship construction, vessels became larger. Now bulk cargoes such as grain from America could flood the European markets and bring down the cost of living, whilst nitrates from Chile and guano from Peru provided European agriculture with much-needed fertilizers.

The steamship was essential in creating a **world economy**, but it was **railways** that had the greatest impact in stimulating the economy of all countries where they were built, as they opened up new markets and made possible the exploitation of natural resources remote from the main centres of population. In the late nineteenth century the bicycle (with pneumatic tyres from 1889) provided increased mobility in local areas, as did the electric tram from 1895 and the building of underground railways around 1900 in capital cities such as London, Paris, Vienna and Berlin. A competitor to the railway appeared with the motor car, powered by a petrol engine, developed in Germany in the 1890s by Gottlieb Daimler and Karl Benz. Mass production of cars began in the USA in 1909 when Henry **Ford** produced his Model T. By 1929 there were twenty-seven million cars in the USA, one for every five Americans. The motor industry was the largest employer (of nearly half a million people) and was producing five million cars a year, which made Detroit America's fourth largest city. Ford's mass-production methods were copied elsewhere, in Britain by **Nuffield**, but most families, except in the USA, were still without a car in 1939. Motor vehicles were also used as taxis, lorries and buses.

Air travel was slow to develop. The Wright Brothers in America made the first brief flight in a heavier-than-air machine in 1903. The Frenchman Blériot flew across the English Channel in 1909, and two Englishmen, Alcock and Brown, crossed the Atlantic in 1919, flying from Newfoundland to Ireland. In that year the first regular air service began between London and Paris and the Dutch airline KLM started passenger services. Surprisingly, these did not commence in the USA, for transcontinental passengers, until 1927, the year in which the American Lindbergh's solo flight across the Atlantic received wide publicity. Imperial Airways had been formed in Britain in 1924 and began regular flights across the Atlantic, by flying boats, in 1937. British Airways, founded in 1936, merged with Imperial Airways in 1940 to form the state-owned British Overseas Aircraft Corporation (BOAC) but only a tiny minority of passengers travelled by air before the **Second World War**.

**Trans-Siberian Railway.** A railway line was begun in 1891 to run from Chelyabinsk in the Urals (where it would link up with the line to Moscow) to Vladivostok on the Pacific. It was built from both ends at the same time. **Witte** hoped that it would open up Siberia, encourage settlement there and enable Russian industry to dominate the huge Chinese market. It also would have great strategic importance, supplying Russian forces in the Far East and extending Russia's influence there. Witte decided that the railway would be hundreds of miles shorter if the final section went through Chinese **Manchuria** rather than over the longer Russian route along the Amur river. Russia therefore leased from China in 1896 a strip of land across Manchuria on which the Russians could build a railway and maintain troops. This shorter route was completed by the end of 1904. The **Russo-Japanese War** (1904-5) showed just how vulnerable to attack the line across Manchuria was, so after the war the all-Russian route was built and was completed during the **First World War**. The railway undoubtedly did transform the Siberian economy. By 1914 it served over ten million people, who grew grain and provided Moscow and St Petersburg with half the meat they ate.

**Trasformismo** ('transformism'). The practice by which Italian governments, from unification (1860) to the beginning of the twentieth century, ensured they had a majority in parliament. As there was a restricted franchise (only three million male Italians had the vote as late as 1912), politics was dominated by the upper middle class, which was divided not by beliefs but by regional rivalries. There was no clear party system, so prime ministers bribed or granted favours to deputies and their constituents in exchange for their votes. **Giolitti** was the last master of this system.

**Trench warfare.** A form of fighting which predominated in the **First World War**, particularly on the Western Front. After the battle of the **Marne** trenches were dug from the Channel to the Swiss frontier. Troops stood in long narrow trenches with barbed wire in front, to protect them from enemy fire. Traverses (kinks in the line) prevented an enemy shooting down the whole length of the line. The front was linked to support and reserve lines by communication trenches. When there was an attack infantry went over the top and across no-man's land to the enemy trenches parallel to their own. An artillery bombardment which preceded the attack was supposed to destroy enemy trenches but this did not happen as dug-outs were deep (German dug-outs were thirty feet below ground) and could survive even direct hits. When the barrage was over, machine-gunners climbed the parapet and could fire 600 rounds a minute at the attacking infantry. In the resulting carnage losses were horrifying: there were 56,000 casualties on the first day of the battle of the **Somme** (1916). Consequently there was stalemate: the line did not move more than ten miles either way between 1914 and 1918. New weapons were introduced to try to break the deadlock: trench mortars which lobbed bombs in a steep trajectory from one trench line to another, hand grenades, poison gas and tanks. None was successful. Tanks had the greatest potential but often broke down or got stuck in the Flanders mud.

**Trianon, Treaty of** (1920). A peace treaty at the end of the **First World War** between Hungary and the Allied Powers. The Hungarian part of the **Austro-Hungarian Empire** consisted of a central core inhabited by Magyars and large areas on the periphery, where Magyars were an economically and politically dominant minority.

All these outlying areas were taken away from Hungary. Ruthenia, inhabited largely by Ukrainians (known in the West as Ruthenians), and Slovakia went to the new state of Czechoslovakia; Croatia to another new state, Yugoslavia, and Transylvania to Romania. Transylvania, which had been promised to Romania to induce her to enter the war on the Allied side, was larger than the territory left to Hungary: a legacy of bitterness remained, which lasted for the next twenty years. One and a half million Magyars lived there, although Romanians were in the majority. As a result of the Treaty, Hungary lost two-thirds of her pre-war territory and her population fell from twenty-one million to eight million. Over a third of Magyars now lived outside Hungary (in Romania, Czechoslovakia and Yugoslavia). Hungary was one of the countries most dissatisfied with the peace settlement. The beneficiaries realized this and so formed the **Little Entente**, to prevent her from overthrowing the Treaty of Trianon.

**Triple Alliance** (1882). A secret treaty between Germany, Austria-Hungary and Italy, who had designs on North Africa and resented France's establishment of a protectorate in Tunis in 1881. Each would assist the other if attacked by France, and Italy would be neutral if there was war between Austria and Russia. The treaty was renewed every five years until 1915 but did not lead to Italy entering the **First World War** on Germany's side, as France was not the aggressor.

**Triple Entente.** The agreements between Russia, France and Britain before the **First World War**. France and Russia had become allies in 1894 with the **Franco-Russian Alliance**. Britain did not make formal alliances with either country until the war began but made an **Anglo-French Entente** in 1904 and an **Anglo-Russian Entente** in 1907.

**Tripoli, invasion of** (1911). Many Italians were convinced that only by acquiring colonies would Italy be regarded as a Great Power. Economic benefits – fertile land, minerals – were also expected from the Turkish provinces of Tripoli and Cyrenaica, which Italians called by the Roman name of Libya. The preoccupation of the other powers with the second **Moroccan crisis** (1911) appeared to provide a favourable opportunity for Italy to invade

Tripoli, though the Italian Prime Minister, **Giolitti**, was not enthusiastic: 'And what if, after we have attacked Turkey, the Balkans begin to stir? And what if a Balkan war provokes a clash between the two power blocs and a European war?' This is precisely what happened. Turkey's preoccupation with Italy prompted the formation of a Balkan League, which began a **Balkan War** against Turkey in 1912. This compelled Turkey to cede Libya to Italy.

**Trotsky, Lev Davidovich** (Leib David Bronstein, 1879–1940). The son of a Jewish farmer in the Ukraine, Bronstein took the name Trotsky (which was the name of one of his jailers) when he first escaped from Siberia. He had been exiled there for his revolutionary activities in 1898 but escaped in 1902 and made his way to Western Europe. When the Russian Social Democrats split in 1903, he first of all sided with the **Mensheviks**, accusing **Lenin** of trying to establish a dictatorship. In the 1905 **Russian Revolution** he played an important role as chairman of the St Petersburg **Soviet**. He was exiled to Siberia for a second time in 1907 but escaped to the West once again. He returned to Russia in May 1917 after the **February Revolution** and found that all his differences with Lenin had disappeared. They both wanted to end Russian participation in the **First World War** and bring about revolution in Russia as quickly as possible, at a time when many of their colleagues doubted the wisdom of a rising. Trotsky, therefore, joined the **Bolsheviks** in July and became chairman of the **Petrograd** Soviet. In this position he organized the Military Revolutionary Committee of the Soviet, the force he used to seize power for the Bolsheviks in the **October Revolution**. After the Revolution the government had two major problems to deal with: the war against Germany and civil war. As Commissar for Foreign Affairs Trotsky led the negotiations at **Brest-Litovsk**, where he adopted the unrealistic attitude of 'neither war nor peace': the Russians would not carry on fighting but would not accept German peace terms. This was shown to be a futile gesture, when the Germans continued their advance. Lenin insisted on accepting German peace terms, whereupon Trotsky resigned as Commissar for Foreign Affairs early in 1918. In the same year he became Commissar for War and was responsible for Bolshevik success in the **Russian Civil War** and therefore for the survival of the Soviet regime. He organized the **Red Army** and made it into an effective fighting force by introducing strict discipline. Trotsky also crushed the **Kronstadt Rising** in 1921, with his customary ruthlessness. He wished to apply military discipline to running the economy too, and proposed that all civilians not called up for army service should be conscripted for labour armies. Lenin supported this idea but it was never fully carried out.

Trotsky's struggle for power began in 1923 during Lenin's last illness. On 4 January Lenin added a postscript to his 'last testament', in which he attacked **Stalin**: 'I propose to the comrades to find a way to remove Stalin from that position [of General Secretary].' Lenin agreed with Trotsky on joint action at the Party Congress to be held in April, but on 9 March he had his third stroke, from which he never recovered. Lenin's death in January 1924 exposed Trotsky's complete isolation in the Bolshevik Party. He was a brilliant orator and theorist but was not liked, even by his brother-in-law **Kamenev**, as he was intellectually arrogant and had a biting wit. He was not trusted either, as he had not become a Bolshevik until 1917. **Zinoviev**, another contender for the leadership, and Kamenev joined with Stalin, whom they regarded as a rather earnest dullard and did not fear, against Trotsky. They persuaded the Central Committee to suppress Lenin's 'last testament'. Trotsky strongly disagreed with Stalin's theory of 'Socialism in one country', put forward in late 1924, by which he meant that Russia could become strong by its own unaided efforts. Trotsky believed that socialism would never survive in Russia unless there was also revolution in Western Europe. In his clash with Stalin, Trotsky had underestimated not only Stalin's political skill but also the significance of the post of General Secretary of the Communist Party, which enabled Stalin to fill Party Congresses with his own supporters. In 1925 Trotsky was forced to resign as Commissar for War and in 1927 he was expelled from the Party, along with others. Stalin offered to readmit them if they would renounce their opposition activities. Trotsky refused to do so and was exiled to Central Asia. In 1928 he was deported from Russia. In one way Trotsky was the centre-piece of the **Great Purges** from 1936–8, as nearly all the victims were accused of acting on his behalf. Trotsky eventually settled in Mexico in 1937 and it was there that he was hunted down and assassinated by a Stalinist agent in 1940.

**Tuileries, attack on the** (10 August 1792). When the French **Legislative Assembly** refused to depose King **Louis XVI**, radicals and *sans-culottes* decided that a rising was necessary. On 9 August *sans-culottes* overthrew the municipal government of Paris and set up a revolutionary Commune. The next morning several thousand National Guards (citizens' militia) and 2,000 *fédérés* (National Guards from the provinces) marched on the Tuileries. The palace was defended by 3,000 troops, 2,000 of whom were National Guards, the rest being Swiss mercenaries. During the morning the King sought refuge in the Assembly to protect his family. The National Guards defending the Tuileries joined the insurgents. When the Swiss began to fire the *fédérés* replied with grapeshot and it seemed that a violent battle was about to take place. At this point the King ordered his Swiss Guards to cease fire. This left them defenceless against the vengeance of the attackers: 600 Swiss were massacred. Of the insurgents ninety *fédérés* and 300 Parisians had been killed or wounded. It was the most bloody *journée* of the **French Revolution**. The rising was as much a rejection of the Assembly as it was of the King. The rebels invaded the Assembly and forced it to recognize the Commune, which had given orders for the attack on the palace. The deputies had to hand over the King to the Commune, which imprisoned him in the Temple, and had to agree to the election of a National **Convention** to draw up a new democratic constitution. The King was suspended, and it was left to the Convention to decide whether or not to dethrone him. It met for the first time on 20 September 1792: the next day it abolished the monarchy.

**Twenty-One Demands** (1915). A Japanese attempt to make China a protectorate. When the **First World War** broke out Japan declared war on Germany, so that she could take over Germany's leased territory in China (see '**Scramble for concessions**'), based on the port of Qingdao in Shandong province. Japanese troops landed and soon took over the port and German railway and mining concessions. The Japanese government then presented **Yuan Shikai** with its 'Twenty-One Demands' and threatened war if they were rejected. They included an extension of Japan's lease of Port Arthur (Lushun) and the South Manchurian railway; the grant of mining, trading and residential rights in South Manchuria and Inner Mongolia; recognition of Japan's dominant position in Shandong; and a promise that China would not make any territorial concessions on her coast to other foreign powers. China was also required to accept a further massive infringement of her sovereignty: she was to have Japanese political and military advisers and a joint Sino-Japanese police force was to be created. Yuan stalled, hoping for support from Britain and the USA. They protested at the last demands, whose application Japan agreed to 'postpone', but they were not prepared to alienate Japan further, so Yuan agreed to the demands on 25 May 1915. This became known to Chinese students as National Humiliation Day and was followed by widespread anti-Japanese demonstrations and a boycott of Japanese goods. The USA, worried about Japanese expansionism, warned her that it would not recognize any infringement of China's political and territorial integrity, but Britain and France gave approval in 1917 to Japanese claims in Shandong.

**T'zu-hsi** (Empress Dowager of China), see **Cixi**

**Uitlanders** (Afrikaans, 'outsiders'). Europeans who came to live in the South African Republic (SAR, or Transvaal) after gold was discovered on the **Rand** in 1885. No one knew how many were there in the 1890s, so President **Kruger** refused to give them the vote in case they formed a majority. 'If we give them the franchise,' he said, 'we may as well give up the republic.' Cecil **Rhodes** tried to arrange for a *uitlander* rising to coincide with the **Jameson Raid** in 1895 but none took place. **Milner**, the British High Commissioner in South Africa from 1897, used *uitlander* grievances to force Kruger into the **South African War** (1899–1902), after which they did get the vote, only to find that they were outnumbered by **Afrikaners**.

**Umar ibn Said Tal** (al-Hajj Umar) (*c.* 1794–1864). Founder of the Tukulor Empire in West Africa. Umar's family had provided political and Muslim religious leaders for the Tukulor in what is now Senegal. In 1836 Umar made a pilgrimage to Mecca and on his return stayed in Sokoto from 1836–7 as the guest of Muhammad Bello, the son of **Uthman dan Fodio**, whose daughter he married. Umar was impressed by Uthman's success in founding the **Fulani Empire** and determined to found his own Muslim Empire when he returned home. He built up a body of devoted followers, created a strong army by buying firearms, and in 1852 declared a *jihad* (holy war) against pagans and lapsed Muslims. He claimed to have divine guidance, took the title of *khalifa* (successor of the Prophet Muhammad) and forbade pagan ceremonies and worship of idols. As he began his *jihad* he came up against the French in the Senegal valley. They defeated Umar in 1857, so in 1860 he made a treaty with them which recognized French influence in Futa Toro and that of Umar in the Bambara kingdoms of Kaarta and Segu. These he conquered, so that he had a large kingdom in the region of the upper Niger and Senegal rivers, but in doing so he made war in the Muslim state of Massina. His enemies denounced this war of Muslim against Muslim and formed a coalition of states against Umar. They defeated and killed him in 1864, though the Empire he founded continued to have a tenuous existence until it became part of the French Empire in 1893.

**Unequal treaties** were imposed on China by force from 1842 to the end of the nineteenth century and granted to other powers privileges that infringed Chinese sovereignty. The Treaty of **Nanjing** opened five ports to foreign trade; another eleven were added by the Treaties of Tianjin (1858) and Beijing (1860) (see **Opium Wars**), and by the end of the century there were fifty such ports. Foreigners enjoyed the privilege of extraterritoriality as a result of these treaties: they could be tried by their own consuls, established in the treaty ports, according to their own laws in both civil and criminal cases. The Chinese had no reciprocal rights abroad. These treaties also granted 'most-favoured nation' status, which meant that any benefits granted to other countries by China would be enjoyed by those who already had treaties with her. Tariffs were another aspect of the treaties – in 1843 China agreed to a low, uniform tariff on British imports, which opened the way to foreign manufactures competing with local handicraft industries. The treaty ports were a sign of China's semi-colonial status, but they did lead China towards modernization and reform. The scholar-officials there played a leading role in the **Self-Strengthening movement**, whilst the merchants provided the capital and managerial skills China needed. China did not recover control of her own tariffs until 1930 and did not get rid of the unequal treaties completely until 1943.

Western powers also enforced unequal treaties on Japan from 1858, and enjoyed the same extraterritorial rights, low tariffs and 'most-favoured nation' status as they did in China. Japan, however, responded more vigorously to the Western threat by acquiring Western skills and technology and had got rid of extraterritorial rights by 1899. She gained tariff autonomy in 1911. As Japanese strength increased, she behaved like the Western imperial powers and imposed unequal treaties on Korea (from 1876) and on China after the **Sino-Japanese War** of 1894–5.

**Union, Act of** (1800). The union of Great Britain and Ireland. When the **Irish Rebellion** occurred in 1798, **Pitt**, the English Prime Minister, decided that the wealthy landowning Anglicans in the Irish parliament could never represent the Irish nation, which was predominantly Catholic. The only way to pacify Ireland, he thought, was to abolish the Irish parliament, unite the two countries and grant **Catholic emancipation**, which would enable Catholics to sit in the parliament in London. The bill was initially rejected by the Protestant Irish parliament in 1799, but widespread bribery and the creation of more Irish peers enabled it to pass. The Irish parliament was abolished: 100 Irish members of parliament were to be elected to the British House of **Commons** and thirty-two Irish peers (including four bishops) were to join the House of **Lords**. Ireland was to contribute 12 per cent to the budget of the United Kingdom, and Irish textile manufacturers were to be protected for twenty years before there was free trade with Britain. Pitt's hopes of Catholic emancipation were dashed, as **George III** refused to accept it and forced Pitt to resign on the issue in 1801. The Act, therefore, did not solve the problems of Irish society, as the Catholic majority was still not treated equally with the Protestant minority. The legacy of the Act was a divided Ireland.

**United Front** (1923–7, 1936–45). Alliance of the **Guomindang** (Nationalist Party) and the Chinese Communist Party (CCP). Since 1917 **Sun Yixian** (Sun Yat-sen) had been seeking support to strengthen his base at Guangzhou (Canton), from where he was twice expelled by local **warlords**. He could expect none from the Western powers, as he fiercely condemned **imperialism**, so he turned to the Soviet Union, as he admired the discipline and dedication of the **Bolsheviks**. In January 1923 he met a **Comintern** representative, Adolph Joffe, who accepted that China was not ready for socialism and that national unification should be the main aim. Sun agreed that CCP members could join the Guomindang as individuals and that the CCP could retain its separate identity, so the first United Front was formed. Leading communists, including **Mao Zedong**, were enthusiastic. Sun now received Soviet military and financial aid. He did not see the CCP as a threat (it had only 300 members in 1923) but thought it would be absorbed by the much larger Guomindang. The communists hoped to use the Front for their own purposes – to gain control of the mass organizations the Guomindang was creating and to take over the leadership of the movement. Sun maintained good relations with the CCP, but when he died the commander of the Nationalist army, **Jiang Jieshi** (Chiang Kai-shek), became the most powerful figure in the Guomindang. Many communists were alarmed when he began a **Northern Expedition** to unite China, as they felt it would increase his power, but **Stalin** insisted that the United Front should be maintained. This was a disaster for the CCP, as in 1927 Jiang carried out a *coup* at **Shanghai**, after capturing the city. He executed all the communists he could find and did the same in other cities. The first United Front came to an end, therefore, with the urban base of the CCP destroyed.

A second United Front was formed after the **Xi'an incident** in 1936, when Jiang was forced by his own troops to abandon his attack on the communists in **Yanan** and to join with them in resisting Japan. The CCP made several concessions: they accepted Jiang as the leader of a united China, promised to stop forming soviets and confiscating landlords' farms, and agreed to put their 30,000 troops under Guomindang command. However, cooperation between the two sides was minimal, as Jiang resented the extension of CCP influence and control in north China during the **Sino-Japanese War** (1937–45). He used half a million troops to impose an economic blockade on Yanan in the early 1940s and there were armed clashes between nationalist and communist forces, the most serious of which was in 1941, when the communist New Fourth Army was attacked by nationalist forces north of the Yangzi. Jiang showed more hostility to the CCP than to Japan, and refused to use his troops in large-scale offensives against the Japanese, as he wanted to preserve them for a future power-struggle with the CCP. When Japan was defeated in 1945, the United Front broke down completely and was followed by a civil war (1945–9), which ended in a communist victory.

**Urabi Pasha** (*c.* 1840–1911). Egyptian army officer and nationalist leader. Ahmad Urabi, the son of a village headman, belonged to a secret nationalist group opposed to Turkish and foreign influence in Egypt, which was part of the **Ottoman Empire**. This was a broadly based group which represented all classes of Egyptian society: peasants, landowners, traders and *ulama* (religious leaders). The discontented army took the lead: the ordinary soldiers hated conscription, whilst Egyptian officers resented the highest ranks being reserved for Turks. Urabi and his followers also opposed the Khedive (King) Tewfiq for being a puppet of foreign powers. In 1881 Urabi's popularity was so great that Tewfiq had to appoint him as Minister for War. The increased influence of Urabi greatly alarmed the British and French, who had great financial interests in Egypt, both in the **Suez Canal** and in loans to the Khedive. When anti-foreign riots broke out in Egypt the British unjustly blamed Urabi. They decided to take joint action with the French to overthrow him, but the French government could not obtain the support of the Chamber of Deputies for this move, so the British acted alone. They bombarded Alexandria. This led to a violent anti-European reaction throughout Egypt and Urabi became a national hero. A British army under General **Wolseley** landed in Egypt and defeated Urabi at Tel el-Kebir in 1882. Egypt came under British occupation and was to remain so for the next fifty years; Urabi was exiled to Ceylon until 1901, when he was allowed to return to Cairo.

**Urbanization.** The growth of towns and cities. In 1800 only twenty-two cities in the world had a population of over 100,000: in 1900 there were 160, most of which had grown up since 1850 (Chicago had 4,000 inhabitants in 1836, 2.2 million in 1910). London was the largest city, with a population of 6.5 million, followed by Paris (4 million) and New York (3.5 million). By 1960 there were twenty-four cities with over 3 million people, thirteen with over 5 million and four with over 10 million. New York and Tokyo had surpassed London in size. In Britain (excluding Ireland) half the population lived in towns by 1850, a figure reached in Germany by 1890 and in the USA in the 1920s. Most people, therefore, at the beginning of the twentieth century still lived in the countryside, though the pattern was changing. The huge increase in the size of towns was a result of the remarkable growth of **population** and of the **Industrial Revolution**. Many conurbations (a word first used in 1915) grew up, which linked one town with another in a seemingly unending chain, as in industrial Lancashire and the Ruhr.

In Britain, the first country where industrial towns grew rapidly, the problems of rapid growth soon became apparent. With governments committed to *laissez-faire* and believing that there should be no interference with property or profit, slums grew up in which there was overcrowding, inadequate sewerage (none at all in the poorer districts) and polluted water, which produced outbreaks of cholera. According to **Haussmann**, 1 million out of 1.7 million people in Paris in 1860 lived in poverty, and even at the end of the century **Rowntree** found 28 per cent of the people of York in a similar situation. Yet in the late nineteenth century conditions in the towns improved considerably. Birmingham, when Joseph **Chamberlain** was mayor in the 1870s, led the way in England with its 'municipal socialism', providing sewers, pure water, public parks, baths and laundries. The quality of life improved, as it did with the advent of public **transport**, first the **railways**, then the electric tram, the electric underground railway and in 1910 the motor bus. Public transport linked the suburbs with the city centre, where large department stores (Harrods and Selfridges in London) grew up. Multiple chain stores appeared in all towns to sell mass-produced goods: Freeman, Hardy and Willis for shoes, Burton's for men's clothing, W. H. Smith for books and magazines, Boots for medicines. Gas and electric street lighting first appeared in the towns, as did various forms of amusement, the theatre, music hall and later the cinema. The service sector (including domestic service) often provided the most employment. As land prices rose, buildings grew higher, until the skyscraper (a building over twenty storeys high) appeared in the USA: by 1929 there were 400 there. In 1931 the tallest of them all, the Empire State Building in New York, was erected: it was 1,250 feet high, with office accommodation for 25,000 people. Whatever its drawbacks − the anonymity of people lost in the large city, the 'lonely crowd' − the city remained a centre of attraction for those wanting a more exciting life or for those seeking to escape from rural poverty, even if they had an equally poverty-stricken existence in the shanty towns, which grew up in places such as São Paulo.

**Uthman (or Usuman) dan Fodio** (1754–1817). Muslim leader and founder of the **Fulani Empire** of Sokoto in Nigeria. Many of the people in Senegal, Gambia, Mali, Guinea and northern Nigeria today are Muslim, largely owing to the *jihads* (holy wars) of the nineteenth century, the earliest and most important of which was that of Uthman. He belonged to a mystical Muslim brotherhood, and as an itinerant preacher he denounced the un-Islamic practices of the Hausa states, some of which accepted pagan ceremonies. He disliked the free socializing of men and women and wanted a strict application of Muslim law. This brought him into conflict with the Sultan of Gobir, who forbade any more conversions to Islam. Uthman therefore began a *jihad* in 1804, supported mainly by Fulani farmers and pastoralists living in the Hausa states but also by some devout Hausa and Tuareg. In the next six years all the Hausa states were conquered by Uthman and his followers. Uthman took the title Commander of the Faithful and made his capital at Sokoto, where he received tribute from the Fulani emirates he had set up in the former Hausa states. His success inspired other *jihads* in the western Sudan, such as that of al-Haji **Umar**, who founded the Tukulor Empire.

**Valmy, battle of** (September 1792). Prussian troops had invaded France and caused panic in the capital, which led to the **September massacres**. The road to Paris seemed open until the troops were held up by a minor military engagement at Valmy. 52,000 French troops confronted 34,000 Prussians but the 'battle' amounted to little more than a desultory exchange of cannon fire: there were 300 French casualties, 180 Prussian. Though of little importance militarily, the skirmish was of great significance politically. If the Prussians had won, Paris would have fallen and that would have been the end of the **French Revolution**. As it was, the cautious Prussian commander, the Duke of Brunswick, retreated to the frontier.

**Van Buren, Martin** (1782–1862). Eighth President of the USA (1837–41). When the old Democratic-Republican Party split in the 1820s into personal and sectional factions, Van Buren put his considerable talent for political organization at the disposal of Andrew **Jackson**. Van Buren wanted to make the new **Democratic Party** a national party and so created a nation-wide chain of newspapers to bring Jacksonian Democracy to the people. He became known as 'the little magician' for his political skills and became Jackson's right-hand man. When Jackson became President in 1828, Van Buren used the **spoils system** to make his position more secure. He became Jackson's Vice-President when Jackson stood for a second term and was the unanimous Democratic choice for President in the 1836 election. He won convincingly but his presidency coincided with a financial and industrial recession, partly brought on by Jackson's policies, which had encouraged land speculation and over-expansion of credit by state banks. Van Buren wanted to make the federal government independent of these banks by erecting an Independent Treasury, which would look after federal funds, but there was considerable opposition and Congress did not pass this measure until 1840. Meanwhile, some banks failed, industry stagnated and there was increased unemployment. Van Buren's popularity declined, especially when he refused to support the Canadian rebellion of 1837, as this might have led to war with Britain. He was also unpopular for refusing to risk war with Mexico by annexing **Texas**. Consequently he was defeated in the presidential election of 1840. He ran in the election of 1848 as a Free Soil anti-slavery candidate but was defeated again. After the **American Civil War** began he supported the **Republican** President Abraham **Lincoln** as the only person who could save the Union.

**Varennes, flight to** (June 1791). **Louis XVI** was a devout man, whose conscience was offended by the **Civil Constitution of the Clergy** (July 1790). He decided to flee to Montmédy in Lorraine, on the border of Luxembourg, and put himself under the protection of the military commander of the area. There he could negotiate with the **Constituent Assembly** from a position of strength, though Louis was aware that his flight might bring about civil war in France. He left Paris with his family on 20 June 1791, but at Varennes, thirty miles short of his goal, he was recognized and stopped. Louis was brought back to Paris amidst an icy silence: he had lost what remained of his popularity, which depended on his being seen to support the **French Revolution**. People began to talk openly about replacing the monarchy with a republic.

**Vargas, Getúlio** (1883–1954). Longest-serving President of Brazil (1930–45, 1951–4). Small, stout and reserved, Vargas became a wealthy cattle rancher and in 1928 Governor of his native state of Rio Grande do Sul. The army became dissatisfied that so much of the nation's wealth went into propping up the export trade in coffee, dominated by one state (São Paulo), and so put Vargas in power in 1930 by a military *coup*. This marked the end of the hegemony of the São Paulo coffee barons. Vargas spent the next five years governing by decree, replacing state governors and building up a patronage network in individual states. He did not have any specific ideology or programme when he came to power but he was a master of political opportunism, constantly changing his policies to suit the moods of the nation and changing circumstances.

In 1937, faced with a slump in coffee prices, a huge balance-of-payments deficit and high inflation, he suspended the Constitution, which would have prevented him staying in office, and proclaimed the *Estado Novo* (New State). Political parties were banned, the parliament closed, civil rights curtailed and the press censored. The *Estado Novo* was an authoritarian **corporate state** based on **Mussolini**'s Italy, but it was never as repressive. Vargas did not create a political party or a paramilitary organization and did little to regiment or indoctrinate Brazilians. The state took the lead in industrialization to make Brazil less dependent on coffee: mining, oil, steel, electricity and chemicals all expanded. The 1943 Labour Code gave many benefits to workers, including an eight-hour day, paid holidays, the right to strike, minimum wages and health and safety regulations. The price the trade unions paid was that they lost their independence and the right to free collective bargaining and came under government control. The new code affected only urban workers: on the *haciendas* (large estates) the old, coercive labour practices continued. Vargas realized that to industrialize Brazil he needed foreign help. When the **Second World War** began in 1939 the USA was the only possible source of assistance, so Vargas allowed them to build bases in Brazil for use in the battle of the **Atlantic**, and in return they erected the huge steel mill at Volta Redonda, the show-piece of Brazilian industry. In 1942 Brazil declared war on the **Axis powers** and by 1945 was the most powerful Latin American state. As the war neared its end and it appeared that Vargas would try to cling to power, the army insisted on his resignation. He was freely elected as President in 1950, taking office in 1951, but he lacked his former dynamism. Prompted by corruption scandals in his government, the army interfered once again and told him to resign or be deposed. In August 1954 Vargas committed suicide by shooting himself.

**Vendean revolt**. When the French government ordered conscription in February 1793, there was a massive rising in four departments south of the Loire, in what became known as the *Vendée militaire*, or simply the Vendée, though the troubles in the Vendée long preceded conscription. Peasants there were paying more in land tax than they had done under the *ancien régime* and so disliked the revolutionary government. Dislike turned into hatred with the sale of Church lands (most of which were bought by the *bourgeoisie* of the towns, who often raised rents) and the **Civil Constitution of the Clergy**. The situation appeared so serious that the government had to bring in 30,000 troops to deal with the rising. Yet the rebels, ill-disciplined and unwilling to move far from their homes, were no real threat to the government in Paris. After the army crushed the rising there was a terrible repression. From January to May 1794 troops moved through the area, shooting almost every peasant they met, burning their farms and crops and killing their animals. When the 'pacifica-tion' was over, the Vendée was a depopulated desert. Thousands who surrendered crammed the prisons and, as they could not be released in case they joined the rebels again, were shot without trial – 2,000 near Angers alone. At Nantes in the dreadful *noyades* (drownings) 1,800 people, nearly half of them women, were put in barges, which were taken to the mouth of the Loire and sunk. 7,000 were condemned by revolutionary courts in the Vendée, half the total for the whole of France. Guerrilla warfare revived in 1794 and was not finally eliminated until 1796, when General Hoche with a huge army of 140,000 sent flying columns across the area.

**Vendémiaire, rising of** (5 October 1795). The last of the *journ-ées* of the **French Revolution**. The constitutional monarchists, who wanted a return to a limited monarchy, had been gaining public support, as they seemed to offer stability. They hoped to win a majority of seats in the legislative Councils set up by the **Conven-tion**, until the Convention decreed that two-thirds of the members of the new Councils should be chosen from the existing deputies of the Convention. In Paris open rebellion broke out on 5 October (13 Vendémiaire), when 25,000 armed Parisians gathered to march on the Convention. They vastly outnumbered the 7,800 government troops, but the latter, unlike the rebels, had cannon, under the command of General **Napoleon Bonaparte**. As over 300 were killed or wounded, this was one of the bloodiest of the revolutionary *journées*. Vendémiaire is usually presented as a royalist rising, yet the largest groups of rebels were artisans and apprentices, suffering from inflation: a third of those arrested were manual workers. Repression was light – only two people were executed. The people of Paris would not again attempt to intimidate an elected assembly until 1830.

**Venizelos, Eleftherios** (1864–1936). Greek statesman. A native of Crete, Venizelos agitated ceaselessly for *enosis* (union) with Greece. When the Military League staged a *coup* in Greece in 1910, following the example of the **Young Turks**, they invited Venizelos to come to Greece as their political adviser. He persuaded the League to withdraw from politics and, after expropriating the remaining large landed estates (a very popular move), he concentrated on foreign affairs. He was the architect of the Balkan alliance, in which Serbia, Bulgaria and Montenegro joined Greece and fought the **Balkan War** of 1912 against the **Ottoman Empire**. Greece captured Salonika, Crete, Jannina and much of Epirus, which the Turks were forced to give up. When Bulgaria turned against her former allies in the second Balkan War (1913), the Greeks took much of Macedonia. Venizelos received the credit for these dramatic gains, which increased the area of Greece by 70 per cent and its population by 2 million (to 4.8 million). Greece needed peace to digest these territories, but when the **First World War** began Venizelos saw that it would lead to the collapse of the Ottoman Empire and give Greece the opportunity to acquire further areas inhabited by Greeks: Macedonia, Thrace, the Aegean islands and Smyrna (Izmir). This was the *Great Idea*. The country was split, as Venizelos wanted to enter the war on the Allied side, whilst King Constantine, married to a sister of Emperor **William II**, wished Greece to be neutral. Venizelos resigned in October 1915, but in August 1916 there was a *coup* of pro-Venizelos officers at Salonika, where Venizelos established his own provisional government. As a result of Allied pressure, Constantine went into exile in June 1917 and Venizelos became Prime Minister again. Greece declared war on Germany and fought successfully in Macedonia. After the war Venizelos gained the reward for his constant support of the Allies. By the Treaty of **Sèvres** (1920) Greece was to occupy Smyrna and she was awarded most of Thrace and the Aegean islands. In spite of great enthusiasm in Greece, Venizelos was crushingly defeated in the election of 1920, as most Greeks were tired of war. The Turks never accepted the Treaty of Sèvres and in 1922 routed the Greek armies in Anatolia. Venizelos, though not a member of the government, led the Greek delegation at **Lausanne**, where Greece lost most of her gains at Sèvres. There was a separate agreement on the exchange of populations between Greece and Turkey: 1.3 million Greeks were removed from Turkey to Greece and ensured that there would be a Greek majority in the newly acquired Macedonia and western Thrace. Venizelos was Prime Minister again in 1928, when he improved relations with Italy and with Greece's neighbours, particularly Turkey, but Greece was badly hit by the **Great Depression** and in 1933 he lost the election. Two attempted *coups* in 1933 and 1935 to restore him to power failed and he fled to France, where he died.

**Verdun, battle of** (February–December 1916). A battle planned by **Falkenhayn**, German Chief of Staff, to 'bleed France white' and so knock her out of the war. He correctly assumed that the French would defend Verdun, which lay in a salient in the south of the French line, at all costs. His plan was to draw the main part of the French army into the salient, where it would be pulverized by German artillery. The Germans concentrated 1,400 guns on an eight-mile front and began the biggest bombardment yet seen on 21 February 1916, when a million shells were fired on the first day. The Germans advanced and came close to a breakthrough, as whole sections of the French line disintegrated. **Joffre**, the French Commander, rushed up reinforcements and sent **Pétain** to take command. The French had great supply problems: their only link with the rear was a minor road, as the railway was put out of action by shelling. Along this *Voie Sacrée* (Sacred Road) Pétain organized a constant stream of trucks, so that he could rotate his front-line units: soldiers were sent back to rest after a short spell at the front. There were continuous German attacks and French counter-attacks, but from July the Germans were on the defensive as they moved troops to counter the **Brusilov offensive** in the east and the British attack on the **Somme**. The French, now under Nivelle, began an offensive in October which recovered some forts and the two miles of ground lost earlier but at a terrible cost. French losses were 542,000, many of whom had never seen the enemy; German casualties were 434,000. Pétain emerged from the battle as a national hero. As the

French forts had held up whole German divisions, the decision was later made to build the **Maginot Line**.

**Vereeniging, Treaty of** (31 May 1902). Ended the **South African War** (1899–1902). The Boer republics of the Transvaal and the Orange Free State gave up their independence and accepted British rule, but they were promised self-government 'as soon as circumstances permitted' (it was granted in 1907). The Boers were promised that 'the question of granting the franchise to natives would not be settled before the introduction of representative government'. This in effect guaranteed that white supremacy would remain in the ex-republics. The Boers were also granted £3 million to repay war debts and were promised considerable relief aid.

**Versailles, Treaty of** (28 June 1919). A treaty between the Allied Powers and Germany after the **First World War**. Germany did not take part in the negotiations which preceded the Treaty, so most Germans regarded it as a dictated peace, which was not morally binding. As a result of territorial changes Germany lost 25,000 square miles, six and a half million people and much of her raw materials. In the west **Alsace-Lorraine** was restored to France and there were some frontier changes in favour of Belgium. North Schleswig went to Denmark after a plebiscite, but the heaviest German losses were in the east. Most of Posen and West Prussia and part of Pomerania were given to Poland. Originally the rich industrial region of Upper Silesia was to go to Poland, but a plebiscite there showed that 60 per cent of the population wanted to be part of Germany, so the area was divided. Danzig, with an almost wholly German population, was made a Free City under a **League of Nations** High Commissioner, so that Poland could have use of a port which was not in Germany. The Polish corridor, which gave Poland access to the sea, cut off East Prussia from the rest of Germany. One and a half million Germans now lived under Polish rule. Memel, another German town, was the only available port for Lithuania, so it was placed under a French High Commissioner and seized by the Lithuanians in 1923. Germany's colonies were also taken from her and became **mandates** of the League of Nations but in fact were handed over to the victorious Allies. There were further territorial restrictions concerning Austria, the **Rhineland**

and the **Saar**. Austria was forbidden to unite with Germany. The left bank of the Rhine and a 50 km strip of the right bank were to be permanently demilitarized: there was to be an Allied army of occupation there, which would be withdrawn in 1935 if Germany fulfilled her treaty obligations. As the Germans had deliberately destroyed French mines when retreating, France was given control of the coal mines in the Saar, which was placed under the League of Nations for fifteen years, when a plebiscite would decide its future.

The disarmament clauses of the Treaty restricted the German army to 100,000 men. Its General Staff was abolished, conscription was forbidden and it was not allowed any tanks. Germany was not allowed to have an airforce or submarines or any ships above 10,000 tons; her navy was limited to 15,000 men. The purpose of the disarmament clauses was 'to render possible the initiation of a general limitation of the armaments of all nations', but as this did not happen the Germans complained bitterly about the restrictions imposed on them. The most resented clause of the Treaty was 231, the so-called 'War-Guilt' clause, which required Germany to admit responsibility for loss and damage sustained by the Allies 'as a consequence of the war imposed on them by the aggression of Germany and her allies'. As a result Germany had to pay **reparations**, which were fixed in 1921 at 132 billion gold marks. The Treaty was regarded as extremely harsh in Germany, although **Clemenceau** had wanted it to be even more severe, with the Rhineland an independent state, the Saar annexed by France and Danzig annexed by Poland. Germans rejected the 'War-Guilt' clause, as they maintained that Russia, not Germany, had started the war (see **July Crisis**) and said that they could not pay the reparations demanded, as these would cripple the German economy. They also claimed that self-determination had been ignored where it would favour Germany: an unofficial plebiscite in Austria had shown that most Austrians wanted *Anschluss* with Germany. The reluctant acceptance of the Treaty of Versailles by Weimar politicians greatly weakened the **Weimar Republic**. After **Hitler** came to power in 1933 the Treaty was increasingly ignored and parts of it (the limitation of the armed forces, demilitarization of the Rhineland, the forbidding of *Anschluss*) were overturned.

**Vichy France** (1940–45). After the fall of **France** the French government signed an armistice with Germany on 22 June 1940. The northern part of France, including Paris, and the whole of the Atlantic coast were to be occupied by German troops. The rest of France was to be independent, with its government in the spa town of Vichy. On 10 July the two houses of the French legislature voted to give full legislative and constitutional powers to **Pétain**, who had requested them. Thus the **Third Republic** came to an end and was replaced by a more authoritarian regime. Pétain, Head of State, disliked parliamentary democracy, which he regarded as corrupt and responsible for the defeat of France. He wanted to get rid of all traces of the Third Republic, so 'French State' replaced 'French Republic', and the slogan 'Liberty, Equality, Fraternity', associated with the **French Revolution**, was replaced by 'Work, Family, Fatherland'. Influenced by **Mussolini**, Pétain wanted a **corporate state**, in which class war would end and people would work in harmony with one another. **Trade unions** and employers' organizations were abolished and a Labour Charter said that industries should be run by 'mixed social committees' of employers and employees. Strikes and lock-outs were illegal. Much of this was more apparent than real, as the government controlled the economy and worked through the employers. 'Foreign' Jews (i.e., those not born in France) were handed over to the Nazis: 75,000 were deported to the death camps. Vichy France was the only territory not occupied by the Germans from which Jews were deported during the **Second World War**. From 10 July 1940 **Laval** was Prime Minister and wanted a more active collaboration with the Germans than Pétain and his colleagues were prepared to contemplate. He was therefore dismissed in December 1940 but returned as head of the government in April 1942, as a result of German pressure. Laval encouraged French men and women to work in Germany, hoping that in return the Germans would release French prisoners of war, and in August compulsory labour began. This made Laval very unpopular, as did German attempts to deport all Jews in France, and led many Frenchmen and women to join the **Resistance**. On 8 November 1942 American forces landed in North Africa (see **North African Campaigns**). When Admiral Darlan in Algiers arranged a cease-fire with them, **Hitler** ordered

German troops to occupy the whole of France. From now on Vichy France was under complete German control, although there was one last act of defiance when the French fleet was scuttled at Toulon on 27 November to prevent the Germans from seizing it.

**Victor Emanuel II** (1820–78). King of Sardinia–Piedmont (1849–61) and first King of Italy (1861–78). Lazy, ignorant and coarse, Victor Emanuel was happiest when hunting or with one of his many mistresses. Pope **Pius IX** complained of his 'inveterate mendacity', whilst the British Foreign Secretary maintained that 'there is universal agreement that Victor Emanuel is an imbecile.' Yet he showed considerable political shrewdness. He became King when his father, Charles Albert, abdicated after being defeated by the Austrians in the **Revolutions of 1848**, and sensibly retained the *Statuto*, the constitution which provided for an elected assembly. In 1852 he made **Cavour** his Prime Minister and saw Piedmont become the most prosperous state in Italy. When **Napoleon III** made peace with the Austrians at Villafranca in 1859, Cavour wanted Piedmont to continue the war alone, but Victor Emanuel wisely accepted the situation. He secretly encouraged **Garibaldi**'s invasion of Sicily and led his troops into the Papal States, after Garibaldi had conquered Naples and Sicily. Victor Emanuel became King of Italy when Garibaldi handed his conquests over to him, though Venetia and Rome were outside the new kingdom. In 1866 he joined Prussia in the **Austro-Prussian War** and, in spite of being defeated on land at Custozza and on the sea at Lissa, he acquired Venetia as Prussia was victorious. When French troops were withdrawn from Rome in 1870, to take part in the **Franco-Prussian War**, Victor Emanuel sent in his army and made Rome his new capital. He thus successfully concluded the *Risorgimento*.

**Victor Emanuel III** (1869–1947). King of Italy (1900–1946). A diminutive figure, Victor Emanuel became King after the assassination of his father Umberto. He kept Italy in the **Triple Alliance** but also sought friendly relations with the **Triple Entente**, so that they would accept his conquest of Libya. Deceitful and secretive, he pursued a policy of what his Prime Minister Salandra called 'sacred egoism' and took several decisions of major importance. The first was to enter the **First World War** on the side of the Allies, in spite of the opposition of a majority in parliament, as he realized that Italy was more likely to acquire South Tyrol, Trieste and Dalmatia by fighting against Austria rather than on her side. The second occasion was when **Mussolini** planned his **March on Rome**. The general commanding in Rome was confident he could deal with the Fascist threat and the Cabinet was united in wanting a declaration of martial law. The King at first agreed but then changed his mind and invited Mussolini to form a government in October 1922, as he disliked **Giolitti** and the Liberals, feared civil war and suspected that the Fascists would replace him with his more popular cousin, the Duke of Aosta, if he resisted. After the murder of **Matteotti** (1924), Victor Emanuel had an opportunity to get rid of Mussolini, but he refused to dismiss him and acquiesced in the establishment of a Fascist dictatorship in 1925. After this he had no influence on events for eighteen years, though he supported Italy's involvement in the **Ethiopian War**, in the **Spanish Civil War** on the side of **Franco** and in the invasion of Albania – he became Emperor of Ethiopia in 1936 and King of Albania in 1939. When Italy was defeated in the **Second World War** Victor Emanuel feared he would lose his throne and began to consider removing Mussolini. After the Fascist Grand Council turned against the *Duce* in 1943, the King dismissed and arrested him and appointed Marshal Badoglio to head a dictatorship. Victor Emanuel would have nothing to do with liberal politicians and wanted 'a Fascism without Mussolini'. On 8 September he made an armistice with the Allies who distrusted him, and a month later was forced to declare war on Germany. In May 1946 he reluctantly abdicated and went into exile in Egypt, where he died. A month after his abdication, the Italians voted in a referendum for a republic.

**Victoria** (1819–1901). Queen of Great Britain and Ireland (1837–1901), Empress of India (from 1876). The only child of **George III**'s fourth son Edward, Duke of Kent, Victoria came to the throne on the death of her uncle William IV but was not able to be sovereign in **Hanover**, as the Salic Law prevented women ruling there. Naive and inexperienced when she became Queen, she relied heavily on the advice of Lord **Melbourne** until she married Prince **Albert** of Saxe-Coburg-Gotha in 1840. The marriage was a very happy one, in which Victoria spent much of her time pregnant (she had nine children) whilst Albert became the uncrowned king. On Albert's death she withdrew to the seclusion of Balmoral and Osborne and refused to perform her ceremonial duties. This aroused much hostile comment and calls for a republic. Obstinate and self-indulgent, Victoria behaved tyranically to those in her Court circle. She never read a newspaper, knew nothing of the lives of her subjects and held reactionary political views. She opposed factory legislation, army reform, examinations for entry into the civil service and 'This mad, wicked folly of "Women's Rights"'. Victoria disapproved of education for the working class which might give them ideas beyond their station and loathed Ireland and **Gladstone**'s reforms there. The political influence of the monarchy declined during her reign. Only when there was no obvious candidate was she able to make her own choice of Prime Minister, as she did with **Aberdeen** in 1852 and Rosebery in 1894. Having written in 1879 that she could never take 'Mr Gladstone as my Minister again', she did take him in 1880, though she persisted in showing her hostility. Her popularity revived in the last quarter of the century, as the symbolic aspects of the monarchy were developed. Magnificent spectacles celebrated her Golden and Diamond Jubilees in 1887 and 1897 as head of the British Empire. By this time Victoria, plain and fat, was a semi-invalid and half blind. She died in 1901 after the longest reign in English history.

**Vienna, Congress of** (October 1814–June 1815). The congress at which a peace settlement for Europe after the **Napoleonic Wars** was arranged. All important decisions were taken by the victors, Britain, Russia, Austria and Prussia, although France was allowed to attend. **Napoleon** had changed the map of Europe extensively, by reducing the number of German states from over 230 to thirty-nine and by annexing much of Germany and Italy for France, as well as the Austrian Netherlands (later to become Belgium) and Holland. France had to give up nearly all her conquests in the Treaty of **Paris** but no attempt was made to revive all the German states. At Vienna a loose **German Confederation** or *Bund* of thirty-nine states was set up under Austrian leadership, but it had no army or real authority: each of its member states retained complete control of its own affairs. Britain regarded Austria as the keystone of the settlement in Central Europe, as she was expected to prevent Russia expanding there and to keep France out of Italy and Germany. This was a role Austria did not have the resources to fulfil. Austria was content to give up the Austrian Netherlands, far removed from her other territories, which were united with Holland to form the United Kingdom of the Netherlands. As compensation Austria acquired Venetia in Italy and the Dalmatian coast. Parma, Modena and Tuscany in central Italy were ruled by Austrians, the Pope returned to the Papal States and the Bourbons to Naples and Sicily. Piedmont in northern Italy acquired the Genoese Republic, so she could be a fairly strong buffer state between the Habsburg Empire and France. Austria's role was to act as policeman in Italy and prevent change there, something she was well able to do.

Russia's main interest was to acquire the whole of Poland, including the parts which had gone to Prussia and Austria in the Partitions of 1793 and 1795. She was prepared in return to let Prussia have Saxony. Austria objected strongly, because Russia would dominate Eastern Europe and Prussia would be given a commanding position in north Germany and would be strong enough to challenge Austria's leadership of the *Bund*. **Castlereagh** supported Austria, as did **Talleyrand**, who saw a chance of dividing the alliance against France and ending French isolation. In January 1815 France, Britain and Austria made a secret defensive alliance and prepared for war. When this was leaked to Russia, she compromised. Prussia would get two-fifths of Saxony; Russia would obtain most but not all of Poland, which would form a separate kingdom ruled by the Tsar of Russia. Russia also gained Finland from Sweden and Bessarabia from Turkey. Prussia probably benefited more than any other power from additional territory. Britain wanted a strong power in west Germany to prevent French encroachment there, so Prussia was given the Rhineland. This was to lay the foundations for her to become the most important German power, although its vast mineral wealth was not realized at the time. Prussia also gained part of wealthy and industrial Saxony and Swedish Pomerania on the Baltic coast (this marked the end of the Swedish Empire). Britain was not interested in acquiring any territory on the Continent but wanted naval bases with which she could control the sea lanes. She therefore acquired Malta, the Ionian islands and Heligoland. Ceylon and the Cape of Good Hope, which had been taken from the Dutch during the Napoleonic Wars, were retained as invaluable bases on the route to India. Britain also supported the transfer of Norway from Denmark to Sweden, so that no one power controlled the entrance to the Baltic. One of Britain's major concerns was to strengthen the states on France's borders, so that they would be strong enough to resist French aggression. She was successful in this, with a United Kingdom of the Netherlands to the north of France, Prussia in the Rhineland to the north-east, a Swiss Confederation, whose integrity was guaranteed by the Great Powers, to the east and a strengthened Piedmont in the south-east.

**Vogel, Sir Julius** (1835–99). Prime Minister of New Zealand (1872–4). A London Jew, Vogel emigrated to Australia in 1852, because of the gold discovered in Victoria, and moved to New Zealand in 1861. Elected to parliament in 1863, he led the opposition from 1865–8 before becoming Treasurer in 1869. This was the beginning of a 'continuous ministry' in which, whatever office he held, Vogel was the real holder of power and picked the leaders of the government for over a decade. He believed that the development of New Zealand was held up by a lack of transport – there were only fifty miles of railway – so that settlement was confined to the coastal strip. Vogel proposed to open up the country by borrowing money to build railways and encourage immigration, using land alongside the railways as security. As there was provincial opposition to this scheme, he abolished provincial governments in 1876 and replaced them by various boards and borough, county and city councils, which have run local government ever since. Between 1870 and 1880 he borrowed £20 million and built 1,100 miles of track, 4,000 miles of telegraph lines and many roads and public buildings. Immigrants from Germany and Scandinavia, as well as from Britain, doubled the population. As land prices increased there was a speculative boom, which burst in 1879. Wool and grain prices had been falling in the 1870s, owing to competition from Russia and America, and New Zealand's long depression (1879–96) began. Yet Vogel had transformed New Zealand and laid the foundations for its future prosperity.

**Wafd Party.** Egyptian political party, formed at the end of the **First World War** when Saad **Zaghlul** requested that a delegation (*Wafd*) should be sent to the **Paris Peace Conference** to put the case for Egyptian independence. When the British rejected this request, the *Wafd* turned into the first real political party in Egypt and one which had mass support. When its leader Zaghlul was arrested and exiled by the British there were widespread riots and demonstrations, some organized by the *Wafd*, in which over a thousand people were killed. In 1922, with unrest continuing, the British granted Egypt her independence, yet retained rights to defend Egypt and the **Suez Canal** and control the Sudan. Egypt was given a parliament and a king, though the British army remained in Egypt and British officers held the highest posts in the Egyptian army. The *Wafd* rejected the British declaration, which it called 'a national catastrophe', as it made a farce of independence. This did not prevent the Party coming to power, which it did in 1924, when it won 190 out of 214 seats in the Egyptian parliament. The *Wafd* continued to be the largest party, usually in conflict with the authoritarian King Fuad, and in 1936 took a major step towards full Egyptian independence, when it made the Anglo-Egyptian Treaty. Britain's occupation of Egypt was to be ended, though she was to retain troops in the Canal Zone and reserved the right of reoccupation in time of war. Egypt regained control of her own forces for the first time since 1882; the legal privileges of foreigners also ended. The leader of the *Wafd*, Nahas Pasha, was made regent during the minority (1936–8) of King Farouk. Nahas and the *Wafd* government were dismissed by the King in 1938 but were restored to power in 1941 on the insistence of the British, who distrusted Farouk's pro-Italian ministers. The *Wafd* remained in power until October 1944, but its cooperation with Britain and its corruption made it unpopular, especially with junior officers like Nasser and

Sadat. After the military revolution of 1952 Farouk was deposed, and the *Wafd* was disbanded, along with all other political parties.

**Wagner Act** (1935). The most important labour legislation of the **New Deal**. The National Labor Relations Act was known as the Wagner Act because it was sponsored by Senator Robert F. Wagner. It upheld the workers' right to form trade unions. No restrictions were placed on labour practices, but several management practices were forbidden as unfair. Employers were not allowed to set up company unions under their own control, stop workers forming their own unions or refuse to bargain with such unions. Employees were to choose their unions in free elections: a union chosen by the majority of workers would be the sole bargaining agent for all employees. The Act also set up a National Labor Relations Board to enforce its provisions and greatly increased the role of government in industrial relations. In 1937 the **Supreme Court** declared the Act valid, overturning previous decisions that had made early New Deal labour legislation illegal. This was the greatest victory labour ever won in the Court. It was followed by a rapid rise in the number of workers in trade unions: 3.5 million in 1935, 15 million in 1947.

**Wahabis.** Followers of an Islamic reform movement, founded by Muhammad ibn Abd al-Wahhab (1703–92) in Nejd, central Arabia. Wahabis sought to return to the pure Islam of the time of the Prophet Muhammad and accepted the authority of the Quran and the *hadith* (the sayings and actions of the Prophet as reported by his companions) alone. All medieval additions to Islamic doctrine were rejected. The Wahabis condemned alcohol and smoking and destroyed shrines, as they encouraged the worship of saints and threatened the oneness of God. Ibn Abd al-Wahhab joined forces with ibn Saud, head of a small tribal dynasty, who led the Wahabis into Iraq in 1802, occupied Karbala, the burial place of Husayn, the Prophet's grandson, and centre of pilgrimage for all Shiite Muslims, and destroyed the shrine. The Wahabis captured Mecca in 1803 and Medina in 1805, the most holy places in Islam, and demolished all the sacred tombs, including that of the Prophet. The Ottoman Sultan sent **Muhammad Ali**, viceroy of Egypt, to deal with the

Wahabis. His son Ibrahim ejected them from Mecca and by 1818 had defeated the Wahabis and razed their capital. Though their military power was broken, many ideas of the Wahabis were accepted by orthodox Islam in the nineteenth and twentieth centuries. They influenced Muhammad **Abduh**, who wanted to purge Islam of medieval innovations, and the **Muslim Brotherhood** in Egypt. A second great Wahabi revival took place in the twentieth century under the leadership of **Abd al-Aziz ibn Saud**, which resulted in the foundation of the state of Saudi Arabia.

**Waitangi, Treaty of** (February 1840). Maoris gathered at Waitangi ('Waters of Lamentation') on North Island, New Zealand, to discuss with a representative of the British Crown the future of their country. Fifty chiefs signed the treaty, which was eventually accepted by over 500. They ceded sovereignty to the Queen, who guaranteed to the Maoris the possession of their lands. Only the Queen had the right to buy Maori lands. The chiefs were given the rights of British subjects. It is difficult to know if they understood what was in the treaty, which prepared the way for the formal annexation of New Zealand in May 1840. The treaty was intended to lay the foundations of a just society in which two races could live peacefully together, but this did not happen. Encroachment by settlers on Maori lands led to the **Anglo-Maori Wars**.

**Wakefield, Edward Gibbon** (1796–1862). British colonialist. Wakefield ran away with one heiress, who died in childbirth, and was imprisoned for three years at Newgate for abducting a second. Whilst in prison he became interested in transportation and colonization and published his *Letter from Sydney* (1829), in which he proposed that Crown lands in Australia should not be given away free but should be sold at a 'sufficient' price in small units. The proceeds from land sales should be used to promote immigration, in which there ought to be a balance of the sexes. Such measures, he thought, would relieve unemployment in Britain and avert the threat of revolution and would provide the free labour the colonies needed. Some of his suggestions were adopted as British colonial policy in 1831 and influenced the South Australian Act (1834), which forbade the use of South Australia as a **penal settlement** and subsidized immigration by the sale of land. 40,000 free immigrants went to Australia in the 1830s. Wakefield was a founder of the New Zealand Company (1838), which sent a party in 1839 to buy land from the Maoris and this led the British government to annex New Zealand in 1840, in order to protect the Maoris. He helped to establish five settlements in New Zealand and spent much of his time trying to gain self-government for the colonists.

**Wall Street Crash.** The collapse of the US financial markets in October 1929. Ever since the end of the post-war depression in 1922 share prices had been rising, and this fuelled a speculative boom. The summer of 1929 was the most frantic in American financial history. Nine million investors in the market bought not for income but in order to sell at a profit, and they bought 'on margin' (with credit, not cash). By the end of the summer, stock prices had quadrupled in four years. But then investors began to sell. Share prices moved down far more quickly than they had gone up, and in October it seemed that everyone was selling. The most terrible days were 'Black Thursday', 24 October, when nearly thirteen million shares were sold, and 'Black Tuesday', 29 October, when investors got rid of sixteen million shares at a loss of $10 billion, twice the amount of money in circulation in the whole country at the time. It was the worst day in the history of the New York stock market: thousands of investors were ruined, and the results of the crash were devastating. Overseas loans came to an end, so that European countries were pushed into a depression. In the USA, investment plans were abandoned, so industry was badly hit, as it was by the removal from the economy of billions of dollars of consumer spending. Investors who had bought shares 'on margin' were now called on to pay cash, which they could do only by selling their possessions, even their homes. Industrial production and house building slumped and unemployment rose – from 1.5 million in 1929 to 3.25 million in March 1930. The **Great Depression** had begun.

**War Communism.** The system in the USSR by which the **Bolsheviks** sought to cope with the disruptive effects of the **Russian Civil War**. It lasted from the spring of 1918 to the spring of 1921. The economy was in chaos, as the richest wheatlands and much of Russia's industry had been lost to the Germans at the

Treaty of **Brest-Litovsk**. There was rampant inflation, with the result that peasants would not sell their grain for worthless money. There was starvation and unemployment in the towns: in 1920 the urban work-force was only half its pre-war size, whilst production was a fifth of its 1913 level. To cope with this situation the Bolsheviks introduced central control and distribution of supplies. All industries were nationalized by late 1920 and private trade was abolished, as were banks. As money was almost worthless, payment in kind and barter largely replaced money. To feed the towns all the peasant's production, except for his own needs, was requisitioned, and Committees of the Village Poor were set up to spy on the richer peasants and introduce class war to the villages. These were so unpopular that they were abolished in November 1918. Without these measures starvation in the towns would have been greater. The peasants responded to requisitioning by cutting down the sown area, and soon turned to violence. There were large peasant risings in 1920–21 in the black-earth regions, the Volga basin and Siberia. Workers too, whose real earnings in 1920 were only 40 per cent of those in 1913, had become disillusioned with the Bolshevik regime. The revolt at **Kronstadt**, the pride and joy of the Revolution, in March 1921 was, said Lenin, 'the flash which lit up reality better than anything else'. He decided to abandon War Communism which, he said, 'was thrust upon us by war and ruin . . . It was a temporary measure'. Other Bolsheviks did not see it simply as the result of the Civil War but had welcomed it ideologically: to them central control and the rejection of the market were indispensable aspects of Communism. They did not welcome Lenin's move to **NEP**.

**Warfare: in the air.** Aircraft came into military service in 1908. Used in the **First World War** (1914–18) for reconnaissance (it was airmen who informed **Joffre** of the German army's change of direction at the battle of the **Marne**), the fighter biplane developed when the French found out how to synchronize firing through the propeller. Germany used Zeppelins to bomb England in 1915–16, but they were an easy target and not very successful: only 1,100 people were killed in England in air attacks in the First World War. Fighters escorted light bombers, in use from 1917, and strafed enemy troops extensively in the 1918 offensives, but aircraft did not make a vital contribution to the outcome of the war.

Between the two world wars the belief arose that the bomber would always get through, so the RAF in the late 1930s concentrated on building monoplane fighters, such as the Spitfire and Hurricane, and radar early warning systems. In the **Second World War** (1939–45) air power was decisive: no operation could be successful without air superiority. The battle of **Britain** (1940) was the first major air battle and showed the crucial importance of air warfare: if the RAF had not been successful Britain would have been knocked out of the war. Aircraft played a vital role in the support of land operations, the Germans deploying dive-bombers as an extension of their artillery in their *Blitzkrieg* on Poland, France and Russia. Before the Normandy landings on **D-Day** (June 1944), Allied air forces prepared the way by destroying German roads, railways and radar installations. Aircraft were also used as transports, to keep troops supplied and to drop paratroopers. German paratroops captured Crete (1941); the Allies dropped them to secure the flanks of the D-Day landings. In Burma (1944–5) 100,000 Allied troops were supplied on an advance of 800 miles mainly from the air. At sea, aircraft were crucial to the success of operations, particularly carrier-based aircraft, which won the battles of **Midway** (1942) and **Leyte Gulf** (1944) for the Americans and so gave them control of the sea in the **Pacific War** (1941–5). Aircraft were essential too in the battle of the **Atlantic**: they were used by Germany to find convoys and by the Allies to look for and destroy submarines. During the Second World War bombers grew in size and range: the Wellingtons and Heinkels of 1940, with their half-ton bombloads and 1,250-mile range, were replaced by planes such as the Lancaster (with its ten-ton bombload) and the American Flying Fortress, which had a 3,000-mile range. They were used in the **strategic bombing offensive** to attack industrial centres and major cities, in order to destroy the enemy's economy and civilian morale: they devastated many German and Japanese towns, without seriously affecting their industrial capacity until the war was nearing its end. Some developments in air warfare – the German supersonic rocket (V2) and Whittle's jet engine – came too late to have much impact on the war, though the dropping of the **atomic bomb** on **Hiroshima** rapidly brought about the surrender of Japan.

**Warfare: on land.** The first conscript armies were raised in France in the **French Revolutionary Wars** and **Napoleonic Wars**. In the nineteenth century most European armies (except Britain's) adopted conscription, though this could usually be avoided by the educated, and only a fraction (a quarter in Prussia in the 1850s) of those eligible for service were called up. The mobility of these troops was vastly increased by **railways**, first used effectively in 1859, when 120,000 French troops reached the front in Italy in eleven days (it would have taken them two months to march). Railways played a vital role in the **American Civil War**, when the weakness of the South in railways was a severe handicap, and in the **Franco-Prussian War** (1870–71), as Prussia mobilized 400,000 troops on the French frontier in twenty-one days, whilst the French could muster only 100,000. The electric telegraph too was invaluable, as it enabled governments and high commands to keep in close touch with armies in the field: **Moltke** ran the **Austro-Prussian War** (1866) almost entirely from his headquarters in Berlin.

New weapons also changed the nature of warfare. The standard weapon in European armies in 1800 was the muzzle-loading musket: the Brown Bess, which British soldiers used until 1852, was little different from the musket used at Blenheim in 1704. It was not very accurate even at 100 yards and took a minute to reload. The rifle which replaced it had spiral grooves on the inside of the barrel and was accurate at 500 yards, but it was still slow to use. The important change came with the breech-loader, which could be loaded quickly and from a position lying down. The first breech-loader was the Prussian needle-gun, effective in the Austro-Prussian War, as the Prussians could fire three times as fast as their enemies. In the 1870s all armies changed over to breech-loaders. The same developments took place in artillery, with steel, rifled, breech-loading cannon developed by **Krupp** and used to devastating effect in the Franco-Prussian War (1870–71). In 1885 smokeless explosives and recoilless carriages were invented, which made it unnecessary to re-sight a gun after each shot and increased the rate and accuracy of fire. Heavy artillery had a range of twenty miles – some howitzers could fire fifty or sixty miles – and could crash through all fortifications. In the 1890s repeating rifles were in general use in European armies, when infantry could fire fifteen rounds in as many seconds. The machine gun was an extension of the repeating rifle. The Gatling gun, hand-cranked, was used in the American Civil War (1861–5), but the first truly automatic repeating gun was the Maxim (1884), a belt-loaded weapon which could fire up to 600 rounds a minute. The machine gun and repeating rifle made cavalry useless as a shock force, though it was still useful for reconnaissance and for raiding, as in the **South African War** (1899–1902). They also made colourful uniforms too easy a target, so the British and Americans adopted khaki, the Germans grey, uniforms. The terrifying fire-power of modern armies, which made the extension of **imperialism** possible, was shown at **Omdurman** (1898), when 11,000 Sudanese were killed for the loss of forty-eight British troops.

'As a result of the improvement of firearms,' Moltke had noted as early as the 1870s, 'the tactical defensive has acquired a great advantage over the offensive.' The **First World War** was therefore dominated on the Western Front by **trench warfare**, which made the front line almost static. Chlorine gas, used by the Germans at Ypres in 1915, and later mustard gas, which could blind and burn, were used by both sides but were not effective weapons, particularly when gas masks were invented. Tanks were another means of trying to break the deadlock, as they gave protection against machine-gun fire, could flatten barbed wire and pass over trenches. When they were used in large numbers at Cambrai in 1917 they had a shattering effect on German morale, but there were not enough reserves to exploit the breakthrough. Yet it was the tank that made the **Second World War** much more mobile than the First, as the Germans used the *Blitzkrieg* to bring quick victories in Poland, France and Russia. Combined operations of land and naval (and later air) forces, first tried at **Gallipoli** in 1915, were used extensively in capturing islands in the **Pacific War** (1941–5), in the invasions of North Africa, Sicily and Italy in 1943 and on **D-Day** in 1944.

**Warfare: at sea.** Nelson's ships were wooden sailing vessels of 2,000 tons displacement, with guns that fired broadside. In a battle, enemy ships were boarded, so ratings were armed with muskets and cutlasses. All this changed in the 1830s with the use of steam engines, which had a great advantage in speed and manoeuvrability over sail. As steamboats did not depend on the wind they could sail up and down rivers, and carried Europeans deep into Africa and Asia: they were used extensively in China in the **Opium War** (1839–42). At first, marine engines were very inefficient and used vast quantities of coal, but the triple-expansion engine in the 1870s and the turbine engine in the 1890s made more efficient use of steam and increased the speed of ships. Just before the **First World War** the switch to oil-fired ships began.

At the same time as steam replaced sail, iron replaced wood. The British navy had its first iron steamer in 1839. As explosive shells superseded solid shot, there was need for more protective armour, so the size of ships increased, as did the calibre of guns. They were too heavy to be mounted broadside, so they were placed in turrets, which could turn through 180°. It was thought that command of the sea would be decided by capital ships, a doctrine disseminated by **Mahan**, so bigger and bigger ships were built, culminating in the **Dreadnought**, which **Tirpitz** copied for the German navy. They were to prove valueless in the **First World War** owing to the development of the torpedo and the submarine. The torpedo, invented in 1860, was followed by the building in France of small, fast torpedo boats. The main use of the torpedo, however, was by submarines, the construction of which was made possible by the development of the electric accumulator battery in the 1890s. Britain ordered its first submarine in 1900, Germany in 1906. Capital ships were vulnerable to submarine attack, so they were kept in port, apart from their one foray at the indecisive battle of **Jutland** (1916). Submarines almost brought victory for Germany in 1917 by cutting off Britain's food supplies, but were thwarted by **convoys**, the interception of their radio communications and by increasingly effective depth charges and location devices.

U-boats again figured prominently in the **Second World War** in the battle of the **Atlantic**, when they took a heavy toll of Allied merchant shipping. The threat they posed was not overcome until 1943 and was not finally eliminated until their bases on the French Atlantic coast were captured towards the end of the war. American submarines had even greater success in the **Pacific War** (1941–5), as nine-tenths of the Japanese merchant marine (over ten million tons in 1941) was sunk, half of it by submarines. The US navy was crucial to success in the Pacific War, as it destroyed Japanese sea-power at the battles of **Midway** (1942) and **Leyte Gulf** (1944) (battles which saw the eclipse of the battleship by the aircraft carrier) and protected troops landing on islands such as **Okinawa**, a stepping stone on the way to Japan. The British navy too played a vital role, keeping the sea lanes open to Malta, the Middle East and Soviet Russia via the North Cape. The aid the Soviet Union received by sea in 1941–2 was of critical importance in her struggle against Germany. The navy also escorted the Allied invasion force to the Normandy landings on **D-Day** (1944), which began the final phase of the war in the West.

**Warlords.** Provincial military rulers in China, whose sole basis of power was their private armies. From the death of **Yuan Shikai** in 1916 until 1928, when **Jiang Jieshi** (Chiang Kai-shek) imposed some semblance of unity on China, hundreds of warlords ruled their particular areas of China. Many of them had been officers in the imperial army, though some were bandit-chiefs. Their troops were recruited from ex-soldiers, landless peasants and the unemployed. Local communities were devastated by the looting of undisciplined troops – soldiers were popularly regarded as little different from bandits – and by the extortions of the warlords. Regular taxes, such as the land tax, were constantly increased and were often collected years in advance. The power of the warlords was unstable, as the area over which they ruled was often not clearly defined, so they fought each other for the wealthy regions, and especially for Beijing (Peking), as whoever controlled the capital would receive the income from the maritime customs and the salt administration. By 1928 Jiang's **Northern Expedition** had forced the warlords to submit to the authority of the **Guomindang**, but it did not crush them. They retained their armies, so the government's control of much of China was very limited. In the west warlords thrived until the 1940s.

**Warsaw Rising** (August–October 1944). In July 1944 the Red Army reached the outskirts of Warsaw. Polish members of the Home Army, loyal to the anti-communist Polish government-in-exile in London, rose up in revolt on 1 August against the Germans occupying Warsaw and seized control of parts of the city. The Red

Army did not move to support them. Stalin would not allow British and American planes to land on Soviet airfields after dropping supplies on Warsaw, though he did allow the Lublin (Communist) Poles to make an (unsuccessful) attempt to relieve Warsaw. The Germans, using tanks, artillery and aircraft, wore down the resistance of the Home Army in two months of ferocious fighting, until its remnants surrendered on 4 October. 200,000 inhabitants of Warsaw had been killed in the battle, and after it the Germans systematically destroyed what remained of the old city. Opinions differ as to why the Red Army remained passive during the rising. Some think Stalin deliberately waited until the Germans had destroyed the Home Army before moving (Russian troops entered Warsaw on 17 January 1945), so that he could then install a communist-dominated government in Poland. Others maintain that the **Red Army** had outrun its supplies by the time it reached the Vistula and that reinforcements did not arrive until 10 September, six weeks after the rising had begun.

**Washington, Booker Taliaferro** (1856–1915). Negro educator and leader in the late nineteenth century USA. Born a slave in Virginia, Washington was the son of a slave mother and a white father. He set forth his ideas in a speech in Atlanta in 1895, which became known as the 'Atlanta Compromise'. 'The wisest among my race,' he said, 'understand that the agitation of questions of social equality is the extremest folly.' He advised Southern Negroes to avoid politics and to be the 'most patient, faithful, law-abiding and unresentful people that the world has seen'. Believing that Negroes could not make political progress until they had made economic progress, he thought they should accept white supremacy and the capitalist values of thrift and hard work. His views were attacked by William **Du Bois**, the leading black intellectual of the day, as a betrayal of black rights and as condemning blacks to a position of permanent inferiority. Yet many blacks accepted the Atlanta Compromise, which pleased the whites too, so that wealthy industrialists like **Carnegie** and **Rockefeller** were prepared to support Washington's educational enterprises. He was the first head of the Tuskegee Institute in Alabama in 1881, which became the best-known Negro educational institution in the USA. Booker T.

Washington became the most influential Negro in the USA, obtaining control of most black organizations and owning several black newspapers; the black churches sought his advice. He also played a political role, in spite of his advice to blacks to keep out of politics. A confidential adviser to Theodore **Roosevelt** on the political appointment of blacks and of white Southerners, he also worked behind the scenes to help Negroes. In 1904 he and others began a successful action against the exclusion of blacks from juries, and in 1911 he obtained a **Supreme Court** ruling that declared peonage (involuntary servitude for debt) illegal.

**Washington Conference** (November 1921–February 1922). This was the first major international conference to be held in the USA and was called to reduce naval armaments in the Pacific. Japan had secured a dominant position in China during the **First World War** and so threatened America's **'open-door' policy** there. After the war she acquired German colonies in the Pacific. Consequently there was a costly naval race between Japan, the United States and Britain, which Charles Hughes, the American Secretary of State, wanted to end. He proposed that there should be a ratio of American, British and Japanese capital ships of 5:5:3, that sixty-six battleships should be scrapped to preserve this ratio and that no capital ships should be built in the next ten years. He also proposed a ratio of 1.75:1.75 for France and Italy. These proposals were accepted in a Five Power Naval Treaty: Japan did not want to accept an inferior position but did so when Britain and the USA agreed not to strengthen their naval bases in Hong Kong and the Philippines. In another treaty the USA, Britain, France and Japan guaranteed each other's possessions in the Pacific and agreed to consult each other if there was a crisis there. A result of these treaties was that the **Anglo-Japanese Alliance** of 1902 was allowed to lapse. A third treaty committed all nine participating nations (Portugal, Belgium, Holland and China in addition to those who signed the Five Power Treaty) to respect China's independence and to maintain the 'open-door' policy. Japan agreed to American requests to restore Shandong to China and to evacuate her troops from Siberia (see **Russian Civil War**). These treaties were an important achievement: they were the first international agreement on arms limitations and reduced tension in the Far East. Yet they had serious weaknesses: they did not apply to armies or air forces and the naval reductions applied only to battleships and aircraft carriers, there was no means provided of enforcing the treaties, and a major Far Eastern Power, the Soviet Union, did not take part. There was great opposition to the treaties in the Japanese navy and in 1934 Japan announced that she was abandoning them.

**Washington, George** (1732–99). First President of the USA (1789–97). Washington, the son of a Virginia planter, fought for Britain in the French and Indian Wars (1754–8) and helped to capture Fort Duquesne (later Pittsburgh) in 1758. A year later he resigned from the army and became a tobacco planter. He became an outspoken opponent of British colonial policies and Commander of American forces in the Revolutionary War (1776–83). Although he was not a great soldier, he had qualities which were needed at the time, particularly determination and courage. Washington managed to make an undisciplined militia into an effective fighting force and kept his army together at Valley Forge in the winter of 1777–8, when a quarter of his 10,000 men died of disease. When French aid came to the colonists' help, Washington trapped the British at Yorktown and forced their surrender in October 1781.

Washington was the obvious choice as President of the Constitutional Convention held in 1787, and helped to secure the adoption of the US Constitution. He was elected unanimously by the state electors as first President of the United States in 1789, although he was very reluctant to become President. One of his strengths as President was that he gathered round him men of great ability though of widely differing views: Alexander **Hamilton** became his Secretary of the Treasury and Thomas **Jefferson** his Secretary of State (Jefferson resigned in 1793, as he was opposed to Hamilton's policies). In his first term Washington was largely concerned with domestic affairs. Here he shared the views of Hamilton: he wanted a stable currency so that he could pay off the national debt and he wanted to encourage the development of industry. Crucial for a sound currency was the establishment of a federal bank, so the Bank of the United States was set up. The money to pay for reforms was to come from tariffs, so James **Madison** introduced the first tariff bill in 1789. Madison was also largely responsible for ten Constitutional amendments, known collectively as the Bill of Rights, of 1791, which guaranteed freedom of religion, speech, assembly and the press and the right to bear arms. These acts helped to reconcile anti-Federalists to the Constitution.

Washington's second term was much more concerned with foreign policy. Just after it began in 1793 France declared war on Britain. The USA had a military alliance with France but Washington was determined to keep the USA out of war and so issued a Neutrality Proclamation. Britain did not help Washington to remain neutral by seizing American ships trading with France and by impressing American sailors into the British navy. It looked as though there might be war, which the USA could ill afford. This was avoided by Jay's Treaty (1794), by which Britain agreed to pay for goods seized from American ships, but it did not stop impressment or British interference with American shipping. The unpopularity of this treaty was offset by an agreement with Spain in 1795, which fixed the northern boundary of Spanish Florida and opened the Mississippi to US shipping. Federal authority was challenged by the Whisky Rebellion of 1794, when Pennsylvania farmers rose up against a tax on rye whisky. Washington used 15,000 militia to crush the rising, making it clear that the federal government would not tolerate any challenge to its authority.

In September 1796 Washington announced his decision to retire in his Farewell Address. In this he stressed the need for national unity, spoke of the 'baneful effects of the spirit of party' and counselled Americans to 'steer clear of permanent alliances'. He had successfully seen the Constitution through its first difficult years, leaving Federal power firmly established and a country that was growing ever more prosperous. Washington became a legendary figure in his lifetime, described by Congressman Henry Lee as 'first in war, first in peace and first in the hearts of his countrymen'.

**Waterloo, battle of** (18 June 1815), was fought by **Wellington**'s Allied army and the Prussians under **Blücher** against **Napoleon Bonaparte**. When Napoleon escaped from his exile in Elba and returned to France, **Louis XVIII** fled and left Napoleon in control of France again. He wanted to defeat the Allied and Prussian armies in Belgium before Russian and Austrian armies could join them, so he hastily moved north. Napoleon wanted to drive a wedge between the Allied army at Brussels and the Prussian army at Namur, before defeating them separately. On 16 June he heavily defeated Blücher at Ligny, and on the same day Wellington fought an inconclusive battle with Marshal **Ney** at Quatre Bras, six miles to the west. Wellington retreated north towards Waterloo on the road to Brussels: Blücher, instead of moving east towards his base at Namur, as Napoleon expected, went north to Wavre, only seven miles from Wellington. If Blücher had not done this, Wellington would have had to fight Napoleon's larger army alone and would almost certainly have been defeated. Wellington took up his position on a low ridge, with most of his men concealed behind reverse (or rearward) slopes, so that they missed much of the impact of the French artillery. Napoleon repeatedly attacked the Allied centre, which held out until 6.30 pm, when French cannon were firing at point-blank range and Wellington's line began to waver. Seeing victory within his grasp, Ney asked Napoleon for reinforcements, but his request was rejected, as most of Napoleon's reserves had been committed to his right flank, which was being attacked by the Prussians. This gave Wellington time to reinforce his centre. When the Imperial Guard was released to attack Wellington's centre it was too late. They were repulsed, to the surprise and despair of the French army, which fled in disorder. The battle was, according to Wellington, 'the nearest run thing you ever saw in your life'. Napoleon's defeat at Waterloo was followed by his second abdication and by the return of Louis XVIII.

**Webb, Sidney** (1859–1947) **and Beatrice** (1858–1943). English social researchers and leading Fabians. Sidney, from the lower middle class, entered the civil service in 1878 and studied in the evenings to become an LL B from London University. In 1885 he joined the **Fabian Society**, rejecting revolution in favour of the 'permeation' of institutions by socialist ideas through persuasion. He was convinced that the 'municipal socialism' of local authorities, shown in the services which they provided such as water, gas and electricity, was bound to spread gradually to the state. In 1892 he made a surprising marriage to the beautiful Beatrice Potter, whose father was a wealthy timber merchant and director of several railway companies. Her strong sense of social guilt had led her to be a research assistant to Charles Booth for his *Life and Labour of the People of London* (1889–1903) and she had become a socialist. She had been infatuated with Joseph **Chamberlain** but not with Sidney, whose shape she unkindly compared to that of a tadpole. 'You I believe in but do not love,' she told him just before they were engaged. In their austere and desiccated marriage they seemed to find pleasure only in work. 'Owing to our concentration on research and municipal administration,' Beatrice wrote in *Our Partnership*, 'we had neither the time nor the energy to listen to music and the drama or to visit picture galleries.'

Beatrice's private income enabled Sidney to leave the civil service, so that they could both concentrate on relentless research, which produced *The History of Trade Unionism* (1894) and eleven volumes on the history of English local government (1903–29). They founded the London School of Economics in 1894 to promote the scientific study of society but did not at first see the need for a **Labour Party**, as they expected their ideas to 'permeate' the **Liberal** and **Conservative** parties. Beatrice was a member of the Royal Commission on the **Poor Laws**: when it reported in 1909 she signed a minority report calling for the abolition of the Poor Laws and the setting up of new ministries of state to provide social services. Disappointment with the **New Liberalism** led the Webbs to join the **Independent Labour Party** in 1912 and a year later to found the *New Statesman*. Sidney became a member of the Labour Party executive in 1916 and drafted much of the party's 1918 constitution, which called for 'common ownership of the Means of Production'. He did not become an MP until 1920, when he was over sixty, and served in the first Labour government (1924) as President of the Board of Trade. In 1929 he did not stand for re-election but moved to the **Lords** as Baron Passmore and became Colonial Secretary in the second minority Labour government. In this post he made many enemies, as he opposed the demands of white settlers in Kenya for the political control of the country and of Jews for increased immigration into Palestine. An opponent of the **General Strike** of 1926, he supported Snowden's reduction of unemployment benefits in 1931.

Sidney refused to serve in **MacDonald**'s **National Government** in 1931 and a year later visited the Soviet Union with Beatrice. Convinced that capitalism was collapsing, they were impressed, as were many left-wingers, by **Stalin**'s ability to avoid unemployment. Beatrice in particular went to absurd lengths to eulogize Stalin, referring coldly and without any reproach to 'Stalin incidentally liquidating the *kulaks*'. 'I think on the whole the Soviet Government has acted in wise restraint,' was her comment on the Moscow Show Trials of 1936. This was an indication of the lack of passion and of compassion which affected all they did. They never understood or mixed with the working men whose lot they cerebrally sought to improve. Their main legacy, and an important one, was their painstaking research into social problems, which greatly increased the understanding of industrial relations and local government and helped to lay the foundations of the **Welfare State**.

**Webster, Daniel** (1782–1852). US politician. With his commanding presence and magnificent voice he made a great reputation as a public speaker, in pleading before the **Supreme Court** in cases which had national significance, especially *McCulloch* v. *Maryland* and *Dartmouth College* v. *Woodward* (see John **Marshall**). For almost forty years from 1813, when he first entered **Congress**, he was New England's greatest orator and defender of national unity. As a supporter of industry he strongly opposed President **Jackson**'s attack on the Second Bank of the United States but backed him in the Nullification Crisis (see **Nullification Doctrine**). It was over the question of states' rights that Daniel Webster made what is regarded as the best speech ever given in Congress. He said that the Constitution was not a contract among states but among people, and could be interpreted only by the Supreme Court. He ended with the call: 'Liberty *and* Union, now and forever, one and inseparable'. He was a founding member of the **Whig Party** in 1834 but failed to win its nomination for President in 1836 and was never given a second chance. From 1841–3 he served as Secretary of State in a nominally Whig administration and concluded the Webster–Ashburton Treaty (1842) with Britain: this fixed the eastern boundary between Canada and the United States. Back in the Senate he opposed the **Mexican–American War**, and as slavery became the dominant issue he tried to prevent it leading to civil war. He believed that Congress could not interfere with slavery where it existed but could, and should, prevent its expansion. He supported Henry **Clay**'s **Compromise of 1850**.

**Weimar Republic** (1918–1933). The German Republic, known after the name of the town where the constituent assembly met in 1919 (it moved to Berlin in 1920). The Republic began on 9 November 1918, when Emperor **William II** abdicated. Unlike the Constitution of the **German Empire** (1871–1918), the Weimar Constitution made the Reich supreme over the states, named *Länder*, with the right of direct taxation, though the states retained their old powers over the police, churches and education. There was to be a bicameral legislature. The **Reichstag** had legislative power and was elected by all men and women over twenty by proportional representation. The Reichsrat represented the *Länder* governments and was less important. The President, elected for seven years, had considerable power, as he appointed all civil and military officials, and was Commander of the armed forces. Clause 48 gave him more power than the Emperor had enjoyed, as in an emergency he could suspend civil liberties and take whatever steps he thought necessary, including the use of armed force, to restore law and order. Proportional representation made government difficult, as it resulted in a multiplicity of parties (none of which had a majority in a German election until 1957) and in unstable coalitions: between 1919 and 1928 there were fifteen governments, none of which lasted for longer than eighteen months.

The Weimar Republic was unpopular from the start, as it was associated with the defeat of Germany in the **First World War**. The **'stab in the back' myth** soon arose: that the German army had not been defeated but that the armistice and the abdication of the Kaiser had been brought about by the 'November criminals', Weimar politicians who were also responsible for signing the humiliating Treaty of **Versailles**, by which Germany lost territory and had limitations imposed on her armed forces. The Republic was hated by the extreme **Left** as well as the **Right**, as Chancellor **Ebert** was faced with the **German Revolution**. To deal with this he made a deal with the army, which crushed the **Spartakist**

**Rising** in Berlin in 1919 and the declaration of a Soviet republic in Bavaria. An attempted right-wing *coup*, the **Kapp *Putsch*** (1920), was thwarted only by the **trade unions** calling a general strike. Inflation was another problem the Republic had to face. This was caused mainly by the imperial government financing the war by printing money rather than by increasing taxes, though it was made worse by the **reparations** demanded by the Allies. When the government defaulted, the French and Belgians occupied the **Ruhr** in 1923. With inflation out of control the middle classes lost their savings, businessmen went bankrupt and civil servants and teachers saw the value of their salaries reduced. It looked as though the Republic would not survive, in spite of the failure of **Hitler**'s **Munich *Putsch***. Recovery came largely through the financial measures of **Stresemann** and the **Dawes Plan**, which brought American loans flowing into Germany and ended the French occupation of the Ruhr. This produced a period of relative stability which lasted for the next five years, during which Germany became a great industrial nation again. She also gained international respectability by signing the treaties of **Locarno** (1925), in which she accepted the permanence of her western frontiers, and by joining the **League of Nations** in 1926.

The **Great Depression** brought both financial and industrial collapse. There were three million German unemployed at the end of 1930, by which time parliamentary government had given way to presidential government. Successive Chancellors (**Brüning**, von **Papen**, and **Schleicher**) could not obtain a majority in the Reichstag and so used Clause 48 of the Constitution, which enabled President **Hindenburg** to rule by decree. Great beneficiaries of the Depression were the extremist parties, the **Nazi** and the Communist. The Nazis had obtained twelve seats in the 1928 election: these rose to 107 in 1930 and 230 in the July election of 1932, when there were over six million unemployed. The Nazis were now by far the largest party, and so in January 1933 Hitler became Chancellor. Two months later an **Enabling Act** was passed which suspended the Weimar Constitution and allowed Hitler to set up the Nazi dictatorship.

**Weizmann, Chaim** (1874–1952). Leading Zionist (see **Zionism**) and scientist. Born in Russian Poland, he studied at German and

Swiss universities before becoming a chemistry lecturer at Manchester in 1904 and a British subject in 1910. As a prominent British scientist in the **First World War** he became a friend of government ministers and played an important part in negotiations which preceded the **Balfour Declaration**, which favoured the establishment of a Jewish home in Palestine. In 1920 he became President of the World Zionist Organization (a post he held from 1920–31 and from 1935–46) and worked hard to raise money and win support, though his caution and belief in a gradual approach did not appeal to extreme Zionists. He approved of the Peel Commission's plan (see **Palestine mandate**), which the extremists opposed, to divide Palestine, acted as scientific adviser to the British Ministry of Supply during the **Second World War** (in which his younger son was killed in the RAF) and denounced terrorist attacks by the **Stern Gang** and Irgun on British officials and installations. In 1948 he held crucial talks with President Truman, which resulted in the USA recognizing the newly formed state of Israel. He was elected as Israel's first President in 1949, a post he held until his death.

**Welfare State.** A state in which the government provides social services, such as education, health, housing and insurance for sickness, unemployment and old age. **Bismarck** in the 1880s was an unlikely progenitor of the Welfare State with his **State Socialism**. In the first decade of the twentieth century his lead was followed by other countries, such as New Zealand, when Richard **Seddon** was Prime Minister, and Uruguay, which **Batlle y Ordóñez** made into the first Welfare State in Latin America.

In Britain some welfare services were provided in the nineteenth century by the state (compulsory elementary education from 1880) and others by local authorities (gas, water, electricity, sewerage, transport) but it was the **Liberal** governments of **Campbell-Bannerman** (1905–8) and **Asquith** (1908–16), who first made a sustained effort to provide a range of social services which laid the basis of the Welfare State. The causes of poverty were attacked by setting up trade boards to deal with low pay in certain industries, by old-age pensions, by labour exchanges, by unemployment and health insurance, to be paid for largely by graduated taxation. The

'New Liberalism' rejected Gladstone's view of a minimalist state and sought more state intervention, as did the Labour Party, but up to 1939 welfare was largely restricted to the poor. During the Second World War an enlarged role for the state in providing welfare was accepted by both the main political parties and was expressed in the Beveridge Report (1942), which recommended welfare benefits 'from the cradle to the grave', where all would be treated equally and services would be above a minimum level. This was the time when the term 'welfare state' was first widely used, though the application of many of the ideas put forward had to await the Labour government of 1945–51.

**Wellington, Arthur Wellesley, 1st Duke of** (1769–1852). British field marshal and Prime Minister (1828–30). The son of an impoverished Irish peer, Wellington joined the army in 1787 and first made his mark when he served in India (1796–1805), defeating Tipu, the Sultan of Mysore, at Seringapatam (1799) and the Marathas in central India between 1802 and 1804, winning great victories against larger forces at Assaye and Argaum, two of the most difficult battles of his career. On returning to England he served as Irish Secretary (1807–8) before going to Portugal in 1808, where he defeated the French at Vimeiro. He was recalled when the French were allowed to evacuate their troops but returned to Portugal in 1809 and remained there or in Spain for the rest of the Peninsular War, skilfully deploying his forces and winning several victories before invading France in 1814. During the Hundred Days, after Napoleon's escape from Elba, Wellington (he was made a Duke in 1814) commanded British forces in Belgium where, with the aid of the Prussians under Blücher, he won his greatest victory at the battle of Waterloo. He then became supreme Allied Commander of the armies of occupation. When these were withdrawn in 1818 he joined Liverpool's government as Master-General of Ordnance and became Commander-in-Chief of the British army in 1827. Wellington resigned both these positions in the same year, when Canning became Prime Minister.

After Canning's death he became Prime Minister himself, the first time a professional soldier had led the government since Cromwell. Wellington proved to be a disastrous leader, ignoring public opinion but also showing great courage in pursuing unpopular policies which he felt were necessary. The Test and Corporation Acts had, since the seventeenth century, prevented Dissenters from holding office in central or local government. They were repealed, with little opposition, in 1828 but **Catholic emancipation** caused an outcry amongst ultra-**Tories** and became law only with **Whig** support in 1829. In the same year **Peel**'s Metropolitan Police Bill set up in London a uniformed, professional police force, who were soon known as Bobbies or Peelers after their founder: it became the model for other police forces throughout the country. The election of 1830 showed that many wanted **parliamentary reform** but Wellington saw no need for this and made a speech in which he unwisely said that 'the legislature and the system of representation possessed the full and entire confidence of the country'. He had split the Tory Party over Catholic emancipation and now the ultras joined with the Whigs to defeat the government. Wellington resigned and was replaced by a Whig government led by Earl **Grey**, which was committed to the reform of parliament. Wellington held office again when he served under Peel briefly as Foreign Secretary (1834–5) and from 1841 as minister without portfolio. He retired from public life in 1846.

**Weltpolitik** ('world policy'). Germany's attempt from 1897 to 1914 to gain influence and possessions abroad. She wanted her industrial and military strength, as the greatest power in Europe, to be reflected in her position in the world. The origins of *Weltpolitik* are to be found in **Social Darwinism**, prevalent at the time, which saw international affairs as a struggle in which each state sought to expand at the expense of others; in social imperialism, by which the **Junkers** and industrialists sought to maintain the status quo at home by diverting the discontent of the masses into expansion abroad; and in the belief that industry, which depended on raw materials from abroad and overseas markets, would not be secure unless Germany was a world power. This involved building a large navy, beginning with the naval laws of 1898 and 1900, which led to the Anglo–German naval race and to Britain making the **Anglo–French** and **Anglo–Russian Ententes**. Germany began her *Weltpolitik* when most of the world had already been divided up amongst the colonial powers, especially Britain and France, so her gains were negligible. She began the '**scramble for concessions**' in China by seizing Qingdao in the Shandong peninsula, as a naval base, in 1897 and during the **Spanish–American War** of 1898 compelled Spain to sell her the Caroline and Mariana Islands in the Pacific. In 1899 she acquired part of the Samoan group of islands. These were meagre acquisitions, indefensible in wartime.

**Westminster, Statute of** (1931), gave freedom to the British **dominions**. After the **First World War** the dominions were accepted as national states in their own right, whilst still being part of the British Empire. They attended the **Paris Peace Conference** and joined the **League of Nations** but there were still limits to their freedom. There was a right of appeal from the dominion courts to the Privy Council in London; and the Governor-General, appointed by the British government, could in theory withhold approval from the Acts of dominion parliaments. At the 1923 Imperial Conference it was agreed that dominions could make their own treaties with other countries and could pursue their own foreign policy. A further step was taken at the 1926 Conference, when the Balfour Report defined the dominions as 'autonomous communities within the British Empire, equal in status, in no way subordinate one to another in any aspect of their domestic or external affairs, though united by a common allegiance to the Crown and freely associated as members of the British Commonwealth of Nations.' The Statute of Westminster aimed at removing the limitations on the freedom of the dominions by applying the principles of the Balfour Report. They could stop the Governor-General withholding consent to their legislation, abolish appeals to the Privy Council and change their own Constitutions. Acts of the British parliament could not apply to the dominions without their consent. Only South Africa and the Irish Free State adopted the Statute in full. Canada renounced her right to alter her Constitution, so that the Anglo-Canadian majority could not interfere with the rights of French Canadians. Australia did not adopt the rights granted until 1942, New Zealand not until 1947.

**Westward expansion** (USA). In 1783, when the American colonies became independent, the population of the USA was three million, most of whom lived east of the Appalachian mountains. US territory expanded in two great movements, the first of which (1803–19) saw the **Louisiana Purchase** and the acquisition of Florida from Spain, partly by force and partly by purchase. Much of the territory acquired by the Louisiana Purchase, between the Mississippi river and the Rockies, was at first regarded as too arid for white settlement and was called the Great American Desert. It was decided to move the Indians living east of the Mississippi to lands west of the great river. The Removal Act of 1830 allowed President **Jackson** to arrange for this and in 1834 what is now the eastern part of Oklahoma was set aside as Indian territory. In ten years the eastern states had been cleared of Indians but they were to find no respite in the west.

The second great expansion of US territory took place between 1845 and 1853, when the present continental boundaries of the USA were fixed. A compromise was reached with Britain over Oregon territory, with the USA taking 285,000 square miles, **Texas** was annexed in 1845, adding another 390,000 square miles and after victory in the **Mexican–American War** of 1846–8, another 529,000 square miles, including New Mexico and California, were added. This territory was rounded off by the **Gadsden Purchase** of 1853. The frontier was moving inexorably west: in 1810 only one in seven Americans lived west of the Appalachians: by 1850 one in two did so. The Great American Desert was still largely unpopulated by whites but this changed in the next decades. Technological advances – the steel plough capable of cutting the tough sod of the prairies, barbed wire for fencing in farms, and machines like the McCormick reaper – made this possible, along with the **Homestead Act** of 1862 and the advance of the **railways**. Without the railways, capable of carrying beef and corn to distant markets, settlement of the Mid-West would have been impossible. The Indians had to be removed and this was done by bribery, threats and force but most effectively by destroying their source of livelihood, the buffalo. The Indians were herded into **Indian reservations**, not without resistance (see **Indian Wars**). The frontier had also moved east from the Pacific, as the quest for gold (see **Gold rushes**) and other minerals quickened. By 1890 the frontier had ceased to exist: white settlement extended from California to the

Atlantic coast, though the westward movement of population continued throughout the twentieth century.

**Whig Party.** American political party, formed in 1834 to oppose President Andrew **Jackson**. Northern financiers and industrialists, led by Daniel **Webster**, condemned Jackson's 'war' on the Bank of the USA. Westerners, led by Henry **Clay**, wanted federal support for improving communications, whilst in the South John C. **Calhoun** was appalled by Jackson's opposition to nullification (see **Nullification Doctrine**). All these groups joined together to form the Whig Party, named after the English **Whigs**, who had opposed the Crown's 'tyranny' just as the American Whigs opposed that of 'King Andrew I'. The party had support from all sections of the population, but it was basically conservative. Only two Whig Presidents were elected, William Henry Harrison in 1840 and Zachary Taylor in 1848: both died shortly after taking office. By this time slavery was the main national issue and it was this that destroyed the Whigs. When the **Kansas–Nebraska Act** was passed in 1854 all the Northern Whigs opposed it; nearly all the Southern Whigs supported it. Most Northern Whigs including **Lincoln** now joined the new **Republican Party**, whilst those in the South became Democrats (see **Democratic Party**). The Whig Party was dead by the end of the 1850s.

**Whigs.** A name which came into use in Britain in the 1670s to describe those who wanted to exclude Charles II's Catholic brother James, Duke of York (later James II), from the succession to the throne. Whigs stressed the importance of parliament as a brake on royal power and were enthusiastic supporters of the Glorious Revolution of 1688, which limited the power of the King and increased that of parliament. The Hanoverian succession (1714) was a disaster for the **Tories**, many of whom became implicated in the Jacobite rebellion of 1715, so Whigs dominated parliament for the next fifty years. They did not form a party but various factions, which gathered round prominent aristocrats who competed for power. Their fortunes changed under **George III**, who sought to increase royal authority, and they were kept out of office from 1783, when **Pitt** the Younger became Prime Minister, until 1830, apart from the brief interlude of the Ministry of All the Talents (1806–7).

Supporters of liberty and religious toleration under Charles James **Fox**, they came to power in 1830 as champions of **parliamentary reform** and in the next eleven years, under **Grey** and **Melbourne**, passed a series of measures, including the **Reform Act** of 1832. Many Whigs in the 1830s referred to themselves as Liberal and, with radicals and Peelites, formed the core of the **Liberal Party** under **Gladstone**. The term Whig then referred to the landowning aristocracy in the Liberal Party, many of whom joined the Tories when the Liberals split over **Home Rule for Ireland** in 1886. Since then the name Whig has ceased to have any political meaning.

**White Australia policy** effectively prevented the immigration of non-Europeans into Australia. In the 1860s Chinese and Kanakas (South Pacific islanders) had entered Australia, as there was a shortage of labour on the Queensland sugar plantations, but by the 1880s the trade unions were objecting, as cheap imported labour was a threat to the standard of living of their members. By 1890 all states had legislation restricting immigration, a policy which had strong public approval. Many supporters spoke in racial terms of preserving purity and of avoiding 'a mongrel' nation. As soon as the new Commonwealth of Australia was formed in 1901, the legislature passed an Immigration Restriction Act, which excluded non-European immigrants by imposing a test in a European language (changed in 1905 to any 'prescribed language' in order to appease the Japanese). At the **Paris Peace Conference** (1919) **Hughes** fought vigorously and successfully against a Japanese amendment to the Covenant of the **League of Nations** providing for racial equality. The White Australia policy was applied to the native Aborigines too. In the 1920s and 1930s reserves were set up where they had to live, unless they were permitted to take employment elsewhere. They were not citizens of the Commonwealth of Australia until 1948 and until then had no legal rights. The White Australia policy was maintained throughout the first half of the twentieth century.

**White Terror** (1794–7) An attack on ex-terrorists, and all who had done well out of the **French Revolution**, by those who had formerly been persecuted. White was the colour of the Bourbons, so 'White Terror' implies that it was a royalist movement, which was only partly true. Most who took part did not want to restore the old regime but sought vengeance on those who had taken part in the **Terror**, or who had benefited from the Revolution by buying Church lands, or by becoming government officials. The White Terror did not cover the whole of France but was confined to a score of departments near the Loire and south of Lyon. In Paris it was limited to the activities of the *jeunesse dorée* ('gilded youth'), middle-class youths who dressed extravagantly with square collars, ear-rings and long hair turned back at the neck, like those about to be guillotined. They formed gangs to beat up **Jacobins** and *sans-culottes* but there was little bloodshed. The White Terror elsewhere was much more violent. In Brittany the Chouan movement (named after its leader Jean Cottereau, known as Chouan) controlled most of the area from 1794–6, and under royalist leaders sought English support. In 1795 3,000 royalist troops were landed at Quiberon Bay and were joined by thousands of Chouans. General Hoche, forewarned, sealed them off and forced them to surrender. Over 700 were shot before Hoche swept across Brittany, wiping out the Chouans. In the south the murder gangs of the White Terror were not such a threat to the Republic, so little use was made of troops to crush them. This allowed them to massacre opponents in the Rhône valley, where there had been a savage repression of the **Federal Revolt**. Here prison massacres reminiscent of the **September massacres** in 1792 took place but this time with Jacobins as victims. Two thousand were killed in the south-east in 1795: the killing continued there throughout 1796 and for much of 1797.

**Wilberforce, William,** see **Evangelical Movement**

**'Wild West'.** A term used to describe frontier society in the USA in the second half of the nineteenth century. Earlier in the century the area between the Missouri river and the Rockies, with its low rainfall and flat, endless plains, was regarded as unsuitable for white settlement. It was known as the Great American Desert, the home of Indian tribes and the buffalo. The first pioneers in this area were miners and cattlemen, followed by farmers after the **American Civil War**. Popular ideas of the 'Wild West' were the product of cheap novels, which began to appear in 1860, and which romanticized the exploits of real people like Billy the Kid, Jesse James,

Buffalo Bill and Calamity Jane. It was a world of stage-coaches, outlaws, Indian attacks, gold rushes and cattle rustling, all made familiar by 'Western' films in the twentieth century. For Americans the 'Wild West' – 'the real genuine America' for Walt Whitman – typified the qualities they admired most: democracy, equality, toughness and self-reliance. It did not last long. By 1890 the Indians had been confined to **Indian reservations**, their hunting grounds were occupied by white settlers (see **Westward expansion**), the 'long drives' had come to an end (see **Cattle trails**) and **transcontinental railroads** criss-crossed the country.

**William I** (1797–1888). King of Prussia (1861–88) and German Emperor (1871–88). William became regent in Prussia in 1858 when his brother, **Frederick William IV**, had a stroke, and did not become King until he was sixty-four. A devout Protestant, he believed that he was responsible only to God but he had a strong sense of honour and was a man of his word: he accepted the Prussian Constitution of 1850 (see Frederick William IV), although he disliked it, because it had been granted by a king. William was a military man, who was deeply suspicious of Austria and wanted to avenge the humiliation of Olmütz, when Austria forced Prussia to abandon the **Erfurt Union**. He therefore asked his War Minister, von **Roon**, to strengthen the army, which he did in 1862 by increasing the length of service from two to three years and by getting rid of the *Landwehr* (a citizen militia with mainly middle-class officers). When the Prussian **Diet** objected to the *Landwehr* changes and refused to pass the bill, there was a constitutional crisis. William would not give way, as he considered that the Diet had no right to interfere with the armed forces, of which he was commander. He thought of abdicating, until Roon persuaded him to make **Bismarck** Minister-President. Bismarck ignored the Diet and carried through the army reforms. After that the King became dependent on his chief minister, though he sometimes disagreed with him (William did not approve of the **Dual Alliance** with Austria in 1879). Bismarck could always get his way by threatening resignation. At the time of the **Hohenzollern candidature for the Spanish throne** the King could see that this would provoke France and pressed Leopold to withdraw, which he did, much to Bismarck's mortification. Bismarck was able to bring about war with France only by distorting, in the **Ems telegram**, an interview William had with the French ambassador. It was this **Franco-Prussian War** which completed the unification of Germany and made William German Emperor in 1871.

**William II** (1859–1941). King of Prussia and German Emperor (1888–1918). The eldest son of Crown Prince Frederick of Prussia (later Emperor Frederick III) and of his wife Victoria, daughter of Queen Victoria, William was born with a left arm that was virtually paralysed and several inches shorter than his right arm. Even as an adult he needed help in dressing and in cutting up his food. William was lazy, disliked routine work and reading lengthy reports, and consequently his knowledge of political affairs was often superficial. His life was an endless round of balls, cruises, hunting trips and parades, which he adored. He was obsessed with the armed forces, invariably appeared in public in military uniform and often chose soldiers as his advisers. When there was a clash between civil and military authority, he took the army's side. Impetuous and volatile, **Bismarck** compared him to a balloon, which had to be held on a string or it would go 'no one knows where'. He was renowned for his intemperate statements, as during the 1905 Ruhr miners' strike, when he declared that: 'First, the socialists must be gunned down . . . in a bloodbath if necessary.' Such remarks alarmed his ministers. 'The phrase current amongst all parties in the **Reichstag**,' wrote Holstein of the Foreign Office in 1896, '"That the behaviour of the Emperor can only be explained pathologically", is taking effect quietly but devastatingly.' 'Such a hot-headed, conceited and wrong-headed young man', was Queen Victoria's stern judgement. The Emperor had considerable powers under the German Constitution: he appointed all ministers, who were responsible to him and not to the Reichstag, was in charge of foreign policy and was Commander of the armed forces. He wanted to rule personally, so he began by dismissing Bismarck. Yet in spite of his boasting that he alone made policy and that Germany 'must follow me wherever I go', his personal rule was a myth. As he suffered from depression and nervous disorders, his ministers invariably had their way. He deferred to them over every major difference of opinion, even when he was unwilling, as in **Caprivi**'s decision in 1890 not to renew the **Reinsurance Treaty** with Russia. In the *Daily Telegraph* **Affair** (1908) he was much criticized, although he had behaved correctly in submitting the text of the interview to Chancellor **Bülow** before publication. During the **First World War** he was ignored more and more, until, deserted by the High Command and his ministers, he was forced to abdicate in 1918. He fled to Holland, where he lived as a country gentleman until his death.

**Wilson, Thomas Woodrow** (1856–1924). Twenty-eighth President of the USA (1913–21). Wilson was born in Virginia, the son of a Presbyterian minister, who was a slave-owner. In 1890 he became a professor at Princeton where he taught history and political science and in 1902 was President of that university. He was elected Governor of New Jersey, where he gained the **Democratic Party** presidential nomination. In the election he promised a New Freedom by smashing the trusts, lowering tariffs and revising the financial system. His appeal was successful, as he was fighting a **Republican Party** split between the supporters of Howard **Taft** and Theodore **Roosevelt**. He was the first Southerner to become President since Andrew **Johnson** and the first Democrat for twenty years. Racial discrimination now entered the federal government: Negroes were segregated from whites in government departments and black office-holders in the South were dismissed or downgraded. Wilson was determined to be a strong Pesident and revived the custom, dropped by **Jefferson** and not used since, of addressing Congress in person on major matters. He had a firmer control over legislation than any of his predecessors and showed great skill and determination in persuading Congress to pass a series of progressive (see **Progressive Movement**) measures. Tariffs were reduced significantly for the first time since the **American Civil War** and a federal income tax was introduced to make up for the loss of revenue. Federal Reserve Banks were created in 1913 to control the money supply and provide credit. The attack on the trusts was spear-headed by the Clayton Act of 1914, which outlawed exclusive sales contracts, rebates, interlocking directorates and price-cutting, if this was aimed at getting rid of competition. The Act also tried to help the **trade unions** by saying they were not illegal combinations in restraint of trade, that peaceful strikes and picketing were legal and that injunctions should not normally be used in labour disputes. Samuel **Gompers** called it 'labor's charter of freedom' but its provisions were made almost meaningless in the 1920s by conservative judges. The same was true of the Federal Trade Commission (1914), formed to act against businesses using unfair methods of competition. In 1916 Wilson supported the Federal Farm Loan Act, which set up banks to supply long-term credit to farmers. He also provided workmen's compensation for federal employees and aided the passage of the first federal child labour law, which limited child labour in factories, and a law that granted an eight-hour day for railroad workers. These laws showed that he had abandoned states' rights and *laissez-faire* and made him one of the most reforming presidents.

In his foreign policy Wilson was determined to abandon Theodore Roosevelt's 'big stick' and Taft's **dollar diplomacy** and said he would deal with Latin American states 'upon terms of equality and law'. Yet he wanted to protect American interests and so found himself intervening more than either Roosevelt or Taft had done. He continued to control Nicaragua's finances and kept Marines there. In 1915, when there was a revolution in Haiti, he sent Marines to take control of the country, and did the same a year later in the Dominican Republic. When the **First World War** began in 1914 he proclaimed American neutrality. The Democrats fought and won the 1916 presidential election with the slogan 'He kept us out of the war' and in January 1917 Wilson affirmed that 'There will be no war.' Yet on 31 January the Germans informed the US government that they would begin unrestricted submarine warfare. This and the **Zimmermann telegram** led Wilson to ask Congress on 2 April to declare war on Germany, which it did. 'The world must be made safe for democracy', said the President.

The President put forward his vision of the world which would follow the end of the war with his **Fourteen Points**, the most important of which was for him the formation of a **League of Nations**, but the congressional elections of 1918 were a severe blow to his hopes, as the Republicans gained control of both Houses of Congress. He spent six months at the **Paris Peace Conference**, where he was rapturously received but the Treaty of **Versailles** was far from being a 'peace without victors', though the League of Nations was set up and for this Wilson was awarded the Nobel Peace Prize in 1919. In July he presented the Treaty for ratification by the Senate but there was much opposition from isolationists and Republicans. In Washington he had a major stroke but still refused to countenance any amendments to the Treaty, which the Senate finally rejected in 1920. For the rest of his presidency he lay in the White House, doing and saying nothing. In the presidential election of 1920 the Republican candidate, Warren Harding, gained one of the biggest victories in US history.

**Windsor, House of.** The name of the British royal family, adopted in 1917 by King **George V** to replace that of Saxe-Coburg-Gotha, derived from Prince **Albert** (1819–61). As there was strong anti-German feeling during the **First World War**, George V felt that an English name was needed for the royal family. This gave Emperor **William II** the opportunity to make one of his rare jokes, when he said that he looked forward to seeing 'The Merry Wives of Saxe-Coburg-Gotha'.

**Witte, Sergei, Count** (1849–1915). Russian Minister of Finance (1892–1903) and Prime Minister (1905–6). Witte realized that Russia would have to industrialize rapidly, if she was to remain a Great Power. If she did not move quickly, she would be in a position of colonial dependence on the countries of Western Europe: an exporter of raw materials and an importer of manufactured goods. The way to industrialize quickly was to borrow foreign capital and expertise. This would be used to develop communications and heavy industry but the state must take the lead to provide a market and money for investment. Witte found it difficult to attract foreign investment, as the rouble was not convertible – its rate fluctuated wildly in terms of gold. He needed therefore a reserve of gold and a stable level of money in circulation. He obtained this by increasing enormously indirect taxes, which fell mainly on the peasantry. In 1897 he issued a new rouble, freely convertible. Foreign loans now flowed into Russia but a price had to be paid: in 1900 20 per cent of the budget was used to service the foreign debt, ten times as much as was spent on education. Much of the investment went into the **Trans-Siberian railway** and other railways, which increased from

13,000 miles of track in 1880 to 33,000 in 1900 and 45,000 in 1917. The coal, oil and iron industries also developed rapidly, especially in the Ukraine, which became the centre of heavy industry. In the 1890s Russia's average annual growth rate was 8 per cent, higher than that of any other industrial country (though starting from a lower base).

Witte's industrialization brought profound strains to all parts of Russian society. The increase in import duties and indirect taxes in the 1890s reduced a standard of living that was already low. 'Your Majesty has 130 million subjects,' Witte wrote to Tsar **Nicholas II** in 1898. 'Of them barely more than half live, the rest vegetate.' Witte was gambling on industrial expansion improving living conditions, before peasants and workers found the burden intolerable. The gamble failed, with famine in the central Volga area in 1898–9, a slump which began in 1899 and the **Russian Revolution of 1905**. Witte's attempts, therefore, to strengthen the autocracy by modernization had precisely the reverse effect. Opposition spread to the Court and his fellow ministers, and he was dismissed in 1903. Nicholas recalled him to negotiate the Treaty of **Portsmouth** with Japan in 1905 and it was largely on Witte's advice that the Tsar issued the October Manifesto. The Tsar never liked Witte – he was too much of a reformer – but made him Prime Minister in 1905, so that he could negotiate a loan from France. Once this was achieved he was dismissed again in 1906. Witte had no illusions about Russia's continuing backwardness and strongly opposed her entry into the **First World War**.

**Wolseley, Garnet Joseph, 1st Viscount** (1833–1913). British field marshal. The son of a shopkeeper, he had to show outstanding ability to rise in the nineteenth-century British army from such lowly origins. Early in his career he saw considerable foreign service in Burma, the **Crimean War**, the **Indian Mutiny** and the second **Opium War** in China. He was soon regarded as one of the most efficient and innovative British officers and collaborated with **Cardwell**, the Secretary for War, in 1871–3 in reforming the army. In 1874 his defeat of the **Asante** in the Gold Coast made him a popular hero in England, where W. S. Gilbert dubbed him 'the very model of a modern major-general'. After the British disaster at

Isandhlwana in the **Zulu Wars** in 1879, Wolseley was sent out to South Africa, where he defeated the Zulu King **Cetshwayo**. In 1882 he was in Egypt, dealing with the rising of **Urabi Pasha**, whom he defeated at Tel el-Kebir and so began the lengthy British occupation of Egypt. Three years later Wolseley was sent to the Sudan to relieve **Gordon**, besieged in Khartoum by the **Mahdi**, but he arrived two days after Gordon had been killed. The rest of his time in the army was spent as a reformer. In 1895 he reached the peak of his success when he became Commander-in-Chief, a post abolished in 1904.

**Women, emancipation of.** Throughout the nineteenth century nearly all women were firmly under the control of men. They had few legal rights or opportunities for education or paid employment. The woman's role was seen as that of a wife and mother, whose place was in the home. In Japan her life was governed by the 'three obediences': in childhood to her father or elder brother, after marriage to her husband, and as a widow to her son. Women had no legal status in the Japanese civil code (1898). More opportunities for the employment of women in the West came with industrialization: in the textile factories, as secretaries (after the invention of the typewriter) and as shop assistants, but most of these jobs were unskilled and were poorly paid. The growth of elementary education expanded the teaching profession, which provided a respectable occupation for unmarried, middle-class women. Yet in the 1890s, 75 per cent of women in the developed countries of Europe were not in paid employment, as women usually stopped work when they married. Women gradually gained more legal rights in Western Europe and access to higher education and the professions in the late nineteenth century: in France in 1903 a woman lawyer pleaded for the first time in a European court. In Britain women were given property rights from 1870 (though they could not hold property on the same terms as men until 1926), whilst the Sex Disqualification Act (1919) removed restrictions on women entering the professions. The first woman MP was elected in 1918, the first woman Justice of the Peace was appointed in 1920 and the first woman called to the Bar in 1922. Women became councillors, magistrates and mayors in slowly increasing numbers.

Socially many European and American women became more emancipated in the first half of the twentieth century (see the '**Roaring Twenties**'): they could go out unchaperoned to the cinema or dance hall and their dress became more daring (hemlines rose and by 1925 were above the knee). Birth control had reduced the size of families and begun to relieve women of the heaviest of their traditional burdens. Yet in 1939 women remained in an inferior position. They were employed in unskilled jobs with half the wages of men and were regarded with great suspicion by male trade unionists, as a threat to jobs and wage levels. Traditional attitudes continued: the place of married women was in the home (women in the British civil service had to leave when they married), so women had to choose between marriage and a career. Few reached the top in professional or political life: there were only nine women MPs in Britain in 1939. In most of the world – in Asia, Africa, Latin America and the peasant societies of southern and eastern Europe – there had been no emancipation of women at all. It was still a man's world.

**Women's suffrage.** The right of women to vote had been demanded by **feminist movements** in Europe and the USA in the nineteenth century but made little headway before the **First World War**, as most males were hostile or indifferent. New Zealand was the first country to give the vote to women in 1893, followed by the states of Australia between 1893 and 1909. In Europe the only countries to enfranchise women before 1914 were Finland and Norway. The important role played by women during the war, far more than the activities of the **suffragettes**, helped to persuade the British parliament to give the vote to women over thirty in 1918 and women over twenty-one in 1928. In the Soviet Union women's suffrage came in 1917, in Germany in 1919. The first state in the USA to give women the vote was Wyoming in 1890 but it was not until 1920, when the **Anthony** Amendment to the US Constitution was ratified, that all American women had the vote. Between 1914 and 1939 twenty-eight countries gave the vote to women, though Catholic countries had to wait longer, as many liberals and socialists feared that women would be influenced by the Church and would vote for conservative parties, as they did in the

**Spanish Second Republic** (1931–6). Women did not get the vote in France, Italy and Japan until 1945.

**Workers' Opposition.** A group within the Russian **Communist Party** who wanted more democracy within the Party and also wanted trade unions to run industry, rather than managers appointed by the Party. Alexandra **Kollontai** drew up their programme, which asked for 'freedom of opinion and discussion, the right to criticize within the Party'. **Lenin** disagreed with them and felt that after the **Kronstadt Rising** all opposition should be barred as 'harmful and impermissible'. He therefore proposed two resolutions at the Tenth Party Congress in March 1921. One condemned the Workers' Opposition: the other forbade the forming of 'factions' within the Party and ordered the immediate dissolution of those already existing. Failure to comply would mean expulsion from the Party. These resolutions suppressed any serious opposition, or even discussion, within the Communist Party, which was regarded as more important than the individual. They also contributed to the dilemma which faced **Bukharin** and others in the **Great Purge** trials of the 1930s: was their loyalty to the Party more important than their own beliefs? This dilemma is brilliantly described in Arthur Koestler's novel *Darkness at Noon.*

**World economy.** The bringing together of different parts of the world into one economic system, in which the separate areas are interdependent. In 1800 most regions of the world had either no contact at all with one another or had only a superficial connection. All this changed in the nineteenth century, as a result of the **Industrial Revolution** in Europe and the technological changes which this brought about. The **railway**, the steamship (see **Transport revolution**) and the electric telegraph (see **Communications revolution**) broke down the isolation of communities within different countries and of one country from another. The fall in shipping charges and the appearance of bulk carriers produced for the first time a world market, governed by world prices. New waterways – the **Suez Canal** (1869) and the **Panama Canal** (1914) – drastically cut the time needed to travel by sea from Europe to India and the Far East and from the east to the west coast of America. European military dominance also helped to bring about a world economy by forcing China to open its ports to foreign trade in the **Opium War** (1839–42), and by forcibly ending the two hundred year isolation of Japan as a closed country (*sakoku*) in 1854. **Imperialism**, particularly the **Scramble for Africa**, brought much of the world into closer contact with Europe.

The technological developments which accompanied industrialization depended on raw materials, which were found all over the world. The motor car required oil and rubber. Oil came mainly from the USA and Russia up to 1914, by which time the reserves of Persia were being exploited. Rubber came wholly from the tropics – the Congo, the Amazon and later Malaya. Tin, needed for plating and canning, also came from Malaya, which increased its trade a hundred-fold between 1874 and 1914 and became the richest of all colonies. The electrical and motor industries needed copper, which came from Chile, Peru, Northern Rhodesia (Zambia), the Belgian Congo (Zaire) and Australia. The largest lead–zinc deposits in the world opened at Broken Hill in Australia in 1883. Nickel was discovered in Canada and gold on the **Rand** in South Africa (1885). There was a demand in Europe not only for metals but also for food, which could be satisfied when refrigeration came into use from 1876. Grain and meat came from the temperate zones (North and South America, Australia, New Zealand), sugar (and tobacco) was grown in Cuba, coffee in Brazil and Colombia, tea in India and Ceylon, cocoa in the Gold Coast. Tropical fruits (the banana was almost unknown in Europe in 1880) also became available from the Caribbean. Soap manufacturers wanted the vegetable oils of West Africa, farmers the nitrates from Chile as fertilizers.

Many countries became dependent on one or two primary products, which they exported to world markets (in 1914 58 per cent of the value of Brazil's exports was in coffee): their economies could, therefore, be devastated if prices fell steeply, as they did during the **Great Depression** (1929–39). The fortunes of farmers in Europe came to depend less on nature (the size of the harvest) than on forces in world markets: as American grain flooded into Europe in the 1870s and 1880s prices fell, causing a great European agricultural depression. All parts of the world were not equally affected by the world economy: in 1940 much of Africa and Asia and most of Latin America still lay outside it.

**Xi'an incident** (1936). In the 1930s **Jiang Jieshi** (Chiang Kai-shek), leader of the **Guomindang**, put the defeat of the Chinese Communist Party (CCP) before everything else. He had forced them out of the **Jiangxi Soviet** and into the **Long March**, which ended in **Yanan** in Shaanxi province in 1935. Meanwhile many Chinese criticized Jiang for not fighting the Japanese, who had occupied **Manchuria** in 1931, and supported CCP calls for a **United Front** to resist Japan. Jiang ignored these calls and in 1936 sent his nationalist troops to attack the communists in Shaanxi. Alarmed at their lack of success and enthusiasm, he flew to Xi'an in December 1936, only to be placed under house arrest by the nationalist commander, Zhang Xueliang, who resented the Japanese seizure of his native Manchuria. Zhang demanded that the campaign against the communists should end and that all Chinese should unite against Japan. If Jiang did not agree, he threatened to execute him as a traitor. **Stalin** was convinced that only Jiang had the prestige to unite all Chinese against Japan, so he urged the CCP to obtain Jiang's release. Zhou Enlai, therefore, negotiated with Jiang to form a second United Front. The CCP agreed to recognize Jiang as head of state and promised to modify its policy of confiscating the land of rich peasants and landlords. When Jiang accepted he was released but the CCP was in a much stronger position than at the time of the first United Front in 1923. Now it had its own army and territory directly under its control.

**Yalta Conference** (4–11 February 1945). The second 'Big Three' summit meeting (the first was the Teheran Conference in 1943) between **Roosevelt**, **Stalin** and **Churchill**, held at Yalta in the Crimea. It dealt mainly with the arrangements to be made after the **Second World War** in Germany, Poland and the Far East. The Allies had agreed in 1944 that Germany should be divided into American, Soviet and British zones of military occupation. This was ratified at Yalta but Churchill persuaded Stalin to accept a French zone too. The unconditional surrender of Germany was again demanded. In Poland, Stalin had already set up a Communist-dominated provisional government. The Western Allies protested at this, so Stalin agreed to include 'democratic leaders from Poland itself and from Poles abroad' and he promised that 'free elections' would be held in Poland. These pledges were not honoured. Stalin wanted to give a large part of eastern Germany to Poland as compensation for the Polish territory the Soviet Union had taken. The Western Allies accepted the **Curzon Line** as the Soviet–Polish frontier and although they were unhappy that the **Oder–Neisse Line** should be the Polish–German boundary, there was little they could do about it, as Russian troops occupied the area. The Soviet Union promised to enter the war against Japan three months after the war with Germany ended and in return would recover what Russia had lost at the Treaty of **Portsmouth** after the **Russo-Japanese War** (1904–5): southern Sakhalin, the Kurile Islands, the lease of Port Arthur and the running of the Manchurian railways. Surprisingly the Russians accepted an American occupation of Japan. The Americans realized that Russian troops would be in Korea before the Americans, so they persuaded the Russians to accept a Russian military occupation of Korea north of the 38th parallel and an American occupation south of it. These were supposed to be temporary measures prior to the unification of Korea.

All agreed to the maintenance of the status quo in Outer Mongolia (i.e. to Russian control). An agreement by the Western Allies to send back to Russia all Soviet citizens caused much controversy later: by September 1945 two million had been returned, many to be shot as collaborators with the Germans and many others to be sent to **forced labour camps**. The Soviet Union agreed to the establishment of the United Nations. The Yalta agreements were much criticized in the USA for making Stalin's position much stronger in both Europe and the Far East but there was little the other powers could do, as Russian troops already occupied much of Germany and Eastern Europe and as Britain and the USA were anxious to obtain Stalin's commitment to war against Japan, which they thought was essential if hostilities there were to be ended quickly. 'I didn't say it was good, Adolf,' Roosevelt told his friend Adolf Berle, 'I said it was the best I could do.'

**Yamagata Aritomo** (1838–1922). Japanese soldier and statesman. A lower *samurai* from Choshu, Yamagata studied military systems in Europe (1869–70) after the **Meiji Restoration** of 1868. He revolutionized the army when he got rid of the *samurai* monopoly of military power and introduced conscription in 1872. All Japanese males over twenty were liable for three years' service in the army and four in the reserves. As War Minister (1872–8) and Chief of Staff (1878–82 and 1904–6), he reorganized the army on German lines, equipping it with modern rifles and artillery and creating a General Staff. His success was shown in the ease with which the Japanese army, under his command, won the **Sino-Japanese War** of 1894–5. As the army was all-important to him, he sponsored the imperial edict of 1900, by which only soldiers or sailors on the active service list could be appointed Minister of War or Navy Minister. This meant that a cabinet could be forced out of office, if the army or navy objected strongly to its policy. Yamagata was Home Minister for most of the time from 1883–90 and Prime Minister from 1889–91 and again from 1898–1900 but he was no admirer of democracy, which he described as 'an evil poison', or of political parties. He thought that opposition to the government was immoral and that political parties promoted sectional interests at the expense of national unity and would, if they had the power, make local and central government into a **spoils system**. He opposed **Ito Hirobumi**'s view that the ruling oligarchy should form its own political party. It was bitter conflict with the **Diet**, first elected during his premiership, that led to his resignation in 1891. When he was Prime Minister for a second time he tried to restrict the activities of political parties by the **Peace Police Law**. From 1905–22 he was President of the Privy Council and a *genro*, an elder statesman, who was a personal adviser to the Emperor and therefore had great influence in appointments to the great offices of state. Yamagata was a major conservative influence in Japanese politics, especially after the death of Ito in 1909, almost until his own death.

**Yamamoto Isoruku** (1884–1943). Japanese admiral. While studying at Harvard and as Japanese naval attaché in Washington he recognized the industrial might of the USA and thought that war with the USA and Britain should be avoided, as Japan could not win a prolonged conflict against both powers. This was an unpopular view in Japan, as was his opposition to an alliance with Germany. In spite of this he was appointed Commander-in-Chief of the Combined Fleet in 1939. As one of the first in Japan to recognize the importance of air power in naval strategy, he pressed for the construction of aircraft carriers rather than of battleships, and drew up plans for action in the Pacific in case of war. The initial Japanese war plan was to seize the Philippines, Malaya and the Dutch East Indies and then defend them against American attack. Yamamato realized that the US fleet would then be able to attack Japan's communications with the conquered territories and so favoured a pre-emptive strike against **Pearl Harbor**, to destroy the American Pacific Fleet. South-East Asia could then be conquered rapidly and Japan's enemies would be forced to make peace within six months of the war starting. Although the attack on Pearl Harbor was a brilliant success, Yamamoto's plans were disrupted, as the American aircraft carriers were not in Pearl Harbor at the time of the attack. He had an opportunity to knock out the US carriers at the battle of **Midway** (June 1942) but made tactical errors in dividing his superior forces, so that they could not support one another, and in attacking the Aleutian Islands at the same time as Midway. The great American victory there was a turning-point in the **Pacific**

**War**; after it Japan's fortunes declined. In April 1943, US planes, working on Japanese wireless messages which were decoded, shot down and killed Yamamato over the Solomon Islands.

**Yamashita Tomoyuki** (1885–1946). Japanese general. In the 1930s Yamashita was a member of the Imperial Way, a nationalist faction dedicated to the establishment of a military government in Japan, which it attempted to set up in the **February Rising** (1936). Yamashita had private knowledge of this, even if he was not directly involved, but it held up his military career only for a short time. When the **Pacific War** (1941–5) began he was put in charge of the invasion of Malaya, where he met with remarkable success. Landing on 8 December 1941 with 70,000 troops in the north, he was outnumbered by the opposing 88,000 Allied troops but he had the inestimable advantage of air and sea superiority. He could therefore outflank Allied strongpoints by sea or by going through the jungle and conquered Malaya in fifty-four days. By this time there were over 130,000 British and Commonwealth troops on the islands of **Singapore**, which was forced to surrender after only a week, the most humiliating defeat ever suffered by the British army. As **Tojo** regarded the 'Tiger of Malaya' as a rival, he was transferred to **Manchukuo** and so took no part in the Pacific Campaigns of 1942–3. After the fall of Tojo (July 1944) Yamashita was put in charge of Japanese forces in the Philippines, just before **MacArthur** invaded. He knew his mission was a hopeless one but aimed to tie down as many US troops for as long as possible. Forced out of Leyte in December 1944 and Manila in February 1945, his tenacious resistance continued in the highlands of the main island, Luzon, until the end of the war. He was charged with allowing members of his command to commit atrocities and though there was no evidence that he was directly responsible, he was sentenced to death and hanged.

**Yanan.** Capital of communist China from January 1937 to March 1947. When the Chinese communists were driven from the **Jiangxi Soviet** by **Jiang Jieshi** (Chiang Kai-shek) they went on the **Long March**, which ended in Shaanxi province. There, protected by mountains from nationalist attack, they established a new base from which they could expand. Membership of the Chinese Communist

Party (CCP) grew from 20,000 in 1936 to 1.2 million in 1945. The Red Army too grew rapidly, from 22,000 in 1936 to 880,000 in 1945. During the **Sino-Japanese War** (1937–45), Yanan became the symbol of national resistance to Japan, when thousands of intellectuals and students flocked from Beijing (Peking) and other cities to Shaanxi. The communists operated behind the Japanese lines in the countryside, which the Japanese were not able to control, and by 1945 dominated an area, mainly in North China, with a population of ninety-six million. From 1936 the CCP was allied to the **Guomindang** in a **United Front** against Japan and so the CCP stressed class harmony and helped the poor by rent and interest reductions rather than by confiscating land. However, Jiang, jealous of CCP influence, imposed a blockade on Yanan from mid-1939 and used half a million troops to enforce it. **Mao Zedong** therefore adopted a more radical style of government. He felt that the higher officials, many with an urban, intellectual background, were becoming divorced from the poor peasants and therefore began a rectification campaign, to 're-educate' officials, who were encouraged to take part in manual labour in a 'to the village campaign'. The 'mass line' was stressed: the need for party officials to keep in close touch with peasants and workers. The army was expected to help on the land, especially at harvest time, scrupulously paid for its food and other necessities and did not molest local women. As a result, the CCP steadily grew in popularity. Schools were set up to promote literacy and, to counter the economic blockade, small-scale industry was encouraged, with peasants involved in iron-smelting and weaving. Many of these practices were revived in the Great Leap Forward (1958) and the Cultural Revolution (1966–76). During the Yanan period Mao became the undisputed leader and theoretician of the CCP. He was elected chairman of the Politburo and of the Central Committee in 1943 and increasing importance was attached to his writings, which marked the beginning of a personality cult. The new party constitution in 1945 said that Mao's thought was the 'single ideological guide' for the CCP. Foreigners who visited Yanan were impressed by the high morale and dedication of the communists, especially the American journalist Edgar Snow, whose *Red Star Over China* was based on his experiences there.

**Yezhov, Nikolai** (1894–1939). Yezhov was head of the Soviet secret police (**NKVD**) from September 1936 to December 1938, at a time when the **Great Purges** reached their height. This period is known in Russia as the *Yezhovshchina* ('the time of Yezhov'). He was responsible for the second and third Moscow show trials and for the secret trial in June 1937, which led to the execution of Marshal Tukhachevsky, Commander-in-Chief of the Red Army, and other senior officers. Soviet estimates indicate that at this time at least seven million people were arrested, including half the Communist Party membership, 70 per cent of the Central Committee and half the officer corps. According to Robert Conquest, 90 per cent of them were either executed or died later in **forced labour camps**. Yezhov was called 'the bloodthirsty dwarf' (he was only five feet tall). His reign of terror came to an end when he, like his predecessor Yagoda, was arrested and shot.

**Young, Brigham** (1801–77). When he took over as Prophet of the **Mormons**, after Joseph Smith's murder in 1844, Young decided that the only way they could avoid persecution was to move to an area where no one else wanted to live. He had heard travellers' reports of the Great Basin, where there were high, barren mountains and a great salt lake but also good farming land. He set off, the first of 16,000 Saints, in February 1846 and crossed the Mississippi. Conditions were atrocious – severe frost, blizzards – but they survived owing to the leadership and strength of will of Brigham Young. They reached what became Salt Lake City in Utah in July 1847. Crops could be grown here only if the land was extensively irrigated, so Young declared that 'there shall be no private ownership of the streams that come out of the canyons, nor of the timber that grows on the hills. These belong to the people: all the people.' The Mormons built irrigation channels and were given land according to the amount they had worked. This system is still used in a modified form today and is the most successful cooperative undertaking ever made in the USA. Young was a dictator – stern, unbending, he loved power and removed all rivals. Though he was 'husband' to seventy women, he emphasized plain living and, in accordance with the original Mormon creed, did not allow the use of alcohol or even of tea and coffee. He became Governor in the new territory of

Utah in 1850 but owing to the violence of Mormons against Gentiles he had to give this up in 1857. He nevertheless continued to be the effective ruler of the territory until his death.

**Young Plan** (1929). The report of a commission on **reparations**, chaired by the American banker Owen D. Young. The **Dawes Plan** (1924) had tried to deal with reparations but by 1929 the German economy was in difficulties again, so the problem was re-examined. Young suggested that the total amount of reparations should be reduced by about three-quarters, that Germany should make annual payments on a sliding scale up to 1988 and that foreign control of reparations should end. This Plan was accepted by all the governments concerned, though in Germany it was attacked by the nationalists, communists and Nazis. Hjalmar **Schacht**, President of the Reichsbank, resigned in protest at the Plan. With the **Great Depression** biting deeply in 1931 the Hoover Moratorium suspended all payments of reparations and war debts for one year. A year later a conference of creditors at Lausanne ended reparations.

**Young Turks**. Turkish officers who wanted to modernize the **Ottoman Empire** and prevent its collapse. They ruled Turkey from 1908-18. In 1908 some army officers, disgusted at the ineffectual government of Sultan **Abdulhamid** and fearful that the Ottoman Empire was about to break up, staged a *coup*. They forced the Sultan to restore the 1876 Constitution, with an elected parliament, abolish censorship and disband his corps of 30,000 spies. The liberalism of the Young Turks did not last long. When Abdulhamid tried to rouse the garrison in Istanbul against them he was deposed and the Young Turks became more authoritarian: from 1912 they ruled by decree. As they believed that the weakness of Turkey was due to the inertia of Islamic society, they continued the secular reforms of the **Tanzimat**. They issued decrees for the emancipation of women and transferred control of Muslim schools and courts to state ministries. They were not able to stem the decline of the Empire, which between 1908 and 1912 lost all its remaining European provinces, except for Eastern Thrace. When the **First World War** began in 1914 the Young Turks joined in on Germany's side and as a result of Allied victories in the Fertile Crescent lost the Arab provinces the Ottomans had acquired 400 years earlier. Far from making the Ottoman Empire stronger, the Young Turks had brought about its complete destruction.

**Yuan Shikai** (1859–1916). Chinese soldier and statesman. His early career was devoted to making his New Army the most modern and efficient in China. He became a favourite of the Empress Dowager **Cixi** and backed her *coup* in 1898 to end the **Hundred Days Reform**. After this he became Governor of Shandong, Governor-General of Zhili province and a member of the Grand Council in Beijing (Peking). When Cixi died, his opponents, jealous of his influence, forced him to retire but he was recalled in 1911 to command government forces, in order to suppress the **Chinese Revolution** of 1911. Instead, he joined the revolution, on being promised that he would become President of the new republic, and arranged for the abdication of the **Qing dynasty** in February 1912. In the elections held for a new bicameral parliament and provincial assemblies **Sun Yixian**'s **Guomindang** (Nationalist Party) became the largest party in both houses, though only 4–6 per cent of the population were entitled to vote. Yuan felt threatened, particularly as military governors of three provinces were supporters of the Guomindang, though he was supported by foreign powers, who arranged for him to have a Reorganization Loan in 1913. In the same year Britain and Russia forced him to recognize the autonomy of Outer Mongolia and Tibet, which had declared their independence during the 1911 Revolution. As Yuan had agreed to the loan without consulting parliament, the Guomindang unsuccessfully tried to impeach him. Yuan responded by dismissing the military governors who supported Sun. They and their Guomindang supporters then rebelled but were crushed in only three months. Sun was forced into exile. Yuan compelled parliament to make him President for five years in 1913 and a year later banned the Guomindang, dissolved parliament and abolished the local assemblies. In January 1915 Yuan became very unpopular when he accepted Japan's **Twenty-One Demands**, which gave Japan extensive rights in China. His centralizing policy to bring the whole of China under his control roused strong opposition from military governors, local gentry and merchants, so Yuan decided to strengthen his authority by declaring himself Emperor in 1915. This led to a public denunciation by **Liang Qichao** and the secession of some southern provinces. Sun, with Japanese support, tried to instigate a rising in Shandong but this failed. The European powers did not support Yuan, as they feared the effect a civil war would have on their economic interests in China, so Yuan abandoned his plan in March 1916 and restored the republic. Even after this, provinces continued to declare their independence and it was only his death in June 1916, from nervous exhaustion, that prevented him from being overthrown. Yuan's disdainful treatment of both parliament and local assemblies was a blow from which the new republic never recovered. After 1916 it was at the mercy of **warlords**.

**Zaghlul, Saad** (*c.* 1860–1927). Egyptian nationalist and leader of the *Wafd* Party. The son of a village headman, he attended al-Azhar University, Cairo, where he came under the influence of **al-Afghani**, an Islamic reformer. He became the most brilliant lawyer of his time and a friend of **Cromer**, the British Agent, who made him Minister of Education in 1906 and Minister of Justice in 1910. Not until 1913, when he was elected to the Legislative Assembly, which mainly represented landowners, did Zaghlul become involved in nationalist agitation. In 1914 the British government declared Egypt a protectorate, when Turkey declared war on Germany's side. The Legislative Assembly, which opposed the British occupation, was prorogued and never met again. At the end of the war Zaghlul was uncompromising in his demand for Egyptian independence. He and other Egyptians were encouraged by Woodrow **Wilson**'s **Fourteen Points**, which supported self-determination for all nations, and by the Anglo-French declaration of November 1918, which promised independence to peoples 'long oppressed by the Turks' and undertook to set up national governments based on the free choice of the population. Zaghlul, supported by the Egyptian government, requested that a delegation, or *Wafd*, should present Egypt's case for independence at the **Paris Peace Conference** but this was turned down by the British. The result was that the delegation, which represented the educated élite, now became a mass political party, the *Wafd*, under the leadership of Zaghlul. When he was arrested and exiled by the British, there were riots, strikes and demonstrations all over Egypt in 1919, in which over 1,000 Egyptians and thirty Englishmen were killed. **Allenby**, sent as High Commissioner to Egypt to restore order, saw that this could be done only by releasing Zaghlul, which he did, and by giving the Egyptians some form of self-government. In 1922 Allenby pushed the British government into declaring the independence of Egypt and the end of the protectorate, but four matters were 'absolutely reserved for the discretion' of the British government: the security of communications in Egypt, the defence of the country, the protection of foreign interests and the Sudan. Zaghlul refused to sign a document which gave Egypt such limited independence. He nevertheless became Prime Minister in the elections of 1923–4, when the *Wafd* gained 190 of the 214 seats.

**Zaibatsu** ('financial clique'). Big-business concerns which dominated Japanese industry until 1945, the largest of which were Mitsui, **Mitsubishi**, Sumitomo and Yasuda. In the early 1880s the Meiji government (see **Meiji Restoration**) sold very cheaply the industries it had founded to a few private companies, which became the *zaibatsu*. Some concentrated on one field of industry or commerce but the largest had a huge range of interests, which included textiles, mining, engineering, heavy industry, insurance and transport. Many had their own banks and controlled all aspects of an industry, from the supply of raw materials to shipping the finished product to its markets. Ownership was usually in one family, though management was increasingly handed over to others. The *zaibatsu* benefited from the boom of the **First World War** and were strong enough to survive the depression which followed it: they alone had enough capital to develop heavy industry, which grew rapidly after 1918. Their drive and efficiency were essential for the development of the Japanese economy but they were unpopular with both **Right** and **Left** in the 1930s. In 1932 the managing director of Mitsui was accused of putting the interests of his company above those of his country and was assassinated. The government came to rely more and more on the new *zaibatsu*, which arose at this time. They specialized in military and chemical industries and made Japan less dependent on imports. In 1938 two companies – Toyota and Nissan – were licensed to make cars and trucks, which had been imported from the USA. The state gave them tax concessions and provided half their capital: by 1939 the Americans had lost their Japanese market. Nissan also founded, with state help, the Manchurian Heavy Industries Corporation to develop **Manchukuo** and by 1938 was larger than any of the *zaibatsu* except for Mitsui and Mitsubishi. The Occupation authorities began to dismantle the *zaibatsu* in 1945, as they regarded them as prime supporters of the Japanese militarism of the 1930s, but many have been re-formed since.

**Zapata, Emiliano** (1879–1919). A hero of the **Mexican Revolution**. A *mestizo* (of mixed race) peasant in the province of Morelos, south of Mexico City, he inherited a little land and livestock. Zapata was a striking figure, with his long moustache, large spurs and wide gold-braided sombrero. He was elected in 1909 head of the defence committee in his village, in order to prevent the *hacendados* (great landowners) taking over village lands. He forcibly recovered land which had been seized by the *hacendados* and distributed it to the peasants. When Madero called for a rising in 1910, Zapata supported him and helped to bring about the fall of Porfirio **Díaz** but when Madero refused to hand over land to the *ejidos* (Indian village communities), Zapata turned against him. Land redistribution was the main purpose of his movement: he had no understanding of the needs of urban workers and had no support from them. After the defeat of his ally Pancho Villa in 1915 he confined his military struggle to Morelos and saw his troops dwindle from 70,000 in 1915 to 10,000 in 1919. In that year he was treacherously murdered.

*Zemstva* (singular *zemstvo*) were set up in Russia in 1864 as one of **Alexander II**'s 'Great Reforms'. The administrative duties of the landlords ended with the **emancipation of the serfs**. Some of them were taken over by the *mir* (peasant commune) but institutions were needed to control areas larger than the village. *Zemstva* were therefore set up: district and provincial councils in European Russia, elected by landlords, peasants and townsmen, although landlords were given the largest representation. They had to provide local services like schools and hospitals, in which they were remarkably successful. In 1856 there were only 8,000 elementary schools in the whole of Russia: by 1880 there were 23,000 in European Russia alone, 18,000 of them provided by the *zemstva*. Doctors, teachers and other specialists employed by the *zemstva* numbered 85,000 in 1912, of whom 80,000 were teachers. They were highly critical of the conditions they saw around them and became the backbone of the liberal opposition to the Tsar.

**Zeng Guofan** (1811–72) Chinese scholar and soldier. Trained as a scholar on the Confucian (see **Confucianism**) classics, he was an official in Beijing (Peking) until he became a general in the 1850s to deal with the **Taiping rebellion**. After the defeat of Manchu imperial generals by the rebels, it was scholar-officials like Zeng who revived **Qing dynasty** fortunes. He built up a well-paid and organized army, bought foreign weapons and was largely responsible for the recapture of Nanjing in 1864 and the defeat of the Taipings. He then went on to repress the Nian rebellion in the North China Plain. He remained a Confucian, completely loyal to the Qing dynasty, and became a leader of the **Self-Strengthening movement** in order to preserve that dynasty. He turned to the West for its military technology, built arsenals and promoted the study of Western technical literature and Western languages but rejected any attempt to copy Western political institutions.

**Zetkin, Clara** (1857–1933). German communist. As a member of the German **Social Democratic Party** (SPD) she represented women workers at the first meeting of the **Second International** (1889) and took part in all its subsequent congresses to 1914. In 1907 she founded and led the Socialist Women's International. She worked closely for a time with Rosa **Luxemburg** and condemned Germany's entry into the **First World War** as an 'imperialist' war. In 1915 she was jailed briefly for trying to organize an international socialist women's conference to oppose the war. Disillusioned with the SPD's support for the war effort, she was a founder of the **Spartakist** League (1916), supported the **October Revolution** (1917) in Russia, became a communist and in October 1919 a member of the Central Committee of the German Communist Party. From 1920–33 she was a communist deputy in the **Reichstag** and a leading opponent of **Hitler**, calling for a united front of workers against **Fascism**. She visited Moscow in 1920 and spent much of the 1920s there, becoming a firm supporter of **Stalin**. After her death, soon after Hitler became Chancellor, her ashes were placed in the wall of the Kremlin.

**Zhang Zuolin.** Manchurian **warlord**. He was supported by the Japanese when he was fighting **Jiang Jieshi** (Chiang Kai-shek) for control of north China in the late 1920s. When Jiang was about to take Beijing in 1928, the Japanese persuaded Zhang to retire to his home base of Manchuria. He left by train for Mukden but just outside the city his train was blown up and he was killed. The Japanese blamed the Chinese Nationalists, although it was well known that junior officers of the Japanese Guandong army were responsible, as they felt that Zhang was too much of a Chinese patriot to be a Japanese puppet. They hoped that his death would force their superiors to take over Manchuria. This did not happen: the Prime Minister Tanaka Giichi and the Emperor were shocked at the assassination. The army conducted an inquiry into the 'grave Manchurian incident': the colonel responsible for the murder was retired. The army insisted that, for its own honour and the morale of the nation, no further action should be taken and nothing should be revealed publicly. This incident showed that the army enjoyed a privileged position in Japan, able to ignore civilian politicians and even the Emperor. Zhang's son, Zhang Xueliang, greatly resented his father's death and joined the Chinese Nationalists to fight against the Japanese. In 1936 during the **Xi'an incident** he captured Jiang Jieshi and forced him to abandon his campaign against the Chinese Communists and to form a **United Front** with them against the Japanese.

**Zhukov, Georgi Konstantinovich** (1896–1974). Soviet field-marshal. The son of a peasant, he was conscripted into the Tsar's army in the **First World War**. After the **October Revolution**, 1917, he joined the **Red Army** as a cavalry commander and became a member of the Communist Party in 1919. By the late 1930s he commanded armoured brigades on the Mongolian–Manchurian border and in 1939 badly mauled a Japanese army at Nomonhan (see **Nomonhan Incident**). In January 1941 he became Chief of the General Staff but was dismissed by **Stalin** after the German invasion in June for advocating a Soviet withdrawal from Kiev. In September he was sent to organize the defence of **Leningrad** but a month later was in Moscow, holding up the German advance there. He launched the first of his counter-offensives, with new troops from Siberia, in December and pushed the Germans back from Moscow, winning the first major Soviet victory of the war. In August 1942 he became Deputy Supreme Commander under Stalin and organized the Soviet offensive which destroyed the German Sixth Army at **Stalingrad**. Zhukov won another major conflict at the battle of **Kursk**, the greatest tank battle of the war, in July 1943 and then broke through in Belorussia. He returned to a field command in March 1944, led his forces into Hungary, and then directed the advance on Warsaw. In April 1945 he launched the final offensive against Berlin, captured the city and accepted the formal German surrender on 8 May. Now he was a national hero and possible rival to Stalin, who banished him to a regional command. After Stalin's death he returned to favour, became Defence Minister in 1955 and a member of the all-powerful Presidium of the Communist Party. When he came into conflict with Khrushchev, who accused him of undermining the Party's control of the army, he was dismissed in 1957. Opinions differ as to his ability as a general. Some regard him highly as the general who never lost a battle: others maintain that his reputation has been inflated and that most of his victories were gained by overwhelming force, by huge concentrations of armour and artillery and by disregarding the human cost. He was certainly harsh and ruthless and shocked **Eisenhower** by telling him that if Russian troops encountered a minefield, they were to attack as if it was not there.

**Zimmermann telegram.** A coded message sent on 19 January 1917 by Arthur Zimmermann, the German Foreign Secretary, to the German minister in Mexico. It said that if there was war between the USA and Germany, the minister should propose a Mexican–German alliance. Mexico should go to war with the USA and would recover her 'lost territory' in Texas, New Mexico and Arizona. She should then persuade Japan to join the alliance and make war on the USA in the Pacific. British naval intelligence intercepted and decoded the message and handed it over to the USA in February, shortly after Germany had told the American government that it was resuming unrestricted submarine warfare against all ships sailing to Allied ports. President **Wilson** did not make the telegram public at first, in case it stimulated demands for war, but when three American ships were sunk without warning in March, he released it to the press. There was an explosion of rage in the USA, even in the isolationist Mid-West, which led to Congress declaring war on Germany on 6 April.

**Zinoviev, Grigori Yevseyevich** (1883–1936). A Jew, whose parents were small farmers, he joined the **Bolsheviks** in 1903 and was **Lenin**'s closest companion in exile from 1909–17. On his return to Russia he was put in charge of the Party organization in **Petrograd** and was chairman of the **Soviet** there. Zinoviev opposed Lenin's call for a rising in October 1917, as he thought it would be premature. After the success of the **October Revolution** he disagreed with the exclusion of non-Bolsheviks from the new Soviet government. This did not prevent him becoming Chairman of the newly formed **Comintern** in 1919 and a full member of the *Politburo* two years later. After Lenin's death he joined with **Kamenev** and **Stalin** to prevent **Trotsky** coming to power, and agreed to the suppression of Lenin's 'last testament', which had suggested that Stalin should be removed from his post of General Secretary of the Communist Party. When it became clear that he had underestimated Stalin's ambition, he formed, with Kamenev, the Left Opposition to Stalin. By this time Stalin controlled all the levers of power, particularly the Secretariat, and forced Zinoviev to resign from the Politburo and the Comintern in 1926. He was expelled from the Party, with Trotsky, in 1927 and was one of the chief victims of the **Great Purges**. In 1936, in the first of the show trials in Moscow, he was spuriously accused of **Kirov**'s murder and of plotting with foreign powers for the overthrow of the Soviet state. He was found guilty and executed.

**Zionism.** A secular and nationalist movement to re-establish a Jewish state in Palestine, which arose as a result of **anti-Semitism** in late nineteenth century Europe. It looked back to the great days of the kings of Israel, when Mount Zion had been the site of the fortress of Jerusalem. Zionism became a political movement when Theodor **Herzl** organized a World Zionist Congress in 1906, though many prominent European Jews before the **First World War** did not support it, as they were more concerned with assimilation. Chaim **Weizmann**, a leading British Zionist, gave a great boost to Zionism when he persuaded the British government to issue the **Balfour Declaration** (1917), favouring the establishment of a Jewish home in Palestine. When the **Palestine mandate** was granted to Britain after the war, it was her duty to prepare Palestine for self-government as quickly as possible but the Zionists opposed this, as the overwhelmingly Arab population would have made Palestine an Arab state. Jewish settlement there developed slowly until the 1930s, when **Hitler**'s persecution of the Jews resulted in increased Jewish immigration. This alarmed the Arabs, who revolted (1936–9) and attacked Jewish settlers. The Arab revolt led to a split in the Zionist movement, when a terrorist wing, led by Irgun and the **Stern Gang**, rejected the cautious approach of leaders like Weizmann and attacked not only Arabs but the British too. The formation of the State of Israel (May 1948) marked the success of the Zionist movement.

*Zollverein* (German customs union). Customs barriers within and between the German states were a serious handicap to economic development. In **Prussia** there were sixty-seven internal tariffs before 1818, when a Prussian customs union was formed, which abolished most of them. By charging heavy duties on goods passing through Prussia, she encouraged other German states to join. In 1834 the German *Zollverein* was formed: it included eighteen states, including Bavaria and Württemberg in the south. By 1852 nearly all German states had joined, though the seaports of Hamburg and Bremen remained outside until the 1880s. The *Zollverein* was an essential precondition of German industrialization: it promoted the standardization of commercial law and a uniform currency, created a large home market with low tariffs and provided tariff protection against foreign competition. Yet the political consequences were perhaps even more important. When Prussia formed her customs union she was not thinking of uniting Germany, yet the *Zollverein* helped her to dominate Germany economically, as Austria was excluded. **Metternich** believed that 'its decisive result' would be 'Prussia's predominance', a point of view shared by the Prussian Minister of Finance, when he wrote that 'unification of these states in a customs and trading union leads to the establishment of a unified political system.' Twice Austria tried to force her way in, after the **Revolutions of 1848** and in the 1860s, but on each occasion she failed.

**Zulu Wars** (1838–1879). Wars fought by Zulus against Boers and later British who were encroaching on their territory. The Zulus had fought many ferocious wars against other African tribes in the *Mfecane* but did not come into conflict with whites in South Africa until Boers invaded Natal in the **Great Trek**. In 1838 the Zulu Chief Dingane treacherously murdered Piet Retief and some Boers who were having discussions in his *kraal* and then slaughtered their defenceless families. Boer revenge was swift: a Boer commando killed 3,000 Zulus at the battle of **Blood River** (December 1838). When the British arrived the Boers moved out of Natal in 1843 and the independence of the Zulu kingdom was recognized by Britain. Trouble arose again in the 1870s, as Zulus blocked the Boers' access to the sea in the Transvaal. Britain supported the Zulu claims to disputed territory until 1877, when the Transvaal was annexed. Now Britain changed sides and backed the Boers. The British High Commissioner in South Africa, Sir Bartle Frere, wanted a confederation in South Africa which would include Zululand and was determined to destroy Zulu power. He gave the Zulu King **Cetshwayo** an ultimatum to disband his army and when this was rejected he invaded Zululand. The British suffered a humiliating defeat at Isandhlwana in 1879 but British fire-power was too great in the end: the military might of the Zulus was destroyed. Zululand was made a British protectorate in 1887 and ten years later was incorporated in Natal. A last Zulu rising was easily put down in 1906.

# READ MORE IN PENGUIN

In every corner of the world, on every subject under the sun, Penguin represents quality and variety – the very best in publishing today.

For complete information about books available from Penguin – including Puffins, Penguin Classics and Arkana – and how to order them, write to us at the appropriate address below. Please note that for copyright reasons the selection of books varies from country to country.

**In the United Kingdom**: Please write to *Dept. EP, Penguin Books Ltd, Bath Road, Harmondsworth, West Drayton, Middlesex UB7 ODA*

**In the United States**: Please write to *Consumer Sales, Penguin USA, P.O. Box 999, Dept. 17109, Bergenfield, New Jersey 07621-0120.* VISA and MasterCard holders call 1-800-253-6476 to order Penguin titles

**In Canada**: Please write to *Penguin Books Canada Ltd, 10 Alcorn Avenue, Suite 300, Toronto, Ontario M4V 3B2*

**In Australia**: Please write to *Penguin Books Australia Ltd, P.O. Box 257, Ringwood, Victoria 3134*

**In New Zealand**: Please write to *Penguin Books (NZ) Ltd, Private Bag 102902, North Shore Mail Centre, Auckland 10*

**In India**: Please write to *Penguin Books India Pvt Ltd, 706 Eros Apartments, 56 Nehru Place, New Delhi 110 019*

**In the Netherlands**: Please write to *Penguin Books Netherlands bv, Postbus 3507, NL-1001 AH Amsterdam*

**In Germany**: Please write to *Penguin Books Deutschland GmbH, Metzlerstrasse 26, 60594 Frankfurt am Main*

**In Spain**: Please write to *Penguin Books S. A., Bravo Murillo 19, 1° B, 28015 Madrid*

**In Italy**: Please write to *Penguin Italia s.r.l., Via Felice Casati 20, I–20124 Milano*

**In France**: Please write to *Penguin France S. A., 17 rue Lejeune, F–31000 Toulouse*

**In Japan**: Please write to *Penguin Books Japan, Ishikiribashi Building, 2–5–4, Suido, Bunkyo-ku, Tokyo 112*

**In South Africa**: Please write to *Longman Penguin Southern Africa (Pty) Ltd, Private Bag X08, Bertsham 2013*

# READ MORE IN PENGUIN

## HISTORY

### London: A Social History  Roy Porter

'The best and bravest thing he has written. It is important because it makes the whole sweep of London's unique history comprehensible and accessible in a way that no previous writer has ever managed to accomplish. And it is angry because it begins and concludes with a slashing, unanswerable indictment of Thatcherite misrule' – *Independent on Sunday*

### Somme  Lyn Macdonald

'What the reader will longest remember are the words – heartbroken, blunt, angry – of the men who lived through the bloodbath ... a worthy addition to the literature of the Great War' – *Daily Mail*

### Aspects of Aristocracy  David Cannadine

'A hugely enjoyable portrait of the upper classes ... It is the perfect history book for the non-historian. Ample in scope but full of human detail, accessible and graceful in its scholarship, witty and opinionated in style' – *Financial Times*

### The Penguin History of Greece  A. R. Burn

Readable, erudite, enthusiastic and balanced, this one-volume history of Hellas sweeps the reader along from the days of Mycenae and the splendours of Athens to the conquests of Alexander and the final dark decades.

### The Laurel and the Ivy  Robert Kee

'Parnell continues to haunt the Irish historical imagination a century after his death ... Robert Kee's patient and delicate probing enables him to reconstruct the workings of that elusive mind as persuasively, or at least as plausibly, as seems possible ... This splendid biography, which is as readable as it is rigorous, greatly enhances our understanding of both Parnell, and of the Ireland of his time' – *The Times Literary Supplement*

# READ MORE IN PENGUIN

## HISTORY

**Frauen**  Alison Owings

Nearly ten years in the making and based on interviews and original research, Alison Owings' remarkable book records the wartime experiences and thoughts of 'ordinary' German women from varying classes and backgrounds.

**Byzantium: The Decline and Fall**  John Julius Norwich

The final volume in the magnificent history of Byzantium. 'As we pass among the spectacularly varied scenes of war, intrigue, theological debate, martial kerfuffle, sacrifice, revenge, blazing ambition and lordly pride, our guide calms our passions with an infinity of curious asides and grace-notes ... Norwich's great trilogy has dispersed none of this magic' – *Independent*

**The Anglo-Saxons**  Edited by James Campbell

'For anyone who wishes to understand the broad sweep of English history, Anglo-Saxon society is an important and fascinating subject. And Campbell's is an important and fascinating book. It is also a finely produced and, at times, a very beautiful book' – *London Review of Books*

**Conditions of Liberty**  Ernest Gellner

'A lucid and brilliant analysis ... he gives excellent reasons for preferring civil society to democracy as the institutional key to modernization ... For Gellner, civil society is a remarkable concept. It is both an inspiring slogan and the reality at the heart of the modern world' – *The Times*

**The Habsburgs**  Andrew Wheatcroft

'Wheatcroft has ... a real feel for the heterogeneous geography of the Habsburg domains – I especially admired his feel for the Spanish Habsburgs. Time and again, he neatly links the monarchs with the specific monuments they constructed for themselves' – *Sunday Telegraph*

# READ MORE IN PENGUIN

## HISTORY

**Citizens**  Simon Schama

The award-winning chronicle of the French Revolution. 'The most marvellous book I have read about the French Revolution in the last fifty years' – Richard Cobb in *The Times*

**The Lure of the Sea**  Alain Corbin

Alain Corbin's wonderful book explores the dramatic change in Western attitude towards the sea and seaside pleasures that occured between 1750 and 1840. 'A compact and brilliant taxonomy of the shifting meanings of the sea and shore' – *New York Review of Books*

**The Tyranny of History**  W. J. F. Jenner

A fifth of the world's population lives within the boundaries of China, a vast empire barely under the control of the repressive ruling Communist regime. Beneath the economic boom China is in a state of crisis that goes far deeper than the problems of its current leaders to a value system that is rooted in the autocratic traditions of China's past.

**The English Bible and the Seventeenth-Century Revolution**
Christopher Hill

'What caused the English civil war? What brought Charles I to the scaffold?' Answer to both questions: the Bible. To sustain this provocative thesis, Christopher Hill's new book maps English intellectual history from the Reformation to 1660, showing how scripture dominated every department of thought from sexual relations to political theory ... 'His erudition is staggering' – *Sunday Times*

**Fisher's Face**  Jan Morris

'*Fisher's Face* is funny, touching and informed by wide reading as well as wide travelling' – *New Statesman & Society*. 'A richly beguiling picture of the Victorian Navy, its profound inner security, its glorious assumptions, its extravagant social life and its traditionally eccentric leaders' – *Independent on Sunday*

# READ MORE IN PENGUIN

## REFERENCE

### The Penguin Dictionary of Literary Terms and Literary Theory
J. A. Cuddon

'Scholarly, succinct, comprehensive and entertaining, this is an important book, an indispensable work of reference. It draws on the literature of many languages and quotes aptly and freshly from our own' – *The Times Educational Supplement*

### The Penguin Spelling Dictionary

What are the plurals of *octopus* and *rhinoceros*? What is the difference between *stationery* and *stationary*? And how about *annex* and *annexe*, *agape* and *Agape*? This comprehensive new book, the fullest spelling dictionary now available, provides the answers.

### Roget's Thesaurus of English Words and Phrases
Edited by Betty Kirkpatrick

This new edition of Roget's classic work, now brought up to date for the nineties, will increase anyone's command of the English language. Fully cross-referenced, it includes synonyms of every kind (formal or colloquial, idiomatic and figurative) for almost 900 headings. It is a must for writers and utterly fascinating for any English speaker.

### The Penguin Dictionary of English Idioms
Daphne M. Gulland and David G. Hinds-Howell

The English language is full of pitfalls for the foreign student – but the most common problem lies in understanding and using the vast array of idioms. *The Penguin Dictionary of English Idioms* is uniquely designed to stimulate understanding and familiarity by explaining the meanings and origins of idioms and giving examples of typical usage.

### The Penguin Wordmaster Dictionary
Martin H. Manser and Nigel D. Turton

This dictionary puts the pleasure back into word-seeking. Every time you look at a page you get a bonus – a panel telling you everything about a particular word or expression. It is, therefore, a dictionary to be read as well as used for its concise and up-to-date definitions.

# READ MORE IN PENGUIN

## REFERENCE

### Medicines: A Guide for Everybody  Peter Parish

Now in its seventh edition and completely revised and updated, this bestselling guide is written in ordinary language for the ordinary reader yet will prove indispensable to anyone involved in health care – nurses, pharmacists, opticians, social workers and doctors.

### Media Law  Geoffrey Robertson QC and Andrew Nichol

Crisp and authoritative surveys explain the up-to-date position on defamation, obscenity, official secrecy, copyright and confidentiality, contempt of court, the protection of privacy and much more.

### The Slang Thesaurus  Jonathon Green

Do you make the public bar sound like a gentleman's club? The miraculous *Slang Thesaurus* will liven up your language in no time. You won't Adam and Eve it! A mine of funny, witty, acid and vulgar synonyms for the words you use every day.

### The Penguin Dictionary of Troublesome Words  Bill Bryson

Why should you avoid discussing the *weather conditions*? Can a married woman be celibate? Why is it eccentric to talk about the aroma of a cowshed? A straightforward guide to the pitfalls and hotly disputed issues in standard written English.

### The Penguin Dictionary of Musical Performers  Arthur Jacobs

In this invaluable companion volume to *The Penguin Dictionary of Music* Arthur Jacobs has brought together the names of over 2,500 performers. Music is written by composers, yet it is the interpreters who bring it to life; in this comprehensive book they are at last given their due.

### The Penguin Dictionary of Third World Terms  Kofi Buenor Hadjor

Words associated with the Third World are rarely subject to analysis and definition. Yet many of these terms are loaded with assumptions and cultural attitudes. As a result, discussion of the Third World can be bogged down in bias, prejudice – and Western self-interest.

# READ MORE IN PENGUIN

## DICTIONARIES

Abbreviations
Archaeology
Architecture
Art and Artists
Astronomy
Biology
Botany
Building
Business
Challenging Words
Chemistry
Civil Engineering
Classical Mythology
Computers
Curious and Interesting Numbers
Curious and Interesting Words
Design and Designers
Economics
Electronics
English and European History
English Idioms
Foreign Terms and Phrases
French
Geography
Historical Slang

Human Geography
Information Technology
Literary Terms and Literary Theory
Mathematics
Modern History 1789–1945
Modern Quotations
Music
Musical Performers
Physical Geography
Physics
Politics
Proverbs
Psychology
Quotations
Religions
Rhyming Dictionary
Saints
Science
Sociology
Spanish
Surnames
Telecommunications
Troublesome Words
Twentieth-Century History